CRITICAL COMPANION TO

Charles Dickens

A Literary Reference to His Life and Work

PAUL DAVIS

Facts On File
An imprint of Infobase Publishing

Critical Companion to Charles Dickens

Copyright © 2007, 1999 by Paul Davis

Facts On File, Inc.
An imprint of Infobase Publishing
132 West 31st Street
New York NY 10001

Library of Congress Cataloging-in-Publication Data

Davis, Paul B. (Paul Benjamin), 1934–
Critical companion to Charles Dickens : a literary reference to his life and
work / Paul Davis.—Rev. ed.
p. cm.
Includes bibliographical references (p.) and index.
ISBN 0-8160-6407-5 (hc : alk. paper)
1. Dickens, Charles, 1812–1870—Criticism and interpretation—Handbooks, manuals, etc. I. Title.
PR4588D37 2006
823'.8—dc22   2006003026

You can find Facts On File on the World Wide Web at http://www.factsonfile.com

Text design by Erika K. Arroyo
Cover design by Cathy Rincon/Anastasia Plé

Printed in the United States of America

VB Hermitage 10 9 8 7 6 5 4 3 2 1

This book is printed on acid-free paper.

For Benjamin, Kate, and Joshua

CONTENTS

ACKNOWLEDGMENTS

I have relied on the work of innumerable scholars and critics in developing the entries for *Critical Companion to Charles Dickens*. Some of my debts are acknowledged in the text, but many more are silent, even unrecognized. I am particularly grateful to generations of Dickensians, writing in journals like *The Dickensian* and *The Dickens Quarterly*, whose devotion to Dickens and his works continues to enlarge our understanding of the man, his times, and his novels. I am indebted to Bob Gish, who originally suggested this project; to Michael Fisher, who provided institutional support for it; and to two graduate assistants, Ann Grigsby and Joyce Flagg, who helped in choosing and chasing down information and in proposing approaches to various entries. I am also grateful to Gary Scharnhorst, Hugh Witemeyer, Gary Harrison, David Johnson, Pat Smith, Tom Linehan, and Bob Fleming for suggestions on particular entries, and to my wife, Mary, for her patience and for her help in preparing the illustrations. I am especially grateful to Bob Wolfe, my first editor at Facts On File, whose careful reading and thoughtful criticism did much to improve many of the entries, and to Jeff Soloway, my current editor. The inevitable mistakes and omissions in a work of this scope are wholly my own.

INTRODUCTION

More than any British writer other than Shakespeare, Dickens has engaged the popular imagination with his crowded gallery of memorable characters and his detailed rendering of the life of his times. His stories and people are familiar even to those who have never read the novels: Oliver Twist, Scrooge, and David Copperfield are as well known as Hamlet, Romeo, or Falstaff.

Adapted for the stage almost as soon as they appeared in monthly parts, Dickens's novels have been public property from the beginning. They have been endlessly retold, adapted, imitated, and pirated on both sides of the Atlantic for a century and a half. The more recent cinematic and television adaptations are just a few examples of this public appropriation of "Dickens," a process that has sometimes created notions about the novels remarkably different from the original texts.

The most important writer of his time, Dickens is often seen as the quintessential Victorian. "Dickens's England" has almost become synonymous with Victorian England. Since he frequently based his characters on real people and used real places—particularly the streets and neighborhoods of London—as settings for his tales, the connections between his fictional world and the actual world of Victorian England have fascinated his readers. Dickens enthusiasts have often applied themselves—sometimes overzealously—to connecting the people and places in the novels with counterparts in the real world. Understanding the historical context in which Dickens worked is especially important to understanding his life and his novels.

Although his favor with the popular audience has never waned, Dickens was, during the modernist decades of the early 20th century, largely dismissed by academics and critics, who ignored his work as vulgar and simplistic. When EDMUND WILSON, in his 1941 essay "Dickens, the Two Scrooges," demonstrated that Dickens was more intellectually challenging than his detractors had allowed, he ushered in an age of serious work on the novelist. Since that time Dickens has been explicated and mythologized, analyzed and psychoanalyzed, constructed and deconstructed in a host of critical and academic studies.

Through both the lean years of critical neglect and the recent decades of academic overcompensation, Dickens has retained the interest and affection of the popular audience. This book, like its predecessor *Charles Dickens A to Z*, is directed to such readers, nonspecialists, students, and others who wish to deepen their experience of Dickens's wonderful novels.

How to Use This Book

Critical Companion to Charles Dickens is a thorough revision and update of *Dickens A to Z*: a guide to the works themselves, to Dickens and the Victorian context in which he worked, and to the vast body of criticism and scholarship about the novels. This volume rearranges the materials in *Dickens A to Z*, revises and updates the entries, and expands the critical discussions, especially those devoted to Dickens's characters. *Critical Companion to Charles Dickens* is arranged in four sections.

Part I: Dickens's Life
The first part presents a concise chronological biography of Dickens.

Part II: Dickens's Works
This part is divided into two sections, Major Works and Minor Works. The first section contains lengthy entries on each of Dickens's 15 novels and the five novellas collected as *The Christmas Books*. Each work is first summarized in a subsection called Synopsis. Since all of Dickens's novels were originally published in either monthly or weekly serial numbers, the synopses are broken down into these original parts. By indicating these part divisions, the synopses show how Dickens constructed multiple plots, created suspense, and gave particular importance to parts 5, 10, and 15 in his standard 20-part structure. The Commentary subsection discusses Dickens's plans for the work, its composition, and some of the important critical issues it raises. The Characters and Related Entries subsection contains subentries in which characters and other important components of the work are described, often in Dickens's own words. Characters' important moments in the story are indicated with parenthetical chapter references. Subentries on the most important characters contain commentary on their significance to the structure and themes of the novel and their connections to other Dickens characters. Other subentries cover concepts unique to particular novels, such as the adjectives *Pickwickian* (*Pickwick*) and *wiglomeration* (*Bleak House*); fictional settings, such as Coketown (*Hard Times*); real settings that appear in one specific novel; and more. Real places that appear in more than one work or that are also important to Dickens's life are covered in Part III instead. The subsection Adaptations describes some important theatrical and cinematic versions of each of the major works. Finally, under Further Reading some of the more important critical commentaries on each novel are described, especially those that indicate its contemporary critical standing. The names of many of the critics mentioned in this section are in SMALL CAPITAL LETTERS, to indicate a cross-reference to the entry on the critic in Part III, where the specific critical work is often discussed in more detail.

The second section of Part II covers Dickens's minor works, including all his short stories, plays, poems, and sketches and most of his journalistic articles and essays. Works that Dickens collected in *Christmas Stories, The Mudfog and Other Sketches, Reprinted Pieces, Sketches by Boz, Sketches of Young Gentlemen,* and *Sketches of Young Couples,* as well as uncollected works or those in later collections, appear individually in the alphabetical listing. Each of these works is briefly summarized, any particular relevance to the novels is indicated, and, for many of the fictional works, the characters are identified and some brief critical commentary is offered. Works included in three important later collections of Dickens's minor writings are indicated with parenthetical markers: Michael Slater's four-volume *Dickens' Journalism* (*Journalism*); B. W. Matz's *Miscellaneous Papers, Plays and Poems* (*Miscellaneous*); and Harry Stone's *Uncollected Writings from Household Words* (*Stone*).

Part III: People, Places, and Topics
The entries in this section include people, such as Dickens's family members, friends, colleagues, and contemporaries; places, such as the houses Dickens lived in and the areas he lived in or visited, especially those that he also used in his fiction; broader social and historical topics, such as the Industrial Revolution, railways, the sensation novel, the early Victorian period, and many more. Critical concepts of especial importance to understanding the novels—such as allegory, satire, or bildungsroman—receive separate entries, as do many of the scholars and critics who have contributed to our understanding of Dickens and to the ongoing conversation about his works.

Part IV: Appendices
The appendices include a chronology of Dickens's life and major works, a list of Dicken's major books, and a bibliography of secondary sources about Dickens and his novels, including all of those mentioned in the main text. Authors indicated with SMALL CAPITAL LETTERS also have entries in Part III.

References
Any reference to an entry in Part III is given in SMALL CAPITAL LETTERS the first time it appears in an entry. Since all of Dickens's works are covered in Part II, they are not specifically cross-referenced.

References to scenes or passages from Dickens's works are indicated with parenthetical chapter numbers. Works identified by the following abbreviated titles appear alphabetically under the longer titles indicated. Short titles not on the list can be found alphabetically among the entries.

Battle = *The Battle of Life*
"Bolton" = "Mr. Robert Bolton"
Boz = Sketches by Boz
    "Beadle" = "The Beadle. The Parish Engine. The Schoolmaster"
    "Broker's" = "The Broker's Man"
    "Christening" = "The Bloomsbury Christening"
    "Curate" = "The Curate. The Old Lady. The Half-pay Captain"
    "Evans" = "Miss Evans and the Eagle"
    "Hackney" = "Hackney-coach Stands"
    "Last Cab-driver" = "The Last Cab-driver, and the First Omnibus Cad"
    "Making a Night" = "Making a Night of It"
    "Milliner" = "The Mistaken Milliner"
    "Minns" = "Mr. Minns and His Cousin"
    "Monmouth Street" = "Meditations in Monmouth Street"
    "Neighbour" = "Our Next-door Neighbour"
    "Pawnbroker's" = "The "Pawnbroker's Shop"
    "Porter" = "Mrs. Joseph Porter"
    "Sparkins" = "Horatio Sparkins"
    "Tottle" = "A Passage in the Life of Mr. Watkins Tottle"
    "Tuggses" = "The Tuggses at Ramsgate"
    "Vauxhall" = "Vauxhall Gardens by Day"
    "Winglebury" = "The Great Winglebury Duel"
Carol = *A Christmas Carol*
Chimes = *The Chimes*
Chuzzlewit = *Martin Chuzzlewit*
Coquettes = *The Village Coquettes*
Copperfield = *David Copperfield*
Cricket = *The Cricket on the Hearth*
Curiosity Shop = *The Old Curiosity Shop*
Dombey = *Dombey and Son*
Dorrit = *Little Dorrit*
"Doubledick" = "The Story of Richard Doubledick"

Drood = *The Mystery of Edwin Drood*
"English Prisoners" = "The Perils of Certain English Prisoners"
Expectations = *Great Expectations*
"Golden Mary" = "The Wreck of the Golden Mary"
"Haunted House" = "The Haunted House" (*Christmas Stories*)
Humphrey = *Master Humphrey's Clock*
Journalism = *Dickens' Journalism*
Lazy Tour = *The Lazy Tour of Two Idle Apprentices*
"Marigold" = "Doctor Marigold"
Miscellaneous = Miscellaneous Papers, Plays, and Poems
    "Bull's Somnambulist" = "Mr. Bull's Somnambulist"
    "Extraordinary Traveller" = "Some Account of an Extraordinary Traveller"
    "Hippopotamus" = "The 'Good' Hippopotamus"
    "Jest-book" = "Proposals for a National Jest-book"
Mudfog = *The Mudfog Papers and Other Sketches*
"Mugby" = "Mugby Junction"
Mutual Friend = *Our Mutual Friend*
Nickleby = *Nicholas Nickleby*
Nightingale = *Mr. Nightingale's Diary*
Notes = *American Notes*
Pickwick = *The Pickwick Papers*
Pictures = *Pictures from Italy*
"Poor Relation" = "The Poor Relation's Story"
Reprinted = *Reprinted Pieces*
    "At Dusk" = "To Be Read at Dusk"
    "Births" = "Births. Mrs. Meek, of a Son"
    "Bore" = "Our Bore"
    "Detective Anecdotes" = "Three 'Detective' Anecdotes"
    "French Folly" = "A Monument of French Folly"
    "French Watering-Place" = "Our French Watering-Place"
    "Inspector Field" = "On Duty with Inspector Field"
    "Poor Man's Tale" = "A Poor Man's Tale of a Patent"
    "Workhouse" = "A Walk in a Workhouse"
Rudge = *Barnaby Rudge*

"Silverman" = "George Silverman's
Explanation"
Stone = *Charles Dickens' Uncollected Writings
from Household Words,* ed. Harry Stone
"Tiddler" = "Tom Tiddler's Ground"
"Tulrumble" = "The Public Life of Mr.
Tulrumble"
Twist = *Oliver Twist*
Two Cities = *A Tale of Two Cities*
Uncommercial = *The Uncommercial Traveller*
    (1) "His General Line of Business"
    (2) "The Shipwreck"
    (3) "Wapping Workhouse"
    (4) "Two Views of a Cheap Theatre"
    (5) "Poor Merchantile Jack"
    (6) "Refreshments for Travellers"
    (7) "Travelling Abroad"
    (8) "The Great Tasmania's Cargo"
    (9) "City of London Churches"
    (10) "Shy Neighbourhoods"
    (11) "Tramps"
    (12) "Dullborough Town"
    (13) "Night Walks"
    (14) "Chambers"
    (15) "Nurse's Stories"

    (16) "Arcadian London"
    (17) "The Italian Prisoner"
    (18) "The Calais Night Mail"
    (19) "Some Recollections of Mortality"
    (20) "Birthday Celebrations"
    (21) "The Short-timers"
    (22) "Bound for the Great Salt Lake"
    (23) "The City of the Absent"
    (24) "An Old Stage-coaching House"
    (25) "The Boiled Beef of New England"
    (26) "Chatham Dockyard"
    (27) "In the French-Flemish Country"
    (28) "Medicine Men of Civilisation"
    (29) "Titbull's Alms-houses"
    (30) "The Ruffian"
    (31) "Aboard Ship"
    (32) "A Small Star in the East"
    (33) "A Little Dinner in an Hour"
    (34) "Mr. Barlow"
    (35) "On an Amateur Beat"
    (36) "A Fly-Leaf in a Life"
    (37) "A Plea for Total Abstinence"
Young Couples = *Sketches of Young Couples*
Young Gentlemen = *Sketches of Young
Gentlemen*

PART I

Biography

Charles John Huffam ("Boz") Dickens

(1812–1870)

Charles Dickens was born on February 7, 1812, in PORTSMOUTH, England, the second child of JOHN DICKENS, a clerk in the Navy Pay Office there, and ELIZABETH BARROW DICKENS. The family moved a good deal during Dickens's childhood, as his father was transferred from one station to another: in 1815 to London while John worked at SOMERSET HOUSE, and in 1817 to CHATHAM in KENT, where the boy spent the happiest years of his childhood. For five years he roamed in the countryside, observed the activities in the bustling seaport town, and began his education with WILLIAM GILES, the son of the local Baptist minister, who thought him an exceptional student. But in 1822, when John Dickens returned to London and the family took up residence at 16 BAYHAM STREET, CAMDEN TOWN, the boy's prospects darkened. The family's straitened finances meant that Charles was not able to continue his education. When his mother undertook to increase the family income by operating a school herself, the family moved, in 1823, to a house suitable for the project at 4 Gower Street, but the school failed to attract any pupils. Meanwhile, Charles, feeling neglected and deprived, envied his older sister Fanny (*see* DICKENS, FRANCES ELIZABETH), who enrolled at the Royal Academy of Music, where she would study until 1827.

Early in February 1824, with the family nearing financial ruin, Charles was sent to work at a shoe polish factory, WARREN'S BLACKING, HUNGERFORD STAIRS, the STRAND, a job obtained for him by his cousin JAMES LAMERT. On February 20, John Dickens was arrested for debt and imprisoned in the MARSHALSEA PRISON. His wife and three of the younger children joined him in the prison; Charles took lodgings with ELIZABETH ROYLANCE, a friend of the family, at her house in Camden Town and continued to work at the blacking factory. He performed his job, pasting labels on the bottles of blacking, while stationed in the front window of the establishment, visible to all who passed by in

Dickens in 1868.

the street; the work was humiliating to the sensitive boy: "No words can express the secret agony of my soul," he later wrote, "as I sunk into this companionship [with his fellow workers]; compared these everyday associates with those of my happier childhood; and felt my early hopes of growing up to be a learned and distinguished man crushed in my breast" (AUTOBIOGRAPHY). In late April, John's mother, ELIZABETH BALL DICKENS, died and left John £450, which paid some of his creditors, and on May 28, after successfully negotiating a settlement, John was released from prison. Later that summer, over his mother's objections, Charles was removed from Warren's Blacking. After leaving Warren's, Charles entered WELLINGTON HOUSE ACADEMY, where he would be a student for the next three years, his only sustained period of formal education. There he won a Latin prize and with his schoolmates wrote and produced plays for a toy theater. The family lived at 29 JOHNSON STREET, SOMERS TOWN during this time, and in 1825, John Dickens retired from the Navy Pay Office with a small pension and went to work as a reporter.

When the family again fell into financial difficulties in 1827, they were evicted from their house for nonpayment of rent. Fanny withdrew from the Royal Academy of Music, and Charles left Wellington House to work as a solicitor's clerk in the offices of ELLIS AND BLACKMORE, GRAY'S INN. There he quickly learned shorthand and in 1828 became a shorthand reporter in Doctors' Commons (*see* COURTS). He became so proficient as a shorthand reporter that in 1831 he moved on to record verbatim the proceedings in PARLIAMENT for the *MIRROR OF PARLIAMENT*, a paper managed by his uncle, John Henry BARROW, and in 1832 became a regular reporter for the *TRUE SUN*. As he covered parliamentary debates, elections, catastrophic events, and other public occasions, he developed an ear for the many class and regional dialects that he

Fred Barnard's vignette of Dickens as a despondent child, sitting in the window of Warren's Blacking, where he pastes labels on the blacking bottles.

heard and an eye for the great variety of people in metropolitan London. When his father was again arrested for debt and held in a sponging house, a kind of way station between freedom and the DEBTORS' PRISON, Dickens moved out of the family house into rooms at FURNIVAL'S INN. From there he roamed the streets of London, acquainting himself with its neighborhoods, its street life, and, in the evenings, its theaters. He even entertained ideas of becoming an actor, but illness forced him to cancel an audition at COVENT GARDEN Theatre in 1832. He also met JOHN FORSTER, drama critic and journalist, who would become his closest friend.

In May 1830, he met MARIA BEADNELL, the flirtatious daughter of a banker, whose family looked with disdain at young Charles, the son of a bankrupt. They sent their daughter to the continent to cool the romance, which waxed and waned over the next three years and was finally broken off in May 1833. This was an eventful year for the young reporter, for his first story, "A Dinner at Poplar Walk," appeared in the December issue of the *MONTHLY MAGAZINE*. Dickens later recalled the moment when he saw his first literary work in print: "My eyes so dimmed with pride and joy that they could not bear the street, and were not fit to be seen" (FORSTER, II:4).

In 1834, Dickens published six more sketches in the magazine and five in the *MORNING CHRONICLE*, a daily newspaper for which he had become a reporter. He also met Catherine Hogarth, the daughter of the music critic on the paper, and began courting her. The Hogarths, unlike the Beadnells, were impressed with the energy and talents of the young reporter, and they encouraged the relationship. Dickens continued to publish his sketches; 20 "Sketches of London" appeared in the *EVENING CHRONICLE* in 1835, 12 in *BELL'S LIFE IN LONDON AND SPORTING CHRONICLE*. In February 1836, the sketches were collected into the first series of *Sketches by Boz*, and their popularity earned him notice as a writer and a contract for a monthly serial, *The Pickwick Papers*, which began its run at the end of March 1836. On the strength of these literary successes, Dickens married Catherine on April 2 and the couple went to CHALK, KENT, for a brief honeymoon. Soon after, although Dickens had been hired to play second fiddle on *The Pickwick Papers* by providing copy to accompany the work of a famous illustrator, ROBERT SEYMOUR, the arrangements changed when Seymour, in the second month of the project, committed suicide. On April 20, Dickens took over the dominant role in the project. He doubled the length of the text for each monthly number and reduced the number of illustrations. After interviewing several candidates to replace Seymour, he selected HABLOT KNIGHT BROWNE, the illustrator who would work with him through most of his career. By November *Pickwick* had become a runaway best seller, and Dickens left the *Morning Chronicle* to devote himself full-time to his literary work.

In January 1837, the month in which his first child, CHARLES CULLIFORD DICKENS, was born, Dickens initiated his first editorial project, BENTLEY'S MISCELLANY, the magazine in which *Oliver Twist* began appearing at the end of the month. For much of the year, both *Pickwick* and *Twist* were appearing monthly. The publication of both novels was suspended for a month in May, however, after the sudden death of Mary Hogarth, Catherine's younger sister who was living with the Dickenses. Dickens was holding her in his arms at the moment of her death and was deeply grieved; he took a ring from her finger which he wore to the end of his life. In his obsessive memories of her, Mary became an angelic ideal, innocent and perfect, the model for many of the fragile young women in his novels, especially for Little Nell in *The Old Curiosity Shop*. Charles and Catherine left their newly acquired house at 48 DOUGHTY STREET and retired to a farm in HAMPSTEAD to recover. Later in the summer they went to BROADSTAIRS, KENT, for the first of many holidays they would spend at that seaside town. By the end of the year the completed *Pickwick* was published in book form.

Having a new project in mind, Dickens went to YORKSHIRE with Browne in January 1838 to observe the infamous YORKSHIRE SCHOOLS there, schools that warehoused and mistreated illegitimate and unwanted children and stepchildren who were banished to them. In March he began the novel *Nicholas Nickleby,* his exposé of such schools. His literary fame had brought him nominations to the

Dickens in 1839, based on the portrait by Maclise.

GARRICK CLUB and the ATHENAEUM CLUB, and his circle of friends included many writers and artists, among them WILLIAM HARRISON AINSWORTH, GEORGE CRUIKSHANK, WILLIAM MACREADY, DANIEL MACLISE, and Forster. Dickens's second child, MARY DICKENS, was also born in March. By the end of the year, *Twist* was completed. *Nickleby* continued its serial run until October 1839, the same month in which his second daughter, KATE MACREADY DICKENS, was born. To house this growing family, Dickens moved from Doughty Street to 1 DEVONSHIRE TERRACE at the end of 1839.

The new project was *Master Humphrey's Clock,* a weekly periodical begun in April 1840 in which Dickens serialized his next two novels, *The Old Curiosity Shop* (1841) and *Barnaby Rudge* (1841). By the end of 1841, Dickens was exhausted, tired and weakened by the two novels; a fourth child, WALTER SAVAGE LANDOR DICKENS, born in February; an active public life that earned him an invitation, which he refused, to stand as the Liberal candidate for Parliament from Reading; and an operation for a fistula in October. He decided to take a trip to the United States to recuperate.

Charles and Catherine sailed from Liverpool on January 4, 1842. Their American journey took them to BOSTON, Worcester, Springfield, HARTFORD, New Haven, NEW YORK, PHILADELPHIA, WASHINGTON, RICHMOND, BALTIMORE, HARRISBURG, PITTSBURGH, Cincinnati, LOUISVILLE, ST. LOUIS, Buffalo, NIAGARA FALLS, Toronto, MONTREAL, and many stops in between. They made many American friends, especially with writers such as WASHINGTON IRVING, RICHARD HENRY DANA, and HENRY WADSWORTH LONGFELLOW. Although Dickens was traveling as a private citizen, he was treated like a celebrity: He was feted nearly everywhere he went and was expected to address the local population. People peered into the windows of his room, scavenged his hair trimmings from the barber's floor, and critiqued his dress and manner in the press. Although he began the trip with high expectations, the draining public schedule and the criticism in the newspapers, prompted in part by his advocacy for an INTERNATIONAL COPYRIGHT agreement, changed his perspective, and he wrote back to Macready that America was "not the republic of [his] imagination." After he and his wife returned to England in July, GEORGINA HOGARTH, Catherine's younger sister, joined the household to help with the housekeeping and the care of the children. Dickens's book describing his travels, *American Notes* (1842), caused little stir in Britain, but it infuriated many Americans, especially for its criticisms of the press. The exaggerated reaction prompted Dickens to plan a satirical account of AMERICA for his next novel, *Martin Chuzzlewit* (1844).

A dark story of money and murder, *Chuzzlewit* did not attract as large an audience as some of the earlier novels, and Dickens's publishers, CHAPMAN & HALL, talked of reducing Dickens's monthly payment. *Chuzzlewit* was planned to be a less improvisational novel than its predecessors and to have as its focus the theme of "self." But the American materials in the middle of the story have seemed to many a divergence from the original purpose, intended to raise sagging sales. In another scheme

to fend off financial troubles, Dickens conceived the idea of writing a story directed to the Christmas market, and the first of the CHRISTMAS BOOKS, *A Christmas Carol,* was published for Christmas 1843. Although it was a critical and popular success, Dickens's production orders were expensive, and it did not bring the hoped-for financial rewards. The birth of Dickens's fifth child, FRANCIS JEFFREY DICKENS, in January 1844, and the continued disappointing sales of *Chuzzlewit* led Dickens to change publishers to BRADBURY & EVANS and to pack up his family to live more cheaply in ITALY. After the novel was completed in July, the Dickenses left for GENOA, ITALY, where they would stay for nearly a year.

In Italy Dickens wrote the next Christmas book, *The Chimes* (1844), and notes for the travel articles that would become *Pictures from Italy* (1846). He also became deeply involved in using MESMERISM to treat the hysteria of AUGUSTA DE LA RUE, a neighbor in Genoa. His attentions to his "patient" aroused Catherine's jealous reprimands, an early sign of deep stresses in their marriage.

After returning to England in summer 1845, Dickens organized the first of his AMATEUR THEATRICALS, playing Bobadil in BEN JONSON's *EVERY MAN IN HIS HUMOUR.* A sixth child, ALFRED D'ORSAY TENNYSON DICKENS, was born, and the third Christmas book, *The Cricket on the Hearth,* appeared. After Christmas Dickens began a short-lived attempt to edit a daily newspaper. The liberal *DAILY NEWS* commenced publication on January 21, but on February 9, burdened by the demands of a daily paper and at odds with some of its sponsors, Dickens gave up the editorship.

In May the restless author again took his family abroad, this time to Switzerland, where he wrote *The Battle of Life,* the Christmas book for 1846, and began *Dombey and Son* (1848), sometimes viewed as the first of the great social novels that characterize the second half of Dickens's writing career. In *Dombey* he subdued the comic strain of his early work, developed a set of working notes in which he planned out the novel in advance, and centered his work on the theme of pride. There are some wonderful comic characters—Captain Cuttle and Mr. Toots, for example—but the novel's focus is a melodramatic critique of the institution of patriarchy in its economic, social, and marital dimensions. In Switzerland, cut off from the sources of his inspiration in London, Dickens found writing *Dombey* difficult, and after three months in PARIS, the family returned to London in February 1847.

His energy restored on home ground, Dickens returned to his characteristic multitasking. He completed *Dombey* in April, the same month in which another child, SYDNEY SMITH HALDIMAND DICKENS, was born. During the summer, Dickens organized another series of amateur theatrical performances. With ANGELA COUTTS he organized URANIA COTTAGE, a philanthropic project to redeem fallen women from the streets, which he opened in November, shortly after the death of his sister Fanny. He planned another Christmas book, but after beginning *The Haunted Man* (1848) he put it off until the next Christmas.

Fanny's crippled son, nine-year-old HENRY BURNETT, the original of Tiny Tim and Paul Dombey, died a few months later in January 1849, the same month in which Dickens's eighth child, HENRY FIELDING DICKENS, was born. By February Dickens had begun work on his "favorite child," *David Copperfield* (1850), an autobiographical novel and his earliest use of first-person narrative in a longer work. Usually viewed as an interlude between the early and late novels, *Copperfield* has also been the favorite of many of Dickens's readers. The closely observed and deeply felt depictions of childhood, the comic hyperbole of Wilkins Micawber, the writhing villainy of Uriah Heep, and the veiled revelations of the author's life, especially of his time in the BLACKING WAREHOUSE, give the novel an appeal transcending both the comedy of the early works and the social analysis of the later ones.

While *Copperfield* was still running in monthly numbers, Dickens initiated another major project, a weekly magazine, HOUSEHOLD WORDS, that began publication in March 1850. He both edited and contributed to the magazine. Meanwhile, his work with Urania Cottage and the amateur theatricals continued. While preparing a theatrical performance at KNEBWORTH, BULWER-LYTTON's country house, Dickens and Lytton came up with the idea for the GUILD OF LITERATURE AND ART, a charity to aid indigent writers and artists through benefit theatrical performances that would tour the country. At the time, *A Child's History of England* (1852–53) was appearing in weekly installments in *Household Words*.

Dickens began work on *Bleak House* (1853), the first of his later social novels, at the end of 1851, a year darkened by a series of personal tragedies. In early March Catherine had suffered a nervous breakdown, and at the end of that month Dickens's father died. His infant daughter, DORA ANNIE DICKENS, born August 16, 1850, died eight months later in April 1851. After a family holiday at Broadstairs, life improved. Catherine recovered her spirits and, under the pseudonym Lady Maria Clutterbuck, wrote a cookbook, *What Shall We Have for Dinner?* The Dickens family moved from Devonshire Terrace to the larger TAVISTOCK HOUSE in Bloomsbury, where their 10th and last child, EDWARD BULWER LYTTON DICKENS, was born on March 13, 1852. Nevertheless, *Bleak House* presents a darkened vision of the times, describing England as a nation shrouded in foggy precedents and ravaged by crippling laws. The COURTS, especially the COURT OF CHANCERY, are identified as the source of England's diseased

Dickens in 1852.

condition, which allows ignorance and want to stalk the streets and haunt the slums. In summer 1853, Dickens took his family to BOULOUGNE, FRANCE, a seaside town on the English Channel where he spent several holidays. After a trip to Italy with WILKIE COLLINS and AUGUSTUS EGG in autumn, Dickens returned to England in time to give the first PUBLIC READING of *Carol* at the BIRMINGHAM town hall just after Christmas.

To research his next novel, *Hard Times* (1854), Dickens traveled up to PRESTON in Lancashire early in the year to observe the manufacturing town during a strike. The novel was serialized in *Household Words,* the briefer weekly format producing a shorter work, with a tighter and simpler structure than the longer novels in monthly parts. Dickens's comment on the industrial revolution, *Hard Times* attacked the mechanistic worldview of the political economists and utilitarians (*see* POLITICAL ECONOMY and UTILITARIANISM), suggesting as an alternative the realm of fancy and imagination.

When he received a letter from Maria Beadnell, now MRS. HENRY WINTER, in February 1855, Dickens had fantasies of reviving their romance after a quarter century, but instead of the flirtatious girl he remembered, Mrs. Winter turned out to be a garrulous and silly middle-aged woman who would provide the model for Flora Finching in his next novel, *Little Dorrit* (1857). He began writing the novel in spring 1855 and continued to work on it during a summer holiday at FOLKESTONE and an extended stay in Paris over the next winter. The first number appeared in December and sold nearly 40,000 copies by the end of the year. Probably the darkest of Dickens's great social novels, *Little Dorrit*'s controlling symbol is the prison, both physical prisons like the Marshalsea and mental prisons such as EVANGELICALISM, which confined the believer in a narrow and vindictive worldview.

After another summer in Boulogne, the Dickens family returned to London in September 1856, and Dickens began preparations to perform in Wilkie Collins's play THE FROZEN DEEP. The first performances in January were held at Tavistock House and included Dickens's daughters as part of the cast, but for the final performances in MANCHESTER in August, Dickens employed some professional

actresses, one of whom was ELLEN TERNAN. Restless, painfully aware of his premature aging, and unhappy in his marriage, Dickens was attracted to the young actress. In September he and Collins took a tour through the north of England, described in *The Lazy Tour of Two Idle Apprentices* (1857), which ended at Doncaster where Ellen was performing.

In spring 1858, Dickens's marital unhappiness reached a crisis. In March, he wrote in a letter to Wilkie Collins that "the domestic unhappiness remains so strong upon me that I can't write, and (waking) can't rest, one minute. I have never known a moment's peace or content, since the last night of The Frozen Deep." In May, he and Catherine agreed to separate. After financial and legal arrangements were worked out by Forster and LEMON, Catherine agreed to move to a separate residence with her son Charley. In June, upset by rumors circulating about his relations with Georgina Hogarth and Ellen Ternan, Dickens, against the advice of his friends and publishers, published a defense of his conduct in *Household Words.* Angered by what he perceived as their lack of support, Dickens turned away from some of his old friends and, over the next few years, surrounded himself with a circle of admiring young men, among them Collins, EDMUND YATES, PERCY FITZGERALD, MARCUS STONE, and CHARLES FECHTER. Because his publishers, Bradbury & Evans, refused to publish his statement in PUNCH, he resigned the editorship of *Household Words* and planned a new magazine with Chapman & Hall. His resentment continued; three years later, he refused to attend the wedding of his son Charley to FREDERICK MULLET EVANS's daughter Bessie. The controversy also led to differences with WILLIAM MAKEPEACE THACKERAY, which erupted in a bitter quarrel between the two novelists over the membership of Edmund Yates in the Garrick Club. The two novelists were not reconciled until 1863, shortly before Thackeray's death.

In the midst of all this turmoil, Dickens began giving public readings from his works as a source of income. After some readings in London in April and May 1858, he undertook an extensive provincial reading tour of 87 performances in the summer

Gad's Hill Place

and fall, reestablishing the relationship with his audience that had been tested by the turmoil in his all-too-public personal life. The new magazine, named ALL THE YEAR ROUND, began publication in April 1859, running weekly installments of *A Tale of Two Cities* (1859). A novel of action rather than character, *Two Cities* translated the turmoil of the French Revolution and the Reign of Terror into a personal mythology. Its divided hero is both domestic exemplar (Darnay) and urban idler (Carton), and in the violence of the revolution the wastrel's sacrifice enables the husband's domestic felicity. When the novel ended late in the year, Dickens began publishing a series of essays in the magazine that would be collected into *The Uncommercial Traveller* (1860) later in the year. He asked other novelists to contribute serial fiction to the new magazine, among them Collins, ELIZABETH GASKELL, CHARLES READE, and GEORGE ELIOT, and in the summer of 1860 he moved his household from Tavistock House in London to take up permanent residence at GAD'S HILL PLACE, a mansion outside Rochester that he had dreamed of owning as a boy.

Dickens concentrated on *All the Year Round* and his public readings. When the magazine's circulation declined during the publication of CHARLES LEVER's *A Day's Ride,* he undertook to restore its audience by replacing Lever's novel with *Great*

Expectations (1861), a story he had originally considered for publication in monthly parts. However, the constraints of the weekly form suited the story, for the resulting novel is probably his most aesthetically satisfying one. Its tight structure, balanced form, and economical presentation contribute to a BILDUNGSROMAN that tells Dickens's own inner autobiography through Pip's first-person narrative. He did a second series of readings in London during the spring of 1861, a second provincial tour later in the year, and another series in London the next spring. Meanwhile, his old friends and associates were dying. ARTHUR SMITH died in 1861 a few days before HENRY AUSTIN, and in 1863–64 Egg, Thackeray, JOHN LEECH, both Dickens's and Catherine's mothers, and their son Walter died within a few months of one another. Georgina suffered a severe illness in 1862, and Dickens himself had pain and lameness in his left foot. His relationship with Ellen Ternan was in the background throughout this period, hinted at occasionally in letters, in unexplained absences from London, and in visits to France. Returning from one of these journeys

Dickens in 1861.

in June 1865, he and Ellen were involved in the STAPLEHURST RAILWAY ACCIDENT. Although they were not injured in the incident, which killed 10 and injured 50 people, Dickens was emotionally shaken by the accident and his experience of caring for the injured and dying.

In mid-1864 Dickens began his last long 20-part novel, *Our Mutual Friend* (1865). A panoramic survey of the condition of England in 1865, the novel reached from the upper levels of society down to the depths, describing relations within society in Darwinian terms as those between predators and prey. After completing the novel and another volume of *Uncommercial Traveller* essays late in 1865, he planned another tour of 50 readings for spring 1866 and toyed with the possibility of giving readings abroad, in Australia or the United States. Although a lingering cold, exhaustion, and sleeplessness plagued him and after the tour he was so drained that he was unable to walk, the promises of huge profits induced him to schedule an American tour. He arrived in Boston in mid-November 1867 and for the next five months, during a severe winter while he harbored a persistent cold, he gave readings up and down the East Coast. Although he made a net profit of about £19,000, the journey left him homesick and exhausted. After six months back in England, however, he undertook another series of readings there. Early in 1869, he introduced into his repertory a new reading, "Sikes and Nancy." A rendering of Nancy's murder and the pursuit of Sikes from *Oliver Twist*, it excited and taxed both the audience and Dickens, and he insisted on performing it despite his physician's advice to the contrary. In April, tired and suffering paralysis on the left side, he was forced to cancel his remaining engagements and return to London.

In spite of failing health, Dickens planned a new series of readings for 1870 and began work on a new novel, *The Mystery of Edwin Drood* (1870). He began his final series of readings in mid-January and on March 15 gave his final performance, a reading of *Carol* and the trial from *Pickwick*. The first installment of the new novel, a story about the disappearance and probable murder of its titular hero, appeared at the beginning of April. On June 9, 1870, after spending the afternoon at work on the novel, he suffered a stroke and died that evening. He was buried in WESTMINSTER ABBEY on June 14.

Forster was Dickens's first biographer. His *Life of Charles Dickens* (1872–74), based on his intimate relationship with Dickens and on the novelist's many letters to him and others, is by far the best account from those who knew Dickens. Forster suppressed what he knew of Dickens's relationship with Ellen Ternan, and his dislike of some of the young men who surrounded Dickens in the 1860s colors his biography, but overall it is a remarkably objective and comprehensive account. The most useful edition of Forster's book is that edited and annotated by J. W. T. LEY (1928). Dickens's active and multifaceted life has also inspired massive biographies. EDGAR JOHNSON's *Charles Dickens: His Tragedy and Triumph* (1952), a detailed and thoroughly annotated version of Dickens's life, remains a valuable scholarly resource. The revisions in Johnson's account necessitated by more recent scholarship are made in FRED KAPLAN's *Dickens, A Biography* (1988), a more contemporary and psychological portrait, and in PETER ACKROYD's lengthy, imaginative, and readable *Dickens* (1990). Among shorter biographies, those by Hibbert (1967), Ackroyd (2002), and Smiley (2002) are especially readable and accessible.

PART II

Works A–Z

MAJOR WORKS

Barnaby Rudge: A Tale of the Riots of Eighty

Dickens's fifth novel, published as a weekly serial in *Master Humphrey's Clock* from February to November 1841, illustrated by BROWNE and CATTERMOLE; issued concurrently in monthly parts; issued in a single volume, 1841. A historical story based on the GORDON RIOTS of 1780, *Rudge* was the first novel Dickens planned to write. He contracted for the story to be published in three volumes in 1836 but then put it aside as *Pickwick* became a popular best seller. He returned to it in 1839 and wrote the first three chapters, but put it down again until 1841 when he completed the novel as a weekly serial. Commentators have considered *Rudge* to be two novels awkwardly put together: a GOTHIC NOVEL about the murder of Reuben Haredale and a HISTORICAL NOVEL about the Gordon Riots, also called the No Popery Riots, of 1780. Although the connections between the two are sometimes strained, Dickens develops similar themes in the two stories, suggesting that the social order reflects the domestic world, where troubled relationships between fathers and sons produce violence and rebellion.

SYNOPSIS

Part I (February 13, 1841)

(1) On the stormy evening of March 19, 1775, a stranger stops at the Maypole Inn near CHIGWELL north of London and asks about the Haredale family, owners of The Warren, a country estate nearby. He learns that the current residents are Sir Geoffrey Haredale, a Catholic landowner, and his niece Emma, the daughter of Reuben Haredale, who was murdered exactly 22 years before, on March 19, 1753. Both the gardener at the Warren and the steward, Barnaby Rudge, disappeared after the crime, so they were the primary suspects in the crime. When a body thought to be that of Rudge was found at the bottom of a well, the gardener was assumed to be the murderer.

Part 2 (February 20, 1841)

(2) On the road to London, Gabriel Varden, a gentle locksmith, is accosted by the stranger from the Maypole, who threatens Varden after his horse collides with Varden's carriage (3). When Varden gets to London, he meets the son of Rudge, young Barnaby, a mentally defective young man, born on the day after the murder. Barnaby is standing over the body of a man who has been robbed, wounded, and left by the road.

Part 3 (February 27, 1841)

(4) Varden takes the wounded man, Edward Chester, to the house of Barnaby's mother, the widow Rudge. (5) The next evening, while Varden is checking on the patient, Mrs. Rudge is called away and frightened by the stranger who threatened the locksmith on the road, but she prevents Gabriel from detaining the man.

Part 4 (March 6, 1841)

(6) Chester tells Varden that his attacker was the stranger from the Maypole.

(7) When Varden returns to his home, the Golden Key, he finds his household in as much disarray as the life in the streets. His temperamental wife, Martha, accuses him of neglecting her.

Part 5 (March 13, 1841)

(8) Varden's apprentice, Simon Tappertit, sneaks out of the house at night to attend a secret meeting of the 'Prentice Knights, a society of disgruntled apprentices who plan to overthrow their masters. (9) When he returns from the meeting, Simon cannot get back into the house because Miggs, Mrs. Varden's maid, has blocked the keyhole so that he cannot get in without her help.

Part 6 (March 20, 1841)

(10) Edward Chester's father, Sir John Chester, engages young Barnaby to carry a message to Geoffrey Haredale asking for a meeting. (11) The regulars at the Maypole speculate that when the two old rivals meet, there will be a fight.

Part 7 (March 27, 1841)

(12) At the meeting, Haredale is irascible and short-tempered, Chester distant and cool, refusing to be ruffled by Haredale's rudeness. Although they dislike each other, they agree that they have a common interest to prevent a match between Edward and Emma. Chester wants his son to marry a wealthy heiress; Haredale wants Emma to marry a Catholic.

Part 8 (April 3, 1841)

(13) On March 25, Joe Willet, son of the Maypole's innkeeper, goes to London to pay the Maypole's annual vintner's bill. He stops at the Vardens' house, hoping to see Dolly, Gabriel's pretty daughter, but Dolly speaks to him only in passing and Mrs. Varden appropriates the bouquet he brought for her daughter. (14) On his way home, Joe meets Edward Chester on the road. They stop by the Warren, but Edward's assignation with Emma there is interrupted by Haredale, who forbids him to see the girl again. When Edward learns that his father has been conferring with Haredale, he returns to the city.

Part 9 (April 10, 1841)

(15) The next day, Edward goes to his father's rooms in the TEMPLE. His father, wishing to live in the luxurious style to which he is accustomed, wants Edward to marry a rich woman in order to replenish the family fortune. Sir John objects to Emma because she is poor, a Catholic, and the daughter of a murdered man.

(16) That evening the widow Rudge is again shadowed by the mysterious and secretive stranger.

Part 10 (April 17, 1841)

(17) The stranger follows the widow home. She recognizes him as her husband, the elder Barnaby Rudge, and shrinks from him, but he warns her against turning him in, and, describing himself as "a spirit, a ghost upon the earth, a thing from which all creatures shrink," he tells her that he will not be taken alive. He hides in a closet when his son returns home and secretly watches the boy with his mother. (18) After Barnaby falls asleep, he leaves and wanders in the streets until dawn.

Part 11 (April 24, 1841)

(19) Edward asks Dolly Varden to take a letter to Emma at the Warren. (20) Dolly delivers the letter, and as she is leaving with Emma's reply, Haredale stops her and offers her a position as Emma's companion.

Part 12 (May 1, 1841)

(21) On her way back to the Maypole, Dolly is assaulted by Hugh, the Maypole's ostler, who comes out of the woods, holds her in his arms, and threatens her. Joe Willet finds her there, upset and

crying; she realizes that she doesn't have the letter or the bracelet that Emma entrusted to her. (22) Joe accompanies her partway back to London.

Part 13 (May 8, 1841)

(23) Hugh takes Emma's letter to Sir John Chester, who chastises him for also stealing the bracelet. (24) Then Simon Tappertit, who is secretly in love with Dolly and jealous of Joe Willet's attentions to her, visits Chester, urging him to stop Dolly from acting as a messenger between Edward and Emma and to "put Joseph Willet down, sir. Destroy him. Crush him."

Part 14 (May 15, 1841)

(25) Fearful of her husband and his power over her, Mrs. Rudge returns to the Warren for the first time in 22 years. She tells Haredale that she can no longer accept an annuity from him because she can no longer control where the money goes. She says that she plans to leave the house in London that he provides for her and to resettle in a secret location. (26) When Haredale asks Gabriel what Mrs. Rudge's motives might be, Varden tells of meeting the stranger at her house. The two men go to the house, but she has left it and Sir John Chester is there instead.

Part 15 (May 22, 1841)

(27) Sir John Chester flatters Mrs. Varden and enlists her help in breaking the engagement between his son and Emma. (28) When Hugh brings him another letter that he has taken from Dolly, Chester warns him to give no public indications of their connection.

Part 16 (May 29, 1841)

(29) At the Warren, Sir John Chester accosts Emma as she walks in the garden. He lies to her, telling her that his son plans to plead poverty and break off their relationship and that he opposes his son's scheme and has tried to dissuade him. Haredale interrupts this conversation and is outraged by Chester's hypocrisy.

(30) When Joe Willet is "put on parole" by his father and not allowed to leave the Maypole, Joe decides that he must leave home.

Part 17 (June 5, 1841)

(31) He calls on Dolly, but she treats him coquettishly and does not admit her love for him, so he

joins the army. (32) The same day Edward defies his father and is disowned.

Part 18 (June 12, 1841)

(33) Five years later, on the stormy night of March 19, 1780, a frightened Solomon Daisy, one of the regulars at the Maypole, tells his drinking companions of hearing a voice in the church and seeing a ghost in the churchyard. (34) Taking Hugh as his guide, John Willet goes to the Warren to tell Haredale what Daisy has seen. Haredale thanks him but seems distracted and distraught.

Part 19 (June 19, 1841)

(35) On their way back to the Maypole, Willet and Hugh meet Lord George Gordon, leader of the No Popery movement. He is on his way to London with Gashford, his opportunistic secretary, and John Grueby, one of his aides. They stop for the night at the Maypole. (36) Before going to bed, Gordon and Gashford discuss their anti-Catholic movement, now 40,000 strong, and mention Sim Tappertit, Mrs. Varden, and Miggs among their London followers.

Part 20 (June 26, 1841)

(37) Gordon and his party are welcomed in London by their supporters. Gashford swears Dennis the hangman into the cause as a future leader. (38) Hugh also joins the movement and becomes a member of Dennis's brigade.

Part 21 (July 3, 1841)

(39) At the Boot Tavern, London headquarters for the No Popery movement, Hugh meets Simon Tappertit, who makes him a member of the United Bulldogs, the latest incarnation of the 'Prentice Knights, one of the groups that has sworn allegiance to the Protestant cause. (40) Leaving the Boot in the middle of the night, Hugh reports back to Sir John Chester, telling him that he has joined the movement and met Dennis. After Hugh leaves, Chester ruminates on how Hugh can serve his ends and bring retribution on Haredale.

Part 22 (July 10, 1841)

(41) Gabriel Varden prepares to take part in the parade of the Royal East London Volunteers. His wife wishes that he would support the No Popery cause, but she is impressed by his uniform nonetheless. (42) When Gabriel returns from the parade, Haredale is waiting for him. He tells Varden of his fruitless search for Mrs. Rudge and Barnaby, missing now for five years. He is staying secretly at their former house in London.

Part 23 (July 17, 1841)

(43) A pistol beside him, Haredale keeps a nightly vigil in Mrs. Rudge's house. One day on his way there from Vauxhall, he meets Gashford, Lord George Gordon, and Sir John Chester in a crowd of Protestants at Westminster Hall. Chester provokes Haredale into expressing his support for the Catholic position and his detestation of Gashford as a snivelling, unscrupulous toady. (44) Gashford tells Hugh and Dennis that any destruction they bring on Haredale's house will be approved.

Part 24 (July 24, 1841)

(45) Stagg, the blind associate of the elder Barnaby Rudge, comes to the village where Mrs. Rudge and Barnaby have lived in secret poverty for five years. He tells the widow that he is allied with the man from whom she fled, and he demands £20. (46) She offers all her savings, but he says that £7 is insufficient. She promises more money in a week. That evening she tells Barnaby that they must disappear into the crowds in London.

Part 25 (July 31, 1841)

(47) Mrs. Rudge and Barnaby make their way to London, getting occasional bits of change by having Grip, Barnaby's pet raven, perform along the way. On June 2, 1780, they arrive in the city. (48) It is the day when Lord George Gordon and his followers have gathered to present their petition to Parliament. As they sit by Westminster Bridge, Barnaby is given the blue cockade of the protestors and is recruited into the movement by Gordon himself. At St. George's Fields, Barnaby meets Hugh and joins his regiment. Banned from the field, Mrs. Rudge loses sight of her son.

Part 26 (August 7, 1841)

(49) The contingents of protestors make their way in four divisions to the House of Commons. Barnaby, bearing the flag of the movement, goes with Hugh and Dennis at the head of one of the

divisions. As they are about to storm their way into the chamber, word comes that soldiers are gathering outside. Barnaby and Hugh confront the Horse Guards. With his flagstaff Barnaby knocks one of the guards from his horse. (50) Later that evening, Gashford tells them that the cause has failed in Parliament by a vote of 192 to 6, and that Barnaby and Hugh are being sought for their attack on the guards. Hugh leads Barnaby and Dennis into the streets, where they join in looting Catholic churches.

Part 27 (August 14, 1841)

(51) Drunk and exhilarated, Sim returns from the riots and gives up his position as Varden's apprentice. Gabriel tries unsuccessfully to detain him. (52) The next morning, Hugh, Dennis, and Sim plan the attack on the Warren. They do not include Barnaby, for fear that he will protect the Haredales. When they go out that evening to raid Catholic houses and churches looking for relics, altar furnishings, and household items to burn, Gashford asks them with annoyance, "Can you burn nothing whole?"

Part 28 (August 21, 1841)

(53) The next day Gashford urges the attack on Haredale's house and counsels "no mercy, no quarter, no two beams of the house to be left standing." Leaving Barnaby on watch at the Boot, Hugh, Dennis, and Sim lead a band of rioters off to Chigwell. Gashford sits on the roof of his house watching for a fiery glow in the night sky to the north. (54) The rioters arrive at the Maypole. They take food and drink and then ransack and vandalize the building. Dennis wants to hang John Willet, but Hugh prevents him. They bind the innkeeper to a chair before setting off for the Warren.

Part 29 (August 28, 1841)

(55) As John Willet sits tied in the chair, the stranger, not recognized as the elder Rudge, enters the inn, takes some food, and inquires about the rioters. He and Willet see a glow in the sky and hear the sounds of the rioting as the mob breaks into the Warren, loots it, and burns it to the ground.

(56) Meanwhile Solomon Daisy and two companions are on their way into London when they meet Mr. Haredale on horseback headed toward his home. Taking Solomon with him, he stops at the Maypole and finds Willet dazed and incoherent, claiming he has seen a ghost. When they get to the Warren, the house is an empty ruin. Everyone seems to be gone, but Haredale discovers the stranger hiding in the tower. Haredale attacks him, names him Barnaby Rudge, accuses him of Reuben Haredale's murder, and takes him captive.

Part 30 (September 4, 1841)

(57) Meanwhile, Barnaby stands watch at the Boot as Lord Gordon and his aide, John Grueby, pass by. Gordon praises him as a hero, but Grueby advises him to hide and warns him that he will be hanged. Barnaby stays at his post until the soldiers arrest him. (58) In spite of his pleas, the soldiers—among them a one-armed man—refuse to give him Grip, his pet raven. But when he is taken in irons to a cell in NEWGATE PRISON, Grip is there.

Part 31 (September 11, 1841)

(59) During the burning of the Warren, Hugh and Dennis have captured Emma and Dolly, taking them to a hideout on the outskirts of London. Sim Tappertit reveals his amorous designs on Dolly, and there is talk of Gashford's similar interest in Emma. (60) When Hugh and Dennis return to the Boot, they are warned that soldiers have occupied it, so they go instead to FLEET MARKET. There a one-armed man, injured and bandaged around his head, tells them that Barnaby has been arrested and taken to Newgate. The rioters plan to attack the prisons and release the prisoners.

Part 32 (September 18, 1841)

(61) Mr. Haredale takes the murderer Rudge into London. He goes to the MANSION HOUSE, but the LORD MAYOR, fearful of the rioters, refuses to hear Haredale's case for having Rudge imprisoned. Magistrate SIR JOHN FIELDING does listen and commits the captive to Newgate. (62) There, in the prison yard, the elder Barnaby meets his son and reveals his identity to him.

Part 33 (September 25, 1841)

(63) The weak Lord Mayor declines to take decisive action against the rioters, and the mob controls the city. That evening the rioters gather to

storm Newgate. On the way they stop to enlist Gabriel Varden to force the locks on the prison gates, but he valiantly refuses to go with the rioters. Miggs, however, helps them gain entry to the house. They capture Varden and his tools and head for the prison. (64) When Gabriel refuses to force the lock, the mob threatens to kill him, but a one-armed man and his accomplice break through the crowd and spirit Gabriel away. Then the rioters set fire to the prison door; slowly it burns away and they gain entry to the prison.

Part 34 (October 2, 1841)

(65) Rudge cowers in a corner of his cell, fearing that the mob will wreak vengeance on him. But they free him along with his son and the other prisoners. Dennis, looking forward to future hangings, tries to prevent the release of four prisoners on death row, but Hugh insists and they too are freed.

(66) Haredale has been searching unsuccessfully for his niece. Tired and dazed from exertion and lack of sleep, he goes to Newgate when he hears of the attack on the prison, but he is too exhausted to prevent Rudge's release. Langdale, a compassionate distiller, takes him to his house and cares for him. Grueby, who has left Gordon and become a servant to Langdale, brings back news of the rioters as they sack and burn the houses of Lord Mansfield and the city magistrates.

Part 35 (October 9, 1841)

(67) The next day there are soldiers in the streets, but the rioters are undeterred. During the day they issue threats; at night they set fires. They attack Langdale's house. Disguised as rioters, Edward Chester and a one-armed Joe Willet rescue Haredale and Langdale as the rioters break into the house.

(68) Meanwhile, freed from Newgate, Barnaby and his father hide in an empty shed in Finchley. Rudge sends his son in search of Stagg, but Barnaby is unable to find the blind man. Drawn by the crowd to the riot at Langdale's house, Barnaby sees Hugh knocked from his horse and wounded, and he takes him back to Finchley.

Part 36 (October 16, 1841)

(69) Before they can escape to the country, however, Dennis, who has turned traitor, turns them over to the soldiers, who arrest Rudge, Barnaby, and Hugh and shoot Stagg as he tries to run away. (70) Then Dennis gets Miggs to aid in Gashford's plan to kidnap Emma and Dolly to the continent.

Part 36 (October 23, 1841)

(71) This scheme is thwarted by Haredale, the Vardens, Joe Willet, and Edward Chester, who rescue Emma and Dolly and arrest the miscreants. (72) Joe is reunited with his father, who has difficulty believing his son has lost an arm. Dolly, changed by her experience, realizes how coquettish she has been. Joe tells her of his idle dream of returning rich to marry her.

Part 37 (October 30, 1841)

(73) By Friday of the week of riots, order has been restored. Recovered from her illness, Mrs. Rudge visits Barnaby in prison and urges him to say nothing about his relationship to his father. She urges the elder Rudge to confess his crime, but he refuses, cursing her and their son. Lord George Gordon is imprisoned in the TOWER OF LONDON for high treason.

(74) Dennis, taken prisoner on the testimony of Gabriel Varden, is locked up in the same cell with Hugh. He fears Hugh's retribution, but Hugh simply wants to live as comfortably as he can until he and Dennis are hanged.

Part 38 (November 6, 1841)

(75) A month later Gabriel Varden has learned that Hugh, who is to hang the next day, is the illegitimate son of Sir John Chester by a gypsy woman who was hanged at Tyburn. He pleads unsuccessfully with Chester to acknowledge his son. (76) At Newgate the prisoners await their execution: Barnaby waits with his mother; Dennis cowers desperately hoping for a last-minute reprieve; Hugh remains exultantly defiant.

Part 39 (November 13, 1841)

(77) On the day of execution, Hugh remains defiant and takes the blame for luring Barnaby into the riots. Barnaby faces death bravely. Dennis remains fearful and cowardly.

(78) Joe tells his father that he plans to go to the West Indies to work there with Edward Chester, but Dolly interrupts the conversation and admits that she loves Joe; the two are reunited.

Part 40 (November 20, 1841)

(79) At the time of the executions, Gabriel Varden's friends gather at the Golden Key, Gabriel's restored house and shop. The distraught Mrs. Rudge is also there. Mr. Haredale asks his niece's forgiveness and blesses her union with Edward Chester. He plans to enter a monastery on the continent. Then Gabriel returns home, bringing Barnaby with him. He and Haredale have secured a last-minute pardon for the boy. Barnaby is restored to his mother. (80) Later, while the Vardens celebrate the reunion of Joe and Dolly, Miggs returns to claim her old place as Mrs. Varden's maid, but they send her away again.

Part 41 (November 27, 1841)

(81) At the end of August, Haredale makes a final visit to the ruins of the Warren. There he meets Sir John Chester and accuses him of engineering the destruction of his house and family. The two duel, and Chester is killed. (82) Haredale escapes to the continent. Sir George Gordon is found not guilty of high treason, but he continues in his fanaticism, finally converting to Judaism. Convicted of libel, he dies in prison. Gashford becomes a government informer, Tappertit a shoeblack, Miggs a prison turnkey. Joe and Dolly Willet restore the Maypole. Barnaby and his mother reside happily on the Maypole farm.

COMMENTARY

It was probably inevitable that Dickens, when planning his first novel in 1836, would choose a historical subject. SIR WALTER SCOTT, who had died only four years earlier, was still the defining novelist in Britain; his influence dominated the 1830s, leading such popular novelists of the period as EDWARD BULWER LYTTON and WILLIAM HARRISON AINSWORTH to specialize in historical romances.

Dickens's choice of the Gordon Riots for his subject may acknowledge a particular indebtedness to Scott. Dickens apparently thought of the Gordon Riots in his novel as similar to the Porteous Riots in Scott's *Heart of Mid-Lothian* (1819), as they brought together historical forces larger than the individual participants. The central figure in Dickens's novel, a fool like Scott's Madge Wildfire, could symbolize the inability of the individual to

control or even understand the historical situation in which he was embroiled. Dickens conceived the idea for the novel in 1836, only 56 years after the events he proposed to relate; there were people still alive who could remember the happenings and give personal accounts of them. In his Scottish history novels, Scott also chose events that were close enough in time to engage this living memory. By doing so, Scott was able to make history relevant to the present concerns of his readers.

Contemporary relevance was particularly important to Dickens, for, as JOHN BUTT and KATHLEEN TILLOTSON (1957) point out, he wanted to link the Gordon Riots with the Chartist agitations and the religious intolerance of his own time. Reactions to the NEW POOR LAW in the late 1830s had prompted petitions to Parliament and mass demonstrations, particularly in the north of England. By 1838 this anti–POOR LAW movement had coalesced into CHARTISM, a working-class movement determined by mass action to force such democratic reforms as universal male suffrage and the secret ballot. One wing of the movement, the "physical force Chartists" led by Fergus O'Connor, advocated violent rebellion as the only means to achieve their ends, and several mass meetings in 1838 and 1839 erupted into violent confrontations between demonstrators and civil authorities.

Religious differences were also becoming more heated in 1839, when the newly founded Protestant Association used mass meetings and petitions to Parliament to oppose legislation that would liberalize restrictions on Catholics. Their organizational tactics and violent rhetoric recalled Gordon's Association of 1779–80. *Barnaby Rudge*—or, as it was originally titled, *Gabriel Varden, the Locksmith of London*—would be a warning of the dangers of religious intolerance and of mob action emerging from mass political movements. Dickens wanted his novel to address the current condition of England by presenting its analogue in the past.

Much of Barnaby's story is clichéd gothic melodrama: He is shadowed by a mysterious stranger who will turn out to be his father and whose crime, committed on the day his son was born, has left the boy a symbolically wounded mental defective. Maimed by his father's crime and abandonment and forced into secretive isolation with his mother, Barnaby acts from instinct rather than reason. He makes Hugh his hero and gets caught up in the public frenzy. Young Barnaby is one of several sons in the novel whose father bears responsibility for his role in the riots.

Maypole Hugh, another son abandoned and denied by his father, leads one of the rebellious battalions. The natural (i.e., illegitimate) son of Sir John Chester by a gypsy woman, Hugh has never known his father and has been abandoned to wildness. An ostler, he lives with animals in the stable and is himself illiterate, savage, and sexually aggressive. Ironically, the father who denies him is as highly civilized as Hugh is wild. Effete, unnaturally restrained and controlled, Chester coolly manipulates others for his own selfish ends.

Chester's other son, Edward, suffers not from neglect but from restraint. His father refuses to sanction his marriage to Emma Haredale, demanding instead that he "must marry well and make the most of [him]self" (15) so that he can enable his father, who has squandered his own inheritance, to live luxuriously. "Every man has a right to live in the best way he can, or he is an unnatural scoundrel" (15), the parasitic father tells his son. So Edward, if he is to recoup his father's losses, must marry against his desire. He escapes this excessive and cynical demand by running off to the West Indies.

Similarly, Joe Willet's father denies his son the chance to choose his own life by treating him as a boy who will never grow up. Old John refuses to give Joe a responsible role at the Maypole Inn, and he does not take Joe's interest in Dolly Varden seriously. Like Sir John Chester, who imposes on Edward to maintain the comforts of his past, so John Willet refuses to allow Joe to grow up in order to maintain the Maypole as an unchanging representative of an idyllic past. The nostalgic picture of the inn that opens the novel suggests the fantasy of "old England" that governs Willet's consciousness. The old house, with "its floors sunken and uneven, its ceilings blackened by the hand of time" and its regular customers who retell its legends, is a reminder of the past, "hale and hearty though, still" (1). Still, but not unchanging, for the storm that

opens the novel presages the storms to come, and the stranger in the Maypole represents the murder of Reuben Haredale, one of several unresolved issues from the past that will lead to the riots and the destruction of the Maypole and the Warren. Like Edward, unnaturally restrained by his father, Joe runs off to the army.

The last of the father-son relationships in the novel leads more directly to the riots. Although Gabriel Varden and Sim Tappertit are not biologically related, their relationship as master and apprentice repeats the issues of freedom and restraint in the other father-son pairs. When we first see Varden in the novel, he is counseling John Willet to treat his son as an adult and not encourage an "ill-timed rebellion" (3). Although Varden treats his apprentice with understanding and forebearance, Tappertit is nonetheless rebellious and unreasonably characterizes Gabriel as one of the "Tyrant Masters (of whose grievous and insupportable oppression, no 'prentice could entertain a moment's doubt)" (8).

Tappertit's disaffection stems from political and personal causes. The secret society of 'Prentice Knights, who have organized to restore "their ancient rights and holidays" (8), encourages him to entertain an idyllic fantasy of the past, similar to the Maypole fantasy, when apprentices were free from restraining masters. But Sim, "little more than five feet high, and thoroughly convinced in his own mind that he was above the middle size" (4), also has a Napoleon complex. He thinks that Varden does not recognize his talents and that Dolly does not acknowledge his physical attractiveness, and the 'Prentice Knights convince him that in the past things would have been different. Sim differs from Edward and Joe in that he, not Gabriel, harbors the fantasy of the past and of himself as victim of arbitrary oppression.

Gabriel is, in fact, the representative of reason and moderation in the novel. While he frequently joins the Maypole community, he does not live in the past. His house is in the center of London and is central to the issues raised by the novel, for as a locksmith, Varden is a technician of restraint. Appropriately, he is a member of the citizen's militia that keeps order in the city, and, at the climax of the novel, he refuses to unlock the gates of Newgate Prison, even under the threat of losing his life. He remains true to his commitment to social order. Thus Varden becomes the primary link between the father-son motif in the first half of the novel and the story of the riots in the second half. His household is a microcosm of the larger social issues: Mrs. Varden and Miggs are fanatical Protestants who sympathize with Gordon and the rioters; Tappertit, a disgruntled "son," is "oppressed" and denied sexual fulfillment by his constraining father/master; Dolly, Varden's "madcap" daughter, softens the harshness of his wife but disturbs the order in the household by attracting Sim's adoration and raising Miggs's jealousy.

Dolly is a key figure in the sexual drama. The object of attentions from Joe Willet, Sim Tappertit, and Hugh, her coquetry increases Joe's frustrations and prompts him to join the army, and her rejection of Sim reinforces his resentment against Gabriel. Dolly also acts as a go-between for Edward and Emma and is sexually attacked and later kidnapped by Hugh. Her presence reveals the sexual energies of the sons that would break the restraints of the fathers and challenge the hegemony of the old order.

These family and sexual issues have seemed to some readers far removed from the political and religious forces that culminate in the riots. *Rudge* seems to be two novels, the first a gothic, domestic romance and the second a historical novel about the riots. If the devices that Dickens uses to connect the two stories are sometimes mechanical or clumsy, they are nonetheless thought out. Dickens believed that the public life is grounded in the private life, the family a microcosm of the larger society. By grounding the riots in the private lives of the participants, he reveals the mixed motives and personal desires that complicate issues of state. At the same time, he knew that history was not always a rational process in which competing interests struggled for control. By making the central figures in the riots fools or madmen or self-serving manipulators, he shows the destruction that results when the irrational mob mirrors its leaders.

The second half of the novel pairs Lord George Gordon with Barnaby Rudge. A historical figure,

Gordon was viewed in his own time as mad, a fanatical Puritan, restless, "wild and ungovernable" (35). Goaded on by Gashford, his cynical, self-serving secretary, and by the adulation of his followers, Gordon does not control the demonstrations and loses sight of the issues that brought him to London. His leaders in the field, Hugh, Barnaby, Simon, and Dennis, exemplify the ungovernable forces he has unleashed. They have no ideological commitment to the Protestant cause. When Gordon leads the mob shouting, "No Popery," Hugh shouts, "No Property!" and Dennis, the renegade hangman, concludes with "Down with everybody, down with everything!" (38). The fury of the mob has no political end. It is simply nihilistic, primitive energy.

Dickens originally planned to use three escapees from Bedlam as leaders of the riot, a way of indicating the insanity of the mob. JOHN FORSTER discouraged that tack, so instead Dickens made the same point with Barnaby and Hugh, mad sons abandoned by their fathers, mentally defective and illiterate. Neither understands nor controls the mob he leads. Dennis the hangman is a somewhat different case, for, as a corrupt and renegade government functionary, he represents the power of the state run amok.

While the mob is a mad monster, the established authority is little better. The Lord Mayor, too frightened to take action to control the mob, in effect encourages the riots. The country magistrate who tries to buy Grip and threatens Barnaby and his mother is an unthinking oppressor (47). Only Varden represents a restrained middle course; he is neither weak nor an oppressor. The Golden Key and its owner are the true representatives of traditional England, but Varden's virtues are insufficient to save the Golden Key from attack during the riots, and his firm heroism cannot prevent the gates of the prison from being breached.

The destruction wrought by the riots purges some stains from the past. Old Rudge the murderer and Sir John Chester, the parasitic aristocrat, are both killed. But Geoffrey Haredale, who brings them both to justice, is vindicated only to retreat to a monastery on the continent, where he will soon die. Barnaby is rescued from the gallows, but he still hears the sounds of the past and remains a fool; Joe Willet, who has lost an arm freeing himself from his father's oppression, restores the Maypole. The toll may be best represented in the destruction of Lord Mansfield's house, especially his extensive law library, for when violence resolves the issues, the rule of law is itself one of the casualties.

CHARACTERS AND RELATED ENTRIES

Black Lion Inn   The inn in WHITECHAPEL freqented by John and Joe Willet (13, 71,72).

Bloomsbury Square   The site of Lord Chief Justice Mansfield's house, which is attacked and sacked by the Gordon rioters (66). Two of the rioters are later hanged here (77).

Boot Inn   The disreputable alehouse that is the headquarters for the Gordon rioters (38).

Bridewell   Workhouse and prison near Blackfriars where Miss Miggs becomes the turnkey.

Bulldogs, The United   The name taken by the 'Prentice Knights during the Gordon Riots (39).

Chester, Edward (Ned)   Son of John Chester, "a young man of about eight-and-twenty, . . . of a somewhat slight figure, gracefully and strongly made. . . . He was well and even richly attired, and without being over-dressed looked a gallant gentleman" (1). He is attacked on his way to London and found by Gabriel Varden and Barnaby lying in the road (3). Disowned by his father for his relationship with Emma Haredale, who is Catholic and lacks wealth, Edward goes off to the West Indies (32), returning at the time of the riots when he and Joe Willet save Geoffrey Haredale, Emma, and Dolly Varden from the vengeance of the mob (67, 71). He marries Emma and returns to the West Indies (79). Edward is one of several sons in the novel who suffer from tyrannical treatment by their fathers.

Chester, John (later Sir John)   A "smooth man of the world, . . . soft-spoken, delicately made, precise and elegant" (12). John Chester hides a ruthless cynicism, selfishness, and hypocrisy behind a mask of affability. The enemy of Geoffrey Haredale from their school days together, Chester seeks to prevent the marriage of his son to Haredale's niece and to force the boy to marry a rich heiress so as to restore the family fortunes, thus enabling his father to live in "luxury and idleness" (15). Using Hugh as his agent, he is also behind the destruction of The Warren (40, 56), though later he refuses to acknowledge Hugh as his illegitimate son by a gypsy woman and thereby perhaps save him from hanging (75). After the No Popery Riots he goes to the ruined Warren where he meets Haredale and is killed in the ensuing duel (81).

Dickens based Sir John Chester on the fourth Earl of Chesterfield (1694–1773), whose *Letters* (1774) to his natural son advised the boy on manners and morals, counseling him to adopt a surface affability while exploiting the weaknesses of others. This advice offended Dickens and many other earnest Victorians. Chester becomes the arch aristocratic villain in the novel, seeking only his own personal gratification while denying both of his sons. His participation in the riots stems from no larger motive than his own self-interest.

Cobb, Tom   General chandler and post-office keeper at CHIGWELL and a regular at the Maypole. When Cobb takes John Willet's side and taunts Joe, the younger Willet "pummeled him with all his might and main" (30).

Conway, General   Historical figure, soldier, and politician Henry Seymour Conway (1721–95). He stands up to the Gordon rioters and prevents their incursion into the House of Commons (49).

Daisy, Solomon   Parish clerk and bell-ringer at CHIGWELL, a regular at the Maypole Inn, who "had little round black shiny eyes like beads; moreover this little man wore at the knees of his rusty black breeches, and on his rusty black coat, and all down his long flapped waistcoat, little queer buttons like nothing except his eyes; . . . he seemed all eyes from head to foot" (1). Daisy tells the story of Reuben Haredale's murder (1), is startled by what he takes to be the ghost of Rudge in the church many years later (33), and accompanies Haredale when he returns to the Warren after its destruction (56).

Dennis, Edward   Public hangman who becomes one of the leaders of the GORDON RIOTS, "a squat, thickset personage, with a low, retreating forehead. . . . A dingy handkerchief twisted like a cord about his neck, left its great veins exposed to view, and they were swoln and starting, as though with gulping down strong passions, malice, and ill-will" (37). Dennis takes an unwholesome pride in his work and relishes the commissions that will be produced by the riots. Although he becomes an informer for the authorities (69), he is arrested and condemned (74), reduced to groveling cowardice by the sentence (77), and eventually hanged (79). Dennis is based on a historical figure who held the post of hangman from 1771 to 1786. He took part in the riots but was not executed.

Duke Street   Off Lincoln's Inn Fields. Location of the Sardinian Chapel destroyed by the Gordon rioters (50).

Fielding, Sir John   (1721–80) Blind half-brother of novelist HENRY FIELDING, who succeeded his brother as chief magistrate at BOW STREET POLICE COURT, where he presided from 1754 to 1780. In the novel he hears the committal of the elder Barnaby Rudge to NEWGATE PRISON (*Rudge,* 58). Dickens stretches historical truth with this incident; Fielding was on his deathbed by the time of the GORDON RIOTS.

Gashford   Lord George Gordon's ruthless and hypocritical secretary, "angularly made, high-shouldered, bony, and ungraceful. . . . His manner was smooth and humble, but very sly and slinking. He wore the aspect of a man who was always lying in wait for something" (35). A former Catholic who was a schoolmate to Geoffrey Haredale and John Chester, Gashford urges the rioters to extreme acts, such as the burning of the Warren (44). He tries to use the riots as a means of seducing Emma Haredale, but his scheme is foiled by Edward Chester and Joe Willet (71). After the riots he deserts Gordon, becomes a government spy, and eventually poisons himself (82).

Gashford's suicide seems to be based on that of Robert Watson, who claimed to have been Gordon's secretary shortly before he strangled himself in 1838. Like John Chester, Gashford is a self-serving hypocrite who has no belief in the Protestant cause.

Gilbert, Mark   Hosier's apprentice and member of the 'Prentice Knights, who, like Tappertit, is in love with his master's daughter. During the riots, he becomes one of Tappertit's lieutenants in the United Bulldogs (8, 39).

Gordon, Colonel   Historical figure, Lord Adam Gordon (1726?–1801), a member of Parliament who opposes his kinsman Lord George Gordon and, with General Conway, prevents the rioters from entering the Houses of Parliament (49).

Gordon, Lord George (1751–1793)   Youngest son of the Duke of Gordon, he was the fanatical leader of the Protestant Association during the No Popery Riots protesting the Catholic Relief Act in July 1780. After he gathered 60,000 supporters in a massive but unsuccessful petition of Parliament for repeal of the bill, mob violence broke out and in several days of rioting 450 people were killed or wounded. After the riots Gordon was arrested for high treason and acquitted. He converted to Judaism and eventually died in NEWGATE PRISON, where he was imprisoned for libel.

Dickens holds to the historical facts of Gordon's life in the novel, presenting Gordon as misguided and muddled rather than malevolent, a man "of a slender make, and sallow complexion, with an aquiline nose, and long hair of a reddish brown, . . . in a full suit of black, quite free of any ornament, and of the most precise and sober cut. The gravity of his dress, together with a certain lankness of cheek and stiffness of deportment, added nearly ten years to his age, but his figure was that of one not yet past thirty" (35). Unlike Sir John Chester, whose malevolence is unfeelingly brutal and self-serving, Gordon is a weak and deluded aristocrat. His character, as Kathryn Chittick (1990) points out, is "summarized rather than dramatized," and he is manipulated by Gash-

Browne's (Phiz's) depiction of Barnaby with his pet raven, Grip.

ford and his other subordinates and overshadowed in action by the power of the mob.

Green, Tom   Alias taken by Joe Willet in the army (58).

Green Lanes   The area in Marylebone that is the meeting place of the Gordon rioters (44).

Grip   Barnaby Rudge's pet raven: "he fluttered to the floor and went to Barnaby—not in a hop, or walk, or run, but in a pace like that of a very particular gentleman with exceedingly tight boots on, trying to walk over loose pebbles" (6).

In a later preface to the novel (1849), Dickens wrote that "the raven in the story is a compound of two great originals, of whom I have been, at different times, the proud possessor," and he told his illustrator, GEORGE CATTERMOLE, that "Barnaby being an idiot my notion is to have him always in company with a pet raven who is immeasurably more knowing than himself." Grip's repeated catch phrase, "I'm a devil!" calls up by contrast Barnaby's innocence and adds to the gothic atmosphere of the story.

Grueby, John   Lord George Gordon's loyal servant, "a square-built, strong-made, bull-necked fellow, of the true English breed, . . . one of those self-possessed, hard-headed, imperturbable fellows, who, if they are ever beaten at fisticuffs, or other kind of warfare, never know it, and go on coolly till they win" (35). He opposes the excesses of Gordon's fanatical followers and helps Haredale escape the wrath of the mob (43). Gordon dismisses him when he says that Barnaby's fanatical devotion to the Protestant cause is madness and implies that Gordon is similarly mad (57). During the riots, he becomes Langdale's servant and later returns to Gordon, tending him in NEWGATE PRISON.

Grueby is contrasted with the conniving Gashford. His devotion to and sympathy with Gordon soften the portrait of the fanatical leader.

Haredale, Emma   Daughter of Reuben Haredale who is raised by her uncle, Geoffrey Haredale, after her father's murder. "So fair . . . so delicately shaped" (20), she loves Edward Chester, but the relationship is opposed by both her uncle and John Chester, who overcome their differences to keep the young couple apart. Dolly Varden, Emma's companion and friend, acts as a go-between for the two lovers. During the riots, Emma and Dolly are captured, vulnerable to the sexual designs of Gashford and Sim Tappertit (59), but they are rescued by Edward Chester and Joe Willet (71). After the riots, Geoffrey blesses Emma's marriage to Edward, and the couple goes off to the West Indies.

Haredale, Geoffrey   Head of a landed Catholic family (*see* CATHOLIC CHURCH) whose country seat, the Warren, is near the Maypole Inn, "a burly square-built man, negligently dressed, rough and abrupt in manner, stern, and . . . forbidding in look and speech" (12). He is at the center of the gothic mystery story that opens the novel, suspected of murdering his brother Reuben. He devotes his life to proving his innocence and caring for Reuben's daughter Emma. When his old enemy, Sir John Chester, enlists his aid to prevent the marriage of Emma to Chester's son Edward, he reluctantly agrees (12), but Chester's excesses make him regret his decision. During the riots, Geoffrey proves his innocence and apprehends the elder Barnaby Rudge for Reuben's murder (56). After the riots, Geoffrey blesses his niece's marriage to Edward (79), duels with Sir John Chester and kills him (81), and retreats to a monastery on the continent, where he lives out his remaining years in penitence (82).

Dickens's sympathetic treatment of the Catholic squire has sometimes been taken as an indication of his tolerance for religious views differing from his own. JOHN R. REED (1995) qualifies this view: "Haredale himself is not a good man. He has lived in error and now, having served as the instrument of God, fate, and the implied author, he must suffer for his own violence."

Herbert, Henry, tenth Earl of Pembroke (1734– 94)   Historical figure who was a member of Parliament at the time of the riots. In the novel he protests Lord Gordon's presence in the chamber wearing the blue cockade of the rioters (73).

Hugh   Wild young ostler at the Maypole Inn who becomes a leader of the Gordon rioters, "a young man, of a hale athletic figure, and a giant's strength, whose sunburnt face and swarthy throat, overgrown with jet black hair, might have served a painter for a model. . . . The negligence and disorder of the whole man, with something fierce and sullen in his features, gave him a picturesque appearance" (11). Hugh acts as an agent for Sir John Chester, stealing Emma Haredale's letters to Edward Chester for him (21, 28). He harbors sexual designs on Dolly Varden, accosting her in the country (21) and later capturing her during the riots (59). Recruited to the No Popery cause by Gashford (38), Hugh leads the rioters in several actions, but he protects Barnaby and takes the blame for leading him into the riots (77). Although Varden discovers that Hugh is the illegitimate son of Sir John Chester and a gypsy woman, Chester refuses to do anything to acknowledge his son or save him from execution (75).

Although Hugh is the Caliban of the story, a misanthropic and untutored natural creature, "more brute than man," he speaks with uncharacteristic eloquence just before his execution (77). GEOFFREY THURLEY (1976) sees Hugh as representative of the proletarian younger generation when contrasted with old John Willet: "If we see in the relationship between old John and Hugh a paradigm of the social structure—the landlord being to the established property-owning class what Hugh is to the (potentially lawless) working class—we observe once again the equation between energy, virility, and lawlessness that obtains throughout the early Dickens."

Jones, Mary   A 19-year-old woman executed in 1771 for shoplifting a piece of cloth. She left behind a husband and two children (37). Dickens uses this historical case to illustrate the harshness of the law and the numerous capital crimes in effect in the 18th century.

Langdale   Based on a historical figure, Thomas Langdale (1714–90), "a very hearty old fellow and a worthy man" (66), this kindly vintner and distiller supplies the Maypole Inn with spirits (13). During the riots, he gives the exhausted Haredale a place to sleep and shelters him from the mob. His house is attacked and burned by the rioters, and he and Haredale escape through the wine cellar (61, 66–68).

Maypole Inn   Inn near Chigwell maintained by John Willet: "an old building, with more gable ends than a lazy man would care to count on a sunny day; huge zig-zag chimneys out of which it seemed as though even smoke could not choose but come in more than naturally fantastic shapes" (1). It is sacked during the Gordon Riots (54). Joe and Dolly Willet restore the inn after the riots (82). The King's Head at Chigwell was the model for the Maypole.

Miggs, Miss   The Vardens' maid, "a tall young lady, . . . slender and shrewish, of a rather uncomfortable figure, and though not absolutely ill-looking, of a sharp and acid visage. As a general principle and abstract proposition, Miggs held the male sex to be utterly contemptible and unworthy of notice; to be fickle, false, base, sottish, inclined to perjury, and wholly undeserving" (7). She slavishly follows her mistress's whims, subscribing to her fanatic Protestantism, and she seeks the attentions of Simon Tappertit, jealously attempting to distract him from Dolly Varden. Out of jealousy and envy, she aids the rioters during the imprisonment of Dolly and Emma Haredale (71). Discharged afterwards by an enlightened Mrs. Varden (80), she spends the rest of her life as a turnkey in a women's prison (82).

Conceived in the tradition of the comic spinster, Miggs takes the emotionalism and self-pity of her mistress to excess. Her language spills out in torrents of malapropisms, misused words, and exaggerations, as when she catalogs her misfortunes: "I am an abject slave, and a toiling, moiling, constant-working, always-being-found-fault-with, never-giving-satisfactions, nor having-no-time-to-clean-oneself, potter's wessel—an't I, miss! Ho yes! My situations is lowly, and my capacities is limited, and my duties is to humble myself afore the base degenerating daughters of their blessed mothers as is fit to keep companies with holy saints but is born to persecutions from wicked relations—and to demean myself before them as is no better than Infidels—an't it, miss! Ho Yes! My only becoming occupations is to help young flaunting pagins to brush and come and titivate theirselves into whitening and suppulchres, and leave the young men

to think that there an't a bit of padding in it nor no pinching ins nor fillings out nor pomatums nor deceits nor earthly wanities—an't it, miss! Yes, to be sure it is—ho yes!" (71).

Paper Buildings   Section of the Temple where Sir John Chester lives, "a row of goodly tenements, shaded in front by ancient trees, and looking, at the back, upon the Temple Gardens" (15).

Parkes, Phil   One of the regulars at the Maypole Inn, a warden in Epping Forest (1).

Peak   Sir John Chester's valet, who, following his master's death and "true to his master's creed, eloped with all the cash and movables he could lay his hands on, and started as a finished gentleman upon his own account" (82).

Percy, Lord Algernon (1750–1830)   Commander of the Northumberland Militia in London during the Gordon Riots (67).

'Prentice Knights   Headed by Simon Tappertit, a secret society of apprentices who are devoted to wresting power from their masters (8). During the Gordon Riots the society allies itself with the Protestant cause and changes its name to the United Bulldogs (36).

Royal East London Volunteers   Gabriel Varden's militia (41–42).

Rudge, Barnaby   Simple-minded young man who wanders the countryside between Chigwell and London with his pet raven, Grip. "He was about three-and-twenty years old, and though rather spare, of a fair height and strong make. His hair, of which he had a great profusion, was red, and hanging in disorder about his face and shoulders, gave to his restless looks an expression quite unearthly. . . . His dress was of green, clumsily trimmed here and there . . . with gaudy lace" (3). Born the day after his father's disappearance and supposed murder in 1753, Barnaby has been raised by his mother. A gentle and imaginative boy, Barnaby goes everywhere with his pet raven Grip, who seems to possess the wit that Barnaby lacks. His mother protects him from knowledge of his father, who pursues them to their hiding place in the country. When they go to London at the time of the riots, Barnaby, over his mother's objections and protests, joins the No Popery movement (48), is allied with Hugh and Dennis, and is arrested, imprisoned, and sentenced to hang (58). He is saved from execution through the efforts of Gabriel Varden and Geoffrey Haredale, and through Hugh's admission before his execution that he was responsible for Barnaby's crimes (79).

As the title character in the novel, Barnaby embodies the energy and confusion that characterizes the rioters, and he gives a sympathetic dimension to their cause. He also underscores the characterization of Gordon as a madman who is as confused in the public realm as Barnaby is privately. Barnaby and Gordon stand as representatives of confusion and disorder; their opposite, the central figure in another title that Dickens considered for the novel, is Gabriel Varden, the clear-thinking locksmith and member of the Royal East London Volunteers, who keep public order.

Many commentators have noted that Barnaby, a character in the tradition of the saintly fool, was probably inspired by Madge Wildfire, a madwoman in Sir Walter Scott's *Heart of Mid-Lothian* (1818), a historical novel about the Porteous Riots in Edinburgh in 1736.

Rudge, Barnaby, Senior   Father of Barnaby and husband to Mary, "a man of sixty or thereabouts, much weatherbeaten and worn by time[,] . . . of a cadaverous hue" (1) with a scarred face. Rudge first appears in the novel as the mysterious stranger at the Maypole Inn (1) who attacks Edward Chester (2) and haunts his wife. She knows him as her husband, thought to have been murdered 22 years earlier. He is, in fact, the murderer who killed his employer, Reuben Haredale, and a gardener. He pursues his wife to extort money from her and is finally captured by Geoffrey Haredale (56). In prison he meets his son (62). Unrepentant, he is hanged for his crimes (76).

The central figure in the gothic mystery story that dominates the first half of the novel, Rudge is only loosely connected to the riots in the second

half by the accident of his capture at the same time that his son is imprisoned for rioting. His crimes and abandonment of his wife and child can be taken as a symbolic cause of his son's mental confusion. He thus contributes to the conflicts between fathers and sons in the novel.

Rudge, Mary   Barnaby's mother: "she was about forty . . . with a cheerful aspect, and a face that had once been pretty. . . . Anyone who had bestowed but a casual glance on Barnaby might have known that this was his mother, from the strong resemblance between them; but where in his face there was wildness and vacancy, in hers there was the patient composure of long effort and quiet resignation" (5). Pursued by her fugitive husband, she disappears with Barnaby into the country (25), for she has devoted her life to keeping father and son apart. When her husband's associate, Stagg, discovers their whereabouts, she attempts to disappear into London with Barnaby, but her son joins the rioters and meets his father in prison. After his release from prison, mother and son retire to the Maypole Farm.

St. George's Fields   Area on the south side of the Thames River around the Obelisk, which was open fields until the beginning of the 19th century. The Gordon rioters gathered here when they came to London to petition Parliament (48).

Stagg   Blind proprietor of the cellar where the 'Prentice Knights gather to drink and plot. "His eyes were closed, but had they been wide open, it would have been easy to tell, from the attentive expression of the face he turned towards them— pale and unwholesome as might be expected in one of his underground existence—and from a certain anxious raising and quivering of the lids, that he was blind" (8). He joins the elder Barnaby Rudge his attempts to extort money from Mrs. Rudge (46). Stagg is killed when he tries to run from the officers arresting Hugh and Dennis (69).

Tappertit, Simon (Sim)   Apprentice to locksmith Gabriel Varden, the narcissistic little man, "little more than five feet high, and thoroughly convinced in his own mind that he was above the middle size" is particularly vain about his legs, "which, in knee-breeches were perfect curiosities of littleness" (4). He is enraptured with his master's daughter Dolly and jealously dislikes Joe Willet as his main rival (24). Leader of the 'Prentice Knights, a drinking society of disaffected apprentices, he changes their name to the United Bulldogs and allies them with the No Popery cause (39). He leaves his employment to join the rioters (51), and during the riots his legs are crushed. He finishes life as a shoe-black with two wooden legs and marries a rag-and-bone man's widow (82).

Tappertit extends the conflict between fathers and sons to one between generations, for he and the 'Prentice Knights challenge the authority of their employers. Dickens makes comedy out of their pretensions, indirectly satirizing the medievalism of the Young England movement and suggesting that working class movements like CHARTISM lack a coherent program of reform and seek only to create public disorder.

Tyburn Site near what is now Marble Arch where public hangings took place from the 12th century to 1783. Maypole Hugh's mother had been executed here (75).

United Bull-Dogs Name taken by the 'Prentice Knights when they ally themselves with the Protestant party during the Gordon riots (36).

Varden, Dolly Daughter of Gabriel and Martha Varden, Dolly has "a roguish face, . . . a face lighted up by the loveliest pair of sparkling eyes; . . . the face of a pretty, laughing girl; dimpled and fresh, and healthful—the very impersonation of good-humour and blooming beauty" (4). A friend of Emma Haredale, she acts as go-between in Emma's relationship with Edward Chester. Attractive and flirtatious, she attracts the unwanted attentions of Hugh and Sim Tappertit and causes her desired suitor, Joe Willet, to join the army because of her frustrating coquetry. During the riots she is captured, along with Emma and Miggs, by Tappertit, Hugh, and Dennis and later rescued by Edward Chester, Joe Willet, and Gabriel. She and Joe marry, take over

the Maypole Inn, and have "more small Joes and Dollys than could easily be counted" (82).

Dickens describes Dolly as fashionably attired, noting especially her dresses and "a little straw hat trimmed with cherry-colored ribbons . . . the wickedest and most provoking head-dress that ever malicious milliner devised" (19). A hat and a dotted dress fabric entered the language as "Dolly Vardens," and a colorful spotted trout was even named the Dolly Varden trout.

Varden, Gabriel A London locksmith, "a round, red-faced, sturdy yeoman, with a double chin, and a voice husky with good living, good sleeping, good humour, and good health, . . . bluff, hale, hearty, and in a green old age" (2). He is a loyal friend to Mrs. Rudge and her son Barnaby, securing a pardon for the boy after the riots (79). A sturdy upholder of law and order during the riots as a member of the Royal East London Volunteers, he heroically refuses the rioters' demand that he unlock the gates of Newgate Prison (63).

Gabriel's household embodies in a small way the conflicts of the time. His wife's fanatical Protestantism, Tappertit's rebellion, Miggs's machinations, and Dolly's flirtatiousness and matchmaking entangle all the members of the household in the larger public events of the time. When order is restored, the Golden Key once again becomes an orderly and happy household. GEOFFREY THURLEY (1976) notes that "the original title of the work was to be *Gabriel Varden, the Locksmith of London*, and Varden remained the book's centre of gravity, a reactionary figure, like Pickwick, yet, like him also, broad-minded, fond of his pint, and in every way opposed to the fanaticism of the sort of Protestantism that has made his wife so hard to live with."

Varden, Martha Gabriel's wife, "a lady of what is commonly called an uncertain temper—a phrase which being interpreted signifies a temper tolerably certain to make everybody more or less uncomfortable. . . . When other people were merry, Mrs. Varden was dull; and . . . when other people were dull, Mrs. Varden was disposed to be amazingly cheerful" (7). A fanatical Protestant, "Mrs. Varden was most devout when most ill-tempered" (4).

She allies herself with the Protestant cause, but she is unsettled by the riots, thinking that her fanaticism has helped to foment the unrest. She is also impressed by her husband's steadfastness and courage. Transformed by these experiences, she overcomes her moodiness, dismisses Miggs, and becomes "in all respects delicious to behold" (80).

Warren, the   The mansion of the Haredale family near Chigwell that is burned down during the Gordon Riots (1, 55).

Welbeck Street   Lord George Gordon lived at No. 64 on this street in Marylebone (37).

Willet, John   "Slow but sure" proprietor of the Maypole Tavern near CHIGWELL, "one of the most dogged and positive fellows in existence—always sure that what he thought or said or did was right, and holding it as a thing quite settled and ordained by the laws of nature and Providence, that anybody who said or did or thought otherwise must be inevitably and of necessity wrong" (1). He exercises this authoritarian perspective over his son Joe, causing him to run away to the army (31). Lord George Gordon and his lieutenants stop at the Maypole on their way into London (35–36), and the rioters ransack the tavern on their way to burn down the Warren, leaving John bound, dazed, and permanently traumatized (54). In the army, young Joe loses an arm but proves his heroism. He returns in time to rescue Mr. Haredale, his daughter, and Dolly Varden during the riots (67, 71). Father and son are reconciled, and Dolly and Joe marry and restore the Maypole, but John never recovers his full sanity (72, 78, 80).

The Willets represent another variation on the father-son theme.

Willet, Joseph (Joe)   Son of John Willet, "a broad-shouldered, strapping young fellow of twenty, whom it pleased his father still to consider a little boy and to treat him accordingly" (1). He leaves home to escape his father's tyranny and declares his love to Dolly Varden, but he is discouraged when she plays hard-to-get so he joins the army (31). After losing an arm at the Battle of Savannah dur-

ing the American Revolutionary War, Joe returns to England to become a hero during the riots. He and others rescue Gabriel from the mob (64), he helps Haredale and Langdale escape (67), and he frees Dolly, Emma, and Miggs from their captors (71). Then he marries Dolly and they restore the Maypole Inn.

ADAPTATIONS

Several stage adaptations were on the boards in London before the novel completed its serial run. Some of these early dramas concentrated on the melodrama of the murder of Reuben Haredale and did not include the riots at all; EDWARD STIRLING's *Barnaby Rudge: or The Riots of London in 1780* (1841) did include the riots, but it did not attract an audience. In most of the early productions women played the role of Barnaby.

Later in the century, stage adaptations focused on Dolly Varden, and many of them, like G. Murray Wood's 1873 adaptation, were titled *Dolly Varden.*

THOMAS BENTLEY made a silent film (1914) notable for its re-creation of the riots using a cast of extras numbering more than 1000. The BBC produced a 13-part television serial of the novel in 1960.

FURTHER READING

Rudge has not engaged the attention of many critics. Those who have written about the novel usually consider it less than successful, finding its melodrama clichéd and its two halves disconnected. It is often viewed as a precursor to Dickens's later historical novel, *A Tale of Two Cities*, especially in its depiction of the mob and the riots, generally thought to be the best section of the novel. STEVEN MARCUS (1965) challenges some of these judgments and finds the novel unified around the theme of fathers and sons. In the most extensive essay on the novel, Myron Magnet (*Dickens and the Social Order*, 1985) makes a convincing case that Dickens's political analysis, grounded in the rationalism of the Enlightenment, is thoughtfully considered and carefully articulated in the novel. Ian Duncan, in *Modern Romance and Transformations of the Novel* (1992), places *Rudge* in the tradition of Scott; JOHN BUTT and KATHLEEN TILLOTSON (1957), and Thomas J. Rice ("The Politics of *Barn-*

aby Rudge," in *The Changing World of Charles Dickens,* ed. Giddings, 1989) describe the composition of the novel and its contemporary relevance.

Battle of Life, The. A Love Story.

Fourth of Dickens's CHRISTMAS BOOKS, published in December 1846, with illustrations by RICHARD DOYLE, JOHN LEECH, DANIEL MACLISE, and CLARKSON STANFIELD. Like the other Christmas books, *Battle* tells of a change of heart, but in this case it is not brought about by a supernatural agency.

SYNOPSIS

(1) On a battlefield that once ran with blood many generations ago, a calm domestic life has now settled in. The memory of the battle and why it was fought is all but forgotten. On the morning of the anniversary of the battle, Doctor Jeddler's two daughters, Grace and Marion, dance in the orchard as pickers take fruit from the trees. When they are done, they join a ceremonial breakfast for Alfred Heathfield, Doctor Jeddler's ward, who is about to set out on a foreign tour. It is both Alfred's and Marion's birthday, and he has just come of age. The lawyers Snitchey and Craggs have come to draw up the legal documents officially ending Jeddler's guardianship. At breakfast they discuss the doctor's philosophy that the world is "a gigantic practical joke: . . . something too absurd to be considered seriously, by any rational man." The lawyers suggest that the law is serious, but the Doctor, using the battle fought on the site as his illustration, insists on the futility of human aspirations and argues that "the same contradictions prevail in everything. One must either laugh or cry at such stupendous inconsistencies; and I prefer to laugh." His servant, Benjamin Britain, echoes his master: "Humanity," he says, "that's the joke."

After breakfast Alfred bids farewell to his love, the younger Jeddler daughter Marion, and asks her calm and serene sister to watch over her for him. As his coach goes off into the distance, Marion falls sobbing on Grace's neck.

(2) Three years later, Snitchey and Craggs are advising one of their clients, Michael Warden, a spendthrift who has burdened his estate in debt through expensive living and now "means to repent and be wise." They counsel him to flee to Europe and live frugally for some time in order to nurse his estate back to financial health. He tells them that he is in love with Marion Jeddler and will agree to follow their advice only after a month has passed so that he has time to save Marion from Alfred's return, which "she dreads, and contemplates with misery."

A month later, during the Christmas season, Warden's departure is set for the same day as Alfred's scheduled return. The doctor plans a grand party to celebrate Alfred's homecoming, but Clemency Newcome, the Jeddlers' maid, has forebodings of disaster when she observes, in the "dark and doubtful night

Maclise's frontispiece for *The Battle of Life* (1846).

that lay beyond the threshold," a secret assignation between Marion and Warden. Alfred plans to surprise the family by arriving on foot at a side door. There he finds a distressed Clemency Newcome with Grace; they announce that Marion is gone.

(3) Six years later, Michael Warden appears at the Nutmeg-Grater, an inn run by Benjamin Britain and his wife, the former Clemency Newcome, who enriches her husband's life with her "plain, straightforward thrift, good-humour, honesty, and industry." Clemency concludes from Warden's black dress and manner that Marion has died and that Grace is to be told of her sister's fate the next day, which is the anniversary of the battle, Marion's and Alfred's birthday, and the anniversary of Grace and Alfred's wedding. Their marriage is a happy one, blessed by Alfred's rewarding medical practice among the poor and by their daughter, Marion. Only the loss of Marion casts a dark shadow on their lives.

At sunset on the anniversary day, Marion returns. She tells them that she left home to enable Grace to marry Alfred, for she knew how much her sister loved him and had sacrificed for her. Warden's flight to the continent had given her a cover for her disappearance; she had actually gone to stay with her Aunt Martha, Doctor Jeddler's sister. Now that her sacrifice has enabled Grace and Alfred to marry, she can return.

Marion's sacrifice changes the doctor. He no longer believes the world a joke. "It's a world full of hearts," he says, "and a serious world, with all its folly, . . . a world on which the sun never rises, but it looks upon a thousand bloodless battles that are set-off against the miseries and wickedness of Battle-Fields, . . . a world of sacred mysteries."

Michael Warden makes Ben Britain the owner of the Nutmeg-Grater, and Britain changes the name to the Nutmeg-Grater and Thimble and posts Clemency's inscriptions in the parlor: "Do as you would be done by!" and "Forget and Forgive!" Michael Warden and Marion marry, and by the time the story is told, they have honored the countryside with their presence for 35 years.

COMMENTARY

The Battle of Life is the least successful of the five CHRISTMAS BOOKS. WILLIAM MAKEPEACE THACKERAY

called it "a wretched affair," and the reviews were generally not laudatory. Even LORD JEFFREY admitted to Dickens, "The general voice, I fancy, persists in refusing it a place among your best pieces."

Though excited by the initial idea for the book, Dickens had difficulty writing it. Away from London and living in Switzerland while also attempting to get *Dombey* under way, he struggled with *Battle,* dreaming for a whole week that the story "was a series of chambers impossible to be got to rights or got out of, through which I wandered drearily all night."

Like the other Christmas books, *Battle* treats a change of heart, but one that involves no supernatural agency. Doctor Jeddler is won to the belief that the world is "serious" and not a joke by the self-sacrificing behavior of his two daughters. First Grace suppresses her love for Alfred Heathfield because she believes her sister loves him. Then Marion, in an even greater sacrifice, disappears for six years to give Grace time to marry Alfred. The melodrama of Marion's disappearance and return is clumsily linked to the story of Michael Warden, otherwise unconnected to the plot. The central characters, especially Alfred and Marion, are notable for their absence. Doctor Jeddler's misguided philosophy lacks the negative energy of Scrooge's miserliness or Redlaw's painful memories.

Battle is also a period piece. Set in the late 18th century, the story was frequently compared to OLIVER GOLDSMITH's *Vicar of Wakefield* by early reviewers. But there is no compelling reason for this historical distance, which also reduced the story's contemporary relevance.

Dickens was right to be excited by his initial idea—linking the historical battlefield with the domestic battlefield of everyday struggles—and the opening scene describing Grace and Marion dancing in a fruitful orchard that centuries before was a bloody field is probably the best thing in the story. But it was, as Dickens later recognized, the germ of a much longer book. In fact, Thackeray's *Vanity Fair,* a very long novel that would begin its run in monthly parts in January 1847, made a similar linkage, connecting the Napoleonic wars and the Battle of Waterloo with the battle of the sexes in the drawing rooms of London and Paris. Dickens just did not have room in a short Christmas book to give his idea adequate development.

The principle that underlay Dickens's idea for the book—that the larger public life is implicit in domestic life—was one that would inform many of Dickens's longer novels, especially such late novels as *Bleak House* and *Our Mutual Friend. Battle* is also interesting for its foreshadowing of characters in the later novels. Marion and Grace prefigure Dora and Agnes in *Copperfield,* though Dora dies to give David the deserving Agnes. Marion's sacrifice also prefigures Sydney Carton's in *Two Cities.* Clemency Newcome, the down-to-earth servant, has long been recognized as an early version of Peggotty in *Copperfield,* less developed and more didactic than her loving successor.

Commentators have been most interested in the biographical elements in the story. Both STEVEN MARCUS (1965) and MICHAEL SLATER (1983) consider Dickens's sisters-in-law, Mary and GEORGINA HOGARTH, as the originals for Marion and Grace. Dickens's idealization of these two women, and his deeply emotional attachment to the memory of Mary, who died in his arms, colors the characterizations of the Jeddler sisters and obscures the relevance of the battle theme. His reluctance to reveal conflict in the sisters' relationship makes the domestic battle unconvincing and diminishes the degree of Marion's sacrifice.

CHARACTERS AND RELATED ENTRIES

Britain, Benjamin ("Little Britain") Doctor Jeddler's manservant, "a small man with an uncommonly sour and discontented face." He matches his master's belief that everything is a joke with the nihilistic philosophy: "I don't know anything; I don't care for anything; I don't make out anything; I don't believe anything; and I don't want anything." After he marries Clemency Newcome and becomes manager of the Nutmeg-Grater Inn, he learns the value of love. The couple have two sons and a daughter, Clem.

Craggs, Mrs. Thomas Craggs's wife, Mrs. Snitchey's closest friend; she is, "on principle," suspicious of Mr. Snitchey.

Craggs, Thomas Law partner in the firm of Snitchey and Craggs, "a cold, hard, dry man, dressed in grey and white, like a flint; with small twinkles in his eyes, as if something struck sparks out of them."

Heathfield, Alfred Doctor Jeddler's ward who is in love with Marion, the Doctor's younger daughter. When she discovers that her older sister Grace also loves Alfred, she disappears and in time Alfred falls in love with Grace and marries her. They have a daughter, Marion. He becomes a village doctor ministering to the poor.

Jeddler, Dr. Anthony A widower who maintains a superficial philosophy of life, unaware of the sacrifices of the soldiers who once died on the battlefield where his house is now located and their possible contributions to his domestic tranquility. "The heart and mystery of his philosophy was, to look upon the world as a gigantic practical joke; as something too absurd to be considered seriously, by any rational man." After seeing the sacrifice that his daughter Marion makes for love of her sister, he takes life more seriously, believing that "love, deep anchored, is the portion of all human creatures."

Although Dr. Jeddler is the central conversion figure in this Christmas book, similar to Scrooge in *A Christmas Carol* or Redlaw in *The Haunted Man,* his transformation is overshadowed by the stories of his daughters. His change from cynicism to seriousness is not well integrated into either the frame story of the battlefield or the melodrama of Marion's disappearance and return.

Jeddler, Grace and Marion Jeddler's daughters, who take life more seriously. Grace, the elder, earnest and self-denying, performs the mother's role in the widower's household. When Marion, the more frivolous younger daughter, realizes that Grace loves her fiancé, Alfred Heathfield, she disappears and by doing so enables Grace and Alfred to marry. Although her disappearance appears to be an elopement, she has actually gone to stay secretly with the Doctor's maiden sister Martha. After six years she returns to clear her reputation and eventually to marry Michael Warden. Marion's sacrifice causes the Doctor to take life seriously and to give up his belief that the world is a joke.

Drawn from Dickens's sisters-in-law, MARY (Marion) and GEORGINA (Grace) HOGARTH, the portraits of Dr. Jeddler's daughters are compromised by Dickens's intense feelings for their originals. Marion's relationship with Warden remains as shadowy to the reader as to her family, and she is presented solely in terms of her sentimental self-sacrifice.

Newcome, Clemency Dr. Jeddler's cheerful, loving, and awkward servant: "She was about thirty years old, and had a sufficiently plump and cheerful face, though it was twisted up into an odd expression of tightness that made it comical. But the extraordinary homeliness of her gait and manner would have superseded any face in the world. To say that she had two left legs, and somebody else's arms, and that all four limbs seemed to be out of joint, and to start from perfectly wrong places when they were set in motion, is to offer the mildest outline of the reality." She is dismissed after Marion Jeddler disappears. She marries Benjamin Britain and the two become proprietors of the Nutmeg-Grater and Thimble Inn, named after objects bearing inscriptions that state her philosophy of life: "Forget and Forgive!" and "Do as you would be done by!" They have three children, Little Clem and two sons.

The most celebrated character in the story, Clemency, whose name bespeaks her thematic role, has often been considered a precursor to Peggotty in *David Copperfield*. Her simple philosophy challenges Dr. Jeddler's cynicism.

Nutmeg-Grater, the Roadside inn kept by Benjamin Britain and Clemency Newcome after they marry. Later the name is changed to the Nutmeg-Grater and Thimble, referring to the two objects whose inscriptions state Clemency's philosophy of life.

Snitchey, Jonathan Dominant partner in the law firm of Snitchey and Craggs; "like a magpie or a raven (only not so sleek)," he refers to the firm as "self and Craggs." They handle the legal affairs of Doctor Jeddler and Michael Warden and advise Warden to flee to the continent on the same night that Marion Jeddler disappears.

Snitchey, Mrs. Like Mrs. Craggs, she distrusts her husband's law partner on principle.

Warden, Michael Spendthrift neighbor of Dr. Jeddler: "a man of thirty, or about that time of life, negligently dressed, and somewhat haggard in the face, but well-made, well-attired, and well-looking." When he runs from his debts to the continent on the same night that Marion disappears, people assume that they have eloped. In time he learns to control his extravagance and eventually he marries her.

ADAPTATIONS

To upstage the pirates, Dickens sold the proof-sheets of *Battle* to ROBERT and MARY KEELEY, actor-managers at the Lyceum Theatre. They secured ALBERT SMITH to write a script, and they opened on December 21, 1846. Six other productions, largely based on Smith's version, appeared in the first few months. George Dibden Pitt's melodramatic adaptation for the Brittania, Hoxton, added a duel between Heathfield and Warden and a suicide attempt by Grace when she learns that Marion is missing. CHARLES CULLIFORD DICKENS, son of the novelist, adapted the story for the theater in 1873, and Walter Ellis's *Marion* was a popular stage adaptation in the 1890s. No films of *Battle* have been made.

FURTHER READING

Battle has received little critical discussion. MICHAEL SLATER (1971) provides a useful introduction to it in his Penguin edition of the CHRISTMAS BOOKS. STEVEN MARCUS (1965) and Slater (1983) develop interesting biographical readings of the story.

Bleak House

Dickens's ninth novel, published in monthly parts in 1852–53, with illustrations by HABLOT KNIGHT BROWNE, issued in one volume in 1853. Often characterized as the first of the late novels, *Bleak*

House describes England as a bleak house, devastated by an irresponsible and self-serving legal system, symbolically represented by the Lord Chancellor ensconced in foggy glory in the COURT OF CHANCERY. Dickens uses two narrators, a third-person narrator who reports on the public life in the worlds of law and fashion and a first-person narrator, Esther Summerson, a young woman who tells her personal history. By this double narration, he is able to connect and contrast Esther's domestic story with broad public concerns. Esther's narrative traces her discovery of her identity as the illegitimate child of Lady Dedlock. Abandoned in infancy and raised by an abusive aunt, Esther is a self-denying, unassertive young woman, grateful for any recognition she receives from the patriarchal society around her. Her situation encapsulates that of the larger society, in which traditions of aristocratic privilege deny human needs and desires and patriarchal institutions like the courts make orphans of society's children, enable slums and disease to flourish, and suppress individual autonomy by a "philanthropy" that makes dependents of its recipients.

SYNOPSIS

Part 1 (March 1852)

(1) A foggy November afternoon. At the heart of the fog, the COURT OF CHANCERY is entangled in the Jarndyce and Jarndyce case, a dispute over a will that has dragged on for several generations. (2) Lady Dedlock is bored to death during the rainy season at Chesney Wold, her place in Lincolnshire, so she and her husband, Sir Leicester Dedlock, a baronet 20 years her senior, come up to London. There they consult with Mr. Tulkinghorn, the family lawyer. When he shows them some inconsequential documents pertaining to the Jarndyce case, she asks who copied them, faints, and is taken to her room.

(3) Esther Summerson begins the story of her life by telling of her lonely and oppressed childhood, raised by Miss Barbary, a "godmother" who tells her that she is her mother's "disgrace" and that it would have been far better had she never been born. After her godmother's death, she is sent to Greenleaf School for six years before being

summoned to London by John Jarndyce, the primary living representative of the Jarndyce family, to become a companion to Ada Clare, one of two wards in the Jarndyce case assigned to the care of Jarndyce by the Court of Chancery. As Esther leaves the court with Ada and the other ward, Richard Carstone, the three young people meet a little madwoman, obsessed with the judgments of the court, who greets them as representatives of "youth, hope, and beauty." (4) Then, Mr. Guppy, a law clerk, conducts them to the house of Mrs. Jellyby, a friend of Jarndyce, where they are to spend the night. The house is in complete disorder: The children are neglected, there is no hot water, stair carpets are loose, dinner is served almost raw. Mrs. Jellyby devotes all of her time and attention to an African mission in Borrioboola-Gha. Her daughter Caddy, who acts as her secretary, complains of the "disgraceful house" and falls asleep with her head in Esther's lap.

Part 2 (April 1852)

(5) The next morning Esther, Ada, and Richard again meet the little madwoman, Miss Flite. She takes them to her room on the top floor of Krook's Rag and Bottle Warehouse, where she shows them the caged birds, with names like Youth, Hope, and Beauty, that she plans to set free when the court decides her case. She leads them past the dark door of another lodger, a law writer called Nemo, and introduces them to her landlord, the junk-dealer Krook, who has earned the nickname "Lord Chancellor" because he collects legal documents and papers among the items in his shop. Although he cannot read, he spells out letter by letter J-a-r-n-d-y-c-e and B-l-e-a-k H-o-u-s-e, words he has learned from his documents.

(6) Then the three young people set out for Bleak House in ST. ALBANS, the home of their guardian. When they arrive, Jarndyce suggests that they meet as old friends even though they have not met before. He shows them their rooms in the irregular house and surprises Esther by giving her the household keys. They also meet a guest in the house, Harold Skimpole, an artist, composer, and doctor who does not work and claims to have no understanding of money. He sponges from Jarndyce and prevails on Esther and Richard to pay a debt to

keep him from being arrested. When Jarndyce finds out that they have given him money, he makes them promise never to do so again.

(7) Mrs. Rouncewell, the housekeeper at Chesney Wold, presides there while the Dedlocks are away. The weather remains wet in Lincolnshire. When Guppy tours the house, he is struck by a portrait of the current Lady Dedlock, who seems strangely familiar to him. He also wants to hear the story of the Ghost's Walk, but Mrs. Rouncewell waits until he leaves before she tells the story to her grandson Watt and the pretty young servant Rosa. The story explains the sound of footsteps on the terrace, the footsteps of a Lady Dedlock of the 17th century who was crippled by her Cavalier husband when she opposed him and aided the Roundheads. She vowed to walk the terrace until the pride of the house was humbled.

Part 3 (May 1852)

(8) At breakfast Skimpole delightfully develops his "philosophy" that drones should be honored over those who are as busy as bees. Jarndyce shows them the Growlery, a room where he retreats when he is out of humor. He talks of the blight of Chancery and urges Richard to choose a profession. One of Jarndyce's acquaintances, Mrs. Pardiggle, a local "philanthropist," recruits Esther and Ada to accompany her to a nearby brickmaker's house. On the way the Pardiggle children complain to Esther that their allowances are taken by their mother for charity. They intrude into the brickmaker's house and discover that an infant child has died. Esther covers the little corpse with her handkerchief. (9) Lawrence Boythorn, an old schoolfellow, visits Jarndyce, filling Bleak House with boisterous superlatives and irrepressible hyperbole. Mr. Guppy also comes to Bleak House. He proposes to Esther, suggesting that he can act on her behalf. She rejects him, but she both laughs and cries over the proposal.

(10) Tulkinghorn asks Snagsby, the stationer who provides copying services for the legal community, who copied the affidavit that Lady Dedlock saw. Together they go to Krook's, and he leads them up to Nemo's room. There is a smell of opium in the darkness and Nemo does not respond to Krook's "Hallo."

Part 4 (June 1852)

(11) They find Nemo dead. While Krook is out of the room, Tulkinghorn removes some papers from Nemo's portmanteau. At the inquest the next day at Sol's Arms, no significant additions are made to the story; the one witness who knew Nemo, Jo, a poor crossing sweeper, is not allowed to testify. Nemo is buried in a pauper's cemetery. Jo sweeps the step into the burial ground. (12) In January Sir Leicester and Lady Dedlock return to Chesney Wold. The weather has cleared. Lady Dedlock arouses the jealousy of Hortense, her French maid, by complimenting the beauty of a local servant girl, Rosa. Tulkinghorn tells Lady Dedlock of Nemo's death. Assuming her characteristic manner, she apparently listens to the story only to divert herself from the tedium of Chesney Wold.

(13) After vaguely considering the navy, the army, and the law, Richard chooses medicine and goes to study with Mr. Bayham Badger. Ada confesses to Esther that she and Richard love each other.

Part 5 (July 1852)

(14) Caddy tells Esther that she is secretly engaged to a dancing master, and Esther goes with her to the academy, where they meet the hardworking Prince Turveydrop and his idle and parasitic father, a latter-day dandy who considers himself the model of deportment. At Miss Flite's, where Caddy has been learning household skills, they meet Jarndyce, Krook, and Allan Woodcourt, the young physician in attendance at Nemo's death. Esther is chilled when she passes the dark room where Nemo died. (15) Skimpole tells Esther and Jarndyce of the death of Neckett, the bill collector, who "has been arrested by the great Bailiff," and they seek out Neckett's orphaned children. They find the two younger ones, Tom and Emma, locked in a tenement room in Bell Yard while Charley, the oldest, is out doing laundry. The neighbors, Mrs. Blinder and Mr. Gridley, keep an eye on the children and tell of their admiration for Charley.

(16) Sir Leicester remains alone in Lincolnshire. In London, Jo, the illiterate crossing sweeper, who was a friend of the dead copywriter Nemo, wonders at his darkened world. He lives in Tom-All-Alone's, a slum blighted because it is caught up in a Chancery suit, and he is surprised when a woman,

dressed as a servant, seeks him out and has him guide her to Snagsby's, Krook's, and the cemetery where Nemo is buried. She gives the boy a golden sovereign before she disappears.

Part 6 (August 1852)

(17) Richard is not committed to medicine. He suggests that the law would be a more engaging pursuit, and Jarndyce agrees to the change, but that evening Esther finds her guardian in the Growlery. There he tells her the little he knows of her personal history. Meanwhile, Allan Woodcourt, a physician devoted to his profession, announces that he is going to the East as a medical man. Caddy brings Esther some flowers that Woodcourt left at Miss Flite's. (18) In midsummer, while visiting Boythorn in Lincolnshire, Esther is disturbed by seeing Lady Dedlock's face, which calls up memories of childhood and a haunting sense that she has seen her before. When they meet in a garden house at Chesney Wold, Lady Dedlock's voice also unsettles Esther.

(19) Taking tea at Snagsby's, Guppy learns that the Reverend Chadband's wife was formerly Miss Rachel, servant to Esther's godmother. When Jo is brought to Snagsby by a constable who has arrested him for not "moving on," Jo tells them of the lady who gave him a sovereign.

Part 7 (September 1852)

(20) Guppy continues to pursue the mysteries surrounding Nemo's death. He convinces his friend Tony Jobling to take Nemo's room at Krook's, so that he can spy on Krook and gather information about Nemo. (21) Nearby, Trooper George, a former soldier, runs a shooting gallery. He has borrowed the money for the business from Grandfather Smallweed, a small-time money-lender, and each month George manages to pay enough interest to renew the loan for the principal amount. (22) Tulkinghorn is also pursuing the Nemo mystery. When Snagsby tells him Jo's story of the lady who gave him a sovereign, the lawyer sends Snagsby and detective Bucket to Tom-All-Alone's to find the boy. When they bring Jo back, there is a veiled lady in Tulkinghorn's rooms. At first Jo thinks it is the woman he guided through the streets, but when she removes her gloves he sees that her hands are not so delicate nor her rings so precious as those on the

woman who gave him the sovereign. This woman is Hortense, Lady Dedlock's former maid. Tulkinghorn and Bucket are pleased to have established that Jo's woman was a lady disguised as Hortense.

Part 8 (October 1852)

(23) Hortense offers herself to Esther as a maid, but Esther turns her down. Richard reveals that he is bored with the law and in debt. Caddy asks Esther to go with her when she informs Mr. Turveydrop and her mother of her engagement. Turveydrop agrees to the marriage when Caddy and Prince promise to take care of him. Mrs. Jellyby, continuing her mission work in spite of her husband's bankruptcy, refuses to take Caddy seriously. Esther is surprised to learn that Mr. Jarndyce has hired Charley as her maid. (24) Richard moves from the law to the army. Jarndyce asks Ada and Richard to break off their engagement because they are too young and unsettled. Richard complies resentfully. To prepare for his new profession, Richard takes fencing and shooting lessons from Trooper George at the shooting gallery where Gridley, the man from Shropshire, now ill and a fugitive from the law, is hiding. Just as Bucket comes to arrest him, Gridley dies.

(25) Mrs. Snagsby has convinced herself that Jo is her husband's son. At an oration by Chadband hinting at this connection, Jo falls asleep. Snagsby quietly gives the boy a half-crown and commends him for saying nothing about the lady with a sovereign.

Part 9 (November 1852)

(26) Grandfather Smallweed asks George for a sample of the handwriting of Captain Hawdon, George's former officer in the army. Smallweed is acting on behalf of Tulkinghorn, and George, reluctant to give it to him until he knows why it is wanted, agrees to go with Smallweed to see Tulkinghorn. (27) The lawyer will not reveal why he wants the writing. George feels vaguely threatened, so he consults with his old army comrade, Mat Bagnet, whose wife advises him to stay out of things he does not understand. George refuses to turn over the writing. (28) Meanwhile, Rouncewell the Ironmaster, the elder son of Mrs. Rouncewell, proposes to remove Rosa from Chesney Wold and educate her to be a fit wife for his son Watt. Sir Leicester

is scandalized to learn that Rouncewell does not value Rosa's training as a servant at Chesney Wold; he knows that "the whole framework of society" has cracked. (29) Guppy tells Lady Dedlock that he has linked her portrait with Esther's face and her story with those of Miss Barbary and Captain Hawdon, that Hawdon was the real name of Nemo the dead law writer, that Esther is his daughter, and that Lady Dedlock herself was the lady who gave Jo the sovereign. He offers to obtain a sheaf of Hawdon's letters for her. After he leaves, she falls on her knees, crying, "O my child!"

Part 10 (December 1852)
(30) Esther serves as Caddy's bridesmaid. On the wedding day, Jarndyce, in good spirits, ignores the differences between Mrs. Jellyby's philanthropic friends, each obsessed with her particular mission, and Turveydrop, who thinks the Jellybys lack deportment. (31) Over Skimpole's objection, Esther and Charley take in Jo, who is sick with fever, but by the next morning Jo has mysteriously disappeared. Charley comes down with the fever and Esther cares for her, but when Charley recovers, Esther contracts the disease. The fever is so bad that Esther goes blind.

(32) Guppy and Jobling wait in Nemo's old rooms for an appointment with Krook at midnight, when he will turn over Nemo's letters to them. They are bothered by an oppressiveness in the air and by oily soot collecting on the windowsills and walls. When the clock strikes 12, they go downstairs and find the cat snarling at a spot on the floor. That is all that remains of Krook, who has died from spontaneous combustion.

Part 11 (January 1853)
(33) Cook's Court can talk of nothing else but the strange events at Krook's. The Smallweeds claim the building as the property of Mrs. Smallweed, Krook's sister. Guppy tells Lady Dedlock that he does not have the letters, that they were probably destroyed. (34) Smallweed demands that George pay the principal of his loan, but George does not have the money, and Mat Bagnet, his cosigner, is threatened. Tulkinghorn agrees to restore matters to their old footing for a sample of Hawdon's writing. George gives in.

(35) After several weeks, Esther awakens from her illness and gradually recovers her sight. She notices that the mirrors in her rooms are gone and realizes that this means that she is scarred by the disease and has lost her "old face." Miss Flite visits and tells of Woodcourt's heroism in saving the survivors of a shipwreck. Esther admits that she used to think Woodcourt loved her, but now she is grateful that she is disfigured and will not have that to worry about anymore.

Part 12 (February 1853)
(36) At Boythorn's house, where she goes to recuperate, Esther finds a mirror in her room with a curtain pulled across it. After Charley has gone to bed, Esther pulls back the curtain, looks in the mirror, and tearfully accepts her changed face. On one of her daily walks in the park at Chesney Wold, Esther is confronted by Lady Dedlock, who reveals that she is Esther's mother and, kneeling before her, asks her forgiveness. Esther is unsettled; walking on the Ghost's Walk and hearing the ghost's hollow footsteps, she thinks she is the calamity in the Chesney Wold legend. Gradually she comes to accept her birth and to believe that she was intended to live. (37) Esther asks Skimpole to discourage Richard's obsession with the Jarndyce case, his distrust of Mr. Jarndyce, and his reliance on his new attorney Vholes. Skimpole says he is incapable of such "responsibility." (38) Esther asks Guppy to abandon his pursuit of her personal history. Guppy, disconcerted by her changed appearance, agrees to do so, and makes her swear that she turned down his original proposal and that she understands that it cannot be renewed.

Part 13 (March 1853)
(39) Tulkinghorn asks Guppy about his business with Lady Dedlock, but Guppy tells him nothing. (40) At Chesney Wold, where the Dedlocks have gathered, Tulkinghorn tells the story of an ironmaster who forbade his daughter to associate with a great lady when he learned that the great lady had suppressed a secret affair and a child she had borne out of wedlock many years before. Lady Dedlock leaves the room. (41) Later she confirms Tulkinghorn's story and tells him of her plan to flee. He threatens her with immediate exposure

Browne's (Phiz's) illustration for the controversial scene in *Bleak House* in which Guppy and Jobling discover that Krook has disappeared by spontaneous combustion.

unless she remains at Chesney Wold and keeps her secret unrevealed. That night Tulkinghorn sleeps unaware of the distraught figure pacing on the Ghost's Walk. (42) When Tulkinghorn returns to the city, Snagsby complains that Mademoiselle Hortense has been lingering near his house and raising Mrs. Snagsby's suspicions. Tulkinghorn threatens to have her thrown in prison if she persists. Hortense demands his aid in securing a new position and leaves threatening revenge.

Part 14 (April 1853)

(43) Esther worries that she will inadvertently reveal her mother's secret. When Sir Leicester Dedlock calls and invites her to visit Chesney Wold, she is disconcerted. She seeks advice from Mr. Jarndyce, telling him that Lady Dedlock is her mother. (43) Jarndyce agrees that she must avoid further meetings with Sir Leicester. Then he asks her to send Charley "this night a week" for a letter from him. The letter turns out to be a proposal asking her to be "mistress of Bleak House." He assures her that nothing will change in his feelings for her, whatever she decides. Esther thinks that devoting her life to Jarndyce's happiness "was to thank him poorly," yet she cries over her good fortune. Then she burns Woodcourt's dried roses. After several days she agrees to be mistress of Bleak House. (45) Esther goes down to Deal, where Richard has sold his commission and is preparing to leave the army. While she is there, Allan Woodcourt returns from India. Esther asks him to be a friend and adviser to Richard.

(46) Back in London, in Tom-All-Alone's, Woodcourt comes upon the sickly Jo. The boy tells him that he was taken from Bleak House by Bucket, who put him in a hospital and then gave him some money and told him to "move on" and stay away from London. He has returned to Tom-All-Alone's to die.

Part 15 (May 1853)

(47) Woodcourt takes the sick boy to George's shooting gallery. There the boy dies as he repeats the Lord's Prayer after Woodcourt. (48) Lady Dedlock turns Rosa over to Rouncewell. Tulkinghorn takes this act as a breach of their agreement, but he will not tell her when he plans to inform Sir Leicester of her secret. That night a shot rings out, and in the morning the people who come to clean Tulkinghorn's rooms discover his body. (49) The next day Bucket appears at Mrs. Bagnet's birthday dinner. He charms the family with his stories and songs and leaves with George, who is white and drawn. On their way home, Bucket arrests George for Tulkinghorn's murder.

Part 16 (June 1853)

(50) After the birth of Caddy's sickly baby, Esther nurses Caddy through an illness. Prince, Mr. Tur-

veydrop, and Woodcourt are frequent visitors to the sickroom. Esther tells Caddy and Ada of her agreement to marry Jarndyce. After Caddy's recovery, Esther returns home and feels a "shade" between herself and Ada. (51) Ada confesses to Esther that she and Richard have married. (52) Esther is now alone in Jarndyce's house. Woodcourt, who serves as both Caddy's and Richard's doctor, tells her of their conditions. When he tells her of George's arrest, they visit the trooper in prison and offer to help him, but he so distrusts lawyers that he refuses any legal aid. Mrs. Bagnet decides to seek out George's mother, whom she believes is still alive and living in Lincolnshire.

(53) Bucket investigates the murder. He observes those attending Tulkinghorn's funeral, studies anonymous letters implicating Lady Dedlock, and learns from Sir Leicester's footman that Lady Dedlock went out walking on the night of the murder.

Part 17 (July 1853)

(54) Bucket reveals the true story of Lady Dedlock to Sir Leicester, advising him to buy Captain Hawdon's letters, now in Grandfather Smallweed's possession. Then he apprehends Hortense and charges her with Tulkinghorn's murder. (55) When Mrs. Bagnet finds George's mother, she turns out to be Mrs. Rouncewell. George has been estranged from his family ever since he ran away from home as a young man. When Mrs. Rouncewell reveals herself to her son, George falls on his knees, asks her forgiveness, and says he is innocent. She asks Lady Dedlock to do anything she can for her son. Guppy tells Lady Dedlock that Hawdon's letters have been found and that Sir Leicester has heard her story. Lady Dedlock writes to Sir Leicester, telling him that she followed Tulkinghorn on the evening of the murder, but that she is innocent of the crime. (56) Sir Leicester collapses on the floor of the library suffering from a stroke. When he learns of Lady Dedlock's disappearance, he summons Bucket and, by writing on a slate, asks the detective to find his wife and forgive her. Bucket hires horses and a carriage, and, at one in the morning, comes to Esther's house to secure her aid in the search.

Part 18 (August 1853)

(57) Bucket and Esther go to a police station where the detective files a description of Lady Dedlock, then to a place by the river where suicides are recovered, and then to the north, picking up a trail that leads to the brickmaker's houses outside St. Albans. There Bucket learns that Jenny, the brickmaker's wife, and Lady Dedlock have gone off in opposite directions. They follow Lady Dedlock's trail to the north, but they lose it about evening. Then Bucket heads back toward London, to follow Jenny's trail.

(58) Meanwhile, Sir Leicester, attended by George, awaits his wife's return.

(59) At three in the morning, Esther and Bucket reach the outskirts of London. They go on to CHANCERY LANE, where they learn from Snagsby's servant that she has directed a ragged woman to the graveyard where Nemo is buried. There they find Lady Dedlock, dressed in Jenny's clothes, dead on the pavement before the cemetery gate.

Part 19–20 (September 1853)

(60) After Lady Dedlock's death, Esther settles in London to be near Ada and Richard. They worry about Richard's declining health. Ada tells Esther that she is pregnant and that she hopes Richard's child will draw him away from his destructive obsession with the Jarndyce case. (61) Esther asks Skimpole to stop seeing Richard. He agrees, seeing no point in making himself part of Richard's unhappy poverty. One evening, Woodcourt, as he accompanies Esther home from Richard's, reveals his love and admiration for her, but Esther turns down his proposal because she is not free to love him. With tears in her eyes, she watches him leave. (62) Esther tells Jarndyce to set the time when she will become mistress of Bleak House. Meanwhile, Grandfather Smallweed has found a Jarndyce will later than any other, which reduces John Jarndyce's interest in favor of Richard's and Ada's.

(63) George visits his brother the ironmaster in the iron district, is welcomed as an honored guest, and is invited to stay there. But George returns to settle at Chesney Wold.

(64) Jarndyce plans to go to Yorkshire to see about Woodcourt's new position there as a physi-cian to the poor. He asks Esther to accompany him. There he shows her a house for Woodcourt furnished like Bleak House, and he tells her that his proposal was a mistake. Both he and Wood-court encourage her to marry Allan and to live in the new Bleak House. She is very happy. Back in London, Guppy renews his proposal and is again refused. (65) Allan and Esther set out for Chancery on the day the Jarndyce will is to be decided. They are late for the session, and when they arrive, the proceedings are already over. Jarndyce and Jarn-dyce is decided. The new will is valid, but all the money has been absorbed in legal costs. Richard, weak, his mouth full of blood, talks of the dream's being over, of beginning in the world. He reconciles with Jarndyce. But he will begin in the next world. As he dies, Miss Flite releases her birds.

(66) Chesney Wold is quiet. Sir Leicester, accompanied by George, can be seen riding by Lady Dedlock's grave and stopping in quiet respect. The house is dark and vacant.

(67) Seven years later, Esther lives a settled life with Allan and her two daughters in Yorkshire, where they are visited by Caddy, by Ada and her son Richard, and by Jarndyce, for whom they have added a growlery to their house.

COMMENTARY

Bleak House, along with *Copperfield* and *Expecta-tions*, is one of the books most often described as Dickens's best novel. A voluminous body of criti-cism attests to its academic popularity. Published in 1852–53, *Bleak House* is often considered the first of the late novels, coming just after the auto-biographical *Copperfield*, which divides Dickens's career. Though there are some comic characters and humorous scenes, it is a dark novel that pres-ents England as diseased and apocalyptically warns of a coming day of judgment. Like the other late novels, it is focused around a central theme and dominant symbol, the fog that represents the per-vasive influence of the COURT OF CHANCERY in all aspects of British life. Dickens began this social critique with a contemporary scandal: In 1850, the *Times* published a series of articles exposing the court, with its endless delays, repetitive proceed-ings, and interminable cases. They cited several cases that had gone on for years and, like Jarn-dyce, ended by exhausting all the resources in court costs. Dickens began with this scandal and turned it into a story, symbolically anatomizing the condition of England in 1852.

The most notable technical feature in Dickens's conception is the use of two contrasting narrations, a third-person narration marked by the usual Dickensian hyperbole and rhetorical effects and a first-person narration by Esther Summerson. Critics have debated at length about why Dickens used this narrative strategy and just how successful it is, particularly in telling Esther's story.

The third-person narration that opens the novel is a generalizing, present tense, highly rhetorical voice with a panoramic view of the world. In the famous description of the fog that begins the first chapter, the narrator links London's present fogginess to Noah's flood, suggesting that it is far more than a weather condition, and then to the Court of Chancery, where the foggy wigs of the judges and lawyers symbolize the pervasive confusion that they bring to the condition of England. Then, in the second chapter, he moves to Lincolnshire and finds that the "waters are out" there as well. Satirical, symbolic, authoritative, these opening chapters present a public view; they are highly stylized reportage of the worlds of Chancery and fashion by a very capable reporter, sure of his effects. The voice is clearly male.

Esther Summerson's voice is just as clearly female. Her narration, which begins in chapter 3, is hesitant, self-deprecating, personal, an account related in the past tense of her life and of the narrow world she inhabits. From her opening sentence—"I have a great deal of difficulty in beginning to write my portion of these pages, for I know I am not clever" (3)—she counters the assurance and objectivity of the male narrator. PHILIP COLLINS (1990) has pointed out that Esther's style and language still have many characteristic Dickensian traits, but many readers have nonetheless found her a tiresome bore. Esther is too passive, too deferential to others, too repressed, too coy; she conceals or withholds her feelings about her mother and about Alan Woodcourt, and she dutifully accepts the role of "little woman." Commentators disagree on

whether Dickens was celebrating Esther as a feminine ideal or using her to show the oppressiveness of patriarchal institutions.

Esther has much in common with Dickens's other "orphan" heroes. Like Oliver Twist, she bears a name that does not indicate her parentage, and her godmother oppresses her psychologically much as Oliver is oppressed by parish authorities. Like David Copperfield, Esther has a host of nicknames, indicative of her uncertainty about her identity and her willingness to accept the identities others give her. Her situation as a woman exaggerates the identity crisis faced by these Dickensian orphans, for the opportunities available to her are fewer than those available to David or Pip. Yet for all her reticence, Esther is not totally passive. She does, for example, resist Mr. Guppy's attempts to claim her and her story.

Esther's "progress" is like that of the title character in Charlotte Bronte's *Jane Eyre* (1847), a popular novel published just a few years before *Bleak House,* which described the stages in Jane's life, from orphanhood through an abusive childhood in the care of an aunt to a position as governess and ultimately a marriage to her master. Like Jane, Esther passes through a series of symbolic bleak houses. She begins in the house of a cruel aunt who tells her, "It would have been far better . . . that you had never been born" (3) and teaches her to use "submission, self-denial, [and] diligent work" as ways to compensate for her guilty presence. After a respite at Greenleaf—a marked contrast to Jane's unhappy Lowood School—Esther is called to be the housekeeper at Bleak House, where she will also be tempted to marry the master of the house. On the way there, she stays at the house of Mrs. Jellyby, whose "telescopic philanthropy" leads to her preoccupation with Africa and to her neglect of her own children. Mrs. Jellyby represents the bleak house of imperial England, engaged around the world but out of touch with the problems at home. Krook's rooming house is another emblem of such waste and neglect. In his rag and bottle shop, he hoards the detritus of legal London that surrounds him, and his apartments house the victims of Chancery, little Miss Flite and the dying law writer Nemo.

In sharp contrast to the poverty and decay in the urban slums is Chesney Wold, the opulent country estate of Sir Leicester Dedlock, but it too has been wasted by the flood that has fogged in London. The floodgates have been opened, Sir Leicester repeatedly complains, and the waters are out in Lincolnshire. Lady Dedlock, "bored to death," acts out the devastation that has been wrought on the landed aristocracy, and the legend of the Ghost's Walk foretells the judgment that will fall upon the house.

Removed from the neglect and decay in London, the actual Bleak House seems far from bleak. Located in ST. ALBANS, an old settlement well away from the city, it provides a refuge in its irregular rooms and gardens where its owner, John Jarndyce, has withdrawn to escape the city and the Jarndyce case. But the devastation of Chancery reaches St. Albans; Jarndyce's attempt to escape to the country proves as illusory as Skimpole's charade as an irresponsible child. Jarndyce must have the Growlery to retreat to when the east wind blows, for the ills of London appear at Bleak House as Skimpole's parasitism, Mrs. Pardiggle's oppressive philanthropy, the sufferings of the brickmakers, and the smallpox that Jo, the diseased child of urban neglect, brings from Tom-All-Alone's to the suburbs.

The bleakness that afflicts all of these houses is in various ways connected to the law and the system of injustice that serves itself but ignores the human effects of its operations. The law is represented by the Lord Chancellor, the interminable Jarndyce suit, and the many lawyers in the novel, especially Tulkinghorn, whose house in LINCOLN'S INN Fields is the bleak house of the law: "Formerly a house of state . . . it is let off in sets of chambers now; and in those shrunken fragments of its greatness, lawyers lie like maggots in nuts. . . . Here, among his many boxes labelled with transcendent names, lives Mr. Tulkinghorn. . . . Everything that can have a lock has got one; no key is visible" (10). The significance of Tulkinghorn is indicated by the ominous figure of Allegory painted on the ceiling of his rooms. Locked up and secretive as an oyster, dressed in rusty black like an agent of fate, his motives for acting are never clear. He seems not to serve the best interests of his clients but rather to seek power for its own sake. His machinations are part of a legal system that simply serves itself, and in doing so wreaks havoc on society. Allegorically, all of England is a bleak house devastated by the law.

The other metaphor that underlies the novel is disease. Here Dickens follows the lead of THOMAS CARLYLE, who coined the phrase "Condition of England" in his essay *Chartism* (1839) to describe the social turmoil of the times as a form of disease (*see* CHARTISM). In *Bleak House* the infection of Chancery is seen in the Jarndyce case (its name suggestively close to jaundice); in Tom Jarndyce, who has blown his brains out before the beginning of the story; and in Richard Carstone, who catches the disease and slowly wastes away and dies. These cases are echoed in the stories of other Chancery suitors: Gridley, the Man from Shropshire, and Miss Flite, for example.

The disease metaphor has its most bizarre expression in the figure of Krook, the illiterate rag and bottle merchant, who acts an underworld parody of the Lord Chancellor. He compulsively collects legal documents and papers, but, unable to understand their contents, he can make no use of them. His papers cannot aid the cause of justice; they are simply instruments of the law. Like the gin that courses through Krook's bloodstream, this narcissistic, self-gratifying use of law is ultimately self-destructive. In Krook's improbable death by spontaneous combustion, an episode that drew much adverse criticism, there is a warning for the established legal system: When the law becomes totally absorbed with itself and its own procedures, it will destroy itself. Dickens defended his use of spontaneous combustion on scientific grounds, citing cases and scientific studies that confirmed the possibility, but his real defense would argue on symbolic grounds. Krook's explosion is a small version of legal England ending in fire. Dickens concluded the preface to the novel by remarking that he had "purposely dwelt upon the romantic side of familiar things." In Krook's improbable death, this romantic focus explodes into magical realism.

The disease metaphor is most fully developed in Jo, the illiterate crossing sweeper. He is the product of Tom-All-Alone's, the slum in the heart of London created by Chancery, for the money that would repair and maintain the houses there is tied up in the Jarndyce case. The child is as neglected as the buildings. In a society with no public education, Jo is allowed "to know nothink," to be less educated than a dog who has at least been trained to herd sheep. This neglected child, forced by the law to "move on," carries the fever from the festering slum to St. Albans. There Esther is exposed, and her illness brings her identity story to its crisis, precipitating the action that leads to Lady Dedlock's death.

Lady Dedlock's death is only the last in a series of deaths that litter the stage of the novel with bodies. From Tom Jarndyce's suicide, which occurs before the action of the story, the novel records the deaths of Miss Barbary, Jenny's baby, Captain Hawdon, Krook, Neckett, Gridley, Tulkinghorn, Jo, and Richard Carstone. All of them are, in some way or other, victims of Chancery.

A constitutional society grounded in the law that neglects its citizens is like an irresponsible parent who neglects or abuses his children. Jo and Esther—and numerous other children in the novel—represent these victims of neglect. The law is not the only bad parent. Dickens also blames religion: the cruel Calvinism that engenders the psychological abuse inflicted by Esther's aunt, the hypocritical EVANGELICALISM of the Chadbands that concentrates on converting street children like Jo rather than feeding their hunger, the "telescopic philanthropy" of those like Mrs. Jellyby who are so obsessed with missionary work in Africa that they neglect the children of England. Dickens also blames "Fashion": the class system that leads Lady Dedlock to suppress her past relationship with Captain Hawdon and "abandon" her child and the dandyism that turns Turveydrop into an imitator of the idle aristocracy and into a parasite who exploits his son. Finally, Dickens blames the artists who, like Skimpole, celebrate beauty and pretend to be children in order to avoid taking responsibility for the ugliness around them.

Faced with such systemic ills—with a national bleak house—Jarndyce's philanthropy seems trivial and ineffective. Indeed, Jarndyce cannot save Richard from Chancery nor Jo from smallpox. His kindness to Skimpole may, in fact, hasten Jo's illness and death. Although he is more enlightened and less self-interested than Mrs. Jellyby and Mrs. Pardiggle, Jarndyce's philanthropy does not represent the solution to bleakness. His strategy is one of retreat and withdrawal; he is basically passive. In spite of his kindness, he is allied with the old order. He can preserve Bleak House, even build a replica of it, but he cannot create a new order.

Jarndyce's inability to change things may account for the unfinished ending of the novel. It breaks off, mid-sentence, in Esther's narrative. She is again revealing her sense of inferiority—or her coyness—and seems not to have been changed at all psychologically by the events of the novel. The scars of parental abandonment are so lasting and the wounds of her childhood are so deep that she will carry them forever, in spite of a happy marriage and loving family. There is ample textual support for this despairing conclusion.

Yet there are also some reasons for hope in the final chapters of the novel. If a self-serving legal system, an obsolete aristocracy, and a narrow and repressive religion collude to deny possibilities for change and growth, there are a few characters in *Bleak House* who are not blinded by self-interest or enfeebled by the past. One such character is Rouncewell the Ironmaster, one of the new captains of industry. He is not intimidated by Sir Leicester's title and position: He challenges the Dedlock candidate in the election and wins, and he removes Rosa from Chesney Wold to better educate her for a useful place in society. Inspector Bucket is also one of the new class, a professional who takes pride in his work and who carries out his duties for his client; he is one of the new Metropolitan Police who represent a new way of administering the law. Finally, Allan Woodcourt, much more than the romantic hero of the novel, is a doctor who serves his patients and ministers to the poor. If anyone can heal the diseased condition of England, it will be such a man.

CHARACTERS AND RELATED ENTRIES

Badger, Bayham Doctor with whom Richard Carstone studies medicine. A cousin of Kenge, John Jarndyce's solicitor, Dr. Badger is "a pink, fresh-faced, crisp-looking gentleman, with a weak voice, light hair, and surprised eyes: some years younger . . . than Mrs. Bayham Badger. He admired her exceedingly, but principally, and to begin with, on the curious ground . . . of her having had three husbands" (13). He is perhaps most notable as Mrs. Bayham Badger's third husband.

Badger, Laura (Mrs. Bayham) Bayham Badger's wife: "She was surrounded in the drawing room by various objects, indicative of her painting a little, playing the piano a little, playing the guitar a little, playing the harp a little, singing a little, working a little, reading a little, writing poetry a little, and botanising a little. She was a lady of about fifty, I should think, youthfully dressed, and of a very fine complexion" (13). In conversation she repeatedly refers to the professional accomplishments of her first two husbands, Captain Swosser of the Royal Navy and Professor Dingo, a naturalist.

The Badgers provide comic relief in the novel, but Mrs. Badger's obsession with the professions of her husbands also draws attention to Richard Carstone's lack of commitment to his medical studies.

Bagnet, Matthew ("Lignum Vitae") Former-artilleryman, bassoon player, and proprietor of a small musical instrument shop at Elephant and Castle. An army friend of George Rouncewell, he acts as guarantor of George's loan from Grandfather Smallweed. "An ex-artilleryman, tall and upright, with shaggy eyebrows, and whiskers like the fibres of a cocoa-nut, not a hair upon his head, and a torrid complexion. His voice, short, deep, and resonant, is not at all unlike the tones of the instrument to which he is devoted. Indeed, there may be generally observed in him an unbending, unyielding, brass-bound air, as if he were himself the bassoon of the human orchestra" (27). Although his nickname from his army days is Lignum Vitae, after a South American hardwood, suggestive of his "extreme hardness and toughness," Bagnet is a gentle family man who defers to his wife in all family decisions. He tells George, "It's my old girl that advises. She has the head. But I never own to it before her. Discipline must be maintained" (27). Their mutual accommodations to this fiction maintain this happy family. When George is unable to repay the loan, Smallweed threatens the meager finances of the

Bagnet family and Mrs. Bagnet acts to rescue the family and George. The Bagnets have three children, Woolwich, Quebec, and Malta, named for the military bases where they were born.

Bagnet, Mrs. ("the Old Girl") "A strong, busy, active, honest-faced woman, . . . so economically dressed (though substantially), that the only article of ornament of which she stands possessed appears to be her wedding-ring; around which her finger has grown to be so large since it was put on, that it will never come off again until it shall mingle with Mrs. Bagnet's dust" (27). She is also recognized by her grey cloak and the umbrella she always carries. Dona Budd ("Langage Couples in *Bleak House*," *Nineteenth Century Literature*, 1994) suggests that the umbrella serves as a kind of scepter, indicating Mrs. Bagnet's assumption of the masculine role in the family. She manages the Bagnet household and makes all the important decisions in her husband's life. When George Rouncewell is arrested for the murder of Mr. Tulkinghorn, she goes to Lincolnshire to find Mrs. Rouncewell and reunites George with his mother from whom he has long been separated (52).

Barbary, Miss Lady Dedlock's stern and cruel sister who lives at WINDSOR, BERKSHIRE; the "godmother" who raises Esther Summerson. "She was a good, good woman! She went to church three times every Sunday, and to morning prayers on Wednesdays and Fridays, and to lectures whenever there were lectures; and never missed. She was handsome; and if she had ever smiled, would have been . . . like an angel—but she never smiled" (3). She tells Esther that "It would have been far better . . . that you had never been born!"

Bell Yard A narrow lane off Fleet Street where Mrs. Blinder cares for the Neckett children (15).

Bleak House Two houses in St. Albans have been suggested as the likely originals of Dickens's Bleak House. Fort House in Broadstairs, Kent, the building where Dickens spent many holidays, has been renamed Bleak House, but it has no connection with the house in the novel.

Blinder, Mrs. The kindly woman in Bell Yard who cares for the Neckett children after their father's death (15).

Blowers, Mr. An eminent attorney involved in the case of Jarndyce and Jarndyce (1).

Bogsby, James George Landlord of Sol's Arms (33).

"Boguey" Weevle's nickname for Krook (32).

Boodle, Lord One of Sir Leicester Dedlock's guests at Chesney Wold, a man of "considerable reputation within his party," who laments the politics of the time. He tells Dedlock that the choices for a new government "would lie between Lord Coodle and Sir Thomas Doodle—supposing it to be impossible for the Duke of Foodle to act with Goodle, which may be assumed to be the case in consequence of the breach arising out of that affair with Hoodle. Then, giving the Home Department and the Leadership of the House of Commons to Joodle, the Foreign Office to Moodle, what are you to do with Noodle? You can't offer him the Presidency of the Council; that is reserved for Poodle. You can't put him in the Woods and Forests; that is hardly good enough for Quoodle. What follows? That the country is shipwrecked, lost, and gone to pieces" (12). This catalog satirizes the do-nothing aristocrats and politicians who maintain the political and social status quo.

Borrioboola-Gha African village that is the focus of Mrs. Jellyby's missionary activities (4).

Boythorn, Lawrence The impetuous and boisterous friend of John Jarndyce, who speaks with a "vigorous healthy voice," spilling out a "very fury of . . . superlatives, which seem . . . to go off like blank cannons and hurt nothing. . . . He was not only a very handsome gentleman . . . with a massive grey head, a fine composure of face when silent, a figure that might have become corpulent but for his being so continually in earnest that he gave it no rest, and a chin that might have subsided into a double chin but for the vehement emphasis which it was constantly required to assist; but he was such a true gentleman in his manner, so chivalrously polite, his face was lighted by a smile of so much sweetness and tenderness, and it seemed so plain that he had nothing to hide, but showed himself exactly as he was" (9). His boisterousness is belied by the pet canary he carries upon his shoulder. He maintains an ongoing litigation over property lines with his neighbor, Sir Leicester Dedlock. He offers his house to Esther Summerson for her recuperation from smallpox (36). In his passionate commitment to principle, GRAHAM STOREY (1987) points out, he is the opposite of Harold Skimpole.

Boythorn was, according to Dickens, "a most exact portrait" of the poet WALTER SAVAGE LANDOR. DORIS ALEXANDER (1991) concludes that Dickens toned down Landor's eccentricities in the portrayal of Boythorn.

Bucket Police detective employed by Tulkinghorn to discover Gridley's whereabouts and to inquire into Lady Dedlock's interest in Hawdon's grave. "With his attentive face, and his hat and stick in his hands, and his hands behind him, [he is] a composed and quiet listener. He is a stoutly-built, steady-looking, sharp-eyed man in black, of about the middle-age" (22). He sizes up those he is questioning or investigating and discovers their interests, using flattery to learn what they might otherwise withhold. After Tulkinghorn's murder, he and his wife work together to solve the crime. Although he initially arrests George for the crime (49), he uses the arrest as a ruse in his scheme to trick Hortense into a confession (54). He is also employed by Sir Leicester Dedlock to follow Lady Dedlock when she runs from Chesney Wold (57).

Although Dickens denied it, Bucket was probably based on INSPECTOR FIELD of the Metropolitan Police.

Bucket, Mrs. Bucket's wife, "a lady of natural detective genius" (53). She keeps tabs on Hortense when the French maid is under suspicion and living as a lodger in the Bucket household.

Buffy, the Rt. Hon. William, M.P. The initial figure in one of Dickens's catalogs satirizing political Dandyism, Buffy is a political ally of Sir Leicester Dedlock. He contends that "the shipwreck of the country—about which there is no doubt . . . is attributable to Cuffy. If you had done with Cuffy what you ought to have done, when he first came into Parliament, and had prevented him going over to Duffy, you would have got him into alliance with Fuffy" (12).

Carstone, Richard Ward of the COURT OF CHANCERY, committed by the court to the charge of John Jarndyce, "a handsome youth, with an ingenuous face, and a most engaging laugh. . . . He was very young" (3). He falls in love with his cousin and fellow ward, Ada Clare. He is kind, trusting, and generous, but also naive and feckless. Jarndyce tries to give direction for his life by encouraging him to enter a profession. Richard tries medicine (13), the law (17), and the Army (24), but he is unable to settle on anything because of his unhealthy preoccupation with the Jarndyce case. Finally he falls into the clutches of the lawyer Vholes, who feeds his obsession with the suit (37). He becomes suspicious and, estranged from Jarndyce, he wastes away. Richard secretly marries Ada (51), but she cannot restore him to health. When the Jarndyce suit ends with all proceeds absorbed in court costs, Richard dies, leaving Ada and his unborn child to the care of Jarndyce (65). Obsessed with the law suit like Gridley, Miss Flite, and Tom Jarndyce, Richard is the most developed portrait of a victim of Chancery.

Chadband, Mrs. (Mrs. Rachael) Esther Summerson's childhood nurse, then known as Mrs. Rachael, "a stern, severe-looking, silent woman" (19).

Chadband, the Reverend Mr. Unctuous dissenting clergyman admired by Mrs. Snagsby, he is the model of cant and hypocrisy: "a large yellow man, with a fat smile, and a general appearance of having a good deal of train oil in his system" (19). He speaks in a homiletic style, asking empty rhetorical questions, exploiting vapid biblical allusions, with a pulpit dialect that transforms "truth" into "terewth." He "never speaks without first putting up his great hand, as delivering a token to his hearers that he is going to edify them" (19). His wife, "a stern, severe-looking, silent woman" (19), turns out to be Mrs. Rachael, Esther Summerson's childhood nurse. Chadband sermonizes Jo on "Terewth" (25). He joins with the Smallweeds in an attempt to blackmail Sir Leicester Dedlock and is thwarted by Bucket (54).

DENNIS WALDER (1981) suggests that the Reverend Edward Irving was the original for Chadband, but DORIS ALEXANDER (1991) identifies a strong physical resemblance between the preacher and the poet John Kenyon.

Charley Nickname of Charlotte Neckett.

Chesney Wold The Dedlocks' house in Lincolnshire (2), where Lady Dedlock's portrait attracts Guppy's attention (7) and where the legend of the Ghost's Walk haunts Lady Dedlock. Dickens based Chesney Wold on Rockingham Castle in Northamptonshire.

Clare, Miss Ada Ward in the COURT OF CHANCERY who is committed by the court to the guardianship of John Jarndyce, "a beautiful girl! With such rich golden hair, such soft blue eyes, such a bright, innocent, trusting face!" (3). Jarndyce chooses Esther Summerson, who refers to Ada as "my beauty," to be her companion. Although Ada is in love with her cousin and fellow ward, Richard Carstone, she is also worried about his restless and suspicious behavior. She secretly marries him shortly before his death (51) and is left with an infant son, Richard, to be cared for by Jarndyce (67).

By repeatedly referring to Ada as "my beauty," Esther calls attention to Ada's role as the figure on whom Esther projects her own physical attractiveness and sexual desires. ALEXANDER WELSH (2000) analyzes her role in these terms as a projection of Esther's repressed self-image.

"Coavinses" Skimpole's name for Neckett, derived from Neckett's employment as an agent for Coavinses' Sponging House (6).

Cook's Court   Street off Chancery Lane where Snagsby has his stationery shop. Based on Took's Court (10).

Crippler, The   Vessel of Captain Swosser in which he fell in love with the future Mrs. Bayham Badger (13).

Darby   Police constable who accompanies Bucket and Snagsby to Tom-All-Alone's (22).

Deal   Seacoast town in Kent where Esther visits Richard Carstone as he is leaving the navy. While there she also meets Allan Woodcourt, who has just returned from the East (45).

Dedlock, Lady Honoria   The proud, beautiful, and cold wife of Sir Leicester Dedlock. Twenty years younger than her husband, "she has beauty still, and, if it be not in its heyday, it is not yet in its autumn. She has a fine face—originally of a character that would be rather called very pretty than handsome, but improved into classicality by the acquired expression of her fashionable state" (2). A celebrated beauty, she conceals her humble origins and her guilt about her past behind a facade of cold condescension, repeatedly protesting that she is "bored to death." Her celebrity and her melodramatic pose draw the curious attentions of several investigators who seek to discover Lady Dedlock's secret. Tulkinghorn wants to discover the reason for her repressed interest in Nemo's handwriting (2), Guppy tries to unravel the physical resemblance between Esther Summerson and Lady Dedlock's portrait, and Bucket investigates her involvement in Tulkinghorn's murder. Tulkinghorn learns of her relationship with Captain Hawdon and of their illegitimate daughter, Esther Summerson. Lady Dedlock reveals herself to Esther and pledges her to secrecy (36), but she runs from Chesney Wold when Sir Leicester learns of her past (56). Disguised as a poor brickmaker's wife, she makes her way to London pursued by Bucket and Esther. They find her dead by the gate to the graveyard where Hawdon is buried (59).

Lady Dedlock's story follows that of the conventional Victorian melodrama of the fallen woman; the novel could easily have been entitled "Lady Dedlock's Secret." Telling it, however, through the two contrasting narrators shifts the interest from the conventional exposé to the psychological implications, both for Lady Dedlock and for those around her. Repressing her secret has frozen her into a state of self-conscious spiritual paralysis, a condition analyzed by J. HILLIS MILLER (1958). She is as deadlocked psychologically as her husband is socially. Seeing her story through the eyes of Esther, who for different reasons represses the truth of her identity, also underscores the degree to which her story is constructed by the men who investigate her, especially Tulkinghorn, Guppy, and Bucket. As her inclusion in the "Galaxy Gallery of British Beauty" indicates, she is a construct of the male gaze. Only Esther, who scrupulously avoids similar attention, has intimations of Lady Dedlock's inner life, knowledge that she is bound to keep secret. Although Esther's narration, in a limited way, defamiliarizes the conventional story, it does not save Lady Dedlock from the inevitable punishment for her sins, a punishment that extends to others, especially Sir Leicester and Tulkinghorn, whose involvement in her story brings suffering and death.

Dedlock, Sir Leicester   Baronet, patriarch of the Lincolnshire Dedlocks and present owner of their landed estate, Chesney Wold. "His family is as old as the hills and infinitely more respectable. He has a general opinion that the world might get on without hills, but would be done up without Dedlocks. . . . He is an honourable, obstinate, truthful, high-spirited, intensely prejudiced, perfectly unreasonable man. Sir Leicester is twenty years, full measure, older than my Lady. He will never see sixty-five again, nor perhaps sixty-six, nor yet sixty-seven. He has a twist of gout now and then, and walks a little stiffly. He is of a worthy presence, with his light grey hair and whiskers, his fine shirt-frill, his pure white waistcoat, and his blue coat with bright buttons always buttoned" (2). At the top of the social scale in the novel, Sir Leicester represents the idle landed aristocracy. He is deadlocked in the past and is totally alienated from his present society, a condition described in the novel as Dandyism (12).

This failure to live in the present is most evident in his interactions with Rouncewell the Ironmaster, who is very much a man of his time (28). Sir Leicester's increasing irrelevance is evident when his candidate loses the election to Rouncewell, and it culminates in his stroke and paralysis when he learns of Lady Dedlock's past. He transcends this largely satiric role at the end of the novel when, loyal to his wife, he offers forgiveness and seeks to save her, prompting the narrator, as GRAHAM STOREY (1987) points out, to a rare accolade: "His noble earnestness, his fidelity, his gallant shielding of her, his generous conquest of his own wrong and his own pride for her sake, are simply honorable, manly, and true" (58).

Dedlock, Volumnia Sir Leicester's cousin, a proud and poor spinster, "a young lady (of sixty) . . . retired to Bath; where she lives slenderly on an annual present from Sir Leicester, and whence she makes occasional resurrections in the country houses of her cousins" (28). After Lady Dedlock's death, she becomes mistress of Chesney Wold.

Dingo, Professor Famous scientist who was the second husband of Mrs. Bayham Badger (13).

Divinities of Albion, or Galaxy Gallery of British Beauty Tony Jobling's prize possession, a collection of copper-plate pictures "representing ladies of title and fashion in every variety of smirk that art, combined with capital, is capable of producing." It includes a picture of Lady Dedlock (20).

Donny, Misses Twin sisters who operate Greenleaf School near Reading, where Esther Summerson was a pupil (3).

Elephant and Castle The district in south London where the Bagnets live (27). Its name comes from the famous public house at its center where the roads to Kent and Surrey come together.

Flite, Miss "A little mad old woman in a squeezed bonnet" (3) who is obsessed by the COURT OF CHANCERY, even though her family has been ruined by it. She believes that a judgment in her case is immi-

nent, a conclusion she confuses with the Last Judgment, describing both events in apocalyptic terms. She befriends Ada, Richard, and Esther (whom she calls Fitz-Jarndyce) and invites them to her lodgings on the top floor of Krook's house (5). There she keeps a cage of birds named Hope, Joy, Youth, Peace, Rest, Life, Dust, Ashes, Waste, Want, Ruin, Despair, Madness, Death, Cunning, Folly, Words, Wigs, Rags, Sheepskin, Plunder, Precedent, Jargon, Gammon, and Spinach, to which she adds the Wards of Jarndyce. When the Jarndyce case is settled, she sets the birds free (65).

One of the victims of Chancery, along with Tom Jarndyce, Gridley, and Richard Carstone, Miss Flite has been driven to madness by her obsession with the court. Appropriately she lives in the house of Krook, the symbolic counter to the Lord Chancellor, her name associating her with the caged birds who catalog the social ills caused by the court. Her confusion over the court's judgment and the biblical Day of Judgment extends her significance beyond social satire to the philosophic theme of living in expectation, a theme Dickens developed in many of his novels, especially *Great Expectations*.

George, Trooper Nickname of George Rouncewell.

Ghost's Walk, the The terrace at Chesney Wold where ghostly footsteps are sometimes heard. Legend has it that they are those of the Lady Dedlock from the 17th century whose sympathy for the Puritan cause made her a traitor to King Charles and the Dedlocks (7).

Greenleaf The school near Reading where Esther Summerson is educated under the tutelage of the Misses Donny (3).

Gridley ("The Man from Shropshire") Another of the victims of the COURT OF CHANCERY whose angry and violent efforts to gain a hearing of his grievances have led to his repeated imprisonment for contempt of court over a period of 25 years. "A tall sallow man with a careworn head, . . . a combative look; and a chafing, irritable manner" (15), he hides out and dies at George's Shooting

Gallery, a place of refuge in the novel, while trying to escape arrest (27).

Growlery, the   John Jarndyce's den at Bleak House to which he escapes when the "east wind" has blown him out of humor.

Grubble, W.   Landlord of the Dedlock Arms, "a pleasant-looking, stoutish, middle-aged man, who never seemed to consider himself cosily dressed for his own fireside without his hat and top-boots, but who never wore a coat except at church" (37).

Guppy, Mrs.   William Guppy's protective and doting mother, "an old lady in a large cap, with rather a red nose and rather an unsteady eye, but smiling all over. Her close little sitting-room was prepared for a visit; and there was a portrait of her son in it" (38). After Esther refuses her son for the last time, Mrs. Guppy refuses to leave Jarndyce's house, indignantly inquiring, "Ain't my son good enough for you?" (64).

Guppy, William   Cockney clerk for Kenge and Carboy, "a young gentleman who had inked himself by accident" (3), Guppy is a brash and vulgar young man who proposes to Esther Summerson and is refused (9). Struck by the likeness between Esther and Lady Dedlock's portrait (7), he investigates Esther's identity and learns Lady Dedlock's secret (29), but Krook's surprising death destroys the corroborating documents that he has arranged to buy (32). After Esther's illness, he formally withdraws his proposal (38), only to renew it later and to be refused again (64). A wonderfully comic figure, Guppy speaks in a mixture of urban slang and legal jargon.

Gusher   One of Mrs. Pardiggle's missionary friends, "a flabby gentleman, with a moist surface, and eyes so much too small for his moon of a face, that they seemed to have been originally made for somebody else" (15).

Guster   Mrs. Snagsby's maid, "a lean young woman from a workhouse by some supposed to have been christened Augusta) . . . really aged three or four and twenty, but looking around ten years older" (10). She is subject to fits.

Hawdon, Captain ("Nemo")   Retired military officer who, using the alias Nemo (Latin for "nobody"), works as a law writer and lives in abject poverty on the middle floor of Krook's house. He is found dead there, probably from an opium overdose (10). His death is mourned only by Woodcourt, the doctor who attended him, and Jo, a ragged crossing sweeper he has befriended. Tulkinghorn and Guppy, suspicious of his identity, discover his secret, that he was Lady Dedlock's lover before her marriage and the father of Esther Summerson. Their investigations lead to the harassment of Trooper George and provoke Lady Dedlock's flight, which ends with her death by the gate of the cemetery in the heart of Tom-All-Alone's, where Hawdon is buried.

Haymarket   Turveydrop likes to dine at a restaurant in this street off Pall Mall in London's West End. George's Shooting Gallery is nearby.

Hortense   Lady Dedlock's passionate French maid, "a large-eyed brown woman with black hair: who would be handsome, but for a certain feline mouth, and general uncomfortable tightness of face, rendering the jaws too eager, and the skull too prominent. There is something indefinably keen and wan about her anatomy; and she has a watchful way of looking out of the corners of her eyes without turning her head, which could be pleasantly dispensed with—especially when she is in an ill-humour and near knives" (12). She becomes insanely jealous when she is supplanted by Rosa. She aids Tulkinghorn's investigation into Lady Dedlock's connection with Hawdon, but when he does not reward her appropriately, she murders him (48). Bucket and his wife pursue and arrest her (54). She is loosely based on Mrs. Maria Manning, the notorious murderess whose execution Dickens witnessed in 1849. Her passionate vengefulness foreshadows that of Dickens's other French villainess, Madame Defarge in *A Tale of Two Cities.*

Jarndyce, John   Present owner of Bleak House and court-appointed guardian to Richard Carstone and Ada Clare, an "upright, hearty and robust" man, "nearer sixty than fifty," who has "a handsome, lively, quick face" (6). Even though he is the principal figure in the Jarndyce case, he avoids any involvement with it and advises others to do the same, advice that would have been useful to his great-uncle, Tom Jarndyce, who "in despair blew his brains out at a Coffee House in Chancery Lane" (1). Although he recognizes the destructiveness of the court, he is not so clear-sighted about the shortcomings of those he helps, especially Harold Skimpole. He is unsuccessful in preventing Richard's entanglement in the case. When such things put him out of humor, he says "the wind's in the east" and retreats to a den in Bleak House he calls his Growlery. He devotes his life to the practice of private philanthropy. He adopts Esther Summerson, sending her to school and then engaging her as a companion to Ada (3). He later proposes marriage to her (44); she accepts out of gratitude and obligation, but when he realizes that she really loves Allan Woodcourt, Jarndyce arranges their marriage, providing a new Bleak House for them in YORKSHIRE (64).

Jarndyce is one of many benevolent gentlemen in Dickens's novels, but his kindness is more conflicted than that of Mr. Brownlow (*Oliver Twist*) or the Cheerybles (*Nicholas Nickleby*). Rather than confront the evils of society, Jarndyce is often driven to retreat into his Growlery. He fails in his attempts to save Richard from ruin and is unable to see the destructive side of Skimpole. His relation to Esther is also more complex than the fatherly affection of the earlier philanthropists and includes an erotic, if repressed, attraction that prompts his quixotic proposal and his diffidence in "courting" her. He hides his inner life from others, a secrecy not probed in Esther's reticent narrative. Finally, in a novel that attacks false philanthropy, Jarndyce also seems reticent to carry out wholeheartedly his role as a representative of positive philanthropy.

Jarndyce and Jarndyce   The lawsuit at the center of *Bleak House* that has been winding on interminably in the Court of Chancery for several generations. John Jarndyce avoids a destructive obsession with the case, but his great-uncle Tom, Richard Carstone, and others are ruined by it. When it is finally settled at the end of the novel, all proceeds from the will have been used up in legal costs. Dickens based the case on actual cases in Chancery

that prompted a movement for court reform at the time the novel was being written.

Jellyby, Caroline (Caddy)   Mrs. Jellyby's eldest daughter, "a jaded and unhealthy-looking, though by no means plain girl" (4), who slaves as her mother's secretary and whose ink-stained hands attest to her drudgery. Caddy resents her mother's neglect in not instructing her in domestic skills or personal grooming, and she resents her mother's exploitation of her. "I wish Africa was dead" (4), she confesses to Esther. Caddy escapes her chaotic home by taking dancing lessons and by marrying Prince Turveydrop, the dance instructor (30). When Prince goes lame, she takes over his duties at the academy. They have one child, a deaf and dumb daughter, Esther.

Welsh (2000) analyzes Caddy's role in the novel as a rival to Esther; Caddy makes her own way out of childhood neglect and struggles to survive, yet she is treated condescendingly in Esther's narrative.

Jellyby, Mr.   Mrs. Jellyby's husband, "a mild bald gentleman in spectacles" who sits "in a corner with his head against the wall, as if he were subject to low spirits" (4). His low spirits and bankruptcy seem to be caused by Mrs. Jellyby's neglect.

Jellyby, Mrs.   "A pretty, very diminuitive, plump woman of from forty to fifty, with handsome eyes, though they had a curious habit of seeming to look a long way off, as if . . . she could see nothing nearer than Africa" (4). Her "mission" is an educational project for "the natives of Borrioboola-Gha, on the left bank of the Niger" (4). This "telescopic philanthropy" causes her to overlook problems at home and to neglect her family and her household, and this negligence is evident in the constant state of chaos in her home. When the African scheme fails, she takes up "the rights of women to sit in Parliament" (67).

Mrs. Jellyby's African project was based on a failed Evangelical missionary effort that Dickens had discussed in "The Niger Expedition" (1848). Mrs. Jellyby's character was based on CAROLINE CHISHOLM, a woman devoted to aiding emigrants to Australia but neglectful of her own family. The satire of feminism in Mrs. Jellyby and Miss Wisk so offended John Stuart Mill, who would write the feminist classic *The Subjection of Women* (1869), that he said *Bleak House* was "much the worst" of Dickens's novels and condemned "the vulgar impudence of this thing to ridicule the rights of women."

Jellyby, Peepy Caddy's younger brother. His mother's neglect is evident in his clothing, which is "either too large for him or too small," and in his frequent scrapes and accidents, such as getting his head caught in the railing in front of his house (4).

Jenny Wife of the violent brickmaker who abuses her. When Esther first visits her house, accompanying Mrs. Pardiggle (8), Jenny has a black eye and is "nursing a poor little gasping baby" who dies during their visit. Esther covers the infant with her handkerchief, an incident recalling Esther's burial of her doll and her own childhood. Lady Dedlock later secures the handkerchief. On her final flight from Chesney Wold, Lady Dedlock exchanges clothes with Jenny (57–59).

Jo ("Toughy") The poor, illiterate crossing sweeper and street urchin at the bottom of the social scale in the novel, "very muddy, very hoarse, very ragged. . . . Name, Jo. Nothing else that he knows on. . . . No father, no mother, no friends. Never

Two crossing-sweepers at work, from Henry Mayhew's *London Labour and the London Poor* (1851).

been to school" (11). Befriended by Nemo, he testifies at the inquest into the law writer's death (11). He lives on the streets of Tom-All-Alone's, suggesting that his utter homelessness and ignorance are the human side of the urban slums created by Chancery. He guides Lady Dedlock to the cemetery where Hawdon is buried (16); carries the smallpox to St. Albans, after he is told to "move on," where it infects Charley and Esther (31); and dies at George's Shooting Gallery attended by Woodcourt (47).

Jo's story is told in a series of famous set pieces: his answers at the inquest into Nemo's death, drawn from an actual case of a crossing sweeper named George Ruby at the Guildhall in January 1850; his breakfast on the steps of the Society for the Propagation of the Gospel in Foreign Parts at which Jo's illiteracy is contrasted to the knowledge of a dog who has been trained to herd sheep (16); his incomprehension as he is sermonized by the hypocritical Chadband (19); and his death repeating the Lord's Prayer following Woodcourt's instruction (47).

The testimony of George Ruby was published in the EXAMINER (January 12, 1850) and later reprinted in HOUSEHOLD WORDS ("Household Narrative," January 1850).

Jobling, Tony ("Weevle") Guppy's friend who "has the faded appearance of a gentleman in embarrassed circumstances; even his light whiskers droop with something of a shabby air" (20). He takes Nemo's rooms after the law writer's death, using the alias "Weevle," in order to keep an eye on Krook for Guppy (20). At the appointed hour when Guppy is supposed to get Hawdon's papers from Krook, Tony and Guppy discover the old man's extraordinary disappearance by spontaneous combustion (32). Tony also goes along when Guppy renews his proposal to Esther (64).

Kenge ("Conversation Kenge") Mr. Jarndyce's solicitor with the firm of Kenge and Carboy: "a portly, important-looking gentleman, dressed all in black, with a white cravat, large gold watch seals, a pair of gold eyeglasses, and a large seal ring upon his little finger. . . . He appeared to enjoy beyond everything the sound of his own voice" (3). He handles Jarndyce's adoption of Esther Summerson and takes

Richard as an assistant when he briefly considers entering the law. Kenge ties the greatness of Britain to her legal system and counters Jarndyce's cynicism about the law with inflated chauvinistic rhetoric: "We are a great country, Mr. Jarndyce, we are a very great country. This is a great system, Mr. Jarndyce, and would you wish a great country to have a little system? Now, really, really!" (62).

Krook ("Lord Chancellor") A drunken and illiterate rag and bone dealer, who amasses miscellaneous artifacts and papers in much the same way as the COURT OF CHANCERY collects documents, earning him the nickname Lord Chancellor. "An old man in spectacles and a hairy cap. He was short, cadaverous, and withered; with his head sunk edgeways between his shoulders, and the breath issuing in visible smoke from his mouth, as if he were on fire within" (5). With his ominous cat, Lady Jane, he presides over an establishment that is a kind of "counter Chancery." Nemo (Captain Hawdon) occupies rooms on the middle floor of Krook's house and Miss Flite the top floor. After Nemo's death, Jobling takes his rooms (20). On the night Krook is to give some of Nemo's papers to Guppy, the old man spontaneously combusts, taking the documents with him (32). When Krook is discovered to have been Mrs. Smallweed's brother, the Smallweeds take over his effects and discover the missing Jarndyce will among his papers (33).

Krook's controversial role in the novel, especially his death, was criticized by many Victorian readers, most notably GEORGE HENRY LEWES, who challenged it as unrealistic and unscientific. Although Dickens cited cases of spontaneous combustion in his preface to the novel, his intent was clearly symbolic. He used the episode as a way of suggesting the fate of Chancery and any institution that so blighted the nation and destroyed those who sought redress in the law.

Lady Jane Krook's tigerish cat (5).

Le Cat, Claude Nicolas (1700–1768) Renowned French surgeon cited by Dickens in the preface to *Bleak House* as the source for a report of a recent case of spontaneous combustion.

Lincolnshire County about 125 miles north of London where Chesney Wold, country seat of the Dedlocks, is located.

Liz Brickmaker's wife and friend of Jenny. "An ugly woman . . . [who] had no kind of grace about her, but the grace of sympathy; but when she condoled with the woman, and her own tears fell, she wanted no beauty" (8).

Lord Chancellor Head of the British judicial system, appointed by the prime minister and a member of his cabinet, and the presiding judge in the COURT OF CHANCERY. He is "at the very heart of the fog" in the opening chapter of *Bleak House* and is the judge who appoints Jarndyce as guardian over Richard Carstone and Ada Clare (3).

Melvilleson, Miss M. "Noted syren" who sings at the Sol's Arms; "she has been married a year and a half, . . . and . . . her baby is clandestinely conveyed to the Sol's Arms every night to receive its natural nourishment during the entertainments" (32).

"Mercury" The Dedlocks' footman (16).

Mooney The beadle who makes arrangements for the inquest into Hawdon's death (11). PETER ACKROYD (1990) identifies his original as Looney, a beadle in charge of Salisbury Square.

Morgan ap Kerrig Mrs. Woodcourt's eminent Welsh ancestor; "He appeared to have passed his life always getting up into mountains, and fighting somebody; and a Bard whose name sounded like Crumlinwallinwer had sung his praises, in a piece which was called, as nearly as I could catch it, Mewlinnwillinwodd" (17).

Mount Pleasant "Ill-favored and ill-savoured neighborhood" in east London where the Smallweeds live (21).

Neckett ("Coavinses") Sheriff's officer who arrests debtors and brings them to Coavinses sponging house (earning him the name "Coavinses" from Skimpole). Esther and Richard stop him from arresting Skimpole by paying Skimpole's debt (6). He dies, leaving three children; Charlotte (age 13) and two younger children, Emma and Tom.

Neckett, Charlotte ("Charley") Neckett's daughter who, after her father's death, provides for herself and her two younger siblings by doing laundry. At 13 she appears "a very little girl, childish in figure but shrewd and older-looking in the face—pretty-faced too—wearing a womanly sort of bonnet much too large for her, and drying her bare arms on a womanly sort of apron" (15). Jarndyce provides for the orphaned children, employing Charley as Esther's maid. After Esther nurses Charley through the smallpox, Charley returns the care and nurses Esther through the illness (31–35, 37). By the end of the story Charley has married a miller.

Charley serves as a kind of double to Esther, repeating the qualities of self-denial, dutifulness, and hard work that earn Esther such nicknames as Dame Durden, Mother Hubbard, and Little Old Woman.

"Nemo" The alias Captain Hawdon uses when in London working as a law writer.

Old Square The section of Lincoln's Inn where the offices of Kenge and Carboy are located (20).

Old Street Road The street in east London, now simply Old Street, where Mrs. Guppy lives "in an independent though unassuming manner" (9).

Pardiggle, Mrs. Philanthropic associate of Mrs. Jellyby; "she was a formidable style of lady, with spectacles, a prominent nose, and a loud voice, who had the effect of wanting a great deal of room. And she really did, for she knocked down little chairs with her skirts" (8). With her intrusive manner, she barges in where she is not wanted to distribute religious tracts rather than aid or comfort.

In Mrs. Pardiggle, Dickens attacked another form of false philanthropy, that of the Tractarians or Puseyites (after the Reverend Edward Pusey), a High Church movement that sought to restore Catholic doctrines to the Anglican church.

Pardiggle, O. A. Mrs. Pardiggle's husband, "an obstinate-looking man with a large waistcoat and stubbly hair, who was always talking in a loud bass voice about his mite, or Mrs. Pardiggle's mite, or their five boys' mites" (30).

Pardiggle children The Pardiggles' five sons, **Egbert, Oswald, Francis, Felix,** and **Alfred,** "weazened and shrivelled" and "ferocious with discontent" (8), are resentful pawns in their mother's philanthropy. Each has his allowance subscribed to various charitable enterprises. Their names are taken from saints of the early Christian church.

Peaks, the Former name of Bleak House (8).

Peffer Snagsby's deceased partner in the law stationer's business (10).

Perkins, Mrs. Resident of the neighborhood around Sol's Arms who, with her neighbor Mrs. Piper, takes a keen interest in the mysterious events at Krook's house.

Piper, Mrs. Anastasia Mrs. Perkins's friend and Krook's neighbor who testifies at the inquest into Nemo's death: "a good deal to say, chiefly in parentheses, and without punctuation, but not much to tell" (11).

Polly Waitress at the restaurant—"of a class known among its freqenters by the denomination Slap-Bang"—who serves Guppy, Jobling, and Chick Smallweed when they go out to dinner. She is "a bouncing young female of forty . . . supposed to have made some impression on the susceptible Smallweed" (20).

Polygon A block of run-down houses in Somers Town where the Dickens family lived 1827. Harold Skimpole lives here (43).

Pouch, Mrs. Joe A widow that Trooper George might once have married. "Joe Pouch's widow might have done me good—there was something in her—and something of her—but I couldn't make up my mind to it" (27).

Priscilla   The Jellyby's maid who "drinks—she's always drinking" (4).

Quayle   A philanthropic associate of Mrs. Jellyby, "a loquacious young man . . . with large shining knobs for temples, and hair all brushed to the back of his head" (4). He praises the missions of Mrs. Jellyby, Mrs. Pardiggle, and others, for his "great power seemed to be his power of indiscriminate admiration" (15). He hopes to marry Caddy Jellyby, but he ultimately settles for Miss Wisk.

Queen Square   Bloomsbury. Jarndyce finds "a neat little furnished lodging in a quiet old house" for Richard Carstone here (18).

Rachael, Mrs.   The name of Esther Summerson's stern nurse who cares for Esther after Miss Barbary dies. She later reappears as the wife of the Reverend Mr. Chadband.

Reading   Greenleaf, the school run by the Misses Donny that Esther Summerson attends, is located near this town in Berkshire (3).

Rolls Yard   A spot in Symond's Inn off Chancery Lane where Mr. Snagsby "loved to lounge about of a Sunday afternoon" (10).

Rosa   "Dark-eyed, dark-haired, shy village beauty" who assists Mrs. Rouncewell, shows visitors around Chesney Wold, and attracts the attentions of Watt Rouncewell. When Lady Dedlock chooses Rosa for her personal maid, she arouses the jealous anger of Hortense (12). After Tulkinghorn uncovers the truth about Lady Dedlock's past, she sends Rosa away to the care of Rouncewell the Ironmaster (48). To correct her "feudal" training at Chesney Wold, he has her reeducated in Germany. She marries Watt (63).

Rouncewell, George ("Trooper George")   Mrs. Rouncewell's younger son who has run away to the army and cut himself off from his family. "He is a swarthy brown man of fifty; well-made, and good-looking; with crisp dark hair, bright eyes, and a broad chest. His sinewy and powerful hands, as

sunburnt as his face, have evidently been used to a pretty rough life. What is curious about him is, that he sits forward on his chair as if he were, from long habit, allowing space for some dress or accoutrements that he has altogether laid aside. . . . Altogether, one might guess Mr. George to have been a trooper once upon a time" (21). After leaving the army he opened a shooting gallery and martial arts academy near LEICESTER SQUARE, borrowing money from Grandfather Smallweed to start the business. Tulkinghorn and Grandfather Smallweed pressure the Trooper to turn over to them a sample of the writing of Captain Hawdon, George's officer in the army (34). George reluctantly does so after they threaten the Bagnets, who have cosigned for the loan. Bucket arrests George for Tulkinghorn's murder (49), but the Bagnets help clear his name and reunite him with his mother (56). He returns to Chesney Wold and becomes Sir Leicester's attendant (63).

Beneath his stiff and military manner, George possesses a simple integrity, a sense of honor, responsibility, and loyalty to his friends and associates. His shooting gallery, in spite of its military character, is a place of refuge where Phil Squod, his assistant, finds affection and where both Gridley and Jo come to die.

Rouncewell the Ironmaster, Mr.   Mrs. Rouncewell's elder son, who has moved away and become an ironmaster; he "would have been provided for at Chesney Wold, and would have been made steward in good season; but he took . . . to constructing steam-engines" (7). "He is a little over fifty perhaps, of a good figure, like his mother; and has a clear voice, a broad forehead from which his dark hair has retired, and a shrewd, though open face. He is a responsible-looking gentleman dressed in black, portly enough, but strong and active. Has a perfectly natural and easy air, and is not in the least embarrassed by the great presence [Sir Leicester] into which he comes" (27). He is not intimidated by the Dedlocks or their conservative, aristocratic traditions. He runs for Parliament representing the interests of the new industrial class and defeats Sir Leicester's candidate (28). He is skeptical at first of Rosa's suitability as a wife for his son Watt, because of her upbringing at Chesney Wold; he agrees to their union after she has been "re-educated" in Germany.

Rouncewell, Mrs. Housekeeper at Chesney Wold, "a fine old lady, handsome, stately, wonderfully neat. . . . It is the next difficult thing to an impossibility to imagine Chesney Wold without Mrs. Rouncewell, but she has only been here fifty years" (7). Mrs. Rouncewell is as much a defining figure of the old-fashioned way of life at Chesney Wold as Sir Leicester Dedlock is. After she is reunited with her vagabond son George, he continues the family connection to this way of life by becoming Sir Leicester's attendant.

The Rouncewell family represents the changes that the Industrial Revolution brought to Britain in the late 18th and early 19th century.

Mrs. Rouncewell was probably drawn from Dickens's grandmother, ELIZABETH BALL DICKENS.

Rouncewell, Watt The ironmaster's son, "out of his apprenticeship, and home from a journey in far countries, whither he was sent to enlarge his knowledge and complete his preparations for the venture of this life" (7). He falls in love with Rosa and ultimately marries her.

Watt is named for the inventor of the steam engine, James Watt (1736–1819).

Skimpole, Harold Friend of John Jarndyce, who, though trained as a physician, practices as a dilettante dabbling in art and music while pretending to be an irresponsible "child." "He was a little bright creature, with a rather large head; but a delicate face, and a sweet voice, and there was a perfect charm in him. All he said was so free from effort and spontaneous, and was said with such captivating gaiety, that it was fascinating to hear him talk" (6). He takes no responsibility for his finances and sponges from Jarndyce and others, establishing a kind of symbiotic relationship with his benefactors. "I don't feel any vulgar gratitude to you," he tells them, "I almost feel as if *you* ought to be grateful to *me*, for giving you the opportunity of enjoying the luxury of generosity" (6). He justifies his parasitic way of life with his "Drone philosophy"(8), which

describes the drone, living on the honey produced by the busy bees, as a necessary counterpart to them. Esther and Richard loan him money to prevent his arrest by Neckett (6). He accepts a bribe from Bucket to disclose the whereabouts of young Jo (31). Vholes gives him five pounds to introduce him to Richard Carstone (57). Later, Jarndyce asks him not to accept money from Richard Carstone (61). Skimpole responds by describing Jarndyce in his memoirs as "the Incarnation of Selfishness" (61). Skimpole has several children and grandchildren, including three daughters, Arethusa, Laura, and Kitty, whom he characterizes as his Beauty daughter, Sentiment daughter, and Comedy daughter (43).

Although Skimpole claims to possess the innocence and openness of a child, he turns out to be more secretive and knowing than he pretends. He colludes with Bucket to "move on" the feverish Jo; he callously ignores the suffering of his wife and children, and his final condemnation of Jarndyce reveals a selfishness that belies his innocent philosophy. His relationship with Jarndyce, who is largely blind to Skimpole's faults, adds an important dimension to the novel's critique of philanthropy, suggesting that philanthropy calls for collusion between the philanthropists and their clients. ALEXANDER WELSH (2000) provides a thoughtful analysis of the relation between Skimpole and Jarndyce.

Skimple was so closely drawn from the writer LEIGH HUNT that Dickens boasted, "I suppose [Skimpole] is the most exact portrait that was ever printed in words! . . . It is an absolute reproduction of the real man." Many of Dickens's contemporaries immediately recognized the portrait.

Skimpole, Mrs. Harold's wife "had once been a beauty, but was now a delicate high-nosed invalid, suffering under a complication of disorders" (43).

Sladdery Proprietor of a bookshop and lending library that caters to a fashionable clientele (2).

Smallweed, Bartholomew (Bart, "Small," "Chick Weed") Joshua Smallweed's grandson, twin of Judy, and one of Guppy's circle of friends. "Whether Young Smallweed (metaphorically called Small and eke Chick Weed, as it were jocularly to express a fledgling,) was ever a boy, is much doubted in Lincoln's Inn. He is now something under fifteen, and an old limb of the law. . . . He is a town-made article, of small stature and weazen features; but may be perceived from a considerable distance by means of his very tall hat. To become a Guppy is the object of his ambition" (20). Bart is less admiring of his idol after Guppy becomes secretive about his investigations into Nemo's identity.

Smallweed, Grandmother   Joshua's senile wife who angers her husband by incoherently referring to his money, so that he throws pillows at her and berates her as "a brimstone idiot" and "an old pig" (21).

Smallweed, Joshua (Grandfather Smallweed) Crippled usurer to whom Trooper George owes money: "the name of this old pagan's God was Compound Interest. He lived for it, married it, died of it" (21). Confined to a chair, under which he keeps his money box, he passes the time berating his wife and throwing cushions at her when she mentions money. Grandfather Smallweed uses George's obligation to him to extract from the trooper a sample of Captain Hawdon's writing for Tulkinghorn (34). After the death of Krook, his brother-in-law, he discovers some papers among Krook's possessions and tries to blackmail Sir Leicester with them, but Bucket foils this scheme (62). He also finds a Jarndyce will that Bucket secures for Jarndyce.

Doris Alexander (1991) suggests that Grandfather Smallweed bears certain resemblances to the poet Samuel Rogers as an old man and Grandmother Smallweed recalls Rogers's wife.

Smallweed, Judy   Bart's twin sister, who keeps house in the Smallweed establishment and reiterates the characteristics of the family. "Judy never owned a doll, never heard of Cinderella, never played at any game. She once or twice fell into children's company when she was about ten years old, but the children couldn't get along with Judy, and Judy couldn't get on with them. She seemed like an animal of another species" (21).

Snagsby   Law stationer who hires Nemo to do occasional work for him as a law writer; "a mild, bald, timid man, with a shining head, . . . he tends to meekness and obesity" (10). He harbors a vague sense of guilt and an anxiety that he is somehow involved in mysteries that he does not understand. He befriends Jo and supplies him with odd half crowns (25).

Snagsby, Mrs. Sarah   Snagsby's wife, a zealous follower of the Reverend Chadband. Her sour temperament, made up of internal "pints of vinegar and lemon-juice" (10), is expressed loudly as she berates her husband whom she suspects of fathering Jo, the poor crossing sweeper, and of a clandestine relationship with Hortense, Lady Dedlock's French maid. She spies on her husband until Bucket finally informs her that her suspicions are groundless (59).

Sol's Arms, the   Public house in Chancery Lane where Little Swills performs and where the inquests into the deaths of Nemo and Krook are held (11, 33). It is based on the Ship Tavern in Chancery Lane.

spontaneous combustion   The controversial manner by which Krook dies (32). Dickens was attacked for believing in superstition and bad science, most notably by George Lewes, after the appearance of the 10th number of the novel, in which the horrific incident occurs. In response, Dickens listed authorities attesting to the authenticity of spontaneous combustion during the inquest in the 11th number, and he defended his use of the incident more fully in the preface to the 1853 edition. Trevor Blout ("Dickens and Mr. Krook's Spontaneous Combustion," *Dickens Studies Annual,* 1970), demonstrates that Dickens believed in the authenticity of the phenomenon and carefully prepared and developed the incident's symbolic role in the novel.

Squod, Phil   Trooper George's assistant at the shooting gallery, "a little man with a face all crushed together, who appears, from a certain blue and speckled appearance that one of his cheeks presents, to have been blown up, in a way of business, at some odd time or times" (21). Originally an itinerant tinker, he goes to live at Chesney Wold with George at the end of the novel.

Stables, the Hon. Bob Sir Leicester Dedlock's cousin, knowledgeable about horses, who is a frequent guest at Chesney Wold. After Lady Dedlock's disappearance, he comments that "although he always knew she was the best-groomed woman in the stud, he had no idea she was a bolter" (58).

Summerson, Esther ("Dame Durden," "Mother Shipton") Narrator of the first-person sections of *Bleak House.* Raised by her aunt, Miss Barbary, as an orphan and told "It would have been far better . . . that you had never been born" (3), Esther is shy and self-deprecating: "I know I am not clever. I always knew that. . . . I had always a rather noticing way—not a quick way. O no!—a silent way of noticing what passed before me, and thinking I should like to understand it better. I have not by any means a quick understanding" (3). After her aunt's death, John Jarndyce sends her to Greenleaf School and then appoints her as his housekeeper at Bleak House in ST. ALBANS and as companion to Ada Clare (6). He praises Esther's industry, thoughtfulness, and maturity, addressing her with nicknames like "Mother Shipton," "Dame Durden," and "Mother Hubbard" that emphasize her role as a sexless housekeeper. He encourages her to learn about her parentage, in spite of Esther's reluctance to do so. In the course of the story, Esther discovers that she is the illegitimate daughter of Lady Dedlock and Captain Hawdon (36). Though Esther is pretty enough to be recognized by Guppy as Lady Dedlock's daughter, she deprecates her own beauty and is pleased when her face, scarred by smallpox, loses its beauty and her resemblance to her mother is disguised. She refuses Guppy's proposal (9) and secretly loves Woodcourt, but she accepts Jarndyce's proposal that she become mistress of Bleak House out of gratitude to him (44). He recognizes her love for Woodcourt, however, and releases her to the doctor, providing a new Bleak House for them in YORKSHIRE (64).

Esther's dual role as both narrator and character has complicated reactions to her. She is praised as narrator for her quick observation and her sound judgments of other characters. She sees through Skimpole's pose, for example, even when Jarndyce does not. She is placed in a difficult position, however, for the openness and self-revelation called for in a narrator goes against the grain of her natural self-denigrating reticence. David Copperfield, as a man, may be expected to write his way to becoming the hero of his own story; Victorian women were expected to be far less assertive. Esther's protestations that she is not clever and her embarrassment at writing about herself emerge from her attempt to reconcile the conflict between her role as narrator and the expectations placed on Victorian women. Her "coyness" is also magnified by the demands of the narrative, so that even though she is writing in the past tense about events that happened several years earlier, she withholds information to enhance the suspense and give more immediacy to the events she describes. Though some commentators find evidence of Dickens's language and inventiveness in her account, her style is still much plainer than the verbal pyrotechnics employed in the third-person narration.

The character Esther's female reticence is increased by her status as an orphan of unknown parentage. She is the child of "no one" and she has been told repeatedly that it would have been better had she never been born. She buries her self-assertiveness with her doll and represses any interest in discovering her parentage. She is comfortable only in a role serving others, as Dame Durden or the Little Old Woman. She projects her self-consciousness onto others, her beauty and sexuality onto Ada, for example, and her anger and resentment onto Caddy. The illness she contracts from Jo and Charley, two of her "outcast" doubles, forces her to confront her self-image, symbolized in the mirrors, and enables her to acknowledge her parentage and her passion.

Nearly every commentator on the novel discusses Esther and her significance. Among extended discussions of her character and psychology LAWRENCE FRANK (1984), J. HILLIS MILLER (1958), and HILARY SCHOR (1999) are particularly noteworthy.

Swills, Little Comic singer at the harmonic meetings at the Sol's Arms; "a chubby little man in a large shirt collar, with a moist eye, and an inflamed nose" (11).

Swosser, Captain, R. N. Mrs. Bayham Badger's first husband, a naval officer (13).

Symond's Inn "A little, pale, wall-eyed, woe-begone inn. . . . It looks as if Symond were a sparing man in his way, and constructed an inn of old building materials, which took kindly to the dry rot and dirt and all things decaying and dismal, and perpetuated Symond's memory with congenial shabbiness" (39). Vholes maintains his offices in this nondescript office building in Chancery Lane.

Tangle Lawyer who "knows more of Jarndyce and Jarndyce than anybody, . . . supposed to have never read anything else since he left school" (1).

Thavies Inn One of the Inns of Chancery near Holborn Circus. The Jellybys' house is located here (4).

Thomas (3) Sir Leicester Dedlock's groom (40).

Tom-All-Alone's "A black, dilapidated street, avoided by all decent people; where the crazy houses were seized upon, when their decay was far advanced, by some bold vagrants, who, after establishing their possession, took to letting them out in lodgings" (16). Jo the crossing sweeper inhabits this slum created because the property is tied up in a Court of Chancery suit. Several locations in St. Giles, Drury Lane, and Bloomsbury have been suggested as the original. The name was taken from the house of a recluse outside Chatham, known to Dickens as a child.

Tulkinghorn Lawyer to the Dedlocks and other important families: "the old gentleman is rusty to look at, but is reputed to have made good thrift out of aristocratic marriage settlements and aristocratic wills, and to be very rich. . . . He is of what is called the old school, . . . and wears knee breeches tied with ribbons, and gaiters and stockings. One peculiarity of his black clothes . . . is that they never shine. Mute, close, irresponsive to any gleaming light, his dress is like himself" (2). Secretive himself, and a keeper of secrets, Tulkinghorn pursues the

Browne's (Phiz's) visualization of Tom-All-Alone's in one of his "dark plates," an engraving technique he developed to render the dark subject matter in *Bleak House*.

mystery of Lady Dedlock's past, seeking Nemo's documents (11) and information from Jo and Hortense (22) and Trooper George (34) before confronting Lady Dedlock (40–41). Shortly after he returns to London from Chesney Wold, he is found murdered (48). Although George is detained for the crime, Hortense, disgruntled by Tulkinghorn's high-handed treatment of her, proves to be his killer (54).

Tulkinghorn represents the darkness at the heart of *Bleak House*. A night creature who resembles a crow, he moves silently between London and Chesney Wold. He reveals nothing of himself and expresses no feelings toward anyone. He is mechanical and misogynistic, storing secrets in locked boxes in his office. He collects secrets, particularly those of women, as a way to power, a power that turns people into objects and brings death. The allegorical painting on the ceiling of his rooms, which points to his death, points more broadly to the killing effects of the law that have made all of Britain a bleak house.

Tulkinghorn's house in LINCOLN'S INN FIELDS was based on JOHN FORSTER's house there.

Turnstile Passage leading from Holborn to Lincoln's Inn Fields, that once, as Snagsby tells his apprentices, led into open countryside (10).

Turveydrop, Mr. Proprietor of a dancing academy and a latter-day Regency dandy who models himself on the Prince Regent: "a fat old gentleman with a false complexion, false teeth, false whiskers, and a wig. . . . He was pinched in, and swelled out, and got up, and stopped down, as much as he could possibly bear. . . . He had a cane, he had an eye-glass, he had a snuff-box, he had rings, he had wristbands, he had everything but any touch of nature; he was not like youth, he was not like age, he was not like anything in the world but a model of Deportment" (14). Vain and indolent, his vocation is his performance as a dandy; he depends on his son to maintain the family income. Turveydrop consents to Prince's marriage to Caddy Jellyby when the couple agree to continue supporting him (23).

NORMAN PAGE (1990) points out that Turveydrop, like Sir Leicester Dedlock, is a survival from an earlier time. Both are equally out of place in the age of ironmasters. Turveydrop complains, "I see nothing to succeed us, but a race of weavers" (14).

Turveydrop, Prince Turveydrop's son, named for the Prince Regent, "a little blue-eyed fair man of youthful appearance . . . [and] a little innocent feminine manner" (14), works himself to the point of exhaustion teaching dancing lessons. He marries Caddy Jellyby (30). However, the burden of running the dancing academy and caring for their deaf and dumb daughter finally falls on Caddy, for Prince becomes lame.

Vholes Richard Carstone's self-serving solicitor, "a sallow man, with pinched lips that looked as if they were cold; a red eruption here and there upon his face; tall and thin; about fifty years of age; high-shouldered and stooping. Dressed in black, . . . there was nothing so remarkable in him as a lifeless manner and a slow fixed way he had of looking at Richard" (37). Introduced to Richard by Skimpole (for a consideration of five pounds), he "puts his shoulder to the wheel" and sucks Richard ever deeper into the toils of Chancery, repeatedly remarking on how hard he works to support his three daughters, Caroline, Emma, and Jane, and his father in the VALE OF TAUNTON.

With a name suggesting a burrowing rodent and his vampirish manner that sucks the life from Richard, Vholes represents the law in its most murderous form.

Walcot Square Just off Kennington Road in Lambeth, South London, this square is the location of the house that Mr. Guppy has obtained, hoping to improve his prospects with Esther Summerson when he renews his marriage proposal (64).

"Weevle" Alias taken by Tony Jobling when he moves into Nemo's rooms in Krook's house (20).

Wiglomeration Jarndyce's term to describe the elaborate procedures and obfuscation of the court. "It's the only name I know for the thing. . . . Counsel will have something to say about it; the Chancellor will have something to say about it; the Satellites will have something to say about it; . . . the whole thing will be vastly ceremonious, wordy, unsatisfactory, and expensive, and I call it, in general, Wiglomeration" (8).

Wisk, Miss A woman with a mission "to show the world that woman's mission was man's mission; and that the only genuine mission, of both man and woman, was to be always moving declaratory resolutions about things in general at public meetings." She marries Quayle (30).

Woodcourt, Allan "Young surgeon, . . . reserved, . . . sensible and agreeable" (13). He signs Nemo's death certificate (11). He falls in love with Esther Summerson before leaving for India, but he does not declare himself. When he returns, Allan becomes a friend and advisor to Richard Carstone and tends Jo in the boy's last illness (45, 47). Jarndyce secures him a practice in Yorkshire and secretly promotes his marriage to Esther Summerson (64).

ALEXANDER WELSH (2000) points out that Woodcourt is present at the deaths of both Esther's father and mother, deaths that are necessary to enable Esther to marry, and thus he becomes a kind of demonic figure who enables Esther's assumption of a mature identity.

Woodcourt, Mrs. Allan's mother, "a pretty old lady, with bright black eyes," who is obsessed with her Welsh heritage from "Morgan ap-Kerrig—of some place that sounded like Gimlet—who was the most illustrious person that ever was known, and all of whose relations were a sort of Royal Family" (17). She warns Esther that the family's proud Welsh heritage makes her son an inappropriate match for someone like Esther (30). However, after Jarndyce arranges the marriage, she drops her objections.

ADAPTATIONS

Nearly all of the early stage adaptations of *Bleak House* concentrated on Jo and were given such titles as *The Adventures of Joe the Crossing-Sweeper, Joe the Orphan, or Outcast Joe; or, The London Arab.* The most famous portrayer of the child was JENNIE LEE, who first played the role in San Francisco in 1875. She continued playing in *Jo; or Bleak House,* a version of the novel done by her husband J. P. Burnett, until 1921. The other frequently dramatized story from the novel was that of Lady Dedlock. Several actresses, the most famous being Fanny Janauschek, played both Lady Dedlock and Hortense in these adaptations.

Four silent films were made from the novel, in 1910, 1918, 1920, and 1922. The last of these films starred Sybil Thorndike as Lady Dedlock. BRANSBY WILLIAMS made a short sound film in 1933 of his characterization of Grandfather Smallweed. The BBC has done three television adaptations of the novel, an 11-part serial by CONSTANCE COX in 1959, an eight-part serial by Arthur Hopcraft,

directed by Jonathan Powell (1985), and a 15-episode adaptation by Andrew Davies with Gillian Anderson as Lady Dedlock (2005).

FURTHER READING

Bleak House has probably generated more criticism than any other Dickens novel, an indication of its importance on academic reading lists. Several collections of criticism, edited by Jacob Korg (*Twentieth-Century Interpretations of Bleak House,* 1968), A. E. DYSON (1969), Harold Bloom (*Bleak House: Modern Critical Interpretations,* 1987), Eliott Gilbert (*Critical Essays on Charles Dickens's Bleak House,* 1989), and Jeremy Tambling (*Bleak House: Charles Dickens, New Casebooks,* 1998), bring together many of the more important articles on the novel published over the last half century. Volume 19 of *DICKENS STUDIES ANNUAL* (1990) contains five articles on *Bleak House,* including one by PHILIP COLLINS, "Some Narrative Devices in *Bleak House,*" that addresses key critical issues in the novel. The Norton Critical Edition of the novel, edited by GEORGE FORD and SYLVÈRE MONOD (1977), includes some critical articles as well as useful background materials. There are also several books that discuss *Bleak House* at length: ROBERT NEWSOM's *Dickens on the Romantic Side of Familiar Things: Bleak House and the Novel Tradition* (1977) analyzes the mixture of romantic and realistic elements in the novel as a way of describing Dickens's work more broadly and his relation to the central tradition of the novel. GRAHAM STOREY (1987) and NORMAN PAGE (1990) survey backgrounds and the critical issues in the novel. ALEXANDER WELSH (2000) provides an extended discussion of character relationships.

Chimes, The. A Goblin Story of Some Bells That Rang an Old Year Out and a New Year In.

Second of the five CHRISTMAS BOOKS, published in December 1844 by CHAPMAN & HALL, with illustrations by DANIEL MACLISE, JOHN LEECH, RICHARD DOYLE, and CLARKSON STANFIELD. More topical than *Carol, The Chimes* addressed controversial social and economic issues of the day.

SYNOPSIS

(1) At his post on a doorstep, Toby ("Trotty") Veck, a poor ticket porter, keeps watch on a windy winter day, the last day in the old year. He is heartened by the sound of the chimes in the church tower, which seem to tell him "Toby Veck, Toby Veck, keep a good heart, Toby!" but he also wonders whether the poor "have any business on the face of the earth," and whether they are intruders who are born bad and "have no right to a New Year." His daughter Meg brings him a dinner of hot tripe, Trotty's favorite dish, and tells him that she and her fiancé Richard, who have been engaged for three years, plan to marry the next morning on New Year's Day. They realize that things will not change for the poor so there is no reason to put off marriage until their lot improves.

Leech's sketch of Toby Veck for *The Chimes* (1844).

As Trotty enjoys his dinner, the door in which he is standing opens and a footman and three gentlemen emerge. One, Mr. Filer, lectures Trotty about political economy, pointing out to him that tripe is an extravagant dish and that by eating it he is depriving widows and orphans of food. The second, Alderman Cute, "puts down" Trotty's belief that people are starving, telling him that "there's a great deal of nonsense talked about Want." He puts down those who are driven by distress to suicide as well. He also condemns Meg and Richard for their imprudent and "wicked" plan to marry. The third gentleman extols "the good old times" and asserts that "its of no use talking about any other times, or discussing what people are in these times." By the end of their harangue, Meg is in tears, Richard is downcast, and Trotty is convinced that he is an intruder who does not belong on earth. The bells now seem to be saying, "Put 'em down! Put 'em down!" Convinced that he has no business with the New Year, Trotty wishes to die.

(2) Alderman Cute dispatches Trotty with a letter to Sir Joseph Bowley, M.P., who is in London for a few hours to clear up his accounts so he can begin the New Year owing nothing to anyone. Bowley calls himself the "Poor Man's Father and Friend" and asserts that the great lesson the poor man must learn is his "entire dependence on myself." He advises Trotty to clear up all his obligations for the new year, but Trotty has some debts that he cannot afford to pay. Cute's letter seeks Sir Joseph's permission to arrest for vagrancy Will Fern, a rural laborer who has come to London looking for a friend and seeking work. Sir Joseph knows Fern in the country as someone who refuses to be dependent, an ungrateful and rebellious troublemaker, so he grants Cute's request. Toby trots back to Cute with Sir Joseph's answer, and then, as he hurries home hoping to avoid hearing the unhappy message of the bells, he meets Fern, who is seeking Alderman Cute so he can clear up his case before the New Year. Trotty warns him that he will be arrested and invites him to his house. With his last sixpence Trotty purchases some tea and a rasher of bacon for Will and his nine-year-old niece Lilian and then provides places for them to spend the night. Helping Will and his niece makes Trotty

happy and hopeful, but when he reads his newspaper, he is again brought to despair by accounts of crime and violence. As the chimes ring they seem to be calling to him and saying, "Haunt and hunt him, break his slumbers." Trotty goes out to the bell-tower and, finding the door open, he climbs up to the top of the belfry, feeling his way in the darkness. There he falls into a swoon.

(3) When Trotty regains consciousness, he sees the many goblin spirits of the bells. The Goblin of the Great Bell accuses him of doubting the message of hope and improvement and of hearing in the bells only a cry of despair. By doing so, the spirit claims, Trotty has wronged the bells. The goblin sends him off with the Spirit of the Chimes, a child who shows Trotty his own corpse lying at the foot of the tower. Then Trotty sees a series of visions of a time nine years after his death: Meg works late into the night to earn enough just barely to survive; Sir Joseph Bowley and his associates are shocked by the suicide of Deedles the banker; Will Fern, a vagabond in and out of prison, gives a revolutionary speech calling for better conditions for the poor; Lilian, now a young woman, has escaped grinding poverty by becoming a prostitute.

(4) In a vision of an even later time, Trotty sees Meg and her drunken husband Richard living in squalor in a room in Mrs. Chickenstalker's house. When Richard dies, Meg, unable to pay the rent, is evicted by Tugby, Mrs. Chickenstalker's husband, formerly Sir Joseph's footman. Meg goes to the river with her infant daughter and is about to plunge in when Trotty pleads with the spirit to save her, protesting that he has learned the message of the bells. "I know that we must trust and hope," he tells the spirit, "and neither doubt ourselves, nor doubt the Good in one another."

Trotty awakens by his hearth as the bells chime in the New Year and Mrs. Chickenstalker brings some celebratory punch. She turns out to be the friend that Will Fern was seeking in the city. They all prepare for the wedding of Meg and Richard.

COMMENTARY

If Dickens set out to make a "sledge-hammer blow on behalf of the Poor Man's Child" in *Carol,* that political message was largely ignored by his readers, so a year later he made his social message more explicit in *The Chimes.* The second Christmas book concentrated on social and political issues. Agricultural distress, Chartist agitation (*see* CHARTISM), and intense debate over the CORN LAWS made these issues especially urgent in the mid-1840s. Sympathetic with the Chartist demands, incensed by the insensitivity of the ARISTOCRACY, and outraged by the Parliamentary reports on the exploitation of children, Dickens became increasingly radical during these years. In *The Chimes* he took up the issue of who was to blame for the distress of the poor.

Trotty Veck, the poor ticket porter at the center of the tale, is a traditional member of the lower orders. Deferential, an errand boy for his superiors, he knows his place; he can always be found at his station on the street corner when he is not on an errand. So deferential is he, in fact, that he takes to heart the cant that the poor are responsible for their lot, that they have "no business on the face of the earth" and "no right to a New Year." He is a victim in a society that blames the victims for their situation.

The gentlemen from the upper classes whom Trotty serves as a messenger represent a cluster of attitudes that combine to "put down" the poor. Filer is the "philosopher," one of the political economists from the school of hard facts that Dickens also attacks in *Twist* and *Hard Times* (*see* POLITICAL ECONOMY). His specious argument that Trotty has stolen his tripe from the mouths of widows and orphans is numerical humbug—or tripe. It echoes a criticism of *Carol* leveled by economist NASSAU SENIOR, who asked how many people went without food so that Scrooge could give Bob Cratchit the prize turkey. Filer also echoes THOMAS ROBERT MALTHUS in counseling Meg and Richard not to marry. The red-faced gentleman in the blue coat who celebrates the past and takes no interest in the present satirizes reactionary Toryism, like that of the Young England Movement, which idealized medieval peasants and ignored the Victorian poor. Alderman Cute is another disciple of Malthus, who, after proving that the population would inevitably outstrip the food supply, argued that the way to reduce the surplus population was to deny charity and welfare to the poor, thus discouraging them from marrying and bearing children. So the sharp-tongued and sharp-witted Cute, based on Sir Peter Laurie, a Middlesex Magistrate, counsels Meg and Richard not to marry, predicting that such imprudence will lead to misery and distress. Then he takes a contradictory position when he asserts his opposition to suicide as a way out of economic distress. The poor who failed to follow his advice would gain no sympathy or support for their imprudence. Finally, Sir Joseph Bowley, "The Poor Man's Friend and Father," represents a paternalism that demands dependency as the price the poor must pay for his support and help. Although Bowley seems to be a Tory landholder, his oppressive paternalism was an attitude found among both Whigs and Tories. Together these men represent the privileged class that takes no responsibility for the poverty around them. They treat the poor as counters or ciphers without individual identity. By blaming them for being poor, they deny their right to a decent life.

The factors that bring about Trotty's conversion from despair to hope are not so clear as those that transform Scrooge. The visions of the bells would seem more calculated to increase his despair, for they show him Meg in an unhappy marriage and then attempting suicide, Lilian surviving by prostitution, and Will Fern radicalized into an incendiary terrorist by the unfair treatment he has received. Nor is Trotty's change brought about by any change in the attitudes of the rich. The separation between rich and poor is not bridged as it was at the end of *Carol.* Trotty chooses hope because he cannot live in despair. His belief that there are things worth living for is supported in the end by the community of the poor who gather round him—Will and Lilian, Mrs. Chickenstalker, Meg and Richard. The vision of *The Chimes* is of England as two nations that have no connection with each other, the separate nations of rich and poor. Trotty hopes that the community among the poor is enough to enable them to survive, in spite of the neglect and irresponsibility of the rich.

CHARACTERS AND RELATED ENTRIES

Bowley, Sir Joseph   An elderly Member of Parliament who poses as "The Poor Man's Friend and Father," but the "one great moral lesson" he would teach the poor is the paternalistic doctrine of their "entire Dependence on myself." He tells Trotty Veck, "your only business in life is with me. You needn't trouble yourself to think about anything. I will think for you; I know what is good for you; I am your perpetual parent."

Bowley, Lady   Sir Joseph's condescending wife, who has introduced eyelet-hole making as an occupation for the men in her village.

Bowley, Master   Sir Joseph's 12-year-old son who is being groomed to take his place in Parliament and continue his father's paternalism.

Chickenstalker, Mrs. Anne   Owner of a general store to whom Trotty Veck owes some small debts, "a good-humoured comely woman of some fifty years of age." In Trotty's dream of the future she has married Tugby, Sir Joseph Bowry's former porter, and he forces Meg to give up the rooms she rents from them when she is unable to pay the rent.

Cute, Alderman   Malthusian city magistrate claiming to be a plain and practical man. He views as cant all talk of poverty, distress, and starvation, denying that they even exist, and he is particularly intent on decrying suicide. He has made his mission in life "putting down" the poor. He warns Trotty against claiming deprivation and lectures Meg and Richard on the imprudence of their marriage plans (1). In a fit of Malthusian irritation, he asserts: "A man . . . may labor all his life for the benefit of such people as those [the poor]; and may heap up facts on figures, facts on figures, facts on figures, mountains high and dry; and he can no more hope to persuade 'em that they have no right or business to be married, than he can hope to persuade 'em that they have no earthly right or business to be born. And *that* we know they haven't."

Dickens based Cute on SIR PETER LAURIE, a garrulous and officious magistrate and LORD MAYOR of London. Cute's Malthusianism would be more fully developed in Gradgrind in *Hard Times* (*see* THOMAS ROBERT MALTHUS).

Deedles   Banker who surprises his friend Alderman Cute by committing suicide.

Fern, Lillian   Will Fern's orphan niece, nine years old when they first come to London. In Trotty's despairing vision of the future, she has been reduced to prostitution.

Fern, Will   A country laborer, "a sun-browned, sinewy, country-looking man, with grizzled hair, and a rough chin," who comes to London with his niece in search of work. He is found sleeping in a shed, arrested for vagrancy, and taken before Alderman Cute, who is "determined to put this sort of thing down." Trotty Veck takes the couple in and they become part of his New Year vision of the future, Will as a rick-burning Chartist (*see* CHARTISM) and Lillian as a prostitute.

Filer   Friend of Alderman Cute, "a low-spirited gentleman of middle age, of a meagre habit, and a disconsolate face; who kept his hand continually in the pockets of his scanty pepper-and-salt trousers; . . . and was not particularly well brushed or washed." He has a political economist's faith in statistics, and he "proves" by numbers that Trotty, by eating tripe, has deprived widows and orphans of sustenance.

In the satiric portrait of Filer, Dickens probably had in mind economist NASSAU SENIOR, who had criticized *A Christmas Carol* for promoting the false doctrine that Cratchit could have a Christmas turkey without depriving others of turkey.

Fish   Sir Joseph Bowley's secretary, "a not very stately gentleman in black."

Red-faced Gentleman   One of two men accompanying Alderman Cute, the Red-faced Gentleman in a blue coat condemns the present "degenerate times" and wistfully recalls "the good old times," ignoring any suggestion that they were not so good as he has made them out to be. Although Dickens toned down his criticism of the medievalism of the Young England movement in the original manuscript for *The Chimes* by changing a character specifically identified as the "Young England Gentleman" to this more generalized old-fashioned Tory, the Red-faced Gentleman represents broadly the backward-looking position of the Young England Tories.

Richard   Meg Veck's fiancé, a blacksmith "with eyes that sparkled like the red-hot drippings from a furnace fire." Engaged to Meg for three years, he and Meg decide that they will wait no longer to marry, since they see little chance that their economic position will get better. In Trotty's dream of the future, Richard has become an unemployed drunk.

Tugby   Sir Joseph Bowry's porter who, in Trotty's dream, has married Mrs. Chickenstalker and evicts Meg from her lodgings when she cannot pay the rent.

Veck, Margaret ("Meg")   Toby Veck's daughter: "Bright eyes they were. Eyes that would abear a world of looking in, before their depth was fathomed. Dark eyes, that reflected back the eyes that searched them; not flashingly, or at the owner's will, but with a clear, calm, honest, patient radiance, claiming kindred with that light which Heaven called into being. With hope so young and fresh; with Hope so buoyant, vigorous, and bright." Told by Alderman Cute that her decision to marry is imprudent, Meg is reduced to despair in Trotty's vision and driven to contemplate suicide.

Veck, Toby ("Trotty")   The cheerful ticket porter or messenger whose dream vision on New Year's Eve is the central story of *The Chimes*. "A weak, small, spare old man, he was a very Hercules, this Toby, in his good intentions. He loved to earn his money. He delighted to believe—Toby was very poor, and couldn't well afford to part with a delight—that he was worth his salt." At his station at the foot of the bell tower, Toby is especially attuned to the sound of the bells, which he hears spreading a message of hope and reminding him to "keep a good heart." Driven to despair by the intimidating teachings of the political economists, he believes that he and other poor people have no right to a place on earth. Then the bells seem send him a different message, repeating Alderman Cute's determination to "put 'em down." His vision of the spirits of the chimes teaches him that he is wrong to blame the poor for their poverty, for society causes their misery. Restored to cheerfulness and hope, he and his daughter plan her wedding and again look forward to the future.

ADAPTATIONS

Compared to *Carol*, *The Chimes* has prompted few adaptations. Its initial production, *The Chimes; a Goblin Story of Some Bells That Rang the Old Year Out and the New Year In,* was staged at the ADELPHI THEATRE. The adaptation was done by Gilbert Abbott à Beckett and MARK LEMON from proof sheets supplied by Dickens. EDWARD STIRLING did a version for ROBERT and MARY KEELEY at the Lyceum, but there were only a few other scattered productions in the 1840s. No other significant production appeared until 1872, when J. L. TOOLE played the lead in *Trotty Veck*, a new version at the Gaiety Theatre in London.

Two silent films of *The Chimes* were produced in 1914 and 1920, but no later film versions have appeared.

FURTHER READING

The most useful work on *The Chimes* is by MICHAEL SLATER in the article "Dickens (and Forster) at Work on *The Chimes*" (1966), in his introduction to the Penguin Edition of the CHRISTMAS BOOKS, and in his article on the topicality of the story (1970). MICHAEL GOLDBERG (1972) discusses the social themes in the story and its indebtedness to THOMAS CARLYLE.

Christmas Carol in Prose, A. A Ghost Story of Christmas.

First of the five CHRISTMAS BOOKS, published in December 1843 by CHAPMAN & HALL, with illustrations by JOHN LEECH. Although Dickens was motivated by the economic controversies of the time to write *Carol*, the book was taken as an affirmation of Christmas rather than as a controversial tract. The best-known of all Dickens's

works, it has become the modern classic of Christmas literature.

SYNOPSIS

(1) Seven years to the day after the death of his partner Jacob Marley, the miser Ebenezer Scrooge works in his counting house on Christmas Eve. The fire is so low and the room so cold that his clerk, Bob Cratchit, attempts to warm his fingers by a candle flame. Scrooge's icy manner chills the office even more than the weather, and his "Bah! Humbug!" dampens the season. He turns down his nephew's invitation to Christmas dinner, drives a caroling boy from his door, and refuses to give anything to charity, suggesting that the poor would be better off dead, thus decreasing "the surplus population." He grudgingly grants Bob a holiday on Christmas, and the clerk plans a grand family celebration on his meager weekly salary of 15 shillings.

Scrooge takes his dinner alone at a "melancholy tavern" and then returns home. As he opens his door, he is surprised to see the face of his late partner, Jacob Marley, in the door knocker. But he checks the house and finds nothing unusual. Then, as he sits by the fire before retiring, he hears the sound of chains rattling and bells ringing, and the Ghost of Marley enters the room. Scrooge tries to dismiss it as a humbug induced by indigestion, but the ghost convinces Scrooge of his reality. He says that he has come to warn Scrooge of his fate and of the chains that his hard-heartedness is forging, and to give him an opportunity to change. Marley tells Scrooge that he will be haunted by three spirits who will show him how to "shun the path I tread." After delivering this message, Marley goes out through the window and joins a crowd of phantoms in the air outside. Scrooge attempts to say "Humbug" but manages only the first syllable. Then he goes to bed.

(2) When the clock strikes one, Scrooge notices a light in his room and sees "a strange figure—like a child: yet not so like a child as like an old man"— standing by his bed. This Ghost of Christmas Past takes Scrooge on a journey to view past Christmases in Scrooge's life: a Christmas when Scrooge as a child was left at school alone for the holidays, taking consolation for his loneliness by reading the

Arabian Nights and *Robinson Crusoe;* a later Christmas when his sister Fan came to the school and took him home for a family celebration; the Christmas in London when Scrooge was apprenticed to old Fezziwig and he and Dick Wilkins helped turn the warehouse into a festive hall for a Christmas dance and party; the Christmas when Belle, Scrooge's fiancée, returned his ring, telling him that he was more interested in money than in her; and finally, a later Christmas when Belle joyfully celebrates the holiday with her husband and children. Shaken by these visions of the past and by what he has lost, Scrooge asks the spirit to haunt him no longer. Then, taking the spirit's extinguisher cap, he snuffs out the light of the spirit as if it were a candle flame and sinks into a heavy sleep.

(3) The clock again strikes one, but Scrooge sees no sign of another spirit. Then, noticing a light coming from the next room, he opens the door to find a blazing fire and a gigantic spirit enthroned atop a cornucopia of Christmas treats. This Ghost of Christmas Present takes Scrooge into the streets and markets filled with the goodwill and abundance of the season. Then he takes him to Bob Cratchit's house, where Mrs. Cratchit and the children are preparing Christmas dinner. After Bob returns from church with Tiny Tim, his crippled son, the family make a feast of their modest board, eating every scrap of goose, mashed potatoes and gravy, applesauce, and Christmas pudding. Then they gather at the hearth and Bob salutes the season— "A Merry Christmas to us all, my dears. God bless us!"—and his toast is echoed by Tiny Tim's "God bless us every one!" Moved by the scene, Scrooge asks the spirit "if Tiny Tim will live" and is told, "If these shadows remain unaltered by the Future, the child will die." Then the Cratchits share family stories and songs and, with some reluctance on Mrs. Cratchit's part, toast Scrooge as the "founder of the feast." The spirit then takes Scrooge on a quick tour of the city streets, a poor miner's cabin, a solitary lighthouse, and a ship at sea where simple celebrations are in progress. Finally, they observe the Christmas party at the house of Scrooge's nephew Fred, where Scrooge wishes he could join in the singing and games, even the game of Yes and No where "Uncle Scrooge" becomes the subject

Leech's well-known illustration of Scrooge confronting the Spirit of Christmas Present.

of some good-natured mockery as the bear who denies the holiday. As the spirit ages and prepares to end his "life upon this globe," Scrooge notices two urchins under the spirit's robe. They are Ignorance and Want, clinging to the spirit because they have been rejected by mankind. As he disappears, the spirit warns Scrooge that these children will bring doom.

(4) In the mist and darkness into which the spirit has vanished, Scrooge sees a phantom "shrouded in a deep black garment, which concealed its head, its face, its form, and left nothing of it visible save one outstretched hand." This Ghost of Christmas Yet to Come shows Scrooge some city businessmen talking unfeelingly about the death of one of their colleagues, a pawnbroker's den where the belongings of the dead man are being sold by his servants, and a darkened room with a corpse laid out on a bed, but Scrooge is unwilling to uncover the face and identify the dead man. When Scrooge

asks if there is anyone moved by this man's death, the spirit shows him a couple rejoicing that it has relieved them of their debts, at least for a time. The spirit then takes Scrooge to the Cratchit house, where the family mourns Tiny Tim. When Scrooge is ready to learn the identity of the dead man, the spirit takes him to a churchyard and shows him his own tombstone. Shaken, Scrooge insists, "I am not the man I was. . . . Why show me this, if I am past all hope?" He promises to honor Christmas in his heart, to "live in the Past, Present, and Future," and, as he kneels before the specter and prays to have his fate reversed, the phantom dwindles into the bedpost on Scrooge's bed.

(5) Scrooge repeats his prayers and his promises and exclaims that "the shadows of the things that would have been, may be dispelled. They will be. I know they will!" He runs to the window and throws open the shutter; it is morning. He learns from a boy in the street below that it is Christmas Day. Scrooge is exultant, for he hasn't missed the holiday. He sends the boy to the poulterer's to buy the prize Christmas turkey for the Cratchits. Going out into the streets, he wishes everyone he sees a merry Christmas, gives a large donation to help the poor, attends a Christmas service at church, and goes to his nephew's house for a "wonderful party, wonderful games, wonderful unanimity, won-der-ful happiness!"

The next morning Scrooge waits in the office for Bob Cratchit, who arrives 18 minutes late, apologizing for his tardiness and promising that it will not happen again. Putting on his stern voice, Scrooge asserts, "I am not going to stand this sort of thing any longer, . . . and therefore I am about to raise your salary!" That afternoon, master and clerk share a bowl of Christmas punch. Scrooge "became as good a friend, as good a master, and as good a man, as the old city knew, . . . [and] he knew how to keep Christmas well, if any man alive possessed the knowledge. May that truly be said of us, and all of us! And so, as Tiny Tim observed, God bless Us, Every One!"

COMMENTARY

Early in 1843, in response to a Parliamentary report on the exploitation of child laborers in the mines and factories, Dickens promised to strike a "sledge-hammer blow . . . on behalf of the Poor Man's Child." That blow turned out to be *A Christmas Carol.* In September, while visiting MANCHESTER, Dickens conceived the specific idea for the story, and by the middle of December it was on the booksellers' shelves, even though he was also writing the monthly numbers of *Chuzzlewit* at the same time.

Many of *Chuzzlewit*'s themes are also found in *Carol.* Both stories are about selfishness. Scrooge, like the Chuzzlewits, particularly Jonas and his father, is obsessed with money. Charity, the virtue preached by the Christmas story, is satirically represented in the novel by Pecksniff's shrewish daughter. Bob Cratchit's mild and deferential manner is exaggerated in Tom Pinch's blind admiration for his hypocritical master. Both stories are about a change of heart: Scrooge's overnight transformation and young Martin's painful recognition of his obsession with himself. However, whereas Scrooge's conversion enables him to join the rest of humanity, giving *Carol* an exultantly positive ending, *Chuzzlewit* remains a much darker story. At the end Martin may enter a caring community with Mary Graham, Tom and Ruth Pinch, and John Westlock, but the unconverted Chuzzlewits remain as selfish as ever. Dickens's intense engagement with the writing of *Carol* may have been due in part to the relief it offered from the dark world of the novel.

At the heart of *Carol,* Dickens had an economic message: A society in which the masters are concerned only with the bottom line and take no responsibility for the general welfare is a death-dealing society. Scrooge knows nothing about Bob Cratchit and his family; he knows only that Bob makes 15 shillings a week and would cheat his employer by demanding a paid holiday on Christmas day. By taking no interest or responsibility for his clerk's situation, Scrooge becomes morally responsible for Bob's inability to afford medical treatment for Tiny Tim; Scrooge's obsession with money has chained him to cash boxes and caged Tim's legs in steel. All this hardware objectifies Scrooge's (screw, gouge) hard heart. Unless he changes, Scrooge and Tiny Tim will both die; their fates are linked. The condition of the poor is the responsibility of the rich.

Although this message arose as a response to the exploitation of children in factories and mines, Dickens does not direct his PARABLE specifically at the abuse of working children. Tim's crippled condition is similar to the injuries sustained by factory children, but Dickens blames people who allow ignorance and want to persist for the maimed children, not the spinning and weaving machines. Charity was needed by the society as a whole.

The celebratory impact of the story was more important to its original readers than its economic message. The wonderful catalogs of the fruits and delicacies in the markets, the descriptions of Fred's Christmas party and the Cratchits' Christmas dinner: These were the striking passages in the story for the Victorian audience. *Carol* proved that one did not need a baronial country house, a burning yule log, and a sumptuous feast to have Christmas. The holiday could be just as festive in Fezziwig's city warehouse, and the modest meal shared by the urban Cratchit family could have its moments of celebration—as when Mrs. Cratchit delivers the Christmas pudding or Tim blesses "every one."

The simplicity of the story, its neat three-part structure, and Scrooge's overnight conversion have bothered some critics, who want a more realistic tale. In the real world, they suggest, Tiny Tim would die. But Dickens's purpose was to take an old nursery tale and give it "a higher form." He uses fantasy in the manner of the FAIRY TALE, giving the story a timelessness that makes it like Cinderella or Little Red Riding Hood, a folk story that seems to have been in the culture forever. The avuncular narrator increases this effect, telling the story as if it is an oral tale passed down from a time before the invention of writing.

Yet for all its simplicity, *Carol* has complexity and ambiguity as well. Even before his conversion, Scrooge is more than the stereotypical miser. He enjoys taking on the believers in Christmas and revels in his own wit, asserting, for example, that "every idiot who goes about with 'Merry Christmas,' on his lips, should be boiled with his own pudding, and buried with a stake of holly through his heart" (1). His zest for the confrontations with Fred and the charity solicitors is not that of a man who merely prefers to be "solitary as an oyster" (1). As we learn something of his life, there are suggestions of painful episodes in the past, like the death of his sister, that may have contributed to his negativism, but Dickens leaves much of this sympathy for Scrooge to the imagination of the reader. Even as he weeps for Tiny Tim, Scrooge is reluctant to reveal the change that is occuring within him. So when the change occurs in Stave 5, the climax is evocative. We share Scrooge's joy as he learns from the boy in the street, a boy he characterizes as "a most intelligent boy," that he has not missed Christmas day.

Dickens imagined his story in musical terms, a carol to be sung or heard, each of its chapters one of five "staves." His timing in this basically oral tale is impeccable, especially the brevity with which he tells the final stave. When he turned it into the first, and the most popular, of his PUBLIC READINGS, the story took to the platform as if it had been written to be performed aloud.

CHARACTERS AND RELATED ENTRIES

Belle Scrooge's fiancée who rejects him because of his love of money.

Cratchit, Belinda Cratchit's second daughter, who assists her mother in preparing the family's Christmas dinner.

Cratchit, Bob Scrooge's poor clerk, "with at least three feet of comforter exclusive of the fringe hanging down before him; and his threadbare clothes darned up and brushed to look seasonable; and Tiny Tim upon his shoulder." On his meager wages of 15 shillings a week, Bob struggles to support his wife and six children, who nonetheless share warm affection for one another in their four-room house in CAMDEN TOWN. There Scrooge observes their Christmas dinner in his vision of Christmas Present. In Christmas Yet to Come, Scrooge observes the family mourning the death of Tiny Tim. A changed Scrooge raises Bob's salary and provides care for his crippled son.

Eytinge's picture of Bob Cratchit and Tiny Tim for an 1867 American edition of *A Christmas Carol* was the first rendering of this iconographic subject.

Bob is central to the message in *Carol,* for Dickens was not simply attacking Scrooge's miserliness. He was even more concerned with Scrooge's irresponsibility as an employer in not providing for the welfare of his employee.

Cratchit, Martha   Cratchit's eldest daughter, who has gone out to work as a milliner and lives away from home. Martha's occupation was significant in 1843, for Parliament released a report detailing the harsh working conditions in which many milliners worked.

Cratchit, Mrs.   Bob's wife, "dressed poorly in a twice-turned gown, but brave in ribbons, which are cheap and make a goodly show for sixpence." She prepares the dinner that Bob calls "the greatest success achieved by Mrs. Cratchit since their marriage."

Cratchit, Peter   Bob's eldest son, who dresses for Christmas in his father's "monstrous shirt collar"; he has just reached an age when he is old enough to go out to work.

Cratchit, Tim ("Tiny Tim")   Bob's crippled son: "Alas for Tiny Tim, he bore a little crutch, and had his limbs supported by an iron frame!" Bob is especially fond of this gentle child, who sings at their fireside and concludes the round of Christmas toasts with, "God bless us every one!" In the vision of Christmas Yet to Come, Scrooge sees the death of Tiny Tim.

In the symbolism of the story, Tim can be taken for the child within Scrooge, crippled by his miserliness and caged in iron chains and cash boxes. When Scrooge frees his inner child on Christmas morning, he chooses to let Tiny Tim live.

Dilber, Mrs.   Scrooge's charwoman, who sells some of his belongings to the pawnbroker Old Joe in Scrooge's vision of Christmas Yet to Come.

Fan   Scrooge's younger sister who comes to take him home from school for Christmas, "a delicate creature . . . [with] a large heart." The mother of Scrooge's nephew Fred, she died before the time of the story. Some adaptors of the story suggest that her death, perhaps at the time of Fred's birth, has embittered Scrooge and turned him against his nephew. She is based on Dickens's sister Fanny (*see* DICKENS, FRANCES ELIZABETH).

Fezziwig, Mr. (Old Fezziwig)   Scrooge's employer when he was a young man, a jovial "old gentleman in a Welsh wig" who turned his warehouse into a Christmas dance hall. After seeing the vision of Fezziwig's Christmas party in Christmas Past, Scrooge acknowledges that Fezziwig modeled the good employer, "He has the power to render us happy or unhappy," Scrooge asserts, "to make our service light or burdensome; a pleasure or a toil. . . .

Leech's familiar rendering of Fezziwig's Ball for *A Christmas Carol* (1843).

The happiness he gives, is quite as great as if it cost a fortune."

Fezziwig, Mrs. Fezziwig's wife, "worthy to be his partner in every sense of the term," is described as "one vast substantial smile." Their daughters, the three Miss Fezziwigs, are "beaming and lovable."

Fred Scrooge's nephew and Fan's son, who thinks of Christmas "as a good time: a kind, forgiving, charitable, pleasant time: the only time I know of, in the long calendar of the year, when men and women seem by one consent to open their shut-up hearts freely" (1). He invites his uncle to Christmas dinner and is refused. The Spirit of Christmas Present shows Scrooge Fred's party and Scrooge regrets his decision not to attend. After his conversion, Scrooge goes to Christmas dinner at Fred's house.

Fred's wife Scrooge observes her at the party, "exceedingly pretty. With a dimpled, surprised-

looking, capital face; a ripe little mouth, that seemed made to be kissed; . . . and the sunniest pair of eyes you ever saw" (3).

Ghosts of Christmas The three spirits of Christmas, who bring about Scrooge's conversion. The Ghost of Christmas Past, "a strange figure—like a child: yet not so like a child as like an old man," dressed in a white tunic and emitting a beam of light from its head, shows Scrooge scenes of his childhood and his early working years (2). The Ghost of Christmas Present, a jolly giant surrounded by a cornucopia of abundance and spreading Christmas cheer, takes Scrooge to the Cratchit's Christmas dinner and his nephew's party (3). The Ghost of Christmas Yet to Come, a hooded specter, shows Scrooge his own and Tiny Tim's deaths (4).

Eytinge's frontispiece to an 1869 American edition of *A Christmas Carol* shows Scrooge confronting the three spirits.

Joe   Receiver of stolen goods who bargains with the charwomen and the undertaker's man for the dead Scrooge's belongings in the vision of Christmas Yet to Come.

Marley, Jacob   Scrooge's deceased partner who died on Christmas Eve seven years before the time of the story. He appears to Scrooge as a ghost, first in the knocker on Scrooge's door and then as an apparition "in his pigtail, usual waistcoat, tights and boots. . . . The chain he drew was clasped about his middle. It was long, and wound about him like a tail; and it was made . . . of cash boxes, keys, padlocks, ledgers, deeds, and heavy purses wrought in steel" (1). He comes with a warning, that Scrooge also bears a chain and will suffer a fate similar to his own unless he heeds the visions of the three spirits and changes his life.

Scrooge, Ebenezer   Sharp-tongued and quick-witted businessman and miser, the surviving partner in the firm of Scrooge and Marley, "a squeezing, wrenching, grasping, scraping, clutching, covetous old sinner! Hard and sharp as flint, from which no steel had ever struck out a generous fire; secret, and self-contained, and solitary as an oyster." Scrooge particularly dislikes Christmas, dismissing the holiday and its celebration with his repeated "Bah humbug!" Haunted by Marley's ghost on Christmas Eve, the seventh anniversary of his partner's death, Scrooge is visited by the three spirits of Christmas, who show him visions of his life in Christmases past, present, and future. Scrooge is changed by the visions and learns "how to keep Christmas well."

Probably Dickens's best-known character, Scrooge has entered the lexicon as a synonym for "miser." His name, suggesting "screw" and "scourge," befits a man who is chained to money and who terrifies his employees and those who owe him money. He has been seen as representing cutthroat capitalism, narrow-minded and dour EVANGELICALISM, obsessive materialism, and selfish individualism. Dickens leaves vague the details of Scrooge's business and the events in his life that have embittered him, giving him a kind of mythic or demonic status as the Spirit of anti-Christmas.

Topper   Bachelor friend of Fred, Scrooge's nephew, he attends Fred's Christmas party and has his eye on one of Fred's wife's sisters.

Wilkins, Dick   Scrooge's fellow apprentice at Fezziwig's.

ADAPTATIONS

Carol has been adapted for stage, screen, and other media more than any other of Dickens's works. Eight stage adaptations were in production within two months of its first publication, and new adaptations continue to appear on an almost annual basis. EDWARD STIRLING (1843), C. Z. BARNETT (1843), J. C. Buckstone (1901), BRANSBY WILLIAMS (1928), Maxwell Anderson (1954), BARBARA FIELD (1977), and Israel Horowitz (1978) are among the playwrights who have adapted the story. Notable film versions include SIR SEYMOUR HICKS's 1935 cinematic version of a role he had played for years on the stage, Alastair Sim's masterful portrayal of a tormented Scrooge (1951), Albert Finney's "counterculture" Scrooge in the 1970 musical, and George C. Scott's 1984 performance in a film for television. Other famous Scrooges include Bransby Williams, LIONEL BARRYMORE, ALEC GUINNESS (also remembered for his portrayal of Marley in the 1970 musical *Scrooge*), Sir Ralph Richardson, Michael Caine, and Patrick Stewart.

Carol has also been a perennial favorite for illustrators. JOHN LEECH's original pictures have been complemented by the later work of SOLOMON EYTINGE, FREDERICK BARNARD, ARTHUR RACKHAM, CHARLES E. BROCK and innumerable others. Noteworthy contemporary illustrators who have pictured the story include Ronald Searle (1960), Michael Foreman (1983), Michael Cole (1985), Lisbeth Zwerger (1988), Roberto Innocenti (1990), and Ida Applebroog (1993). The story is so embedded in the popular culture that it is annually translated, parodied, and adapted in various ways to speak to changing times. The Muppet version (1982), Disney's *Mickey's Christmas Carol* (1983), and Bill Murray's modernization in *Scrooged* (1988) are among the most recent in the ongoing folk process of adapting the story.

FURTHER READING

MICHAEL SLATER's edition of the CHRISTMAS BOOKS includes a good introduction to *Carol.* Paul Davis, in *The Lives and Times of Ebenezer Scrooge* (1990), discusses the many adaptations of the story and the ways they articulate different readings of it. In its Winter 1993 issue, the DICKENSIAN devoted the entire issue to *Carol* to celebrate the 150 years since its initial publication. Fred Guida's *A Christmas Carol and Its Adaptations* (2000) discusses the film and television versions of the story.

Cricket on the Hearth, The. A Fairy Tale of Home.

Dickens' third Christmas book, published by BRAD-BURY & EVANS in December 1845, with illustrations by DANIEL MACLISE, RICHARD DOYLE, JOHN LEECH, SIR EDWIN HENRY LANDSEER, and CLARKSON STAN-FIELD. Returning to a domestic story from the politics of *The Chimes,* Dickens puts the conversion of the hard-hearted man in the background and focuses this Christmas story on a humble couple and the threat to their marriage.

SYNOPSIS

(1) Dot Peerybingle puts the kettle on as she waits for her husband John, a carrier and delivery man, to return from work. The kettle hums and a cricket chirps. Dot believes that the cricket brings them luck. "To have a Cricket on the Hearth," she says, "is the luckiest thing in all the world!" When John arrives, he surprises his wife by bringing with him a stranger, a deaf old white-haired man he has found sitting by the roadside. The stranger thinks Dot is John's daughter, because she seems so much younger than her husband. Dot is also surprised by one of the packages John is delivering, a wedding cake for the gruff and selfish old toy maker, Tackleton, who plans to marry in three days, on the first anniversary of John and Dot's wedding. When Tackleton comes to collect the cake, he offends the Peerybingles by comparing his impending marriage to theirs, for he, like John, is marrying a much

younger woman. He also urges them to get rid of the annoying cricket. Dot is briefly overcome by some unexplained terror, but she returns to herself and goes about her household tasks as John smokes his pipe and meditates on the cricket's visions of his happy hearth and home.

(2) Caleb Plummer, Tackleton's assistant, and his blind daughter Bertha work together in their toy-making workshop. He makes Noah's arks and rocking horses; she is a doll's dressmaker. Caleb acts as her eyes, making their lot seem far happier than it really is. He describes their shabby rooms as colorful and happy, his own ragged clothes as new and stylish, and their hard-hearted employer as benevolent and good-natured. He assures Bertha that all of Tackleton's cynicisms are merely jokes, and Bertha believes Tackleton to be a kind and noble man. She is pleased that he is to marry her friend, May Fielding, but she admits that she envies May, for she too loves Tackleton. Caleb regrets that he has deceived his daughter about the harsh old man.

The stranger, who has taken lodgings with the Peerybingles, accompanies them on their weekly picnic with Caleb and his daughter. Bertha senses something familiar in his step and Dot is distracted and agitated in his presence. During the gathering, Tackleton takes John Peerybingle to the toy warehouse to enable him to spy on an assignation between Dot and the stranger, who has removed his white-haired wig and is now a handsome young man. On their way home, John cannot ride in the cart with Dot. He walks beside his horse, brooding on what he has seen.

(3) John spends the night before the fire, thinking about Dot, about the difference in age between them, about the "shadow of the stranger" in their home. He seeks guidance from the spirit of the cricket on the hearth, and he concludes that he was not understanding enough of Dot's situation. He decides to release her from the marriage to return to her parents' home if she should choose to do so. John surprises Tackleton in the morning when he tells him of this decision. He is in turn surprised to discover that the stranger is missing from his room.

Caleb admits to his daughter that he has deceived her, and he enlightens her about their situation and their employer. When the stranger returns, he is revealed to be Edward Plummer, the son that Caleb thought had died in South America. He has claimed May as his bride and they have just been married. Dot and John also renew their vows on this anniversary of their wedding day. When Tackleton learns what has happened, he sends them the wedding cake, for he has been changed by observing the generosity of John Peerybingle during his trial. Everyone joins the celebration of Edward and May's marriage and John and Dot's anniversary as the cricket chirps on the hearth.

COMMENTARY

In its review of *Cricket*, *Chambers's Edinburgh Journal* remarked: "We are happy to find that Mr. Dickens . . . has left the question of social wrongs and rights to the discussion of those who can consider them in a calmer and less partial spirit and turned his attention to a subject of purely moral interest." Many Victorian readers shared this view. The politics of *The Chimes* had seemed contentious and inappropriate for a Christmas book. Like the reviewer, they preferred *Cricket*'s "picture of humble life, contemplated in its poetic aspects, and at its more romantic crises"; they bought, according to JOHN FORSTER's somewhat exaggerated figures, more than twice as many copies of *Cricket* than of the earlier Christmas books. Seventeen dramatic productions of the story were staged within a month of its publication. It was a runaway best seller.

Modern readers, however, have agreed with Lenin, who, according to GEORGE ORWELL, walked out of a dramatic production of *Cricket* because he "found Dickens's 'middle-class sentimentality' so intolerable." The idealization of home and hearth that led Dickens's Victorian readers to canonize him as, in Margaret Lane's words, "a humorous but Puritan god of the domestic hearth," makes modern readers remark on his hypocrisy and turn to his other works that treat marriage more realistically.

Dickens's idea for *Cricket* began as the name for a magazine that would promote the "*Carol* philosophy, cheerful views, sharp anatomization of humbug, jolly good temper, . . . a vein of glowing, hearty, generous, mirthful, beaming reference in everything to Home and Fireside." When he aban-

doned the magazine project, he used the idea for this Christmas book, making "the Cricket a little household god—silent in the wrong and sorrow of the tale, and loud again when all went well and happy."

The central action of the story occurs at the Peerybingles' hearth, the residence of the cricket. There the stranger is introduced who will disrupt Tackleton's marriage plans and threaten the Peerybingles' happiness. There John broods through the night as he considers Dot's supposed infidelity. There Tackleton learns of John's heroic decision and himself abandons his claim to May Fielding. The cricket is a chirping or silent presence as these crises are faced and overcome. It is the supernatural agency in this fairy tale, comparable to the spirits in *Carol*.

The dramatic plot on which the story turns, set off by the arrival of the white-haired stranger, is clichéd and predictable, as is the story of blind Bertha Plummer, who is predictably enlightened by the events of the tale. The more interesting story involves the threat to Dot and John's marriage, an action doubled in the marriage of Tackleton and May Fielding scheduled to take place on the first anniversary of the Peerybingles' wedding. Both are January and May unions, bringing together a young woman and a much older man. But Tackleton irritates Dot when he presumes to call attention to their similarity, for she had not thought of her own marriage as unequal or unfulfilling, and she—and everyone else except blind Bertha Plummer—knows that Tackleton is not an appropriate husband for young May, Dot's former schoolmate.

Tackleton is a relative of Scrooge. A man who should have been a money-lender or a sharp attorney, he became instead a toy maker and "a domestic Ogre, who had been living on children all his life, and was their implacable enemy" (1). Like Scrooge, he also exploits his worker, Caleb Plummer, yet he expects gratitude and obedience from him. Tackleton's interest in May is not explained, but there are suggestions that he is indulging an unhealthy desire to control the young woman. We do not know enough of Tackleton to understand his character; he is presented in terms of his external contradictions rather than his interior desires.

reactions of most recent critics with a sympathetic reading of *Cricket* as a January/May story.

David Copperfield, The Personal History of. (Serial Title: The Personal History, Adventures, Experience & Observation of David Copperfield the Younger, of Blunderstone Rookery. [Which He never meant to be Published on any Account.])

Dickens's eighth novel, published in monthly parts by BRADBURY & EVANS from May 1849 to November 1850, with illustrations by HABLOT KNIGHT BROWNE. Published in one volume, 1850. Written at the midpoint in Dickens's career, *Copperfield* uses materials from the author's life in David's fictional autobiography. The novel is usually considered the dividing point in Dickens's career between the early and late novels. Although it appears to have the formlessness of the 18th-century "personal histories" on which it is modeled, *Copperfield* is a carefully crafted and unified novel, presenting its hero as a Victorian everyman seeking self-understanding.

SYNOPSIS

Part 1 (May 1849)

(1) "Whether I shall turn out to be the hero of my own life, or whether that station will be held by anybody else, these pages must show." With these words David Copperfield begins the story of his life. He tells of his birth six months after his father's death, a "posthumous child," born into a loving household composed of his sweet and doting mother, Clara Copperfield, and her housekeeper, Clara Peggotty. His father's sister, his aunt Betsey Trotwood, comes for the occasion, but when she learns that the child is a boy and not the girl she expected, "she vanished like a discontented fairy … and never came back any more." (2) David remembers his early childhood, his house, his visits to church, and Mr. Murdstone, who accompanies his mother home from church. (3) When his mother has Peggotty take David on a holiday to Yarmouth, they visit her brother, Daniel Peggotty, and stay in his house, a boat turned upside down on the beach. There David meets Ham and Mrs. Gummidge and spends long hours playing by the sea with Little Em'ly, Daniel's orphaned niece. When he returns to Blunderstone, he discovers that Mr. Murdstone has married his mother.

Part 2 (June 1849)

(4) Murdstone suppresses his wife's sympathy for her son and introduces a regime of "firmness," bringing in his steely sister, Miss Jane Murdstone, to oversee the household. David finds secret solace reading the books his father left in a little room upstairs. When Murdstone beats him for confusing his lessons, David bites him on the thumb and is locked in his room for five days. Through the keyhole, Peggotty sends kisses and tells him that he will be sent away to school. (5) As he sets off to school, the carrier, Mr. Barkis, asks him to tell Peggotty that "Barkis is willin'." In London, David is met by Mr. Mell, a master at Salem House. On the way to the school, they stop at an almshouse where Mell visits his mother and plays the flute for her. When they arrive at Salem House, deserted for the school holiday, David is directed to wear a placard stating, "Take care of him. He bites." (6) Mr. Creakle, the headmaster, warns David that he is "a Tartar," but the boys are more friendly. The head boy, James Steerforth, takes charge of David's seven shillings, spending the money for a late-night supper at which he promises to be young David's protector (6).

Part 3 (July 1849)

(7) David idolizes Steerforth, who encourages him to tell nightly stories to the other boys, based on the stories he had read in his father's library. One day Steerforth challenges Mr. Mell as an "impudent beggar." When Steerforth reveals that Mell's mother is in an almshouse, something he has learned from David, Creakle fires the schoolmaster. David feels

implicated in Steerforth's mean action, but he keeps silent, and when Mr. Peggotty and Ham visit the school, he introduces them to Steerforth.

(8) On his way home for the Christmas holiday, David promises Barkis that he will tell Peggotty that "Barkis is waitin' for an answer." When he arrives, the Murdstones are out and David spends an idyllic afternoon with his mother, Peggotty, and his new baby brother. But after the Murdstones return, the regime of firmness is reinstated and David is miserable until it is time to go back to Salem House. (9) In March, on his birthday, David is called to Creakle's office and told that his mother has died. On his way home he stops at the shop of Mr. Omer, the undertaker, where he is fitted for funeral clothes as he listens to the hammer constructing his mother's coffin. Peggotty describes his mother's death, her gradual decline under the rule of firmness, her concern for her "fatherless boy," and her desire to have her baby buried with her should he die at the same time. After the funeral David ruminates, "The mother who lay in the grave, was the mother of my infancy; the little creature in her arms, was myself, as I had once been, hushed for ever on her bosom."

Part 4 (August 1849)

(10) Murdstone dismisses Peggotty, but she arranges to take David to Yarmouth. There David renews his ties with Little Em'ly and the others, and, on a "wonderful day" when David and Em'ly accompany Peggotty and Barkis to their wedding, David dreams of marrying Em'ly. Back at Blunderstone, David is idle and neglected until Murdstone announces that he is not returning to school but rather is to be sent to London to work at Murdstone and Grinby's, a wine business.

(11) In London David begins life on his own account, washing and pasting labels on wine bottles. He contrasts his fellow workers, Mick Walker and Mealy Potatoes, to his former companions at Salem House and describes the "secret agony," "misery," and "shame" that he feels in his new situation. He is introduced to Mr. Micawber, with whom he has lodgings. He soon learns of Micawber's financial difficulties, offers to lend the family money from his meager wages, and helps them by taking items to the pawnbroker's. When Micawber is imprisoned for debt, David takes lodgings

near the prison. (12) After his release from prison, Micawber decides to go to Plymouth, where he hopes something will "turn up." David also decides to leave London and to seek out his Aunt Betsey in DOVER. After work on a Saturday evening, David puts his plan into effect, but the young man he hires to carry his box to the coach steals the box and the half-guinea David has borrowed from Peggotty for travel expenses. So David begins his journey on foot, "taking very little more out of the world, towards the retreat of my aunt, Miss Betsey, than I had brought into it, on the night when my arrival gave her so much umbrage."

Part 5 (September 1849)

(13) On his six-day journey, David sustains himself by selling his vest and coat. He sleeps outside—one night in a field near Salem House—and arrives in Dover ragged and tired. His aunt, acting on the advice of her weak-minded lodger, Mr. Dick, bathes and feeds the boy. (14) The Murdstones come to Dover and make it quite clear that they will have nothing more to do with David if he does not return to Blunderstone. Aunt Betsey castigates them and sends them away. She becomes David's guardian and decides to call him Trotwood Copperfield. (15) David soon becomes best friends with Mr. Dick. They fly kites made from pages of Mr. Dick's Memorial, an autobiographical memoir he writes to seek redress from the Lord Chancellor, but he inevitably gets entangled in discussing his obsession with King Charles's head and must discard each successive draft. When Aunt Betsey decides that David should go to school in CANTERBURY, KENT, he stays at the home of Mr. Wickfield, her solicitor, and meets Wickfield's daughter, Agnes, and his clerk, Uriah Heep. As she leaves to return to Dover, Aunt Betsey counsels David: "Never . . . be mean in anything; never be false; never be cruel. Avoid these three vices, Trot, and I can always be hopeful of you."

Part 6 (October 1849)

(16) David begins at Doctor Strong's school, where he meets the old scholar and his young wife Annie. David senses some uneasiness between Mr. Wickfield and Doctor Strong when they talk of Jack Maldon, Annie's cousin, and he observes Annie's

distress when Maldon goes off to India. (17) Mr. Dick visits David in Canterbury regularly and becomes a good friend of the doctor. He tells David of a strange man who loiters outside Betsey Trotwood's house and gets money from her. David also gets to know the fawning Uriah Heep. When he goes to tea at Uriah's house, David is "pumped" by the clerk and his mother about his former life. While he is there, Mr. Micawber passes the open door, sees David, and introduces himself to Heep. The Micawbers are in Canterbury seeking employment. David is uneasy when he sees Heep with Micawber the next day. He enjoys a lavish dinner with the Micawbers before they return to London, but Micawber leaves David a letter detailing his desperate financial situation.

(18) In a retrospective chapter—the first of four such chapters (*see also* 43, 53, and 64) in which David sums up a stage in his life and prepares for an important change—David remembers the infatuations of his schooldays: his love for Miss Shepherd, his fight with a young butcher over her, and later on, when he has become head boy at Doctor Strong's, his infatuation for the eldest Miss Larkins. These retrospective chapters stress the importance of memory in the novel.

Part 7 (November 1849)

(19) David finishes school and plans a vacation at Yarmouth before settling into a profession. Before he leaves, Agnes reveals her worry about her father's alcoholism and Uriah Heep's role in encouraging it. David also learns that Maldon wants to return from India, and he observes Mr. Wickfield's distrust of Annie Strong. On his way to Yarmouth, David unexpectedly meets Steerforth in London. (20) He spends a few days at Steerforth's home in HIGHGATE, where he meets Steerforth's mother, who dotes upon her son, and Rosa Dartle, her contrary and volatile companion who bears a scar across her lip. She got the scar as a child when Steerforth threw a hammer at her. (21) David also meets Littimer, Steerforth's respectable servant, whose condescending manner makes David feel young. David takes Steerforth to Yarmouth and introduces him to the Daniel Peggotty household. They celebrate Ham's engagement to Em'ly, and

Steerforth charms the company with his stories and affability.

Part 8 (December 1849)

(22) When Steerforth falls into a spell of dejection, he confesses to David that he lacks purpose in his life and wishes he had a father who would help him "guide [himself] better." He tells David that he has bought a boat that he plans to call "The Little Em'ly." Miss Mowcher, a dwarf hairdresser, gossips with Steerforth as she fixes his hair.

Em'ly befriends Martha Endell, one of her coworkers, who has been ruined and wants to run off to London. Afterward, Em'ly tearfully tells Ham that she is unworthy of him.

(23) David follows Aunt Betsey's suggestion that he become a proctor at Doctors' Commons (*see* COURTS). As they go together to Mr. Spenlow's office to arrange his articles, Aunt Betsey is accosted by a strange man who gets money from her. She arranges rooms for David at Mrs. Crupp's. (24) David invites Steerforth and two of Steerforth's college friends to a housewarming. After drinking too much wine at dinner, they go to the theater, where the drunken David sees Agnes. He awakens the next morning bitterly remorseful.

Part 9 (January 1850)

(25) Agnes warns David of Steerforth's influence. She also tells him that her father is about to make Uriah Heep his partner. Uriah boasts of his changed relationship with Wickfield and outrages David when he reveals his desire to marry Agnes.

(26) When David spends a weekend at Mr. Spenlow's, he falls hopelessly in love with Spenlow's daughter Dora. He is disconcerted to find Miss Murdstone acting as Dora's companion, but they agree to keep confidential their past relationship.

(27) David meets Traddles, a former schoolmate at Salem House, who tells David of his struggle to establish himself as a lawyer and of his engagement to a curate's daughter. David is surprised to learn that Traddles lodges with Micawber.

Part 10 (February 1850)

(28) At a dinner in David's lodgings, Mrs. Micawber urges her husband to advertise for work and David learns that Micawber's financial difficulties

have entangled Traddles. Afterward Steerforth brings a letter from Peggotty informing David that Barkis is dying. David plans to go to Yarmouth after spending a day at Steerforth's home, (29) where Rosa Dartle questions him to learn what she can of Steerforth's movements. (30) In Yarmouth, David sees Barkis as he "goes out with the tide," and he notices that Em'ly seems restless. (31) After the funeral Ham receives a letter from Em'ly saying that she is running off with Steerforth. Daniel Peggotty resolves "to seek [his] niece through the wureld . . . and bring her back."

Part 11 (March 1850)
(32) Miss Mowcher tells David of Steerforth's treachery. When David and Daniel Peggotty call on Mrs. Steerforth, she is haughty and unsympathetic. Rosa Dartle too scorns Em'ly. Daniel Peggotty sets out on his journey.

(33) David spends an ecstatic day at Dora's birthday picnic. Afterward, with the help of Miss Mills, Dora's friend, he arranges a tryst with Dora. They are engaged but decide to keep it secret from Mr. Spenlow. (34) David returns home to find Betsey Trotwood with Mr. Dick, two birds, a cat, and all her worldly belongings "like a female Robinson Crusoe," sitting in the middle of his apartment. She tells David that she is ruined.

Part 12 (April 1850)
(35) David is determined to help his aunt out of her difficulties, and he tries unsuccessfully to resign his articles and recover some of the premium. Agnes suggests that he apply to work as a secretary for Doctor Strong, who has retired to London. (36) Doctor Strong hires David for £70 a year. David also decides to learn shorthand with an eye to becoming a Parliamentary reporter. Mr. Dick takes up legal copying and proudly contributes his earnings to Betsey Trotwood. Heep, now the dominant partner in Wickfield and Heep, hires Micawber as a clerk. Before he leaves for Canterbury, Micawber "repays" Traddles with an IOU. (37) David tries to explain to Dora his changed circumstances, but she refuses to listen.

Part 13 (May 1850)
(38) Traddles helps David learn shorthand by reading Parliamentary speeches for him to copy.

When Mr. Spenlow learns of David's relationship with Dora from Miss Murdstone, who has discovered one of David's letters, he demands that the affair be broken off. The same evening he dies suddenly, without a will, his affairs in disarray. Dora goes to live with her two maiden aunts in Putney.

(39) At Canterbury David finds Micawber unwilling to speak about Heep, Wickfield lamenting his partner's interest in his daughter, and Heep suspicious of David, whom he considers a rival for Agnes's affections.

(40) One snowy night David meets Daniel Peggotty, who tells of his unsuccessful search for Em'ly in France, Italy, and Switzerland. David notices that Mr. Peggotty is being followed by Martha Endell.

Part 14 (June 1850)
(41) Dora's aunts, Miss Clarissa and Miss Lavinia Spenlow, agree to allow David to visit Dora on certain stated conditions. Aunt Betsey becomes a regular caller at their house. David worries that all, including his aunt and himself, treat Dora "like a plaything." (42) When the Wickfields come to London to visit the Strongs, David introduces Agnes to Dora.

Heep tells Doctor Strong that he suspects Annie of infidelity with Maldon and indicates that David and Wickfield share his suspicions. The Doctor refuses to believe Annie unfaithful and blames himself for any unhappiness she feels. Afterwards David angrily strikes Heep for involving him.

(43) In a retrospective chapter, David remembers his 21st birthday and how his career changes from successful shorthand reporter to successful author. He remembers his wedding to Dora.

Part 15 (July 1850)
(44) David and Dora begin housekeeping and Dora proves utterly incapable of managing a home. David asks his aunt to counsel her, but she refuses to interfere in their lives. Dora asks David to think of her as his "child-wife."

(45) Mr. Dick notices the "cloud" between Doctor Strong and his wife and tells David that he will set things right. A few weeks later, Dick escorts Annie into the presence of her husband. She kneels before the Doctor, reiterates her love and respect for him, and tells of the awkward position she has

been in because of the dishonorable behavior of Jack Maldon. David ruminates on two things she says: "There can be no disparity in marriage like unsuitability of mind and purpose," and "I should be thankful to him for having saved me from the first mistaken impulse of my undisciplined heart."

(46) About a year after his wedding, David is summoned to Steerforth's house. There Littimer tells him that Steerforth has left Em'ly and that she has disappeared. Rosa Dartle exults over Em'ly's suffering.

Part 16 (August 1850)

(47) David goes with Daniel Peggotty to seek out Martha Endell and enlist her aid in locating Emily should she come to London. They trace Martha to the edge of the THAMES RIVER and prevent her from drowning herself.

When David returns home he sees Aunt Betsey give some money to a man in her garden. She tells David that the man is her husband.

(48) David gives up parliamentary reporting and takes up writing full time. Dora sits by his side as he works, but they quarrel about domestic issues. David attempts to "form Dora's mind," but the effort is unsuccessful, so he accepts her limitations and loves her as his "child-wife." During the second year of their marriage, Dora's health begins to fail so that David must carry her up and down the stairs.

(49) Mr. Micawber has become secretive, irritable, and depressed. When David and Traddles meet him in London, he is so troubled that he is unable even to make punch. Suddenly he explodes with a denunciation of his employer, "HEEP," and then, just as abruptly, he leaves. He makes an appointment to meet them in Canterbury in a week, when he will expose the villain.

(50) Martha conducts David to her rooms, where they find Rosa Dartle berating Em'ly. Knowing that Daniel Peggoty has been told of Em'ly's whereabouts, David does not interfere. Just as Rosa leaves, Daniel arrives and Em'ly faints into his arms.

Part 17 (September 1850)

(51) Mr. Peggotty recounts the story of Em'ly's escape from Steerforth, her illness and recupera-

tion in Italy, and her return to England. He plans to emigrate to Australia with her and "begin a new life over there." Ham confesses that he feels partly responsible for Em'ly's ruin because she was trying to avoid marrying him. He asks David to tell Em'ly of his feelings.

(52) On the appointed day, David, Aunt Betsey, and Traddles meet Micawber in Canterbury. At the office of Wickfield and Heep, Micawber reads off his accusations against the "HEEP of Infamy," charging him with forgery, misrepresentation, and embezzlement. Aunt Betsey learns that Heep, not Wickfield, was responsible for her losses. Traddles takes over the legal prosecution and assembles the evidence that Micawber has gathered. Although his mother urges him to "be 'umble and make terms," Uriah is defiant. He attacks David as the one responsible for his comeuppance: "I have always hated you. You've always been an upstart, and you've always been against me."

(53) In a retrospective chapter, David recalls Dora's decline and how, in her final hours, she regretted their childish marriage and asked to speak with Agnes while David meditated on his "undisciplined heart." As her dog Jip expired in his Chinese house, Dora passed away upstairs.

Part 18 (October 1850)

(54) Traddles and Micawber sort out Wickfield's business and Heep's schemes. They recover Aunt Betsey's money and liquidate Wickfield's firm without bankruptcy. Betsey praises David for meeting the test of financial hardship, "nobly—persevering, self-reliant, self-denying." She arranges to pay off Micawber's debts and enable him to settle in Australia. Back in London, she reveals that her husband has died.

(55) David decides to deliver Em'ly's reply to Ham in person. At Yarmouth he finds himself in a tumultuous storm, "the greatest ever known to blow upon that coast," and it jumbles his thoughts and recollections. Drawn to the beach by news that a schooner is breaking up just off shore, David finds Ham preparing to attempt to rescue the lone sailor who clings to the mast of the sinking ship. But the attempt fails, and, "beaten to death by a great wave," Ham's generous heart is stilled forever. The

body of the lone sailor also washes up on the shore. It is Steerforth. (56) David returns to London with Steerforth's body. Mrs. Steerforth's spirit is broken, but Rosa Dartle's pride and anger rise to a fever pitch and she curses David and the "evil hour that you ever came here."

(57) David bids farewell to the Micawbers and Mr. Peggotty as they leave for Australia. Daniel is taking Martha, as well as Em'ly and Mrs. Gummidge, with him.

Part 19–20 (November 1850)

(58) While David spends three years in a Swiss village where he overcomes the "brooding sorrow . . . that fell on my undisciplined heart," he realizes that he loves Agnes and he thinks he has "thrown away the treasure of her love."

(59) Back in England, David learns that Traddles has married and Murdstone has driven his new wife mad. He is reunited with Betsey, Dick, and Peggotty, who is now Miss Trotwood's housekeeper. (60) At Canterbury, David finds Agnes running a school for girls, but he is troubled by the thought that she is not happy.

(61) When David accepts an invitation to visit a model prison from Mr. Creakle, now a Middlesex Magistrate, he is surprised to find Littimer and Uriah Heep among the model prisoners. Littimer forgives Em'ly "her bad conduct toward myself" and Heep hopes that "Mr. W. will repent, and Miss W., and all of that sinful lot." David leaves the prison convinced that the system merely encourages hypocrisy and false humility.

(62) David seeks to learn the secret of Agnes's unhappiness. He confesses to her his hope that she might be "something more than a sister" to him. She breaks into tears of joy and reveals that she has loved him all her life. Two weeks later, on their wedding day, Agnes tells David that Dora on her deathbed had given her "this vacant place."

(63) Ten years later Mr. Peggotty surprises the Copperfields with a visit. He reports his success as a farmer, Em'ly's goodness and kindness to others, Martha's marriage, and Micawber's rise to become Port Middlebay District Magistrate. David also reads in an Australian paper of Doctor Mell of Colonial Salem House Grammar School.

(64) David closes with a final retrospect. He describes Aunt Betsey, a firm and upright woman of 80; Peggotty teaching his youngest son to walk as she taught him; and Mr. Dick continuing work on his memorial. He also remembers Mrs. Steerforth, whose life stopped on the day of her son's death; Julia Mills and Jack Maldon, who are "in society"; Doctor Strong, who still works on his dictionary; and Traddles, successful in the law, now a judge, and happy in his marriage to Sophy. Most of all, David tells of Agnes, "one face shining on me like a heavenly light by which I see all other objects."

COMMENTARY

In his 1867 preface to *Copperfield*, Dickens described the novel as his "favourite child" and spoke of the difficulty of "dismissing some portion of himself into the shadowy world." The book may have had such personal importance to him because it was the most autobiographical of all his novels, and some of the most painful episodes of his life were only thinly disguised in the novel. These oblique revelations contained in *Copperfield* gave it a special place for him and contribute to its truthfulness and power as a novel.

The most important autobiographical materials involve the months he spent at WARREN'S BLACKING, his courtship of MARIA BEADNELL, and his journalistic and writing career. As JOHN FORSTER and others have pointed out, these episodes are essentially factual. The descriptions of David's labor at Murdstone and Grinby's repeat verbatim much of Dickens's description of his experiences at the BLACKING WAREHOUSE in the fragmentary AUTOBIOGRAPHY he gave to Forster. David's fascination with Dora Spenlow draws on Dickens's own attraction to the flirtatious Maria Beadnell, and the outlines of David's career—from Doctors' Commons (*see* COURTS) to shorthand reporter to novelist—follow that of his creator.

Yet all these episodes—as well as the other autobiographical materials in the novel—are also transformed by art. The villainous Murdstone is very different from the well-intentioned JAMES LAMERT, Dickens's cousin who was responsible for placing him at Warren's Blacking. David's resolution to run away from the wine-bottling warehouse ends his time there on a courageous note; Dickens, embittered by his mother's desire that he continue working, was saved by his father, who removed him from the factory to attend school. In the story of Maria Beadnell, re-created as Dora Spenlow in the novel, David marries the girl who spurned Dickens, and, perhaps indulging in some *ex post facto* wish fulfillment, Dickens "kills" the father who has frustrated the courtship. David's literary career seems far less hectic and demanding than Dickens's and David's achievement far less spectacular. David's modesty about such matters would not alone account for these differences in temperament and achievement. Some of these transformations may be explained as the result of Dickens telling his life as he wished it might have been, but they must also be seen as indications of Dickens's conscious artistry, taking the materials of autobiography and giving them thematic relevance and coherence. In the end, *Copperfield* is David's autobiography, not Dickens's.

David begins his account by stating, "Whether I shall turn out to be the hero of my own life, or whether that station will be held by anybody else, these pages must show" (1), suggesting that even he is unsure of the resolution of this issue and that the test of his heroism will come in the writing of his story. In this Victorian quest narrative, the pen will be mightier than the sword, and the reader left to judge those qualities of the man and the writer that constitute heroism.

David's opening statement implies one of the standards by which to judge his heroism: that he, rather than someone else, will determine his life. The form of David's narrative exaggerates this test. Even though he narrates the story, David often seems to disappear. Other characters have a physical presence that he lacks. By contrast to Micawber, Heep, or Steerforth, he often appears colorless and passive. Several commentators have noted that we have no clear physical impression of David; in the illustrations he tends to be out of the center of the picture, often facing away from the viewer. To judge whether he becomes the hero of his life, then, we need to read his story in a different way from the way we would read a hero's saga. Instead of measuring David's great deeds, we need to study his refractions in other characters. What

does Steerforth, or Micawber, or Heep, or Dora tell us about David? And we must look at the narration itself for signs of the writer's heroism.

David's difference from two other writers in the story may suggest some of the tests for heroic narrative. Doctor Strong and Mr. Dick are both engaged in writing projects. Strong's dictionary will never be completed; by the end of the novel he is laboring "somewhere about the letter D" (64). Like the project of writing one's life, the dictionary will be "finished" only with the death of the author. Mr. Dick—whose name and connection with King Charles links him to Dickens—is engaged on an explicitly autobiographical project. His memorial gives surreal exaggeration to the test David faces as a writer. Can he overcome incoherence and inconclusiveness as he attempts to tell his life? Can he take control of his story? Can he unify it, give it a beginning, middle, and end? Can he transcend the traumas of the past—the severing of King Charles' head—to make sense of the present and give direction to the future? David's ability as a storyteller to pull together an account of his whole life, including the painful and traumatic episodes as well as his successes, is one measure of his heroism as a writer.

The pull of the past is especially strong on David. Born "a child of close observation" (2), he is an adult of extraordinary memory. His account of his childhood is so concretely realized that we forget, as he sometimes seems to, that he is remembering the past rather than describing events as they happen. He remarks on the powers of memory and marks the passages in his life with "retrospective" chapters. In many ways, *Copperfield* is a novel about memory and the ways in which it provides the imagination with the materials to make experience whole.

GEORGE ORWELL remarked on Dickens's ability to enter into the child's point of view, "to stand both inside and outside the child's mind." The opening chapters of *Copperfield* are a beautiful example of this double vision, combining the child's perspective with that of the narrator who knows that David's innocence and security will pass. Even before Murdstone intrudes as his stepfather or his mother dies, young David has intimations of his mortality in such scenes as the "Brooks of Sheffield" episode (2), and he knows that childhood has ended when he sees his infant brother, the image of himself, dead on his mother's breast (9).

David's life is in a way a series of lives, each one of them ending in a radical disjunction from what follows. The boy who goes to work at Murdstone and Grinby's is a different person from the child of Blunderstone Rookery or the boy at Salem House, and David seems to think his survival depends on keeping these parts of himself disconnected. When, as a schoolboy in Canterbury, for example, he meets Micawber again while he is having tea at Uriah Heep's house (17), he is terrified that Heep might connect him with the waif the Micawbers knew in London. These radical breaks in David's life are often marked by his changing name. When he runs away to Dover and begins a new life as Trotwood Copperfield under his aunt's protection, he remarks, "Thus I began my new life, in a new name, and with everything new about me. Now that the state of doubt was over, I felt, for many days, like one in a dream. . . . The two clearest things in my mind were, that a remoteness had come upon the old Blunderstone life—which seemed to lie in a haze of an immeasurable distance; and that a curtain had for ever fallen on my life at Murdstone and Grinby's" (14). In remembering and telling his story, David must connect these separate lives into one.

Sometimes the connections force themselves upon him, as when the Micawbers disconcert him by appearing at the door of Uriah Heep's house (17), when Traddles reappears at the Waterbrook's dinner party (25), or Miss Murdstone turns up as Dora Spenlow's companion (26). Such coincidences may test the limits of realism, but they make perfect sense in a narrative where all the characters enact various dimensions of the hero. Dora, for example, engages both David's longing for his mother and his Murdstonian need for firmness. The disreputable Micawber inevitably "turns up" when David most wishes to appear respectable. Coincidence makes visible the contradictions within himself that David must resolve if he is to be the hero of his life.

"A posthumous child" (1), David is born after his father's death. His aunt acts out his identity problem, his "orphanhood," on the day of his birth

when she abandons him because he was supposed to be a girl. His early years, spent in a community of women, centering on his mother, Clara Copperfield, and his nurse, Clara Peggotty, further undermine his sense of masculine identity. He develops a feminine sensibility, trusting, unworldly, innocent, and insecure like his orphan mother. Young David is characterized as Daisy, Steerforth's feminine nickname for him. If he is to avoid his mother's fate and survive in the world with a masculine identity, he must find a father figure to replace the father he never knew.

Murdstone is the first of his male role models. He darkens David's childhood with "firmness," a principle missing in David's parents and in his life up to the time Murdstone appears. Murdstone and his metallic spinster sister bring order to the household, but they stifle and eventually kill its love and care. David's resistance to Murdstone is both a challenge to the usurper who has stolen his mother's love and an act of rebellion that liberates him from the regime of firmness. In Micawber David finds another ineffectual father, one very different from Murdstone. Micawber lacks firmness and responsibility; he does not lack imagination and love. His marriage is grounded in fidelity and devotion, and, in spite of the recurrent setbacks in his life, his outlook is one of eternal optimism; he always believes that something will "turn up." As a member of the Micawber household, David must himself adopt a semiparental role and help the Micawbers with their financial difficulties.

Among David's other male role models are Heep, Traddles, and, especially, Steerforth. Heep acts as a kind of negative mirror to David, magnifying qualities that David represses or denies. Heep exploits his humble origins with a false humility as a way of evoking sympathy and disguising his ruthless ambition. Although David suppresses his humble past and hides his ambition under a veneer of genteel diffidence, he is also a self-seeking social climber. Heep's ambition, like Murdstone's firmness, is unbalanced by any tempering feminine qualities.

Steerforth appears to David to be everything that Heep is not. He has been born to his place as a gentleman, and even though he has no visible ambition, no apparent purpose in life, he is a commanding and charismatic person. His unacceptability as a male ideal, however, is suggested long before he steals Em'ly from Yarmouth to ruin her in Italy. It appears in his brutality to Rosa Dartle, which has scarred her for life, and in his cruelty to Mr. Mell. His condescending attitude and selfish exploitation of others is contrasted to Daniel Peggotty's selflessness and love. Although David comes to realize Steerforth's villainy, he is still drawn to Steerforth's charismatic gentility, even as he sees him lying dead on the sands at Yarmouth, "lying with his head upon his arm, as I had often seen him at school" (55).

Though he lacks Steerforth's charisma, Traddles is, in the long run, a far better model for David. In many ways, Traddles and David are alike, but Traddles is less easily manipulated by others. He possesses a moderation and restraint that David sometimes lacks. Born neither to humbleness nor wealth, he too must find his own place in the world. Love tempers Traddles's ambition, patience restrains his passion, and justice is more important to him than social position.

David's personal history makes it harder for him to achieve such balance in his life, for he seems fated to reenact the mistakes of his parents. He is inevitably attracted to Dora, for she possesses the same delicate and captivating femininity as his mother, and she is just as frivolous. The chapters describing their courtship and marriage are among the most successful in the novel, for they capture David's painful ambivalence. He is both infatuated with Dora and frustrated by her helplessness, incompetence, and lack of discipline. While he loves her, he attempts to change her and "form her mind." In doing so, he is forced to recognize his own need for "firmness" and his discomfiting kinship with Murdstone.

David's Aunt Betsey dramatizes the struggle to achieve a balance between firmness and softness, rationality and sympathy, the male and female dimensions of the self. Aunt Betsey, whose repressed personal history has forced her into a masculine role, is a proponent of firmness and discipline tempered with love. Often described as David's fairy godmother, she may also be the best

of his surrogate father figures. Her tough-mindedness prompts her to abandon the infant David and to decry the weakness of his parents, but it is tempered by her own experience of suffering and by her sympathy for Mr. Dick, who modifies her rationality with his irrational foolishness and down-to-earth advice. In spite of her rationality, Aunt Betsey cannot control her world: She cannot make the infant David a girl, save herself from Heep's machinations, or resist her husband's entreaties for money. She can see David's "blindness," but she cannot prevent his marriage to Dora. Ironically, it is Mr. Dick, prompted by intuition and feeling, who can act to aid Micawber in exposing Heep or to heal the misunderstandings between the Strongs.

The story of Doctor Strong's marriage to his young wife Annie, which counterpoints David's marriage to Dora, illustrates the mixture of firmness and feeling necessary to take control of one's life. While Dora is dying and David attempting to understand his role in his marriage, he watches the Strongs sort out their relationship. Two statements by Annie Strong lodge in his memory. When she tells why she rejected Jack Maldon, she thanks her husband for saving her "from the first mistaken impulse of my undisciplined heart" and asserts that "there can be no disparity in marriage like unsuitability of mind and purpose" (45). David repeats these words to himself, acknowledging their relevance to his life and his marriage to Dora and underscoring their thematic importance in the novel. Discipline must be tempered with love, firmness balanced with feeling.

This recognition and the painful memories that he suffers after Dora's death enable David to overcome his blindness and acknowledge his love for Agnes, the woman Dickens identified in his notes for her first appearance in the story as the "true heroine" of the novel. She may also be, as HILARY SCHOR (1999) suggests, the novel's hero, for she inspires David's writing, and the story he tells brings together the stories of the many women who shape his life. Nevertheless, Agnes, with the saintly aura of the stained-glass window surrounding her, has disappointed many readers. She is more of a conscience or ideal than a real person; she brings discipline and responsibility into David's life, but she seems to lack the human qualities that make Dora so attractive.

The ending has also annoyed some readers, who find the Micawbers' exile to Australia a convenient but unconvincing way to "clean up" David's identity, allowing him to achieve respectable maturity by removing them from his presence. If David has achieved a "disciplined heart" by the end of his autobiography, he has done so, these critics suggest, by diminishing the richness and complexity of his life, for he sacrifices Dora to death and the Micawbers and Peggottys to emigration. It is not the details of the story that one remembers, but the tone of its telling that lingers. In the narration David's success as a novelist and his happy marriage to Agnes are mixed with memories of his losses. Whatever heroism there is for him by the end of his story, he has not been left unscathed achieving it.

Some critics find David unconvincing as a portrait of the artist. David tells us little about the books that he writes, and he is not self-dramatizing in the manner of the Inimitable Boz. In spite of the novel's autobiographical passages, Dickens does not seem to be presenting David as his own self-portrait in the novel. In some ways, Micawber comes closer to filling that role. The most triumphant creation in *Copperfield,* he is the character who possesses the power of self-creation. He does so through language, and we remember him not for his story but for his words. His story is inconsistent: Who can believe that Heep would hire him, that this perennially unsuccessful man could pull together the case against Heep, or that he could achieve such success in Australia? It is Micawber's grandiloquent and inflated rhetoric that transforms the world, even if it inevitably ends, like Micawber, unable to sustain itself and, in short, deflated. His most famous speech exemplifies this self-creating, self-affirming, and deflating rhetorical pattern:

> "My other piece of advice, Copperfield," said Mr. Micawber, "you know. Annual income twenty pounds, annual expenditure nineteen nineteen six, result happiness. Annual income twenty pounds, annual expenditure twenty pounds ought and six, result misery. The blossom is blighted, the leaf is withered, the God of day goes down upon the dreary scene, and—and in short you are for ever floored. As I am." (12)

If Dickens was "floored" in ending this novel, unable to sustain the richness of the story he had spun, nevertheless, we remember the wonderful invention in the telling and accept the inevitability in the end.

CHARACTERS AND RELATED ENTRIES

Adams   Head boy at Dr. Strong's school in Canterbury when David is in attendance there: "He looked like a young clergyman in his white cravat, but was very affable and good-humored" (16).

Babley, Richard   The given name of Mr. Dick.

Bailey, Captain   David's presumed rival for the attentions of the eldest Miss Larkins (18).

Barkis   The carrier between Blunderstone and Yarmouth, "a man of phlegmatic temperament, and not at all conversational" (5). As he is taking David off to school, after eating a piece of Peggotty's cake, he entrusts David with the message "Barkis is willin'" to deliver to Peggotty (5). Barkis and Peggoty marry at a ceremony observed by David and Little Em'ly (10). Although he is tight with his money, keeping close watch on the cash box he keeps under his bed, he is a loving husband and leaves Peggotty comfortably well off after he goes "out with the tide" (30).

Barkis was based on a carrier named Barker who lived at Blundestone, a town near Yarmouth.

Blue Boar, Aldgate   The coaching inn in Whitechapel where David first arrives in London and is met by Mr. Mell (5).

Blunderstone   The village in Suffolk where David spends his earliest years, based on the village of Blundestone, which Dickens visited in 1848.

Buckingham Street, Strand   A street in the Adelphi where David Copperfield takes rooms in Mrs. Crupp's house at No. 15 (23), the rooms Dickens himself occupied in 1834.

Castle Street   Street in Holborn where Traddles has lodgings (36).

Charley   Secondhand clothing dealer at CHA-THAM to whom David sells his jacket on his way to DOVER. He frightens the boy by intoning "oh—goroo" and chasing the boys who taunt him for selling himself "to the devil" (13).

Chestle   Hop grower from KENT who marries the eldest Miss Larkins (18).

Chillip   Blunderstone doctor who attends David's birth, "the mildest of little men" who carries "his head on one side, partly in modest deprecation of himself, partly in modest propiation of everybody else" (1). After his second marriage, Chillip moves his practice to BURY ST. EDMUNDS, where his wife has some property (59). He tells David of Murdstone's second marriage to a young woman whose "spirit has been entirely broken since her marriage" (59).

Clickett ("The Orfling")   "A dark-complexioned young woman, with a habit of snorting" who serves as the Micawber's maid. She is an orphan from St. Luke's Workhouse (11).

Copperfield, Clara (later Mrs. Murdstone)   David's mother, described by Quinion as "bewitching Mrs. Copperfield" and "the pretty little widow" (2). A nursery governess before her marriage, Clara was the "child bride" of David's father, who died before David was born. Youthful, weak, vain, and sickly, she is described by Aunt Betsey as "a very Baby" (1), but to David she is a loving, caring, and indulgent parent. She marries a second husband, Mr. Murdstone (3), but she fades under his regime of "firmness" and, with her infant son from the second marriage, dies while David is still a boy (9).

Her marriage to David's father sets the pattern for her son; his first marriage to Dora repeats his father's. With Dora and Annie Strong, Clara Copperfield is one of the "child wives" in the novel. Of the three, only Annie grows up and survives into maturity.

DORIS ALEXANDER (1991) suggests that Dickens "put into Clara the best of his early memories of his mother."

Copperfield, David   Author who narrates his personal history to let his readers decide "whether [he] shall turn out to be the hero of [his] own life" (1). He is the "posthumous son" of David Copperfield of Blunderstone, who died before he was born, and Clara, a young, pretty, and weak widow. David dislikes his mother's second husband, Murdstone; challenges his authority; and bites his thumb (4). He is sent away to Salem House School, where he is mistreated and forms a close friendship with James Steerforth (5–9). After his mother's death, he is withdrawn from the school and sent to London to work in Murdstone and Grinby's wine-bottling warehouse (10). Fleeing from London to Dover, he seeks refuge with his Aunt Betsey Trotwood (12), who sends him to school in Canterbury (15). After school he is apprenticed to the law (23); unwisely marries Dora Spenlow, his boss's daughter (42); and gradually becomes a well-known author. After the deaths of his wife (53) and Steerforth (55), and after learning the pain of "an undisciplined heart," he eventually settles his life and marries the steady Agnes Wickfield (62).

David is the most autobiographical of Dickens's characters; his initials reverse those of the author, and many of the episodes in Copperfield's history are based on Dickens's own experiences.

Freud's favorite novel, *David Copperfield* could be David's account to an analyst of his life or, with its coincidences and bizarre characters, of his dream life. Especially observant, David has the capacity to remember the past, even his infancy, in vivid detail. The traumas of his childhood—of the father dead when he was born, his Oedipal competition with Murdstone for his mother's love, the deaths of his mother and infant brother, his humiliation and loss of class as a worker at the wine-bottling warehouse—set the patterns for his later life. He searches unsuccessfully for a replacement for his deceased father. He is as susceptible to "wax doll" women as his father was, and he repeats his father's mistake when he marries Dora. His fears of losing class contribute to his uneasiness with Micawber, his abhorrence of Heep, and his admiration for Steerforth. Just as Dombey's "son" turns out to be a daughter, David's search also seems to end with the discovery of the feminine. His best father substitute

Browne's (Phiz's) illustration of the boy David ordering his lunch at a London pub exaggerates David's youth in contrast to the towering adult world of the city.

is his Aunt Betsey, and the mixture of discipline and love that he achieves by the end is modeled for him by Agnes who is, HILARY SCHOR (1999) suggests, the "hero" of David's story. The criteria for heroism are set by the female characters: Aunt Betsey's desire that he become "a firm fellow, with a will of [his] own" and her injunction "never . . . be mean in anything, never be false; never be cruel . . . and I can always be hopeful of you" (15) set the goals for his life. Annie Strong observes the danger of "disparity" in marriage, and she states the ideal of the "disciplined heart." Agnes models these virtues, enables David finally to bring together the parts of his life, and inspires his writing. His success as a novelist, however, is less significant than his marriage, for his heroism is achieved in the domestic, not in the public sphere. In the end all of his names—Davy, Brooks of Sheffield, Master Murdstone, Young Copperfield, "the little Gent," Trotwood Copperfield, Daisy, Mr. Copperfull, Doady,

Master/Mister Copperfield, David Copperfield, author—become part of the single story that Agnes inspires him to tell.

Copperfield, Dora David's loving and feckless first wife, "She had the most delightful little voice, the gayest little laugh, the pleasantest and most fascinating little ways, that ever led a lost youth into hopeless slavery. She was rather diminutive altogether. So much the more precious, I thought" (26). David is infatuated with Dora at first sight: "She was a Fairy, a Sylph, I don't know what she was—anything that no one ever saw, and everything that everybody ever wanted. I was swallowed up in an abyss of love in an instant" (26). When David and Dora's secret engagement is discovered by Dora's companion, Miss Murdstone, Mr. Spenlow objects to the relationship and is killed in a carriage accident the same day (38). Aunt Betsey, after warning David that he is "blind, blind, blind" (35), nevertheless aids him in courting Dora and, after their marriage, refuses to interfere and instruct Dora in domestic discipline. She accepts Dora for what she is, calling her "Little Blossom." Educated for idleness with such accomplishments as playing the guitar, Dora has no domestic skills. Raised indulgently by her widower father and lacking a mother's guidance, Dora is spoiled and playful, and capable only of being David's "child-wife." Her domestic disasters are presented comically, but David still attempts to "form her mind" and bring some discipline into their household. Even though this project is a hopeless failure, David's love for Dora continues to the time of her early death (53). David may realize that his marriage was imprudent, the result of his "undisciplined heart," but he loves Dora in spite of her failings.

The complexity in the character of Dora belies the criticism sometimes made that Dickens was capable of creating only women who were either angels in the house or demonic villainesses. Dora embodies both a criticism of the Victorian ideal that reduced women to childish playthings and a fascination with her enchanting sexuality. She has a vitality lacking in the more perfect and idealized Agnes Wickfield, also the daughter of a widower, who serves as a contrasting DOUBLE to Dora.

Dickens has been accused of literary wish fulfillment in his portraits of Dora and Mr. Spenlow. Based on MARIA BEADNELL and her father, the characters in the novel give David a chance to marry the woman Dickens was denied in life, and Mr. Spenlow suffers an end Dickens may have wished for Mr. Beadnell.

County Inn Inn where Mr. Dick stays on his visits to David in Canterbury. Based on the Royal Fountain Hotel.

Creakle Sadistic headmaster of Salem House School, a brutal man who delights "in cutting at the boys, which was like the satisfaction of a craving appetite" (5). He has almost no voice and speaks in a whisper, confiding to David and the other students that he is "a Tartar." His daughter, whom young David considers "of extraordinary attractions," is thought by the boys to be in love with Steerforth. Creakle later becomes a Middlesex Magistrate and warden of the prison where the hypocritical Heep and Littimer are his model prisoners (61). Creakle was based on WILLIAM JONES, headmaster of WELLINGTON HOUSE ACADEMY.

Creakle, Mrs. Creakle's wife, "thin and quiet"; she informs David of his mother's death (9).

Crewler, Sophy Tommy Traddles's fiancée, "the dearest girl," one of ten daughters of the Reverend Horace Crewler, a poor curate in Devonshire. Traddles has difficulty securing his consent to the marriage because Sophy helps care for her mother, an invalid, and her many sisters. Traddles and Sophy finally marry after a long engagement (59). Dickens contrasts Traddles's patience and his and Sophy's acceding to her father's wishes with the precipitous courtship of David and Dora and their challenge to Mr. Spenlow's desires.

Crupp, Mrs. David Copperfield's landlady in the ADELPHI, when he begins his life in London as a clerk in Spenlow's office. She suffers from "the spazzums," a complaint relieved by David's brandy (26). When David falls in love with Dora, she is aware that there is "a lady in the case" (26), and in

an oblique warning to "Mr. Copperfull," her name for David, she tells him of "the gentleman which died here before yourself, . . . that fell in love—with a barmaid—and had his waistcoats took in directly, though much swelled by drinking." Her tyranny over the youthful David is ended by Betsey Trotwood, who terrifies the obsequious landlady.

Dartle, Rosa Mrs. Steerforth's tormented and vindictive companion and distant relative; "she had black hair, and eager black eyes, and was thin, and had a scar upon her lip. It was an old scar—I should rather call it, seam, for it was not discolored, and had healed years ago—which had once cut through her mouth, downward towards the chin, but was now barely visible across the table, except above and on her upper lip, the shape of which it had altered. I concluded in my own mind that she was about thirty years of age, and that she wished to be married. . . . Her thinness seemed to be the effect of some wasting fire within her, which found a vent in her gaunt eyes" (20). The scar, inflicted by Steerforth with a hammer when they were much younger, is a visible manifestation of the wounds she bears from their past passion and his denial of affection. When Steerforth elopes with Em'ly, Rosa vows revenge upon the girl, and when Em'ly returns to London, Rosa pursues her and heaps contempt upon her (50). After Steerforth's death, for which she blames his mother, she nonetheless remains as Mrs. Steerforth's companion.

Rosa's angry and vindictive love for Steerforth articulates a darkened version of the irrational passion in David's playful infatuation with Dora. JOHN R. REED (1995) describes Rosa's worldview as "a secular version of the Murdstones' wrathful theology."

Demple, George Pupil at Salem House, a doctor's son (5).

Dick, Mr. Name by which Richard Babley is known, but which he cannot bear to hear spoken: "Mr. Dick . . . was grey-headed and florid: I should have said all about him, in saying so, had not his head been curiously bowed—not by age; it reminded me of one of Mr. Creakle's boys' heads after a beating—and his grey eyes prominent and large, with a strange kind of watery brightness in them that made me, in combination with his vacant manner, his submission to my aunt, and his childish delight when she praised him, suspect him of being a little mad" (13). A harmless lunatic and distant connection of Betsey Trotwood, whom she has rescued from the asylum where he was placed by his brother, she describes him as "the most friendly and amenable creature in existence" (14) and relies on his good advice. He keeps busy writing a memorial of his life for the lord chancellor, always trying to avoid mention of King Charles's head, which inevitably finds its way into his account. Then he makes kites of the manuscripts spoiled by his obsession. Though mad, he advises Betsey to keep and care for David and to educate him at CANTERBURY. He also sorts out the misunderstandings between Doctor Strong and his wife Annie (45).

Mr. Dick, a character in the tradition of the wise fool, is in some ways a parody of the project undertaken by David Copperfield—to write an account of his life so as to learn whether he will be the hero of it. Dick (whose name suggests the author's) is inevitably frustrated by the appearance of King Charles's head, extending the parody to a comment on Dickens's project as well.

Dolloby   Dealer in used clothing to whom David sells his waistcoat for ninepence while on the road to DOVER (13).

Ely Place   Street in the City off Holborn Hill. Agnes stays here with the Waterbrooks when she visits London (25).

Em'ly, Little   Daniel Peggotty's orphaned niece who is raised in his boathouse on the Yarmouth sands and is David's infant sweetheart, "a most beautiful little girl (or I thought her so), with a necklace of blue beads on, who wouldn't let me kiss her when I offered to, but ran away and hid herself" (3). Even as a child Em'ly wishes she were a lady and risks danger by walking out on an old jetty over the sea (3). She goes to work as a seamstress in Omer's shop and is about to marry her cousin Ham when David introduces Steerforth into the Yar-

mouth circle (21). Steerforth seduces Em'ly, running off to Italy with her on the eve of her marriage (31). Daniel spends years searching for the girl, and the two are reunited when Em'ly returns to London after Steerforth tires of her (50). She emigrates to AUSTRALIA with Daniel, Mrs. Gummidge, and Martha Endell (57), but she never marries.

Although Dickens was involved in the URANIA COTTAGE project to rescue girls from the streets and hoped "to do some good" for such women by his portrait of Little Em'ly, his treatment of her does not significantly differ from the conventions of this repeated story in Victorian fiction. Her desire to be a lady, her good and honest working-class fiancé, and her seduction by an upper-class wastrel are all clichéd elements of the theme. Even though she is saved from the streets or from drowning in the Thames, she is "punished" by being denied the fulfillments of marriage and children.

Endell, Martha   A schoolmate of Little Em'ly who also works as an apprentice at Omer's. After she is seduced and disgraced, she runs off to London using money given to her by Em'ly (22). There she becomes a prostitute (46), contemplates drowning herself in the Thames (47), but redeems herself by helping Daniel Peggotty in his search for Em'ly. Eventually she emigrates with the Peggottys to AUSTRALIA, where she marries a farm laborer (57).

Martha doubles Little Em'ly, even shadowing her in Yarmouth and searching her out in London. Her story foreshadows Em'ly's in some instances and shows alternative courses that Em'ly's might have taken in others.

Fibbitson, Mrs.   The old woman who sits by the fire like "a bundle of old clothes" during Mr. Mell's visit to his mother at the BLACKHEATH almshouse (5).

George   Guard on the coach that takes David to Salem House (5).

Grainger   One of Steerforth's friends who attends David's bachelor dinner party at his rooms in Mrs. Crupp's house (24).

Grayper, Mr. and Mrs. Neighbors of Mrs. Copperfield at Blunderstone at whose house she meets Murdstone (2).

Gregory Foreman at Murdstone and Grinby's warehouse (11).

Gulpidge, Mr. and Mrs. Dinner guests of the Waterbrooks. Mr. Gulpidge has "something to do . . . with the law business of the Bank" (25).

Gummidge, Mrs. Widow of Daniel Peggotty's fishing partner who serves as his housekeeper. Of a "fretful disposition, . . . she whimpered more sometimes than was comfortable for other parties," repeating the complaint, "I am a lone lorn creetur' . . . and everythink goes contrairy with me" (3). She remains at Daniel's house when he goes off in search of Em'ly (32) and acts as "the prop and staff of Mr. Peggotty's affliction" (32). Her transformation during the family crisis holds true to the end, when she refuses to be left in England, cheerfully accompanying the Peggottys to Australia.

Heep, Mrs. Uriah's mother, "the dead image of Uriah, only short" (17). She is as "'umble" as her son and as devoted to him as Mrs Steerforth is to her son.

Heep, Uriah Wickfield's clerk and eventual partner, "a red-haired person . . . whose hair was cropped as close as the closest stubble; who had hardly any eyebrows, and no eyelashes, and eyes of a red-brown, so unsheltered and unshaded, that I remember wondering how he went to sleep. He was high-shouldered and bony; dressed in decent black, with a white wisp of a neckcloth; buttoned up to the throat; he had a long, lank, skeleton hand" (15). He is a writhing, hypocritical opportunist who repeatedly protests that "we are very 'umble" while he contrives to take over Wickfield's business, marry his daughter, and defraud the firm's clients. His schemes ruin Betsey Trotwood (34), but Micawber eventually exposes his villainy (52). Imprisoned for fraud, he becomes a model prisoner, still asserting his humility and offering forgiveness to David with the pious hope that David will "curb [his] passions in future" (61).

One of Dickens's great villains, Uriah, as JOHN REED (1995) points out, inverts the Christian teachings at the heart of *David Copperfield*. His "humility" is a hypocritical mask for his class envy and calls attention to the upper-class snobbery of Steerforth, his mother, and Rosa Dartle. Heep's false forgiveness contrasts with the true forgiveness of Daniel Peggotty and Doctor Strong. Most important, Uriah serves as a DOPPELGANGER, a dark DOUBLE, to David. His ambition to rise in the world is a ruthless and hypocritical version of David's desire for a secure and respectable position, and his sexual aggressiveness, nicely analyzed by HARRY STONE (1994), more openly expresses David's similar desires.

Barnard's portrait of Uriah Heep.

DORIS ALEXANDER (1991) suggests that Dickens derived Heep's physical characteristics and his obsequiousness from HANS CHRISTIAN ANDERSEN.

Hill, Mrs. Jane Seymour   Dickens's contemporary, a dwarf chiropodist who recognized herself as the original for Miss Mowcher, the dwarf hairdresser in *Copperfield* (22). She wrote to Dickens objecting to the portrait, and in response, Dickens radically changed Miss Mowcher's character on her next appearance in the novel (32).

Hopkins, Captain   Fellow inmate with Micawber in KING'S BENCH PRISON, a prisoner "in the last extremity of shabbiness, with large whiskers, and an old brown greatcoat with no other coat below it" (11).

Janet   Betsey Trotwood's maidservant, "a pretty blooming girl, of about nineteen or twenty, . . . one of a series of protégées whom my aunt had taken into her service expressly to educate in the renouncement of mankind, and who had generally completed their abjuration by marrying the baker" (13). She marries a tavern-keeper (60).

The relation of Betsey and Janet is a comic foreshadowing of Miss Havisham's with Estella in *Great Expectations.*

Jip (short for Gypsy)   Dora Spenlow's spoiled little spaniel, who has a little pagoda for a doghouse and who dies at David's feet at the same moment as his mistress dies upstairs (53).

Jones, Master   CANTERBURY schoolboy, "a boy of no merit whatever," who is David Copperfield's rival for the attentions of Miss Shepherd (18).

Joram   Assistant to Omer the undertaker who marries Minnie, Omer's daughter, and becomes a partner in the business (9).

Jorkins   Spenlow's partner in the law firm of Spenlow and Jorkins, "a mild man of a heavy temperament, whose place in the business was to keep himself in the background, and be constantly exhibited by name as the most obdurate and ruth-

less of men" (23). After Spenlow's death David discovers that Jorkins is "an easy-going, incapable sort of man" who lets the business decline (39).

Kentish Town   An area in north London, home of Mrs. Kidgerbury, the Copperfields' charwoman (44).

Kidgerbury, Mrs.   "The oldest resident of Kentish town," hired by David and Dora Copperfield as a charwoman, even though she is "too feeble to execute her conceptions of that art" (44).

Kitt, Miss   The "young creature in pink" at Dora's birthday picnic with whom David flirts when Dora's attentions are monopolized by "Red Whisker." Her "mother in green" also attends the picnic (33).

Larkins, the eldest Miss   Object of the youthful David Copperfield's romantic fantasies, "a tall, dark, black-eyed, fine figure of a woman" of about 30 (18). David is distressed to learn that she is going to marry Mr. Chestle, a hop grower. Her father is "a gruff old gentleman with a double chin, and one of his eyes immovable in his head" (18).

Littimer   Steerforth's smug, deferential, and respectable manservant: "He was taciturn, soft-footed, very quiet in his manner, deferential, observant, always at hand when wanted, and never near when not wanted; but his great claim to consideration was his respectability. He had not a pliant face, he had rather a stiff neck, rather a tight smooth head with short hair clinging to it at the sides, a soft way of speaking, with a peculiar habit of whispering the letter S so distinctly, that he seemed to use it oftener than any other man; but every peculiarity that he had he made respectable. . . . He surrounded himself with an atmosphere of respectability, and walked secure in it. It would have been next to impossible to suspect him of anything wrong, he was so thoroughly respectable" (21). His demeanor intimidates David, making him feel "particularly young in this man's presence" (21). It also provides cover for his machinations to arrange Steerforth's affair with Em'ly. He tells David of Steerforth's wanderings on the continent (46) and relates how Steerforth offered Em'ly to him when he tired of her. After he embezzles from another master and his villainy is discovered by Miss Mowcher, he ends up as a "model" prisoner awaiting transportation (61).

JOHN REED (1995) comments that Littimer serves to reveal David's moral sensitivity: "What David does not realize as a young man is that he feels 'found out' because he has a strong moral sense and is aware of his own faults no matter how small they are. Littimer, on the other hand, is devoid of any genuine morality and thus is not troubled by his conscience."

Lowestoft   Costal town in Suffolk where Murdstone takes young David (2).

Maldon, Jack   Annie Strong's cousin, "rather a shallow sort of young gentleman . . . with a handsome face, a rapid utterance, and a confident bold air" (16). He had a youthful affair with Annie and sponges off Doctor Strong, who sponsors his trip to India (16). Maldon returns without having established himself in a profession and pursues a flirtation with Annie that leads to malicious gossip about the doctor's young wife. Mr. Dick arranges a reconciliation between Annie and her husband. Her revelation about her relationship with Maldon exonerates her from suspicion and states one of the primary themes of the novel, especially applicable to David's relationship with Dora: "We had been little lovers once. If circumstances had not happened otherwise, I might have come to persuade myself that I really loved him, and might have married him, and been most wretched. There can be no disparity in marriage like unsuitability of mind and purpose" (45).

Markham   One of Steerforth's Oxford friends, "youthful looking . . . not more than twenty" (24), who is invited to David's housewarming dinner. His awkward habit of speaking of himself in the third person as "a man," calls attention to his uncomfortable stage of life between boyhood and adulthood, which is shared by David.

Markleham, Mrs. ("the Old Soldier")   Annie Strong's mother, called "the Old Soldier" by the boys in the school "on account of her generalship,

and the skill with which she marshalled great forces of relations against the Doctor" (16). Her machinations embarrass Annie and increase the suspicions about her daughter's relations with Jack Maldon; her selfish indulgence in her own pleasures makes her insensitive to Annie's suffering (45).

Betsey Trotwood, who refuses to interfere in David's relationship with Dora, sums up the significance of Mrs. Markleham's meddling: "There never would have been anything the matter, if it hadn't been for that old Animal. . . . It's very much to be wished that some mothers would leave their daughters alone after marriage, and not be so violently affectionate" (45).

"Mealy Potatoes"   Nickname of one of the boys David works with at Murdstone and Grinby's wine-bottling warehouse. His complexion is "pale or mealy" (11).

He is based on Paul Green, the son of a fireman, who worked with Dickens at WARREN'S BLACKING.

Mell, Charles   Assistant schoolmaster at Salem House; "a gaunt, sallow young man, with hollow cheeks, . . . and his hair, instead of being glossy, was rusty and dry. He was dressed in a suit of black clothes which were rather rusty and dry too, and rather short in the sleeves and legs" (5). Mell meets David at the coach when he first arrives in London; on their way to the school they visit Mell's mother in an almshouse, where Mell plays the flute for her (5). Mell is dismissed when Steerforth reveals that his mother is in an almshouse, a fact he has learned from David (7). Mell later becomes Dr. Mell of the Colonial Salem-House Grammar School, Port Middlebay, Australia; he presides at the dinner for Micawber there, which is also attended by his fourth daughter, Helena (63). The original for Mell was Mr. Taylor, a master at WELLINGTON HOUSE ACADEMY when Dickens was a student there.

Micawber, Emma   Micawber's wife, "a thin and faded lady, not at all young" (11). She has married beneath her social station and recalls more prosperous days before her marriage, but she is intensely loyal to her improvident husband, repeatedly asserting, "I never will desert Mr. Micawber!" The Micawbers have six children, Wilkins Jr., Emma, a girl and a boy under five, and a pair of infant twins. Mrs. Micawber supports her husband's optimism that "something will turn up" with analyses of the possibilities.

J. B. PRIESTLEY (1925) remarks, "Mrs. Micawber is one of the severest logicians with whom we have ever been acquainted; but she is not really reasoning about this world at all: she lives in Micawber's world, and, indeed, represents the logical and scientific point of view in that world." She is loosely based on Dickens's mother, Elizabeth Dickens, a more sympathetic portrait than that of Mrs. Nickleby.

Micawber, Emma the younger   The Micawbers' second child. She ultimately marries Ridger Begs of Port Middlebay, Australia.

Micawber, Wilkins   One of Dickens's great comic characters. David lodges with him and his family in Windsor Terrace when David is sent to London to work for Murdstone and Grinby (11). "A stoutish, middle-aged person, in a brown surtout and black tights and shoes, with no more hair upon his head . . . than there is upon an egg. . . . His clothes were shabby, but he had an imposing shirt-collar on. He carried a jaunty sort of stick, with a large pair of rusty tassels to it; and a quizzing-glass hung outside his coat,—for ornament, I afterwards found, as he very seldom looked through it, and couldn't see anything when he did" (11). Micawber, a model of shabby gentility, has an easygoing and accepting way of life that is the opposite of Murdstone's regime of firmness. Self-dramatizing, Micawber speaks with oratorical flourish in ornate and hyperbolic language, as when he directs David to his new lodgings: "Under the impression . . . that your peregrinations in this metropolis have not as yet been extensive, and that you might have some difficulty in penetrating the arcane of the Modern Babylon in the direction of the City Road—in short . . . that you might lose yourself—I shall be happy to call this evening, and install you in the knowledge of the nearest way" (11). After Micawber is released from the KING'S BENCH PRISON, where he was imprisoned for debt (12), he and his family set out for Plymouth with the hope that some

Mr. Micawber, by Kyd (Joseph Clayton Clarke).

employment for him will "turn up." Eternally optimistic, from there he goes to CHATHAM to explore opportunities in the coal trade; to CANTERBURY, where he embarrasses David by appearing at Uriah Heep's door (17); and then back to London, where Traddles becomes his lodger (27). He ultimately finds work in the office of Wickfield and Heep in Canterbury (36), where he exposes Heep's villainy (52). In gratitude Betsey Trotwood pays his debts and enables the family to settle in Australia (54), where Micawber rises to become district magistrate for Port Middlebay (63). His classic advice to David, "that if a man had twenty pounds a year for income, and had spent nineteen pounds nineteen shillings and sixpence, he would be happy, but that if he spent twenty pounds one he would be miserable" (11), may have been advice given to the young Charles Dickens by his own father, on whom Micawber is based.

G. K. CHESTERTON (1911) expatiates on his own speechlessness in the presence of Micawber: "Micawber is not a man; Micawber is the superman. We can only walk round and round Micawber wondering what we shall say. All the critics of Dickens, when all is said and done, have only walked round and round Micawber wondering what they should say. I am myself at the moment walking round and round Micawber wondering what I shall say. And I have not found out yet." J. B. PRIESTLEY (1925) describes Micawber as "not only the greatest of Dickens' comic figures, but, with the one exception of Falstaff, he is the greatest comic figure in the whole range of English literature." GEORGE BERNARD SHAW (1937), however, takes a different view. Comparing Micawber with William Dorrit, he concludes, "Micawber suddenly becomes a mere marionette pantaloon with a funny bag of tricks which he repeats until we can bear no more of him, and Dorrit a portrait of the deadliest and deepest truth to nature."

Micawber, Wilkins, Jr.   Eldest of the Micawber's six children, he sings at public houses.

Mills, Julia   Dora Spenlow's romantic and self-dramatizing bosom friend and confidante who acts as an intermediary during David's courtship of Dora; "Miss Mills having been unhappy in a misplaced affection, and being understood to have retired from the world on her awful stock of experience, but still to take a calm interest in the unblighted hopes and loves of youth" (33). She is taken to India (42) and returns as the wife of "a growling old Scotch Croesus, . . . is steeped in money to the throat, and talks of nothing else" (64).

Mithers, Lady   She, along with her husband, is one of Miss Mowcher's clients (22).

Montague Square   Area in Marylebone where Mr. Jorkins "lived by himself in a house . . . which was fearfully in want of painting" (35).

Mowcher, Miss   Dwarf hairdresser and manicurist who includes Steerforth among her fashionable clients; "a pursy dwarf, of about forty or forty-five, with a very large head and face, a pair of roguish grey eyes, and such extremely little arms, that, to enable herself to lay a finger archly against her snub nose as she ogled Steerforth, she was obliged to meet the finger half-way, and lay her nose against it" (22). She repeatedly exclaims, "Ain't I volatile?" Although, when she first enters the novel, she clearly seems to be someone who will aid Steerforth in his seduction of Em'ly (22), she is outraged when she hears of it and offers to help Daniel Peggotty in his search for his niece (32). She captures Littimer as he is trying to escape to America (61).

The change in Miss Mowcher's character was prompted by the objections of Mrs. Jane Seymour Hill, a dwarf chiropodist who complained to Dickens after the initial appearance of the character. Dickens may have gone a bit overboard in responding to her complaint and redeeming the character of Miss Mowcher. In chapter 32 he makes her the devoted supporter of her brother and sister, both of whom, like their father, are also dwarfs.

Murdstone, Edward   Clara Copperfield's second husband, David's stepfather, whose name suggests his hard philosophy and its killing effects on the Copperfield family. Yet even as a boy David can see that Murdstone is handsome as well as fearsome: "He had that kind of shallow black eye . . . which, when it is abstracted, seems from some peculiarity of light, to be disfigured, for a moment at a time, by a cast. . . . His hair and whiskers were blacker and thicker, looked at so near, than even I had given them credit for being. A squareness about the lower part of his face, and the dotted indication of the strong black beard he shaved close every day, reminded me of the waxwork that had travelled into our neighbourhood some half-a-year before. This, his regular eyebrows, and the rich white, and black, and brown, of his complexion—confound his complexion, and his memory!—made me think him, in spite of my misgivings, a very handsome man" (2). Murdstone's oppressive EVANGELICALISM institutes a regime of firmness in the Copperfield household, prompting David to bite the firm hand that punishes him (4). Murdstone then sends him to Salem House school (5) and later, after his mother's death, to work at Murdstone and Grinby's wine-bottling warehouse (10). Murdstone offers to take back David "unconditionally" from Betsey Trotwood and is refused (14). He later marries again and again breaks his wife's spirit (59).

Although David resists everything that Murdstone stands for, he unconsciously adopts some of Murdstone's "philosophy" when he attempts to form the mind of Dora, his "child-wife" who is much like his mother. The result, Dora's death, recalls his mother's similar decline and death. The effect of this repetition is to soften Murdstone's villainy and to suggest that at least some of his murderousness stems from the gender roles adopted at the time.

Murdstone, Jane Murdstone's spinster sister, installed by him as housekeeper to manage his household with "firmness": "Like her brother, whom she greatly resembled in face and voice; and with very heavy eyebrows, . . . she brought with her two uncompromising hard black boxes, with her initials on the lids in hard brass nails. When she paid the coachman she took her money out of a hard steel purse, and she kept the purse in a very jail of a bag which hung upon her arm by a heavy chain, and shut up like a bite" (4). Jane Murdstone reenters David's life as Dora Spenlow's companion (26); she discovers David's letters to Dora and informs Mr. Spenlow of them (33).

Murdstone and Grinby Wine-bottling business partly owned by Murdstone where David is sent to work after his mother's death (10–11). David describes the "secret agony of [his] soul" when he is reduced to the menial labor of pasting labels on wine bottles in the company of working-class boys from the streets of London (11).

This traumatic episode in David's life is based on the most painful episode in Dickens's own childhood, when he was sent to work at WARREN'S BLACKING while his father was imprisoned for debt in the MARSHALSEA PRISON. The description follows nearly verbatim that of the fragmentary AUTOBIOGRAPHY that Dickens gave to JOHN FORSTER.

Nettingall, Misses Proprietors of a girls' school in Canterbury attended by Miss Shepherd, who infatuates David (18).

New River Head Uriah Heep takes lodgings in this section of Islington while he is staying in London (25).

Obelisk, the A London landmark that in Dickens's time stood in the center of St. George's Circus in south London. David Copperfield meets the young man who steals his box and money near the Obelisk as he heads out of London toward Dover (12).

Old Kent Road The road David takes from London to Dover in search of his aunt (13).

Omer "Tailor, Haberdasher, Funeral Furnisher" in Yarmouth who arranges the funeral of Clara Copperfield Murdstone (9). "A fat, short-winded, merry-looking, little old man in black" (9), he employs Little Em'ly as an apprentice dressmaker before she runs off with Steerforth.

Omer, Minnie Omer's daughter, who marries Joram, the shop foreman in her father's establishment who later becomes a partner and then the proprietor of the business.

Paragon, Mary Anne The first in a series of impossible servants employed by David and Dora Copperfield, "a woman in the prime of life; of a severe countenance; and subject (particularly in the arms) to a sort of perpetual measles or fiery rash." David harbors the belief that "she must have been Mrs. Crupp's daughter in disguise," for she drinks herself under the kitchen table, pilfers teaspoons, and hides her cousin, a deserter from the Life Guards, in the Copperfield coal cellar (44).

Passnidge Murdstone's friend whom David meets at Lowestoft (2).

Peggotty, Clara Daniel's sister, David Copperfield's devoted nurse, "with no shape at all, and eyes so dark that they seemed to darken their whole neighbourhood in her face, and cheeks and arms so hard and red that I wondered the birds didn't peck her in preference to apples" (2). She warmly loves David and is forever popping the buttons on the back of her gown when she hugs the boy. While David's mother is marrying Murdstone, she takes David to Yarmouth to the converted boat where her brother Daniel lives (3). Known as "Peggotty" because she bears the same first name as David's mother, she is a kind of surrogate mother to David, especially comforting him when Murdstone denies his mother the opportunity to comfort the boy after he rebels against the regime of firmness: "She did not replace my mother; no one could do that; but she came into a vacancy in my heart, which closed upon her, and I felt towards her something I have never felt for any other human being" (4). When Murdstone dismisses Peggotty after Clara Copperfield's death, she marries the "willin'" Barkis and settles in Yarmouth (10). After Barkis dies (30), she returns to live with David and his aunt (34). She serves as Aunt Betsey's housekeeper, known as "Barkis," because Betsey objects to Peggotty as a "South Sea Island name."

Peggotty, Daniel Clara's "bacheledore" brother, a "rough-and-ready" fisherman, who lives in a house made from an overturned boat on the shore at Yarmouth, where he has taken in his orphaned niece and nephew, Little Em'ly and Ham, and the widow of his partner, Mrs. Gummidge. He refuses to be thanked for his generosity in taking them in, and "if it were ever referred to, by any one of them, he struck the table a heavy blow with his right hand . . . and swore a dreadful oath that he would be 'Gormed' if he didn't cut and run for good, if it was ever mentioned again" (3). When Em'ly abandons her fiancé Ham and runs off with Steerforth, Daniel makes it his mission to find her and restore her to the family (31). After seeking her unsuccessfully throughout Europe, he and Little Em'ly are reunited with the help of Martha Endell (50). In the end, Daniel, Em'ly, Mrs. Gummidge, and Martha resettle in Australia (57).

Peggotty, Ham Daniel's nephew and Em'ly's cousin, taken in by Daniel after he is orphaned. "He was, now, a huge, strong fellow of six feet high, broad in proportion, and round-shouldered; but with a simpering boy's face and curly hair that gave him quite a sheepish look. He was dressed in a can-

vas jacket, and a pair of such very stiff trousers that they would have stood quite well alone, without any legs in them" (2). Ham is betrothed to Little Em'ly and is left devastated and angry when she elopes with Steerforth, vowing vengeance on Steerforth should he ever catch him (31). Ironically, Ham loses his life in a terrible storm while trying to rescue a sailor who turns out to be Steerforth (55).

Port Middlebay Town in Australia where Mr. Peggotty, Mell, and the Micawbers settle after leaving England. Mr. Micawber becomes its magistrate (63).

Pyegrave, Charley One of Miss Mowcher's aristocratic clients (22).

Quinion Manager of Murdstone and Grinby's wine-bottling warehouse who employs David Copperfield and introduces him to Mr. Micawber (11). David first meets him at Lowestoft when he and Murdstone obliquely refer to David as "Brooks of Sheffield" (2).

Roman Bath The bath off the Strand where David Copperfield has "had many a cold plunge" and to which he goes after learning of his Aunt Betsy's bankruptcy (35).

Rookery, the The name of the house where David Copperfield was born, the choice of David's father even though the nests had long been deserted (1).

St. Luke's Workhouse Located opposite the Eagle Inn in the City Road, the workhouse is the home of "the Orfling," the little servant girl who works for the Micawbers when they are in Windsor Terrace (11).

Salem House Mr. Creakle's school in Blackheath where Murdstone sends David Copperfield and where David meets Steerforth (5–7, 9, 13). It is based on Wellington House Academy.

Sharp First master at Salem House, "a limp, delicate-looking gentleman . . . with a good deal of nose, and a way of carrying his head on one side, as if it were a little too heavy for him. His hair was very smooth and wavy; but I was informed by the very first boy who came back that it was a wig (a second-hand one *he* said), and that Mr. Sharp went out every Saturday afternoon to get it curled" (6).

Shepherd, Miss   A boarder at the Misses Nettingalls' school who infatuates young David Copperfield. "She is a little girl, in a spencer, with a round face and curly flaxen hair. . . . I am sometimes moved to cry out, 'Oh, Miss Shepherd!' in a transport of love" (18).

Spenlow, Clarissa and Lavinia   Dora Spenlow's maiden aunts who take in Dora after her father's death: "There was a disparity of six or eight years between the two sisters; and . . . the younger appeared to be the manager of the conference. . . . They were dressed alike, but this sister wore her dress with a more youthful air than the other; and perhaps had a trifle more frill, or tucker, or brooch, or bracelet, or some little thing of that kind, which made her look more lively. They were both upright in their carriage, formal, precise, composed, and quiet" (41). With the help of his aunt, David arranges to court Dora while she is under their supervision.

Spenlow, Dora   Francis Spenlow's daughter, David Copperfield's "child-wife." *See* Copperfield, Dora.

Spenlow, Francis   Partner in the firm of Spenlow and Jorkins; proctor in Doctors' Commons (*see* COURTS) to whom David was articled. "He was got up with such care, and was so stiff, that he could hardly bend himself; being obliged, when he glanced at some papers on his desk, after sitting down in his chair, to move his whole body, from the bottom of his spine, like Punch" (23). He uses Jorkins as his "bad guy," blaming him for refusing to release David from his articles after Aunt Betsey's financial difficulties (35). When he invites David to his home in NORWOOD for his daughter's birthday party, David is immediately infatuated with Dora, but when Miss Murdstone, Dora's com-

panion, discovers their courtship and reveals it to Mr. Spenlow, he demands that the affair be broken off and then dies that evening after falling from his carriage (38). Spenlow was based on MARIA BEADNELL's father.

Spenlow and Jorkins   Firm of Doctors' Commons (*see* c o u r t s) proctors to which David Copperfield is articled. Spenlow uses Jorkins, his invisible partner, as his excuse in difficult decisions, as, for example, in refusing to allow David to resign his articles after Betsey Trotwood's financial difficulties (35).

Spiker, Mr. and Mrs. Henry   Dinner guests of the Waterbrooks: he is a solicitor, "so cold a man, that his head, instead of being grey, seemed to be sprinkled with hoar-frost," she, "a very awful lady in a black velvet dress, and a great black velvet hat, whom I remember as looking like a near relation of Hamlet's—say his aunt" (25).

Steerforth, James   Head boy at Salem House School, charming, arrogant, manipulative, and David's boyhood hero, who was "reputed to be a great scholar, and was very good-looking, and at least half-a-dozen years my senior" (6). Steerforth acts as David's protector at the school, but he uses information that David has given him about Mell to publicly humiliate the schoolmaster and have him dismissed (7). David meets him again in London when Steerforth is a student at Oxford (24), and he takes Steerforth to Yarmouth and introduces him to Daniel Peggotty and Little Em'ly (21). Steerforth seduces Em'ly, runs off with her to Italy, and then abandons her. David is disillusioned but forgiving: "In the keen distress of the discovery of his unworthiness, I thought more of all that was brilliant in him, I softened more towards all that was good in him. . . . Deeply as I felt my own unconscious part in his pollution of an honest home, I believed that if I had been brought face to face with him, I could not have uttered one reproach. I should have loved him so well still—though he fascinated me no longer—I should have held in so much tenderness the memory of my affection for him, that I think I should have been as weak as a spirit-wounded child, in all but the entertainment of a thought that we could ever be re-united" (32). David does not see Steerforth again until his body is washed ashore at Yarmouth during a terrible storm in which Ham also dies while trying to save Steerforth (55).

Although he enacts a villainous role in David's life, David's final judgment of him is qualified by his admiration and love. Like David, Steerforth lacks a father figure in his life, but his social position has not left him to fend for himself in order to rise in society. He has been left, however, with a sense of his shallowness and a lack of conscience that leads to his selfish and callous treatment of others, from Mr. Mell and Rosa Dartle to Little Em'ly. Another of David's DOPPELGANGERS, Steerforth draws out the feminine in David, calling him "Daisy," a dimension to their relationship that some commentators see as homoerotic.

John (2001) analyzes Steerforth as a Byronic hero, cast in that role by his mother. His shallow cynicism, callous disregard for the feelings of others, and sense of lacking a moral center express this romantic sensibility that both charmed the Victorians and aroused their moral outrage.

Steerforth, Mrs. James Steerforth's mother, "an elderly lady, though not very advanced in years, with a proud carriage and a handsome face" (20). She dotes on her son and then disowns him when he elopes with a lower-class girl. She vows that "he never shall come near me, living or dying, while I can raise my hand to make a sign against it, unless, being rid of her for ever, he comes humbly to me and begs for my forgiveness" (32). She arrogantly rejects Daniel Peggotty's appeal for aid and understanding (32). Estranged from her son, she ages almost overnight and suffers from "a fretful wandering of the mind" (64). Mrs. Steerforth's class arrogance and inability to forgive is contrasted with Daniel Peggotty's humility and forgiveness.

Strong, Annie Doctor Strong's young wife, "a very pretty young lady" (16) whom David at first mistakes for Strong's daughter. She is 40 years younger than her husband, and David, Mr. Wickfield, Uriah Heep, and others suspect her of a secret affair with her cousin, Jack Maldon. Annie puts such suspicions to rest by her passionate avowal of love and respect for her husband (45), and Dickens gives her the responsibility of stating one of the central themes of the novel. Reflecting on her childish infatuation for Maldon, she asserts, "There can be no disparity in marriage like the unsuitability of mind and purpose," and she thanks her husband "for having saved me from the first mistaken impulse of my undisciplined heart" (45). These reflections are especially applicable to David's marriage to Dora.

HILARY SCHOR (1999) points out the gendered discrepancy between the suspicions of David and other men that Annie has been sexually unfaithful to her husband and her view that she is suspected of marrying Strong for his money. GRAHAM STOREY (1991) calls the Strong subplot "unconvincing" because the melodramatic language Annie uses in her defense is inflated and "self-indulgent," and both she and the Doctor are "too good to be true."

Strong, Doctor Kind headmaster of the school in CANTERBURY that David Copperfield attends. An elderly man preoccupied with his Greek dictionary, Strong "looked almost as rusty, . . . as the tall iron rails and gates outside the house; and almost as stiff and heavy as the great stone urns that flanked them. . . . He was in his library . . . with his clothes not particularly well brushed, and his hair not particularly well combed; his kneesmalls unbraced; his long black gaiters unbuttoned; and his shoes yawning like two caverns on the hearth-rug. Turning upon me a lusterless eye, that reminded me of a long-forgotten blind old horse who once used to crop the grass, and tumble over the graves, in Blunderstone churchyard, he said he was glad to see me: and then he gave me his hand; which I didn't know what to do with, as it did nothing for itself" (16). His age and his preoccupation with his dictionary—which he will never complete—lead to suspicions that his young wife is having a secret affair with her cousin, Jack Maldon, whom Strong has aided by securing a position for him in India. Mr. Dick, who has become friendly with the doctor, puts these suspicions to rest (45). Doctor Strong's January/May marriage develops at greater length the theme of the Peerybingle marriage in *The Cricket on the Hearth*. After Betsey

Trotwood's financial losses, David goes to work as Doctor Strong's secretary (36).

Tiffey Senior clerk at Spenlow and Jorkins: "a little dry man . . . who wore a stiff brown wig that looked as if it were made of gingerbread" (23).

Tipp Red-jacketed carman who works for Murdstone and Grinby (11).

Topsawyer Mythical patron of the inn where David stops on his way to London, who, according to the waiter, drank "a glass of this ale . . . and fell dead." The waiter protects David from a similar fate by drinking David's glass of ale himself (5).

Traddles, Thomas David Copperfield's schoolmate at Salem House who spends his time drawing skeletons on his slate: "the merriest and most miserable of all the boys. He was always being caned" (7). He is the "soul of honor" and defends Mr. Mell against Steerforth's aspersions (7). Traddles's life parallels David's in several ways. When David is learning to be a proctor in Doctors' Commons, Traddles is studying the law in London (25). David's hasty courtship of Dora is contrasted to Traddles's interminable engagement to Sophy Crewler, "the dearest girl" (27). Traddles also lodges with the Micawbers, and he assists Micawber in exposing Heep (52). He is the best man at David's wedding and acts as David's legal adviser. Eventually he marries Sophy and becomes a successful lawyer (59).

Characterizing him as "simple-hearted, generous, and amiable," GRAHAM STOREY (1991) describes Traddles as "perhaps the most attractive character in the novel." If Steerforth and Heep are doubles articulating repressed dimensions of David, Traddles is the double who represents David's best sense of himself.

Trotwood, Betsey David Copperfield's strong-minded great-aunt who deserts him on the day of his birth because she was expecting the child to be a girl (1). Disappointed in this expectation, she "vanished like a discontented fairy" (1), seeming to turn her back on the role of "fairy godmother" that she will later play in David's life. When David

runs from Murdstone and Grinby and seeks her out in DOVER, he discovers that her formidable masculine manner conceals a caring heart. "There was an inflexibility in her face, in her voice, in her gait and carriage, . . . but her features were rather handsome than otherwise, though unbending and austere. I particularly noticed that she had a very quick, bright eye. . . . Her dress was of a lavender color, and perfectly neat; but scantily made, as if she desired to be as little encumbered as possible. I remember that I thought it, in form, more like a riding-habit with the superfluous skirt cut off, than anything else. She wore at her side a gentleman's gold watch, if I might judge from its size and make, with an appropriate chain and seals; she had some linen at her throat not unlike a shirt-collar, and things at her wrists like little shirt-wristbands" (13). She has already taken the distracted Mr. Dick into her household (13), and she agrees to become David's guardian (14). She chases the Mursdstones' donkeys from her lawn and sends the Murdstones back to Blunderstone without David (14). She sends him to Doctor Strong's school in CANTERBURY (15) and starts him on the way to becoming a proctor in Doctors' Commons (*see* COURTS) (23). When she loses her money through Heep's machinations, she moves to London (24, 25). Although she realizes that David is "blind, blind, blind" (35) in his infatuation for Dora, she wisely refuses to interfere in their marriage and is a true friend to Dora (44). Her own life is shadowed by a bad marriage and a scapegrace husband who reappears periodically to demand money from her before he eventually dies (54), a circumstance that leads her to instruct Janet, her maid, and other young women to a "renunciation of mankind" (13).

Betsey Trotwood is especially important in contributing to the theme of "firmness" that runs through the novel. Although she challenges the Murdstones and their loveless regime of firmness, she instructs David to be "a fine firm fellow, with a will of your own. . . . with strength of character that is not to be influenced except on good reason, by anybody, or by anything—that's what I want you to be. That's what your father and mother both might have been, Heaven knows, and been the better for it" (19). This desire is tempered by love, for even when she sees Dora's lack of firmness, she refuses to join David's efforts to form Dora's mind.

Pearl Solomon (*Dickens and Melville in Their Time,* 1975), noting the masculine dimensions in Betsey's character and dress, suggests that Betsey is the "most satisfactory" of the surrogate fathers that David seeks out in his quest for identity.

Tungay   Creakle's assistant at Salem House; "a stout man with a bull-neck, a wooden leg, overhanging temples, and his hair cut close all round his head" (5). He interprets Creakle's whispered words in his own strong voice.

Walker, Mick   "Oldest of the regular boys" who work with David at Murdstone and Grinby's, "he wore a ragged apron and paper cap. He informed me that his father was a bargeman, and walked, in a black velvet head-dress, in the LORD MAYOR's Show" (11).

Waterbrook, Mr. and Mrs.   A genteel solicitor and his wife with whom Agnes Wickfield stays in London. He is "a middle-aged gentleman, with a short throat, and a good deal of shirt collar, who only wanted a black nose to be the portrait of a pug-dog," and his wife is "a very awful lady in a black velvet dress, and a great black velvet hat, whom I remember as looking like a near relation of Hamlet's—say his aunt" (25).

Wickfield, Agnes   Wickfield's daughter and housekeeper, who brings a measure of tranquility into her father's life. When he first meets her, David associates her with the memory of a stained glass window: "Although her face was quite bright and happy, there was a tranquility about it, and about her—a quiet, good, calm spirit,—that I never have forgotten; that I never shall forget. . . . I cannot call to mind where or when, in my childhood, I had seen a stained glass window in a church. Nor do I recollect its subject. But I know that when I saw her turn round, in the grave light of the old staircase, and wait for us, above, I thought of that window; and I associated something of its tranquil brightness with Agnes Wickfield ever afterwards"

(15). The association continues to the end of the novel, when David and his "good angel" finally marry. In the meantime, Agnes cares for her father; rebuffs the attentions of Heep; counsels David against Steerforth, his "bad angel"; tends Dora on her deathbed, receiving Dora's secret blessing for Agnes's marriage with David; and sustains David by mail as he grieves in Switzerland after Dora's death. Through it all David remains, in Betsey Trotwood's eyes, "blind, blind, blind," viewing Agnes only as a sister in whom he can confide. When he finally admits his love for her, she confesses, "I have loved you all my life!" (62)

Although Dickens knew from her first appearance in the novel that Agnes was the "real heroine" of the story, most readers, even JOHN FORSTER, have found her wooden and far less attractive than Dora. GEORGE BERNARD SHAW (1937) called her "the most seventh rate heroine ever produced by a first rate artist," and GEORGE ORWELL (1939) described her as "the real legless angel of Victorian romance." HILARY SCHOR (1999) suggests that Agnes appears so unconvincing because we have only David's version of her story, which stresses "her goodness, and her lack of erotic interest." Her story "not only revises and supplements, his novel, but suggests that he has been a lousy narrator, indeed, reader, of his own life; that he is hardly fit to write his own autobiography."

Wickfield, Mr.   Betsey Trotwood's lawyer with whom David stays while in CANTERBURY attending Dr. Strong's school: "His hair was quite white now, though his eyebrows were still black. He had a very agreeable face, and, I thought, was handsome. There was a certain richness in his complexion, which I had been long accustomed, under Peggotty's tuition, to connect with port wine; and I fancied it in his voice too, and referred his growing corpulency to the same cause. He was very cleanly dressed, in a blue coat, striped waistcoat, and nankeen trousers; and his fine frilled shirt and cambric neckcloth looked unusually soft and white, reminding my strolling fancy (I call to mind) of the plumage on the breast of a swan" (15). A widower whose grief has led to alcoholism and an obsessive love for his daughter Agnes, Wickfield has become neglectful of his business and vulnerable to the schemes of his clerk, Uriah Heep, who manipulates his affairs, becomes a partner in the firm, and hopes to marry Agnes (35). After Heep's schemes ruin Aunt Betsey's fortune and Wickfield's reputation and place Heep as the dominant partner (34), Micawber, acting as a clerk for the firm, exposes Heep and restores order (52).

William (1) The "twinkling-eyed, pimple-faced" waiter who drinks David's ale and eats most of his dinner at the inn where David stops on the way to Salem House (5).

William (2) Coachman who drives David to London from CANTERBURY (19).

Willing Mind Tavern Public house to which Daniel Peggotty goes (3).

Windsor Terrace Street in Finsbury, north London, where David lodges with the Micawbers (11).

Yarmouth, Norfolk Seaside town in Norfolk where Daniel Peggotty has his boathouse and where many crucial scenes in *David Copperfield* take place, most notably, perhaps, the drowning of Ham and Steerforth (55).

Yawler Schoolmate of David and Traddles at Salem House who helps Traddles enter the legal profession (27).

ADAPTATIONS

MALCOLM MORLEY claims that after *Twist* and *Cricket, Copperfield* has inspired more dramatic adaptations than any other work by Dickens. During the 1850s alone there were at least 25 productions. The first stage adaptation, *Born with a Caul* by George Almar, produced before the serial had completed its run, took great liberties with the story; he saved Steerforth from drowning to marry Little Em'ly and added a character named Hurricane Flash whose role was to kill Murdstone. Most other early adaptations were more faithful to the text.

Later in the Victorian period, ANDREW HALLIDAY's *Little Em'ly* (1869) provided a model for many

other adaptations. Telling only the story of Em'ly, Halliday's play and its imitations replaced nearly all other adaptations in the last three decades of the 19th century.

In the 20th century, Mr. Micawber has proved a more engaging focus. He was central in Louis Napoleon Parker's 1914 stage adaptation, in which Sir Herbert Beerbohm Tree played both Micawber and Daniel Peggotty. BRANSBY WILLIAMS doubled in the same two roles (1923). Williams, famous for his one-man shows of characters from Dickens, also included Uriah Heep in his repertory.

The popularity of the story is attested to by the seven silent film adaptations of the novel that appeared early in the century, but the two great cinematic versions were sound films made in 1934 and 1969. The first, produced for MGM by David O. Selznick and George Cukor, starred Edna May Oliver as Aunt Betsey, LIONEL BARRYMORE as Dan-

Mr. Micawber (W. C. Fields) and David Copperfield (Freddie Bartholomew) in the 1935 movie adaptation *David Copperfield. Courtesy of PhotoFest.*

iel Peggotty, Maureen O'Sullivan as Dora, W. C. FIELDS as Micawber, and Freddie Bartholomew as the child David. The 1969 film had an equally distinguished cast. Directed by Delbert Mann for Fox, it included Edith Evans as Aunt Betsey, Susan Hampshire as Agnes, Lawrence Olivier as Mr. Creakle, Michael Redgrave as Daniel Peggotty, EMLYN WILLIAMS as Mr. Dick, and Ralph Richardson as Micawber.

Several television adaptations of the novel have appeared: a 13-part adaptation by Vincent Tilsley, produced twice for the BBC (1956, 1966); Hugh Whitemore's six-part adaptation (1974); James Andrew Hall's 10-part version (1986); and Simon Curtis's adaptation (1999) with Bob Hoskins and Maggie Smith. Adaptations have also been produced for American (1954, 2000), French (1967), and Australian (1985) television.

FURTHER READING

Overall *Copperfield*, Dickens's favorite of all his novels, has been his readers' favorite as well. Its unity of style and tone, its serious theme leavened by the wonderful comic scenes with the Micawbers, and its fundamentally optimistic view of life have made it a perennial favorite. The vivid account of David's childhood has also given it recognition as a story for children, though its popularity as a school text is probably due at least as much to its moral earnestness.

Three good general introductions to *Copperfield* are SYLVÈRE MONOD (1967), whose chapters on the novel are particularly good on the part structure and the style; PHILIP COLLINS (1977), who compares David's life to Dickens's life and discusses David as child, adult, and narrator of the novel; and GRAHAM STOREY (1991), who is especially good at analyzing the characters in the novel. Q. D. LEAVIS (1970) compares *Copperfield* with *War and Peace*, making a case for Dickens's novel as an important influence on Tolstoy and analyzing the serious and adult insights in both novels. Leavis is especially good on David's relationship with Dora. Gwendolyn Needham's classic essay, "The Undisciplined Heart of David Copperfield" (*Nineteenth Century Fiction*, 1954), analyzes a central theme in the novel. JEROME BUCKLEY (1974) discusses *Cop-*

perfield along with *Expectations* as examples of the BILDUNGSROMAN. ALEXANDER WELSH (1987) spends several chapters exploring the novel as the culmination of Dickens's autobiographical attempt in the middle works to come to terms with his role as a novelist. Finally, J. B. PRIESTLEY's discussion of Micawber (1925) explains his conclusion that "with the one exception of Falstaff, [Micawber] is the greatest comic figure in the whole range of English literature."

Dombey and Son. (Full Title: Dealings with the Firm of Dombey and Son, Wholesale, Retail, and for Exportation)

Dickens's seventh novel, published in monthly parts by BRADBURY & EVANS, October 1846 to April 1848, with illustrations by HABLOT KNIGHT BROWNE. Published in one volume, 1848. Conceived by Dickens as a novel about pride, *Dombey* exhibits more careful planning and execution than the novels that precede it. Its characters and situations all contribute to the development of the main theme, which the novel expresses in the symbolic opposition of the railway and the sea. This overall organization and symbolic centering have led some critics to consider it the first of the later novels.

SYNOPSIS

Part 1 (October 1846)

(1) Dombey, 48 years old, sits in front of the fire with his son, 48 minutes old. He exults that the house will once again be Dombey and Son, for his cosmos is predicated on the perpetuation of the male line and his marriage has produced no other issue except a daughter, Florence, "a piece of base coin that couldn't be invested—a bad Boy—nothing more." Meanwhile, Mrs. Dombey's life ebbs away, and she drifts out upon the "dark and unknown sea that rolls round all the world." (2) A nurse must be found for the new baby. Polly Toodle, mother of a large family, is hired with the

stipulations that she take the name Richards and that after her job is done she will sever all ties with the Dombeys. (3) Polly feels imprisoned in Dombey's house, a blank tomb of a building where the furniture is shrouded in dust covers. When Polly encourages Florence to play with young Paul, Susan Nipper, Florence's nurse, objects because she has been instructed to keep Florence out of her father's sight. But Polly convinces Dombey to allow the two children to play together by suggesting that young Paul will benefit from the interaction.

(4) At the Wooden Midshipman, an old-fashioned marine instruments shop that does little business, Sol Gills celebrates the first day that his nephew, Walter Gay, has worked at Dombey and Son. They share the next-to-last bottle of some special Madeira with Captain Cuttle, tell sea stories, and imagine Walter's progress to the top of the firm. They even imagine Walter marrying Dombey's daughter as they toast the future of "Dombey—and Son—and Daughter."

Part 2 (November 1846)
(5) To thank Miss Tox, a spinster friend of the family, for her help in securing a nurse, Dombey considers making her young Paul's godmother, but he doesn't want his gesture misunderstood. He has no intention of marrying again, for with a son his life is complete. On the cold day of the christening, the house is icy and the church cold and funereal. Dombey bestows chilly compliments and calculated gifts—a bracelet to Miss Tox, and a place in the Charitable Grinder's School for Rob, Polly's eldest son. (6) The next day Polly and Susan take Florence and Paul to Stagg's Gardens, where the Toodle family live in a jerry-built row of houses in the midst of railway construction. Polly visits her younger children, and then, hoping to see Rob on his way home from school, she takes a roundabout route home. As they are rescuing Rob from some bullies and evading a runaway coach, they lose Florence, who is "found" by an old crone, Good Mrs. Brown. She leads the child back to her hovel, where she takes her clothes and considers cutting off her hair. Afterwards she abandons Florence in the streets of the City, where, two hours later, Walter Gay discovers her. When Dombey learns

of the episode, he dismisses Polly for endangering his son.

(7) Miss Tox inhabits a dark little house in a dead-end street in a neighborhood of illustrious people. The situation is especially important to Miss Tox's neighbor, Major Joey Bagstock, who boasts of his neighbors at his club, carries on a vague flirtation with Miss Tox, and is annoyed that young Paul has diverted her attention from him. Meanwhile Miss Tox studies Dombey's bracelet, apparently entertaining romantic notions about the giver.

Part 3 (December 1846)
(8) As Paul grows up, he becomes a curious mixture of youth and age. Sitting in his small armchair, he often seems more an old philosopher than a child. One day he asks his father, "What is money?" When Dombey replies, "Money, Paul, can do anything," the boy wishes to know why it didn't save his mother and cannot make him as strong as Florence. The doctor recommends sea air for the boy's frail health, so Paul is sent to stay with Mrs. Pipchin, who keeps a juvenile boarding house in Brighton. Paul strikes up a curiously frank relationship with the old woman, and he enjoys being pushed in his wheelchair out by the ocean to listen to the waves.

(9) When a broker takes possession of the Wooden Midshipman for a debt of £370 that Sol is unable to pay, Captain Cuttle advises Walter to ask Mr. Dombey for help. Seeing Walter's request as a chance to show Paul "how powerful money is," Dombey asks the boy to decide. Paul watches Florence's tears turn to joy as he grants the loan.

Part 4 (January 1847)
(11) When Paul is six, Dombey places him in Dr. Blimber's Academy in Brighton to get the boy past his "childish life." Florence is to remain in Brighton for a term so that Paul can be gradually "weaned" from her. Paul enters Blimber's educational "hothouse" as an uncultivated plant ready for forcing, but when his father and Florence leave him there, he feels very old, "weary, weary! very lonely, very sad." (12) Dr. Blimber lectures the boys on Roman history as they eat; after dinner they loiter outside for half an hour but do nothing "so vulgar as play." Paul's tutor, Cornelia Blimber, confuses the boy with lengthy assignments,

but with the help of Florence, who buys copies of his books and studies the assignments ahead of him, he begins to learn. Paul watches at the window for Florence, who passes the school each evening. Occasionally Dombey himself does the same.

(13) When Dombey needs to fill a junior position in Barbados, he sees it as an opportunity to get rid of Walter Gay, who reminds him of his daughter. Walter has also annoyed James Carker, Dombey's second-in-command, by unwittingly mentioning his brother, Mr. Carker the Junior, a clerk kept in a lowly position as a punishment and reminder of his youthful mistake of stealing from the firm. Both Dombey and Carker thus have reasons to want Walter out of the way.

Part 5 (February 1847)

(14) As the boys at Blimber's Academy prepare for their summer holiday, Cornelia gives Paul his "analysis," noting that he has a tendency to be singular or "old-fashioned" in his character and conduct. By the end-of-term dance, Paul is so ill that he just sits and watches the party. Afterwards he must stay at Mrs. Pipchin's for several days to regain strength before returning to London.

(15) Unable to tell his uncle that he is to go to Barbados, Walter asks Cuttle to break the news, but the Captain delays until he can first urge Mr. Dombey to change his mind. (16) Meanwhile Paul is fading. From his bed he watches the sunlight, the "golden water" as it ripples on the walls of his room. He asks Florence, "Are we all dead, except you?" and urges his father to "remember Walter. I was fond of Walter." Then he goes out to that "old, old fashion—Death."

Part 6 (March 1847)

(17) Paul's illness has prevented Cuttle's proposed interview with Dombey, and when Walter returns to the Wooden Midshipman, Cuttle has not managed to break the news to Sol. When he finally does tell Sol, describing it as a grand chance for Walter, Sol is dispirited. As the time for Walter's departure nears, Cuttle seeks out Carker to confirm his sense of Walter's bright future. Flattered by the urbane manager, Cuttle thinks that he gains Carker's agreement about Walter's prospects, even his prospect of winning Florence.

(18) Dombey orders a tombstone describing Paul as his "only child" and withdraws into his darkened rooms. Upstairs alone, Florence watches a family across the street. A motherless family of daughters, the eldest replacing the mother in her attentions to her loving father, they become a symbol of what Florence wishes her life would be. Although she goes down in the darkness to her father's rooms, his door is always shut. One evening Florence finds his door open. She goes in to him, but he retreats from her and sends her back upstairs. Then he locks the door and cries for his lost boy.

(19) Before Walter leaves for Barbados, Florence asks him to be her "brother" and presents him with a purse she had made for Paul. Sol and Cuttle take Walter to his ship, the *Son and Heir*.

Part 7 (April 1847)

(20) To recuperate from his son's death, Dombey goes to Leamington Spa with Joey Bagstock. On the train, Dombey feels blighted and, haunted by the memory of Florence's face the night before, he wishes that she, rather than Paul, had died. (21) At Leamington they meet Mrs. Skewton and her beautiful widowed daughter, Edith Granger. Dombey admires Edith's accomplishments as artist, harpist, and pianist, but he does not recognize the song Florence used to sing to Paul when Edith performs it.

(22) Back in London, James Carker takes charge of Dombey and Son. He goes through the mail, reading a letter from Mr. Dombey very carefully and noting the impossibility of carrying out Dombey's request to prevent Walter from sailing. He secures a place for Rob Toodle with Sol Gills and tells the boy that he wants to know the details of Sol's life and his connections with Florence. As Carker passes Dombey's house, Florence's dog barks and growls at the catlike manager.

Part 8 (May 1847)

(23) Alone in the dark and empty house, Florence meditates on loving her father and winning his heart. When no news of Walter comes, she seeks out Sol Gills and finds him restless and distracted. (24) Florence spends her time observing other children to see if she can learn the secret of their loving relationships with their parents. She longs for such parental love and blames herself for its denial. Her

Browne's (Phiz's) illustration of the Dombey wedding party for the 10th number of the novel recalls Hogarth's crowd scenes, such as the execution of Tom Idle from *Industry and Idleness*.

life is a greater trial than an orphan's, for "not an orphan in the wide world can be so deserted as the child who is an outcast from a living parent's love." When Carker offers to take a message to her father, she sends only her love. She reads in Carker's manner or smile that nothing is yet known of Walter's ship, and when Carker leaves, she shudders.

(25) Cuttle learns that Sol has disappeared, so he takes charge of the Midshipman, keeping it against the return of either Walter or Sol.

Part 9 (June 1847)

(26) At Leamington, while Carker reports to Dombey, Bagstock and Mrs. Skewton arrange the marriage of Edith and Dombey. (27) On a walk in the countryside early the next morning, Carker sees a woman whose face suggests intense internal struggle. Later he recognizes Edith as the troubled woman he had seen on his walk.

After touring Warwick Castle with Carker as their guide, Edith sketches for Dombey, plays the piano, and sings to his command. Later she tells her mother that "he has bought me," comparing herself to a slave and a racehorse, objects traded in the market.

(28) When Dombey introduces Edith to his daughter, Florence thinks that perhaps she can learn from "her new and beautiful Mama, how to gain her father's love."

Part 10 (July 1847)

(29) Mrs. Chick, Dombey's sister who had sponsored Miss Tox in Dombey's house, so surprises Miss Tox when she tells her about Dombey's impending marriage that Miss Tox faints. Mrs. Chick acts shocked and surprised to "learn" that Miss Tox had entertained hopes of an alliance with her brother, and she snobbishly breaks off any connection with her.

(30) During the week before the wedding, Florence stays with Edith and her mother, but when Mrs. Skewton surprises Dombey by suddenly revealing Florence hidden under her shawl, Dombey is speechless and Florence distressed by his discomfort. Edith's insistence that Florence go home after the ceremony and not stay to be corrupted by Mrs. Skewton causes a rift between Edith and her mother. (31) After the ceremony, Dombey and Edith depart for Paris. Florence returns to the newly refurbished room where Paul once slept.

Part 11 (August 1847)

(32) Cuttle goes to Dombey and Son to verify a newspaper report of the sinking of the *Son and Heir*. Carker confirms the news, refuses to say a good word for Walter, and, after accusing Cuttle and Sol of dark schemes, ejects the Captain from his office. Shaken, Cuttle goes back to the Midshipman and commits Walter's body to the deep.

(33) James Carker's house is luxuriously furnished with books, paintings, and games; a parrot who sits in a hoop that looks like a great wedding ring; and, most notably, a portrait of a woman resembling Edith Dombey. On the other side of London, John Carker and his sister Harriet occupy a modest cottage surrounded by vines and flowers. When a stranger who knows John's story comes to the door and offers to help them, Harriet refuses his aid, saying that John's reward is the self-respect he has achieved by his repentance. That afternoon, Harriet comforts a weary traveler who resembles Edith Dombey. She takes her in out of the rain, washes her bleeding feet, and gives her some money.

(34) As Good Mrs. Brown huddles before the fire in her hovel in the heart of London, the traveler enters and identifies herself as Mrs. Brown's daughter Alice, returned from a sentence of transportation; she is resentful of her mother's neglect and bitter about her betrayal by James Carker. When she realizes that the woman who gave her the money was Harriet Carker, she returns to the cottage and throws the money on the ground in front of the startled sister and brother.

Part 12 (September 1847)

(35) Florence asks Edith to instruct her how to become the loving child of her father, but Edith tells

her that she is not a good teacher of love. That night Florence dreams of trying to help her father but not being able to set him free. Then she dreams that she sees Paul, the river, and a grave with the body of Edith at the bottom. (36) At the housewarming, Dombey's guests do not mix with Edith's guests. Afterward, in Carker's presence, Dombey criticizes Edith for not being a better hostess. (37) The next day, Carker apologizes to Edith for his helplessness the night before, professing that as Dombey's "mere dependent," he was powerless to leave. Then, insinuating his influence over Dombey, he warns her that Florence's continued association with Cuttle and the group at the Midshipman will bring her husband's displeasure. After he leaves, Edith learns that her mother has had a paralytic stroke.

(38) Miss Tox, abandoned by Mrs. Chick, seeks out Polly Toodle, hoping to learn from her about the Dombeys.

Part 13 (October 1847)

(39) A year after Sol's disappearance, Cuttle, living alone at the Midshipman like Crusoe on his island, opens the letter that Sol left. It is Sol's will, leaving everything to Walter—or to Cuttle in lieu of Walter. Cuttle notes that he opened the letter and then puts it away again.

(40) Proud Dombey hates Florence in his heart because she has stolen his bride as she stole his son. Resolved to show his wife that he is supreme, he tells her she displeases him by her treatment of his guests, by her extravagance, and by the company she keeps. He requires that she defer to him and threatens to use Carker as an emissary to see that his demands are met. Edith, thinking of Florence, suppresses her anger, but she tells him that she will never pay him homage. She reminds him that their lives are bound up with others'. Dombey repeats his ultimatum.

Attended by Edith and Florence, Mrs. Skewton is sent to Brighton for her health. On the Downs outside Brighton, Edith and her mother meet another mother and daughter—Mrs. Brown and Alice—who appear as DOUBLES to them. Mrs. Skewton gives some money to Mrs. Brown, telling her that she is an "excellent woman, and a good mother." Alice tells Edith that good looks and pride will not save them. (41) Florence tearfully visits Paul's old school. Mrs. Skewton dies. Dombey goes to Brighton for the funeral.

Part 14 (November 1847)

(42) Back in London, Dombey asks Carker to tell Edith that any show of devotion to his daughter displeases him. As he rides back to the City, Dombey is thrown from his horse and injured. Florence is shaken by the news, but Edith accepts it calmly. (43) When Dombey is brought home, he is guarded by Mrs. Pipchin, and Florence is unable to see him. One night she slips downstairs, finds him alone, and stares at his sleeping face, unclouded by any consciousness of her. When she returns upstairs, she finds Edith still awake, bearing a self-inflicted wound on her hand and wondering what her life might have been had she not been tormented by pride and self-hatred. As dawn breaks, Edith seeks comfort in the company of Florence, watching over her as she sleeps. (44) Later that morning, Susan Nipper tells Dombey of Florence's kindness, gentleness, and love for him and is dismissed from his service. (45) Meanwhile, Carker informs Edith that she has displeased Dombey by being unsubmissive and that Florence will suffer if Edith remains partial to her. Insinuating his control over her, Carker kisses her gloved and wounded hand as he leaves.

Part 15 (December 1847)

(46) Carker rides through the street attended by Rob Toodle and observed by Alice and Mrs. Brown, who question Rob about his master. At the office Carker tells his brother that everyone there secretly wishes to see Dombey humbled; then he returns to Dombey's house thinking of his growing power over Edith.

(47) Florence worries that she has caused Edith to be more distant and cold to her, but Edith tells her the change is on the surface only. Florence is alone again, living with the images of the people she loves rather than the people themselves. When Dombey humiliates Edith because she refuses to attend his dinner for their second wedding anniversary, Edith asks to be released from the marriage and Carker supports her request for a separation. Later that evening, Florence sees Carker slip out of Edith's rooms and then she meets Edith on the staircase, as Edith

cringes against the wall and descends past Florence without touching her. The next morning Dombey finds Edith gone and all the clothes and ornaments from her marriage scattered about the floor of her room. He feels utterly dishonored. Florence goes to him with outstretched arms, but he strikes her across the heart, knocking her to the floor. She runs out of the house with "no father upon earth." (48) Sobbing and confused, Florence goes into the streets at dawn, wanders to the Wooden Midshipman, and there faints into the arms of Captain Cuttle. He prepares a room at the top of the house for her.

Part 16 (January 1848)

(49) The Captain cares for Florence, but she is troubled by the "darkening mark of an angry hand" on her breast. On her second evening there, Cuttle tells the story of a shipwreck and of the survival of three members of the crew, one of them a boy beloved of all his shipmates. As Florence realizes that it is Walter's story, he appears and "brother and sister" are restored to each other. (50) Learning from Florence the reasons for her "exile," Walter realizes that he cannot urge her to return home. He confesses that he loves her. She returns his love.

(51) Dombey retreats from the world, refusing help from Mrs. Chick, Feenix, and Bagstock. He is unaware of Miss Tox's interest in his condition, of the gossip in the servant's quarters, and of the speculation at the office about who will fill Carker's position.

Part 17 (February 1848)

(52) From Mrs. Brown and Alice, who have wormed the information out of Rob Toodle, Dombey learns that Carker and Edith have gone abroad separately and plan to meet in Dijon.

(53) When Dombey dismisses John Carker the Junior from the firm because his presence reminds him of the unfaithful manager, Harriet tells her brother of a stranger who has promised to help them. The stranger turns out to be Mr. Morfin, one of Dombey's assistants. He offers to help John find another position and tells him of James's reckless and self-serving investments in the name of the firm. Regretting that she helped Dombey learn Carker's whereabouts, Alice asks Harriet to warn her brother that he is in danger.

(54) When Carker and Edith meet at midnight in a luxurious apartment in Dijon, she resists his advances, telling him that she only used him to humiliate her husband. She wished Dombey to think her unfaithful so that she could humble him. She also wanted to compromise Carker so that he could not reveal the truth without humiliating himself. When Dombey knocks on the door, Edith disappears into another room and slips out a secret passage. Carker, discovering her gone, escapes by the same route.

Part 18 (March 1848)

(55) Pursued by Dombey, Carker flees back to England. He stops at a country inn beside the railway, but he is tormented by visions and by the noise of passing trains and cannot sleep. Arising at dawn to continue his journey, he sees Dombey, steps back onto the tracks into the path of a passing train, and is torn limb from limb.

(56) Walter and Florence plan their wedding. On the day before the wedding, Sol Gills returns and joins the celebration. (57) Florence and Walter visit Paul's grave on their way to the church in the City where they are to be married. After the ceremony they set out on a year-long journey to China.

Part 19–20 (April 1848)

(58) A year later, the world buzzes with talk of the failure of Dombey and Son. Meanwhile, Harriet asks Mr. Morfin to arrange for James Carker's money—which she and John have inherited because James died without a will—to be secretly used to give a life income to Mr. Dombey. Then she calls on Alice, who is gravely ill, and learns

Carker's death, depicted here in Barnard's illustration for the Household Edition of *Dombey and Son* (1877), makes the railway a murderous agent of social and technological change.

that Alice is the child of Edith's father's brother. Harriet reads to her of Christ's compassion for the woman taken in adultery. After she leaves, Alice dies. (59) The fall of Dombey and Son causes the breakup of the household. The servants leave and the furnishings are sold at auction. Polly Toodle is employed to occupy the house and watch over Dombey, who has retreated into the darkness of his rooms. Dombey broods on his life and on what he has given up. In particular he is aware that he has lost Florence. In the dead of the night, he climbs the stairs to the children's room and lies on the bare floorboards weeping. At daybreak he goes downstairs again, returning again the next night. Seeing his wasted image in a mirror, he wonders how long it would take for a trickle of blood from a dying man to be discovered in the empty house. Suddenly his daughter returns, asks forgiveness, and tells him of her own child. She leads him out of the house. Polly closes up the mansion and goes home.

(60) A series of marriages takes place: Cornelia Blimber marries Mr. Feeder, schoolmaster at the Academy; Susan Nipper marries Toots; Cuttle's friend, Captain Jack Bunsby, marries Mrs. MacStinger.

(61) Weak, incoherent, and distracted, Dombey gradually regains his senses under Florence's care, but he has very little strength. One evening, Feenix takes Florence to meet Edith. Edith rejects Florence's offer to secure Dombey's forgiveness for her. She tells Florence she is innocent and intends to resettle in the south of Italy. (62) The group at the Wooden Midshipman, including Mr. Dombey, drink the last bottle of Madeira to celebrate Walter and his wife. Mr. Dombey lives on a sum that arrives each year anonymously. Mr. Morfin has married Harriet, and John Carker lives with them. The Wooden Midshipman—now Gills and Cuttle—prospers. Walter has an important position with the shipping firm that sent him to China and is helping build a new "edifice," a new Dombey and Son. An old man, Dombey walks on the beach with his grandchildren—his grandson, who is a strong version of young Paul, and his granddaughter, for whom he has profound and unspoken affection.

COMMENTARY

Dickens told JOHN FORSTER while he was at work on *Dombey* that the novel "was to do with Pride what [*Chuzzlewit*] had done with Selfishness." *Dombey* is, however, a considerable advance over its predecessor in terms of structure and control. KATHLEEN TILLOTSON (1956) has shown how carefully Dickens planned and worked out the novel. The extravagant comic invention of a Mrs. Gamp may be missing in *Dombey,* but each of the characters and episodes in the novel is made relevant to its developing theme. *Dombey* is the first novel for which Dickens wrote out detailed plans. It is clear from these notes—and from Dickens's letters to Forster—that he had the story well in mind from the beginning, especially the central action involving Mr. Dombey, young Paul, and Florence. At the same time, Dickens's notes also indicate that he changed his mind about things as the story developed. He altered his plans for both Edith and Walter Gay as he worked on the story and saved both of them from the deaths he had planned. He also prevented Walter from falling into idleness and ruin, a story he saved for Richard Carstone in *Bleak House.*

Dickens's careful planning for the novel, his subordination of character and incident to the development of theme, and his use of the contrasting symbols of the railway and the sea to center the novel make *Dombey* more akin to the later novels—those following *Copperfield*—than to the novels that preceded it. Even though Dickens's career has traditionally been divided at *Copperfield* into early and late periods, there are strong reasons, as several critics have argued, for making *Dombey* the turning point.

The novel's title, as the brilliant opening chapter makes clear, perfectly links the domestic and the public spheres, for *Dombey and Son* refers both to the 48-year-old father with his infant son and to the family business. As a business magnate, Dombey thinks of his new son not as a human child but as the continuation of the firm. On the one hand, he reduces everything to its commercial value: Young Paul counts only as the "and Son" and his sister doesn't count at all, for she is "merely a piece of base coin that couldn't be invested—a bad Boy—nothing more" (1). On the other hand, Dombey grandiosely inflates his own importance to a blasphemous extreme: Dombey and Son, "those three words conveyed the one idea of Mr. Dombey's life. The earth was made for Dombey and Son to trade in, and the sun and moon were made to give them light. Rivers and seas were formed to float their ships; . . . stars and planets circled in their orbits, to preserve inviolate a system of which they were the centre. Common abbreviations took new meanings in his eyes, and had sole reference to them: A.D. had no concern with anno Domini, but stood for anno Dombei—and Son" (1). Dombey's pride, based in wealth and social position, raises him above the rest of mankind to live in a delusion of divine power beyond the reach of mortal limitation. He is the controlling figure in his "House"—the firm Dombey and Son—and in his household—both a merchant prince whose underlings feed his pride and a patriarch who rules his family. At the end of chapter 1, mortality appears to upset his rule when his wife dies, but Dombey is untouched. She has served her purpose in bearing his son and has no further usefulness. She leaves his temporal and mechanical world—symbolized by the watches in the opening chapter—and drifts "out upon the dark and unknown sea that rolls round all the world" (1).

By the end of the opening chapter, Dickens has established several of the crucial oppositions on which the novel turns. The spheres of business and family, public and private, male and female are established and contrasted. The public sphere of business recognizes external achievement and denies or represses the private world of internal feeling. Material, mechanical, and male, it opposes the immaterial, natural, and female. After Fanny's death, the Toodle family enter as representatives of the "other" side. Humble people who are as low in the social scale as Dombey is high, the Toodles are devoted to their children—both male and female—and their love and concern for one another is apparent in the interview with Dombey and in their natural "apple" faces. Even though Dombey tries to control Polly's relationship with his son by restraining her in the terms of their

contract and by giving her a male name, Richards, Polly's natural feelings come out.

Dickens ends the first monthly number with a chapter introducing the Wooden Midshipman, the household of sea people that symbolically counters Dombey's destructive commercial empire. There Sol Gills and Captain Cuttle nurture Walter Gay on stories about the sea, stories that Walter will reenact as he rescues Florence from the kidnapping and later as he returns from the sea to rescue and marry her. Walter is a creature of legend, particularly the legend of DICK WHITTINGTON, the story of a poor boy who, through trading ventures, rose to become LORD MAYOR of London. His miraculous return and fairy-tale romance are, as HARRY STONE (1979) has shown, part of the fairy-tale method of the CHRISTMAS BOOKS that Dickens adapts to a longer novel in *Dombey*.

But the sea people and Walter are elaborations on the central story of Mr. Dombey and Florence. As he began the novel, Dickens described his plan to Forster in the following terms:

> I design to show Mr. D. with that one idea of the Son taking firmer and firmer possession of him, and swelling and bloating his pride to a prodigious extent. As the boy begins to grow up, I shall show him quite impatient for his getting on, and urging his masters to set him great tasks, and the like. But the natural affection of the boy will turn towards the despised sister. . . . When the boy is about ten (in the fourth number), he will be taken ill, and will die; and when he is ill, and when he is dying, I mean to make him turn always to the sister still, and keep the stern affection of the father at a distance. So Mr. Dombey—for all his greatness, and for all his devotion to the child—will find himself at arm's length from him even then, and will see that his love and confidence are all bestowed upon his sister. . . . The death of the boy is a death-blow, of course, to all the father's schemes and cherished hopes; and "Dombey and Son," as Miss Tox will say at the end of the number, "is a Daughter after all."

Dickens moved Paul's death to the fifth number, and Miss Tox's observation comes much later, in chapter 59, but the focus of the story on Mr. Dombey is clear in Dickens's summary and in the novel itself.

Dombey is a difficult hero. Icy, remote, reserved, and unfeeling, he presents only surfaces and hides whatever depths are within him. We get only brief and infrequent glimpses of the man beneath the surface in such scenes as the one in which he secretly watches Florence as he sits in the drawing room with a handkerchief over his head (35). Withdrawn from the world, he acts through intermediaries: Bagstock arranges his wedding; Carker manages his business and negotiates the terms of his marriage. His decline and fall elicits little sympathy from the reader, who may agree with Hippolyte Taine, a French critic of the Victorian period, who commented that when Dombey is transformed at the end "he becomes the best of fathers, and spoils a fine novel" (PHILIP COLLINS, 1971).

Florence, on the other hand, is a sympathetic figure, but the SENTIMENTALITY in her presentation has put off many modern readers. Like David Copperfield and Little Nell, Florence seems small for her age; even when she is in her late teens and runs from home, she is described as if she were a much younger child. This appearance of childlike innocence, though it may increase the pathos in her presentation, does not endear her to her father. For him she is, as ALEXANDER WELSH (1987) points out, an angel of death. She is at her mother's side and at Paul's side when each dies. Her name and its contraction, Floy, suggest flowing and thus her connection with the waters of death and immortality, but Dombey, who denies death and whose only notion of immortality involves the longevity of the firm, blames her for his son's death. The more she seeks his love, the more he resents and hates her. A passive victim of her father's neglect, she never abandons her hopeless love for him, even after he strikes her and drives her out of the house. Her devotion strains credulity, even though we may recognize in her the abused child who blames herself for the treatment she receives. The episodes in which Florence studies other children in order to learn how to gain her father's love and asks Edith to teach her how to love him embody painful psychological truth.

The story of Dombey and daughter seems headed toward the tragic conclusion that Taine expected and preferred, a 19th-century version of *King Lear* in which Dombey would recognize too late that the child he treasured was "a daughter after all." But Dombey is saved from Lear's fate at the last minute. After financial ruin, madness, and an attempt at suicide, he is rescued by Florence, removed from his funereal house, and granted a chance to walk by the sea with his grandchildren. This final moment in the novel, narrated as if it is dream or vision rather than reality, suggests how close Dombey came to completing the tragedy his life appeared to be reenacting. So tenuous, in fact, is this ending, that ANNY SADRIN (1994) has suggested that the real point of the novel is that the patriarchal succession is preserved as the family line is passed down to grandson Paul. Thus the novel, in Sadrin's view, turns out to be not Dombey and daughter but Dombey and son after all.

Dombey's mythic story of father and daughter and its parable of pride is embedded in the 1840s, a period of rapid social and material change. The Whigs, who assumed power after the passing of the Parliamentary REFORM BILL OF 1832, introduced a long agenda of legislation designed to reform governmental and social institutions and to respond to industrialization and urbanization. The railway boom during the period made the INDUSTRIAL REVOLUTION visible and turned England from a horse-and-coach nation to one run on steam. Beneath the story of Dombey's progress and redemption is an embedded historical fable on the theme of social change. A merchant prince who has inherited the family trading business from his father and grandfather, Dombey represents the mercantile era of the 17th and 18th centuries. He is not one of the new captains of industry, not a member of Marx's bourgeoisie controlling the means of production. He comes from a preindustrial society where merchants may have had money but power reposed in the hands of landed aristocrats who looked down on those like Dombey who acquired their riches in trade. Indeed, Dombey's rigid pride may derive in part from his sense of inferiority in a society based on aristocratic rules, an inferiority that makes him easily manipulated by Bagstock and attracted to

Edith, both of whom have a tincture of the nobility he lacks. It also makes him incapable of seeing Mrs. Skewton for what she is, an embodiment of the artificial, false, and outmoded aristocracy.

Trapped in outmoded habits of mind, Dombey not only overvalues the past but is incapable of understanding the present and dealing in it. He employs intermediaries like Bagstock to manage his life and his business, and they in turn manage him. James Carker represents a new class of professional managers, replacing the former owner-operators of the CITY. Ambitious, manipulative, class-conscious, and resentful, Carker asserts that there is no one of Dombey's employees "who wouldn't be glad at heart to see his master humbled: who does not hate him, secretly: who does not wish him evil rather than good: and who would not turn upon him, if he had the power and boldness" (46). Expressed at the same time that Marx and Engels were composing *The Communist Manifesto* (1848), Carker's world-view also envisions society as class war. Carker may manage and manipulate, but he does not own the means of production and he does not control the course of history—or his own destiny. Appropriately, he is killed by a train, a symbol of the new industrialism that was radically changing Victorian England.

The famous description of the railway construction at Staggs' Gardens in chapter 6 compares the turmoil to "a great earthquake" in its destruction and to the Tower of Babel in its confusion. It is both a source of "dire disorder" and of "civilization and improvement." For Dombey and for Carker, the railway will become "the remorseless monster, Death" (20), but for Toodles, it offers opportunity. He rises to become an engineer, and even though his old neighborhood is "cut up root and branch" (15), a new neighborhood emerges from the destruction and confusion:

> There were railway patterns in its drapers' shops, and railway journals in the windows of its newsmen. There were railway hotels, office-houses, lodging-houses, boarding-houses; railway plans, maps, views, wrappers, bottles, sandwich-boxes, and time-tables; railway hackney-coach and cabstands; railway omnibuses, railway streets

and buildings, railway hangers-on and parasites. . . . There was even railway time observed in clocks, as if the sun had given in. . . . To and from the heart of this great change, all day and night, throbbing currents rushed and returned incessantly like its life's blood. (15)

The Toodle family thrives by adapting their natural energy to this new life force. Dombey cuts himself off; his class pride even causes him to reject Mr. Toodle's sympathetic condolences after Paul's death (20).

If Dombey's pride is in part a product of a consciousness that fails to adapt to changes in his society and its class system, it is also an expression of patriarchal power in a radically gendered society. In a world based on what THOMAS CARLYLE called "the cash nexus," where all relationships are defined by contract in monetary terms, Dombey values his son as "capital" for what he represents to the business, and he devalues his daughter as a "base coin" (1). His marriages are contracts, and when he hires a wet nurse to nurture his son, the terms of the relationship are strictly contractual. Most of the women in the novel collude with this system of male power, which turns them into commodities on the market. Many become sycophantic hangers-on like Miss Tox or Mrs. Chick. A few, like Alice Marwood and Edith, resent their degraded position. Edith defines the limits of her contract when she tells her mother, "There is no slave in a market; there is no horse in a fair: so shown and offered and examined and paraded, mother, as I have been, for ten shameful years. . . . He sees me at the auction, and he thinks it well to buy me. Let him! . . . When he would have me show one of [my accomplishments], to justify his purchase to his men, I require of him to say which he demands, and I exhibit it. I will do no more" (27). She resentfully acquiesces to the system and accepts the marriage contract contractually.

To acquiesce to patriarchy and reduce all relationships to money is to choose death over life. The precocious young Paul uncovers this truth when he asks his father, "What is money?" and elicits the answer, "Money, Paul, can do anything." The boy's response, "If it's a good thing, and can do anything

. . . I wonder why it didn't save me my Mama" (8), underscores the impotence of a culture that divides the world, placing thought, action, and material control on one side and feeling, acceptance, and spiritual understanding on the other, elevating the former and devaluing the latter. Dombey's systematic decline, Carker's destruction, Edith's self-destructive resentment, Mrs. Skewton's sycophantic emptiness, and Alice Marwood's obsessive bitterness are among the casualties of this divided civilization. The power to heal the division and restore some balance flows from the waters of immortality, is heard in the voice of the waves, and returns from a honeymoon at sea to unite a broken old man with his grandchildren. The tenuous account and the sentimental distance in the final pages make the novel seem much more assured in its analysis of the disease than in its expectations for a cure.

CHARACTERS AND RELATED ENTRIES

Anne   Dombey's housemaid who, when the House of Dombey crashes, marries Towlinson the butler; together they open a grocery store (59).

Bagstock, Major Joseph (Joey B.)   Retired army officer who lives across the way from Miss Tox; "a wooden-featured, blue-faced major, with eyes starting out of his head, . . . [who] tickled his vanity with the fiction that [Miss Tox] was a splendid woman, who had her eye on him. This he had several times hinted at the club: in connexion with little jocularities, of which old Joe Bagstock, old Joey Bagstock, old J. Bagstock, old Josh Bagstock, or so forth, was the perpetual theme. . . . 'Joey B., Sir,' the Major would say, . . . '[is] tough, Sir, tough and de-vil-ish sly!'" (7). He keeps an Indian servant whom he abuses and calls "the Native." Reactionary and self-absorbed, Bagstock seeks to repay Miss Tox for ignoring him by worming his way into Dombey's confidence. He accompanies Dombey to Leamington, where he promotes Dombey's marriage to Edith Granger and negotiates arrangements with Mrs. Skewton (26), goes with Dombey to Dijon in pursuit of Carker, but then he abandons Dombey after the bankruptcy (58).

Bagstock assumes a role in Dombey's personal life comparable to Carker's role in Dombey's business

life. Both manage Dombey's affairs. Bagstock's leering sexuality is sometimes said to express Dombey's repressed libido, but the marriage he negotiates for Dombey is childless and dysfunctional. LAWRENCE FRANK (1984) compares his role to that of the unnatural Mrs. Skewton: "Mrs. Skewton becomes imprisoned in her habitul pose as Cleopatra, evading the romantic imperative to change and self-creation, while Major Bagstock denies the realities of time, change, and death through those verbal repetitions by which he seeks to perpetuate himself. . . . His 'stone dead' personal language, addressed primarily to an absent self, reveals the extent to which 'Bagstock is [not] alive, Sir,' in any genuine sense. Like Mrs. Skewton in her role as Cleopatra, he has chosen paralysis—until Paralysis chooses him—to avoid the romantic pilgrimage of being. Each becomes a self-plagiarist, with a version of the self constructed upon an originally specious and now outmoded pose."

Baps   The dancing master at Dr. Blimber's academy, "a grave gentleman, with a slow and measured manner of speaking" (14).

Baps, Mrs.   Baps's wife, who attends the school going-away party with her husband (14).

Berenthia (Berry)   Mrs. Pipchin's middle-aged niece "and devoted slave, . . . possessing a gaunt and iron-bound aspect, and much afflicted with boils on her nose" (8).

Bishopsgate   The street in the City of London where Brogley, the broker who takes possession of the Wooden Midshipman, has his shop (9).

Bitherstone, Bill   One of Paul Dombey's fellow boarders with Mrs. Pipchin in Brighton, "whose relatives were all in India" (8). Major Bagstock knew his father in the army.

Black Badger, the   The pub frequented by the Game Chicken (22).

Blimber, Cornelia   Daughter of Doctor and Mrs. Blimber and her father's assistant in the school.

"There was no light nonsense about Miss Blimber. She kept her hair short and crisp, and wore spectacles. She was dry and sandy with working in the graves of deceased languages. None of your live languages for Miss Blimber. They must be dead—stone dead—and then Miss Blimber dug them up like a Ghoul" (11). She is assigned to be Paul's tutor and concludes in her report on his work that "he is singular (what is usually termed old-fashioned) in his character and conduct" (14). Ultimately, Cornelia, "in a new pair of spectacles," marries Mr. Feeder, B.A., who inherits the Blimber Academy (60).

Blimber, Doctor   Pompous and egotistical headmaster of the school that Paul Dombey attends in Brighton, "a portly gentleman in a suit of black, with strings at his knees, and stockings below them. He had a bald head, highly polished; a deep voice; and a chin so very double, that it was a wonder how he ever managed to shave into the creases. He had likewise a pair of little eyes that were always half shut up, and a mouth that was always half expanded into a grin, as if he had, that moment, posed a boy, and were waiting to convict him from his own lips. Insomuch, that when the Doctor put his right hand into the breast of his coat, and with his other hand behind him, and a scarcely perceptible wag of his head, made the commonest observation to a nervous stranger, it was like a sentiment from the sphinx. And settled his business" (11). His school is "a great hothouse in which all the boys blew before their time. . . . Every description of Greek and Latin vegetable was got off the driest twigs of boys under the frostiest circumstances" (11). Blimber's "forcing system" speaks to Mr. Dombey's desire to rush his son into adulthood, but it does not work in Paul's case. The boy gradually declines during his time at Blimber's, and when he leaves at the end of the autumn term, he is too ill to dance at the Christmas party (14). At retirement, Blimber turns his school over to his son-in-law, Mr. Feeder, B.A.

In Blimber's school Dickens satirizes the public school education of his time, which overemphasized the classics, paid little attention to the differences among students, and gave no encouragement to the imagination. Blimber is not cruel or physi-

cally abusive as some of Dickens's other schoolmasters are, but despite his good nature and good intentions, his system is partly responsible for Paul's decline.

Blimber, Mrs.   Doctor Blimber's wife, who "was not learned hserself, but she pretended to be, and that did quite as well. She said at evening parties, that if she could have known Cicero, she thought she could have died contented. It was the steady joy of her life to see the Doctor's young gentlemen, in the largest possible shirt-collars, and the stiffest possible cravats. It was so classical, she said" (11).

Blockitt, Mrs.   The nurse who attends Mrs. Dombey at the birth of Paul, "a simpering piece of faded gentility" (1).

Bokum, Mrs.   Mrs. MacStinger's "dearest friend," who keeps a close watch on Bunsby to see that he does not run off on the way to his wedding with Mrs. MacStinger, for whom she acts as bridesmaid (60).

Briggs   Student at Blimber's Academy with whom Paul shares a room. His assignments in the classics are for him "a nightmare" (14).

Brig Place, India Docks   "On the brink of a little canal near the India Docks" (9), this street is the site of Mrs. MacStinger's house, where Captain Cuttle lodges.

Brogley, Mr.   Secondhand furniture dealer and broker, "a moist-eyed, pink-complexioned, crisp-haired man, of a bulky figure and an easy temper" (9), who takes possession of the Wooden Midshipman when Sol Gills cannot pay his debts. Walter Gay stays with Brogley after he returns from overseas (48–49).

Brown, Alice (aka Alice Marwood)   Daughter of Good Mrs. Brown, the child of her seduction by Edith Granger's uncle. Seduced by James Carker, Alice is abandoned by him and reduced to crime. Transported for theft, she returns to England embittered and determined to avenge her mistreatment by Carker. Her passionate anger prompts her to reject aid from Harriet, James Carker's sister (34), and to reveal to Dombey the secret of Carker's whereabouts after Carker runs off with Edith, an act she later regrets (52, 53). She dies repentant, reconciled with Harriet Carker (58).

Alice bears a striking physical resemblance to her cousin Edith, a connection that underscores their importance in the commodification theme. Although Dombey considers his daughter worthless, merely a "base coin," both Mrs. Brown and Mrs. Skewton recognize their daughters' commercial value in the marketplace. Alice's open and passionate anger contrasts with Edith's frozen and repressed demeanor, but the doubling helps reveal Edith's suppressed rage.

William Palmer (*Dickens and the New Historicism*, 1997) notes the similarity of Alice Brown's alias, Marwood, to Millwood the conniving prostitute in GEORGE LILLO's *The London Merchant* (1731), a play upon which Dickens drew in several novels.

Brown, "Good Mrs."   The ironic name of the thief and receiver of stolen goods who kidnaps Florence Dombey in the street; "a very ugly old woman, with red rims around her eyes, and a mouth that mumbled and chattered of itself when she was not speaking" (6). She is the mother of Alice, the child of her seduction by Edith Granger's uncle, and Alice bears a striking physical resemblance to Edith. Mrs. Brown hates James Carker, who has ruined Alice, and she aids Dombey's discovery of Carker to avenge this wrong (52).

Mrs. Brown and Alice are doubled by Mrs. Skewton and Edith, a connection that emphasizes the theme of the reduction of human beings to commodities, mirroring Alice's prostitution and Mrs. Brown's intent to sell Florence's hair with the more polite transactions in the upper levels of society carried out by Mrs. Skewton and Edith.

Bunsby, Captain Jack   Friend of Captain Cuttle and skipper of the *Cautious Clara*, "a bulk head—human and very large—with one stationary eye in the mahogany face, and one revolving one, on the principle of some lighthouses" (23). Cuttle seeks

his advice, which is inscrutable and laced with nautical terminology. Bunsby enables Cuttle to escape Mrs. MacStinger, only to be caught himself by the widow, whom he marries in the end.

Burgess and Co.   Mr. Toots's tailors (12).

Carker, Harriet   Sister of the Carker brothers who lives with her disgraced brother John, a "slight, small, patient figure, . . . who . . . went over to him [John] in his shame and put her hand in his, and with a sweet composure and determination, led him hopefully upon his barren way" (33). Harriet also befriends Alice Marwood, but she is rebuffed when Alice learns that she is James Carker's sister (33, 34). Nevertheless, she nurses Alice in her last illness (58). During their years of humiliation, John and Harriet are befriended by Mr. Morfin, who ultimately marries Harriet (62). When they inherit James's fortune, they use the money to provide an annuity for the bankrupt Dombey (58).

Carker, James   Manager at Dombey and Son, "thirty-eight or forty years old, of a florid complexion, and with two unbroken rows of glistening teeth, whose regularity and whiteness were quite distressing. It was impossible to escape the observation of them, for he showed them whenever he spoke; and bore so wide a smile upon his countenance . . . that there was something in it like the snarl of a cat. He affected a stiff white cravat, after the example of his principal, and was always closely buttoned up and tightly dressed" (13). Sybaritic and self-serving, Carker is obsequious to Dombey but secretly resents his authority. When Dombey employs him as a go-between to negotiate the terms of his relationship with Edith (42), Carker insinuates himself into a position of power over her and elopes with her to Dijon (47). There she rejects him, revealing that she loathes him and simply used him to humiliate him and her husband (54). Fleeing from Dombey, who has discovered his whereabouts from Alice Marwood, his former mistress, Carker falls in front of a passing train and is torn limb from limb (55).

In the historical myth that underlies the story, Carker represents the managerial class that has displaced the owner-operators of an earlier era. Ambitious and manipulative, he resents Dombey's power, derived from ownership, and seeks to usurp it. But Carker, in turn, does not comprehend the new industrialism, represented by the railway, or the anger of women unafraid of patriarchy. In his own ways he is just as short-sighted as Mr. Dombey.

Carker, John (Carker Junior) James Carker's elder brother, called "Carker Junior" because he occupies an inferior position in the firm. "He was not old, but his hair was white; his body was bent, or bowed as if by the weight of some great trouble: and there were deep lines in his worn and melancholy face. The fire of his eyes, the expression of his features, the very voice in which he spoke, were all subdued and quenched, as if the spirit within him lay in ashes. He was respectably, though very plainly dressed, in black; but his clothes, moulded to the general character of his figure, seemed to shrink and abase themselves upon him, and to join in the sorrowful solicitation which the whole man from head to foot expressed, to be left unnoticed, and alone in his humility" (6). His humility is the result of a lifelong role of penitence demanded of him by his brother for the youthful mistake of stealing money from the firm. His sister supports him in his sincere penitence. He befriends Walter Gay.

Dickens's original intent to trace the degeneration of Walter Gay may account for the presence of John Carker as a warning example of a misspent life, but the novel ultimately challenges such simple moral dichotomies as that between the industrious and idle apprentices. John's humiliation is less an indication of a deserved punishment than a result of his brother's exercise of power. The successful brother in the end proves to be the villain in a reversal of the conventional story.

Cautious Clara, The Captain Jack Bunsby's ship (23).

Charitable Grinders Charity school to which Mr. Dombey sends Polly Toodle's eldest son, earning the boy the nickname Rob the Grinder. The uniform that Rob wears, "a nice, warm, blue baize tailed coat and cap, turned up with orange-coloured binding; red worsted stockings; and very strong leather small-clothes" (5), was characteristic of charity school uniforms of the day.

Chick, John Mrs. Chick's husband, "a stout bald gentleman, with a very large face, and his hands continually in his pockets, and who had a tendency in his nature to whistle and hum tunes" (2).

Chick, Mrs. Louisa Mr. Dombey's sister, "a lady rather past the middle age than otherwise, but dressed in a very juvenile manner, particularly as to the tightness of her bodice" (1). She claims that Mrs. Dombey died in childbirth because she was not a true Dombey and did not "make an effort" (3). She invites her friend, Miss Tox, to aid in finding a nurse for young Paul and encourages her to entertain hopes of Dombey's matrimonial interest, but when Dombey selects Edith, she ends her friendship with Miss Tox (29). She explains Dombey's ruin as the result of his not making an effort.

Clark Wharf manager who turns over Florence Dombey to Walter Gay after she has been kidnapped by Mrs. Brown and is lost in the streets of London (6).

Cuttle, Captain Edward (Ned) Retired sea captain and loyal friend to Sol Gills, Walter Gay, and Florence, "a gentleman in a wide suit of blue, with a hook instead of a hand. . . . He wore a loose black silk handkerchief round his neck, and such a very large coarse shirt collar, that it looked like a small sail" (4). He is intimidated by the matrimonial ambitions of his landlady, the widow MacStinger, but he escapes her clutches to care for the Wooden Midshipman when Sol Gills goes off in search of Walter Gay (25). He is fond of aphorisms which, along with seagoing language, salt his speech: "In the Proverbs of Solomon," he tells Walter, "you will find the following words, 'May we never want a friend in need, nor a bottle to give him!' When found, make note of" (15). He adds to this store of somewhat confusing wisdom by seeking the cryptic advice of his seagoing colleague, Captain Bunsby. When Florence runs from her father (44), Cuttle shelters her and cares for her at the Wooden Midshipman. After Gills's return, he becomes a partner in the business (66).

Daws, Mary   Dombey's kitchen maid, who worries that her wages will not be paid after the bankruptcy (59).

Dijon   The city in France to which Carker and Edith Dombey elope (52).

Diogenes   Florence Dombey's "blundering, ill-favoured, clumsy, bullet-headed dog" (18). A gift from Toots, the dog formerly belonged to the Blimbers and was especially friendly with young Paul. Toots secures the Bimbers's permission to give the dog to Florence.

Dombey, Edith (Edith Granger)   Mrs. Skewton's daughter, the beautiful and statuesque young widow with aristocratic connections who becomes Dombey's second wife, "very handsome, very haughty, very willful, [she] tossed her head and drooped her eyelids, as though, if there were anything in all the world worth looking into, save a mirror, it certainly was not the earth or sky" (21). She interests Dombey as a "trophy wife" for her beauty and her aristocratic pedigree, and because she proved fertile during her first marriage by bearing a son who later drowned. She is as proud as her new husband, though her pride is mixed with self-loathing: "There was a difference even in the pride of the two, that removed them farther from each other, than if one had been the proudest and the other the humblest specimen of humanity in all creation. He, self-important, unbending, formal, austere. She, lovely and graceful in an uncommon degree, but totally regardless of herself and him and everything around, and spurning her own attractions with her haughty brow and lip, as if they were a badge or livery she hated" (27). Cold as a "frozen statue," she, like Dombey, represses her feelings, especially her seething anger at being prostituted on the marriage market. "There is no slave in a market," she tells her mother, "there is no horse in a fair: so shown and offered and examined and paraded, mother, as I have been, for ten shameful years" (27). Edith challenges

Dombey's dominance, and their marriage becomes a protracted struggle for control. Her husband especially resents her relationship with Florence. Dombey humiliates Edith by employing Carker, his business manager, to negotiate the terms of their marriage. Edith humiliates Dombey by running away to France with Carker, and in turn humiliates Carker by rejecting his advances (54). At the end, Edith is an outcast sheltered in the house of Lord Feenix, but when Florence offers to seek Dombey's forgiveness for her, she refuses the offer and protests her innocence (61).

A complex character who prompts a feminist analysis of the Victorian patriarchy and its treatment of women, Edith is also treated conventionally in terms of the melodramatic stereotypes of the bought bride and the fallen woman. At her best, as in the scenes where she condemns her mother's pimping (27), Edith reveals a passionate cynicism that shapes her contentious relationship with her husband and raises her above the clichés of melodrama.

Doris Alexander (1991) argues that Edith is based on the notorious Mrs. Caroline Norton, accused by her husband of infidelity with Lord Melbourne, the prime minister. Although she was exonerated at trial, her reputation was permanently stained.

Dombey, Fanny   Dombey's first wife, mother of Florence and Paul, who, after giving birth to her son, "clinging fast to that slight spar within her arms, . . . drifted out upon the dark and unknown sea that rolls round all the world" (1).

Dombey, Florence (Floy)   Dombey's daughter, six years old at the time of her brother's birth: "There had been a girl some six years before. . . . But what was a girl to Dombey and Son! In the capital of the House's name and dignity, such a child was merely a piece of base coin that couldn't be invested—a bad Boy—nothing more" (1). Dombey neglects and abuses Florence, resenting the close relationship she has with her brother, and after Paul's death Dombey wishes that it had been Florence who died. Florence blames herself for his neglect and desperately wishes for his approval, hoping that Edith can show her the way to her father's heart, but her relationship with Edith merely increases Dombey's resentment of both of them. When Dombey strikes her a bruising blow (47), Florence runs away to the Wooden Midshipman and there is reunited with Walter Gay, whom she marries. She and her father are reconciled only after his business fails and he, a broken man, is nearly brought to suicide (59, 61).

If, as many commentators have suggested, *Dombey and Son* turns out to be the story of Dombey and daughter after all, then Florence is the central figure in the novel, a position complicated by what is often seen as the cloying sentimentality in her treatment. She is not presented realistically, as Dombey is, nor melodramatically, like Edith. She is, as KATHLEEN TILLOTSON (1956) and HARRY STONE (1979) have proposed, a creature out of fairy tale. She is the sleeping princess or the lost heir who is released from the spell cast upon her and restored to her rightful place. The fairy-tale mode, however, is complicated by its placement in the context of a realistic narrative anatomizing the contradictions within the Victorian patriarchy. LYN PYKETT (2002) points out that "Florence exposes some of the contradictions of the ideology of the separate masculine and feminine spheres, and of the contemporary worshipping of the angel in the house. Paradoxically, Florence is most hated by her father when she most closely approximates the Victorian feminine ideal of exerting moral influence and inspiring love and devotion through her own self-sacrificial love. Conversely, she is most loved by him, most influential in his moral redemption, and most effective as a domestic angel when she has rebelled against the law of the father, left the patriarchal home, married a man from a lower class, spent her honeymoon on a trading voyage to China, and helped her husband to build up his business—and, it should be added, when she has also become a mother, the mother of a son (another Paul, but crucially not another Dombey." HILARY SCHOR (1999) suggests that the transformation brought about in the novel is not that of Dombey but that of the daughter who is brought into accord with the expectations of the patriarchy: "The daughter here begins by being *alien* to the paternal order, outside of it. She must

come to understand that order through her passage through the mother's plot (in this case, the far more interesting plot of the stepmother, Edith Granger) and then, having left the father's house in disgrace and anger, return to it as domestic angel."

Dombey, Paul Current head of the firm Dombey and Son, a reserved, distant, and controlling man, whose wealth is a sign that he possesses the Dombey trait, characterized by his sister Mrs. Chick as "making an effort" (1). He is a model of patriarchy: "rather bald, rather red, and though a handsome, well-made man, too stern and pompous in appearance, to be prepossessing" (1). Dombey's inflated pride and self-importance derive from his position as Dombey of Dombey and Son: "Those three words conveyed the one idea of Mr. Dombey's life. The earth was made for Dombey and Son to trade in, and the sun and moon were made to give them light. Rivers and seas were formed to float their ships; rainbows gave them promise of fair weather; winds blew for or against their enterprises; stars and planets circled in their orbits, to preserve inviolate a system of which they were the centre. Common abbreviations took new meanings in his eyes, and had sole reference to them: A. D. had no concern with anno Domini, but stood for anno Dombey—and Son" (1). His pride is increased by the birth of a son and heir, but he despises his daughter, thinking her worthless, "a base coin." This misogyny extends to his first wife, whose death does not disturb him, for she has served her sole function of bearing him a male child; it extends further to the realm of feminine concerns—love, relationship, family—all of which he rejects. He marries Edith to get a son to replace the son he lost and to enhance the public display of his wealth and power. Dombey may seem blind to everything that does not confirm his arrogant, self-centered worldview, but, in his preface to the novel, Dickens contends that Dombey was aware of his denial and chose to live in bad faith: "Mr. Dombey undergoes no violent change, either in this book, or in real life. A sense of injustice is within him, all along. The more he represses it, the more unjust he necessarily is. Internal shame and external circumstances may bring the contest to a close in a week, or a day; but, it has been a contest for years, and is only fought out after a long balance of victory." Dombey's stubbornness causes Edith to leave and humiliate him, causes Florence to seek refuge with Cuttle (47), and enables Carker to ruin Dombey's business. Even after all these setbacks, Dombey resists admitting his culpability. He is saved by Florence's intervention only when it is almost too late.

Commentators debate about whether Dombey qualifies as a tragic figure. ALEXANDER WELSH (1987) compares him to King Lear, a tragic hero of the 19th century blinded by the adulation universally accorded to him as an important businessman. Others, however, find his stubborn arrogance a cover for his repressed awareness of the injustice of his position. His suffering is, in their view, deserved and not cathartic.

Dombey, Paul, Jr. Dombey's son, born in the opening chapter of the novel: "Dombey was about eight-and-forty years of age. Son about eight-and-forty minutes. Dombey was rather bald, rather red, and though a handsome well-made man, too stern and pompous in appearance, to be prepossessing. Son was very bald, and very red, and though (of course) an undeniably fine infant, somewhat crushed and spotty in his general effect, as yet. On the brow of Dombey, Time and his brother Care had set some marks, . . . while the countenance of Son was crossed and recrossed with a thousand little creases, which the same deceitful time would take delight in smoothing out and wearing away with the flat part of his scythe, as preparation of the surface for his deeper operations" (1). Dombey exults that his son will carry on the firm, but the sensitive and sickly boy, who has "a strange, old-fashioned, thoughtful way . . . of sitting brooding in his miniature armchair, when he looked (and talked) like one of those terrible beings in fairy tales, who, at a hundred and fifty or two hundred years of age, fantastically represent the children for whom they have been substituted" (8), cannot adapt to the monetary mundanity of the Dombey world. He disconcerts his nurse, Mrs. Pipchin, with his uncanny questions and comments and his father by questioning the value of money and why it failed to save his mother's life (8). As his health gradually declines, Paul spends an indifferent term at Dr. Blimber's Academy, listening to the tick-

ing of the clock rather than to Blimber's lectures on Greece and Rome. He prefers to listen to the waves by the sea and to the sea stories of Old Glubb. He returns to London an invalid, and, at age six, watching the waves of light play on the walls of his room, he dies, held in the loving arms of his sister (16).

From his birth Paul's old-fashioned ways reveal the imbalance in Dombey's world. He is a "wise child," a changeling old beyond his years. NEWSOM (2001) analyzes the accumulating meanings of the term "old fashioned" as they apply to Paul and reveal the limitations of his childish understanding of his situation and the world.

Feeder, Mr. B.A. Assistant master to Dr. Blimber, "he was a kind of human barrel-organ, with a little list of tunes, at which he was continually working over and over again, without any variation. He might have been fitted up with a change of barrels, perhaps, in early life, if his destiny had been favourable; but it had not been; and he had only one, with which, in a monotonous round, it was his occupation to bewilder the young ideas of Doctor Blimber's young gentlemen" (11). He drills the boys in Greek and Latin grammar. After Blimber retires, Feeder is married to Cornelia Blimber and takes over the management of the school.

Feenix, Lord (Cousin Feenix) Edith Dombey's aristocratic cousin, "a man about town forty years ago" (31), he now makes his home in Baden-Baden. He is fond of referring to such friends as Conversation Brown, Billy Jopler, Tommy Screwzer, and others in his conversation, assuming that his listeners will know these luminaries he talks about. He represents Edith's family at her wedding and takes her in after she leaves her husband (61).

Finchbury, Lady Jane Amateur painter mentioned by cousin Feenix, a "woman with tight stays" who has sketched the village church (41).

Flowers Mrs. Skewton's maid, who presides over the mysteries of "Cleopatra's" cosmetics and dress.

"Game Chicken, The" Boxer employed by Mr. Toots to teach him to fight by "knocking him about the head three times a week for the small consideration of ten and six a visit" (22).

Gay, Walter Sol Gills's nephew, "a cheerful looking, merry boy, . . . fair-faced, bright-eyed, and curly-haired" (4). He is employed by the House of Dombey as a junior clerk and is instrumental in returning Florence to her home after she is abducted by Mrs. Brown (6), an act that earns him the friendship of young Paul and the displeasure of Mr. Dombey. At the instigation of James Carker, who fears Walter as a rival for Florence's affections, Dombey sends Walter to Barbados (13), but the ship, *Son and Heir,* is lost at sea. Unwilling to give up hope, Sol Gills goes off in search of Walter, who has survived the wreck. He returns to London (49), marries Florence (57), and goes to sea again with his bride. When they return, Dombey, a ruined and broken old man, lives with them and loves their children.

Dickens originally intended to make Walter's story that of "the idle apprentice," and, as he wrote to JOHN FORSTER, "to show him gradually and naturally trailing away, from a love of adventure and boyish light-heartedness, into negligence, idleness, dissipation, dishonesty, and ruin." Forster apparently advised him otherwise, for Walter enacts a positive version of the DICK WHITTINGTON legend. Julian Moynahan (1962) finds Walter unconvincing, "simply not of executive caliber."

Gills, Solomon (Old Sol) Walter Gay's uncle and the proprietor of The Wooden Midshipman, a nautical instrument shop, "a slow, quiet spoken, thoughtful old fellow, with eyes as red as if they had been small suns looking at you through the fog. . . . He wore a very precise shirt-frill, and carried a pair of first-rate spectacles on his forehead, and a tremendous chronometer in his fob, rather than doubt which precious possession, he would have believed in a conspiracy against it on the part of all the clocks and watches in the City, and even of the very Sun itself" (4). This old-fashioned dress suggests that Sol is past his time. When his old-fashioned instrument business fails, Walter borrows money from Mr. Dombey to res-

cue his uncle (10). When Walter is lost at sea, Sol goes off in search of him, leaving Captain Cuttle, his closest friend, in charge of the shop (25). Sol comes back after a long absence to find that Walter has returned and is about to marry Florence (56). In the end, Sol makes Cuttle his partner in the business.

Sol and the group at the Wooden Midshipman constitute an alternative "family" to the many dysfunctional families in the novel, especially the Dombeys. Their association with water (Gills, Cuttle) enables them to know what the waves are saying, and their "old fashioned" business also connects them with the natural and organic as opposed to the mechanistic and linear. The bonds between the members of the Wooden Midshipman group are bonds of love, not of commodification.

Glubb, Old The old sailor—"a weazen, old, crab-faced man, in a suit of battered oilskin, who had got tough and stringy from long pickling in salt water, and who smelt like a weedy sea-beach when the tide is out" (8)—who pushes Paul's invalid chair and tells him stories of the sea. His name identifies him as one of the water creatures who speaks to Paul's old-fashioned desire to understand what the waves are saying.

Granger, Edith Edith Dombey's name before she marries Mr. Dombey.

Howler, the Reverend Melchisedech Evangelical preacher who acts as Mrs. MacStinger's spiritual guide and performs the wedding ceremony when she marries Bunsby (60): He "announced the destruction of the world for that day two years, at ten in the morning, and opened a front-parlour for the reception of ladies and gentlemen of the Ranting persuasion" (15).

Jemima Polly Toodle's unmarried sister who takes over the care of Polly's children when Polly goes to work for the Dombeys (2, 6).

John An unemployed laborer, pitied by Florence. During her visit to the Skettles, Florence observes him, especially noting his kindness to his unresponsive daughter, and she compares this loving father to her own (24).

Johnson One of Dr. Blimber's pupils, who disrupts the doctor's lecture on the Romans with convulsive fits of coughing (12).

Johnson, Tom Acquaintance of Cousin Feenix, the "man with cork leg from White's" (41).

Kate An orphan girl who visits the Skettles' house in FULHAM when Florence is staying there. She is loved by the aunt who cares for her and wonders why Florence's father neglects her (24).

"Larkey Boy, The" Prizefighter who demolishes "The Game Chicken" (44).

Leamington Dickens and Hablot Knight Browne stayed at Copps's Royal Hotel at this spa in Warwickshire in 1838. Dombey and Major Bagstock have the same accommodations when Dombey meets Edith Granger (20).

Long's Hotel Fashionable hotel in BOND STREET where Cousin Feenix stays (31).

MacStinger, Alexander Mrs. MacStinger's infant son, given to fits of crying so much that he "passed a piebald childhood, forasmuch as he was black in the face during one half of that fairy period of existence" (39).

MacStinger, Charles ("Chowley") Mrs. MacStinger's elder son.

MacStinger, Juliana Mrs. MacStinger's daughter, "the image of her parent," who observes the wedding of her mother to Captain Bunsby with such intense concentration that Cuttle "saw in this a succession of man-traps stretching out infinitely; a series of ages of oppression and coercion, through which the seafaring line was doomed" (60).

MacStinger, Mrs. Captain Cuttle's landlady, "a widow lady, with her sleeves rolled up to her shoulders, and her arms frothy with soap-suds and smok-

ing with hot water" (9), who holds Cuttle captive at 9 Brig Place near the India Docks, terrifying him with her matrimonial intentions. After he escapes to the Wooden Midshipman (25), she tracks him down, but he is saved by Captain Bunsby, who eventually marries her (60).

Martha "Ugly, misshapen, peevish, ill-conditioned," but "best-beloved" daughter of John, the laborer whom Florence meets while she is at the Skettleses' (24).

Marwood, Alice Alias used by Alice Brown. The name suggests a connection with Millwood, the courtesan who corrupts George Barnwell, the hero of GEORGE LILLO's *The London Merchant* (1731).

'Melia A maid at Doctor Blimber's Academy who is kind to young Paul: "a pretty young woman in leather gloves, cleaning a stove. The young woman seemed surprised at his appearance and asked him where his mother was. When Paul told her she was dead, she took her gloves off, and did what he wanted [helped him dress]; and furthermore rubbed his hands to warm them; and gave him a kiss; and told him whenever he wanted anything of that sort—meaning in the dressing way—to ask for 'Melia (12).

Miff, Mrs. Attendant and pew opener in the church where Dombey is married, "a mighty dry old lady, sparely dressed, with not an inch of fulness anywhere about her"; she has a "vinegary face . . . and a mortified bonnet, and eke a thirsty soul for sixpences and shillings" (31).

Morfin, Mr. Assistant manager, "an officer of inferior state," at Dombey and Son, "a cheerful-looking hazel-eyed bachelor: gravely attired, as to his upper man, in black; and as to his legs, in pepper-and-salt colour. His dark hair was just touched here and there with specks of grey" (13). A loyal member of the firm, but not a flatterer or deceiver like James Carker, Morfin anonymously offers aid to John Carker (33) and eventually marries Harriet Carker.

Native, the   Joey Bagstock's servant, "a dark servant . . . who Miss Tox was quite content to classify as a 'native,' without connecting him with any geographical idea whatever" (7). He is treated with contempt and is physically abused by the Major. Although he has only an incidental role in the novel, many postcolonial commentators see in him a trenchant criticism of British imperialism.

Nipper, Susan ("Spitfire")   Florence Dombey's sharp-tongued maid: "a short brown womanly girl of fourteen, with a little snub nose, and black eyes like jet beads . . . who was so desperately sharp and biting, that she seemed to make one's eyes water" (3). A loving defender of Florence in the Dombey household, Susan is nonetheless "a disciple of that school of trainers of the young idea which holds that childhood, like money, must be shaken and rattled and jostled about a good deal to keep it bright" (3). When she speaks up for Florence to Mr. Dombey, she is discharged (44), but she later returns to Florence's service. She marries Mr. Toots (60).

Oxford Market   Dombey's footman Towlinson hopes to lead "an altered and blameless existence as a serious greengrocer" at this market north of Oxford Street between Great Tichfield Street and Great Portland Street (18).

Pankey, Miss   Paul Dombey's fellow boarder at Mrs. Pipchin's, "a mild little blue-eyed morsel of a child, who was shampoo'd every morning" (8).

Peckham   South London suburb, east of Camberwell, where Walter Gay attends a weekly boarding school (4) and Mr. Feeder plans to board with his two maiden aunts while he explores "the dark mysteries of London" (14).

Peps, Dr. Parker   Doctor with an "immense reputation for assisting at the increase of great families" who attends Paul Dombey's birth and death (1, 16).

Perch   Messenger for Dombey and Son, "whose place was on a little bracket, like a time-piece" (13)

outside Dombey's office. He is so deferential and accommodating to Mr. Dombey that "if he might have laid himself at Mr. Dombey's feet, or might have called him by some such title as used to be bestowed upon the Caliph Haroun Alraschid, he would have been all the better pleased" (13). After the fall of the house of Dombey, Perch continues to perform his former duties in spite of Dombey's absence, and he recounts his somewhat fictional version of the events that led to the changes at the firm to those who will ply him with drinks to hear his tearful account (58).

Perch, Mrs.   Perch's wife, who presides over the Perch household at BALL'S POND and raises their many children. She interests herself in the below-stairs gossip in the Dombey household.

Pilkins   Dombey family physician who calls in Dr. Parker Peps for consultation (1, 8).

Pipchin, Mrs.   Ogress and child queller who operates a children's boarding house in Brighton, where Paul and Florence Dombey are sent to stay; "a marvellous ill-favoured, ill-conditioned old lady, of a stooping figure, with a mottled face, like bad marble, a hook nose, and a hard grey eye, that looked as if it might have been hammered at on an anvil without sustaining injury. Forty years at least had elapsed since the Peruvian mines had been the death of Mr. Pipchin; but his relict still wore black bombazeen, of such a lusterless, deep, dead, somber shade, that gas itself couldn't light her up after dark, and her presence was a quencher to any number of candles. She was generally spoken of as 'a great manager' of children; and the secret of her management was, to give them everything they didn't like, and nothing that they did" (8). However, she fails to intimidate young Paul, who surprises and disconcerts her with his direct and innocent questions (9). After his marriage to Edith, Mr. Dombey hires Mrs. Pipchin as his housekeeper (42). After Dombey's fall, she returns to her ogress's castle and child-quelling business in Brighton (59). Mrs. Pipchin is based on ELIZABETH ROYLANCE, Dickens's landlady in London when his father was in the MARSHALSEA PRISON.

Princess's Place The mews in London's fashionable West End where Miss Tox and Joey Bagstock live across the way from each other (7).

Queen Charlotte's Hospital Miss Tox inquires at this maternity hospital in Marylebone Road when seeking a wet nurse for Paul Dombey (2).

"Richards" The name Dombey assigns to Polly Toodle when she is working in his household. The name denies her individuality and womanliness, even though she is employed to be a wet nurse for young Paul.

Robinson Clerk in Dombey's counting house (51).

"Rob the Grinder" Nickname of Robin Toodle, derived from his attendance at the school of the Charitable Grinders.

Saxby, Long A tall friend—"six foot ten"—of Cousin Feenix (51).

Screwzer, Tommy One of Cousin Feenix's many acquaintances—a "man of an extremely bilious habit" (61).

Skettles, Barnet, Jr. Son of Barnet Skettles who is to be a pupil at Doctor Blimber's Academy in the term following Paul's departure; "he did not appear to Paul to be particularly happy, or particularly anything but sulky" (14).

Skettles, Sir Barnet, M.P. Pompous and imposing member of Parliament who "expressed his personal consequence chiefly through an antique gold snuff-box, and a ponderous silk pocket-handkerchief, which he had an imposing manner of drawing out of his pocket like a banner, and using with both hands at once. Sir Barnet's object in life was constantly to extend the range of his acquaintance" (24). He and Lady Skettles invite Florence to stay with them in Fulham after Paul's death while Mr. Dombey is in Leamington (24).

Skewton, the Hon. Mrs. ("Cleopatra") Edith Dombey's mother, a woman of 70 who is pushed about in a wheeled chair. "The discrepancy between Mrs. Skewton's fresh enthusiasm of words, and forlornly faded manner, was hardly less observable than that between her age, which was about seventy, and her dress, which would have been youthful for twenty-seven. Her attitude in the wheeled chair (which she never varied) was one in which she had been taken in a barouche, some 50 years before, by a then fashionable artist who had appended to his published sketch the name of Cleopatra: in consequence of a discovery made by the critics of the time, that it bore an exact resemblance to that Princess as she reclined on board her galley" (21). She repeatedly protests that she is "inspired by the sight of nature" as she settles "her false curls and false eyebrows with her fan, and showing her false teeth, set off by her false complexion" (21). She is all artifice, turning herself into a painted object, just as she turns her daughter into an object and peddles her on the marriage market.

Mrs. Skewton contributes another variation on the theme of turning human beings into objects. Like Dombey, who objectifies Florence as a "base coin," Mrs. Skewton turns herself into a painted work of "art," a Cleopatra, and her daughter into a woman peddled on the marriage market. Edith's role as a "frozen statue" symbolizes her objectification.

Mrs. Skewton is doubled with Good Mrs. Brown, making explicit the connection between literal pimping and prostitution and the allegedly more polite versions in the marriage market.

Smalder Girls, the Acquaintances of Cousin Feenix (47).

Son and Heir, the Ship on which Walter Gay sails to Barbados; it sinks on the way (13, 32).

Sownds "Portentous" beadle at the church where Paul Dombey is christened (5) and his father married (31).

Stagg's Gardens Fictitious area in Camden Town where the Toodles family live amidst the chaos of railway construction. Although the inhabitants consider it "a sacred grove not to be withered by railroads" (6), the area is so utterly transformed that when Susan Nipper seeks out Polly's house a few years after her first visit there, it seems to have "vanished from the earth" (15) in the wake of the railroad.

Toodle, Mr. "Apple-faced" husband of Polly Toodle, "a strong, loose, round-shouldered, shuffling, shaggy fellow" (2) who works as a stoker on the new railway and later becomes an engine driver. He arouses Mr. Dombey's class snobbery when he presumes to express his condolences to Dombey after Paul's death and compares it to his own loss of a child (20).

In the historical scheme that informs the novel, Toodle represents the new class of working men who control the new railway, a class that will displace the old mercantile class (Dombey) and the managerial class (James Carker). The vitality and warmth of the relationships in this working-class family contrast with the cold, emotionless calculations of the Dombeys and the Carkers.

Toodle, Polly ("Richards") Paul Dombey's wet nurse; "a plump, rosy-cheeked wholesome apple-faced young woman" (2) who is hired by Dombey on the conditions that she take the name Richards and sever all connection with the Dombey family after she leaves (2). She is dismissed when she endangers Paul by taking him with her when she visits her family (6). On his deathbed Paul asks to see Polly again (16). Polly is employed to tend Dombey after he is ruined (59).

Commentators dispute whether Mrs. Hayes, a servant in the household of Dickens's sister, Fanny (*see* DICKENS, FRANCES ELIZABETH) was the original for Polly.

Toodle, Robin ("Rob the Grinder," "Biler") Eldest of the five Toodle children, he is placed in the Charitable Grinders School by Mr. Dombey (5). A "youth of the streets," Biler resents having to wear the uniform of the Grinders School. He later becomes a servant for James Carker, spying on Gills and Cuttle for him.

Toots Oldest student at Blimber's Academy, who, "when he began to have whiskers, left off having

brains" (11). Obsessed with clothes and boxing, Toots aspires to become a young man of fashion; he repeatedly remarks, "It's of no consequence." Although slow-witted, Toots is a gentle and loving friend to Paul and Florence. He brings the dog Diogenes to Florence after Paul's death and falls hopelessly in love with her. In the end he settles for Susan Nipper and regards her as a "most extraordinary woman" (62). He and Susan have three children: Florence, Susan, and another daughter. DORIS ALEXANDER (1991) identifies HENRY BURNETT, husband to Dickens's sister Fanny, as the original for Toots.

Towlinson, Thomas Dombey's footman who leaves the Dombey household after Dombey's ruin, marries Anne the maid, and enters the grocery business.

Tox, Lucretia Spinster friend of Mrs. Chick, "a long, lean figure, wearing such a faded air, that she seemed not to have been made in what linen-drapers call 'fast colours' originally, and to have, by little and little, washed out" (1). Although her neighbor, Joey Bagstock, flatters himself that she has designs on him, she transfers her interest to Mr. Dombey after he becomes a widower. She finds Polly Toodle as a nurse for young Paul (2) and attends his christening, but she faints when she learns of Dombey's marriage (29). Disowned by Mrs. Chick for her presumption and banished from the Dombey household, Miss Tox nonetheless remains loyal to Dombey and his children. Miss Tox's sincere emotional attachment to Dombey and his children serves as a pathetic contrast to the many relationships in Dombey's world based only on power and money.

Tozer Paul Dombey's roommate at Blimber's Academy, "a solemn young gentleman, whose shirt-collar curled up the lobes of his ears" (12).

Warwick Castle Dombey makes an excursion to this castle south of Coventry with Edith Granger and Mrs. Skewton (27). Dickens visited the castle with Hablot Knight Browne in 1838.

Wickam, Mrs. Paul Dombey's nurse after Polly Toodle is dismissed, "a meek woman . . . who was always ready to pity herself, or to be pitied, or to pity anybody else; and who had a surprising natural gift of viewing all subjects in an utterly forlorn and pitiable light" (8). She later nurses Alice Brown in her last illness (58).

Wiggs and Co.   Owners of the ill-fated ship *Polyphemus* in one of the sea stories recounted by Walter Gay (4).

Withers   "Tall, and wan, and thin" page who pushes Mrs. Skewton's wheeled chair (21).

ADAPTATIONS

The first play from the novel, T. P. Taylor's *Dombey and Son, or Good Mrs. Brown the Child Stealer* (1847), appeared in London when the novel had completed only half of its serial run; a male actor played Mrs. Brown. W. Sydney's *Dombey and Son* (1849), produced after the completion of the novel, nonetheless amplified the story by adding three visions of Christmas to it. Early American adaptations usually featured Captain Cuttle. W. E. Burton's performance of the part in JOHN BROUGHAM's adaptation (1848) was popular for more than two decades; other adaptations, including ANDREW HALLIDAY's popular *Heart's Delight* (1873), gave similar prominence to the Captain.

Two silent films were based on the novel: the very early *What Are the Wild Waves Saying Sister?* (1903) and *Dombey and Son* (1917), adapted by Eliot Stannard. A sound film, *Rich Man's Folly* (1931), directed by John Cromwell and adapted by Grover Jones and Edward Paramore Jr., modernized the story, making Dombey into a rich shipbuilder.

The BBC produced a 13-episode television version written by Hugh Leonard in 1969, and a 10-part serial adapted by James Andrew Hall in 1983.

Sir Harry Johnston's novel *The Gay-Dombeys* (1919), in which the title figures are descendants of Dickens's characters, derives many of its characters from *Dombey* and other Dickens novels.

FURTHER READING

KATHLEEN TILLOTSON (1954; 1957) describes Dickens's careful planning and composition of the novel and the resulting unity in theme, character,

and incident. STEVEN MARCUS (1965) treats the novel as "a comprehensive, unified presentation of social life by depicting how an abstract principle conditions all experience. That principle is change, and the novel's key words, so to speak, are change, alteration and time." RAYMOND WILLIAMS (Introduction, 1970) discusses the historical context of these changes as expressed in the novel, seeing Dickens's characters and incidents as expressions of a popular urban culture. HARRY STONE (1979) analyzes the images and motifs from fairy tales that run through the novel as part of a much fuller and more integrated use of such materials than in the earlier novels. SUSAN HORTON (1979) employs *Dombey* as a case study in which she explores the role of the reader in the process of interpretation. Denis Donoghue ("The English Dickens and *Dombey and Son*," *Nineteenth Century Fiction*, 1970) considers the novel in Wordsworthian terms as a celebration of the primacy of feeling. Nina Auerbach's feminist analysis ("Dickens and Dombey, a Daughter after All," *Dickens Studies Annual*, 1976) discusses the novel as an exploration of the separation between male and female spheres and suggests that Dickens failed to connect the two, arriving in the end only at a "troubled, tragic awareness of the gulf between the sexes." HILARY SCHOR (1999) expands this feminist analysis in a reading that centers on Florence's thematic and structural roles in the novel.

Great Expectations

Dickens's 13th novel, published in 36 weekly parts in ALL THE YEAR ROUND (December 1, 1860–August 3, 1861), unillustrated. Published in three volumes by CHAPMAN & HALL, 1861. A BILDUNGSROMAN narrated in the first person by its hero, *Great Expectations* recalls *David Copperfield*, but Pip's story is more tightly organized than David's and Pip is more aware of his shortcomings. Pip tells his story in three equal parts, casting his life as a journey in three stages: his childhood and youth in KENT, when he wishes he could overcome his humble origins and rise in the world; his young manhood in London after he receives his great expectations; and his disillusionment when he learns the source of his good fortune and realizes the emptiness of his worldly values. The novel's concise narration, balanced structure, and rich symbolism have made it the most admired and most discussed of Dickens's works.

SYNOPSIS

Stage I

Part 1 (December 1, 1860)

(1) Philip Pirrip, known as "Pip," remembers the day when he was seven and gained his "first most vivid and broad impression of the identity of things." Then, while visiting the graves of his parents in the churchyard on a dreary Christmas Eve, the child Pip is surprised by an escaped convict who threatens to kill him if he does not bring him food and a file. (2) Back at the house of his sister, who has brought him up "by hand," Pip is punished for getting home late for supper, but he has the sympathetic companionship of his sister's husband, Joe Gargery the blacksmith. At supper Pip secretly saves his bread, and early on Christmas morning, after taking a pork pie and some brandy from the larder and a file from the forge, he slips out of the house and onto the marshes.

Part 2 (December 8, 1860)

(3) There he is surprised by another escaped convict, a young man with a scar on his face. When he finds the ragged man who scared him the day before, Pip watches compassionately as he devours the food and files the manacle from his leg, but he arouses the convict's anger when he tells him of the other escapee on the marshes. (4) At Christmas dinner, while he guiltily awaits the discovery of the theft from the larder, Pip is admonished by his Uncle Pumblechook and the other guests to "be grateful" and to overcome the tendency of boys to be "naterally wicious." As his sister goes to the larder to fetch the pork pie that he stole for the convict, a troop of soldiers appears at the door.

Part 3 (December 15, 1860)

(5) The soldiers ask Joe to repair some handcuffs. Then Joe and Pip follow them as they pursue the convicts. The two escapees are captured as they fight with each other on the marshes. Before he is returned to the prison ship anchored in the Thames, Pip's convict confesses to stealing some food from Mrs. Joe's larder. Joe forgives him, saying, "We don't know what you have done, but we wouldn't have you starved to death for it, poor miserable fellow-creatur.—Would us, Pip?"

Part 4 (December 22, 1860)

(6) Pip is unable to tell Joe the truth about the theft from the larder. (7) As he awaits the time when he will be apprenticed to Joe, Pip gets some rudimentary education from Mr. Wopsle's great aunt and her granddaughter Biddy, enough to realize that Joe cannot read. Then, about a year after the convict episode, Mrs. Joe announces that her Uncle Pumblechook has arranged for Pip to play at the house of Miss Havisham, a rich recluse in the nearby market town.

Part 5 (December 29, 1860)

(8) Pumblechook delivers the boy to Satis House the next morning. There Pip meets Estella, a supercilious young woman not much older than he, and Miss Havisham, an old woman in a tattered bridal dress, inhabiting rooms in the ruined house where everything is yellowed with age and all the clocks have stopped at 20 minutes to nine. Miss Havisham orders Pip and Estella to play cards and urges

Estella, Pip, and Miss Havisham, as portrayed in the 1946 movie adaptation of *Great Expectations. Courtesy of PhotoFest.*

Estella to break Pip's heart. Pip fights back tears when Estella ridicules him as coarse and common, and he escapes into the garden to cry. There he has a sudden vision of Miss Havisham in the abandoned brewery, hanging from a beam and calling to him.

Part 6 (January 5, 1861)

(9) When Pumblechook and Mrs. Joe ask about Miss Havisham, Pip caters to their imaginings by telling them a fantastic tale about a black velvet coach, four dogs, and a silver basket of veal cutlets. Later he confesses to Joe that he made up the story because he felt "common," but Joe assures him that he is "oncommon small" and an "oncommon scholar." (10) Pip enlists Biddy's help in teaching him to be "uncommon." One Saturday evening, Pip finds Joe at the Jolly Bargeman with a "secret-looking" stranger who stirs his drink with a file and gives Pip a shilling wrapped up in two one-pound notes. Pip fears that his connection with the convict will come to light.

Part 7 (January 12, 1861)

(11) When Pip returns to Miss Havisham's, her relatives have gathered at Satis House for her birthday. Estella insults him, slaps him, and dares him to tell. Miss Havisham shows him a table spread with a decaying feast, including the remains of a wedding cake, where she will be laid out when she dies. She points out the places her relatives will occupy at this table when she is dead. Again she orders Pip to play cards with Estella and to admire her beauty. When he goes out into the garden, Pip meets a pale young gentleman there who challenges him to fight. Pip reluctantly enters the match, but he knocks the young man to the ground and gives him a black eye. After the fight, Estella invites him to kiss her.

Part 8 (January 19, 1861)

(12) Pip's visits to Satis House become more frequent. He pushes Miss Havisham around her rooms in a wheelchair and plays cards with Estella as the old lady murmurs, "Break their hearts, my pride and hope!" One day, Miss Havisham, noting that Pip is growing tall, asks him to bring Joe Gargery to Satis House. (13) Two days later, in his Sunday clothes, Joe accompanies Pip to Miss Havisham's. She asks Joe whether Pip has ever objected to becoming a

blacksmith and if Joe expects a premium for taking Pip on as an apprentice. Joe, speaking through Pip, replies no to both questions, but she gives him 25 guineas anyway to pay for Pip's apprenticeship. The Gargerys celebrate the occasion with a dinner at the Blue Boar, but Pip is wretched, convinced he will never like Joe's trade.

Part 9 (January 26, 1861)

(14) Pip does not tell Joe of his unhappiness, but as he works at the forge he remembers his former visits to Satis House and sees visions of Estella's face in the fire. (15) Although Joe advises against it, Pip takes a half-holiday to visit Miss Havisham. His fellow worker, Dolge Orlick, a surly and contrary man, envies Pip and demands equal time off, but when he offends Joe with some derogatory remarks about Mrs. Joe, the blacksmith knocks him to the ground. At Satis House, Pip learns that Estella has gone abroad to be educated. Miss Havisham tells him that he can visit her each year on his birthday, but he is to expect nothing from her. Back at the forge, he discovers that someone has broken into the house and Mrs. Joe has been knocked senseless by an unknown assailant.

Part 10 (February 2, 1861)

(16) The weapon was an old convict's leg-iron. Convinced that it is the manacle from his convict's leg, Pip feels guilty, as if he struck the blow himself. Mrs. Joe is left unable to speak and partly paralyzed, but she changes character and becomes good-tempered. Although Orlick is suspected of the crime, Mrs. Joe is conciliatory to him. Biddy, Pip's schoolmate and teacher, moves to the forge to take over housekeeping duties. (17) On his birthday Pip visits Miss Havisham, receives a guinea, and is told to come again next year. It becomes his regular custom. Meanwhile, Pip and Biddy develop a close friendship and he confesses to her his desire to become a gentleman "on Estella's account." She wisely asks him whether he wants "to be a gentleman, to spite her or to gain her over?" As Pip and Biddy walk through the countryside, Orlick follows them.

Part 11 (February 9, 1861)

(18) In the fourth year of his apprenticeship, Pip is surprised by Mr. Jaggers, Miss Havisham's law-

yer from London, who announces that Pip has "great expectations." If Joe will release him from his apprenticeship, Pip is to move to London and become a gentleman. He is to be known as Pip and not to ask the identity of his benefactor. Joe refuses any compensation for Pip's release, but there is a touch of sadness in his celebration of Pip's good fortune. (19) After they burn the apprenticeship papers, Pip talks of what he will do to raise Joe up. He bids farewell to Pumblechook, who takes credit for Pip's good fortune, and to Miss Havisham. After an awkward parting from Joe, Pip sets out for London.

Stage II

Part 12 (February 23, 1861)

(20) In London, Jaggers, a criminal lawyer, is to act as the representative of Pip's unnamed benefactor. At Jaggers's office near SMITHFIELD Market, Pip finds a host of shady characters clamoring for the lawyer's attention. While he waits, Pip visits NEW-GATE PRISON nearby. (21) Jaggers has his clerk, John Wemmick, take Pip to Barnard's Inn, where he is to stay with Herbert Pocket, the son of his tutor. When he meets Herbert, Pip recognizes him as the pale young gentleman he fought in Miss Havisham's garden.

Part 13 (March 2, 1861)

(22) Herbert teaches Pip the manners of a gentleman and nicknames him "Handel" (in honor of the composer's "Harmonious Blacksmith"). Herbert tells Pip of Estella, adopted by Miss Havisham to wreak vengeance on men. He also recounts the story of Miss Havisham's own past: The daughter of a wealthy brewer, she, with her half-brother, inherited their father's business. She fell in love with a fast-talking con-man who proposed to marry her and convinced her to buy her brother's share in the brewery at a high price. Then he split the proceeds with her brother and jilted her on her wedding day, the day she stopped the clocks at 20 minutes to nine and withdrew into Satis House.

Part 14 (March 9, 1861)

(23) At the home of Matthew Pocket, Herbert's father, who is to act as Pip's tutor, Pip meets his

fellow pupils: Drummle, a disagreeable young man from a wealthy family, and Startop, a delicate and friendly fellow. The Pocket household is in disarray. Matthew, educated at Harrow and Cambridge, is impractical and a poor manager; his wife Belinda, daughter of a knight, is obsessed with social position and pays no attention to housekeeping. (24) When Pip goes to secure Jaggers's approval for his plan to live at Barnard's Inn with Herbert, he has an opportunity to watch the lawyer's intimidating courtroom manner and to become further acquainted with Wemmick, Jaggers's clerk. Wemmick shows Pip the death masks of some of their former clients; advises him to "get hold of portable property"; and tells him, when he goes to Jaggers's house for dinner, to observe the housekeeper, whom he describes as "a wild beast tamed." He also invites Pip to visit his home in the suburbs.

Part 15 (March 16, 1861)

(25) Although some of the Pockets resent Pip, thinking that he has intruded on their rightful portion of Miss Havisham's fortune, Matthew, who has refused to curry favor with Miss Havisham, bears him no ill will. Pip's studies progress nicely. When he visits Wemmick at his home in WAL-WORTH, he finds him very different from the hard and materialistic clerk he met in the City. Wemmick lives in a bucolic little castle, surrounded by a moat, gardens, and animal pens, and he maintains a domestic establishment with his Aged Parent. Jaggers knows nothing of Wemmick's private life, for Wemmick's policy is to keep office and home totally separate. (26) When Pip goes to Jaggers's house for dinner with Startop and Drummle, the lawyer makes his housekeeper, Molly, display her strong and scarred wrists. Fascinated with Drummle, Jaggers calls him "the Spider" and provokes him to boast of his strength and to reveal his dislike for Pip. As they leave Jaggers advises Pip to keep clear of Drummle.

Part 16 (March 23, 1861)

(27) Joe visits Pip in London. Dressed uncomfortably in his best clothes and intimidated by Pip's formality and servant boy, he addresses his old companion as "sir." He tells Pip that Wopsle has

come to London to be an actor, that Estella has returned to Satis House and would be glad to see him, and that Pip is always welcome at the forge. Then he leaves. (28) Pip immediately sets out to see Estella. On the coach going to his hometown, he rides with two convicts, one of whom talks of once delivering two one-pound notes to a boy in the town. Pip is shaken by this coincidence. Once he is home, Pip decides to stay at the Blue Boar Inn rather than at the forge.

Part 17 (March 30, 1861)
(29) Pip is disturbed to find Orlick working as the porter at Satis House, but Estella is more beautiful than ever. She warns him that she has "no heart," but Miss Havisham urges him to "Love her, love her, love her!" Pip is convinced that Miss Havisham has chosen him for Estella. He is uneasy that he has not gone to visit Joe.

Part 18 (April 6, 1861)
(30) As Pip walks through town, the tailor's boy mocks his snobbery and elegance in the street by pretending not to know him. Pip warns Jaggers about Orlick, and the lawyer promises to dismiss him from Miss Havisham's service. Back in London, Pip confesses to a dubious Herbert that he loves Estella. Herbert reveals that he is secretly engaged to Clara Barley, the daughter of a ship's purser. (31) Pip and Herbert see Mr. Wopsle, the parish clerk from Pip's village who has ambitions for the stage, perform Hamlet. After the wretched but hilarious production, they invite the actor, whose stage name is Waldengarver, to dinner.

Part 19 (April 13, 1861)
(32) When Estella asks Pip to meet her coach in London, he arrives hours early. While he is waiting, Wemmick takes him through Newgate Prison. He returns just in time to see Estella's hand waving to him in the coach window. (33) She tells him that she is going to be introduced into society and that he may visit her in RICHMOND. Pip takes this as part of Miss Havisham's plan for them (33).

Part 20 (April 20, 1861)
(34) Pip falls into lavish spending habits. He and Herbert list their debts, but then, with the other members of their club, the Finches of the Grove,

they get even further into debt. When Pip learns that his sister has died (35), he returns home for the funeral. There Biddy tells him that his sister's last words were "Joe," "Pardon," and "Pip." Pip is annoyed when Biddy doubts his promise to come often to see Joe.

Part 21 (April 27, 1861)
(36) On his 21st birthday, Pip receives £500 from Jaggers to pay his debts. Jaggers says that he will receive the same sum each year until his benefactor reveals himself. Pip asks Wemmick to help him use some of the money to advance Herbert's prospects. When Wemmick gives his "deliberate opinion in this office" against doing so, Pip asks to solicit his opinion at home. (37) There Wemmick suggests that Pip buy Herbert a position with Clarriker, an up-and-coming shipping broker. Wemmick has Skiffins, his fiancée's brother, arrange it so that Herbert will not know the source of his good fortune.

Part 22 (May 4, 1861)
(38) Pip visits Estella frequently. Although she warns him to beware of her, she also drives him to jealous distraction. When the two of them visit Satis House, Miss Havisham delights to hear of Estella's conquests, but she accuses her of being cold and indifferent to her. "I am what you have made me," Estella replies, proud and hard. Unable to sleep that night, Pip observes Miss Havisham walking the halls of Satis House moaning. Back in London, he is outraged when Drummle toasts Estella at a meeting of the Finches. Pip warns her against him; she says that she is simply out to "deceive and entrap" him. Pip tells the story of the sultan who, at the height of his power, is crushed by a great stone from the roof of his palace, and Pip says that "the roof of [his] stronghold" is about to fall on him.

Part 23 (May 11, 1861)
(39) A week after his 23rd birthday, late on a stormy night while Herbert is away, Pip is surprised by someone calling his name on the stairs outside his door. It is a man about 60 years old with iron-grey hair, dressed like a sea voyager. When the man holds out his hands, as if to embrace him, Pip recog-

nizes the convict from the marshes. He has been a sheep farmer in New South Wales and reveals that he is the source of Pip's expectations. The convict looks about Pip's rooms with the pride of ownership, especially at his gentleman. "I'm your second father," he tells Pip, but Pip is horrified and speechless and troubled by knowing that the convict will be hanged if he is discovered in England. Gradually he realizes that all his ideas about Miss Havisham and Estella were a dream and that he deserted Joe and Biddy to be linked with a criminal.

Stage III

Part 24 (May 18, 1861)

(40) The next morning Pip learns that his benefactor is Abel Magwitch, going by the name Provis, and that he has returned to England for good, even though he will be sentenced to death should he be caught. Pip dresses him like a prosperous farmer and secures rooms for him in a nearby lodging house. Jaggers confirms Magwitch's identity as Pip's benefactor by not denying it; the lawyer says that he warned Magwitch not to return to England. When Herbert returns to London, Magwitch swears him to silence.

Part 25 (May 25, 1861)

(41) Pip and Herbert agree that Pip should take no more of Magwitch's money and that Magwitch must be gotten out of England. (42) Magwitch tells them the story of his life: about 20 years earlier he became an accomplice of a gentleman named Compeyson, a forger and swindler who, with a Mr. Arthur, had just bilked a rich lady of her fortune. Arthur, near death at the time, had nightmares about a woman in white who tried to cover him with a shroud. When Magwitch and Compeyson were arrested and tried for their crimes, Magwitch was sentenced to 14 years. Compeyson, presenting himself as a gentleman, received a light sentence, and Magwich resentfully vowed revenge. Finding himself on the same prison ship with Compeyson, he struck him, scarring his face, and then escaped from the ship, only to learn that Compeyson had also escaped. In ensuring Compeyson's recapture, Magwitch was also taken and sentenced to transportation for life. He does not know what happened to Compeyson. After hearing the story, Herbert tells Pip that Arthur was Miss Havisham's brother and Compeyson her lover.

Part 26 (June 1, 1861)

(43) Pip returns home to see Estella. At the Blue Boar, he finds Drummle attended by Orlick. Drummle is also there to see Estella. (44) Pip accusingly tells Miss Havisham and Estella of his benefactor. Miss Havisham admits to leading him on, but tells him he made his own snares. She justifies her actions as a way of tormenting her avaricious relatives. Pip pours out his love for Estella, but she says he touches nothing in her breast and tells him that she plans to marry Drummle. Distraught, Pip walks back to London, arriving late at night. The watchman at the gate to his rooms has a note for him from Wemmick. It reads, "Don't go home."

Part 27 (June 8, 1861)

(45) After a restless night in a hotel, Pip learns from Wemmick that his rooms are being watched by Compeyson and that he must get Provis out of the country. (46) Pip arranges with Provis, now known as Mr. Campbell, to watch for him as he rows on the river. He and Herbert plan to keep a boat at the Temple stairs and to make a regular practice of rowing up the Thames. When the time is right, they will get the convict from his hiding place and take him to the Continent.

Part 28 (June 15, 1861)

(47) As Pip waits for the signal from Wemmick that the time has come to take Magwitch out of the country, he and Herbert regularly row down the river. One evening after attending one of Wopsle's dramatic performances, Pip learns from the actor that the second convict taken on the marshes was sitting behind him in the theater. Pip knows that Compeyson is watching him, and he writes to Wemmick of the growing danger. (48) During dinner at Jaggers's house, Pip notices Molly's hands. They remind him of Estella's hand as she waved from the coach window on her arrival in London. Wemmick tells him what he knows of Molly's story: that she was tried for the strangulation murder of a woman much larger than herself; that Jaggers concealed the strength of her hands during the

trial and argued that she was physically incapable of the crime; that she was suspected of destroying her three-year-old daughter at the time of the trial to avenge herself on the father; and that, after her acquittal, she went to work for Jaggers.

Part 29 (June 22, 1861)

(49) Pip goes to Satis House to learn more of Estella's story. A remorseful Miss Havisham tells Pip how she took the child supplied by Jaggers and turned the girl's heart to ice, that she knows nothing of Estella's parentage, and that Estella is now married and in Paris. She supplies Pip with money to pay for Herbert's position with Clarriker's and asks him to forgive her. As he walks in the ruined garden outside the house, Pip again sees the vision of Miss Havisham hanging from a beam. When he returns to bid her farewell, her dress is suddenly set afire by the flames in her grate. Pip extinguishes the flames, burning his hands in the process. That evening, as he leaves for London, the seriously injured old woman mutters distractedly, "What have I done?" (50) Herbert cares for Pip's burns and tells him what he has learned of Magwitch's story: Magwitch had a daughter of whom he was fond, but he lost touch with her when he went into hiding during the trial of the child's mother. Compeyson controlled him by threatening to reveal his whereabouts to the authorities. The child, had she lived, would be about Pip's age. Pip is sure that Magwitch is Estella's father.

Part 30 (June 29, 1861)

(51) Pip challenges Jaggers to confirm his suspicion about Estella's parentage. Jaggers obliquely does so, telling Pip that he hoped to save one of the many lost children by giving Estella to Miss Havisham. Jaggers asserts that it will do no one any good—not Molly, nor Magwitch, nor Estella—to reveal the truth now, and he advises Pip to keep his "poor dreams" to himself. (52) When Wemmick signals that the time has come to smuggle Magwitch to the continent, Pip's hands are still too badly burned to row the boat. He enlists Startop's aid. Before they can set out, however, Pip receives a mysterious letter telling him to come that evening to the limekiln on the marshes near his former home if he wants "information regarding *your uncle Provis.*"

Part 31 (July 6, 1861)

(53) In the dark sluice house, Pip is suddenly attacked and bound by a noose. The attacker is Orlick, who plans to kill him. Orlick accuses Pip of causing him to lose his job with Miss Havisham and of coming between him and Biddy. He admits that he struck Mrs. Joe with the manacle, but claims "it warn't Old Orlick as did it; it was you." He knows about Magwitch. As he is about to strike Pip with a hammer, Startop, Herbert, and Trabb's Boy come to the rescue. Exhausted and ill from the ordeal, Pip is now very concerned about Magwitch's safety.

Part 32 (July 13, 1861)

(54) The next morning, Pip, Startop, and Herbert set out on the river. After picking up Magwitch, they go to an isolated inn to spend the night before rowing out to meet the Hamburg packet steamer the next morning. Pip is uneasy when he sees two men examining their boat. The next morning, they are followed by another boat and ordered to turn over Abel Magwitch. Compeyson is in the other boat. In the confusion that follows, Compeyson and Magwitch go overboard, locked in struggle. Only Magwitch surfaces. Afterward, Pip accompanies Magwitch, injured and having difficulty breathing, back to London. He no longer feels any aversion to the wretched man who holds his hand in his. Pip knows that all Magwitch's property will be forfeited to the Crown.

Part 33 (July 20, 1861)

(55) Magwitch's trial is set for a month from the time of his arrest. Meanwhile, Herbert, now a shipping broker, prepares to go to Egypt, where he will be in charge of Clarriker's Cairo office. He offers Pip a clerk's position there. Jaggers and Wemmick both deplore Pip's failure to secure Magwitch's property. Wemmick invites Pip to breakfast at Walworth. Afterward, they walk to a country church, where Wemmick and Miss Skiffins are married in an apparently impromptu ceremony. (56) Pip visits Magwitch daily in the prison hospital and holds his hand at the trial when he is condemned to hang. But Magwitch is gravely ill and dies with Pip at his side before the sentence is carried out. On his deathbed, he thanks Pip for not deserting him. Pip tells him that his daughter lives and that he loves her.

Part 34 (July 27, 1861)

(57) Pip, deeply in debt, is very ill. When the arresting officers come, he is delerious and loses consciousness. He awakens from the fever to discover Joe, gentle as an angel, caring for him. As he slowly recuperates he learns from Joe that Miss Havisham has died, leaving all of her property to Estella except for £4,000 left to Matthew Pocket. He also learns that Orlick is in jail for assaulting Pumblechook. As Pip recovers, Joe becomes more distant. After Joe returns home, Pip learns that Joe has paid his debts. Pip considers his options: to return to the forge and ask Biddy to take him back or to go to Cairo to work with Herbert.

Part 35 (August 3, 1861)

(58) No longer a man of property, Pip gets a cool reception at the Blue Boar and from Pumblechook. When he returns to the forge, he discovers that it is Joe and Biddy's wedding day. He asks their forgiveness, promises to repay the money that Joe spent to pay his debts, and goes off to Egypt. There he lives with Herbert and Clara and rises to become third in the firm. Only then does Clarriker tell Herbert that Pip had originally paid for his position. (59) After 11 years in Egypt, Pip returns home to visit Joe, Biddy, and their son Pip. At the ruins of Satis House, he finds Estella, a widow who suffered at the hands of an abusive husband. She asks Pip's forgiveness "now, when suffering has been stronger than all other teaching, and has taught me to understand what your heart used to be." They vow friendship, and as they leave the ruined garden, Pip takes her hand and sees "no shadow of another parting from her."

COMMENTARY

Although Dickens's original plan seems to have been to publish *Great Expectations* in monthly numbers, he opted to write it as a weekly serial for ALL THE YEAR ROUND when the magazine's sales slipped during the run of CHARLES LEVER's tedious *A Long Day's Ride*. *Expectations* restored the audience for the magazine, but it changed Dickens's novel from what it would have been in monthly parts. Each weekly number comprised only one or two short chapters, and like the other novels in the magazine,

it was unillustrated. This format forced Dickens to adopt concise and focused chapters, to concentrate on a single story line, and to work out, almost mathematically, the overall structure of the novel. He divided the story into three equal "stages," with 12 of the 36 weekly parts devoted to each. The three-stage structure reinforces the underlying metaphor of the novel, which casts life as a journey.

As he began work on the novel, Dickens wrote to JOHN FORSTER that "the book will be written in the first person throughout, and during these first three weekly numbers, you will find the hero to be a boy-child, like David." Dickens reread *Copperfield* just to make sure that there were "no unconscious repetitions" of the earlier novel. There are many similarities. Both boys are essentially orphans and both suffer from a feeling of hopelessness as they labor at pasting labels on bottles or working at a forge. Blacksmithing is the later novel's version of the BLACKING WAREHOUSE, for both novels are essentially autobiographical.

The first-person narrator of *Great Expectations* is more fully identified than the narrator of *David Copperfield*. Philip Pirrip, a middle-aged businessman who has spent several years in Egypt, tells the story of his earlier life. He also has an ironic perspective and greater awareness of his shortcomings than David, but his growth does not alter his situation. Whatever happens after the novel is over, in the final chapter he is still an outsider.

Expectations is more realistic than its autobiographical predecessor. Written at a time when novels like GEORGE ELIOT's *Adam Bede* (1859) were in vogue, *Expectations* is more restrained stylistically and more consistent in tone than many of the earlier novels. GEORGE GISSING (1898) defined its difference from earlier works by comparing Joe Gargery and Daniel Peggotty: "if we compare the two figures as to their 'reality,' we must decide in favor of Gargery. I think him a better piece of workmanship all round; the prime reason, however, for his standing out so much more solidly in one's mind than Little Em'ly's uncle, is that he lives in a world, not of melodrama, but of everyday cause and effect."

Although *Expectations* has no Daniel Peggotty and no Mr. Micawber, it is not lacking humorous scenes or memorable characters. The descriptions of Pip's Christmas dinner (4), Wopsle's *Hamlet* (31), or Wemmick's wedding (55) are among the great comic scenes in the novels. Its unforgettable characters include the lawyer Jaggers, with his intimidating forefinger, his habit of washing his hands with scented soap, and his conversation by cross-examination; the divided Wemmick, at the office smiling mechanically with his "post-office" mouth as he advises Pip to secure "portable property," and at home in his castle a loving son who refuses to talk business; and Miss Havisham, the bizarre recluse who lives in a ruined mansion, dressed in the tattered bridal gown that she has worn since she was left standing at the altar many years before. Neither the comic scenes nor the eccentric characters are independent of the story. They are absolutely organic to the plot and theme of the novel.

Great Expectations achieved realism in spite of its status as one of the SENSATION NOVELS of the 1860s, novels that relied on melodrama, sensational incidents, and surprises to achieve their "special effects." Dickens advertises these attractions with the title of his story, promising that he will fulfill his readers' expectations for the sensational. He begins by surprising them—and Pip—in the very first chapter, when Magwitch appears like a ghost in the churchyard, and surprise forms the center of the story, when Magwitch reappears. Even a bizarre character like Miss Havisham expresses the uncanny dimensions of Pip's illusions, exaggerated to surreal surprise in Pip's visions of her as the hanging woman.

In *Copperfield*, David defines himself by establishing his difference from the other characters in his life. Although he sees himself as a victim of others' cruelty—of Murdstone's tyranny and neglect, for example—he is more industrious than Pip in pursuing a career and establishing a place for himself in society. David admires Steerforth's genteel indolence, but he does not adopt it as a way of life. When the tempest comes, he is able to view Steerforth's body on the beach with only a twinge of regret. He does not consciously connect his own undisciplined heart with Steerforth or link Steerforth's death to Dora's. Implicitly, the novel sug-

gests that David survives and is successful because he is not Steerforth.

Pip's is a more interior story. His expectations make him passive, waiting to discover what others have in store for him. He adopts a life of idleness and is frequently made aware of his connections with Drummle, Orlick, and the convict. He is also more present in the narrative as an older and wiser man judging the mistakes of his past. The stormy night that brings Magwitch to Pip's door in the TEMPLE forces Pip to acknowledge his connection with the convict, to abandon his illusions, and to reconstruct his life on totally different assumptions. David seems unconscious of the losses and rejections that have been necessary to secure his respectable position as a successful novelist; Pip is painfully aware of what he has left behind or lost, and *Great Expectations* has a pervasive mood of disillusionment. Joe articulates one of the central themes of the novel when he tells Pip that "life is made of ever so many partings welded together" (27). If David's story is truer to the outward facts of Dickens's life, Pip's may be more revealing of Dickens's inner autobiography.

The difference is apparent in the opening chapters of the two novels. *Copperfield* begins with an account of David's birth; *Expectations* opens with Pip's psychological "birth," when, at age seven or so, he comes to his "first most vivid and broad impression of the identity of things." The setting is bleak: an empty churchyard at dusk on a cold and grey winter day, a "wilderness," "overgrown with nettles," where the only distinguishing features are a gibbet and a beacon. A "small bundle of shivers," Pip is delivered into consciousness by an escaped convict who picks him up, turns him upside down, places him on a tombstone, fills him with fear and terror, and makes him promise to bring food and a file. Every detail in this short chapter simultaneously contributes to the realistic picture of the marsh country on a bleak December evening and to the primal story of Pip's psychological birth.

Appropriately, this encounter takes place on Christmas Eve, and together the first five chapters of the novel—the first three numbers published in the first three weeks of December 1860—form a kind of Christmas story, similar to the CHRISTMAS

BOOKS that Dickens published in the mid 1840s. It includes Pip's stealing the Christmas pie from the larder and delivering it to the convict, and a wonderfully humorous Christmas dinner at which the guilty child awaits exposure while the adults at the table lecture him about the ingratitude and natural viciousness of boys. This Christmas story culminates with the pursuit on the marshes, which ends with Pip's being exonerated by the captured convict, who confesses to stealing the pie himself. Joe states the Christmas theme of the story when he assures the convict, "we don't know what you have done, but we wouldn't have you starved to death for it, poor miserable fellow-creature.—Would us, Pip?" (5).

This Christmas story and its message of empathy and compassion is pushed into the background as Pip goes on to tell the main story of his life, which begins with his introduction to Satis House (8). Although he is occasionally reminded of the odd and terrifying incident in his childhood—by the man who stirs his drink with a file (10), for example—Pip treats the Christmas story as if it were an unusual and bizarre event, part of the story of his life but unconnected with its plot.

Pip divides his life between external reality and interior wishes. The realities include his abuse by Mrs. Joe, who brings him up "by hand"; his apprenticeship to Gargery, the blacksmith, and the likelihood of his becoming Joe's partner and successor; and his humiliating visits to the decaying Satis House, where he is taunted and abused. His wish is to be a gentleman, and in his fantasies he is Miss Havisham's heir, chosen to inherit her money and to marry Estella, her adopted daughter. By the time Jaggers announces Pip's "great expectations" (18), Pip has so internalized these wishes and elaborated their implications in his mind, that he is not surprised. He accepts his elevation to gentility as inevitable and deserved, and he rejects his humble beginnings, the forge, and Joe and represses his memory of the traumatic Christmas on the marshes.

Pip's wishes so control his consciousness that he is unable to see the truth. Joe appears to him an illiterate country bumpkin, and Pip condescendingly tells Biddy how he will educate Joe and "remove [him] into a higher sphere" (19). Only much later does Pip recognize Joe for the "gentle Christian man" (57) he is. While Pip is unable to see the depths in Joe's character, he cannot see the surfaces in Miss Havisham's either. In spite of the decay, ruin, and madness at Satis House and the harsh teaching that makes Estella his tormentor, Pip wishes for the old woman's riches and hopes to be selected, like Estella, as her protégé. By rejecting Joe's true gentility and idealizing Miss Havisham's sham, Pip abandons himself to illusions.

This division indicates Pip's fractured sense of self. In Wemmick, Pip can observe someone who divides his life into public and private parts, surviving in both worlds by keeping them separate. Pip is unable to do so. He attempts to repress the dark and humble sides of his life, but Orlick and Drummle shadow him, and criminals remind him of the "taint of prison and crime" (32) that seems to cling to him. When he rejects Joe and avoids the forge on his visits to his hometown, Trabb's boy follows him in the streets and taunts him as a snob with the refrain, "Don't know yah" (30). In the novel's psychological parable, many of the characters in the story can be seen as fragments of Pip's self that he has failed to integrate into a full understanding of who he is.

Herbert Pocket acts as Pip's foil during his years in London. Although he is not Pip's equal in strength or expectations, he has a more realistic view of the world. He recognizes Miss Havisham's madness and Estella's cruelty, and he has no unwarranted hopes of inheriting Miss Havisham's money, even though he is related to her. His modest ambition is based on a realistic view of his situation and expectations.

The story reaches its crisis in chapter 39 when Pip, alone in his apartment on a stormy winter evening, is forced in a way to reenact the traumatic Christmas Eve on the marshes. Suddenly the story that seemed merely a curious and disconnected episode in his childhood becomes the defining text for his life. Pip's surprise mirrors that of the reader, who has also constructed Pip's rags-to-riches tale as a fairy-tale romance. The convict's revelation redirects the reader's expectations in this sensational turn of events in the novel. By making our reading of the story mirror Pip's self-understanding,

Dickens engages our wishes and expectations. The romance that Pip has imagined his life to be is the romance that we wish for him—and for ourselves. But Magwitch's revelation strips Pip of his wishes and of the fairy-tale scenario he has constructed for himself. In the final stage of his life, Pip must redefine the relationships that he has taken for granted, such as his friendship with Herbert, his business relationship with Jaggers, and, especially, his relationships with Miss Havisham and Estella; he must also come to terms with those parts of himself that he has repressed and rejected—with Drummle, Orlick, Magwitch, and Joe.

In the novel's psychological theme, Pip's reconciliation with Joe is linked with his acceptance of Magwitch. They represent two related aspects of the father that have both contributed to Pip's identity. When he denied his criminal father, he also rejected Joe, the companion with whom he could share "larks." Pip's acceptance of Magwitch has several stages: At first Pip hopes to get him out of the country; then he plans to go with him to the continent; after the failed escape attempt, Pip accompanies him back to London, appears beside him in court, and attends him as he dies. Critics debate just how complete Pip's final acceptance of Magwitch is; his refusal to secure Magwitch's money seems to indicate that he still believes that he can be free of the taint of Newgate, and his final prayer at Magwitch's bedside, "O Lord, be merciful to him a sinner!" (56), can be read as the condescending words of a Pharisee. But Pip also publicly acknowledges his connection with Magwitch by holding the convict's hand as he is sentenced to hang (56). By such acts Pip gives up his great expectations and can be reconciled with Joe. Though he is no longer young enough or innocent enough to share larks with the blacksmith, he can recognize Joe's true gentility and prepare to start life on his own in Egypt.

Jaggers, the novel's third father figure, embodies aspects of both Joe and Magwitch and represents a darkly realistic assessment of the human condition. As a criminal lawyer, he knows that the taint of Newgate is pervasive and that darkness and violence define the human psyche. Cynical, secretive, and pessimistic, he has abandoned whatever illusions, or, as he calls them, "poor dreams," that he may once have had. Nevertheless, he acts in ways to redress injustice and impose order. He "saves" Magwitch's daughter from abandonment, for example, and controls Molly's violent strength. Yet his cynical realism, his lack of expectations, makes him a discomfiting and morally ambiguous figure.

Pip's relationships with the women in his life are, if anything, even more complicated than those with the men. Just as Joe, Magwitch, and Jaggers represent for Pip various aspects of the father, Mrs. Joe, Miss Havisham, Estella, and Biddy represent various aspects of the feminine. Mrs. Joe's harsh abuse may teach Pip resentment and cause him subconsciously to wish for the blow that Orlick inflicts on her, as Orlick suggests when he is taunting Pip in the sluice house (53). She also has a share in introducing Pip to Miss Havisham and encouraging him to think of the madwoman in white as a potential benefactress, thus prompting both his illusions and his masochism as Pip seeks the pain of his visits to Satis House as exquisite testimony to his desires. Pip may wish that Mrs. Joe and Miss Havisham suffer for the pain they cause him. He is indirectly implicated in both of their deaths and painfully burned while attempting to extinguish the fire that mortally injures Miss Havisham (49). Only Estella survives the suffering that Pip may subconsciously wish for her. At their final meeting she acknowledges a changed understanding of him; "suffering has been stronger than all other teaching," she tells him, "and has taught me to understand what your heart used to be" (59).

Estella's statement appears in both versions of the final chapter that Dickens wrote for the novel and would seem to be central to his final thematic point. Dickens changed the original ending after EDWARD BULWER LYTTON read the proofs and urged him to do so. In the original ending, which is included as an appendix in many editions of the novel, Pip returns to England after eight years in Egypt, and while he is walking with little Pip, Joe and Biddy's child, on a street in London, he meets Estella, who has married a Shropshire doctor after her unhappy marriage to Drummle. She

Pip and Joe by the hearth at the forge in McLenan's illustration for the original American serial of *Great Expectations* in *Harper's Weekly*. The simultaneous British serial in *All the Year Round* was unillustrated.

assumes that the child is Pip's, and he does not tell her otherwise; then she confides that suffering has changed her. Pip concludes the original ending by remarking, "I was very glad afterwards to have had the interview; for, in her face and in her voice, and in her touch, she gave me the assurance, that suffering had been stronger than Miss Havisham's teaching, and had given her a heart to understand what my heart used to be." This tough ending has seemed to many readers more consistent with the tone of the novel than the revised ending. John Forster described it as "more consistent with the drift, as well as natural working out, of the tale."

Forster does not take note of the imagery in the second ending, however, that makes it, as GEORGE BERNARD SHAW put it, "artistically much more congruous than the original." In many ways, *Great Expectations* is a poetic novel, constructed around recurring images: the desolate landscape of the marshes; twilight; chains binding us to home, the past, and painful memories; fire; hands that manipulate and control; wishes as remote and distant as stars; the river linking past, present, and future. In the second ending, Dickens changed the meeting place from London to Satis House at twilight as evening mists are rising, mists that recall the mists as Pip left for London at the end of stage one, an allusion to the rising mists in Milton's *Paradise Lost* as Adam and Eve leave Eden. The imagery in the altered ending, then, seems to suggest a new beginning for Pip and Estella, and many readers consider it a "happy" ending, promising the union of the two lovers. But Dickens's words are more ambiguous than that. The imagery of rising mists and the broad expanse of light may suggest a new beginning, but Pip only concludes that at that moment, "I saw no shadow of another parting from her." Even if Pip and Estella remain together, the ending seems to suggest that the human condition, so aptly symbolized in the bleak graveyard of the opening chapter, will remain bleak in the ruined garden that was once Satis House. Shaw, who recognized that the atmosphere that Dickens added to the second ending improved it, nevertheless objected to the happy, marital implication. The perfect ending, he suggested, would consist of a sentence added to the revised ending, "Since that parting I have been able to think of her without the old unhappiness; but I have never tried to see her again, and I know I never shall." If, as the ambiguity in the final sentence allows, Pip and Estella make a final parting as they leave Satis House, never again to see each other—or part from each other—then the second ending confirms the disillusioning note with which the novel began and is the novel's final statement of Joe's theme, that "life is made of ever so many partings welded together." In either case, the final sentence does not describe a historical fact but rather an expectation: "as the morning mists had risen long ago when I first left the forge, so, the evening mists were rising now, and in all the broad expanse of tranquil light they showed to me, I saw no shadow of another parting from her" (59). This concluding sentence confirms a central truth in the novel, that humans, in spite of all suffering, survive by expectation.

CHARACTERS AND RELATED ENTRIES

"Aged P, the" Short for the Aged Parent. Wemmick's father, who lives with his son in the castle at WALWORTH; "a very old man in a flannel coat: clean, cheerful, comfortable, and well cared for, but intensely deaf" (25). Wemmick entertains him with the sound of a cannon, which he can hear in spite of his deafness. Wemmick's kindness and solicitude for the old man exemplify his Walworth persona.

Amelia The wife of Bill, a criminal defendant being represented by Jaggers. She is so persistent in pleading with Jaggers for his help that the lawyer threatens to drop her husband as his client if she does not stop bothering him (20).

"Avenger, The" Pip's nickname for his servant boy, Pepper (27).

Barley, Clara Herbert Pocket's fiancée, a "pretty, slight, dark-haired girl of twenty or so" (30), who arranges to hide Magwich, under the name of Campbell, in her father's house until he can be smuggled abroad. "A captive fairy whom that truculent Ogre, Old Barley, had pressed into his service" (46), Clara does not marry Herbert until after her father, who objects to her marrying for fear she will stop taking care of him, has died.

Barley, Old Bill Clara's invalid father, a retired ship's purser who is "totally unequal to the consideration of any subject more psychological than Gout, Rum and Purser's Stores" (46). He speaks in nautical language, comparing his bedridden situation "lying on the flat of his back" to "a drifting old dead flounder" (46).

Barnard's Inn One of the Inns of Court, now defunct. Located in Holborn, it is "the dingiest collection of buildings ever squeezed together in a rank corner as a club for Tom Cats"; where Herbert Pocket and Pip share rooms when Pip first arrives in London (21).

Bartholomew's Close A back street near Jaggers's office in Little Britain where Pip observes Jaggers's clients waiting to see the lawyer (20).

Biddy Wopsle's great aunt's granddaughter. An orphan like Pip, she assists in the dame school where Pip receives his earliest education: "her hair always wanted brushing, her hands always wanted washing, and her shoes always wanted mending and pulling up at heel" (7). After Pip's sister is injured, Biddy comes to look after the Gargery house and Mrs. Joe. She becomes Pip's close friend and confidante, but Pip does not recognize her love for him and treats her with snobbish condescension (17–19). "She was not beautiful—she was common, and could not be like Estella—but she was pleasant and wholesome and sweet-tempered" (17). She gently reprimands Pip for his condescending treatment of Joe. After losing his fortune, Pip plans to propose to her, but he arrives home to discover that she has just married Joe Gargery (57–58).

Biddy and Joe Gargery define the ideals of simplicity, honesty, and love in the novel. JEROME MECKIER (2002) describes her as the true Cinderella figure in the book and contrasts her to Estella and Miss Havisham as false Cinderellas. Blinded by his relationships to these two pretenders, Pip is unable to appreciate Biddy until too late in the novel.

Bill Criminal defended by Jaggers, husband of Amelia (20).

Bill, Black Inmate of NEWGATE PRISON among Jaggers's clients visited by Pip and Wemmick on their tour of the prison (32).

Blue Boar Inn near the forge where Pip and Joe sign Pip's apprenticeship papers and where Pip stays when he returns from London to his hometown (13, 28, 30, 43).

Brandley, Mrs. Society woman with whom Estella stays in RICHMOND and who sponsors her coming out in London. She has a daughter, Miss Brandley, who is considerably older than Estella. "The mother looked young, and the daughter looked old; the mother's complexion was pink, and the daughter's was yellow; the mother set up for frivolity, and the daughter for theology" (38).

Camilla, Mrs. Matthew Pocket's sister and one of the parasitic Pocket relatives who gather at Miss Havisham's, hoping for inclusion in her will (11). She claims that her concern for Miss Havisham keeps her awake at night, so she receives £5 in the will "to buy rushlights to put her in spirits when she wake[s] in the night" (56).

Clarriker Young shipping broker who is looking for a partner and from whom Pip buys the place for Herbert Pocket (52). After his own loss of expectations, Pip himself joins the firm (58).

Coiler, Mrs. Neighbor to Matthew and Belinda Pocket, "a widow lady of that highly sympathetic nature that she agreed with everybody, blessed everybody, and shed smiles and tears on everybody, according to circumstances" (23).

Compeyson Fast-talking forger, swindler, and con man, the arch-villain of the novel. He escapes from the prison ship on the same day as Magwitch and is captured on the marshes as he fights with Magwitch, whose desire for vengeance overcomes his will to escape (5). As Magwitch describes him, "He set up fur a gentleman, this Compeyson, and he'd been to a public boarding-school and had learning. He was a smooth one to talk, and was a dab at the ways of gentlefolks. He was good-looking too" (42). When they are caught, Compeyson uses his boarding-school polish and good looks—in spite of the scar on his face—to cast blame on Magwitch and get himself a lighter sentence, thus prompting Magwitch's vengeance and desire to create a gentleman of his own. It is Compeyson, in a scheme with Arthur Havisham, who deceives Miss Havisham to secure her money and then jilts her on the day of the wedding. Compeyson learns of Magwitch's return to England and aids the police in capturing him, though he drowns in the struggle with Magwitch (53–55). He is married to Sally, whom he physically abuses.

Compeyson is central to the plot of the novel, for he has driven Miss Havisham into angry seclusion and inspired Magwitch's desire for revenge. Scarred on his face, he plays Cain to Magwitch's Abel, though, in a reversal of the biblical story,

he dies in the struggle between them. Self-serving, cruel, with "no more heart than an iron file" (92), Compeyson represents a totally materialistic version of the "gentleman." Lacking feeling for others and any capacity for friendship, he is wholly defined by money.

Drummle, Bentley ("The Spider") Pip's fellow student at Matthew Pocket's; from a rich family in Somersetshire, "the next heir but one to a baronetcy" (23), he is "heavy in figure, movement, and comprehension . . . idle, proud, niggardly, reserved, and suspicious" (25). To Jaggers, who cultivates those in the criminal underworld, he seems one of "the true sort" (26), and he names him "the Spider." Estella marries him for his money, but he beats and abuses her. He is, in turn, kicked and killed by a horse that he has ill-treated (58).

Born a gentleman and a member of the aristocracy, Drummle helps articulate the theme that true gentility is not something one is born with. Described by Julian Moynahan ("The Hero's Guilt: The Case of *Great Expectations*," *Essays in Criticism*, 1960) as "a reduplication of Orlick at a point higher on the social-economic scale," Drummle expresses the dark, vengeful side of Pip and is contrasted to Startop, the idealist.

Dunstable During Christmas dinner Pumblechook describes this village butcher's especially adept method of killing a pig as a good reason for Pip to be glad that he was not born a pig (4).

Essex Street The street between the Strand and the river where Pip finds lodgings for Magwich (40).

Estella The child provided by Jaggers whom Miss Havisham adopts to be the agent of her vengeance against men. When Pip is recruited as a child to play with her (8), Estella, "beautiful and self-possessed," taunts and humiliates him, mocking his "coarse hands" and "thick boots." She inspires Pip's desire to be "oncommon." When Pip receives his expectations (18), he believes that Miss Havisham is their source and that she also plans for him to marry Estella. While Pip lives as a gentleman in London, Estella continues to tantalize and torment him (32, 33, 38), though at the same time warning him that she has "no heart, . . . no softness there, no—sympathy—sentiment—nonsense" (29). Proud, cold, and disdainful, she also denies Miss Havisham's request for love, reminding her, "I am what you have made me" (38). Even after he learns that she is not his intended, Pip remains masochistically devoted to her, and he tells Magwitch, after learning that Estella is his and Molly's daughter, that he loves her (56). Pip is distressed when she plans to marry Bentley Drummle (44), who abuses her so that she separates from him. In the revised ending that Dickens wrote for the novel (59), Estella meets Pip at the ruins of Satis House, and as they leave "the ruined place," Pip says that he sees "no shadow of another parting from her." But in the suppressed original ending, Pip and Estella meet and part on a London street with no suggestion that they will meet again.

Estella's name, from the Latin for "star," places her as the remote ideal on which Pip hangs his desires. In many ways her story parallels Pip's: Both are tainted by Newgate as "children" of Magwitch; both of their lives are manipulated by the expectations of others. We know of Pip's suffering because he tells his own story, but we know Estella's story only in Pip's version and must question its reliability. The two endings, as HILARY SCHOR points out, suggest that Pip and Estella emerge from their ordeals with very different understandings of their relationship. EDMUND WILSON's (1941) suggestion that ELLEN TERNAN was the inspiration for Estella has been seconded by many later biographers and critics, but DORIS ALEXANDER (1991) makes a persuasive case that she was based on MARIA BEADNELL.

Finches of the Grove   Dining club to which Pip, Herbert Pocket, Drummle, and Startop belong. "The object of which institution I have never divined, if it were not that the members should dine expensively once a fortnight, to quarrel among themselves as much as possible after dinner, and to cause six waiters to get drunk on the stairs" (34).

Flopson   One of Mrs. Pocket's nursemaids who cares for the distracted mother's seven children (22, 23).

Gargery, Georgiana Maria (Mrs. Joe)   Pip's older sister, "tall and bony" with "such a prevailing redness of skin, that I sometimes used to wonder whether it was possible she washed herself with a nutmeg-grater instead of soap" (2), she resentfully brings up Pip "by hand" and indulges in "Rampages" at the boy and her husband Joe. With Joe's Uncle Pumblechook, she arranges Pip's visitations to Miss Havisham and encourages his false expectations. Her meanness is stilled after she is struck over the head by an unknown assailant (16), a wound that partly paralyzes her, leaves her speechless, makes her much more patient, and leads to her early death (34).

Gargery, Joe   Blacksmith and husband of Pip's older sister Georgiana: "a fair man, with curls of flaxen hair on each side of his smooth face, and with eyes of such a very undecided blue that they seemed to have somehow got mixed with their own whites. He was a mild, good-natured, sweet-tempered, easy-going, foolish, dear fellow—a sort of Hercules in strength, and also in weakness" (2). "This gentle Christian man" (57) is ruled by his shrewish wife, who makes him and Pip "fellow-sufferers" (2). He befriends Pip as a boy and speaks of the "larks" they will share together as they grow older, "ever the best of friends." Pip confesses to Joe his lies about Miss Havisham (9), and as Joe's apprentice he regretfully learns the trade of blacksmith (13). Although Pip is snobbish and condescending to him, Joe remains loyal to Pip (27) and nurses him when he falls ill after Magwitch's death (57). After his wife's early death, Biddy takes over Mrs. Joe's duties as housekeeper and eventually marries Joe (58). They have one son, Pip.

Joe defines the moral message of the novel, representing the ideal of the "gentle Christian man" (57) in contrast to the false ideal of the gentleman that Pip pursues in London. Although he is illiterate and inarticulate, repeating his apologetic "which I meantersay," he speaks directly and honestly many of the home truths in the novel. Using the language of a blacksmith, he tells Pip that "life is made of ever so many partings welded together," a theme traced through to the last sentence of the book in images of chains and the motif of life as a journey. Joe's love and friendship forms one of the chains of gold in Pip's life, binding the two of them together just as the iron chain from the leg iron symbolically binds Pip to Magwitch.

Gerrard Street   The street in Soho where Jaggers lives (26).

"Handel"   Herbert Pocket's nickname for Pip, an allusion to George Frederick Handel's "Harmonious Blacksmith" (1718); "We are so Harmonious, and you have been a Blacksmith, would you mind Handel for a familiar name?" (22).

Harrow   Famous public school in Middlesex, just west of London. Matthew Pocket was an old Harrovian (23).

Havisham, Arthur   Miss Havisham's deceased half brother, a drunken ne'er-do-well who conspired with Compeyson to defraud his sister of her inheritance.

Havisham, Miss   Eccentric old woman who lives as a recluse in Satis House and who hires Pip to play with her adopted protégée, Estella. "She was dressed in rich materials—satins, and lace, and silks—all of white. Her shoes were white. And she had a long white veil dependent from her hair, but her hair was white. . . . I saw that everything within my view which ought to be white, had been white long ago, and had lost its lustre, and was faded and yellow" (8). She retreated into seclusion after being jilted by Compeyson, stopping all the clocks there at 20 minutes before nine, the hour of her betrayal; leaving the wedding feast to decay on the table; and wearing her tattered wedding gown. She is training Estella to carry out her revenge by despising and spurning men. She brings Pip to Satis House as a victim for Estella to practice on (8), and she also uses him to taunt her relatives into thinking him a rival for her money (11). She pays for his apprenticeship (13), leading Pip to believe that

she is the source of his great expectations. After he learns otherwise, she asks for his forgiveness and gives him £900 to pay for Herbert's position at Clarriker's. Pip rescues her from burning (49), but her injuries prove fatal. She leaves most of her money to Estella (57).

Miss Havisham's name suggests her contributions to the illusions (have a sham) that Pip harbors and to the guilt (have a shame) that troubles him. Encouraged by his sister and Pumblechook, Pip takes her for the godmother in the fairy-tale version of his life, ignoring the decay and misery at Satis House. DOROTHY VAN GHENT (1953) describes Estella and Miss Havisham as "not two characters but a single one, or a single essense with dual aspects. . . . For inevitably wrought into the fascinating jewel-likeness of Pip's great expectations, as represented by Estella, is the falsehood and degeneracy represented by Miss Havisham."

Furniss's illustration of the recluse Miss Havisham for his edition of *Great Expectations*.

Many sources have been suggested for Miss Havisham: WILLIAM WILKIE COLLINS's novel *The Woman in White* (1860) and the White Woman of Dickens's essay "Where We Stopped Growing" have been proposed by several commentators. DORIS ALEXANDER (1991) proposes Dickens's godmother and great aunt Elizabeth Charlton as his inspiration for both Miss Havisham and David Copperfield's aunt Betsey Trotwood.

Higham The village in Kent which, along with Chalk, was the original for the village of Joe Gargery and his forge in *Great Expectations.*

Hubble, Mr. and Mrs. Friends of the Gargerys who attend Christmas dinner at the blacksmith's house. Mr. Hubble is the village wheelwright "with his legs extraordinarily wide apart: so that in my short days I always saw some miles of open country between them when I met him coming up the lane" (4). Pip describes his wife as "a little curly sharp-edged person in sky-blue, who held a conversationally junior position, because she had married Mr. Hubble . . . when she was younger than he" (4).

Hummums Hotel The inn in Covent Garden where the Finches of the Grove hold their meetings and where Pip spends the night after being warned by Wemmick not to go home (33, 45).

Jack The man of all work at the riverside inn where Pip and Magwich stay as Pip attempts to spirit Magwich out of England. His shoes, "taken . . . from the feet of a drowned seaman," and his certainty about the Custom House officers make his brief appearance in the novel memorable (54) and led ALGERNON C. SWINBURNE (1913) to describe him "as great among the greatest of the gods of comic fiction."

Jaggers Lawyer with offices in Little Britain who serves both Miss Havisham and Magwich. "He was a burly man of an exceedingly dark complexion, with an exceedingly large head and a corresponding large hand. . . . His eyes were set very deep in his head, and were disagreeably sharp and suspicious" (11). As a lawyer with an extensive criminal practice, he carries on conversations through cross-examination and questioning. He also has a habit of washing his hands frequently with scented soap. Pip first meets him at Miss Havisham's house (11). Later, Jaggers announces to Pip his great expectations (18) and represents Pip's secret benefactor. After successfully defending Molly, Estella's mother, on a murder charge, he hired her as his maid. He explains his decision to place Estella in the care of Miss Havisham as a way of saving at least one child from a life in the criminal underworld (51). Jaggers is wholly defined by his professional life. Unlike Wemmick, he has no private domestic world separate from the office. A bully with his clients, Jaggers avoids knowing the truth about their crimes. He adopts an intimidating and aloof manner to control every situation and escape being tainted by the evil he manipulates daily.

The ambivalences in Jaggers's character provoke contradictory responses to him. Nicholas Bentley, MICHAEL SLATER, and Nina Burgis (1988), for example, describe him as "a humane man made cynical by his professional experience"; BERT G. HORNBACK (1987) characterizes him as "a sinister and intellectually selfish man."

Lazarus, Abraham Thief whom Jaggers is engaged to prosecute for stealing a plate; his brother tries unsuccessfully to bribe Jaggers to represent him (20).

Little Britain Street in the City where Jaggers's office is located (20).

Magwitch, Abel (a.k.a. Provis and Campbell) Unnamed escaped convict for whom Pip steals the Christmas pie from his sister's larder (2): "a fearful man, all in coarse grey, with a great iron on his leg. A man with no hat, and with broken shoes, and with an old rag tied round his head. A man who had been soaked in water, and smothered in mud, and lamed by stones, and cut by flints, and stung by nettles, and torn by briars; who limped and shivered; glared and growled; and whose teeth chattered in his head" (1). He is recaptured on Christmas Day with Compeyson, another escapee who is Magwitch's former accomplice and now his enemy (5). Out of gratitude to the boy and a desire to get even with the gentlemen who imprisoned him, Magwitch, who has been transported to Australia for life, secretly uses his earnings as a sheep farmer to provide Pip's great expectations. When he illegally returns to England to see his gentleman, he surprises Pip and repels him with his commonness and his claim to be Pip's "second father" (39). While Pip makes plans to smuggle him out of England, he takes the aliases Provis and Campbell and tells Pip the story of his life (42), of his entanglement with Compeyson, of his relationship with Molly, and of their daughter, who turns out to be Estella. He is arrested during Pip's abortive attempt to escape with him to the continent (54). Sentenced to hang, he dies in the prison hospital before the sentence can be carried out (56).

In the novel's inversion of the Cinderella story, Magwitch, whose name suggests magic and witchery, is the dark fairy godmother, or, as J. HILLIS MILLER (1958) describes him, "a nightmare permutation of Mr. Brownlow and Mr. Jarndyce," the benefactors in *Oliver Twist* and *Bleak House.* Magwitch's harsh treatment and hardships as a child have led to his criminality, just as Pip's mistreatment by Mrs. Joe has left him with a guilty conscience and a self-image as naturally vicious. The similarities between the lonely, shivering man and the orphaned, shivering boy in the opening chapter establish the identification between Magwitch and Pip. Magwitch's crass assumption that money can make a gentleman embodies Dickens's criticism of the money society that fails to appreciate the true gentility of a common man like Joe Gargery.

Mary Anne Wemmick's "neat little" maidservant (25).

Mike "Gentleman with one eye, in a velveteen suit and knee-breeches" who is one of Jaggers's clients (20).

Millers One of Belinda Pocket's nursemaids (22).

Molly Jaggers's maid, "a woman of about forty . . . [whose] face looked to me as if it were all disturbed by fiery air, like the faces I had seen rise out of the Witches' caldron [in *Macbeth*]" (26). Jaggers

had successfully defended her in a murder case and then taken her as his maid. She is very strong and has deeply scarred wrists. Jaggers relishes his control over this powerful woman, whom Wemmick describes as "a wild beast tamed" (24). After Pip notices a likeness between Molly's hands and Estella's, he confirms that Molly is Estella's mother (48).

Orlick, Dolge Joe Gargery's journeyman blacksmith, "a broad-shouldered loose-limbed swarthy fellow of great strength, never in a hurry, and always slouching" (15). He holds grudges against Pip, whom he thinks Joe favors, and against Mrs. Joe, who has called him a fool and a rogue. He secretly attacks and maims her (16), and these injuries lead to her early death (35). When Miss Havisham hires him as a porter, Pip has him dismissed (29–30). Finally, he falls in with Compeyson and plots to murder Pip by luring him to the limekiln on the marshes, a scheme foiled by Herbert Pocket, Startop, and Trabb's Boy (53).

While the evil machinations of Compeyson and Drummle are explained in the plot of the novel, Orlick's attempts to destroy Pip are more mysterious. He appears as a kind of evil alter ego to Pip, expressing the resentment or violence that Pip suppresses. Like Pip, he seems to have named himself, for the narrator tells us that the name Dolge is a "clear impossibility" (15). His first role is as the "idle apprentice" in contrast to Pip's "industrious apprentice," a traditional folk-story motif that is developed in GEORGE LILLO's play, *The London Merchant* (1731), with which Wopsle taunts Pip (15). In this role, Orlick fights with Joe and maims Mrs. Joe. He shadows Pip and Biddy, an apparent rival for Biddy's attentions, and later becomes the doorkeeper to Satis House, symbolically blocking Pip's access to Estella, his presence there a reminder to Pip of his unsuitability as a former blacksmith's apprentice. Orlick makes explicit his role representing Pip's suppressed anger at the limekiln, when he admits to killing Mrs. Joe but blames Pip: "But it warn't old Orlick as did it. You was favoured, and he was bullied and beat. . . . You done it" (53). In a more comic vein, his treatment of Pumblechook—"tied him up to his bedpost, and . . . stuffed his mouth full of flowering annuals"

(57)—also carries out Pip's desire for revenge on this hypocritical relative. In light of all his crimes, Orlick's punishment—imprisonment in the county jail—seems unusually indulgent.

Pepper ("The Avenger")   Pip's servant boy. "I had even started a boy in boots—top boots—in bondage and slavery to whom I might be said to pass my days. For, after I had made this monster (out of the refuse of my washerwoman's family) and had clothed him with a blue coat, canary waistcoat, white cravat, creamy breeches, and the boots already mentioned, I had to find him a little to do and a great deal to eat" (27).

Pip   Name by which Philip Pirrip Jr. is generally known. His "infant tongue" could make of his given name "nothing longer or more explicit than Pip" (1). His benefactor later makes keeping the name a condition for receiving his great expectations (18). It is a name Pip gives himself, suggesting his orphan status and the necessity to make his own way in the world. The name also suggests that Pip is a "seed" or a "hatchling."

Pirrip, Philip, Jr. (Pip)   Narrator and protagonist of *Great Expectations*. He is the orphan son of Philip Sr. and Georgiana, who are buried in the local churchyard with five of their children, Alexander, Bartholomew, Abraham, Tobias, and Roger. Pip is raised by his sister, Mrs. Joe Gargery. Pip's story begins on a Christmas Eve when he is about seven and befriends an escaped convict by stealing for him some food from his sister's larder and a file from the forge (3). Pip assumes that this episode was simply something unusual that happened to him, and he represses his memory of the convict and his sense of identification with him. Sometime later he is taken to play with Estella, rich Miss Havisham's ward, who scorns him, makes him discontented with his common life and prospects, and inspires his hopeless adoration (8). While he serves his apprenticeship to his brother-in-law the blacksmith, Pip wishes for a better life, a wish that seems to come true when he is notified that he is the recipient of "great expectations" (18). His unnamed benefactor—assumed by Pip to be Miss Havisham—supports his life as an idle gentleman in London. Pip also assumes that Miss Havisham has chosen him to marry Estella. When his benefactor reveals his identity several years later, he turns out to be Abel Magwitch, the convict Pip befriended as a child (38). At first Pip is repelled, but as he plans Magwitch's escape from London and then witnesses his arrest, trial, and death, he realizes the shallowness of his expectations and the value of the life he rejected when he left Joe and the forge and went to the city. By the time of Magwitch's death, Pip has learned to love the convict who gave so much of himself to advance Pip's fortunes. In the end, Pip gives up Magwitch's money, works for his living, and is reconciled with Joe (59).

Pip's character is complicated by the fact that there are at least two Pips—Pip the narrator and Pip the character at the center of the story. Although the narrator does not reveal a great deal about his present life, we do know that he is a moderately successful, middle-aged businessman who has spent several years in Egypt. His ability to laugh at some of his earlier foolishness and to achieve ironic distance on his mistakes, as well as his occasional comments on his former short-sightedness, suggests that the narrator has become wiser and has realized the emptiness of his former expectations and the value of the forge. There are also, however, several reasons to conclude that Pip may not have learned as much as he thinks he has. His confession to the dying Magwitch that he loves Estella (56), his prayer identifying the convict and not himself as the sinner in need of mercy (56), and his final sentence in the novel, in which he still harbors expectations (59), suggest that Pip may not have overcome his condescension and his habit of "expecting." These ambivalences in the narration seem to indicate that Philip Pirrip cannot be taken as a wholly reliable narrator.

The ambivalences also reveal a tension in the novel between the conventional BILDUNGSROMAN, in which Pip grows and learns of his mistaken values, and a satiric novel in which Pip fails to overcome his illusions. The ambiguities in the ending, especially the revised ending that Dickens chose at the urging of EDWARD BULWER LYTTON, and the shifting point of view that moves between that of

Philip Pirrip the middle-aged businessman and that of the younger Pip present a multifaceted character developed with psychological complexity who has both strengths and weaknesses.

The psychological portrait of Pip, nicely analyzed by Bernard J. Paris in *Imagined Human Beings* (1997), presents a guilt ridden, imaginative boy who harbors suppressed anger, especially toward his sister. The events of his childhood—his orphanhood, his association with criminals, his mistreatment by Mrs. Joe—make him secretive and susceptible to Miss Havisham's illusions and Estella's humiliations. By suppressing his guilt and projecting his violent anger onto characters like Orlick and Drummle, Pip is able to maintain the illusion that he is worthy of his elevation to the status of young gentleman. But he is not able, like Wemmick, to keep the two sides of his bifurcated character separated, and he is frequently troubled by reminders of criminality, guilt, and violence. His acceptance of Magwitch and his rejection of Magwitch's money suggest that he finally comes to terms with this separation and integrates disparate parts of himself, but he does not seem fully able to achieve psychological wholeness. He still has not come to terms with his feelings about Estella. In the original ending, his satisfaction in Estella's suffering and in her mistaken assumption that young Pip is his child suggests that he has not overcome his resentment at her earlier humiliations. The revised ending implies that Pip still harbors expectations that involve Estella, however one reads the ambiguities in the final sentences of the novel. In both endings the voice is that of a chastened middle-aged bachelor, still a lonely outsider and a psychological orphan.

Pocket, Belinda Matthew's wife, a knight's daughter, "had grown up highly ornamental, but perfectly helpless and useless" (23). She is so obsessed with social position that she pays no attention to housekeeping or to her young children Alick, Jane, Charlotte, Fanny, Joe, and an unnamed baby, who "tumble" in the care of two neglectful nursemaids. DORIS ALEXANDER (1991) suggests that she was based on CATHERINE HOGARTH DICKENS.

Pocket, Herbert Pip's roommate at Barnard's Inn after Pip comes into his expectations. Son of Matthew Pocket, Herbert is the "pale young gentleman" who fought with Pip over Estella (11). He has "a frank and easy way" and "a natural incapacity to do anything secret and mean" (22). He names Pip "Handel," reflecting Pip's background as a blacksmith and celebrating their harmonious relationship, and he instructs Pip in manners (22). He helps Pip hide Magwitch and plan the escape. Pip secretly secures a position for Herbert with Clarriker's (37). Herbert marries Clara Barley after a long engagement, manages the Cairo office for the firm, and hires Pip as his clerk there (58).

Pocket, Matthew Miss Havisham's cousin, Herbert's father, and Pip's tutor when he comes to London to become a gentleman. A graduate of Harrow and Cambridge, he was "a young-looking man, in spite of his perplexities and his very grey hair, and his manner seemed quite natural. I use the word natural, in the sense of its being unaffected; there was something comic in his distraught way, as though it would have been downright ludicrous but for his own perception that it was very near being so" (23). He is kind and unselfish but feckless and impractical, and he has a habit of pulling his hair as a sign of frustration. He is the only one of Miss Havisham's relatives who speaks honestly to her, so he has been banished from her presence. Pip later tells Miss Havisham of Matthew's good character, and she leaves Matthew £4000 in her will (59).

Pocket, Sarah Miss Havisham's "little dry brown corrugated" cousin (11), who hopes for a share of the old woman's money. After Estella leaves Satis House, Sarah Pocket serves as Miss Havisham's companion. Miss Havisham leaves her a bequest of £25 for pills (57).

Potkins, William Waiter at the Blue Boar, ROCHESTER, where Pip dines with Pumblechook (58).

Provis Alias assumed by Magwitch when he returns illegally to England (40), a name that suggests his role as the provider of Pip's fortunes.

Pumblechook, Uncle Joe Gargery's uncle, a prosperous and hypocritical corn chandler and seed merchant: "a large hard-breathing middle-aged slow man, with a mouth like a fish, dull staring eyes, and sandy hair standing upright on his head, so that he looked as if he had just been all but choked" (4). He arranges Pip's initial meeting with Miss Havisham and Estella (7) and subsequently takes credit for being the founder of Pip's great expectations (19), toadying to Pip's new-found wealth. But when Pip loses his prospects, Pumblechook treats him with patronizing pity, suggesting that Pip's downfall is a result of his ingratitude to him, his "earliest benefactor" (58). He receives his comeuppance when Orlick breaks into his house, ties him to a bedpost, and stuffs his mouth full of flowers (57).

As a seed merchant, Pumblechook is responsible for selling Pip (a seed) to Miss Havisham and introducing him to the materialistic illusions that she fosters. DORIS ALEXANDER (1991) connects Pumblechook with John Willett in *Barnaby Rudge* and suggests that both characters are based on John Porter Leigh, the father of MARY ANN LEIGH.

Raymond Husband of Camilla, one of Miss Havisham's toadying relatives (11).

Restoration House Elizabethan mansion in Rochester, south of the cathedral, said to be the original of Satis House in *Great Expectations.*

Satis House Miss Havisham's decaying mansion. The name, taken from a house in Rochester, derives from the Latin for "enough." Estella explains the name to Pip as signifying "whoever had this house could want nothing else" (8). The house itself is based on another mansion in Rochester, Restoration House, where Charles II spent a night when returning to London.

Ship, the Riverside inn below Gravesend where Pip, Herbert, and Magwitch spend the night before attempting to board a steamship for the Continent (54). It was based on the Ship and Lobster Inn.

Skiffins, Miss Woman of "wooden appearance" and uncertain age and in possession of portable property, who first appears at Wemmick's castle wearing an orange dress and green gloves. She marries Wemmick in a country church in what is planned to appear an impromptu ceremony (37, 55).

Startop Pip's fellow pupil at Matthew Pocket's. Optimistic, spoiled, and delicate, he is the opposite of Bentley Drummle. He joins Herbert in rescuing Pip from the limekiln (53), and he rows the boat during the abortive attempt to spirit Magwitch out of England (54).

Three Jolly Bargemen Inn, the Village pub that Joe Gargery frequents and where Pip gets two one-pound notes from the strange man who stirs his drink with a file (10).

Trabb Obsequious tailor who provides a new suit of clothes when Pip learns of his great expectations (19).

Trabb's Boy Trabb's assistant, "the most audacious boy in all that country-side" (19), who mocks Pip's snobbery by pretending to be overcome by Pip's mere presence and then aping Pip's apparent nonchalance by chanting, "Don't know yah!" (30) Although Pip writes a letter to Trabb objecting to the behavior of the boy and declining to do further business with Trabb, the boy is instrumental in rescuing Pip from Orlick at the limekiln (53). Orlick's antagonism to Pip is the product of intense class consciousness; Trabb's Boy's antics seem to arise from jealous envy.

Waldengarver The stage name used by Mr. Wopsle when he plays Hamlet in London (31).

Wemmick, John, Jr. Jaggers's clerk, "a dry man, rather short in stature, with a square wooden face, whose expression seemed to have been imperfectly chipped out with a dull-edged chisel. . . . He wore at least four mourning rings . . . [and] several rings and seals hung at his watch chain, as if he were quite laden with remembrances of departed friends" (21). These items of "portable property" are gifts from the firm's executed former clients. With his "post office of a mouth," Wemmick hides his feelings behind a mechanical smile as he advises Pip repeatedly to value "portable property." At his home in WALWORTH, Wemmick has a personal life that he keeps totally separated from his business life. There he cares for his deaf and aged father in a castle complete with a moat and a cannon (25) and courts Miss Skiffins, his fiancée whom he marries in a wonderfully comic ceremony (55). He aids Pip in secretly setting up Herbert Pocket in business (37), warns him of Compeyson (45), and aids him in planning Magwitch's escape (48).

Wemmick's response to the corruption of the world is to live two separate lives, a solution he recommends to Pip. But Pip is unable to hide or deny Magwitch's presence and importance in his life. When Pip sits by Magwitch holding his hand at the trial and when he makes no attempt to secure Magwitch's money, he implicitly rejects Wemmick's "split personality" solution and follows the example of Joe, who refuses to take money for releasing Pip to Jaggers. Although Wemmick does much to aid Pip, especially in the attempt to get Magwitch to the Continent, he is, as BERT G. HORNBACK (1987) points out, "finally corrupted by his preference for money."

Whimple, Mrs. Landlady of the house where old Bill Barley and his daughter lodge and where Magwitch hides (46).

Wopsle Parish clerk and friend of the Gargerys, he unites "a Roman nose, . . . a large shining bald forehead, . . . [and] a deep voice which he was uncommonly proud of" (4). He aspires to enter the church, but he ends up in the theater where he takes the stage name of Waldengarver. Pip sees him perform Hamlet in an obscure London theater (31), and later, when he has been reduced to playing miscellaneous bit parts, Pip sees him at an even more obscure venue along the river (47). Wopsle's desires to escape his provincial origins and seek success in the theater in London act as a comic parody of Pip's similar pretensions to gentility.

ADAPTATIONS

Although several theatrical adaptations of *Great Expectations* appeared in the United States during the 1860s, the first British adaptation was W. S. Gilbert's *Great Expectations*, produced at the Court Theater in London in 1871. In this production and in some of the American versions, the role of Pip was played by an actress; Adah Isaacs Menken became famous while touring the United States as Pip in her adaptation of the story. Noteworthy among later stage versions are those by ALEC GUINNESS (1939), in which Guinness played Herbert Pocket, and BARBARA FIELD (1983). An opera by Dominick Argento and John Olon-Scrymgeour, *Miss Havisham's Fire,* premiered in 1979.

Paramount produced a silent film based on the novel in 1917, and in 1921 a Danish company filmed an adaptation by Laurids Skands. Universal made a talking picture in 1934, an adaptation by Gladys Unger directed by Stuart Walker, in which the grotesque elements in the novel are given realistic treatment; Miss Havisham wears her wedding dress, for example, only on each anniversary of the day on which she was jilted. DAVID LEAN's 1947 film for Cineguild, one of the great cinematic adaptations of Dickens, stars JOHN MILLS (Pip), Bernard Miles (Joe Gargery), Martita Hunt (Miss Havisham), FRANCIS L. SULLIVAN (Jaggers), Alec Guiness (Herbert Pocket), and Findlay Currie (Magwitch). Mexican director Alfonso Cuaron's 1997 *Great Expectations,* starring Ethan Hawke, Gwyneth Paltrow, Anne Bancroft, and Robert De Niro, transposes the story to contemporary Florida and New York City.

The BBC produced a 13-part serial in 1959, a 10-part serial written by Hugh Leonard in 1967, and a 12-part version by James Andrew Hall in 1981. NBC has produced two American television adaptations: a 1954 production, with Roddy McDowall as Pip, and Sherman Yellen's 1974 adaptation, starring James Mason as Magwitch. A six-hour serial produced in Britain in 1989 featured Anthony Hopkins as Magwitch and Jean Simmons, who played the young Estella in Lean's 1947 film, as Miss Havisham.

Several late 20th-century novelists have taken *Great Expectations* as a starting point for their own work: Kathy Acker, *Great Expectations* (1982); Michael Noonan, *Magwitch* (1982); and Peter Carey, *Jack Maggs* (1998).

FURTHER READING

The criticism on *Great Expectations* is voluminous. Several collections bring together significant critical essays on the novel: Richard Lettis and W. E. Morris, *Assessing Great Expectations* (1960), includes DOROTHY VAN GHENT's (1953) classic discussion of the novel's modes of characterization and Julian Moynahan's "The Hero's Guilt: the Case of *Great Expectations*" (*Essays in Criticism*, 1960), a psychological analysis of Pip and his doubles. Edgar Rosenberg's (1999) authoritative edition supplements its carefully established text and thorough explanatory footnotes with a selection of critical essays, among them Peter Brooks's (1984) Freudian analysis of the plot, "Repetition, Repression, and Returns: The Plotting of *Great Expectations*." Janice Carlisle's (1996) edition also includes Brooks's essay, as well as others illustrating several contemporary approaches to the novel. Of particular interest among them is HILARY SCHOR's feminist reading, "'If He Should Turn to and Beat Her': Violence, Desire, and the Woman's Story in *Great Expectations*." Harold Bloom's (2000) volume in the *Modern Critical Interpretations* series is a good selection of recent essays. The autobiographical roots of the story are discussed by ADA NISBET in "The Autobiographical Matrix of *Great Expectations*" (*Victorian Newsletter*, 1959). F. R. LEAVIS and Q. D. LEAVIS (1970) provide a close reading of the novel as an example of psychological realism. Many commentators write on Pip as narrator, including Robert B. Partlow, "The Moving I: A Study of Point of View in *Great Expectations*" (*College English*, 1961), ROBERT E. GARIS (1965), and STEVEN CONNOR (1985). Beth Herst (*The Dickens Hero: Selfhood and Alienation in the Dickens World*, 1990) discusses Pip as an example of the alienated hero in Dickens's later novels. Three book-length discussions of the novel are especially noteworthy: BERT G. HORNBACK (1987) and ANNY SADRIN (1988) provide extended critical introductions to the novel; JEROME MECKIER (2002) considers the novel in comparison to other works of Victorian fiction.

Great Expectations was first published as a serial in ALL THE YEAR ROUND and, consistent with the format of that magazine, was unillustrated. Some critics, most notably F. R. Leavis and Q. D. Leavis (1970), have suggested that the realism of the novel made illustrations—especially caricatures in the manner of HABLOT KNIGHT BROWNE—inappropriate. However, there have been many successfully illustrated later editions of the novel. The first American edition—the serial published in *Harper's Weekly*—was illustrated by John McLenan. Since it was printed from advance proofs sent from England and appeared a week before the English serial, this edition could be said to be the first edition of the novel. Dickens had MARCUS STONE illustrate the LIBRARY EDITION of the novel in 1862. Especially noteworthy among later illustrators of the novel are F. W. Pailthorpe (1885), HARRY FURNISS (1910), and Gordon Ross (1937).

Hard Times, for These Times

Dickens's 10th novel, serialized weekly in HOUSEHOLD WORDS (April 1–August 12, 1854), unillustrated. Published in one volume by BRADBURY & EVANS, 1854. This controversial book, the shortest of Dickens's novels, takes up the issues of industrialism and education and offers a moral fable challenging some of the dominant ideologies of the Victorian era.

SYNOPSIS
I. Book the First. Sowing.

Part 1 (April 1, 1854)
(I:1) Mr. Gradgrind instructs schoolmaster M'Choakumchild that the one thing needful in life is facts. (I:2) Sissy Jupe is the only "little vessel" in Gradgrind's school that is not filled with facts. Bitzer, the star pupil, shows off his ability to recite all the physical characteristics of a horse. These children are "regulated and governed" by fact; they are never to imagine. M'Choakumchild, a factory-produced teacher, will fill them with facts and kill any harmful fancy lurking within them. (I:3) On his way home to Stone Lodge, Thomas Gradgrind passes the circus and discovers his children Tom and Louisa peeping into the tent. He reprimands them by repeating, "What would Mr. Bounderby say?"

Part 2 (April 8, 1854)

(I:4) Banker and manufacturer, Mr. Bounderby, the "Bully of Humility," is bullying Mrs. Gradgrind, a woman of surpassing feebleness, with the story of his neglected and abused childhood. Bounderby ascribes Louisa and Tom's deliquency to the influence of Sissy Jupe, a circus performer's daughter who is a student at Gradgrind's school. He and Gradgrind decide to ask Signor Jupe to persuade his daughter to refrain from encouraging the idle curiosity of the Gradgrind children. As they leave to find Jupe, Bounderby kisses Louisa goodbye and she tries to rub off the mark of the kiss. (I:5) Coketown, a red-brick town founded upon fact, is totally utilitarian and functional—blackened by the "serpentlike" smoke from factory chimneys. On the way to Pod's End, Gradgrind and Bounderby meet Sissy, who is being chased through the streets by Bitzer. They halt the pursuit and go on with the girl.

Part 3 (April 15, 1854)

(I:6) When they get to the Pegasus' Arms, Jupe is not there. The circus people tell them that Jupe has probably "cut," run off because his talents were slipping, and deserted both the circus and his daughter. Bounderby berates Jupe's irresponsibility. Grandgrind offers to take Sissy into his home if she will promise to cut herself off from the circus. Sissy tearfully agrees. As they leave, Sleary, the circus manager, counters Gradgrind's harsh judgment of the circus by reminding him that "People must be amuthed," and asking him to "make the betht of uth, not the wurtht."

Part 4 (April 22, 1854)

(I:7) Mrs. Sparsit, grandniece to Lady Scadgers, acts as Bounderby's housekeeper. He exploits her privileged background as a contrast to his story of deprivation. She tolerates, but inwardly resents, this vulgar exploitation. Sissy is told to pay proper deference to Mrs. Sparsit, to forget her own past and the circus, and to begin her life anew as a servant to Mrs. Gradgrind. (I:8) The keynote of Gradgrind's system is "never wonder," but Tom and Louisa sit before the fire and wonder about the "something missing" in their lives and about the future. Tom wants to leave home and join Bounderby's bank, where he plans to manage Bounderby

by playing on the banker's affection for his sister. When Mrs. Gradgrind discovers the two children "wondering," she reprimands them for disobeying their father.

Part 5 (April 29, 1854)

(I:9) Sissy does not do well in school. She cannot take facts seriously and cannot remember them. Given statistical problems, she ignores the percentages and attends only to individuals who are suffering, no matter how small their numbers. She tells Louisa of her father, a clown, and of the stories she read to him from the *Arabian Nights*. She continues to hope for his return.

(I:10) After work, Stephen Blackpool, a weaver in Bounderby's mill, walks home with Rachael, the woman he loves, telling her of his unhappiness and of his belief that life is a muddle. When he gets to his own apartment, he discovers that his wife of many years has returned and is lying drunk on his doorstep.

Part 6 (May 6, 1854)

(I:11) Stephen seeks Bounderby's advice about getting a divorce. Bounderby warns him not to be a malcontent and tells him that he married for better or worse and that there is no way that he, a poor man, can dissolve the bond. Stephen's response, "Tis a muddle," shocks Mrs. Sparsit and prompts Bounderby to assert, "I see traces of turtle soup, and venison, and gold spoon in this." (I:12) Outside Bounderby's house, Stephen meets an old woman who tells him that she comes to town once a year to look at Bounderby. Later, as he works at his loom, Stephen sees the old woman in the street, looking at the factory building with admiration.

Part 7 (May 13, 1854)

(I:13) At home Stephen finds Rachael attending his ailing wife. He sleeps fitfully in a chair, dreaming that he is on stage and everyone in the world shuns him. Then, half awake, he sees his wife get up from the bed and take a bottle of poison from the table. He is powerless to stop her, inwardly wishing to be free of her. Just as she is about to drink it, Rachael awakens and takes the bottle away from her. As Rachael leaves, Stephen blesses her as "an angel" who "changest me from bad to good."

(I:14) Some years later, Mr. Gradgrind has become a member of Parliament, Sissy has been dismissed from school but is liked by Gradgrind in spite of her academic failings. Tom works in Bounderby's bank. When her father makes an appointment to talk with Louisa about marriage, Tom urges her to remember him. Louisa looks into the "factory" of her self and finds it mute, noiseless, and secret.

Part 8 (May 20, 1854)

(I:15) Gradgrind tells Louisa that Bounderby has proposed to marry her. When she asks if she is expected to love Bounderby, Gradgrind advises her just to look at the facts: she is 20; Bounderby is 50. There is disparity in their ages but not in their means or positions. In sum, he says, Bounderby has asked her to marry him. The question now is whether she will. Louisa observes the smoke pouring from the Coketown chimneys, wonders about the shortness of her life, and then accepts the proposal. "Let it be so," she says. "What does it matter?" Sissy looks at Louisa in wonder, pity, and sorrow. Mrs. Gradgrind worries about what she will call her son-in-law. (I:16) When Bounderby announces his intentions to Mrs. Sparsit, she responds with compassion, simultaneously wishing him happiness and treating him as "a Victim." She accepts his offer of a position at the bank. At the wedding, Bounderby speaks of Louisa as deserving of him, and Tom bids her goodbye as "a game girl" and a "first-rate sister."

Book the Second. Reaping.

Part 9 (May 27, 1854)

(II:1) On a hot summer day, Mrs. Sparsit and Bitzer, now the bank's light porter, look out of her window above the bank and see a stranger with an "air of exhaustion." He brings an introduction to the Bounderbys from Mr. Gradgrind and inquires if Mrs. Bounderby is quite the formidable philosopher her father makes her out to be.

Part 10 (June 3, 1854)

(II:2) Bored with serving in the Dragoons and the foreign service, traveling to Jerusalem, and yachting about the world, the stranger, James Harthouse, has decided to go in for hard fact. He flatters Boun-

derby by agreeing with him on the necessity of smoke, the pleasantness of the work in the mills, and the unreasonable demands of the "hands." But he is puzzled and challenged by the cold, unrevealing face of Louisa. He believes any set of ideas as good as any other; she seems to believe in nothing. Only when Tom arrives does Harthouse discover something that will "move that face." So he cultivates "the whelp" and secures him as a guide back to his hotel. (II:3) Harthouse plies Tom with cigars and liquor and pumps him for the truth about his sister, who married Bounderby for Tom's sake. He also asks about Mrs. Sparsit, who had her cap set for Bounderby herself, and, inadvertently, about Tom himself. The whelp leaves in a fog, not remembering what he has revealed.

Part 11 (June 10, 1854)

(II:4) Slackbridge, the union organizer, urges the workingmen of Coketown to shun Blackpool as a traitor for refusing to join them. Stephen defends himself before the men, saying that he remains their friend and will work by himself among them, but the loneliness of being shunned is difficult, for Stephen is afraid even to contact Rachael. After four lonely days, Bitzer informs Stephen that Bounderby wishes to see him. (II:5) Bounderby asks him why he refuses to join the union, but Stephen declines to reveal his reason. He defends the men against Bounderby's charges that they are rebellious, and, taking courage from looking at Louisa's face, he describes "the muddle" and condemns the rich, who blame everything on the workingmen. By the end of the interview, Bounderby is so angry he fires Stephen.

Part 12 (June 17, 1854)

(II:6) In the street, Stephen meets Rachael and the old lady he met once before outside Bounderby's house. Stephen tells Rachael he has been fired and that he plans to leave Coketown to search for work. She knows it was because of his promise to her not to join the union. They go to Stephen's home, where Mrs. Pegler, the old woman, questions Stephen about Bounderby's wife. Their tea is interrupted by Louisa and Tom. Louisa offers Stephen help for his journey. Tom engages him to wait outside the bank on the evenings before he sets out, telling him that he hopes he can do something for him and that Bitzer will bring a message. But no message comes. After the third night, Stephen sets out on his journey.

Part 13 (June 24, 1854)

(II:7) Harthouse gains the trust of Gradgrind and Bounderby and takes an increasing interest in Mrs. Bounderby. He visits her at the country house that Bounderby has acquired by repossession. There he learns that she has given Tom a good deal of money to cover his gambling debts, but Tom is short with her because she has refused him more money. In a private interview with Tom, Harthouse offers to help him with his debts and urges him to be nicer to his sister. That evening, Tom is indeed much nicer to her. Harthouse observes the gratitude in her face.

Part 14 (July 1, 1854)

(II:8) During the night, the bank is robbed by someone using a forged key. Bitzer and Mrs. Sparsit had seen Blackpool loitering outside the bank, and the disgruntled hand is suspected. After this "explosion," Mrs. Sparsit comes to stay at the Bounderby country house; she pays particular attention to Bounderby, playing cards with him and fixing his favorite drinks. Louisa is shocked by the news of the robbery. When she asks Tom if he has anything to tell her, she gets only a sullen and resentful reply.

Part 15 (July 8, 1854)

(II:9) Mrs. Sparsit takes over her old role as Bounderby's housekeeper. Louisa is indifferent, but Mrs. Sparsit's involvement with Bounderby frees Louisa to spend more time with Harthouse. When Louisa is called back from the country to the bedside of her gravely ill mother, Mrs. Gradgrind tries to tell her daughter of something that has been missing from her life, but she dies without communicating her message. (II:10) Mrs. Sparsit imagines a staircase and, as she contemplates this mental image, she watches Louisa descending. Bounderby informs Mrs. Sparsit that Blackpool and an old woman are the prime suspects in the robbery. That evening Mrs. Sparsit watches Harthouse and Louisa talking in the garden. They are talking about Blackpool:

Harthouse found him "dreary," but Louisa believed in him.

Part 16 (July 15, 1854)

(II:11) Mrs. Sparsit continues to watch Louisa's descent. When she learns that Harthouse, who is away hunting in Yorkshire, will return while Bounderby is away on business, she hastens to the country house and, hiding in the heavy shrubbery, spies on the couple as Harthouse presses his suit. Louisa resists but appears finally to give in. Mrs. Sparsit cannot overhear the arrangements, however, for a thunderstorm drowns out their words. In the rain, she follows Louisa to the train, but she loses track of her when they arrive in Coketown. (II:12) Louisa goes to her father and tells him that his training has made her empty and confused, that she has left a husband she despises, that Harthouse has proposed to elope with her, and that she has not disgraced her father. She tells him that his philosophy has brought her to this pass and asks him to save her. Then she collapses at his feet.

Book the Third. Garnering.

Part 17 (July 22, 1854)

(III:1) Shaken by his daughter's revelations, Gradgrind tells Louisa the next morning that he has neglected the wisdom of the heart for the wisdom of the head. Sissy, who has brought such understanding into the Gradgrind household, offers to help Louisa. (III:2) That evening Sissy goes to Harthouse and tells him that he should forget Louisa and leave Coketown. Harthouse is struck by how "absurd" and "ridiculous" he will appear if he just walks away from Coketown, but he is "vanquished" by Sissy and decamps for Egypt and the pyramids.

Part 18 (July 29, 1854)

(III:3) When Bounderby appears at Stone Lodge with Mrs. Sparsit to inform Gradgrind that Louisa has run off, he learns that she is in her father's house. Although Gradgrind tells Bounderby that Louisa is suffering from the education he gave her and needs time with Sissy to recuperate, Bounderby demands that she return to his house by noon the next day. When she does not appear, he gets rid of her things and resumes his bachelor life. (III:4)

Bounderby pursues his investigation into the bank robbery. Rachael assures him that Stephen will return to clear his name; she sends a letter to Stephen telling of the accusations against him, but he does not return.

Part 19 (August 5, 1854)

(III:5) Sissy assures Rachael that the people of Stone Lodge still believe in Stephen. The two women plan to walk in the countryside to search for him on the route he would take back to Coketown. Meanwhile, Mrs. Sparsit has apprehended the old lady who is suspected along with Stephen. The woman turns out to be Bounderby's mother, Mrs. Pegler. She humiliates her son by giving a very different account of his childhood from the story he tells.

(III:6) In the country, Sissy and Rachael find Stephen's hat lying on the ground near the entrance to an abandoned mine—the Old Hell Shaft. With help they find Stephen at the bottom, injured but still alive. Stephen tells of hurrying to return to Coketown, cutting across open country at night, and falling into the pit. He also tells of a star he has watched from the bottom of the pit and of his wish that all men might live together peacefully. He tells Gradgrind of Tom's request that he wait outside the bank. Then he dies.

Part 20 (August 12, 1854)

(III:7) Tom disappears from the group gathered around the Old Hell Shaft. Gradgrind realizes his son's guilt and Sissy tells him that she directed Tom to go to Sleary's circus. There they find Tom, dressed as a clown, taking part in the show. He blames Louisa for his crime, for she did not give him the money he needed, and he excuses himself by citing figures to prove his dishonesty was predictable. They prepare to send him abroad, but just as he is about to leave, Bitzer arrives to arrest him. (III:8) Gradgrind tries to appeal to Bitzer's good nature, which is lacking, and to his self-interest, but Bitzer thinks he can take over Tom's position at the bank only if he apprehends him. Finally Sleary distracts Bitzer and Tom is spirited away. Sleary explains the circus philosophy to Gradgrind: Sissy's faith that her father will return is a sign, he says, that there is love in the world and "not all [is] self

interest after all." His other message to Gradgrind is that "People mutht be amuthed. They can't be alwayth a-learning, nor yet they can't be alwayth a-working." Thus Sleary challenges the two central propositions of Gradgrind's shattered worldview.

(III:9) Bounderby, outraged by the Mrs. Pegler episode, dismisses Mrs. Sparsit and sends her off to live with her relation, Lady Scadgers. The future shows Bitzer rising in business; Bounderby dying of a fit in the street; Gradgrind adopting the philosophy of Faith, Hope, and Charity and exonerating Blackpool; Tom dying penitent abroad; Sissy marrying and raising a loving family; and Louisa, remaining unmarried, loving Sissy and her children.

COMMENTARY

Dickens wrote *Hard Times* for HOUSEHOLD WORDS, and the novel seems almost tailored to articulate the aims of the magazine, stated in its first issue: "No realities, will give a harsh tone to our *Household Words*. . . . We would tenderly cherish that light of Fancy which is inherent in the human breast; which, according to its nurture, burns with an inspiring flame, or sinks into a sullen glare, but which (or woe betide that day!) can never be extinguished."

Yet Dickens had difficulty with the short installments called for in the weekly magazine, and as he worked on the novel, he thought of it in terms of monthly parts. Compared with the other monthly serials, however, *Hard Times* is a very short novel. Its five monthly numbers (two for "Sowing," two for "Reaping," one for "Garnering") make it only a quarter of the standard length. Even when compared with the other weekly serials, such as *A Tale of Two Cities* or *Great Expectations*, *Hard Times* is a short novel. Its spare and unembellished prose, its simple fable, and its overt didacticism reinforce the impression that the shortest of Dickens's novels is also the simplest. So uncharacteristic is it that many Dickensians have considered it insignificant; FREDERIC G. KITTON (1900), for example, placed it along with the magazine articles, travel books, and CHRISTMAS BOOKS among Dickens's "minor writings."

The novel's controversial subject matter has put off many readers like the Whig historian and politician Thomas Babington Macaulay, who dismissed it as "sullen socialism," but *Hard Times* has also had defenders; John Ruskin considered it the most important of Dickens's novels and in *Unto This Last* (1862) called its view of industrialism "the right one, grossly and sharply told." This Victorian controversy, which pitted the novel's detractors, who decried its lack of Dickensian humor, against those who praised its social insights, has continued to the present, supercharged in 1948 by what may be the single most controversial essay on Dickens in the 20th century, F. R. LEAVIS's "Note" on *Hard Times* in *The Great Tradition.* After excluding Dickens from the great tradition of the English novel as an "entertainer" in whose works "the adult mind doesn't as a rule find . . . a challenge to an unusual and sustained seriousness," Leavis added an appendix describing *Hard Times* as a "masterpiece" and an exception to this rule. He praised the tight construction of the novel as a "moral fable," its systematic critique of UTILITARIANISM, and its poetic expression. His eccentric evaluation—reprinted in slightly revised form in 1970 in *Dickens the Novelist*—aroused many Dickensians to respond. Many made the case for the greatness of the other novels, often at the expense of *Hard Times*, which was frequently described as misinformed on the issues, humorless, and lacking convincing and engaging characters.

Certainly Dickens's intent in the novel was serious. When he dedicated it to THOMAS CARLYLE, he told him, "I know it contains nothing in which you do not think with me." The critique of industrialism and utilitarianism in the novel is as Carlylean as the history of the French Revolution in *Two Cities.* Carlyle described Victorian times as diseased, hardened by a belief in "mechanism" and "machinery," and he attacked the economic philosophers of the day for using an analytic method that reduced everything to numbers and statistics. The utilitarians, he asserted, did not consider individuals, and they denied the truths of intuition and spirit.

Gradgrind represents the utilitarians in the novel. Appropriately, he schools his own children to become creatures of fact like himself. He sees these children not as living creatures filled with wonder but rather as empty vessels to be stuffed with facts. The contrast between the living, organic world that he stifles and the deadly realm of fact that drains life from the children is presented in the contrast between Sissy Jupe and Bitzer as they are caught in a shaft of sunlight entering the schoolroom. Sissy "was so dark-eyed and dark-haired, that she seemed to receive a deeper and more lustrous colour from the sun, when it shone upon her, the boy was so light-eyed and light-haired that the self-same rays appeared to draw out of him what little colour he possessed. . . . His skin was so unwholesomely deficient in the natural tinge, that he looked as though, if he were cut, he would bleed white" (I:2). This contrast between the natural and unnatural is fundamental to Dickens's analysis in the novel. By reducing everything to material fact, utilitarianism is unnatural and destructive. It fragments the world into unnatural pieces—like the "facts" in Bitzer's definition of a horse—and fails to see anything whole as it naturally appears in the world.

Dickens is sometimes criticized for creating an unrecognizable caricature of utilitarianism, the rational-empiricist philosophy of Jeremy Bentham (1748–1832), James Mill (1773–1836), and Mill's son, the great political philosopher John Stuart Mill (1806–73). Bentham based his philosophy on a binary opposition between sensations of pleasure and pain and on the principle of maximizing pleasure and minimizing pain. The philosophy's quantifiable social goal was to achieve the greatest happiness of the greatest number of people. Bentham and his followers were particularly interested in principles of social organization that facilitated progress toward this goal. While Gradgrind's philosophy may not be intellectually rigorous, it is grounded in a binary opposition between fact and fancy, and it constructs "reality" from analytically derived pieces.

Gradgrind's educational program has often been compared to the one James Mill developed for his son, a rigorous discipline in mathematics, logic, and language, instilled from early childhood, but Gradgrind's system, with its commitment to the "-ologies," may be more scientific than the one Mill devised. Both schemes, however, were unsuccessful. In his *Autobiography* (1873), John Stuart

Mill described a nervous breakdown he suffered in his 20s when he realized that he really did not care about the social and rational principles he had been taught; he overcame the depression only when he allowed the truths of feeling, especially as expressed in Wordsworth's poetry, to counter the absolute rationalism of his upbringing. In the novel, Louisa, Tom, and Bitzer also discover that their EDUCATION in Gradgrind's school, by denying feeling and imagination, has not prepared them to live fulfilling lives.

Louisa has no resources to enable her to respond to Bounderby's proposal of marriage. When she asks her father's advice, he can only suggest that she treat the issue "simply as one of Tangible Fact," and then he reduces the fact to numbers, to the 30-year difference in their ages that he then evaluates statistically. Although Louisa has a vague sense that something more should be at issue, she does not know what it might be and acquiesces to the marriage, saying, "What does it matter?" (II:15). Tom, who has learned the principle of self-interest and who has no empathy for anyone but himself, robs Bounderby's bank and frames Blackpool. Bitzer, the model analyst who reduces the world to bits, also evaluates everything in terms of self-interest. When Gradgrind tries to bribe him to allow Tom to escape arrest, the calculating Bitzer responds from pure self-interest: "Knowing that your clear head would propose that alternative," he tells Gradgrind, "I have gone over the calculations in my mind; and I find that to compound the felony, even on very high terms indeed, would not be as safe and good for me as my improved prospects in the Bank" (III:8).

The reductionism inherent in Utilitarianism was exaggerated in the principles of POLITICAL ECONOMY, the popular economic philosophy of the time that reduced all human relationships to economic self-interest. The names of Gradgrind's younger children—Adam Smith and MALTHUS—suggest the alliance between the utilitarians and political economists whom Dickens was attacking. Coketown and Mr. Bounderby are the most blatant expressions of the new economics in the novel. A town of red brick, smoke and ashes, machinery, and tall chimneys, Coketown articulates the philosophy that created it: "Fact, fact, fact, every-

where in the material aspect of the town; fact, fact, fact, everywhere in the immaterial" (I:5). Like the schoolchildren who are reduced to "vessels," Coketown's inhabitants are reduced to "hands," "people equally like one another, who went in and out at the same hours, with the same sound upon the same pavements, to do the same work, and to whom every day was the counterpart of the last and the next" (I:5). What signs there are of imagination have been perverted into repetitive madness by the iron laws of economics that define the town's existence: from the chimneys "interminable serpents of smoke trailed themselves for ever and ever, and never got uncoiled. . . . [and] the piston of the steam engine worked monotonously up and down like the head of an elephant in a state of melancholy madness" (I:5).

Bounderby, the captain of industry who represents the triumph of economics, also perverts imagination. Like Dickens's great comic figures—Micawber, Tony Weller, or Sarah Gamp, for example—Bounderby claims to be self-created, but his rags-to-riches story of rising from abandonment to become Josiah Bounderby of Coketown is not a triumph of imagination. It is a clichéd narrative, produced to affirm the ideology of laissez-faire, and it is a lie. Unlike Gradgrind, who is humbled and changed by Louisa's fall, Bounderby is simply reinforced in his fatuous dishonesty. He bullies Gradgrind's humility and rejects Louisa.

Stephen Blackpool's double bind shows how the "laws" of Coketown constrain and oppress the worker. When he seeks to escape "the muddle," Bounderby accuses him of rebelliousness and of being a dupe of some "mischievous stranger" (I:11), but when Stephen refuses to go along with Slackbridge and join the LABOR UNION, he is shunned by his fellow workmen. The marriage laws and the laws of political economy conspire to deny Stephen love, community, and identity. Although Stephen can imagine a better life for himself, he dies as an industrial martyr, killed by falling into the hell shaft of industrial England. He cannot escape the muddle.

Harthouse's cynical fatalism—"What will be will be" (II:8)—is an apt expression of the fundamental truth of a world without imagination, and it echoes Louisa's "What does it matter?" If fact rules everything, then human choice and action can have no effect. Harthouse is ironically named, for he is as empty inside as Bounderby, but he does act as a catalyst to make Louisa aware of her own heart and inner needs. Their climactic rendezvous takes place outside Coketown in a natural setting during a cleansing rainstorm (II:11), and it releases Louisa's natural impulses that have been so long repressed.

Sissy Jupe is the real representative of heart. She acts from a higher law than the law of fact, and she alone can reduce Harthouse to absurdity and convince him to leave Coketown. She affirms the centrality of love. Her loyalty to her father, even after he abandons her, is in marked contrast to Bounderby's immediate rejection of Louisa after she returns to her father. Sissy's connections with the circus also enable Tom to escape the inevitability of "the law."

The CIRCUS embodies the alternative to Coketown's philosophy of fact. Its world of illusion expresses its commitment to FANCY, to imagination. Its horses are not fettered to mechanical routines like the melancholy elephants in Coketown; the circus people know and understand them from experience, not from textbook definitions of them, so a real horse can dance rings around Bitzer and foil his attempt to arrest Tom (III:8). There is a community among the circus people, derived from another power of the imagination, the power to empathize with others, to imagine oneself in another's place. Sleary sums up the philosophy of fancy when he tells Gradgrind "that there ith a love in the world, not all Thelf-interetht after all" and that fancy "hath a way of ith own of calculating or not cálculating, whith Thomehow or another ith at leatht ath hard to give a name to" (III:8). These mysterious powers of love, empathy, and imagination offer hope, comfort, and amusement.

The circus has sometimes been criticized as an inadequate symbol to represent the alternative to fact. Certainly the amusing circus vagabonds were a less-established social institution than the factories and schools of fact in Victorian England. The circus's power to counteract the destructive effects of industrialism is very limited. It saves Tom from arrest, but he will soon die far from home. It may be the basis of Sissy's ability to achieve happiness, but it cannot remove the taint of Coketown from Louisa, who will never know the happiness of having her own family. Coketown has blighted Tom's and Louisa's lives and the lives of every other inhabitant. The circus changes Gradgrind, but he is scorned by his former associates and Coketown goes on as before. The marginality of the circus may suggest just how important its presence was in Victorian England, even if its unspoken philosophy of fancy was accessible only to those who could translate the truths in Sleary's boozy prose.

CHARACTERS AND RELATED ENTRIES

Bitzer Star pupil at Mr. Gradgrind's school, he goes to work for Bounderby's bank. There he spies on Tom Gradgrind and reports his illegal activities. "His skin was so unwholesomely deficient in the natural tinge, that he looked as though, if he were cut, he would bleed white" (I:2).

Bitzer's name—especially apt today in the age of computer bits—identifies him as an example of the fact school that fails to see things whole and instead cuts them up analytically into bits and pieces. His education has left him with only one motivation, self-interest. His opposite in the novel is Sissy Jupe, who is as colorful as he is white. She thinks only of individuals, not averages or numbers, and her primary motivation is love for others.

Blackpool, Mrs. Stephen's wife of 19 years, "a disabled, drunken creature . . . so foul to look at, in her tatters, stains, and splashes, but so much fouler than that in her moral infamy, that it was a shameful thing even to see her" (I:10). A shadowy figure who has left her husband, she reappears periodically, disrupting his life and his hopes of marrying Rachael.

Blackpool, Stephen A power-loom weaver in Bounderby's mill, he is "a rather stooping man with a knitted brow, a pondering expression on his face, and a hard-looking head sufficiently capacious, on which his iron grey hair lay long and thin" who finds life "a muddle" (I:10). He loves Rachael, another Coketown factory hand, but he is unable to marry her because he is already married. When he seeks advice from Bounderby about how to obtain a divorce, he is rebuffed by his employer as a trouble-maker (I:11), and when he refuses to join the union he is ostracized by his fellow workers (II:4). When Stephen leaves Coketown to look for work, Tom Gradgrind manages to throw suspicion for the bank robbery on him (III:4). As he returns to clear his name, Blackpool falls into an empty mineshaft, the Old Hell Shaft, and dies shortly after he is rescued by Sissy and Rachael (III:6).

Stephen's name, combining allusions to Stephen, the first Christian martyr, and Blackpool, a town in Yorkshire, suggests the tension between his symbolic role as a victim of industrialism and his realistic role as a Yorkshireman. He has been criticized as sentimental and impossibly good, and he has been praised by Ruskin and others as an accurate portrait of a workingman.

Bounderby, Josiah   Coketown banker and mill owner and friend of Mr. Gradgrind: "A big, loud man, with a stare, and a metallic laugh. A man made out of coarse material, which seemed to have been stretched to make him. . . . A man who could never sufficiently vaunt himself a self-made man. . . . A man who was the Bully of humility" (I:4). To maintain the myth that he is self-made, Bounderby hides his mother, Mrs. Pegler, who has sacrificed to give him an education and a place in the world. He bullies his employees, convinced that they are a rebellious lot who want to "be set up in a coach and six, and . . . fed on turtle soup and venison, with a gold spoon" (I:11). He pursues Stephen Blackpool, one of his mill hands who is accused of robbing his bank, and later the actual robber, Tom Gradgrind, who works in the bank. His marriage to Louisa Gradgrind is a loveless union that ends when she leaves him and returns to her father's home (II:12). The truth about his origins is revealed at the close of the novel (III:5).

A satiric portrait of a "Manchester Man"—the composite of the generation of mill owners that emerged in the early decades of the INDUSTRIAL REVOLUTION—Bounderby has often been considered one of the great achievements in *Hard Times*. Described by James Marlow (*Charles Dickens: The*

Uses of Time, 1994) as "an archetypal character of capitalistic civilization," Bounderby represents the practical captains of industry who often allied themselves with the philosophic radicals like Gradgrind to promote their interests and doctrines of laissez-faire. Typical of this new class, Bounderby combines ownership of the factory with that of the bank to control the economy of Coketown; he celebrates his economic ascendancy by hiring as his housekeeper Mrs. Sparsit, a lady with upper-class relations, and by acquiring in a liquidation sale a country house formerly owned by a member of the gentry. Most of all, Bounderby concocts a clichéd rags-to-riches story, attributing his success solely to his own hard work. The novel exposes him as a bounder and fraud and his story as a lying misuse of the power of fiction.

Childers, E. W. B.   Equestrian performer with Sleary's Circus, "a remarkable sort of Centaur . . . celebrated for his daring vaulting act as the Wild Huntsman of the North American Prairies" (I:6). He stands up to Gradgrind and Bounderby when they disparage Sissy's father (I:6), and he later helps Tom escape to LIVERPOOL (III:7, 8). He is married to Sleary's daughter Josephine, and their three-year-old son is billed as "The Little Wonder of Scholastic Equitation" (III:7). His name is associated with the childlike qualities of the imagination that are represented by the circus and threatened by industrialism.

Coketown   Industrial town that serves as the setting for *Hard Times;* "a town of machinery and tall chimneys, out of which interminable serpents of smoke trailed themselves for ever and ever, and never got uncoiled. It had a black canal in it, and a river that ran purple with ill-smelling dye, and vast piles of building full of windows where there was a rattling and trembling all day long, and where the piston of the steam-engine worked monotonously up and down like the head of an elephant in a state of melancholy madness" (I:5). Commentators have disagreed whether the original of Coketown was Manchester or Preston; it is safe to say that it is neither but rather a town based on Dickens's visits to both places and to other industrial towns in the north of England.

Gordon, Emma   Tightrope walker in Sleary's Circus who comforts Sissy after her father abandons her (I:6). She marries an admiring cheesemonger (III:7).

Gradgrind, Louisa   Gradgrind's daughter, whose emotional life and imagination are blighted by her father's philosophy. She is vaguely aware that something is missing in her upbringing and her life: "struggling through the dissatisfaction of her face, there was a light with nothing to rest upon, a fire with nothing to burn, a starved imagination keeping life in itself somehow, which brightened its expression." Taught to consult only her head and not her heart, she marries Bounderby because she can think of no reason not to, because her father provides no help with her decision (I:15), and because Tom asks her to. She is wholly unprepared to encounter the seductions of James Harthouse who, by playing on her affection for her brother, convinces her to leave her husband (II:11–12). She does not run off with Harthouse but instead returns to her father, whose transformation is inspired by her fall. She is denied the joys of motherhood but becomes a loving nurturer to Sissy's children (III:9).

Gradgrind, Mrs.   Thomas Gradgrind's wife. So much in the shadow of her husband, Mrs. Gradgrind lacks even the identity of a Christian name. She is "a little, thin, white, pink-eyed bundle of shawls, of surpassing feebleness, mental and bodily; who was always taking physic without any effect, and who, whenever she showed any symptom of coming to life, was invariably stunned by some weighty piece of fact tumbling on her" (I:4). Gradgrind's philosophy has so drained her of life that she is reduced to near transparency and idiocy. She dies unenlightened before Louisa returns home (II:9).

Gradgrind, Thomas   Retired merchant and member of Parliament for Coketown, he is the sponsor of a school devoted to teaching his philosophy of hard facts and a representative of the UTILITARIAN point of view in Parliament. "A man of realities—a man of facts and calculations—a man who proceeds upon the principle that two and two are four, and nothing over, and who is not to be talked into allowing

Portrait of Gradgrind by Furniss (1910).

for anything over" (I:2). Gradgrind's educational system discourages imagination, stresses fact, and encourages such rote memorization as Bitzer's definition of a horse (I:2). The children are told to "never wonder" (I:8). This heartless philosophy has its harshest effects on his children: Louisa accepts a loveless marriage, and Tom is consummately selfish. The names of the other Gradgrind children, Jane, Adam Smith, and Malthus, bespeak their father's philosophical commitments. The coldness, hardness, and lack of imagination in Gradgrind's philosophy is caricatured in Stone Lodge, his home, which expresses the same qualities as its owner: "A great square house, with a heavy portico darkening the principal windows, as its master's heavy brows overshadowed his eyes" (I:3).

Gradgrind is not a wholly unsympathetic figure. His motives, unlike Bounderby's, are not self-interested, and his remorse when Louisa leaves her husband and Tom robs a bank generates a natural sympathy for him not unlike that for the converted Scrooge. Gradgrind has often been criticized, especially in the 19th century, as a shallow and ignorant depiction of UTILITARIANISM, but the story recounted in John Stuart Mill's *Autobiography* (1873) of his nervous breakdown after he underwent a one-sided utilitarian curriculum gives credence to Dickens's critique.

Gradgrind, Thomas, Jr. ("the Whelp") Son of Thomas Gradgrind whose education leaves him totally selfish and unconcerned for others: "It was very remarkable that a young gentleman who had been brought up under one continuous system of unnatural restraint, should be a hypocrite; but it was certainly the case with Tom. It was very strange that a young gentleman who had never been left to his own guidance for five consecutive minutes, should be incapable at last of governing himself; but so it was with Tom. It was altogether unaccountable that a young gentleman whose imagination had been strangled in its cradle, should be still inconvenienced by its ghost in the form of groveling sensualities; but such a monster, beyond all doubt, was Tom" (II:3). Tom urges Louisa to marry Bounderby to forward his own career at Bounderby's bank (I:14). Later, he robs the bank after framing Stephen Blackpool to appear guilty (II:6–8). He hides in Sleary's circus, and Sleary helps him escape to Liverpool and from there to America.

Harthouse, James A good-looking gentleman of 35 who comes as a potential parliamentary candidate to look over Coketown. "Had tried life as a Cornet of Dragoons, and found it a bore; and had afterwards tried it in the train of an English minister abroad, and found it a bore; and had then strolled to Jerusalem, and got bored there; and had then gone yachting about the world, and got bored

everywhere" (II:2). He insinuates his way into Louisa Bounderby's affections by his apparent interest in her brother Tom, whom he calls "the Whelp" (II:7). When Bounderby is away, he meets Louisa in the garden of her country house and urges her to run off with him, but she returns instead to her father's home (II:11–12). Representing Louisa, Sissy Jupe confronts him and persuades him to leave Coketown (III:2).

Described by GEORGE BERNARD SHAW (1985) as the typical Victorian "swell," Harthouse is the catalyst who prompts Louisa's transformation, even as he fails to engage her affections. He is less sympathetically treated than some others among Dickens's dandies, characters such as Sydney Carton in *A Tale of Two Cities* or Eugene Wrayburn in *Our Mutual Friend.* Diffident, fashionable, and smooth, he is described as satanic and devilish, and he uses his diabolical smoothness to take in Gradgrind, corrupt Tom, and seduce Louisa. In the end, his schemes come to nothing, and he leaves Coketown "a great Pyramid of failure . . . to go up the Nile" (III:2).

Jupe, Cecelia (Sissy) Daughter of the circus clown and dog trainer Signor Jupe, she is adopted into the Gradgrind household when her father runs off and abandons her. There she is unsuccessfully educated, as "Girl number twenty," at Gradgrind's school. A foil to Bitzer, whose whiteness reveals his lack of human feeling and warmth, Sissy "was so dark-eyed and dark-haired, that she seemed to receive a deeper and more lustrous color from the sun, when it shone upon her" (I:2). She is wholly incapable of making sense of statistics, which she calls "stutterings." Her loving-kindness counters the "hard fact" utilitarianism in the Gradgrind household. She cares for Louisa after her separation from Bounderby, convinces Harthouse to leave Coketown (III:2), discovers the dying Stephen Blackpool in the Old Hell Shaft (III:6), and accompanies Gradgrind and Louisa when they go to Sleary's circus in search of Tom (III:7).

Jupe, Signor Circus clown and dog trainer who disappears from the circus when he thinks himself too old to perform (I:6). Although Jupe's fate remains unknown, Sleary assumes that he has died when his dog, Merrylegs, returns to the circus on his own (III:8).

Kidderminster "A diminutive boy with an old face" who assists E. W. B. Childers in his equestrian act in Sleary's Circus. "Made up with curls, wreaths, wings, white bismuth, and carmine, this hopeful young person soared into so pleasing a Cupid as to constitute the chief delight of the maternal part of the spectators; but in private, where his characteristics were a precocious cut-away coat and an extremely gruff voice, he became of the Turf, turfy" (I:6). Like that of his colleague Childers, Kidderminster's name suggests the childlike imagination that is symbolized by the circus.

M'Choakumchild Schoolmaster in Gradgrind's school of hard facts. "He and some one hundred and forty other schoolmasters, had been lately turned out at the same time, in the same factory, on the same principles, like so many pianoforte legs. He had been put through an immense variety of paces, and had answered volumes of head-breaking questions. Orthography, etymology, syntax, and prosody, biography, astronomy, geography, and general cosmography, the sciences of compound proportion, algebra, land-surveying and levelling, vocal music, and drawing from models, were all at the ends of his ten chilled fingers. . . . If he had only learnt a little less, how infinitely better he might have taught much more!" (I:2).

In M'Choakumchild, Dickens satirizes the generation of teachers produced—mechanically, he thought—by the new teachers' colleges. M'Choakumchild's Scottish ancestry alludes to the importance of the Scots as political economists and hard-facts philosophers. GEORGE H. FORD and SYLVÈRE MONOD (1966) suggest that M'Choakumchild was based on the Scottish schoolmaster and textbook writer J. M. McCulloch, headmaster of Circus-Place School, Edinburgh.

Merrylegs Signor Jupe's performing dog. The dog disappears with its master (I:6) but later returns to the circus to die, an event Sleary takes as a sign that Jupe is also dead (III:8).

Nickits The former owner of Bounderby's country house whose improvidence caused the bank to foreclose on his mortgage (II:7). Bounderby contrasts Nickits's public-school background with his own allegedly deprived childhood.

Old Hell Shaft The abandoned mine shaft where Stephen Blackpool is found after his disappearance (III:6).

Pegasus Arms, the The inn where the Sleary circus troupe stays in Coketown (I:6).

Pegler, Mrs. The mysterious old country woman who occasionally appears in the streets of Coketown looking at Bounderby's house or factory: "The flutter of her manner, in the unwonted noise of the streets; the spare shawl, carried unfolded on her arm; the heavy umbrella, and little basket; the loose long-fingered gloves, to which her hands were unused; all bespoke an old woman from the country" (I:12). She is revealed to be Bounderby's mother (III:5). He has given her 30 pounds a year on the condition that she keep secret her relationship to him so that he can maintain the fiction of being a self-made man.

Powler Family to which Mrs. Sparsit boasts of being connected through her late husband; they "could trace themselves so exceedingly far back that it was not surprising if they sometimes lost themselves" (I:7).

Rachael Coketown factory hand and faithful friend to Stephen Blackpool: "She turned . . . and showed a quiet oval face, dark and rather delicate, irradiated by a pair of very gentle eyes, and further set off by the perfect order of her shining black hair. It was not a face in its first bloom; she was a woman of five-and-thirty years" (I:10). Although she and Stephen love each other, his inability to secure a divorce from his drunken wife prevents their marrying. She tends Stephen's wife during her illness (I:13). Stephen's promise to her not to join the trade union causes the other workmen to shun him (II:4). With Sissy, she discovers the injured Blackpool at the bottom of Old Hell Shaft (III:6).

Scadgers, Lady Mrs. Sparsit's great aunt, "an immensely fat old woman, with an inordinate appetite for butcher's meat, and a mysterious leg which had now refused to get out of bed for fourteen years" (I:7).

Slackbridge Union organizer in Coketown who publicly castigates Blackpool for refusing to join the association. "An ill-made, high-shouldered man, with lowering brows, and his features crushed into an habitually sour expression, he contrasted most unfavourably, even in his mongrel dress, with the great body of his hearers in their plain working clothes" (II:4).

GEORGE BERNARD SHAW (1985) considers Slackbridge Dickens's "one real failure in the book," revealing the author's bourgeois mistrust of unions. Slackbridge's characterization is vague, and his language, as STEVEN CONNOR (1985) points out, has an "elaborately 'written' quality."

Sleary Proprietor of an equestrian circus, "a stout man . . . with one fixed eye, and one loose eye" and a lisping, asthmatic voice "like the efforts of a broken pair of bellows, . . . and a muddled head which was never sober and never drunk" (I:6). He cares for Sissy Jupe after her father deserts her (I:6), and he shelters Tom Gradgrind after he runs from Coketown (III:7). Sleary's philosophy, summed up in his assertion "People mutht be amuthed" (III:8), expresses Dickens's views that imagination must temper hard facts and that amusement is essential even in the most earnest life. Many commentators consider Sleary's circus inadequate as a symbol to represent the realm of imagination and counter the factualism of Gradgrind's philosophy.

Sleary, Josephine The circus owner's daughter, "who had been tied on a horse at two years old, and had made a will at twelve, which she always carried about with her, expressive of her dying desire to be drawn to the grave by the two piebald ponies" (I:6). She marries E. W. B. Childers.

Sparsit, Mrs. Bounderby's housekeeper. A widow with aristocratic pretensions and "a Coriolanian style of nose" (I:7), she trades on her connections with the Powler and Scadgers families and hopes to marry Bounderby. When he marries Louisa, she is relegated to a position at Bounderby's bank where, resentfully, she sets out to undermine his marriage, creating the fantasy of a great staircase that she sees Louisa descending. She spies on Louisa, brings news of Louisa's rendezvous with Harthouse (III:3), and uncovers the identity of Mrs. Pegler as Bounderby's mother (III:5), an act for which she is dismissed from Bounderby's service (III:9). Critics have generally admired Mrs. Sparsit as an unerring portrait of aristocratic snobbery, satirically balanced to Bounderby's bourgeois pretensions. Each is, in a way, the undoing of the other.

ADAPTATIONS

Very few dramatic versions of *Hard Times* have been produced. The first, a melodramatic adaptation by FREDERICK FOX COOPER, appeared at the close of the novel's serial run, but it radically changed the story by rehabilitating nearly every character: Tom returned the stolen money to the bank, Blackpool lived through his accident to marry Rachael, and Louisa was reunited with Bounderby, who ended the play bestowing gifts on everyone.

THOMAS BENTLEY made a silent film version (1915) with BRANSBY WILLIAMS as Gradgrind. Arthur Hopcraft's four-part television adaptation appeared on Granada TV in 1977. A four-part serial for the BBC (1994), directed and written by Peter Barnes, presented Bob Peck as Gradgrind and Alan Bates as Bounderby.

FURTHER READING

F. R. LEAVIS's essay, first included in *The Great Tradition* (1948) and later in slightly revised form in *Dickens the Novelist* (1970), defined many of the critical issues in *Hard Times* and threw down a gauntlet to other critics by describing the novel as a "masterpiece." John Holloway ("*Hard Times*: A History and a Criticism," *Dickens and the Twentieth Century*, edited by John Gross and Gabriel Pearson, 1962) responded to Leavis by arguing that the novel was a shallow and simplistic rendering of utilitarianism. Robin Gilmour ("The Gradgrind School: Political Economy in the Classroom," *Victorian Studies*, 1967), on the other hand, showed that Dickens understood in some depth the educational philosophy and schools that he was attacking. MICHAEL GOLDBERG (1972) discusses Dickens's debt to THOMAS CARLYLE in the novel. PAUL SCHLICKE (1985) describes Victorian circuses and analyzes the symbolism of the circus in the novel. STEVEN CONNOR (1985) deconstructs the novel by analyzing the tensions between metaphor and metonymy. KATE FLINT (1986) suggests that Dickens failed to confront the structural and social issues in his critique of industrial capitalism and chose instead to offer a sentimental vision of Sleary's circus as an anarchic alternative to Coketown. GEORGE H. FORD and SYLVÈRE MONOD (1966), in their edition of the novel, include a selection of contemporary background pieces and responses to the novel as well as Leavis's essay and some responses to it. Margaret Simpson's *Companion to Hard Times* (1997) provides exhaustive notes to the text, its sources, contexts, and backgrounds.

Haunted Man and The Ghost's Bargain, The: A Fancy for Christmas-Time

Fifth and last of the CHRISTMAS BOOKS, published for Christmas 1848 by BRADBURY & EVANS, with illustrations by JOHN TENNIEL, FRANK STONE, CLARKSON STANFIELD, and JOHN LEECH. Returning to a story of a Christmas conversion, Dickens tells how Redlaw, a chemist who is given a gift that enables him to eradicate painful memories, learns how important such memories are in enabling love and understanding between people.

SYNOPSIS

(1) Redlaw, a professor of chemistry, sits before his fire on Christmas Eve, brooding on the past and looking like a haunted man. It is a cold and windy night, and even in his vaultlike dwelling, part library and part laboratory, he is chilled and depressed in the gathering darkness. The keeper of the college, William Swidger, comes to stir the fire and lay the table for dinner. As he does so, he

talks of his wife, Milly, and of her concern for a sick student and for a street urchin she has taken in. When she arrives with the dinner, her father-in-law, 87-year-old Philip Swidger, comes with her, bringing bunches of holly to decorate the college rooms for Christmas. He remembers past Christmases, even the painful ones, and the memories make him "merry and happy."

After they leave, Redlaw is troubled by painful memories of his own—of his sister's death and of a friend who betrayed him by jilting his sister and stealing his fiancée. He finds that each Christmas only adds "more figures in the lengthening sum of recollection that we work and work at to our torment." As he ruminates, his double appears out of the gloom and stands behind his chair. This phantom rehearses the wounds of Redlaw's past, and when the chemist wishes to "forget my sorrow and my wrong," the specter offers him the opportunity to do so. He even goes a step further: Since the chemist has recognized that "the memory of sorrow, wrong, and trouble is the lot of all mankind," he will also be granted the power to erase the memories of those he meets. After the specter

Tenniel's frontispiece for *The Haunted Man* (1848) shows Redlaw encircled by contending angels and devils.

melts away, the chemist hears a cry in the lecture hall adjoining his rooms. He finds there the ragged waif that Milly has taken in; the child is looking for her.

(2) At the Tetterby house in Jerusalem Buildings, Mr. Tetterby lovingly tends his rambunctious children. When Mrs. Tetterby comes home with supper, she is upset and tells her husband that she envies those in the market with more money and resents being poor. But after she is at home for a while, she remembers their trials together as a family and her heart is softened. The Tetterbys are surprised by Redlaw, who comes to their flat seeking the sick student. As he leaves, the once-happy family, influenced by his power to erase their softening memories, begins fighting.

The student turns out to be Edmund Denham, the quietest and most retiring of all Redlaw's students. He explains that his real name is Edmund Longford and that he is the son of the woman whom Redlaw once loved. He chose another name in order to be judged only on his own merits. After telling Redlaw of his admiration for him, Denham steps forward to touch the chemist, but Redlaw, to avoid physical contact with the boy, backs away, throwing a purse to him as he does so. Hurt and insulted, Denham returns the purse, but Redlaw grasps him by the arm and the student forgets his past, his obligations, and his resentments. When Milly comes to visit Denham, he is curt with her, suggesting that she makes more of his illness than it deserves and asking what payment she expects for her attentions. Hurt and rejected, Milly leaves.

Redlaw is distressed by his influence on others. "I am infected," he cries, "I am infectious! I am charged with poison for my own mind, and the minds of all mankind. Where I felt interest, compassion, sympathy, I am turning into stone." Hating his new power, Redlaw seeks solitude. Then he remembers the urchin, the one person who would seem able only to benefit from his powers. He finds the boy and asks to be taken to the slum where the boy comes from. As they go along, Redlaw realizes that "the expression on the boy's face was the expression on his own," that they are doubles. Redlaw believes that taking away the memories of sorrow, wrong, and trouble that torment those in

Stone's illustration of Milly Swidger with the Tetterby children for *The Haunted Man* (1848).

the slum can do no harm. But his power affects an abused woman so that she is not softened by memories of her family, and it hardens a repentant George Swidger against reconciliation with his father and brother. Old Philip, denied his softening memories, becomes instantly senile, aware only that he is 87. Alarmed by the destructiveness of his power, Redlaw rushes back to his flat with the boy and locks himself in. Milly comes to the door begging him to help her deal with the sorrowful changes that have occurred, but he refuses. He prays for the phantom to return and take back the gift.

(3) Back in his rooms with the boy, Redlaw again confronts the phantom. When he asks that the curse he has laid on others be withdrawn, the phantom tells him to seek out Milly. Then the phantom explains that the boy is the one creature who is not changed by Redlaw, because he has no softening memories to lose.

The next morning the Tetterbys are still fighting, regretting that they ever married and ever had children. But when Milly comes to their house, they are reconciled and restored to a loving family. Milly tells them that Redlaw came to her very early on Christmas morning, and together they went to the slum, where the abused woman regained soothing memories of her family and George Swidger again became penitent. Now at the Jerusalem Buildings the Tetterbys are reconciled and Edmund Longford asks forgiveness for his cruel treatment of Milly. Redlaw can see in those around him how much is lost with the loss of memories.

Back at the Swidgers' rooms, Milly restores the good feeling in her family and reunites Redlaw with Mr. Longford, who, many years before, had wronged Redlaw by jilting his sister and stealing his fiancée. Now a penitent, Longford has returned to seek Redlaw's forgiveness and that of Edmund, the son that he abandoned. Edmund is also reunited with his fiancée, reminding Redlaw of his own love many years before. In the end all are brought together in the old college hall, where they celebrate Christmas dinner beneath the portrait of the college founder. After the events of Christmas Eve, the prayer of the founder has taken on new meaning for Redlaw: "Lord, keep my memory green."

COMMENTARY

Dickens began *Haunted Man* in the fall of 1847, but he found that it diverted his attention from *Dombey and Son* and quickly abandoned his original plan to release the book for Christmas. As a result, 1847 was the first year in five in which Dickens did not write a Christmas book. When he resumed work on the story in autumn 1848, he found the writing difficult, and the manuscript, now in the collection of the Pforzheimer Foundation in New York, shows considerably more revision than usual. One of the original reviewers, writing in *Macphail's Edinburgh Ecclesiastical Journal* (January 1849), was so displeased with the tale that he advised the author to "quit the *twenty-fifth of December,* and take to the *first of April.*" Many modern readers have also been unmoved by the story, described by EDGAR JOHNSON (1977) as "feeble," "slapdash," "sentimental," and "overmoralistic."

Haunted Man follows Dickens's plan for all of the CHRISTMAS BOOKS of giving a "higher form" to an "old nursery tale." The presence of ghosts and phantoms that turn Redlaw's wishes into magical

and destructive powers; the countering effect of the "fairy godmother," Milly Swidger; and the sudden transformations of the chemist and of several other characters are all elements that Dickens took from FAIRY TALES, especially from the stories of E. T. A. Hoffmann. In this use of fairy-tale conventions and motifs, *The Haunted Man* is, of all the Christmas books, most like *A Christmas Carol.*

Dickens shapes his fairy tale to a higher form by injecting into the story realistic commentary on the social conditions of his time, especially through the figure of the orphan waif. This neglected slum child has never experienced love or caring from others and thus has no humanizing memories to counter his brutish ignorance. He is a warning to Victorian England of the results of social neglect. He is also a DOUBLE to Redlaw, a perverse projection of the scientist's wish to alleviate human suffering by suppressing painful memories of the past.

Haunted Man also achieves its higher form by using the fairy story to explore the psychology of the chemist and his wish to free himself and humanity from painful memories. That wish—one of the central desires of scientific rationalism—is shown to lack psychological and spiritual understanding of the human condition. Deprived of such memories, mankind loses community; relationships formerly based on shared suffering are reduced to cash transactions.

The opening chapter, "The Gift Bestowed," presents the haunted man, the chemist Redlaw, inhabiting his college fortress like an ogre in his castle. His apartment and his laboratory are separated only by a curtain. His rooms suggest that his inner life is all mind, "part library and part laboratory." Nevertheless, Redlaw is not an enlightened man; instead he is surrounded by darkness and gloom, engulfed in a paralytic cloud of despair and self-pity. As the darkness of Christmas Eve descends, his depression deepens. The good nature of the Swidgers and their preparations for Christmas cannot penetrate his gloom. Unlike old Philip Swidger, who hangs Christmas greens while keeping green the memories of his long life, Redlaw is tormented by his painful memories.

As he dwells on these memories, Redlaw's gloom deepens until it calls up a phantom, the chemist's double, who grants Redlaw's wish to cast out the poisonous memories in his mind just as a chemist might counter poisons in the body with a chemical antidote. But the phantom's gift will not be limited to Redlaw alone. Articulating the benevolent scientist's desire to aid mankind with his knowledge, the phantom also gives Redlaw the power to be mankind's benefactor: "Your wisdom has discovered that the memory of sorrow, wrong, and trouble is the lot of all mankind, and that mankind would be happier, in its other memories, without it. Go! Be its benefactor! Freed from such remembrance, from this hour, carry involuntarily the blessing of such freedom with you."

This gift turns out to be a Faustian bargain rather than a blessing. The second chapter, "The Gift Diffused," shows its effects on Redlaw and others. He blights the loving Tetterby family, similar to the Cratchits in *Carol,* who, lacking the memories of shared suffering symbolized by the remnants of their past occupations in their shop window, focus on present distress and blame each other for their difficulties. Redlaw's presence also prevents George Swidger's reconciliation with his family, for without memory, George lacks reasons for penitence and the family lacks sources for forgiveness. And with his own memories gone, Redlaw loses his former benevolence; when he unfeelingly offers money to minister to the sick student's illness, mechanical charity has replaced fellow feeling.

Only two characters remain untouched by Redlaw's power. The urchin child has no healing memories to counter the unrelenting pain of his life. He has no ties to others. By the end of the second chapter, Redlaw, locked in his rooms with the urchin, realizes that he is like the child: Stripped of his memories, he has lost his ties to others. His gift, in its effects on himself and on those he touches, is revealed to be a curse. Milly Swidger is the other person untouched by Redlaw's power. Her love for those around her, from her family to the students who affectionately call her "Swidge," derives from her memories, especially from the painful memory of a lost child. In the final chapter, "The Gift Reversed," her counterinfluence restores the Tetterbys to a loving family, reconciles George Swidger and his family, restores Longford to health, and

reconciles him with Redlaw. Milly also restores Redlaw's repressed memories and, by bringing them to light, frees him from the neurotic denial that has paralyzed him and darkened his life. By the end he has discovered the truth of the founder's prayer for his own life, "Lord, keep my memory green."

The higher form that Dickens's tale takes, then, is one that challenges Redlaw's enlightenment rationalism, showing its one-sidedness in its stress on intellect and its denial of emotion. Redlaw is not just wrong in his rationalism; he is also emotionally paralyzed, unable to act positively or lovingly. In the fable of freeing the chemist from these psychological neuroses, Dickens foreshadows the Freudian analysis of Redlaw's condition. For Dickens, however, the final form that the fable takes is spiritual. Milly represents more than psychological liberation, more than an embodiment of Redlaw's emotional "better wisdom." When Redlaw thanks Milly, "who through the teaching of pure love, has graciously restored me to the memory which was the memory of Christ upon the cross, and of all the good who perished in His cause," he is reminded of the Christian doctrine of suffering, and the story becomes a Christmas Christian ALLEGORY.

CHARACTERS AND RELATED ENTRIES

Denham, Edmund Name taken by Edmund Longford to maintain his anonymity as Redlaw's student.

feral boy A boy who is rescued from the slums by Molly Swidger and discovered by Redlaw in his rooms: "A bundle of tatters, held together by a hand, in size and form almost an infant's, but, in its greedy, desperate little clutch, a bad old man's. A face rounded and smoothed by some half-dozen years, but pinched and twisted by the experiences of a life. Bright eyes, but not youthful. Naked feet, beautiful in their childish delicacy,—ugly in the blood and dirt that cracked upon them. A baby savage, a young monster, a child who had never been a child, a creature who might live to take the outward form of man, but who, within, would live and perish a mere beast." He guides Redlaw to the slums from which he comes; there the chemist sees the effects of his gift on the urchin and on George Swidger.

This feral urchin has no softening memories to be affected by Redlaw's gift. As a double to Redlaw, he is the child within so traumatized by the painful experiences of his past that he is unable to grow through acknowledging them. But he has been touched, as Redlaw will be, by Milly's power to teach forgiveness and growth through pain.

Jerusalem Buildings The row of shops that houses the Tetterbys' shop and lodgings and the rooms of the poor student, Edmund Longford.

Longford, Edmund Redlaw's student, he takes the name Edmund Denham to conceal his identity as the son of Redlaw's one-time fiancée. Poor and ailing, he is cared for by Molly Swidger. When Redlaw's gift releases him from his memories, he turns against Milly, but her loving influence restores him to his better self.

Longford, Mr. Edmund's father, formerly Redlaw's friend and the fiancé of Redlaw's sister. He jilted Redlaw's sister and ran off with Redlaw's fiancée, embittering the scientist. Milly shows Redlaw the reduced situation of Longford since: "He has long been separated from his wife and son—has been a stranger to his home almost from his son's infancy, I learn from him—and has abandoned and deserted what he should have held most dear. In all that time he has been falling from the state of a gentleman, more and more."

Redlaw Protagonist of *Haunted Man*, a professor of chemistry who is visited by a phantom double on Christmas Eve. He is a popular teacher and a benevolent man, but his life is darkened by past sorrows. "Who could have seen his hollow cheek, his sunken brilliant eye; his black attired figure, indefinably grim, although well-knit and well-proportioned; his grizzled hair hanging, like tangled sea-weed about his face,—as if he had been, through his whole life, a lonely mark for the chafing and beating of the great deep of humanity,—but might have said he looked like a haunted man?" The phantom offers to rid him of these painful memories on the condition

that the chemist will also pass this gift on to those he touches. The gift turns out to be a curse, for without the capacity to remember past hurts and sorrows, Redlaw and those he influences lose their compassion, their ability to feel for the troubles of others. Redlaw's power is countered and reversed by Milly Swidger, his "better wisdom," who restores community to those affected by Redlaw by restoring the healing power of memory.

Redlaw's desire to suppress painful memories may have been prompted by Dickens's desire to do the same, for at about the time he was working on *Haunted Man*, he wrote the autobiographical fragment describing his painful experiences at the BLACKING WAREHOUSE. Just a month before he began writing the story, his sister FANNY DICKENS died. Redlaw's role as a scientist extends these personal issues to the broader question of scientific progress and its contribution to human happiness. Seeing the destructive impact of his power on others makes Redlaw recognize the necessity of accepting and forgiving his past pains rather than simply repressing them.

Redlaw's name may also suggest his role as a scientist, for at the time scientists were studying the processes of the natural world and the struggle for existence among species. Only two years after *The Haunted Man*, ALFRED TENNYSON, in *In Memoriam* (1850), would characterize the "law" of the natural world as described by the scientists as "red in tooth and claw."

Swidger, George Old Philip's dissolute eldest son. On his deathbed he is repentant, but when touched by Redlaw's gift, he loses his penitence and dies unreconciled with his family.

Swidger, Milly ("Mrs. William," "Mouse," "Swidge") William's wife: "Mrs. William, like Mr. William, was a simple, innocent-looking person, in whose smooth cheeks the cheerful red of her husband's official waistcoat was very pleasantly repeated. But whereas Mr. William's light hair stood on end all over his head, and seemed to draw his eyes up with it in an excess of bustling readiness for anything, the dark brown hair of Mrs. William was carefully smoothed down, and waved away under a trim tidy cap, in the most exact and quiet manner imaginable. Whereas Mr. William's very trousers hitched themselves up at the ankles, as if it were not in their iron-grey nature to rest without looking about them, Mrs. William's neatly-flowered skirts—red and white, like her own pretty face—were as composed and orderly, as if the very wind that blew so hard out of doors could not disturb one of their folds." Her "better wisdom," rooted in her own sorrows and especially in the memory of her dead child, restores the memory and compassion of those affected by Redlaw's curse.

Swidger, Philip (Old Philip) Eighty-seven-year-old father of George and William, "who don't know what forgetting means." He is the former custodian of the school where Redlaw teaches.

Swidger, William Philip's youngest son, Milly's husband. He is Redlaw's servant and the keeper of the college, "a fresh-colored busy man."

Tetterby, Adolphus A struggling newsagent, husband to Sophia and the father of eight children. "The small man who sat in the small parlor, making fruitless attempts to read his newspaper peaceably in the midst of this disturbance, was the father of the family, and the chief of the firm described in the inscription over the little shop front, by the name and title of A. Tetterby and Co., Newsmen. Indeed, strictly speaking, he was the only personae answering to that designation; as Co. was a mere poetical abstraction, altogether baseless and impersonal." Under the influence of Redlaw's power to erase memory, Adolphus's usual good spirits are lost, but they are restored again on Christmas morning by Milly Swidger.

Tetterby, Adolphus, Jr. ('Dolphus) The eldest son in the Tetterby family, a newspaper boy "at a railway station, where his chubby little person, like a shabbily disguised Cupid, and his shrill little voice (he was not much more than ten years old), were as well known as the hoarse panting of the locomotives, running in and out."

Tetterby, Johnny The Tetterbys second son, who minds the baby of the family: "another little boy—the biggest there, but still little—was tottering to and fro, bent on one side, and considerably affected in his knees by the weight of a large baby, which he was supposed to be hushing to sleep."

Tetterby, Sally ("Little Moloch") The youngest Tetterby child, an infant, the first daughter after seven sons.

Tetterby, Sophia "The process of induction, by which Mr. Tetterby had come to the conclusion that his wife was a little woman, was his own secret. She would have made two editions of himself, very easily. Considered as an individual, she was rather remarkable for being robust and portly; but considered with reference to her husband, her dimensions became magnificent."

ADAPTATIONS

Haunted Man has not been as popular with theatrical and film adaptors as most of Dickens's other works. Although about 14 stage versions appeared between 1848 and 1850, there have been few later adaptations. The first adaptation, by MARK LEMON, "by express permission of the author," was staged for 42 performances at the ADELPHI THEATER, London, between December 20, 1848 and February 7, 1849. Among other early stage adaptations was one by EDWARD STIRLING, the last of Dickens's works that he adapted. Stirling's version does not seem to have been performed. No film or television adaptations of the story have been made.

BRET HARTE's parody of Dickens's CHRISTMAS BOOKS, "The Haunted Man. A Christmas Story. By CH_R_S D_CK_N_S," in his *Condensed Novels* (1867), is partly based on *Haunted Man.*

FURTHER READING

HARRY STONE analyzes the style and structure of the story in "Dickens' Artistry and *The Haunted Man*" (*South Atlantic Quarterly*, 1962) and later discusses its fairy-tale techniques (1979). Deborah Thomas (*Dickens and the Short Story*, 1982) discusses the ways in which reading contributes to humanizing memory. Stanley Tick ("Autobiographical Impulses in *The Haunted Man*," *Dickens*

Quarterly, 2001) explores the painful memories that haunted the author.

Little Dorrit

Dickens's 11th novel, published in monthly numbers (December 1855–June 1857) by BRADBURY & EVANS, illustrated by HABLOT KNIGHT BROWNE. Published in one volume, 1857. *Little Dorrit* may be the most difficult of Dickens's novels. Its passive hero and heroine, obscure and complex inheritance plot, and unremittingly bleak picture of society make it a dark and ambiguous story. It anatomizes Victorian Britain as a nation obsessed with wealth and power, imprisoned by traditions of class privilege, and diminished by oppressive and negative religion. Arthur Clennam and Amy Dorrit struggle to overcome these imprisoning forces, and the novel ends on a redemptive and hopeful note as they seem to begin a more authentic and fulfilling way of life.

SYNOPSIS
Book I: Poverty

Part 1 (December 1855)
(I:1) On a bright August day in MARSEILLE 30 years ago, two prisoners linger in a dark cell, Monsieur Rigaud, charged with murdering his wife, and Italian John Baptist Cavalletto, a small-time smuggler. (I:2) At the same time, several English travelers returning from the East are in quarantine in Marseille: the Meagleses (a retired banker and his wife), their pampered daughter Pet, and her servant Tattycoram; Miss Wade, a bitter and unforgiving spinster; and Arthur Clennam, returning to London after many years working in his family business in China. Clennam speaks of his lack of purpose and will. (I:3) Arthur arrives in London on Sunday and remembers the oppressive Sundays of his childhood. He finds his mother's house unchanged: decaying and rusting, blackened by the smoke of the city, and propped up by huge timbers. His invalid mother, confined to a chair in an upper room, is also unchanged. She greets him coldly. (I:4) Meanwhile, Affery Flintwinch,

Mrs. Clennam's maid, sees her husband with his double in the middle of the night. After sending the double away, Flintwinch tells her she has been dreaming.

Part 2 (January 1856)
(I:5) The next day Arthur offends his mother by withdrawing from the family business and by asking if his late father had any guilty secret that he might have wanted to set right. Mrs. Clennam takes Flintwinch into the business in Arthur's place. Arthur wonders if his family's guilty secret has to do with his mother's servant, Amy Dorrit.

(I:6) Amy, also known as Little Dorrit, was born in the MARSHALSEA PRISON, a debtors' prison where her father, William Dorrit, has been a prisoner longer than any other inmate and is known as "the Father of the Marshalsea." Other inmates and visitors acknowledge his importance by giving him small monetary tributes. (I:7) Amy grew up as "the Child of the Marshalsea." After her mother died when she was eight, she became the "mother" of the family, keeping the accounts and providing for her ungrateful older sister Fanny and her ne'er-do-well brother Tip. Amy goes out to work each day for Mrs. Clennam. (I:8) Curious about Amy, Arthur follows her and discovers that she lives in the Marshalsea. There he meets her father, William Dorrit; pays his respects; and leaves a tribute. He asks Little Dorrit's forgiveness for intruding in her life. When he attempts to leave the prison, he discovers that the gates have been closed and he must spend the night.

Part 3 (February 1856)
(I:9) Arthur's interest in Amy and her family continues. Amy tells him that getting her father out of prison is hopeless and, in any case, she worries that he could not survive outside the Marshalsea. After learning that Dorrit's primary creditor is Tite Barnacle of the Circumlocution Office, Arthur seeks him out to learn more (I:10) Devoted to the process of How Not To Do It, the Circumlocution Office has long been the preserve of the Barnacle family. After inquiring for Tite Barnacle several times and never seeing him, Arthur is finally introduced to Barnacle Junior who, after aimless conversation, sends him to Tite Barnacle's home in Mews

Street behind GROSVENOR SQUARE. There Arthur finds Tite Barnacle posing for a portrait; after more fruitless questioning Arthur is sent back to the Circumlocution Office, where he is given a lot of forms. As he leaves, Arthur meets Meagles with Daniel Doyce, an inventor who has unsuccessfully attempted to secure support for his invention at the Circumlocution Office. Instead of helping Doyce, the bureaucrats treat him as a public offender.

(I:11) The scene shifts to the Break of Day, a small inn in Chalons, France, where Rigaud and Cavaletto, the two prisoners from Marseille, meet again. Since they are both on their way north, Rigaud suggests that they travel together, but at dawn Cavaletto slips out of the inn and goes off on his own.

Part 4 *(March 1856)*

(I:12) Seeking information about the Dorrits, Clennam goes to Bleeding Heart Yard, a slum tenement, and there engages Plornish, an unemployed plasterer, to act as his agent in securing the release of Tip, Amy's brother, from the Marshalsea. (I:13)

Arthur finds Mr. Casby, landlord of the tenement and father of his childhood sweetheart, Flora. Now the widow of Mr. Finching, Flora has gained weight, but she is still silly, garrulous, and flirtatious. After an uncomfortable dinner with them, Arthur leaves with Pancks, Casby's rent collector. In the street they aid a foreigner—Cavaletto—who has been run over by a mail van. After this eventful day, Arthur ruminates on his life: "From the unhappy suppression of my youngest days, through the rigid and unloving home that followed them, through my departure, my long exile, my return . . . down to . . . this day with poor Flora, . . . What have I found!" As he asks this question, Little Dorrit appears at his door. (I:14) She tells him that Tip has been released from prison by the good agency of an unknown benefactor whom she is not allowed to thank. She asks Arthur to give no more money to her father. Then she spends the cold night in the streets, the first night she has ever spent outside the Marshalsea.

In "The Marshalsea Becomes an Orphan," Browne (Phiz) depicts the Dorrits leaving the prison after Mr. Dorrit comes into his fortune.

Part 5 (April 1856)

(I:15) Affery overhears her husband and Mrs. Clennam quarreling. Flintwinch accuses Mrs. Clennam of not putting Arthur's doubts about his father to rest. He warns her that he will not submit to being ruled by her. He also tries to discredit Little Dorrit, but Mrs. Clennam refuses to hear him out. Affery is convinced that something is wrong in the house.

(I:16) Arthur and Daniel Doyce go to the Meagleses' country place for a weekend. Arthur thinks about courting Pet and offering to become Doyce's business partner. (I:17) Arthur takes an immediate dislike to Henry Gowan, an arrogant and unsuccessful painter who comes to visit Pet. Doyce tells Arthur that Meagles dislikes Gowan so much that he took Pet away to Europe.

(I:18) Meanwhile, young John Chivery, son of the Marshalsea turnkey who looks to the Dorrits as the aristocracy of the prison, is infatuated with Amy. One Sunday, after bringing his tribute of cigars to Mr. Dorrit, he seeks out Amy on the Iron Bridge, a place where she goes seeking solitude, and asks her if he "may say it." She tells him that he should never say it and never again seek her out on the bridge. She wishes him happiness and a good wife. He goes home imagining the epitaph on his tombstone.

Part 6 (May 1856)

(I:19) The Dorrit brothers are a study in contrasts. William, the prisoner, is strong and healthy; Frederick, who lives outside the prison and works as a musician, is weak and depressed. William wonders whether his brother would have been better off in prison, but he decides that he would not have had the strength of character for it.

When Chivery, the turnkey, is short with him, William blames Amy for rejecting Chivery's son. As he eats the meal she has prepared for him, he pities himself and asks, "What am I worth to anyone?" She is so upset that she sits up the whole night, watching over him as he sleeps. (I:20) When Amy asks her sister about a bracelet she is wearing, Fanny takes her to Mrs. Merdle's house in Harley Street, CAVENDISH SQUARE. There Amy learns that Mrs. Merdle has offered Fanny presents—the bracelet, dresses, money—to prevent a romance between

Fanny and her son, Edmund Sparkler. Fanny justifies making Mrs. Merdle pay for her class snobbery, and she accuses Amy of acting in ways that encourage such people to despise them as paupers. (I:21) Later, at a dinner party at the Merdles' home, Bar and Bishop, Treasury and Admiralty, flatter their host, Mr. Merdle the financier, and speculate about his wealth. Mrs. Merdle displays her husband's jewels on her bosom. But there is a shadow over the party: Merdle has a physical complaint, even though his doctor can find nothing wrong with him.

(I:22) Once he stops paying tribute to Mr. Dorrit, as Amy has requested, Clennam does not rise in the estimation of the Father of the Marshalsea. Nevertheless he continues to visit. One Sunday Clennam sees young John Chivery, disconsolate and melancholy, pining for Little Dorrit. Clennam is surprised, for he has not thought of Little Dorrit in romantic terms. When he breaks his promise and sends some money to her father, Clennam is puzzled by the intensity of Amy's distress.

Part 7 (June 1856)

(I:23) Arthur buys a partnership in Doyce's factory in Bleeding Heart Yard, and he recruits Pancks to secure information about the Dorrits. (I:24) Flora wants to employ Little Dorrit, but she makes Amy uncomfortable by spilling out the story of her life and her relationship to Arthur. Amy is also intimidated by Pancks, who observes her closely and tells her fortune. After he describes her family with uncanny accuracy and tells her that she "shall live to see," she retreats to her room. There she tells Maggy, a retarded woman who regards Amy as her "Little Mother," the story of a princess and a little woman who works at her wheel and has a secret shadow hidden in her closet. When the little woman dies, the princess cannot find the shadow and believes that it has gone, as the little woman said it would, into her grave with her. (I:25) Cavalletto moves into Bleeding Heart Yard, where the residents teach him English and notice that he peers out into the streets as if he is fearful of someone.

Part 8 (July 1856)

(I:26) Had Arthur decided to court Pet, he would have intensely disliked Henry Gowan. Gowan does bother Mr. Meagles. When Clennam goes with Gowan to visit the artist's mother at Hampton Court, Arthur meets a group of condescending aristocratic parasites. Mrs. Gowan asserts that Pet is just a social climber trying to "catch" her son, but Arthur, angered by her snobbery and condescension, assures her that Mr. Meagles is not pleased by the courtship. (I:27) When Meagles asks Clennam to help him search for Tattycoram, who has run away, they find the girl living with Miss Wade. She tells Tattycoram that Meagles wants to take her back to be "a foil to his pretty daughter, a slave to her pleasant wilfulness, and a toy in the house showing the goodness of the family," and the girl refuses to go. (I:28) After several attempts to change her mind, Meagles decides that Tattycoram is irrecoverable. Meanwhile Gowan continues to pursue Pet. When Pet confides to Arthur that she is going to marry Gowan, he goes to the edge of the river at night and scatters some roses on the flowing water.

(I:29) Back in the city, Mrs. Clennam wonders why Pancks is inquiring into Little Dorrit's life; she questions the girl about her situation and seems to be consoled by Amy's uncomplaining answers.

Part 9 (August 1856)
(I:30) Rigaud, the Marseille prisoner, who now calls himself Blandois and describes himself as a man of no country, arrives at Mrs. Clennam's door with a letter of credit to Clennam and Co. He flatters Mrs. Clennam, admires her husband's portrait and watch, and learns that the initials on the watch—DNF—stand for "do not forget." She tells him that her monotonous existence does not allow her to forget "to be sensible of having (as we all have every one of us, all the children of Adam!) offences to expiate and peace to make."

(I:31) Little Dorrit walks from Bleeding Heart Yard to the Marshalsea with Old Nandy, a workhouse resident. Fanny is scandalized that her sister would be seen in the streets with a pauper. Her father is also distressed and tells her that he has been humiliated and that she lacks "Spirit," but a letter from Clennam containing a banknote puts him in a better frame of mind. At tea, he is obse-

quious with Clennam; patronizing with Nandy, who sits on a window ledge like a serf in a baronial hall; and angered by Tip, who shows his "proper spirit" by insulting Clennam. (I:32) Arthur tells Amy not to be concerned over the "insults" he has suffered; he would gladly suffer them to see her. When he asks her to rely on him, she weeps uncontrollably. He confides to her his realization, prompted by his loss of Pet, that he is too old for love and romance; he asks her to confide similarly in him. Maggy suggests that she tell the story of the princess, but Amy tells Arthur it is merely a fairy story. Pancks informs Arthur that he is on the verge of a breakthrough in the search for Little Dorrit's story.

Part 10 (September 1856)
(I:33) Although Meagles will pay Gowan's debts, Mrs. Gowan still considers her son's marriage a demeaning alliance in society's eyes. Mrs. Merdle complains that her husband does not accommodate himself to Society, that he is preoccupied with business. She wants him to "seem to care about nothing." Merdle wanders through his house as if he does not belong there. (I:34) Gowan complains that he is a disappointed man. But then, he philosophizes, we are all disappointed. Even his impending marriage does not diminish his disappointment. At the wedding, the differences between the high-society Barnacles and the business-class Meagles cause uneasiness.

(I:35) Pancks discovers that Mr. Dorrit is heir to a landed fortune. When Arthur breaks the news to Little Dorrit, she faints. When they tell Mr. Dorrit, he is so upset that he just shakes. Little Dorrit wonders that her father "should have lost so many years and suffered so much, and at last pay all the debts as well. It seems to me," she remarks, "hard that he should pay in life and money both." (I:36) On his last day in prison, Mr. Dorrit gives a baronial dinner for the inmates and then, at noon, leads his family out to a waiting coach. Little Dorrit is not with them. She has fainted in her room. Clennam finds her and carries her to the carriage, where Fanny is scandalized because Amy is wearing her old dress. The carriage drives off, leaving Clennam behind in the street.

Book II: Riches

Part 11 (October 1856)

(II:1) The Dorrits—William, Frederick, Fanny, Tip, and Amy—who are traveling from SWITZERLAND to ITALY stop for the night at the monastery at the Pass of the Great Saint Bernard. There they meet the Gowans and Blandois, who are on their way to Rome. Amy comforts Pet after the young bride faints during dinner. Blandois watches Amy, disconcerting her. (II:2) Traveling with the Dorrits is Mrs. General, daughter of a clerical dignitary and widow of a commissariat officer, who has been engaged to "form the minds" of Fanny and Amy. (II:3) As the Dorrits make their descent into Italy, Little Dorrit is haunted by the image of Blandois watching their carriage. At Martigny, Mr. Dorrit is offended because the hotel room he has reserved has been taken by Mrs. Merdle and her son Edmund Sparkler. Mrs. Merdle does not acknowledge either Fanny or Amy, but as her coach pulls away Sparkler peers at them through the back window.

In Italy, cut off from familiar people and places, Amy lives in her memories. At VENICE she becomes known as the little English girl who sits alone on her balcony looking out on the canal. (I:4) Amy writes to Arthur from Venice to tell him that she has met Pet and that she senses something is not right in the marriage, something that even Pet may not be aware of. She thinks Pet needs a husband more "steadfast and firm." She tells him of the "unreality" of her trip and how she thinks about the people in England. She asks him not to think of her as in any way different from the poor girl he knew in the prison.

Part 12 (November 1856)

(II:5) Mrs. General reports to Mr. Dorrit that Amy has no force of character and no self-reliance. He directs Amy to submit to Mrs. General's instruction and says that she alone of the family reveals the taint of the prison. Frederick defends Amy and confronts the family: "I protest against pride. I protest against ingratitude. I protest against any one of us here who have known what we have known, and have seen what we have seen, setting up any pretension that puts Amy at a moment's disadvantage, or to the cost of a moment's pain." The other Dorrits are outraged

and agree that he is crazy. (II:6) When Little Dorrit visits the Gowans, she finds Henry painting in his studio with Blandois as his model. After his dog growls at Blandois, Gowan knocks the animal to the floor and kicks it. On the way home, Little Dorrit observes that Gowan treats his wife like a child. Fanny notices Sparkler following their gondola and says that she will make a slave of him. (II:7) When Little Dorrit sees Pet again, they are shadowed by Blandois and Pet tells her that Blandois has poisoned Gowan's dog. Fanny astounds Amy with the news that Mrs. General has designs on their father. Little Dorrit realizes that Society in Italy is a "superior sort of Marshalsea." From Venice they go on to ROME, where they meet the Merdles again.

Part 13 (December 1856)

(II:8) Back in London, Arthur seeks support for Doyce's invention and sorely misses Little Dorrit. (II:9) One day he sees Tattycoram in a London street with a foreigner; he secretly follows them and observes their clandestine meeting with Miss Wade. (II:10) A few days later Arthur is disturbed to meet the insolent foreigner, now identified as Blandois, at his mother's house.

(II:11) Little Dorrit writes to Arthur of Pet's devotion to her husband, of their new son, and of the Meagleses' discomfort with Gowan. She also tells of Fanny's suitor and of her own homesickness.

Part 14 (January 1857)

(II:12) Merdle's wealth gives him power. He uses his influence with Sir Decimus Barnacle to secure a position in the Circumlocution Office for Edmund Sparkler. (II:13) His influence spreads throughout England, and there is a boom in Merdle's enterprises and an epidemic of speculation in Merdle's shares. Even Pancks has invested £100. Arthur is cautious, but he considers placing the Doyce and Clennam money in Merdle's stock. (II:14) In Rome, Sparkler's new position is the talk of the English community. Fanny must make up her mind about marrying him and returning to England with him. She recognizes that she is a willful person who would not submit to a clever husband; Sparkler's dull-wittedness suits her desire to rule her husband. Marriage to Sparkler also offers her a chance to get back at Mrs. Merdle.

Part 15 (February 1856)

(II:15) Fanny asks Amy whether she should rush her marriage or delay it. Amy counsels delay, but Fanny sees a quick marriage as a way to get one up in her struggle with Mrs. Merdle. So she marries quickly and returns to London with her husband, accompanied by Mr. Dorrit. Amy is left behind with Mrs. General. (II:16) In London, the Sparklers take over Mrs. Merdle's rooms in the Merdles' house. Mr. Dorrit buys into Merdle's securities and becomes increasingly aware that Fanny's marriage has moved him ahead in the world. (II:17) Before he leaves London, Mr. Dorrit goes to Mrs. Clennam to learn what he can about the disappearance of Blandois, but she tells him very little. Dorrit is unsettled by her secrecy, by Affery's fear of noises in the house, by Flintwinch's dispatch, and by the realization that the house is being watched. (II:18) He is also upset by a visit from young John Chivery, who reminds him of his prison days. On the way back to Rome, Dorrit builds castles in his mind, contemplating marriage to Mrs. General.

Part 16 (March 1856)

(II:19) Mr. Dorrit is unwell. He is prepared to propose to Mrs. General, but he does not find an opportune moment. At Mrs. Merdle's going-away party, crowded with all the important English people in Rome, he seems confused. When he rises to deliver a speech, he reverts to his old manner as Father of the Marshalsea. He thinks he is back in the prison. Amy manages to get him home. She cares for him, but he continues in his old identity and dies 10 days later attended by Frederick, who also dies, kneeling at his brother's bedside.

(II:20) Hoping to learn something about Blandois, Arthur Clennam seeks out Miss Wade, who is sequestered in CALAIS with the unhappy Tattycoram. She suggests that Arthur ask Gowan about Blandois, her sarcasm revealing her hatred for the artist and his wife, and she gives Arthur a document. (II:21) The document is Miss Wade's life story, "The History of a Self-Tormentor." An orphan who became a governess, Miss Wade learned in childhood to distrust others who patronized and condescended to her. She is insanely jealous and distrustful of friends and lovers and hateful

toward those who abandoned her or interfered in her life. She especially detests Gowan, a former lover, and Pet, who stole him from her. She sees in Tattycoram an orphan as patronized and mistrusted as she was.

(II:22) Unsuccessful in securing support for his work in England, Doyce goes abroad to work for a "barbaric" power that believes in getting things done. He leaves the financial affairs of Doyce and Clennam in Arthur's hands, advising Arthur only to avoid speculation. Clennam learns that his employee, Cavaletto, knows Blandois as Rigaud, an accused murderer.

Part 17 (April 1856)

(II:23) Arthur tells his mother that Blandois is an accused murderer, and even though she is taken aback, she will reveal nothing about her dealings with the foreigner. Affery tells him of noises, rustlings, and tremblings in the house, but is afraid to tell him its "secrets."

(II:24) Three months after the deaths of the Dorrit brothers, the Sparklers spend a hot summer evening alone in London. They were calculated to "shine in society," Fanny asserts, but now that she is pregnant, she is incapable of shining. She vows that she will guard against their being alone anymore. Mr. Merdle appears at their door. He is distracted, speaks of having much to do, borrows a penknife, and sets out for home. (II:25) A little while later, at a dinner party where the guests are speculating on rumors circulating about Merdle's finances, Merdle's physician is called away to the baths down the street. There he finds Merdle, a suicide, lying in a pool of blood. A note to the physician indicates that Merdle's complaint was simple forgery and robbery. (II:26) Arthur had invested all of his company funds in Merdle's enterprises. He sends a letter to the company's creditors, telling them that payment will be stopped and exonerating Doyce from any blame. He is arrested for debt, taken to the Marshalsea, and placed in the Dorrits' former rooms.

Part 18 (May 1857)

(II:27) In the Marshalsea, John Chivery attends Arthur, but Arthur senses an undercurrent of anger in Chivery's manner. Finally John accuses Arthur of not being honest and insists that he admit that he loves Little Dorrit. He tells Arthur that Little Dorrit loves him. Arthur is stunned. He broods on Little Dorrit's importance in his life. (II:28) Ten or 12 weeks later, Cavalletto and Pancks bring Blandois to the prison. Blandois admits that he sells anything that commands a price—that he sold information about the Gowans to Miss Wade, that he has something to sell to Mrs. Clennam, and that she has a week to respond to his offer. (II:29) Arthur, stifled and despondent, is unable to sleep for the next week. On the sixth day he finds a bouquet of flowers beside his bed. He is vaguely aware of a quiet figure in the room. It is Little Dorrit. He weeps and embraces her. She offers him all of her money, but he cannot accept that sacrifice. John Chivery escorts her home and returns with the message that she sends Arthur her undying love.

Part 19–20 (*June 1857*)

(II:30) On the seventh day, Pancks and Cavalletto bring Blandois to Mrs. Clennam's house. Blandois reveals that he knows Mrs. Clennam's secret: Arthur is not her child but is her husband's child by another woman. She has suppressed the truth and brought up Arthur in a spirit of revenge, "that the child might work out his release in bondage and hardship." She has also suppressed a codicil to Arthur's uncle's will that made Little Dorrit an heiress. Blandois has given copies of the papers he has to Little Dorrit, instructing her to open them if no one claims them before the gates of the Marshalsea close. In shock, Mrs. Clennam rises out of her chair for the first time in 15 years and runs out of the house. (II:31) She runs through the unfamiliar streets, crosses LONDON BRIDGE, and goes to the Marshalsea. There she asks Little Dorrit to read the papers and learn how she has been wronged. But Amy forgives Mrs. Clennam and promises not to tell Arthur until after Mrs. Clennam is dead. As they return to the house, it crumbles into a ruin, killing Blandois, who is sitting inside. Mrs. Clennam falls paralyzed to the street. She lives for three years but is unable to speak or move.

(II:32) Pancks blames himself for recommending Merdle's shares to Clennam, and the more unhappy he is with himself, the more unhappy he becomes with Casby. When Casby tells him that he is not squeezing enough from the tenants, Pancks resigns his position, knocks off Casby's hat, cuts off his long flowing locks, and leaves the patriarch standing in the middle of Bleeding Heart Yard looking foolish and not in the least venerable.

(II:33) Amy worries that the originals of Blandois's documents will come to light, so she asks Meagles to retrieve them. The search ends at Miss Wade's in Calais, but she denies having any documents. Afterwards Tattycoram appears in London with the papers. She asks to become part of the Meagles family once again.

(II:34) On an autumn day after Arthur has recovered, Little Dorrit tells him he must leave the prison. When he learns that they have both been ruined in Merdle's collapse and are poor, he embraces her. The next morning they are married in the church next to the prison. Then they go down together into the roaring streets.

COMMENTARY

Little Dorrit is a complex novel, the epitome of the later Dickens works that Lionel Stevenson characterized as the "dark novels." Its inheritance plot is so intricate that John Wain has described the novel as "plotless" and "a labyrinth," and the editor of the Penguin Edition provides an unravelling summary of its intricacies in an appendix. Yet even when these plot complications are clarified, the novel remains a puzzling and disturbing book.

The devices from gothic melodrama used to resolve the plot—the fall of Mrs. Clennam's house, for example, and the machinations of Blandois—seem to break with the realistic temper of much of the rest of the novel and do not really resolve the story. The reader, with a little help, learns the details of Arthur's parentage and Little Dorrit's inheritance, but Arthur is never fully informed about the facts, and the lack of knowledge that contributed to his sense of guilt at the beginning of the novel continues even after its apparently "happy" conclusion. The human situation, the novel seems to suggest, is an imprisoning muddle.

Many of Dickens's initial readers found these frustrations in the story daunting. *Frazer's Magazine* declared it "decidedly the worst" of Dickens's novels, and E. B. Hanley characterized the novel as a "wilderness." These early reviewers usually attributed their disappointment to the lack of comedy in the novel and called for Dickens to return to such figures as Pickwick and Mrs. Gamp.

Modern critics, however, have been as positive as the original reviewers were negative. Lionel Trilling's classic introduction (1955) in *The Opposing Self* declared *Little Dorrit* "one of the three great novels of Dickens's great last period," along with *Bleak House* and *Our Mutual Friend*. Many others have suggested that the ambiguities in the plot and irresolution at the end are part of Dickens's Dostoyevskian strategy to respond to the condition of England in the wake of the Crimean War.

Although the novel is set in the mid-1820s, it directly addresses several topical issues of the 1850s. The Circumlocution Office, for example, is an attack on the abuses brought to light by a Parliamentary inquiry of 1853, which criticized the incompetence of the Civil Service during the Crimean War and the methods for recruiting civil servants. Merdle's story drew on the case of JOHN SADLEIR, a bank director and member of Parliament, who committed suicide in 1856 after falling heavily into debt. The MARSHALSEA PRISON, the main symbol in the novel, however, comes from an earlier period. Imprisonment for debt had been declining since the mid-1840s, and the prison itself had been closed in 1849.

Trilling describes the novel as "about society in its very essence." The social range of the novel is very broad, reaching from the aristocratic Barnacles and Gowans at the top down to Nandy's workhouse and the proletarian housing complex at Bleeding Heart Yard at the bottom. The figure most representative of English society in the 1850s is Merdle, the speculator and securities dealer who attracts attention and money from all quarters. His wife is the epitome of a society matron, a statuesque bust where Merdle displays his wealth in jewels, and his dinners are attended by representatives of all the dominant institutions. These dinner guests are not individualized but are identified only by their roles in society: Bar, Treasury, Bishop, and so forth. Yet Merdle, in spite of financial power and adulation from all sectors of established society, suffers from "some deep-seated recondite complaint" (I:21), a feeling of unease that his doctor cannot diagnose.

Merdle's complaint and his power to infect so many others have prompted Edwin B. Barret ("*Little Dorrit* and the Disease of Modern Life," *Nineteenth Century Fiction*, 1970) to suggest that the controlling metaphor in the novel is disease. Disease links the speculators with the paralyzed, like the guilty Mrs. Clennam; with the depressed, like Arthur Clennam; and with the neurotic, like the self-tormenting Miss Wade. The novel's diagnosis of the condition of England finds the whole society infected with Merdle's complaint. The more accepted analysis, however, identifies the prison as the novel's controlling symbol.

The Marshalsea, the debtors' prison where Dickens's father was imprisoned in 1824, crystallizes the prison imagery in the novel. William Dorrit has been held there so long that his youngest child, who is 17 at the start of the novel, was born there. She is the Child of the Marshalsea and he, its longest inmate, the Father. He sees his position as one of honor, a belief reinforced by the deference and monetary tributes he receives from other inmates and visitors. He thinks of himself as the patriarch of the prison and as a father who provides for his family; he cannot acknowledge that his children work outside the prison to provide for him. These patriarchal delusions echo those of the society outside the prison that admires the idle gentleman as a social ideal and establishes a class hierarchy with idle aristocratic parasites like the Barnacles or wealthy swindlers like Merdle at the top.

Dickens mocks the absurdity of the bureaucracy in the Circumlocution Office and attacks the pretensions of the Barnacles. There was a sharp and bitter edge to his satire in 1856, for the inefficiency, incompetence, and infighting among various departments of the Civil Service had produced a series of fatal disasters during the Crimean War. The army was inadequately fed and clothed, supplies did not reach the troops, and the medical care for the wounded was insufficient and unsanitary. The unnecessary suffering and deaths caused by administrative mismanagement were tallied daily in the British press from reports telegraphed from the front. Dickens was in the vanguard of those calling for reform of the Civil Service; for purging unnecessary departments, paperwork, and red tape; and for choosing bureaucrats on the basis of their competence rather than their family connections. Edmund Sparkler's appointment to a government job and the incompetent Barnacle dynasty at the Circumlocution Office represent abuses that Dickens thought needed correction. His critique goes well beyond the shortcomings of aristocratic privilege. When even such good people as the Meagleses collude to keep such incompetents as the Barnacles in positions of power, more than the Civil Service needs to change. The class system itself imprisons people, blinding them to the truth and leading to delusion, loneliness, and despair.

Nearly all of the settings in the novel elaborate the theme of imprisonment: the quarantine station in Marseille where the novel opens, the prison where Rigaud and Cavaletto share a cell, the crumbling house in which Mrs. Clennam is confined to her wheelchair, the slum tenement in Bleeding Heart Yard, the convent at the top of the Simplon Pass, the palaces in Venice. Each in its own way articulates an imprisoning mode of consciousness. Dark, haunted by unnerving sounds and secretive strangers, Mrs. Clennam's house, for example, contains the repressed secrets of the Clennam family, secrets that threaten to undermine the building; the house, like its occupant, must rely on crutches to avoid collapse. The house is more than simply a projection of Mrs. Clennam's paralyzing and debilitating psychology. It also represents the oppressive Calvinism that afflicts her to the point of paralysis, blights the lives of all around her, and makes Sunday in England a day of oppressive monotony, where "melancholy streets in a penitential garb of soot, steeped the souls of the people who were condemned to look at them out of windows, in dire despondency" (I:3).

Arthur is one of the victims of this imprisoning Calvinism, which has left him with a large measure of guilt and little sense of self-worth. His lack of will is rooted in this cultural ideology that causes Mrs. Clennam's paralysis, but Arthur, unlike his mother, refuses to live in bad faith. He gives up his place in the family business and, convinced that he and his family have some responsibility for William

Dorrit's situation, sets out to release Dorrit from prison. With Pancks's help, he does liberate the Dorrits, but that accomplishment does not free him from the debilitating sense of guilt that eventually leads him to acquiesce to his own imprisonment as a just punishment for his mishandling of the funds of Doyce and Clennam.

For many readers, Arthur is not an engaging hero. A middle-aged failure, burdened by a sense of guilt into depression and passivity, he withdraws from life, giving up his place in the family business, his courtship of Pet, and his hopes for Doyce and Clennam. His diffidence and self-punishment are not extraordinary. He is, rather, a Victorian everyman at midlife, uncertain of his origins, wounded and guilt-ridden as a result of a harsh Calvinistic upbringing, alienated from the dishonesty and hypocrisy in his materialistic society, and incapable of acknowledging and acting from spontaneous feeling. He is, as several chapter titles suggest, "a Nobody" (I:16, 17, 26, 28). Dickens's original title for the novel, *Nobody's Fault,* suggested, along with its sarcasm about the buck-passing in the Circumlocution Office, Clennam's debilitating sense of guilt as the central theme of the novel. By changing the title to *Little Dorrit,* Dickens stressed some of the more positive aspects of his theme.

Amy Dorrit may be, as Trilling describes her, "the Beatrice of the *Comedy,* the Paraclete in female form," but her redemptive role in the story does not make her without conflict or flaws, an innocent untouched by the imprisoning society in which she lives. She is the Child of the Marshalsea and a product of the prison that nurtured her. She rejects the pretenses adopted by her father, Tip, and Fanny and accepts the need to work for a living, but Amy also supports her father's delusions and pretensions and worries that he could not survive outside the prison, a concern that his death in Rome proves to be justified. Little Dorrit's concern for her father is also a concern for herself, for she is, to use a contemporary term, codependent with him. She justifies her life by caring for him and by maintaining the lies that feed his delusions. Clennam's project to free Mr. Dorrit threatens Amy as well as her father. Her inability to adapt to a life of idle gentility in Italy mirrors her father's inability to suppress his memories of the prison and Arthur's inability to overcome his guilt. Amy and Arthur are both imprisoned by their parentage and their pasts. If Arthur suffers from midlife crisis, Amy reveals arrested development, her childlike "littleness" at odds with the adult responsibilities she assumes and the complex mixture of truth and complicity that forms her character. She may be unbelievable, but she is not simplistically boring, as some commentators have suggested.

Paradoxically, it is the acceptance of imprisonment that finally liberates Amy and Arthur. She does not respond to the teaching of Mrs. General, and she embarrasses her family by failing to develop "a truly refined mind [which] will seem to be ignorant of anything that is not perfectly proper, placid, and pleasant" (II:5). She remains true to an inner sense of self and to the truth of her situation: She is a child of the Marshalsea. Similarly, Arthur's guilt causes him to seek imprisonment, even though Daniel Doyce does not blame him for losing the firm's money by speculating in Merdle's enterprises. By acknowledging his responsibility and refusing to deny or repress his guilt, Arthur acknowledges that he too is a child of the Marshalsea. Once he is there he can recognize and accept his love for Little Dorrit. Both Amy and Arthur go through imprisonment in order to transcend it.

Most of the other characters in the novel lack the inner resources to enable them to admit and go beyond their imprisonment. Fanny resists Mrs. General but gives herself to a loveless marriage with Sparkler in order to establish her power over Mrs. Merdle. Though good-hearted, Mr. and Mrs. Meagles alienate Tattycoram by their condescending treatment of her, and their toadying to the Barnacles may enable Pet's disastrous marriage to Gowan. Although Frederick Dorrit has managed to eke out a living outside the prison and is more clear-sighted than William about the family's position, he cannot survive the death of his defining brother-double. William Dorrit and Arthur's father represent the dishonesty and delusions of patriarchy; Casby dramatizes it as a patriarchal impostor who grinds the faces of the poor into the soil of Bleeding Heart Yard. Pancks, his agent, has been turned into a machine, a "laboring steam-engine,"

to carry out Casby's oppression; even though he helps free the Dorrits from prison and publicly humiliates Casby in the end, Pancks is not saved from ruin when Merdle's financial bubble bursts. Merdle, the avatar of this diseased society, fraudulent and vacuous, destroys himself, a victim of his own lies and delusions, the most extreme of the many characters in the novel who are, in Miss Wade's term, "self tormentors."

Two characters stand out as free spirits. The inventor Daniel Doyce receives no support from English institutions and clearly has little head for business, but he continues his creative work in spite of frustrations with the Circumlocution Office. When he is discouraged from working in England, he finds opportunities abroad. He does not succumb to despair and paralysis. When Arthur, against Doyce's instructions, speculates with the firm's money, Doyce nonetheless forgives him and maintains their partnership. His energy, creativity, and independence help sustain Arthur and bring him out of the prison of despair.

Flora Finching is the other notable exception to the rule of passivity and vacuousness in the novel. She too is inventive, and in her profusions of language she connects in a random and associative way the disparate pieces of her life. She blends absurdity with benevolence, shrewdness with excess; in a novel notably short on comedy, she is one of Dickens's great comic figures. Like Doyce, she is a figure of energy, overwhelming the passive and reserved Clennam with her physical and vocal presence. She also intimidates Little Dorrit by ignoring the social distance between them and spilling out the details of her life to her. In garrulous middle age, Flora may be a peony rather than a lily, but she brings a natural energy to a novel in which many of the characters have been reduced to objects or machines; her organic presence—indicated by her botanic and ornithological name—blesses the wedding of Arthur and Amy (II:34). Unlike the roses that Arthur tosses on the river when he gives up any notion of courting Pet (I:28), Flora is a flower that he retains, one of the autumn blooms flourishing when Arthur is restored to health (II:34).

Neither Arthur nor Amy has the extraordinary creative powers of Doyce and Flora. Both are products of their time and place, children of the Marshalsea who have been wounded in childhood and have struggled to free themselves. Theirs is a victimhood that cannot be transformed by the discovery of forgotten parents or lost wills. These staples of the inheritance plots that produced the happy endings in so many of Dickens's earlier novels are parodied in the grotesque exaggerations in the story of Arthur's parentage and the codicil that improbably makes Amy an heiress. Dickens sends up such conventions as sources for happiness in life, for, the novel shows, human misery is produced by family connections and money. By burning the codicil so that they have no money, by forgiving those who have trespassed against them, and by being forgiven their debts, Amy and Arthur are free to leave the Marshalsea and also the mental prisons in which they have lived. By doing so, they transcend the very conventions of the novel that enable happy endings. It is this transcendence that makes the justly famous final paragraphs of the novel so moving. These paragraphs celebrate Amy and Arthur's existential choice to transcend the past, leave the prison, go into the streets, and live as fully as they can in the here and now:

> They paused for a moment on the steps of the portico, looking at the fresh perspective of the street in the autumn morning sun's bright rays, and then went down.
>   Went down into a modest life of usefulness and happiness. . . . They went quietly down into the roaring streets, inseparable and blessed; and as they passed along in sunshine and shade, the noisy and the eager, and the arrogant and the froward and the vain, fretted, and chafed, and made their usual uproar. (II:34)

CHARACTERS AND RELATED ENTRIES

Antwerp, Belgium Rigaud meets Jeremiah Flintwinch's twin brother Ephraim here when Ephraim brings the iron box containing the Clennam papers from London (II:30).

aunt, Mr. F's The crazy old lady who lives with Flora Finching, the aunt of Flora's deceased husband: "an amazing little old woman, with a face

Mr. F's Aunt intimidates Arthur Clennam in Browne's (Phiz's) rendering of a scene from Little Dorrit.

like a staring wooden doll too cheap for expression, and a stiff yellow wig perched unevenly on top of her head, as if the child who owned the doll had driven a tack through it anywhere, so that it only got fastened on. Another remarkable thing in this little old woman was, that the same child seemed to have damaged her face in two or three places with some blunt instrument in the nature of a spoon; her countenance, and particularly the tip of her nose, presenting the phenomena of several dints, generally answering to the bowl of that article" (I:13). She is marked by "extreme severity and grim taciturnity; sometimes interrupted by a propensity to offer remarks in a deep warning voice, which, being totally uncalled for by anything said by anybody, and traceable to no association of ideas, confounded and terrified the mind."

Her irrationality can be taken as a disturbing and comic indication of the irrational world she finds herself in. Her anger and resentment seem to be an expression of the resentment that Flora suppresses at being rejected by Arthur. Lionel Trilling, in *The Opposing Self* (1955), describes her as "one of Dickens's most astonishing ideas, the embodiment of senile rage and spite, flinging to the world the crusts of her buttered toast."

Bangham, Mrs. The charwoman and messenger in the MARSHALSEA PRISON who attends Mrs. Dorrit at the birth of her daughter Amy (I:6). Her garrulousness and, as JAMES KINCAID (1971) points out, her ability "to twist every occasion into pleasantness and comfort" are reminiscent of Sairey Gamp in *Martin Chuzzlewit*.

Barbary, Mrs. Captain, of Cheltenham   Owner of a horse that Captain Maroon attempts to sell (I:12).

Barnacle family   The important and extensive family that controls the Circumlocution Office, Dickens's satiric representation of aristocratic privilege in the higher levels of the government bureaucracy. "The Barnacles were a very high family, and a very large family. They were dispensed all over the Public Offices, and held all sorts of public places" (I:10). "Wherever there was a square yard of ground in British occupation under the sun or moon, with a public post upon it, sticking to that post was a Barnacle" (I:34). Arthur Clennam goes to the Circumlocution Office in an unsuccessful attempt to secure information about the Dorrits' debts. There he meets Daniel Doyce, whose search for support for his invention is similarly frustrated by these bureaucratic aristocrats. Lord Decimus Tite Barnacle, cabinet Minister of Circumlocution, considers his duties "to set bounds to the philanthropy, to cramp the charity, to fetter the public spirit, to contract the enterprise, to damp the independent self-reliance" of the people (I:34). His nephew Tite Barnacle is a senior official in the Circumlocution Office, an "altogether splendid, massive, overpowering, and impracticable" man, "the express image and presentment of How not to do it." He "wound and wound folds of white cravat round his neck, as he wound and wound folds of tape and paper round the neck of the country" (I:10). His son Clarence Barnacle (Barnacle Junior) is also an official in the Office, an empty-headed and callow young man, "the born idiot of the family" (I:26): "Such a downy tip was on his callow chin, that he seemed half fledged like a young bird. . . . He had a superior eye-glass dangling round his neck, but unfortunately had such flat orbits to his eyes, and such limp little eyelids, that it wouldn't stick in when he put it up, but kept tumbling out against his waistcoat buttons" (I:10). Although Ferdinand Barnacle, private secretary to Lord Decimus, comes from "the more sprightly side of the family"

and is "an agreeable young fellow" (I:12), he nonetheless advises Clennam that the Circumlocution Office "is not a wicked Giant to be charged at full tilt; but, only a windmill showing you, as it grinds immense quantities of chaff, which way the country wind blows. . . . We must have humbug, we all like humbug, we couldn't get on without humbug. A little humbug, and a groove, and everything goes on admirably, if you leave it alone" (II:28). Gowan is a distant relation to the Barnacles, who gratify Meagles's snobbishness by attending the wedding of Gowan and Minnie Meagles (I:34). Among the family members at the wedding is William, a member of Parliament "who had made the ever-famous coalition with Tudor Stiltstocking" (I:34). Edmund Sparkler, through the influence of Merdle, is made one of the lords of the Circumlocution Office (II:12).

Tite Barnacle was thought at the time to be based on Sir James Stephen, father of JAMES FITZJAMES STEPHEN, the harshest of Dickens's contemporary critics. He was especially critical of *Little Dorrit* and its presentation of the Circumlocution Office.

Barroneau, Madame   The young widow of a Marseille innkeeper who married Rigaud. Although he claims she leaped to her death from the top of a cliff, he is generally believed to have murdered her (I:1).

Beadle, Harriet ("Tattycoram")   Orphan companion and maid to Pet Meagles, whose nickname combines the diminutive of Harriet with an allusion to Coram's Hospital, the orphanage from which she comes. "A sullen, passionate girl," she is subject to fits of rage and is instructed by Mr. Meagles to count to 10 before speaking. In one of these fits, she runs from the Meagleses and joins Miss Wade as her companion (I:27), but the relationship sours and Tattycoram returns penitently to the Meagleses, bringing with her the papers concerning Little Dorrit and Mrs. Clennam that had been in Miss Wade's possession (II:33).

Although only a minor figure, Tattycoram's divided character is indicative of the division in many characters in the novel, especially characters who suppress deep emotional pain or resentment. Tattycoram is also an important member of a group of characters; she is, as Brian Rosenberg (1996) points out in *Little Dorrit's Shadows*, a double to both Pet Meagles and Miss Wade, revealing in her explosive self-division the more repressed divisions in the other women. As a "child of Coram's Hospital" she provides a contrasting commentary on Amy Dorrit, "the Child of the Marshalsea." She also brings out both the caring and condescending sides in Dickens's ambivalent presentation of the Meagleses.

Bilberry, Lady Jemina   Wife of Lord Decimus Tite Barnacle and the daughter of the 15th Earl of Stiltstocking and the Honorable Clementina Toozellem (I:17).

Blandois, Monsieur   The alias adopted by Rigaud in England.

Bleeding Heart Yard   An urban tenement in Holborn, situated in "a maze of shabby streets," that takes its name from the Bleeding Heart Pub. The property is owned by Casby, and the rents are collected by Pancks. Plornish lives here, and his wife has her small shop here; Doyce and Clennam's factory is also located in the yard.

Bob   Turnkey at the Marshalsea and godfather to Amy Dorrit. Although he wants to will his property to Amy, he cannot discover a way to do so without making it also available to her father.

Break of Day Inn, the   The inn at Chalons-sur-Saone where Rigaud and Cavaletto are briefly reunited as they are traveling northward (I:11).

A view of Bleeding Heart Yard, the tenement compound in *Little Dorrit* where the Plornishes live and where Arthur Clennam has his business.

Casby, Christopher ("Patriarch") Father of Flora Finching and the slumlord of Bleeding Heart Yard and other properties, his "shining bald head, . . . the long grey hair at its side and back, like floss silk or spun glass . . . looked so benevolent . . . that various old ladies spoke of him as The Last of the Patriarchs. . . . His smooth face had a bloom upon it, like a ripe wall-fruit. What with his blooming face, and that head, and his blue eyes, he seemed to be delivering sentiments of rare wisdom and virtue. In like manner, his physiognomical expression seemed to teem with benignity. Nobody could have said where the wisdom was, or where the virtue was, or where the benignity was, but they all seemed to be somewhere about him" (I:13). He employs Pancks as his unforgiving rent collector, enabling the odium that properly should fall on him to be directed instead at his agent and enabling Casby to maintain his benign appearance. In the end, Pancks exposes his hypocritical employer by cutting his locks and leaving him shorn in the middle of Bleeding Heart Yard, "a bare-polled, goggle-eyed, big-headed lumbering personage . . . not in the least venerable" (II:32).

Cavaletto, Signor John Baptist ("Altro") Petty Italian smuggler imprisoned with Rigaud in MARSEILLE (1): "A sunburnt, quick, lithe, little man, though rather thick-set. Earrings in his brown ears, white teeth lighting up his grotesque brown face, intensely black hair clustering about his brown throat, a ragged red shirt open at his brown breast. Loose, seamanlike trousers, decent shoes, a long red cap, a red sash round his waist, and a knife in it" (I:1). He makes his way to London, where he is aided by Arthur Clennam after being hit by a mail cart in the street (I:13). Clennam employs him and calls him "Altro," an Italian word meaning "certainly," which Cavaletto uses as "a confirmation, an assertion, a denial, a taunt, a compliment, a joke, and fifty other things" (I:1). Cavaletto aids in the search for Rigaud in London and nurses Clennam in the MARSHALSEA.

Chalons, France Rigaud and Cavaletto meet briefly at the Break of Day Inn near this town on the Marne east of Paris (I:11).

Chivery, John The turnkey at the MARSHALSEA during William Dorrit's time there, "a man of few words, . . . he had imbibed a professional habit of locking everything up. He locked himself up as he locked up the Marshalsea debtors" (I:25).

Chivery, Mrs. Chivery's wife, a "comfortable-looking woman, much respected about HORSEMONGER LANE for her feelings and her conversation" (I:22). She has a small tobacconist's shop. Young John brings Dorrit cigars from the shop as a form of tribute.

Chivery, Young John Chivery's "sentimental son," who is hopelessly in love with Amy Dorrit. Young John is "small of stature, with rather weak legs, and very weak light hair. . . . But he [is] great of soul. Poetical, expansive, faithful" (I:18). After Amy declines to hear his proposal, he pines for her by sitting alone amid the laundry (I:22), but he is faithful to her to the end, aiding Pancks in uncovering her history (I:35) and forcing Arthur to see how much Amy loves him (II:27).

Circumlocution Office, the Dickens's satiric representation of the Civil Service in *Dorrit*, written in the wake of the bureaucratic bumbling during the Crimean War. Staffed on the principles of nepotism and aristocratic privilege and entangled in red tape, the Circumlocution Office is the special preserve of the Barnacle family: "No public business of any kind could possibly be done at any time, without the acquiescense of the Circumlocution Office. . . . Whatever was required to be done, the Circumlocution Office was beforehand with all the public departments in the art of perceiving—HOW NOT TO DO IT" (I:10). The office makes it impossible for Daniel Doyce to secure a patent for his invention, a theme Dickens also develops in "A Poor Man's Tale of a Patent."

Clennam, Arthur The diffident hero of the novel, Arthur is "the son . . . of a hard father and mother. . . . The only child of parents who weighed, measured, and priced everything; for whom what could not be weighed, measured, and priced, had no existence. Strict people as the phrase is, professors of a stern religion, their very religion was a gloomy sacrifice of tastes and sympathies that were never their own, offered up as part of a bargain for the security of their possessions" (I:2). At the beginning of the novel, Arthur returns from 20 years in China, where he has been working unhappily in the family business until the death of his father. His harsh upbringing in a Calvinistic religion has left him with an unspecific sense of guilt, and in middle age he has no direction or purpose in his life, a condition he describes as lacking "a will," and would now be described as depression. In this state of mind he thinks of himself in the third person as "Nobody." He suspects that his parents have a guilty secret, and when he sees Little Dorrit working as his mother's servant, he intuitively links her with the supposed secret and undertakes to learn her story, which will ultimately reveal his own. Arthur leaves the family business (I:5), becomes a partner to Daniel Doyce (I:23), and encourages the investigation by Pancks that uncovers Mr. Dorrit's inheritance (I:35). He has a disillusioning reunion with his garrulous childhood sweetheart, Flora Finching (I:13), half-heartedly considers courting Pet Meagles but withdraws in the face of Henry Gowan's interest in her (I:28), and only after convincing himself that he is too old for romantic impulses realizes that he loves Little Dorrit (II:29). Although he blames himself for losing Doyce's money by speculating in Merdle's investment schemes and also for his family's treatment of the Dorrits, he is freed from guilt—and from prison—by both Doyce's and Amy's forgiveness. He also learns that he is the love child of his father and a singer and the adopted son of his "mother," Mrs. Clennam, who has suppressed the truth about his parentage. Finally free and forgiven, and without any inheritance, he marries Amy and they begin life anew.

Arthur Clennam is Dickens's most sympathetic and interior study of the diffident man who appears in many of the later novels—as James Harthouse in *Hard Times*, Sydney Carton in *A Tale of Two Cities*, and Eugene Wrayburn in *Our Mutual Friend*. Clennam possesses psychological complexity and at the same time reflects the social and religious context which has sapped him of his will and contributed

Arthur Clennam's imprisonment in the Marshalsea externalizes the imprisoning inner guilt that defines his character. An illustration for the Household Edition by Mahoney.

to his guilt. Brian Rosenberg (*Little Dorrit's Shadows*, 1996) suggests that the fullness in Dickens's portrait of Clennam derives in part from his role in a cluster of characters, the "House of Clennam," which includes his mother, Flintwinch, and Affery, all of whom help illuminate dimensions of Arthur's character and situation. DORIS ALEXANDER (1991) traces autobiographical sources for many aspects of Arthur's character and situation.

Clennam, Gilbert   Arthur's father's uncle who, for financial reasons, arranged the Clennams' loveless marriage. Knowing that Arthur's mother has gone mad and died, the guilty Gilbert added a codicil to his will leaving £1000 to the youngest daughter or cousin of her benefactor, Frederick Dorrit, a provision that makes Little Dorrit the beneficiary of the will. Mrs. Clennam has suppressed this codicil.

Clennam, Mr.   Arthur's father, a businessman who spent 20 years in China, where Arthur was his business associate. This "exile" abroad is in part a punishment for his infidelity to his wife with a singer who was Arthur's natural mother.

Although the nature of Clennam's business is not specified in the novel, recent commentators have suggested that Mr. Clennam was likely to have had some involvement with the opium trade that led to the Opium Wars between China and Britain in the middle decades of the 19th century. Arthur's sense of guilt, then, might also have derived from involvement in the opium trade.

Clennam, Mrs.   Arthur's "mother," who controls the family business from her invalid chair in a crumbling house in London: "On a black bier-like sofa in this hollow, propped up behind with one great angular black bolster, like the block at a state execution in the good old times, sat his mother in a widow's dress. She and his father had been at variance from his earliest remembrance. To sit speechless himself in the midst of rigid silence, glancing in dread from the one averted face to the other, had been the peacefullest occupation of his childhood. She gave him one glassy kiss, and four stiff fingers muffled in worsted" (I:3). She has been confined to the house and her chair for 12 years by the time Arthur returns from China. Her rigid Calvinism sees life as sin and punishment and allows for no love or forgiveness. She has exiled her husband to China for his infidelity and has adopted Arthur to raise him in righteousness and retribution. She attempts to keep the stories of the past suppressed, but Arthur's suspicions, the investigation that he promotes, and the machinations of Rigaud (Blandois), who has obtained the codicil and other Clennam papers, finally reveal the truth. Confronted with his threat to reveal the truth, Mrs. Clennam rises from her paralysis, goes to the Marshalsea, secures the forgiveness of Little Dorrit, and escapes the collapse of her house—which kills Blandois. She lives on speechless and paralyzed for three more years.

Clive   Clerk at the Circumlocution Office (I:10).

Cripples, Mister   Proprietor of a night school in the building where Frederick Dorrit lives. His son, "a little white-faced boy," lives with him (I:9).

Dawes, Mary   Nurse in the household where Miss Wade works as a governess. Miss Wade is convinced that Mary will turn the children against her (II:21).

Dorrit, Amy ("Little Dorrit," "Child of the Marshalsea")   Youngest child of William, she was born in the prison, earning the nickname "Child of the Marshalsea." After her mother dies when she is eight, she goes out to work and with self-denying industry provides for her father and the rest of the family. "Her diminutive figure, small features, and slight spare dress gave her the appearance of being much younger than she was. A woman, probably of not less than two-and-twenty, she might have been passed in the street for little more than half that age" (I:5). Her self-denying concern for others extends beyond her family to include Maggy, a mentally retarded Marshalsea inmate who calls Amy "Little Mother." When Arthur returns from China, Amy is working in the Clennam household, where she draws Arthur's interest; he learns that she lives in the Marshalsea, believes that his family is somehow responsible for her situation, and seeks to have the Dorrits released from prison. When the family comes into an inheritance, discovered through the efforts of Arthur and Pancks, Amy is reluctant to change from her prison dress and leave the Marshalsea (I:36), and she is unhappy living in luxury in Italy (II:4). After her father's death and the financial collapse of the family, Amy returns to England, where she cares for Arthur Clennam in prison. Even though she has distressed John Chivery, the turnkey's son, by rejecting his proposal of marriage, he gets Arthur to see that Little Dorrit loves him. After she refuses a legacy of her own, she marries Arthur and the two start life anew together.

Little Dorrit suffers from the judgments that nearly all such good characters arouse, that she is unbelievably good and hence not interesting. There is, however, more complexity to her character than may at first be evident. Her extreme self-denial, her collusion with her father's delusions, her unwillingness to leave the prison, and her fear that her father cannot survive outside the prison all seem to confirm the judgment by Fanny and others that she is truly "the child of the Marshalsea" and has developed a prisoner's mentality. This tainted perspective also enables her to reject delusions of gentility, to harbor no resentment or bitterness, and to accept that she is owed nothing and must work for what she wants. These attitudes liberate her from the delusions of her father, brother, and sister; from the belief in money that elevates the Merdles into prominence; and from the bitterness that infects familial and social relationships. Paradoxically, it is the Child of the Marshalsea who turns out to be free, and her power to forgive can also free Arthur of the guilt that has driven him into depression.

Dorrit, Edward ("Tip") Amy's brother, a restless ne'er-do-well, who ruins himself with drink. Although Arthur secures his release from prison (I:14), Tip returns to hang out in questionable company in the prison and ultimately to become a prisoner on his own account. After the family fortunes are reversed, Tip adopts a spendthrift life and loses everything in Merdle's collapse.

Dorrit, Fanny Amy's older sister, a gold digger who works as a dancer in the theater where Frederick plays clarinet in the orchestra: "a pretty girl of a far better figure and much more developed than Little Dorrit, though looking much younger in the face when the two were observed together" (I:3). She attracts the attentions of Sparkler and is bought off with a bracelet from Mrs. Merdle, but she resents Mrs. Merdle's condescension and after the change in the family's fortunes, she captures Sparkler and marries him for his social position and as a way of wreaking revenge on his mother. The couple move to London where Sparkler takes a position in the Circumlocution Office. After Merdle's fall, Fanny must live on her husband's salary.

Dorrit, Frederick William Dorrit's brother: "He was dirtily and meanly dressed, in a threadbare coat, once blue, reaching to his ankles and buttoned to his chin, where it vanished in the pale ghost of a velvet collar. A piece of red cloth with which that phantom had been stiffened in its lifetime was now laid bare and poked itself up, at the back of the old man's neck, into a confusion of grey hair and rusty stock and buckle which altogether nearly poked his hat off. A greasy hat it was, and a napless; impending over his eyes, cracked and crumpled at the brim, and with a wisp of pockethandkerchief dangling out below it. His trousers were so long and loose, and his shoes so clumsy and large, that he shuffled like an elephant; though

how much this was gait, and how much trailing cloth and leather, no one could have told" (I:8). Ruined in the financial collapse of his brother, Frederick makes a meager living playing the clarinet at the theater where Fanny is a dancer. He is patronized by William, who dislikes his brother's humility and unpretentious poverty. In Italy, Frederick is out of place, unable to adopt the pretenses that his brother and Fanny assume after the change of fortune. He defends Amy against their condescension: "I protest against pride. I protest against ingratitude. I protest against any one of us here who have known what we have known, and have seen what we have seen, setting up any pretension that puts Amy at a moment's disadvantage, or to the cost of a moment's pain" (II:5). He dies at his dead brother's bedside (II:19). Frederick acts as a DOUBLE to William, revealing the broken man without pretenses that William suppresses.

Dorrit, William ("Father of the Marshalsea") Patriarch of the Dorrit family, father of Little Dorrit, Fanny, and Edward, "a very amiable and very helpless middle-aged gentleman" (I:6), Imprisoned in the MARSHALSEA for more than 20 years, longer than any other prisoner, he has earned the epithet "Father of the Marshalsea." "A shy, retiring man; well-looking, though in an effeminate style; with a mild voice, curling hair, and irresolute hands . . . which nervously wandered to his trembling lip a hundred times" (I:6), he punctuates his halting speech with interjections of "ha" and "hum." He patronizes the other inmates as his inferiors, accepting monetary "testimonials" from them and from visitors to the prison. Brought up a gentleman, he is incapable of providing for himself and he refuses to acknowledge that he survives by depending on others, particularly his daughter Amy, who works as a servant for Mrs. Clennam to support him. She colludes with his denial by not telling him that she works outside the prison, that Fanny is a dancer, and that Tip is imprisoned on his own account. He accuses Amy of ingratitude when she refuses John Chivery's proposal (I:19), and after Clennam and Pancks discover that he is heir to a large fortune, he criticizes her unwillingness to adopt a lavish way of life. He dies suddenly in Rome, however, imagining that he is back in the prison (II:19), and the family then learns that he has lost his fortune by investing in Merdle's financial schemes.

Dorrit articulates the recognition that the human situation is not changed by riches or poverty; he maintains his delusions of his prerogatives and his superiority both in and out of prison. This imprisonment in delusion and denial defines the lot of many characters in the novel. JAMES KINCAID (1971) observes, for example, that "after his release [from prison], Mr. Dorrit becomes a truer copy of Merdle, similarly afraid of servants, similarly powerful, and similarly alienated from his own home. Though still a partially humorous figure, he becomes more and more representative of a generalized condition of man, 'so full of contradictions, vacillations, inconsistencies, the peevish perplexities of this ignorant life'" (II:19).

Doyce, Daniel Engineer and inventor, friend of Meagles; he takes Arthur Clennam as a partner in his business: "a short, square, practical looking man, whose hair had turned grey, and in whose face and forehead there were deep lines of cogitation. . . . He had a spectacle-case in his hand, which he turned over and over . . . with a certain free use of the thumb that is never seen but in a hand accustomed to tools" (I:10). According to Meagles, Doyce is "a very ingenious man" who has perfected "an invention (involving a very curious secret process) of great importance to his country and his fellow creatures" (I:10). Clennam tries and fails to secure support for Doyce's invention from the Circumlocution Office (II:8). While Doyce is abroad, where his work is more appreciated, Clennam disastrously invests the firm's assets in Merdle's ruinous ventures (II:26). When Doyce returns to England, he forgives his partner and helps secure his release from prison.

Challenging Lionel Trilling's assertion in *The Opposing Self* (1955) that Doyce "stands for the creative mind in general," JAMES KINCAID (1971) finds him "too limited to represent the creative mind; he is, in many ways, its antithesis. He is merely clear; he is not joyous, resilient, imaginative, or, in any real sense creative. It is a key to the desperation and bitterness informing this novel that something

so very limited as pragmatic clarity, attacked over and over again in earlier novels, is admired. It suggests that *Little Dorrit* is, at least in one major strain, deeply reactionary in its celebration of the practical and in its implicit disenchantment with the powers of the liberating and extroverted imagination."

Finching, Flora Widowed daughter of Casby and childhood sweetheart of Arthur Clennam before he went to China. In middle age, she has become garrulous and silly: "Flora, always tall, had grown to be very broad too, and short of breath; but that was not much. Flora, whom he had left a lily, had become a peony; but that was not much. Flora, who had seemed enchanting in all she said and thought, was diffuse and silly. That was much. Flora, who had been spoiled and artless long ago, was determined to be spoiled and artless now. That was a fatal blow" (I:13). Flora's speech—which runs on mixing past and present, illusion and shrewdly realistic observations, hopes and fears—acts as a vocal bulwark against the loneliness and isolation that is the lot of so many characters in the novel. Her desperate volubility often seems on the edge of tears, but her words enable her to triumph over the disappointments and losses in her life—the death of her husband, Arthur's rejection, the hypocrisy of her father, the resentful shadow represented by the mad Mr. F's aunt. In spite of all, she is kind to Amy, whom she employs at Arthur's request; forgiving of Arthur; and accepting of Mr. F's aunt. Like Micawber in *David Copperfield* or Sairey Gamp in *Martin Chuzzlewit*, she is a character who creates herself through language. In the end she blesses the relationship of Arthur and Amy. Flora was modeled on MARIA BEADNELL, who resurfaced in Dickens's life in 1855 as the middle-aged Maria Winter.

Flintwinch, Affery Arthur Clennam's nurse, "a tall hard-favoured sinewy old woman, who in her youth might have enlisted in the Foot Guards without much fear of discovery" (I:3), she has married Jeremiah Flintwinch during Arthur's absence in China. She is troubled and bewildered by the strange noises and puzzling occurrences in Mrs. Clennam's household, especially by the dark dealings of her husband with Mrs. Clennam, whom she refers to as the "two clever ones." She does not know that her husband has a twin brother, and she does not understand the machinations he is involved in, taking much that she sees as bewildering and frightening bad dreams. In the end she realizes that what she has overheard were the schemes of Mrs. Clennam and her husband and that his dream double was actually his brother; she adds what she knows to Rigaud's revelations (II:30).

Flintwinch, Ephraim Jeremiah's twin and DOUBLE. He takes the papers relating to Arthur's identity and Little Dorrit's inheritance to Europe where, somehow, Rigaud secures them.

Flintwinch, Jeremiah Confidential clerk and business partner of Mrs. Clennam. "A short, bald old man, in a high-shouldered black coat and waistcoat, drab breeches, and long drab gaiters. . . . There was nothing about him in the way of decoration but a watch. . . . His head was awry, and he had a one-sided, crab-like way with him, as if his foundations had yielded at about the same time as those of the house, and he ought to have been propped up in a similar manner" (I:3). He has an intimate knowledge of Mrs. Clennam's affairs, including her suppression of the codicil to Gilbert Clennam's will. When Arthur returns from China, Jeremiah gives documents concerning Arthur and Little Dorrit to his twin brother and double, Ephraim, to take abroad for safekeeping (I:3), but Rigaud gets possession of the papers and blackmails Mrs. Clennam (I:30). When Rigaud's scheme is foiled by the collapse of the house, Flintwinch escapes to Holland. Jeremiah's wife Affery is bewildered by his activities.

General, Mrs. The "dignified and imposing" widow of a commissariat officer, employed as a chaperone and "polisher" to "form the minds" of Amy and Fanny Dorrit: "In person, Mrs. General, including her skirts which had much to do with it, was of a dignified and imposing appearance; ample, rustling, gravely voluminous; always upright behind the proprieties. . . . If her eyes had no expression it was probably because they had nothing to express. . . . Mrs. General had no opinions. Her way of forming a mind was to prevent it from forming opinions"

(II:2). She counsels her charges to practice their elocution by repeating "Papa, potatoes, poultry, prunes and prism" (II:15). Mr. Dorrit's death thwarts her design to secure him as her second husband.

Describing her as a "humorous *and* dangerous agent of falsification," JAMES KINCAID (1971) observes, "Her dedication to surfaces and to the proprieties ties her, ironically, to Blandois and to the novel's deep distrust of the basic assumption of the realistic comedy of manners: that surfaces reflect depths. In *Little Dorrit* the surface either falsifies the real or simply varnishes an emptiness."

Gowan, Henry An indolent and snobbish young gentleman, a distant connection of the Barnacles, "well-dressed of a sprightly and gay appearance, a well-knit figure, . . . a rich dark complexion . . . [and] an air of cruelty" (I:17). He takes up a career as an artist for lack of something better to do and pursues his art in a careless, offhand, and cynical way. He courts Pet Meagles and marries her, much to the distress of her parents. After the wedding the couple travels to Italy, where Gowan does portraits of the rich expatriates, including Mr. Dorrit; neglects his wife and child; and associates with Blandois, a relationship indicative of his repressed cruelty. When the couple returns to England, Gowan snubs his wife's parents while condescending to accept an annual allowance from them.

Although WILLIAM MAKEPEACE THACKERAY is not in every way a model for Gowan, his aristocratic diffidence and his cavalier attitude toward his art especially annoyed Dickens, so Gowan is often considered Dickens's verdict on these attitudes in his great rival.

Gowan, Mrs. Widow of "a commissioner of nothing in particular," she is as snobbish and condescending as her son. She lives on a small pension in Hampton Court Palace. She objects to her son's marriage to a woman so far beneath him in social standing, but she is pleased by the financial rewards it brings.

Great St. Bernard Pass The pass over the Alps between Switzerland and Italy where the hospice of St. Bernard is located. The Dorrits, traveling from England, meet the Gowans and Rigaud at the hospice when their journeys cross there (II:1).

Haggage   Drunken doctor in the Marshalsea who delivers Amy Dorrit (I:6, 7).

Hampton Court Palace   This royal palace, presented to Henry VIII by Cardinal Wolsey in 1526, was, in the 19th century, a residence for royal pensioners. Mrs. Gowan has apartments here on the strength of her husband's diplomatic post (I:17, 26).

Harley Street   The Merdles live in "the handsomest house" on this fashionable street north of Cavendish Square (I:20).

Hawkins   Middle-aged baker of PENTONVILLE whom Miss Rugg successfully sues for breach of promise (I:25).

Iron Bridge   Southwark Bridge over the Thames, built in 1818, a favorite walking place of Little Dorrit (I:9, 18).

Jenkinson   Messenger at the Circumlocution Office (I:10).

Jerusalem Coffee House   One of the oldest such establishments in the City of London, this coffeehouse was frequented by merchants, like Jeremiah Flintwinch, who were engaged in trade with China, India, and Australia (I:29).

Lagnier   Alias used by Rigaud at Chalons (I:11).

Lion   Henry Gowan's Newfoundland dog. After Gowan punishes him for attacking Blandois, the dog is later found poisoned, probably by Blandois (I:17, II:6).

Little Gosling Street   Street near the London docks where Flora and Mr. Finching "settled down" at no. 30 after their honeymoon on the continent (I:24).

London Coffee House   Tavern in Ludgate Street where Arthur Clennam stays when he first returns to England from China (I:3).

Maggy   Mentally retarded granddaughter of Mrs. Bangham; an inmate in the MARSHALSEA with Amy Dorrit, to whom she is devoted. She calls Amy, who cares for her, "Little Mother." "She was about eight-and-twenty, with large bones, large features, large feet and hands, large eyes and no hair. Her large eyes were limpid and almost colourless; they seemed to be very little affected by light, and to stand unnaturally still. There was also that attentive listening expression in her face, which is seen in the faces of the blind but she was not blind, having one tolerably serviceable eye. Her face was not exceedingly ugly, though it was only redeemed from being so by a smile" (I:9). Her retardation is the result of brutal treatment from her grandmother, described by Maggy as "Gin . . . Broom-handles and pokers" (I:9). After the Dorrits go off to Italy, Maggy is cared for by the Plornishes (II:4). Another child of the Marshalsea, Maggy acts as a DOUBLE to Little Dorrit, externalizing the wounds that Amy carries within, eliciting Amy's story of the little woman and the shadow (I:24), and engaging Amy's adult, maternal side.

Maroon, Captain   Horse trader to whom Tip Dorrit owes money: "gentleman with tight drab legs, a rather old hat, a little hooked stick, and a blue neckerchief" (I:12).

Martin, Captain   MARSHALSEA prisoner whom Mr. Dorrit uses as an example to Amy, implicitly urging her to "lead on" to John Chivery's proposal; Martin had encouraged his sister to tolerate the attentions of the turnkey's brother (I:19).

Meagles, Lillie   Pet's twin sister, who died in childhood.

Meagles, Minnie ("Pet")   The surviving daughter of the Meagles twins, "round and fresh and dimpled and spoilt, and there was in Pet an air of timidity and dependence which was the best weakness in the world, and gave her the crowning charm a girl so pretty and pleasant could have been without" (I:2). Arthur considers courting her, but he gives up his interest when he meets Henry Gowan (I:28), who marries her, is snobbish and contemptuous of her parents, and treats Pet with indifference.

Meagles, Mr. An "honest, affectionate, and cordial" (I:16) retired banker, who exemplifies the virtues and limitations of the British bourgeoisie. He lives in an idyllic country cottage by the Thames near TWICKENHAM, which is filled with mementos from his many travels abroad. Clennam has met him at the quarantine station in MARSEILLE while returning from China (I:2). There Meagles complained about the French, as he always does about foreign ways while abroad, only to remember his travels positively when at home. This combination of cosmopolitan experience and insularity is present also in his mixture of acceptance of and snobbery with others. He takes Tattycoram into his family but treats her with a measure of condescension that leads to the contradictions in her relationship with the family. Even though Meagles champions the work of Daniel Doyce, he treats the inventor condescendingly, and he is gratified by Gowan's connections with the Barnacles, even though he recognizes that Gowan is a cad. A "practical" man, Meagles helps Arthur in the search for the papers stolen by Blandois. He and Doyce are also responsible for delivering Arthur from prison.

Meagles, Mrs. Meagles's wife, "comely and healthy, with a pleasant English face which had been looking at homely things for five-and-fifty years or more, and shone with a bright reflection of them" (1:2).

Merdle, Mr. Financier, speculator, forger, and swindler; his enterprises are the bubble that engages all of England and ruins Clennam, Doyce, Pancks, and the Dorrits. "He was a reserved man, with a broad, overhanging, watchful head, . . . and a somewhat uneasy expression about his coat-cuffs, as if they were in his confidence, and had reasons for being anxious to hide his hands" (I:21). He has a habit of "clasping his wrists as if he were taking himself into custody (I:33). Surrounded by power-

ful representatives of society, Merdle suffers from a vague complaint that his physician is unable to diagnose (I:21). After his enterprises fail, he cuts his throat in a Turkish bath (II:25). His schemes bring financial ruin to many characters in the novel, including Clennam, Pancks, and the Dorrits. The original of Merdle was JOHN SADLEIR.

Merdle, Mrs. Merdle's wife, a society matron, who provided "a capital bosom to hang jewels upon, . . . and he bought it for the purpose" (I:21). By her first marriage she is the mother of Edmund Sparkler; she thwarts her son's interest in Fanny Dorrit by buying Fanny off with a bracelet (I:20), but when the Dorrits come into money, she seeks out their company in Italy.

Nandy, John Edward Mrs. Plornish's father, "a little reedy piping old gentleman, like a worn-out bird; who had been in what he called the music-binding business, and met with great misfortunes, and who . . . had retired of his own accord to the Workhouse" (I:31). While visiting Plornish in the Marshalsea, Nandy meets Mr. Dorrit and occasionally comes to visit him. Dorrit treats him with great condescension, as if he is his feudal retainer. When Mr. Dorrit enables Mrs. Plornish to set up a shop, Nandy leaves the workhouse and moves in with his daughter (II:13).

Nobody's Fault Dickens's original working title for *Little Dorrit* when he conceived of the central emphasis in the book as the impersonality of the social and political system. He changed the title to *Little Dorrit* shortly before the first number was published.

Pancks Casby's agent and rent collector, a "short dark man . . . dressed in black and rusty iron grey; [who] had jet black beads of eyes; a scrubby little black chin; wiry black hair striking out from his head in prongs, like forks or hair-pins; and a complexion that was very dingy by nature, or very dirty by art, or a compound of nature and art. He had dirty hands and dirty broken nails, and looked as if he had been in the coals; he was in a perspiration, and snorted and sniffed and puffed and blew, like a little labouring steam engine"

(I:13). This energetic and hard-working man works as Casby's agent, squeezing the tenants in Bleeding Heart Yard and taking the blame for Casby's avarice. On his own he recruits Rugg and John Chivery and leads the effort to discover the Dorrit fortune (I:35). He invests his money in Merdle's enterprises and leads Arthur to do the same, bankrupting Doyce and Clennam (II:13). He aids in exposing Rigaud (II:30) and he cuts Casby's patriarchal locks in the middle of Bleeding Heart Yard (II:32). He goes to work for Doyce and Clennam, eventually becoming a partner.

Like Mr. Lorry in *Two Cities* and Wemmick in *Great Expectations*, Pancks divides his business life from his personal life and is another of Dickens's commentaries on the corrupting force of 19th-century capitalism.

Physician One of the allegorically named guests in Merdle's circle of important people, he serves as Merdle's personal physician but is unable to diagnose Merdle's complaint (I:21). He is called in to deal with Merdle's suicide (II:25).

Plornish, Sally Plornish's wife, "a young woman, made somewhat slatternly in herself and her belongings by poverty; and so dragged at by poverty and the children together, that their united forces had already dragged her face into wrinkles" (I:12). She has a habit, when questioned, of beginning her reply with "not to deceive you." With Mr. Dorrit's aid, she establishes a small grocery shop in her house and has the building painted to look like a country cottage. The Plornishes have two children.

Plornish, Thomas Frequently unemployed plasterer who lives in Bleeding Heart Yard, "a smooth-cheeked, fresh-coloured, sandy-whiskered man of thirty. Long in the legs, yielding at the knees, foolish in the face, flannel-jacketed, lime-whitened" (I:12). When he is imprisoned in the Marshalsea, he meets the Dorrits and offends Mr. Dorrit with the small size of his tribute (I:6). Clennam employs him to sort out Tip Dorrit's debts (I:12) and to provide Cavaletto a place to stay (I:25).

Rigaud (alias Blandois, alias Lagnier) Adventurer, murderer, and blackmailer, "his eyes, too close together, . . . had no depth or change. . . . He had a hook nose, handsome after its kind, but too high between the eyes, by probably just as much as his eyes were too near to one another. For the rest, he was large and tall in frame, had thin lips, where his thick moustache showed them at all, and a quantity of dry hair, of no definable colour" (I:1). Son of a Swiss father and French mother and born in Belgium, Rigaud is "European," "a cosmopolitan gentleman. . . . He had a certain air of being a handsome man, which he was not; and a certain air of being a well-bred man, which he was not; it was mere swagger and challenge" (I:1). He is imprisoned in MARSEILLE charged with murdering his wife (I:1), but he is released for lack of evidence, and he hypocritically vows revenge on society for the wrongs done to him. Posing as a gentleman named Blandois, he shows up in London and then disappears, leading Arthur to think that his mother is somehow guilty of disposing of him. In Italy he attaches himself to the Gowans (II:1). After he obtains documents implicating Mrs. Clennam in the suppression of her uncle's will, he attempts to blackmail her, but his attempts are foiled when Mrs. Clennam's house collapses on him (II:33).

According to ALEXANDER WELSH (1971), Rigaud is a DOUBLE to Arthur Clennam, serving a role in *Little Dorrit* similar to that of Orlick in *Great Expectations*. DORIS ALEXANDER (1991) suggests that Dickens took Rigaud's physical appearance from his friend and fellow novelist EDWARD BULWER LYTTON.

Rugg Pancks's landlord, a debt collector and accountant "who had a round white visage, as if all his blushes had been drawn out of him long ago, and who had a ragged yellow head like a worn-out hearth-broom" (I:25). He aids in the investigation that leads to the discovery of the Dorrit fortune, and he takes care of Clennam's financial affairs when Arthur is imprisoned for debt (II:26).

Rugg, Anastasia Rugg's middle-aged daughter who lives on the proceeds of a successful breach-of-promise suit against a baker named Hawkins (I:25).

Slingo Horse trader who employs Tip Dorrit (I:7).

Sparkler, Edmund Mrs. Merdle's "chuckle-headed" son by her first marriage. An idler and dandy, "he had given so few signs of reason, that a by-word went up among his companions that his brain had been frozen up in a mighty frost which prevailed at St. John's, New Brunswick, at the period of his birth there, and had never thawed from that hour. . . . [He was] monomaniacal in offering marriage to all manner of undesireable young ladies" (I:21). He pursues Fanny Dorrit when she is just a poor dancer; Mrs. Merdle buys her off with a bracelet (I:20), but when the Dorrits come into money, he is allowed to marry Fanny (II:15), who has renewed her pursuit as a way of getting revenge on Mrs. Merdle and treats him with disdain. He gets a sinecure in the Circumlocution Office in spite of his obvious incompetence.

Stiltstalking, Lord Lancaster One of the residents at Hampton Court with Mrs. Gowan. He is "a noble refrigerator" (I:26).

St. George's Church, Southwark Church adjoining the Marshalsea where Little Dorrit is christened and married (I:6, II:34).

"Tattycoram" Nickname of Harriet Beadle, derived from the diminutive for Harriet, "Tatty," and the name of the founder of the orphanage from which she comes, Coram's Foundling Hospital.

Tickit, Mrs. The Meagleses' housekeeper and cook: "When they went away, she . . . established herself in the breakfast-room, put her spectacles between two particular leaves of Doctor Buchan's Domestic Medicine, and sat looking over the blind all day until they came back again" (I:16).

Tinkler Mr. Dorrit's valet, who travels with the family to Italy.

Treasury One of Merdle's powerful dinner guests (I:21).

Wade, Miss Discontented, angry, distrustful, and "self-tormenting" woman whose paranoia leads her to distrust all offers of friendship and to consider any kindness to her as a trap. Her cynicism matches that of Henry Gowan, who courted and jilted her. Miss Wade is one of the travelers in quarantine (I:2), and, as a friend of the Meagles, she convinces Tattycoram to leave them and live with her. Her primary role in the plot is to obtain from Rigaud the documents relating to Little Dorrit's identity, which Tattycoram returns when she leaves Miss Wade. Her interpolated autobiography, "The History of a Self-Tormentor" (II:21) tells of her painful illegitimacy, of her jealous and distrustful relationship with a schoolmate, and of her abusive relationship with Gowan.

Recent critics have devoted far more attention to Miss Wade than her inconsequential role in the novel seems to demand. As the inverse of Amy Dorrit, Miss Wade resents every deprivation and imagined slight by others. Although she is an independent woman, she is caught in a prison of the self, consumed by bitterness and resentment. Miss Wade appeals to the darker side of the divided Tattycoram, who is split between gratitude and resentment, drawing her away from the Meagles. Her "independence" and apparent lesbianism have made her interesting as a reflection of the alienation of women in patriarchal Victorian culture. HILARY SCHOR (1999) makes the most convincing case for her role in the novel, analyzing her story as a Browningesque monologue complementing several other women's stories (e.g., Amy's, Mrs. Clennam's) that embody the central issues of the novel.

Wobbler Rude and desultory clerk at the Circumlocution Office who passes the buck to another clerk when Clennam is referred to him (I:10).

ADAPTATIONS

The least dramatized of all Dickens's novels, *Little Dorrit* prompted only one unsuccessful adaptation, by FREDERICK FOX COOPER, during its initial appearance. James Albery's *The Two Roses* (1870) starred HENRY IRVING as Digby Grant, a character modeled on William Dorrit. Albery's play was a popular production during the rest of the 19th century and was probably the basis for a silent film (1910). Four more silent films—one American (1913), one

German (1917), one British (1920), and one Danish (1924)—were produced. A German adaptation, *Klein Dorrit*, appeared as a sound film in 1934, and the Stanislavsky Theater in Moscow produced a Russian adaptation in 1953. The most successful dramatization of the novel is the film adaptation written and directed by Christine Edzard (1987). The most ambitious cinematic adaptation of any Dickens novel, Edzard's film echoes the structure of the novel in its two three-hour sections. The first part, "Nobody's Fault," tells Arthur's version of the story; the second half is "Little Dorrit's Story." Major roles are played by Sarah Pickering (Amy), Derek Jacobi (Arthur), Joan Greenwood (Mrs. Clennam), and ALEC GUINNESS (William Dorrit).

FURTHER READING

Lionel Trilling's Introduction to the novel (reprinted in *The Opposing Self*, 1955) is the classic essay on *Little Dorrit*. He describes society's effect on the individual will as the central concern of the novel, an analysis he compares to Freud's theory of neurosis. J. C. Reid's *Charles Dickens: Little Dorrit* (1967) is a useful general introduction to the novel; JAMES KINCAID (1971) finds the novel so "deeply rooted in pessimism" that it turns all its comic effects ultimately into an "attack on comedy." George Holoch analyzes the interlocking mystifications that constitute the novel's social order in "Consciousness and Society in *Little Dorrit*" (*Victorian Studies*, 1978). F. R. LEAVIS and Q. D. LEAVIS (1970) offer a controversial analysis of the novel that compares Dickens to Blake and describes Little Dorrit as an agent of the real. P. J. M. Scott (*Reality and Comic Confidence in Charles Dickens*, 1979) extends and modifies the Leavises' view in an essay that characterizes the novel as Dickens's "triumph of reality." David Holbrook (*Charles Dickens and the Image of Woman*,

A scene that directly reflects one of Browne's (Phiz's) original illustrations in the novel, called "Little Dorrit's Party." Little Dorrit and Maggy are huddled in the street on the night that they are locked out of the Marshalsea Prison after the gates have been closed. From the 1987 film adaptation of *Little Dorrit*. *Courtesy of PhotoFest.*

1993) also takes issue with the Leavises' praise of Amy Dorrit and Arthur Clennam; he finds them representatives of "duty" rather than spokespersons for the reality principle. Kathleen Woodward ("Passivity and Passion in *Little Dorrit*," *Dickensian*, 1975) discusses the women characters in the novel; she finds Amy "unconvincing and boring" as a portrait of a mature woman and Miss Wade "the only woman in the book who possesses sexuality and mystery." HILARY SCHOR (1999) challenges many similar recent interpretations of the novel that exaggerate the importance of Miss Wade with a reading that compares the life stories of the various women in the novel and their attitude toward women's ownership of property, celebrating Amy's story of fulfillment through renunciation of property and love.

Martin Chuzzlewit, The Life and Adventures of. (Serial title: *The Life and Adventures of Martin Chuzzlewit, his Relatives, Friends and Enemies: Comprising all his Wills and his Ways, with an Historical Record of What he did, and What he didn't; showing, moreover, who inherited the Family Plate, who came in for the Silver Spoons, and who for the Wooden Ladles: the Whole forming a Complete Key to the House of Chuzzlewit,* edited by "Boz")

Dickens's sixth novel, published in monthly parts (January 1843 to July 1844), with illustrations by HABLOT KNIGHT BROWNE. Published in one volume by CHAPMAN & HALL, 1844. A transitional novel between the loosely structured early works and the more carefully planned later ones, *Chuzzlewit* combines improvisation and indulgent characterization with the more consciously developed central theme of selfishness. To expose the materialism of the Chuzzlewits and, by extension, of Victorian society, Dickens mixed humors comedy—comedy based on the exaggeration of single obsessive traits—with satire, sentimental comedy, and the comedy of the absurd to create two of his most memorable characters, Seth Pecksniff and Sairey Gamp.

SYNOPSIS

Part 1 (January 1843)

(1) The Chuzzlewit family is one of extreme antiquity, "descended in a direct line from Adam and Eve." Their importance renders them "highly improving and acceptable acquaintance to all right-minded individuals."

(2) On a windy afternoon in late autumn, Seth Pecksniff, an architect, arrives home, only to have the wind blow shut his front door and knock him to the ground; there he is rescued by his younger daughter, Mercy. At tea, Pecksniff's assistant, Tom Pinch, tries unsuccessfully to reconcile architect Pecksniff with his student, John Westlock, but as he leaves for London Westlock tells Pinch, who defends his employer, that Pecksniff is a self-serving hypocrite.

(3) At the Blue Dragon, the local inn, a sick old man and a young woman have taken refuge. Since the apothecary is unavailable, Mrs. Lupin, the innkeeper, asks Pecksniff as a prominent member of the community to visit the sick man. She tells Pecksniff that she thinks the old man's illness stems from guilt over his association with an unmarried young woman. Pecksniff discovers the invalid to be his relative, old Martin Chuzzlewit. When the old man awakens, he tells Pecksniff that he is pursued by greedy relatives and has no friends because his wealth dooms him "to try the metal of all other men and find it false and hollow." He says that he trusts only Mary Graham, the young orphan who travels with him. He has told her that she will inherit nothing from him, so she has nothing to gain by his death. Pecksniff advises old Martin to provide for his grandson, young Martin. The old

Martin Chuzzlewit (Paul Scofield) is attended by Mary Graham (Pauline Turner), an orphan whom he adopts as his nurse and companion, in this movie adaptation of *Martin Chuzzlewit. Courtesy of PhotoFest.*

man assumes Pecksniff's pleading is "a new plot," and as the architect leaves, old Martin mutters, "Oh self, self, self! at every turn nothing but self!"

Part 2 (February 1843)

(4) Rejected by old Martin, Pecksniff nonetheless is determined "to return good for evil," so he keeps watch over the old man, peering in on him though the keyhole of his room. One day he finds a vagabond dressed in grandiloquent and tattered clothes at the keyhole before him. It is Montague Tigg, a friend of Chuzzlewit's nephew Chevy Slyme. Tigg asserts Slyme's claim upon old Martin and tells Pecksniff that other relatives have discovered the old man's whereabouts and are gathering in the town. Soon all available accommodations are taken by Chuzzlewits, each suspicious of the others and of Tigg and Mary Graham, who are not members of the family. Pecksniff calls them all together at his house, where they agree that Mary Graham "casts a shadow of disgrace and shame upon this family," but they fight about everything else. Meanwhile old Martin secretly slips away.

(5) On his way to Salisbury, Tom Pinch gives a ride to Mark Tapley, the man-of-all-work at the Blue Dragon who is going off to seek work elsewhere that will present more of a challenge to his good humor. Tom has gone to town to meet young Martin Chuzzlewit, grandson of the old man, who is to be Pecksniff's new architectural pupil. In pleading the young Chuzzlewit's case to old Martin, Pecksniff had been indirectly pleading his own. Tom and young Martin quickly become friends. Tom even confides to Martin his joy in playing the organ at the parish church and reveals how smitten he is by a beautiful young woman who listens to him play, and, with tears in his eyes, he tells Martin of Pecksniff's goodness. When they arrive at Pecksniff's house, the architect and his two daughters, Charity and Mercy, appear to be unprepared for their arrival, but Tom notes that the supper is unusually lavish. The girls pay particular attention to the new student.

Part 3 (March 1843)

(6) The next morning Pecksniff announces that he and his daughters are going to London for a week; he leaves Martin in charge of the household, instructing him to design a grammar school while he is gone. Martin is disconcerted to have his education interrupted so soon. That evening Martin tells Tom of his expectations from his grandfather and of the old man's obstinacy and selfishness in opposing his love for Mary Graham. Obstinacy and selfishness, Martin asserts, are Chuzzlewit traits, and he promises to respond to his grandfather's obstinacy with "firmness." He has come to study with Pecksniff because of his grandfather's "inveterate dislike" for the architect.

(7) While Martin works on the grammar school and Tom goes over Pecksniff's accounts, Montague Tigg comes to Pecksniff's house as an ambassador from Chevy Slyme. They are being detained at the Dragon because they cannot pay their bill, so Martin pays Mrs. Lupin just to get the two out of town. Tigg coaxes an extra 10 shillings out of Pinch.

(8) Meanwhile, on the London coach Pecksniff and his daughters are joined by Anthony Chuzzlewit, old Martin's brother, and his son Jonas, who are returning home to London.

Part 4 (April 1843)

(9) At the heart of the labyrinth of London streets, not far from the MONUMENT, is the boardinghouse for gentlemen presided over by Mrs. Todgers. The men of the house, led by Jinkins, the senior resident, plan a festive dinner to honor the visiting Pecksniffs. Meanwhile, Pecksniff, his daughters, and Mrs. Todgers deliver a letter from Tom Pinch to his sister Ruth, who is working as a governess in CAMBERWELL. Pecksniff condescends to Ruth, hoping for an introduction to the snobbish copper founder for whom she works, but he is only asked to stay off the grass and leave the premises. At the dinner party, Charity and Mercy are honored by the gentlemen of Todgers's; Pecksniff drinks too much, makes up to Mrs. Todgers, falls into the fireplace, and is carried upstairs. There he is subdued and locked in his room. Young Bailey, the energetic houseboy of the establishment, keeps watch at his door.

(10) Pecksniff's business in London is to meet with old Martin Chuzzlewit, who urges the obsequious architect to dismiss the ungrateful young Martin as his student.

Part 5 (May 1843)

(11) At the end of the week Jonas calls on Charity, arousing the jealous envy of Mercy. He takes the two girls on a miserly sightseeing tour to the free attractions in London. Although he is ostensibly interested in Charity, he keeps inquiring about "the other one." Jonas's interest in his cousins throws the gentlemen of Todgers's into despair. They serenade the girls on their last night in town and then bid their coach farewell the next morning. Jonas and his father also come to see the Pecksniffs off.

(12) While Pecksniff is in London, Martin works on the design for the grammar school and treats Pinch with condescension. John Westlock, to celebrate coming into an inheritance, invites Pinch and Martin to dine with him at the best hotel in Salisbury. There Martin learns that John, much to the consternation of the naive Tom Pinch, thinks

Pecksniff "the most consummate scoundrel on the face of the earth." After Martin tells John how Tigg imposed on Pinch, John returns the loan and advises Tom to lend no more money to Tigg.

On his return from London, Pecksniff snubs Martin and refuses to speak to him. When Martin demands an explanation, Pecksniff renounces him and charges him with deception and depravity. Martin leaves abruptly, telling Tom that he will go to America.

Part 6 (June 1843)

(13) Out in the rain, Martin looks into the book that Tom has given him as a parting gift and finds the half-sovereign that Tom had once lent Tigg. He makes his way to London, pawning his belongings to get by. Five weeks after arriving in the city, penniless and despairing of ever reaching America, Martin receives a letter with £20 in it, and at the same time, Mark Tapley appears at his door and offers to go to America with him as his servant. Mark tells Martin that Mary Graham is in London. (14) When the two meet in ST. JAMES'S PARK, Martin tells Mary that he has asked Tom Pinch to protect her while he is away. She gives him a diamond ring as a parting gift, and he smugly asserts that "she is worthy of the sacrifices I have made." (15) During the crossing to America, Mark cares for other passengers in the steerage of the *Screw*, especially helping a mother with three small children who is on her way to join her immigrant husband. Martin reprimands Mark for not paying more attention to him, and he spends the whole voyage inside the cabin because he does not want to be seen on deck as someone who could only afford to travel in steerage.

Part 7 (July 1843)

(16) When the *Screw* arrives in NEW YORK, newsboys and newspaper editors meet the ship and Martin goes off with Colonel Diver, editor of the New York *Rowdy Journal*. At the newspaper offices, Martin meets Jefferson Brick, the paper's youthful war correspondent, who is presented to him, like every other American, as "one of the most remarkable men" in the country. (17) At Pawkins's Boarding House, Martin meets an exception to this rule, Mr. Bevan, who is simply a kind physician from

BOSTON. When Mark hires a former slave to help him with their luggage and is outspoken about the contradiction in a country that is devoted to liberty and yet harbors slavery, Bevan warns them that Mark's frankness may get him into trouble. They visit the Norrises, a family of abolitionists who nevertheless believe in the necessity of separating the races. The Norrises also preach the superiority of American liberty but are obsessed with the British aristocracy. When they learn that Martin crossed in steerage, they snub him. After less than a day in AMERICA, Martin begins to despair about his plan to establish himself as an architect.

Part 8 (August 1843)

(18) Back in London, Jonas taunts his father for not dying and leaving his money to him. The old man delights in his son's tight-fisted ways. While Pecksniff negotiates with Anthony a possible marriage between Jonas and his daughter, the old man falls ill. Jonas tells Pecksniff that the architect's fortunate presence in the house means that people will not be able to accuse Jonas of causing his father's illness. But neither Pecksniff nor Jonas nor Chuffey, Anthony's old clerk who genuinely cares for his master, can prevent Anthony from dying.

(19) Pecksniff seeks out Mrs. Gamp, the nurse and midwife recommended by the undertaker, to prepare the body for burial. Jonas orders an expensive and elaborate funeral and appears to the undertaker to be the very model of a bereaved son. Only old Chuffey's sobbing mars the ceremony and unsettles Jonas. (20) After the funeral, Jonas plans to spend some time at Pecksniff's house in the country. On the way there he elicits a promise that Pecksniff will provide a dowry of £4,000 should either of his daughters marry. But when Jonas proposes to Mercy, Pecksniff is surprised and Charity is beside herself. Jonas asks Pecksniff for an extra £1,000 for choosing the more difficult daughter, but their negotiations are interrupted when Pinch announces that old Martin and Mary Graham are approaching the house.

Part 9 (September 1843)

(21) Back in the United States, on a train going west, Martin and Mark meet General Choke, who introduces them to Mr. Scadder, agent for the Valley of Eden Land Corporation, which he operates out of a small shed containing a grand map of the settlement. Assured that there is work for an architect in the developing town of Eden, Martin buys into the scheme, in spite of Mark's skepticism. Using Mark's money for the purchase, Martin makes him an equal partner in the firm of Chuzzlewit and Co. Then they go to a meeting of the Watertoast Sympathisers, a group devoted to putting down the British lion and celebrating liberty. When the group learns that an Irish politician they have supported because of his anti-British position also opposes slavery, they renounce him and disband the organization. (22) Captain Kedgick, proprietor of the National Hotel, where they are staying, requires Martin to hold a levee, a reception for nearly everybody in town, including Mrs. Hominy, an authoress of moral sentiments who attaches herself to Martin for the next two days. Meanwhile, Mark gathers supplies for their new life in Eden. As they are about to set off on the steamboat for the settlement, Mark asks Kedgick why they hold the levees. "Our people like ex-citement," Kedgick tells him, and "nobody as goes to Eden ever comes back a-live." (23) As the steamboat goes farther and farther on its journey, the settlements become increasingly rude and primitive. Eden is simply a few rotting cabins set in a fetid swamp. Most of the settlers have left or died, and the few who remain are weak and sickly. Martin cries, expecting to die there; Mark tries to set things in order and raise Martin's spirits.

Part 10 (October 1843)

(24) Back in England, old Martin and Mary Graham are again staying at the Blue Boar and visiting Pecksniff. The architect has difficulty presenting a harmonious household to old Martin. Charity, jealous and resentful that Jonas has chosen her sister, is at odds with Mercy. Jonas, described by Pecksniff as a model son, nonetheless is suspicious and hostile to everyone around him. When Tom escorts Mary and the old man back to their inn, his praise of Pecksniff convinces Martin that Tom is just another of Pecksniff's toadies. When Tom confronts the surly Jonas and knocks him to the ground, he earns Charity's grateful approval.

Old Martin asks Mercy whether she loves Jonas. She says she hates him and will marry to tease him and get the better of him. After she toys with Jonas about a date for the wedding, he vows to punish her once they are married.

(25) Mrs. Gamp has been hired to care for Chuffey while Jonas is in Wiltshire. She also holds a second position as a night nurse for a young man at the Bull Inn. On her first night there, the patient surprises her by feverishly exclaiming in the middle of the night, "Chuzzlewit! Jonas! No!" (26) Later, when the newly married Jonas and Mercy return to the city, Mrs. Gamp does not think that the bride looks very merry. Old Chuffey raises his trembling hands above his head saying, "Oh! woe, woe, woe, upon this wicked house!"

Part 11 (November 1843)

(27) Jonas meets with Tigg Montague (formerly Montague Tigg), who has established the Anglo-Bengalee Disinterested Loan and Life Assurance Company, an operation whose lavish appearance conceals several confidence schemes. He impresses Jonas with his head for business and invites him to buy into the company. After Jonas leaves, Tigg employs Nadgett, his private investigator, to find out as much about Jonas as he can. (28) Later, at an opulent dinner at Montague's house, Jonas is plied with liquor until he agrees to join the firm. Young Bailey, formerly Mrs. Todgers's houseboy and now Montague's liveried footman, takes the drunken Jonas home at three in the morning. There the boy finds Mercy looking broken and dispirited and hears Jonas threaten her.

(20) As Mrs. Gamp prepares Lewsome, her patient from the Bull, for a journey to the country to recuperate from his illness, the sick man asks his friend John Westlock if he can confide a terrible secret to him. Westlock invites him to do so, but Lewsome is not yet ready to reveal his secret.

Part 12 (December 1843)

(30) Charity leaves home for London, so Pecksniff invites old Martin to move into his house with him. To improve his chances for the old man's money, Pecksniff decides he must marry Mary. When he meets her alone in the woods, however, she rejects him and threatens to tell old Martin

of his unwanted advances. Pecksniff promises to injure young Martin should she do so. (31) After this confrontation, Pecksniff goes into the church to rest and, while he hides in one of the pews and listens to Tom Pinch playing the organ, he also overhears a conversation between Tom and Mary. She tells him of Pecksniff's treachery, and Tom is finally convinced that Pecksniff is not the man he thought him. That evening, in the presence of old Martin, Pecksniff dismisses Tom, accusing him of making overtures to Mary Graham. Tom leaves for London, adjusting to a world in which "there was no Pecksniff; there never had been a Pecksniff."

(32) Ensconced at Todgers's, Charity works on the affections of Augustus Moddle, the youngest of the gentleman boarders, who was driven to thoughts of suicide by Mercy's marriage. Although

Browne's (Phiz's) illustration of Pecksniff discharging Tom Pinch depicts the central theme of *Martin Chuzzlewit*—the struggle between selfishness and altruism.

he is interested in Charity only because she reminds him of "Another," he finally offers her "a blighted heart," which she accepts.

Part 13 (January 1844)

(33) Back in America, on the day after his arrival in Eden, Martin falls ill of fever. When Mark goes to the neighbors for help, they turn out to be the family he cared for on the ship. They help him tend Martin, who is so ill he nearly dies. When Martin finally begins to recover, Mark falls ill. Martin and the neighbors care for him. Mark has at last found a situation that challenges his ability to maintain his good spirits, and Martin, during his illness, realizes how selfish he has been. Desperate to leave Eden, he writes to Mr. Bevan asking for help. Several weeks later a letter arrives with money in it, and Martin and Mark begin their journey home. (34) On the steamboat back to New York, they meet Elijah Pogram, a member of congress and another remarkable man. Mr. Bevan offers them money for their passage back to England, but Mark arranges to pay for it by signing on as a cook on the ship. As they leave, Mark speculates on how he would represent the American eagle: "like a Bat, for its shortsightedness; like a Bantam, for its bragging; like a Magpie, for its honesty; like a Peacock, for its vanity; like an Ostrich, for putting its head in the mud." Martin adds, "and like a Phoenix, for its power of springing from the ashes of its faults and vices, and soaring up anew into the sky." (35) A year after they left, Martin and Mark arrive back in England. Surprised to see Pecksniff in the port town, they learn that he is there to lay the cornerstone for his new building. Martin is outraged to discover that the building is the grammar school he designed.

Part 14 (February 1844)

(36) In London, Tom finds his unhappy sister patronized and put down by the copper founder she works for, so he gives the man a piece of his mind and takes Ruth away from her demeaning job. They find a flat in ISLINGTON. (37) Tom meets Charity Pecksniff and Augustus Moddle and goes with them to Todgers's. There he finds Mercy looking much altered. Tom is grateful for Mrs. Todgers's concern for the girl.

(38) After shadowing Jonas for some time, Nadgett reports to Montague. When Montague whispers something to Jonas after this interview, Jonas looks disturbed and agrees to put more money into the enterprise.

Part 15 (March 1844)

(39) John Westlock comes to Tom's Islington flat with news that Tom has been offered a position at £100 per annum. At the dark and dusty offices of Mr. Fips, an attorney in Austin Friars, Tom learns that he is to catalog a room full of books for an unnamed employer. (40) Tom regularly collects his wages from Fips, but he learns nothing more about his employer.

On one of his regular morning walks to the steamboat piers, Tom is asked to deliver a letter to a person boarding the steam packet for Antwerp. The passenger turns out to be Jonas, and the letter shocks him, calling him off the boat to meet Montague, who is waiting to take him to the CITY. (41) Jonas admits to Montague that he was trying to escape. Threatening to disclose Jonas's secret that Nadgett has uncovered, Montague demands that he put more money into the firm and help in a scheme to fleece Pecksniff.

Part 16 (April 1844)

(42) Reluctantly, Montague undertakes a journey to the country with Jonas. It is a stormy night, and Montague imagines that Jonas is about to attack him with a bottle. Then the coach overturns, and Montague is just barely saved from having his head crushed by the horses that Jonas is manuevering. Young Bailey, who has accompanied them on the coach, is badly injured in the accident and is left in the road for dead.

(43) Meanwhile, Mark and Martin arrive at the Dragon to a joyful reunion with Mrs. Lupin, who tells them all that has transpired in their absence. The next morning they go to Pecksniff's, where Martin unsuccessfully seeks reconciliation with his grandfather, who seems to be under Pecksniff's influence. After a brief reunion with Mary, Martin leaves Pecksniff's house just as Jonas is arriving. (44) Jonas arouses Pecksniff's greed with his surly talk of Montague's scheme, and by evening Pecksniff has agreed to commit nearly all his money to

the Anglo-Bengalee. While Montague stays in the country to close the deal with the architect, Jonas returns to London alone.

Part 17 (May 1844)

(45) John Westlock advises Tom to inform Jonas that he was innocent in his involvement in delivering the letter on the packet ship, (46) but when Tom and Ruth go to see Jonas, he is away in the country, so they have tea with Mercy and her sister. While they are there, old Chuffey distractedly wonders who is dead upstairs. As they are about to leave, Jonas returns home, berates his wife for holding parties while he is gone, and refuses to hear Tom's apology. After Tom leaves, Mrs. Gamp frightens Jonas when she tells him of Chuffey's ranting. He hires her to watch the old man. Then he goes to a downstairs bedroom to sleep, ordering that he not be disturbed for the next day and a half. In the middle of the night he puts on the clothes of a country laborer and slips out into the street. (47) After riding all night on a coach to the west, Jonas gets off in the country and hides in a wood where he knows Montague will pass on his way back to London. Then, with a club fashioned from a fence post, he leaps out at Montague, clubs him to death, and leaves the body in the wood. Making his way back to London that night, he is frightened but feels no regret. He returns to the small downstairs room at five in the morning. When Mercy awakens him, he learns that Nadgett has been inquiring about him.

Part 18 (June 1844)

(48) Martin is in London with John Westlock when Lewsome reveals his secret. It is simply that Lewsome, a physician, supplied Jonas with some poisons in exchange for forgiving a gambling debt; shortly after he did so, Anthony Chuzzlewit died. (49) John and Martin go to Sarah Gamp to see if she can enable them to talk to Chuffey to corroborate Lewsome's suspicions, but she has been drinking, and before they can question her about Chuffey she falls asleep.

(50) The next morning Martin breaks off his friendship with Tom Pinch, regretfully accusing Tom of failing to keep his promise to protect Mary. Tom is disappointed and asserts that Martin will

regret what he has done, but Ruth, who knows her brother's heart, gets Tom to admit that he loves Mary himself. The next day at work, Tom's employer finally reveals himself. It is old Martin Chuzzlewit.

Parts 19–20 (July 1844)

(51) When Mrs. Gamp comes to take charge of Chuffey, she is followed by old Martin, John Westlock, Lewsome, and Mark Tapley. They accuse Jonas of killing his father, but Chuffey, in a moment of lucidity, says that Anthony discovered his son's plot to poison him and destroyed the poison. He died of natural causes, grieving and blaming his own greed as the cause of Jonas's cruelty. His final words to Chuffey were "Spare him." On learning that he is not guilty of his father's death, Jonas gloats and orders his accusers to leave. But Nadgett and Chevy Slyme, now a policeman, are at the door. They charge Jonas with Montague's murder. Jonas offers Slyme £100 for five minutes alone in which to poison himself. Slyme takes the money, but he gives it back when Jonas is still alive some time later. Placed under arrest, Jonas takes the poison in the cab on the way to the police station.

(52) At a meeting of the Chuzzlewits and those associated with them, old Martin announces that "the curse of our house . . . has been the love of self; has ever been the love of self." He reconciles with many of the family members and particularly with his grandson, young Martin, and he blesses Martin's love for Mary. He rejects Pecksniff as a consummate fraud and hypocrite, beating him over the head with his walking stick. Hypocritical to the end, Pecksniff forgives him. After the denunciation of Pecksniff, young Bailey appears before the assembly, miraculously recovered from his wounds. (53) John Westlock proposes to Ruth Pinch; they plan to move to the country, where John can practice architecture and hire Tom to work with him. Tom will also live with them. At a celebratory dinner, the happy couples—John and Ruth, Martin and Mary, Mark and Mrs. Lupin—honor Tom Pinch, for whom the day has been one of unutterable joy.

(54) On the morning of Charity's wedding, old Martin tries unsuccessfully to elicit some sympathy from Charity for her widowed sister. As she waits for her wedding to begin, Charity learns that

Augustus Moddle has avoided the marriage at the last minute by running away to the South Seas.

COMMENTARY

In his 1844 Preface to *Chuzzlewit*, Dickens noted a change in his manner of composition. "I have endeavored in the progress of this Tale," he wrote, "to resist the temptation of the current Monthly Number, and to keep a studious eye upon the general purpose and design." Although he did not write down his plans for each part—a practice he would initiate with *Dombey*—he did consciously relate everything in his narrative to a central theme, which, in the preface to the CHEAP EDITION, he described as follows: "My main object in the story was, to exhibit in a variety of aspects the commonest of all the vices; to show how Selfishness propagates itself."

The extended title for the serial parts of the novel suggests that this thematic center was to be grounded in the story of old Martin Chuzzlewit and his extended family, whose lineage, in the opening chapter, is traced all the way back to Adam and Eve. But the narrative proper, which begins with the second chapter, seems to make Pecksniff the central character. JOHN FORSTER's account confirms this as Dickens's intent: "The notion of taking Pecksniff for a type of character was really the origin of the book," Forster wrote, "the design being to show, more or less by every person introduced, the number and variety of humours and vices that have their root in selfishness."

With Pecksniff as its central figure, *Chuzzlewit* becomes a kind of comedy of humors, in the manner of BEN JONSON. JOHN LUCAS (1970) identifies some of the humors, the obsessions that preoccupy various characters, as, for example, selfish greed (Anthony, Jonas), hypocrisy (Pecksniff), and expectations (young Martin, Slyme). Pecksniff, the exemplar of hypocrisy, may take in the innocent Tom Pinch for much of the novel, but he fools neither old Martin, the good-hearted "Volpone" of this Jonsonian comedy, nor the evil con men, Tigg and Jonas. The structure of the story also recalls humors comedy, beginning with the gathering of the selfish Chuzzlewits, going on to their dispersal into the world to exercise their various obsessions,

and ending with another gathering, where rewards and punishments are meted out and Pecksniff's villainy is finally exposed.

As Jonsonian comedy, the novel is concerned with the external aspects of the characters, with their dramatic presence. Pecksniff is an apt center in this drama, for he is wholly defined by external appearances. All that is inside him, the narrator suggests, are the trite moral sentiments that frequently drop from his lips:

> It has been remarked that Mr. Pecksniff was a moral man. So he was. Perhaps there never was a more moral man than Pecksniff: especially in his conversation and correspondence. It was once said of him by a homely admirer, that he had a Fortunatus's purse of good sentiments in his inside. In this particular he was like the girl in the fairy tale, except that if they were not actual diamonds which fell from his lips, they were the very brightest paste, and shone prodigiously. (2)

Pecksniff has no guilt about his hypocrisy, because he believes in his own fraud and does not admit his greed, his megalomania, or his lasciviousness. His story does not involve introspection and moral growth. It is rather a series of dramatic actions, each overreaching those that precede it, until his hypocritical scheming is finally exposed. His progress is marked by scenes of physical comedy: his wind-blown entrance into the novel, his drunken collapse into Mrs. Todgers's fireplace, his exit from the novel as old Martin Chuzzlewit beats him with a walking stick. Appropriately, Pecksniff is an architect whose most fully executed designs are the schemes he devises to make money; his greatest construction is his own public character. Pecksniff stands with such great dramatic hypocrites as Tartuffe and Malvolio; the humors comedy that presents his story is the central focus of what R. C. CHURCHILL (1982) has described as "not only Dickens' best comic novel but the greatest work of comic genius in the whole of English literature."

Chuzzlewit is more than a comedy of humors. Several other comedic strands are woven into the novel. The social satire that begins the novel by tracing the genealogy of the Chuzzlewit family back to Adam and Eve runs throughout, especially in the chapters exposing the self-serving greed and hypocrisy of the liberty-loving Americans that Martin encounters on his journey to Eden at the heart of the American darkness, the site of his loss of innocence. If young Martin is seen as the novel's central figure, it becomes a comic BILDUNGSROMAN describing the hero's growth from immature self-centeredness to an awareness of and concern for others. Tom Pinch, the novel's central figure for many Victorian readers, adds a strand of sentimental comedy to the tough moralism of the Jonsonian story. His unworldly innocence is rewarded with a place in the hearts of the other characters, but he is not worldly enough to win the hand of Mary Graham. Mrs. Gamp, probably the greatest comic character in the novel, transcends generic containment and exists as one of Dickens's great comic figures, along with Pickwick, Micawber, and Scrooge, in a realm of pure imagination. Much of the comedy involving this attendant at the rites of birth and death is "black comedy," drawing humor from her garrulously outrageous defenses of her negligent disregard for the lives of her patients. So complex is the mix of comedic strands in the novel that many critics have wondered whether *Chuzzlewit* is really less of an improvisation than the novels that preceded it and whether its stated thematic center can really bring together all of these disparate parts.

Just what Dickens meant by selfishness has prompted a good deal of discussion. Anthony and his son Jonas most fully represent the usual definition of the term. Business and the pursuit of wealth completely dominate their lives. They live in their place of business; the bedroom and dining furniture of their domestic life occupies corners in their warehouse. The "pursuit of wealth" has become for them "the one affair of life," and their philosophy is expressed in Jonas's perverse version of the golden rule, "Do other men, for they would do you" (11). Jonas never pretends to seek anything other than his own self-interest; he carries the principle to the rapacious extreme of patricide when his father does not die and leave him the family wealth soon enough to suit him.

Most of the other characters do more to disguise their selfishness. Tigg Montague's insurance scam pretends to be a legitimate business providing protection against the vicissitudes of fortune. His luxurious clothes and offices are part of a charade that promises the security of wealth to his clients, but he is more honest with the greedy Jonas, telling him, "Why should I disguise what you know so well, but what the crowd never dream of? We companies are all birds of prey: mere birds of prey" (27). The differences between Anthony Chuzzlewit and Son and The Anglo-Bengalee Disinterested Loan and Life Assurance Company seem to be only those of appearance and scale. Both ruthlessly pursue economic self-interest.

Selfishness, when applied to Martin Chuzzlewit or his grandfather, however, seems to have a very different meaning. Old Martin's refrain, "Oh self, self, self! at every turn nothing but self!" seems to extend beyond selfish greed to include self-obsession or self-centeredness. Young Martin's failing is not that he is rapaciously greedy. Although he hopes and expects to inherit his grandfather's money, he is not among the fawning and obsequious relatives, and his love for Mary Graham appears to lessen his chances of keeping the old man's favor. His fault, rather, is self-centeredness, an egotistical assumption that everything revolves around him. He takes Tom Pinch and Mark Tapley for granted. In his relationship with Mary Graham, he assumes that all sacrifice is his, and he fails to understand why she gives him the ring. His egotism and class arrogance lead him to think that others exist to serve him. These are failings of a very different sort from the capitalistic rapaciousness of Jonas and Tigg or the hypocrisy of Pecksniff.

Old Martin is similarly self-obsessed, feeding his paranoia with the belief that everyone is out to get his money. He is not a hypocrite; his unconcern for appearance is evident in his open relationship with Mary Graham, which others, even Mrs. Lupin, view scandalously. But the contract he has made with Mary, giving her no hopes of inheriting his money, is a sign of an egotistical paranoia that takes no one on trust. While young Martin is off in America, learning through sickness and suffering of his common humanity, old Martin is learning that there really are disinterested and selfless Tom Pinches in the world.

The notion of self that is at the center of the novel, then, ranges from the rapacious self-interest of Anthony and Jonas on one extreme to the selflessness of Tom Pinch and Mark Tapley on the other. In between are the two Martins, self-centered egotists who are transformed by their experiences, and the various hypocrites whose pretenses of charity, mercy, and respectability mask their self-interest. Pecksniff is their prophet.

This moral continuum shapes the overall structure of the novel, but it is occasionally forgotten in the details of the story. Inconsistencies in character and plot undermine the thematic focus. For example, there are, as Lucas (1970) points out, two accounts of Anthony Chuzzlewit's death. The first, which Jonas himself believes, makes Anthony the victim of Jonas's poison, an end gruesomely consistent with the unmitigated self-interest in their do-or-be-done-to philosophy. But Chuffey's later account claims that Anthony, aware of Jonas's scheme, escaped the poison and died of a broken heart. This revised version calls for the reader to accept a very different notion of Anthony's character from that presented earlier in the novel.

Several other characters make noteworthy changes in the course of the story, thematically reinforcing, perhaps, the central conversion of young Martin from egotism to altruism. Martin may be given enough interior development to make his transformation believable, but the changes in some of the others are harder to accept. Montague Tigg's transformation into Tigg Montague plays a wonderful counterpoint to Pecksniff's frauds. Appropriately, Pecksniff's final comeuppance is brought about by an even bigger fraud than himself, but it is hard to believe the vagabond of chapter 3 capable of such a compelling impersonation. Mercy Chuzzlewit's transformation from the frivolous and conniving schemer who outwits her sister to win Jonas into the sympathetic victim after her marriage asks the reader to shift uncomfortably from the vigorous morality of the Jonsonian comedy to the sympathetic identification of sentimental fiction.

Perhaps the most difficult transformation to accept is that of old Martin Chuzzlewit, for by the end of the story it is not clear whether he was changed by experience or whether from the beginning he was a pious fraud who schemed to test his grandson and manipulate others so that the story would turn out as he wished. Since both versions of his story are left unresolved in the end, one is tempted to think that Dickens, as he improvised the story, may have changed his own sense of Martin's role midway through the novel.

Forster indicates that the American sections of the novel also were not planned from the beginning. Dickens introduced the American journey as a way to lift sales, for the novel was not selling as well as either he or his publishers had expected. Although some readers find these American chapters extraneous, an unnecessary interpolated tale taking up nearly one-sixth of the novel, most have seen them as extending and exaggerating the thematic issues in the British sections of the book. In America Martin finds a whole society devoted to self-interest and egotism but preaching a mythology of liberty, equality, and opportunity. Martin's journey of discovery is like a fifth voyage of Gulliver to discover a land where liberty excuses slavery, equality idolizes the British aristocracy, and opportunity offers only a chance to die in a fetid swamp named New Eden. In *Chuzzlewit*'s America, as STEVEN MARCUS (1965) points out, "the private self [was converted] into public property and into something wholly externalized." Martin notes that every American he meets has a title and is "one of the most remarkable men" in the country. These Americans do not converse; they orate. Their speeches invariably boast about the superiority of the United States over anywhere else. They are all surfaces; their personalities can be read in their faces. In Dickens's Dantesque description, Zephaniah Scadder, the land salesman who sells Martin a piece of Eden, has his hypocrisy and double-dealing written into the features of his face:

> He was a gaunt man in a huge straw hat, and a coat of green stuff. The weather being hot, he had no cravat, and wore his shirt collar open; so that every time he spoke something was seen to twitch and jerk up in his throat, like the little hammers in a harpsichord when the notes are struck. Perhaps it was the Truth feebly endeavouring to leap to his lips. If so, it never reached them.

Two grey eyes lurked deep within this agent's head, but one of them had no sight in it, and stood stock still. With that side of his face he seemed to listen to what the other side was doing. Thus each profile had a distinct expression; and when the movable side was most in action, the rigid one was in its coldest state of watchfulness. It was like turning the man inside out, to pass that view of his features in his liveliest mood, and see how calculating and intent they were.

Each long black hair upon his head hung down as straight as any plummet line; but rumpled tufts were on the arches of his eyes, as if the crow whose foot was deeply printed in the corners had pecked and torn them in a savage recognition of his kindred nature as a bird of prey. (21)

Scadder is literally two-faced, just as the Eden on the architect's plan in his office maps a very different place from the swamp where Martin nearly dies.

Although rendered in satiric caricature, America is the site of Martin's conversion. He recovers from his illness to attend Mark through his and to realize how his preoccupation with himself has made him unaware and uncaring of others. Similar changes are taking place in other characters. Mark has met the extreme test of his good spirits, and he will recover ready to return to the comforts of the Blue Dragon. Back in England, Mercy has met her match in marrying Jonas, and his brutality has intimidated and subdued her. And young Bailey, elevated from Mrs. Todgers's houseboy to become Montague's footman and a savvy young man about town, is shocked by seeing Mercy's degradation. His near death and "resurrection" after the coach accident is a baroque parody of Martin's recovery story.

Over this black, life-and-death comedy, Mrs. Gamp presides like a ruling goddess. Her role in the plot is tangential: She is called in only to lay out Anthony's body and to nurse Lewsome and old Chuffey. As a nurse, midwife, and preparer of bodies for burial, she presides over both birth and death, but her care is more for herself than for her patients, and she is adept at obtaining a medicinal flask of gin or the clothes of the deceased persons she lays out. Her self-interest expresses her instinct for survival in the face of death, violence, and brutality. But most of all it is her language—wholly her own and at times incomprehensible—that identifies her. She repeatedly describes herself as "living in a wale," both the biblical "vale of tears" and also, perhaps, the belly of Jonah's whale. In what is probably her most famous speech, she explains to undertaker Mould her reasons for agreeing to work a double shift with two different patients: "I will not deny . . . that I am but a poor woman, and that the money is a object; but do not let that act upon you Mr. Mould. Rich folks may ride on camels, but it ain't so easy for 'em to see out of a needle's eye. That is my comfort, and I hope I knows it" (25). This idiosyncratic speech, characteristically larded with obscure and confused biblical allusions, makes no sense, but it nonetheless contributes to the theme of selfishness in its oblique comment on the difficulties of the rich in transcending this "wale" to enter the Kingdom of Heaven.

Mrs. Gamp confirms her idiosyncratic view of things by appealing to the authority of Mrs. Harris, an imaginary friend she can call up to support her anecdotes or to provide corroborating evidence for her argument. Thus she lives in a self-created world, peopled by characters from her own imagination. The climax of Mrs. Gamp's story comes when Betsey Prig, her nursing partner, announces, "I don't believe there's no sich a person [as Mrs. Harris]." Mrs. Gamp responds with a spirited defense of her fantasy friend:

"What!" said Mrs. Gamp, "you bage creetur, have I know'd Mrs. Harris five and thirty year, to be told at last that there ain't no sech a person livin'! Have I stood her friend in all her troubles, great and small, for it to come at the last to sech an end as this, which her own sweet picter hanging up afore you all the time, to shame your Bragian words! But well you mayn't believe there's no sech a creetur, for she wouldn't demean herself to look at you, and often has she said, when I have made mention of your name, which, to my sinful sorrow, I have done, 'What, Sairey Gamp! debage yourself to *her*!' Go along with you!" (49)

By the end of this defense, Mrs. Gamp's reasoning has come full circle, using Mrs. Harris herself to demolish Betsey Prig's skepticism. She has used the powers of imagination and language to survive the confusion and isolation of the city.

James Kincaid (1971) points out that old Martin's Jonsonian "punishment" of Mrs. Gamp—that she drink less, have more regard for her patients, and not depend on him as a witness to her character—does not restrain the comic energy that she has introduced into the novel. After Martin's admonitions, she goes off in search of some gin. Even Pecksniff rises up from old Martin's humiliation and beating to forgive the old man for his treatment of him. In the city the patriarchal authority needed to support these Jonsonian sanctions no longer holds sway. The seat of the new order is Todgers's.

Dorothy Van Ghent's (1950) classic essay describes the view of the city from the roof of Todgers's as one characterizing "the Dickens world." From the roof, London appears as a "wilderness," a world in which inanimate objects take on life and appear to have nervous energy like the city itself. The city is a "maze" or "labyrinth," and to find Todgers's at the heart of this maze, "you groped your way for an hour through lanes and bye-ways, and court-yards, and passages" (9). The maze of Mrs. Gamp's language also mirrors this city; her creation of Mrs. Harris provides a way to counter the isolation and loneliness of urban life. Mrs. Harris offers Mrs Gamp the illusion of community, just as Todgers's offers a fragile place of human refuge at the heart of the London labyrinth. Van Ghent asserts that "the Todgers' world requires an act of redemption," as does the world of *Chuzzlewit*—redemption from parricide, from Mercy's brutalization, from the frauds of Tigg and Pecksniff, from the dark obsession with money. The conversions and transformations that end the novel seek to redeem *Chuzzlewit*'s darkness, but they are not altogether satisfactory to counter the cruelty of urban life. Old Martin's domestic despotism may have just been part of a pious fraud and his softening a premeditated end to his story. Young Bailey's miraculous reappearance strains credulity. Though Mrs. Gamp desperately clings to her belief in Mrs. Harris, she too is troubled by Betsey Prig's realistic assessment of the truth.

CHARACTERS AND RELATED ENTRIES

Anglo-Bengalee Disinterested Loan and Life Assurance Company The fraudulent investment company promoted by Montague Tigg and David Crimple, with investment capital amounting to "two and as many noughts after it as the printer can get in the line" (27).

Austin Friars The street in the City where Mr. Fips, old Martin Chuzzlewit's solicitor, has his office (39).

"Bailey Junior" Houseboy at Todgers's, "a small boy with a large red head and no nose to speak of" (8). His protean energy is mirrored in the number of names the men at Todgers's have for him: "Benjamin was supposed to be the real name of this young retainer, but he was known by a great variety of names. Benjamin, for instance, had been converted into Uncle Ben, and that again had been corrupted into Uncle; which, by an easy transition, had again passed into Barnwell, in memory of the celebrated relative in that degree who was shot by his nephew George, while meditating in his garden at Camberwell. The gentlemen at Todgers's had a merry habit, too, of bestowing upon him, for the time being, the name of any notorious malefactor or minister; and sometimes when current events were flat, they even sought the pages of history for these distinctions; as Mr. Pitt, Young Brownrigg, and the like. At the period of which we write, he was generally known among the gentlemen as Bailey junior; a name bestowed upon him in contradistinction, perhaps, to Old Bailey" (9). A streetwise and resiliant cockney, he leaves Todgers's to become a groom for Tigg Montague (27), is left for dead in the coach accident (42), and is "resurrected" at the end to become a partner in Poll Sweedlepipe's bird business (52).

Bailey's cockney wit, his skill at pantomime, and his ability to create and re-create himself link him with the great self-creating comic figures in Dickens, including both major characters like Sam Weller (*Pickwick*), the Artful Dodger (*Oliver Twist*), and Dick Swiveller (*Curiosity Shop*) and more incidental figures like Trabb's Boy (*Expectations*). P. N. Furbank (Introduction to the Penguin Edition, 1968) sees Bailey as emblematic of the comedy in the novel, his transformation enabling him to overcome even so dark a threat as death.

Bald-Faced Stag, the A coaching inn where Tom Pinch stops on the road to London from Salisbury (36).

Bevan Kindly American physician whom Martin Chuzzlewit meets at Pawkins's Boarding House in New York: "a middle-aged man with a dark eye and a sunburnt face, who had attracted Martin's attention by having something very engaging and honest in the expression of his features" (16). Bevan is far less chauvinistic than his fellow countrymen, and he is embarrassed by their boastfulness. He sends Martin money to enable him to leave Eden and return to England.

Bib, Mr. Julius Washington Merryweather Boarder at the National Hotel, "a gentleman in the lumber line" who is present at the levee for Elijah Pogram that Martin Chuzzlewit attends in America (34).

The disjunction between his weighty Christian names and his ridiculous surname is characteristic of the names of the Americans Martin meets. It reinforces the satiric point of view that contrasts the exaggerations of the Americans with the reality of their situation. (*See* Philip V. Allingham, "The Names of Dickens's American Originals in *Martin Chuzzlewit*," *Dickens Quarterly*, 1990.)

Black Bull Inn The inn in Holborn where Sarah Gamp and Betsey Prig nurse Lewsome (25).

Blue Dragon, the The inn near Salisbury, owned by Mrs. Lupin, where old Martin Chuzzlewit stays when he is hounded by relatives. Mark Tapley plans to change the name to "The Jolly Tapley" after he marries Mrs. Lupin (3, 53).

Brick, Jefferson War correspondent of the New York *Rowdy Journal*, "a small young gentleman of very juvenile appearance, and unwholesomely pale in the face; partly, perhaps, from intense thought, but partly, there is no doubt, from the excessive use of tobacco," who is convinced that "the aristocratic

circles of England quailed before the name of Jefferson Brick" (16).

Brick, Mrs. Jefferson Brick's wife, "a sickly little girl . . . with tight round eyes" (16), cares for two young children and attends lectures on the Philosophy of the Soul and the Philosophy of Vegetables.

Buffum, Oscar Leader of the group at the National Hotel in America that holds the levee for Elijah Pogram (34).

Bull, the, Holborn Also known as the Bull and Gate and the Black Bull, this is the coaching inn at 121 HOLBORN where Mrs. Gamp tends Lewsome (25).

Bullamy Porter in the offices of the Anglo-Bengalee Assurance Company: "A wonderful creature in a vast red waistcoat and a short-tailed pepper-and-salt coat" (27), his dress is part of the luxurious facade that disguises the fraudulence of the company. After the collapse of the company, he and Crimple abscond with the remaining assets.

Chiggle "Immortal" American sculptor who, Martin is told, "made the celebrated Pogram statter in marble, which wrose so much con-test and preju-dice in Europe" (34).

Choke, General Cyrus General in an American militia, member of the Watertoast Association of United Sympathizers, and another "one of the most remarkable men in the country." He introduces Martin to Scadder, agent for the Eden Land Corporation (21).

Chollop, Major Hannibal American frontiersman in Eden, "esteemed for his devotion to rational liberty; for the better propagation whereof he usually carried a brace of revolving pistols in his coat pocket. . . . He always introduced himself to strangers as a worshipper of Freedom; was the consistent advocate of Lynch law, and slavery" (33).

Chuffey Anthony Chuzzlewit's devoted and senile clerk, "a little blear-eyed, weazen-faced, ancient man. . . . He was of a remote fashion, and dusty, like the rest of the furniture; he was dressed in a decayed suit of black; with breeches garnished at the knees with rusty wisps of ribbon, the very paupers of shoe-strings; on the lower portion of his spindle legs were dingy worsted stockings of the same colour. He looked as if he had been put away and forgotten half a century before, and somebody had just found him in a lumber-closet" (11). Although he is so old that he seems totally out of touch with reality, he brightens with a word from Anthony. After Anthony's death, he lives with Jonas and Mercy and transfers his loyalty to Mercy. To silence him, Jonas places him in the care of Mrs. Gamp (46), but after Jonas is exposed, Chuffey tells of the young man's abortive attempts to poison his father (51), thus revealing Jonas's intent but absolving him from the crime of parricide. Comparing Chuffey with Melville's Bartleby, STEVEN MARCUS (1965) notes that "in Chuffey, that distinctively modern possibility, the loss of self, of a sense of being somebody with a separate identity, is prefigured."

Chuzzlewit family Old family at the center of *Martin Chuzzlewit* that is "descended in a direct line from Adam and Eve" (1). Dickens satirically traces their lineage through British history, including the Chuzzlewit who arrived with William the Conqueror and Chuzzlewit Fawkes of the Gunpowder Plot. Their claim to aristocratic connections derives from Diggory, who "was in the habit of perpetually dining with Duke Humphrey" (i.e., going without food), and Toby, whose dying words identified his grandfather as "Lord No Zoo" (1). In the present generation the family is represented by the central figures in the plot, as well as by several members of an extended clan, all of whom are focused on old Martin Chuzzlewit's money. Among these lesser Chuzzlewit relatives are George, "a gay bachelor cousin . . . inclined to corpulency" (4); Mrs. Ned, widow of old Martin's brother, and her three daughters; MRS. SPOTTLETOE, a niece; CHEVY SLYME, a nephew; and an unnamed grandnephew, "very dark and very hairy."

Chuzzlewit, Anthony Old Martin's younger brother and father of Jonas, a miserly old business-

man who delights in sharp dealing: "the face of the old man so sharpened by the wariness and cunning of his life, that it seemed to cut him a passage through the crowded room" (4). He takes particular pride in the ruthlessness and cunning of Jonas, so that when he discovers that Jonas has been plotting to poison him to hasten his inheritance, he blames himself for Jonas's intended crime: "It began when I taught him to be too covetous of what I have to leave, and made the expectation of it his great business! . . . I have sown, and I must reap" (51). Although he dies a natural death, he leaves Jonas and others believing that his son has poisoned him.

Chuzzlewit, Jonas Anthony's son, who "had so well profited by the precept and example of the father, that he looked a year or two the elder of the twain" (4). In raising his son, Anthony has overreached himself: "The education of Mr. Jonas had been conducted from his cradle on the strictest principles of the main chance. The very first word he learnt to spell was 'gain,' and the second (when he got into two syllables), 'money.' But for two results, which were not clearly foreseen perhaps by his watchful parent in the beginning, his training may be said to have been unexceptionable. One of these flaws was, that having been long taught by his father to over-reach everybody, he had imperceptibly acquired a love of over-reaching that venerable monitor himself. The other, that from his early habits of considering everything as a question of property, he had gradually come to look, with impatience, on his parent as a certain amount of personal estate, which had no right whatever to be going at large, but ought to be secured in that particular description of iron safe which is commonly called a coffin, and banked in the grave" (8). There is a rough humor to Jonas's cunning one-upmanship in negotiating his marriage to Pecksniff's daughter, in which he extracts a larger dowry from the hypocrite and shocks Charity by choosing Mercy. But his cunning sours when he brutally abuses his wife, whom he has married only to take sadistic revenge. Jonas overreaches himself, however, in his dealings with Tigg Montague, who discovers Jonas's plot to poison his father and uses this knowledge to blackmail Jonas into investing in the insurance scam and then into helping Montague trap Pecksniff. Fearing exposure, Jonas tries unsuccessfully to escape to the Continent (50) and then murders Montague (47), only to be tormented by an even greater fear of exposure. After he is arrested, he poisons himself (51).

In his preface to the CHEAP EDITION of the novel (1849), Dickens defended his presentation of Jonas against charges that it was extreme or unnatural: "so born and so bred; admired for that which made him hateful, and justified from his cradle in cunning, treachery, and avarice; I claim him as the legitimate issue of the father upon whom those vices are seen to recoil. And I submit that their recoil upon that old man, in his unhonoured age, is not a mere piece of poetical justice, but is the extreme exposition of a plain truth." Although JOHN LUCAS (1970) finds Jonas's change from "blustering bully to panic-stricken coward" one of the novel's inconsistencies, other modern critics have been impressed by the gradual interiorization of Jonas's character and the development of the oedipal contest between father and son and share SYLVÉRE MONOD's (1985) view that Jonas is "one of Dickens's most interesting criminal figures." KATE FLINT (2001) analyzes the ways in which Dickens uses Jonas's room to present his repressed subconscious fear and anger, and STEVEN MARCUS (1965) and Monod (1985) analyze the dimensions of the oedipal conflict.

Chuzzlewit, Martin, Junior The eponymous hero of the novel, Martin senior's grandson: "He was young—one-and-twenty, perhaps—and handsome; with a keen dark eye, and a quickness of look and manner" (5). Turned out by his grandfather who raised him because of his love for Mary Graham, Martin signs on as an architectural student with Pecksniff, whom his grandfather detests. At old Martin's request, Pecksniff dismisses Martin, and the young man decides to seek his fortune in America. There he purchases land in New Eden, which turns out to be a swamp; contracts a fever and nearly dies; and, through these experiences and the example of Mark Tapley's selflessness, comes to realize just how selfish and self-absorbed he has been. Before his conversion, he took his role

as his grandfather's heir for granted; condescended to those beneath him, like Tom Pinch; and failed to appreciate the sacrifices of others, like Mary and Tom, for him. After returning from America, he earns his grandfather's respect and his inheritance by appreciating those he formerly took for granted and by assuming the responsibilities of his station. He marries Mary Graham.

Although Martin Chuzzlewit has a position in this novel similar to those of Nicholas Nickleby or David Copperfield in theirs, he is not so interesting or sympathetic a "hero" as either of them. His self-absorption works against the heroic impulsiveness that makes Nicholas sympathetic, and he lacks the lively awareness of others and of his surroundings that gives David's life substance. There is little to engage the reader's interest in him as the central figure of the novel, and the predictability of his story decenters the reader's attention to the darker aspects of the novel.

Chuzzlewit, Martin, Senior Young Martin Chuzzlewit's grandfather and the patriarch of the Chuzzlewit clan, "a strong and vigorous old man with a will of iron and a voice of brass" (4), who obstinately believes that everyone is out to secure his money. He trusts no one. He has secretly sworn his young companion, Mary Graham, to the agreement that she will expect nothing from him in his will. Even the grandson that he has groomed to become his heir earns his distrust when he disobeys his grandfather and falls in love with Mary. He prompts the toadying Pecksniff to dismiss Martin as his student (12), and by moving in with Pecksniff he encourages the hypocrite's expectations (30). However, he attempts to make Mercy aware of her mistake in agreeing to marry Jonas (24), and he anonymously provides Tom Pinch with a job in London (39–40). When young Martin returns from America a changed man, his grandfather also seems to be changed, realizing how his suspicions and his need for control soured his relations with others. He is reconciled with young Martin and blesses the young man's marriage to Mary Graham (52), but he remains a stern judge of Pecksniff's hypocrisy. He exposes the architect to the rest of the family and beats him with his cane (52).

Although JAMES KINCAID's (1971) judgment that old Martin is "the most unsatisfactory character in all of Dickens" may overstate the case, there is a vagueness about his role and his motivation that leaves the reader dissatisfied. At the heart of his presentation is the unresolved mystery over whether he is changed by his experiences during the novel or whether he is a pious fraud who manipulated others for their own good. The reader is forced to wonder about his paranoia (Does he sense Pecksniff's hypocrisy from the start?), his relationship to Mary Graham (Has he chosen her for young Martin's wife?), and his involvement in Martin's reformation in America (Did he set up the trip? Provide the ring? Prompt Mark to seek out Martin?). At the end, he takes on a godlike role, meting out rewards and punishments, that suggests he was in control all along, but the mechanical worldview implied by this role seems to be at odds with the vital energy of such characters as Young Bailey, Sarah Gamp, and even Pecksniff.

Cicero   Former slave whom Mark Tapley meets in New York who bears the physical scars from his mistreatment as a slave. When he got too old to work, his master allowed him to buy his freedom (17).

Codger, Miss   One of the two "transcendental" literary ladies presented to Elijah Pogram. "Sticking to [her] forehead, . . . by invisible means, was a massive cameo, in size and shape like the raspberry tart which is ordinarily sold for a penny, representing on its front the Capitol at Washington" (34).

Crimple, David   A pawnbroker, then known as Crimp (13), who becomes Tigg Montague's cohort in the Anglo-Bengalee insurance scam (27). After Montague's murder, he and Bullamy leave the country with the remaining funds (51).

Diver, Colonel   Editor of the New York *Rowdy Journal*, "a sallow gentleman, with sunken cheeks, black hair, small twinkling eyes, and a singular expression hovering abut that region of his face, which was not a frown, nor a leer, and yet might have been mistaken at the first glance for either. Indeed it would have been difficult, on a much closer acquaintance, to describe it in any more satisfactory terms than as a mixed expression of vulgar cunning and conceit" (16). He meets the *Screw* at the dock and introduces Martin to Pawkins's Boarding House.

Dunkle, Dr. Ginery   Spokesman for the deputation at the National Hotel that waits on Elijah Pogram, "a shrill boy . . . of great poetical elements" (34).

Eden   The town on the Mississippi River where the Eden Land Corporation is selling lots. Martin Chuzzlewit buys land here sight unseen from General Choke and Mr. Kettle, only to discover that the place is a swamp "choked with slime and matted growth" (23). Martin's dream of setting up an architectural firm in Eden ends when he contracts fever and nearly dies (33). Dickens based Eden on a settlement in Cairo, Illinois, that he saw on his American trip in 1842.

Esau Slodge, The   The riverboat that takes Martin Chuzzlewit's appeal for help from Eden to Mr. Bevan in New York (33).

Fips, Mr.   Old-fashioned lawyer of Austin Friars, "a small and spare" man who "looked peaceable, and wore black shorts and powder" (39). He is retained anonymously by old Martin Chuzzlewit to employ Tom Pinch to catalog a library for an annual salary of £100.

Fladdock, General   American militia officer who has just returned from Europe on the *Screw*. He is introduced to Martin Chuzzlewit by the Norrises. After he condemns the pride and "the artificial barriers set up between man and man" in Europe, he is outraged to be considered a "fellow" passenger with Martin when he learns that Martin was traveling in steerage (17).

Fountain Court   One of the courtyards in The Temple where Ruth Pinch and John Westlock rendezvous (45, 53).

Gamp, Mrs. Sarah (Sairey)   Nurse and midwife who attends Anthony Chuzzlewit, Lewsome, and old Chuffey: "She was a fat old woman . . . with a husky voice and a moist eye, which she had a remarkable power of turning up, and only showing the white of it. Having very little neck, it cost her some trouble to look over herself, if one may say so, at those to whom she talked. She wore a very rusty black gown, rather the worse for snuff, and a shawl and bonnet to correspond. . . . The face of Mrs. Gamp—the nose in particular—was somewhat red and swollen, and it was difficult to enjoy her society without becoming conscious of a smell of spirits. Like most persons who have attained to great eminence in their profession, she took to hers very kindly; insomuch that, setting aside her natural predilections as a woman, she went to a lying-in or a laying-out with equal zest and relish" (19). She carries a patched and faded umbrella. Above all, Sarah Gamp is a triumph of language. Her garrulous, vaguely cockney speech is peppered with malapropisms, mispronunciations, exaggerations, mixed metaphors, confused allusions, and endless anecdotes and aphorisms. Her profusion and confusion of language, described by ANGUS WILSON in *The World of Charles Dickens* (1970) as "the greatest triumph in literature of verbal collage," both illuminates and obscures the "wale of tears" in which she lives. In one of her justly famous aphorisms, she opines, for example, "Rich folks may ride on camels, but it ain't so easy for'em to see out of a needle's eye" (25). Her humor is often darkened by her associations with the rites of both birth and death, as when she looks at one of her patients and remarks, "he'd make a lovely corpse" (25). She supports her observations by appealing to Mrs. Harris, who supplies gossip and anecdote and attests to the truth of Mrs. Gamp's often outrageous claims. In a great comic scene, she defends Mrs. Harris against Betsey Prig's presumptuous assertion that "There's no sich a person!" (49). She prepares the body of Anthony Chuzzlewit for burial (19), tends Chuffey while Jonas is in the country (25, 26), and, splitting her duties with Betsy Prig, cares for Lewsome at the Bull Inn (29). She aids Westlock in securing Chuffey's testimony at the final exposure of Jonas (51).

One of Dickens's most celebrated comic characters, Mrs. Gamp has been described by STEVEN

Mrs. Gamp shares a toast with Betsey Prig.

MARCUS (1965) as "a kind of pagan, cockney goddess" and compared with Joyce's Molly Bloom. As a priestess at the rites of birth and death, she is an elemental presence in the novel, articulating an archetypal humor that informs the comedy in the midst of cruelty, murder, and death. SYLVÉRE MONOD (1985) offers an insightful analysis of her role in the novel, especially her language, which is also discussed in some detail by JOHN BOWEN (2000). Marcus is especially insightful on her archetypal role, describing her as "that rare phenomenon, the character as creative artist, an imaginary person endowed with the same kind of vitality that imagined her, impelled to invent her own imaginary person in order to define and celebrate herself and the world she lives in."

Gander, Mr. Gentleman "of a witty turn" who boards at Todgers's (9).

Gill, Mrs. A client of Sarah Gamp. Mrs. Gill is noteworthy for her ability to "name the very day and hour" when she will give birth. She had predicted the time for the births of all of her six children, and her husband, according to Mrs. Gamp, "would back his wife agen Moore's Almanack, to name the very day and hour, for ninepence farden" (29).

Graham, Mary   The heroine of the novel, "very young; apparently no more than seventeen; timid and shrinking in her manner, and yet with a greater share of self-possession and control over her emotions than usually belongs to a far more advanced period of female life. . . . She was short in stature; and her figure was slight, as became her years; but all the charms of youth and maidenhood set it off, and clustered on her gentle brow" (3). She accompanies old Martin Chuzzlewit, raising suspicions about their relationship and about her designs on the old man's money. She has, however, agreed to be his companion on the understanding that she will inherit nothing. She falls in love with young Martin, gives him a diamond ring as he leaves for America, and remains loyal to him during his absence. Meanwhile, Pecksniff presses his opportunistic attentions on her and Tom Pinch adores her from afar. When Martin returns, Pecksniff is exposed, and Mary and young Martin marry.

Groper, Colonel   A member of the group that welcomes Mr. Elijah Pogram (34).

Half Moon and Seven Stars, the   An obscure alehouse in Pecksniff's village where Anthony, Jonas, Tigg, and Slyme stay (4).

Hominy, Mrs. Major   Pretentious and conceited American "philosopher and authoress" who is a fellow traveler with Martin on the way to New Eden: "She was very straight, very tall, and not at all flexible in face or figure. On her head she wore a great straw-bonnet, with trimmings of the same, in which she looked as if she had been thatched by an unskilful labourer" (22). "A writer of reviews and analytical disquisitions," who signs her letters from abroad "The Mother of the Modern Gracchi" (22), she makes heavy use of capitals and italics and looks on "foreign countries with the eye of a perfect republican hot from the model oven" (22).

Izzard   One of the welcoming committee for Elijah Pogram (34).

Jane   Pecksniff's maidservant (31).

Jinkins   The oldest boarder at Todgers's "of a fashionable turn, . . . a fish-salesman's book-keeper, aged forty" (9).

Jobling, Dr. John   Physician who attends the dying Anthony Chuzzlewit and Lewsome, Mrs. Gamp's patient at the Bull Inn. He later acts as the medical officer for the Anglo-Bengalee Disinterested Loan and Life Assurance Company. "He had a portentously sagacious chin, and a pompous voice. . . . His neckerchief and shirt-frill were ever of the whitest, his clothes of the blackest and sleekest, his gold watch-chain of the heaviest, and his seals of the largest. His boots, which were always of the brightest, creaked as he walked. . . . Exactly the sort of person whom the Anglo-Bengalee Company wanted for a medical officer. But Jobling was far too knowing to connect himself with the company in any closer ties than as a paid (and well-paid) functionary, or to allow his connexion to be misunderstood abroad" (27).

Jodd   Member of the welcoming committee for Elijah Pogram (34).

Kedgick, Captain   Proprietor of the National Hotel, where Martin Chuzzlewit stays on his way to and from Eden. Kedgick insists that Martin, as "a public man," must hold a levee at the hotel (22), but he berates Martin when he returns from Eden for misleading the expectations of "our people" (34).

Kettle, La Fayette   Secretary of the Watertoast Association of United Sympathisers whom Martin meets on the train on his way to Eden. He is languid, listless, and suspicious. "He had bright dark eyes, which he kept half closed; only peeping out of the corners, and even then with a glance that seemed to say, 'Now you won't overreach me: you want to, but you won't'" (21, 22).

Kingsgate Street   Street in Holborn where Mrs. Gamp lives "at a bird-fancier's next door but one to the celebrated mutton-pie shop, and directly opposite to the original cat's-meat warehouse" (19).

Lewsome Physician's assistant and former schoolmate of John Westlock, who hires Mrs. Gamp to attend Lewsome during a serious illness. She is intrigued by his delirious mutterings. After his recovery he confesses to Westlock that, in exchange for forgiving a gambling debt, he supplied Jonas Chuzzlewit with poison, which he believes Jonas used to murder his father (48).

Lummy Ned Guard on the Salisbury coach whose emigration to the United States prompts Martin to consider taking the same course (13).

Lupin, Mrs. Landlady of the Blue Dragon Inn, "just what a landlady should be: broad, buxom, comfortable, and good-looking, with a face of clear red and white, which by its jovial aspect, at once bore testimony to her hearty participation in the good things of the larder and cellar, and to their thriving and healthful influences. She was a widow, but years ago had passed through her state of weeds, and burst into flower again. . . . She had still a bright black eye, and jet black hair; was comely, dimpled, plump, and tight as a gooseberry" (3). Her admiration for Pecksniff is destroyed when he dismisses Tom Pinch (31). She welcomes Martin and Mark back from AMERICA (43); she marries Mark, and they rename the Blue Dragon the Jolly Tapley (53).

Moddle, Augustus Shy and melancholy "youngest gentleman" at Todgers's, who wallows in his "lonely, melancholy state" and seems always on the verge of tears, "more like a Pump than a man," observes Mrs. Todgers (32). He falls in love with Mercy Pecksniff and is devastated when she marries Jonas. Charity Pecksniff overcomes his scruples, but he agrees to marry her as a man with "a blighted heart" who will always love "Another" (32). On the day of the ceremony, however, he runs away to Van Dieman's Land, leaving a melancholy letter for the "Ever-injured Miss Pecksniff" (54).

Montague, Tigg Name adopted by Montague Tigg when he becomes director of the Anglo-Bengalee Disinterested Loan and Life Assurance Company (27).

Mould Undertaker who buries Anthony Chuzzlewit and recommends Mrs. Gamp for the laying-out of the body (19); "a little elderly gentleman, bald, and in a suit of black, . . . [with] a face in which a queer attempt at melancholy was at odds with a smirk of satisfaction" (19).

Mould, Mrs. Mould's wife, whose plump and contented presence seems at odds with her husband's melancholy profession.

Mould, the Misses Mould's two daughters: "So round and chubby were their fair proportions, that they might have been bodies once belonging to the angels' faces in the shop below, grown up, with other heads attached to make them mortal" (25).

Mourning Coach-Horse Inn House of call for undertakers in the City where Nadgett pursues his investigation into the death of Anthony Chuzzlewit (38).

Mullit, Professor American professor of education whom Martin meets at Pawkins's Boarding House. Brick tells Martin that "He felt it necessary at the last election for President, to repudiate and denounce his father, who voted on the wrong interest. He has since written some powerful pamphlets, under the signature of 'Suturb', or Brutus reversed" (16).

Nadgett, Mr. Private investigator employed by Montague to check out policyholders in the Anglo-Bengalee Assurance Company. "He was the man at a pound a week who made the inquiries—he was born to be secret. He was a short, dried-up, withered old man, who seemed to have secreted his very blood. How he lived was a secret, where he lived was a secret" (27). He uncovers Jonas's attempt to poison his father (38) and proves Jonas's guilt in the murder of Tigg (51). He is also Tom Pinch's landlord in ISLINGTON.

A precursor to Bucket in *Bleak House*, Nadgett is probably the first detective in English fiction. His secrecy and involvement in Tigg's insurance scam seem to ally him with the villains of the novel when he first appears, but he later becomes an agent of justice in exposing Jonas.

Norris Family   Mr. Bevan's New York relatives, a family of six—the parents, two daughters, a college student son, and a grandmother—who match Pecksniff for hypocrisy. Although they boast of living in a land of "brotherly love and natural equality," they are obsessed with the British aristocracy and French fashion. They profess to be abolitionists, but they consider Negroes "such a funny people, so excessively ludicrous in their manners and appearance, that it was wholly impossible for those who knew them well, to associate any serious ideas with such an absurd part of the creation" (17). When they learn that Martin has crossed the ocean in steerage, they are "disgraced" that he has entered their home.

Pawkins, Major   Mrs. Pawkins's husband, "distinguished by a very large skull, and a great mass of yellow forehead; in deference to which commodities it was currently held in bar-rooms and other such places of resort that the major was a man of huge sagacity." He is a "politician," "patriot," and "bold speculator": "In plainer words he had a most distinguished genius for swindling, and could start a bank, or negotiate a loan, or form a land-jobbing company (entailing ruin, pestilence, and death, on hundreds of families), with any gifted creature in the Union" (16).

Pawkins, Mrs.   Proprietor of the boardinghouse where Martin stays in New York: She is "very straight, bony, and silent" (16).

Pecksniff, Charity (Cherry)   The elder of Pecksniff's two daughters. Although her public persona is one of "fine strong sense and . . . mild, yet not reproachful gravity" (2), beneath her surface mildness is a shrewish and vindictive disposition: "the tip of that feature in the sweet girl's countenance [her nose] was always very red at breakfast time. For the most part, indeed, it wore, at that season of the day, a scraped and frosty look, as if it had been rasped, while a similar phenomenon developed itself in her humour, which was then observed to be of a sharp and acid quality, as though an extra lemon (figuratively speaking) had been squeezed into the nectar of her disposition, and had rather damaged the flavour" (6). Cherry is twice disappointed: when Jonas proposes to Merry rather than

to her (20) and when she is jilted by Augustus Moddle (54). She is left to bitter spinsterhood, tending to the needs of her father.

Charity combines two stereotypical roles: as a hypocritical repetition of her father presenting a public face that hides her shrewish disposition, and as the old maid embittered by loneliness and rejection. Unchanged by her experiences, she maintains these stereotypical roles to the end and is punished by Moddle's rejection and by her banishment with her father in the final chapter.

Pecksniff, Mercy (Merry)   Pecksniff's younger daughter: "She was all girlishness, and playfulness, and wildness, and kittenish buoyancy. She was the most arch and at the same time the most artless creature, was the youngest Miss Pecksniff, that you can possibly imagine. It was her great charm. She was too fresh and guileless, and too full of child-like vivacity, was the youngest Miss Pecksniff, to wear combs in her hair, or to turn it up, or to frizzle it,

Mercy Pecksniff (Julia Sawalha) and her father Seth Pecksniff (Tom Wilkinson), from the movie adaptation of *Martin Chuzzlewit. Courtesy of PhotoFest.*

or braid it. . . . Moderately buxom was her shape, and quite womanly too; but sometimes—yes, sometimes—she wore a pinafore; and how charming *that* was! Oh! She was indeed 'a gushing thing'" (2). As frivolous as her sister is serious, Mercy marries Jonas Chuzzlewit to triumph over her sister and to best Jonas in marital quarrels (24), but he physically and psychologically abuses her, arousing the sympathy of Mrs. Todgers, who gives her refuge after Jonas's death. She is reformed by her experience and accepts the care and protection of old Martin Chuzzlewit (54). Unlike her sister, who is her contrasting DOUBLE, Mercy is transformed by her harsh marriage; by the end she has abandoned her coquettish ways and her role as a frivolous young thing.

Pecksniff, Seth Architect and surveyor, the very model of the hypocrite, who lives with his two daughters in Wiltshire near Salisbury. He is old Martin Chuzzlewit's cousin. "Perhaps there never was a more moral man than Mr. Pecksniff: especially in his conversation and correspondence. It was once said of him by a homely admirer, that he had a Fortunatus's purse of good sentiments in his inside. In this particular he was like the girl in the fairy tale, except that if they were not actual diamonds which fell from his lips, they were the very brightest paste, and shone prodigiously. He was a most exemplary man: fuller of virtuous precept than a copybook. . . . His very throat was moral. You saw a good deal of it. You looked over a very low fence of white cravat . . . and there it lay, a valley between two jutting heights of collar, serene and whiskerless before you. It seemed to say, on the part of Mr. Pecksniff, 'There is no deception, ladies and gentlemen, all is peace, a holy calm pervades me'" (2). Pecksniff supports his limited architectural practice by taking on students whose talents and ideas he exploits for his own gain. Expecting to promote his scheme of obtaining old Martin Chuzzlewit's money, he accepts young Martin as a student and then, when the old man demands it, repudiates and dismisses him (12). He arranges the marriage of his vain and frivolous daughter Mercy to Jonas Chuzzlewit, who brutally abuses her. He takes old Martin into his house and schemes to marry the old man's companion, Mary Graham,

Fred Barnard's iconographic representation of Pecksniff for the Household Edition of *Martin Chuzzlewit* (1872).

in hopes of gaining Chuzzlewit's money. Only then does his assistant and former student, Tom Pinch, his most loyal admirer, discover his hypocrisy (31). After Jonas convinces Pecksniff to invest in the Anglo-Bengalee Assurance scam, he loses his money and is exposed and denounced by old Martin, who beats him with his cane (52). Pecksniff leaves the gathering, forgiving the old man, to become a begging letter writer.

Pecksniff has often been compared to Moliere's Tartuffe as a great literary portrait of hypocrisy. Tartuffe uses religion to camouflage his villainy, but Pecksniff—even though he speaks in a language Norrie Epstein in *The Friendly Dickens* (1998) describes as "Bible-ese"—relies simply on his performance as a moral and upright man. His pieties and pretenses are those of the British bourgeoisie; JOHN FORSTER (1872) describes Pecksniff's vices as quintessentially English and as a sufficient counterweight to the exposure of duplicity in the American sections of the novel. STEVEN MARCUS (1965) describes Pecksniff as "a totalitarian of the moral life; it is not excessive to say that he sees morality in a grain of sand—not to speak of anything so gross as eggs: 'eggs . . . even they have their moral. See how they come and go! Every pleasure is transitory. We can't even eat, long. If we indulge in harmless fluids, we get the dropsy; if in exciting liquids, we get drunk. What a soothing reflection is that.'"

In the Jonsonian conclusion to the plot, Pecksniff is beaten by old Martin and deflated, even physically reduced, in his exposure and humiliation: "Not only did his figure appear to have shrunk, but his discomfiture seemed to have extended itself even to his dress. His clothes seemed to have grown shabbier, his linen to have turned yellow, his hair to have become lank and frowsy; his very boots looked villainous and dim, as if their gloss had departed with his own" (52). JAMES KINCAID (1971) points out, however, that there is a counter to this Jonsonian conclusion in a "comedy of accommodation," which celebrates the life-affirming survival instincts of such characters as Young Bailey and Sarah Gamp: "Though old Martin, in one of the few truly bungled scenes in Dickens, actually clubs Pecksniff, the real verdict on him is quietly suggested by a person much closer to the moral norm, Mrs. Lupin, who remains loyal to this 'noble-spoken gentleman' (XLIII). In responding to Pecksniff's mastery of speech, Mrs. Lupin is, in fact, displaying the true sensitivity; for in this novel Mr. Pecksniff's hypocrisy is ultimately judged to be almost trifling; his style is his salvation." Pecksniff rises from the floor and, consummate in his hypocrisy to the end, adjusts to his new situation and forgives old Martin for his mistreatment of him.

Although the original of Pecksniff is usually identified as journalist and editor Samuel Carter Hall (1800–89), Nancy Aycock Metz ("Dickens, *Punch*, and Pecksniff," *Dickens Quarterly*, 1993) has suggested that Sir Robert Peel (1788–1850), Tory prime minister when *Chuzzlewit* appeared, was the model for Pecksniff.

Pinch, Ruth Tom Pinch's sister: "she had a good face; a very mild and prepossessing face; and a pretty little figure—slight and short, but remarkable for its neatness. There was something of her brother, much of him indeed, in a certain gentleness of manner, and in her look of timid trustfulness" (9). She is employed in a demeaning position as a governess in the household of a condescending copper founder in CAMBERWELL (36). When Tom comes to London after being cast out by Pecksniff, he rescues Ruth from her humiliating employment, and the two set up housekeeping together, supported by Tom's employment as a librarian (39). Tom introduces Ruth to his friend and former fellow pupil John Westlock, and the two eventually marry (53).

Ruth's innocence and domesticity make her one of the many doll-like "little women" who appear in Dickens's novels. Most modern readers find them cloyingly sentimental versions of the Victorian ideal of the "angel in the house." In Dickens's case they also owe something to his idealized memory of MARY HOGARTH.

Pinch, Tom Pecksniff's former pupil and general assistant and the organist at the parish church: "An ungainly, awkward-looking man, extremely short-sighted, and prematurely bald, . . . he was far from handsome certainly; and was drest in a snuff-coloured suit, of an uncouth make at the best, which being shrunk with long wear, was twisted and tortured into all kinds of odd shapes; but notwithstanding his attire, and his clumsy figure, which a great stoop in his shoulders, and a ludicrous habit he had of thrusting his head forward, by no means redeemed, one would not have been disposed (unless Mr. Pecksniff said so) to consider him a bad fellow by any means. He was perhaps about thirty, but he might have been almost any age between sixteen and sixty" (2). Gentle and unselfish, he is a loyal friend to young Martin, who treats him condescendingly, and a devoted admirer of Pecksniff, blind to all his master's faults. When Tom discovers Pecksniff's scheme to seduce Mary Graham, with whom Tom is secretly in love, he is disillusioned and Pecksniff dismisses him (31). Tom goes to London and there rescues his sister and catalogs a library in a job anonymously provided by old Martin. After Ruth marries John Westlock, Tom lives with them and remains devoted to his friends—Ruth and John, young Martin and Mary Graham and their children—and to playing the organ (54).

Although Tom is untouched by the hypocrisy, greed, and selfishness that afflict most of the characters and was seen by many Victorian readers as the "true hero" of the novel, his simple innocence makes him something of a fool in the eyes of many modern readers. How can he remain so blind for so long to Pecksniff's chicanery? Like Mark Tapley, Tom is a foil to Martin, his concern for others contrasting with Martin's self-absorption. Martin's insensitivity is revealed when Tom gives him a half sovereign as he leaves for London and Martin concludes, "what a winning fellow he [Martin] must be to have made such an impression on Tom" (13), and also when Martin asks Tom to protect Mary Graham while he is in America. In America, Martin loses his innocence by discovering that the New Eden is a false paradise; at the same time, Tom loses his innocence as he sees Pecksniff attempt to seduce Mary Graham. Although his story has strong parallels to Martin's, Tom is not rewarded with the hand of the heroine in the end. That goes to his DOUBLE, Martin.

Pip   Theatrical man invited to Tigg Montague's dinner for Jonas Chuzzlewit (28).

Piper, Professor   Member of the committee that interviews Elijah Pogram at the National Hotel (34).

Pogram, the Hon. Elijah   Member of Congress whom Martin meets on the steamboat he takes when leaving Eden: "A faint gentleman sitting on a low camp stool, with his legs on a high barrel of flour, as if he were looking at the prospect with his ankles. . . . He was about five and thirty; was crushed and jammed up in a heap, under the shade of a large green cotton umbrella; and ruminated over his tobacco-plug like a cow." Pogram is renowned as "one of the master minds of our country" for his "Defiance" which "defied the world in general to com-pete with our country upon any hook; and devellop'd our internal resources for making war upon the universal airth" (34).

Prig, Betsey   Professional nurse who is Mrs. Gamp's friend and associate: She "was of the Gamp build, but not so fat; and her voice was deeper and more like a man's. She had also a beard" (25). She divides the duties of caring for Lewsome with Mrs. Gamp and would have been part of a similar arrangement with Chuffey had she not challenged

the existence of Mrs. Harris, asserting, "I don't believe there's no sich person" (51). Mrs. Gamp casts her off forever for this act of disbelief.

Salisbury   Wiltshire cathedral town near the village where Pecksniff lives. Tom Pinch, who considers Salisbury "a very desperate sort of place; an exceeding wild and dissipated city" (5), meets Martin Chuzzlewit there. He and Martin go to dinner at the best restaurant in town as the guests of John Westlock (12).

Scadder, Zephaniah   Duplicitous agent for the Eden Valley Land Company who sells Martin worthless property in the development. The two sides of his face present totally different profiles: "Two grey eyes lurked deep within this agent's head, but one of them had no sight in it, and stood stock still. With that side of his face he seemed

General Choke Zephaniah Scadder from the American scenes in *Chuzzlewit* as seen by American illustrator Eytinge.

to listen to what the other side was doing. Thus each profile had a distinct expression; and when the movable side was most in action, the rigid one was in its coldest state of watchfulness" (21).

Screw, The   Steamship on which Martin Chuzzlewit and Mark Tapley travel—in steerage—to America (15).

Simmons, William   Van driver who gives Martin a lift from Salisbury to Houndslow after he is dismissed by Pecksniff (13).

Slyme, Chevy   Indolent and sullen nephew of old Martin Chuzzlewit who hangs out with Montague Tigg. Although Tigg describes him as "the most thoroughly Shakespearian, if not Miltonic, and at the same time the most disgustingly-unappreciated dog I know," when he first appears "his sharp features being much pinched and nipped by long waiting in the cold, and his straggling red whiskers and frowsy hair being more than usually dishevelled from the same cause, he certainly looked rather unwholesome and uncomfortable than Shakespearian or Miltonic" (4). He and Tigg are small-time scam artists and panhandlers who try to use Slyme's Chuzzlewit connections to secure small sums of money. Slyme turns up at the end of the novel, somewhat improbably, as the police officer who arrests Jonas. Jonas gives Slyme £100 to allow him time to take poison, but Slyme returns the money (51).

Smif, Putnam ("America Junior")   Clerk in an American dry goods store who writes to Martin asking his help in finding someone in England who will pay his passage there and his living expenses so that he can pursue his fame (22).

Sophia   Ruth Pinch's disrespectful pupil, the daughter of a copper founder (9, 36).

Spottletoe, Mr.   One of the Chuzzlewit clan "who was so bald and had such big whiskers, that he seemed to have stopped his hair, by the sudden application of some powerful remedy, in the very act of falling off his head, and to have fastened it irrevocably on his face" (4). He is among the relatives who follow old Martin into the country

with designs on his money (4). He and his wife are also present for Charity Pecksniff's abortive wedding (54).

Spottletoe, Mrs.   Old Martin Chuzzlewit's niece, "much too slim for her years, and of a poetical constitution" (4).

Sweedlepipe, Paul ("Poll")   Barber and bird fancier who is Mrs. Gamp's landlord; "a little elderly man, with a clammy cold right hand, from which even rabbits and birds could not remove the smell of shaving soap. Poll had something of the bird in his nature" (26). With a "small treble voice" and a "tender heart," Poll is a gentle friend to Young Bailey and is devastated by the boy's apparent death. After Bailey's surprising reappearance, the two go into partnership (52).

Tacker   Assistant to Mould the undertaker, "an obese person, with his waistcoat in closer connection with his legs than is quite reconcilable with established ideas of grace. . . . He had been a tender plant once upon a time, but, from constant blowing in the fat air of funerals, had run to seed" (19).

Tamaroo   Bailey Junior's successor as Mrs. Todgers's servant: "She was a very little old woman, and aways wore a very coarse apron with a bib before and a loop behind, together with bandages on her wrists, which appeared to be afflicted with an everlasting sprain. She was on all occasions chary of opening the street-door, and ardent to shut it again; and she waited at table in a bonnet" (32).

Tapley, Mark ("Co.")   Ostler at the Blue Dragon; he "walked with a light quick step, and sang as he went. . . . He was a young fellow, of some five or six-and-twenty perhaps, and was dressed in such a free and fly-away fashion, that the long ends of his loose red neckcloth were streaming out behind him quite as often as before; and the bunch of bright winter berries in the buttonhole of his velveteen coat was . . . visible" (5). His self-defined mission in life is to remain "jolly" in the most trying circumstances: "I don't believe there ever was a man as could come out so strong under circumstances that would make other men miserable, as I could, if I could only get a chance" (5). Even though he is expected to marry Mrs. Lupin and settle in Wiltshire, he leaves the Dragon because he is too comfortable and there is no challenge to his optimism (5). Later he comes to Martin in London and volunteers to serve him in AMERICA (13), expecting that Martin's selfishness and the duplicity of the Americans will severely test his optimism. His selfless concern for others—for the family on the ship, for Martin in his illness—keeps him jolly, and his own illness and Martin's conversion enable him to return to England in changed circumstances. He blames Martin for "deceiving" him by overcoming his selfishness, and he "abandons [himself] to despair" by marrying Mrs. Lupin, "a dear, sweet creetur, as is wery fond of me" (46). They rename the Blue Dragon the Jolly Tapley.

Mark acts as a foil to Martin, his concern for others countering Martin's tendency to self-pity and despair. Although his search for "credit" is sometimes thought to be overdone, most readers would agree with SYLVÉRE MONOD (1985): "On the whole Mark Tapley is a satisfactory and reassuring embodiment of moral health in a world—or in two worlds, the Old and the New—where corruption and vices like selfishness and pride are rampant."

Tigg, Montague Vagabond and confidence man who fronts for Chevy Slyme in his attempts to extract money from his Chuzzlewit relatives. "He was very dirty and very jaunty; very bold and very mean; very swaggering and very slinking; very much like a man who might have been something better and unspeakably like a man who deserved to be something worse" (4). After leaving Slyme, the fast-talking Tigg appears to be something better when he establishes the fraudulent Anglo-Bengalee Disinterested Loan and Life Assurance Company, takes luxurious offices and lodgings, and changes his name to Tigg Montague (27): "He had a world of jet-black shining hair upon his head, upon his cheeks, upon his chin, upon his upper lip. His clothes, symmetrically made, were of the newest fashion and the costliest kind. . . . And yet, though changed his name, and changed his outward surface, it was Tigg. Though turned and twisted upside down, and inside out, as great men have been sometimes known to be; though no longer Montague Tigg, but Tigg Montague; still it

was Tigg; the same Satanic, gallant, military Tigg" (27). He blackmails Jonas to put his money into the scheme (38) and to help con Pecksniff into becoming an investor (44). Jonas murders Tigg to escape his clutches (46).

With his powers of language, Tigg, like Jingle in *Pickwick* or Micawber in *Copperfield*, is one of Dickens's self-creators, characters whose rich and imaginative use of words enables them to define (and, in Tigg's case, redefine) themselves. Although JOHN LUCAS (1970) finds his transformation from "comic trickster" to "frightened victim" inconsistent and unconvincing, most critics share STEVEN MARCUS's (1965) view: "Tigg is one of Dickens's most seductive and amiable scoundrels; his charm consists in the flamboyant style of his fraudulence, and although he is continually embellishing, inflating, dramatizing and imposing his utterly fabricated self upon the world, the activity is at the same time the one utterly genuine thing about him, his sole absolute."

Todgers, Mrs. M. Proprietor of a boardinghouse for commercial gentlemen known simply as Todgers's: "A bony and hard-featured lady, with a row of curls in front of her head, shaped like little barrels of beer; and on top of it something made of net—you couldn't call it a cap exactly—which looked like a black cobweb," she is "the presiding deity of the establishment" (8). She puts up the Pecksniffs when they first come to London (8) and fends off Pecksniff's drunken advances at the dinner party (9). She offers Charity a place to stay when she comes to London on her own (30), and she is especially kind to Mercy, offering her a refuge from her marriage; "in some odd nook in Mrs. Todgers's breast, up a great many steps, and in some corner easy to be overlooked, there was a secret door, with 'Woman' written on the spring, which, at a touch from Mercy's hand, had flown wide open, and admitted her for shelter" (37).

By offering a boardinghouse that is a place of refuge in the city and a place where the individuality of each of the boarders is respected and nurtured, Mrs. Todgers is one of the positive figures in the novel whose generosity counters the selfishness of other characters. SYLVÉRE MONOD (1985), in contrast to most critics, sees Mrs. Todgers as one of the characters transformed during the story from a "hard" and "calculating" woman when she is first introduced to a saintly caretaker at the end.

Todgers's   The boardinghouse near the Monument in London run by Mrs. Todgers in *Chuzzlewit*. In the novel it becomes symbolic of the city and the urban community. A place of refuge for single gentlemen in the heart of the urban "labyrinth," it is contrasted with Pawkins's boardinghouse in New York where Martin is introduced to America. Van Ghent's classic essay, "The Dickens World: The View from Todgers's" (1950), has given the boardinghouse broader significance in Dickens criticism as symbolic of a worldview in which the inanimate takes on a life of its own.

Toppit, Miss   American literary lady wearing "a brown wig of uncommon size" at the levee for Elijah Pogram (34).

Watertoast Association of United Sympathisers   An Anglophobic association of pro-Irish Americans encountered by young Martin on his American journey, headed by General Cyrus Choke. "The Watertoast Association sympathised with a certain Public Man in Ireland [Daniel O'Connell], . . . because they didn't love England at all—not by any means because they loved Ireland much." However, when they learn that O'Connell opposes slavery, they disband the organization (21).

Westlock, John   Pecksniff's pupil before Martin, "a good-looking youth, newly arrived at man's estate" (2), who leaves Pecksniff resentful of the treatment he has received and convinced that the architect is a hypocritical scoundrel. He is a staunch friend to Tom Pinch, even though they disagree about Pecksniff. He befriends both Martin and Tom when they come to London. He marries Ruth Pinch, and Tom lives with them (54).

Wolf   Associate of Tigg Montague who attends the dinner for Jonas Chuzzlewit: "literary character— . . . remarkably clever weekly paper—oh, remarkably clever!" (28).

ADAPTATIONS

EDWARD STIRLING and Charles Webb wrote competing adaptations that were staged in London as soon as *Chuzzlewit* completed its serial run. In both of these productions and in the 20 or so other adaptations produced by 1850, the lead actress played Young Bailey and the leading male comedian Mrs. Gamp. The focus of much dramatic interest, Mrs. Gamp inspired farces and playlets of her own as well as playing an important role in adaptations of the novel. *Mrs. Sarah Gamp's Tea and Turn Out* (1846) by Benjamin Webster and *Dealings with the Firm of Gamp and Harris* (1846) by FREDERICK FOX COOPER were two of the plays that exploited the popularity of Dickens's boozy nurse.

Only one American adaptation of the novel appeared in the 1840s, an indication of the disaffection with Dickens brought on by his criticism of the United States in *American Notes* and *Chuzzlewit*.

Most later adaptations continued to feature Mrs. Gamp, but Pecksniff sometimes displaced Young Bailey from his earlier prominence. An adaptation from the 1880s, *Tom Pinch*, departed from the established version and told only the story of Tom and Ruth. A German production in 1864 by H. Chr. Klein, *Tartuffe Junior; oder Martin Geldermann und sein Erben*, linked Pecksniff with Moliere's famous hypocrite.

Two silent films appeared in 1912 and 1914. The BBC has made two adaptations, CONSTANCE COX's (1964) 13-part version and David Lodge's (1994) more recent adaptation directed by Pedr James, with Paul Scofield (old Martin, Anthony), Tom Wilkinson (Pecksniff), Pete Postlethwaite (Montague), Elizabeth Spriggs (Mrs. Gamp), and JOHN MILLS (Chuffey). A sound film, *Greedy* (1994), vaguely derived a modern story from the relationship of the two Martins in *Chuzzlewit*.

FURTHER READING

ALEXANDER WELSH (1987) discusses the biographical origins of *Chuzzlewit* and considers several of the characters—Jonas, Tigg, Pinch, Pecksniff, and the two Martins—as projections of the author.

Nearly all the critics agree that *Chuzzlewit* is both a great comic novel and a seriously flawed one. JOHN BOWEN (2000) describes it as "the strangest, most demanding, and funniest of Dickens's earlier fictions, and one of the most important of all nine-teenth-century novels." R. C. CHURCHILL's (1982) claim that it is "the greatest work of comic genius in the whole of English literature" is perhaps the most extravagant assertion of its virtues. SYLVÉRE MONOD's (1985) *Martin Chuzzlewit* is an excellent book-length critique of the novel with individual chapters devoted to the text and context, to the style and structure, and to important characters. In the most sustained analysis of its comic structures and themes, JAMES KINCAID (1971) describes *Chuzzlewit* as a novel that begins with the didactic intent of presenting varieties of selfishness and develops into a "comedy of accommodation" in which Mrs. Todgers and Mrs. Gamp model ways to survive positively in society. JOHN LUCAS (1970) writes of *Chuzzlewit* as a flawed novel, in which Dickens was unable to bring together his realistic rendering of Victorian society with the moral fable he was tell-ing at the same time. This lack of a coherent center to the novel is evident in loose ends in the plot and inconsistencies in the characters. STEVEN MARCUS (1965), while admitting the novel's contradictions, finds its characters and social analysis a marked advance on the earlier novels. His archetypal read-ing is particularly interesting for its discussion of the American scenes and Martin's transformation in the "anti-Paradise" of New Eden. JOSEPH GOLD (1972) also takes an archetypal approach, tracing Dickens's use of the story of Jonah in the whale as the archetype underlying the novel. F. S. SCHWAR-ZBACH (1979) takes on the realistic elements in the book, discussing the city in the novel as a physical and symbolic representation of industrial society in the Victorian age. DOROTHY VAN GHENT's (1950) classic essay, "The Dickens World: A View from Todgers's," takes Todgers's as a touchstone to dis-cuss the central features of Dickens's sensibility, especially his animation of the inanimate and his objectification of the human.

Mystery of Edwin Drood, The

Dickens's 15th novel, left unfinished at the time of his death in June 1870, when he had nearly completed six

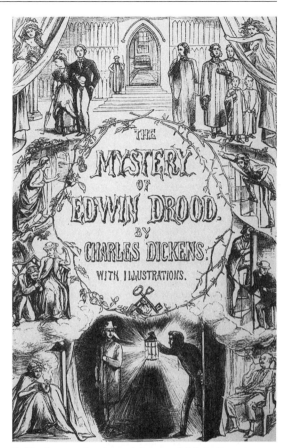

Collins's cover for the serial parts of *Edwin Drood*, completed before illness forced him to abandon the project, has fed speculation about Dickens's intentions for the unfinished portions of the story.

of the projected 12 monthly parts. The six parts were published from April to September 1870 by CHAPMAN & HALL, with illustrations by LUKE FILDES. CHARLES ALLSTON COLLINS provided the cover illustration for the monthly numbers. Published in one volume, 1870. Although most of the commentary has attempted to explain how Dickens would have finished the novel, *Drood* can also be read as the culmination of themes and motifs in his earlier works.

SYNOPSIS

Part 1 (April 1870)
(1) At dawn three men lie in an opium den run by an old woman in the East End of London. John

Jasper awakens from a drug-induced stupor and from incoherent oriental visions. He checks his wretched companions and, satisfied that their mutterings are "unintelligible," places some money on a table and leaves. That afternoon he arrives late for the cathedral service in Cloisterham, puts on his choir robe, and joins the procession as the words "Where the Wicked Man . . ." are intoned in the sanctuary.

(2) The Reverend Septimus Crisparkle worries that Jasper, music master and lay precentor of Cloisterham Cathedral, is ill. Jasper assures him that it is nothing, but he confides to his nephew, Edwin Drood, a young man nearly as old as his uncle, that "the cramped monotony of [his] existence grinds [him] away by the grain" and he has been taking opium. At dinner Jasper and Drood toast "Pussy," Jasper's music student and Drood's

In *London, A Pilgrimage* (1872), Gustave Doré connected this woodcut of an opium den with the opening scene in *Edwin Drood*.

fiancée, whose portrait hangs over the fireplace in Jasper's rooms. (3) The next day Edwin visits Pussy, whose real name is Rosa Bud, at Miss Twinkleton's School. Pretty, spoiled, and willful, she is uncomfortable with her position as an "engaged orphan," bequeathed by her father's will to marry Edwin. Had they not been willed to each other, she says, they might have been friends. As it is, they try each other. She is not really interested in his career as an engineer or in going with him to Egypt to engage in developing an undeveloped country.

(4) Thomas Sapsea, a pompous, conceited auctioneer, invites Jasper to comment on the epitaph he has written for his wife's tomb. It celebrates the way she "looked up to him" and admonishes those who read it to "with a blush retire" if they cannot do likewise. Jasper finds the epitaph "striking characteristic, and complete." Durdles, the maker of tombstones, measures the inscription for size and asserts, "It'll come in to an eighth of an inch." He takes the key to the Sapsea tomb and goes off to contemplate his carving. (5) On his way home, Jasper comes upon Durdles in the churchyard and asks him how he discovers forgotten tombs. Durdles taps with his hammer, demonstrating the different sounds by which he can distinguish the contents of the tombs. At midnight, back at his gatehouse rooms, Jasper fills a pipe with opium before going to bed.

Part 2 (May 1870)
(6) The Reverend Luke Honeythunder, a large and overbearing philanthropist, brings to Cloisterham his two wards, the twins Neville and Helena Landless. Septimus Crisparkle has his mother arrange a dinner in honor of their arrival, but Honeythunder dominates the conversation and all the guests are glad to see him return to London. (7) Neville tells Crisparkle, his tutor, of his unhappy childhood in Ceylon. Orphaned as children, he and Helena were abused by their stepfather and tried several times to run away. Neville became "secret and revengeful," hating his stepfather to the point of wanting to kill him; Helena developed courage and resourcefulness, disguising herself as a boy and acting without fear. Neville asks Crisparkle to bear with them and help them. When Neville and his tutor return

to the drawing room, Rosa is singing to Jasper's accompaniment. Suddenly she breaks off, saying she cannot continue. Later she tells Helena that she feels assaulted by Jasper and is afraid of him. (8) After escorting Rosa and Helena back to Miss Twinkleton's school, Edwin and Neville quarrel over Rosa. Jasper joins them just as they are about to come to blows. Although he separates them, he also encourages their dispute, and the quarrel breaks out again over Rosa's portrait when they get to Jasper's rooms. Neville throws the dregs of his wine at Edwin, tells him that he might appreciate Rosa properly had he known some hardships, and then leaves abruptly. The next day, after Edwin has left Cloisterham, Jasper reports to Crisparkle that the two are "murderous" toward each other. (9) Rosa's guardian, Mr. Grewgious, tells her that she is not bound by the will to marry Edwin. Rosa seems relieved but indicates no unwillingness to go on with the wedding. She asks Grewgious to come back at Christmas, when Edwin will again be in Cloisterham, so that they can discuss their marriage plans with him.

Part 3 (June 1870)

(10) Crisparkle urges a reluctant Neville to apologize for his behavior toward Drood. Meanwhile Crisparkle gets Jasper to elicit an apology from Drood. Edwin writes asking Jasper to arrange a Christmas Eve dinner with Neville where the differences can be forgiven and forgotten.

(11) Meanwhile, Edwin goes to Grewgious's rooms in STAPLE INN on a foggy evening to ask if he can take any communication to Rosa when he goes to Cloisterham. Grewgious tells him that there can be "no coolness, no lassitude, no doubt, no indifference . . . in a real lover," and gives him a diamond-and-ruby ring that belonged to Rosa's mother. The ring was left for Rosa should she and Edwin marry. The ring makes Edwin consider just how serious his love for Rosa is.

(12) Jasper has arranged to visit the crypts under the cathedral with Durdles. He brings a bottle of liquor and gives it to Durdles, and the tombstone carver gradually becomes drunk. By the end of their tour, Durdles has fallen asleep in the crypt. He dreams that he hears Jasper's footsteps fading in

the distance and the clink of a key falling from his hand. When Durdles awakens at 2 A.M., Jasper is gone and the key to the crypt is on the ground.

Part 4 (July 1870)

(13) Edwin comes to Cloisterham for Christmas. His conscience has been pricked by Grewgious, and he intends to speak earnestly to Rosa. She too has been thinking about their relationship and proposes that they be brother and sister to each other rather than lovers. He accepts her suggestion and thinks better of telling her about the ring.

(14) On Christmas Eve, Neville prepares for a solitary walking tour. He has purchased boots and a heavy ironwood walking stick. He is uneasy about the dinner that evening at Jasper's house, where he will meet Edwin again. Edwin spends a solitary day thinking about what to tell Grewgious, whom he will ask to inform Jasper of the broken engagement. At dusk in the street he meets an old woman, Princess Puffer, the opium dealer from London, who begs money from him. She tells him that someone named Ned is in danger. Jasper, meanwhile, spends the day preparing for his dinner guests.

On Christmas morning, Jasper comes to the cathedral, where workmen are inspecting damage from a storm during the night. He is looking for Edwin, who went out with Landless during the storm and did not return. Neville has already set out on his trek. (15) As he is walking down a cart track several miles from Cloisterham, Neville sees eight men following him. He allows four to pass, but the other four follow behind. Without explaining the reason, they surround and apprehend him. When they are joined by Crisparkle and Jasper, Neville learns that Edwin is missing and that he was the last person known to have seen him alive. Neville claims that Edwin returned to Jasper's gatehouse and Crisparkle believes him, but Jasper suspects him of murdering Drood. As crews drag the river searching for a body, Grewgious tells Jasper that Edwin and Rosa have decided not to marry. Jasper turns white and collapses. (16) When Edwin's body is not found, Jasper thinks Edwin may have gone away to avoid embarrassment over his change of plans, but when Crisparkle finds Edwin's watch and shirt pin by Cloisterham Wier, Jasper is convinced that Edwin has been murdered. There is insufficient evidence to hold Neville, but he remains the primary suspect in the crime. He leaves Cloisterham and goes to London.

Part 5 (August 1870)

(17) Mr. Honeythunder annoys Crisparkle by judging Neville guilty, giving up his guardianship of the boy, and condemning Neville's defenders. At Staple Inn, where Neville has taken a room, Crisparkle visits Grewgious, who keeps an eye on Neville. Grewgious tells him that Jasper has been lingering outside the inn.

(18) A stranger, Dick Datchery, appears in Cloisterham, rents rooms from Mrs. Tope next to Jasper's gatehouse, and goes on a tour of the cathedral with Mayor Sapsea. He takes particular interest in the disappearance of Edwin Drood.

(19) Six months after Drood's disappearance, Jasper calls on Rosa for the first time. They are both dressed in mourning, for they have given up hope of Edwin's return. Rosa tells Jasper that she does not plan to begin music lessons with him again. He tells her, vehemently and repeatedly, that he loves her and implies that no one else can admire her and live. After he leaves, Rosa faints. (20) When she regains consciousness, Rosa flees to London, where Grewgious takes care of her. Helena Landless has also come to London, and Grewgious arranges a meeting between the two girls in the rooms of Lieutenant Tartar, Neville's neighbor at Staple Inn.

Part 6 (September 1870)

(21) Grewgious takes lodgings for Rosa with Mrs. Billickin and asks Miss Twinkleton to come to London and act as her chaperone.

(22) Jasper spends the night in the opium den where the old woman guides his fantasies and prompts him to speak during his opium trance. At dawn she shadows him as he leaves, following him to Cloisterham and to his gatehouse. There she learns his identity from Datchery. The next morning, she attends the service in the cathedral and, from the shadows behind a pillar, shakes her fist at him.

COMMENTARY

Dickens began *Drood*, his last novel, in the spring of 1870, four and a half years after he completed *Mutual Friend*. This is the longest gap between any two books in Dickens's career, a sign perhaps of his failing health and of his intense involvement with the PUBLIC READINGS during the final years of his life. He planned the new novel for only 12 monthly numbers, about two-thirds the length of his usual monthly serials, but he completed only half of them. When he died on June 9, 1870, he was working on the final pages of the sixth number.

He was excited by his idea for the book, telling JOHN FORSTER that it was "not a communicable idea (or the interest in the book would be gone), but a very strong one, though difficult to work." The difficulties began in the first number, which he underwrote by 12 pages. He remedied the shortfall by pulling a chapter from the second number and including it in the first. His notes for the novel also indicate that he had difficulty following his plan in later numbers and introduced several episodes earlier than he expected to. Though most of his original readers were not aware of these difficulties as they read the story, WILKIE COLLINS, in a harsh judgment of the book, described it as "Dickens's last laboured effort, the melancholy effort of a worn-out brain."

Collins may have been reacting to Dickens's subject matter, which, with its oriental themes, opium trances, and mystery genre, seemed to be challenging Collins's own novel, *The Moonstone*, which had completed its serial run in ALL THE YEAR ROUND in 1868. Many of the commentators who have attempted to suggest the ways in which Dickens planned to complete the novel assume that the book was to be more on the order of a Collins mystery thriller than like Dickens's own earlier works. Dickens's initial inspiration, however, sounds a lot like the idea for some of his own earlier novels: "Two people, boy and girl, or very young, going apart from one another, pledged to be married after many years—at the end of the book. The interest to arise out of the tracing of their separate ways, and the impossibility of telling what will be done with that impending fate." Although Dickens dropped this plan or transformed it into the story of Rosa and Edwin, there is in their arranged relationship echoes of John Harmon and Bella Wilfer's arranged marriage (*Mutual Friend*) and of Pip's expectations for his marriage to Estella (*Expectations*).

In many ways *Drood* reminds its readers of Dickens's earlier novels. The intriguing opening chapter with its contrast between the opium den in London and the cathedral in Cloisterham recalls the contrast between city and country in *Bleak House* and the opposition of the private and public spheres in that novel's two narratives. In *Drood,* the opium den may have connections to the East, but its primary function seems to be to represent the repressed inner world of Jasper, so different from his respectable outer appearance as the choirmaster of the cathedral, a contrast not unlike that between Bradley Headstone's controlled and mechanical respectability as schoolmaster and his passionate and murderous suppressed self in *Mutual Friend.* The cathedral is a projection of one side of Jasper's character; it also represents a way of life that has often been compared to the ecclesiastical world of ANTHONY TROLLOPE's Barsetshire novels. But Dickens is not concerned with the politics of Cloisterham or with the ways in which worldly concerns affect the religious community. He is more interested in the ways religious mysteries attempt to explain the human situation and the presence of evil in the world. *Drood* seems closer to the world of GRAHAM GREENE than to that of Trollope.

The cathedral and the opium den act as the symbolic centers in *Drood,* as the MARSHALSEA PRISON does in *Dorrit* or the dustheaps and the river do in *Mutual Friend.* The DOUBLES in the novel also continue one of Dickens's repeated motifs. Like Sydney Carton in *Two Cities,* Harmon/Rokesmith in *Mutual Friend,* or Pip, who is both blacksmith and gentleman, Jasper is a divided figure whose separate lives are part of his mystery. This doubling in the central character is echoed in the Landless twins and, in comic parody, in Miss Twinkleton, who is described as having "two distinct and separate phases of being" (3).

What Dickens planned to make of these materials has been a matter of considerable dispute. The commentators can be broadly placed into two camps. The first group argues that *Drood* was to be a novel like Dickens's earlier ones, relating private and public realms; finding parallels in the domestic sphere to the larger public world. His interest was not so much in the mystery or the murder at the heart of his story as in the psychology of the characters involved in it, particularly John Jasper, who would be presented from the inside as a portrait of a murderer. The other school looks at *Drood* as something new in the Dickens canon, a mystery thriller in the manner of Collins, relying on a sensational plot with surprising turns at the end of the story. Adherents of this view often read the novel as if it were by Agatha Christie, looking for details in the text that provide clues to the surprises Dickens had planned. Several key questions have focused much of the discussion: What, exactly, is the central "mystery" in *Edwin Drood?* Is it Drood's disappearance, the identity of his presumed killer, or something about Jasper and his connection with Princess Puffer? What role was the ring that Grewgious gave to Edwin intended to play in the unraveling of the mystery? How would Durdles and his knowledge of the tombs underneath the cathedral figure in the story? Who are the Landless twins and why are they in Cloisterham? Is Datchery a detective come to Cloisterham to solve the mystery of Edwin's disappearance, or is he one of the other characters in disguise, as his mismatched hair and eyebrows suggest?

Besides the text itself, literary detectives have the illustrations by LUKE FILDES and CHARLES ALLSTON COLLINS to work from; reports of Dickens's intent from the illustrators, his family, and Forster; a fragment, known as "The Sapsea Fragment," that may have been planned for a future number but was probably a discarded passage from the existing text; Dickens's other works; and numerous contemporary works by other authors that provide parallels to *Drood* or offer suggestions for interpreting Dickens's intentions. Forster (1872) offers the most clues: "The story," he writes, "was to be that of a murder of a nephew by his uncle; the originality of which was to consist in the review of the murderer's career by himself at the close, when its temptations were to be dwelt upon as if, not he the culprit, but some other man, were the tempted. The last chapters were to be written in the condemned cell, to which his wickedness, all elaborately elicited from him as if told to another, had brought him. Discovery by the murderer of the utter needlessness of the murder for its object, was to follow hard upon commission of the deed; but all discovery of the murderer was to be baffled till towards the close, when, by means of a gold ring which had resisted the corrosive effects of the lime into which he had thrown the body, not only the person murdered was to be identified but the locality of the crime and the man who committed it. . . . Rosa was to marry Tartar, and Crisparkle the sister of Landless, who was himself, I think, to have perished in assisting Tartar finally to unmask and seize the murderer."

Forster's account is consistent with the existing text and with Dickens's usual interest in the psychology of the characters rather than in the elaborations of plot. His account identifies Edwin as the victim and Jasper as the murderer, the most probable directions suggested in the existing text. The very probability of Forster's solution disappoints those who want more mystery or who expect the story to turn upon unexpected events, but such surprises would not be characteristic of an author who "solved" the Harmon murder halfway through *Mutual Friend* and who was more interested in Headstone's criminality than in his crime.

Forster's account makes Jasper the puzzling center of the story, and commentators have wondered just what sort of man this murderer would reveal himself to be in his final meditations in the condemned cell. Is he a consciously malevolent man who conceals his villainy behind a mask of clerical respectability? A passionately out of control man insanely jealous of Edwin's relationship with Rosa? A person who must control others and who uses the powers of drugs and hypnotism to do so? A killer with ties to the Eastern cult of Kali who has a mission to murder Edwin? A man so deeply divided within himself that the respectable choirmaster is not even aware of the murderous activities of the opium addict? Commentators have advanced all of these interpretations to explain his character.

Clearly Jasper is a kind of Jekyll/Hyde figure. Both sides of his character appear in the opening chapter, where his murderous visions in London are countered by his singing later the same day in the cathedral service. The narrator's description of the doubleness in Miss Twinkleton's character may provide some important clues to understanding Jasper: "As, in some cases of drunkenness, and in others of animal magnetism, there are two states of consciousness which never clash, but each of which pursues its separate course as though it were continuous instead of broken (thus, if I hide my watch when I am drunk, I must be drunk again before I can remember where), so Miss Twinkleton has two distinct and separate phases of being" (3). Jasper the opium addict may be a totally separate person from Jasper the choirmaster; his murderous side may be unaware of his loving side that dotes on Edwin and later actively seeks to discover his nephew's murderer. Jasper is clearly subject to spells of drugged drunkenness and seems to be practicing animal magnetism when he frightens Rosa at the piano (7) and "suggests" to Crisparkle the location of Edwin's watch (16). There is a good deal of evidence, both in the novel and in external sources, leading to the suggestion that he is a Thug, a member of an Eastern cult of murderers, who kills Edwin in a ritual murder to avenge an earlier wrong. The surprising scene that was to end the novel might have been Jasper's realization and confession of his hidden side or Dickens's sympathetic interior portrait of the murderer coming to recognize his divided self and admitting the evil he has done.

EDMUND WILSON (1941) suggested that the divided Jasper was also a portrait of his creator: "Mr. Jasper is, like Dickens, an artist: he is a musician, he has a beautiful voice. He smokes opium, and so, like Dickens, leads a life of imagination apart from the life of men. Like Dickens, he is a skilful magician, whose power over his fellows may be dangerous. Like Dickens, he is an alien from another world; yet, like Dickens, he has made himself respected in the conventional English community." Jasper's final revelation, then, was also to be the author's revelation of his own self-division, that he was, to use Wilson's phrase, "two Scrooges." If W. W. Robson's suggestion that Datchery was to be revealed as Dickens himself ("'The Mystery of Edwin Drood': The Solution?" *Times Literary Supplement*, November 11, 1983), then *Drood* might have become for Dickens what *The Tempest* was for Shakespeare, his final affirmation of his magical artistry and his revelation that imagination itself was the solution to the mystery.

If *Drood* was to be Dickens's most complete self-revelation, there is reason to believe that Jasper may not be fully aware of his crime—even in his murderous persona—or that he may, like Pip, carry the guilt of his relative's death without being guilty of actually carrying out the crime. Several commentators have suggested that Edwin, after becoming aware of Jasper's intent to murder him, ran off and disappeared or that Jasper failed in his attempt to kill Edwin. According to this view, the surprise at the end of the novel—a surprise for both the reader and Jasper—was to be Edwin's reappearance, his resurrection from his presumed death. The power of the cathedral to renew life is suggested in the pages Dickens wrote on the day before he died. After an episode in the murky visions of the opium den, Cloisterham is bathed in the redeeming light of the morning sun: "A brilliant morning shines on the old city. Its antiquities and ruins are surpassingly beautiful, with the lusty ivy gleaming in the sun, and the rich trees waving in the balmy air. Changes of glorious light from moving boughs, songs of birds, scents from gardens, woods, and fields—or, rather, from the one great garden of the whole cultivated island in its yielding time—penetrate into the Cathedral, subdue its earthy odour, and preach the Resurrection and the Life" (23). The resurrection theme recurs in all of the later novels, from Sydney Carton's sanctified execution to the baptismal drownings in *Expectations* and *Mutual Friend*. Edwin's return would have provided a surprising turn to end Dickens's last fable and a fulfillment consistent with the resurrection theme in all of his later novels.

CHARACTERS AND RELATED ENTRIES

Bazzard Grewgious's gloomy clerk: "A pale, puffy-faced, dark-haired person of thirty, with big dark eyes that wholly wanted luster, and a dissatisfied doughy complexion that seemed to ask to be sent to the baker's, this attendant was a mysterious being, possessed of some strange power over Mr. Grewgious. . . . A gloomy person with tangled locks, and a general air of having been reared under the shadow of that baleful tree of Java which has given shelter to more lies than the whole botanical kingdom, Mr. Grewgious, nevertheless, treated him with unaccountable consideration" (11). He is the author of the unproduced tragedy, which Grewgious asserts will never be produced. Since he is absent from Grewgious's office later in the story, some commentators have speculated that Datchery is Bazzard in disguise.

Billickin, Mrs. ("The Billickin") Landlady of the London lodging house in Southampton Street, Bloomsbury Square, where Rosa Bud and Miss Twinkleton are placed by Mr. Grewgious. She takes Miss Twinkleton to be her "natural enemy" and maintains an ongoing feud with her. "Personal faintness and overpowering personal candor" were her distinguishing characteristics (22).

Brobity, Ethelinda Mrs. Sapsea's maiden name.

Bud, Rosa (Rosebud, Pussy) "Pet pupil" at Miss Twinkleton's school, "wonderfully pretty, wonderfully childish, wonderfully whimsical" (3). An orphan, she has been "willed" in marriage to Edwin Drood by her father, who was a friend to Edwin's father. Because their fate is decided for them, she acts with pettish childishness toward Edwin, and he condescendingly takes her for granted. Before it is too late, both of them reevaluate their relationship and in an earnest consultation agree to be "brother and sister" to each other rather than husband and wife (13). She studies music with Jasper and is intimidated by a seeming hypnotic power he holds over her, stimulated perhaps by one repeated musical note as he accompanies her on the piano. After Edwin's disappearance and presumed death, Rosa flees from Jasper, who frightens her with his vehement protestations of love for her (19). As the novel breaks off, she seems to be attracted to Tartar (20). JOHN FORSTER (1872) claims that in Dickens's plan for the novel "Rosa was to marry Tartar."

Paired with Edwin Drood as the fair and childish couple who are contrasted with the Landless twins, the dark and knowing couple, Rosa, like her portrait, is "unfinished." Spoiled and childish, she is drawn to Helena, whose dark understanding of Rosa's situation recognizes that Rosa is not merely threatened by Jasper but also, as LAWRENCE FRANK (1984) points out, sexually attracted to him.

Fildes's picture of Edwin and Rosa for the first number of *Edwin Drood* is characteristic of the realistic illustrations of the 1860s.

Chinaman, Jack Opium den proprietor who operates his business across the court from that of Princess Puffer (1).

Cloisterham Cathedral town that is the setting for *Drood*, a thinly disguised version of Rochester.

Crisparkle, Mrs. The reverend Septimus Crisparkle's widowed mother: "What is prettier than an old lady—except a young lady—when her eyes are bright, when her figure is trim and compact, when her face is cheerful and calm, when her dress is as the dress of a china shepherdess: so dainty in its colours, so individually assorted to herself, so neatly moulded on her?" (6). She shares a house with Septimus, her seventh and only surviving son.

Crisparkle, the Reverend Septimus Minor canon of the Cloisterham Cathedral, a 35-year-old muscular Christian who is "fair and rosy, and per-petually pitching himself head-foremost into all the deep running water in the surrounding county, . . . early riser, musical, classical, cheerful, kind, good-natured, contented, and boy-like" (2). He agrees to tutor Neville Landless, seeks to curb the wildness in the boy's character, and tries to reconcile Neville and Edwin after the two quarrel. When Neville is suspected of murdering Drood, Crisparkle remains convinced of the boy's innocence.

Although Crisparkle is a good man, his innocent misunderstanding of the darker impulses that drive Neville and Jasper inadvertently contributes to Jas-per's crime. LAWRENCE FRANK's (1984) judgment sums up his limitations: "Crisparkle, far more than Drood, remains the embodiment of conventional consciousness in the novel. He succeeds, at best, in drawing the veil of conventional consciousness over the volatile energies of the brother and sister, once so like 'beautiful barbaric captives . . . from some wild tropical dominion.'"

Crozier Inn Cloisterham inn where Datchery stays when he first comes to town. Based on the Crown Inn, Rochester (18).

Datchery, Dick Mysterious stranger who announces his intention of settling in Cloisterham: "a white-haired personage with black eyebrows. Being buttoned up in a tightish blue surtout, with a buff waistcoat and gray trousers, he had something of a military air. . . . This gentleman's white head was unusually large, and his shock of white hair was unusually thick and ample" (18). He takes lodgings with the Topes, apparently to keep an eye on Jasper, who lives in the gatehouse next door.

Commentators have speculated that he is one of the other characters in disguise who would have become instrumental in solving the mystery. Those suggested most often are Drood, Bazzard, Helena Landless, and Tartar. W. W. Robson in "'The Mystery of Edwin Drood': The Solution?" (Times Literary Supplement, Nov. 11, 1983) has offered the intriguing suggestion that Datchery is Dickens himself, the author's identity to be revealed in a surprising conclusion to the story.

Dean of Cloisterham Dignitary of the cathedral in Cloisterham, "a modest and worthy gentleman" (4). The highest ecclesiastical official at the cathedral, the Dean is a cautious and politic man. After Neville Landless is suspected of killing Drood, he counsels Crisparkle to send Neville away and not to defend the young man's innocence (16). Appropriately Sapsea, who aspires to an ecclesiastical presence, admires the Dean and models himself on him (4).

Deputy ("Winks") The "hideous small boy" who identifies himself as a "man-servant up at the Travellers' Twopenny in Gas Works Garding" (5), a cheap lodging house for transients. He is hired by Durdles to pelt him with stones and drive him home when he is wandering aimlessly under the influence of drink.

Drood, Edwin John Jasper's nephew, a fair young orphan who has been destined by his father's will to marry Rosa Bud. He describes himself as "a shallow, surface kind of fellow" (2).

Trained as an engineer, he plans to go to Egypt to help develop an undeveloped country. He arrogantly assumes the superiority of the British over the darker races, just as he takes for granted his relationship with Rosa. His imperialistic arrogance, racism, and male superiority are simply aspects of his thoroughly conventional character. His condescension toward Rosa and his taking her for granted bother both John Jasper and Neville Landless, who are both infatuated with the girl. After earnestly discussing their relationship, Edwin and Rosa decide to be brother and sister rather than husband and wife (13), but they do not tell either Jasper or Landless of their decision. Jasper jealously provokes a quarrel between Landless and Drood (8) that makes Neville a prime suspect in Drood's disappearance (14).

Edwin's disappearance has generally been thought to be the result of his murder by Jasper, as in the plot outlined by JOHN FORSTER (1872), but some completions of the unfinished novel have Drood reappearing in the denouement of the story. For some versions of this latter point of view, see FELIX AYLMER (1964) and Gwen Watkins, *Dickens in Search of Himself* (1987).

Durdles ("Stony Durdles") Drunken stonemason who carves the tombstones for Cloisterham Cathedral; "in a suit of coarse flannel with horn buttons, a yellow neckerchief with draggled ends, an old hat more russet-colored than black, and laced boots of the hue of his stony calling, Durdles leads a hazy gipsy sort of life, carrying his dinner about with him in a small bundle" (4). Sapsea employs him to carve his wife's epitaph (4), and Jasper gets him to lead him on a guided tour of the catacombs beneath the cathedral and to demonstrate how he identifies which of the old tombs contain bodies (12). Datchery appears to be interested in taking a similar tour (18).

Ferdinand, Miss A lively girl at Miss Twinkleton's school who "surprised the company with a sprightly solo on the comb-and-curlpaper" (13).

Giggles, Miss A pupil, "deficient of sentiment," at Miss Twinkleton's (9, 13).

Grewgious, Hiram Lawyer of STAPLE INN and Rosa Bud's guardian. An angular "man of incorruptible integrity" that nature seems to have left unfinished, "with an awkward and hesitating manner; with a shambling walk and with what is called a near sight—which perhaps prevented his observing how much white cotton stocking he displayed to the public eye, in contrast with his black suit—Mr. Grewgious still had some strange capacity in him of making on the whole an agreeable impression" (9). His gentle questioning leads Edwin to consider seriously whether he wants to marry Rosa (11). He supplies the heirloom ring (11) that Edwin decides not to give to Rosa and that probably would have become an important clue to identifying Edwin's corpse. After Edwin's disappearance, he tells Jasper of Edwin and Rosa's decision to break off their engagement (15). He cares for Rosa when she flees to London and finds a place for her to stay with Mrs. Billickin (21). With Crisparkle and Tartar, he is committed to clearing Neville Landless of suspicion (20). He also seems to suspect Jasper of the presumed murder.

Honeythunder, the Reverend Luke Professional philanthropist, director of the Haven of Philanthropy, brother-in-law of Mrs. Crisparkle, and guardian of Neville and Helena Landless; a bullying, overbearing man whose "philanthropy was of that gunpowderous sort [so] that the difference between it and animosity was hard to determine" (6). His aggressive manner belies his Christian vocation and his professed philanthropy. He is quick to assume Neville's guilt and to give up his guardianship of the Landless twins (17). DORIS ALEXANDER (1991) suggests that he was modeled on "the appearance and character" of Thomas Babington Macaulay, who was known for the loudness and vehemence of his manner.

Jasper, John (Jack) Edwin Drood's uncle, "a dark man, of some six-and-twenty, with thick lustrous, well-arranged black hair and whiskers. . . . His voice is deep and good, his face and figure are good, his manner is a little sombre" (2). Although he is choir director at Cloisterham Cathedral and a respected member of the ecclesiastical establish-

ment there, he is also an opium addict and a frequenter of Princess Puffer's den in London's East End. Under the influence of opium, he envisions sensual oriental fantasies and seems to reenact a dream of murdering one he loves; in Cloisterham he suffers from occasional fits and terrifies Rosa Bud with what seems to be a hypnotic power over her. He is devoted to his nephew Edwin, but he is also secretly in love with Rosa, Edwin's fiancée. After Edwin's disappearance, he confesses his passionate love to Rosa, prompting her to seek refuge in London. The devotion and jealousy in Jasper's relationship with Edwin, the ambiguous hints in his opium dreams, his interest in the tombs under the cathedral, and his attempts to throw suspicion on Neville Landless all seem to confirm JOHN FORSTER's (1872) assertion that in Dickens's plan, the novel told of an uncle murdering his nephew. The end, according to Forster, was to be the murderer's confession in his condemned cell.

Although most commentators consider Jasper the villain of the novel—see FELIX AYLMER (1964) for an exception—the nature of his crimes and the motivations for his villainy have been very differently described. Most agree that his jealous rivalry with Edwin is one motivation, but there is considerable dispute over just how conscious Jasper is in his villainy. He is clearly a conflicted and divided man, torn between the opium den and the cathedral. Some have suggested that Jasper is a precursor to Stevenson's Doctor Jekyll and Mr. Hyde, himself unaware of the two sides of his personality. His final revelation, then, was to be an act of self-discovery as well as a confession. Several commentators have argued that Jasper was a follower of Kali, the Indian goddess of destruction, who carried out the murder of Drood as a Thugee ritual. This line of reasoning is nicely summarized by EDMUND WILSON (1941). Others have considered a homosexual attraction to Drood in conflict with his heterosexual attraction to Rosa as the ultimate source of conflict in Jasper's character (see GEOFFREY THURLEY [1976] and Eve Kosofsky Sedgwick, *Between Men: English Literature and Male Homosocial Desire* [1985]). Dickens's final hero-villain continues the study of self-division that has characterized such important male figures in his works as Steerforth (*Copperfield*), Sydney Carton (*Two Cities*), and Eugene Wrayburn/Bradley Headstone (*Mutual Friend*). The dimensions of the conflict within Jasper are analyzed at length by LAWRENCE FRANK (1984) and Thacker (*Edwin Drood: Antichrist in The Cathedral,* 1990).

Jennings, Miss   Pupil at Nun's House, Miss Twinkleton's school (9).

Joe   Driver of the Cloisterham bus.

Landless, Neville and Helena   Orphaned twins, born in Ceylon and raised there by a brutal and abusive stepfather: "an unusually handsome lithe young fellow, and an unusually handsome little girl; much alike; both very dark, and very rich in color; she of almost the gipsy type; something untamed about them both" (6). They are in England under the guardianship of the Reverend Honeythunder, who places them in Cloisterham to be educated and "civilized." Helena is enrolled at Miss Twinkleton's school, where she becomes Rosa Bud's roommate and close friend; Neville is placed under the tutelage of the Reverend Crisparkle. When Drood's patronizing way with Rosa annoys Neville, who is also attracted to her, the two men quarrel (8), and when Drood disappears, Neville becomes the prime suspect in his presumed murder (15–16). Supported by Crisparkle and Grewgious, he leaves Cloisterham and takes lodgings in London. There he is joined by Helena as well as by Crisparkle, who has followed her to London (21). JOHN FORSTER (1872) says that Helena and Crisparkle were to marry and Neville was to perish "in assisting Tartar to unmask and seize the murderer."

   Neville and Helena form a dark couple contrasting the fair Edwin and Rosa. Their dark complexion and Asian roots suggest sources for their violent and passionate vitality, characteristics that contrast with the death-in-life civilized and respectable Cloisterham and thus accentuate the "oriental" side of Jasper. Postcolonial critics see them as an important part of Dickens's critique of xenophobic complacency and imperial racism.

Lobley   Tartar's servant in charge of Tartar's yacht: "a jolly-favoured man, with tawny hair and whiskers, and a big red face. He was the dead image of the sun in old woodcuts, his hair and whiskers answering for rays all around him" (22).

Nuns' House   Miss Twinkleton's "Seminary for Young Ladies," housed in a former convent (3).

Porters   A suitor of her youth at TUNBRIDGE WELLS recalled by Miss Twinkleton as "foolish Mr. Porters" (3).

Puffer, Princess   The "haggard woman" (1) who presides at the opium den in the East End of London frequented by John Jasper. Late in the afternoon of Christmas Eve, Edwin encounters her as he is walking; she tells him ominously that "Ned" is "a threatened name. A dangerous name" (14). Six months after Edwin's disappearance, she reappears in Cloisterham in the final chapter, having followed Jasper from London (23).

Reynolds, Miss   One of Miss Twinkleton's pupils at Nuns' House (9).

Rickitts, Miss   Pupil at Miss Twinkleton's school, "a junior of weakly consitution" (13).

Sapsea, Thomas   Pompous and bombastic auctioneer and mayor of Cloisterham; "the purest Jackass in Cloisterham. . . . He possesses the great qualities of being portentous and dull, and of having a roll in his speech, and another roll in his gait. . . . Much nearer sixty years of age than fifty, with a flowing outline of stomach, and horizontal creases in his waistcoat; reputed to be rich; voting at elections in the strictly respectable interest; morally satisfied that nothing but he himself has grown since he was a baby" (4). He hires Durdles to carve his epitaph to his late wife, Ethelinda Brobity Sapsea, which celebrates her appreciation of his importance and ends with a charge to those who read it: "STRANGER, PAUSE / And ask thyself the Question / CANST THOU DO LIKEWISE? / If Not, / WITH A BLUSH RETIRE" (4).

Southampton Street   Mrs. Billickin's boarding-house is located in this street, which connects High Holborn with Bloomsbury Square (22).

Tartar, Lieutenant, R. N.   Retired navy man who was once Crisparkle's school chum and is Neville Landless's neighbor at STAPLE INN after Landless comes to London: "a handsome gentleman, with a young face, but with an older figure in its robustness and breadth of shoulder; say a man of eight-and-twenty, or at the utmost thirty; so extremely sunburnt that the contrast between his brown visage and the white forehead shaded out of doors by his hat, and the glimpses of white throat below the neckerchief, would have been almost ludicrous but for his broad temples, bright blue eyes, clustering brown hair, and laughing teeth" (17). By the end of the unfinished novel, he is aiding Crisparkle and Grewgious in their defense of Landless. He would probably have been instrumental in solving the mystery.

Tilted Wagon, the   Inn near Cloisterham where Neville Landless stops for breakfast as he sets out on his walking tour (15).

Tisher, Mrs.   Miss Twinkleton's assistant at Nuns' House, "a deferential widow with a weak back, a chronic sigh, and a suppressed voice, who looks after the young ladies' wardrobes, and leads them to infer that she has seen better days" (3).

Tope   Chief verger at Cloisterham Cathedral. He is landlord to both Jasper in the gatehouse and Datchery, who rents rooms at the Topes' house next door.

Tope, Mrs.   Tope's wife; she also serves as Jasper's housekeeper.

Twinkleton, Miss   Principal of the Seminary for Young Ladies at Nuns' House in Cloisterham attended by Rosa Bud and Helena Landless. She has "two distinct and separate phases of being": a scholastic model of decorum during the day and a "sprightlier" persona each evening (3). As a school-mistress she avoids saying anything that might

bring a blush to the cheeks of her young ladies, so she bowdlerizes the stories she teaches them. In the evening she indulges in gossip with Mrs. Tisher. She becomes Rosa's chaperone in London after Rosa flees from Jasper (21). There, in spite of her differences with "the Billickin," she reaches "a happy compromise between her two states of existence" (22).

"Winks"   Nickname for Deputy (23).

ADAPTATIONS

Before his death Dickens had raised with DION BOUCICAULT the possibility of making a play from *Drood*. After Dickens's death, Boucicault considered going through with the project but thought better of it. The first stage production was by T. C. De Leon, produced in October 1870 in Chicago and offering a solution received spiritualistically "direct from the shade of the deceased novelist." When his first adaptation was unsuccessful, De Leon rewrote the script and restaged the play in New York as *Jasper*. The first English production, Walter M. Stephens's adaptation at the Surrey Theatre, opened in November 1871. In this production Neville Landless, disguised as Datchery, pursues Jasper, who takes poison to escape capture. Datchery also pursues Jasper in G. H. MacDermott's 1872 production, but in this play he is Bazzard in disguise. In another frequent solution to the mystery employed in the production at the Britannia Theatre in 1872, Jasper turns out to have botched the murder, and Drood turns up alive, causing Jasper to suffer a fatal heart attack before the final curtain. Drood also reappears in Robert Hall's *Alive or Dead* (1876), disguised as the lawyer who defends Jasper in court. An adaptation by Joseph L. Hatton and Dickens's son CHARLES CALLIFORD DICKENS ends with the guilty Jasper taking poison. Although scheduled for production in 1880, it never reached the stage.

Notable among later stage versions are Beerbohm Tree's production of J. Comyns Carr's adaptation, in which the addict Jasper, played by Tree, deliriously believes himself guilty of a murder he did not commit. An adaptation by Jane Bacon and FELIX AYLMER (1951) represents an early version of Aylmer's ingenious defense of Jasper. A musical adaptation by Rupert Holmes (1985) in the style of a Victorian music hall offers the audience an opportunity to vote on possible endings for the story.

The two best-known film versions, a silent film by Gaumont British (1914) with Tom Terriss as Edwin and a Universal sound film (1935) with Claude Raines (Jasper), Valerie Hobson (Helena), and Francis Sullivan (Crisparkle), both end with Jasper's death. There were two other silent film versions (1909, 1912); another sound film was produced in Britain in 1993, which repeats the version of the story from the 1935 film.

Two television adaptations have appeared: a two-part American production for CBS (1952) and an eight-part serial for British independent television (1960).

FURTHER READING

Nearly all of the commentary on *Drood* has been concerned with how the novel was to end, a topic that especially obsessed Dickensians around the turn of the century. The bibliographies of *Drood* commentaries compiled by BERTRAM W. MATZ and his daughter (*Dickensian*, 1911, 1928, 1929) list hundreds of books and articles offering solutions to the plot. Among the more influential later suggestions are Howard Duffield's "John Jasper—Strangler" (*Bookman*, 1930), which proposed that Jasper was connected to the Thugee cult of Kali and that the murder was a ritual killing for revenge. EDMUND WILSON (1941) accepted Duffield's conclusion but extended his reading of the novel to describe Jasper as a projection of a divided and Dostoyevskian Dickens. FELIX AYLMER (1964) also found evidence for an Eastern

Scene in the crypt from the 1935 adaptation of *The Mystery of Edwin Drood*. *Courtesy of Photofest.*

connection to the murder, but in Egypt rather than India, and he offers an ingenious argument that Jasper is innocent of the crime and that Drood is not really dead.

Two recent completions of the story by Charles Forsyte (*The Decoding of Edwin Drood*, 1980) and Leon Garfield (*The Mystery of Edwin Drood Concluded*, 1980) develop conclusions more consistent with Forster's account of Dickens's plans for the story. Forsyte finds in Jasper a Jekyll/Hyde character: One of his selves loves Edwin and pursues the murderer; the other murders him. Garfield ends his Dickensian retelling with Jasper's dramatic confession of guilt to Crisparkle and then his execution. John Thacker, in *Edwin Drood: Antichrist in the Cathedral* (1990), analyzes the characters and themes of the novel in the light of Dickens's other works and finds the religious concerns of the late novels reaffirmed in *Drood*. Addressing another of the *Drood* conundrums, the identity of Datchery, W. W. Robson ("'The Mystery of Edwin Drood': The Solution?" *Times Literary Supplement*, November 11, 1983) suggests that the surprise at the end of the novel would reveal that Datchery was Dickens himself. Two Italian mystery writers, Carlo Fruttero and Franco Lucentini, make a grand send-up of the Drood industry in *The D. Case or the Truth about The Mystery of Edwin Drood* (1992) when they gather a convention of literary detectives to decide how the novel was going to end. Of course, the detectives, all working in their own characteristic ways, arrive at different conclusions.

Noteworthy among commentaries not attempting to solve the mystery is Charles Mitchell's "The Mystery of Edwin Drood: The Interior and Exterior of Self" (*ELH*, 1966), which analyzes psychological themes in the existing text, and STEVEN CONNOR's deconstructive reading, "Dead? Or Alive?: *Edwin Drood* and the Work of Mourning," (*Dickensian*, 1993), which accepts the novel's inconclusiveness as part of its meaning. Wendy S. Jacobson's *Companion to The Mystery of Edwin Drood* (1986) provides exhaustive textual and explanatory notes to accompany the text, as well as maps and plans of the settings.

Nicholas Nickleby, The Life and Adventures of (Serial title: The Life and Adventures of Nicholas Nickleby, containing a Faithful Account of the Fortunes, Misfortunes, Uprisings, Downfallings and the Complete Career of the Nickleby Family. Edited by Boz.)

Dickens's third novel, published in monthly parts from April 1838 to October 1839, with illustrations by HABLOT KNIGHT BROWNE. Published in one volume by CHAPMAN & HALL, 1839. Dickens improvised this picaresque story, bringing together elements from TOBIAS SMOLLETT, theatrical melodrama, journalistic realism, and social satire. Although the novel lacks a strong central theme, it offers interesting scenes and characters and shows Dickens in the process of discovering his own novelistic voice.

SYNOPSIS

Part 1 (April 1838)

(1) When Godfrey Nickleby inherited £5,000 from his Uncle Ralph, he bought a small farm in Devonshire where he settled with his wife and two sons, Ralph and Nicholas. When Godfrey died, £5,000 went to Ralph, who entered business in London, and £1,000 and the farm went to Nicholas. Nicholas married and there raised his two children, Nicholas and Kate, but he speculated with the money and lost it. He died penniless, leaving his wife and adolescent children to the protection of his brother.

(2) As the story begins, Ralph Nickleby pursues his business, a business of no clear definition or professional description but one concerned with money, in a spacious house on GOLDEN SQUARE, in a section of London on its way down. At a public meeting of the United Metropolitan Improved Hot Muffin and Crumpet Baking and Punctual Delivery

Squeers, the Yorkshire schoolmaster, at the Saracen's Head recruiting students for his school, in Browne's (Phiz's) illustration for the original edition of *Nicholas Nickleby* (1838).

Company, Ralph and the other directors consider a petition to Parliament calling for the abolition of the existing muffin trade by forbidding street sellers, an action that will favor their enterprise. When Newman Noggs, Ralph's clerk, brings him a letter announcing his brother's death and the arrival of his brother's widow and children in London, Ralph proceeds to his sister-in-law's lodgings at the establishment of Miss La Creevy, a painter of miniatures. He warns Miss La Creevy that his relative is poor and that he will not be responsible for her rent, and he offers to aid Kate and Mrs. Nickleby only if Nicholas will go off to teach in a YORKSHIRE SCHOOL. Although Ralph clearly dislikes Nicholas, the boy is determined to prove his mettle and to help his mother and sister. Kate is skeptical about this plan, but Mrs. Nickleby is grateful to her brother-in-law for his help. (4) Later, at the Saracen's Head in Snow Hill, Mr. Wackford Squeers interviews potential students and possible tutors. In his negotiation with Snawley, a potential client, Squeers makes it clear that most of his boys are illegitimate or stepchildren who are exiled to Yorkshire by their parents, and Snawley commits his two

stepsons to the school. Ralph, who has dealt with Squeers in the past, comes to the inn with Nicholas and Noggs and convinces the schoolmaster to hire his nephew for £5 a year. Nicholas is excited by his prospects, but Noggs seems strangely disturbed by Nicholas's optimism.

Part 2 (May 1838)

(5) As Nicholas leaves on the Yorkshire coach, Noggs slips a note into his hand. Riding on the outside of the coach in cold winter weather, Nicholas is suddenly awakened when the coach overturns. (6) The other passengers praise him for his quick response in taking the reins of the horses while the coachman cut the traces. As they wait for another coach at a nearby inn, the passengers tell stories. A grey-haired man tells "The Five Sisters of York," a legend behind a stained-glass window in YORK Cathedral. A merry-faced gentleman then tells "The Baron of Grogswig," the tale of a medieval German baron and his scolding wife. When the new coach arrives, they set out again, arriving the next evening at GRETA BRIDGE in Yorkshire. (7) There at Dotheboys Hall Mrs. Squeers greets her husband with a steak dinner, while Nicholas is served short rations and has fears of what is to come. Smike, the boy of all work, reduced to near idiocy by mistreatment, hopes for a letter, but Squeers has brought none for him. Nicholas discovers the letter from Noggs in his pocket offering him aid should he need it. It brings tears to Nicholas's eyes.

Part 3 (June 1838)

(8) The next morning Nicholas watches as Mrs. Squeers administers treacle and brimstone to the boys and Squeers assigns their "lessons," various chores around the school. The boys are not the young gentlemen that Nicholas had imagined but rather a group of maimed and abandoned waifs. Their meals are poor porridge, and their schooling is limited and ignorant. After dinner, Squeers distributes the mail, berating the boys as he does so and driving them to tears. Smike tells Nicholas of a boy who died at the school, and Nicholas finishes his first day in despair, but he is determined to go on for the sake of his mother and Kate. He is convinced that his uncle is angry only at him. (9) When Miss Fanny Squeers, the schoolmaster's

daughter, returns home and hears of the new young master, she goes into the schoolroom, pretending to need her pen sharpened, and immediately falls in love with Nicholas. She arranges a tea for him and invites her friend, Matilda Price, and Matilda's beau, John Browdie. At the tea Nicholas flirts with Tilda, angering both John and Fanny.

(10) Meanwhile Ralph finds a position for Kate with Madame Mantalini, a milliner. At her interview Kate is disturbed by Mr. Mantalini's flirtatiousness and refuses to acknowledge him. She insists that she live at home with her mother, and Ralph reluctantly agrees. He tells her that they can stay in a house he owns near the river.

Part 4 (July 1838)

(11) Kate has misgivings about her job, but Mrs. Nickleby talks of rich milliners. Noggs guides them to the dilapidated house near the river; he has furnished it with a few broken pieces of furniture.

(12) In Yorkshire, Nicholas angers Fanny Squeers by vowing that he has no romantic interest in her. (13) When Smike runs away from the school, Mrs. Squeers captures him. Squeers prepares to beat the boy before the whole school, but after the first blow, Nicholas intervenes and beats the schoolmaster. Then he packs up his belongings and sets out on foot for London. John Browdie, impressed by Nicholas's boldness, gives him some money for his journey. On the second morning, Nicholas awakens to see Smike watching him. The boy has followed him from the school.

(14) In London Noggs attends an anniversary party for his neighbors the Kenwigses, where the honored guest is Mrs. Kenwigs's uncle, Mr. Lillyvick, a collector of water rates. The high point in the evening comes when Miss Petowker of the Theatre Royal, DRURY LANE, performs "The Blood-Drinker's Burial." As Noggs prepares punch for the party, he is called away to meet two strangers who have arrived at his lodgings.

Part 5 (August 1838)

(15) The strangers are Nicholas and Smike. Nicholas tells Newman his story and is outraged to hear of the lies that Fanny Squeers has written about him to Ralph Nickleby. He is diverted from his anger, however, by the cries of the Kenwigses'

baby. He rushes downstairs to rescue the infant and impresses the Kenwigses with his aristocratic manner. (16) The next morning Nicholas seeks employment in London. He turns down a degrading position as secretary to Mr. Gregsbury, M.P., but later, under the pseudonym Mr. Johnson, he agrees to tutor the Kenwigses' daughters in French for five shillings a week.

(17) On her first day at Madame Mantalini's, Kate overhears a quarrel between Madame and her husband and is humiliated by some snobbish customers. At home, Mrs. Nickleby imagines Kate as Madame Mantalini's partner and Nicholas as Dr. Nickleby of Westminster School.

Part 6 (September 1838)

(18) At first Kate is befriended by Miss Knag, Madame Mantalini's forewoman, but when customers prefer Kate to her, Miss Knag takes out her jealous anger on Kate. (19) Ralph asks Kate to preside at a dinner at his house, and Mrs. Nickleby is delighted. The dinner is attended by Lord Frederick Verisopht, a naive young aristocrat whom Ralph intends to fleece, and several of Ralph's disreputable aristocratic acquaintances, Mr. Pyke, Mr. Pluck, Mr. Snobb, and Colonel Chowser. When Kate is humiliated by the advances of Verisopht's rakish companion, Sir Mulberry Hawk, Ralph intervenes and seems to show some compassion for his niece.

(20) Nicholas finally locates Ralph at his mother's lodgings, where his uncle is recounting Fanny Squeers's lies about him and announcing that "this boy, headstrong, wilful, and disorderly as he is, should not have one penny of my money, or one crust of my bread, or one grasp of my hand, to save him from the loftiest gallows in all Europe." Warning his uncle that he will hold him responsible for any wrongs done to his mother or sister, Nicholas leaves London so that he will not be a burden on them.

Part 7 (October 1838)

(21) When Madame Mantalini's business fails and the establishment is closed, Kate must seek employment elsewhere. She takes a position as companion to Mrs. Wititterly, a delicate and snobbish woman.

(22) Nicholas and Smike set out for PORTS-MOUTH with the vague idea of going to sea. At an

inn along the way, they meet Mr. Vincent Crummles, manager of a traveling theatrical troupe, who recruits them for his company. (23) The next day they meet their fellow actors, including Crummles's daughter, an aging "Infant Phenomenon" who plays child roles. Nicholas is made playwright for the company and instructed to translate some French works and put them into English under his own name. He is also given roles in several of the troupe's repertory of plays.

Part 8 (November 1838)

(24) Nicholas (as Mr. Johnson) has a leading role in his first effort, playing opposite Miss Snevellicci, the leading lady of the company. He, Miss Snevellicci, and the Infant Phenomenon canvass Portsmouth for patrons, and their opening is a great success. (25) When Miss Petowker joins the company, Nicholas discovers that Lillyvick, smitten with the actress, has secretly followed her from London. They are married in a theatrical ceremony. Meanwhile, in the company's production of *Romeo and Juliet,* Nicholas plays Romeo, Smike the apothecary.

(26) Back in London, Verisopht and Hawk are both pursuing Kate. Ralph, to forward his scheme to fleece Verisopht, tells him where Kate lives. Sir Mulberry flatters Mrs. Nickleby to gain the same information.

Part 9 (December 1838)

(27) With the aid of his confederates Pyke and Pluck, Hawk contrives to get Mrs. Nickleby to the theater where Kate and Mrs. Wititterly have a box. There Mrs. Nickleby and Mrs. Wititterly are both awed by the men's aristocratic company, and Kate is abandoned to the unwanted attentions of Sir Mulberry. She spurns him and tells him that her brother will resent his "unmanly persecution" of her. (28) Hawk and Verisopht make regular calls at Mrs. Wititterly's, who is flattered to have aristocratic visitors, but she becomes jealous of Kate and accuses her of being forward with them. When Kate appeals to her uncle for protection, Ralph says he can do nothing.

(29) In Portsmouth, Nicholas has risen to the head of Crummles's company, arousing the jealousy of his fellow actors. Noggs writes that Kate needs her brother's protection, so Nicholas prepares to cut short his successful theatrical career and return to London.

Part 10 (January 1839)

(30) After a farewell dinner with the company and a final performance in the theater, Nicholas rushes back to London in response to another letter from Noggs telling him to return instantly. (31) When he arrives on the evening after Kate's futile appeal to her uncle, (32) Nicholas cannot find either Noggs or his mother, and he wanders into a luxurious hotel near Hyde Park. There he overhears a stranger at an adjoining table speak insultingly about "Little Kate Nickleby." Nicholas challenges him and demands to know his name, but the stranger, Sir Mulberry, disdains him and as he leaves strikes him with his carriage whip. Nicholas grabs the whip, breaks it, and strikes Hawk across the face with the handle, leaving an open wound from eye to lip. (33) The next morning Nicholas removes Kate from Mrs. Wititterly's and breaks off relations with his uncle.

Part 11 (February 1839)

(34) When the financially strapped Mantalinis come to borrow money from Ralph, they tell him of Nich-

In this scene from the 1947 movie adaptation, Nicholas accuses Sir Mulberry Hawk of defaming his sister's name and reputation. After they leave the restaurant Nicholas will attack Hawk and strike him with the handle of a coach whip, leaving a permanent scar. *Courtesy of PhotoFest.*

olas's altercation with Hawk. Ralph is pleased to learn that Nicholas is in trouble. Squeers, recovered from the wounds that Nicholas gave him, tells Ralph about Smike, the boy he claims Nicholas abducted when he left Dotheboys Hall. Ralph suggests that they may get revenge on Nicholas through Smike. (35) After placing his mother, Kate, and Smike at Miss La Creevy's, Nicholas goes to the employment office to find work. There he meets Charles Cheeryble, a benevolent businessman who listens to his story and introduces him to his twin brother Edwin. They hire him to assist Tim Linkinwater, their aging clerk. They also provide a cottage for the Nicklebys at Bow.

(36) When Nicholas informs the Kenwigses of Lillyvick's marriage to Miss Petowker, they are deeply disappointed and despair about their children's prospects.

Part 12 (March 1839)

(37) Nicholas and Tim Linkinwater become comrades, and Tim proudly shows Nicholas's work to their employers. At Bow, Mrs. Nickleby is "courted" by a strange gentleman in small clothes in the next cottage, who tosses cucumbers and other vegetables to her over the garden wall.

(38) One day when Smike is returning to Bow from Miss La Creevy's house in town, he meets Squeers and young Wackford in the street. Squeers grabs him and holds him captive at Snawley's house in Somers Town. (39) John Browdie, in London on his honeymoon, learning of Smike's imprisonment, slips into the house at night and frees the boy.

Part 13 (April 1839)

(40) Noggs and the Nicklebys are overjoyed to have Smike back. Nicholas is determined to find out if his uncle was behind Smike's capture, but he is diverted from this pursuit when he sees a young woman in the Cheerybles' office who had first caught his attention at the employment office. He becomes obsessed with finding out who she is. He engages Noggs to discover her identity and arrange a meeting with her. Noggs tracks down a Miss Cecelia Bobster, but she turns out to be the wrong person. (41) Meanwhile, Mrs. Nickleby's suitor comes over the garden wall and proposes

to her before his keepers arrive to take him back. (42) While Nicholas is dining with John and Tilda Browdie at the Saracen's Head, Squeers, Fanny, and young Wackford appear. Fanny jealously attacks Tilda, and Squeers accuses John and Nicholas of abducting Smike.

Part 14 (May 1839)

(43) When Nicholas steps in to quell a disturbance at the inn, one of the disputants turns out to be Frank Cheeryble, nephew of the Cheeryble brothers, who has been defending the good name of a young woman of his acquaintance against the aspersions of another patron. Frank turns out to be a "good-humoured, pleasant fellow" and shows an immediate interest in Kate.

(44) Ralph's hatred of Nicholas is intense, nearly as powerful as his avarice. As he makes his rounds to the Mantalinis and others, Ralph plans his revenge. (45) With Squeers and Snawley, he goes to the Nicklebys' cottage and produces papers proving that Smike is Snawley's son. Smike refuses to go with them. Nicholas and John Browdie protect him from being forcibly taken away.

Part 15 (June 1839)

(46) The Cheerybles support Nicholas's effort to keep Smike from Snawley. They also ask Nicholas to act as their representative in dealing with a young woman, Madeline Bray, whom they have supported by buying drawings from her. She is the daughter of a debtor detained under the rules of the King's Bench Prison for a debt to Ralph Nickleby. Madeline turns out to be the young woman Nicholas has been seeking. (47) Meanwhile, an old moneylender, Arthur Gride, conspires with Ralph Nickleby to marry the girl, for Gride has learned that she stands to inherit some property. Ralph broaches the proposition to Mr. Bray, offering to forgive his debt if he agrees to the marriage. (48) Unaware of Ralph's scheme, Nicholas admires Madeline's sacrificial concern for her father, but he despairs of winning the heart of so noble a woman. By chance he again meets the Crummleses, who are in London on their way to a theatrical tour in America, and he attends their farewell dinner.

Part 16 (July 1839)

(49) Nicholas worries about Smike's failing health, a condition worsened, it seems, by Frank Cheeryble's attentions to Kate. Meanwhile, Mrs. Nickleby's lunatic suitor emerges from her chimney during a family party and outrages Mrs. Nickleby by shifting his attentions from her to Miss La Creevy.

(50) After recovering from his injuries at the hand of Nicholas, Hawk returns from Belgium, where he has been recuperating. He vows to avenge his injury, but he gets into an altercation with Verisopht, kills the young lord in the ensuing duel, and is forced to escape again to the Continent.

(51) Noggs learns of Ralph Nickleby's scheme for Arthur Gride and Madeline Bray to marry. When Nicholas tells him that Madeline is the young woman he has been seeking, Noggs tells Nicholas of the scheme and indicates that the wedding is scheduled to take place in two days.

Part 17 (August 1839)

(52) Although Nicholas despairs of preventing the marriage, Noggs encourages him to "hope, hope, to the last." Noggs meets Lillyvick, who has returned to London after Miss Petowker abandoned him to run off with a half-pay captain. Their hopes restored, the Kenwigses are reunited with their disconsolate relative. (53) Nicholas finds Mr. Bray eagerly anticipating the wedding that is to take place the next day, and he fails to dissuade Madeline from her determination to sacrifice herself for her father. In a last attempt to prevent the marriage, Nicholas tells Gride what he knows of the scheme, threatens him, and attempts to buy him off, but Gride rejects his offers and throws him out of his house. (54) The next morning Nicholas and Kate confront Gride and Ralph Nickleby before the wedding. Although their opposition only incites Ralph's determination, the ceremony is prevented by Mr. Bray's sudden death. Nicholas carries off the insensible Madeline to the Nickleby cottage at Bow.

Part 18 (September 1839)

(55) Attended by Kate, Madeline slowly recovers. As Frank Cheeryble courts Kate, Smike's condition worsens, and Nicholas takes him to Devonshire hoping to effect his recovery there.

(56) Ralph blames Nicholas for thwarting his scheme and vows revenge, but fortune has turned against him. Gride learns that his housekeeper, Peg Sliderskew, has absconded with the documents and papers relating to Madeline's property, and Ralph discovers that he has lost £10,000. He engages Squeers to recover Gride's papers, and he plans his revenge on Nicholas. (57) As Squeers is about to secure the documents from Peg Sliderskew, Noggs and Frank Cheeryble intercede and take the papers themselves.

(58) Smike is not cured by going to Devonshire. He continues to decline. During his last days, he is alarmed by seeing the man who left him as a child many years before at Squeers's school, and just before he dies he confesses to Nicholas his hopeless love for Kate.

Parts 19, 20 (October 1839)

(59) Ralph's schemes unravel and are exposed. Squeers, his factotum, is imprisoned, and his cohorts—the Snawleys and Gride—turn him away. In addition to this, the Cheerybles, aided by Noggs, are closing in on a truth unknown even to Ralph. (60) Summoned to the Cheerybles', Ralph is confronted by a former clerk, Brooker, who reveals that Smike was Ralph's son from a clandestine marriage. In revenge for maltreatment, Brooker had secretly left the child at Dotheboys Hall after telling Ralph that the boy had died.

(61) Meanwhile, Nicholas returns from Devonshire. He has admitted to Kate his love for Madeline, and she has admitted to him her love for Frank, but they have agreed that they are not the social equals of those they love and have resolved not to marry. (62) Haunted by grief and remorse, Ralph wanders the streets, slowly making his way back to his house in Golden Square. There, in the attic, he hangs himself. (63) The Cheeryble brothers bless the unions of Frank and Kate, Nicholas and Madeline, and Tim Linkinwater and Miss La Creevy. (64) When Nicholas carries the news to Yorkshire that Squeers has been sentenced to transportation, the boys at Dotheboys riot and rebel, and the school is disbanded. (65) The good are rewarded, the bad punished, and the firm of Cheeryble and Nickleby continues into the next generation.

COMMENTARY

Although *Nickleby* is Dickens's third novel, it is, in many ways, still an apprentice work in which he is experimenting with the novel form and seeking his own place in the tradition he inherited. An exuberant story, filled with incident and invention and told with energy, *Nickleby* is Dickens's first attempt at a novel with a young man as its hero, a story that he repeated with variations in many of the later works, especially in *Chuzzlewit, Copperfield, Expectations,* and *Mutual Friend.*

The early years of Dickens's writing career were full of intense activity and experimentation. He often had several projects going at the same time and would begin a new novel while he was still at work on the old one. *Pickwick* and *Twist* overlapped for nine months in 1837, and *Twist* overlapped for nine months with *Nickleby* in 1838. When he began work on *Nickleby* in February 1838, Dickens was also finishing *Sketches of Young Gentlemen* and editing *Memoirs of Grimaldi* and the monthly magazine BENTLEY'S MISCELLANY. With so many irons in the fire, he had trouble meeting his deadline on the 15th of the month for each installment of the novel, and he had no time to plan the whole story beforehand. Interpolated tales like "The Five Sisters of York" in the second number suggest that Dickens may have filled out the monthly part with a previously written story, and the desultory progress of the whole novel suggests that Dickens improvised the story as he wrote it.

Dickens's early novels can be seen, in part, as interpretations of his childhood reading: *Pickwick* of *Don Quixote, Twist* of WILLIAM HOGARTH's Progresses, and *Nickleby* of TOBIAS GEORGE SMOLLETT's picaresque tales. *Nickleby*'s alliterative title recalls *Roderick Random* and *Peregrine Pickle,* and its story of a young man seeking his place in the world recalls the similar journeys of Smollett's heroes. Roderick, Peregrine, and Nicholas are externally defined, physical heroes who gain their places in the world by conquest. Nicholas's fights with Squeers and Hawk recall the two-fisted assertiveness of Smollet's picaros. Yet even though he is physically assertive, Nicholas, also like Smollett's heroes, is more acted upon than acting. His uncle, Crummles, and the Cheeryble Brothers do more to determine the course of his life than he does himself.

The improvisatory character of the novel is evident from the beginning. The first chapter sets up the PICARESQUE situation when the young Nicholas is left on the edge of adulthood, fatherless and without financial resources, and must fend for himself. The second chapter satirizes parliamentary meetings and business speculation in its account of the United Metropolitan Improved Hot Muffin and Crumpet Baking and Punctual Delivery Company, but it adds nothing to the story of Nicholas and Kate. They return in the final chapters of the first number, which introduce the attack on YORKSHIRE SCHOOLS as Nicholas is employed by Squeers as an assistant master for Dotheboys Hall. From its first number, the novel has the character of a miscellany, mixing the picaresque with satire and social reform.

Dickens's initial idea for the novel was to attack Yorkshire schools in the way he had attacked the POOR LAW and workhouses in *Twist.* At the beginning of February 1838, he and HABLOT KNIGHT BROWNE went to visit some of the infamous schools where unwanted children were banished by uncaring parents. Using "a plausible letter to an old Yorkshire attorney from another attorney in town, telling him how a friend had been left a widow, and wanted to place her boys at a Yorkshire school in hopes of thawing the frozen compassion of her relations," Dickens interviewed an attorney who advised him to tell the widow not to send her son to Yorkshire. His visits to the schools confirmed the advice, particularly in the case of Bowes Academy, which was run by WILLIAM SHAW. Shaw, who had been prosecuted for mistreating his students, has often been identified as the original of Squeers, but Dickens claimed that his schoolmaster was "the representative of a class, and not of an individual. . . . Mr. Squeers and his school are faint and feeble pictures of an existing reality, purposely subdued and kept down lest they should be deemed impossible."

The chapters on Dotheboys Hall addressed a specific social grievance, and Dickens, in his 1848 preface to the novel, took some credit for the decline in the number of Yorkshire schools in the 1840s. But Dotheboys Hall also represented broader social concerns. It extended Dickens's interest in children begun with his exposé of the mistreated children in the workhouses and baby farms in *Twist*. While he was writing *Nickleby*, the mistreatment of children in the factories of northern England was a hotly debated issue. Pamphleteers and novelists like Mrs. Trollope in *Michael Armstrong* (1840) described the maimed and deformed children who worked on the cotton machines. Dickens's description of the physical infirmities suffered by the inmates at Dotheboys Hall links them with the controversial factory children:

> Pale and haggard faces, lank and bony figures, children with the countenances of old men, deformities with irons upon their limbs, boys of stunted growth, and others whose long meagre legs would hardly bear their stooping bodies, all crowded on the view together; there were the bleared eye, the hare-lip, the crooked foot, and every ugliness or distortion that told of unnatural aversion conceived by parents for their offspring. (8)

The implicit connection between the factory children and the students at Dotheboys Hall extends the specific abuses in the schools to the mistreatment of children generally in Victorian England. The neglectful parents who abandoned their illegitimate or unwanted sons to Squeers's cruelties were representative of a society that provided no schools for the young and allowed children to work for 14 hours a day in the mines and factories.

When Dickens used up his material on the Yorkshire schools, he had Nicholas attack Squeers and desert Dotheboys Hall. Then he took up Kate's parallel story of working in Madame Mantalini's millinery establishment. The factory children and the young women who worked as dressmakers and milliners would become the subjects of important Parliamentary investigations in the early 1840s, but in his treatment of Kate's story Dickens abandoned social reform and took up stage melodrama. He does not dwell on the ill health or the working conditions of the milliners. There is no equivalent of Smike at Madame Mantalini's. Instead he describes Kate as a victim of sexual exploitation. In the millinery showroom and in Ralph Nickleby's drawing room, she is not a case study for a parliamentary report but rather an embattled melodramatic heroine.

Appropriately, Nicholas follows her lead and soon finds himself a member of a traveling theater company. In the second quarter of the novel, Dickens comes closest to finding its thematic center, for *Nickleby* is, in many ways, a novel about life as theater. Handsome and active in defending the downtrodden Smike or his unprotected sister, Nicholas is a stage hero; he has little inner awareness and does not seem to grow as a result of his experiences. The villains, too, seem to be born to their theatrical roles as avaricious uncle (Ralph), aristocratic rake (Hawk), or miserly satyr (Gride). It may be this very theatricality that made the Royal Shakespeare Company's hugely successful 1980 dramatic adaptation so much more effective than the novel itself. In the stage melodrama we are not so aware of the lack of psychological depth as we are in reading the novel.

The Crummles episodes in Portsmouth act as a kind of play within the play, turning episodes from the rest of the novel into harmless theatrical illusion. In the theater the exploitation and oppression of children is not really exploitation, for the Infant Phenomenon is not really a child. The disagreements between the actors may lead to duels, but no one really dies in these altercations, unlike Sir Frederick Verisopht, who is killed by Sir Mulberry Hawk in the larger story. Even the theatrical marriage of Miss Petowker and Mr. Lillyvick proves to be a sham, an unreal interlude between his life as a water-rate collector and her affair with the half-pay captain. As playwright and leading man, Nicholas (as Mr. Johnson) has a chance to author his own life and play its leading role, but that too proves illusory, for his plays are merely plagiarisms of French plays. Back in London, his challenge to Hawk is a brief theatrical gesture. It does not change the direction of his life; that will be left to the Cheerybles.

While Nicholas is on stage in Portsmouth, Kate is attending the theater in London, where she is "assaulted" by Sir Mulberry Hawk, the rakish stage villain. As an attendant to Mrs. Wititterly, Kate cannot withdraw from her public role and retreat to a more private sphere. The conventions of melodrama demand that she be trapped in her vulnerable position until Nicholas returns, challenges the villainous Hawk, and rescues her.

The second half of the novel is less interesting than the first. Dotheboys Hall, the Mantalini millinery establishment, and Crummles's theatrical troupe, despite the staginess in their presentation, were all based on realities of early Victorian England. Dickens's visits to the Yorkshire schools and provincial theaters provided him with realistic observation to ground the melodrama in the story, but the heroes and villains of the second half have only a stage life. Nicholas's fight with Hawk and Frank Cheeryble's similar altercation at the Saracen's Head give both young heroes opportunities to defend the honor of the heroines. The machinations of the villains, from the seductions of the aristocratic rake and his accomplices Pyke and Pluck to the document shuffling of the old miser Gride, have a basis only in theater. Even though the Cheeryble twins were drawn from real people—the benevolent WILLIAM AND DANIEL GRANT of Manchester—their role in the novel is out of fairy tale or pantomime. They are, in GEORGE ORWELL's (1939) words, "two gruesome old Peter Pans" who take over the direction of the story and arrest any chance Nicholas has of becoming the hero of his own life.

The most interesting characters in the novel are grounded in reality. For all his ogreish exaggeration, Squeers was drawn from schoolmaster WILLIAM SHAW, who had a bad eye and had been sued by some of his clients for grossly mistreating their children. Crummles, typical of many theater people of the day, was inspired by T. D. Davenport, who advertised his daughter Jean as "the most celebrated Juvenile Actress of the day." Although the originals of the Kenwigs family have not been identified, Dickens's descriptions of them are grounded in the social realism that distinguished Boz's *Sketches*. And he based Mrs. Nickleby, probably the most memorable character in the book, on his mother. Garrulous and self-absorbed, she is identified in her speech by her wishful thinking, associative logic, and digressive style. Her delusions make her diverting and sometimes dangerous to her children but of no consequence in the plot. Her assessment of her lunatic neighbor is characteristic:

"There can be no doubt," said Mrs. Nickleby, "that he *is* a gentleman, and has the manners of a gentleman, and the appearance of a gentleman, although he does wear smalls and grey worsted stockings. That may be eccentricity, or he may be proud of his legs. I don't see why he shouldn't be. The Prince Regent was proud of his legs, and so was Daniel Lambert, who was also a fat man; *he* was proud of his legs. So was Miss Biffin: she was—no," added Mrs. Nickleby, correcting herself, "I think she had only toes, but the principle was the same." (37)

Though her incoherence is comic, it also serves to veil the class snobbery, self-absorption, and egotism that makes Mrs. Nickleby incapable of recognizing or responding to the needs of her children.

Mrs. Nickleby is only one of several irresponsible parents in the novel, a motif that will become an important theme in many of the later novels. In *Nickleby*, as in *Twist,* Dickens seems still to be searching for this theme. The most interesting development in this exploration in *Nickleby* emerges in the role of Smike as a shadowing DOUBLE to Nicholas. Many readers have noted the seeming contradiction at the heart of *Twist,* in which, on the one hand, Dickens describes the corrupting effect of a social system that leads children into deliquency and, on the other hand, presents Oliver as totally untouched by his environment. While Nicholas seems similarly unaffected by his weak father, dithering mother, and malevolent uncle, Smike shows the effects of childhood abuse and neglect in his maimed mind and body. As Nicholas's shadow and companion, Smike exaggerates and makes visible the inner wounds that Nicholas suppresses. Smike's uncertain parentage complements Nicholas's anonymity as Mr. Johnson; his unspoken love for Kate parallels Nicholas's reticence with Madeline Bray. Appropriately, Smike turns out to be Nicholas's cousin, and his death, in the Nickleby home country in Devonshire, frees Nicholas to marry Madeline and Kate to marry Frank. Smike's doubling relationship with Nicholas is one of Dickens's initial explorations of a technique that would become, in later works, an increasingly important way to give dramatic expression to the inner life of his characters.

Even Ralph Nickleby is touched by the transforming power of Smike. Although he is the malevolent stage villain through most of the novel, Ralph becomes a novelistic character with an inner life as he faces the revelation that he is Smike's father and that the maimed boy is also a maimed part of himself. Like Scrooge recognizing his connection to the maimed Tiny Tim or Dombey coming to understand his responsibility for his son's illness and death, Ralph retreats to the attic room of his consciousness, where he stores the suppressed memories of his past, the room where Smike spent his childhood. There, alone with his thoughts and memories, he is transformed from a stage villain into a self-conscious novelistic character before he takes his own life (62). Smike plays an important part in enabling Dickens to reach beyond the theatrical conventions that dominate the novel and to experiment with their novelistic possibilities.

CHARACTERS AND RELATED ENTRIES

Adams, Captain Lord Frederick Verisopht's second in the duel with Sir Mulberry Hawk (50).

Alice Youngest of the five sisters of York: "how beautiful was the youngest, a fair creature of sixteen!" With her four sisters she is working on an embroidery, which is represented in the "Five Sisters" window at York Minster (6).

Alphonse Mrs. Wititterly's little page boy, "so little indeed that his body would not hold, in ordinary array, the number of small buttons which are indispensable to a page's costume, and they were consequently obliged to be stuck on four abreast. . . . If ever an Alphonse carried plain Bill in his face and figure, that page was the boy" (21).

Belling, Master One of Squeers's pupils, "a diminutive boy, with his shoulders drawn up to his ears," who travels up to YORKSHIRE with Nicholas (4, 5).

Belvawney, Miss Member of Crummles's theatrical company, "who seldom aspired to speaking parts, and usually went on as a page in white silk

hose, to stand with one leg bent and contemplate the audience" (23).

Blockson, Mrs. Miss Knag's charwoman (18).

Bobster, Cecilia The girl that Newman Noggs confuses with Madeline Bray. He arranges a secret meeting between Nicholas and the girl, and the mistake is discovered just in time for Nicholas to avoid her tyrannical father (40, 51).

Bolder One of Squeers's pupils at Dotheboys Hall, "an unhealthy-looking boy, with warts all over his hands" (8).

Bonney Promoter of the United Metropolitan Improved Hot Muffin and Crumpet Baking and Punctual Delivery Company: "a pale gentleman in a violent hurry, who, with his hair standing up in great disorder all over his head, and a very narrow white cravat tied loosely round his throat, looked as if he had been knocked up in the night and had not dressed himself since" (2).

Boroughbridge, Yorkshire A town that Nicholas passes through on his return to London after beating Squeers. Smike joins him here (13).

Borum, Mrs. A patron of Crummles's theater company who subscribes for a box and brings her husband and some of her six children to see Crummles's productions (24).

Bow The rural district in east London where the Nicklebys live in the cottage rented to them by the Cheeryble brothers. The mad Gentleman in Smallclothes lives next door (35).

Bravassa, Miss Member of Crummles's theatrical company, "who had once had her likeness taken 'in character' by an engraver's apprentice, whereof impressions were hung up for sale in the pastrycook's window, and the green-grocer's, and at the circulating library, and the box-office" (23).

Bray, Madeline The girl Nicholas falls in love with when he first sees her at the employment office: "a young lady who could be scarcely eighteen, of very slight and delicate figure, but exquisitely shaped, who . . . disclosed a countenance of most uncommon beauty, although shadowed by a cloud of sadness" (16). Later, when she seeks help from the Cheerybles, they employ Nicholas to act as their agent in aiding the girl and her father (46). Nicholas discovers that Bray has agreed to marry his daughter to the old miser, Arthur Gride, in exchange for having his debts forgiven (47). Gride alone knows that Madeline is to inherit £12,000 from her grandfather. On the wedding day, Nicholas rescues Madeline and takes her away to his mother's home (54). They eventually marry (65). A DOUBLE to Kate Nickleby, Madeline is similarly burdened with the cares caused by an improvident father.

Bray, Walter   The embittered, petulant, and tyrannical father of Madeline: "He was scarce fifty, perhaps, but so emaciated as to appear older. . . . His looks were very haggard, and his limbs and body literally worn to the bone, but there was something of the old fire in the large sunken eye notwithstanding, and it seemed to kindle afresh as he struck a thick stick, with which he seemed to have supported himself in his seat, impatiently on the floor twice or thrice, and called his daughter by her name" (46). A debtor living within the rules of the KING'S BENCH PRISON, Bray agrees to marry his daughter to the old miser, Arthur Gride, who has learned that Madeline is heiress to a considerable fortune. In exchange for his daughter, Bray's debts to Ralph Nickleby will be forgiven, but he falls dead on the day of the wedding, saving his daughter from the unwanted marriage (54).

Broad Court   Off Bow Street, Covent Garden, the home of Mr. Snevellicci (30).

Brooker   Ralph Nickleby's former clerk who took Smike to Dotheboys Hall. He has returned from transportation abroad to try to blackmail his former employer with his knowledge that Smike is Ralph's son: "a spare, dark, withered man . . . with a stooping body and a very sinister face" (44).

Browdie, John   The hearty Yorkshireman who meets Nicholas at Fanny Squeers's tea party: "something over six feet high, with a face and body rather above the due proportion than below it. . . . Mr. Browdie was not a gentleman of great conversational powers" (9), though when he speaks he does so in a broad Yorkshire accent. He helps Nicholas escape Dotheboys Hall and gives him some money for his journey (13). On his wedding trip to London with his bride Matilda Price, he arranges Smike's escape from Squeers (39).

Browndock, Miss   Nicholas Nickleby's father's cousin's sister-in-law who, according to Mrs. Nickleby, "was taken into partnership by a lady that kept a school at Hammersmith, and made her fortune in no time at all; I forget, by the bye, whether that Miss Browndock was the same lady that got the ten thousand pounds prize in the lottery, but I think she was; indeed, now I come to think of it, I am sure she was" (17).

Bulph   The pilot at whose house the Crummleses stay in PORTSMOUTH (23, 30).

Cadogan Place   Fashionable street in west London where the Wititterlys live, "the connecting link between the aristocratic pavements of Belgrave Square, and the barbarism of Chelsea" (41).

Carnaby Street   Near Oxford Circus, the street where the Kenwigses live.

Cheeryble, Charles and Edwin (Ned)   Twin brothers, wealthy and benevolent merchants who hire Nicholas Nickleby and become his benefactor. Charles, "a sturdy old fellow in a broad-skirted coat, . . . with . . . a pleasant smile playing about his mouth, and . . . a comical expression of mingled slyness, simplicity, kind-heartedness, and good-humour, lighting up his jolly old face" is matched by his brother whose "slight additional shade of clumsiness in his gait and stature formed the only perceptible difference between them" (35). They are benefactors who seek out people who need their help, among them Madeline Bray. It is through working for them that Nicholas meets Madeline

(46). When they retire, they leave the business to Nicholas and their nephew Frank.

Although the Cheeryble brothers are so impossibly benevolent as to seem unbelievable, Dickens based them on real people, WILLIAM AND DANIEL GRANT, calico merchants in MANCHESTER whom Dickens met in 1838. He commented on them in the preface to the novel: "Those who take an interest in this tale will be glad to learn that the Brothers Cheeryble live; that their liberal charity, their singleness of heart, their noble nature, and their unbounded benevolence, are no creations of the Author's brain; but are prompting every day (and oftenest by stealth) some munificent and generous deed in that town of which they are the pride and honour."

Cheeryble, Frank Nephew of the Cheeryble brothers, a "sprightly, good-humoured, pleasant fellow" who reminds Nicholas of his uncles (43). He and Newman Noggs foil Squeers's plot to secure the papers relating to Madeline Bray's inheritance (57). He marries Kate Nickleby (63) and becomes Nicholas's business partner after they inherit the Cheeryble's business.

Chowser, Colonel One of Ralph Nickleby's questionable dinner guests: "Colonel Chowser of the Militia—and the race-courses" (19).

Clark, Mrs. Potential employer to whom the employment agency sends Madeline Bray (16).

Cobbey Pupil at Dotheboys Hall who receives 18 shillings in pocket money from his sister that is appropriated by Mrs. Squeers (8).

Cropley, Miss Friend of Mrs. Nickleby at Exeter (33).

Crowl Newman Noggs's neighboring garret-dweller, "a hard-featured square-faced man, elderly and shabby, . . . [who] wore a wig of short, coarse, red hair, which he took off with his hat, and hung upon a nail" (14).

Crown Inn, Golden Square Newman Noggs's favorite inn (7).

Crummles, Charles and Percy Vincent Crummles's two sons, "a couple of boys, one of them very tall and the other very short, both dressed as sailors—or at least as theatrical sailors, with belts, buckles, pigtails, and pistols complete—fighting what is called in play-bills a terrific combat with two of those short broad-swords with basket hilts which are commonly used at our minor theatres" (22).

Crummles, Mrs. Vincent's wife and partner in the theatrical business: "a stout, portly female, apparently between forty and fifty, in a tarnished silk cloak, with her bonnet dangling by the strings in her hand, and her hair (of which she had a great quantity) braided in a large festoon over each temple" (23).

Crummles, Ninetta ("The Infant Phenomenon") Vincent Crummles's daughter, known on the stage as "The Infant Phenomenon." He claims that she is 10 years old, "though of short stature, [she] had a comparatively aged countenance, and had moreover been precisely the same age—not perhaps to the full extent of the memory of the oldest inhabitant, but certainly for five good years. But she had been kept up late every night, and put upon an unlimited allowance of gin-and-water from infancy, to prevent her growing tall, and perhaps this system of training had produced in the infant phenomenon these additional phenomena" (23). Ninetta was probably based on JEAN DAVENPORT (1829–1903), daughter of T. D. Davenport.

Crummles, Vincent Manager of a touring repertory company whom Nicholas meets on the road to PORTSMOUTH, a large man with "a very full under-lip, a hoarse voice, as though he were in the habit of shouting very much, and very short black hair, shaved off nearly to the crown of his head—to admit . . . of his more easily wearing character wigs of any shape or pattern" (22). Known as "bricks and mortar" by the actors in his company because "his style of acting is rather in the heavy and ponderous way" (23), Crummles acts leading roles in many of the company's productions. He hires Nicholas to play Romeo and to write scripts for the company and engages Smike to play the apothecary in *Romeo* *and Juliet.* He uses Nicholas's departure as a pretext for special farewell performances, and he bids Nicholas a public farewell as he boards the coach for London with a series of stage embraces (30). Later Nicholas bids farewell to the Crummleses as the family leaves for America (48). The original for Crummles was the actor-manager T. D. Davenport (1792–1851).

Although Nicholas's adventures in the theater are sometimes said to have little thematic relevance to the novel and are more a reflection of Dickens's lifelong fascination with the theater, others have suggested that performance as a way of self-creation is the central issue in the novel. J. HILLIS MILLER (1958), for example, characterizes "the central action of *Nicholas Nickleby*" as theatrical, "the elaborate performance of a cheap melodrama, complete with sneering villains, insulted virginity, and a courageous young hero who appears in the nick of time." LYN PYKETT (2002) suggests that "*Nickleby* is about performance: the performance of class, gender, familial and emotional roles. . . . The characters in *Nicholas Nickleby* form their identity or become themselves by impersonating real or imaginary models of those they wish to be."

Curdle, Mr. A literary critic in PORTSMOUTH who has "written a pamphlet of sixty-four pages, post octavo, on the character of the Nurse's deceased husband in Romeo and Juliet, [and who] . . . likewise proved, that by altering the received mode of punctuation, any one of Shakespeare's plays could be made quite different, and the sense completely changed" (24).

Curdle, Mrs. Curdle's wife, "supposed, by those who were best informed on such points, to possess quite the London taste in matters relating to literature and the drama" (24). The Curdles subscribe to Miss Snevellicci's "bespeak" performance.

Cutler, Mr. and Mrs. Friends of the Kenwigses who attend their anniversary party (14).

David Cheeryble's butler, "of apoplectic appearance, and with very short legs" (37).

Dibabs, Jane Acquaintance of Mrs. Nickleby who married a man much older than herself. Mrs. Nickleby uses her example to justify the appropriateness of Madeline Bray's marrying Gride (55).

Dick (1) Guard on the coach that takes Nicholas to YORKSHIRE (5).

Dick (2) Tim Linkinwater's blind blackbird: "there was not a bird of such methodical and business-like habits in all the world, as the blind blackbird, who dreamed and dozed away his days in a large snug cage, and had lost his voice, from old age, years before Tim first bought him" (37).

Dorker Pupil at Dotheboys Hall who dies in spite of Squeers's last-minute attempts to save him (4).

Dotheboys Hall School run by Squeers in the YORKSHIRE village of Dotheboys in "a long cold-looking house, one story high, with a few straggling outbuildings behind, and a barn and stable adjoining" (7). Like the notorious YORKSHIRE SCHOOLS that Dickens was attacking, Dotheboys takes unwanted and illegitimate children, keeping them far away from their families in the south of England. Dotheboys was based on William Shaw's Bowes Academy at GRETA BRIDGE, which Dickens visited in 1838.

Dowdles, Misses "The most accomplished, elegant, fascinating creatures," according to Mrs. Nickleby, at the school Kate attended in Devon (26).

Eel-Pie Island An island in the Thames River that Morleena Kenwigs proposes to visit (52).

Exeter The town in Devon where Mrs. Wititterly danced at the election ball with the baronet's nephew (21).

"Five Sisters of York, The" Interpolated tale told by a grey-haired passenger on the London-to-York coach that explains the origins of the famous stained-glass windows in York Minster. During the reign of Henry IV, the five sisters are reprimanded by a monk for spending their time frivolously embroidering. He urges them to enter a convent, but they refuse. Gradually they leave the garden of their youthful happiness to marry. Their husbands, knights and courtiers, die, and then their youngest sister, Alice, the most beautiful and innocent of them all, also dies. The monk repeats his advice, but they again refuse. As they die, their embroideries are made into stained glass that becomes the window in the cathedral known as the Five Sisters (6).

Fluggers   Member of Crummles's theatrical company who does the "heavy business" (30).

Folair, Augustus (Tommy)   Pantomimist and dancer with Crummles's theatrical company, "a shabby gentleman in an old pair of buff slippers" (23). He "delights in mischief" (29) and tries to instigate a feud between Lenville and Nicholas.

Gallanbile   Sabbatarian Member of Parliament who advertises for a cook: "Fifteen guineas, tea and sugar, and servants allowed to see male cousins, if godly. . . . No victuals whatever, cooked on the Lord's Day, with the exception of Dinner for Mr. and Mrs. Gallanbile, which, being a work of piety and necessity, is exempted" (16).

Gazingi, Miss   Member of Crummles's theatrical company, "with an imitation ermine boa tied in a loose knot round her neck, flogging Mr. Crummles, junior, with both ends in fun" (23).

Gentleman in Small-clothes, the   The madman who lives with his keeper next door to Mrs. Nickleby at Bow. He courts her by throwing vegetables over the garden wall (37) and makes a dramatic entrance into her cottage by coming down the chimney. But when he sees Miss La Creevy, he deserts Mrs. Nickleby for the artist (49).

George   "A young man . . . bearing the reputation of a rake" present at the Kenwigses' dinner party (14).

George and New Inn   The inn at GRETA BRIDGE, YORKSHIRE, where the coach leaves

Squeers and his party when they arrive from London (*Nickleby,* 6).

Glavormelly, Mr.   A deceased actor and friend of Mr. Snevellicci (30).

Graymarsh   Pupil at Dotheboys Hall whose aunt thinks Squeers "too good for this world" (8).

Gregsbury   A member of Parliament, "a tough, burly, thick-headed gentleman, with a loud voice [and] a pompous manner," who offers Nicholas a position as his secretary, which Nicholas turns down (16).

Gride, Arthur   An old miser and moneylender who is involved with Ralph Nickleby in underhanded schemes, "a little old man of about seventy or seventy-five years of age, of a very lean figure, much bent and slightly twisted. . . . The whole expression of the face was concentrated in a wrinkled leer, compounded of cunning, lecherousness, slyness and avarice" (47). He has illegally obtained a document indicating that Madeline Bray will inherit £12,000 when she marries, and with Ralph's help, he gets Mr. Bray's consent to marry his daughter in return for paying off Bray's debts (47). But Bray dies on the wedding day, and Nicholas carries off the bride (54). Gride's housekeeper, Peg Sliderskew, steals the documents that will reveal his duplicity, but Gride is murdered by burglars before he can be called to account (65).

Grimble, Sir Thomas   An acquaintance of Mrs. Nickleby. She unrealistically speculates that Smike may have dined with this wealthy YORKSHIRE landowner while he was a pupil at Dotheboys Hall (35).

Grogzwig, Baron of   The title of the Baron von Koëldwethout in the interpolated tale told by the "merry-faced gentleman" on the London-to-York coach (6).

Grudden, Mrs.   Member of Crummles's theatrical company who "assisted Mrs. Crummles in her domestic affairs, and took money at the doors, and dressed the ladies, and swept the house, and held the prompt book when everybody else was on for the last scene, and acted any kind of part on any emergency without ever learning it, and was put down in the bills under any name or names whatever that occurred to Mr. Crummles as looking well in print" (23).

Ham House   This baroque mansion in Surrey across the Thames from Twickenham is the site of the duel between Sir Mulberry Hawk and Lord Frederick Verisopht that leaves the latter dead (50).

Hannah   Miss La Creevy's servant girl "with an uncommonly dirty face" (3).

Hawk, Sir Mulberry   A dissolute aristocrat, dandy, and gambler who lives by fleecing rich young men: "Sir Mulberry Hawk was remarkable for his tact in ruining, by himself and his creatures, young gentlemen of fortune—a genteel and elegant profession, of which he had undoubtedly gained the head" (19). While he and Ralph Nickleby are engaged in taking Lord Frederick Verisopht's money, he meets Kate Nickleby and determines to seduce her in spite of her disdain (19). Nicholas thwarts this scheme by beating Hawk with a whip handle and marking his face for life (32). Hawk kills Verisopht in a duel and then flees to France (50). After living many years abroad, Hawk returns to England where he dies in prison (65).

Hawkinses, the   A family in the VALE OF TAUNTON whom Mrs. Nickleby visited while she was in school.

Kenwigs, Lillyvick   The Kenwigses' infant son, named for the water-rate collector from whom they hope to inherit.

Kenwigs, Morleena   The Kenwigses' eldest daughter. Her uncommon Christian name "was invented by Mrs. Kenwigs previous to her first laying-in, for the special distinction of her eldest child" (14).

Kenwigs, Mr.   Husband and father of the family that occupies the first floor in the building where

Newman Noggs lodges: "a turner in ivory, who was looked upon as a person of some consideration on the premises, inasmuch as he occupied the whole of the first floor, comprising a suite of two rooms" (14). He kowtows to Lillyvick, his wife's uncle, in expectation that the old man will leave money to the five Kenwigs children, and he is distressed when Lillyvick marries Miss Petowker.

Kenwigs, Mrs. Susan   Wife and mother of the family on the first floor of Noggs's lodging house, "quite a lady in her manners, and of a very genteel family, having an uncle who collected a water-rate; . . . so stately that you would have supposed she had a cook and housemaid at least, and nothing to do but order them about, she had a world of trouble with the preparations [for the anniversary party]; more indeed than she, being of a delicate and genteel constitution, could have sustained, had not the pride of housewifery upheld her" (14). Her aspirations for her children are evident in her groveling attendance on Lillyvick and her hiring Nicholas to give French lessons to her daughters. Dickens maintains sympathy for the desperately social-climbing Kenwigs family, Norrie Epstein (*The Friendly Dickens*, 1998) points out, by making them "beguiling rather than repellent [because] . . . they honestly don't see themselves as motivated by greed."

Knag, Miss   Madame Mantalini's forewoman, "a short, bustling, over-dressed female, . . . marvelously loquacious and marvelously deferential to Madame Mantalini" (17), who punctuates her conversation with "hems." At first she is friendly with Kate Nickleby, but then she becomes jealous when Kate displaces her in the eyes of customers (20, 21). After the Mantalinis' bankruptcy, she takes over the business (44).

Knag, Mortimer   Miss Knag's brother, the proprietor of a small circulating library near TOTTENHAM COURT ROAD (18): "a tall lank gentleman of solemn features, wearing spectacles, and garnished with much less hair than a gentleman bordering on forty or thereabouts usually boasts" (18). Disappointed in his romantic infatuation for Madame

Mantalini, according to his sister, he "took to scorning everything, and became a genius" (18), expressing his melancholy by writing novels.

Koëldwethout, Baron von, of Grogzwig Subject of the tale told by the merry-faced gentleman to his fellow passengers when the Yorkshire coach breaks down (6).

La Creevy, Miss A painter of miniatures, "a mincing young lady of fifty" (3), with whom the Nicklebys take lodgings when they first come to London. A bright and cheerful optimist, she idealizes the subjects of her miniature portraits, painting clerks, for example, in military uniforms. She stands by Kate in her troubles and eventually marries Tim Linkinwater (63). STEVEN MARCUS (1965) comments that through her "idealized portraits of depressed, lonely persons . . . [s]he understands that these people too have a despairing need to create themselves, to improvise some concrete image of their own aspirations, and her art serves these illusions of self-realization."

Lane, Miss Distracted governess tending the unruly Borum children (24).

Ledrook, Miss Member of Crummles's theatrical company, a special friend of Miss Snevellicci. She serves as a bridesmaid at Miss Petowker's wedding (25).

Lenville, Mrs. Thomas Lenville's wife, "in a very limp bonnet and veil" (23), is also a member of the theatrical company.

Lenville, Thomas Member of Crummles's theatrical company; "his age did not appear to exceed thirty, although many at first sight would have considered him much older, as his face was long and very pale, from the constant application of stage paints" (33). When Lenville's professional jealousy is aroused by Nicholas, Folair directs him to challenge Nicholas and threaten to "pull his nose" in retaliation (29). Nicholas knocks Lenville down and forces him to apologize publicly.

Lillyvick Mrs. Kenwigs's uncle, a collector of water rates with an inflated view of his own importance and his position; "a short old gentleman, in drabs and gaiters, with a face that might have been carved out of *lignum vitae*" (15). He imagines the world in terms inspired by the water service, and he manipulates the attentions of the Kenwigses, who are obsessed with the desire to inherit his money. Smitten by Miss Petowker, the actress, he follows her to PORTSMOUTH, where she is playing with Crummles's company, and marries her, much to the disappointment of the Kenwigses (25). After she abandons him for a half-pay captain, he returns to London, restoring the hopes of the Kenwigses that their children will inherit his money (52).

Linkinwater, Miss Tim's sister, "a chubby old lady" who attends the birthday party for her brother (37).

Linkinwater, Timothy "Fat, elderly, large-faced clerk, with silver spectacles and a powdered head" (35), who has loyally served the Cheeryble brothers for 44 years. Nicholas is hired to relieve him of some of his duties (35). He has a blind blackbird, Dick, that he keeps in a cage in the countinghouse. He befriends the Nicklebys and through them meets Miss LaCreevy, whom he eventually marries (65).

Lukin One of the suitors of Mrs. Nickleby's youth (41).

Lumbey, Dr. Doctor who delivers Mrs. Kenwigs's baby; "a stout bluff-looking gentleman, with no shirt-collar, to speak of, and a beard that had been growing since yesterday morning; for Doctor Lumbey was popular, and the neighbourhood was prolific; and there had been no less than three other knockers muffled, one after the other, within the last forty-eight hours" (36).

Mallowford, Lord Arthur Gride's former client who, on the day Gride first wore his bottle-green suit, burned to death in his bed, bringing Gride repayment of several loans to him. Gride thus considers the suit lucky and plans to wear it for his wedding (51).

Kenny Meadows's portrait of Mr. Mantalini from his set of extra illustrations, "Heads from Nicholas Nickleby" (1839).

Mantalini, Alfred Madame Mantalini's much younger husband, an idler and parasite, whose "name was originally Muntle. . . . [He] had married on his whiskers; upon which property he had previously subsisted, in a genteel manner, for some years" (10). He supports himself by flattering his vain wife and comparing her to the countess he gave up to marry her. But after his extravagance, gambling, and embezzling bankrupts the firm, his wife leaves him and he is imprisoned. He is last seen mangling for the laundress who pays to release him from DEBTORS' PRISON (64).

Mantalini, Madame Fashionable dressmaker whose indulgence of her ne'er-do-well younger husband Alfred gets her financially entangled with Ralph Nickleby, who induces her to hire Kate (10). Her husband's extravagance bankrupts the business (21), so Madame Mantalini, "a buxom person, handsomely dressed and rather good-looking, but much older than the gentleman in the Turkish

trousers, whom she had wedded some six months before" (10), finally immune to Alfred's blandishments, turns the business over to her assistant, Miss Knag (44). Madame Mantalini's millinery establishment, where Kate works long hours (9 A.M. to 9 P.M., plus frequent overtime), is Dickens's condemnation of the exploitation of young women in the dressmaking and millinery industries, a concern of his day.

Matthews Servant boy to Mr. Gregsbury, "looking as if he had slept underground from his infancy, as very likely he had" (16).

Mobbs Pupil at Dotheboys Hall who cannot eat fat (8).

Muntle Mr. Mantalini's real name.

Nickleby family Family at the center of the inheritance and identity plot of the novel. The two sons of Godfrey Nickleby, a Devonshire landholder and gentleman, inherit his property: Ralph, the elder son, takes his money and goes into business; Nicholas, who inherits the family farm, speculates with his inheritance and dies, leaving nothing for his wife and two children, Nicholas Jr. and Kate, "a . . . beautiful girl of about seventeen." Mrs. Nickleby and the two children appeal for help to Ralph, who grudgingly provides a house for Mrs. Nickleby, places Nicholas in a YORKSHIRE SCHOOL as an assistant master, and secures a position for Kate in a millinery establishment. Nicholas eventually foils his uncle's plots.

Nickleby, Kate Sister of Nicholas Jr., "a slight but very beautiful girl of about seventeen" (3), she is the pure and virtuous heroine of the story. Her uncle Ralph places her in Madame Mantalini's millinery establishment, where she arouses the jealousy of Miss Knag when she models hats for the customers and displaces Miss Knag in that role. She is also used by Ralph as a "hostess" at a dinner party where she is subjected to the unwanted advances of Sir Mulberry Hawk (19). After she leaves Madame Mantalini's, she secures humiliating employment as a companion to Mrs. Wititterly, who becomes jealous of Kate because of the attentions paid to her by Hawk. Nicholas then leaves his position with a traveling theatrical company, returns to London, confronts and wounds Hawk (32), and removes Kate from her position as companion to Mrs. Witterly. In the end, Kate marries Frank Cheeryble.

Nickleby, Mrs. Mother of Nicholas and Kate, "a well-meaning woman enough, but rather weak withal" (3). Although she loves her children, she is a distracted and garrulous woman who fails to appreciate the dangers her children face and always expects things to turn out for the best. She is therefore unable to see the potential pitfalls in Nicholas's position at Squeers's school or to protect Kate from the attentions of Hawk and Verisopht. Her naive belief in gentility and in the virtues of the class system, opposite to Ralph's cynical reduction of all relationships to selfish monetary ones, endangers her children and distorts her view of the world around her. She even imagines that the lunatic who throws vegetables to her over her garden wall is an eccentric but acceptable gentleman suitor (37).

Most of all, Mrs. Nickleby is characterized by her language, "one unbroken monotonous flow" (18) following an associative logic that strings past and present into a meandering discourse of digressions. Testifying to Miss Knag of Kate's intelligence, for example, she characteristically gets entangled in recollections of Kate's godfather, Mr. Watkins: "'Why, that Mr. Watkins, my dear,' said Mrs. Nickleby slowly, as if she were making a tremendous effort to recollect something of paramount importance; 'that Mr. Watkins—he wasn't any relation, Miss Knag will understand, to the Watkins who kept the Old Boar in the village; by the bye, I don't remember whether it was the Old Boar or the George the Fourth, but it was one of the two, I know, and it's much the same—that Mr. Watkins said, when you were only two years and a half old, that you were one of the most astonishing children he ever saw. He did indeed, Miss Knag, and he wasn't at all fond of children, and couldn't have had the slightest motive for doing it. I know it was he who said so, because I recollect, as well as if it was only yesterday, his borrowing twenty pounds of

her poor dear papa the very moment afterwards'" (18). One of Dickens's great comic characters, the voluble and garrulous Mrs. Nickleby mitigates some of the melodramatic excesses of the story and provides a foretaste of her comic successors Sarah Gamp (*Chuzzlewit*) and Flora Finching (*Dorrit*). She was loosely based on Dickens's mother.

Nickleby, Nicholas Titular hero of *Nickleby* whose youth and inexperience are contrasted with the worldly cynicism of his uncle Ralph, the villain of the novel:

> The face of the old man was stern, hard-featured, and forbidding; that of the young one, open, handsome, and ingenuous. The old man's eye was keen with the twinklings of avarice and cunning; the young man's bright with the light of intelligence and spirit. . . . However striking such a contrast as this may be to lookers-on, none ever feel it with half the keenness or acuteness of perception with which it strikes to the very soul of him whose inferiority it marks. It galled Ralph to the heart's core, and he hated Nicholas from that hour. (3)

Nicholas, anxious to prove himself to his uncle, accepts a position as an assistant master at Dotheboys Hall, but his good-hearted sympathy for the mistreated boys, especially for Smike, prompts him to beat Squeers, the headmaster, and he is forced to leave the school (13). As Nicholas walks back to London, he is joined by Smike, who becomes his companion on his further adventures. After a spell with Crummles's theatrical company in PORTSMOUTH, where Nicholas (as Mr. Johnson) is an actor and playwright, he returns to London to defend his sister Kate from the lecherous attentions of Sir Mulberry Hawk. He impetuously assaults Hawk and wounds him (32). Nicholas finds work in London as a clerk for the Cheeryble brothers, who befriend him and his family (35). They support him as he saves Smike, who turns out to be Ralph's illegitimate son (60), from the persecutions of Ralph and Squeers. The Cheerybles also introduce him to Madeline Bray, whom he eventually marries.

In his 1848 preface to the novel, Dickens wrote of Nicholas: "If Nicholas be not always found to be blameless or agreeable, he is not always intended to appear so. He is a young man of an impetuous temper and of little or no experience; and I saw no reason why such a hero should be lifted out of nature." Nicholas's flaws—impulsiveness, naivete, and a tendency to employ violent solutions to his problems—are those of a sympathetic young man, more forgivable than, for example, Martin Chuzzlewit's self-absorption. Unlike Martin, Nicholas usually errs while defending others.

Nickleby, Ralph   Nicholas's uncle, who takes an instant dislike to his nephew and plots against him: "Mr. Ralph Nickleby was not, strictly speaking, what you would call a merchant: neither was he a banker, nor an attorney, nor a special pleader, nor a notary. He was certainly not a tradesman, and still less could he lay any claim to the title of a professional gentleman; for it would have been impossible to mention any recognized profession to which he belonged" (2). He is, rather, a particularly cruel usurer who lives on GOLDEN SQUARE: "He wore a sprinkling of powder upon his head, as if to make himself look benevolent; but if that were his purpose, he would perhaps have done better to powder his countenance also, for there was something in its very wrinkles, and in his cold restless eye, which seemed to tell of cunning that would announce itself in spite of him" (2). Ralph banishes Nicholas by securing him an appointment as an assistant master at a YORKSHIRE SCHOOL (4). He places Kate in Madame Mantalini's Millinery business (17) and subjects her to the unwanted attentions of Sir Mulberry Hawk (19). After Nicholas foils his plots, rescues Kate, saves Smike from capture, and reveals that Smike is Ralph's illegitimate son (60), Ralph hangs himself in the attic of his house (62).

A precursor to the selfish Chuzzlewits and Scrooge, Ralph combines avarice with hatred and lacks the capacity to imagine others as different from himself. Thus he is incapable of growing in self-awareness as Chuzzlewit does or of converting as Scrooge does. His narrow, single-minded worldview inevitably leads to suicide when the forces that oppose him discover the secrets of his life. STEVEN MARCUS (1965) suggests that in Ralph, Dickens specifically condemns usury, a "profession"

traditionally outlawed by the Christian faith but approved in the puritanical value sustem that promoted work and prudence and attacked improvidence. JOHN BOWEN (2000) argues that Ralph more broadly represents "business" and "capitalism" in his reduction of all relationships to monetary ones.

Noggs, Newman   Ralph Nickleby's clerk, "a tall man of middle-age, with two goggle eyes whereof one was a fixture, a rubicund nose, a cadaverous face, and a suit of clothes . . . much the worse for wear, very much too small . . . [who] rubbed his hands slowly over each other: cracking the joints of his fingers, and squeezing them into all possible distortions" (2). From a well-to-do family in the north of England, Noggs has fallen into drink and debt and is forced to take on menial work. Remembering a kind loan from Nicholas's father, Noggs befriends Nicholas and acts as his "spy" into Ralph Nickleby's schemes. He warns Nicholas of the danger to Kate from Hawk (29) and provides information that enables the Cheerybles to expose Ralph. Noggs is said to be based on Newman Nott, whom Dickens met when he worked for ELLIS AND BLACKMORE.

Peltirogus, Horatio   Childhood playmate of Kate Nickleby, described by Mrs. Nickleby as a suitor for her daughter's hand (55).

Petowker, Henrietta   Minor actress and friend of the Kenwigses "able to sing and recite in a manner that brought the tears to Mrs. Kenwigs's eyes" (14). She joins Crummles's company; marries Mr. Lillyvick, the water-rate collector (25); and rules his life mercilessly before leaving him to run off with a half-pay captain (52).

Phoebe (Phib)   Fanny Squeers's maid, "a small servant girl with a hungry eye" (12).

Pitcher   A sickly pupil at Dotheboys Hall (7).

Pluck   One of Sir Mulberry Hawk's "toads in ordinary," "a gentleman with a flushed face and a flash air" (19). He and Pyke flatter Mrs. Nickleby into telling them Kate's whereabouts as part of Hawk's scheme to seduce Kate (27).

Price, Matilda ('Tilda) Lively Yorkshire miller's daughter who encourages Nicholas Nickleby to take a romantic interest in her friend Fanny Squeers (9). She marries John Browdie and brings her bridesmaid Fanny along on her wedding trip to London (39).

Pugstyles "Plump gentleman in a violent heat" who leads a deputation of constituents of Mr. Gregsbury, M.P., demanding that he resign (16).

Pupker, Sir Matthew, M.P. Chairman of the United Metropolitan Improved Hot Muffin and Crumpet Baking and Punctual Delivery Company (2).

Pyke A "sharp-faced" cohort of Pluck, one of Sir Mulberry Hawk's "toads in ordinary" (19).

Regent Street Fashionable street connecting Oxford Circus and Picadilly Circus, completed in 1820 following a design by John Nash. Lord Frederick Verisopht has a suite of apartments here (10).

Saracen's Head, Snow Hill Coaching inn next to St. Sepulchre's Church, "just at that particular part of Snow Hill where omnibus horses going eastward seriously think of falling down on purpose, and where horses in hackney cabriolets going westward not unfrequently fall by accident" (4). A terminal for coaches going north to Yorkshire, this inn serves as Squeers's London headquarters.

Scaley One of the bailiffs who takes possession of Madame Mantalini's establishment (21).

Simmonds, Miss One of Madame Mantalini's employees who apologizes to Kate for criticizing her black shawl before she realized that Kate was in mourning (17).

Sliderskew, Peg Arthur Gride's housekeeper, "a short thin weasen blear-eyed old woman, palsy-stricken and hideously ugly" (51). On the day Gride is to marry, Peg, resenting Gride's plan to dismiss her, steals the documents relating to Madeline Bray's inheritance (56); Ralph Nickleby hires Squeers to retrieve the papers from her, but his attempt to do so is foiled by Nicholas and Frank Cheeryble (59). Peg is sentenced to transportation for her crimes (65).

Smike Ralph Nickleby's son; unbeknownst to his father, who thinks him dead, Smike was left at Dotheboys Hall by Brooker. There Squeers employs him as a drudge, and Smike is maimed in both body and mind by his mistreatment. "Although he could not have been less than eighteen or nineteen years old, and was tall for that age, he wore a skeleton suit, such as is usually put upon very little boys. . . . Heaven knows how long he had been there, but he still wore the same linen which he had first taken down; for, round his neck, was a tattered child's frill, only half concealed by a coarse, man's neckerchief. He was lame; . . . and . . . so dispirited and hopeless, that Nicholas could hardly bear to watch him" (7). After Nicholas defends him from Squeers's abuse, Smike follows him to London (13). Together they travel to PORTSMOUTH and join Crummles's troupe, where Smike (as Digby) plays the apothecary in *Romeo and Juliet* (23, 25). After they return to London, Smike is captured by Squeers but rescued again by John Browdie (38, 39). He develops a hopeless love for Kate Nickleby and pines away his life, dying in Devonshire (58). After his death, Brooker informs Ralph that Smike was his son (61).

As cousins, Smike and Nicholas are among Dickens's earliest treatments of the DOUBLE. In his characterization of Nicholas as his "home," his love for Kate, and his challenge to Ralph, Smike articulates parts of Nicholas that are shadowy or suppressed. Both STEVEN MARCUS (1965) and JOHN BOWEN (2000) analyze these connections between Nicholas and Smike. Smike also has broader significance to the social themes of the novel, representing the abused children of early Victorian England who, denied education and proper sustenance, become "Ignorance" and "Want" in the vision of Christmas Present in *A Christmas Carol*. In his physical deformities, Smike is a precursor to Tiny Tim and calls up the images circulating at the time that *Nickleby* was published of abused factory children from mills hidden, like the schools, in Yorkshire and Lancashire.

Snawley   Sanctimonious hypocrite who places his two stepsons in Squeers's school; "a sleek, flat-nosed man, clad in sombre garments, and long black gaiters, and bearing in his countenance an expression of much mortification and sanctity" (4). He poses as Smike's father in Ralph Nickleby's scheme to recover the boy (45). Prompted by his shrewish wife, Snawley confesses his involvement in Ralph Nickleby's plot (59).

Snevellici, Miss   Daughter of the Snevellicis, the leading lady in Crummles's troupe, "who could do anything, from a medley dance to Lady Macbeth, and also always played some part in blue silk knee-smalls" (23). She is enamored with Nicholas, but he does not reciprocate her flirtatious attentions. Eventually she marries a tallow chandler (48).

Snevellici, Mr.   Miss Snevellici's father, dignified and addicted to drink, he plays "military visitors and the speechless noblemen" (23) in the troupe's productions and occasionally beats his wife.

Snevellici, Mrs.   Miss Snevellici's mother, "still a dancer, with a neat little figure and some remains of good looks" (30).

Snewkes   Friend to the Kenwigses who attends their anniversary party (14).

Snobb   Guest at Ralph Nickleby's dinner party (19).

Snuffim, Sir Tumley   Physician who attends Mrs. Wititterly. She is, according to her husband, his "favorite patient" (28).

Spigwiffin's Wharf   Fictional address along the Thames River in east London, between Billingsgate and the Custom House, where Ralph Nickleby provides a run-down house for Mrs. Nickleby and Kate (11).

Squeers, Fanny   Daughter of Wackford, "in her three-and-twentieth year. . . . She was not tall like her mother, but short like her father; from the former she inherited a voice of harsh quality, and from the latter a remarkable expression of the right eye,

something akin to having none at all" (9). She attempts to induce a romantic interest in Nicholas, but when he rebuffs her she becomes vindictive (12). She expresses her frustration by jealously quarreling with her friend Matilda Price, who has found a suitor in John Browdie, and by writing a letter to Ralph Nickleby cataloging Nicholas's transgressions (15), a letter, PETER ACKROYD (1990) points out, that has "with some justice been described as the funniest letter in English literature."

Although Fanny, as the desperate woman in search of a mate, is the butt of much of the humor in the Dotheboys Hall chapters, she does elicit some sympathy. Norrie Epstein (*The Friendly Dickens*, 1998) comments: "Her predicament is very moving. . . . Of course you care about her, that's why you laugh! You only laugh at someone you care about. I don't think Dickens is ever cruel without also being kind."

Squeers, Mrs.   Wackford's wife and partner in the administration of Dotheboys Hall: "a large raw-boned figure, . . . about half a head taller than Mr. Squeers" (7), who "waged war against the enemy [the boys] openly and fearlessly" (8). She is particularly feared by the boys for her administration of "brimstone and treacle," which she explains: "if they hadn't something or other in the way of medicine they'd be always ailing and giving a world of trouble, and partly because it spoils their appetites and comes cheaper than breakfast and dinner" (8). At the breakup of the school, the boys force Mrs. Squeers to swallow a spoonful of her own medicine (64).

Squeers, Wackford   Ogreish headmaster of Dotheboys Hall, "he had but one eye, and the popular prejudice runs in favour of two. The eye he had was unquestionably useful, but decidedly not ornamental: being of a greenish grey, and in shape resembling the fan-light of a street door. The blank side of his face was much wrinkled and puckered up, which gave him a very sinister appearance, especially when he smiled, at which times his expression bordered closely on the villainous. His hair was very flat and shiny, save at the end, where it was brushed stiffly up from a low protruding forehead, which assorted well with his harsh voice and coarse manner" (4). He views his pupils as "natural enemies" (8), appropriates their clothing and pocket money for his own uses, and assigns them to menial labor at the school. When Nicholas whips the schoolmaster to stop him from beating Smike (13), he is forced to leave the school. Squeers later comes to London and captures Smike (38), who he claims that he is Snawley's son. He is also employed by Ralph Nickleby to secure the papers that Peg Sliderskew has taken from Arthur Gride (57). In the end he is imprisoned and transported (65).

The Squeers family is one of several families in the novel that combine their domestic life with a business. Like the Mantalinis, the Crummleses, and the Cheerybles, the Squeers family is a business. Mrs. Squeers is an equal partner in running the school, Wackford Junior is groomed as a walking advertisement for it. The whole family contributes to the image of Squeers as what MICHAEL SLATER (1978) describes as "the schoolmaster of our nightmares" in "our national folklore." Squeers was based on WILLIAM SHAW of BOWES Academy in GRETA BRIDGE, who had been sued by some of his clients for mistreating and blinding their children.

Squeers, Master Wackford   Squeers's look-alike son, kept plump and well fed as an advertisement for the school. Squeers dresses the vindictive boy in clothes sent for the schoolboys, and young Wackford looks forward to the day when he can cane the boys himself. He helps his father capture Smike in London (42). After his father's downfall, the schoolboys immerse his head in a bowl of brimstone and treacle (64).

Swillenhousen, Baron and Baroness von   Parents of the Baroness von Koëldwethout in the interpolated tale of the Baron of Grogswig (6).

Thomas   Mortimer Knag's servant boy (18).

Threadneedle Street   Street in the City running from Mansion House to Bishopsgate, in which the Bank of England, "The Old Lady of Threadneedle Street," is located. The offices of the Cheerybles are located off this street (35).

Timberry, Snittle   Member of Crummles's theatrical troupe who chairs the farewell dinner for the Crummleses as they leave for AMERICA. He was especially adept at the "gymnastic performances" required by the writhings of a dying man (48).

Tix, Tom   Bailiff who, with Scaley, takes possession of Madame Mantalini's; "a little man in brown, very much the worse for wear, who brought with him a mingled fumigation of stale tobacco and fresh onions" (21).

Tomkins   Pupil at Dotheboys Hall who tells Squeers that Smike has run away (13).

Trimmers   Friend of the Cheeryble brothers who brings to their attention cases deserving of their aid (35, 61).

United Metropolitan Improved Hot Muffin and Crumpet Baking and Punctual Delivery Company   A company promoted by Mr. Bonney to corner the market in muffins and crumpets. Ralph Nickleby is one of its directors (2).

Verisopht, Lord Frederick   Foppish young aristocrat who "exhibited a suit of clothes of the most superlative cut, a pair of whiskers of similar quality, a moustache, a head of hair, and a young face" (19). He is a companion to Sir Mulberry Hawk who schemes to fleece him. He and Hawk both pursue Kate Nickleby, but when he threatens to interfere with Hawk's plan to seek revenge on Nicholas, whom he admires for his defense of Kate, the two men duel and Verisopht is killed (50).

Watkins   Kate Nickleby's godfather. Kate's father paid £50 bail for him, which he did not repay before he ran away to the United States (18).

Westwood   Hawk's second in the duel with Verisopht (50).

Wititterly, Henry   Mrs. Wititterly's husband, "an important gentleman of about eight-and-thirty, of rather plebian countenance and with a very light head of hair" (21). He is especially solicitous about his wife's health and her delicate constitution.

Wititterly, Julia The languid and insipid lady from Belgravia to whom Kate Nickleby becomes secretary and companion after leaving Madame Mantalini's: "The lady had an air of sweet insipidity, and a face of engaging paleness; there was a faded look about her, and about the furniture, and about the house altogether" (21). She is jealous of the attentions paid to Kate by Sir Mulberry Hawk and Sir Frederick Verisopht. Nicholas removes Kate from the house of Mrs. Wititterly after his fight with Hawk (33).

Wrymug, Mrs. Client of the employment agency that Nicolas consults who requires her servants to be "serious" and join the Little Bethel Congregation: "each female servant required to join the Little Bethel Congregation three times every Sunday—with a serious footman. If the cook is more serious than the footman, she will be expected to improve the footman; if the footman is more serious than the cook, he will be expected to improve the cook" (16).

ADAPTATIONS

Nickleby has been one of the most popular of Dickens's novels on the stage, partly because of Vincent Crummles and his theatrical troupe. The first adaptations, however, were produced so early in the novel's serial run that Crummles had not yet entered the story. EDWARD STIRLING's adaptation, which opened in November 1838, was modified over the following months to incorporate material from later parts of the novel as they appeared, and when the serial was completed, he produced another version, *The Fortunes of Smike, or, A Sequel to Nicholas Nickleby* (March 1840). H. Philip Bolton (*Dickens Dramatized*, 1987) counts twenty-five stage adaptations produced before the novel finished its serial run, including WILLIAM MONCRIEFF's *Nicholas Nickleby and Poor Smike; or, the Victim of the Yorkshire School* (1839). Moncrieff, who had annoyed Dickens with an earlier dramatization of *Pickwick*, was probably the model for the plagiarist that Nicholas meets in chapter 48 who has adapted 247 novels for the stage.

Nickleby has remained popular on the stage in the 20th century. Bolton (1987) documents a number of stage versions leading up to the Royal Shakespeare Company production in 1980. That eight-hour performance by an ensemble cast was based on a script by David Edgar developed collaboratively with the company. It was directed by TREVOR NUNN and John Caird, and the cast included David Trefall (Smike), Roger Rees (Nicholas), Edward Petherbridge (Noggs), and Susan Littler (Kate). Filmed for television in 1982, this celebrated production is available on videotape. Leon Rubin tells the story of the production in *The Nicholas Nickleby Story* (1981).

Three silent films were based on the novel: perhaps the earliest film adaptation of Dickens, a scene from Dotheboys Hall made by American Biograph in 1903; an Edison version of the Yorkshire school in 1910; and another adaptation by Thanhouser in 1912. Ealing Studios produced Alberto Cavalcanti's version in 1947, with a screenplay by John Dighton, and a cast including Sir Cedric Hardwicke (Ralph Nickleby), Bernard Miles (Noggs), and Stanley Holloway (Crummles). A recent film version (2002), directed by Douglas McGrath, included Christopher Plummer, Jim Broadbent, and Anne Hathaway in the cast. Three British television serials have appeared: Vincent Tilsey's 10-part adaptation in 1957, Hugh Leonard's 13-part serial in 1968, and Martyn Hesford's version in 2000. Saxon Lucas and D. Corr's "pop opera" *Smike* was broadcast on BBC-TV in 1973.

FURTHER READING

MICHAEL SLATER (1978), in the introduction to his facsimile edition of the novel, provides a comprehensive discussion of the composition and sources for the work, especially for Dotheboys Hall and Crummles's theatrical troupe. His introduction to the Penguin Edition of the novel (1978) discusses the novel critically and includes some excellent analyses of the major characters. Kathryn Chittick (*Dickens and the 1830s*, 1990) surveys the contemporary reception of the novel, generally more positive than later criticism of it. Describing *Nickleby* as "the most undisciplined of all [Dickens's] novels," JOHN LUCAS (1970) discusses the parts that will be developed in the characters and themes of later works. Challenging those who find no thematic unity in *Nickleby*, STEVEN MARCUS (1965) considers it a novel about prudence and imprudence, in which Nicholas, victimized by the imprudence of his father and the false prudence of his uncle, must seek an identity for himself. Bernard Bergonzi's essay on the novel ("*Nicholas Nickleby*," *Dickens and the Twentieth Century*, edited by John Gross and Gabriel Pearson, 1962) is especially good on the picaresque and theatrical elements in the novel. JOHN BOWEN (2000) offers an especially good analysis of the familial and economic relationships in the novel. Leon Rubin's (*The Nicholas Nickleby Story*, 1981) description of "the making of the historic Royal Shakespeare Company production" offers insights into the themes of the novel and its theatrical character along with a fascinating account of the highly successful theatrical production.

Old Curiosity Shop, The

Dickens's fourth novel, published weekly in *Master Humphrey's Clock* (April 25, 1840 to February 6, 1841), with illustrations by HABLOT KNIGHT BROWNE, GEORGE CATTERMOLE, DANIEL MACLISE, and SAMUEL WILLIAMS. Issued simultaneously in monthly numbers. Published in one volume by CHAPMAN & HALL, 1841. One of the most controversial of Dickens's novels, *Old Curiosity Shop* has been praised as one of his most moving works and vilified as morbidly sentimental. Using contrast as its organizing principle, the novel's formal structure pits the innocent and pure Nell against the carnal and corrupt Quilp. Dick Swiveller emerges as a kind of synthesis of these opposed forces, suggesting the possibilities for change and growth.

SYNOPSIS

Part 1 (April 25, 1840)

(1) One night while he is out walking, Master Humphrey meets a lost young girl. He guides her to her home, an old curiosity shop. There he reprimands the girl's grandfather for neglecting her, but the old man responds by affirming his love for the girl. As Master Humphrey leaves, the grandfather leaves too, disturbing Humphrey by his apparent neglect. Afterwards Humphrey is unable to forget the girl who "seemed to exist in a kind of allegory."

Part 2 (May 16, 1840)

(2) When he next visits the curiosity shop, Humphrey finds Nell's grandfather with his wastrel grandson Fred. Although Fred says he is there to see his sister Nell, he and his friend Dick Swiveller seem more interested in the old man's money. (3) When Nell arrives with the dwarf Quilp, she tells Fred that she loves him. The grandfather confesses to Humphrey his dream of riches for Nell.

Part 3 (May 23, 1840)

(4) At the Quilp house on Tower Hill, Mrs. Quilp and her mother Mrs. Jiniwin gather with a group of women to discuss the tyranny of men. When Quilp returns, he drives the women away and threatens his wife, advising her to have nothing to do with the women.

Part 4 (May 30, 1840)

(5) The next morning the tyrannical dwarf torments his wife and mother-in-law before crossing the river to his warehouse and wharf, where he torments the boy who works for him. Nell interrupts these recreations when she brings him a letter.

Part 5 (June 6, 1840)

(6) Quilp reads the letter but does not answer it. Instead, he asks Nell if she would like to be the second Mrs. Quilp and marry him when his present wife dies. She shrinks from him. As they leave, Quilp's boy is fighting with Kit Nubbles, the shopboy from the curiosity shop who is devoted to Nell. At Quilp's house, the dwarf eavesdrops as Nell tells Mrs. Quilp of her worries about Nell's grandfather, who has taken to staying out all night.

(7) As a way of getting to his grandfather's money, Fred Trent convinces Dick Swiveller to marry Nell. Swiveller plans to initiate the scheme by being cool to his current girlfriend, Sophy Wackles.

Part 6 (June 13, 1840)
(8) Meanwhile Sophy has decided to pressure Dick by making him jealous of her attentions to Cheggs, a market gardener. Dick makes an early departure from Sophy's party, leaving Sophy to Cheggs.

Part 7 (June 20, 1840)
(9) Worried about her grandfather's unhappiness, Nell urges him to leave with her, even if they only become wandering beggars. Quilp refuses to lend the old man any money and tells him that Kit Nubbles says he has been gambling away all he has. (10) The grandfather sends Nell to inform Kit that his services are no longer needed and that he never again is to come to the curiosity shop.

Part 8 (June 27, 1840)
(11) Grandfather falls ill. Meanwhile Quilp and his lawyer, Sampson Brass, take possession of the curiosity shop, and Quilp takes over Nell's room. Kit keeps watch in the street and offers Nell and her grandfather his house as a refuge. (12) When the old man has barely recovered, Quilp tells him to prepare to leave. Nell and her grandfather slip out of the house at night and set out on their wanderings.

Part 9 (July 4, 1840)
(13) When Quilp discovers that they are gone, he is angry. Swiveller too is disconcerted, his plan to marry Nell thwarted before it has begun. Quilp removes everything from the house; Kit takes Nell's bird. (14) Kit needs to work to help support his widowed mother and brother Jacob. He offers to hold the Garlands' horse while they are signing apprenticeship papers for their son Abel in the office of notary Witherden.

Part 10 (July 11, 1840)
(15) Nell and her grandfather go into the country-side. Her grandfather urges them on so they can get as far as possible from the city. (16) They stop at a country churchyard where they meet Tommy Codlin, proprietor of a traveling Punch and Judy show.

Part 11 (July 18, 1840)
(17) The next morning Nell meditates on those buried in the churchyard. Then she and her grandfather join Codlin and his partner Short, who are on their way to a race meeting. (18) The next evening they stop at the Jolly Sandboys Inn, where many traveling performers have gathered.

Part 12 (July 25, 1840)
(19) As they approach the race meeting, Nell gathers wild roses into nosegays to sell, but she worries that Codlin will betray them, so, at an opportune moment when he is engaged with his puppets, she and her grandfather slip away.

(20) Kit daily expects Nell to return, but after she has been gone a week, he accepts his mother's conclusion that they have escaped to a foreign country. He again minds the Garlands' horse while they are in Witherden's office.

Part 13 (August 1, 1840)
(21) The Garlands offer Kit £6 a year to be their servant. Quilp tries to discover Nell's whereabouts. After learning nothing from Kit, he plies Swiveller with liquor and learns of Dick's scheme to marry Nell. (22) Kit goes to Abel Cottage in Finchley to serve the Garlands.

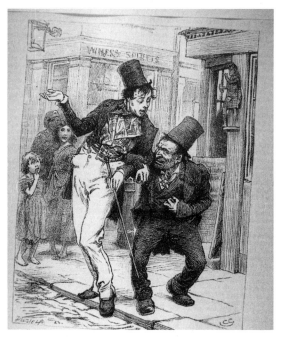

Green's rendering of Quilp and Dick Swiveller for the Household Edition of *The Old Curiosity Shop* (1876).

Part 14 (August 8, 1840)

(23) When Swiveller tells Fred Trent that he revealed their scheme to Quilp, Fred persuades Quilp to join them in their efforts to find Nell and her grandfather.

(24) Even though they are well away from the race meeting, Nell and her grandfather still fear being followed. They stop in an out-of-the-way village at the house of a poor schoolmaster who is troubled by the illness of his favorite pupil.

Part 15 (August 15, 1840)

(25) The next day the sick child dies. (26) Nell notes that the child left behind a loving grandparent who cared for him. Nell and her grandfather set out again and come upon a caravan whose hospitable owner, Mrs. Jarley, invites them to take tea and to travel with her.

Part 16 (August 22, 1840)

(27) The proprietor of a traveling waxworks, Mrs. Jarley hires Nell as a guide to the exhibition. In the town where they stop for the night, Nell is surprised to see Quilp in the street at midnight. He troubles her dreams. (28) The next morning, while the poet Slum writes verses to advertise the exhibition, Mrs. Jarley instructs Nell about each of the figures. Nell learns quickly.

Part 17 (August 29, 1840)

(29) Nell feels safe and happy working for the kind Mrs. Jarley. One day, while they are out walking, Nell and her grandfather are caught in a thunderstorm and take refuge at the Valiant Soldier Inn, where some gamblers are playing cards. The grandfather takes Nell's purse and joins the game. (30) He spends all the money in the purse, so Nell must take some money from a secret cache in the hem of her dress to pay for their night at the inn. In the middle of the night, the rest of her hidden money is taken by a figure who slips into her room in the dark. It is her grandfather.

Part 18 (September 5, 1840)

(31) The next morning Nell tells her grandfather that their money was taken during the night. He does not confess.

Mrs. Jarley sends Nell to Miss Monflathers's school to advertise the exhibition; the snobbish schoolmistress presents Nell to her pupils as a person debased by her association with the waxworks. (32) Meanwhile, her grandfather gambles away all the money that Nell makes; she fears that if she does not give him money he will steal from Mrs. Jarley.

Part 19 (September 12, 1840)

(33) In their law office in Bevis Marks, Sampson and Sally Brass discuss Quilp's proposal that they hire Dick Swiveller as a clerk. Sally opposes the idea, but Sampson says they must cater to such an important client as Quilp. Dick is hired and placed under the supervision of the intimidating Sally Brass. (34) When Miss Brass goes out, leaving Swiveller in charge of the office, a diminutive servant girl emerges from the cellar and asks Dick to show the apartment for rent on the first floor. Dick rents it on good terms to a single gentleman, who moves in immediately and goes to bed.

Part 20 (September 19, 1840)

(35) Brass is pleased with Dick's negotiation, but Sally thinks he should have bargained for even more. When the single gentleman sleeps for 26 hours straight, they bang on his door to rouse him. He takes Dick inside and tells him he does not want to be disturbed or spied on. He will not give his name. (36) All relations with the lodger are henceforth undertaken by Swiveller. Dick gains Sampson's respect and shares an affectionate camaraderie with Sally. He wonders about the little servant. One day he secretly follows Sally to the cellar, where he sees her mete out a meager lunch to the girl and then beat her.

Part 21 (September 26, 1840)

(37) The single gentleman takes an unusual interest in Punch and Judy shows and invites the puppeteers to perform in the street in front of the Brasses' house. When Codlin and Short perform for him, he learns of their connections with Nell and her grandfather and offers to pay them for any information they can give of Nell's whereabouts.

Part 22 (October 3, 1840)

(38) Kit Nubbles is called into Mr. Witherden's office. There the single gentleman inquires about Nell and her grandfather, telling Kit that he

intends only good for them and asking him to keep their meeting secret. Swiveller tries unsuccessfully to learn from Kit about his connection with the single gentleman. (39) Kit and Barbara, the Garlands' maid, celebrate the half-holiday when they receive their quarter's pay by taking their mothers to ASTLEY'S ROYAL EQUESTRIAN AMPHITHEATRE and then to an oyster supper.

Part 23 (October 10, 1840)

(40) The next morning Mr. Garland tells Kit that the single gentleman wants to hire him, pay him more than the Garlands do, and improve his prospects, but Kit refuses to go. So the Garlands lend him to the single gentleman, who needs Kit to go with him to fetch Nell and her grandfather. Kit, because of his falling-out with the grandfather, proposes that his mother go in his place. (41) When Kit finds his mother at the Little Bethel Chapel, Quilp is also there. Kit rushes her off to Witherden's office, where a coach is waiting to leave.

Part 24 (October 17, 1840)

(42) Meanwhile Nell has discovered that her grandfather plans to rob Mrs. Jarley's cash box. Telling him that she has had a troubling dream of his scheme, she gets him to slip away with her. (43) After walking through the night, they get a ride on a dirty canal boat, which takes them to an industrial city in the middle of the BLACK COUNTRY.

Part 25 (October 24, 1840)

(44) There they spend the night in the factory town, befriended by a laborer who gives them a place to sleep by the warmth of a factory furnace. As they leave, the laborer presses two pennies into Nell's hand. (45) Passing through the industrial wasteland, Nell becomes sick and feverish. They run out of food and money. Everywhere they look, they see distress and death.

Part 26 (October 31, 1840)

(46) Tired and sick, Nell collapses in the road just as they meet Mr. Marton, the poor schoolmaster with whom they stayed earlier. He carries her to an inn and orders a room, food, and care for her. The schoolmaster is on his way to a new post as clerk in a remote village to the north. After Nell recovers, she and her grandfather go there with him.

(47) Meanwhile, the single gentleman and Mrs. Nubbles arrive at their destination, the town where the waxworks are on exhibition. Mrs. Jarley and William, her driver, are being married. She tells them that Nell and her grandfather have disappeared and she has been unable to discover where they have gone.

Part 27 (November 7, 1840)

(48) Quilp has followed Mrs. Nubbles to the country. After learning of her destination, he took the night stage. On the stage back to London, he rides on the roof and torments Mrs. Nubbles, who is inside. When the coach arrives in London, Kit accuses him of being a "little monster." (49) At his home, Quilp discovers his wife and Mrs. Jiniwin holding a wake for him, assuming that he has drowned in the river. He surprises those who have gathered for the occasion by walking into the room "like a dismounted nightmare."

Part 28 (November 14, 1840)

(50) Quilp accuses his wife of being a "widow in anticipation," and he chooses to become a "bachelor in earnest" by moving down to the wharf. At Brass's office, he hypocritically commiserates with Swiveller, who laments Sophy's marriage to Cheggs as he eats a piece of their wedding cake. Quilp ruminates on when might be the appropriate time to disclose to the single gentleman Dick's scheme to marry Nell. (51) At tea, Quilp tells Sampson and Sally Brass that Kit is interfering with his plans and asks them to get the boy out of the way.

Part 29 (November 21, 1840)

(52) Meanwhile, the schoolmaster arrives at the rural village with Nell and her grandfather. He arranges a house for them and a job for Nell as keeper of the keys to the church. The bachelor, a patriarch of the community, introduces them to the people and schoolchildren of the village. (53) Nell meets the old sexton of the church, who is both gravedigger and gardener. She finds peace among the tombs in the old, moldering church.

Part 30 (November 28, 1840)

(54) The bachelor and the sexton tell Nell about the town, the church, and those buried in the churchyard. She grieves for those who die and are

forgotten, but the schoolmaster tells her that everyone lives in the memories of those who loved them. Nell decides to make tending graves one of her projects. (55) Everyone in the village is fond of her. The bachelor and the schoolmaster read to her in the evenings. Her grandfather, realizing how much she has done for him, devotes himself to her. The schoolchildren know and love her.

Part 31 (December 5, 1840)
(56) When Kit comes to deliver a letter to the single gentleman living above Sampson Brass's office, Brass surprises him with praise and gives him two half crowns.

(57) Left alone in the office, Dick Swiveller discovers the little servant peeking from behind the cellar door. He invites her in, orders a dinner, names her "the Marchioness," and recruits her as a cribbage partner.

Part 32 (December 12, 1840)
(58) As Dick and the Marchioness play cribbage, she describes the deprivation inflicted on her by the Brasses and tells him of their suspicion that he is not to be trusted. Later when Sally and Sampson complain that some money is missing from the office, Dick suspects the Marchioness. (59) Then Sampson secretly hides a £5 note in Kit's hat and arranges it so that Dick discovers it there. Kit is charged with theft, and Dick becomes the material witness.

Part 33 (December 19, 1840)
(60) Kit protests his innocence and asks to be taken to Witherden's office. On the way they meet a gloating and exultant Quilp. Though neither the Garlands nor Witherden believe the charge, the Brasses get Swiveller to corroborate the evidence against the boy, and Kit is taken to jail. (61) In his cell, Kit remembers his happy days with Nell and weeps. His mother, brother Jacob, and Barbara's mother tearfully visit him in prison. Swiveller sends him a mug of beer.

Part 34 (December 26, 1840)
(62) Sampson visits Quilp at his wharf and is worried that the dwarf, who is singing exultantly about Kit's imprisonment, is being indiscreet. Undaunted, Quilp orders Sampson to fire Swiveller. (63) A

clever prosecutor wins his case, and Kit is found guilty of the crime. Swiveller takes Mrs. Nubbles home after the trial, and when he returns to Bevis Marks, Brass pays him off and tells him not to return. That night Dick falls ill with a raging fever.

Part 35 (January 2, 1841)
(64) For three weeks Swiveller is delirious. When he regains consciousness, the Marchioness is caring for him. She has run away from the Brasses and has pawned all of Swiveller's clothes to buy medicine for him. She tells him that Kit has been sentenced to transportation and that she heard the Brasses, acting on instructions from Quilp, conspiring to frame the boy. (65) Swiveller has the Marchioness tell Abel Garland about the Brasses' plot.

Part 36 (January 9, 1841)
(66) The next morning, the Garlands, Witherden, and the single gentleman come to Swiveller's lodgings, bringing him food and people to care for him. They decide to try to get Sally Brass to testify against her fellow conspirators, but Sally is immovable. Sampson, however, agrees to testify against Quilp, and while he is writing his confession, Sally slips away. That evening Dick learns that he has inherited an annuity of £150 a year from his aunt.

Part 37 (January 16, 1841)
(67) At his wharf on a very foggy night, Quilp receives a letter of warning from Sally Brass. He curses Sampson, but he realizes that every "trouble and anxiety I have had of late times, springs from that old dotard and his darling child." Quilp plans his escape, but when he hears knocking at his gate, he panics, gets lost in the fog, falls into the river, and drowns.

(68) The Garlands hold a party to welcome Kit home from jail. His mother, his brother Jacob, Barbara's mother, and the single gentleman are all there. The pony Whisker nuzzles Kit, and Barbara kisses him. Mr. Garland tells him to prepare for a journey to the village where Nell and her grandfather have been found.

Part 38 (January 23, 1841)
(69) The next morning in the carriage, the single gentleman tells Mr. Garland a story, revealing that he is the estranged younger brother of Nell's grandfather. The two brothers had loved the same girl,

and he had gone abroad, giving up the girl to his brother. Now, after many years, he has returned to be reunited with him. (70) In the middle of a snowy night on the second day of their journey, they arrive at the village and rouse the sexton, who points the way to the ruin where Nell and her grandfather are living. Kit, carrying Nell's birdcage, goes to the house, drawn by a light in the window. As he knocks at the door, he hears a low moaning within.

Part 39 (January 30, 1841)

(71) Inside he finds Nell's grandfather huddled before the ashes of a dying fire. Nell is asleep in an adjoining room. Neither Kit nor the grandfather's younger brother can rouse the old man from his preoccupation with Nell. When they go into the little room, they discover that Nell is dead. (72) She has been dead two days. On the Sunday of the funeral, the townspeople get a small boy to take the grandfather into the country. Then they bury Nell in the church she loved. When the grandfather returns, he searches for her. Distracted and despairing, he takes his pack and staff and spends each day sitting by her grave waiting for her to return so they can resume their journey. One day they find him there dead.

Part 40 (February 6, 1841)

(73) Sampson Brass is sent to prison. Sally becomes a vagrant slum dweller. Mrs. Quilp, enriched with her husband's money, marries an out-pensioner. Abel Garland marries a bashful young lady, and the bachelor leaves the village and comes to London to live with Mr. Garland, his brother. Dick Swiveller renames the Marchioness Sophronia Sphynx, pays for her education, marries her, and moves to Hampstead. Fred Trent is drowned in Paris. The single gentleman seeks out all who were kind to Nell and his brother. Kit marries Barbara and tells his children, Barbara, Abel, and Dick, "the story of good Miss Nell who died."

COMMENTARY

The Old Curiosity Shop has been rated as both the best and the worst of Dickens's novels, but no matter the verdict the novel almost always receives critical consideration. It has provoked strong reac-

Cattermole's illustration of the most memorable event in *The Old Curiosity Shop*—the death of Little Nell.

tions from its first appearance to the present. The idea for the story came to Dickens when he was visiting WALTER SAVAGE LANDOR in March 1840; the old poet became one of young Nell's greatest admirers, suggesting that the "divine Nelly" was the best creation since Shakespeare's Cordelia. The story had its detractors as well; Edward Fitzgerald condemned "Boz's sham pathos," and politician Daniel O'Connell threw the book out of a train window in indignation when he realized that Nell was going to die. Most of Dickens's contemporaries, whether sophisticated readers or part of his broad popular audience, were deeply moved by the book. American readers are said to have gathered on the pier in New York as the ship arrived with the next installment to the serial to ask, "Is Little Nell dead?"

Many later critics have been less kind. Oscar Wilde is said to have quipped, "One must have a heart of stone to read the death of Little Nell without laughing," and Aldous Huxley chose Little Nell as a prime example of "vulgarity in literature"; her suffering, he claimed, lacked a context to give it significance. As a result it became merely bathetic SENTIMENTALITY. Although many contemporary critics continue to condemn the novel as overwritten and sentimental, others find significant ALLEGORY and a probing critique of Victorian culture in

Nell's story. There is still no consensus about the quality or significance of the book.

Dickens began *Curiosity Shop* as a short story to be completed in six chapters, but as he worked with the idea, it called for more expansive treatment. At the time, he was seeking a way to give more continuity to *Master Humphrey's Clock,* for its miscellaneous and desultory character was turning away readers. As the story grew into a novel, Dickens knew that he had discovered the means to sustain reader engagement with his magazine. He found the weekly deadlines and the shorter installments in the first of his weekly serials much more confining than the longer monthly parts in the earlier novels. After he got a feel for the weekly format and moved into the PICARESQUE journey narrative, the novel almost wrote itself. The only real difficulty Dickens encountered was telling the death of Little Nell.

JOHN FORSTER takes credit for suggesting to Dickens, when he was about halfway through the novel, that Little Nell should die, but the idea seems present in the text from the start, as the paired illustrations by SAMUEL WILLIAMS of the sleeping Nell and by GEORGE CATTERMOLE of the dead Nell from the beginning and the end suggest. Dickens clearly improvised much of the novel, and even if he had not consciously worked out the plot from the beginning, he had a least a subconscious awareness of the morbid logic at the heart of his story. Nell's death is foreshadowed throughout. Yet when he came to the final scenes, his grief for MARY HOGARTH, who had died three years earlier, made the writing difficult and painful. "It is very painful to me," he wrote to Forster, "that I really cannot express my sorrow. Old wounds bleed afresh when I think of this sad story." Yet Dickens, like many of his readers, sought the painful indulgence. As he was writing about Nell's death, he refused all invitations to social engagements for fear of "disturbing the state I am trying to get into." Although he grieved Mary's memory, his letters reveal that he was animated and lively at the same time.

The idea of an innocent young girl surrounded by old curiosities and old men immediately established the principle of contrast that pervades the novel. Youth and age, innocence and experience,

good and evil, beauty and ugliness, passivity and violence, female and male are just a few of the polarities that are implicit from the opening scene. By the time he finished the story, Dickens realized that this principle of contrast was also the basis of allegory. A passage added to the opening chapter when the novel was published as a single volume in 1841 comments: "As it was, she seemed to exist in a kind of allegory; and having these shapes about her, claimed my interest so strongly, that . . . I could not dismiss her from my recollection, do what I would" (1). At several points later in the story, the narrator refers to Bunyan's *Pilgrim's Progress,* and some episodes on Nell's journey recall scenes from that well-known allegory.

Even though Nell is usually accepted as an allegorical rather than a realisitic character, she is nonetheless often dismissed as sentimental, a character for whom Dickens attempted to generate sympathy in excess of the facts of her situation. Certainly the narrator's clumsy attempts to heighten the effect of the narrative by preaching to the reader, as in his homily on sleep and death in chapter 12, often have an effect opposite the one intended. But Dickens also shows considerable restraint in dealing with his highly charged subject matter. Nell's death, for example, occurs "offstage";

Worth's illustration of Nell and her grandfather for the American Household Edition (1872–73) depicts the pair as pilgrims in the allegorical tradition of Bunyan's *Pilgrim's Progress.*

Dickens does not belabor the event itself. The modern reader must also remember the context in which the novel was produced. Victorian children, especially those who worked in mines and factories or scavenged with the street arabs of London, were endangered by industrialization and urbanization in ways that have been corrected by the social legislation of the last century and a half. The facts of Victorian life made many children endangered species.

The novel does not attempt to treat these perils realistically. Even the scenes in the industrial BLACK COUNTRY are presented as surreal nightmare. The novel has more in common with FAIRY TALES, melodrama, pastoral, allegory, and such popular forms as PUNCH AND JUDY shows than with journalistic coverage or official reports. The young child leading the old man out of the corrupt city into the peacefulness of the country is an archetypal image, but it does not describe a sociological reality of the time. It articulates the ideal of a pastoral quest.

The simple journey plot is grounded in the opposition between city and country. The city—man-made and materialistic, corrupted by money, crowded and dangerous—threatens to draw innocence into its destructive vortex. By escaping to the peaceful countryside, Nell hopes to save her grandfather from destruction at the gambling table and to preserve her own innocence. But the problem is not defined by this simple dichotomy. When Quilp pursues them or when they fall in with companions like Codlin and Short who threaten to expose them, the dangers of the city reach into the country. Also, the countryside—a place of graveyards, dying schoolchildren, moldering churches—achieves peacefulness at the expense of vitality. Rural villages are populated by old people on the edge of death; vitality and energy reside in the cities.

The dream allegory is dialectically structured around three groups of characters. Nell, the novel's thesis, is supported in her virtue by the Garland and Nubbles familes. She is characterized by contrast to the old curiosities that surround her. From her first appearance lost on the streets of London, she is "little," an adjective used five times on the first page as she is introduced into the story. The curiosities around her include the old men—Master Humphrey and her grandfather—as well as the antique objects in the shop. She is solitary, "the only pure, fresh, youthful object in the throng" (1). Isolated amid the darkness and corruption of the city, Nell is abandoned by Grandfather and forced to plan her own retreat from Quilp's aggression.

The threat to Nell's innocence is not only external. As a girl of 13, Nell is on the edge of adulthood; her emerging sexuality also compromises her innocence. She responds to the threat of sexual maturation by retreat and denial. Withdrawing into her bower in the curiosity shop, she becomes, while sleeping, a prophetic image of the dead child at the end of the novel. She runs from Quilp, from her grandfather's weakness, and from real and imagined threats of disclosure, and she denies herself comfort and food to provide for her grandfather. Her anorexic withdrawal is a gradual suicide to preserve her innocence and virtue. She is devoted to death. On her journey she seeks out graveyards, identifies with the schoolmaster's dying pupil, and becomes a guide to a collection of corpselike waxwork figures; she is "a wax-work child" herself, as Miss Monflathers describes her (31). Nell is a childish, fairy-tale version of Richardson's Clarissa.

Yet for all her weakness and passivity, Nell also has strength. On the journey she is a parent to the old man, sustaining and providing for the two of them. The narrator ascribes her endurance to her virtue: "Nature often enshrines gallant and noble hearts in weak bosoms—oftenest, God bless her, in female breasts—and when the child, casting her tearful eyes upon the old man, remembered how weak he was, and how destitute and helpless he would be if she failed him, her heart swelled within her, and animated her with new strength and fortitude" (24). The journey stresses Nell's allegorical role; she becomes "the child" who shall lead her grandfather and others into the paths of righteousness. In the country, drawn to peace in country churchyards, Nell pursues the logic of her retreat from life as a choice of death.

Quilp represents the antithesis to Nell's death-wishing thesis. While she is passive, he is aggressively active, constantly seeking confrontations with his wife, his mother-in-law, and his business contacts. Misogynous and sadistic, he describes his wife as "timid, loving Mrs. Quilp" (3) and delights in tormenting her. Even though she conspires with her female friends at tea "to resist that [male] tyranny" (4), she masochistically invites his mistreatment. He is a living version of Punch, the puppet who carries a stick to beat his wife and child. Quilp is as aggressively male as Nell is passively female. While Nell starves, he eats: "he ate hard eggs, shell and all, devoured prawns with the heads and tails on, chewed tobacco and water-cresses at the same time and with extraordinary greediness, drank boiling tea without winking" (5). But as a deformed dwarf, he is an ugly parody of patriarchal power, capitalist greed, sexual oppression, and urban corruption, all aspects of his allegorical significance. As an impish ogre out of fairy tale, he embodies Nell's childish fears more than he represents the social realities of the time. He is "a perpetual nightmare to the child, who was constantly haunted by a vision of his ugly face and stunted figure" (29), a projection of her fears of the city and her own sexuality.

Quilp's threat to Nell is explicitly sexual. He proposes to make her the second Mrs. Quilp, "to be my wife, my little cherry-cheeked, red-lipped wife" (6), and when he moves into the curiosity shop, he takes over Nell's "little room" for himself (11). The sexual threat posed by Quilp is a more assertive version of Fred Trent's scheme to marry the diffident Swiveller to her and a precursor to her grandfather's stealing into her room in the middle of the night to take money hidden in her clothes, a scene interpreted by some critics as a symbolic rape.

If Quilp is a monster of evil, a grotesque and deformed representation of aggression, violence, energy, capitalistic greed, and patriarchal oppression, Nell is a monster of virtue—innocent, selfless, otherworldly, suicidal. They represent such extremes—such absolutes—that they become separated from the other characters. Although Kit, the Garlands, and the Bachelor are members of Nell's camp of virtue, their goodness is more realistic and more compromising than hers. Kit is capable of transferring his affections to Barbara and surviving after Nell's death. Likewise, Quilp's villainy is of a different order from that of Fred Trent or the Brasses. They inhabit the more realistic domain of con men and shady lawyers. Nell's isolation in the rural village inhabited by old men is mir-

rored by Quilp's solitary existence on the wharf by the Thames. They are polarized DOUBLES: energy versus passivity, city versus country, male versus female, adult experience versus childish innocence. Inevitably they die on the same night, Nell passing peacefully in her sleep, Quilp drowning as he tries to escape into the fog.

In the novel's dialectic, Dick Swiveller is the character who synthesizes the polarities of Nell and Quilp to the possibilities of compromise. He enters as a dissipated cohort of Fred Trent; in Trent's scheme to get his grandfather's money, Dick is to marry Nell. But Dick is too diffident to pursue that plot. He drops Sophy Wackles, but he makes no serious play for Nell. He is too intent on rosy wine and the songs that run through his head to pay serious attention to anyone else. Although he seems, like Quilp, to threaten Nell's virtue, he puts no energy into that scheme or into his job with the Brasses. He lacks Quilp's aggressiveness and greed. If Quilp pursues self-interest, Dick could be said to pursue self-indulgence.

Dick swivels when he meets the Marchioness, the little kitchen drudge who emerges from the cellars of the Brasses' house in Bevis Marks. She is little like Nell, but she is not a child of innocence; in a cancelled passage Dickens suggested that she was the illegitimate child of Quilp and Sally Brass. But she draws Dick out of himself, focuses his antagonism to the Brasses, and makes his self-indulgent way of life useful as he teaches her to play cribbage and share a drink. By the end he has named, educated, and married her, and she has nursed him back to health. He did not drink himself to death while repeating old songs; she did not die in the tombs under the house in Bevis Marks. Together, they transcend their separateness and isolation. Dick began as one of Dickens's self-creating comic figures who by imagination alone can transform gin into rosy wine and expand his single room into elaborate chambers. In the end, his imagination has expanded to name the mysterious Sophronia Sphynx and establish a new world for himself and his bride.

The Old Curiosity Shop is a flawed novel, but it does not deserve STEVEN MARCUS's (1965) description as "Dickens's least successful novel, a work in which he seems to have lost much of his intellectual control, abandoning himself to all that was weakest and least mature in his character as a writer." Certainly Dickens searches for his theme and is vague about the allegorical significance of such characters as the schoolmaster and Mrs. Jarley, but the central opposition between Nell and Quilp is clear and powerful. If Dick Swiveller seems less clearly defined and the nature of his achievement by the end not fully realized, he nevertheless remains one of Dickens's great comic characters, a novelistic figure whose ability to adapt to changing circumstances enables him to survive and grow. Meanwhile, both Nell and Quilp, fixed as allegorical absolutes, are destroyed by their inability to learn from experience and change their lives.

CHARACTERS AND RELATED ENTRIES

bachelor, the Kindly old gentleman who lives with the clergyman in the rural village where Nell and her grandfather end their wanderings. In the village, he is known only as the bachelor, "the active spirit of the place, the adjuster of all differences, the promoter of all merry-makings, the dispenser of his friend's bounty, and of no small charity of his own besides; the universal mediator, comforter, and friend" (52). He turns out to be Mr. Garland's brother, and one of his letters reveals the location of Nell and her grandfather to those who are searching for them (68).

Barbara The Garland's servant girl, "tidy, modest and demure, but very pretty too" (22). She is jealous of Kit Nubbles's devotion to Little Nell, but later marries him. Her mother becomes friendly with Mrs. Nubbles on the excursion to ASTLEY'S ROYAL EQUESTRIAN AMPHITHEATRE (39) and later goes with her daughter to visit Kit in prison (63).

Beadnell Wolverhampton The description of the BLACK COUNTRY in the industrial midlands of England (45) is based on Dickens's experience of the countryside between BIRMINGHAM and this industrial town in Staffordshire.

Bevis Marks A street off Whitechapel in east London where Sampson Brass has his house and office (33).

Brass, Sally Sampson's sister, an "amazon at common law," acts as his housekeeper, partner, clerk, and co-conspirator: "a lady of thirty-five or thereabouts, of a gaunt and bony figure, and a resolute bearing, which if it repressed the softer emotions of love, and kept admirers at a distance, certainly inspired a feeling akin to awe in the breasts of those male strangers who had the happiness to approach her" (33). Masculine in appearance and manner, she looks enough like her brother to be mistaken for him. But she is tougher than he, refusing to give in when their schemes are discovered (66). The Marchioness is probably her child by Quilp, a relationship Dickens included in the manuscript for the novel but removed from the final text. In the end, she escapes the clutches of the law and becomes a vagrant (73). The Brasses are the children of Old Foxey, a lawyer as unscrupulous as they are (36).

Brass, Sampson Quilp's obsequious legal advisor, "an attorney of no very good repute from Bevis Marks, . . . a tall, meagre man, with a nose like a wen, a protruding forehead, retreating eyes, and hair of a deep red. . . . He had a cringing manner but a very harsh voice, and his blandest smiles were so extremely forbidding, that . . . one would have wished him out of temper that he might only scowl" (11). He manipulates Quilp's possession of the curiosity shop (11), hires and fires Swiveller as his clerk on Quilp's instructions (33), and frames Kit Nubbles for robbery (59). But after their schemes are discovered, he testifies against Quilp (66). Disbarred as lawyer and imprisoned for some time, Sampson ends his life wandering the London streets with Sally, searching for "refuse food, . . . the embodied spirits of Disease, Vice, and Famine" (73). In his physical characteristics, obsequious manner, and profession, Sampson is the precursor of one of Dickens's most famous villains, Uriah Heep in *David Copperfield*.

Cheggs, Alick Market gardener who is Dick Swiveller's rival for the hand of Sophy Wackles. She tries to heighten Swiveller's interest by her attentions to Cheggs just as Dick is scheming to marry Nell (8). Cheggs wins the contest and marries Sophy (50).

Cheggs, Miss Sophy Wackles's close friend who disparages Swiveller to Sophy and promotes her brother's suit.

Chuckster Witherden's clerk who is jealously resentful of Kit Nubbles's favor in the eyes of the Garlands. He distrusts the boy, condemning him as "snobby." Chuckster considers himself a man-about-town, and he shares the "fashionable intelligence" as he gossips with his fellow Glorious Apollo, Swiveller.

Codlin, Thomas Proprietor of an itinerant Punch and Judy show and partner of Harris, or Short, with whom Nell and her grandfather travel in their wanderings. A misanthrope, devious and suspicious, he plans to sell Nell's secret to anyone who will pay for it, but Nell slips away from him at the races before he is able to do so (19). Later he tells the single gentleman of his association with her (37).

David, Old Sexton's assistant and gravedigger in the village where Little Nell dies (54).

Duke's Place Street of secondhand clothing shops near Sampson Brass's office in Bevis Marks, Aldgate (33).

Edwards, Miss A teaching apprentice at Miss Monflathers's school: "This young lady, being motherless and poor, was apprenticed at the school—taught for nothing—teaching others what she learnt, for nothing—boarded for nothing—lodged for nothing—and set down and rated as something immeasurably less than nothing, by all the dwellers in the house" (31). Nevertheless, she befriends Little Nell, a kindness Nell also sees in her loving treatment of her younger sister (32).

Evans, Richard One of Marton's pupils at the school in the village where Nell ends her days: "An amazing boy to learn; blessed with a good memory; with a good voice and ear for psalm-singing," who has a habit of sleeping during the sermons (42).

Foxey, Old Father of Sampson and Sally Brass, whose maxim is "always suspect everybody" (66).

Garland, Abel The Garlands' 28-year-old son, who resembles his father "in face and figure, though wanting something of his full round cheerfulness, and substituting in its place a timid reserve" (14). Like his father, he has a club foot. He is employed by Witherden and eventually becomes his partner. He is a duplicate of his father.

Garland, Mr. and Mrs. A kindly old couple—he, "a little fat placid-faced old gentleman," she, "a little old lady, plump and placid like himself" (14)—who befriend Kit Nubbles and hire him as their groom. With the help of attorney Witherden they defend Kit from the false charges made by Quilp and Sampson Brass. They release him from their employment to enable him to help the single gentleman search for Nell. Mr. Garland's long-estranged brother, the bachelor, is discovered in the village where Nell and her grandfather have gone, and he informs Garland of their whereabouts. The Garlands counterpoint the evil duplicates Sampson and Sally Brass. JOHN FORSTER reports that Dickens told him that the Garlands were based on the family with whom Dickens lodged while his parents were in the MARSHALSEA PRISON. He remarked on their kindness to him at that time.

George Driver of Mrs. Jarley's touring van who eventually marries her (26, 28, 47).

George, Mrs. One of the guests at Mrs. Quilp's tea party, who says of her hostess: "Before I'd let a man order me about as Quilp orders her, . . . I'd kill myself, and write a letter first to say he did it!" (4).

Glorious Appollers "A select convivial circle" devoted to drinking and glee singing. Dick Swiveller is Perpetual Grand Master and Chuckster a member (13).

grandfather, Little Nell's Nell's maternal grandfather, "a little old man with long grey hair, [in] whose face and figure, . . . though much altered by age, I fancied I could recognize in his spare and slender form something of that delicate mould which I had noticed in the child" (1). A dealer in pictures and antiquities, the old man's addiction to gambling ruins him. After he loses his shop to Quilp (11), Nell leads him out of the city on a series of wandering adventures (12) as they run to escape Quilp's pursuit and the grandfather's addiction to gaming. They go to the races with some traveling performers (19), stay in the house of a poor schoolmaster (24–26), join Mrs. Jarley and her waxworks (27–28), pass through the BLACK COUNTRY (44–45), and, after meeting the schoolmaster again, end their journey in a remote rural village (52). There, in tranquility, both Nell and her grandfather die (71–72). After the conclusion of the story, Master Humphrey, also known as the single gentleman, reveals that Nell's grandfather is his long-lost older brother. Throughout the novel, however, he is identified only as Nell's grandfather, emphasizing his allegorical role as the figure of experience and age who is paired with Nell, the innocent and pure child.

Great Queen Street   The street in Holborn where Dick Swiveller has bought a pair of shoes on credit, so he can take it only after the shops have closed (8).

Grinder   A traveling showman with a small company consisting of himself, a young gentleman, and young lady on stilts. Little Nell and her grandfather meet them on the road (17).

Groves, James (Jem)   Landlord of the Valiant Soldier and the leader of a group of gamblers who lure Nell's grandfather into gambling, take his money, and persuade him to rob Mrs. Jarley (29, 30, 73). Fred Trent joins this band of conspirators; they are ultimately disbanded by the law.

Harris, Mr. (a.k.a. "Short Trotters," "Short," "Trotters")   Codlin's partner in the itinerant Punch and Judy show with whom Nell and her grandfather travel to the race meeting. "A little merry-faced man with a twinkling eye and a red nose, who seemed to have unconsciously imbibed something of his hero's character" (16). His nicknames derive from the shortness of his legs, and he is conveniently known as either "Short" or "Trotters."

Harry   Marton's favorite pupil, a young boy who falls ill and dies: "His hair still hung in curls about

his face, and his eyes were very bright; but their light was of Heaven, not earth" (25).

Jarley, Mrs.   Proprietor of a traveling waxworks, "a Christian lady, stout and comfortable to look upon, who wore a large bonnet trembling with bows" (26). She befriends Little Nell and her grandfather and employs Nell as a guide to her "calm and classical" exhibit, which she adapts to the different audiences that come to view it: "by altering the face and costume of Mr. Grimaldi as clown to represent Mr. Lindley Murray as he appeared when engaged in the composition of his English Grammar, and turning a murderess of great renown into Mrs. Hannah More. . . . Mr. Pitt in a nightcap and bedgown, and without his boots, represented the poet Cowper with perfect exactness; and Mary Queen of Scots in a dark wig, white shirt collar, and male attire, was such a complete image of Lord Byron" (29). She marries George, the driver of her caravan (47). PAUL SCHLICKE (1985) identifies Madame Tussaud, who had published her memoirs in 1838, as the inspiration for Mrs. Jarley.

Jerry   "A tall, black-whiskered man, in a velveteen coat" who manages a troupe of performing dogs (18, 19, 37).

Jiniwin, Mrs.   Mrs. Quilp's mother, "laudably shrewish in her disposition and inclined to resist male authority" (4). Even though she is terrified of Quilp, she encourages her daughter to rebellion. When her daughter remarries after Quilp's death, her new husband requires that Mrs. Jiniwin will not be part of the household (73). Some commentators have suggested that Mrs. Jiniwin is based on Dickens's mother-in-law, with whom he had verbal sparring sessions similar to Quilp's.

Jolly Sandboys, the   "A small road-side inn of pretty ancient date" where Nell and her grandfather stay on the recommendation of Codlin and Short (18).

Jowl, Joe   A gambler, "a burly fellow, of middle age; with black whiskers, broad cheeks, a coarse wide mouth, and bull neck," who, with others at the Valiant Soldier pub, fleeces Nell's grandfather and tries to persuade him to rob Mrs. Jarley (29, 42).

List, Isaac One of the group of gamblers at the Valiant Soldier who fleece Nell's grandfather and persuade him to rob Mrs. Jarley. He "was of a more slender figure—stooping, and high in the shoulders—with a very ill-favoured face, and a most sinister and villainous squint" (29, 30, 42).

"Marchioness, The" Dick Swiveller's nickname for the nameless little servant kept locked in the cellar at Bevis Marks by the Brasses: "a small slipshod girl in a dirty coarse apron and bib, which left nothing visible but her face and feet. She might as well have been dressed in a violin-case" (34). Illiterate and half-starved from her imprisonment, she knows only what she can gather by peering through keyholes at the world outside her subterranean cage. Dick gives her food and beer to make up for the short rations that Sally Brass allows her and teaches her to play cribbage (57). When Dick is dismissed by Sampson and falls ill, she runs away from Bevis Marks to care for him (64). Her testimony about the Brasses' and Quilp's scheme to frame Kit Nubbles leads to Sampson's imprisonment and Kit's pardon (66). After coming into his inheritance, Dick names her Sophronia Sphynx, pays for her education, and marries her (73). Dickens's manuscript indicates that the Marchioness was the child of Sally Brass by Quilp, but he removed the relevant passage before publication, leaving her parentage ambiguous.

The Marchioness's story counterpoints that of Nell, for as Nell sinks inexorably toward death, the fortunes of the orphan girl from the Brass's cellar gradually rise. Unlike the static, iconographic Nell, whose destiny seems fixed from the outset, the Marchioness is capable of change and growth. If Nell's story is a fairy-tale version of Richardson's *Clarissa*, the story of the Marchioness is a novelistic version of Cinderella. JOHN FORSTER claims that the Marchioness is based on the workhouse orphan who was a servant to the Dickens family during their time in the MARSHALSEA PRISON.

Marton Village schoolmaster with whom Nell and her grandfather stay on their wanderings, "a pale, simple-looking man, of a spare and meagre habit, [who] sat among his flowers and beehives, smoking his pipe" (24). He is unjustly blamed for causing the death of Harry, his favorite pupil, who feared him and was driven to overwork. As he goes to a new teaching post, Nell and her grandfather meet him again in the BLACK COUNTRY and go with him to the remote village where Nell dies (52–54, 73).

Maunders, Old Showman remembered by Vuffin; he "had in his cottage in Spa Fields in the winter time, when the season was over, eight male and female dwarfs setting down to dinner every day, who was waited on by eight old giants in green coats, red smalls, blue cotton stockings, and highlows" (19).

Monflathers, Miss Snobbish principal of a girls' school whose pupils tour the waxworks with Nell as their guide. She uses Nell as an example to the girls of the vulgar people associated with such entertainments (29, 31).

Morgan, Becky Old woman whose age is a topic of discussion between the sexton and old David as the latter digs her grave. Nell listens to their conversation (54).

Nell, Little The name by which Nell Trent, the 13-year-old heroine of the novel, is better known. A gentle, angelic girl, whose "very small and delicate frame imparted a peculiar youthfulness to her appearance" (1), Nell lives with her grandfather, a dealer in antiquities, surrounded by old people and antique objects. When their lives are threatened by the grandfather's addiction to gambling and the schemes of Quilp to take over the business and seduce Nell, she leads her grandfather out of the city on a wandering pilgrimage through the countryside and the industrial midlands that finally ends in a small village where Nell, exhausted by her exertions, dies.

In the 1848 preface to the novel, Dickens described his intent to "surround the lonely figure of the child with grotesque and wild, but not impossible companions, and to gather about her innocent face and pure intentions, associates as strange and uncongenial as the grim objects about her bed when her history is first foreshadowed." He carried this contrast between youth and age, innocence and experience, through the novel, surrounding Nell initially with old curiosities and ultimately with the moldering stones of the village church and its graveyard. In the "kind of allegory" that emerged from this initial idea, Nell is often called simply "the child," and her grandfather has no name other than "Grandfather." The journey they undertake recalls that of John Bunyan's Christian in *The Pilgrim's Progress* (1678), second only to the Bible in popularity during the Victorian era. Those she meets along the way after escaping the city are often identified by type as much as name, as the sexton, for example, the schoolmaster or the mill worker. Their significance thereby is generalized.

A static figure representing the innocent and pure child, Nell is characterized by contrast, especially with Quilp, whose corruption, roughness, sexual aggressiveness, gluttonous cannibalism, and energy define her purity, smoothness, asexuality, anorexia, and passivity. Comparisons with the Marchioness, also a child surrounded by corruption and darkness, underscore Nell's angelic otherworldliness. Although Dickens did not envision her death when he began her story, he realized its inevitability when JOHN FORSTER pointed it out about halfway through. After writing of her death, which recalled for Dickens the death of MARY HOGARTH three years earlier, he realized that Mary was the subconscious inspiration for Little Nell.

Many of Dickens's contemporaries found Nell's death as harrowing as the author did, FRANCIS JEFFREY comparing it, for example, to the death of Cordelia in *King Lear*. At the end of the century, however, readers were not so moved. ALGERNON C. SWINBURNE described Nell as "a monster as inhuman as a baby with two heads," and Oscar Wilde quipped that one would need to "have a heart of stone to read the death of Little Nell without laughing." Modern critics have almost universally objected to the morbid sentimentality in her passive acceptance of suffering and death. In a reading

that seeks to recover a more Victorian perspective on Little Nell, Nina Auerbach (*Woman and the Demon*, 1982) challenges many of these characterizations of Nell by stressing the heroic and positive dimensions of her character.

Nubbles, Christopher (Kit) Shopboy at the curiosity shop, "a shock-headed shambling awkward lad with an uncommonly wide mouth, very red cheeks, a turned-up nose, and certainly the most comical expression of face I ever saw" (1). Devoted to Nell, who teaches him to write, he is dismissed by her grandfather, who suspects him of disclosing his employer's addiction to gambling to Quilp (11). After Nell disappears, Kit secures employment with the Garlands, tending their pony Whisker (21), but Quilp conspires against him and has the Brasses accuse him of stealing five pounds (59); Kit is sentenced to transportation (64) and is saved only at the last minute by the testimony of the Marchioness (66). With Mr. Garland and the single gentleman, he travels to the village where Nell has been found, but he arrives too late to see her alive (68–71). After Nell's death, he marries Barbara, the Garlands' maid; they have three children, Barbara, Abel, and Dick (73).

Nubbles, Jacob Kit's younger brother, "a sturdy boy of two or three years old" (10).

Nubbles, Mrs. Kit's mother, a kind-hearted widow and hard-working laundress, who is occasionally misguided and upset by the preaching at the Little Bethel chapel that she attends (41).

old curiosity shop Several sites in London have been proposed as the original for the one in the novel; the popular tourist attraction in Portsmouth Street, however, is not among them.

Owen, John Pupil at Marton's school, "a lad of good parts, . . . but too thoughtless, too playful, too light-headed by far" (52).

Quilp, Betsy Quilp's abused wife: "a pretty, little, mild-spoken, blue-eyed woman, who having allied herself in wedlock to the dwarf in one of those strange infatuations of which examples are by no means scarce, performed a sound practical penance for her folly, every day of her life" (4). Intimidated by her husband's misogynous criticism, she helps in his schemes by prying information from Nell. In spite of Quilp's treatment of her, she admires her abuser; "Quilp has such a way with him," she tells her women friends, "that the best-looking woman here couldn't refuse him if I was dead, and she was free, and he chose to make love to her" (4). Nevertheless, after Quilp's death, she marries "a smart young fellow" who was not, as Quilp was, selected by her mother (73).

Quilp, Daniel Malevolent dwarf who lends money to Nell's grandfather, takes over the old curiosity shop in payment, and then pursues Little Nell and her grandfather when they flee from him. "His head and face were large enough for the body of a giant. His black eyes were restless, sly, and cunning; his mouth and chin, bristly with the stubble of a coarse hard beard; and his complexion was of that kind which never looks clean or wholesome. But what added most to the grotesque expression of his face, was a ghastly smile, which . . . revealed the few discoloured fangs that were yet scattered in his mouth, and gave him the aspect of a panting dog. His dress consisted of a large high-crowned hat, a worn dark suit, a pair of capacious shoes, and a dirty white neckerchief sufficiently limp and crumpled to disclose the greater portion of his wiry throat. Such hair as he had, was of a grizzled black, cut short and straight upon his temples, and hanging in a frowzy fringe about his ears. His hands, which were of a rough coarse grain, were very dirty; his fingernails were crooked, long, and yellow" (3). Sadist and misogynist, he delights in tormenting his wife and other women; a voracious eater with cannibalistic tendencies, "he ate hard eggs, shell and all, devoured gigantic prawns with the heads and tales on, chewed tobacco and water-cresses at the same time and with extraordinary greediness, drank boiling tea without winking" (5). He schemes to seduce Nell, ruin Nell's grandfather, and have Kit Nubbles thrown into prison. Finally, his plots discovered after Sampson Brass confesses (66), he flees from the police to his wharf along the Thames, where he

Nell (Sally Walsh) is constantly pursued by the menacing Quilp (Tom Courtenay), as portrayed in this scene from the Disney Channel's *The Old Curiosity Shop* miniseries. *Courtesy of PhotoFest.*

sets the building afire and drowns as he runs from the police and the fire in the fog (67).

One of Dickens's great villains, the grotesque Quilp melds elements of a gargoyle, a fairy-tale demon, a savage, a pantomime villain, and Punch. HARRY STONE (1979) describes him as "a nightmare kin of Shakespeare's Richard III." He concentrates evil in the ALLEGORY as Nell does saintly purity. His age and experience counter her innocence; his energy challenges her passivity; his cannibalism her self-starvation. He is as fixed a definition of evil as she is of innocent goodness, and their simultaneous deaths are both inevitable.

Quilp's Wharf "A small, rat-infested dreary yard" on the Surrey side of the river near Tower Hill where Quilp carries on his numerous occupations as ship breaker, smuggler, moneylender, and so on (4).

Scott, Tom Quilp's "amphibious boy," an "eccentric spirit" with an addiction to standing on his head (5). After mourning Quilp's death he becomes a professional tumbler and takes an Italian name (73).

"Short" or "Short Trotters" Nickname of Harris, Codlin's partner in the itinerant PUNCH AND JUDY show.

Simmons, Mrs. Henrietta Mrs. Quilp's neighbor and sympathizer (4).

single gentleman, the Mysterious lodger who moves into the apartment on the upper floor of the Brasses' house in Bevis Marks in order to spy on the Brasses (34). A man of reclusive habits, he takes particular interest in Swiveller and in traveling PUNCH AND JUDY shows. He turns out to be the younger brother of Nell's grandfather, who has returned from many years wandering abroad to be reunited with his brother just shortly before his death (71–72). After his brother's death, he becomes himself a kind of pilgrim; "it was his chief delight to travel in the steps of the old man and the child (so far as he could trace them from her last narrative), to halt where they had halted, sympathise where they had suffered, and rejoice where they had been made glad" (73).

In the frame story in *Master Humphrey's Clock,* Humphrey surprisingly claims to be the single gentleman (6). JOHN REED (1995), in his analysis of the modes of narration in the novel, challenges the notion that Humphrey and the single gentleman could be the same character.

Slum Ragged poet who writes advertising verses for Mrs. Jarley's Waxworks (28). He is disappointed when she marries William (47). EDWIN PUGH (1912) suggests that Slum was based on the "poets" who wrote advertising jingles for WARREN'S BLACK-ING whom Dickens observed when he worked there as a boy.

Spa Fields Open area in Clerkenwell, east London, surrounding Spa Fields Chapel. In the 19th century, traveling showmen like Old Maunders made the area their winter quarters (19).

Sphynx, Sophronia Name that Dick Swiveller gives to the Marchioness.

Sweet William One of the travelling performers—a conjurer who can put lead lozenges on his eyes and bring them out his mouth—that Nell meets at the Jolly Sandboys (19).

Swiveller, Dick Dissolute and feckless associate of Fred Trent who has "the fire of his soul . . . kindled at the taper of conviviality" (2). In his initial appearance in the novel, "his wiry hair, dull eyes, and sallow face" suggest that he has just arisen from a night of dissipation, and his clothing "in a state of disorder . . . induced the idea that he had gone to bed in it" (2). He agrees to Fred Trent's scheme that he marry Nell so that Fred can get his grandfather's money (7) and so that he can enjoy the pleasures of rosy wine, tobacco, and singing with his companions in the Glorious Apollers. Dick gives up Sophy Wackles to forward this scheme (8). Thinking that Dick may be useful in his plots against Nell and her grandfather, Quilp has the Brasses hire him as a clerk (33), and Dick enlivens their office with his happy-go-lucky attitude and his quotations from popular songs (36). His life takes a turn toward the serious when he befriends the Brasses' little servant girl, whom he calls "the Marchioness," teaching her the pleasures of beer and cribbage (57). When he is dismissed and falls ill, she runs away to him, nurses him through his fever, and provides him with the evidence to exonerate Kit Nubbles (64). With a small inheritance from an aunt, Dick educates her, names her Sophronia Sphynx, and marries her (73).

Like many of Dickens's other great comic characters, Swiveller is a self-creator; he imagines the world around him and himself, using flowery language and uncontrolled metaphor to turn his narrow circumstances into poetry and song. His first name suggests a connection with his author, for both re-create the world with language. Dick, for example, imagines his small room as "chambers," remaps London according to the locations of his creditors, and remakes a ragged urchin into a Marchioness through the power of words. In the allegorical context of the story, in which Nell and Quilp are unchanging polarities in the allegory of good and evil, Dick is a novelistic figure who turns from dissipated fatalism at the beginning of the story to take responsibility for himself and his choices by the end. His relationship with the Marchioness prompts this swiveling and enables his growth. His illness, attended by the Marchioness, completes his transformation and rounds out the novelistic story that complements the allegorical main story in the novel. J. B. PRIESTLEY (1925) puts Swiveller into the company of Shakespeare's Falstaff and Fielding's

Parson Adams as one of the great "English comic characters." GARRETT STEWART (1974) analyzes his pivotal role in the novel.

Tomkinley Schoolmaster with whom Abel Garland goes to MARGATE (14).

Tong Village in Shropshire, three miles east of Shifnal, which was the original of the village where Little Nell dies. The Church of St. Bartholomew in Tong was the original for George Cattermole's engraving. There is, in the churchyard, a grave bearing the inscription, "Reputed Grave of Little Nell."

Trent Surname of Little Nell and her brother Frederick.

Trent, Frederick Nell's brother, a wastrel and gambler, "a young man of one-and-twenty or thereabouts; well made, and certainly handsome, though the expression of his face was far from prepossessing, having in common with his manner and even his dress, a dissipated, insolent air which repelled one" (2). He conspires to get the fortune he believes his grandfather has hoarded and to marry his sister to Swiveller (7). After Nell disappears, he goes abroad, and his body ultimately turns up in the PARIS MORGUE (73).

Valiant Soldier Inn, the Public house and gambling den run by Jem Groves where Nell's grandfather is lured into gambling (29).

Vuffin Traveling showman whose exhibits include a giant and a limbless lady (19).

Wackles, Mrs. "An excellent, but rather venomous old lady of three-score," who maintains a small school for young ladies in CHELSEA. Her daughters teach the various subjects; Mrs. Wackles handles "corporal punishment, fasting, and other tortures and terrors" (8).

Wackles, Sophia "A fresh, good-humoured, buxom girl of twenty," Dick Swiveller's first love. She and her sisters Melissa and Jane teach in their mother's "very small day school for young ladies

of proportionate dimensions," Sophy instructing in "dancing, music, and general fascination" (8). When Sophy tries to encourage Dick's interest by her attentions to Cheggs, a market gardener, he leaves her, with some regrets, to pursue Fred Trent's scheme to marry him to Nell (8).

West, Dame Grandmother of Mr. Marton's favorite scholar, young Harry, who dies while Nell is staying with the schoolmaster. She unjustly blames Marton for overworking the willing student and thus causing his death (25).

Whisker Mr. Garland's independent pony who follows commands "after his own fashion, or not at all" (25).

Wilderness, the Riverside tavern near the wharf where Quilp takes Dick Swiveller (21) and Sampson and Sally Brass (51).

Witherden, Mr. Notary to whom Abel Garland is apprenticed, "short, chubby, fresh-coloured, brisk and pompous" (14). He aids the single gentleman in tracing Nell and her grandfather (40) and brings about the comeuppance of the Brasses and Quilp (66).

ADAPTATIONS

There were surprisingly few early theatrical adaptations of *Curiosity Shop,* in spite of Little Nell's popularity. EDWARD STIRLING adapted the story for the Adelphi Theatre while the novel was still running in serial, providing an ending in which Nell lives happily ever after. MALCOLM MORLEY reports the probably apocryphal story that "such anticipation of her fate by the dramatist . . . annoyed Dickens so much that, having still several more chapters of the work to write, he reversed the Stirling pronouncement and killed the poor girl off."

The story came into its own theatrically in the late 1860s and 1870s, when several versions of Nell's story appeared. JOHN BROUGHAM's "Little Nell and the Marchioness" was first performed in America in 1867 with Carlotta Crabtree playing both Nell and the Marchioness. Several other actresses combined the two roles during the following decade in plays that concentrated on the story of the child heroine, "An Angel on Earth," as one adaptation presented her. After the turn of the century, several theatrical adaptations appeared that gave Quilp or Dick Swiveller top billing.

There were several silent films from the novel, in 1903, 1911, 1912, and 1914, and, most important, THOMAS BENTLEY's 1921 version. Bentley also made the first sound picture from the novel in 1935, described by *The DICKENSIAN* as "the first British talking picture." Although there have been few theatrical adaptations of the novel since World War II, a musical film, directed by Michael Tucker with music by Anthony Newley, appeared in 1975. Newley also starred in the role of Quilp, with David Hemmings as Swiveller, Sara Jane Varley as Nell, and Michael Hordern as the grandfather.

The BBC has presented several radio and television adaptations of the novel, most notably a version in 13 episodes for television (1963) and William Trevor's nine-part television adaptation in 1980.

FURTHER READING

The Old Curiosity Shop is the most discussed of the early novels. GEORGE H. FORD (1955) and Loralee MacPike ("'The Old Curiosity Shape': Changing Views of Little Nell," *Dickens Studies Newsletter*, 1981) survey the widely differing responses to the novel and its heroine from the time of its publication. Since it evokes such divergent reactions, *Curiosity Shop* has been particularly interesting to reader-response critics: MICHAEL STEIG has explored responses to the novel in several articles on Nell and, especially, Quilp, and on the role of grotesque comedy in the reader's reaction to the novel. In "Abuse and the Comic Grotesque in *The Old Curiosity Shop*: Problems of Response," (*Dickens Quarterly*, 1994), he reevaluates his earlier work in light of the differences between male and female responses to the novel. Analyzing the dynamics in reading the novel, Nicholas Morgan (*Secret Journeys: Theory and Practice in Reading Dickens*, 1992) finds the reader caught between the allegorical poles of angel and imp. The logic of the lives of both Nell and Quilp leads to death, he argues, and the reader must transfer sympathy from these

allegorical figures to the survivors—Kit, Barbara, Swiveller, and the Marchioness.

Gabriel Pearson's classic essay on the novel (*Dickens and the Twentieth Century*, 1962) established the structural analysis that most later critics have followed. He is especially good on Dick Swiveller, whose ability to develop and adapt places him in sharp contrast to the unchanging Nell and Quilp. GARRETT STEWART (1974) uses Swiveller as the "pivotal" figure in the novel and in Dickens's work generally, one of Dickens's "men of fancy" who re-create the world in their imagination. S. J. Newman (*Dickens at Play*, 1981) sees incoherence as "the principle of narrative energy" in the novel and Swiveller as a figure who transforms the world in play.

The historical context of the novel is discussed by PAUL SCHLICKE (1985), who considers the role of the traveling entertainers. In "The True Pathos of *The Old Curiosity Shop*" (*Dickens Quarterly*, 1990), he discusses the historical background more broadly. SUSAN HORTON ("Swiveller and Snivellers: Competing Epistemologies in *The Old Curiosity Shop*," *Dickens Quarterly*, 1990) considers the novel in relation to changing modes of shopping and popular entertainment. Ella Westland ("Little Nell and the Marchioness: Some Functions of Fairy Tale in *The Old Curiosity Shop*," *Dickens Quarterly*, 1991), interprets the story as an allegory of economics in which Quilp represents "early-nineteenth-century capitalism; Nell comes to stand for capitalism's many victims," and the Marchioness offers a fairy tale of survival and modest triumph over the oppressive economic forces of the time. Sue Zemka ("From the Punchmen to Pugin's Gothics: The Broad Road to a Sentimental Death in *The Old Curiosity Shop*," *Nineteenth-Century Literature*, 1993) also analyzes the economics of the novel, finding it "symptomatic of contradictions inherent in the ideological intertwining of Protestantism and capitalism in early Victorian England."

In a feminist reading, Gail Houston (*Consuming Fictions*, 1994) treats Nell and Quilp as representatives of the polarized gender roles in Victorian society. Characterized by his voracious appetite, Quilp is the "ultimate consumer who insists on possessing everything in the world around him," but anorexic

"Nell's bodily desires must be contracted, and the Victorian narrative must transform her eros into thanatos." Deirdre David (*Rule Brittania: Women, Empire, and Victorian Writing,* 1995) explores feminist and economic issues in a postcolonial reading of the novel that constructs Nell as a victim of Quilp's savage imperialism.

Dickens Quarterly ran a 150th anniversary issue (March 1990) containing several articles on various aspects of the novel.

Oliver Twist, or, The Parish Boy's Progress

Dickens's second novel, serialized in 24 monthly installments in BENTLEY'S MISCELLANY between February 1837 and April 1839 (no installments June, October 1837; September 1838), with illustrations by GEORGE CRUIKSHANK. In *Twist,* Dickens seemed to choose subject matter that turned *Pickwick* on its head. As his central figure, he replaced the retired businessman with a child, and the innocent world of the earlier novel gave way to the dark criminal underworld of Sikes and Fagin. Although he was not fully successful in giving coherence to this story, it does evoke a compelling vision of childhood haunted by a mythic struggle between the forces of good and evil.

SYNOPSIS

Part 1 (February 1837)

(1) Oliver Twist is born in a workhouse. His mother dies before she makes her identity known to anyone there. (2) Oliver is brought up "by hand" in the workhouse for a year. Then he is sent to Mrs. Mann's baby farm, where he is systematically starved for the next eight years. On Oliver's ninth birthday, Mr. Bumble, the parish beadle, takes the boy back to the workhouse to learn a useful trade—picking oakum. The inmates there are also systematically starved. The hungry boys draw lots, and Oliver is "chosen" to ask for a second bowl of gruel. His innocent request of the master, "Please, sir, I want some more," so astonishes and horrifies the workhouse authorities that they predict he "will be hung" and advertise his availability to apprentice to a trade.

Part 2 (March 1837)

(3) Mr. Gamfield, a chimney sweep, applies to take the boy. After some haggling, the board agrees to turn Oliver over to him, but Oliver pleads with the magistrate, who refuses to approve the papers. (4) The next applicant is Mr. Sowerberry, an undertaker. Oliver, by this point "reduced . . . to a state of brutal stupidity and selfishness," makes no objection. Mrs. Sowerberry assigns Oliver a place to sleep among the coffins.

Part 3 (April 1837)

(5) The next day Oliver meets Noah Claypole, a charity boy also employed by Sowerberry. He taunts Oliver with the epithet "Work'us." After a month or so, Oliver is promoted to serve as a mute, a silent mourner supplied by the undertaker. His first funeral in this capacity is for a poor woman who starved to death while her husband was imprisoned for begging. After this sad event, Sowerberry tells

Cruikshank's rendering of the most famous moment in *Oliver Twist*—Oliver asking for more.

Oliver that he'll "get used to it in time." (6) Resentful of Oliver's favored place, Claypole tells him, "yer must know, Work'us, yer mother was a regular right-down bad 'un." Furious, Oliver attacks Noah and knocks him to the floor, but Mrs. Sowerberry and the maid Charlotte subdue him and lock him in a cellar. Noah is sent to fetch Mr. Bumble.

Part 4 (May 1837)

(7) When Bumble arrives, Oliver is still defiant. Bumble cannot calm him, and asserting, "It's meat. . . . You've over fed him, ma'am," he advises Mrs. Sowerberry to starve Oliver into submission. When the undertaker returns, he beats Oliver. Early the next morning, Oliver runs away and sets out for London. On the way he says good-bye to Little Dick, one of his companions at Mrs. Mann's baby farm. (8) Oliver walks the 70 miles to London in six days, sleeping under hayricks along the way. On the seventh day, he arrives in BARNET. There he meets "one of the queerest looking boys" he has ever seen, a short, ugly boy wearing a top hat and a man's overcoat with the sleeves folded back. Jack Dawkins, or "the Artful Dodger," buys some food for the hungry Oliver and then takes him into the city to the den of Fagin, a receiver of stolen goods, an old Jew who maintains a gang of juvenile pickpockets. There he is given supper and a place to sleep.

Part 5 (July 1837)

(9) The next morning Oliver sees Fagin going through the treasures in a little strongbox. When Fagin realizes the boy is watching him, he is alarmed and tells him the things in the box are his savings. Later the Dodger and Charley Bates return from working the crowd at an execution; they bring handkerchiefs and pocketbooks to Fagin. The boys play a game of picking Fagin's pockets that brings Oliver such laughter that tears run down his face. (10) After many days in the hideout, Oliver is allowed to go out with the Dodger and Bates. When they see an old gentleman outside a bookshop absorbed in reading, the Dodger steals his handkerchief, gives it to Charley, and then the two of them run off. In an instant Oliver realizes what the gang is up to and he too begins running. The cry of "stop thief" goes up. Oliver is pursued

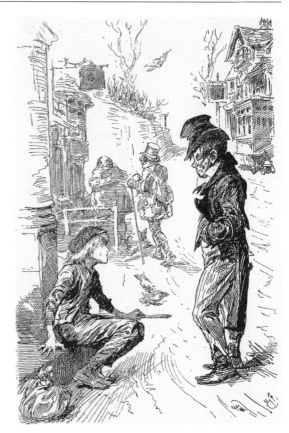

The Artful Dodger greets Oliver Twist as he arrives in London. Illustration by Furniss (1910).

through the streets. Even the Dodger and Bates join the chase. Finally, his strength spent, Oliver is knocked to the ground and arrested. The other two boys have disappeared. (11) Weak and faint, Oliver is unable to give his name, so he stands trial as "Tom White." Even though the old gentleman does not press charges, Oliver is convicted by Magistrate Fang. When the bookstore owner exonerates him, Fang reluctantly releases Oliver into the custody of the old gentleman, Mr. Brownlow.

Part 6 (August 1837)

(12) Brownlow takes Oliver to his home in PENTONVILLE and puts the feverish child to bed. Mrs. Bedwin, a kind housekeeper, nurses him back to health. As he convalesces in the housekeeper's room, he is fascinated by a portrait of a young

woman. Brownlow is startled to notice that Oliver is a "living copy" of the picture.

Meanwhile, the Dodger and Bates return to Fagin's den after the robbery. (13) The Jew is enraged when he hears what has happened. He throws a mug of beer at Bates, but it hits instead a dark, unkempt fellow, Bill Sikes, who has just entered the room. Fearful that Oliver will expose the gang, Fagin recruits Nancy, a prostitute who is Sikes's companion, to recover the boy. Posing as Oliver's sister, she learns the general location of Brownlow's house.

Part 7 (September 1837)

(14) When Oliver recovers, Brownlow buys him a new suit. One evening he asks the boy to give an account of his life, but before Oliver can tell his story, Mr. Grimwig, Brownlow's cynical chess companion, comes to visit. Later, when Brownlow wants to return some books to the bookseller, Oliver offers to go. Brownlow agrees, convinced that the boy will refute Grimwig's assumption that Oliver, with "a suit of clothes on his back, a set of valuable books under his arm, and a five-pound note in his pocket," will not return. (15) Oliver gets lost on the way to the bookstore. In a side street he meets Nancy, who, with the help of Bill Sikes and the support of the crowd that gathers, overpowers him. Meanwhile Brownlow and Grimwig sit in the dark awaiting Oliver's return.

Part 8 (November 1837)

(16) Nancy and Sikes take Oliver to Fagin's new den, where the Dodger and Bates mock his fancy clothes. Fagin beats the boy, but Nancy takes away Fagin's club and vows that the Jew "will be the worse for it" if he harms the boy. The thieves take Oliver's new suit and restore the identical rags he had worn before, which they have found at a rag dealer's shop.

(17) The narrator compares the alternation of tragic and comic scenes on the stage to similarly abrupt changes in real life. Then the narrative shifts back to Oliver's birthplace, where Bumble has stopped at Mrs. Mann's on his way to London. There he learns that little Dick is ill. The boy, whose limbs have "wasted away, like those of an old man," asks the Beadle to convey a message of love and good wishes to Oliver Twist. Bumble is outraged; "that out-dacious Oliver has demogalized them all," he exclaims. In London, Bumble sees Brownlow's advertisement offering five guineas for information about Oliver. Bumble's account of the boy's "vicious parent, . . . treachery, ingratitude, and malice" saddens Brownlow, who forbids Oliver's name to be mentioned again in his household. Nevertheless, Mrs. Bedwin continues to believe in the boy.

Part 9 (December 1837)

(18) Fagin holds Oliver in solitary confinement. After several lonely weeks, Oliver is advised by the Dodger and Bates to join them in the "trade," but Oliver resists. Finally, Fagin decides to educate Oliver to the trade by placing him in the constant company of the other two boys. (19) When Sikes and his accomplice Toby Crackit need a small boy for a robbery, Nancy proposes Oliver. Fagin likes the idea of implicating Oliver in a crime as a way to silence him. He is also convinced that his uneasiness about Nancy was unwarranted.

Part 10 (January 1838)

(20) Fagin warns Oliver that Sikes is a "rough man." When Nancy comes to fetch him, Oliver senses that he has "some power over the girl's better feelings," but she tells him that "this is not the time" to attempt to escape from Fagin. Sikes holds a pistol to Oliver's temple and warns him to do exactly as he is told. (21) Then Sikes and Oliver go westward out of the city, stopping on the way at an old ruined house. (22) Within they find Toby Crackit and Barney, a waiter from SAFFRON HILL. They rest until 1:30 in the morning and then set off again. After passing through CHERTSEY, they silently approach a large house. When Oliver realizes what is afoot, he pleads with Sikes to let him go. But Sikes cocks his pistol, removes the shutter from a small window at the back of the house, and tells Oliver to go through the house and unlock the street door. Then he lifts Oliver through the window and drops him inside. Oliver thinks of raising an alarm, but suddenly he sees two men, "a flash—a loud noise—a smoke—a crash somewhere." Sikes pulls him back through the window, and as Sikes carries him off, Oliver loses consciousness.

Part 11 (February 1838)

(23) Bumble visits Mrs. Corney, the matron of the workhouse, and enunciates his welfare principle: "The great principle of out-of-door relief is, to give the paupers exactly what they don't want; and then they get tired of coming." Mrs. Corney agrees and invites him to tea. Bumble moves his chair until he can put his arm around Mrs. Corney's waist and kiss her. This domestic scene is interrupted when she is summoned to the deathbed of an inmate. While she is gone Bumble inventories the items in her china closet. (24) The dying pauper confesses to Mrs. Corney that years earlier she stole a gold object from the young woman who bore a child named Oliver. Mrs. Corney leaves the room reporting, "Nothing to tell, after all."

(25) When Crackit tells Fagin that the robbery was bungled and that he and Sikes left the boy bleeding in a ditch, Fagin rushes out of the house "twining his hands in his hair."

Part 12 (March 1838)

(26) Fagin finds Nancy, apparently stupefied from drink, but she has no information about Sikes or Oliver. When Fagin arrives back at his den at midnight, a mysterious man named Monks is there waiting for him. The two discuss the bungled robbery, and Monks asserts that Fagin could have made a thief of the boy and had him transported for life. They are startled by the shadow of a woman on the wall, but when they search they find no one.

(27) Meanwhile, Bumble evaluates the contents of Mrs. Corney's room, exclaiming to himself, "I'll do it." When the matron returns, Bumble calls her "a angel" and proposes, envisioning them as the codirectors of the workhouse. Mrs. Corney accepts her "irresistible duck."

Part 13 (April 1838)

(28) After the robbery Sikes leaves the wounded Oliver in a ditch. The boy recovers consciousness early the next morning and, weakened by loss of blood, he stumbles to the nearest house, the one they had attempted to rob. He knocks on the door and collapses on the front steps. The servants in the house, including Giles and Brittles, the two who had surprised him the night before, answer his knock and "capture" the thief. (29) Mr. Losberne,

a doctor, examines Oliver and (30) discovers that the robber is a "mere child." Convinced that the boy is innocent, Losberne, Mrs. Maylie, and her niece Rose are determined to save him. That evening, Losberne encourages Oliver to tell them his "simple history." The doctor confounds Giles and Brittles, making them uncertain of their identification of Oliver as the robber.

Part 14 (May 1838)

(31) The investigating officers from London, Blathers and Duff, get an evasive account from Losberne and hear contradictory stories from Giles and Brittles. By the time they question Oliver, the boy is feverish, and they return to London without an arrest. (32) After Oliver recovers, Losberne offers to go with him in search of Mr. Brownlow. As they pass the ruined house where Oliver and Sikes stopped on the way to the robbery, Losberne impetuously goes into the building, but he finds only an old humpbacked man who claims that he has lived there for 25 years. In London they discover that Brownlow has gone to the West Indies. Disappointed, Oliver goes to the country with Mrs. Maylie and Rose.

Part 15 (June 1838)

(33) Oliver thrives in the country, but Rose falls ill. When she takes a turn for the worse, Mrs. Maylie asks Oliver to mail letters to Losberne and to her son, Harry, telling them of Rose's condition. As he is leaving the inn after dispatching the letters, Oliver stumbles against a tall man in a dark cloak who curses him, shakes his fist as if he is about to hit him, and then falls to the ground in a fit. Oliver's astonishment and fear are soon forgotten, however, in his concern about Rose, who hovers on the brink of death. Finally Losberne reports that Rose has passed the crisis and will live. (34) When Harry arrives, Oliver tells him the good news, and Harry informs his mother that he loves Rose and plans to marry her, even though her birth is clouded by scandal.

One evening as Oliver is reading in a small room with a window opening on the garden, he dozes off and dreams that he is back in Fagin's den. He hears the Jew say, "It is he, sure enough," and awakens to see two figures in the window, Fagin and the man who cursed him at the inn. They vanish as Oliver calls for help.

Part 16 (July 1838)

(35) Harry Maylie, Losberne, and Giles respond to Oliver's cry, but they can find no sign of the intruders. As Rose recovers she urges Harry to forget her, telling him that the stain on her name would blight his prospects. Harry gets her permission to press his suit once more within a year. (36) As he sets out for London, Harry secures Oliver's promise that he will write regularly and tell about himself and Rose.

(37) Meanwhile, Bumble has married Mrs. Corney and become master of the workhouse. Although he has been married for eight weeks, "it seems a age." Mrs. Bumble refuses to take his orders. She pummels him and humiliates him in front of the paupers. Bumble seeks solace at a public house and there meets a stranger who is seeking information about Oliver's mother. Bumble arranges to introduce the stranger, Monks, to someone who can throw some light on the subject of his inquiry.

Part 17 (August 1838)

(38) The next evening the Bumbles meet Monks at a ruined warehouse by the river. For £25, Mrs. Bumble reveals the things that Oliver's mother left, a locket containing "two locks of hair, and a plain gold wedding ring" inscribed with the name "Agnes." Monks drops the trinkets through a trap door into the river. Then he pledges the Bumbles to secrecy.

(39) Ravaged by illness, Sikes abuses Nancy and accuses his cronies of neglecting him. He sends Nancy to get some money from Fagin. While she is at Fagin's den, she overhears a private conversation between Fagin and Monks. She collects the money and then runs out into the street, crying and wringing her hands. By the time she delivers the money to Sikes, she has recovered her equanimity.

Part 18 (October 1838)

The next day Nancy has "the nervous manner of one . . . on the eve of some bold and hazardous step." She puts opium in Sikes's gin to make him sleep. Then she goes to a hotel near Hyde Park, where she asks to see Rose Maylie. (40) Nancy tells Rose that she would be murdered if her where-

abouts were known. She tells of overhearing Monks offer Fagin money to make Oliver a thief and then, just last night, of hearing Monks tell Fagin that all traces of Oliver's identity had been destroyed. She reports that Monks wants to destroy Oliver, his half-brother. Monks also told Fagin that Mrs. Maylie and Rose would pay a fortune to know Oliver's identity. Rose offers to help Nancy escape from her dangerous life, but Nancy refuses all help. She arranges to walk on London Bridge on Sunday evenings between 11:00 and midnight should Rose want to communicate further with her.

(41) Oliver and Mr. Brownlow are reunited. Brownlow is overjoyed to see Oliver and learn his story. He and Rose plan to pursue Monks, but they agree not to tell Oliver.

Part 19 (November 1838)

(42) Noah Claypole and Charlotte come to London after taking money from Sowerberry's till. Fagin recruits Noah to steal coins from children. (43) Fagin sends Noah, now using the pseudonym Morris Bolter, to observe the Artful Dodger's trial for picking pockets. The Dodger makes a mockery of the court, but he is formally indicted and taken off to jail. Noah takes the news back to Fagin.

Part 20 (December 1838)

(44) Fagin enlists Noah to spy on Nancy. The next Sunday evening, Bill Sikes remains at home, so Nancy, nervous and hysterical, cannot go out. (45) A week later, Noah follows her to London Bridge. (46) There she meets Rose and Brownlow and takes them down some stairs at the end of the bridge. She offers to help Brownlow capture Monks on the conditions that Fagin not be involved and her identity as informer be kept secret. When she describes "a broad red mark, like a burn or scald" on Monks's neck, Brownlow indicates that he knows Monks's identity. Brownlow offers to help Nancy go to a safe haven, but she refuses. After Rose and Brownlow leave, she sinks down on the stairs and sobs. Then she returns to the street, soon followed by Noah, who has overheard the conversation on the stairs.

Part 21 (January 1839)

(47) After Fagin gets Noah to tell Sikes what he saw and heard on the bridge, Sikes, wild with

anger, rushes back to his rooms, awakens Nancy, and accuses her. She pleads with him to take up Brownlow's offer and go off with her to some distant place. But Sikes beats her twice across her upturned face with his pistol, knocking her to the ground. Then he seizes a heavy club and delivers the killing blow. (48) As the morning sunlight comes into the room, Sikes turns his back on the body, but he cannot get the horror out of his mind or forget the eyes staring at him. He burns the club, washes the bloodstains from his clothes, and leaves the house with his dog Bull's Eye. He goes to the countryside north of London, but wherever he goes he is haunted by the "widely staring eyes." Finally he decides to return to the city. Afraid that his dog will give him away, he attempts to drown the animal, but the dog escapes and runs off.

(49) Meanwhile Brownlow has captured Monks. Brownlow knows Monks is Edward Leeford, the son of his oldest friend, Edwin Leeford. He tells Monks the story of his father's unhappy first marriage, the separation from his wife (Monks's mother), and the later relationship with Oliver's mother. He describes the will that Monks's mother destroyed after Edwin Leeford's death and the proofs of Oliver's identity that Monks destroyed. Threatening to prosecute Monks as an accessory to Nancy's murder, Brownlow gets Monks to write a confession, which will restore Oliver as their father's heir.

Part 22 (February 1839)

(50) Fagin and Noah Claypole have been arrested. Three fugitives—Toby Crackit, Chitling, and Kags—have holed up in a derelict dwelling on Jacob's Island, a repulsive slum near the Thames. Sikes's dog arrives there mud-covered and lame. A little while later Sikes appears, his blanched face buried in a handkerchief. When Charley Bates arrives, he backs away from Sikes and vows to turn him over to the mob that has gathered outside. Bates calls to the police from an open window. Sikes gets a rope and crawls out onto the roof of the house. The mob, directed by Bates's cries, breaks down the door. Sikes loops the rope around a chimney, but when he loses his balance and falls from the roof, the rope forms a noose around his neck. Bates sees the murderer's body swinging outside the window. Bull's Eye jumps from the roof to his master, but misses the body and is dashed to death on a stone in the ditch below.

Part 23 (March 1839)

(51) Mr. Brownlow takes Oliver to his birthplace. There Monks corroborates the story of Edwin Leeford and Agnes Fleming, Oliver's parents, and gives an account of Edwin Leeford's will, which had left his estate to Oliver if "in his minority he should never have stained his name with any public act of dishonor, meanness, cowardice, or wrong." Monks paid Fagin to arrange Oliver's corruption. The Bumbles admit their complicity in suppressing Oliver's identity. Bumble tries to place the blame on his wife, but Brownlow informs him that under the law he is the more guilty party, because the law "supposes that your wife acts under your direction." Bumble responds by asserting, "If the law supposes that, the law is a ass—a idiot." Then Brownlow reveals the identity of Rose Maylie as the younger sister of Agnes Fleming, hence Oliver's aunt. Harry renews his suit for her hand, telling her that he has chosen to become a village parson so that he will be her social equal. The engaged couple join the others for a celebratory supper, but Oliver is sad, for he has learned that Little Dick is dead.

Part 24 (April 1839)

(52) Fagin is found guilty and condemned to death by hanging. In his cell he vacillates between stupefaction, defiance, and dementia. When Oliver comes with Brownlow to visit Fagin in his cell, at first the old thief shrinks from the boy, but then he imagines that the child can get him out of prison. As Oliver and Brownlow leave, Fagin sends up "cry upon cry that penetrated even those massive walls, and rang in their ears until they reached the open yard." By the time they leave, it is dawn and the crowd is gathering for the execution.

(53) Three months later Rose and Harry marry and settle in the country. Brownlow adopts Oliver and they settle nearby. Oliver gives half of his father's estate to Monks so he can start a new life in the New World, where he squanders the money and dies in prison. Noah Claypole, pardoned for testifying against Fagin, takes up a career as a police informer. Charley Bates abandons crime to become

a sheepherder in Northamptonshire. The Bumbles, relieved of their parochial positions, are inmates in the workhouse they once managed. The community of Brownlow and the Maylies, augmented by the frequent visits of Losberne and Grimwig, is "truly happy"; the two orphans, Oliver and Rose, "tried by adversity, remember its lessons in mercy to others, and mutual love, and fervent thanks to Him who had protected and preserved them." In the village church there is a white marble tablet inscribed with one name, "Agnes."

COMMENTARY

In *Twist*, Dickens explores territory very different from that in *Sketches by Boz* or *Pickwick*. It represents a third kind of experiment by a novelist still in the process of learning his craft and discovering his voice. The novel does not follow Oliver's life long enough to make this a BILDUNGSROMAN, for we do not see how Oliver's childhood experiences shape his character as an adult, but the beginnings of that learning process are present in Oliver's story. *Twist* is one of the earliest novels to employ a child hero, a figure that will reappear in several of Dickens's later novels and in the works of other Victorian novelists. In its time, *Oliver Twist* was an experimental novel.

Like Dickens's other early works, *Twist* was not carefully planned. A monthly serial for BENTLEY'S MISCELLANY, a magazine Dickens was editing at the time, *Twist* began appearing while *Pickwick* was in the midst of its serial run. The two novels overlapped for nine months, and Dickens devoted half of the month to composing each of the monthly installments for the two books. After only a few months' respite at the end of *Pickwick*, Dickens began *Nickleby* in February 1838; that novel overlapped the last nine months of *Twist*'s serialization. At the same time, Dickens was editing the *Miscellany* and undertaking other writing and editorial projects. With so many demands, he had little time to plan his novels or to revise the monthly numbers. There are extensive revisions for some later editions of *Twist*, suggesting that Dickens was aware, at least later on, of the limitations to his demanding schedule. The revisions also reveal a more mature writer at work, for they toned down

the sentimentality, cut some of the strong language, and removed some of the apparent anti-Semitism in the presentation of Fagin.

Dickens also dealt with stresses in his personal life while working on the novel. The many projects he undertook and his unsettled contractual arrangements with various publishers indicate the financial pressures that Dickens faced as a young husband and father establishing himself as a professional writer. Some commentators have suggested that Oliver's vulnerability reflects the insecurity that Dickens felt at this early stage in his career. Only a few months after he began the novel, MARY HOGARTH, his young sister-in-law, died. Overcome with grief, Dickens suspended the publication of the monthly installments of his novels, one of the rare times that he failed to meet his publication schedule. Rose Maylie, the first in a series of young women in the novels who were inspired by Dickens's memories of Mary Hogarth, is arrested in angelic innocence.

Oliver Twist, too, may be the first novel in which Dickens imaginatively re-created his experiences as a child working in the BLACKING WAREHOUSE. Kidnapped from his respectable life with Brownlow and forced by Fagin to take part in Sikes's crimes, Oliver, like the young Dickens, feels helplessly trapped in an alien world. Several commentators have suggested that *Twist* is the first of the "autobiographical" novels, the initial statement of Dickens's orphan myth that will be developed most fully in *Copperfield* and *Expectations*.

Dickens began the novel with topical satire, taking on the controversial NEW POOR LAW and the workhouse system that it instituted. In 1837–38 there were massive protests against the law, especially in the north of England. By abolishing outdoor relief, that is, payments from the parish to supplement otherwise inadequate wages, and by requiring those who received benefits to enter a workhouse, the Poor Law was widely regarded as oppressive, making poverty a crime and imprisoning the pauper in "Poor Law Bastilles," workhouses made uninviting to discourage any but the most desperate from entering.

Bumble, Mrs. Corney, Mrs. Mann, and the workhouse board of supervisors are the heartless representatives of the workhouse system in the novel.

To them, Oliver is simply an "item of mortality" (1), his name merely the next one on an alphabetical list that Bumble uses to identify infant paupers. These nameless orphans have no history, no life story; if they survive the deprivation of the baby farm and the workhouse, they are sold as apprentices to the least-demanding bidder. Oliver's innocence saves him from being released as a chimney sweep—an occupation notorious at the time for endangering and maiming the boys who worked at it—when the magistrate accidentally looks into his face and understands his fear. But the Board of Poor Law Guardians shows no similar humanity or understanding. They are convinced that Oliver is a "bad 'un" who will surely end up being hung.

Besides his attacks on the workhouse system, the law that established it, and the bureaucracy that administered it, Dickens also satirized—in Magistrate Fang—the legal system that supported it. Fang was based on Magistrate Laing of HATTON GARDEN, notorious for his harshness and insolence. Dickens, who knew Laing only by reputation, visited his courtroom before writing of Oliver's hearing. His satire of the trial is said to have prompted the home secretary to remove Laing from the bench.

Dickens's subtitle, "The Parish Boy's Progress," suggests a larger satiric context for the topicalities in the opening numbers of *Twist*. Although STEVEN MARCUS (1965) and others have argued that Dickens had Bunyan's *Pilgrim's Progress* in mind as a model for his story, the progresses of WILLIAM HOGARTH were a more likely inspiration, for Dickens knew Hogarth's visual stories well, and he shared the satiric and moralistic vision that prompted Hogarth's art. *Twist* begins as a story that promises to expose the ways in which oppressive social institutions corrupt children and turn them into thieves and criminals; Oliver's progress seems destined to follow a course much like that of Hogarth's idle apprentice: from idleness to crime and ultimately to the gallows. That Hogarthian theme governs the stories of the Artful Dodger, Noah Claypool, and most of the underworld characters in the novel, but Dickens was not so cynical as his mentor, nor, at this early stage of his career, so philosophically consistent in developing his satiric theme. When Oliver leaves the country and goes to London, the novel seems to shift from satiric exposé to mythic allegory. Instead of describing Oliver's progress to the gallows, the novel pits the innocent Oliver against the satanic Fagin and transforms his progress into a quest for identity.

Although *Twist* was attacked when it first appeared as one of the corrupting NEWGATE NOVELS, the Oliver of the quest story is very different from such Newgate figures as WILLIAM HARRISON AINSWORTH's Jack Sheppard, with whom he was often linked. The fictional biography of a notorious criminal from the *Newgate Calendar,* Jack's story is a realistic account, a downward progress from idleness to thievery to transportation and, finally, to the gallows. By the time Oliver reaches London, Dickens thinks of his child hero not as a realistic figure but rather as the allegorical "principle of Good surviving through every adverse circumstance, and triumphing at last" (1843 preface). Although Oliver gradually comes to recognize and understand the presence of evil in the world, he is not corrupted by it. As an allegorical figure, he is not changed by experience; he remains angelic to the end, representative of innocence and goodness.

Although Dickens defended Fagin as a realistic representation of a whole class of criminal receivers of stolen goods, his allegorical intent is also apparent from Fagin's first appearance. Standing "before the fire. . . . with a toasting-fork in his hand . . . [his] villainous-looking and repulsive face . . . obscured by a quantity of matted red hair" (8), Fagin is satanic from the outset. Ironically, he is almost the first person to treat Oliver kindly and to take some "parental" interest in him. He provides food and lodging for the boy and devotes himself to Oliver's education. That Fagin should provide what the indifferent representatives of the parish have denied to Oliver heightens the satiric message and describes a world in which an indifferent society colludes with the powers of darkness to destroy the innocent. Evil has a metaphysical presence in the novel; goodness is less convincing. GRAHAM GREENE (1951) describes the Manichaean allegory in *Twist* as "a world without God, . . . [where] we can believe in evil-doing, but goodness wilts into philanthropy."

Oliver has moments of epiphany when he loses his intellectual innocence, as, for example, when he realizes during the bookshop robbery that he is one of a gang of thieves and that the handkerchief game was part of his instruction in picking pockets (10). But Oliver is not changed by this knowledge. The more he knows of Fagin, Sikes, and Monks, the more evident is the contradiction between the assumptions behind the satire and those behind the allegory. Satire is existential; it assumes that experience molds and changes people, that oppression and deprivation will turn an innocent child into a criminal. Allegory takes an essentialist view; its static characters represent fixed ideas and ideals. These contradictory modes at the heart of the novel create what has sometimes been formulated as a version of the nature/nurture conflict, asking whether criminals are born or made. Dickens seems to take both sides of the issue, depending on whether he is writing about the Artful Dodger or about Oliver.

Dickens may recognize the contradiction at the heart of his story when he introduces chapter 17 with a discussion of the principle of alternation between tragic and comic scenes in the drama as one that is also true to life offstage. But moving back and forth between satiric and allegorical modes, and between the light world of Brownlow and the dark underworld of Fagin, his story sometimes seems headed in two different directions. He does use alternation effectively to provide suspense when he leaves Oliver lying wounded in a ditch for three numbers while he narrates the comedy of Bumble's courtship. But the novel loses coherence when Oliver takes up permanent residence with the Maylies and is no longer part of Fagin's urban hell. As long as Oliver was present in both allegorical dimensions, he provided a coherent center to the alternations between the light and dark worlds in the novel. But when he exited from Fagin's realm, Dickens was forced to turn the allegorical quest narrative into an inheritance story.

This difficulty may have resulted from Dickens's choice of a child hero. Even with his allegorical power to resist evil, there are limits to Oliver's experience. When Brownlow takes him to Fagin's cell on the night before the old man is to hang, the jailer warns him, "It's not a sight for children,

sir." Brownlow replies that "This child has seen him in full career of his success and villainy, I think it as well—even at the cost of some pain and fear—that he should see him now" (52). But Dickens was unwilling to expose his child hero to the murder of Nancy and the death of Sikes. There were some things beyond the limits of even Oliver's innocence.

While the dark side of the novel careens out of control with the account of Sikes and Nancy, Oliver is in protective custody at the Maylies' country house. Oliver's existential quest to reconcile the bifurcation in his experience is replaced by Brownlow's manipulation of Oliver's origins and identity. Oliver becomes the passive recipient of an 18th-century inheritance plot rather than the 19th century hero who defines the terms of his own life. Earlier in the novel, he asserts himself to ask for more in the workhouse dining room, to resist being apprenticed to the chimney sweep, to defend his mother's honor against Noah Claypole's aspersions, to run away from Sowerberry, and to resist becoming a thief. But by the end he has lost his assertiveness, and he simply accepts Brownlow's version of his story.

Yet even in Eden, Oliver is not wholly without contradiction. In one of the most memorable and puzzling scenes in the novel, Oliver sees Fagin and Monks at the window of his country retreat, but when he raises the alarm no trace of their presence can be found (34, 35). We are left to wonder whether the experience was dream or reality and to speculate about whether the evil represented by the intruders is outside the window or within Oliver. The novel provides no answer either to these questions or to some of the other mysteries in Oliver's story. Losberne, for example, cannot confirm Oliver's account of the house where he and Sikes spent the night on their way to Chertsey (32).

Even the formulaic inheritance plot cannot fully replace the experiential account of Oliver's search for identity. His father's will, which made Oliver's inheritance contingent on his incorruptibility, may explain Monk's motivation and Fagin's interest in the boy, but it cannot comprehend the depths of betrayal and fear that motivate the evil characters or the goodness that protects Oliver and prompts Nancy to give her life for him. The mysteries of good and evil at the heart of the allegory are beyond novelistic explanation. Nor can the inheritance plot provide Oliver with a fully acceptable identity. He remains an illegitimate child, bearing his workhouse name, son of a mother identified on her tombstone only as "Agnes." In the end he is still a kind of social orphan.

In spite of its inconsistencies and contradictions, *Oliver Twist* contains a number of memorable scenes and characters, many of them rendered in the compelling original illustrations by GEORGE CRUIKSHANK. The success of these pictures suggests that Dickens may have thought of his story as a literary version of one of Hogarth's progresses. Especially memorable scenes include Oliver asking for more gruel at the workhouse, his arrival at Fagin's den, the robbery at Chertsey, Monks and Fagin at the window, Sikes's death, and Fagin in the condemned cell. These scenes do represent a downward progress from the workhouse to the gallows, even though Oliver is not the prisoner waiting to be hung at the end of the story.

While Oliver is usually criticized as a simplistic allegorical character and a passive pawn in the inheritance plot, the contradictory modes in the novel make many of the characters around him, particularly those from the criminal underworld, intriguingly complex figures. Fagin has sometimes been viewed simply as an anti-Semitic stereotype. Certainly he is a product of anti-Semitic tradition, which Dickens seems to have accepted uncritically. Yet Dickens's revisions of later editions of *Twist* and his inclusion of Riah in *Mutual Friend* indicate his willingness to redress a wrong when the injustice of his portrayal was pointed out to him. Even in his original depiction, Fagin does, in significant ways, transcend the stereotype. A mixture of satanic evil and sympathy complicates his character. His kindness to Oliver contrasts with the inhumane bureaucracy of the Poor Law administrators, and when Fagin instructs Noah Claypole in the principle of looking out for number one (43), he articulates the "philosophy" shared by the respectable proponents of laissez-faire who created the workhouse system and those in criminal underworld. But Fagin's

application of the principle of self-interest—using hanging as a way of getting rid of those who know too much—takes the cruelty of the system to a brutal extreme. As the avatar of satanic evil, the vehicle for exposing the inhumanity of the system, and the scapegoat of society's attempt at self-preservation, Fagin elicits complicated responses and some limited sympathy.

The Artful Dodger is similarly complex. His criminality demands that he be punished, but his oversized clothes remind us that he is a child forced into adult responsibilities by a society that neglects and abuses its children. His unrepentant assertiveness, especially at his trial (43), allies him with characters like Sam Weller in *Pickwick* and Young Bailey in *Chuzzlewit,* who survive by assertive self-creation. He commands admiration as much as condemnation.

Sympathy does not complicate our response to Sikes, even though we get an interior glimpse of him after the murder. But Nancy, the only interesting woman in the novel, elicits sympathy for her simultaneous compassion for Oliver and her loyalty to Sikes, a complexity characterized by Dickens as "a contradiction, an anomaly, an apparent impossibility, but it is a truth" (preface). None of the good characters embody such intriguing contradictions.

Bumble, one of Dickens's great comic figures, comes from a different world from that of Fagin and Sikes. Their evil is metaphysical; his is earthly and opportunistic. He serves his own self-interest by trying to serve those in power, the perfect representative for an inhumane system that victimizes the poor while pretending to serve them. His stupidity makes him foolish and ineffective, causing him, for example, to misread Brownlow's interest in Oliver and to miscalculate Mrs. Corney's willingness to subordinate her own interests in marriage. His marital persecution may transform his role as satiric butt into clichéd domestic comedy as the henpecked husband, but his classic response to Brownlow's warning that the law will hold him accountable for his wife's actions is one of the most memorable—and most quoted—passages in all of Dickens: "If the law supposes that . . . the law is a ass—a idiot" (51). At moments like this, Dickens redefines the tradition.

CHARACTERS AND RELATED ENTRIES

Angel, Islington Coaching inn at ISLINGTON on the northern route out of London that Oliver Twist and Noah Claypole pass as they enter the city (8, 42).

Anny An old pauper who summons Mrs. Corney, the matron of the workhouse, to the death-bed of Sally, another pauper, who attended Oliver's mother on her deathbed. Sally gives Mrs. Corney a locket and information essential to unraveling Oliver's parentage (24, 51).

"Artful Dodger, the" The nickname of Jack Dawkins.

Barker, Phil One of Fagin's cohorts, drunk at the Three Cripples (26).

Barney Jewish waiter at the Three Cripples who helps Fagin and Sikes plan the Chertsey robbery.

Bates, Charley Member of Fagin's kennel of pickpockets, he exhibits "some very loose notions concerning the rights of property" (10). He advises Oliver to "put [himself] under Fagin" so as to make himself "able to retire on [his] property and do the genteel" (18), as Bates intends to do. But, horrified by the murder of Nancy, Bates aids in the exposure of Sikes, reforms, and becomes "the merriest young grazier in all Northamptonshire" (53). Several recent commentators see a double entendre in the name "Master Bates," suggesting that it hints of a repressed sexual dimension in the gang of thieves and reinforces veiled allusions to Fagin's homoerotic involvement with his gang of boys.

Bayton, Mrs. A pauper who dies of starvation, requiring Bumble to arrange the "porochial" funeral that Oliver Twist attends as an apprentice to undertaker Sowerberry (5).

Bedwin Mr. Brownlow's housekeeper, "a motherly old lady," who cares for Oliver after he faints in Magistrate Fang's courtroom (12). She remains a staunch believer in Oliver's innocence, even when Grimwig and Brownlow doubt him.

Bet (Betsy) Prostitute and companion to Nancy, "gaily . . . attired, in a red gown, green boots, and yellow curl papers" (13), she is Tom Chitling's girl. After identifying Nancy's body, she goes mad.

Blathers BOW STREET RUNNER summoned with Duff to investigate the robbery at Mrs. Maylie's house: "a stout personage, of middle height, aged about fifty, with shiny black hair cropped pretty close, half whiskers, a round face, and sharp eyes" (31). Losberne frustrates their investigation so that they leave without arresting Oliver.

Bolter, Morris Noah Claypole's alias in London as a member of Fagin's gang.

Brittles Mrs. Maylie's man-of-all-work, "who entered her service a mere child and was treated as a promising boy, though he was something past thirty" (28). He is the younger of the two servants who surprise Oliver when Sikes lowers the boy into the house in CHERTSEY.

Brownlow The kindly old man who befriends Oliver Twist, "a very respectable-looking personage, with a powdered head and gold spectacles" (10). He is as idealistic and trusting as his friend Grimwig is cynical. After Oliver is arrested for picking his pocket, he believes in the boy's innocence, refuses to testify against him, and takes him into his home (10–12). When Oliver is retaken by Sikes and Nancy and seems to have run away, Brownlow briefly doubts the boy, but Mrs. Bedwin's unwavering belief in Oliver restores Brownlow's trust. After the Maylies reconnect Oliver with him, Brownlow becomes a detective who constructs the story of Oliver's identity. He adopts Oliver as a son.

Bull's Eye Bill Sikes's "white shaggy dog, with his face scratched and torn in twenty different places" (13), wounds indicative of his owner's mistreatment. After Nancy's murder, Sikes, fleeing from the law, attempts to drown the dog (48), but Bull's Eye escapes and shows up at Jacob's Island just before his owner arrives (50). When Sikes falls from the roof of the hideout and hangs himself, the dog leaps for his body, misses, and dashes his brains out on a stone (50).

Bumble   Self-important parochial beadle of the workhouse where Oliver Twist is born. "A fat man and a choleric [who] had a great idea of his oratorical powers and his importance" (2). He wears a cocked hat and a coat with gold-laced cuffs. He names the parochial "fondlings" in alphabetical order, following "Swubble" with "Twist," who will be succeeded by "Unwin" and "Vilkins," a responsibility that leads Mrs. Mann to remark of him, "Why, you're quite a literary character, Sir!" Bumble oversees Oliver's childhood and apprenticeship. After taking an inventory of the china cabinet of Mrs. Corney, matron of the workhouse, he marries her with an eye to "a joining of hearts and housekeepings" (27), but she rules him in an unequal marriage. When the two are being questioned about their involvement in suppressing Oliver's identity, Brownlow prompts Bumble's most famous speech by stating that the law supposes that Mrs. Bumble acts under the direction of her husband. "If the law supposes that," Bumble responds, "the law is a ass—a idiot. If that's the eye of the law, the law is a bachelor; and the worst I wish the law is, that his eye may be opened by experience" (51). The Bumbles lose their positions as a result of their actions in Oliver's case and end their lives as inmates in the workhouse they once administered.

For much of the novel, Bumble is the butt of Dickens's satire of self-important bureaucrats who wield their petty power arbitrarily and who indulge in all the perquisites of office. A pompous bully and a toady to his superiors, Bumble becomes more sympathetic as the victim of Mrs. Corney's marital tyranny. JAMES KINCAID (1971) suggests that Dickens pushes the comeuppance of Bumble "past the humorous point" by piling on one humiliation after another.

Charlotte   The Sowerberrys's maidservant, "a slatterly girl, in shoes down at heel, and blue worsted stockings very much out of repair" (4). Infatuated with Noah Claypole, she feeds him food from the master's table while feeding Oliver scraps. She steals money from her employers and runs off to London with Noah Claypole.

Chickweed, Conkey   Subject of an anecdote told by Blathers, he was the keeper of a tavern near BATTLE BRIDGE who faked a burglary in order to solicit public sympathy and donations (31).

Chitling, Tom   Member of Fagin's gang who has recently returned from prison and taken up with Betsy. At 18, he is older than the Dodger, but he is deferential to him as a superior thief. "He had small twinkling eyes, and a pock-marked face; wore a fur cap, a corduroy jacket, greasy fustian trousers, and an apron" (18). He is at Jacob's Island when Sikes is killed.

Claypole, Noah   Charity boy who is Sowerberry's assistant, "a large-headed, small-eyed youth, of lumbering make and heavy countenance" (5). Noah bullies and taunts Oliver as "Work'us," lower on the social scale than a charity boy. When he calls Oliver's mother "a right-down bad 'un" (6), Oliver strikes back. Noah runs off to London with Charlotte (42), joins Fagin's gang (43), and, using the alias Morris Bolter, spies on Nancy for Fagin (46). He testifies against Fagin and takes up a profession as a police informer (52). Noah's "progress" from bully to thief to police informer describes a Hogarthian pattern of downward movement. It confirms the satiric point that deprivation and mistreatment produce juvenile delinquents and criminals.

Corney, Mrs.   Widow who is matron of the workhouse where Oliver Twist is born. She complains about her solitary life and manages to entrap Bumble into marrying her (27), only to make his life miserable with her domination of him. She secures from a dying pauper the trinkets that confirm Oliver's parentage (24) and sells them to Monks (38). Ultimately, she and her husband, dismissed from their parochial positions, become inmates in the workhouse they once ran (53).

Crackit, Toby ("Flash Toby")   Member of Fagin's gang, Flash Toby is Sikes's accomplice in the attempted break-in at Mrs. Maylie's house (22): He "had no very great quantity of hair, either upon his head or face; but what he had, was of a reddish dye, tortured into long corkscrew curls, through which he occasionally thrust some very dirty fingers, ornamented with large common rings. He was a trifle above the middle size, and apparently rather weak in the legs; but this circumstance by no means detracted from his own admiration of his top-boots, which he contemplated . . . with lively satisfaction" (22). His hideout on Jacob's Island is where Sikes seeks refuge in the end (50).

Craven Street   Street near Charing Cross where Mr. Brownlow takes up residence after returning from the West Indies (41).

Dawkins, John ("The Artful Dodger")   Youthful pickpocket who is a member of Fagin's gang and recruits Oliver Twist: "one of the queerest looking boys that Oliver had ever seen. He was a snub-nosed, flat-browed, common-faced boy, . . . but he had about him all the airs and manners of a man. He was short of his age: with rather bowlegs, and little, sharp, ugly eyes. . . . He wore a man's coat, which reached nearly to his heels. He had turned the cuffs back, half-way up his arm, to get his hands out of the sleeves: apparently with the ultimate view of thrusting them into the pockets of his corduroy trousers; for there he kept them. He was, altogether, as roistering and swaggering a young gentleman as ever stood four feet six, or something less, in his bluchers" (8). He and Charley Bates rob Brownlow at the bookstore, the crime for which Oliver is arrested (10). When the Dodger is apprehended and tried for stealing a silver snuff box, he appears in court and gamely tries to put the judge and the court itself on trial, but his strategy fails and he is sentenced to transportation for life. He leaves the courtroom heroically unrepentant (43).

Described by Richard Dunn (*Oliver Twist: Whole Heart and Soul*, 1993) as "a Dickensian free spirit," the Dodger is the successor to Sam Weller in *Pickwick*, the articulate product of the London streets who creates himself in colorful and clever language. His insolent and defiant wit challenges the corrupt institutions that make boys into criminals, but, unlike Sam, he is not triumphant. In spite of his verbal ability to turn the courtroom on its head, he is sentenced to transportation and

cast out of the story, an indication of the narrative shift away from the satire that opens the novel to the romantic fairy tale that ends it. In the Artful Dodger, Dickens comes closest to one element of the NEWGATE NOVEL that his critics disliked, the heroic portrayal of the outlaw, but in spite of his wit and defiance, the Dodger is ultimately defeated by the system.

Dick   Orphan friend of Oliver Twist at Mrs. Mann's baby farm. He blesses Oliver as he leaves to go to London (7). When Bumble interviews the sick and dying boy before he goes to London, Dick requests someone to write down that he leaves his "dear love to Oliver Twist," prompting Bumble's assertion "that out-dacious Oliver has demogalized them all!" (17).

Duff   BOW STREET RUNNER and colleague of Blathers: "a red-headed, bony man, in top-boots; with a rather ill-favoured countenance, and a turned-

Fagin (Ron Moody) and the Artful Dodger (Jack Wild) sing "Reviewing the Situation" while picking pockets in *Oliver!*, the popular 1968 musical movie adaptation of *Oliver Twist. Courtesy of PhotoFest.*

up sinister-looking nose" (31). He investigates the CHERTSEY robbery.

Fagin Receiver of stolen goods and leader of a gang of young thieves and pickpockets, "a very old shrivelled Jew, whose villainous-looking and repulsive face was obscured by a quantity of matted red hair" (8). The Artful Dodger introduces Oliver Twist into Fagin's gang (8), and Oliver's half-brother, Monks, employs Fagin to corrupt his innocent sibling. To this end, Fagin teaches Oliver to pick pockets and involves him in Sikes's robbery of Mrs. Maylie's house (22). Fagin attempts but fails to recapture Oliver after the Maylies take him in, and as his own capture approaches, he desperately urges Sikes to murder Nancy (47). After his capture, as he awaits execution, Fagin is visited in prison by Oliver and Mr. Brownlow. Mad with fear, he attempts to leave his cell with the boy (52).

Although the novel is titled *Oliver Twist*, Fagin is really its central figure and focus of energy. Both fearful and fascinating, Fagin brings together traditional anti-Semitic stereotypes with more sympathetic characteristics—his wit and playfulness, for example. The matted red hair and the toasting fork that Fagin is holding when Oliver is first introduced to him begin the satanic allusions that create his character. He is also bestial: "As he glided stealthily along, creeping beneath the shelter of the walls and doorways, the hideous old man seemed like some loathsome reptile, engendered in the slime and darkness through which he moved: crawling forth, by night, in search of some rich offal for a meal" (19). This characterization concludes in the condemned cell, where he sits "with a countenance more like that of a snared beast than the face of a man" (52). But Fagin is also sympathetic, the first person to offer food and comfort to Oliver ungrudgingly. JAMES KINCAID (1971) points out that "More often than 'sinister' even, the words 'gentle' and 'soft' are associated with Fagin, and the over-emphasized and obvious satanic connections should not obscure the fact that there is something maternal as well about the recurring image of Fagin bending over the fire and about his favourite phrase, 'my dear.'" This effeminacy has led some recent critics, Epstein (1998), for example,

Cruikshank's famous rendering of Fagin awaiting execution for the original edition of *Oliver Twist* (1839).

to detect "hints of homosexuality" in Fagin and his gang of boys. Even if Dickens was unaware of this dimension to his portrayal, he was aware of the irony in the contrast between the torments of the workhouse and the playful games in Fagin's den that bring Oliver to tears of joyful laughter, perhaps for the first time in his life. With similar irony, Fagin's expatiation to Noah Claypole on the philosophy of "number one" (43) draws ironic parallels to the doctrine of economic self-interest that inspired the work of the Poor Law reformers.

Dickens took Fagin's name from Bob Fagin, a boy who worked with him at WARREN'S BLACKING in 1824. Fagin has often been considered an anti-Semitic caricature, based on a stereotype. ALEC GUINESS's portrayal of the Jew in DAVID LEAN's 1948 film was censored before it could be shown in the United States. After ELIZA DAVIS, a Jewish acquaintance of Dickens's, communicated her objections to Dickens, he removed many references to "the Jew" from the CHARLES DICKENS EDITION of the novel in 1867 and included Riah in *Mutual Friend* as a way of redressing the balance in his depictions of JEWS.

Fang Magistrate who hears the case against Oliver Twist for picking Mr. Brownlow's pocket. "His face was stern, and much flushed. If he were really not in the habit of drinking rather more than was exactly good for him, he might have brought an action against his countenance for libel, and have recovered heavy damages" (11). He bullies Oliver, browbeats Mr. Brownlow, and sentences the boy to three months in prison. When the bookseller exonerates Oliver, Fang threatens to bring charges against Brownlow. Fang was modeled on the notorious magistrate Allan Stewart Laing of HATTON GARDEN Police Court.

Fleming, Agnes Oliver Twist's mother and the sister of ROSE MAYLIE. Seduced by Edwin Leeford, "she was weak and erring" (53), but her gravestone is a shrine for the son who never knew her. Her portrait, which hangs in Brownlow's house, is an important clue in aiding Brownlow establish Oliver's identity, for the boy is a "living copy" of the picture (12).

Gamfield Cruel chimney sweep "whose dark and villainous face was a regular stamped receipt for cruelty" (3). He observes to the magistrate that "boys is wery obstinit, and wery lazy, gen'lmen, and there's nothink like a good hot blaze to make 'em come down with a run. It's humane too, gen'lmen, acause, even if they've stuck in the chimbley, roasting their feet makes 'em struggle to hextricate theirselves'" (3). The magistrate, noting Oliver's fear of the man, refuses to approve the apprenticeship papers drawn up by the workhouse guardians.

Gentleman with the White Waistcoat One of the governors of the workhouse who is especially representative of the hard-hearted attitude of the board. When Oliver asks for more gruel, he asserts, "That boy will be hung" (2).

Giles Mrs. Maylie's butler, who raises the alarm about the robbery and fires the shot that wounds Oliver (22).

Grannett Overseer in the workhouse where Oliver Twist is born, admired by Bumble and Mrs. Corney for his harsh treatment of the paupers (23).

Grimwig Mr. Brownlow's cynical lawyer friend who is as suspicious of Oliver as Brownlow is trusting, "a stout old gentleman, rather lame in one leg, who was dressed in a blue coat, striped waistcoat, nankeen breeches and gaiters, and a broad-brimmed white hat" (14). He underscores his cynical predictions with the hyperbolic promise to "eat my head" should they not come true. He appears to be delighted when his suspicions are confirmed by Oliver's disappearance with Brownlow's books and money (16), but underneath he is good-hearted and wishes the best for the boy. By the end of the story, he and Dr. Losberne have become close friends (53).

Harry Peddler selling stain remover who, after Nancy's murder, meets Bill Sikes in a pub and offers to remove the bloodstain from his hat (48).

Hendon A village on the outskirts of London to which Sikes escapes after murdering Nancy, but "all the people he met—the very children at the doors—seemed to view him with suspicion" (48).

Hockley-in-the-Hole A slum area in Clerkenwell through which the Artful Dodger leads Oliver on his way into London (8).

Hosier Lane A street beside Smithfield Market along which Oliver goes with Bill Sikes (21).

Jacob's Island Island in the Thames River off Bermondsey where Toby Crackit's house is located in a festering slum. Sikes ends his life here (50).

Kags Convict who has returned illegally from transportation and is hiding in Toby Crackit's house on Jacob's Island when Sikes comes to hide out there: "a robber of fifty years, whose nose had been almost beaten in some old scuffle, and whose face bore a frightful scar" (50).

Laing, Allan Stewart A real-life magistrate from HATTON GARDEN whose "harshness and insolence" made him the model for Magistrate Fang in *Oliver Twist*.

Leeford, Edward ("Monks")   Villainous half brother of Oliver Twist. "A tall man wrapped in a cloak" (33), he is described by Nancy as "a strongly made man, but not stout; he has a lurking walk; and as he walks, constantly looks over his shoulder, first on one side, and then on the other. . . . His face is dark, like his hair and eyes; and, although he can't be more than six or eight and twenty, withered and haggard. His lips are often discoloured and disfigured with the marks of teeth; for he has desperate fits, and sometimes even bites his hands and covers them with wounds" (46). There is also on his neck "a broad red mark, like a burn or a scald" that he covers with a neckerchief. Monks plots with Fagin to corrupt Oliver into a life of criminality (26). If he succeeds, Monks will inherit the estate of their father, whose will otherwise left most of his property to Oliver on the condition that he remain uncorrupted. Monks plotted with his mother to suppress the will, but after he robbed and deserted her, she revealed the truth before dying. Nancy reveals his dealings with Fagin to Brownlow (46), and Monks is forced to leave the country. He dies in prison in America (52). Monks bears the physical signs of his moral degeneracy on his body in the marks on his face and hands, perhaps scars from syphilis, and in the mark of Cain, indicating his exclusion from society, that he bears on his neck.

Leeford, Edwin   Father of Oliver and Monks, who seduced Agnes Fleming, Oliver's mother, and died before he could marry her. He was Brownlow's close friend and brother to Brownlow's fiancée, who died before they could marry.

Limbkins   Chairman of the Board of Guardians at the workhouse where Oliver is born, "a red-faced gentleman in the high chair" (2).

Lively   Receiver of stolen goods on SAFFRON HILL, "a salesman of small stature, who had squeezed as much of his person into a child's chair as the chair would hold" (26).

Losberne   Physician and friend of the Maylies; he believes Oliver innocent and protects him from the inquiries of the BOW STREET RUNNERS; "known . . . as 'the doctor,' [he] had grown fat, more from good humour than from good living: and was as kind and hearty, and withal as eccentric an old bachelor, as will be found" (29). When he retires from his practice, he settles near Rose and Harry (53).

Mann, Mrs.   Operator of the baby farm, "a branch workhouse . . . where twenty or thirty other juvenile offenders against the poor laws, rolled about the floor all day, without the inconvenience of too much food or too much clothing" (2), where Oliver lives until he is nine. "A woman of wisdom and experience; she knew what was good for the children; and she had a very accurate perception of what was good for herself. So, she appropriated the greater part of the weekly stipend to her own use, and consigned the rising parochial generation to an even shorter allowance than was originally provided for them" (2). JAMES KINCAID (1971) observes that "Mrs. Mann and her double, Mrs. Corney, are much more vicious characters than Bumble. They have about them a frightening competence which is born of deep cynicism; they are far more rigid than Bumble; they are both frozen into the role of a monster."

Martha   Palsied old workhouse inmate who sees Mrs. Corney get from Sally the pawn ticket that leads to the locket proving Oliver's identity (23–24).

Maylie, Harry   Mrs. Maylie's son, "about five-and-twenty years of age, and was of the middle height; his countenance was frank and handsome; and his demeanour easy and prepossessing" (34). He gives up a career in politics to marry Rose Maylie. He chooses instead to become a country parson.

Maylie, Mrs.   An upright and stately woman, "dressed with the utmost nicety and precision, in a quaint mixture of by-gone costume with some slight concessions to the prevailing taste" (29), whose house in CHERTSEY is the target of Sikes's robbery. When the wounded Oliver is found on her doorstep, the kind and sympathetic woman takes him in (30). Years before, she had rescued from poverty her adopted daughter Rose.

Maylie, Rose Seventeen-year-old adopted daughter of Mrs. Maylie: "So mild and gentle; so pure and beautiful; that earth seemed not her element, nor its rough creatures her fit companions" (29). Rose interests herself in Oliver's story and arranges the meeting with Nancy on LONDON BRIDGE that leads to Nancy's murder (46). Rose is discovered to be the sister of Agnes Fleming, Oliver's mother (50). Although she considers herself unworthy, because of the obscurity and presumed illegitimacy of her birth, of the love of Harry, Mrs. Maylie's son, he prevails upon her to marry him (50).

Rose's perfection makes her the female counterpart to the innocent Oliver. Based on MARY HOGARTH, whose death forced the distraught Dickens to suspend publication of the novel temporarily, Rose is described in the same superlatives that Dickens applied to Mary. Her spirit dominates the second half of the novel; Oliver is never again in danger after he joins the Maylie circle. Dickens saw Rose and Nancy as contrasted counterparts in this part of the novel, two women whose lives go in different directions, but who are both responsible for saving Oliver from destruction.

Monks The name by which Edward Leeford is known.

Mutton Hill The back door to Mr. Fang's police court led out of this street (also known as Mutton Lane), running between Hatton Garden and Clerkenwell Green (11).

Nancy Prostitute and member of Fagin's gang, she is the mistress of Bill Sikes. She and Bet, the other female member of the gang, "wore a good deal of hair, not very neatly turned up behind, and were rather untidy about the shoes and stockings. They were not exactly pretty, perhaps; but they had a great deal of colour in their faces, and looked quite stout and hearty" (9). After Brownlow takes Oliver in, she recaptures the boy for Fagin by pretending to be his sister (15), but later, disturbed by

Fagin's schemes, she provides Brownlow with information about Monks and Oliver (46). This leads to her murder by Sikes, who has been informed of her betrayal and beats her to death with a club (47).

In his preface to the novel, Dickens defended his portrayal of Nancy as "true": "It is emphatically God's truth, for it is the truth He leaves in such depraved and miserable breasts; the hope yet lingering there; the last fair drop of water at the bottom of a weed-choked well." The same principle, magnified hyperbolically, helps explain Oliver's innocence in spite of his childhood in the workhouse and the streets of London. John Bayley ("Oliver Twist: 'Things as They Really Are.'" *Dickens and The Twentieth Century,* edited by John Gross and Gabriel Pearson, 1962) sees Nancy and Sikes as the central figures in the novel, which he describes as a "gothic nightmare." For Dickens himself, the violence and psychological intensity of the stories of Sikes and Nancy prompted his nearly compulsive need to perform the reading "Sikes and Nancy" in the final months of his life, in spite of the doctors's warning that it caused dangerous stress on his mind and body. JOHN BOWEN (2000) discusses the complexity in the characterization of Nancy, her hysteria, and the contradictory love she bears for both Sikes and Oliver.

Ned Chimney sweep who has, in the past, hired out his small son on burglaries with Sikes, but "then the Juvenile Delinquent Society comes, and takes the boy away from a trade where he was earning money, teaches him to read and write, and in time makes a 'prentice of him" (19).

Sally Workhouse inmate who assists at the delivery of Oliver Twist and steals from Oliver's dead mother the locket and ring that later establish Oliver's identity (1, 23, 24).

Sikes, Bill Brutal thief and murderer; Fagin's accomplice; lover and murderer of Nancy; "a stoutly-built fellow of about five-and-thirty. . . . He had a brown hat upon his head, and a dirty belcher handkerchief round his neck: with the frayed ends of which he smeared the beer from his face as he spoke. He disclosed, when he had done so, a broad heavy countenance with a beard of three days' growth, and two scowling eyes; one of which displayed various parti-coloured symptoms of having been recently damaged by a blow" (13). He is always accompanied by his dog, Bull's Eye. He undertakes to carry out Fagin's scheme to corrupt Oliver by involving the boy in the CHERTSEY robbery (20–22). After Fagin tells him of Nancy's meeting with Brownlow, Sikes, enraged by her betrayal, clubs her to death (47). Then, haunted by a vision of her eyes, he wanders in the countryside around London (48) before returning to Jacob's Island, where he accidentally hangs himself while attempting to escape from the mob (50).

Some critics find in Sikes's haunting memory of Nancy's eyes indications that he is not so irredeemably evil as he otherwise seems to be. John Bayley ("Oliver Twist: 'Things as They Really Are,'" *Dickens and The Twentieth Century*, edited by John Gross and Gabriel Pearson, 1962) suggests that this glimpse into his inner feelings makes him human, and JOHN REED (1995) sees just the glimmerings of "something like" a conscience in this haunting. Dickens, in his 1841 preface, however, defended his characterization in starker terms: "I fear that there are in the world some insensible and callous natures that do become, at last, utterly and irredeemably bad. . . . There are such men as Sikes, who, being closely followed through the same space of time, and through the same current of circumstances, would not give, by one look or action of a moment, the faintest indication of a better nature."

Slout Bumble's predecessor as master of the workhouse where Oliver Twist was born (27).

Sowerberry Undertaker who takes on Oliver Twist as an apprentice; "a tall, gaunt, large-jointed man, attired in a suit of threadbare black, with darned stockings of the same colour, and shoes to answer. His features were not naturally intended to wear a smiling aspect" (4). He carries a snuff box shaped like a small coffin. He employs Oliver as a mute for children's funerals, but he is dominated by his wife and is unable to protect the boy from her harsh treatment.

Sowerberry, Mrs. Sowerberry's wife, "a short, thin, squeezed-up woman, with a vixenish countenance" (4), who feeds the boy scraps for the dog, makes him sleep among the coffins, and locks him in the coal cellar for attacking Noah Claypole. After fighting with Claypole and being held captive by Mrs. Sowerberry, Oliver runs away to London (8).

Spyers, Jem Police officer who arrested Conkey Chickweed, the fraudulent publican in the story told by Blathers (31).

Three Cripples Inn, the Tavern in Saffron Hill frequented by Fagin and his associates (26).

Twist, Oliver "Parish boy" hero of the novel that bears his name. Even though he is born in a workhouse (1), is apprenticed to an undertaker from whom he runs away (4), and falls into Fagin's den of thieves in London (8), Oliver maintains his innocence. His face convinces Brownlow that he is not a thief (11). Even after he is identified as one of the robbers at Mrs. Maylie's house, he convinces her and Doctor Losberne of his innocence (30). Fagin's attempts to corrupt Oliver are encouraged by Monks, who is revealed to be Oliver's half brother and stands to receive Oliver's inheritance should the boy be corrupted. After piecing together Oliver's parentage as the illegitimate child of Edwin Leeford and Agnes Fleming, and hence the nephew of Rose Maylie, Brownlow adopts the boy (50).

In his preface, Dickens declared: "I wanted to shew, in little Oliver, the principle of Good surviving through every adverse circumstance, and triumphing at last." This aim with his hero would seem at odds with the satiric intention to show how children raised in the workhouse and in the streets of London were driven into criminality. Commentators almost inevitably remark on the inconsistency in the novel's apparent position on the relative importance of nature and nurture in forming the individual. Noah Claypole may have learned his toadyism, cowardice, and meanness, but Oliver is a born innocent. He is an emblematic or allegorical figure, not a realistic one. John Bayley ("Oliver Twist: 'Things as They Really Are,'" *Dickens and*

The Twentieth Century, edited by John Gross and Gabriel Pearson, 1962) describes him as "a true everyman. . . . It is logical that he has no character, because he has no physical individuality—he is the child element in a nightmare which is otherwise peopled by animals, and precariously by men."

Oliver's passivity has also bothered many readers, for his innocence is preserved largely through his refusal to engage the forces of evil, and his identity is provided for him through the efforts of Brownlow. Oliver does not act to become the hero of his life; his identity is a gift, not an achievement. Even his moments of assertion—asking for more or attacking Noah Claypole—are compromised. He is put up to asking for more, for example, when the parish boys draw lots. His passive innocence, H. M. DALESKI (1970) points out, is uncomfortably close to stupidity. He is very slow to realize that Fagin's games provide schooling in picking pockets.

ADAPTATIONS

One of the most dramatized of Dickens's novels, *Twist* spawned 10 adaptations before it completed its serial run, the first opening after only 12 of the 24 monthly numbers had appeared. The most noteworthy of these early productions was J. Stirling Coyne's at the ADELPHI THEATRE, starring as Oliver MARY KEELEY, who would become famous for her portrayal of Jack Sheppard, and as Sikes O. SMITH, who also performed Scrooge and the monster in *Frankenstein*. Dickens was distressed by some of the stagings and considered adapting the novel himself, but he was discouraged from doing so by WILLIAM MACREADY, who thought the novel would not make good theater.

There were also nontheatrical pirates who produced prose mutations of the novel in cheap serial format, usually for working-class readers. The best-known of such piracies was by "Bos" (T. P. Prest), *The Life and Adventures of Oliver Twiss, the Workhouse Boy* (1839).

H. Philip Bolton (*Dickens Dramatized,* 1987) counts more than 200 stage versions by 1900 and estimates that there were probably double or triple that number. Oliver was most often played by actresses, among them MARIA HONNER and Mary Keeley. On rare occasions the role was taken by a child actor. Among the famous stage Fagins were ROBERT HONNER, FREDERICK YATES, E. E. Saville, Beerbohm Tree, and BRANSBY WILLIAMS. J. L. TOOLE was famous for his portrayal of the Artful Dodger.

At least 23 film versions have been made, from the early silent *Modern Oliver Twist; or the Life of a Pickpocket* (1906) to Lionel Bart's musical *Oliver!*, adapted for the screen by Vernon Harris and directed by Carol Reed (1968). At least 18 silent films appeared, including French, Italian, and Hungarian versions. Best known of the silent films is Sol Lesser's *Oliver Twist* (1922), starring Jackie Coogan as Oliver and Lon Chaney as Fagin. The first sound version appeared in 1933 with Dickie Moore as Oliver. The best of the film adaptations, DAVID LEAN's 1948 version for Cineguild, starred John Howard Davies as Oliver, ALEC GUINNESS as Fagin, and Anthony Newley as the Artful Dodger. This film, censored in the United States for the stereotypical anti-Semitism in its portrayal of Fagin when it first appeared, continued the controversial history of stage production of the story. Early adaptations were often linked with *Jack Sheppard,* and several of them were scrutinized or censored for their portrayal of crime. Modern adaptations are occasionally criticized or cut for their anti-Semitism. The most recent film version (2005), directed by Roman Polanski with a script by Ronald Harwood, is a faithful rendering of the story, especially its darker elements. Ben Kingsley plays a sympathetic interpretation of Fagin.

The single most popular dramatic version of the novel has probably been Bart's musical *Oliver!*, which opened on the London stage in 1960 and on film in 1968. Among television adaptations are CONSTANCE COX's 13-part serial for the BBC (1962); James Goldman's version, directed by Clive Donner for CBS (1982); Monte Merrick's adaptation for American television starring Richard Dreyful (1997); and Alan Bleasdale's free adaptation for British television, which expanded the details in the inheritance plot (1999).

FURTHER READING

Two classic essays by English novelists provide quite different introductions to *Twist*. GRAHAM GREENE's

"The Young Dickens" (1951) is a personal account of reading the novel as a child, "its simple and terrible explanation of our plight, how the world was made by Satan and not by God, lulling us with the music of despair"; ANGUS WILSON's introduction to the Penguin Edition (1966) discusses the literary sources for the story, its historical context, and the literary qualities of the text itself. J. HILLIS MILLER (1962, 1991) treats *Twist* as a novel about surviving threats of extinction, suffocation, hanging, drowning, enclosure, and starvation, as Oliver journeys to the heart of the urban labyrinth seeking to discover his identity. In the end his identity is recovered for him, a resolution, Miller points out, with which Dickens will soon become dissatisfied in the novels that follow.

William T. Lankford ("'The Parish Boy's Progress': The Evolving Form of *Oliver Twist*," PMLA, 1978) explains the inconsistencies and contradictions in the novel by analyzing Dickens's changing ideas as he worked on it. STEVEN CONNOR ("'They're All in One Story': Public and Private Narratives in *Oliver Twist*," *Dickensian*, 1989) traces the thematic importance of the various stories within the novel and the role of storytelling itself. STEVEN MARCUS (1965) provides an especially useful discussion of Dickens's religion and the relation of the novel to *Pilgrim's Progress*. In a special issue of the *DICKENSIAN* on the novel, MICHAEL SLATER (1974) analyzes its structure and satire. KENNETH J. FIELDING (1987), in a special issue of the *DICKENS QUARTERLY*, provides a thorough discussion of *Twist*'s anti-UTILITARIAN satire, showing how it responded to the contemporary understanding of Bentham's philosophy of self-interest. Richard J. Dunn's *Oliver Twist: Whole Heart and Soul* (1993) provides an extended introduction to the novel, its contexts, characters, themes, and adaptations.

Our Mutual Friend

Dickens's 14th and last completed novel, published in 20 monthly numbers from May 1864 to November 1865 by BRADBURY & EVANS, with illustrations by MARCUS STONE. Published in two volumes, February and November 1865; one volume, 1865. A panoramic novel set in the present, *Our Mutual Friend* satirizes the superficiality of society; the corrupting power of money; the waste of urban, materialistic existence; and the predatory relations among human beings. Dickens represents this blighted world symbolically in the dust heaps of material wealth, the Thames River polluted with dead bodies, and the human birds of prey who scavenge in the wasteland. The parallel stories of John Harmon and Eugene Wrayburn offer a process of death and resurrection as a way of achieving a deeper, more spiritual sense of self.

SYNOPSIS

Part 1 (May 1864)

(I:1) In society's depths, at twilight, a boat with two figures in it floats on the Thames. Gaffer Hexam watches the water while his daughter Lizzie handles the oars. He discovers a floating corpse and takes it in tow. (I:2) Shortly afterwards, on the surface of society, at the brand new home of the Veneerings, the fashionable members of society have gathered. Mortimer Lightwood, a lawyer, tells the story of "the man from Somewhere," young John Harmon, son of a wealthy and vindictive dust contractor. The rich old man had disowned his daughter for marrying against his wishes, and he bequeathed his whole

Gaffer and Lizzie Hexam scavenging on the Thames in Mahoney's illustration for the first number of the Household Edition of *Our Mutual Friend* (1874).

estate to his son on the condition that he marry Bella Wilfer, a girl chosen because of her petulance. The dinner party is interrupted when Lightwood is informed that young Harmon, returning to England to claim his late father's fortune, has drowned. (I:3) Lightwood and his friend, the diffident Eugene Wrayburn, a lawyer with no practice, go with Charley Hexam, son of Gaffer, to Limehouse to view the corpse. There they meet Julius Handford, a stranger also inquiring about the dead man.

(I:4) A few days later, the Wilfer family, at their house in Holloway, discuss Bella, who has suddenly become a "widow." As they do so, a stranger, John Rokesmith, takes rooms in the Wilfers' house.

Part 2 (June 1864)

(I:5) Silas Wegg, a one-legged street seller of ballads and miscellaneous items, is at his regular post outside the corner house near CAVENDISH SQUARE. He imagines himself an employee of the house, hired to run errands. Mr. Boffin, Harmon's former employee who has inherited the Harmon estate in lieu of young Harmon, greets Wegg. After some casual conversation, Boffin hires Wegg to read to him at his house, Boffin's Bower, formerly Harmony Gaol, the house of the elder John Harmon the dust contractor. On his first evening at Boffin's, Wegg begins reading, with little understanding, *The Decline and Fall of the Roman Empire.*

(I:6) Abbey Potterson, proprietor of the Six Jolly Fellowship Porters, a riverside pub in Limehouse, rules the inn like an abbess. She has excluded both Gaffer Hexam and Rogue Riderhood, another river scavenger, from the pub because of rumors about their unsavory work. She tries to convince Lizzie Hexam to stop working for her father and to set out on her own, but Lizzie politely refuses to follow Abbey's advice. She does, however, give her brother some money and sends him away to pursue an education. When Gaffer returns home and discovers Charley gone, he is angry and disowns him.

(I:7) On his way to Boffin's Bower, Wegg stops at the shop of Mr. Venus, a taxidermist and articulator of bones. He hopes to negotiate for the bone of his amputated leg, which Venus has obtained. Venus confesses to Wegg that he is in love, but that the woman has refused him because of his profession.

Part 3 (July 1864)

(I:8) A simple and illiterate man, Nicodemus Boffin was the faithful employee of John Harmon for many years. He plans to use his newfound wealth to become cultured by having Wegg read to him. On the day that the Harmon property is to be turned over to him, Boffin asks Mortimer Lightwood, his lawyer, to make a "tight will," leaving all of his property to Mrs. Boffin. Later, in the street, he meets Rokesmith, the stranger who took lodgings at the Wilfers', who offers to serve as his secretary. (I:9) The Boffins decide to use some of their money to adopt an orphan and call him John Harmon, in remembrance of the drowned man whose fortune they have inherited and whom they last saw as a seven-year-old child. They also decide to offer the disappointed bride, Bella Wilfer, a place in their home.

(I:10) The Veneerings prepare for a society wedding between "a mature young gentleman," Alfred Lammle, and "a mature young lady," Sophronia Akershem, who is reputed to have property. The ceremony is followed by a wedding breakfast at the Veneerings' house. On their honeymoon at SHANKLIN Sands, Sophronia and Alfred bitterly confess that each has been misled about the financial situation of the other. Then they conspire to deceive the rest of the world as they have mutually deceived each other.

Part 4 (August 1864)

(I:11) The Podsnaps, the very models of the Philistine nouveau riche, hold a funereal party for their daughter Georgiana's 18th birthday. There the Lammles plot to exploit their relationship with Georgiana and insinuate themselves into the shy "young person's" confidence.

(I:12) At their cottage in HAMPTON, Wrayburn and Lightwood are interrupted by Rogue Riderhood, Gaffer Hexam's former partner, who is seeking Lightwood in order to claim Boffin's £10,000 reward for information about Harmon's murderer. Rogue asserts that Gaffer Hexam confessed the crime to him on the night that it occurred. (I:13) With the police inspector, the three men wait in Limehouse for Gaffer to return from his work on the river. When he does not appear, Rogue sets out

Marcus Stone's picture of the Lammles on their disillusioning honeymoon for the original edition of *Our Mutual Friend* (1864).

to find him and returns to say that he has found only Gaffer's empty boat with a broken oar. There was no sign of Gaffer.

Part 5 (September 1864)

(I:14) When Gaffer's boat is brought to shore, they discover Gaffer's body at the end of the towrope.

(I:15) Mr. Boffin hires Rokesmith to be his secretary and, since he plans to move into a fashionable house on Cavendish Square, he offers Wegg a post as caretaker at Boffin's Bower. One evening, Mrs. Boffin interrupts Wegg's reading of *Decline and Fall* to tell Boffin that she has been frightened by seeing the ghostly faces of old Harmon and his two children. (I:16) As Boffin's secretary, Rokesmith is exemplary and puts all of Boffin's affairs in order. He is only difficult about one thing: He refuses to deal with Lightwood. He takes charge of the search for an adoptable child and accompanies the Boffins to the house of Betty Higden, where they meet her grandson, little Johnny, and arrange to take him in. When Rokesmith tells Bella that he is Boffin's

secretary, she is unimpressed. (I:17) The Boffins move into their fashionable new house, where they are visited by members of society, invited to join charitable efforts, and solicited by all kinds of beggars, who are attracted by their gold dust.

Part 6 (October 1864)

(II:1) Charley Hexam, accompanied by his teacher Bradley Headstone, visits Lizzie at her new lodging in Smith Square. They meet the "person of the house," Fanny Cleaver, known as Jenny Wren, a precocious and crippled 13-year-old who makes dolls and acts as parent to her alcoholic father. Charley urges Lizzie to find another lodging, but she is content with her place because it is near the river. On their way home, Charley and Bradley meet Eugene Wrayburn on the VAUXHALL BRIDGE. Charley, who introduced Eugene to his sister when he brought the lawyer to view Harmon's body, worries that Eugene is on his way to see Lizzie. (II:2) His concern is not unfounded. Eugene offers to educate Lizzie. She reluctantly accepts, after he argues that she should do it for her father's sake. After Eugene leaves, Jenny's drunken father comes home from work and is berated by his daughter.

(II:3) Veneering pays £5000 for the privilege of running for the seat in Parliament for the borough of Pocket-Breaches. With the help of his friends, who "do a piece of work" for him, he is elected to the uncontested seat.

Part 7 (November 1864)

(II:4) Mrs. Lammle pursues her friendship with Georgiana Podsnap. She and her husband encourage a relationship between the girl and Fascination Fledgeby, an awkward young gentleman of apparently independent means. (II:5) After a difficult evening at the opera with the two reluctant lovers, Lammle tries first to insinuate his way into Fledgeby's confidence and then to bully him, but the secretive Fledgeby resists Lammle's manipulation. That afternoon Fledgeby goes to Pubsey and Co., his secret moneylending business in St. Mary Axe, where Mr. Riah, a Jew, fronts for him. He finds Riah there with Jenny Wren and Lizzie Hexam in a small roof garden. Jenny taunts Fledgeby with the enigmatic invitation to "Come up and be dead!"

(II:6) Mortimer senses that something is troubling Eugene, and when Charlie Hexam and Bradley Headstone demand that Eugene end his relationship with Lizzie, Lightwood realizes what has been preoccupying his friend. He asks Eugene whether it is his "design to pursue her." Eugene responds diffidently: "I don't design anything. I have no design whatever. I am incapable of designs. If I conceived a design, I would speedily abandon it, exhausted by the operation."

Part 8 (December 1864)

(II:7) At Boffin's Bower, where he is now the caretaker, Wegg is visited by Mr. Venus, who brings him his lost leg bone. Venus is distraught because Pleasant Riderhood, Rogue's daughter who runs a pawnbroking business, has rejected his marriage proposal. Wegg proposes that they should collaborate in searching the dust mounds for valuables. He agrees to join Wegg in this "friendly move."

(II:8) Rokesmith chides Bella, who is now living with the Boffins, that she seems to have forgotten her family. To prove him wrong, Bella orders the coach and visits home, but her grand entrance spurs Mrs. Wilfer's haughtiness. With a bank note for £50 from Boffin, Bella buys her father a new wardrobe, goes with him for a secret dinner in GREENWICH, and turns the balance of the money over to him at the end of the evening. She tells him that she has become mercenary and is seeking a rich husband. (II:9) Soon after, on learning that little Johnny is very ill, the Boffins, Rokesmith, and Bella get the sick child from Betty Higden's house and take him to the Children's Hospital. But the illness is too far advanced; that evening, as Rokesmith watches over him, the child dies. (II:10) At a family conference the next day, Mrs. Boffin proposes that they not try to name another orphan child John Harmon, for the name has proved unfortunate. They choose instead to help Sloppy, another of Betty Higden's boys, in spite of his ungainliness (II:10).

Part 9 (January 1865)

(II:11) Bradley Headstone urges Lizzie to break off her relationship with Wrayburn and to be guided by her brother and himself, but she rejects his advice. Headstone is reluctant to leave her house until he secures her promise that she will meet with him again.

(II:12) At her pawnshop and rooming house for sailors, Pleasant Riderhood is confronted by a sailor who wants to speak with her father. The stranger accuses Rogue of lying about Gaffer's involvement in the Harmon murder and promises to return with a paper for Rogue to sign relating the true facts of the case. (II:13) The stranger then goes out into the streets of Limehouse Hole, removes his disguise, and reveals himself as John Rokesmith. As he looks about him, he reconstructs the story of his death as John Harmon. Uneasy about the terms of his father's will, he conspired to exchange identities with George Radfoot, a mate on the ship on which he was returning to England, so he could observe Bella anonymously. But Radfoot conspired with Riderhood to poison Harmon, a plot that failed when Harmon did not die and when Radfoot, dressed in Harmon's clothes, did. Harmon then decided to assume the identity of Rokesmith and honestly win the affections of Bella, to whom he is devoted. When he returns to the Boffins' house after his evening in Limehouse, Rokesmith proposes to Bella, but she rejects him. He promises to bother her no more.

Part 10 (February 1865)

(II:14) Rokesmith decides that bringing Harmon back to life would do no good for Bella, the Boffins, or himself, so he buries him still deeper. Meanwhile, Betty Higden asks for help to outfit herself as an itinerant seller of sewing supplies so that she can leave London and free Sloppy to accept the opportunity offered by the Boffins. Mrs. Boffin reluctantly agrees to help her.

(II:15) Charley and Bradley intercept Lizzie by a churchyard in the CITY on her way home from work. There Headstone confesses to Lizzie: "You are the ruin—the ruin—the ruin—of me. I have no resources in myself, I have no confidence in myself, I have no government of myself when you are near me or in my thoughts. And you are always in my thoughts now. I have never been quit of you since I first saw you. Oh, that was a wretched day for me! That was a wretched, miserable day!" When she refuses him, he accuses her of an interest in Wrayburn. Afterward, Charley berates her and tries unsuccessfully to change her mind. She is discovered in tears by Riah and Wrayburn, who both accompany her home. Wrayburn quizzes himself about his interest in her.

(II:16) On the first anniversary of the Lammles' marriage, society gathers to celebrate the occasion. Twemlow, a timid man with aristocratic connections who is a regular guest at the Veneerings' dinner parties, is introduced to Fledgeby, his distant kinsman. Sophronia Lammle secretly asks Twemlow to intercede with Mr. Podsnap to save Georgiana from her scheme. Mortimer reports the latest news in the story of the man from Somewhere—that Lizzie Hexam has disappeared.

Part 11 (March 1865)

(III:1) While Riah waits for Fledgeby's instructions, Fledgeby warns Lammle to avoid the clutches of Pubsey and Co. Then Fledgeby instructs Riah to buy up bad debts, especially those of the Lammles. He also tries to learn from Riah where Lizzie is hidden. (III:2) That evening Riah and Lizzie take Riderhood's affidavit that Gaffer Hexam was not responsible for the Harmon murder to the Six Jolly

Fellowship Porters. While they are at the pub, the body of Riderhood is brought in, drowned in a river accident. (III:3) Efforts to resuscitate Rogue succeed, and he returns to life as belligerent as he was before, threatening to sue the steamer that ran him down and blaming his rescuers for not preserving his fur hat.

(III:4) At the Wilfers' wedding anniversary dinner, Mrs. Wilfer is uncomfortable and unhappy. Afterward, Bella tells her father that Rokesmith proposed to her and was refused, that Lightwood would propose were she to encourage him, that Boffin has promised a good marriage settlement for her, and that Mr. Boffin daily "grows suspicious, capricious, hard, tyrannical, unjust" in his escalating love for money.

Part 12 (April 1865)

(III:5) Boffin has, in fact, become obsessive about money. He sets Rokesmith's wages at £200 per annum and demands that the secretary be available around the clock; he tells Bella that her good looks are worth money. Meanwhile, Mrs. Lammle takes an increasing interest in Bella.

(III:6) One evening, when Boffin does not appear for one of his reading sessions, Wegg invites Venus into the Bower. Boffin startles the two conspirators by showing up late with a collection of books about misers. He then goes out to the mounds alone and digs up a bottle. As he leaves, he informs Wegg that he has sold the mounds and that their removal will begin in the morning. (III:7) After Boffin is gone, Wegg confides to Venus that he has found a will of old John Harmon. Venus, distrusting his partner, insists on keeping the document; Wegg reluctantly gives in.

Part 13 (May 1865)

(III:8) Betty Higden continues her pilgrimage, plying her wares along the upper reaches of the Thames. Several times she faints and is near death, but the threat of being sent to the workhouse spurs her on. Once she is found by Rogue Riderhood, who is working as a deputy lockkeeper; he takes her money and then allows her to go on. Finally, near death, she is found by Lizzie Hexam. (III:9) When Bella, Rokesmith, Sloppy, and the Milveys come up to the mill town where Lizzie is working to pay for the funeral of Betty Higden, Lizzie asks them to keep her whereabouts secret. She tells Bella that her disappearance had nothing to do with the charges against her father, and she confides that she is running from the attentions of Bradley Headstone and Eugene Wrayburn. Bella is moved by Lizzie's honesty and depth of feeling; she tells Rokesmith that meeting Lizzie has changed her.

(III:10) Eugene visits Jenny Wren, hoping to learn Lizzie's whereabouts from her, but Jenny will not tell him. Afterwards Jenny's drunken father comes to Eugene's rooms and offers to get Lizzie's address in exchange for drink. Meanwhile, Bradley Headstone follows Eugene through the streets, hoping that Eugene will lead him to Lizzie. Eugene taunts Bradley by leading him on long, pointless peregrinations.

Part 14 (June 1865)

(III:11) Thinking that Lizzie may be hiding at Wrayburn's rooms, Bradley slips into the TEMPLE late at night and listens outside his antagonist's door, but he hears no woman's voice. As he leaves, he meets Riderhood. They share their dislike of Wrayburn, and Bradley gives Rogue five shillings to inform him should he discover Lizzie's whereabouts.

(III:12) In desperate financial straits, the Lammles plan to make a move on Boffin by informing him of Rokesmith's proposal to Bella. They hope he will fire Rokesmith and replace him with Alfred. Riah, representing Pubsey and Co., pursues the Lammles to repay their debts. Although they plead with him, Riah is adamant, for he has been instructed by Fledgeby, the secret owner of the firm, to go after them. (III:13) Even Twemlow, who has cosigned a note for a friend, finds himself in the clutches of Pubsey and Co. Riah demands payment from him. Jenny is disgusted by Riah's hard-heartedness and calls him "the wicked wolf."

(III:14) Troubled by his involvement with Wegg, Venus discloses their scheme, the "friendly move," to Boffin and allows Boffin to overhear Wegg's tirade against him as a "minion of fortune and worm of the hour." Boffin asks Venus to keep his change of heart secret from Wegg for the time being. As he goes home, Boffin meets Sophronia Lammle, who asks to speak to him in confidence.

Part 15 (July 1865)

(III:15) She tells him about Rokesmith's proposal to Bella, and the next morning Boffin fires the secretary for his "insolence" to Bella and for his mercenary designs on her and on Boffin's money. Bella is humiliated to be implicated in Boffin's meanness; she leaves his house and gives up the money the Boffins promised her. (III:16) Then she goes to her father's office and tells him what she has done. Rokesmith joins them there, proposes again, and this time is accepted. The "three hobgoblins," Bella, John, and Mr. Wilfer, share a celebratory tea.

(III:17) The Lammles' belongings are auctioned off to pay their debts. Sophronia warns Twemlow that Fledgeby is the owner of Pubsey and Co. and that Riah is just Fledgeby's "mask." At the Veneerings' dinner party, the members of society disparage the Lammles for living beyond their means. In the middle of supper, Wrayburn is called away from the table to get some information from Mr. Dolls, Jenny's father.

Part 16 (August 1865)

(IV:1) At the Plashwater Weir Mill Lock on the upper Thames, where Riderhood is the lockkeeper, Eugene Wrayburn comes through rowing a small boat. When he recognizes Rogue, he insults him. Eugene is being shadowed by Bradley, who, dressed like Rogue, follows Eugene until he sees him meet Lizzie. Then, exhausted and suffering from unexplained nosebleeds, he returns to Rogue's lock house to spend the night.

(IV:2) The Lammles attempt to secure positions with the Boffins, replacing Rokesmith and Bella, but Mr. Boffin pays them £100 for their "service" of exposing Rokesmith and then dismisses them. Boffin also prevents Georgiana Podsnap from turning over £15 and her heirloom necklace to aid the Lammles.

(IV:3) Silas Wegg makes his move and comes down on Boffin, threatening to reveal the will he has found if Boffin will not share his wealth with him.

(IV:4) Bella and her father go off to Greenwich, where Bella and John are married. The three spend the rest of the day celebrating.

Part 17 (September 1865)

(IV:5) John and Bella settle down to happy married life. Bella reconciles her mother and sister to her "mendicant husband" and dismisses John's questions about whether she would be happier if they were rich.

(IV:6) Eugene meets Lizzie by the river near the mill town where she has been in hiding. She pleads with him to leave her alone, but he also gets her to admit her love for him. After they separate, Eugene, in tears, goes down to a quiet spot by the river to settle his thoughts. There he is attacked by a man wearing a red neckerchief, beaten, and pushed into the river. Lizzie, who has also been settling her emotions by the river, hears the struggle and, finding a boat by the riverbank, pulls the nearly lifeless body into the boat and prayerfully takes it to an inn. There the doctors see little chance that Eugene will live. (IV:7) After the attack, Bradley, dressed like Rogue Riderhood, returns to Plashwater Weir Mill Lock. There Rogue feeds him and

Bella Wilfer (Jane Seymour) and John Rokesmith (John McEnery) in a 1978 PBS adaptation of *Our Mutual Friend. Courtesy of PhotoFest.*

watches him suspiciously as he sleeps. At their meal together, Bradley accidentally cuts his hand and spatters blood over Rogue's clothes. When Bradley leaves the lock, Rogue follows him and watches him change into his schoolmaster's clothes and throw the clothes he was wearing into the river. Rogue fishes the bundle of clothes from the river and returns to his lock. Back at school, Charley Hexam hears of the attack on Eugene Wrayburn and dissociates himself from Bradley.

Part 18 (October 1865)

(IV:8) Before he leaves England, bankrupt Alfred Lammle beats Fledgeby. When Jenny finds the moneylender wounded and sore, she adds pepper to the vinegar plaster that she places on his wounds. (IV:9) Jenny now believes in Riah's innocence, and when Fledgeby fires the old man, he returns with her to her house, where they find Mr. Dolls dead from drink. After the funeral, Jenny is summoned to the bedside of Eugene Wrayburn. (IV:10) She and Mortimer attend Eugene on his deathbed. In his rare moments of consciousness, Eugene, to save Lizzie from public humiliation, asks that Bradley not be pursued. Many days later he asks Mortimer to propose to Lizzie for him. (IV:11) Mortimer goes to London to get John and Bella for the wedding, but John will not allow Lightwood to see him. At the train station Bradley Headstone meets Bella and Mortimer on their way to the wedding. When he hears that Lizzie is to be married, he falls to the platform in a fit. Although Eugene is semiconscious and apparently close to death, during the ceremony Lizzie's love keeps recalling him to consciousness.

Parts 19–20 (November 1865)

(IV:12) When Lightwood accidentally meets the Rokesmiths and recognizes John as Julius Handford, the stranger he first met when he was inquiring about the drowned Harmon, Rokesmith must extricate himself from suspicion in the murder of John Harmon. He is identified for the police inspector as John Harmon. The next day John announces to Bella that they must move, and he takes her to the Boffins' house, where they are reconciled with their old friends. (IV:13) The Boffins tell Bella how Mrs. Boffin discovered John Harmon's identity and how Boffin pretended to be a miser in order to make Bella aware of what she really wanted. Then they show Bella her new home.

(IV:14) Wegg comes down on Boffin, but Boffin, Venus, and Harmon expose Wegg's villainy, and Sloppy throws the covetous balladmonger into a dustcart.

(IV:15) Several months later, Rogue appears at Bradley's school with the bundle of clothes. He insists that Bradley come to the lock. There Rogue tries to blackmail him; Bradley, desperately cornered, grabs Rogue around the waist and pulls him into the lock, where both men drown.

(IV:16) Mrs. Wilfer makes a grand visit to her daughter's grand house; Sloppy and Jenny share their humor together; the Wrayburns visit the Harmons; Eugene, much recovered, vows his love and loyalty to Lizzie and rejects society.

(IV:17) The members of society gather one last time at the Veneerings' house, before Mr. and Mrs. Veneering will escape from their creditors by running to the continent. When Lady Tippins canvasses the assembled guests about the marriage of Eugene and Lizzie, they all agree that it was inappropriate, ill-advised, and a violation of society's rules. Only Mortimer and Twemlow dissent from the general chorus. Twemlow rises to the occasion, challenging Podsnap and describing Eugene as "the greater gentleman" for marrying Lizzie and making her "the greater lady."

COMMENTARY

When *Our Mutual Friend* began its run in monthly numbers in May 1864, it had been nearly a decade since Dickens had completed his last monthly serial, *Little Dorrit*. In the meantime he had published two novels in weekly parts in ALL THE YEAR ROUND, but they were much shorter and required a different discipline from that required by the longer monthly numbers. Distracted by his PUBLIC READINGS and magazine editing and weakened from illness, Dickens found it difficult getting started again on a long novel. Although he began working on the germ ideas for *Mutual Friend* in the early 1860s, it took him over two years to write the first five numbers, the goal he set for himself before beginning publication.

JOHN FORSTER reports that Dickens mentioned in his letters four years before publication "three leading notions" for the novel: "a man, young and perhaps eccentric, feigning to be dead, and *being* dead to all intents and purposes external to himself; . . . a poor impostor of a man marrying a woman for her money; she marrying *him* for *his* money; after marriage both finding out their mistake, and entering into a league and covenant against folks in general; [and] . . . some Perfectly New people." To these germs for Harmon, the Lammles, and the Veneerings, Dickens added "the uneducated father in fustian and the educated boy in spectacles" whom he had seen in CHATHAM, the models for Gaffer Hexam and his son. But the writing went very slowly, and he worried that he had lost his creative power.

Influenced perhaps by his personal knowledge of the author's struggles to get the story on paper, Forster concluded that the novel "wants freshness and natural development." Henry James, one of the book's early reviewers, claimed that it was contrived and artificial, "a book so intensely *written*, so little seen, known, or felt." James also found the book lacking "philosophy," despite its overly conscious creation. Other critics were kinder, but few of Dickens's contemporaries ranked the book with his best work.

Modern critics, particularly Marxist and social critics, have been much more positive, considering it one of the great social novels of Dickens's later period, along with *Bleak House*, *Little Dorrit*, and *Great Expectations*. Arnold Kettle ("Our Mutual Friend," *Dickens and The Twentieth Century*, edited by John Gross and Gabriel Pearson, 1962) praised the "profundity and consistency of the artistic structure," and JACK LINDSAY (1950) called it a "supreme work . . . one of the greatest works of prose ever written. A work which fully vindicates Dickens's right to stand, as no other English writer can stand, at the side of Shakespeare."

A satiric anatomy of Victorian society, *Mutual Friend* explores some of the same themes as WILLIAM MAKEPEACE THACKERAY's *Vanity Fair*, another panoramic satire of the period. Like the characters in Thackeray's novel, the Lammles demonstrate how to "live on nothing a year," Podsnap reigns in patriarchal tyranny over his bourgeois household, and the Veneerings hold fashionable dinner parties that are all surfaces and superficialities. Thackeray distanced his readers from his satire by setting *Vanity Fair* during the Napoleonic wars, 30 years before the time he was writing. In *Our Mutual Friend* Dickens writes about his own time. Beginning with the words, "In these times of ours," he goes on to anatomize life in the present, much as ANTHONY TROLLOPE would do a decade later in *The Way We Live Now* (1874–75). Dickens's subject is the emptiness and corruption of society in his time, which he surveys from top to bottom.

The first two chapters establish the range of Dickens's broad social canvas. He begins at the bottom with the lumpen proletarians, Hexam and Rogue Riderhood, who scavenge bodies from the Thames for a living. Hexam, the narrator tells us, is "allied to the bottom of the river rather than the surface" (I:1), a realm in which human life is reduced to elemental, physical terms. A kind of urban cannibal, he responds to Lizzie's repulsion at their occupation by asserting: "As if it wasn't your living! As if it wasn't meat and drink to you!" (I:1). One of the lower orders of humanity, he is reduced to the animal, a bird of prey who survives by feeding on his fellow man.

If Hexam is confined to the depths, the nouveau riche Veneerings in the next chapter, as their name implies, are all surface. The circle gathered at their supper table only appear to be friends, for they hardly know each other. Their relationship is summed up in the superficial image of their gathering in the mirror above the table. But there is a note of foreboding in this fashionable world as well; a "fatal freshness" (I:2) clings to the Veneerings, and their gloomy butler serves the wine as if it is a form of chemical poison.

As these two chapters establish the oppositions between high and low, surface and depth, they also connect them. The body that Hexam drags from the Thames turns out to be that of "the man from Somewhere," the subject of the shallow and disembodied dinner conversation at the Veneerings. Until that time, John Harmon has been a kind of legal fiction, a creation of the story about his father's contrary will. With the news of his drowning, he becomes a physical presence, linking the river people with the society people as the "mutual friend" of the title. He is the subject that the two worlds have in common, even though they view him very differently. To the river people he is a corpse and a source of their physical survival. To the members of society he is merely the subject of a diverting story. The task of the novel will be to bridge this gulf in perception and attempt to reconnect the mental and physical, the animal and the human, surface and depth.

T. S. ELIOT derived his original title for *The Waste Land*, "He do the police in different voices," from *Our Mutual Friend*. Although Eliot seems to have been thinking of the novel as a source for the many urban monologues in his poem, its images of waste and decay may have been suggested by some of the images in Dickens's novel. The novel has sometimes been called Dickens's *Waste Land*, for its central symbols of the dust heaps and the river are the dominant features of a blighted urban landscape, symbols of an entropic society in its final days. There is no spiritual meaning to life in here. The rich, like Lady Tippins and the Veneerings, who take their physical comforts for granted, are bored and vacuous. Things have only monetary worth; the silver on the Veneerings' supper table is only valued "melted down." All value is reduced to its lowest physical terms. A human life is worth the money in its pockets or the price of its body parts to an articulator like Mr. Venus. Worth is determined in terms of salvage value as it is pulled from the river, scavenged from the dust heaps, or melted into its original form.

Written only five years after the first publication of Charles Darwin's *Origin of Species* (1859), the novel's world is, in Tennyson's words, "red in tooth and claw." The river scavengers are "birds of prey" who compete with each other for the carrion they recover from the river; there is no "partnership," no mutual aid, between Gaffer Hexam and Rogue Riderhood. Mr. Venus's taxidermy business symbolically institutionalizes this predatory culture, his name ironically calling attention to the absence of love in this struggle for existence. The rich—indolent and idle—are similarly isolated. The Veneerings' debased notion of "friendship" calls attention to their lack of ties to others. Pushing out of existence anything they do not wish to know about, as

Podsnap does, they reject "mutual understanding." The natural selection of the competitive marketplace that has created them makes mutuality and sharing alien concepts:

> Traffic in shares is the one thing to have to do with in this world. Have no antecedents, no established character, no cultivation, no ideas, no manners; have Shares. . . . Where does he come from? Shares. Where is he going to? Shares. What are his tastes? Shares. Has he any principles? Shares. What squeezes him into Parliament? Shares. Perhaps he never of himself achieved success in anything, never originated anything, never produced anything! Sufficient answer to all; Shares. O mighty Shares! (I:10)

Like friendship, the idea of sharing has been ironically redefined as its opposite. Dickens's critique of this Darwinian world presages that of Peter Kropotkin, whose *Mutual Aid* (1902) challenged Darwin's conclusion that struggle rather than cooperation was the fundamental biological fact of creation. By satirically reducing life to elemental terms and denying mutuality, Dickens was similarly challenging Darwin.

Dickens depicts a society disintegrating into pieces and returning to its original elemental forms. Mud and ooze form the substratum in the realm of the river people; dust and detritus provide the riches of the well-to-do. The novel itself seems fragmented, its abrupt transitions from one scene to the next suggesting the disconnectedness of the fragmented world it describes. JULIET MCMASTER (1987) suggests that the fragmentation in the novel is based on the division of labor in 19th-century capitalism, which broke apart societal bonds and divided people within themselves. Reduced to their elemental economic value, human beings become the bodies Gaffer fishes from the Thames, the skeletons for which Venus has cornered the market, the bride willed to her husband like so many spoons.

Even if all men do not share in the shares, they do share a common fate. Death is a constant attendant on the characters in *Mutual Friend*, low and high alike. Besides the death of Harmon/Radfoot that opens the story, several other important characters die along the way: Gaffer Hexam, Young Johnny, Betty Higden, Bradley Headstone, and Rogue Riderhood (twice). In the end, death, or virtual death, will give meaning and value to life.

The preoccupation with physical death in the "low" world is matched by a kind of spiritual death in the "high." Emptiness and vacuity characterize such figures as Lady Tippins. Eugene Wrayburn, the gentleman hero, is caught in a kind of living death, a paralysis induced by his relationship with his overbearing father and expressed in his cynicism, indolence, and sadism. The Darwinian world that has been reduced to an instinctive struggle for existence leaves Eugene with no sense of "design." There is no plan, no direction for his life. When Mortimer questions him about his intentions with Lizzie, Eugene responds: "I don't design anything. I have no designs. I am incapable of designs. If I conceived a design, I should speedily abandon it, exhausted by the operation" (II:6). While the "half-savage" river scavengers are reduced to an instinctive level of behavior to survive, the civilized members of society live aimless lives in a world without design.

These polarized ways of life articulate the two dominant responses to Darwinism in the 1860s. On the one hand, Darwin was accused of reducing human beings to animals; on the other hand, he was accused of describing a universe without design. Godless and without purpose, it was a universe without spiritual dimensions, ruled by struggle and death. In the surreal imagery of the novel, life is reduced to a semiliterate reading circle listening to nightly installments of "Decline-and-Fall-Off-The-Rooshan-Empire."

A few of the characters challenge this domination of meaninglessness, materialism, and death. Betty Higden, who chooses to die rather than be reduced to dependency in the workhouse, provides a vision of a purposeful existence. The Boffins, although they later seem to succumb to the temptations of miserliness and fashion, begin the novel by attempting to use their inheritance to aid other people. Abbey Potterson seeks to maintain a small community at the Six Jolly Fellowship Porters, even though she is not altogether successful in keeping the taint of Limehouse out of her public house. Lizzie Hexam, in spite of her impoverished childhood and her tyrannical father, maintains a sense of her own worth and continues to see visions in the fire. Her even more visionary companion, Jenny Wren, in spite of physical deformities, an alcoholic father, and impoverishment, makes "art" of her suffering by making dolls of the people she observes around her. It is Jenny who articulates the paradoxical message at the heart of the story. In a scene where she and Lizzie have gone up to the roof of Pubsey and Co. to have a picnic and escape the turmoil of the city, she invites Fledgeby to join them and "come up and be dead!" (II:5). Her invitation suggests that "death" is a kind of liberation from the material life below, a transcendence of suffering into a realm of peace and joy.

The parallel plots of the novel—the John Harmon and Eugene Wrayburn stories—both elaborate the message in the rooftop picnic scene. Both Harmon and Wrayburn go through death experiences to discover more meaningful lives. Harmon's death, which begins the novel, frees him from his identity as his father's son and heir. His disguise enables him to test Bella, but more important, it enables him to discover and establish his identity for himself. By the time he proposes to Bella, it is not because she has met his test but rather because he has come to know his own heart. As the prince in a kind of fairy tale, Harmon is not very interesting. Bella, especially before her conversion into Harmon's little wife, is a more engaging character. Her name, with etymological roots suggesting both "beauty" and "war," describes her complexity. The child of a divided family in which the accepting father, R. W. Wilfer, is countered by his snobbish and irritable wife, Bella inherits these parental contradictions and speaks of herself as "always at war with myself" (III:5). She is petulant and money grubbing as well as caring and self-denying. She is both the minx admired by old Harmon and the "boofer lady" loved by young Johnny.

Bella is one of several divided characters in the novel. Besides Harmon/Handford/Rokesmith, whose multiple names indicate the instability of his identity, there is Boffin the benefactor and Boffin the miser; Fanny Cleaver/Jenny Wren, the sharp-tongued and visionary doll's dressmaker; Fledgeby and Riah, whose public personae reverse the hidden truths about them; the two Bradley Headstones, the mechanical teacher and the impassioned murderer; and the two Eugene Wrayburns, the aimless, cynical, sometimes sadistic man-about-town and, after his struggle in the river, the gentle and loving man.

Eugene's story, the engaging center of the novel, repeats in many ways that of John Harmon. Both young men are burdened by the dominance and expectations of their fathers. Harmon "dies" to escape his father's perverse will, and Eugene adopts cynicism and idleness to thwart the expectations of his M.R.F. (Most Respected Father). Both refuse to accept their fathers' "designs" for their lives, but both are left without design when they choose to break away from paternal domination.

While Harmon becomes a shadowy figure caught up in the complications of the plot, Wrayburn emerges as a complex personality whose struggle to achieve personal independence and self-understanding is linked to the divisions in society that separate rich from poor, high from low, the governors from the governed. To Eugene's upper-class compatriots at the Veneerings', John Harmon is a character from another world—from "Somewhere"—whose story provides only a passing diversion. By entering that world, Eugene bridges the gulf between rich and poor and explores what the two worlds have in common—their mutuality. His quest is not purposeful; it lacks design, and he is intolerant of much that he finds in the underworld, particularly of Bradley Headstone, whose energy, passion, and single-mindedness are the qualities that Eugene has repressed in himself in his rebellion against his father. Eugene's taunting of Headstone matches Headstone's angry confrontations with the lawyer; their reciprocal games of cat and mouse mirror the mutuality between the two men who are "set against one another in all ways" (II:6). Their mutual struggle for dominance—to become, in a play on Riderhood's name for Eugene, the "other's governor"—is a life-and-death confrontation. It destroys Headstone and nearly destroys Eugene.

The difference between them is Lizzie, who is one of several characters who can be described as the "mutual friend" in the title. Like Boffin, Harmon, and Eugene, she bridges the gulf between high and low and facilitates mutual understanding. When she rescues Eugene from the river, she saves him from his destructive competition with Headstone and, with Jenny's aid, nurses him to health. The novel seems to suggest that Eugene's recovery depends on strength from the working class, spiritual vision from Jenny, and mutuality from the community of women. By marrying Lizzie, he transcends his upper-class diffidence and isolation, his male need for competition, and his purposeless engagement in games of mutual destruction.

As a counter to the Darwinian world of competition and struggle, mutuality seems largely to reside in the community of women. Male partnerships—like those between Riderhood and Hexam or Wegg and Venus—are grounded in distrust and become mutually destructive. Women, who reject the predatory principle of competition, can create sites of nurture and cooperation. Abbey Potterson, "abbess" of the community at the Six Jolly Fellowship Porters, has made such a place; Lizzie and Jenny support each other and provide a refuge for society's outcasts, like Riah and Betty Higden; in their marriages, Bella and Lizzie enable their husbands to leave behind dangerous struggles. Their community is apparent in the relationship between Jenny and Lizzie, the influence of Mrs. Boffin that makes Bella young Johnny's "boofer lady," and their mutual aid to Betty Higden. Lizzie's independence provides Bella with a model for her own transformation, and the meeting of the two women after Betty Higden's death (III:9) is an important turning point in the "long lane" of the novel.

The marriages represent modest achievements in establishing mutual understanding. They do not transform society. They do not save Rogue and Headstone from mutual destruction or the Lammles and Veneerings from bankruptcy and exile. The community presided over by the Golden Dustman and his wife at the end of the novel exists in the realm of fairy tale. The pious fraud by which Boffin pretends to be a miser in order to change Bella is manipulative and unconvincing, lacking even the minimal ambiguities that characterized its earlier telling in the story of the two Martin Chuzzlewits.

In the end, the realistic voice of society has not been silenced. Lady Tippens, Podsnap, and their friends condemn Eugene for marrying beneath his class. Only Twemlow objects and praises Eugene's "feelings of gratitude, of respect, of admiration, and affection, [that] induced him . . . to marry the lady. . . . I think he is the greater gentleman for the action and makes her the greater lady" (IV:17). By recognizing the mutual love between Eugene and Lizzie, Twemlow transcends his isolation and reification. He is no longer just a leaf in the Veneerings' dining table, but a distinctly human voice, differentiated from the other voices in the social chorus.

CHARACTERS AND RELATED ENTRIES

Akershem, Sophronia Sophronia Lammle's maiden name.

"Analytical Chemist, the" The Veneerings' butler who "goes round like a gloomy Analytical Chemist; always seeming to say, after 'Chablis, sir?'—'You wouldn't if you knew what its made of'" (I:2).

Anglers' Inn The riverside inn where Lizzie Hexam takes Eugene Wrayburn after he is attacked by Bradley Headstone (IV:10). The original is the Red Lion Hotel in Henley-on-Thames.

Blight, Young Mortimer Lightwood's "dismal" office boy.

Bocker, Tom A 19-year-old orphan suggested by Milvey for adoption by the Boffins (I:9).

Boffin, Henrietta ("Henrietty") The kind and simple wife of Nicodemus, who befriends Bella Wilfer and discovers in Rokesmith the John Harmon she had loved when he was a child. "A stout lady of rubicund and cheerful aspect," she pretends to be a "highflyer at Fashion" (I:5), but she is at heart a down-to-earth, commonsensical woman. She advises her husband to move to CAVENDISH SQUARE to a house more appropriate to their changed circumstances, asks Bella to live with them, and promotes the plan to adopt a child to replace John Harmon.

Boffin, Nicodemus (Nick or Noddy Boffin; "the Golden Dustman") Unlettered former employee of old John Harmon, the dust contractor, who inherits his master's wealth when Harmon's son, the primary heir, is presumed drowned in the THAMES. "A broad, round-shouldered, one-sided old fellow. . . . Both as to his dress and to himself he was of an overlapping, rhinoceros build, with folds in his cheeks, and his forehead, and his eyelids, and his lips, and his ears; but with bright, eager, childishly-inquiring grey eyes, under his ragged eyebrows and broad-brimmed hat" (I:5). To make up for his illiteracy, he hires Silas Wegg to read to him (I:5) and Rokesmith to act as his secretary (I:8). To make up for Bella's loss of a chance at fortune, he invites her to live with them (I:9), and he and his wife adopt a child to replace the John Harmon who was lost. His kindness appears to be undermined when he develops an obsession with misers and their money (III:4–5) and dismisses Rokesmith for his mercenary intentions in proposing to Bella (III:15), changes that prompt Bella to leave his house and give up her mercenary ways. His change in character, however, proves to have been a pious fraud, a pretense to bring Bella to her senses and make her into a desirable wife for John Harmon, whom his wife has recognized in his disguise as Rokesmith (IV:13).

Boffin has probably been the most controversial character in the novel. GRAHAME SMITH (1968), in a view shared by many readers, asserts, "One of the biggest disappointments in literature occurs in *Our Mutual Friend* at the moment when we discover that Boffin's moral degeneration has been nothing but a well-intentioned sham." The fraud, these critics argue, undermines Boffin's moral authority and the theme of the corrupting power of money that Boffin seems to exemplify. On the other hand, ANNY SADRIN (1994) argues that Boffin's simplicity as a character complements the complexity of his role in the novel because "Boffin has no need of the subtleties of the inner life since he lives only for others." Boffin is probably based on Henry Dodd, a dust contractor in ISLINGTON who was said to have given his daughter a dustheap as a wedding present.

Boffin's Bower Formerly Harmony Gaol when it was occupied by the elder John Harmon, this house among the dust heaps in *Our Mutual Friend* is where the Boffins live before moving to their fashionable house on Cavendish Square. Boffin hires Wegg to live at the Bower and be its caretaker.

Boots Always linked with Brewer; these two guests, apparently indistinguishable from each other, attend the Veneerings' dinner parties, where they reiterate the banalities of "the social chorus."

Brewer One of the pair of Veneering sycophants, Boots and Brewer.

Church Street Jenny Wren and Lizzie Hexam share lodgings in this street off Smith Square in Westminster.

Cleaver, Fanny ("Jenny Wren") The crippled doll's dressmaker, granddaughter of one of the drowning victims pictured on Gaffer Hexam's wall, with whom Lizzie Hexam takes lodgings after her father's death: "a child—a dwarf—a girl—a something. . . . The queer little figure, and the queer but not ugly little face, with its bright grey eyes, were so sharp, that the sharpness of the manner seemed unavoidable" (II:1). Although she is only an adolescent, she is "sharp" beyond her years and sharp-tongued. Tormented by other children because of her deformities, she imagines tormenting them in return: "And I'll tell you what I'd do to punish 'em. There's doors under the church in the Square— black doors, leading into black vaults. Well! I'd open one of those doors, and I'd cram 'em all in, and then I'd lock the door and through the keyhole I'd blow in pepper" (II:1). She has the manner and responsibilities of an adult, earning a living by her craft and, as "the person of the house," caring for and berating her alcoholic father as if he were her child. These "sharp" characteristics articulate the Fanny Cleaver side of her character. But Jenny is also a visionary who imagines a world free of pain, unsullied by materialistic reality, that is symbolized by Riah's roof garden, where she invites others to "come up and be dead" (II:5). With Riah, she aids Lizzie's escape from London and keeps the secret of Lizzie's whereabouts. She is called to Eugene's bedside after his beating, attends his recuperation, and translates his messages from the other side into his desire to marry Lizzie (IV:9). The final chapters suggest that a marriage to Sloppy is in her future.

Jenny Wren is one of the most intriguing characters in Dickens, for she both restates and revises persistent motifs in his work. Like Little Nell (*Curiosity Shop*), Florence Dombey (*Dombey*), and Lucie Manette (*Two Cities*), she is the wise daughter who cares for her older relative, but Jenny's care has a cruel and sharp edge. The ambiguities in her character (child/adult, caretaker/pain giver, visionary seer/immobilized cripple) articulate the complexities in her role. She is both the realistic Victorian child crippled by abuse and neglect, like Smike (*Nickleby*), and the creative visionary who imaginatively enters the lives of others to create her dolls or to translate messages from the spirit world. J. HILLIS MILLER (1996) and HILARY SCHOR (1999) find in Jenny a representative of Dickens as artist imaginatively transforming his own biography and the life of his time.

Cleaver, Mr. ("Mr. Dolls") Jenny Wren's alcoholic father, whom she treats as if he were a child, berating him as "a bad old boy! . . . [a] naughty, wretched creature!" (II:2) He responds to her with pathetic groveling: "The shaking figure, unnerved and disjointed from head to foot, put out its two hands a little way, as making overtures of peace and reconciliation. Abject tears stood in its eyes, and stained the blotched red of its cheeks. The swollen lead-colored under-lip trembled with a shameful whine. The whole indecorous threadbare ruin, from the broken shoes to the prematurely-grey scanty hair, groveled" (II:2). Wrayburn bribes him with money for rum to reveal the secret of Lizzie's whereabouts (III:17). He dies in the street outside Wrayburn's lodgings, where he has come in search of more rum money (IV:9).

"Dolls, Mr." Nickname of Jenny Wren's father, Mr. Cleaver, ascribed to him by Wrayburn.

Duke Street (2) A quiet street off Piccadilly where Mr. Twemlow has his lodgings over a livery stable (I:2).

Elwes, John (1714–1789) Historical figure, one of the misers on whom Boffin supposedly models his change to miserliness. Through scrimping and saving, Elwes cleared an encumbered estate from debt and left a fortune worth £500,000. (III:5).

Exchequer Coffee-house The address that John Harmon gives when posing as Julius Handford (I:3). Supposed to be in Palace Yard, Westminster, but probably fictitious.

Fenchurch Street The street in the City where, at the corner of Mincing Lane, Bella Wilfer waits for her father to come from his office (II:8).

Fledgeby, "Fascination" "An awkward sandy-haired, small-eyed youth, . . . prone to self-examination in the articles of whisker and moustache" (II:4). Although he appears to be a man of independent means, Fledgeby is secretly a moneylender who operates as Pubsey & Co. and employs Mr. Riah to front for him. His father had also been a moneylender, and his mother, one of the Snigsworth family, married her husband when she was unable to repay a loan. "The meanest cur existing, with a single pair of legs . . . this young gentleman (for he was but three-and-twenty) combined with the miserly vice of an old man, any of the open-handed vices of a young one. . . . He was sensible of the value of appearances as an investment, and liked to dress well; but he drove a bargain for every moveable about him, from the coat on his back to the china on his breakfast-table; and every bargain, by representing somebody's ruin or somebody's loss, acquired a peculiar charm for him" (II:5). He offers the Lammles £1000 if they can arrange a marriage with Georgiana Podsnap, but Mrs. Lammle finally regrets her involvement in the scheme and warns the Podsnaps, through Twemlow, of Fledgeby's designs on their daughter's money. When Mrs. Lammle realizes that Riah is just a front for Fledgeby, who has called in their loans, her husband beats Fledgeby and rubs salt into the wounds. Jenny Wren adds some pepper (IV:9).

JAMES KINCAID (1971) describes Fledgeby as "a pure economic creation and a true nineteenth-century man, with a real genius in money matters and complete idiocy otherwise. His nickname refers sarcastically to his anti-social qualities: other people must actually talk for him, and Dickens flays this offshoot of the commercial society with deeply aggressive and emasculating wit, continually making the frightening and funny point that this impotent non-being is sure to succeed in this mad Podsnappian world."

foreign gentleman A guest at Georgiana Podsnap's birthday party. Podsnap condescendingly dismisses him as "not English" (I:11).

Glamour, Bob Regular patron at the Six Jolly Fellowship Porters.

Gliddery, Bob The potboy at the Six Jolly Fellowship Porters.

"Golden Dustman, the" Nickname of Nicodemus Boffin.

Goody, Mrs. The grandmother of a child that the Reverend Milvey suggests the Boffins might adopt, but his wife objects that she is "an inconvenient woman," who "it would be impossible to keep . . . from Mrs. Boffin's house" (I:9).

Grapes Inn Tavern in Narrow Street, Limehouse, original of the Six Jolly Fellowship Porters.

"Greenwich, Archbishop of" Head waiter at the restaurant in GREENWICH where Bella Wilfer and John Rokesmith have their wedding dinner (IV:4).

Grompus The "ogre" that Mrs. Podsnap presents as a dancing partner for Georgiana at her 18th birthday party. During the dance, "like a revolving funeral," he gives her an extended account of an archery tournament (I:11).

"Gruff and Glum" An old pensioner with two wooden legs who is present at the marriage of Bella Wilfer and John Rokesmith (IV:4).

Handford, Julius The pseudonym used by John Harmon when he goes to view the body believed to be his own (I:3).

Harmon, John (a.k.a. Julius Handford, John Rokesmith, "the Man from Somewhere") The "mutual friend" of the title whose several identities indicate his alienation from his father and his uncertainty about his own place in the world. When he inherits his father's estate on the condition that he marry Bella Wilfer, he decides to return to England from South Africa in disguise in order to size up his potential bride, but his scheme to switch identities with Radfoot, a mate on the ship, is foiled when Radfoot double-crosses and attempts to murder him. Harmon survives, but Radfoot is drowned. Taking the alias Julius Handford, Harmon identifies Radfoot's body as Harmon (I:2). Then, taking the alias John Rokesmith, he takes rooms at the Wilfers' house (I:4) and becomes secretary to Mr. Boffin, who has inherited the Harmon estate in John's place (I:15). As Rokesmith, Harmon falls in love with Bella, proposes to her, and is refused (II:13). Although his identity as Harmon is confirmed for the reader at this point in the story, it is not revealed to Bella and the others until after his proposal is finally accepted and he is married (IV:4). Only after he is cleared of the suspicion of murdering Harmon and is recognized by the Boffins does he finally reveal his identity to Bella and accept his fortune (IV:12).

Dickens has been criticized for his awkward handling of the mystery at the heart of *Our Mutual Friend*, but he anticipated this criticism. In his postscript to the novel, he commented:

When I devised this story, I foresaw the likelihood that a class of readers and commentators would suppose that I was at great pains to conceal exactly what I was at great pains to suggest: namely, that Mr. John Harmon was not slain, and that Mr. John Rokesmith was he. Pleasing myself with the idea that the supposition might in part arise out of some ingenuity in the story, and thinking it worth while, in the interests of art, to hint to an audience that an artist (of whatever denomination) may perhaps be trusted to know what he is about in his vocation, if they will concede him a little patience, I was not alarmed by the anticipation.

His title is not "The Mystery of John Harmon," but one that calls attention to Harmon's role in linking the many disparate parts of the novel. He is, as Boffin comments, "the mutual friend" of both the Boffins and the Wilfers and a character who links, as Arnold Kettle ("*Our Mutual Friend*," *Dickens and The Twentieth Century*, edited by John Gross and Gabriel Pearson, 1962) points out, the dust mounds with the river, the world of wealth with that of poverty. Although his story is not as engaging as that of Wrayburn and his character is simpler and less revealed, he is, nonetheless, the character whose story provides the reference point for the rest of the novel. His drowning, for example, foreshadows those of Headstone and Riderhood and the near-drowning of Wrayburn. In his problematic relationship with his father is echoed in the relationships of Charley Hexam and Gaffer, Eugene and M. R. F., Georgiana and Podsnap, even Jenny and Mr. Dolls. In his role as secretary, as James Davies (*The Textual Life of Dickens's Characters*, 1990) has suggested, he brings order out of the numerous documents that establish the network of relationships in the novel.

Harmon, old John "A tremendous old rascal who made his money by Dust, . . . and lived in a hollow in a hilly country entirely composed of Dust. On his own small estate the growling old vagabond threw up his own mountain range, like an old volcano, and its geological formation was Dust. Coal-dust, vegetable-dust, bone-dust, crockery-dust, rough dust, and sifted dust—all manner of Dust" (I:2). He cast out his daughter when she wished to marry against his will, and he cast out his son when he defended his sister. Before he died, however, he reconsidered and left his wealth to his son—who had become a small farmer in South Africa—on the condition that he marry Bella Wilfer, a girl chosen because on the one occasion on which he saw her as a child she was angry and petulant.

Harmony Jail The name by which Boffin's Bower was known in the days of old John Harmon.

Harrison Orphan suggested by Reverend Milvey as suitable for the Boffins to adopt, but rejected by his wife because he "squints so *much*" (I:9).

Hawkinson, Aunt Georgiana Podsnap's aunt, who left her the necklace that she offers to the Lammles to help them out of their financial difficulties (IV:2).

Headstone, Bradley Schoolmaster who trains Charley Hexam and then falls in love with Lizzie, Charley's sister. "In his decent black coat and waistcoat, and decent white shirt, and decent formal black tie, and decent pantaloons of pepper and salt, with his decent silver watch in his pocket, and his decent hair guard round his neck, [he] looked a thoroughly decent young man of six-and-twenty. He was never seen in any other dress, and yet there was a certain stiffness in his manner of wearing this, as if there were a want of adaptation between him and it, recalling some mechanics in their holiday clothes. He had acquired mechanically a great store of teacher's knowledge. He could do mental arithmetic mechanically, sing at sight mechanically, blow various wind instruments mechanically, even play the great church organ mechanically. From his early childhood up, his mind had been a place of mechanical stowage. . . . There was a kind of settled trouble in the face. It was the face belonging to a naturally slow or inattentive intellect that had toiled hard to get what it had won, and that had to hold it now that it was gotten" (II:1). By such schooling, Bradley has risen from low origins to his position as schoolmaster, but his learning is insufficient to enable him to control his passion and jealousy. Against his will, he falls in love with Lizzie Hexam and confesses to her that she is "the ruin" of him (II:15); she rejects his proposal. When he meets Eugene Wrayburn, he is intensely aware of his social inferiority (III:6). The two become rivals for Lizzie's affections, shadow each other in the streets of London, and feverishly compete with each other to discover Lizzie's whereabouts. Bradley pursues Eugene up the THAMES (IV:1), spies on his assignation with Lizzie, and murderously attacks and nearly kills him (IV:6). Rogue Riderhood uncovers Headstone's guilty secret and attempts blackmail, and the two of them drown together as they struggle in each other's arms (IV:15).

Headstone's funereal name suggests that his attempts to achieve "decency" by suppressing his passionate inner self have been a death-dealing enterprise, turning him into a kind of walking corpse. (Appropriately, the important scene in which Bradley makes his tortured proposal to Lizzie (II:15) takes place beside a cemetery.) JULIET MCMASTER (1987) explores the imagery associated with this death-in-life theme as it relates to Bradley. His struggle to rise to a better position is portrayed as characteristic of the upward movement of the working class through education to positions on the margins of the middle class, a process requiring the suppression of working-class energy to adopt the superficial values of the middle class. JULIET JOHN (2001) explores Bradley's role in representing some of these changes demanded by 19th-century capitalism.

Bradley also acts as a DOUBLE to several other characters. Charley Hexam repeats Bradley's rise from obscure origins through education, a process that strips them both of conscience and an authentic inner life. Rogue Riderhood articulates Bradley's suppressed working-class origins; primitive and elemental, he is implicated in the attempt to murder Harmon, an act that foreshadows Headstone's attack on Wrayburn. Appropriately, Headstone dresses in Riderhood's clothes while carrying out the attack and ultimately drowns in Riderhood's arms. Headstone is also a contrasting double to Wrayburn. Passionately energetic in contrast to the bored and indifferent Eugene, Bradley is enraged by Eugene's patrician condescension and diffidence, but this obsessive cat-and-mouse contest ultimately makes Eugene recognize his own "designs" on Lizzie and explore the depths beneath his surface boredom. GRAHAME SMITH (1968) suggests that Bradley is a "self-projection" of Dickens, reflecting his rise from obscure origins, his obsessive relationship with ELLEN TERNAN, and his "desire to escape from the complexities of his existence."

Henley This village along the Thames in Oxfordshire is the original of the town where Eugene Wrayburn is attacked by Bradley Headstone. The Angler's Inn, where he recuperates, is based on the Red Lion Inn. Hurley Lock, about six miles downriver from Henley, became Plashwater Weir Mill Lock.

Hexam, Charley Gaffer's ambitious and selfish son: "There was a curious mixture in the boy, of uncompleted savagery and uncompleted civilization. His voice was hoarse and coarse; but he was cleaner than other boys of his type; and his writing, though large and round, was good; and he glanced at the backs of the books, with an awakened curiosity that went below the binding. No one who can read, ever looks at a book, even unopened on a shelf, like one who cannot" (I:3). Over Gaffer's objections, Lizzie helps Charley escape from home to become a pupil-teacher under Bradley Headstone. Desiring respectability above all else, Charley objects to Lizzie's association with Jenny Wren; he resents Eugene's offer to educate Lizzie because he has planned to undertake that task himself. When Lizzie rejects Headstone's marriage proposal (II:15), Charley rejects her, just as he later turns on Headstone when he learns of his complicity in the maiming of Wrayburn. He sums up his character himself when he tells Headstone: "I have made up my mind that I will become respectable in the scale of society, and that I will not be dragged down by others. I have done with my sister as well as with you" (IV:7).

JOHN REED (1995) describes Charley as "a parody of the prodigal son," who leaves home and whose "father refuses to forgive," because Charley "does not want to waste his substance and swill with pigs."

Hexam, Jesse ("Gaffer") "The nightbird of the Thames" and former partner of Rogue Riderhood, Gaffer is a waterman who patrols the river looking for corpses: "a strong man with ragged grizzled hair and a sun-browned face" (I:1). He finds the body that is taken to be John Harmon's (I:1). Rogue, resentful that Gaffer has dissolved their partnership, identifies Gaffer as Harmon's murderer, but when Lightwood, Wrayburn, and the Inspector go in search of Gaffer, they find him dead, entangled in the rope by the side of his boat (I:14). James Davies (*The Textual Life of Dickens's Characters*, 1990) analyzes Gaffer as a character who incorporates several themes of the novel: birds of prey, death by drowning, hostile social relationships, and problems with parenting. He even suggests that Gaffer can be viewed as an "inverted Christ figure."

Hexam, Lizzie Gaffer's daughter, "a dark girl of nineteen or twenty" (I:1) who rows the boat as her father observes the water. Out of loyalty to her father, she refuses to leave this unsavory occupation even though she is discomfited by the work and is offered chances to do so, but she does enable her brother to leave home and go to school (I:6). After her father's death, Lizzie moves in with Jenny Wren and works with a seamen's outfitter (II:1). She attracts both Wrayburn and Headstone, who compete for her attention, and both offer to educate her. She angers her brother by rejecting Headstone's proposal of marriage. To escape the attentions of the two men, she is driven into seclusion and, aided by Riah, finds refuge in a mill town up the Thames. There she comes upon Betty Higden, who dies in her arms (III:8), and meets Bella, who is changed by the honesty and simplicity in Lizzie's account of her life (III:9). When Wrayburn discovers her there (IV:1), he is attacked by Headstone and saved from death by Lizzie (IV:6), who nurses him back to consciousness and finally marries him (IV:11).

Although Lizzie shares the self-denying goodness of many of Dickens's "little women," she is not the typical "angel in the house" who devotes herself to self-denying domesticity. As HILARY SCHOR (1999) points out, she is an independent woman who works for a living, an independence she guards jealously. Her working-class origins and commitment to working act as obstacles to both Headstone, who is anxious to leave behind his own obscure background, and Wrayburn, who, unconsciously perhaps, assumes the stereotypical role of the upper-class seducer. Although the voices of society in the final chapter condemn the marriage of Eugene and Lizzie as a violation of the rules of social class, some commentators see Twemlow's closing approval of the couple as an optimistic note. GRAHAME SMITH (1968), however, describes their union as "despairing romanticism," commenting that "theirs is the solidarity of figures who are otherwise in utter isolation, and their marriage is without content except on the personal level. . . . Twemlow's stand is a personal one. Indeed, by placing his plea for humanity in the mouth of such an ineffectual vessel, Dickens only emphasizes the enormity of the forces ranged against that humanity."

MICHAEL SLATER (1983) compares Lizzie to Charlotte Brontë's Jane Eyre, seeing Eugene as a Rochester who would take her independence and make her "into a doll" and seeing Bradley's offer of marriage as one, like the marriage St. John Rivers offers to Jane, that would kill her. But Slater finds Lizzie "idealized" and lacking "the emotional and intellectual complexity" of Brontë's heroine.

Higden, Mrs. Betty An old woman, "one of those old women . . . who by dint of an indomitable purpose and a strong constitution fight out many years, though each year has come with its new knock-down blows fresh to the fight against her, wearied by it; an active old woman, with a bright dark eye and a resolute face, yet quite a tender creature too; not a logically-reasoning woman, but God is good, and hearts may count in Heaven as high as heads" (I:16). She keeps a "minding school" and does ironing on a mangle operated by Sloppy, one of the boys she has taken in. Mrs. Boffin wants to adopt her great-grandson Johnny (I:16), but the child dies before the adoption can be arranged (II:9). When the Boffins decide to take Sloppy instead, Betty, knowing that Sloppy will not willingly leave her, runs away. She takes to the road as a peddler of needlework supplies (II:14). Determined to stay out of the workhouse, she dies by the side of the road in the arms of Lizzie Hexam (III:8).

In Betty Higden, Dickens renewed his attacks on the POOR LAW begun in *Oliver Twist*. In his postscript to the novel, Dickens addressed his critics who had challenged his portrayal of the old woman:

In my social experiences since Mrs. Betty Higden came upon the scene and left it, I have found Circumlocutional champions disposed to be warm with me on the subject of my view of the Poor Law. . . . I have been called upon to admit that I would give Poor Law relief to anybody, anywhere, anyhow. Putting this nonsense aside, I have observed the suspicious tendency in the champions to divide into two parties; the one contending that there are no deserving Poor who prefer death by slow starvation and bitter weather, to the mercies of some Relieving Officers and some Union Houses; the other admitting that there are such Poor, but denying that they have any cause or reason for what they do. . . . That my view of the Poor Law may not be mistaken or misrepresented, I will state it. I believe there has been in England, since the days of the Stuarts, no law so infamously administered, no law so often openly violated, no law so habitually ill-supervised. In the majority of the shameful cases of disease and death from destitution that shock the Public and disgrace the country, the illegality is quite equal to the inhumanity—and known language could say no more of their lawlessness.

Holloway   Rural suburb north of London where the Wilfer family lives. (I:4).

inspector, the   Policeman in charge of the THAMES station who investigates the death of John Harmon and later the death of Gaffer Hexam.

Joey, Captain   "A bottle-nosed person in a glazed hat" (I:6), a regular patron at the Six Jolly Fellowship Porters.

Johnny   Betty Higden's great-grandson whom the Boffins wish to adopt and name John Harmon. He dies at the CHILDREN'S HOSPITAL watched over by Rokesmith and Bella Wilfer, whom he calls "the boofer lady" (II:9).

Jonathan   Patron "in a faded scarlet jacket" at the Six Jolly Fellowship Porters, sent home by Abbey Potterson to meet his wife's demand that he be punctual (I:6).

Jones, George   A regular patron at the Six Jolly Fellowship Porters.

Kibble, Jacob   A passenger with John Harmon on the voyage back from South Africa who gives testimony at the inquest into the death of Harmon (IV:12).

Lammle, Alfred and Sophronia   "A mature young gentleman with too much nose on his face, too much ginger in his whiskers, too much torso in his waistcoat, too much sparkle in his studs, his eyes, his buttons, his talk, his teeth" (I:2). An opportunistic friend of Veneering and an unscrupulous adventurer, he marries Sophronia Akershem, a "mature young lady," for her money. Equally opportunistic, she has married him for his money, and on the honeymoon they discover that each has been deceived about the financial situation of the other. So they join forces to dupe others as they have been duped (I:10). Sophronia, however, has misgivings about their scheme to marry Georgiana Podsnap to Fascination Fledgeby, and she secretly asks Twemlow to warn the Podsnaps (II:16). Later the Lammles seek to replace Rokesmith and Bella Wilfer in the Boffin household (IV:2), but they fail to fool Boffin, who pays them £100 to enable them to escape overseas from their debts. Before they go, Alfred, who has learned that Fledgeby is the moneylender who has ruined them, beats Fledgeby and rubs salt into the wounds (IV:8).

Lightwood, Mortimer   Lawyer and intimate friend of Eugene Wrayburn with whom he shares rooms in the TEMPLE. Unlike Eugene, who has no clients, Mortimer has one, the Harmon will. He opens the plot of the novel (I:2) by telling the story at the Veneerings' dinner table of "the man from Somewhere," the younger John Harmon who is returning to England to claim his inheritance. At subsequent gatherings, Lightwood continues and updates this story. Although he does not narrate the novel, he could be said to frame it, for his ongoing narrative punctuates the novel, and he ends the story by appreciating Twemlow's defense of Eugene and Lizzie and accompanying him home (IV:17). Lightwood also serves as a foil to Eugene, challenging his desultory pursuit of Lizzie and his taunting of Headstone. He serves as Boffin's lawyer and investigates Fledgeby's secretive financial dealings. After Eugene is attacked, Mortimer attends his injured friend, arranges the wedding with Lizzie, and tells the injured Eugene that he is a "friend who has always loved you, admired you, imitated you, founded himself upon you, been nothing without you, and who, God knows, would be here in your place if he could" (IV:10).

Limehouse Dockside area in east London, site of the Grapes Inn, original of the Six Jolly Fellowship Porters. Rogue Riderhood and the Hexams live nearby in Limehouse Hole. Pleasant Riderhood's leaving shop is also located here.

Mary Anne Miss Peecher's favorite pupil, who always raises her hand before speaking. She "sufficiently divined the state of Miss Peecher's affections [for Bradley Headstone] to feel it necessary that she herself should love young Charley Hexam" (II:1). Mary Anne doubles Charley Hexam, relating to Miss Peecher as Charley does to Bradley Headstone.

Milvey, the Reverend Frank Young clergyman, "expensively educated and wretchedly paid, with quite a young wife and half-a-dozen quite young children. He was under the necessity of teaching and translating from the classics, to eke out his scanty means, yet was generally expected to have more time to spare than the idlest person in the parish, and more money than the richest. He accepted the needless inequalities and inconsistencies of his life, with a kind of conventional submission that was almost slavish; and any daring layman who would have adjusted such burdens as his, more decently and graciously, would have had small help from him" (I:10). He arranges the adoption of young Johnny by the Boffins (I:16), conducts the funeral service for Betty Higden (III:9), and marries Eugene Wrayburn and Lizzie Hexam (IV:11). Dickens presents the Milveys as earnest do-gooders who accept, even welcome, the hardships of a clergyman's life with a touch of graceless masochism.

Milvey, Margaretta The clergyman's young wife, "a pretty, bright little woman, something worn with anxiety, who had repressed many pretty tastes and bright fancies, and substituted in their stead

schools, soup, flannel, coals, and all the week-day cares and Sunday coughs of a large population, young and old" (I:10).

Mincing Lane On this street in the City between Fenchurch Street and Eastcheap, the center of the tea trade, R. W. Wilfer works in the offices of Chicksey, Veneering and Stubbles (II:8).

Mullins, Jack A regular customer at the Six Jolly Fellowship Porters.

Palace Yard Part of the Westminster Hall complex. John Harmon, disguised as Handford, gives his address as Exchequer Coffee House, Old Palace Yard (I:3).

Peecher, Emma Schoolteacher in the female division of the school where Bradley Headstone is master. "Small, shining, neat, and methodical, and buxom was Miss Peecher; cherry-cheeked and tuneful of voice. A little pincushion, a little housewife, a little book, a little workbox, a little set of tables and weights and measures, and a little woman all in one. She could write a little essay on any subject, exactly a slate long, beginning at the left-hand top of one side and ending at the right-hand bottom of the other, and the essay should be strictly according to rule. If Mr. Bradley Headstone had addressed a written proposal of marriage to her, she would probably have replied in a complete little essay on the theme exactly a slate long, but would certainly have replied yes. For she loved him" (II:1).

Plashwater Weir Mill Lock The lock where Rogue Riderhood is the keeper and where he and Bradley Headstone drown together (IV:15). It is probably based on the Hurley Lock, six miles downriver from Henley.

Podsnap, Georgiana Podsnap's 17-year-old daughter: "an under-sized damsel, with high shoulders, low spirits, chilled elbows, and a rasped surface of nose, who seemed to take occasional frosty peeps out of childhood into womanhood, and to shrink back again" (I:11). When the Lammles scheme to marry her to Fascination Fledgeby, her snobbish and self-satisfied father is unaware of the danger to his daughter. She is saved from the union only when a conscience-stricken Mrs. Lammle warns Podsnap through Twemlow (II:16). She naively maintains a pathetic loyalty to the Lammles and, after their ruin, offers to give £15 and a heirloom necklace to help them out of their financial difficulties (IV:2).

Podsnap, John A pompous, self-satisfied insurance man who symbolizes the PHILISTINISM of the Victorian middle class: "Mr. Podsnap was well to do, and stood very high in Mr. Podsnap's opinion. . . . He never could make out why everybody was not quite satisfied, . . . being particularly well-satisfied with most things, and, above all other things, with himself" (I:11). He ignores anything that would upset his complacency by denying it and pushing it away with a flourish of the right hand. He is the model for "Podsnappery," or middle-class complacency and condescension.

> Mr. Podsnap's world was not a very large world, morally; no, nor even geographically: seeing that although his business was sustained upon commerce with other countries, he considered other countries, with that important reservation, a mistake, and of their manners and customs would conclusively observe, 'Not English!' when, Presto! with a flourish of the arm, and a flush of the face, they were swept away. Elsewhere, the world got up at eight, shaved close at a quarter-past, breakfasted at nine, went to the City at ten, came home at half-past five, and dined at seven. Mr. Podsnap's notions of the Arts in their integrity might have been stated thus, Literature; large print, respectively descriptive of getting up at eight, shaving close at a quarter-past, breakfasting at nine, going to the City at ten, coming home at half-past five, and dining at seven. Painting and Sculpture; models and portraits representing Professors of getting up at eight, shaving close at a quarter-past, breakfasting at nine, going to the City at ten, coming home at half-past five, and dining at seven. Music; a respectable performance (without variations) on stringed and

wind instruments, sedately expressive of getting up at eight, shaving close at a quarter-past, breakfasting at nine, going to the City at ten, coming home at half-past five, and dining at seven. Nothing else to be permitted to those same vagrants the Arts, on pain of excommunication. Nothing else To Be—anywhere! (I:11)

Podsnap sums up his xenophobic world view by affirming "that there is in the Englishman a combination of qualities, a modesty, an independence, a responsibility, a repose, combined with the absence of everything calculated to call a blush into the cheek of a young person, which one would seek in vain among the Nations of the Earth" (I:11). His voice dominates the "voice of society" that pontificates at the Veneerings' dinner parties. In the closing chapter, he condemns the marriage of Eugene and Lizzie: "Then all *I* have to say is . . . that my gorge rises against such a marriage—that it offends and disgusts me—that it makes me sick—and that I desire to know no more about it" (IV:17). Dickens's friend JOHN FORSTER is said to be the model, at least in some respects, for Podsnap.

Podsnap, Mrs. Podsnap's wife, "a fine woman" with a "quantity of bone, neck and nostrils like a rocking horse," who wears a majestic headdress on which she displays the "golden offerings" from her husband (I:2). She is wholly consumed with her social position, with her appearances in society, and with arranging her daughter's social life. The shy Georgiana confides to Mrs. Lammle, "You are not ma. I wish you were." (II:4)

Portman Square The Podsnaps live "in a shady angle adjoining" this fashionable square in Marylebone (I:11).

Potterson, Abbey Proprietor of the Six Jolly Fellowship Porters, the pub along the THAMES in Limehouse near where John Harmon's body was found. "A tall, upright, well-favoured woman, though severe of countenance" (I:6), she rules the pub like an abbess governing a convent: She advises Lizzie to separate herself from her father and his work; on the basis of rumors about their unsavory activities, she excludes both Gaffer Hexam and Rogue Riderhood from the fellowship in the inn; and she presides over the resuscitation of Rogue when he is pulled from the river. After Rokesmith forces Rogue Riderhood to admit that his accusations against Gaffer were fabricated, she admits that she was wrong in her judgment of Gaffer.

Potterson, Job   Abbey's brother, steward on the ship on which John Harmon returned to England from South Africa; he identifies the drowned man as Harmon (I:3).

Pubsey and Co.   The moneylending business in St. Mary Axe that is run by Riah as a front for Fascination Fledgeby.

Riah ("Aaron")   "An old Jewish man, in an ancient coat, long of skirt and wide of pocket. A venerable man, bald and shining at the top of his head, and with long grey hair flowing down at its sides and mingling with his beard. A man who with a graceful Eastern action of homage bent his head and stretched out his hands with the palms downward, as if to deprecate the wrath of a superior" (II:5), who is employed by Fascination Fledgeby to act the stereotype of a Jewish moneylender and be the front for Fledgeby's business, Pubsey and Co. Underneath his stereotypical disguise, Riah is a loving and caring man who befriends Jenny Wren and Lizzie and finds a job for Lizzie in the upriver mill town when she wants to hide from Headstone and Wrayburn. After he breaks with Fledgeby, he and Jenny Wren, who calls him "godmother," suggestive of his fairy-tale role in the story, make a home together.

In part, Riah was Dickens's response to ELIZA DAVIS's objection to the anti-Semitic stereotyping in the portrayal of Fagin. G. K. CHESTERTON (1911) overstated the dissatisfaction that many critics have expressed about Riah's characterization: "The impeccable old Aaron stands up in the middle of this ironic carnival with a peculiar solemnity and silliness. He looks like one particularly stupid Englishman pretending to be a Jew, amidst all that crowd of clever Jews who are pretending to be Englishmen."

Riderhood, Pleasant   Rogue's 24-year-old daughter, an unlicensed pawnbroker and proprietor of a leaving shop in Limehouse Hole, who has a jaded view of life and "had it in the blood, or had been trained, to regard seamen, within certain limits, as her prey" (II:12). She is the object of Mr. Venus's frustrated affections, and, in the end, she overcomes her aversion to Venus's business when he agrees to confine himself "to the articulation of men, children, and the lower animals" so that she, as a woman, would not be "regarded in a bony light" (IV:14). Then she marries him. HILARY SCHOR (1999) analyzes Pleasant's unusual position among the women of the novel as a woman of property whose small inheritance gives her an independence that many of the other women lack.

Riderhood, Roger ("Rogue")   A Thames waterman, formerly Gaffer Hexam's partner, he has a "squinting leer" and fumbles at his "old sodden fur cap" as he speaks: "I am a man as gets my living and seeks to get my living by the sweat of my brow" (II:12). He attempts to implicate Hexam in Harmon's murder in order to claim the reward offered by Boffin (I:12), but Rokesmith makes him sign a confession confirming his own involvement in the murder (II:12). After he escapes from drowning (III:2), he takes a position as a deputy lockkeeper at Plashwater Weir Mill Lock (IV:1), where he becomes aware of Headstone's plan to murder Wrayburn and throw the blame on him. He shadows Headstone, retrieves the clothes that Headstone discards into the Thames, and attempts to blackmail the schoolmaster. The enmity between the two leads to a struggle at the lock in which the two men drown, locked in one another's arms (IV:15). Riderhood's return from his near-drowning unchanged has convinced many commentators that the resurrection theme in the novel is not simplistic, for all who go through near-death experiences in the river are not changed by the experience.

Rokesmith, John   Pseudonym taken by John Harmon while he serves as Boffin's secretary and into the initial year of his marriage, before his true identity is revealed.

Sackville Street Fashionable street off Piccadilly where Alfred Lammle lives (I:10).

St. James's Church Christopher Wren church in Piccadilly where the Lammles are married (I:10).

St. Mary Axe The area in the City of London where Fledgeby has the office of Pubsey and Co. Here Riah has the roof garden visited by Lizzie Hexam and Jenny Wren (II:5).

St. Peter's Church In the churchyard of this church in Cornhill, Bradley Headstone makes his impassioned proposal to Lizzie Hexam (II:15).

Sampson, George Young man who, disappointed in his love for Bella Wilfer, transfers his affections to her sister Lavinia. "He put the round head of his cane in his mouth, like a stopper, when he sat down. As if he felt himself full to the throat with affecting sentiments" (I:9). She rules him with "stinging discipline" as a way, perhaps, of reminding him of his initial mistake.

Six Jolly Fellowship Porters (The Porters) The riverside pub in Limehouse where Abbey Potterson presides like an abbess over a community institution. It was probably based on the Grape Inn.

Sloppy An orphan from the poorhouse taken in by Betty Higden, "a very long boy, with a very little head, and an open mouth of disproportionate capacity that seemed to assist his eyes in staring at the visitors" (I:16). He operates the mangle for Betty and reads to her from the police reports in the newspaper. After Johnny's death, the Boffins decide to take in Sloppy but not to rename him John Harmon. Boffin assigns Sloppy the task of keeping an eye on Wegg at the dust mounds (IV:3), and after Wegg's schemes are exposed, Sloppy dumps him into a dustman's cart (IV:14). At the end of the novel his particular attentions to Jenny Wren suggest a future marriage (IV:16).

Smith Square, Westminster Now Dean Stanley Street, the site of the house where Lizzie Hexam lived with Jenny Wren.

Snigsworth, Lord Twemlow's aristocratic cousin who serves as Twemlow's calling card in society.

Sprodgkin, Mrs. Sally Parishioner of the Reverend Milvey who torments the clegyman "by conspicuously weeping at everything, however cheering, said by the Reverend Frank in his public ministrations" (IV:11).

Swoshle, Mrs. Henry George Alfred Mrs. Tapkins's married daughter, who calls on the newly-rich Boffins at their fashionable house on CAVENDISH SQUARE (I:17).

Tapkins, Mrs. Representative of an extensive and socially prominent family who, with her five daughters, is among the first to call and leave her card for the newly-rich Boffins at their house on CAVENDISH SQUARE (I:17).

Tippins, Lady Widow of Sir Thomas Tippins who was "knighted in mistake for somebody else" (I:10), she is a friend of the Veneerings and one of the voices of society. Old and ugly, she has "an immense obtuse drab oblong face, like a face in a tablespoon, and a dyed Long Walk up the top of her head, as a convenient approach to the bunch of false hair behind," and there is "a certain yellow play in Lady Tippins's throat, like the legs of scratching poultry" (I:2). She maintains "a grisly little fiction concerning her lovers" (I:2), dressing and presenting herself as much younger than she is; "you could easily buy all you see of her, in Bond Street: or you might scalp her, and peel her, and scrape her, and make two Lady Tippinses out of her, and yet not penetrate to the genuine article" (I:10). A later version of Mrs. Skewton from *Dombey*, Lady Tippins reinforces the vision of society as all surfaces and of its members as being more dead than alive.

"Toddles" Pet name of a boy in Betty Higden's minding school.

Tootle, Tom A regular customer at the Six Jolly Fellowship Porters who tells Abbey Potterson that Rogue Riderhood's boat has been run down by a steamer (III:2).

Twemlow, Melvin A member of society, this mild-mannered gentleman, "grey, dry, polite, susceptible to east wind, First-Gentleman-in-Europe collar and cravat, cheeks drawn in as if he had made a great effort to retire into himself some years ago, and had got so far and had never got any farther" (I:2). He is claimed by Veneering as one of his "oldest friends" because he is a cousin of Lord Snigsworth, who provides him with the small annuity on which he lives. Sophronia Lammle confides to him her scheme to entrap Georgiana Podsnap into a marriage with Fledgeby (II:16), and Twemlow in turn warns Podsnap. At the end of the novel, Twemlow separates himself from the other voices of society by defending Wrayburn as "the greater gentleman" for marrying Lizzie Hexam and making her "the greater lady" (IV:17). Although many commentators discover a hopeful note for society's reform in Twemlow's final approval of Eugene, JAMES KINCAID (1971) considers that Dickens shows something "close to contempt" for Twemlow's "passive goodness."

Veneering, Hamilton and Anastasia Nouveau riche family, the principal representatives of high society in *Mutual Friend*; "bran-new people in a bran-new house in a bran-new quarter of London. Everything about the Veneerings was spick-and-span-new. . . . For, in the Veneering establishment, . . . all things were in a state of high varnish and polish. And what was observable in the furniture, was observable in the Veneerings—the surface smelt a little too much of the workshop and was a trifle sticky" (I:2). They have a "bran-new baby." Their dinner parties, which occur regularly through the novel, gather the members of society—Mortimer Lightwood, Eugene Wrayburn, the Podsnaps, Lady Tippins, Twemlow, Boots, and Brewer—to share the gossip of the day, hear the ongoing story of John Harmon, and provide a social chorus to the novel. Veneering buys his way into Parliament, representing the borough of Pocket Breaches (II:3). In the end, bankrupt and despised, they escape to France. JULIET JOHN (2001) points out that the Veneerings are abstractions and lack a distinct physical appearance. They are "an idea summed up by a name," characters who only pretend "to be human, to be real."

Venus, Mr. A morose, 32-year-old bachelor, taxidermist, and articulator of bones in "a little dark greasy shop" in Clerkenwell (I:7): "a sallow face with weak eyes, surmounted by a tangle of reddish-dusty hair. . . . His eyes are like the over-tried eyes of an engraver; . . . his expression and stoop are like those of a shoemaker" (I:7). He makes Wegg's acquaintance when Wegg seeks to recover his amputated leg bone, which Venus has obtained from a hospital attendant (I:7). The two men enter into a compact, the "friendly move," to blackmail Boffin (II:7). But Venus repents his involvement, reveals the plot to Boffin (III:14), and helps incriminate Wegg. Venus is in love with Pleasant Riderhood, who finds his occupation distasteful and objects to being regarded "in that bony light"; she overcomes her objections when he agrees not to work on female skeletons (IV:14).

JULIET MCMASTER (1987), who describes *Our Mutual Friend* as a novel about social fragmentation, sees Venus as a "force for integration" because he puts things together. His comic love affair with Pleasant Riderhood justifies his comic name and parodies the relationship between Eugene and Lizzie, which is shadowed by "the long light" of death. PETER ACKROYD (1990) identifies a Mr. Willis, a taxidermist in St. Andrew's Street near SEVEN DIALS, as the original of Venus.

Walton, Surrey One of the towns along the Thames that Betty Higden passes through on her final journey (III:8).

Waterloo Station Railway station, opened in 1846, where Bradley Headstone learns of Lizzie Hexam's impending marriage from her friends who are going to the wedding (IV:11).

Wegg, Silas Semiliterate balladmonger and street vendor hired by Boffin to be his "literary man" and read to him (I:5) and to be caretaker of Boffin's Bower (I:15). "A knotty man, and a close-grained, with a face carved out of very hard material, that had just as much play of expression as a watchman's rattle. When he laughed, certain jerks occurred in it, and the rattle sprung. Sooth to say, he was so wooden a man that he seemed to have taken his wooden leg naturally, and rather suggested to the fanciful observer, that he might be expected—if his development received no untimely check—to be completely set up with a pair of wooden legs in about six months" (I:5). His comic villainy echoes many of the main themes in the novel. Like the living-dead members of society, he literally has one foot in the grave. His reading of the "Decline-and-Fall-Off-the-Rooshan-Empire" is a ritual of the social disintegration that surrounds him, and his prodding investigations of the dust mounds with his wooden leg repeat the occupations of the many characters who live off the dead. His "friendly move" with Venus to blackmail Boffin is foiled when Venus confesses the plot to Boffin and another will is discovered. Wegg's comic comeuppance occurs when Sloppy picks him up, carries him out of Boffin's house, and throws him into a dust cart (IV:14).

Wilfer, Bella   The petulant and capricious young woman chosen by old John Harmon as the appropriate bride to will to his son. Describing herself as "a kind of widow who was never married" (I:4), Bella decries old Harmon's will, which treats her "like a dozen of spoons" (I:4), willing her to someone she has never met. But she admits that "those ridiculous points would have been smoothed away by the money, for I love money, and want money—want it dreadfully. I hate to be poor, and we are degradingly poor, offensively poor, miserably poor, beastly poor" (I:4). When she is disinherited by the presumed death of young Harmon, the Boffins take her into their house, where she indulges her mercenary tendencies, encouraged by Boffin himself, who pretends to be a miser to teach her the bad effects of being mercenary. She rejects Rokesmith's first proposal of marriage, indignant at his presumption (II:13), but when he is harshly treated by Boffin and dismissed, she recognizes the shallowness of Boffin's (and her own) mercenary values, and a meeting with Lizzie Hexam shows her another way of being a woman. A changed person, Bella runs off with Rokesmith and marries him (IV:4). She is not informed of the real identity of her husband until many months later.

The other central figure in the main plot of the novel, Bella has been praised as possessing a depth and complexity beyond that of many of Dickens's earlier heroines, a complexity suggested by her name: Bella (beautiful, warlike) Wilfer (Willful, willed to Harmon). Her growth and transformation, however, has been criticized (e.g., by MCMASTER [1987] and KINCAID [1971]) as brought about by Boffin's fraud and an ambiguous meeting with Lizzie. The resulting transformation is also somewhat disconcerting, for Bella becomes domesticated and is rewarded with the wealth that she has abjured.

Wilfer, Cecelia   Bella's married sister, who, three months after her wedding, learns that she must take into her house her husband's poor aunt. Mrs. Wilfer asserts that Cecelia's "self-sacrifice . . . reveals a pure and womanly character" (I:4).

Wilfer, Lavinia ("Laavy")   Bella's "audacious" younger sister who challenges Bella's position in the family and talks back to everyone, even her majestic mother. She commandeers George Sampson, who has previously courted Bella, but she unsettles his affections with her mercurial behavior.

Wilfer, Mrs.   Bella's mother, she is as majestic as her husband is modest:

> a tall woman, and angular. Her lord being cherubic, she was necessarily majestic, according to the principle which matrimonially unites contrasts. She was much given to tying up her head in a pocket-handkerchief, knotted under the chin. This head-gear, in conjunction with a pair of gloves worn within doors, she seemed to consider as at once a kind of armour against misfortune (invariably assuming it when in low spirits or difficulties), and as a species of full dress. (I:4)

Feeling herself above the station to which marriage has reduced her, she complains about her poverty and of being ill-used. Gloomy and pompous, she rules her husband and her family, but nonetheless suffers Lavinia's barbs and Bella's neglect. She is not invited to Bella's secret wedding party with her husband (IV:4), nor does she share the tender relationship Bella has with her father.

Wilfer, Reginald (R. W.; "the Cherub," "Rumty") Bella's father, a henpecked clerk for Chicksey, Veneering, and Stobbles. His cherubic appearance, "chubby, smooth, innocent," bespeaks his gentle and self-effacing manner: "shy, and unwilling to own to the name of Reginald, as being too aspiring and self-assertive a name, . . . he used only the initial R., and imparted what it really stood for to none but chosen friends" (I:4). He is so poor that "the modest object of his ambition [is] to wear a complete new suit of clothes, hat and boots included, at one time" (I:4). The Wilfers have many children, but R. W.'s favorite child is Bella. She confides in him, buys him a new suit, and goes with him for a private dinner in Greenwich (II:8). He attends her secret wedding to Rokesmith (IV:4).

Williams, William A regular customer at the Six Jolly Fellowship Porters.

Wrayburn, Eugene Mortimer Lightwood's close friend, a lawyer who has been in the profession seven years without work, "in susceptibility to boredom . . . the most consistent of mankind" (I:12). An upper-class idler, melancholy and cynical, with no direction in his life, he is nonetheless uneasy about the expectations of his M.R.F. (Most Respected Father) that he should establish himself and marry well. He interests himself in the Harmon murder case, meets Lizzie Hexam (I:2), and pursues her but has no clear acknowledgment or understanding of his intentions (II:6). Over the objections of her brother he educates her, and he engages in a cat-and-mouse contest with her other suitor, the schoolmaster Bradley Headstone. When Lizzie runs off to escape his attentions and those of Bradley Headstone, he follows her, learning her whereabouts from Mr. Dolls (III:16). At the mill town on the upper THAMES where she is living, he confesses his love to her, is attacked by Headstone, and is rescued by Lizzie (IV:6), whom he marries during his gradual recovery. Her love brings more than his physical recovery; it gives purpose and meaning to his life.

A more interesting and complex character than John Harmon, Wrayburn, hero of the plot that parallels the main plot, repeats many of the motifs in John Harmon's story. Near-murder by drowning is at the center of both plots, but the effects on character are more profoundly studied in Eugene's case than in Harmon's. Both men are uneasy about the control exerted by their fathers, but Eugene's escape through denial and repression is more engaging than Harmon's masquerade. When he pleads boredom to avoid self-understanding and uses his cynical wit to fend off serious challenges, Eugene seems to be "light wood" floating on the surface of life, doubling his friend, or at least his friend's name. He claims to have "no designs" in his relationship with Lizzie, and he does not reflect on the roots of the self-destructive sadism that drives him to taunt Headstone to murder. These contradictions and complexities in his character surface in the drowning and rescue, which finally release his capacity to love and to choose the depths of loving Lizzie over the superficialities of society.

"Wren, Jenny" The name by which Fanny Cleaver is known.

ADAPTATIONS

Like the other late novels, *Mutual Friend* inspired fewer stage adaptations than the earlier works. No stage versions appeared until six months after the novel completed its serial run, when two versions were staged, one in New York and the other in London. The latter, Henry Brougham Farnie's *Golden Dustman,* proved to be the most successful of the eight stage versions produced in the 1870s, especially after several long speeches were cut to reduce the four-and-a-half–hour playing time. The American adaptation, George Fawcett Rowe's *Our Mutual Friend; or, Found Drowned* (1866), also played in London in 1871. Two silent films, one by Edison (1911) and one by a A. W. Sandberg (1919), were derived from the novel, but no sound films have appeared. Three BBC television serials have dramatized the novel, one by Freda Lindstrom in 12 parts (1959), with David McCallum as Wrayburn; another by Julia Jones in seven parts (1976), with Leo McKern as Boffin; and one by Sandy Welch in four parts (1998), with Anna Friel as Bella, Paul McGann as Wrayburn, and David Morrissey as Headstone.

FURTHER READING

The contemporary setting of *Mutual Friend* has made the background of the novel particularly interesting to historical critics. Richard Altick (1974) discusses the education controversies of the time as they affect the novel, and HUMPHRY HOUSE (1941) and HARVEY PETER SUCKSMITH ("The Dust-Heaps in *Our Mutual Friend*," *Essays in Criticism*, 1973) consider the actual contents of Victorian dustheaps and their symbolic significance in the novel. Arnold Kettle's (1962) Marxist analysis ("*Our Mutual Friend.*" In *Dickens and The Twentieth Century*, edited by John Gross and Gabriel Pearson, 1962) also locates the symbols in the novel in the realities of bourgeois Victorian culture. Jonathan Arac (*Commissioned Spirits: The Shaping of Social Motion in Dickens, Carlyle, Melville, and Hawthorne*, 1979), on the other hand, finds the novel incoherent and lacking in organic connections between the characters and their social world.

J. HILLIS MILLER, who has written about *Mutual Friend* on several occasions, argues (1958) that the novel, which seems to present merely "a collection of unrelated lives," in fact relates them in an "immense network of interrelations." He goes on to analyze the symbolism of money, dust, and regeneration. In his afterword to the Signet Edition (1964; 1991), Miller stresses the insubstantiality of money and the superficial values it imposes. Only those characters who "confront material and emotional depths, and then return to live their surface lives in terms of those depths can reconcile 'Society' and reality." ANDREW SANDERS (1982) also finds the theme of regeneration important; he analyzes Eugene's baptismal resurrection from a life of idle boredom and spiritual death as the emblematic center of the novel. In *The Form of Victorian Fiction* (1968), Miller analyzes the use of the mirror above the Veneerings' dining table as a symbol of the way art reflects and transforms social reality. John Romano (*Dickens and Reality*, 1978) also uses the mirror to introduce his extended discussion of the realism in the novel. Connecting the mirror with Lightwood's story of the "man from Somewhere," Romano shows the inadequacy of art to fully comprehend the truth of what it reflects.

Beth Herst (*The Dickens Hero: Selfhood and Alienation in the Dickens World*, 1990) considers the various heroes and villains of the novel—Harmon, Wrayburn, Headstone—as culminating versions of the hero Dickens has developed from the earlier novels. Gail Houston (*Consuming Fictions: Gender, Class, and Hunger in Dickens's Novels*, 1994) analyzes the ways in which Victorian society's consuming greed valued waste and objectified human beings. She finds a contradiction in the resolution, in which the novel's commodified heroines are sacrificed to the growth and well-being of the heroes. HILARY SCHOR (1999) develops a reading of the novel that concentrates on the roles of the female characters.

Pickwick Papers, The. (Serial title: The Posthumous Papers of the Pickwick Club, containing a Faithful Record of the Perambulations, Perils, Travels, Adventures and Sporting Transactions of the Corresponding Members, edited by Boz.)

Dickens's first novel, published in 20 monthly numbers by CHAPMAN & HALL, April 1836 to November 1837 (omitting June 1836), illustrated by ROBERT SEYMOUR (Parts 1 and 2); ROBERT WILLIAM BUSS (Part 3), and HABLOT KNIGHT BROWNE. Published in one volume, 1837. Dickens was commissioned by WILLIAM HALL to write the letterpress for a series of sporting sketches by Seymour, but after the artist's suicide, Dickens chose a new illustrator, took direction of the project, and gave the narrative more prominence. Gradually, what began as essentially a series of comic sketches (*see* SKETCH) developed into a novel, and the novel, especially after the introduction of Sam Weller, became a runaway best seller. By the end, *Pick-*

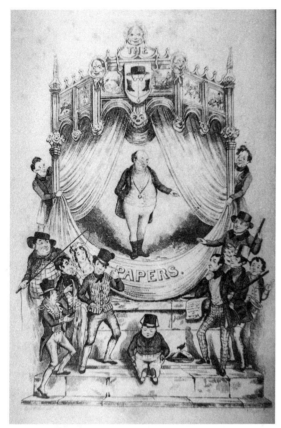

Alfred Crowquill's iconographic frontispiece for an 1852 edition of *The Pickwick Papers*.

wick had turned into a kind of comic BILDUNGS-ROMAN in which the innocent protagonist learns to compromise principle and affirm life. Although he experiences pain and suffering, Pickwick is not diminished or hardened by his trials.

SYNOPSIS

Part 1 (April 1836)

(1) At its meeting on May 12, 1827, the Pickwick Club forms a corresponding society to travel about the country and report its findings back to the group in London. The traveling group will be led by Samuel Pickwick, founder of the club and noteworthy for his theory of tittlebats. Three other gentlemen—Tracy Tupman, an admirer of the fair sex; Augustus Snodgrass, a poet; and Nathaniel Winkle, a sportsman—will accompany him. As Pickwick addresses the meeting, his speech is interrupted by Mr. Blotton, who calls him a "humbug." The dispute is resolved when Blotton agrees that he used the term only in its "Pickwickian sense." (2) As the Pickwickians set out on their travels the next day, Pickwick offends a cabdriver by taking down notes of his conversation. He is rescued from the altercation by a stranger in a green coat who is also going to ROCHESTER. That evening Tupman lends their traveling companion, Mr. Alfred Jingle, Mr. Winkle's Pickwick Club suit so the two of them can attend a dance. There Jingle offends Dr. Slammer of the local regiment, and the next morning Slammer's second delivers a challenge to Mr. Winkle, believing that he was the offending young man. But at the duel Slammer does not recognize Winkle as his antagonist and the engagement is called off. (3) The next morning Jingle introduces to the Pickwickians a strolling actor, who offers to tell them a story.

Part 2 (May 1836)

(3) The actor, Dismal Jemmy, tells "The Stroller's Tale," an account of a pantomime clown who abuses his wife and family and falls into an alcohol-induced dementia on his deathbed. When Dr. Slammer and his friends arrive, they are taken aback to see Tupman and the stranger in the green coat, who was the offending party at the ball. When Jingle is identified as a strolling actor, however, Slammer declines to renew his challenge. (4) At a military exercise the next day, Pickwick gets caught between the opposing lines. He also meets the Wardles, who have come to view the proceedings. Mr. Wardle, a country squire, invites the Pickwickians to Manor Farm. (5) On the way to the farm, they manage to frighten their horses and overturn their carriage, and they therefore arrive late and tired after walking the last seven miles.

Part 3 (June 1836)

(6) The Pickwickians join the Wardles and their friends for cards and other games. Tupman pays his attentions to Rachael, the spinster sister of Mr. Wardle. The local clergyman recites his poem, "The Ivy Green," and then tells the story "The Convict's Return." John Edmunds, one of his parishioners, after a childhood of abuse and mistreatment, is

transported for 17 years for robbery. When he returns, he is unrecognized by all in the village except his abusive father, who dies from a ruptured blood vessel when he recognizes his son. Edmunds, "contrite, penitent, and humbled," served the vicar for three years before he died. (7) On a morning shooting expedition, Winkle wounds Tupman slightly, much to the consternation of Wardle's spinster sister. In the afternoon, the Pickwickians attend the Dingley Dell/Muggleton cricket match and the dinner that follows the game, where they again meet Mr. Jingle. (8) While his friends are at the cricket dinner, Tupman courts Rachael in the garden. There they are discovered by Joe, Wardle's sleepy servant boy. After the drunken group returns from the cricket celebration, Jingle charms the ladies with his stories. He learns that Tupman's courtship has been discovered, and he advises Tupman to ignore Rachael and to be attentive instead to Emily, her niece. Meanwhile, Jingle pursues Rachael.

Part 4 (July 1836)

(9) When Rachael runs off with Jingle, Wardle and Pickwick give chase, but their carriage overturns just as it reaches the fleeing pair. Jingle sneers back at their misfortune. (10) In London, at the White Hart Inn, Sam Weller is cleaning shoes when Wardle and Pickwick pay him to show them the room where Rachael and Jingle are staying. Wardle pays Jingle £120 to give up Rachael. As Jingle leaves he gives Pickwick the marriage license he has obtained, telling him it is "for Tuppy." Pickwick is outraged. (11) Back at Dingley Dell, Pickwick discovers that Tupman has left the farm and retreated in suicidal humiliation to the Leather Bottle in COBHAM. There they find him eating supper and looking well. They also find a stone with a strange inscription. Before going to bed, Pickwick reads "A

Pickwick gets into a scuffle with the cabdriver, before being rescued from the fight by Alfred Jingle, in this scene from the 1952 movie adaptation. *Courtesy of PhotoFest.*

Madman's Manuscript," a document given to him by the clergyman at Dingley Dell, which purports to be a madman's account of his illness, his plot to murder his wife and children, and his capture before the scheme can be carried out. The next day the Pickwickians return to London to report to the club on the inscribed rock that they have found.

Part 5 (August 1836)

(12) Pickwick surprises his landlady, the widow Bardell, with what she misconstrues as a proposal of marriage. She throws herself into his arms just as the other Pickwickians arrive at his rooms. Pickwick has really been asking Mrs. Bardell about the advisibility of hiring a servant; that afternoon he engages Sam Weller, the bootblack from the White Hart. (13) The Pickwickians go down to Eatanswill to observe the election between the BLUES AND BUFFS. (14) Pickwick and Winkle stay at the home of Mr. Pott, the irascible editor of the *Eatanswill Gazette*. At the Peacock Inn, where the rest of the Pickwickians stay, a traveling salesman tells them "The Bagman's Story." Tom Smart, a traveling salesman, stops at a country inn, where a "grim-looking high-backed chair" in his room turns into an old man during the night and advises him to expose Jinkins, the adulterous suitor of the widow who owns the inn, and to marry the widow himself.

Part 6 (September 1836)

(15) The Pickwickians are invited to Mrs. Leo Hunter's fête champêtre, a fancy-dress affair where they will meet clever people and hear the hostess recite her "Ode to an Expiring Frog." When Jingle appears at the affair as Mr. Charles Fitz-Marshall, Pickwick is astonished and pursues him to the ANGEL, BURY ST. EDMUNDS. (16) There Sam learns from Jingle's servant, Job Trotter, that his master has a plan to elope that evening with one of the girls from Miss Tomkins's school. To foil the scheme, Pickwick hides in the school courtyard so that he can inform Miss Tomkins when the elopement is taking place. But he is discovered in the courtyard and no one at the school knows anything of Fitz-Marshall or his scheme. Sam and Wardle rescue Pickwick from this compromising situation. (17) Beset by rheumatism for three days after this escapade, Pickwick passes the time writing the story

"The Parish Clerk" and reading it to Wardle. It tells of Nathaniel Pipkin, a parish clerk and schoolmaster who dreams of marrying Maria Lobbs. She flirts with him and he confesses his desire to her father, Old Lobbs, the local saddler, who rejects the idea out of hand. Maria marries her cousin, and Nathaniel and Old Lobbs become friends.

Part 7 (October 1836)

(18) Winkle is surprised when Mr. Pott calls him a "serpent" and shows him an article in the rival newspaper implying that there is an affair between Pott's wife and Winkle. The misunderstanding is cleared up just as Pickwick is served notice informing him that Mrs. Bardell has filed suit against him for breach of promise. (19) On a hunting expedition with Wardle, Winkle's reckless handling of the gun frightens Pickwick. After a picnic lunch, Pickwick, who has drunk too much cold punch, is left sleeping in a wheelbarrow. There he is discovered by Captain Boldwig, who takes him for a trespasser and carts him off to the village pound. He is again rescued by Sam and Wardle. As they take him away, he threatens to sue Boldwig. (20) Back in London, Pickwick goes to Mrs. Bardell's attorneys, Dodson and Fogg, and becomes so incensed that he accuses them of being scoundrels. His own attorney, Mr. Perker, is out of town, so Pickwick seeks out Perker's clerk, Mr. Lowten, at the Magpie and Stump tavern.

Part 8 (November 1836)

(21) An old man, Jack Bamber, in the group of law clerks gathered at the Magpie and Stump tells "The Tale of the Queer Client," about George Heyling, a debtor in the MARSHALSEA PRISON, who vengefully pursued his cruel father-in-law because he blamed him for the deaths of his wife and child. (22) Sam and Pickwick go to Ipswich in a coach driven by Sam's father, Tony Weller, in search of Jingle. On the way Pickwick meets Peter Magnus, who is going to Ipswich to propose to Miss Witherfield, a lady he knows only through correspondence. At the inn, Pickwick and Peter Magnus eat dinner together. That night, Pickwick loses his way in the inn and ends up in the wrong bedroom, where he surprises a middle-aged woman. (23) The next morning Sam runs into Job Trotter, who tells him that Jingle

has another nefarious plot. Sam plans to foil the scheme.

Part 9 (December 1836)

(24) When Peter Magnus meets Miss Witherfield, he follows Pickwick's advice about the romantic strategy to follow; his suit is almost immediately successful. But when he introduces Pickwick to his prospective bride, she turns out to be the woman Pickwick surprised the night before. Neither Pickwick nor Miss Witherfield will reveal what happened, and their reticence inflames the jealousy of Peter Magnus. Fearing that a duel will ensue, Miss Witherfield files a complaint against Pickwick and Tupman with the local magistrate, Mr. Nupkins. They are arrested and taken through the streets. When Sam tries to rescue Pickwick, he is apprehended as well. (25) Sam has figured out that Jingle's plot involves the magistrate's daughter, and when Pickwick reveals the scheme to Nupkins, the magistrate dismisses the case against them. Together they expose Jingle's villainy. (26) Back in London, Pickwick sends Sam to Mrs. Bardell's to pay the rent, give notice of his intention to leave his rooms, and find out her feelings about the suit. Sam learns that she intends to go forward with the suit.

Part 10 (January 1837)

(27) Sam goes down to the Marquis of Granby in Dorking to visit his father and stepmother. There he also finds Mr. Stiggins, Mrs. Weller's spiritual guide, who spends his time at the pub drinking and borrowing money from Tony. Sam advises his father to get rid of Stiggins, but Tony rejects his son's advice, telling Sam that he does not understand the intricacies of marriage. (28) The Pickwickians go down to Dingley Dell for Christmas, bringing with them a large codfish and several barrels of oysters. There they celebrate the wedding of Wardle's daughter Isabella to Mr. Trundle and join in the Christmas festivities, playing games, drinking wassail, and kissing under the mistletoe. (29) At the end of Christmas Eve, Wardle tells "The Story of the Goblins Who Stole a Sexton." Gabriel Grub, a morose sexton and gravedigger, drinks himself into a stupor as he digs a grave on Christmas Eve and dreams that he is tormented

by goblins. The dream changes his life: Ashamed of his misanthropy, he leaves his village and wanders for 10 years before returning as a ragged and repentant man.

Part 11 (February 1837)

(30) Christmas Day is cold, and there are plans for skating. Two new guests, both medical students, arrive: Benjamin Allen, brother of Arabella, who has caught the eye of Mr. Winkle, and Bob Sawyer. At breakfast, they talk about the details of surgery. Later, Bob Sawyer proves to be an accomplished figure skater, but Winkle is thoroughly incompetent and Pickwick calls him a "humbug." Pickwick does some sliding on the ice, falls through, and is thoroughly soaked. When the Christmas party breaks up, Bob Sawyer invites Pickwick to a bachelor party at his rooms in London. (31) Back in town, Winkle, Snodgrass, Tupman, and Sam are served subpoenas by Dodson and Fogg to be witnesses for Mrs. Bardell. Pickwick is incensed at the unscrupulous lawyers, and he tells Perker that he will pay no money to Dodson and Fogg, no matter what the outcome of the trial, which is scheduled for February 14. Perker assures him that the best defense is planned and that Serjeant Snubbin will represent him in court. Pickwick tells Snubbin that he wants him as a lawyer only if Snubbin believes him innocent. (32) The Pickwickians attend Bob Sawyer's party in LANT STREET. By the end, their drunken songs are awakening the neighborhood in the wee hours of the morning, and Sawyer's landlady, Mrs. Raddle, who is angry with her tenant for not paying his rent, throws all the revelers out into the street.

Part 12 (March 1837)

(33) Sam composes a valentine for Mary, the Nupkinses' maid, and signs it with Pickwick's name. Tony gets Sam to go with him to the branch of the United Grand Junction Ebenezer Temperance Association, where they expose the drunken Stiggins as a hypocrite. (34) On St. Valentine's Day, the trial of Bardell *v.* Pickwick takes place. The Pickwickians who came upon Mrs. Bardell in the arms of Pickwick prove to be damaging witnesses, for they are easily confused by the sharp lawyers.

Sam tries to save the day for Pickwick with his smart and evasive answers, but the jury finds for Mrs. Bardell and awards her £750 damages. Pickwick vows never to pay the fine.

Part 13 (April 1837)

(35) Pickwick decides to go off to BATH. On the way he meets Mr. Dowler, who introduces him to Angelo Cyrus Bantam, M.C., the dandified master of ceremonies in the Assembly Rooms at Bath. (36) The Pickwickians and the Dowlers take a house together on the Royal Cresent. In a drawer in his room, Mr. Pickwick finds a manuscript telling "The True Legend of Prince Bladud," describing the founding of Bath. Prince Bladud, broken-hearted because his love has married another, wandered tearfully to the site of Bath, where he wished that his tears "might flow forever." When "his hot tears welled up through the earth," his wish was granted, and the springs at Bath have been warm ever since. After everyone has gone to bed except Mrs. Dowler, Winkle is awakened by Mrs. Dowler's cabmen, who are bringing her home at three in the morning from a party. Winkle answers the door, but the wind blows it shut and he is left outside in his nightshirt with Mrs. Dowler. When the others in the house are finally awakened, Dowler accuses Winkle of running away with his wife, and he chases Winkle around the crescent in the middle of the night. (37) Sam is invited to a "swarry" of Bath footmen. The splendor of their uniforms is matched only by their snobbery and condescension. Sam deflates the gathering with his racy language and apt epithets. The next morning, Pickwick tells Sam that Winkle has disappeared, and he asks Sam to find him.

Part 14 (May 1837)

(38) Winkle has gone to the Bush Inn at BRISTOL. While walking about the town he runs into Bob Sawyer, who, with Ben Allen, has set up a medical practice there. Bob, Ben, and Winkle spend the day drinking with Benjamin Allen, and Winkle learns that Ben's sister Arabella is also in Bristol. When he returns to the Bush, Dowler is there, asking forgiveness and wishing to be reconciled. Sam also arrives and insists on taking Winkle back to Bath, but Winkle convinces Sam to stay with him in Bristol while they seek out Arabella Allen. (39)

When Pickwick learns of Winkle's whereabouts, he joins the search for Arabella. Sam runs into Mary, the Nupkinses' maid, who has taken a new place in Bristol, and learns from her that Arabella is kept in seclusion in a neighboring house. Sam climbs a pear tree into Arabella's garden when she is on her evening walk and arranges an interview for Winkle the next evening. Winkle, Pickwick, and Sam all go on the expedition. Winkle is successful in speaking with Arabella, but the three must make a run for it when they are taken for robbers. (40) After they return to London, Pickwick is arrested by a sheriff's officer. Perker advises him to pay the fine, but Pickwick is adamantly opposed to paying money that will enrich Dodson and Fogg, so he chooses instead to enter the FLEET PRISON.

Part 15 (July 1837)

(41) At the Fleet, Pickwick is horrified by the dungeons where some of the prisoners are housed. He rents a bed from the warden for his first night and is awakened by three drunken prisoners, Mivens, Smangle, and an unnamed third man, who convince him to buy drink and cigars. (42) The next morning Pickwick is assigned a close, dirty room with a drunken clergyman and a butcher. When he discovers that he can pay to get a room of his own, he arranges to do so. He pays a pound a week to the prisoner whose room it is, and to hire furniture for the room he pays 27 shillings a week to the jailer, Mr. Roker. When he visits the poor side of the Fleet, the part of the prison for those who cannot afford to pay for their accommodations, Pickwick finds Jingle and Job Trotter among the prisoners. Shedding a tear, Pickwick gives Job some money. Then he returns to his quarters and dismisses Sam for the duration of his confinement. (43) Sam gets his father to issue an order to have him arrested for debt, and he arrives at the prison accompanied by an entourage of coachmen. As a matter of principle, Sam refuses Pickwick's help in satisfying his creditor. He says he does not want to enrich an evil man.

Part 16 (August 1837)

(44) The Pickwickians visit the prison. Winkle says that he must go away for a while and that he

The racket-ground in the yard of Fleet Prison. The groups of prisoners who congregate here are described in Pickwick as "worth looking at, if it were only in idle curiosity" (45).

had hoped to take Sam with him, but now that Sam is a prisoner, he cannot do so. (45) Tony Weller, Susan, and Stiggins visit Sam. Stiggens gets sustenance from the prison bar and then sermonizes Sam. Pickwick takes Sam to see Jingle and Job Trotter, and Sam learns that his master, an "angel in tights and gaiters," has provided them with a room and with food and clothing. The misery in the prison so depresses Pickwick that he decides to confine himself to his rooms. He stays there for three months. (46) On a day late in July, Mrs. Bardell and several of her friends make an excursion to the Spaniards Inn in HAMP-STEAD for tea. While they are there, Mr. Jackson of Dodson and Fogg's appears and takes Mrs. Bardell off for an appointment, which turns out to be at the Fleet, where she is also imprisoned for the costs of the trial. Pickwick and Sam see her enter. Pickwick turns away without speaking; Sam sends for Perker.

Part 17 (September 1837)

(47) The next morning at 10 o'clock, Perker arrives at the Fleet. He tells Pickwick that he is the only person who can release Mrs. Bardell from prison. He counters Pickwick's angry resistance by suggesting that Pickwick will be recognized as the one who showed up the sharp practices of Dodson and Fogg. Then he produces a letter from Mrs. Bardell that absolves Pickwick and puts the blame for the action on the lawyers. When Winkle and his new bride, Arabella Allen, arrive, they ask Pickwick to reconcile Benjamin Allen and Mr. Winkle senior to their marriage. At last, Pickwick is convinced to pay the costs and leave the Fleet. As he goes, he takes steps to release Jingle and Job Trotter. (48) Bob Sawyer and Ben Allen are discussing the possibility of Bob's marrying Arabella as a way to get out of financial difficulties, when they learn of Arabella's marriage. Allen is incensed. It takes a little liquor and a lot of convincing from Pickwick to reconcile Ben and

Bob Sawyer to the union. In the end, Allen agrees to go with Pickwick to inform Winkle's father of the marriage. (49) Back at his inn, Pickwick meets the one-eyed bagman again and hears "The Story of the Bagman's Uncle." After drinking too much one evening in Edinburgh, Jack Martin, the Bagman's uncle, falls asleep in a derelict coach and imagines himself back in the 18th century, a passenger in a mail coach from Edinburgh to London. With him in the coach is a beautiful young woman; the son of the Marquess of Filletoville, who has abducted her; and the Marquess's henchman. Jack rescues the girl and races off with her in the coach, pursued by the villains. Before they can catch him, he wakes up to find himself sitting in a derelict coach on a cold and rainy morning in Edinburgh.

Part 18 (October 1837)

(50) The next morning, Pickwick, Sam, Ben Allen, and Bob Sawyer head for BIRMINGHAM on a journey marked by frequent stops to eat and drink. When they tell Mr. Winkle of the marriage, he receives the news stolidly, showing no emotion. They leave angry and disappointed. (51) On their return to London, rain forces them to stop for the night at the Saracen's Head in Towcester. There they find Pott, editor of the *Eatanswill Gazette,* and Slurk, the rival editor of the *Eatanswill Independent.* The two editors engage in a brawl, which is broken up by Sam. (52) In London, Sam learns that Tony's wife has died, and he goes to console his father. Tony tells him that Susan recognized before she died how her religion had interfered with her life and her relationship with Tony. He also tells Sam how he has been beset since Susan's death with widows seeking his attentions. Stiggins inquires about what Susan has left him, and he refuses to believe that he has been excluded from her will. Tony picks him up, carries him outside, and tosses him into a horse trough.

Part 19–20 (November 1837)

(53) Early the next morning, Pickwick goes to Perker's office. There he accepts the gratitude of Jingle and Job Trotter as they set off for the West Indies. Then Dodson and Fogg come to be paid off. Although they are civil to him, Pickwick's anger mounts; he follows them as they leave, yelling

"Robbers!" after them several times. He returns to Perker's office with a great weight removed from his mind. (54) When Wardle learns that Snodgrass and his daughter Emily are in love, he is at first upset and irritable, but then he accepts the match. (55) Sam goes with Tony Weller to attorney Solomon Pell to execute Susan Weller's will. She has left £200 to Sam and the rest of her estate to Tony. After Pell proves the will, stockbroker Wilkins Flasher liquidates Tony's funds. When Tony puts together all of his money at the end of the day, he has £1,180. (56) He takes the money to Pickwick and asks him to take charge of it for him. At first Pickwick refuses, but then he calls Tony back, tells him of Sam's affection for Mary, and agrees to do some good with Tony's money. He offers to set up Sam and Mary in business, but Sam is committed to serving Pickwick. Meanwhile, Mr. Winkle goes anonymously to see his new daughter- in-law. He is thoroughly pleased with her and is reconciled with his son. (57) Pickwick gives up traveling, disbands the Pickwick Club, and settles down in a house in Dulwich. There the wedding of Emily and Snodgrass is held, and there he gathers together his many friends and colleagues. Sam and Mary marry, have children, and serve in Pickwick's house; the Winkles live nearby. Pickwick is known and respected by all in the neighborhood.

COMMENTARY

The Posthumous Papers of the Pickwick Club, or *The Pickwick Papers,* the shortened title by which it is usually known, is Dickens's first novel, published in serial form in 1836–37. In it, one can trace the transition in Dickens's work from the journalistic sketches with which he began his writing career to the more sustained narrative that made him the great comic novelist of the century. *Pickwick* also contains some indications of Dickens's darker vision and of the concern with social issues that would stamp his work as characteristically Victorian.

The novel began as a project of artist ROBERT SEYMOUR and young publisher WILLIAM HALL to produce a series of sporting prints depicting the exploits of the Nimrod Club, which would be accompanied by some prose narrative commentary. After Hall failed to interest several other authors in the project, he approached Dickens, a 24-year-old writer whose newspaper sketches, soon to be collected and published as *Sketches by Boz,* had brought him some favorable notice. Although Dickens was unfamiliar with the sporting themes in the original idea, he was quick to see opportunity in the proposal, and he suggested that the subject matter not be limited to sporting scenes. The contract was agreed to in early March—Dickens was to receive about £14 for each 12,000-word monthly number—and Dickens submitted the first installment to Hall three weeks later.

Mr. Winkle is the character who is most clearly a product of the sporting design that inspired the project. He is a literary relative to the popular figures in the SPORTING NOVELS of R. S. SURTEES and Pierce Egan. But Pickwick and the wonderful, fast-talking villain of the early numbers, Mr. Jingle, carry a Dickensian stamp from the beginning. Seymour had to modify his original idea of a lean hero when Dickens decided, in the first number, to make his hero a fat, older man. For the second number, Seymour had difficulty with the illustration of the dying clown, a subject far afield from the sporting scenes he was accustomed to drawing. The tension between illustrator and author may have contributed to Seymour's distress. In any case, on April 20, he shot himself, after completing the illustrations for the second number.

Dickens, who had married in April on the strength of the contract for *Pickwick,* was determined that the project not be abandoned. He took an active role in redesigning the format and hiring a new illustrator. The number of illustrations for each monthly part was reduced from four to two, and the number of pages of text was increased from 24 to 32. After working for a month with an interim illustrator, R. W. BUSS, Dickens interviewed applicants in May for an illustrator to replace Seymour. He chose a man younger even than himself, 20-year-old HABLOT K. BROWNE, the artist who would become Dickens's most consistent collaborator, using "Phiz" as his artistic name to match Dickens's "Boz." Among the applicants for the position whom Dickens did not choose was WILLIAM THACKERAY, who had recently returned to London from art school in Paris.

The new plan gave more prominence to the writer and less to the illustrator. By reducing the number of pictures and increasing the number of words, Dickens was able to include fewer episodes in each number and to develop them more fully. This change in format was important in enabling him to grow from a writer of brief sketches into a novelist following a continuing plot. By the fourth number a more unified story began to take shape with the introduction of Sam Weller and the beginning of the Bardell versus Pickwick story, the most sustained plotline in the book.

The episodic character of *Pickwick Papers* was influenced by other factors than its mode of publication. Dickens's models for the story were the novels of the PICARESQUE tradition, works like ALAN RENÉ LESAGE's *Gil Blas* and especially such 18th-century English novels as DANIEL DEFOE's *Robinson Crusoe,* HENRY FIELDING's *Tom Jones* and *Joseph Andrews,* and TOBIAS SMOLLETT's *Roderick Random* and *Peregrine Pickle,* works he had pored over as a child. These episodic picaresque novels were filled with practical jokes, slapstick situations, and physical comedy, scenes that provided prototypes for many of the comic episodes in *Pickwick.* MIGUEL DE CERVANTES's *Don Quixote* and OLIVER GOLDSMITH's *The Vicar of Wakefield* were also key influences, contributing to the idealism and the sentiment in Dickens's novel. Dickens was especially indebted to Goldsmith's novel for the prison scenes in *Pickwick.*

As Dickens gained assurance with his story, he also gained readers. Only 1,000 of the first number were printed, but sales began to pick up with the appearance of Sam Weller in the fourth number, and after a year 20,000 copies of each part were being produced. By the end of its run in November 1837, nearly 40,000 copies of each part were being sold, a phenomenal number for a Victorian novel. Its success was more than literary. Pickwick was a cultural event that became an industry. ROBERT PATTEN (1978) describes the frenzy: "There were Pickwick hats, canes, cigars, fabrics, coats, song books, china figurines, Weller corduroys and jest books, and Boz cabs. There were imitations, plagiarisms, parodies, sequels, extra illustrations, Pickwick quadrilles, stage piracies, and adaptations." ELIZABETH GASKELL gently satirized this literary mayhem in *Cranford* (1853) with a newspaper report that describes a man being run over by a train because he is so engrossed in the current installment of the novel.

From the beginning, as PHILIP COLLINS (1971) has commented, Pickwick was a "cult novel," having an appeal similar to the Sherlock Holmes stories. The ATHENAEUM described Dickens's recipe during the novel's initial run as "two pounds of Smollett, three ounces of Sterne, a handful of Hook, a dash of grammatical Pierce Egan—incidents at pleasure, served with an original sauce piquante." The sauce is what has sustained *Pickwick*'s special appeal, the quality that makes the world of the novel unique and that introduces in the very first number a new word into the language, the adjective "Pickwickian." Readers who get caught up in the Pickwickian worldview may become members of the cult or the club, but not everyone is smitten. In her inauguration speech as president of the Dickens Fellowship, Margaret Lane admitted that *Pickwick* was the one Dickens novel she did not enjoy and could not finish. There may be some evidence to suggest that the Pickwick Club, the novel's celebration of male bonding, and the depiction of many of its women characters as predatory has more appeal to men than to women, though the Pickwick Club formed by Louisa May Alcott's little women seems to be evidence to the contrary.

If *Pickwick* initiated the Victorian novel by introducing serial publication as an appropriate mode for other novelists, it also articulated a Victorian consciousness. Appropriately, the novel was being published as Victoria took the throne. While it drew on 18th-century models, it transformed them, turning the crude bawdy humor of the picaresque into playful innocence. Mary Russell Mitford, recommending the novel to a friend, specifically pointed to the "Victorian" sensibility in the book:

So you never heard of the "Pickwick Papers"! . . . It is fun—London life—but without anything unpleasant: a lady might read it all *aloud*; and it is so graphic, so individual, and so true, that you could courtsey to all the people as you met them in the streets. I do not think

there had been a place where English was spoken to which "Boz" had not penetrated. . . . It seems like not having heard of Hogarth, whom he resembles greatly, except that he takes a far more cheerful view, a Shakespearean view, of humanity. It is rather fragmentary, except the trial (No. 11 or 12), which is as complete and perfect as any bit of comic writing in the English language. You must read the "Pickwick Papers." (*The Life of Mary Russell Mitford*, ed. A.G.L. L'Estrange, 1870, III: 78)

Mitford's observation that the novel is fragmentary highlights a frequent criticism of the book. Many readers think that Dickens's object for the novel, stated in the preface as "to place before the reader a constant succession of characters and incidents," is achieved at the expense of unity. The incoherence may be most evident in the INTERPOLATED TALEs, stories that Dickens inserted into the novel, particularly in the first half. Their presence suggests that Dickens may have met his monthly deadlines by including material that he had written previously and had not published.

This view has been effectively challenged. Several critics, most notably Patten (1967), have pointed out how the dark and gloomy subject matter of the interpolated tales contrasts with the light and sunny story of "the immortal Pickwick," who rises with "the first ray of light" and converts "obscurity" into "a dazzling brilliancy." The contrast between light and darkness that runs through the novel becomes central to the main line of the action in the last third of the book during the prison scenes. In the second half of the novel, the interpolated tales nearly disappear, as a more coherent worldview, melding light and dark, emerges in the main action.

The Bardell versus Pickwick story has long been recognized as the main element of plot in what often seems a meandering story, but SYLVÈRE MONOD (1968) has identified three subplots that also contribute to what Dickens described as "one tolerably harmonious whole": (1) the relationship between old Wardle and Pickwick, (2) the pursuit of Jingle, and (3) the "Weller saga." Monod goes on to point out a number of episodes that have no relation to any of these plots, suggesting that the whole may not be quite as coherent as some ingenious commentators have suggested. Dickens, in the 1847 preface, seems to want it both ways: "I could perhaps wish now that these chapters were strung together on a stronger thread of general interest, still, what they are they were designed to be."

If *Pickwick* began as a novel designed by committee, this collaborative inspiration seems to be reflected in the collective hero of the opening numbers, the members of the peripatetic Pickwick Club. Each of the four corresponding members begins the novel as a "humors" character, a person defined by a single dominating obsession: Winkle is the sportsman, Snodgrass the poet, Tupman the lover, and Pickwick the scientific investigator. They are equally inept at their professions, and the opening sketches suggest that the story will progress by mocking their pretensions. Winkle proves to know nothing about hunting, Snodgrass never writes a poem, Tupman loses Rachael Wardle to Jingle, and Pickwick—even with his spectacles on—is stumped by Bill Stump's stone.

Although he is satirized for his scientific pretensions, Pickwick, from the moment he first appears, differs from the other members of the club. If Winkle, Snodgrass, and Tupman are defined as latter-day representatives of the humors tradition, Pickwick redefines that tradition and begins a new one. His age makes him anomalous as a candidate for education in a collective BILDUNGSROMAN. He is, as the opening paragraph suggests, the sun itself, and his foolish quarrel with Blotton makes him a humbug only in a Pickwickian sense. By the end of the opening chapter, Dickens has already defined a unique Pickwickian world where the rules of the Smollettian picaresque and the comedy of the sporting novels no longer apply.

Pickwick is paradoxical. As an older man, a scientific observer, a former man of business, and the mentor to a group of young men seeking to establish themselves in the world, he is expected to represent wisdom and experience, but he is as innocent as a child, and his innate goodness makes him incapable of imagining the world in anything other than the most benevolent and optimistic terms.

His inflated language, often grounded in a parody of the public utterances of politicians and academics, indicates how he transforms reality. Jingle can outwit him because Pickwick is incapable of seeing or imagining Jingle's villainy. The interpolated tales that he hears, which describe a world darkened by pain and suffering, are just tales, separate from the real experience of his life.

The protean Jingle, who cons his victims by impersonating their wishes, appears to Pickwick as a seasoned traveler, a man of the world whose knowledge of people and places enables him to speak with authority on any topic. Jingle's telegraphic manner of speaking, so opposite from Pickwick's prolix and airy generalizing, reduces experience to a series of discrete sensory data and his language to a series of nouns and verbs. He appears to be the voice of experience, to model the empiricism to which Pickwick has pretensions, but, as Pickwick painfully discovers, Jingle lacks benevolence and has no notion of serving others. When Pickwick is confronted with Jingle's selfishness, in the scene where Wardle rescues Rachael and buys off her "abductor," Pickwick is enlightened into anger; in a blind rage he stumbles into the arms of Sam Weller, the cockney boots of the White Hart Inn who will replace Jingle as the representative of experience in the novel.

A product of the London streets and the son of a coach driver, Sam combines the knowledge of the traveler with that of the city boy. He is every bit as clever as Jingle, but his wit emerges in exemplary tales—like the story of the man who survived on crumpets—and in "Wellerisms," apt analogies from his experience that relate to the situations in which he finds himself. When he is urging the Ipswich magistrate to restrain his deputies and enjoy the company of the Pickwickians, for example, Sam comes up with the following analogy: "Business first, pleasure arterwards, as King Richard the Third said wen he stabbed t'other King in the Tower, afore he smothered the babbies" (25). His stories are more coherent than Jingle's, and they point to a moral. He uses his wit to serve others, not just himself. Appropriately, he becomes Pickwick's servant. In the course of the story—as his name, which repeats his master's, indicates—he becomes Pickwick's alter ego, playing experience to

Pickwick's innocence. His entrance into the story changes the novel. The Pickwick Club is replaced, and the central focus shifts to Samuel Pickwick and Samuel Weller, the idealistic Victorian Quixote and his cockney Sancho Panza.

With the introduction of Sam Weller, *Pickwick* found its center. Dickens may have begun the novel thinking of the project as a series of magazine sketches similar to those collected in *Sketches by Boz.* The sketches became a connected story when the chemistry between Samuel Pickwick and Sam Weller focused the action. Dickens's original audience responded to this change, for with the fourth number, in which Sam first appears, sales of the novel markedly increased, the beginning of the mania that would make *Pickwick* a runaway best seller.

The fifth number opens with the scene between Pickwick and Mrs. Bardell that begins the central action of the novel, the Bardell versus Pickwick

Browne's (Phiz's) rendering of the "First Appearance of Mr. Samuel Weller" depicts the cockney servant who is often given credit for the runaway popularity of *The Pickwick Papers* in 1836–37.

trial. It clearly draws the differences between master and man. Pickwick is incapable of realizing how his evasive language misleads Mrs. Bardell. Although he is soliciting her opinion on the wisdom of keeping a servant, he puts the question abstractly: "Do you think it a much greater expense to keep two people, than to keep one?" (12) Mrs. Bardell misconstrues his meaning and faints into his arms. Sam Weller will not be similarly misled. When Pickwick asks him whether he has "any reason to be discontented with your present situation," Sam insists on knowing "whether you're goin' to purwide me with a better," and he goes on to negotiate the terms of his employment and his wages at £12 a year with two suits of clothes. There is no room for misunderstanding in Sam's dealings with Pickwick.

Pickwick comes to rely on Sam to extricate him from awkward situations, Sam to admire and love Pickwick. The story of their relationship becomes the story of the novel, but even Sam's confusing testimony at the trial cannot save Pickwick from himself. Appearances and the lawyers are against his master. While Pickwick chooses to go to jail as a matter of principle, Sam has himself imprisoned as a matter of love. In the Fleet, Pickwick must deal with darkness and suffering in fact—not just as part of an interpolated story. When Mrs. Bardell is also locked up because of his principles, Pickwick realizes that benevolence is more important to him than principle. He pays the fine, extricating all of the imprisoned Pickwickians, and he settles in Dulwich, a benign spirit presiding over a little community. Darkness and suffering are real in *Pickwick,* but they can be banished in the end to restore the Eden of Pickwick's imagination. The pattern of *Pickwick* will be repeated in several of the later novels, but never again will paradise be so completely regained.

CHARACTERS AND RELATED ENTRIES

Allen, Arabella "A black eyed young lady in a very nice pair of boots with fur round the top" (28) who captivates Mr. Winkle. Although her brother hopes to marry her to Bob Sawyer, Arabella elopes with Winkle and marries him (48).

Allen, Benjamin Arabella's brother, a medical student, he is a friend and drinking companion of Bob Sawyer, "a coarse, stout, thick-set young man, with black hair cut rather short, and a white face cut rather long. . . . He presented, altogether, rather a mildewy appearance, and emitted a fragrant odour of full-flavoured Cubas" (30). Later, he and Bob set up unsuccessfully in a medical practice in BATH. His plan that Bob marry his sister is foiled when she elopes with Winkle (48). Pickwick reconciles Allen to his sister's marriage. Ben and Bob ultimately secure appointments in Bengal as physicians for the East India Company (57).

Ayresleigh, Mr. Debtor whom Pickwick meets at Namby's sponging house: "a middle-aged man in a very old suit of black, who looked pale and haggard, and paced up and down the room incessantly; stopping, now and then, to look with great anxiety out of the window as if he expected somebody" (40).

bagman, the one-eyed The traveling salesman, "a stout, hale personage of about forty, with only one eye—a very bright black eye, which twinkled with a roguish expression of fun and good humour" (14), who tells two of the INTERPOLATED TALES in *Pickwick*, "The Bagman's Story" (14) and "The Story of the Bagman's Uncle" (49). The Pickwickians meet him at the Peacock Inn in Eatanswill (14) and again at the Bush Inn at BRISTOL (48).

Bagman's Uncle *See* Martin, Jack.

Bamber, Jack One of the law clerks Pickwick meets at the Magpie and Stump (20), "a little, yellow high-shouldered man [with a] . . . shrivelled face, . . . remarkable features, . . . [and] a fixed grim smile." He tells "The tale of the Queer Client" (21). He reappears in *Master Humphrey's Clock*, where Pickwick proposes him for membership in Master Humphrey's circle (*Humphrey*, 4).

Bantam, Angelo Cyrus The master of ceremonies in the Pump Room at BATH, a dandy, "a charming young man of not much more than fifty, dressed in a very bright blue coat with resplendent buttons, black trousers, and the thinnest possible pair of highly-polished boots. . . . His features were contracted into a perpetual smile; and his teeth were in such perfect order that it was difficult at a small distance to tell the real from the false" (35). He introduces Pickwick to the society at Bath and is a central figure in Dickens's satirical treatment of the town as a society of appearances.

Bardell, Mrs. Martha Pickwick's landlady in Goswell Street. "A comely woman, of bustling manners, and agreeable appearance; with a natural genius for cooking" (12), she is the widow of a government clerk who was "knocked on the head with a quart pot in a public house cellar" (34). After she misconstrues Pickwick's questions about keeping a servant as a proposal of marriage (18), she files a breach-of-promise suit against him and is represented in the action by the unscrupulous lawyers Dodson and Fogg. When Pickwick refuses to pay the costs of the trial, the lawyers turn on her, and she too is imprisoned in the FLEET (47). She is released when Pickwick agrees to pay the costs.

Bardell, Tommy Mrs. Bardell's spoiled 10- or 11-year-old son. He is used by the lawyers to elicit sympathy for his mother at the Bardell versus Pickwick trial (34).

Bell Alley, Coleman Street A "narrow and dark street" in the City, the location of Namby's sponging house (40).

Beller, Henry Former toastmaster who drank a great deal of foreign wine and is reported to be a convert to the Brick Lane branch of the United Grand Junction Ebenezer Temperance Association (33).

Belle Sauvage Inn Coaching inn on Ludgate Hill, west of St. Paul's Cathedral, that is the headquarters of Tony Weller, who calls it "my nat'ral-born element."

Berkeley Heath, Gloucestershire Pickwick's coach changes horses at the Bell Inn here on his journey from Bristol to Birmingham (50).

Betsy Mrs. Raddle's "dirty, slipshod" servant girl who waits on Bob Sawyer's dinner party (36).

Bill Prison turnkey in the story Sam tells of Prisoner Number Twenty (41).

Black Boy Inn, the The inn at Chelmsford where Tony Weller picks up Jingle and Trotter (20).

Bladud, Prince The mythical founder of the town of BATH and its public baths whose story Pickwick finds in his hotel room there (36).

Blazo, Sir Thomas Jingle describes playing in a cricket match in the West Indies with him: "Played a match once—single wicket—friend the Colonel—Sir Thomas Blazo—who should get the greatest number of runs" (7).

Blotton, Mr. The member of the Pickwick Club who calls Mr. Pickwick "a humbug." The controversy is resolved when Blotton agrees that he meant the term only "in its Pickwickian sense" (1). He is expelled from the club for revealing the truth about Bill Stumps's stone (11).

Blue Boar, Leadenhall Market One of Tony Weller's hangouts. While waiting for his father here, Sam writes his valentine to Mary (33).

Blue Lion Inn, Muggleton The dinner that follows the great Muggleton versus Dingley Dell cricket match is held here (7, 9).

Boffer A stockbroker expelled from the Exchange whose ruin prompts Wilkins Flasher and Frank Slimmery to bet on the chances of his suicide (55).

Boldwig, Captain A neighbor of Sir Geoffrey Manning, an imperious and self-important property owner who has Pickwick wheeled to the village pound when he finds him on his property in a wheelbarrow, sleeping off the effects of cold punch. "A little fierce man in a stiff black neckerchief and blue surtout" (19).

Bolo, Miss An ancient spinster who is Pickwick's card partner at BATH. She becomes so distressed by his play that she "rose from the table considerably agitated and went straight home, in a flood of tears, and a sedan chair" (35).

Brick Lane Street in Whitechapel that is the site of the meeting hall of the United Grand Junction Ebenezer Temperance Association (33).

Brooks Sam Weller's former fellow lodger, a pieman who makes pies from cats. "I seasons 'em for beefsteak, weal, or kidney 'cordin' to the demand" (19).

Brown Shoemaker who made Rachael Wardle's shoes. His name on her shoes enables Wardle and Pickwick to discover where she and Jingle are staying in London (10).

Budger, Mrs. Widow "whose rich dress and profusion of ornament bespoke her a most desirable addition to a limited income" (2). Dr. Slammer is courting her when Jingle cuts in on him at the ball in ROCHESTER. As a consequence, Slammer challenges Winkle to a duel.

Bulder, Colonel Commander of the ROCHESTER garrison, he attends the ball at the Bull with his wife and daughter (2) and commands the review of the troops (3).

Bull, the, Aldgate This coaching inn in Whitechapel in London's East End is the starting point for Tony Weller's coach going to Ipswich (20).

Bullman Plaintiff represented by Dodson and Fogg in the case of Bullman and Ramsey (20).

Bunkin, Mrs. Mrs. Bardell's neighbor, who is cited by Mrs. Sanders in her testimony at the trial as the source of the information that Pickwick is engaged to Mrs. Bardell (34).

Burton, Thomas One of the converts to teetotalism mentioned at the Brick Lane Temperance meeting, "a purveyer of cat's meat to the Lord Mayor and Sheriffs" (33).

Bush Inn, Bristol This inn, owned by Moses Pickwick, operator of the London-to-Bath coach, is where both Winkle and Pickwick stay when they are in Bristol (38, 39, 48, 50).

Buzfuz, Serjeant The barrister "with a fat body and a red face" who represents Mrs. Bardell in court. He bullies the witnesses at the trial, especially confusing Winkle into giving incriminating testimony. He does not, however, faze Sam Weller (34). He is thought to be based on Serjeant Bompas, a prominent lawyer of the period.

Cateaton Street Street in the City—now Gresham Street—where the warehouses of Tom Smart's employers, Bilson and Slum, are located (49).

Chancery Prisoner, the "A tall, gaunt, cadaverous man . . . with sunken cheeks, and a restless, eager eye" who sublets his room in the Fleet Prison to Pickwick (42).

chaplain, drunken One of Pickwick's fellow prisoners in the FLEET (42).

Charley "Shambling pot-boy, with a red head" at the Magpie and Stump (20).

"Christmas Carol, A" Song celebrating the Christmas season sung by Wardle in *Pickwick* (28). It was set to music when the novel first appeared and was later included in *The Book of British Song*.

Clarke, Susan Maiden name of Susan Weller, Tony Weller's second wife.

Clifton, Gloucestershire Suburb of Bristol where Arabella Allen is sequestered with her aunt (38).

Clubber, Sir Thomas Commissioner of the Chatham Dockyard who creates "a great sensation" when he enters the charity ball at the Bull Inn, ROCHESTER, with his wife and his two daughters (2).

Cluppins, Mrs. Elizabeth A friend of Mrs. Bardell and the sister of Mrs. Raddle. "A little, brisk, busy-looking woman," she gives evidence supporting Mrs. Bardell at the Bardell versus Pickwick trial (34).

Craddock, Mrs. Landlady of the house in the Royal Crescent in BATH where Pickwick and the Dowlers take lodgings (36).

Crawley Young man at BATH who, because his father has "eight hundred a-year, which dies with him," is turned down when he seeks to dance with Miss Wugsby (35).

Cripps, Tom Shop boy for Bob Sawyer and Ben Allen. He advertises Sawyer's apothecary business by leaving bottles of pills at the wrong addresses (38).

Crookey Attendant at Namby's lockup who "looked something between a bankrupt grazier, and a drover in a state of insolvency" (40).

Crushton, the Honorable Mr. Lord Mutanhed's obsequious friend "in the red under waistcoat and dark moustache" at the Assembly Rooms in BATH (35).

Cummins, Tom The man "in the chair" during an adventurous evening of drinking described by one of Dodson and Fogg's clerks (20).

Dingley Dell Village in Kent where Wardle's Manor Farm is located. The Pickwickians first visit the farm on their initial journey (4–9) and later celebrate Christmas there (28–30). The original is thought to be the village of Sandling near Maidstone.

Dodson, Mr. Partner in the firm Dodson and Fogg; "a plump, portly, stern-looking man, with a loud voice" (20), he always acts as the spokesman for the firm.

Dodson and Fogg The firm of unscrupulous attorneys, "mean, rascally, petifogging robbers" (53), who take on speculation Mrs. Bardell's breach-of-promise suit against Pickwick. When Pickwick refuses to pay the costs of the trial because of his outrage at these lawyers, they imprison Mrs. Bardell in the Fleet, where Sam Weller discovers her; his kindhearted master pays the fine so that she can be released (53).

Dorking Town in Surrey where Mrs. Weller maintains an inn, the Marquis of Granby (27, 33, 52).

Dowler, Mr. A retired army officer who, with his wife, travels to BATH on the coach with Pickwick; they share lodgings there in the Royal Crescent with the Pickwickians. "A stern-eyed man of about five-and-forty, who had a bald and glossy forehead, . . . and large black whiskers," the irascible Dowler is fierce in the middle of the night, threatening to cut Winkle's throat when he thinks the young man has pursued his pretty wife. But the next morning he is cowardly and timorous (35–38).

Dowler, Mrs. Dowler's "agreeable and fascinating" wife, "a rather pretty face in a bright blue bonnet" (35). When Winkle, in his nightshirt, accidentally ends up with her in the street, Mr. Dowler accuses him of attempting to run off with his wife and pursues him, vowing to cut his throat (36).

Dubbley A constable at Ipswich, "a dirty-faced man, something over six feet high, and stout in proportion," who helps in the arrest of Mr. Pickwick during the confrontation with Peter Magnus (24–25).

Dulwich Village south of London where Pickwick settles in retirement (57).

Dumkins, Mr. Star batsman for the All-Muggleton Cricket Club (7).

Dunchurch The Warwickshire village where Pickwick stops on his way to London from Birmingham (51).

"Dying Clown, The" Alternative title for "The Stroller's Tale." Robert Seymour was working to meet Dickens's objections to his illustration for this tale just before he committed suicide.

Eatanswill Fictitious town in East Anglia where the Pickwickians observe the election between the Blues and Buffs, respectively, Tories and Whigs (13). Although it is generally thought to be based on Sudbury, where Dickens covered an election as a reporter in 1834, Ipswich, Bury St. Edmunds, and Norwich have also been suggested as models. The contentiousness of the election is apparent

Seymour's illustration for "The Stroller's Tale" in the second number of *The Pickwick Papers*. His difficulties with the unfamiliar subject matter and Dickens's objections to his work troubled the artist shortly before his suicide.

in the town's two rival newspapers, the *Eatanswill Gazette*, edited by Pott, and the *Eatanswill Independent*, edited by Slurk, a rivalry that comes to blows between the two editors (51).

Edmunds, John The subject of "The Convict's Return," the tale told by the clergyman at Dingley Dell (6). Abused by his father, Edmunds is transported for robbery. When he returns, contrite and penitent, and confronts his father, the old man dies.

Emanuel Chapel The church in Dorking where Stiggins is an official (52).

Emma One of the servant girls at Dingley Dell; Pickwick kisses her under the mistletoe (28).

Filletoville, son of the Marquis of The young man in "The Bagman's Story" who abducts the lady rescued by the bagman's uncle (49).

Fitz-Marshall, Captain Charles Alias that Jingle adopts in Ipswich.

Fizkin, Horatio The Buff candidate for Parliament in Eatanswill who is defeated by the Hon. Samuel Slumkey (13, 18).

Fizzgig, Christina In Jingle's account, this daughter of the Spanish Grandee, Don Bolaro Fizzgig, commits suicide when her father refuses to consent to her marriage to Jingle (2).

Flasher, Wilkins The stockbroker who transfers the securities left to Tony Weller by his wife (55).

Fogg Silent partner in the firm Dodson and Fogg, the unscrupulous lawyers who represent Mrs. Bardell. "An elderly, pimply-faced, vegetable-diet sort of man, . . . who seemed to be an essential part of the desk at which he was writing, and to have as much thought or sentiment" (20).

Freeman's Court On the north side of Cornhill in the City of London, site of Dodson and Fogg's offices.

George and Vulture Inn Inn on Lombard Street in the City where Pickwick takes rooms when he comes to London to deal with Mrs. Bardell's suit (26). He is also arrested and taken to the Fleet from here (40) and returns here when he is released from prison (50). The Winkles also stay here after their marriage (54).

Goblins, King of the The leader of the pack of goblins who capture and torment Gabriel Grub in Wardle's Christmas story, "The Goblins Who Stole a Sexton" (29).

Goodwin Mrs. Pott's maid, who "rendered herself useful in a variety of ways, but in none more so than in the particular department of constantly aiding and abetting her mistress in every wish and inclination opposed to the desires of the unhappy Pott" (18).

Goswell Street Now known as Goswell Road, this street in the city is the site of Mrs. Bardell's

house, where Pickwick has his lodgings. As Pickwick surveys his neighborhood, "Goswell Street was at his feet, Goswell Street was on his right hand— as far as the eye could see Goswell Street extended on his left; and the opposite side of Goswell Street was over the way" (2).

Granby, Marchioness of Tony Weller's nickname for Mrs. Weller, proprietor of the Marquis of Granby.

Griggs family Social rivals to the Nupkins family in Ipswich (25).

Groffin, Thomas A druggist who is called for jury duty in the Pickwick and Bardell trial and who asks unsuccessfully to be relieved for fear his errand boy may poison one of his customers while he is gone (34).

Grub, Gabriel The "ill-conditioned cross-grained surly" sexton and gravedigger who is the subject of Wardle's Christmas story. Tormented by goblins in a dream on Christmas Eve, he is made ashamed of his misanthropy. After wandering for years, he returns to his home village a ragged but repentant man (29). Grub is the Scrooge figure in this tale, which is often considered a precursor of *A Christmas Carol.*

Grummer, Daniel Constable at Ipswich, "an elderly gentleman in top boots, who was chiefly remarkable for a bottle-nose, a hoarse voice, a snuff-coloured surtout, and a wandering eye, . . . who had been a peace officer, man and boy, for half a century at least" (24). He arrests Pickwick and Tupman for breach of the peace and brings them before Magistrate Nupkins.

Grundy One of the law clerks Pickwick meets at the Magpie and Stump (20).

Guildhall Seat of civic government on Gresham Street in the City of London, where the statues of Gog and Magog are housed in the great hall. The Court of Common Pleas was held here until 1873. The trial of Bardell *v.* Pickwick takes place here (34).

Gunter   One of the guests at Bob Sawyer's bachelor party, "a gentleman in a shirt emblazoned with pink anchors." After a drunken exchange of insults with Mr. Noddy, the two shake hands and declare their admiration for each other (32).

Gwynn, Miss   The writing and ciphering teacher at Westgate House, the school in BURY ST. EDMUNDS where Pickwick is caught after hours hiding in the courtyard (16).

Harris   Greengrocer in BATH whose shop is the site of the footmen's "swarry" attended by Sam Weller (37).

Henry   Cousin of Maria Lobbs in "The Parish Clerk," a tale told by Sam Weller to Mr. Pickwick. He is Nathaniel Pipkin's rival for Maria's affections, and he eventually marries her (17).

Heyling, George   Subject of Jack Bamber's "Tale about the Queer Client." After his wife and his infant son die while he is in debtor's prison, he devotes his life to wreaking revenge on his wife's father, whom he blames for the tragedy (21).

Hopkins, Jack   Fellow medical student with Bob Sawyer who, at the bachelor party, "wore a black velvet waistcoat, with thunder-and-lightning buttons; and a blue striped shirt, with a white false collar" (32). He tells the story of the child who swallows a necklace bead by bead, until his stomach rattles when he arrives at the hospital (32).

Hop Pole Inn, Tewkesbury   Inn in Gloucestershire where Pickwick, Bob Sawyer, and Ben Allen stop on their way to Birmingham (50).

Horn Coffee House   The establishment near the Fleet Prison to which Pickwick sends for wine to celebrate Winkle's marriage (44).

Humm, Anthony   "A converted fireman, now a schoolmaster, and occasionally an itinerant preacher" who is the president of the Brick Lane branch of the United Grand Junction Ebenezer Temperance Association. He presides at the meet-ing of the association attended by Sam and Tony Weller (33).

Hunt   Captain Boldwig's gardener (19).

Hunter, Mr. Leo   Mrs. Leo Hunter's "grave" husband (15).

Hunter, Mrs. Leo   Poetess, "lion hunter," and literary hostess of "The Den" in Eatanswill. Pickwick and his followers attend her fancy dress "fête champêtre," where they meet the literary lions of Eatanswill and hear Mrs. Hunter, dressed as Minerva, recite her "Ode to an Expiring Frog" (15).

Hutley, Jemmy ("Dismal Jemmy")   A strolling actor who tells "The Stroller's Tale" to the Pickwickians in ROCHESTER (3). Jingle later identifies him as Job Trotter's brother, a "clever fellow" who has since emigrated to America (53).

Insolvent Debtors' Court   Court in Portugal Street, west London, where Solomon Pell practices (43). Here insolvent debtors who could prove that their personal belongings were worth less than £20 could appeal for relief from imprisonment. The court was abolished in 1861.

Ipswich   The town in Suffolk where Pickwick, in pursuit of Jingle, is brought before Magistrate Nupkins after his misunderstanding with Miss Witherfield and Peter Magnus at the White Hart Inn (22–25).

Isaac   Sheriff's officer, "a shabby man in black leggings," who takes Mrs. Bardell to the FLEET PRISON (46).

"Ivy Green, The"   A poem written by the clergyman at Dingley Dell (6).

Jackson   Dodson and Fogg's clerk, "an individual in a brown coat and brass buttons, whose long hair was scrupulously twisted round the rim of his napless hat, and whose soiled drab trousers were so tightly strapped over his Blucher boots, that his knees threatened every moment to start from their concealment" (31). He delivers the writs to the Pickwickians (31) and later arrests Mrs. Bardell (46).

Jane (1) Wardle's maidservant (5).

Jane (2) Mrs. Pott's maidservant (13).

Jingle, Alfred A strolling actor and adventurer "of No Hall, Nowhere." "The thinness of his body and the length of his legs gave him the appearance of being much taller. The green coat had been a smart dress garment in the days of swallowtails, but had evidently in those times adorned a much shorter man, for the soiled and faded sleeves scarcely reached to his wrists. . . . His face was thin and haggard, but an indescribable air of jaunty impudence and perfect self-possession pervaded the whole man" (2). He enters the novel when he rescues Pickwick from an altercation with a cabdriver (2), and he entertains the Pickwickians with his telegraphic speech on the journey to ROCHESTER:

> Ah! you should keep dogs—fine animals—sagacious creatures—dog of my own once—Pointer—surprising instinct—out shooting one day—entering enclosure—whistled—dog stopped—whistled again—Ponto—no go; stock still—called him—Ponto, Ponto—wouldn't move—dog transfixed—staring at a board—looked up, saw an inscription—"Gamekeeper has orders to shoot all dogs found in this enclosure"—wouldn't pass it—wonderful dog—vauluable dog that—very. (2)

In Rochester his outrageous behavior prompts a challenge to a duel from Dr. Slammer (2). Introduced to Wardle by Pickwick, he elopes with Rachael (9), Wardle's sister, and is bought off by Wardle (10). In Eatanswill, he appears at Mrs. Leo Hunter's party as Captain Fitz-Marshall (15) and is pursued by Pickwick to BURY ST. EDMUNDS, where his scheme to seduce Nupkins's daughter is exposed (25). Jingle and his servant, Job Trotter, eventually turn up in the FLEET, imprisoned for debt (42). The two are given a chance to begin life anew in the West Indies when Pickwick pays their debts and releases them from prison (53).

Dickens seems to have begun with the idea of Jingle as the villain of the story, but the pursuit of the fast-talking actor peters out after the events at Ipswich (25). This seeming change of plan is often taken to indicate the spontaneity in Dickens's development of the story line for the novel. However, Jingle has a continuing role as a foil to Pickwick and his companions. At the beginning of the novel his shape-shifting flexibility contrasts with the static qualities of the Pickwickians, who are characterized by their humors as lover, poet, hunter, and philosopher. With the introduction of Sam Weller into their circle, the Pickwickians are gradually forced to realize that Jingle's adaptability and fluidity are not necessarily villainous qualities. As Sam educates them into changing themselves, finally forcing Pickwick's capitulation to abandon principle and save Mrs. Bardell, he enables Pickwick to see Jingle and himself as victims rather

Kyd's (Joseph Clayton Clarke's) rendering of Mr. Jingle.

than as villains. Although Jingle is not assimilated into the Dulwich circle at the end, Sam is and, in a sense, acts as Jingle's surrogate in affirming the comic values of flexibility and laughter.

Jinkins "A tall man—a confoundedly tall man—with black whiskers," the suitor of the widow innkeeper in "The Bagman's Story," who is exposed by Tom Smart as already married with six children (14).

Jinks The "pale, sharp-nosed, half-fed, shabbily-clad clerk, of middle age" who serves Magistrate Nupkins, Mayor of Ipswich (24).

Joe ("The Fat Boy") Wardle's page, a "red-faced boy in a state of somnolency," who is always either eating or sleeping. He is awake, though, when he spies on Tupman courting Rachael Wardle in the garden at Dingley Dell, and he reports what he sees to Mrs. Wardle, preparing her for the news by announcing, "I wants to make your flesh creep" (8).

Although he has an incidental role in the novel, Joe is important as, in Barbara Hardy's (*The Moral Art of Dickens*, 1970) words, "a kind of parody of Pickwick." He exaggerates Pickwick's plump enjoyment of food and drink to an unhealthy obsession tinged with an edge of cannibalism. For the Pickwickians, eating and drinking are convivial social activities; for Joe they are solipsistic indulgences. Diagnosed as a case of acute narcolepsy, Joe's obesity, fatigue, and sleep apnea is medically known as "the Pickwickian syndrome." James Davies (*The Textual Life of Dickens's Characters*, 1990) provides an extended analysis of Joe's character and role in the novel.

John (1) The dying pantomime clown who is the subject of "The Stroller's Tale" (3).

John (2) Waiter at the Saracen's Head, Towcester (51).

Kate Maria Lobbs's "arch, impudent, bewitching little" cousin in the interpolated tale "The Parish Clerk" (17).

Leather Bottle Inn, the Inn at Cobham, Kent, where Tupman retreats after he is deserted by Rachel Wardle (11). The inn has become a site of Dickensian pilgrimage.

Lobbs, Maria The daughter of a rich saddler, who is the object of the secret affections of Nathaniel Pipkin, a parish clerk, in Pickwick's tale "The Parish Clerk" (17).

Lobbs, Old Maria's father, a rich saddler who resists his daughter's desire to marry the parish clerk in Pickwick's tale "The Parish Clerk" (17).

Lowten Perker's "puffy-faced young" clerk, who introduces Pickwick to the society of law clerks at the Magpie and Stump (20).

Lucas, Solomon Eatanswill costume dealer from whom the Pickwickians rent costumes for Mrs. Leo Hunter's fancy-dress breakfast. "His wardrobe was extensive—very extensive—not strictly classical perhaps, nor quite new, nor did it contain any one garment made precisely after the fashion of any age or time, but everything was more or less spangled; and what *can* be prettier than spangles!" (16).

Lud Hudibras, King King of Britain and father of Prince Bladud in "The True Legend of Prince Bladud": "He was a mighty monarch. The earth shook when he walked; he was so very stout" (36).

Luffey Star player for the Dingley Dell Cricket Club (7).

Magnus, Peter The "red-haired man, with an inquisitive nose and blue spectacles," who travels with Pickwick to Ipswich, where he plans to propose to Miss Witherfield (22). After Pickwick inadvertently stumbles into Miss Witherfield's room in the middle of the night, the jealous Magnus is so enraged that she fears a duel between Magnus and Pickwick, so she has Pickwick arrested by Nupkins the magistrate (24).

Magpie and Stump Gathering place for Lowten and his fellow law clerks, this tavern could have been based on either the George IV or the Old Black Jack, which were both located in Portsmouth Street, LINCOLN'S INN FIELDS (20, 21).

Maidstone   Village in Kent generally believed to be the original of Muggleton (7).

Mallard   Serjeant Snubbin's elderly law clerk, "whose sleek appearance, and heavy gold watchchain, presented imposing indications of the extensive and lucrative practice of Mr. Serjeant Snubbin" (31).

Manning, Sir Geoffrey   Wardle's neighbor on whose lands the Pickwickian hunting party takes place (18).

Manor Farm   Wardle's home at Dingley Dell where the Pickwickians visit (2–4) and later spend Christmas (29–30).

Marlborough Downs   Old inn on the downs in Wiltshire. Tom Smart, in "The Bagman's Story," meets the mysterious chair that turns into an old man at his room in the inn (14).

Marquis of Granby   Tavern in Dorking kept by Tony Weller's second wife; "a model of a roadside public-house of the better class—just large enough to be convenient, and small enough to be snug" (27).

Martin (1)   Sir Geoffrey Manning's gamekeeper (19).

Martin (2)   Surly groom employed by Arabella Allen's aunt (39, 48).

Martin, Betsy   One-eyed charwoman converted by the Brick Lane branch of the United Grand Junction Ebenezer Temperance Association, who "thinks it not impossible that if she had always abstained from spirits, she might have had two eyes by this time" (33).

Martin, Jack   The bagman's uncle, "one of the merriest, pleasantest, cleverest fellows that ever lived" (49).

Mary   The Nupkinses' housemaid, who later serves as Arabella Allen's maid and facilitates the courtship of Winkle and Arabella. She eventually becomes Pickwick's housemaid, on the condition that she marry Sam Weller, who has courted her from the time he first saw her at Ipswich. In the March 1837 number, Sam composes his famous valentine for Mary (33).

Matiner, Misses   Two single ladies at the Assembly Rooms in BATH, "in hope of getting a stray partner now and then" (35).

Miller   Guest at Dingley Dell, "a little, hardheaded, Ribston-pippen-faced man" (6, 28).

Mivins ("The Zephyr")   A prisoner in the FLEET, "a man in a broad-skirted green coat, with corduroy knee smalls and grey cotton stockings" (41), who introduces Pickwick to the prison by dancing a hornpipe and grabbing Pickwick's nightcap off his head.

Montague Place   Fashionable street in Bloomsbury, off Russell Square, where Mr. Perker lives (47).

Mordlin, Brother   Musical member of the Brick Lane branch of the United Grand Junction Ebenezer Temperance Association who has put the words of Dibden's "Who Hasn't Heard of a Jolly Young Waterman?" to the tune of the Old Hundredth. He justifies his adaptation by "expressing his firm persuasion that the late Mr. Dibden, seeing the errors of his former life, had written that song to show the advantages of abstinence" (33).

Mudberry, Mrs.   According to the testimony of Susannah Sanders at the trial, this neighbor of Mrs. Bardell, "which kept a mangle," informed her that Pickwick would marry Mrs. Bardell (34).

Mudge, Jonas   Secretary of the Brick Lane branch of the United Grand Junction Ebenezer Temperance Association, "an enthusiastic and disinterested vessel, who sold tea to the members" (33).

Mutanhed, Lord The "richest young man in Baath . . . the one with the long hair, and the particularly small forehead" (35).

Muzzle Mr. Nupkins's "undersized footman, with a long body, and short legs," who challenges Job Trotter for attempting to steal the affections of the cook, who is Muzzle's sweetheart (24, 25).

Namby The sheriff's officer, who arrests Pickwick for refusing to pay the costs of Bardell versus Pickwick: "a man of about forty, with black hair, and carefully combed whiskers. He was dressed in a particularly gorgeous manner, with plenty of articles of jewellery about him—all about three sizes larger than those which are usually worn by gentlemen—and a rough great-coat to crown the whole" (40).

Neddy A man "of a taciturn and thoughtful cast" (42) who is one of the turnkeys in the FLEET PRISON.

Noddy "A scorbutic youth" who attends Bob Sawyer's party and gets into a drunken quarrel with Mr. Gunter (32).

"Number Twenty" Subject of a story Sam tells of prisoner number twenty, who convinces the turnkey to allow him to leave the prison briefly after he has been there for 17 years (41).

Nupkins, George Mayor of Ipswich, principal magistrate and "grand personage," who hears the case against the Pickwickians for disturbing the peace; he dismisses the charges when they reveal that Charles Fitz-Marshall, who is courting his daughter, is the scoundrel Jingle.

Nupkins, Henrietta The Nupkinses' daughter, who "possessed all her [mother's] haughtiness without the turban, and all her ill-nature without the wig" (25); she is the object of Jingle's amorous schemes in Ipswich, where he courts her as Captain Fitz-Marshall.

Nupkins, Mrs. Nupkins's wife, "a majestic female in a pink gauze turban and a light brown wig" (25), who laments that her husband blames her and their daughter for bringing shame on the family by socializing with Jingle.

Payne, Doctor Army doctor who is present at the interrupted duel between Dr. Slammer and Winkle (2, 3).

Peacock Inn Eatanswill inn where Snodgrass and Tupman stay (13–14).

Pell, Solomon Shady lawyer of the Insolvent Court who arranges Sam Weller's imprisonment in the FLEET (43) and proves Susan Weller's will for Tony (55). "A fat flabby pale man, in a surtout which looked green one minute and brown the next: with a velvet collar of the same cameleon tints. His forehead was narrow, his face wide, his head large, and his nose all on one side, as if Nature, indignant with the propensities she observed in him in his birth, had given it an angry tweak which it had never recovered" (43).

Perker Pickwick's and Wardle's solicitor, "a high-dried man, with . . . small restless black eyes, that kept winking and twinkling on each side of his little inquisitive nose." He arranges the payoff for Jingle in the Rachel Wardle affair (10), represents Pickwick in the Bardell suit, and negotiates Pickwick's release from the FLEET (45–47). Perker is said to be based on Ellis of the firm ELLIS AND BLACKMORE, who employed Dickens in his youth as a clerk.

Phunky Assistant barrister and second to Serjeant Snubbin in Pickwick's defense. "Although an infant barrister, he was a full grown man" (31).

Pickwick, Moses Operator of the coaches running between London and BATH and proprietor of several hotels in Bath, notably the White Hart, where the Pickwickians stay (35). Dickens took the name for his hero from Moses Pickwick.

Pickwick, Samuel The retired businessman and confirmed bachelor who is the founder and chairman of the Pickwick Club. With his "bald head and circular spectacles" and dressed in old-fashioned "tights and gaiters," the rotund Pickwick presides at the meeting of the club, a position justified by his "academic" achievements: tracing the source of the Hampstead ponds and promulgating his "theory of tittlebats." He proposes to lead a group of young men—Winkle, Snodgrass, and Tupman—on a series of journeys around England to observe the world and report back to the club about their excursions. After a series of misadventures, in which Pickwick's innocence and naiveté make him the butt of the humor and the dupe of the schemes of Jingle, Pickwick takes a manservant, Sam Weller, who is as savvy about the world as Pickwick is innocent (12). Sam usually manages to rescue his master from the difficulties he finds himself in, but even Sam's clever testimony is unable to save Pickwick in the case of Bardell versus Pickwick (34). Outraged by the unscrupulousness of the lawyers, Pickwick refuses to pay the costs in the case as the court has ordered, so he is sent to FLEET PRISON, where this sunny and benevolent man confronts the darker side of humanity (40). When Mrs. Bardell is also imprisoned in the Fleet, Pickwick's goodheartedness overcomes his principles and he pays the money that releases Mrs. Bardell and himself from the prison (47). At the same time he arranges the release of Jingle and Job Trotter. Once out of prison, he settles down in Dulwich with Sam Weller and his bride as his servants (57).

Dickens said that the germinating idea for the novel was the character of Pickwick: "I thought of Mr. Pickwick," he wrote in the 1847 preface to the novel, "and wrote the first number." The name was drawn from the proprietor of a Bath coach, Moses Pickwick, mentioned in chapter 35 as the Pickwickians go to Bath on one of his coaches. At the beginning, Pickwick seems to be a vehicle for satire: of "scientific" pretensions and of self-importance. His pontificating to the club is challenged by Blotton's assertion that he is a "humbug" (1); his hyperbolic awakening the next morning as "another sun" (2) is quickly undercut by his inept interaction with a cabman. If he begins, in LYN PYKETT's (2002) words, as "a man of sentiment masquerading as a man of science," we soon learn that his sentiment is more important than his science and his innocence more

Nast's Pickwick, for the American Household Edition (1873).

profound than simple näiveté. By the end of the novel, he has abandoned his role as a passive observer of humanity to become an active participant; his innocence has become benevolence, and he, in Sam Weller's words, an "angel in tights and gaiters" (45). He gives up the pretensions of principle to save Mrs. Bardell from prison, an act that in turn releases Sam and himself from the Fleet, enabling him to establish the community in Dulwich, and to promote Winkle's and Sam Weller's marriages, and to free Jingle and Job Trotter.

Pickwick has often been described as a character who changes in the course of the novel, losing his innocence as a result of his experiences, especially his time in prison. But Dickens suggested that the change was not so much in Pickwick as in the reader: "I do not think this change will appear forced or unnatural to my readers," he wrote, "if they will reflect that in real life the peculiarities and oddities of a man who has anything whimsical about him, generally impress us first, and that it is not until we are better acquainted with him that we usually begin to look below these superficial traits, and to know the better part of him."

Pickwickian This adjective for an uncomplimentary word that has lost its derogatory connotations comes from the episode in chapter 1 of *Pickwick,* where Mr. Blotton calls Pickwick a "humbug" and then explains that the word was not to be taken as derogatory because he had not used it "in a common sense," but rather "in its Pickwickian sense."

Pipkin, Nathaniel Parish clerk, "a harmless, inoffensive, good-natured being, with a turned-up nose, and rather turned-in legs: a cast in his eye, and a halt in his gait," who is in love with Maria Lobbs in Sam Weller's story "The Parish Clerk" (17).

Podder One of "the most renowned members" of the All-Muggleton Cricket Club (7).

Porkenham, Mr. Sidney and family The Porkenham family are friends and rivals to the Nupkins family in Ipswich society. Nupkins is terrified lest the Porkenhams discover that Captain Fitz-Marshal, whom he introduced into Ipswich society, is a fraud (25).

Pott, Mr. Editor of the *Eatanswill Gazette,* "a tall, thin man, with a sandy-coloured head inclined to baldness, and a face in which solemn importance was blended with a look of unfathomable profundity" (18). He is a contentious man, obsessed with his rivalry with Slurk, editor of the *Eatanswill Independent.* He attacks Winkle when Slurk implies in print that his wife is infatuated with the Pickwickian (18). Later, his wife leaves him, and the Pickwickians find him brawling with Slurk at the Saracen's Head in Towcester (51).

Pott, Mrs. Pott's controlling wife: "All men whom mighty genius has raised to a proud eminence in the world, have usually some little weakness which appears the more conspicuous from the contrast it presents to their general character. If Mr. Pott had a weakness, it was, perhaps, that he was *rather* too submissive to the somewhat contemptuous control and sway of his wife" (18).

Price One of the debtors whom Pickwick meets at Namby's sponging house, "a coarse vulgar young man [with a] captivating freedom of manner, which is to be acquired in public-house parlours and at low billiard tables" (40).

Pruffle Servant to the scientific gentleman at Clifton (39).

Queen Square Bath site of the house of Angelo Cyrus Bantam, the master of ceremonies in the Pump Room, whom Pickwick visits (35).

Raddle, Mrs. Mary Ann Bob Sawyer's landlady in LANT STREET and the sister of Mrs. Cluppins. "A little fierce woman," she shrewishly orders about her husband, a "faint-hearted, timorous wretch" (32).

Rogers, Mrs. Mrs. Bardell's genteel lodger (46).

Roker, Tom The turnkey who arranges Mr. Pickwick's rooms at the FLEET PRISON (40–44).

St. Clement's, Ipswich Church next to the Nupkinses' residence. Sam Weller meets Job Trotter in the churchyard (23).

Sam Cabdriver who resents Pickwick's questions, suspecting that Pickwick is taking down his number to report him (2).

Samba, Quanko The last member of the West Indian cricket side left standing, who, in Jingle's account, finally bowls out Jingle in a cricket match: "Quanko Samba—last man left—sun so hot, but in blisters—ball scorched brown—five hundred and seventy runs—rather exhausted—Quanko mustered up last remaining strength—

bowled me out." He is ultimately killed by the heat (7).

Sanders, Susannah Mrs. Bardell's friend, "a big, fat, heavy-faced personage," who testifies at the trial that her husband had often called her "duck" but never "tomata sauce," and that she "believed that Pickwick would marry Mrs. Bardell" (34).

Sandling Village in Kent near Maidstone generally thought to be the original of Dingley Dell in *Pickwick*.

Sawyer, Bob Medical student at GUY'S HOSPITAL and bosom friend of Benjamin Allen. He has "that sort of slovenly smartness and swaggering gait, which is peculiar to young gentlemen who smoke in the streets by day, shout and scream in the same by night, call waiters by their Christian names, and do various other acts and deeds of an equally facetious description. He wore a pair of plaid trousers, and a large rough double-breasted waistcoat; out of doors, he carried a thick stick with a big top. He eschewed gloves, and looked, upon the whole, something like a dissipated Robinson Crusoe" (30). He holds a bachelor party in his rooms in LANT STREET, which is disrupted by his landlady, Mrs. Raddle, who is angry with him because he has not paid his rent (32). After finishing medical school, he and Ben Allen buy the practice of Nockemorf at BRISTOL, where they desultorily and unsuccessfully follow their profession (38–39). Although Benjamin Allen plans to marry his sister Arabella to Bob, Winkle marries her first (50). In the end Bob and Ben start life afresh as medical officers with the East India Company in Bengal (57).

Serjeant's Inn An inn of Chancery in Chancery Lane to which Pickwick is taken as he is being committed to the Fleet Prison (40).

Simmery, Frank "A very smart young gentleman who wore his hat on his right whisker, and was lounging over the desk, killing flies with a ruler" in the office of stockbroker Wilkins Flasher. The two men gossip and bet on the lives of their acquaintances, on whether, for example, one of them will commit suicide within 10 days (55).

Simpson One of Pickwick's fellow prisoners in the FLEET, who is originally assigned as one of Pickwick's cellmates (42).

Skimpin, Mr. Junior barrister to Sergeant Buzfuz, representing Mrs. Bardell in the trial of Bardell *v.* Pickwick (34).

Slammer, Dr. The fiery little surgeon of the 97th, "a little fat man, with a ring of upright black hair round his head and an extensive bald plain on the top of it" (2). He challenges Jingle to a duel when the actor, wearing Winkle's coat, dances with the widow Budger, whom Slammer has been courting. The challenge, however, is delivered to Winkle by mistake (2–3).

Slasher Surgeon, described by Jack Hopkins as the "best operator" at ST. BARTHOLOMEW'S HOSPITAL, "took a boy's leg out of the socket last week—boy ate five apples and a ginger bread cake—exactly two minutes after it was all over, boy said he wouldn't lie there to be made a game of, and he'd tell his mother if they didn't begin" (32).

Slumkey, the Hon. Samuel Successful Blue candidate who defeats Horatio Fizkin in the election at Eatanswill (13).

Slummintowkens, the Friends and social rivals to the Nupkins family in Ipswich society (25).

Slurk Editor of the *Eatanswill Independent*, organ of the Buff (Whig) party, and the archrival of Pott. "His manner was peremptory; his eyes were sharp and restless; and his whole bearing bespoke a feeling of great confidence in himself, and a consciousness of his immeasurable superiority over all other people" (51). The rival editors end up fighting with each other at Towcester, a fight stopped by Sam Weller, who puts a meal sack over Pott's head (51).

Smangle A prisoner for debt in the FLEET PRISON, "a rakish vagabond" with a "kind of boastful rascality" (41).

Smart, Tom A traveling salesman and the hero of "The Bagman's Story." He exposes Jinkins's scheme to marry the buxom widow innkeeper (14).

Smauker, John Angelo Cyrus Bantam's footman who invites Sam Weller to the footmen's "swarry" at BATH (35, 37).

Smiggers, Joseph Perpetual Vice-President of the Pickwick Club (1).

Smithers, Miss Schoolgirl at Westgate House who is incited "into hysterics of four young lady power" by the discovery of Mr. Pickwick in the school's courtyard (16).

Smithie family Family attending the ball in ROCHESTER (2).

Smorltork, Count The foreign visitor whom Pickwick meets at Mrs. Leo Hunter's fête champêtre, who is collecting materials for a work on England. He was based on Count Pückler-Moskau and Friedrich von Raumer, who had both written books giving their observations of the English (15).

Smouch Assistant to Namby the sheriff; "a shabby-looking man in a brown great-coat shorn of divers buttons" (40).

Snicks Life office secretary, a guest at Perker's dinner party (47).

Snipe, The Hon. Wilmot Ensign in the 97th Regiment who attends the ball at ROCHESTER (2).

Snodgrass, Augustus One of the members of the traveling Pickwick Club; "the poetic Snodgrass poetically enveloped in a mysterious blue cloak with a canine skin collar" (1). He secretly falls in love with Emily Wardle, marries her, and lives happily at Dingley Dell (57).

Snubbin, Serjeant Mr. Pickwick's barrister in the breach-of-promise trial, "a lantern faced, sallow-complexioned man of about five-and-forty. . . . He had that dull-looking boiled eye, which is often to be seen in the heads of people who have applied themselves, during many years, to a weary and laborious course of study" (31). He was probably based on Serjeant Arabin, a well-known barrister of the time.

Snuphanuph, Dowager Lady "A fat old lady" who is Pickwick's whist partner at BATH (35–36).

Spaniards Historic inn at the edge of Hamstead Heath where Mrs. Bardell is having tea with her friends in the tea garden when Jackson apprehends her to take her off to prison (46).

Staple Supporter of the Dingley Dell cricket team, "a little man with a puffy Say-nothing-to-me-or-I'll-contradict-you sort of countenance," who toasts Dunkins and Podder at the dinner following the match with Muggleton (7).

Stareleigh, Mr. Justice The judge who presides over the Bardell versus Pickwick case, "so fat that he seemed all face and waistcoat. . . . All you could see of him was two queer little eyes, one broad pink face, and somewhere about half of a big and very comical-looking wig" (35). Dickens's character is said to have been based on Sir Stephen Gazelee and to have contributed to his retirement from the bench.

Stiggins, the Rev. Mr. The drunken hypocrite who preaches temperance as the "deputy shepherd" of the Brick Lane branch of the United Grand Junction Ebenezer Temperance Association: "he was a prim-faced, red-nosed man, with a long thin countenance, and a semi-rattlesnake sort of eye—rather sharp, but decidedly bad" (27). Susan Weller, Tony's second wife, is one of the women taken in by his piety. At a meeting of the temperance society, Tony exposes his hypocrisy (33) and later kicks him into a horse trough (52).

Struggles Member of the Dingley Dell cricket team (7).

Sun Court Street off Cornhill, location of the George and Vulture, the inn where Dodson and Fogg's clerk seeks out Pickwick (31).

Tadger, Brother Member of the Brick Lane branch of the United Junction Ebenezer Temperance Association, "the little man in the drab shorts," whom a drunk Stiggins accuses of being drunk (33).

Tappleton, Lieutenant Dr. Slammer's second in the abortive duel with Winkle (2).

Tewkesbury Town in Gloucestershire where Pickwick, Ben Allen, and Bob Sawyer stop for dinner at the Hop Pole Inn on their way from Bristol to Birmingham (50).

Thomas Waiter in Sam Weller's story of the man who killed himself by eating crumpets (44).

Tomkins, Miss Head mistress of the Westgate House School, BURY ST. EDMUNDS, where Pickwick is caught in the courtyard in a compromising situation (16).

Tomlinson, Miss Post-mistress at ROCHESTER who attends the ball at the Bull Inn (2).

Towcester Stopping at this town in Northamptonshire on their way back to London from Birmingham, Pickwick and his friends observe the fight between the rival editors from Eatanswill, Pott and Slurk (51).

Town Arms Headquarters of the Blue faction during the Eatanswill election (13).

Trotter, Job Jingle's manservant, "a young fellow in mulberry-coloured livery . . . who had a large, sallow, ugly face, very sunken eyes, and a gigantic head, from which depended a quantity of lank black hair" (16). He aids Jingle in his schemes, and his ability to call up hypocritical tears fools Sam twice. He is loyal to his master, accompanying him to the FLEET and, in the end, to the West Indies.

Pickwick and Sam are mirrored by Jingle and Trotter. Sam's street savvy is matched by Trotter's scheming cleverness. Each master/servant pair follows a similar course, ending up in the Fleet Prison at the same time.

Trundle Speechless young man "in high feather and spirits, but a little nervous withal," who marries Wardle's daughter Isabella during the Christmas festivities at Dingley Dell (28).

Tuckle A footman who presides at the Bath "swarry": "a stoutish gentleman in a bright crimson coat with long tails, vividly red breeches, and a cocked hat" (37).

Tupman, Tracy One of Pickwick's traveling companions, a middle-aged bachelor whose "ruling passion" is "admiration of the fair sex." "The too susceptible Tupman who, to the wisdom and experience of maturer years, superadded the enthusiasm and ardour of a boy, in the most interesting and pardonable of human weaknesses—love" (1). After his courtship of Rachel Wardle is foiled by Jingle (8), Tupman withdraws from such pursuits, eventually retiring to RICHMOND, where he is much admired by "elderly ladies of single condition" (57).

Although he begins the novel as a "humors" character, defined by his interest in the "fair sex," Tupman (despite the double entendre in his name) is foiled in his amorous pursuits by the fat boy and Jingle, who make him aware of the absurdity of his middle-aged obsession. Changed by his experience, he becomes a respectable single gentleman, while his younger associates, Winkle and Snodgrass, become lovers and marry in the end.

United Grand Junction Ebenezer Temperance Association The temperance society of which Stiggins is a leading member of the Brick Lane branch and Mrs. Weller an ardent member. Sam and Tony visit a meeting of the association (33). Later in the novel, Dickens, apparently forgetting the name, changes Ebenezer to Emmanuel (52).

Upwich, Richard Greengrocer who serves as a juryman at Pickwick's trial (34).

Walker, H. Tailor who is converted to teetotalism and recruited into the Brick Lane branch of the United Grand Junction Ebenezer Temperance Association. "When in better circumstances, owns to having been in the constant habit of drinking ale and beer, . . . is now out of work and penniless; thinks it must be the porter" (33).

Wardle, Emily Wardle's daughter who is secretly in love with Snodgrass through much of the novel, eventually marrying him after Pickwick's release from prison. The couple then settle at Dingley Dell.

Wardle, Isabella Wardle's daughter, "a very amiable and lovely girl," who marries Mr. Trundle during the Christmas festivities at Dingley Dell (28).

Wardle, Mr. The jolly old yeoman and owner of Manor Farm at Dingley Dell, "a stout gentleman, in a blue coat and bright buttons, corduroy breeches and top boots" (4). The Pickwickians meet Wardle at the military review in Chatham (4). He invites them to Manor Farm, where Tupman courts Wardle's spinster sister and is outwitted by the unscrupulous Jingle, who elopes with Rachael, hoping to gain her small fortune (5–9). With Pickwick, Wardle pursues the couple to London, where he buys off Jingle for £120 and recovers Rachael. While at Manor Farm, the Pickwickians participate in a shooting party and a cricket match. They later return for CHRISTMAS and the wedding of Isabella.

Wardle, Mrs. Wardle's deaf old mother, who "occupied the post of honour on the right-hand corner of the chimney-piece" in the manor house.

Wardle, Rachael Wardle's spinster sister, over 50 and desperate to find a husband. Tupman's courtship of her is foiled when they are observed by Joe in the arbor and when she elopes with Jingle. Although she resists Wardle's attempt to rescue her, he buys off Jingle and returns with her to Manor Farm. Rachael is portrayed as the stereotypical desperate spinster, occasioning what JAMES KINCAID (1971) describes as "the harshest and most aggressive" humor in the novel.

Watty Bankrupt client who pesters Mr. Perker, "a rustily-clad, miserable-looking man, in boots without toes and gloves without fingers. There were traces of privation and suffering—almost of despair—in his lank and care-worn countenance" (31).

Weller, Samuel Tony's son and Pickwick's manservant who matches Pickwick's innocence with worldly savvy. He is working as the boots at the White Hart in the BOROUGH when Pickwick first meets him: "he was habited in a coarse striped waistcoat, with black calico sleeves, and blue glass buttons, drab breeches, and leggings. A bright red handkerchief was wound in a very loose and unstudied style round his neck; and an old white hat was carelessly thrown on his head" (10). Sam is the embodiment of cockney wit; he tells bizarre tales and has a "Wellerism," an outlandish comparison, for nearly every occasion: "'That's the pint, sir,' interposed Sam; 'out with it, as the father said to the child, wen he swallowed a farden'" (12). Sam extricates his master from many embarrassing situations and uses his experience in the streets to compensate for Pickwick's naiveté. But even his cockney wit and clever testimony at the Bardell *v.* Pickwick trial cannot prevent Pickwick from being sent to prison, so Sam contrives to have himself sent to the FLEET for debt (43), and he does not leave until Pickwick chooses to leave as well. In the end Sam marries Mary, the pretty housemaid whom he first met in Ipswich, and he and his wife and their two sons, Sam Junior and Tony Junior, settle down in Dulwich as Pickwick's servants.

Even more than Pickwick, Sam Weller is the character on whom the greatness of *The Pickwick Papers* rests. The overwhelming success of the book in its own time began with the introduction of Sam in the fourth number; he has continued to delight readers as one of Dickens's great comic characters, along with Dick Swiveller (*Curiosity Shop*), Sarah Gamp (*Chuzzlewit*), and Wilkins Micawber (*Copperfield*). All of these comic figures are distinguished by their powers of self-creation through language. Weller transforms experience into wonderfully bizarre stories, like those of the man who dies from eating crumpets and of the pieman who makes meat pies from cats, or into "Wellerisms," outlandish similes, such as "Avay with melincholly, as the little boy said ven his school missis died." He is, in Tony's words, his father's "prodigy son."

Although he enters the story as the opposite of Pickwick—young, poor, and working class in contrast to Pickwick's age, wealth, and bourgeois identity—he is the cunning voice of experience who counters his master's innocence. But by the end of the novel, the two transcend the differences of servant and master to become loving friends identified as one by their shared Christian name.

Sam reappears in *Master Humphrey's Clock,* in which he and his father preside over "Mr. Weller's Watch," a circle of servants who gather below stairs while the circle of Master Humphrey gathers upstairs. SAM VALE, the cockney actor, is said to be the original from whom Dickens drew his character.

Weller, Susan Tony Weller's second wife, "a rather stout lady of comfortable appearance" (27). Formerly the widow Susan Clarke, she is the proprietress of the Marquis of Granby, a public house in Dorking. She is partly responsible for Tony's reservations about "widders," for she has made him miserable with her involvement with Stiggins and the Brick Lane Temperance Association. She apologizes for doing so as she is dying, and Tony responds by telling her, "You've been a wery good vife to me, altogether." Her will leaves Tony enough to provide some capital for Sam and Mary and for his own comfort.

Weller, Tony Sam's father, a coachman, a stout red-faced man who lives to eat, drink, and smoke; "his face . . . had expanded under the influence of good living, and a disposition remarkable for resignation; and its bold fleshy curves had so far

Tony Weller advises Sam about writing a valentine in this famous illustration by Browne (Phiz) for *The Pickwick Papers.*

extended beyond the limits originally assigned them, that unless you took a full view of his countenance in front, it was difficult to distinguish more than the extreme tip of a very rubicund nose" (23). Like his son, Tony is a repository of cockney wit and stories, many having to do with the evils of matrimony, especially the danger posed by predatory "widders." He is plagued by the involvement of his wife—Tony's second wife and hence Sam's stepmother or, in the parlance of the day, his mother-in-law—with Stiggins and the Brick Lane Temperance Association. With Sam's help, he attends one of their meetings and exposes the hypocritical Stiggins (33). After the death of his wife, he inherits enough from her to live comfortably. When Stiggins inquires what Susan has left for him, he tosses the preacher into a horse trough (52). Both Sam and Tony reappear briefly in *Master Humphrey's Clock.*

Westgate House Jingle and Job Trotter trick Pickwick into hiding in the courtyard of this school for young women in Bury St. Edmunds, leading to his embarrassing discovery there in the middle of the night (16).

Whiffers A Bath footman at the "swarry" who has resigned his position because he has been asked to eat cold meat (37).

Whiffin Town crier at Eatanswill (13).

White Hart Inn (1) Bath inn where the Pickwickians stay, operated by Moses Pickwick, probably the source for Dickens's hero's name (35).

White Hart Inn (2) In the Borough, one of the old coaching inns of London—"Great, rambling, queer, old places they are, with galleries, and passages, and staircases, wide enough and antiquated enough to furnish materials for a hundred ghost stories" (10)—where Jingle and Rachael Wardle put up and where Sam Weller is the boots.

Wicks Clerk to Dodson and Fogg (20).

Wildspark, Tom Tony Weller's acquaintance who got off a manslaughter charge with "a alleybi" (33).

Wilkins One of Captain Boldwig's gardeners (19).

Winkle, Nathaniel One of the traveling Pickwickians, Winkle's pretense of being a sportsman gets him repeatedly into trouble and causes Pickwick to call him a "wretch" after one particularly inept performance with a gun (7). Winkle's confused testimony at the trial helps convict Pickwick (34), but while Pickwick is in prison, Winkle marries Arabella Allen and, with Pickwick's help, secures his father's blessing for the union (56). His father, Winkle, Senior, a BIRMINGHAM wharf owner, is "a little old gentleman in a snuff-coloured suit, with a head and face the precise counterpart of those belonging to Mr. Winkle, Junior, excepting that he was rather bald" (50).

Witherfield, Miss The middle-aged lady in curl papers who is surprised to find Pickwick in her hotel room in Ipswich in the middle of the night. The altercation that arises the next morning between Pickwick and her suitor, Peter Magnus, leads to Pickwick's arrest for disturbing the peace (22, 24).

Wugsby, Mrs. Colonel One of the whist players at Bath (35, 36).

"Zephyr, The" Nickname of Mivins, one of Pickwick's fellow prisoners in the FLEET.

ADAPTATIONS

Three stage adaptations appeared in London while the novel was still appearing in parts, one by EDWARD STIRLING, one by William Leman Rede, and one by WILLIAM MONCREIFF. All of them included much that was not in the novel, but only the last achieved some success in the theater, perhaps because it featured Sam Weller, played by W. J. HAMMOND. When Dickens protested against the play, Moncreiff defended his plagiarism by attacking the novel with praise: "to meddle with so extraordinary a writer, therefore, is as dangerous as it is enticing; the desultory nature of the adventures in which he has revelled, & the absence of that continuity of plot so essential in a dramatic piece, has also been the subject of much embarassment and has led the adaptor to draw on his own resources very frequently, when he would more gladly have availed himself of the superior material of his master."

The Pickwick mania prompted a great many sequels and other derivative works based on Dickens's novel. PHILIP COLLINS (1969), in the *New* *Cambridge Bibliography of English Literature,* provides a substantial list of these stepchildren. Many of them are described in William Miller's "Imitations of Pickwick" (DICKENSIAN, 1936).

Pickwick has also been very popular as a source for dramatic material; its episodic nature has prompted many short pieces. Among later plays of note, John Hollingshead's *Bardell v. Pickwick* (1871) claimed to be based on Dickens's popular PUBLIC READING. It starred J. L. TOOLE as Buzfuz and Miss E. Farren as Sam Weller. Cosmo Hamilton's and Frank C. Reilley's *Pickwick* (1927–28) played in Washington, D.C.; New York; and London with CHARLES LAUGHTON in the title role. Wolf Mankowitz's musical *Pickwick*, with music by Cyril Ornadel and lyrics by LESLIE BRICUSSE, opened in London in 1963.

Of the six silent films based on *Pickwick,* THOMAS BENTLEY's 1921 adaptation was the most ambitious. It featured Frederick Volpe as Pickwick, a role he had played many times on stage, and BRANSBY WILLIAMS as Sergeant Buzfuz. The only sound film based on the novel is NOEL LANGLEY's 1952 version, starring James Hayter (Pickwick), Nigel Patrick (Jingle), and Harry Fowler (Sam Weller).

On television, *Pickwick* has appeared in numerous versions. Michael Pointer (*Charles Dickens on the Screen*, 1996) lists 15 adaptations based on the novel. The earliest, a 25-minute excerpt from Anthony Coates's opera, *Mr. Pickwick*, was telecast in 1936. *Pickwick* was also the first of Dickens's novels serialized on the BBC, in seven parts in 1952. The BBC also produced a 12-part serial in 1985 starring Nigel Stock in the title role. The novel has also been adapted for French and Italian television.

FURTHER READING

Pickwick established the serial as a standard mode of publication for later Victorian novels, and its format, 20 parts (18 plus a final double number), was the one most often adopted. The story of how Dickens came to work in the serial form and how it developed as the novel went along is told by JOHN BUTT and KATHLEEN TILLOTSON (1957) and ROBERT PATTEN (1978). Patten's introduction to the Penguin Edition of the novel (1972) adds critical commentary to his account of the novel's composition.

In a classic essay on *Pickwick*, W. H. Auden ("Dingley Dell and the Fleet," in *The Dyer's Hand,*

1962) describes the novel as an archetypal fable about the fall of man. When the innocent Pickwick discovers the presence of evil and suffering in the world during his time in the FLEET PRISON, he loses his innocence. When Mrs. Bardell is imprisoned, he must give up his principles, sacrifice his honor, and collude with the evil system to end her suffering and his own imprisonment.

Barbara Hardy (*The Moral Art of Dickens,* 1970) challenges critics like Auden who find a mythic unity in the book. Describing it as a work of parts—some of them tedious and disconnected from the whole—she finds the power of the novel in its comedy and especially in the Pickwickian innocence that comes to terms with the harsh realities of Victorian England by denying and transforming them.

STEVEN MARCUS (1965) characterizes the novel's unique power as "transcendence . . . a representation of life which fulfills that vision, which men have never yet relinquished, of the ideal possibilities of human relations in community, and which, in the fulfillment extends our awareness of the limits of our humanity." This ideal is most fully realized, Marcus contends, in the bonds between Pickwick, Sam, and Tony Weller. JAMES KINCAID (1971) describes Pickwick's transcendence as a result of his education at the hands of Sam Weller, who introduces him to pain and poverty and teaches him the limitations of principle and the virtues of flexibility and realism.

GARRETT STEWART (1974) devotes a third of his book to an analysis of parody and style in *Pickwick* as it sets a paradigm for the liberating power of imagination that Dickens explores in many of his novels.

JOHN BOWEN (2000) sees the book as a work that initiates many themes and ideas that Dickens will develop in his later works. His discussions of writing in the novel and of the theme of imposture are especially illuminating.

Tale of Two Cities, A

Dickens's 12th novel, serialized unillustrated in weekly parts in ALL THE YEAR ROUND (April 30 to November 26, 1859). It was simultaneously issued in eight monthly numbers by CHAPMAN & HALL, illustrated by HABLOT KNIGHT BROWNE. Published in one volume, 1859. Dickens's second historical novel, largely based on THOMAS CARLYLE's *The French Revolution, Two Cities* was intended, Dickens said, to make that "terrible time" more "popular and picturesque." Departing from his accustomed manner to concentrate on the incidents and myth in his story rather than on the characters, Dickens attempted to reconcile his historical theme with the personal story of Sydney Carton, whose sacrifice challenges historical inevitability.

SYNOPSIS
Book One. Recalled to Life

Part 1 (April 30, 1859)
(I:1) The year 1775, "it was the best of times" and "the worst of times." In England, its American colonies on the verge of revolution, public order is maintained with muskets. In France, the Woodman, Fate, and the Farmer, Death, are already silently at work preparing for the revolution.

(I:2) As the London-to-Dover coach labors up a muddy hill on a dark November night, a horseman brings a message for one of the passengers, Mr. Jarvis Lorry of Tellson's Bank. Lorry reads the brief note and sends the messenger back with the answer, "Recalled to Life." The coachmen speculate on the cryptic reply. The narrator comments that Jerry Cruncher, the messenger, who works as a "resurrection man" on the side, stealing bodies from graves, would be "in a Blazing bad way" should recalling to life come into fashion. (I:3) Jerry is uneasy about the message. Jarvis Lorry, sleeping fitfully in the coach, dreams of digging someone out of a grave who has been buried for 18 years.

Part 2 (May 7, 1859)
(I:4) At Dover, Lorry meets Miss Lucie Manette, a young woman of 17 who has been informed that there is news respecting the property of her father, whom she has never seen. Lorry tells her how he handled the financial affairs of a physician of Beauvais and his English wife. When their child, Miss Manette, was allegedly orphaned 15 years ago, he brought her to England. But, Lorry tells her, Doctor Manette did not die; he was a prisoner in the BASTILLE, and he has recently been released and is

in the care of a former servant in Paris. Their secret mission is to bring him out of France. On hearing this news Miss Manette faints.

Part 3 (May 14, 1859)

(I:5) A mob of the poor has gathered in front of a wineshop in the St. Antoine section of Paris to sop up wine from a cask that has broken and spilled into the cobblestone street. During the desperate revelry, one of the celebrants writes "Blood" in wine on the wall. Meanwhile, in the wineshop, Madame Defarge, the owner's wife, watches and knits; her husband sends three customers, all named Jacques, into a tower off the courtyard. When Lorry and Miss Manette arrive, Defarge directs them to the same tower. At the door of a garret room, they find the three Jacques peering into the darkened garret, where Doctor Manette is busily making shoes.

Part 4 (May 21, 1859)

(I:6) Yellowed from so many years in prison, like a creature revived from the grave, Manette does not recognize Lorry or his daughter. When Defarge asks him his name, he says, "One Hundred and Five, North Tower." When he sees his daughter's golden hair, he shows some signs of recognition. He takes some similar hairs from a locket around his neck, compares the two and asks, "Was it you?" Gradually he allows her to embrace him. A few hours later Lorry and Miss Manette set off in a coach, taking the broken old man and his shoe-making equipment with them.

Book Two. The Golden Thread

Part 5 (May 28, 1859)

(II:1) Five years later, Jerry Cruncher, Tellson's bank messenger, stands at his post outside the London office with young Jerry, his look-alike son. (II:2) He is sent to the OLD BAILEY court, where a treason case is in progress, and he is told to wait there for any message that Lorry may wish to send. In the dock, Charles Darnay, a French émigré, stands accused of giving the French information about British troop movements. Everybody in the room is focused on the prisoner except Sydney Carton, a lawyer who lounges at the side of the room, looking at the ceiling and showing little interest in the proceedings.

Part 6 (June 4, 1859)

(II:3) The crowd has gathered in the courtroom like flies around carrion, expecting Darnay to be sentenced to death. Two witnesses for the prosecution, John Barsad and Roger Cly, testify that they saw Darnay deliver information to the French. The Manettes, who met Darnay on the channel boat as the doctor was being brought out of France five years earlier, are called to testify. The doctor remembers nothing, but Lucie is forced to testify that Darnay had jokingly suggested that George Washington would probably surpass George III in history. She had also seen him confer with some Frenchmen. Then Stryver, lawyer for the defense, points out his associate, Sydney Carton, and asks a prosecution witness to identify Carton as definitely not the gentleman in question. Carton's resemblance to Darnay is so remarkable that the witness cannot do so. The jury deliberates and delivers its verdict. Jerry receives the note from Lorry, "Acquitted." He speculates that "Recalled to Life" would again have been appropriate. The flies disperse.

Part 7 (June 11, 1859)

(II:4) The doubles, Carton and Darnay, dine together. Carton's cynicism and despair clash with Darnay's optimistic integrity. During the meal, Carton drinks too much and becomes insolent, and he describes himself as "a disappointed drudge" who cares "for no man on earth." After Darnay leaves, Carton studies himself in a mirror, seeing in his self-hatred the reasons for his dislike of Darnay, who looks so much like him.

(II:5) Carton goes to Stryver's office, where the two work through the night. Carton does the hard work, prepping Stryver on the issues in the cases for the next day. He drinks as he works. Stryver observes that Sydney has always been a background figure; even when they were schoolboys together at Shrewsbury, Carton did the assignments for the other boys. At dawn, Sydney leaves the office to wander through the wasteland of the city, which seems to echo the "waste forces within him." He falls asleep in tears.

Part 8 (June 18, 1859)

(II:6) In London on a July afternoon, Lorry walks to SOHO to visit the Manettes. Only Miss Pross, Lucie's companion who is bothered by the "hundreds" of unworthy people interested in her "ladybird," is at home. When Lorry asks if Doctor Manette ever thinks of his time in prison, Pross says that Lucie sometimes walks in the night with her father till he recovers from such memories. Standing in the window of the Manettes' corner house, Lorry can hear the Manettes' footsteps approaching. Later, Charles Darnay joins them. As they sit under the plane tree in the yard, Darnay tells a story about a prisoner who left the letters DIG carved on the wall in his cell; in the floor under the letters, a manuscript he had buried there was found. The story upsets Doctor Manette. By tea time Carton has arrived, and an approaching storm sounds like hundreds of footsteps coming toward the house.

Part 9 (June 25, 1859)

(II:7) In Paris the rich gather for a reception at the house of Monseigneur, the powerful representative of the French aristocracy. In his private rooms, Monseigneur has four men to prepare his chocolate before he appears briefly to greet the fawning company. As the Marquis St. Evrémonde, who has attended the affair, sets off for the country, his speeding carriage runs over and kills a boy in the street. The Marquis worries about injury to his horses and berates the boy's father for not protecting the child. Defarge, the wineshop owner, consoles the boy's father with the thought that the child did not live to suffer poverty. The Marquis gives Defarge and the father gold coins, but as he sets out again, a coin comes flying in the carriage window. He demands to know who threw it, but Defarge and the grieving father have disappeared. Meanwhile, a woman sits knitting while the carriages of the aristocracy continue to pass by the poor in the streets. (II:8) In the country the Marquis stops in the village near his chateau and asks a road mender why he was staring at the carriage. The man explains that he was staring at a figure covered in dust underneath the carriage who is no longer there. The Marquis goes on to his castle, where he asks whether his nephew, Monsieur Charles, has arrived from England.

Part 10 (July 2, 1859)

(II:9) His nephew has not come, so the Marquis dines alone. He thinks he sees something or some-

one outside the window, but the servant finds no one. When his nephew, Charles Darnay, arrives, they have an uncomfortable meeting. Charles knows his uncle was responsible for the trial in London and has tried to silence him "for the honor of the family." Charles urges the Marquis to right the wrongs done by the family, but his uncle says that to be feared and hated by the vulgar is a mark of respect. Charles renounces his family and France and tells the Marquis that he plans to work rather than take any tainted family money. He also indicates that he knows the Manettes. The Marquis ends this chilly conversation muttering, "So commences the new philosophy!" The next morning the body of the Marquis is found, stabbed to death, with a note: "Drive him fast to his tomb. This, from Jacques."

Part 11 (July 9, 1859)

(II:10) A year later, Charles Darnay is earning his living as a French-language tutor in London. The chateau in France has faded into a dream. When he tells Doctor Manette that he loves Lucie but that he is reluctant to come between father and daughter, the doctor assures him that he will not stand in their way. Charles starts to reveal his identity, but the doctor stops him, saying that if his suit prospers the revelation can wait until the wedding morning. Later Lucie hears the sound of hammering coming from her father's room, but when she knocks at the door the noise ceases.

(II:11) Darnay is not Lucie's only suitor. Stryver confides to Carton as they are drinking together that he plans to propose to Lucie, even though he has criticized her in the past as only a golden-haired doll.

Part 12 (July 16, 1859)

(II:12) Stryver heads for Soho to propose, stopping on the way to test his plan on Mr. Lorry. Speaking in his personal and not his business capacity, Lorry advises against it. Stryver is offended but agrees to let Lorry sound out the situation and report back. By the time Lorry returns, the lawyer has convinced himself that he was never serious. Lorry repeats his earlier counsel.

(II:13) Sydney haunts the streets outside Lucie's house. One day he confesses to her that she has given him a sense of how his life might have been better. She urges him to allow her to help him achieve a better life, but he says it is too late. He makes her promise to keep his confession secret, telling her that he "would embrace any sacrifice for you and for those dear to you."

Part 13 (July 23, 1859)

(II:14) Outside Tellson's, Cruncher and his son watch the funeral procession for Roger Cly, the spy who testified against Darnay. Cly has staged his funeral in order to escape the wrath of the mob and secretly slip off to France. Because it is a spy's funeral, the mob in the streets riots, chases away the mourners, and forms a celebratory mob. They climb on the hearse and, led by a dancing bear, turn the procession into a parade. Jerry Cruncher joins the mob and goes to the cemetery. That evening, Jerry plans a "fishing trip" to exhume Cly's corpse, warning his wife not to spoil it by "flopping," that is, by kneeling down and praying. At one in the morning, he collects his tools and slips out of the house, unknowingly followed by his son. With two cohorts he goes to a dark cemetery, and his son watches as the three men fish Cly's coffin from a grave, only to find it empty. The next morning young Jerry asks his father, who is in a foul mood, what a "resurrection man" is, and he says he hopes to become one.

Part 14 (July 30, 1859)

(II:15) At the Parisian wineshop, in the tower room formerly occupied by Manette, Defarge, who calls himself Jacques Four, and the road mender, Jacques Five, who observed the Marquis's carriage, meet with Jacques One, Two, and Three. The road mender tells this group of revolutionaries of seeing a gaunt man, the father of the dead child, hanging underneath the coach of the Marquis and then, many months after the Marquis's murder, seeing the same man apprehended, taken to prison, and then hanged in the village square. The Defarges take Jaques Five to Versailles to see the King and Queen, his "natural prey."

Part 15 (August 6, 1859)

(II:16) A confederate on the police force secretly tells Defarge that Barsad, the Englishman who testified with Cly against Darnay, has been assigned to St. Antoine as a spy. When Barsad appears at the

Furniss's portrait of Madame Defarge at her knitting.

wineshop, Madame Defarge signals his presence to the patrons by placing a rose in her hair. He introduces several topics—oppression, the execution of the Marquis's assassin Gaspard, and so on—but he fails to get any expressions of revolutionary sympathy from them. He does suprise Defarge with the information that Lucie Manette is to marry the Marquis St. Evrémonde. Madame Defarge, who keeps a list of the enemies of the French people to be executed during the revolution by knitting them into a "shroud," records this information with her fateful needles.

Part 16 (August 13, 1859)

(II:17) On the evening before her wedding, Lucie asks her father for assurance that her marriage does not disturb him. He tells her for the first time how, while he was in prison, he imagined the child he had never seen. Sometimes he envisioned a son who would seek vengeance, but more often he imagined a daughter. In one of these visions, she was married and kept her father's picture in her house. She would show the picture to her children, but she could not deliver him from prison. (II:18) Before the wedding Charles Darnay meets with Doctor Manette in his room to reveal his identity as a member of the St. Evrémonde family. When they emerge, Manette is deathly pale. After Charles and Lucie leave for their honeymoon, the doctor relapses into his role as shoemaker-prisoner. For nine days, watched over by Pross and Lorry, he works at his bench and does not recognize them. Lorry's efforts to communicate with him are unsuccessful.

Part 17 (August 20, 1859)

(II:19) On the 10th morning, Lorry finds Manette restored to himself. Lorry consults with Manette, disguising the doctor's case to him as the story of someone else and asking if there is danger of a relapse. The doctor says that the attack was brought on by "a strong and extraordinary revival of the train of thought and remembrance that was the first cause of the malady," that the subject would not remember that cause, and that there was hope it would not recur. Lorry asks whether the tools of his traumatic trade—say, a blacksmith's tools—should be gotten rid of. This question makes Manette anxious. He finally agrees to the destruction of the shoemaker's tools for the sake of his daughter. When Manette leaves to visit Lucie and Charles, Lorry destroys the cobbler's bench.

(II:20) Sydney tells Darnay that he wishes to become his friend, but Darnay tells him that he already considers him a friend. When Charles tells Lucie of Sydney's request, he speaks of Sydney "as a problem of carelessness and recklessness." Lucie says that Sydney deserves more consideration and respect and "is capable of good things, gentle things, even magnanimous things."

Part 18 (August 27, 1859)

(II:21) For several years the Darnays live peacefully in their corner house in Soho, which is still filled with the sound of echoing footsteps. They have a son who dies and a daughter who lives. Sydney visits them six times a year and is a favorite of their child. By July 1789, when the child is six, Lorry tells them that French depositors are lining up to put their money into an English bank. As they sit in the window that evening, the echoing footsteps seem particularly loud.

Meanwhile, in France the mob led by the Jacquerie storms the Bastille. When they get into the prison, Defarge goes to One Hundred and Five North Tower and finds there a stone with A.M. on it. He searches the room, looking for a hiding place. The mob plans to take the governor of the prison to the Hotel de Ville, the city hall, for judgment, but they kill him on the way and Madame Defarge decapitates him. The mob carry the prisoners released from the Bastille into the confusion of the streets. Above it all, carried aloft on poles, are the heads of seven decapitated officials.

Part 19 (September 3, 1859)

(II:22) In Paris, the mob from St. Antoine converges on the Hotel de Ville. Defarge announces that Foulon, an old man who suggested that starving people could eat grass, has been captured. They take Foulon into the street and hang him from a lamppost. His head is displayed, his mouth stuffed with grass. Next they capture and execute Foulon's son-in-law and parade with his head through the streets.

(II:23) In the country village near the chateau of the St. Evrémonde family, everything is brown and wasted. The mender of roads directs a stranger to the chateau. That evening the castle burns and the townspeople refuse to fight the fire. They ring the town bell for joy, light candles in their windows, and threaten the local tax collector, Gabelle, who hides in his attic.

Part 20 (September 10, 1859)

(II:24) Three years later, in August 1792, Lorry has received a letter addressed to the Marquis St. Evrémonde, and he inquires among the French emigrés if any of them has knowledge of the Marquis. Although Darnay has promised Doctor Manette that he will never reveal his identity without the doctor's permission, he admits to Lorry that he knows the Marquis and takes the letter. The letter is from Gabelle, whom Charles employed to aid the tenants of the St. Evrémonde estates after his uncle's murder. Gabelle has been imprisoned and needs Charles's testimony to prove that he has the people's best interests at heart. Charles decides he must go to France. Leaving letters to Lucie and the doctor to be delivered after he is gone, he sets out.

Book 3. The Track of a Storm
Part 21 (September 17, 1859)
(III:1) Charles passes through barricades at each town as he moves closer to Paris. Finally he is forced to hire an escort to take him into the city. When they arrive at the walls of the city, he is addressed by the gatekeepers as "the prisoner" and is taken into custody. He asserts his status as a free man, but a recently passed law has made all émigrés felons. He is taken to La Force Prison and placed in a dungeon where many aristocrats are being held.

Part 22 (September 24, 1859)
(III:2) Tellson's in Paris is in Monseigneur's former house, the same building that now also serves as a kind of revolutionary headquarters. The Jacquerie have put a grindstone in the courtyard to sharpen their swords. Lorry, in Paris on bank business, looks into the courtyard with trepidation. After he thanks God that he has no friends in Paris, Lucie and Doctor Manette arrive and tell him that Charles is imprisoned in La Force. Lorry points out the revolutionaries in the courtyard to Manette, and the doctor goes to see what he can do for Charles. (III:3) Defarge appears at Tellson's with a letter from Charles to Lucie. He is accompanied by his wife and The Vengeance, her lieutenant. In Madame Defarge's presence, Lucie feels a shadow come over her. Lorry is troubled.

Part 23 (October 1, 1859)
(III:4) At first Manette believes he can get Charles released quickly. He manages to secure a hearing, but just as it looks as if Charles will be freed, the court changes its mind.

Manette becomes the doctor to the prisons. He can visit Charles, but cannot get him released. Working among the carnage for more than a year, the doctor realizes that his suffering has given him strength. (III:5) Manette tells Lucie of a spot on

the sidewalk outside a wood sawyer's yard where Charles can see her from a prison window. She stands there each afternoon as the sawyer, the former road mender, who calls his saw La Guillotine, torments her with his ritual of pretending the pieces of wood he cuts are heads. One wintry day she is on the corner as Madame Defarge and a revolutionary mob dance in the street doing the Carmagnole. She hides her eyes in horror. When she uncovers them, her father is there to tell her that Charles's trial is scheduled for the next day.

Part 24 (October 8, 1859)
(III:6) Darnay defends himself by telling how he gave up his French citizenship many years before in order to disown his family. He came back only to testify for Gabelle. The doctor testifies about Charles's life, ideas, and trial in England. Charles is released; he and his father-in-law are escorted home by a cheering mob. (III: 7) That evening the family plans a quiet celebration. While Pross and Jerry go out to get wine and food, four rough men in red caps appear at the door to arrest Evrémonde again, as he has been denounced by Citizen Defarge and his wife.

Part 25 (October 15, 1859)
(III:8) At the wineshop, Pross is startled to meet her brother Solomon, who is working as a spy in the prisons. Cruncher recognizes him as Barsad, the English spy, and Carton, who arrived secretly in Paris the night before, threatens to denounce Solomon to the tribunal. They know that he gave false testimony at Darnay's trial in London and that he helped fake the funeral of Roger Cly. Carton uses this knowledge to secure Pross's assistance.

Part 26 (October 22, 1859)
(III:9) Cruncher confesses to Lorry his other life as a resurrection man and says that the horrors he has seen in France have made him penitent.

Meanwhile, Carton makes a deal with Solomon Pross to have access to Darnay, and he asks that Lucie not be told of the arrangement. Then he walks the streets all night, stopping briefly to purchase some drugs. The next morning, he goes to the court and hears the announcement that Darnay has been charged by the Defarges and by Doctor Alexander Manette. Defarge describes how he found Doctor Manette's manuscript hidden in One Hundred and Five North Tower during the storming of the Bastille. An account of how he came to be imprisoned, the doctor's manuscript describes the crimes of the St. Evrémonde family.

Part 27 (October 29, 1859)

(III:10) Manette's narrative, written in prison in December 1767, is an account of Christmas week in 1757. On December 22, he was accosted by the St. Evrémonde twins, the Marquis St. Evrémonde, Charles's father, and his brother, who was later assassinated by Gaspard. They took the doctor to a house outside Paris to attend two patients. One was a young woman of 20 or so, pregnant and crazed. She kept repeating: "My husband, my father, and my brother!" Then she would count to 12 and say "Hush!" The other patient was her brother, dying from a stab wound inflicted by one of the twins. As he died he told Manette that his sister had become crazed after her husband, worked to death by the twins, died in her arms. Then she was sexually violated by the younger brother. Following her brother's death, she lived a week, attended by Manette. After the deaths of the two young peasants, the doctor was released by the St. Evrémonde brothers and allowed to return home. There he wrote an account of the events he had witnessed and sent it to a minister of the crown. Soon afterward he was imprisoned in the Bastille.

Manette's manuscript unlooses the fury of the court. Charles Darnay, the current Marquis St. Evrémonde, is sentenced to die within 24 hours.

Part 28 (November 5, 1859)

(III:11) After the courtroom empties, only the Manettes, Barsad, and Carton remain. Lucie is allowed one last embrace from Charles. Dr. Manette begins to kneel before them, as if to ask their forgiveness, but they prevent him. Charles acknowledges his fate as the inevitable end of his family's crimes. As he is taken away, Lucie faints onto her father's breast. Carton carries her to the coach and escorts her home. There he embraces little Lucie, urges Manette to do everything he can to save Charles, and admits to Lorry that he has lost hope.

(III:12) Carton goes to the wineshop in St. Antoine. There the Defarges observe how much he

looks like Darnay. He overhears Madame Defarge identify the violated peasant family in Manette's story as her own. She vows vengeance on Lucie, her daughter, and the doctor as well as on Charles. When the doctor returns from the prison, he has reverted to his shoemaker self. They know he has failed. Carton tells Lorry to prepare a coach to leave Paris the next afternoon at two.

Part 29 (November 12, 1859)

(III:13) Fifty-two people are scheduled to die in the group with Darnay. In his cell Charles accepts his impending death and writes letters to those he loves—to all except Carton. He dreams of being with Lucie. Shortly after noon on the day of the execution, Sydney Carton appears in Darnay's cell. Carton exchanges clothes with him and then, knowing that Darnay will resist, drugs him unconscious. Solomon Pross carries Charles away. Left behind, Sydney is led to the room where the condemned are waiting. He meets a seamstress there, and they plan to go the guillotine together. Outside the prison, the waiting carriage admits the drugged Darnay. As it passes through the checkpoints going out of Paris, Lucie worries that they are being pursued.

Part 30 (November 19, 1859)

(III:14) Madame Defarge plans to arrest Doctor Manette, Lucie, and little Lucie. She does not tell Defarge, for she thinks him softhearted about the doctor. Only Pross is at the Manette apartment when she arrives. Pross knows that the longer Madame Defarge thinks that Lucie is there, the more time Lucie and the others will have to escape, so she prevents Madame Defarge from looking into the rooms of the apartment. In the struggle between the two women, Madame Defarge is killed with her own pistol. Pross locks the apartment, drops the key in the river, and leaves Paris with Cruncher.

Part 31 (November 26, 1859)

(III:15) The tumbrils proceed to the Guillotine. In the back of the third wagon are Sydney and the seamstress, speaking to each other and paying no attention to the crowd. Madame Defarge has not arrived for the execution; The Vengeance calls for her. Sydney and the seamstress give each other

Sydney Carton and the seamstress on their way to the guillotine, in the 1958 movie adaptation of *A Tale of Two Cities. Courtesy of PhotoFest.*

strength. If Sydney could have written his thoughts as he went to the knife, he would have described a vision of the happy family that his sacrifice has preserved and the years to come of their lives together. "It is a far, far better thing that I do, than I have ever done; it is a far, far better rest that I go to than I have ever known."

COMMENTARY

Dickens wrote *A Tale of Two Cities* in weekly numbers to inaugurate ALL THE YEAR ROUND. A tale of revolution, it emerged from a revolutionary period in Dickens's own life when he separated from his wife, initiated the affair with ELLEN TERNAN, changed publishers, and began a new magazine.

Just as he had turned his personal life into public event by publishing the statement "Personal" about his marital breakup in HOUSEHOLD WORDS, so the novel sought to connect public and private events and to explain the FRENCH REVOLUTION in personal terms.

One of Dickens's favorite books was THOMAS CARLYLE's *The French Revolution* (1837), a history he had read many times. Carlyle's idiosyncratic and impressionistic work broke from the tradition of rationalist historiography and stressed the irrational aspects in the revolution, what he called the "daemonic" element. Dickens's intention was not to question Carlyle's history by turning it into fiction but rather "to add . . . picturesque means of understanding that terrible time." To achieve this end, he planned a very different kind of novel from those he was accustomed to writing. Instead of allowing the characters to generate the story, he "fancied a story of incident . . . pounding the characters in its own mortar, and beating their interest out of them" (FORSTER, 1872). This violent narrative strategy called for concentrated description, very limited dialogue, and a reliance on incident. The voice of the usual Dickensian narrator is subdued as the action itself takes precedence. Although Dickens relied on Carlyle's history for the incidents in his story and shared Carlyle's apocalyptic view of the revolution and its significance, he effaced his narrator, removing the voice of the prophetic interpreter who narrates Carlyle's account, to concentrate on the action itself.

The picturesque story Dickens planned to tell was one of extreme personal sacrifice. The idea of dying to save the life of a rival was suggested to him by WILKIE COLLINS's play THE FROZEN DEEP, in which the hero, RICHARD WARDOUR, discovers that one of his companions on an arctic expedition is his rival for the love of Clara Burnham. Overcoming his desire for revenge, he chooses instead to save the life of his rival, Frank Aldersley, and in the final scene he carries Frank to safety before dying himself. When playing Wardour in 1857, Dickens was deeply moved, especially by this final scene.

Dickens had developed similar themes in several of his stories, most notably in the sacrifices of Marion Jeddler, who gives up her fiancé to her sister (*Battle of Life*), and Gill Davis, who risks his life, inspired by his admiration and love for Marion Maryon ("English Prisoners"). But these characters had not been called upon to die. The French Revolution offered an extreme situation that made stories of such ultimate sacrifice believable. It was the same SETTING that inspired similar stories by WATTS PHILLIPS in *The Dead Heart* (1859) and EDWARD BULWER LYTTON in *Zanoni* (1842). As he contemplated his novel for the year and a half before he began writing, Dickens jotted down a series of possible titles, suggesting some of the themes that he planned to develop: *Buried Alive, Recalled to Life, The Thread of Gold, The Doctor of Beauvais, Memory Carton,* and *A Tale of Two Cities.*

Dickens's version of the French Revolution is "a picturesque story." Scenes like the breaking of the wine cask in the streets of St. Antoine (I:5); Darnay's English trial, resolved by his visual doubling with Sydney Carton (II:3); Cly's anarchic funeral procession (II:14); the murder and beheading of Foulon (II:22); and the frenzied dancing of the Carmagnole (III:5) concentrate history into vivid pictorial events. Murray Baumgarten ("Writing the Revolution," *Dickens Studies Annual,* 1983) has compared particular scenes in *Two Cities* with their counterparts in *The French Revolution* to show how Dickens made Carlyle's history visual.

Dickens's narrative is also filled with visual imagery. The cold-hearted Marquis is a man of stone whose face and philosophy are as inhuman as the stone faces that embellish his chateau. Images of natural catastrophe—of lightning, storms, floods, and earthquakes—communicate the inevitability of revolution. Christian images, especially of water and blood, foretell the transformation of Carton and prepare his sacrifice. Most pervasive, perhaps, are the contrasted images of darkness and light. Night journeys like the one that begins the story, darkened prison cells, the shadowy activities of Cruncher, and the nighttime labors of Carton are countered by visions of a bright heavenly city and, especially, by Lucie's thread of gold, which links the Manette circle in bonds of love and challenges the death-dealing threads of Madame Defarge's knitting.

The novel also includes some of Dickens's most quotable prose. The antitheses and repetitions of the opening paragraph, beginning with "It was the best of times, it was the worst of times," and Sydney Carton's closing speech as he goes to the guillotine are two of the best-known and most often quoted passages in all of Dickens's work.

In spite of its vivid pictorial scenes and quotable passages, *Two Cities* has received much unfavorable criticism. Carlyle called it "wonderful," but many of Dickens's contemporaries were less impressed. Sir James Fitzjames Stephen, offended by Dickens's justification of the revolution, if not its excesses, was prompted by the novel to write one of the most telling attacks on any Dickens work; he faulted the structure and style, but he was most annoyed by the exaggerations in Dickens's history, especially in his descriptions of the excesses of the French aristocracy. Modern critics, for different reasons, have also been unkind to the novel. They have praised its structure and plotting but decried its tedious characters and SENTIMENTALITY. The reservations of the critics, however, have not been shared by the broader popular audience. The novel has been a perennial best seller, not only because it does double duty for English and history teachers, but also for its moving story. The sacrifice that so engaged Dickens has also moved many of his readers, and the scenes describing Sydney Carton's final hours have lodged themselves in the popular memory.

The famous passages that open and end the novel suggest its character and appeal. The antitheses at the beginning—"It was the best of times, it was the worst of times, it was the age of wisdom, it was the age of foolishness, it was the epoch of belief, it was the epoch of incredulity, it was the season of Light, it was the season of Darkness. . . ." (I:1)—present a pattern of opposition that will explode into revolution. These unqualified antitheses establish the tone of inevitability that supports Dickens's historical theme: "Crush humanity out of shape once more, under similar hammers, and it will twist itself into the same tortured forms. Sow the same seed of rapacious license and oppression over again, and it will surely yield the same fruit according to its kind" (III:15). Ironically, the antitheses draw attention to the similarities between the two cities of the title, which, despite the suggestion that they are opposed, are essentially similar: "In both countries it was clearer than crystal to the lords of the State . . . that things in general were settled forever" (I:1).

The generalizing effect of the opening chapter introduces the abstract character of the novel. *Two Cities* is, after all, based on history. Its particular story is intended to show the inevitable consequences of oppression and carries an implicit warning to its English readers about the dangers of upper-class indifference to the plight of the poor. Thus, its plot embodies the inevitability of history, but the characters, even those based on actual persons, are representative figures. They are creatures of MYTH, and the novel is more an ALLEGORY than

a history. The Woodman Fate and the Farmer Death, who emerge at the end of the first chapter to visualize the theme of historical inevitability, are just the first of many allegorical figures. Monseigneur represents the French aristocracy, the many Jacques the oppressed peasantry. The very name St. Evrémonde carries the bilingual suggestion that its bearer is an "everyman," a representative of all the world.

Much in the personal story of Doctor Manette, his daughter Lucie, and her husband Charles Darnay, although intended to individualize these historical generalizations, is less interesting than the allegory. Dickens's decision to concentrate on incident rather than character made his actors pawns rather than complex figures. Lucie is identified by her resemblance to her mother, her golden hair, and the allegorical suggestion in her name, meaning light. Charles is simply a secret aristocrat turned into an earnest bourgeois. The most intriguing thing about him seems to be the connection of his initials to those of his creator. Doctor Manette, though he enacts a somewhat mechanical version of repressed memory, holds one of the keys to the novel, for buried in his memory—and in the manuscript hidden in the stones of the Bastille—is the myth that explains the revolution and opens up depths of character beyond the roles determined by history.

In what appears to be a kind of second beginning to the novel in the third chapter, Dickens defines the personal dimension of his story in the narrator's reflections on the theme of the buried life:

. . . every human creature is constituted to be that profound secret and mystery to every other. A solemn consideration, when I enter a great city by night, that every one of those darkly clustered houses encloses its own secret; that every room in every one of them encloses its own secret; that every beating heart in the hundreds of thousands of breasts there, is, in some of its imaginings, a secret to the heart nearest it! Something of the awfulness, even of Death itself, is referable to this. No more can I turn the leaves of this dear book that I loved, and vainly hope to read it all. No more can I look into the depths of this unfathomable water, wherein, as momentary lights glanced into it, I have had glimpses of buried treasure and other things submerged. . . . My friend is dead, my neighbour is dead, my love, the darling of my soul, is dead; it is the inexorable consolation and perpetuation of the secret that was always in that individuality, and which I shall carry in mine to my life's end. (I:3)

This passage introduces some of the thematic implications of Doctor Manette's story, that each individual has a buried life, forever unknown to others and perhaps even to himself. The passage also calls attention to a technical problem that Dickens faced. Because the truth about Manette is buried, he is incapable of revealing it, except in the somewhat mechanical performance of switching between his two personae. The manuscript that he has left buried in the wall of the Bastille seems inconsistent with the idea underlying his character, for it requires that he remember the traumatic events for at least a decade before repressing them into the depths of his consciousness. Doctor Manette represents an extreme example of the buried lives that many of the characters lead. Darnay has buried his French past, and Jerry Cruncher keeps secret his avocation as a resurrection man; even Mr. Lorry keeps his personal feelings from intruding into his business life.

The only character whose submerged depths complicate the surface of his personality is Sydney Carton. A diffident, self-denigrating man, Carton is one of Dickens's wastrels, like Harthouse (*Hard Times*), Henry Gowan (*Dorrit*), or Eugene Wrayburn (*Mutual Friend*). Self-hating, dissipated, and cynical, he finds nothing to value in life, but he does work at his profession as Stryver's legal devil, and he has occasional moments of vision when his suppressed self rises to the surface of his personality. In one such moment, Carton, after a night in Stryver's office, goes out into the city, which appears to him "like a lifeless desert," a projection of the "waste forces within him." Then he has a vision: "a mirage of honourable ambition, self-denial, and perserverance. In the fair city of this vision, there were airy galleries from which

the loves and graces looked upon him, gardens in which the fruits of life hung ripening, waters of Hope that sparkled in his sight. A moment and it was gone" (II:5). Called up from the depths of Carton's better self, this buried vision, along with his hopeless and self-denying love for Lucie, inspires his ultimate sacrifice.

The other "buried treasure" that *Two Cities* uncovers is Manette's manuscript, the "dear book" that reveals the depths of Manette's story and develops the myth that explains the revolution. That myth is a darkened version of the New Testament story, beginning at Christmas and ending with an Easter sacrifice, that explains the extreme violence of the revolution, the hysteria of Madame Defarge, and the need for Carton's sacrifice to "redeem the time."

The myth begins at Christmas 1757, when Doctor Manette is commandeered by the Marquis St. Evrémonde and his twin brother to attend two victims, a young man who has been stabbed in a sword fight with the Marquis and the wounded man's sister, whom the Marquis has raped. The Marquis is Charles Darnay's uncle; the victims are the brother and sister of Thérèse Defarge. Their deaths give birth to the cycle of violence that begins during that Christmas season and culminates in the revolution and Carton's sacrifice 35 years later. In this inversion of the gospel story, the rough beast that slouches to Paris to be born in 1757 is the vengeance of the peasantry provoked by the violence and class hatred of the ancien régime, which murdered Madame Defarge's brother and sister and buried the secret of the crime in the Bastille. Paris has become Babylon in the era of the beast; the self-indulgent brutality of the aristocracy and the resentment of the peasants foretells the revolution. Madame Defarge, an 18th-century sister to the Fates, symbolizes the inevitable vengeance to come as she knits her death list.

Both Paris and London are in the grip of the beast. In a mad parody of the Christian sacrament that turns wine into blood, the poor in the streets of St. Antoine write "Blood" on the wall with wine from the broken casks (I:5). In London, Jerry

Cruncher, a "resurrection man" with the same initials as Jesus Christ, performs a parody of the Easter story when he digs up Cly's grave only to find the tomb empty (II:14). The bloodlust that will drive the Jacquerie into the streets attends Darnay's trial in London, where the spectators take a ghoulish interest in his punishment: "he'll be drawn on a hurdle to be half hanged, and then he'll be taken down and sliced before his own face, and then his inside will be taken out and burnt while he looks on, and then his head will be chopped off, and he'll be cut into quarters" (II:1). In this latter-day, apocalyptic novel, the two cities of the title are not very different from one another.

On an allegorical level, the contrasting cities, as JOSEPH GOLD (1972) points out, are the Earthly City—represented by both Paris and London—and the City of God, the latter present in the novel in "the fair city" of Sydney Carton's visions, his earlier moment of epiphany in London repeated in Paris just before he goes to the guillotine. In his memorable final scene, cast as a vision of the future rather than an account of past and present, Carton imagines a city that will replace the two cities of the title: "I see a beautiful city and a brilliant people rising from this abyss, and, in their struggles to be truly free, in their triumphs and defeats, through long long years to come, I see the evil of this time and of the previous time of which this is the natural birth, gradually making expiation for itself and wearing out" (III:15). His self-sacrifice, which culminates this vision, the novel suggests, will break the hold of historical inevitability and start the process that will engender this "beautiful city."

Two Cities is memorable not because it makes history picturesque, but because it challenges the very idea of history. Carton's final scene replaces historical fact with vision and culminates the translation of history into myth. Dickens took many of the historical facts in his novel from Carlyle's *The French Revolution*, but his interpretation of "that terrible time" relies on a buried story, on the manuscript hidden in the wall of the Bastille by Doctor Manette and on the biblical story that breaks the hold of history with the sacrifice of a "truly free" individual. Carton's sacrifice provides the "Easter" ending to the novel's redemption myth.

Gold (1972) describes Carton's death as the culmination of Dickens's "translation of the Christian metaphysic into humanistic terms." Carton is drawn to the "loadstone rock" by his earthly love for Lucie, who has become the guiding light in his life, and by his vision of the beautiful city that will redeem the wasteland within him. Although before changing places with Darnay he meditates on the biblical promise, "I am the resurrection and the life, saith the Lord; he that believeth in me, though he were dead, yet shall he live: and whosoever liveth and believeth in me, shall never die," he is not really a Christ figure. He is more like the deeply flawed whiskey priest in GRAHAM GREENE's *The Power and the Glory* (1940), whose martyrdom arises from despair and an awareness of the darkness of his situation. A self-denigrating libertine, hopelessly in love with Lucie, Carton becomes an everyman in spite of himself. His vision of the future describes his blessedness as an immortality of influence on the Darnays and their descendants, who will remember his sacrifice. His final words state an optimistic challenge to historical fatalism, a challenge that may over time enable the two earthly cities to recover from the excesses of the best and the worst of times.

CHARACTERS AND RELATED ENTRIES

Barsad, John   Alias of Solomon Pross.

Beauvais, France   Birthplace of Doctor Manette and a stopping point on Charles Darnay's return journey to France (III:1, 10).

Carton, Sydney   The dissipated barrister who works as a researcher for Mr. Stryver. The "idlest and most unpromising of men," he lounges about the court "with his hands in his pockets, staring at the ceiling" (II:5). His physical resemblance to Charles Darnay enables Stryver to confuse the witnesses at Darnay's trial and secure his acquittal. Carton falls hopelessly in love with Lucie Manette and tells her that he "would embrace any sacrifice for you and for those dear to you" (II:13). His opportunity comes when Darnay, now her husband, is arrested in France and sentenced to execution. He uses his likeness to Darnay to change places with him in prison and take his place at the guillotine. As he goes to his death, Carton states the famous closing lines of the novel, "It is a far, far better thing that I do, than I have ever done; it is a far, far better rest that I go to than I have ever known" (III:15).

Carton's sacrifice, suggested by the similar sacrifice of Richard Wardour in *The Frozen Deep*, Wilkie Collins's play in which Dickens played the lead role, was the germ that inspired *A Tale of Two Cities*. For many Victorians, Carton was "one of the noblest characters in the whole literature of fiction" (Edwin Whipple, *Charles Dickens*, 1912), and his concluding moments were viewed as tragedy of the highest order. Many modern critics, however, have viewed the final pages of the novel as gross sentimentality. The linking of Carton's death with Christ's crucifixion, underlined by the repetition of "I am the Resurrection and the Life," such critics suggest, overstates the signifi-

Barnard's idealized portrait of Sydney Carton (1894).

cance of Carton's sacrifice. His death does nothing to change the course of the revolution; it merely serves to keep intact one relatively uninteresting bourgeois family. Carton is not really a Christ figure, such interpreters contend, for his death lacks the transforming power of the crucifixion. The best that Carton can hope for, his final vision suggests, is to have his story told to Lucy and Charles Darnay's descendants.

Cly, Roger   The former servant of Charles Darnay who gives questionable evidence against his employer at the trial in England (II:3). A petty thief, spy, and criminal associate of Barsad, Cly stages a sham funeral that enables him to escape the resentful mob (II:14). In Carton's final vision of the future, Cly is counted as one who dies by the guillotine (III:15).

Conciergerie   Ancient French prison in which Charles Darnay is held when Sydney Carton changes places with him (III:13).

Cruncher, Jeremiah (Jerry)   Messenger for Tellson's Bank and a "RESURRECTION MAN," one who takes bodies from graves and sells them as anatomical specimens. He has "stiff black hair, standing jaggedly all over" his head, "more like the top of a strongly spiked wall than a head of hair" (I:3). His sideline as a grave robber enables him to know that Roger Cly is not really dead (II:14). Despite his protestations that he is an "honest tradesman," his wife is distressed by his clandestine activities. When Jerry accompanies Mr. Lorry to Paris, the Reign of Terror so frightens him that he vows to give up his resurrection business and to be kinder to his wife (III:14). Although sometimes seen as a comic figure in a novel that contains little of Dickens's usual humor, Cruncher's abusive treatment of his wife and his role as a resurrection man is at best black comedy, a dark and disturbing inversion of the love and resurrection themes of the novel.

Cruncher, Jerry, Jr.   Jerry's look-alike son who spies on his father's grave robbing and wants to take up the same profession.

Cruncher, Mrs. Jerry's wife, whose evangelical fervor irritates her husband. He accuses her of being an "Aggerawayter" and objects to her "flopping herself down and praying agin me" (II:1).

Darnay, Charles The English name taken by Charles D'Aulnais, "a young man of about five-and-twenty, well-grown and well-looking, with a sunburnt cheek and a dark eye. His condition was that of a young gentleman" (II:2). Although he is heir to the title Marquis St. Evrémonde after the death of his father and the assassination of his uncle, Charles renounces his title and chooses to live in England and earn his living there as a teacher. Through the machinations of his servant Roger Cly and the influence of his uncle, Charles is tried for treason in London but acquitted because of his physical resemblance to Sydney Carton (II:3). He marries Lucie Manette, and they have a daughter, also named Lucie. During the revolution, he returns to France to testify for a family servant, Gabelle, and is himself arrested as an émigré. Through the efforts of Doctor Manette, he is released (III:6), only to be rearrested and convicted, largely on the basis of a manuscript condemning the St. Evrémonde family written by the doctor while he was in prison (III:10). Sydney Carton substitutes himself for Darnay in Darnay's prison cell, and Darnay returns with his wife and daughter to England.

Both French aristocrat and English bourgeois, Darnay links the two cities of the novel's title in a role largely determined by the plot. He is more acted upon than acting. He is tried in England on a trumped-up charge and acquitted by an accidental resemblance to Carton. His family ties bring about his imprisonment in France, despite his rejection of his title and citizenship.

His role as a double to Sydney Carton creates some interest in this otherwise colorless and impossibly good young man. He gains depth from the contradictions and complexities in Carton, so that the hero of the novel is probably best described as Darnay/Carton. Darnay's initials, C. D., the same as those of his creator, suggest Dickens's own psychic engagement with this doubled hero.

Defarge, Ernest A leader of the revolutionary Jacquerie, Defarge keeps a wineshop in the St. Antoine section of Paris, which is a center for revolutionary activity. Formerly a servant of Doctor Manette, he takes in the old man when he is released from prison. During the storming of the Bastille, he goes to the cell formerly occupied by Manette, One Hundred and Five North Tower, and finds the manuscript left there by the doctor (II:21) that will later be used to convict Charles Darnay (III:10). "A bull-necked, martial-looking man of thirty," identified in his revolutionary role as Jacques Four, "he was a dark man altogether, . . . good-humoured looking on the whole, but implacable-looking, too" (I:5). Unlike his wife, he shows some compassion for Doctor Manette and Lucie.

Defarge, Madame Thérèse Ernest's wife and partner in the wineshop, described by her husband as "a frightfully grand woman" (II:16), she symbolizes the ruthlessness and vengeance of the revolution. She is "a stout woman, . . . with a watchful eye that seldom seemed to look at anything," and she records the atrocities of the aristocracy by knitting them into a list that condemns them to the guillotine. More violent than her husband, she beheads the governor of the Bastille (II:21) and leads the mob of vengeful women at the execution of Foulon (II:22). Her thirst for vengeance is personal, a vendetta inspired by the rape and death of her sister and the murder of her brother by the Marquis, Darnay's uncle. Determined that none of the St. Evrémonde family shall live, she pursues Darnay's execution and attempts to detain Lucie before she flees from Paris, but when she arrives at the Darnay apartment all but Miss Pross have fled. In a struggle with Pross, Madame Defarge is killed by her own gun (III:14).

One of Dickens's most remembered iconic characters, Madame Defarge symbolizes Dickens's view of history and centers his mythic explanation of the origins of the revolution. Her unremitting thirst for vengeance expresses Dickens's own view that the oppression visited upon the French peasantry by the aristocracy inevitably led to revolutionary retribution. Her knitting, which alludes to the Fates in classic mythology who spin the thread of life and cut it off, symbolizes this inevitability. The story of her family's violation by the Evrémonde brothers individualizes this historical principle and grounds the revolution in a myth of sexual violation and murder.

Foulon A historical figure, Joseph-François Foulon (1715–89), a financier who was hated by the Jacquerie for asserting, "The people may eat grass" and was later assassinated. Dickens bases his description of Foulon's death on THOMAS CARLYLE's account in *The French Revolution.*

Gabelle, Théophile Postmaster in the village near the St. Evrémonde chateau. After the murder of the Marquis, Charles Darnay puts Gabelle in charge of some of the business affairs of the estate. When Gabelle is arrested by the revolutionary court, Darnay returns to France to testify for him and is arrested himself.

Gaspard French peasant whose child is run over and killed by the Marquis St. Evrémonde's carriage (II:7). He murders the Marquis (II:9) and is hanged for his crime (II:15).

George III The "King with a large jaw" described in the opening paragraphs of *Two Cities* who is on the English throne at the time of the French Revolution.

Jacques The name used by the revolutionaries, the "Jacquerie" connected with Monsieur Defarge, which identifies them as representatives of the revolutionary peasantry of France. Jacques Four is the epithet assumed by Defarge himself. Jacques Five is the road mender who watches the Marquis St. Evrémonde, reports on the imprisonment and death of Gaspard, and later becomes a wood sawyer in Paris.

Joe Coachman who drives Mr. Lorry from London to Dover (I:2).

King's Bench Walk An area in the Temple where Sydney Carton walks before going to his job at Stryver's office (II:5).

La Force Parisian prison in which Charles Darnay is incarcerated before he is taken to La Conciergerie.

Lorry, Jarvis A confidential clerk in Tellson's Bank, he served as Doctor Manette's financial advisor before his imprisonment. After Mrs. Manette died, he brought their two-year-old daughter Lucie to England, and he undertakes the mission to reunite the daughter with her father when Doctor Manette is "recalled to life" (I:2). He remains a close friend and adviser to the doctor. In Paris on bank business during the revolution, he assists the Manettes and brings Lucie and Charles back to England after Sydney Carton takes Darnay's place on the guillotine (III:13).

Although he claims to speak only as a man of business, repressing any personal feelings or opinions, he is a loyal friend to the Manettes and often acts from deep emotional commitment to them. In separating his business life from his personal feelings, Lorry foreshadows Wemmick of *Great Expectations.*

Manette, Doctor Alexandre French physician who becomes entangled in the revolution through his connections with the aristocratic St. Evrémondes and the revolutionary Defarges. In 1857, as a physician in Beauvais, he was taken by the Marquis St. Evrémonde and his twin brother and forced to attend to a peasant girl, who has been raped by the younger brother, and to the girl's brother, wounded while defending his sister's honor. After both patients died, the St. Evrémondes had the doctor thrown into the Bastille to keep him quiet (III:10). There he remained for 18 years. The novel begins when Manette is released from prison and "recalled to life." Lorry escorts 17-year-old Lucie, who has never seen her father, to Paris to bring the doctor back to England (I:2–6). The doctor, who has worked as a shoemaker in prison, is a confused and broken man who continues to work at his cobbler's bench: "He had a white beard, raggedly cut, but not very long, a hollow face, and exceedingly bright eyes. The hollowness and thinness of his face would have caused them to look large, under his yet dark eyebrows and his confused white hair, though they had been really otherwise; but, they were naturally large, and looked unnaturally so. His yellow rags of shirt lay open at the throat, and showed his body to be withered and worn. He, and his old canvas frock, and his loose stockings, and all his poor tatters of clothes, had, in a long seclusion from direct light and air, faded down to such a dull uniformity of parchment-yellow, that it would have been hard to say which was which. . . . He sat with a steadfastly vacant gaze" (I:6). He fails to recognize Lorry or his daughter, but her loving care and her physical resemblance to his wife, especially her golden hair, gradually restore him. When Lucie marries Charles Darnay, a French émigré in England, however, the doctor temporarily reverts to his prison occupation as a shoemaker on learning that Darnay is the nephew of the Marquis who had him imprisoned (II:18). Later, when Charles is arrested in Paris, Manette works to save him, but when a manuscript he wrote in prison condemning the crimes of the St. Evrémondes comes to light, Darnay is condemned to death (III:10).

A study of the psychological effects of trauma, Doctor Manette represses his memories of the past, leaving him a character divided between his physician self, active and capable of healing, and his shoemaker self, imprisoned and isolated from others. These two sides of Manette restate the double theme most fully developed in Charles Darnay and Sydney Carton. Manette is also a central figure in the conflict between fathers and sons, a theme discussed at length by LAWRENCE FRANK (1984), which leads to his becoming the inevitable, even if unwilling, voice that finally condemns Darnay to death.

Manette, Lucie   Doctor Manette's daughter. Born while her father is in prison and "orphaned" in infancy when her mother died, Lucie was taken by Jarvis Lorry to be raised in England. Years later, Lorry escorts her to Paris to bring the father she has never seen back to England (I:2–6): "a young lady of not more than seventeen, in a riding cloak and still holding her traveling-hat by its ribbon in her hand. As his eyes rested on a short, slight, pretty figure, a quantity of golden hair, a pair of blue eyes that met his own with an inquiring look, and

a forehead with a singular capacity (remembering how young and smooth it was) of lifting and knitting itself into an expression that was not quite one of perplexity, or wonder, or alarm, or merely of a bright fixed attention, though it included all the four expressions" (I:4). Lucie's resemblance to her mother, particularly her golden hair, awakens her father's memory of his wife, and Lucie's love and care restore his health, but when she marries Charles Darnay (II:18), her father temporarily reverts to his prison self on learning Darnay's identity as a St. Evrémonde. When her husband is imprisoned, Lucie and her daughter, also Lucie, go to Paris to seek his release. Madame Defarge goes to arrest them for execution as members of the St. Evrémonde family (III:14), but they are already on their way back to England. In Carton's final vision of the future, the Darnays have a second child, a son named Sydney.

Lucie, whose name means "light," stands as the opposite to the dark Madame Defarge. The "golden thread" of her love (and her hair)—in contrast to the death-dealing threads of Madame Defarge's knitting—reawakens her father's memories of his wife, inspires Carton's love and promise of service to her, and illuminates his visions of a beautiful city and a peaceful future. Although she has often been criticized as a vapid character, Glancy (A *Tale of Two Cities: Dickens's Revolutionary Novel*, 1991) points out her "strength, dedication, patience, and bravery" as qualities that form her healing power in the novel.

Manette, Madame   Lucie's English mother, who died when Lucie was just an infant. Lucie was then taken to England by Jarvis Lorry.

Pross, Miss   Lucie Manette's maid, a thoroughly loyal servant to her "Ladybird" who "beneath the surface of her eccentricity [is] one of those unselfish creatures—found only among women" (II:6). She accompanies Lucie to Paris, where she is surprised to meet her brother Solomon (also known as John Barsad), who is working as a spy in the French prisons. Earlier in the novel, as Barsad, he testified against Charles Darnay at the trial in London (II:3). At the end of the story, Miss Pross is in the Manette's apartment in Paris when Madame Defarge comes in search of Lucie. In the struggle between the two women, Madame Defarge's gun fires, killing its owner (III:14).

Pross, Solomon (aka John Barsad) Miss Pross's brother, "a heartless scoundrel who had stripped [Miss Pross] of everything she possessed, as a stake to speculate with, and had abandoned her in her poverty for evermore, with no touch of compassion" (II:6). As John Barsad, he works as a spy and gives false testimony at the English trial of Charles Darnay (II:3). Later, he aids in Roger Cly's sham funeral (II:14), enabling Cly to escape to France. In France, Barsad becomes a "Sheep of the Prisons," spying on those captive there. Carton, aware of Pross's crimes, is able to blackmail him into aiding in Darnay's escape from the guillotine.

Royal George Hotel Inn at Dover where Mr. Lorry meets Lucie Manette on their way to Paris to retrieve her father (I:4).

St. Antoine, Paris Poor district near the Bastille where Defarge's wineshop is located. Many in the mob of revolutionaries are recruited from the hungry and unemployed people who live here.

St. Evrémonde Three men qualify for the title of Marquis St. Evrémonde. Charles Darnay's father, the elder of twins, first holds the title. He abuses the peasants on his estate and aids his brother's scheme to abduct and rape the daughter of one of their tenants. When the girl's brother attempts to defend his sister's honor, he is wounded by the younger twin, and Dr. Manette is called in to tend the brother and sister. Both of the peasants die, the boy from his wound, the girl from brain fever (III:10). When the doctor later attempts to reveal the crimes of the St. Evrémondes, they have him imprisoned in the Bastille (III:10). After the death of Charles's father, the younger twin, Charles's uncle, becomes marquis. A tyrant "with a face like a fine mask, . . . very slightly pinched at the top of each nostril," he is murdered in his sleep after his carriage runs over a child in the streets of Paris (II:7–8). Although Charles Darnay renounces the title, he is tried and convicted by the revolutionary court as an émigré and as the current Marquis St. Evrémonde (III:9–10).

Symbolically, the St. Evrémondes, especially Charles's uncle, represent the oppressive aristocracy of the ancien regime, the social system in France prior to the Revolution. Their social position and power, exercised irresponsibly and without compassion, has hardened into stone. When the Marquis's carriage kills a child in the streets, he expresses concern only about the condition of his horses and offers a coin to compensate the child's distressed father. His abuse of Madame Defarge's sister and brother is "justified" by the laws of feudal privilege, which give the lord the power of life and death over his tenants. Similarly, an aristocrat could have someone imprisoned without charge or trial, as Doctor Manette is, simply by requesting such imprisonment. When Charles rejects his title, his uncle characterizes him as a radical espousing "the new philosophy" (II:9), which rejects these powers of the old regime.

seamstress "A young woman, with a slight girlish form, a sweet spare face in which there was no vestige of colour, and large widely opened eyes" (III:13), who accompanies Sydney Carton to the guillotine.

Stryver London barrister who defends Charles Darnay, "stout, red, bluff, and free from any drawback of delicacy" (II:4). He employs his old school friend Sydney Carton as his devil. He briefly considers proposing marriage to Lucie Manette but is dissuaded from doing so by Mr. Lorry (II:12).

Tellson's Bank The long-established bank in Fleet Street near Temple Bar for which Jarvis Lorry is a senior clerk and Jerry Cruncher a messenger. "It was very small, very dark, very ugly, very incommodious. It was an old-fashioned place, moreover, in the moral attribute that the partners in the House were proud of its smallness, proud of its darkness, proud of its ugliness, proud of its incommodiousness" (II:1). There is also a Paris branch where Lorry conducts business during the revolution.

Tom Coachman on the DOVER mail coach (I:2).

Eytinge's rendering of The Vengeance for an American edition of *A Tale of Two Cities*.

"Vengeance, The" Madame Defarge's chief associate among the female revolutionaries, a "short, rather plump wife of a starved grocer" (II:22). She personifies the ruling principle of Madame Defarge's life and of the Reign of Terror.

ADAPTATIONS

Although Dickens contemplated playing Sydney Carton on stage himself, he did not do so. The first production, which he authorized and supervised, opened at the Lyceum Theatre in London shortly after the novel completed its serial run. This production, with a script by Tom Taylor and starring Fred Villiers as Carton, had a successful run, even though it ended anticlimactically with the death of Madame Defarge rather than that of Carton. Another 1860 adaptation, *The Tale of Two Cities; or, The Incarcerated Victim of the Bastille,* changed the novel even more, ending with Sydney Carton's escape from the guillotine after

a second change of clothes, this time with Barsad, who replaces him under the knife. Although there were several later 19th-century productions, the most famous adaptation, described by MALCOLM MORLEY as the "most successful of all plays taken from Dickens," did not appear until 1899. With a script by two clergymen, Freeman Wills and Frederick Langbridge, commissioned by the actor John Martin-Harvey, this play, *The Only Way,* dominated the dramatizations of the novel for the first half of the 20th century. Martin-Harvey played Carton for 36 years on the stage in both England and America, as well as in a silent film version (1925). *The Only Way* was also the basis of the first television adaptation of the novel (1948). F. Dubrez Fawcett (*Dickens the Dramatist,* 1952) reports that Martin-Harvey played Carton, the role that defined his theatrical career, "as an intellectual study, and a psychological one, gradually revealing him with ever-increasing power till he held the audience spellbound."

Silent films derived from the novel appeared in 1908, 1911, 1917, 1920, and 1925. Two sound films have been produced: David O. Selznick's 1935 version, with Ronald Colman as Carton, and a 1957 British version (J. A. Rank), starring Dirk Bogarde and directed by Ralph Thomas.

The story was frequently adapted for radio in the 1940s and 1950s. Notable television productions include a 1958 adaptation for CBS with a cast including Agnes Moorehead and Denholm Elliott, CONSTANCE COX's 10-episode BBC adaptation (1965), and Pieter Harding's eight-part serial (1980), also for the BBC. A joint English/French television production made in 1989 for the anniversary of the revolution starred James Wilby as Carton, Xavier Duluc as Darnay, and JOHN MILLS as Lorry. The script by Arthur Hopcraft was directed by Philippe Monnier for Granada TV (Britain) and DUNE (France).

Susanne Alleyn's novel *A Far Better Rest* (2000) fills out the story of Sydney Carton, imagining his earlier life, which is not discussed in Dickens's novel.

FURTHER READING

The most thorough discussion of *Two Cities* as an example of a historical novel is by ANDREW SANDERS (1979); he compares the later novel with *Rudge* and discusses Dickens's fascination with the power of the mob.

Dickens's debt to THOMAS CARLYLE in the novel has been thoroughly explored by MICHAEL GOLDBERG (1972) and by William Oddie (*Dickens and Carlyle,* 1972), who provides a detailed listing of Dickens's borrowings from *The French Revolution.* Oddie also points to important differences between the two works, especially to the fatalism in Dickens's novel, which is not present in Carlyle's history.

SYLVÈRE MONOD (1968), the premier French scholar working on Dickens, praises Dickens's use of the two trial scenes to give structural symmetry to the story and his "conveying the emotions and evolutions of crowds and mobs," but he finds Dickens's history untrustworthy, the Anglo-French spoken by the French characters wearisome, and the story excessively pathetic and melodramatic.

JOSEPH GOLD (1972) offers a provocative reading of the mythic dimensions of the novel and of Dickens's use of Christian symbolism. Chris Brooks (*Signs for the Times,* 1984) interprets the novel, especially the resurrection theme, in light of Christian biblical typology. ALBERT D. HUTTER (1978) analyzes the generational conflict and its links to the revolutionary history in psychological terms. Ruth Glancy's *A Tale of Two Cities: Dickens's Revolutionary Novel* (1991) is an informative and intelligent general introduction.

Volume 12 of *Dickens Studies Annual* (1983) includes several articles discussing aspects of Carlyle's influence on the novel. A recent collection of essays edited by Michael A. Cotsell, *Critical Essays on Charles Dickens's A Tale of Two Cities* (1998), offers a wide range of critical perspectives on the novel.

Minor Works

"Address of the English Author to the French Public"

Dickens's preface to the French translation of *Nicholas Nickleby* by P. Lorain (1857). Uncollected.

"Agricultural Interest, The"

Article from the MORNING CHRONICLE (March 9, 1844) challenging the idea that those calling for repeal of the CORN LAWS were simply a conspiracy of manufacturers. Dickens identifies many other sectors of society calling for repeal. *Journalism.*

"American in Europe, An"

Dickens's review for the EXAMINER (July 21, 1849) of Henry Colman's *European Life and Manners, in Familiar Letters to Friends.* Dickens criticizes Colman's sycophantic fascination with the British aristocracy and his misrepresentations of English life, resulting from his concentration on the luxurious life at country estates. *Miscellaneous.*

American Notes for General Circulation

Dickens's account of his American journey in 1842, largely based on his letters to JOHN FORSTER. The Dickenses sailed from LIVERPOOL on January 3 and visited BOSTON, Springfield, HARTFORD, New Haven, NEW YORK, PHILADELPHIA, WASHINGTON, Fredericksburg, Richmond, BALTIMORE, HARRISBURG, PITTSBURGH, Cincinnati, LOUISVILLE, CAIRO (ILLINOIS), ST. LOUIS, LEBANON (Illinois; the LOOKING-GLASS PRAIRIE), Columbus, Sandusky, Cleveland, Erie, Buffalo, NIAGARA FALLS, Toronto, KINGSTON, MONTREAL, QUEBEC, Albany, West

Nast's frontispiece for an American edition of *American Notes* (1872–73) depicts the confrontation between Britain and America that angered many American readers of the book.

Point, and a Shaker settlement in LEBANON Springs (New York) before leaving for England from New York City on June 7.

Although Dickens made many friends on the tour, particularly among the literati of Boston, he found the public attentions of the Americans exhausting, and his speeches endorsing international COPYRIGHT alienated some of his American readers. His growing disillusion with America during the journey finds its way into *American Notes* in his critical remarks on the American press, sanitary conditions in the cities, slavery, and American manners, especially the practice of spitting in public. Ironically, *Notes* first appeared in the United States in a pirated version in the periodical *Brother Jonathan*. The book so angered some American readers that it was publicly burned at a theater in New York.

Characters and Related Entries

Britannia, The The steamship on which Dickens crossed the Atlantic on his way to America in 1842. After a sometimes rough and stormy crossing, the other passengers selected Dickens to present Captain Hewitt with an engraved plate commending his courage and competence during a hazardous journey (1).

Crocus, Doctor Scotch phrenologist on a lecture tour of America whom Dickens meets in Belleville, Illinois (13).

Pitchlynn Choctaw Indian chief, "a remarkably handsome man . . . with long black hair, an aquiline nose, broad cheek-bones, a sun-burnt complexion, and a very bright, keen, dark, and piercing eye," with whom Dickens discusses the decline of his people as they travel from LOUISVILLE, Kentucky, to ST. LOUIS (12).

Planter's House St. Louis hotel where Dickens stayed on his first American journey, "a large hotel . . . built like an English hospital" (12).

Tremont House "Very excellent" hotel in Boston where Dickens stayed during his 1842 visit.

Catlin's portrait of Pitchlynn, an Indian chief whom Dickens met on his American journey in 1842.

"It has more galleries, colonnades, piazzas and passages than I can remember, or the reader would believe" (2).

"American Panorama, The"

Article for the EXAMINER (December 16, 1848) recommending "the largest picture in the world," a three-mile long panorama of the MISSISSIPPI and Missouri rivers from New Orleans to Yellowstone by Mr. Banvard that was currently on display in PICCADILLY. *Miscellaneous, Journalism.*

"Amusements of the People, The"

Two-part article for HOUSEHOLD WORDS (March 30 and April 13, 1850) describing working-class theaters and arguing for their support and improvement. They should not be closed, Dickens argues much like Sleary in *Hard Times*, because "the people . . . *will be* amused somewhere." Viewing the exhibits at the Polytechnic Institution and reading are not reasonable substitutes for these melodramatic plays in working-class theaters and saloons. *Miscellaneous, Journalism.*

Characters and Related Entries

Whelks, Joe Representative working-class theatergoer in Dickens's descriptions of "The Amusements of the People."

"Another Round of Stories by the Christmas Fire"

Extra Christmas number of HOUSEHOLD WORDS, 1853. Dickens contributed "The Schoolboy's Story" and "Nobody's Story." Among the other contributors were Eliza Lynn, ADELAIDE ANN PROCTER, and GEORGE SALA.

"Appeal to Fallen Women, An"

Privately printed leaflet by Dickens (1850) in aid of the URANIA COTTAGE project to rescue prostitutes from the streets.

"Aspire"

Poem in HOUSEHOLD WORDS (April 25, 1851) urging the reader to affirm the power "in thyself alone . . . / Which strives to reach the light."

"Bardell and Pickwick"

Along with *A Christmas Carol*, this reading from *Pickwick* was the most popular of Dickens's PUBLIC READINGS. Dickens first performed this reading, also entitled "The Trial from Pickwick," in 1858.

"Bastille Prisoner, The"

A public reading from *A Tale of Two Cities* that Dickens prepared in 1861 but never performed.

"Best Authority, The"

In this article for HOUSEHOLD WORDS (June 20, 1857) Dickens describes his search for the Best Authority, a personification of the source for much of the gossip that is purveyed in London society. When he finally captures the person purported to be Best Authority, he turns out to be the narrator's cousin Cackles, "the most amiable ass alive." *Miscellaneous, Journalism.*

Characters and Related Entries

Cackles Cousin of the narrator of "The Best Authority," the "most amiable ass alive."

Flounceby An especially obstinate purveyor of gossip in "The Best Authority."

O'Boodleom Irish Member of Parliament who passes on information to the narrator from "The Best Authority."

Pottington Friend who challenges the narrator's news by appealing to "The Best Authority."

"Betting-Shops"

An article for HOUSEHOLD WORDS (June 26, 1852) describing the betting shops in London and some of their questionable practices. *Miscellaneous, Journalism.*

Characters and Related Entries

Cheerful Proprietor of a betting shop in the vicinity of the offices of HOUSEHOLD WORDS.

"Black Eagle in a Bad Way, A"

Description of the state of Vienna in 1851, divided by class differences, dominated by the presence of the military, and characterized as "the most inhospitable capitol in Europe." An article for HOUSEHOLD WORDS (November 22, 1851) written with E. C. Grenville Murray and Henry Morley. *Stone.*

"Blacksmith, The"

Poem celebrating "the iron Blacksmith," whose work shows "what A MAN can do." Published in ALL THE YEAR ROUND (April 20, 1859).

"Bob Sawyer's Party"

One of the most popular of Dickens's PUBLIC READINGS, based on chapter 32 of *Pickwick*.

"Boots at the Holly Tree Inn"

One of Dickens's PUBLIC READINGS, derived from the Christmas story for 1855, "The Holly-Tree Inn."

"Boys to Mend"

Article by HENRY MORLEY and Dickens for HOUSE-HOLD WORDS (September 11, 1852) on juvenile offenders, with an extensive description of the system of reformation employed at the Farm School at Red Hill in East Surrey. *Stone.*

"British Lion, The"

Satirical verses Dickens wrote for the DAILY NEWS in 1846, characterizing the old aristocratic order as a lion by repute that turns out to be a boar.

"Bundle of Emigrant's Letters, A"

Article for HOUSEHOLD WORDS (March 30, 1850) describing the efforts of Mrs. CAROLINE CHISHOLM—who became the model for Mrs. Jellyby in *Bleak House*—and the Family Colonisation Loan Society, to enable English working-class families to emigrate to the colonies. The article reprints the letters of several emigrants to Australia supplied by Mrs. Chisholm. *Stone.*

"By Rail to Parnassus"

Article for HOUSEHOLD WORDS (June 16, 1855) by Henry Morley and, perhaps, Dickens. It describes the imaginings of the narrator, prompted by reading LEIGH HUNT's *Stories in Verse,* as he rides on the train to Southampton on a dismal day for a job interview. The implicit praise it gives to Hunt may have been Dickens's way of making up for his portrayal of Hunt as Skimpole in *Bleak House. Stone.*

"Cain in the Fields"

Article by R. H. Horne for HOUSEHOLD WORDS (May 10, 1851) with some significant additions and revisions by Dickens. It describes several recent murders in the countryside, suggests the social conditions—ignorance, poor education, poverty—that prompt these murders, and attacks the barbarism of the public executions held in the countryside. *Stone.*

"Card from Mr. Booley, A"

Note in HOUSEHOLD WORDS (May 18, 1850) from Booley recognizing the contributions of several artists to the panoramas described in his earlier article, "Some Account of an Extraordinary Traveller." *Miscellaneous.*

"Cheap Patriotism"

A retired civil servant, Mr. Tapenham, tells of his experiences in the government bureaucracy and of the reforms that came with each new government. These reforms were, however, "cheap patriotism," for they always went after junior bureaucrats and never changed anything at the top of the department. Originally appeared in HOUSEHOLD WORDS (June 9, 1855). *Miscellaneous, Journalism.*

Characters and Related Entries

Baber Junior clerk in Tapenham's department who "represented the Turf, . . . made a book, and wore a speckled blue cravat and top-boots."

Fitz-Legionite, Percival One of the aristocratic junior members of Tapenham's government department.

Gritts, Right Honorable Mr. Member for Sordust whose administration of Tapenham's department is noteworthy for corrupt appointments.

James, Sir Jasper "Remarkable man of business" who is twice appointed with changes in govermnents to reform Tapenham's department.

Meltonbury Son of Lady Meltonbury, who used her influence to secure him a government job.

O'Killamollybore One of Tapenham's colleagues when he was a junior member of the government bureaucracy.

Random, Honorable Charles Lord Stumpington's official private secretary.

Scrivens Dandy who dresses like the Prince Regent and is a junior clerk in Tapenham's government department.

Stumpington, Lord Political appointee who takes over Tapenham's department with a change in government.

Tapenham Retired civil servant who narrates "Cheap Patriotism," describing the circumlocutions of the bureaucracy and the reforms that do not change anything.

Topham's frontispiece for the first volume of *A Child's History of England* (1852).

Child's History of England, A

Dickens's narrative history of England from its beginnings in 55 B.C. to the Glorious Revolution of 1688, written for children and published serially in HOUSEHOLD WORDS from January 25, 1851, to December 10, 1853, and issued in three volumes with frontispieces by F. W. TOPHAM in 1854. Based on Thomas Knightley's *History of England* (1839), Dickens's work is particularly Protestant—sympathetic to Cromwell while attacking Popish plots and Catholic kings like James I, who is called "his sowship." Dickens characterizes the rule of William and Mary, when the Protestant religion was estab-

lished in England, as the time when "England's great and Glorious Revolution was complete."

"Chinese Junk, The"

Article describing the junk anchored in the THAMES that offers Londoners an instant visit to China. From the EXAMINER (June 24, 1848). *Miscellaneous, Journalism.*

"Chips"

Corrections, additions, or clarifications to articles in HOUSEHOLD WORDS appeared under the rubric "Chips." Dickens was responsible for several such pieces in relation to "A Free (and Easy) School" (December 6, 1851), "'Household Words' and English Wills" (November 16, 1850), "The Samaritan Institution" (May 16, 1857), and "Small Beginnings (April 5, 1851). *Stone.*

"Chips: The Individuality of Locomotives"

A note on the individual peculiarities of railroad locomotives, calling for different ways of handling each of them. From HOUSEHOLD WORDS (September 21, 1850). *Journalism.*

Christmas Books

Dickens gave this title to the volume in the CHEAP EDITION collecting the five stories he had written for Christmas between 1843 and 1848: *A Christmas Carol* (1843), *The Chimes* (1844), *The Cricket on the Hearth* (1845), *The Battle of Life* (1846), and *The Haunted Man* (1848). Although later editions sometimes call them CHRISTMAS STORIES, Dickens used that title for the stories collected from Christmas numbers of HOUSEHOLD WORDS and ALL THE YEAR ROUND.

"Christmas in the Frozen Regions"

Article by Dickens and Robert McCormick, surgeon aboard the Antarctic expedition in 1834–43, describing Christmas on the expedition. For the Christmas number of HOUSEHOLD WORDS (December 21, 1850).

Characters and Related Entries

McCormick, Dr. Robert (1800–1890) Surgeon on the *Erebus* during Sir James Clark Ross's expeditions, described in his *Voyages of Discovery in the Arctic and Antarctic Seas, and Round the World* (1884). He described the Christmas celebration

aboard the *Erebus* for the Christmas number of HOUSEHOLD WORDS (1850), an article that Dickens edited and expanded.

Christmas Stories

Title given to collections of Dickens's stories for the Christmas numbers of HOUSEHOLD WORDS and ALL THE YEAR ROUND. Typically Dickens wrote a frame narrative and then invited other writers to submit stories fitting the frame. The collections include only the frame narratives and the stories that Dickens wrote, except for "No Thoroughfare," which he wrote with Wilkie Collins. The following stories were included in the CHARLES DICKENS EDITION and the LIBRARY EDITION: "The Seven Poor Travellers," "The Holly Tree," "The Wreck of the Golden Mary," "The Perils of Certain English Prisoners," "Going into Society," "The Haunted House," "A Message from the Sea," "Tom Tiddler's Ground," "Somebody's Luggage," "Mrs. Lirriper's Lodgings," "Mrs. Lirriper's Legacy," "Doctor Marigold," "Two Ghost Stories" ("To Be Taken with a Grain of Salt" and "No. 1 Branch Line: The Signalman"), "The Boy at Mugby," and "No Thoroughfare." Later editions added the rest of "Mugby Junction," "What Christmas Is as We Grow Older," "A Christmas Tree," "The Poor Relation's Story," "The Child's Story," "The Schoolboy's Story," "Nobody's Story," and "The Lazy Tour of Two Idle Apprentices." Stories included as *Christmas Stories* in this volume follow the contents for the OXFORD ILLUSTRATED EDITION.

"A CHRISTMAS TREE"

Dickens's essay for the Christmas number of HOUSEHOLD WORDS, 1850. As he looks at a Christmas tree, he remembers the Christmases of his childhood: the toys he played with, the toy theaters and the pantomime, fairy tales and Arabian Nights stories, and ghost stories told around the Christmas fire.

"WHAT CHRISTMAS IS AS WE GROW OLDER"

Essay for the Christmas number of HOUSEHOLD WORDS (1851), a meditation on the meaning of

Christmas. Though he begins by remembering the Christmases of his childhood and young manhood, Dickens focuses the essay on remembering, with gentle comfort and peaceful reassurance, those who have died.

"THE POOR RELATION'S STORY"

One of two contributions Dickens made to the Christmas number of HOUSEHOLD WORDS, 1852. Michael, the poor relation who narrates the story, tells his relatives a "castle-in-the-air" version of his life—his happy marriage to Christiana, his success in business with his partner John Spatter, and his affection for his cousin Little Frank. In fact, Michael is a penurious bachelor, living on the edge in Clapham Road after being defrauded by his business partner.

Characters and Related Entries

Chill, Uncle   Miserly uncle of Michael, the poor relation, who disinherits his nephew when he wants to marry a poor woman.

Christiana   Sweetheart of Michael, she gives him up when his Uncle Chill disinherits him.

Frank, Little   "A diffident boy," the young cousin that Michael imagines as his loving companion.

Michael   Narrator of "The Poor Relation's Story," who gives an idealized account of his life and suppresses the truth of his lonely poverty.

Snap, Betsy   Uncle Chill's housekeeper, "a withered, hard-favoured, yellow old woman."

Spatter, John   Business partner of Michael who defrauds him and steals their business.

"CHILD'S STORY, THE"

Allegorical story describing the journey of life from childhood to old age. One of Dickens's two contributions to *A Round of Stories by the Christmas Fire*, the Christmas number of HOUSEHOLD WORDS, 1852.

Characters and Related Entries

Fanny   "One of the prettiest girls that ever was seen," sweetheart of the narrator as a young man.

"SCHOOLBOY'S STORY, THE"

One of Dickens's contributions to the Christmas number of HOUSEHOLD WORDS, 1853, *Another Round of Stories by the Christmas Fire*. It tells of Old Cheeseman, a former student and master at the school who had been neglected as a child and exploited as a master, but he becomes a benefactor to the boys when he inherits a fortune. Then he marries Jane Pitt, his loyal friend in his school days. This story was one of Tennyson's favorites among Dickens's works.

Characters and Related Entries

Cheeseman, Old   Subject of "The Schoolboy's Story." He had been a student at the school who was left there, like Scrooge, to spend the holidays alone. Then he had been hired as second Latin master and was considered a traitor by the other boys, who organized a society to torment him. But when he inherits a fortune and is kind to the boys, they change their mind about him.

Pitt, Jane   Only friend of Old Cheeseman the Latin master. "Uncommonly neat and cheerful, and uncommonly comfortable and kind," she eventually marries him.

Tartar, Bob   President of the Society of Schoolboys, the group that decides to torment Old Cheeseman as a traitor. Tartar was thought to be the son of a wealthy West Indian planter.

"NOBODY'S STORY"

One of two stories that Dickens wrote for the Christmas number of HOUSEHOLD WORDS, 1853, this allegorical tale describes the suffering of Nobody and his oppression by the Bigwigs, who blame him for social ills.

Characters and Related Entries

Bigwig family   The "stateliest" family, devoted to ruling those beneath them.

Nobody   The hero of "Nobody's Story," a representative of the ordinary working person.

"SEVEN POOR TRAVELLERS, THE"

Christmas number of *HOUSEHOLD WORDS*, 1854. Dickens wrote the opening chapter, in which the narrator becomes a seventh traveler at Watts's Charity and provides a dinner for the six travelers stopping there for the night. After supper the travelers tell stories; the narrator's is "The Story of Richard Doubledick." In the concluding chapter, also by Dickens, the narrator takes leave of the travelers and walks from ROCHESTER to GREENWICH, meditating on the significance of Christmas.

Characters and Related Entries

Watts, Richard   Founder, in 1579, of the ROCHESTER charity that provides a bed and fourpence for six travelers each night.

"STORY OF RICHARD DOUBLEDICK, THE"

After being jilted, Richard Doubledick joins the army and is redeemed from a life of dissipation by Captain Taunton, an officer to whom he becomes a loyal friend and comrade-in-arms during the Napoleonic campaigns. When Taunton is killed, Doubledick vows to kill the French officer responsible for his death, but he is wounded, reunited with his love, and, through the influence of Taunton's mother, learns to love his enemies, including the French officer.

Characters and Related Entries

Doubledick, Richard   Young man who joins the army after being jilted and is saved from a life of dissipation by his commanding officer. After the death of his officer, he is restored to the woman he loved by the mother of his officer friend.

Exmouth   Town in Devon where Richard Doubledick was born.

Frome   The quiet town in Somerset where Dick Doubledick goes to tell Mrs. Taunton that her son has died at Badajoz.

Marshall, Mary   Richard Doubledick's sweetheart, who jilts him and then marries him many years later, after he has been wounded in battle and is near death in Brussels.

Taunton, Captain   Richard Doubledick's officer and comrade-in-arms, who saves him from a life of dissipation. After Taunton is killed in battle, Doubledick visits Mrs. Taunton, the Captain's mother, learning from her to love his enemies.

"HOLLY-TREE, THE"

The Christmas number of *HOUSEHOLD WORDS* for 1855. Dickens wrote three parts of this five-part story, retitling them "The Holly Tree: Three Branches" when he reprinted them in *CHRISTMAS STORIES*. "The Guest" tells of Charley, a jilted lover, who gets snowed in at the Holly Tree Inn on his way to LIVERPOOL to sail for AMERICA. He spends his time there remembering stories about the many inns where he has stayed. In the second section, Cobbs, the boots of the inn, tells Charley "The Boots," a story of two children, Harry Walmers and Norah, who try to elope to GRETNA GREEN. In "The Bill," Charley learns that he has not been jilted, and he is reunited with his sweetheart.

Characters and Related Entries

Charley   Bashful narrator of "The Holly Tree" who, thinking himself jilted by Angela Leath, sets off for AMERICA, but he gets snowed in at the Holly Tree Inn on the way and there learns that Angela really loves him.

Cobbs   Boots at the Holly Tree who tells Charley, the narrator, the story of Master Harry Walmers and Norah.

Edwin   Charley's schoolmate and his supposed rival for the affections of Angela Leath. They meet at the Holly Tree Inn when Edwin is on his way to GRETNA GREEN to marry Angela's cousin Emmeline.

Emma   The waitress "with the bright eyes and the pretty smile" at an English angler's inn.

Emmeline   Angela Leath's cousin, a young woman of property who elopes with Edwin. They marry and have seven children.

George Guard on the coach that Charley takes to the Holly Tree Inn.

Henri Employee of a Swiss Inn who disappeared during the night and turned out to have been murdered, in Charley's memories of inns where he has stayed.

Holly Tree Inn, the Inn on the Yorkshire moor that is the setting for "The Holly Tree." It is thought to be based on the George and New Inn in Greta Bridge, where Dickens had stayed in 1838.

Leath, Angela Fiancée of Charley, the bashful narrator of "The Holly-Tree." When he thinks she has left him for his friend Edwin, Charley plans to run off to America, but he learns that she has not jilted him and they are reunited and married, becoming the parents of eight children.

Louis Employee of a Swiss inn who murdered Henri, a fellow employee who discovered him stealing from their employer, in Charley's memories of inns where he has stayed.

Norah Harry Walmer's seven-year-old cousin with whom he elopes, intending to go to GRETNA GREEN. As an adult she marries an army captain and dies in India.

Walmers, Harry Eight-year-old gentleman whose elopement with Miss Norah is the subject of a tale told by Cobbs, the boots of the Holly Tree Inn. Harry is the only son of Mr. Walmers of the Elmses, Cobbs's former employer.

"THE WRECK OF THE *GOLDEN MARY*"

Christmas number of *HOUSEHOLD WORDS*, 1856. Dickens wrote the opening chapter describing the *Golden Mary*, a ship on its way from Liverpool to California that is rammed by an iceberg off Cape Horn. The passengers, led by Captain Ravender, survive 27 days in lifeboats before being rescued, but during that time a child, Lucy Atherfield, dies. WILKIE COLLINS collaborated with Dickens on the mate's narrative in this opening chapter and also wrote the final chapter, "The Deliverance,"

describing the rescue. Other writers contributed interpolated tales to the number.

Characters and Related Entries

Atherfield family Mrs. Atherfield and her daughter Lucy are passengers on the GOLDEN MARY, the ship that collides with an iceberg. Lucy dies at sea after they abandon ship.

Coleshaw, Miss Passenger on the *Golden Mary* who is on her way to California to join her brother.

Golden Mary Cargo ship carrying emigrants bound for California that collides with an iceberg and sinks off Cape Horn.

Mullion, John Brave member of the crew of the *Golden Mary*.

Rames, William Second mate of the *Golden Mary*.

Rarx "A sordid and selfish" passenger on the *Golden Mary* who is obsessed with gold and loses his mind after the wreck.

Ravender, William George The courageous captain of the *Golden Mary*, who saves many of his passengers but dies himself in the effort.

Smithick and Watersby LIVERPOOL ship owners of the *Golden Mary*, who hire Ravender to sail the ship to California.

Snow, Tom Captain Ravender's black steward.

Steadiman, John Chief mate of the *Golden Mary*, "aged thirty-two, . . . a perfect sailor," who takes command when Captain Ravender dies.

"THE PERILS OF CERTAIN ENGLISH PRISONERS"

Christmas number of *HOUSEHOLD WORDS*, 1857. Dickens wrote chapters 1 and 3, WILKIE COLLINS, chapter 2. The story is narrated by Gill Davis, a private in a Royal Marine detachment dispatched to the English colony on Silver-Store Island to deliver supplies and bring out the annual production of silver from the mines in Honduras, which is stored on the island. Aided by a native turncoat, Christian George King, a band of pirates attack the island, divide the residents and the soldiers, kill many of the colonists and take the rest prisoner, and abscond with the silver. The prisoners are taken into the interior of Honduras and eventually, under the heroic leadership of Davis, manage to escape and reunite with their British protectors.

Characters and Related Entries

Carton, Captain George Commanding officer of the expedition to Silver-Store Island. He leads the expedition against the pirates and shoots Christian George King. He marries Marion Maryon and later becomes Admiral Sir George Carton, Bart.

Charker, Corporal Harry Gill Davis's comrade-in-arms who is killed in the battle to protect the colony of Silver-Store Island from pirates. "He had always one most excellent idea in his mind. That was, Duty."

Davis, Gill Illiterate retired private in the Royal Marines who narrates "The Perils of Certain English Prisoners" to Lady Carton, one of the former colonists whom he has been instrumental in rescuing from the pirates on Silver-Store Island. A poor and ignorant man, he envies the comfortable life of the colonists, but his admiration and love for Marion Maryon prompts his heroic efforts on their behalf. He tells the story late in his life when he has become a "poor, old, faithful, humble" retainer of Lord and Lady Carton.

Drooce, Sergeant Royal Marine Sergeant on the expedition to Silver-Store Island, "the most tyrannical non-commissioned officer in His Majesty's service."

Fisher, Mr. and Mrs. Fanny Members of the English colony on Silver-Store Island who are attacked and taken captive by pirates. At the end of the story they are reunited with their child, who they thought had been killed in the raid.

King, Christian George Native pilot of the sloop *Christopher Columbus* who betrays the colonists to the pirates. He is shot by Captain Carton.

Kitten Vice-commissioner at Silver-Store Island, "a small, youngish, bald, botanical and mineralogical gentleman."

Linderwood, Lieutenant Officer in command of the 24 Royal Marines dispatched to Silver-Store Island who is ill when they arrive at the colony.

Macey, Mr. and Mrs. A mine owner and his wife who are residents on Silver-Store Island. Mrs. Macey is the sister of Marion Maryon.

Maryon, Captain and Marion Commander of the sloop *Christopher Columbus* on the expedition to Silver-Store Island, Captain Maryon is taken ashore ill when they arrive at the island. His sister Marion, one of the colonists and the "life and spirit of the Island," acts heroically during the pirate attack. Although Gill Davis loves and admires her, she is far above him in social station. She marries Lord Carton, and Gill becomes one of the family retainers.

Packer, Tom Private in the Royal Marines who fights against the pirates invading the Silver-Store colony.

Pordage, Mr. Commissioner Representative of the British government on Silver-Store Island, "a stiff-jointed, high-nosed old gentleman, without an ounce of fat on him, of a very high temper and a very yellow complexion. Mrs. Commissioner Pordage, making allowance for difference of sex, was much the same." He becomes governor of the island and a KCB.

Silver-Store A British colony on an island off the Mosquito Coast of Honduras, established as a "safe and convenient place" to store the silver taken from mines on the mainland.

Snorridge Bottom Town between Chatham and Maidstone that is Gill Davis's hometown.

Tott, Mrs. Isabella ("Mrs. Belltott")   One of the colonists on Silver-Store Island, widow of a non-commissioned officer. "A little saucy woman, with a bright pair of eyes. . . . The sort of young woman, I considered at the time, who appeared to invite you to give her a kiss, and who would have slapped your face if you accepted the invitation."

Venning, Mrs.   A British colonist on Silver-Store Island, Fanny Fisher's mother. She is murdered by pirates during the raid.

"GOING INTO SOCIETY"

Dickens's story for *House to Let*, the Christmas number of *HOUSEHOLD WORDS*, 1858. Toby Magsman, former tenant of the house to let and proprietor of Magsman's Amusements, tells of Mr. Chops, a performing dwarf, who won the lottery and left the show to go into society. After spending all his money, he learned that society is itself a kind of sideshow, and he returned to the show and died soon after.

Characters and Related Entries

Chops   Dwarf in a sideshow whose real name is Stakes and who performs as Major Tpchoffki of the Imperial Bulgraderian Brigade. After he wins £12,500 in a lottery, he goes into society, fulfilling a lifelong ambition, but he learns that performing in society is no different from performing in a sideshow, so he returns to the show, where he dies.

Jarber   The man who reads aloud the story "House to Let."

Magsman, Robert (Toby)   Proprietor of the sideshow where Mr. Chops the Dwarf performs, "a grizzled personage in velveteen, with a face so cut up by varieties of weather, that he looked as if he had been tattooed"; the narrator of "Going into Society."

Normandy   Gaming booth operator and con man, with "a very genteel appearance," who goes into society with Chops and ruins him.

Stakes   Real name of Mr. Chops, the dwarf.

Tpschoffki, Major   Professional name of Chops, the dwarf.

Trottle   Member of the group listening to the story of Mr. Chops, the dwarf.

"THE HAUNTED HOUSE"

Christmas number of *ALL THE YEAR ROUND*, 1859. Dickens wrote two of the eight chapters, "The Mortals in the House" and "The Ghost in Master B.'s Room." John, the narrator of the story, rents a house in the north of England, even though he is told that it is haunted. After all of his servants are frightened away by various supernatural happenings and their own imaginings, he invites a group of his friends to spend the Christmas season in the house with him. They plan to share their supernatural experiences at the close of their stay. John takes Master B.'s room and there encounters the ghost of "my own childhood, the ghost of my own innocence, the ghost of my own airy belief," as he remembers the innocent re-creation of Haroun Alraschid's seraglio he enacted with his schoolmates and the traumatic death of his father.

Characters and Related Entries

B., Master   Ghost in the haunted house, a projection of the lost youth of John the narrator.

Bates, Belinda   One of the guests in the haunted house, "a most intellectual, amiable and delightful girl, . . . [who] 'goes in' . . . for Women's mission, Women's rights, Woman's wrongs, and everything that is woman's with a capital W."

Beaver, Nat   A sea captain, with "a world of watery experiences in him," and a guest in the haunted house.

Bottles   John's stableman, "a phenomenon of moroseness not to be matched in England," whose deafness makes him untouched by the ghosts in the house.

Bule, Miss   A girl of eight or nine, the leading lady in John's memories of his childhood "seraglio" at Miss Griffin's School.

Doylance, Old   John's former schoolmaster.

Goggle-eyed Gentleman   Madman on the train that John the narrator takes to the north.

Governor, Jack   One of the visitors to the haunted house and an old friend of the narrator, "a portly, cheery, well-built figure of a broad-shouldered man, with a frank smile, a brilliant dark eye, and a rich dark eyebrow."

Greenwood   One-eyed tramp who has seen the ghost in the haunted house. His name is Joby, but he answers to Greenwood.

Griffin, Miss   Principal of the school where John the narrator had secretly played Haroun Alraschid as a child: "We knew Miss Griffin to be bereft of human sympathies."

Herschel, John   Cousin of the narrator of "The Haunted House." He and his wife are part of the group assembled to investigate the hauntings.

Ikey   Stableboy at the inn near the haunted house.

Joby   One-eyed tramp also known as Greenwood.

John   Narrator and lessee of the Poplars, the haunted house where he gathers his friends together.

"Mesrour"   Name given to Tabby by the children engaged in the seraglio fantasy.

Odd Girl, the   City girl whose first visit to the country is to the haunted house.

Patty   Spinster sister of the tenant of the haunted house.

Perkins   Resident of the village near the haunted house who "wouldn't go a-nigh the place."

Pipson, Miss   "Fair Circassian" at Miss Griffith's school and a member of John's "seraglio."

Poplars, the   Haunted house in the north of England rented by John, the narrator of the story.

Starling, Alfred   Financially independent young man "who pretends to be 'fast'"; one of John's guests at the haunted house.

Streaker   Housemaid at the haunted house, capable of producing "the largest and most transparent tears."

Tabby   Serving drudge at Miss Griffin's school.

Turk   John's pet bloodhound. Dickens owned a bloodhound with the same name.

Undery   A solicitor who is one of those assembled at the haunted house. His name plays on that of Dickens's own solicitor, FREDERIC OUVRY.

"A MESSAGE FROM THE SEA"

Christmas number of ALL THE YEAR ROUND, 1860. Dickens and WILKIE COLLINS wrote the first, second, and fifth chapters. The story tells of Captain Jorgan, who brings a message in a bottle to Alfred Raybrock in the fishing village of Steepways in north Devon. The message, from Alfred's brother Hugh, seems at first to interfere with Alfred's planned marriage, but eventually it restores the lost brother, clears the bride's father of a robbery charge, and facilitates the marriage.

Characters and Related Entries

Barnstaple, Devon   Coastal town at the mouth of the Taw Estuary in north Devon; setting of "A Message from the Sea."

Clissold, Lawrence   Clerk who embezzles £500 from his employer and lays the blame on Tregarthen.

Dringworth Bros.   Firm in America Square, London, that employs Tregarthen and Clissold.

Jorgan, Captain Silas Jonas   Native of Salem, Massachusetts, "American born . . . but he was a citizen of the world," who finds Hugh Raybrock's message.

Parvis, Arson Resident of Lanrean.

Penrewen Old resident of the village of Lanrean.

Pettifer, Tom Captain Jorgan's steward whose hat contains the papers that explain the message from the sea.

Polreath, David Elderly resident of Lanrean.

Raybrock family Family in Steepways burdened with a long-standing suspicion of guilt and loss. Mrs. Raybrock, draper and postmistress of the village, believes her eldest son Hugh lost at sea, but when Captain Jorgan brings a message from him found in a bottle, the family is rescued from disgrace. The message enables Hugh's younger brother Alfred to marry Kitty Tregarthen. They have an infant son Jorgan. Hugh also returns to his wife Margaret and his daughter.

Steepways Fictional name for Clovelly, a seaside village in Devon that steps down a steep hillside to the sea.

Tredgear, John Resident of Landrean.

Tregarthen, Kitty Fiancée of Alfred Raybrock. Their marriage is made possible by the message from the sea, which clears Kitty's father from complicity in the embezzlement committed by Lawrence Clissold.

"TOM TIDDLER'S GROUND"

Christmas story for ALL THE YEAR ROUND, 1861. Dickens wrote the frame chapters and one of the stories, "Picking Up Miss Kimmeens." A Traveller comes to a remote rural village to visit Mopes the Hermit, who is said to be a miser who leaves coins about his property for passersby to pick up. When the Traveller gets to Mopes's ruined homestead, however, he finds a misanthropic man, dirty and surly, who justifies himself as a model of misanthropy. The Traveller, refusing to be intimidated by him, calls him "a Nuisance" and promises to show him that "every man must be up and doing, and that all mankind are made dependent on one another." Several passersby prove that humans are social beings, including the lonely child Miss Kimmeens, who ventures onto Tom Tiddler's ground in search of human contact.

Characters and Related Entries

Bella Miss Pupford's housemaid who leaves Miss Kimmeens by herself.

Kimmeens, Kitty Pupil of Miss Pupford who, left alone at Miss Pupford's school, seeks out human contact and comes upon the Traveller, who takes her to Tom Tiddler's Ground.

Linx, Miss "Sharply observant" pupil in Miss Pupford's Lilliputian College.

Mopes Dirty, indolent, and surly hermit visited by the Traveller, Miss Kimmeens, and the Tinker at his decayed and ruined homestead, Tom Tiddler's ground. The Traveller tries to counter his misanthropy by proving to him that people must work and depend on each other. Dickens based the character on James Lucas, the notorious Hertfordshire Hermit, who attracted many visitors, including Dickens, to the family mansion at Stevenage where he barricaded himself away from the world outside.

Peal of Bells, the Village alehouse where Mr. Traveller stays.

Pupford, Miss Euphemia Principal of the Lilliputian College attended by Miss Kimmeens.

Tinker A wanderer resting on Tom Tiddler's ground who, like the Traveller, refuses to take Mopes's misanthropy seriously.

Traveller, Mr. Narrator of "Tom Tiddler's Ground," he has come to visit the misanthropic Mopes with the intent of proving that human beings need one another.

"SOMEBODY'S LUGGAGE"

Christmas number of ALL THE YEAR ROUND, 1862. Dickens wrote the frame chapters, narrated by

Christopher, a hotel waiter who acquires some luggage left by a former guest to the hotel. In the luggage he discovers some manuscripts, which he submits for publication. When the stories are about to be published, the owner of the luggage, an aspiring author who had no luck in placing his work, returns to the hotel and is so overjoyed to learn that the stories are in print that he gives Christopher £20. Dickens also wrote two of the stories. The first, "His Boots," tells of Langley, an Englishman who retreats to the French village of Vauban to forget a daughter that he has disowned. There he observes the love of Corporal Théophile for the orphan child Bebelle. When the corporal is killed in a fire, Langley adopts the child and forgives his daughter. The narrator of the second story, "His Brown-Paper Parcel," is a sidewalk artist who is so diffident and antisocial that he hires others to pretend that his work is theirs.

Characters and Related Entries

Baptiste Soldier billeted on the poor water carrier in the French town where Langley, the misanthropic Englishman, stays.

Bebelle Pet name of Gabrielle, the orphan girl loved and cared for by Corporal Théophile and later adopted by Langley.

Bishops Older waiter who acts as a mentor to Christopher as he learns the trade.

Bouclet, Madame Langley's French landlady, "a compact little woman of thirty-five or so." Her husband, Monsieur Bouclet, is "great at billiards."

Charles, Old Waiter in a West Country Hotel, by some considered the "Father of Waitering."

Christopher Sixty-one-year-old waiter who "comes from a family of Waiters"; he narrates "Somebody's Luggage." He acquires some luggage left by a hotel guest, discovers some manuscripts in the bags, and gets them published.

Click Gas-fitter and fellow lodger of the sidewalk artist who narrates "His Brown-Paper Parcel."

Cour, Capitaine de la Commander of the soldiers stationed in Vauban, the French village where Langley goes.

Dick The name by which Christopher's father is known.

Emile The soldier billeted at the clock maker's in the French town where Langley goes.

Eugène Solder billeted at the tinman's in the French town where Langley goes.

Gabrielle Orphan known by her pet name, Bebelle.

Henrietta Sweetheart of Tom, the pavement artist, who agrees to "walk" with him "on the understanding that softer sentiments may flow." She does not know that Tom is the artist who created the pictures on the pavement in PICCADILLY that she admires. When Tom criticizes the impostor who claims the pictures as his own, Henrietta rejects him. She later marries the impostor.

Hyppolite, Private Soldier billeted at the perfumer's in Vauban.

Joseph Head waiter at the Slamjam Coffee-house.

La Cour, Capitaine de French officer billeted at Madame Bouclet's.

Langley (M. L'Anglais or "Mr. The Englishman") English visitor who has come to the French town of Vauban to forget the daughter he has rejected. While he is there he watches Corporal Théophile, a soldier stationed in the town, as he loves and cares for a small orphan girl, Bebelle. When the corporal is killed in a fire, Langley adopts the child and forgives his daughter.

Martin, Miss Bartender and bookkeeper at the hotel where Christopher works.

Mutuel, Monsieur "A spectacled, snuffy, stooping old gentleman" with a "walnut-shell countenance" who is a friend of Madame Bouclet and is pleased by Langley's generous act in adopting Bebelle.

Pratchett, Mrs. Head chambermaid in the hotel where Christopher, the narrator of "Somebody's Luggage," works. Her husband is in AUSTRALIA in "the Bush."

Théophile, Corporal French soldier in Vauban who lovingly cares for the orphan Bebelle. After Théophile is killed in a fire, Langley finds the child lying on his grave.

Tom Sidewalk artist who narrates "His Brown-Paper Parcel."

Valentine, Private Orderly to Captaine de la Cour, the "sole housemaid, valet, cook, steward, and nurse in the family of his Captain."

Vauban French village where Langley goes and discovers the orphan Bebelle.

"MRS. LIRRIPER'S LODGINGS"

Christmas number of ALL THE YEAR ROUND, 1863. Dickens wrote the first chapter, in which Mrs. Lirriper tells of her 38 years as a lodging-house keeper, of the servants she has employed, and of her adopted son, Jemmy, whose mother died shortly after giving birth to him in the lodging house. She and her parlor boarder, Major Jackman, raised the boy. In the final chapter, also by Dickens, Jackman tells of Jemmy's achievements and retells Jemmy's story, the boy's fictional account of his life.

Characters and Related Entries

Betley One of Mrs. Lirriper's first lodgers.

Bobbo The best friend of the hero of Jemmy's story, "the cleverest and bravest and best-looking and most generous of all the friends that ever were."

Edson One of Mrs. Lirriper's lodgers who deserts his pregnant wife, Peggy. She dies shortly after, and Mrs. Lirriper adopts their infant son. Years later,

Mrs. Lirriper takes the boy to France, where he meets his father on his deathbed.

Jackman, Major Jemmy Mrs. Lirriper's lodger, a good-hearted but irregular man who becomes joint guardian to Jemmy Lirriper.

Jane Miss Wozenham's maidservant.

Lirriper, Mrs. Emma ("Gran") Narrator of "Mrs. Lirriper's Lodgings" and "Mrs. Lirriper's Legacy." Widowed in the second year of her marriage and left with her husband's debts, she opened the lodging house at 81 NORFOLK STREET, STRAND, that she has managed for 38 years. Kind and good-natured, she is irritated only by her rival lodging-house keeper, Miss Wozenham, but after she saves her rival from bankruptcy the two become friends. She tells of the servants who have worked for her and of her lodgers, especially Major Jackman, her parlor boarder, and the Edsons, a young married couple whose child she adopts and names Jemmy Jackman Lirriper after Mrs. Edson is abandoned and dies giving birth to the boy. She and the major dote upon Jemmy, who loves them in return, telling them a fictionalized version of his life. In "Legacy," Mrs. Lirriper and the Major take the boy to Sens, France, where he meets his dying father.

Maxey, Caroline A bad-tempered girl who worked as a maid for Mrs. Lirriper and was sent to prison for assaulting two of the lodgers.

Perkinsop, Mary Anne One of Mrs. Lirriper's maids, "worth her weight in gold, as overawing lodgers without driving them away." Miss Wozenham lures her away with higher wages.

St. Clement Dane's Church Church in the St r a n d where Mrs. Lirriper was married.

Seraphina Schoolmaster's daughter, "the most beautiful creature that ever was seen," who is the heroine of Jemmy Lirriper's tale.

Sophy One of Mrs. Lirriper's servants.

Wozenham, Miss Rival lodging-house keeper to Mrs. Lirriper. Although there has been "a little unpleasantness" between the two rivals over the years, they become good friends after Mrs. Lirriper saves Miss Wozenham from bankruptcy.

"MRS. LIRRIPER'S LEGACY"

Christmas number of ALL THE YEAR ROUND, 1864, continuing the story of "Mrs. Lirriper's Lodgings." (1) In her opening monologue, Mrs. Lirriper tells of Major Jackman's friendship with Jemmy and of the model train they made together; of Joshua Lirriper, her husband's younger brother, a victim of drink and debt; of taking in Mr. Buffle, the tax collector, and his family after their house burned down; of saving a grateful Mrs. Wozenham from bankruptcy; and of traveling to Sens, France to learn the identity of a dying Englishman who has left her a small legacy. There they find Mr. Edson, Jemmy's father, on his deathbed. (2) In the final chapter, Jemmy, who does not know that the dying man is the father who abandoned him, makes up an idealized account of the man's life.

Characters and Related Entries

Buffle family A disagreeable tax collector who is taken in, with his wife and daughter Robina, by Mrs. Lirriper and Major Jackman after their house burns down.

Edson Jemmy's father, who is visited by Mrs. Lirriper and Jemmy in Sens, France, where he is on his deathbed.

George Clerk to Buffles, the tax collector.

Gran, Mrs. Jemmy Lirriper's name for Mrs. Lirriper in the story he tells.

Jackman, Major James See "Mrs. Lirriper's Luggage."

Madgers, Winifred One of Mrs. Lirriper's serving maids, a Plymouth Sister who goes off with a Plymouth Brother.

Norfolk Street This street leading from the Strand to the river is the site of the lodging houses of Mrs. Lirriper and her rival Miss Wozenham.

Rairyganoo, Sally One of Mrs. Lirriper's maids, suspected of "Irish extraction."

Sens, France "A pretty little town with a great two-towered cathedral and the rooks flying in and out of the loopholes" where Mrs. Lirriper and Major Jackman take Jemmy to meet his father, Edson, on his deathbed.

Wozenham, Miss See "Mrs. Lirriper's Luggage."

"DOCTOR MARIGOLD'S PRESCRIPTIONS"

Christmas number of ALL THE YEAR ROUND, 1865. The narrator of the frame narrative, Doctor Marigold, is a cheap jack, a traveling peddler and auctioneer, who adopts a deaf-and-dumb girl after his own daughter dies. He teaches her to read and write and then places her with a tutor for two years. While she is away, he makes a special "library cart" for her. But she falls in love with a deaf-and-dumb young man at the school, and, even though she chooses to return to Marigold, she is clearly denying her love. Marigold unites the two young lovers. They go off to China, returning with their daughter on Christmas Eve, 1864, to be reunited with Marigold.

"TO BE TAKEN WITH A GRAIN OF SALT"

Dickens's contribution to the stories in "Doctor Marigold's Prescriptions," a collection of stories that Marigold prepared for his adopted daughter. Dickens's story is a ghost story told by the jury foreman in a murder trial, who sees the ghost of the murdered man throughout the trial until a guilty verdict is returned and the ghost disappears.

Characters and Related Entries

Derrick, John Valet to the narrator of the ghost story "To Be Taken with a Grain of Salt."

Harker Officer in charge of the jury for the murder trial.

Marigold, Doctor, and family   Cheap jack—a traveling peddler and auctioneer—who follows the profession of his father, Willum. He narrates an account of his life: "I was born on the Queen's highway, but it was the King's at that time. A doctor was fetched to my own mother by my own father, when it took place on a common; and in consequence of his being a very kind gentleman, and accepting no fee but a tea-tray, I was named Doctor, out of gratitude and compliment to him. There you have me. Doctor Marigold." His temperamental wife abuses their daughter Sophy. After his wife, daughter, and dog die, Marigold adopts a deaf-and-dumb girl, names her Sophy after his daughter, educates her, and blesses her marriage to a deaf-and-dumb young man.

Mim   Traveling showman who exhibits Pickleson the Giant. He sells his deaf-and-dumb daughter to Marigold for six pairs of braces.

Pickleson ("Rinaldo di Velasco")   Giant, performing under the name Rinaldo di Velasco, who tells Doctor Marigold of the deaf-and-dumb child Sophy and of the young man she eventually marries.

Sophy   Doctor Marigold's daughter, a loving child who dies young. When he later adopts a deaf-and-dumb girl, he names her Sophy. He lovingly educates her and makes a wagon stocked with books for her to read, including a special book, *Doctor Marigold's Prescriptions,* that he has written for her himself.

"MUGBY JUNCTION"

Christmas number of ALL THE YEAR ROUND, 1866. Dickens wrote the first four chapters. (1) "Barbox Brothers" tells of Young Jackson, who has just retired as the head of Barbox Brothers, a notary and bill-brokering firm. On an unplanned journey to Mugby Junction, he meets Lamps, a porter at the station who makes up songs for his invalid daughter Phoebe. Lamps becomes a guiding spirit for Jackson. (2) In "Barbox Brothers and Co.," Jackson, also known as "Barbox Brothers," considers which of the seven train lines to take out of Mugby. Phoebe advises him to take the one to the city. There, on his birthday, he meets Polly, the daughter of Tresham, a friend from his young manhood who ran off with Beatrice, the one woman Jackson loved. He forgives them and returns to settle at Mugby Junction. (3) "Main Line: The Boy at Mugby" is narrated by Ezekiel, the boy from the refreshment room at Mugby Station, where inedible food is served and the customers are treated with contempt. Our Missus, who manages the operation, goes to France and returns to tell of the "despicable" practices in French refreshment rooms, which serve edible food at moderate prices with polite service. (4) "No. 1 Branch Line: The Signal-man," the last of Dickens's contributions, is a ghost story. The narrator visits a signalman in an isolated cutting along the railway and learns that the man is troubled by an apparition that has appeared twice under his warning light. Tragedies followed both appearances. After the apparition appears for a third time, the narrator learns that the signalman has been killed by an engine. Four other chapters were contributed by other writers.

Characters and Related Entries

Barbox Brothers   A bill-brokering house off LOMBARD STREET with a reputation for hard dealing. When Young Jackson, the last remaining member of the firm, retires, the firm is closed down. He is known by the nickname "Barbox Brothers."

Ezekiel   The name of the serving boy at Mugby Junction.

guard, the   Attendant on the train that leaves Young Jackson at Mugby Junction.

Jackson, Young   He works his way up in the firm of Barbox Brothers until he is the only member. Then he dissolves the firm.

"Lamps"   Porter at Mugby Junction who is devoted to his crippled daughter Phoebe, composing comic songs to sing to her.

Melluka, Miss   Polly Tresham's name for the doll given to her by Jackson.

"Missus, Our" Ferocious and disdainful manager of the refreshment room at Mugby Junction. She operates her "model establishment" as a "constitutional check upon the public."

Mugby Junction Train station where the newly retired Young Jackson starts a new life by choosing to take one of the seven lines leading from the junction. Mugby is based on Rugby in Warwickshire.

Papers Boy working at Smith's bookstall.

Phoebe The crippled 30-year-old daughter of Lamps, who makes lace and is contented in spite of her disability.

Piff, Miss One of the attendants in the Mugby Junction refreshment room.

signal-man, the A careful and professional employee of the railway, "whose post was in as solitary and dismal a place as ever I saw"; he tells Young Jackson of the troubling apparitions that appear by his warning light. Twice they have appeared preceding tragic accidents. A third appearance occurs just before the signalman himself is run down by a train.

Sniff, Mrs. One of the disdainful attendants at the Mugby Refreshment Room. Her husband, "a regular insignificant cove," is so "disgustingly servile" to the public that her associates cannot understand how she ever "come so far to lower herself as to marry him."

Tresham Young Jackson's former colleague. Tresham stole and married Beatrice, the woman Jackson loved. Years later the retired Jackson is reunited with Tresham, now a very sick man, through Tresham's daughter Polly. Jackson forgives Tresham and Beatrice.

Whiff, Mrs. An attendant at the Mugby Junction refreshment room.

"NO THOROUGHFARE"

Christmas story for *ALL THE YEAR ROUND* (1867) by Dickens and Wilkie Collins. Dickens wrote all of the "Overture" and Act 3; Collins wrote all of Act 2; they collaborated on Acts 1 and 4. They also collaborated on a stage version of the story.

SYNOPSIS

(1) 1835. Sally, a nurse from the FOUNDLING HOSPITAL is stopped in the street by a woman who asks her the name given to a child recently taken into the institution. Sally tells her "Walter Wilding."

1847. The same woman visits the hospital and asks the matron to point out Walter Wilding to her.

1861. At the offices of Wilding and Co., the bachelor head of the firm, Walter Wilding, is hiring a housekeeper and making George Vendale a partner in the firm. Wilding's late mother established him in the business after reclaiming him from the Foundling Hospital. Now he has idealistic plans to make the firm like a family. When he hires Sarah Goldstraw as his housekeeper, he learns from her that he is not really his mother's son. Sarah was Sally, the nurse from the hospital; she knows that the real Walter Wilding was another child who was adopted shortly before the present Wilding was given his name. Wilding decides to seek out the real Walter and turn the wine business over to him, but every lead that he finds to the man's identity ends in a "no thoroughfare."

Meanwhile, Vendale carries on the firm's business dealings with Jules Obenreizer, a representative of the Swiss wine merchants Defresnier et Cie. As he does so, he falls more and more in love with Obenreizer's niece Marguerite.

Binfrey, Wilding's attorney, and Vendale advise Wilding to give up the search for the real Wilding and to keep Sally's information secret, but he rewrites his will to leave everything to the real Wilding should he be discovered within two years of his death. Then, weakened by the stress of his situation and increasingly depressed, he dies.

(2) When Vendale asks Obenreizer's permission to marry Marguerite, he is refused because of the social distance between an English gentleman and the daughter of a Swiss peasant. Obenreizer relents and says he will agree to the marriage should Vendale's income reach £3,000 a year. As Vendale goes over his accounts, he discovers that his firm has

received a fraudulent receipt from Defresnier et Cie; to clear up the crime he must take the receipt to SWITZERLAND. Obenreizer arranges to travel with him. As they leave, Marguerite pleads with George, "Don't go!"

(3) On the journey, Vendale is concerned about protecting the receipt. Obenreizer, who is guilty of the forgery, makes secret plans to steal it from him. He drugs Vendale and steals into his room in the night, but he cannot secure the document. Finally, as the two men cross the Simplon Pass in a dangerous February snowstorm, Obenreizer drugs Vendale and pushes him into a chasm, leaving him for dead, but the Englishman is rescued from an icy ledge by Marguerite, who has followed the two men to Switzerland.

(4) In April, two months after the episode on the mountain, Obenreizer, who has been dismissed by Defresnier et Cie, is working as a clerk for Maître Voigt, a Neuchâtel attorney. He uses his position to gain access to the lawyer's files on a client named Vendale. When Obenreizer and Voigt are summoned to Brieg to meet with the English attorney Binfrey, they learn that Vendale did not die. Binfrey demands that Obenreizer give up his guardianship of Marguerite in exchange for not being prosecuted for attempted murder. Obenreizer reveals the secret from the files that Vendale is really Walter Wilding, a bastard adopted from the Foundling Hospital, and thus heir to Wilding and Co.

On the day of Marguerite and George's wedding in Brieg, the body of Obenreizer is brought down from the mountain, where he died in a snowstorm.

Characters and Related Entries

Bintrey Walter Wilding's solicitors who helps track down and expose Obenreizer.

Break-Neck Stairs Stairs leading to the THAMES at the foot of the street where Wilding and Co. is located.

Brieg, Switzerland Town at the foot of the Simplon Pass, the starting point for Vendale's and Obenreizer's journey over the mountains and the site of Vendale's marriage to Marguerite.

Cripple Corner Courtyard where Wilding and Co. is located.

Defresnier et Cie Swiss wine merchants, represented in England by Jules Obenreizer.

Dick Fiancé of Sally, nurse at the FOUNDLING HOSPITAL.

Dor, Madame Obenreizer's Swiss housekeeper; Marguerite's friend and protector.

Ganz, Dr. Physician at Neuchâtel who helps prove George Vendale's identity.

Goldstraw, Mrs. Sarah (Sally) Nurse at the FOUNDLING HOSPITAL who later becomes Wilding's housekeeper and tells him of his mistaken identity.

Harker, the Reverend John Vicar of Groombridge Wells who acts as a reference for Mrs. Miller when she adopts Walter Wilding.

Jarvis Clerk to the wine merchants, Wilding and Co.

Jean Marie An Alpine guide in the drama *No Thoroughfare,* but not the story.

Jean Paul An Alpine guide in the drama *No Thoroughfare,* but not the story.

Ladle, Joey Superstitious cellarman for Wilding and Co. who accompanies Marguerite Obenreizer on her journey to SWITZERLAND to rescue Vendale.

Miller, Jane Ann Widow who negotiates the adoption of Walter Wilding from the Foundling Hospital for the Vendales.

Obenreizer, Jules Agent for a firm of Swiss wine merchants, Defresnier et Cie.; "the great Obenreizer peculiarity was, that a certain nameless film would come over his eyes—apparently by the action of his own will—which would impenetrably veil ... every expression save one of attention" (1). He fears that Vendale will expose his fraud and embezzlement, so he tries to murder him in an Alpine pass. He is killed in an avalanche.

Obenreizer, Marguerite Jules's niece, daughter of Swiss peasants, with "a wonderful purity and freshness of colour in her dimpled face and bright grey eyes, [who] seemed fraught with mountain air" (1). She foils her uncle's plot, saves Vendale's life, and later marries him (4).

Pebbleson Nephew Firm of London wine merchants purchased by Mrs. Wilding and renamed Wilding and Company.

Rolland Junior partner of Defresnier et Cie. who writes to Vendale concerning a forged receipt.

Vendale, George Partner in Wilding and Co. and fiancé to Marguerite Obenreizer; "a brown-cheeked handsome fellow" (1). He goes to Switzerland to investigate a fraud by Marguerite's uncle Jules, who attacks him and leaves him in the mountains for dead. He is rescued by Marguerite and learns that he is the legitimate heir to the Wilding business.

Voigt, Maître Neuchâtel notary who holds the documents that reveal Vendale's identity and facilitates the unmasking of Obenreizer. In the dramatized version of the story he is given the name Father Francis.

Wilding, Walter Head of Wilding and Co., London wine merchants, a firm he has inherited from his mother. As a child he was an orphan. His mother recovers him from the Foundling Hospital thinking him her child, but after her death he learns that she was mistaken. He sets out to find her rightful heir but dies in the attempt.

"Clause for the New Reform Bill, A"

Article by Dickens and WILKIE COLLINS for HOUSEHOLD WORDS (October 9, 1858) proposing a new reform bill that would instruct mayors not to decorate their cities for a visit from the Queen, thus allowing the Queen to see her people "in *their* natural characters." *Stone.*

"Common Sense on Wheels"

Article for HOUSEHOLD WORDS (April 12, 1851) by Dickens, W. H. WILLS, and E. C. GRENVILLE MURRAY discussing the need for reforms of the hackney coach trade and describing the regulations in several European cities. *Stone.*

"Court Ceremonies"

Article for the EXAMINER (December 15, 1849) commenting on the death of Adelaide, the Queen Dowager, and her request for a simple funeral. Her request makes this an appropriate occasion on which to note how outdated and preposterous most ceremonies of the English court are and how much they are in need of being updated. *Miscellaneous, Journalism.*

"Crisis in the Affairs of Mr. John Bull, A"

In this essay from HOUSEHOLD WORDS (November 23, 1850), Dickens writes an allegorical fable in which Mrs. John Bull instructs her children on the dangers of associating with Master Wiseman, Young England, and the Bulls of Rome, who "perpetuate misery, oppression, darkness, and ignorance." The article was written in response to the restoration of the Catholic hierarchy in England on September 29, 1850. When the Pope returned the English divisions of the Catholic Church to the status of regular dioceses and named Bishop Wiseman Cardinal and Bishop of Westminster, his action, which seemed to ignore the authority of the Anglican hierarchy, aroused English Protestants and prompted a bill in Parliament that prohibited the assumption of ecclesiastical titles already held by the clergy in the Church of England. In a letter to ANGELA COUTTS, Dickens condemned the restoration of Catholic titles in even stronger terms: "*Now*, a war between the Roman Catholic Religion—that curse upon the world—and Freedom, is inevitable." *Miscellaneous, Journalism.*

"Cruikshank's 'The Drunkard's Children'"

Dickens's "gentle protest" at GEORGE CRUIKSHANK's pictorial analysis of the effects of gin chides the artist for ignoring the social misery that produces drunkenness while blaming the gin. Although Dickens praised the art and the observation of social reality in the pictures, his criticism strained his relationship with the artist. The article first appeared in the EXAMINER (July 8, 1848). *Miscellaneous, Journalism.*

"Curious Dance round a Curious Tree, A"

Article for HOUSEHOLD WORDS (January 17, 1852) written with W. H. WILLS, describing a visit to a holiday party for the inmates of St. Luke's Hospital for the insane and showing the positive effects of humane and loving treatment of the patients. *Stone.*

"Curious Misprint in the 'Edinburgh Review'"

Article for HOUSEHOLD WORDS (August 1, 1857) in which Dickens challenges the *Edinburgh*'s reviewer for suggesting that novelists were not qualified to discuss social issues, and, in particular, his claim that the Post Office and Rowland Hill's career there show that the Circumlocution Office does not exist. Dickens describes the obstacles to reform

that Hill faced for many years from the government establishment. *Miscellaneous, Journalism.*

"December Vision, A"

Article for HOUSEHOLD WORDS (December 14, 1850) describing the Spirit of Death coming over the world through Ignorance, Disease, and Injustice. Those who recognize that these social ills need to be overcome nonetheless acquiesce to despair, remarking that "it will last my time." The spirit points out that their time is in eternity and that they will be forever condemned for doing nothing to change things. The essay allegorizes the criticism of the COURT OF CHANCERY that Dickens develops in *Bleak House*. *Miscellaneous, Journalism.*

"Demeanour of Murderers, The"

Article for HOUSEHOLD WORDS (June 14, 1856) in which Dickens comments on the trial of murderer William Palmer (1824–56), a case that aroused intense public interest. Known as the Rudgeley Poisoner, Palmer was convicted in 1856 of poisoning his friend John Parsons, as well as his wife and brother. Although people have been surprised by the complete self-possession of Palmer during his recent trial, Dickens observes, such equanimity is characteristic of ruthless killers who have lost all natural human feeling and are confident of acquittal. *Miscellaneous, Journalism.*

"Demoralisation and Total Abstinence"

Article for the EXAMINER (October 27, 1849) in which Dickens challenges the advocates of total abstinence for grossly oversimplifying the role of drunkenness in contributing to crime and social misery. Dickens sees drunkenness as a symptom of ignorance and want among the lower orders and argues that addressing these root causes is called for rather than blindly advocating total abstinence. *Journalism.*

"Dinner at Poplar Walk, A"

Dickens's first published story appeared in the MONTHLY MAGAZINE (December 1833). In *Sketches by Boz* it was retitled "Mr. Minns and His Cousin."

"Discovery of a Treasure near Cheapside"

Article written with HENRY MORLEY for HOUSEHOLD WORDS (November 13, 1852) describing the smelting of gold and other precious metals at Wingrove's Wood Street Smelting Works. *Stone.*

"Doctor Dulcamara, M.P."

Article for HOUSEHOLD WORDS by Dickens and WILKIE COLLINS (December 18, 1858) expressing their dislike of the formalism and dogmatism of the Oxford Movement, which sought to reform the Church of England by returning to the rituals of the CATHOLIC CHURCH and by reconciling Anglican and Catholic doctrines. The article challenges the quackery of Mr. Sidney Herbert, who promulgates the outlandish idea that Charlotte Yonge's Puseyite (after Edward Pusey, one of the leaders of the Oxford Movement) novel, *The Heir of Redclyffe* (1853), is a work second only to the Bible. *Stone.*

"Doctor Marigold"

Title given to the two framing chapters Dickens wrote for "Doctor Marigold's Prescriptions" when they were collected in *Christmas Stories.*

"Doom of English Wills, The"

Article by Dickens and W. H. WILLS for HOUSEHOLD WORDS (September 28, 1850) calling attention to the deplorable state of public records in England. Antiquarian William Wallace, a fictional character based on William Downing Bruce, searches for documents in the registry at an unnamed cathedral based on Lincoln and Litchfield. There he confronts officious and uncooperative clerks, uncovers neglected and rotting documents, and discovers some unrecognized treasures. *Stone.*

"Doom of English Wills: Cathedral Number Two, The"

A second article by Dickens and W. H. WILLS for HOUSEHOLD WORDS (October 5, 1850) on the deplorable state of public records in England. William Wallace goes to the Registry of Public Documents at York, where he finds the papers stored in a totally inadequate building, ill-cataloged and unprotected. Some documents have even been sold to private parties. *Stone.*

Characters and Related Entries

Wallace, William Fictional character based on William Downing Bruce (1824–75), an antiquarian scholar who exposed the deplorable state of the public records in England.

"'The Dream at Sea' by J. B. Buckstone"

Theater review for the MORNING CHRONICLE (November 24, 1835). In this review of Buckstone's melodrama, Dickens describes the absurdities of the plot but praises the production; he ends by saying, "we should be more happy to see [a play] in his old pleasant domestic style, where the situations are not wholly improbable, nor the incidents palpably absurd." *Journalism.*

"Drooping Buds"

Essay by Dickens and HENRY MORLEY for HOUSE-HOLD WORDS (April 3, 1852), occasioned by the opening of the Hospital for Sick Children in Great Ormond Street. It describes the problem of infant mortality at the time and a visit to the new hospital. In the middle of the essay Dickens reflects on the deaths of some children—and some adults he had known as children—who had been close to him: his infant daughter DORA ANNIE DICKENS; his sister Fanny (see DICKENS, FRANCES ELIZABETH) and her son, HENRY BURNETT JR.; and MARY HOGARTH. *Stone.*

"Duelling in France"

Article for HOUSEHOLD WORDS (June 27, 1857), by ELIZA LYNN LINTON and Dickens, though Dickens's contribution was small. The article gives a historical account of duelling in France by telling the stories of a number of duels. *Stone.*

"Edinburgh Apprentice School Association"

Article from the EXAMINER (December 30, 1848) reporting on the success of the Edinburgh night school for apprentices and working men. *Miscellaneous.*

"Enlightened Clergyman, An"

Note from ALL THE YEAR ROUND (March 8, 1862) reporting on the objections raised by two clergymen to public readings of WILKIE COLLINS's story "Picking up Waifs at Sea" and Dickens's "The Bloomsbury Christening," which, according to the clergymen, "trifles with a sacred ordinance." *Miscellaneous, Journalism.*

"Epsom"

Article by W. H. WILLS and Dickens for HOUSE-HOLD WORDS (June 7, 1851) describing a tour of Epsom Downs, its stables and track, before race day and concluding with Dickens's masterful set piece on race day at Epsom. *Stone.*

"Familiar Epistle from a Parent to a Child"

See *Mudfog.*

"Fast and Loose"

Allegorical essay for HOUSEHOLD WORDS (March 24, 1855) describing the lies by which the rich and powerful control those beneath them, whom they tell that their situation is the result of "Providence" and that it would be "unparliamentary" to attempt to change it. *Miscellaneous.*

"Few Conventionalities, A"

Humorous article for HOUSEHOLD WORDS (June 28, 1851) in which Dickens lists conventional phrases and actions used in government, in the theater, at public dinners and meetings, and in social discourse. Such phrases, he suggests, disguise and soften the truth. *Miscellaneous.*

"Finishing Schoolmaster, The"

Article from HOUSEHOLD WORDS (May 17, 1851) commenting on the applicants who volunteered to stand in for the regular hangman, who was unavailable for the execution of Maria Clarke. Their letters of application, which Dickens reprints, are testimony to their illiteracy and to the education offered by a society that cannot agree to teach the Lord's Prayer but can agree on the educational efficacy of public hanging. *Miscellaneous, Journalism.*

Characters and Related Entries

Calcroft Executioner for the county of Suffolk who was unavailable to carry out the execution of Maria Clarke.

Clarke, Maria Woman scheduled for hanging on Easter Tuesday, 1851, a "decent compliment to the festival of Easter," Dickens satirically remarks.

"Fire and Snow"

Essay for HOUSEHOLD WORDS (January 21, 1854) describing a Christmastime visit to Wolverhampton, when the factories are shut down for the holiday and the BLACK COUNTRY is covered with snow. *Miscellaneous, Journalism.*

"First Fruits"

Article by Dickens and GEORGE AUGUSTUS SALA for HOUSEHOLD WORDS (May 15, 1852) describing "primaries," first experiences in life. Dickens records his first picture book, first oyster, first visit to the theater, and the first time he was taken for a man. *Stone.*

"Five New Points of Criminal Law"

Satirical article for ALL THE YEAR ROUND (September 24, 1859) describing five ways in which the proposed revisions in the criminal law embody the underlying assumption "that the real

offender is the Murdered Person." *Miscellaneous, Journalism.*

"Foreigners' Portraits of Englishmen"

To this article for HOUSEHOLD WORDS (September 21, 1850), written with W. H. WILLS and E. C. MURRAY, Dickens contributed descriptions of some absurd depictions of Englishmen in continental theaters. *Stone.*

"Frauds on the Fairies"

Dickens's critical review in HOUSEHOLD WORDS (October 1, 1853) of GEORGE CRUIKSHANK's retellings of classic FAIRY TALES to promote teetotalism. Dickens argues that we nurture our imagination on such stories, and to make them serve such political causes removes the FANCY from them; "a nation without fancy, without some romance, never did, never can, and never will, hold a great place under the sun." Then he presents a retelling of "Cinderella" according to the politically correct principles of the day in support of his final admonition: "The world is too much with us, early and late. Leave this precious escape from it, alone." *Miscellaneous, Journalism.*

"Free (and Easy) School, A"

Article for HOUSEHOLD WORDS (November 15, 1851) by Dickens and HENRY MORLEY, who investigated the operation of free grammar schools by visiting Queen Elizabeth's Royal Grammar-school at Thistledown. There the narrator finds the master of the school, Dr. Laon Blose, separating the free pupils from his private pupils, a common violation of the intent of such schools brought about by allowing the masters to supplement their inadequate salaries by taking private students. *Stone.*

Characters and Related Entries

Blose, Dr. Laon Headmaster of Queen Elizabeth's Royal Free Grammar-school at Thistledown; "he is stout, but every limb betrays his laxity of fibre; his coat is fluffy; his hands are unclean. He evidently lives in an unwholesome atmosphere."

"Friend of the Lions, The"

While painting Dickens as a rat catcher in one of his paintings, EDWIN HENRY LANDSEER complains about how the lions at the London Zoo are housed and fed. An article for HOUSEHOLD WORDS (February 2, 1856). *Miscellaneous, Journalism.*

"From the Raven in the Happy Family"

Three articles for the first volume of HOUSEHOLD WORDS (May 11, June 8, and August 24, 1850) in the voice of a raven, who complains of Buffon's characterization of ravens as gluttons and thieves and retaliates by describing human beings from a raven's point of view (1). Then he satirizes ostentatious funerals and identifies undertakers as the ravens among humankind (2). He completes his natural history of human beings with a horse's view of man's stupidity, irrationality, and conceit (3). *Miscellaneous.*

"Gaslight Fairies"

Article for HOUSEHOLD WORDS (February 10, 1855) on the actors who play the walk-on roles in the theaters, like the fairies in the PANTOMIME. Dickens wonders about their lives between pantomime seasons and, by imagining the Fairy family, supported by the meager earnings of the 23-year-old daughter who plays one of the fairies, urges his readers not to condemn the shabby people who take these parts. *Miscellaneous, Journalism.*

"George Silverman's Explanation"

Short story written for the ATLANTIC MONTHLY (January–March 1868; also in ALL THE YEAR ROUND, February 1, 15, and 29, 1868). George Silverman, an elderly clergyman, tells the story of his life, from his harsh childhood in a PRESTON cellar to his early orphanhood and youth under the guardianship of Brother Hawkyard, an enthusiastic and hypocritical chapel preacher; to his success at Cambridge as a scholarship student and tutor; to his modest living in a parish in Devon controlled by Lady Fareway. There he fell in love with Adelina Fareway, but he eschewed so unequal a marriage and encouraged her relationship with Granville Wharton. When he married them secretly, Lady Fareway accused him of profiting from the union and he resigned the living. Throughout his life Silverman has been accused of worldliness and self-seeking, but his "explanation," told when he is 60, reveals that the judgments of others fail to understand a diffident, self-denying, and unworldly man.

Characters and Related Entries

Fareway family Aristocratic family that determines the course of George Silverman's life. After he tutors the second son of the family, a young man whose "abilities were much above the average; but he came of a rich family, and was idle and luxurious," Lady Fareway, "a handsome well-preserved" and manipulative woman offers Silverman a small living in north Devon on the condition that he will also serve as her secretary and tutor her daughter. In Devon he secretly falls in love with the daughter, Adelina, but, considering himself unworthy, he marries her to Granville Wharton instead of claiming her for himself.

Gimblet, Brother An "expounder" in the dissenting congregation to which he and Brother Hawkyard, his rival expounder, belong.

Hawkyard, Brother Verity Dissenting preacher and dry salter who acts as George Silverman's guardian. The story implies that he has appropriated properties that rightfully belong to Silverman, but the self-denying Silverman writes a letter exonerating Hawkyard from any guilt.

Parksop, Brother George Silverman's grandfather.

Silverman, the Rev. George Sixty-year-old clergyman who explains his life in "George Silverman's Explanation." Abused by his mother, who calls him "a worldly little devil," in the Preston cellar where he spent his early childhood, he becomes a self-denying and self-effacing adult. Even when he gives up the woman he loves and marries her to another man, he is accused of doing so for monetary gain. His story explains how his childhood prompted his otherworldliness, which in turn has isolated him from "the world."

Sylvia Girl at the farm where Silverman stays after he is orphaned. He avoids her for fear of giving her the fever from which his parents died.

Wharton, Granville George Silverman's pupil, "a young gentleman near coming of age, very well connected, but what is called a poor relation." Silverman promotes his marriage to Adelina Fareway.

"Gone Astray"

In this article from HOUSEHOLD WORDS (August 13, 1853), Dickens describes an experience when he was eight or so of being separated from the person he was with and finding himself lost in the CITY. He spent the day visiting London's landmarks, imagining himself as DICK WHITTINGTON, and going to a play. In the evening he went to a police station, and his father was called to rescue him. The essay is echoed in Florence Dombey's "kidnapping" and

in David Copperfield's wanderings in the streets of London. *Miscellaneous, Journalism.*

"Gone to the Dogs"

Article for HOUSEHOLD WORDS (March 10, 1855) in which Dickens describes the ways in which his own life and that of the nation have gone to the dogs. The only competitor Posterity has for the treasures that may be handed down to them, he asserts, are the Dogs. The romantic castles he once built in the air have gone to the dogs; Bob Temple, friend of his youth, has succumbed to gambling; whole streets of buildings have fallen into ruin; the nation is sending its soldiers to vanish in Balaklava. The "romantic castles" obliquely allude to Dickens's infatuation with MARIA BEADNELL. *Miscellaneous, Journalism.*

Characters and Related Entries

Amarinta "Bright-eyed" lady "with the obdurate parents" in the narrator's youthful castle in the air. Probably an allusion to MARIA BEADNELL. *Miscellaneous.*

"'Good' Hippopotamus, The"

Article for HOUSEHOLD WORDS (October 12, 1850) satirizing the use of public funds to provide for idle aristocrats in its description of the proposed subscription to erect a monument to H.R.H (His Rolling Hulk) the Hippopotamus. *Miscellaneous.*

Characters and Related Entries

Cannana, Hamet Safi Arabian gentleman organizing the subscription campaign to erect a monument to the Good Hippopotamus.

"Grand Colosseum Fête"

An anonymous news article for the MORNING CHRONICLE (July 10, 1835) reporting on the grand opening of the Colosseum near Regent's Park after its renovations. Dickens commends the charitable purpose of the benefit—to support London's hospitals; he describes the distinguished company, the dinner, and the ball: "like all other public balls—that there were matchmaking mamas in abundance—sleepy papas in proportion—unmarried daughters in scores—marriageable men in rather smaller numbers—greedy dowagers in the refreshment room—flirting daughters in the corners—and envious old maids everywhere." *Journalism.*

"Great Baby, The"

Article from HOUSEHOLD WORDS (August 4, 1855) opposing proposals to close taverns on Sunday. The members of Parliament who intend to do so are under the influence of Monomaniacs who view the People as a Great Baby, influenced by strong drink and bad company in taverns, and thus incapable of acting responsibly. *Miscellaneous, Journalism.*

"Great Exhibition and the Little One, The"

Essay by Dickens and R. H. HORNE for HOUSEHOLD WORDS (July 5, 1851) contrasting the Great Exhibition at the Crystal Palace with a little exhibition of Chinese articles at the Chinese Gallery in HYDE PARK. It is a "comparison between Stoppage and Progress," between a Chinese culture "crippled by conceited absolutism and distrust" and the Western industrial culture, which is "moving in a right direction towards some superior condition of society—politically, morally, intellectually, and religiously." *Stone.*

"H. W."

Article by Dickens and HENRY MORLEY for HOUSEHOLD WORDS (April 16, 1853) describing the process by which the magazine is produced, from choosing the contents to preparing the plates and running the steam presses to distributing it to news dealers. *Stone.*

"Haunted House, A"

Satiric article for HOUSEHOLD WORDS (July 23, 1853) describing Mr. Bull's haunted house in Westminster, a scene of confused babbling made worse by members of Bull's family who go into the countryside, into towns like Burningshame, bringing ill-will, depravity, and corruption. *Miscellaneous, Journalism.*

"Heart of Mid-London, The"

Article for HOUSEHOLD WORDS (May 4, 1850) by W. H. WILLS and Dickens, describing the overcrowding and brutality at the SMITHFIELD Livestock Market and recommending that a suburban market replace it. A description of a mad bull rampaging through the streets is reminiscent of the scene of Florence's kidnapping in *Dombey. Stone.*

"Hidden Light"

Poem in HOUSEHOLD WORDS (August 26, 1854) by ADELAIDE ANNE PROCTER and Dickens proclaiming the goodness inherent in "the soul of all mankind." *Stone.*

"Hiram Power's Greek Slave"

Poem from HOUSEHOLD WORDS (October 26, 1850) saluting Powers's statue of a shackled Greek slave as a work of art that can "shame the strong" and overthrow serfdom.

"Holiday Romance"

A collection of four short stories, supposedly written by four children, that Dickens wrote for the American magazine OUR YOUNG FOLKS; they appeared there between January and May, 1868, and simultaneously in ALL THE YEAR ROUND. Eight-year-old William Tinkling tells of his "marriage" to seven-year-old Nettie Ashford and of his unsuccessful attempt to save her and her friend, seven-year-old Alice Rainbird, from imprisonment in school. Alice tells the story of a magic fishbone that the Princess Alicia uses to save her father's fortunes. Nine-year-old Robin Redforth tells the story of Captain Boldheart and his struggles with the Latin-grammar master. Nettie tells of a utopia where adults obey the children.

Characters and Related Entries

Alicia, Princess   Eldest daughter of King Watkins the First and heroine of Miss Alice Rainbird's story.

Alicumpaine, Mrs.   A friend of Mrs. Orange in Nettie's story.

Ashford, Nettie   The young lady, "aged half-past six," who is the author of the story of Mrs. Orange in "Holiday Romance," a fantasy about a world where adults and children exchange roles.

Black, Mrs.   One of Mrs. Lemon's pupils in Nettie's topsy-turvy world, where adults have children's roles.

Boldheart, Captain   Pirate and captain of the schooner *Beauty* and the nine-year-old hero of the story told by nine-year-old Robin Redforth. He enters a life of piratical adventure after being "spited by a Latin-grammar master."

Boozey, William   Captain of the foretop on the schooner *Beauty* in the tale of Captain Boldheart.

Brown   One of Mrs. Lemon's pupils.

Certainpersonio, Prince   Alicia's bridegroom in Alice Rainbird's tale.

Chopper   William Tinkling's great uncle who brings a "shabby" gift to the christening of William's baby brother.

Drowvey, Miss   Coproprietor with Miss Grimmer of the school that Alice Rainbird and Nettie Ashford attend.

Emilia   Mrs. Orange's baby in Nettie's story.

Grandmarina, Fairy   Princess Alicia's godmother from whom she receives the magic fishbone.

Greedy   One of Mrs. Lemon's pupils.

Grimmer, Miss   Miss Drowvey's partner in managing the school where Nettie Ashford is a pupil.

Jane   Mrs. Orange's maidservant.

Latin-grammar master, the   Antagonist to Captain Boldheart in Robin Redforth's tale of piratical adventure.

Lemon, Mrs.   Friend of Mrs. Orange who takes in all of Mrs. Orange's "children" in Nettie Ashford's tale. She is the mother of Tootleumboots.

Orange, Mrs.   "A truly sweet young creature," friend of Mrs. Lemon, and wife of James in Nettie Ashford's tale.

Peggy   Lord Chamberlain to King Watkins the First.

Pickles   Fishmonger who provides King Watkins the First with the salmon containing the magic fishbone.

Rainbird, Alice   One of the four child narrators of the stories in "Holiday Romance," she tells the story of Princess Alicia and her magic fishbone, which enables her to provide for the struggling family of King Watkins the First.

Redforth, Lt.-Col. Robin   One of the four child authors in "The Holiday Romance." He tells the story of Captain Boldheart, a pirate who defeats his enemy the Latin-grammar master and a band of cannibals, and then rescues his sweetheart from a bathing machine at Margate.

Scorpion, The   Ship of the Latin-grammar master, Captain Boldheart's enemy.

Tinkling, William Eight-year-old narrator of the "Holiday Romance." He is "married" to Nettie Ashford and writes out the tales of the other three tellers.

Tom Captain Boldheart's cousin.

"Tootleum-Boots" Mrs. Lemon's baby.

Watkins the First, King Father of Princess Alicia in Alice Rainbird's story.

White A "pale, bald child, with red whiskers" who is one of Mrs. Lemon"s pupils.

"Home for Homeless Women"

Article for HOUSEHOLD WORDS (April 23, 1853) describing the operation and philosophy of a successful home for women from the streets. Although it is not named in the article, the institution was URANIA COTTAGE, a charitable enterprise in which Dickens was a guiding hand. *Miscellaneous, Journalism.*

"Household Narrative of Current Events, The"

Monthly supplement to HOUSEHOLD WORDS, begun in April 1850 and discontinued in December 1855, providing a chronicle of the important events during the preceding month. Dickens wrote the announcement describing the narrative for the April 13, 1850, issue. *Stone.*

"House to Let, A"

Christmas number of HOUSEHOLD WORDS for 1858. Dickens contributed the third chapter, "Going into Society"; he collaborated with WILKIE COLLINS on another, "Let at Last."

"Hunted Down"

Short story published in the NEW YORK LEDGER (August 20 and 27 and September 3, 1859) and in ALL THE YEAR ROUND (April 4 and 11, 1860). Based on the case of the notorious poisoner Thomas Wainewright, the story is narrated by Mr. Sampson, an insurance man who holds a policy on the life of Alfred Beckwith, an intended victim of Julius Slinkton, the beneficiary. Beckwith is, in fact, Meltham, an insurance actuary in disguise, determined to trap Slinkton for the earlier murder of his niece, the girl Meltham loved. After the crimes are brought to light, Slinkton commits suicide and Meltham fades and dies of a broken heart.

Characters and Related Entries

Adams Clerk to Mr. Sampson, narrator of "Hunted Down."

Banks, Major Meltham assumes the disguise of this retired East India Company Director to trick Julius Slinkton.

Beckwith, Alfred Alias adopted by Meltham in his scheme to trick Julius Slinkton.

Meltham Insurance actuary, described by Sampson as "the most profound, the most original, and the most energetic man I have ever known connected with Life Assurance." He pursues Julius Slinkton for the murder of the girl he loved, Slinkton's niece. Disguising himself as Alfred Beckwith and Major Banks, he exposes Slinkton's poisoning schemes and saves Margaret Niner, Slinkton's other niece, from dying like her sister. After he succeeds in exposing Slinkton, Meltham dies of a broken heart.

Niner, Margaret Niece of Julius Slinkton, whom he plans to poison to get the insurance on her life. His plot is foiled by Sampson and Meltham.

Sampson, Mr. Insurance man who narrates the story of Julius Slinkton, a poisoner he has helped Meltham capture.

Scarborough Seaside resort in Yorkshire where Meltham pursues Slinkton.

Slinkton, Julius Poisoner who has murdered his niece and plots to murder Margaret Niner and Alfred Beckwith. He commits suicide when his schemes are discovered. Slinkton was based on the notorious poisoner Thomas Wainewright, whom Dickens had met.

"Hymn of the Wiltshire Labourers, The"

Verses by Dickens, published in the *DAILY NEWS* in 1846, expressing sympathy for the distressed agricultural workers in Wiltshire, who were suffering from hunger and oppression.

"Idea of Mine, An"

Article for *HOUSEHOLD WORDS* (March 13, 1858) proposing to reconnect the fine arts with reality by withdrawing all artists' models from service, an action that might force the artists to concentrate on the "telling of stories and conveying of ideas." *Miscellaneous.*

"Idiots"

Article for *HOUSEHOLD WORDS* (June 4, 1853) by W. H. WILLS and Dickens, describing current knowledge about "idiocy" and advocating humane institutions for the care and instruction of the mentally ill. A visit to the Asylum for Idiots in HIGHGATE shows the effectiveness of such institutions. *Stone.*

"Ignorance and Crime"

Article for the *EXAMINER* (April 22, 1848) reporting on the figures released by the government indicating how many of those convicted of various crimes in 1847 had no occupational skills and were illiterate. Ignorance, Dickens suggests, is almost always allied with crime, disease, and misery. *Miscellaneous, Journalism.*

"Ignorance and Its Victims"

Article for the *EXAMINER* (April 29, 1848) following up on "Ignorance and Crime." Dickens reports on a young woman, educated in a national school, who is tricked into giving away money and clothing by a gypsy astrologer who promises to change her fortunes by controlling the stars. Dickens suggests that the rote learning promulgated by the schools produces ignorant people who are easily victimized by such scams. *Journalism.*

"In and Out of Jail"

Review of Frederic Hill's *Crime: Its Amount, Causes, and Remedies* (1853) for *HOUSEHOLD WORDS* (May 14, 1853) by HENRY MORLEY, with considerable revisions and additions by Dickens. The essay concludes with a strong statement of Dickens's views that prisons should punish and that the lives of prisoners should not be more comfortable than those of the poor. *Stone.*

"In Memoriam. W. M. Thackeray"

A eulogy for his fellow novelist, published in the *CORNHILL* (February 1864). Dickens recalls his interactions with WILLIAM MAKEPEACE THACKERAY from the time Thackeray applied to become the illustrator of *Pickwick* to a meeting just a week before his death. *Journalism.*

"Insularities"

Article for *HOUSEHOLD WORDS* (January 19, 1856) describing patterns of unreasonable or ridiculous behavior that the English fail to question: resistance to innovative dress and beards, denigration of "theatrical" paintings, contempt for the innocent recreations of the poor, and servile adulation of aristocracy and royalty. *Miscellaneous, Journalism.*

"International Copyright"

Letter that appeared in the EXAMINER (July 16, 1842) and in other English papers, discussing the issue of INTERNATIONAL COPYRIGHT and urging Dickens's fellow English writers not to deal with American publishers who opposed an agreement. *Miscellaneous.*

Is She His Wife? or Something Singular

A one-act farce performed at the St. James's Theatre, March 6, 1837. It deals with the misunderstandings that arise when two married couples, the Lovetowns and the Limburys, and a neighboring squire, Felix Tapkins, misrepresent their marital status and flirt with one another.

Characters and Related Entries

Limbury, Mr. and Mrs. Peter Friends of the Lovetowns who are caught up in their mutual attempts to make each other jealous.

Lovetown, Mr. and Mrs. Alfred Recently married couple who are bored with each other. They reawaken each other's romantic interest by flirting with others, Alfred with Mrs. Limbury and Mrs. Lovetown with Felix Tapkins.

Tapkins, Felix Bachelor friend of the Lovetowns who flirts with Mrs. Lovetown.

"It Is Not Generally Known"

Article for HOUSEHOLD WORDS (September 2, 1854) arguing against Sunday closing laws. Such laws are

promoted, Dickens suggests, by those who base legislation on the worst members of society and justify closing public amusements on Sunday because the notorious criminal Sloggins declares that "Amusements done it." *Miscellaneous, Journalism.*

"Judicial Special Pleading"

Article for the EXAMINER (December 30, 1848) chiding Mr. Baron Alderson, judge in the trial of the physical force Chartists (*see* CHARTISM), for his gross oversimplification of the situation that brought on the FRENCH REVOLUTION. Such special pleading, Dickens argues, can easily be challenged by the Chartists. *Miscellaneous, Journalism.*

Lamplighter, The

Farce written by Dickens for WILLIAM MACREADY in 1838. The astrologer Stargazer, convinced that the stars have predicted the marriage of his niece to Tom Grig, a cockney lamplighter, has his scheme thwarted by Betsy Martin, his maid, who convinces him that he has misread the omens and that his son, Galileo Isaac Newton Flamstead, is the predicted suitor. Macready, unconvinced of the play's commercial potential, did not produce it. Dickens turned it into a short story. "The Lamplighter's Story" (1841), for *The Pic-nic Papers.*

Characters and Related Entries

Barker, Fanny The name given to Fanny Brown in "The Lamplighter's Story," the prose adaptation of Dickens's play, *The Lamplighter.*

Brown, Fanny Stargazer's niece; he thinks she is destined to marry Tom Grig.

Grig, Tom Poor lamplighter who Stargazer thinks is the person predicted by the stars to marry his niece.

Martin, Betsy Stargazer's servant who foils the astronomer's misguided scheme to marry his niece to Tom Grig.

Mooney   Stargazer's scientific partner, an absent-minded astronomer who can only be brought down to earth by electric shocks. Stargazer wants him to marry his daughter, but Mooney declines the opportunity.

Stargazer family   Astronomer, astrologer, and alchemist whose reading of the stars convinces him that the lamplighter Tom Grig is destined to marry his niece, Fanny Brown. He tries to marry his daughter Emma to his laboratory partner Mooney, but his maid Betsey Martin foils that scheme and enables the marriage of Fanny to Stargazer's son, Galileo Isaac Newton Flamstead.

"The Lamplighter's Story"

See *The Lamplighter*.

"Landor's Life"

Review of JOHN FORSTER's biography of WALTER SAVAGE LANDOR for ALL THE YEAR ROUND (July 24, 1869). Dickens writes of his associations with the poet, giving a portrait that shows how fully Lawrence Boythorn in *Bleak House*, who was based on Landor, embodies the qualities Dickens saw in his friend. *Miscellaneous, Journalism.*

"Last Words of the Old Year, The"

Article for HOUSEHOLD WORDS (January 4, 1851) written in the vein of Carlylean prophesy. On his deathbed, the year 1850, a venerable old man catalogs his accomplishments and failures, particularly noting his failure to do anything to educate the 45% of English children who are illiterate, and he bequeaths to the new year "a vast inheritance of degradation and neglect in England." *Miscellaneous, Journalism.*

Lazy Tour of Two Idle Apprentices, The

Semifictional account by WILKIE COLLINS and Dickens of their tour of the north of England in August 1857. The story appeared in five parts in HOUSEHOLD WORDS (October 1857). (1) Two apprentices to the trade of writing set out on an idle walking tour. Taking their names, Francis Goodchild (Dickens) and Thomas Idle (Collins), from WILLIAM HOGARTH's *Industry and Idleness*, they walk five miles out of London before turning around and taking the train to Carlisle. They go into the Cumberland highlands and climb Carrock Mountain on a misty day. There Idle sprains his ankle on the way down. (2) The travelers go on, stopping at Wigton and then at an unnamed town, where Doctor Speddie is called to examine Tom's injury. Goodchild returns to the doctor's surgery with him and hears the story of Arthur Holliday, the son of a manufacturer, who stopped one night in Doncaster, where the only room he could find turned out to have a dead man in the second bed. As Arthur, unable to sleep, watched the body, he saw signs of life and called in Speddie, then a doctor in Doncaster, who revived the man. Now, many years later, Speddie thinks that his strange assistant, Lorn, resembles the young man that he revived in Doncaster. (3) The apprentices go on to Allonby on the Cumberland coast to give Tom a healing rest, but the town is so boring that they leave and spend time at a railway station instead. (4) Going on to LANCASTER, they take a room at an inn, where Goodchild hears the story "The Bride's Chamber" from the ghost of the man who murdered both the bride and the young man who tried to save her. (5) Then the two go on to Doncaster for race week, where Goodchild gets caught up in the crowds and activity while Idle nurses his foot at the hotel, the one idler in Doncaster not involved with the races.

Characters and Related Entries

Allonby   Seaside town in Cumberland where the two idle apprentices find nothing to keep them occupied.

Ben   Servant at the Two Robins Inn.

Goodchild, Francis One of the two idle apprentices—Dickens himself—who "would take upon himself any amount of pains and labour to assure himself that he was idle."

Holliday, Arthur The "reckless, rattle-pated, open-hearted, and open-mouthed" son of a rich manufacturer who is the protagonist of Doctor Speddie's story of the dead medical student who comes back to life.

Idle, Thomas One of the two lazy apprentices, based on WILLIAM HOGARTH's apprentices from *Industry and Idleness*. Idle is a thinly disguised version of WILKIE COLLINS.

Jock Serving boy at the Cumberland inn where Idle's sprained ankle is treated.

Lorn Dr. Speddie's pale assistant; he is probably the medical student that Speddie revived many years before.

Speddie, Dr. Cumberland doctor who attends Thomas Idle's sprained ankle and tells Goodchild the story of Arthur Holliday.

"Leech's 'The Rising Generation'"

Review of JOHN LEECH's collection of 12 drawings from *Punch* for the EXAMINER (December 30, 1848). Describing Leech as "the very first English caricaturist . . . who has considered beauty as being perfectly compatible with his art," Dickens concentrates on the humor, rather than the satire, in Leech's pictures. *Miscellaneous, Journalism.*

"Legal and Equitable Jokes"

Satiric article for HOUSEHOLD WORDS (September 23, 1854). The narrator, a barrister, rejects Graham Willmore's proposed legal reforms on the grounds

that what they address are just practical jokes played by the legal system about which Willmore has no sense of humor. *Miscellaneous, Journalism.*

"Leigh Hunt. A Remonstrance."

Article for ALL THE YEAR ROUND (December 24, 1859) reviewing the biography of LEIGH HUNT by his son. In the article, Dickens admits that he based the delightful side of Skimpole in *Bleak House* on Hunt, but he claims that Skimpole's vices were not drawn from the poet. *Miscellaneous, Journalism.*

Life of Our Lord, The

Narrative life of Jesus that Dickens wrote for his own children in 1846 under the title *The Children's New Testament*. When it was first published in 1934—after the death of his last surviving child, HENRY—it was given the title by which it is now known. The narrative is cast in simple language and emphasizes the parables and the moral teachings in the gospels.

"Little Dombey, The Story of"

Dickens's PUBLIC READING from *Dombey and Son*. Developed in 1858, the first reading from one of the longer novels, it presented the life and death of Paul Dombey. A sad reading, it was not performed as often as many of the others.

"Lively Turtle"

Satiric article for HOUSEHOLD WORDS (October 26, 1850) celebrating the virtues of the turtle—who enjoys comfort and desires to be left alone—as the virtues of England. Snoady, the narrator, sees a similarity between his friend Groggles, a member of the London City Council, and the turtles kept by a restaurant for soup, and he deduces the political significance of the turtles. *Miscellaneous, Journalism.*

Characters and Related Entries

Groggles Member of the Common Council who recommends a restaurant where Snoady can get turtle soup. There Snoady sees the resemblance between the turtle and his friend.

Skim, Mrs. Proprietor of the Commercial Lodging House near ALDERSGATE STREET, where Snoady stays when he comes up to London. *Miscellaneous.*

Snoady Narrator of "The Lively Turtle," a smug and parsimonious man who splurges on a dinner of turtle soup and tender steak. Afterward he realizes that the turtle is representative of the best English virtues—a belief in comfort and a desire to be left alone—which oppose the radicals' desire for change.

"Lost Arctic Voyagers, The"

Two-part article for HOUSEHOLD WORDS (December 2 and 9, 1854) in which Dickens responds to Dr. John Roe's conclusion that the members of the Franklin expedition to the Arctic resorted to cannibalism in their attempts to survive. Dickens points out that Franklin was prepared to die on an earlier expedition and did not consider cannibalism then. He also questions the veracity of the Eskimo stories on which Roe based his conclusions. In the second article, Dickens reviews many cases of alleged cannibalism to show how uncommon and unnatural the practice is, particularly for civilized Europeans. *Miscellaneous, Journalism.* Roe answered Dickens's objections in a letter printed in HOUSEHOLD WORDS on December 23, 1854 (*Stone*). WILKIE COLLINS's play THE FROZEN DEEP (1856), prompted by an idea from Dickens and written in collaboration with him, was based on the Franklin expedition.

"Loving Ballad of Lord Bateman, The"

Cockney version of a traditional ballad, illustrated by GEORGE CRUIKSHANK and published by Charles Tilt in 1849. Dickens wrote a preface and some notes for the volume.

"Magic Fishbone, The"

Children's story told by Alice Rainbird in "Holiday Romance." Given a magic fishbone by Fairy Grandmarina, Princess Alicia knows when to use the charm to save her father, King Watkins the First, from financial ruin. She is rewarded with the hand of Prince Certainpersonio.

"Martyr Medium, The"

Article for ALL THE YEAR ROUND (April 4, 1863) attacking the spiritualist Daniel Dunglas Home by reprinting passages from his book, *Incidents in My Life,* and then debunking them. *Miscellaneous.*

Master Humphrey's Clock

Weekly periodical edited and written by Dickens. Begun on April 4, 1840, it was planned to be a collection of stories and sketches produced by Master Humphrey and his circle of friends. The group gathered weekly to hold readings of manuscripts found in the case of Master Humphrey's clock. The original scheme was not successful, and Dickens altered the format to make the Master Humphrey material a frame narrative for two of his novels, *The Old Curiosity Shop* and *Barnaby Rudge.*

(1) In the opening chapter, Master Humphrey, a reclusive and crippled old man, and his three friends—a deaf gentleman, Jack Redburn, and Owen Miles—hear the first of the Giant Chroni-

cles, "Magog's Tale" of Hugh Graham and Mistress Alice. (2) The second story, "A Confession Found in a Prison . . . ," chronicles a murder during the Restoration period in the 17th century. (3) When Pickwick applies for membership in the group, he offers a tale of witchcraft (4) and proposes Jack Bamber for the other vacant place in the circle. (5) Meanwhile, below stairs, Sam and Tony Weller and Humphrey's servants form a similar storytelling group, "Mr. Weller's Watch," where Sam tells two anecdotes involving barbers. (6) Tony Weller introduces his mischievous grandson, little Tony, to the group; Master Humphrey tells of visiting ST. PAUL'S CATHEDRAL; in the end the deaf gentleman finds Master Humphrey dead in his chair before the fire. The final installment of *Humphrey* appeared on December 4, 1841. The *Master Humphrey* material was first collected for the CHARLES DICKENS EDITION. The individual stories are discussed below.

Characters and Related Entries

The following are characters in the frame story of *Master Humphrey's Clock.*

Belinda   A lovelorn young woman from Bath who writes to Master Humphrey seeking help in finding her lover.

Benton, Miss   Master Humphrey's housekeeper. Briefly the object of Tony Weller's affections, she later marries Slithers.

Blinder, Bill   The hostler who dies and leaves his lantern to Tony Weller.

deaf gentleman   Companion to Master Humphrey who is like a brother to him even though he has never told him his name.

Etc. Etc.   "Devilish gentlemanly fellow" who requests admission for himself and a friend to Master Humphrey's circle. His application is refused.

Gog and Magog   Two giant figures in the Guildhall—guardian spirits of the CITY of London—who come to life and tell stories and legends of the city's past.

Humphrey, Master   Narrator of *Master Humphrey's Clock*, "a misshapen, deformed old man"; he gathers a group of friends around him who contribute manuscripts that they read to each other and store in his clock case. He extends his role, in what must be an authorial afterthought, when he identifies himself as the "single gentleman," the brother of Nell's grandfather, in *Curiosity Shop*. After Dickens completed *Barnaby Rudge*, the deaf gentleman, one of the circle of friends, tells of Master Humphrey's peaceful death.

Miles, Owen   Fourth member of Master Humphrey's circle, a rich retired merchant who is Jack Redburn's constant companion.

Pickwick, Samuel   A diminished figure in this reappearance, Pickwick joins Humphrey's circle and tells the story of John Podgers.

Redburn, Jack   Member of Master Humphrey's circle and a Jack of many trades, he acts as "librarian, secretary, steward, and first minister; director-general of all my affairs, and inspector-general of my household" (2). He and the deaf gentleman are Master Humphrey's heirs.

Slithers   Master Humphrey's barber, one of the members of "Mr. Weller's Watch."

Toddyhigh, Joe   Childhood friend of the incoming LORD MAYOR of London. He falls asleep in the Guildhall during the Lord Mayor's banquet and awakens to overhear Gog and Magog telling stories in the night.

Weller, Sam and Tony   Accompanying Pickwick when he joins Humphrey's circle, Sam and Tony Weller become the central figures in a below-stairs circle, "Mr. Weller's Watch," in which the servants imitate their masters and share stories among themselves.

"MAGOG'S TALE"

Story of Hugh Graham, apprentice to a wealthy bowyer at the time of Elizabeth. He falls in love with Mistress Alice, his employer's daughter, but she runs off with a gentleman and is ruined. When she returns, Hugh protects her, kills her seducer, and is killed himself in the ensuing riot.

Characters and Related Entries

Alice, Mistress Heroine of Magog's tale, the only daughter of the bowyer.

bowyer, the The rich man who is Mistress Alice's father and Hugh Graham's master in Magog's story.

Graham, Hugh The hero of Magog's tale, a 16th-century apprentice who is in love with his master's daughter, Mistress Alice. After she is seduced and ruined by a nobleman, Hugh protects her, kills the offending nobleman, and is himself killed in the ensuing riot.

"A CONFESSION FOUND IN A PRISON IN THE TIME OF CHARLES THE SECOND"

Story included in *Master Humphrey's Clock*, narrated by an officer in the army of King Charles II as he awaits execution for murdering his nephew. He tells how the murder came about, of his guilt after committing it, and how he was caught by two bloodhounds, who entered his garden and exposed the grave where he had buried the boy.

"MR. PICKWICK'S TALE"

Story told to Master Humphrey by Mr. Pickwick. John Podgers, a well-to-do burger of Windsor during the reign of James I, is asked to watch through the night for some witches that have been disturbing citizens in the neighboring town of KINGSTON. He turns down the opportunity, but his brash young nephew, Will Marks, accepts, and he becomes involved in a Cavalier intrigue to transport the body of a hanged cavalier from Kingston to the Church of ST. DUNSTAN in London. After his secret mission, he tells the citizens of Kingston of his wild adventure with witches.

Characters and Related Entries

Marks, Will John Podgers's nephew, "a wild, roving young fellow of twenty" who accepts the com-

mission to watch for witches and becomes involved in a Cavalier conspiracy to bury one of their hanged comrades.

Podgers, John A comfortable and lazy citizen of Windsor in Mr. Pickwick's tale of the 17th century, who refuses an opportunity to watch through the night for witches.

SAM WELLER'S TALES

Sam tells two anecdotes about barbers. The first tells of Jinkinson, a barber so obsessed with barbering that he even cuts his own hair just before he dies. In his second story, also about a barber, William Gibbs, a hairdresser, is so enamored of the dummies that he has placed in his window that he vows he will not marry until he meets a woman to match the model. When he meets such a woman, she refuses his proposal because she has become enamored of the male dummy and finds Gibbs less attractive.

Characters and Related Entries

Gibbs, William Hairdresser who is the subject of Sam Weller's story. He vows never to "enter into the bonds of wedlock . . . until I meet with a young 'ooman as realizes my idea o' that 'ere fairest dummy with the light hair."

Jinkinson Barber in Sam Weller's tale—"easy shavin' was his natur', and cuttin' and curlin' was his pride and glory"—who spent all his money on bears.

Memoirs of Grimaldi

These memoirs of JOSEPH GRIMALDI (1778–1837), the great clown of Regency PANTOMIME, were written during the last years of his life. At the request of the publisher RICHARD BENTLEY, Dickens selected the most engaging parts of Grimaldi's story, changed the first-person narration to third-person, and added a preface in which he described his own fascination with clowns. The *Memoirs*, "Edited by Boz" and with illustrations by GEORGE CRUIKSHANK, were published in two volumes in 1838. A modern edition, edited by Richard Findlater, appeared in 1968.

"Metropolitan Protectives, The"

Article for HOUSEHOLD WORDS (April 26, 1851) by W. H. WILLS and Dickens about a night they spent at a police station. They describe the various cases that come before the police, many of them involving drunkenness, and how the police deal with them. The article was intended to assure readers of the magazine that they would be well protected during the upcoming Great Exhibition. *Stone.*

Miscellaneous Papers

Collection of previously uncollected articles, plays, and poems by Dickens, put together by B. W. MATZ in 1908 as volumes 35 and 36 of the National Edition of Dickens's works. It contains 21 articles from the EXAMINER, 1838–49; 83 articles from HOUSEHOLD WORDS, 1850–59; 12 articles from ALL THE YEAR ROUND, 1859–69; 6 plays; and 19 poems. Matz's collection has been expanded by later work done by WALTER DEXTER for the NONESUCH EDITION, by HARRY STONE, by MICHAEL SLATER and John Drew, and by various other scholars, who have identified other works. The four-volume scholarly edition of Slater and Drew's *Dickens' Journalism* (2000) is now the standard source for such material, but it does not include all of the materials in the collections by Matz and Stone.

Misnar, the Sultan of India

This play, written by Dickens when he was a boy of nine, is the earliest known work by him. It was based on one of the Tales of the Genii, but no known copy of it has survived.

"Mr. Bendigo Buster on Our National Defences against Education"

Satiric article for HOUSEHOLD WORDS (December 28, 1850) by HENRY MORLEY and Dickens in which an old boxer, Bendigo Buster, describes the German educational system and warns his English readers, particularly those of the misguided journal for which he is writing the article, of the demoralizing effects of education. Do not follow the Germans, he counsels; stand with Turkey, Russia, Spain, Portugal, and southern Italy, which, like Britain, do not educate their children. *Stone.*

"Mr. Bob Sawyer's Party"

One of Dickens's two PUBLIC READINGS from *Pickwick*. (The other was the Bardell *v.* Pickwick trial.) This reading was based on chapter 32 of the novel and was one of the most effective and popular of the comic pieces he performed.

"Mr. Booley's View of the Last Lord Mayor's Show"

An allegorical interpretation of the LORD MAYOR's parade by Dickens's representative Englishman, Mr. Booley, the retired gentleman from ISLINGTON. From HOUSEHOLD WORDS (November 30, 1850). *Miscellaneous.*

"Mr. Bull's Somnambulist"

Political satire on the Crimean conflict for HOUSEHOLD WORDS (November 25, 1854), in which Mr. Bull's household is afflicted with the somnambulism of its housekeeper, Abby Dean (Lord Aberdeen,

Prime Minister at the time). Her condition causes her to do nothing and to allow Bull's mortal enemy Nick (Russia) to steal a Turkey. *Miscellaneous, Journalism.*

Characters and Related Entries

Dean, Abigail Mr. Bull's sleepwalking housekeeper, a satiric representation of the earl of Aberdeen, prime minister from 1852 to 1855: "Abby Dean. Phlegmatic temperament. Bilious habit. Circulation, very sluggish. Speech, drowsy, indistinct, and confused. Senses, feeble. Memory, short. Pulse, very languid. A remarkably slow goer. At all times a heavy sleeper, and difficult to awaken."

"Mr. Chops the Dwarf"

PUBLIC READING based on "Going into Society," Dickens's Christmas story for HOUSEHOLD WORDS, 1858. Although he prepared the reading text in 1861, he did not perform it until 1868, and then only rarely.

Mr. Nightingale's Diary

One-act farce by Dickens and MARK LEMON in 1851. The hypochondriacal Mr. Nightingale is saved from Slap's schemes to defraud him of his money by Gabblewig and Rosina Nightingale, who foil Slap by assuming various disguises. They are rewarded for their efforts when Nightingale blesses their marriage.

Characters and Related Entries

Bit, Charley Under this name (short for Blitheringtonfordbury), Gabblewig disguises himself as an actor who once played in the same company as Slap.

Blower, Captain R. N. One of Gabblewig's disguises, he has presumably been made ill by taking Slap's mustard-and-milk cure.

Formiville Slap's stage name.

Gabblewig Lawyer who, by a series of impersonations, promotes his claim to Rosina Nightingale's affections and saves her uncle from Slap's extortion schemes.

Lithers, Thomas Landlord of the Water-Lily Hotel at Malvern, where Nightingale comes to take the water cure.

Malvern Wells Spa in Worcestershire where the hypochondriacal Mr. Nightingale comes to take the water cure.

Nightingale family Family at the center of the farce in *Mr. Nightingale's Diary.* Christopher, a hypochondriac who is the victim of Slap's schemes, opposes the marriage of his niece Rosina to Gabblewig. When she and her suitor save her uncle from Slap's plots, they win his consent to the marriage.

Poulter, Mr. and Mrs. Gabblewig and Rosina disguise themselves as Mr. and Mrs. Poulter, a couple who have benefited so from the water cure at Malvern that they cannot stop walking.

Sexton A deaf old man, one of Gabblewig's impersonations in his scheme to expose Slap.

Slap Actor, known professionally as Formiville, who concocts several schemes to take Mr. Nightingale's property.

Susan Rosina Nightingale's maid.

Tip Gabblewig's servant. Slap recruits him to pretend to be Mr. Nightingale's son in one of his schemes.

Trusty, Mrs. Rosina disguises herself as Mrs. Trusty, Captain Blower's nurse, in one of Gabblewig's impersonations.

"Mr. Robert Bolton"
See *Mudfog*

"Mrs. Gamp"

Dickens's PUBLIC READING from *Martin Chuzzlewit,* first performed in 1858. Although Mrs. Gamp was one of Dickens's most popular characters, he had difficulty developing a suitable text for the reading, and this piece underwent more revision than any other in his repertory. Still it was a mixed success. His portrayal of Mrs. Gamp was generally applauded, but Betsey Prig and Pecksniff were regarded as disappointing.

Mudfog Papers, The

Collection of Dickens's early sketches from BENTLEY'S MISCELLANY, 1837–38, published by RICHARD BENTLEY in 1880. The collection included "The Public Life of Mr. Tulrumble," "Full Report of the First Meeting of the Mudfog Association . . . ," "Full Report of the Second Meeting . . . ," "The Pantomime of Life," "Some Particulars concerning a Lion," and "Mr. Robert Bolton." Later editions also included "Familiar Epistle from a Parent to a Child."

"PUBLIC LIFE OF MR. TULRUMBLE, THE"

Sketch describing the rise to eminence of Nicholas Tulrumble, a coal dealer who becomes mayor of Mudfog and for an unhappy six weeks surrounds himself with pomp and pretension until he realizes that he was much happier as just one of the regulars at the Jolly Boatman. First published in BENTLEY'S MISCELLANY (January 1837).

Characters and Related Entries

Jennings Secretary to Nicholas Tulrumble, mayor of Mudfog.

Jolly Boatman Public house in Mudfog that is denied a license by Mayor Tulrumble, who has statistically figured out that the number of beer patrons served by the pub contributes to the increasing depravity of the town.

Lighterman Arms Public house in Mudfog where Nicholas Tulrumble spends the evenings with his friends before he becomes mayor.

Mudfog "A pleasant town" in a hollow by the river, "from which river Mudfog derives an agreeable scent of pitch, tar, coals, and rope-yarn, a roving population in oilskin hats, a pretty steady influx of drunken bargemen, and a great many other maritime advantages." The setting for several of Dickens's early sketches, it is based on Chatham.

Sniggs Mayor of Mudfog who dies at 85, leaving the position vacant for Nicholas Tulrumble.

Tulrumble family Nicholas, a prosperous coal merchant of Mudfog Hall who is appointed mayor of Mudfog. Impressed by the LORD MAYOR's installation ceremony in London, he creates a grand ceremony for himself in Mudfog, but the occasion is disrupted by the drunken Ned Twigger, who reels into the procession in a suit of armor. Tulrumble gives up the position after six weeks when he realizes he was happier as just one of the group of men who gathered at the local pub. Mrs. Tulrumble and Nicholas Jr. are not so ready to give up the magnificence of the mayoral life as Tulrumble is.

Twigger, Edward ("Bottle-nosed Ned") Dissolute idler in Mudfog who is recruited by Mayor Tulrumble to appear in the mayoral procession in a suit of armor, but who is too drunk to perform sedately. He disrupts the procession and finally is chased home by his wife.

"FULL REPORT OF THE FIRST MEETING OF THE MUDFOG ASSOCIATION"

Second of three sketches published in BENTLEY'S MISCELLANY (October 1837). Boz's report of the proceedings in the zoology and botany, anatomy and medicine, statistics, and mechanical science sections of the Conference at Mudfog satirizes the proceedings of the British Association for the Advancement of Science.

"FULL REPORT OF THE SECOND MEETING OF THE MUDFOG ASSOCIATION"

This second satirical report of the proceedings of the Mudfog Association appeared in BENTLEY'S

MISCELLANY (September 1838) and added a section on umbugology and ditchwateristics.

Characters and Related Entries

Augustus The dog, "named in affectionate remembrance of a former lover of his mistress to whom he bore a striking personal resemblance," dissected by Professors Muff and Noggs.

Black Boy and Stomach-ache Oldcastle inn where the second meeting of the Mudfog Association is held.

Blank An exhibitor at the mechanical science section of the Mudfog Association.

Blubb Member of the Mudfog Association.

Blunderbore, Captain Officer in the Horse Marines and an authority on horses.

Blunderum Member of the Mudfog Association who contributes a paper on the last moments of the learned pig.

Boot-jack and Countenance Oldcastle inn where the second meeting of the Mudfog Association is held.

Brown Member of the Mudfog Association.

Buffer, Dr. Member of the Mudfog Association.

Carter Head of the mechanical section of the Mudfog Association.

Coppernose Member of the Mudfog Association.

Crinkles Exhibitor at the meeting of the Mudfog Association who has invented a machine to pick pockets.

Doze, Professor Member of the Mudfog Association.

Drawley, Mr. Member of the Mudfog Association.

Dull Vice president of the umbugology and ditchwateristics section of the Mudfog Association.

Dummy Member of the Mudfog Association.

Fee, Dr. W. R. A medical member of the Mudfog Association.

Flummery Member of the Mudfog Association.

Foxey Member of the Mudfog Association.

Grime, Professor A member of the mechanical section of the Mudfog Association.

Grub, Mr. President of the umbugology and ditchwateristics section of the Mudfog Association.

Grummidge, Dr. Member of the medical section of the Mudfog Association.

Jobba Member of the Mudfog Association who invents a machine for bringing "railway shares prematurely to a premium."

Joltered, Sir William President of the zoology section of the Mudfog Association.

Ketch, Professor John Member of the Mudfog Association who exhibited the skull of a notorious murderer, James Greenacre.

Knight Bell, Mr. Member of the Mudfog Association who exhibits the interior of a man who has swallowed a door key.

Kutankumagen, Dr. Member of the medical section of the Mudfog Association.

Kwakley Member of the statistical section of the Mudfog Association.

Leaver Member of the Mudfog Association.

Ledbrain, X. Member of the statistics section of the Mudfog Association.

Long Ears, the Hon. and Revd. Member of the Mudfog Association.

Mallet Member of the Mudfog Association.

Misty, X. X. Speaker who addresses the second meeting of the Mudfog Association on the disappearance of dancing bears from the streets of London.

Mortair Member of the medical section of the Mudfog Association.

Muddlebranes, Mr. A vice president of the zoology and botany section of the Mudfog Association.

Mudfog Association for the Advancement of Everything Dickens's satirical version in BENTLEY'S MISCELLANY of the British Association for the Advancement of Science, an organization founded in 1831, with sections devoted to many scientific specialties. Dickens included two reports of the Mudfog Association in the magazine.

Muff, Professor Member of the medical section of the Mudfog Association, a hard drinker who claims that infinitesimal doses of drugs are just as effective as regular doses.

Mull, Professor Member of the Mudfog Association.

Neeshawts, Dr. Member of the Mudfog Association.

Noakes Member of the statistical section of the Mudfog Association.

Nogo, Professor Member of the medical section of the Mudfog Association.

Pessell Member of the medical section of the Mudfog Association.

Pig and Tinderbox Inn Inn where Professors Snore, Doze, and Wheezy are expected to stay during the meeting of the Mudfog Association.

Pipkin, Mr., M. R. C. S. Speaker at the anatomy and medicine session of the Mudfog Association.

Prosee, Mr. Participant in the display of models and mechanical section of the Mudfog conference.

Pumpkinskull, Professor Member of the Mudfog Association.

Purblind Member of the Mudfog Association.

Queerspeck, Professor Member of the mechanical section of the Mudfog Association.

Rummun, Professor Member of the Mudfog Association.

Scroo Vice President of the display of models and mechanical science section of the Mudfog Association.

Slug Member of the Mudfog Association.

Smith, Mr. Member of the Mudfog Association.

Snivey, Sir Hookham Member of the Mudfog Association.

Snore, Professor President of the zoology section of the Mudfog Association, an "ingenious gentleman [who] proposed to open a communication with fleas . . . so that they might be thoroughly imbued with a sense of the advantages they must necessarily derive from changing their mode of life, and applying themselves to honest labour."

Snuffletoffle, Q. J. Speaker at the umbugology and ditchwateristics section of the Mudfog Association.

Soemup, Dr. President of the anatomy and medicine section of the Mudfog Association.

Sowster Oldcastle beadle who has "a very red nose, which he attributes to a habit of early rising—so red, indeed, that but for this explanation I should have supposed it to proceed from occasional inebriety."

Styles   Member of the statistics section of the Mudfog Association.

Thom   Practitioner of homeopathy and member of the Mudfog Association.

Tickle   Inventor of "spectacles, which enabled the wearer to discern, in very bright colours, objects at a great distance, and rendered him wholly blind to those immediately before him."

Timbered   Vice-president of the statistics section of the Mudfog Association.

Toorell, Dr.   Member of the anatomy and medicine section of the Mudfog Association.

Truck   Member of the mechanical science section of the Mudfog Association.

Waghorn   Member of the Mudfog Association.

Wheezy, Professor   Vice president of the zoology and botany section of the Mudfog Association.

Wigsby   Member of the Mudfog Association.

Woodensconce   Member of the Mudfog Association.

"PANTOMIME OF LIFE, THE"

Article from BENTLEY'S MISCELLANY comparing the types from PANTOMIME on the stage to people in real life.

Characters and Related Entries

Do'em   Captain Fitz-Whisker Fiercy's servant, a pantaloon.

Fiercy, Captain the Hon. Fitz-Whisker   A swaggering officer who, with his servant Do'em, operates a con game in which they take goods on credit and sell them for cash.

"SOME PARTICULARS CONCERNING A LION"

Facetious article for BENTLEY'S MISCELLANY (May 1837) comparing the lion in the zoo with a literary lion and concluding that the latter is superior.

"MR. ROBERT BOLTON— THE 'GENTLEMAN CONNECTED WITH THE PRESS'"

At a gathering of the regulars at the Green Dragon, Robert Bolton, a shorthand writer for the press, tells the story of Sawyer, a brutal baker who killed his son by boiling him in a laundry kettle. First published in BENTLEY'S MISCELLANY (August 1838).

Characters and Related Entries

Bolton, Robert   Shorthand writer for the press who engrosses his audience at the Green Dragon pub with his account of a baker who murdered his son.

Clip   Hairdresser who is among the group listening to Robert Bolton's tale.

Green Dragon   Public house in Westminster where Robert Bolton holds forth.

Murgatroyd   A regular at the Green Dragon, an undertaker.

Sawyer   Drunken baker who abuses his wife and then, when his son objects, murders the boy by boiling him in a laundry copper.

Thicknesse   A regular at the Green Dragon; "a large stomach surmounted by a man's head, and placed on the top of two particularly short legs."

"FAMILIAR EPISTLE FROM A PARENT TO A CHILD"

Dickens's letter to the readers of BENTLEY'S MISCELLANY (February 1839) as he turned over to WILLIAM HARRISON AINSWORTH the editorship of the magazine, his child.

"Murdered Person, The"

Article for HOUSEHOLD WORDS (October 11, 1856) criticizing the public sympathy for the murderer and the lack of concern for the victim, even to the extent of blaming the victim. Dickens begins with the case of Mr. Dove, a penitent "pet prisoner," whose self-justifying statements reveal no remorse for the wife he killed. Similarly, those who support strict divorce and Sunday closing laws ignore the victims who suffer or are driven to crime by these constraining laws. Dickens develops this theme again in "Five New Points of Criminal Law," in which he suggests that the underlying principle behind the points is "that the offender is the Murdered Person." *Miscellaneous, Journalism.*

"Murderous Extremes"

Article for HOUSEHOLD WORDS (January 3, 1857) lamenting the failure of bystanders to stop a murder in progress and suggesting that such passivity is the result of the public's being told that they should not take the law into their own hands and that to do so is to risk being accused of interfering with the rights of the criminal. *Miscellaneous, Journalism.*

"My Mahogany Friend"

Article for HOUSEHOLD WORDS (March 8, 1851), by MARY BOYLE, considerably reworked by Dickens. It tells of life at the Chase, the old house near the narrator's "Den," that the narrator gleans from a mahogany hat rack. *Stone.*

"My Uncle"

Article for HOUSEHOLD WORDS (December 6, 1851) by W. H. WILLS and Dickens, describing the pawn-

broker and the people who patronize his business, a fuller and more sympathetic picture than that in *Boz,* "Pawnbroker's Shop." *Stone.*

"Narrative of Extraordinary Suffering, A"

Article for HOUSEHOLD WORDS (July 12, 1857) describing Mr. Lost, a retired businessman from Ware who gets lost in the maze of the railway system and Bradshaw's railway schedule. In his diary, Lost records an extraordinary series of railway journeys throughout Britain on which he is continually shunted from one line to another, never reaching his intended destinations. The whole experience reduces him to babbling idiocy. *Miscellaneous.*

Characters and Related Entries

Flay, George   John Lost's manservant.

Lost, John   Retired businessman of the Maze, Ware, who becomes lost in Bradshaw's railway schedule and goes mad trying to find his way home.

Mag, Mary Anne   John Lost's confidential domestic who purchases the Railway Guide that drives her employer mad.

"New Song"

Verses Dickens wrote in 1849 to his friend MARK LEMON, urging Lemon to join him on holiday in Brighton. *Miscellaneous.*

"New Year's Day"

Article for HOUSEHOLD WORDS (January 1, 1859) in which the narrator remembers several New Year's Days. On the first he was taken as a child to the

World of Toys near SOHO SQUARE, where he chose a magic wand, but he was disappointed when he could not transform anything with it. Then the day itself becomes a kind of wand, calling up memories of New Year's Days past: a party where all adults were lined up against a wall simultaneously drinking punch from glass cups; a day when he and his sister hid a man with a wooden leg behind the coal cellar; the day when he challenged Paynter, his rival for "the youngest Miss Clickett but one," to a duel; several New Year's Days spent at Miss Boles's country house; a day in an Italian villa; a cold day in Paris going to the theater. *Miscellaneous, Journalism.*

Characters and Related Entries

Boles   Inhabitant of a "high, bleak" house "in the Down-country" and father of Miss Boles, "a blessed creature, a Divinity," whom the narrator visits on several New Year's Days.

Clickett, Miss   "The youngest Miss Clickett but one" is the object of the boyish affections of the narrator and his rival, "the Fiend Paynter."

Paynter   The narrator's "enemy" in the competition for the attentions of "the youngest Miss Clickett but one." Although they arrange to duel, the two end up avoiding a fight and agreeing on the perfidy of Miss Clickett.

Pipchin, Mrs.   "An unsympathetic old personage of the female gender, flavoured with musty dry lavender, dressed in black crepe," who accompanies the narrator as a child to a toy market and buys a Harlequin's wand for him. Although Dickens does not explicitly connect this Mrs. Pipchin with the character in *Dombey*, the two women have similar roles and characteristics.

"Nicholas Nickleby at the Yorkshire School"

Dickens's PUBLIC READING from *Nickleby*, it included the comic scene of Fanny Squeers's tea party and reached a triumphant climax in Nicholas's thrashing of Squeers.

"Niger Expedition, The"

Article from the EXAMINER (August 19, 1848) in which Dickens reviews Captain William Allen's report of the failed expedition up the Niger in 1841. The expedition set out with three ships, intending to negotiate with the tribal chiefs along the river to end the slave trade, open up commerce with Britain, establish an agricultural colony, and promulgate Christianity. After entering into some naive agreements with double-dealing tribal chiefs, the expedition was ravaged by fever, which killed nearly all of the Europeans. Dickens concludes that "no amount of philanthropy has a right to waste such valuable life as was squandered here. . . . Between the civilized European and the barbarous African there is a great gulf set." Looking forward to his satire of Mrs. Jellyby in *Bleak House*, he suggests that missionary efforts must begin in England: "the work at home must be completed thoroughly, or there is no hope abroad." *Miscellaneous, Journalism.*

"Nightly Scene in London, A"

Article for HOUSEHOLD WORDS (January 26, 1856) describing the narrator's experience outside the workhouse in WHITECHAPEL, where he found five young women lying in rags in the street because there was no more room in the casual ward of the workhouse. He was told that there were starving people lying outside the workhouse every night, usually more than five. After giving each one some money for food and lodging, the narrator attacks "demented disciples who use arithmetic and political economy beyond all bounds of sense. . . . I utterly renounce and abominate them in their insanity; and I address people with respect for the spirit of the New Testament, who mind such things, and who think them infamous in our streets." *Miscellaneous, Journalism.*

"No. 1 Branch Line: The Signal-man"

Short story about an apparition that appears to a railway signalman. See *Christmas Stories*, "Mugby," 4.

"Nobody, Somebody, and Everybody"

Article for *HOUSEHOLD WORDS* (August 30, 1856), attacking "Nobody . . . the great, irresponsible, guilty, wicked, blind giant of this time," who is accomplished at failure, takes no responsibility for his inaction or incompetence, and is responsible for bringing about the many fiascos of the recent Crimean War. "I want Somebody to be clever in doing business, not clever in evading it," the narrator asserts. "I want to see the working Somebody in every responsible position which the winking Somebody and Nobody now monopolize between them." This article helps explain the "nobody's fault" theme, which Dickens developed in *Dorrit*. *Miscellaneous, Journalism*.

"North American Slavery"

Article for *HOUSEHOLD WORDS* (September 18, 1852) by HENRY MORLEY and Dickens. The authors praise HARRIET BEECHER STOWE's *Uncle Tom's Cabin* as "a noble work; full of high power, lofty humanity; the gentlest, sweetest, and yet boldest, writing," and a work that prompts a desire to abolish slavery. They compare the cruel slavery in Cuba to the much more benign institution in the United States, pointing out that few slaves in the United States attempt to escape to freedom. The harsh treatment of free Negroes in the North also discourages slaves from attempting to escape. Efforts to educate Negroes and to create colonies such as the one in Liberia will enable the Americans to end slavery in a much more positive way than the British did. *Stone*.

"Old Lady in Threadneedle Street, The"

Article for *HOUSEHOLD WORDS* (July 6, 1850) by W. H. WILLS and Dickens describing a visit to the BANK OF ENGLAND in Threadneedle Street. Characterizing the visit as if to the household of "a dear, kind, liberal, benevolent Old Lady," they describe the activities in each of the rooms in the bank, comparing the institution to a publishing firm and a large circulating library. *Stone*.

"Old Lamps for New Ones"

Article for *HOUSEHOLD WORDS* (June 15, 1850) attacking the medievalism of such groups as the Young England Movement and, especially, the PRE-RAPHAELITE Brotherhood that disdained the progress of the preceding 300 years and, repeating the bargain made by the evil magician to obtain Aladdin's wonderful lamp in *THE ARABIAN NIGHTS*, traded modern lamps for medieval ones. Dickens may also have had Ruskin, whose *Seven Lamps of Architecture* (1849) was current, in mind when he chose the title for the article. Although Dickens apparently did not read Ruskin's book until later in the summer of 1850, Ruskin had already published one defense of the Pre-Raphaelites in a letter to the *Times* in May, shortly before Dickens published this article attacking them. Dickens begins with a famous attack on JOHN EVERETT MILLAIS's painting *Christ in the House of His Parents*, in which he claims that realism reduces a subject that should prompt "tender, awful, sorrowful, ennobling, sacred, grateful, or beautiful associations" into one that reveals "the lowest depths of what is mean, odious, repulsive, and revolting." Dickens then satirically suggests several other movements that might similarly promote retrogressive ideas. Pre-Perspective, Pre-Newtonian, Pre-Galileo, Pre-Harvey, Pre-Gower, and Pre-Chaucer brotherhoods could apply similarly misguided principles to various scientific and humanistic studies and to literature, "cancelling all the advances of nearly four hundred years, and reverting to one of the most disagreeable periods . . .

when the Nation was yet very slowly emerging from barbarism." *Miscellaneous, Journalism.*

"One Man in a Dockyard"

Article for *HOUSEHOLD WORDS* (September 6, 1851) by R. H. HORNE and Dickens, describing the visit of John Strongitharm, "a man of good average size and strength," to ROCHESTER and CHATHAM. After visiting the Castle and Cathedral in Rochester and the military barracks, parade grounds, and fortifications in Chatham, he tours the dockyard with its sawmill, rolling mill, and shipbuilding activities. Awed by the scale of achievement, Strongitharm realizes that only "well-devised combinations of men [could] produce this majestic result." The power resides in all who contribute to the project and should not be ceded to "two or three genteel families." *Stone.*

"On Her Majesty's Service"

Article for *HOUSEHOLD WORDS* (January 7, 1854) by E. C. GRENVILLE MURRAY, edited by Dickens, that fictionalized Murray's experience as a consular official in Turkey and included an especially biting and bitter portrait of Sir Stratford Canning, Ambassador to Turkey, under the name Sir Hector Stubble. *Stone.*

"On Mr. Fechter's Acting"

Article for the *ATLANTIC MONTHLY* (August 1869) enthusiastically describing the dramatic talents of CHARLES FECHTER, Dickens's friend and protégé, when the actor was beginning his theatrical tour of America.

"On Strike"

Article for *HOUSEHOLD WORDS* (February 11, 1854) in which Dickens describes his visit to PRESTON during the bitter and prolonged strike of the cotton weavers. In the train on his way there, he argues with a fellow traveler he calls Mr. Snapper. Dickens expresses his reservations about POLITICAL ECONOMY and his desire not to take sides in the strike; Snapper sides with the masters and asserts that one cannot be neutral. In Preston, Dickens reads the bills posted by the workers and attends one of their meetings; he is impressed with their restraint, the orderliness of the proceedings, and the "absence of anything like sullen discontent." He ends the article urging mediation between masters and men. *Miscellaneous, Journalism.*

Characters and Related Entries

Snapper   The name Dickens gives to a fellow traveler on the train to PRESTON who supports the masters in the Preston strike.

"Our Almanac"

Dickens's announcement in *HOUSEHOLD WORDS* (November 24, 1855) of the first issue of the *The Household Words Almanac*. The project was not successful, and only two issues of the almanac appeared, in 1856 and 1857. *Stone.*

"Our Commission"

Satirical article for *HOUSEHOLD WORDS* (August 11, 1855). Following a commission report on the adulteration of food, the article describes a report on the adulteration of government, public offices, and the representative chamber. The report finds all of these institutions adulterated by "unprincipled wholesale dealers. . . . When one of these dealers succeeded to a business or 'came in,' according to the slang of the trade—his first proceeding, after the adulteration of Public Office with Noodledom, was to consider how he could adulterate and lower his Representative Chamber." The solution, Dickens suggests, is for the public to reject all adulteration whatsoever. *Miscellaneous, Journalism.*

"Our Wicked Mis-statements"

Article for HOUSEHOLD WORDS (January 19, 1856) by HENRY MORLEY and Dickens, responding to HARRIET MARTINEAU's pamphlet *The Factory Controversy: A Warning against Meddling Legislation* (1855), in which she argued against a proposal to require cotton manufacturers to fence off their machinery to prevent accidents. Martineau accused HOUSEHOLD WORDS of "unscrupulous statements, insolence, arrogance, and cant" in its statements of support for the proposal. After expressing esteem for Martineau, the authors challenge her misstatements and accuse her of special pleading for the Lancashire Association to Prevent the Fencing of Machinery, the organization that issued the pamphlet. Morley and Dickens challenge her figures for the number of accidents and go on to state the case for fencing machinery, pointing out that the manufacturers in Lancashire have been especially recalcitrant in taking preventive measures. *Stone.*

"The Pantomime of Life"

See *Mudfog.*

"Paper Mill, A"

Article for HOUSEHOLD WORDS (August 31, 1850) by MARK LEMON and Dickens describing a visit to a paper mill at Dartford in KENT. As the narrator describes the process of making paper, he imagines himself as the rags that go through several stages of transformation to become writing paper. *Stone.*

"Paradise at Tooting, The"

A bitter article for the EXAMINER (January 27, 1849) sarcastically attacking Mr. Drouet, proprietor of a baby farm in Tooting where a cholera epidemic had ravaged the infant population of 1,400, so that the "Tooting churchyard became too small for the piles of children's coffins." Dickens charges Drouet with neglect, overcrowding, and physical cruelty to the children. He charges the POOR LAW Guardians and inspectors with responsibility for the scourge. They allowed Drouet to maintain his vile establishment, which was "brutally conducted, vilely kept, preposterously inspected, dishonestly defended, a disgrace to a Christian community, and a stain upon a civilized land." Drouet's baby farm is a large-scale version of Mrs. Mann's establishment in *Twist,* where Oliver spends his early years and where his friend, young Dick, dies. Dickens addressed the Drouet case in two further articles. "The Tooting Farm" and "The Verdict for Drouet." *Miscellaneous, Journalism.*

"Perfect Felicity"

First in a series of articles for HOUSEHOLD WORDS (April 6, 1850) written in the voice of a raven who objects to being caged and misunderstood by humans who think he is happy and a "member of a Happy Family." He tallies his dislike of other family members—owl, pigeon, dogs, children, sparrows—and reveals his disgust with his situation in writing. *Miscellaneous, Journalism. See also* "From the Raven in the Happy Family."

"Personal"

Dickens's statement in HOUSEHOLD WORDS (June 12, 1858) responding to rumors regarding his marital difficulties and his relationships with GEORGINA HOGARTH and ELLEN TERNAN. Addressed to those of his readers "who know me through my writings, and who do not know me otherwise," the statement concludes with the following declaration: "I most solemnly declare, then—and this I do, both in my own name and in my wife's name—that all the lately whispered rumours touching the trouble at which I have glanced, are abominably false." When his publishers, BRADBURY & EVANS, refused to publish the statement in PUNCH, Dickens broke off his relationship with them and began a new magazine to replace HOUSEHOLD WORDS. *Stone, Journalism.*

"Pet Prisoners"

Article for *HOUSEHOLD WORDS* (April 27, 1850) on PRISONS, criticizing the separate system of imprisonment currently in effect at the model prison in PENTONVILLE. Dickens objects to the expense of the experiment, pointing out that the prisoners are better fed and have better accommodations than workhouse inmates or the working poor. The money being spent on model prisons would be better spent, he suggests, on education for the honest poor and emigration for the criminals. He also argues that the separate system encourages false penitence, a criticism repeated in his portrayal of Littimer and Uriah Heep as prisoners in *Copperfield* (61). The separate system is also unnatural: By isolating naturally gregarious creatures from one another, the system induces both mental and physical illness. The silent system, which does not isolate prisoners but rather enforces a discipline of silence, is a better system, Dickens asserts, and it is considerably cheaper. *Miscellaneous, Journalism.*

Characters and Related Entries

Styles, John Prisoner held up as a model of repentance by the proponents of the separate system of imprisonment. Dickens shows that his written statements are self-serving and hypocritical.

Pic-Nic Papers, The

Miscellany of poems, short stories, sketches, and so forth by various writers, edited and introduced by Dickens for the benefit of the widow and children of JOHN MACRONE, Dickens's first publisher. Dickens contributed the story "The Lamplighter." The three-volume work was published by HENRY COLBURN in 1841.

Pictures from Italy

Dickens's travel book based on the letters he wrote to JOHN FORSTER during the year he spent with his family in GENOA from July 1844 to July 1845. The book describes their travels through France to get to Italy and those through northern Italy. Dickens was particularly taken with VENICE, NAPLES, POM-

Palmer's panoramic drawing of Pompeii for *Pictures from Italy.*

PEII—including an ascent of Vesuvius—and ROME. He comments on the places and people he sees, on the art, and on the Roman CATHOLIC CHURCH, vigorously expressing his belief that the poverty and oppression in Italy are largely due to the influence of the Church. The letters were originally published in the DAILY NEWS between January 21 and March 11, 1846, and, in revised form, as a single volume by BRADBURY & EVANS in May 1846, with illustrations by SAMUEL PALMER. DAVID H. PAROISSIEN (1974) has edited and annotated an edition of *Pictures*.

"Plate Glass"

Article for *HOUSEHOLD WORDS* (February 1, 1851) by Dickens and W. H. WILLS, one of several on various manufacturing processes. The article describes a tour of a plate-glass factory near Blackwall. *Stone*.

"Please to Leave Your Umbrella"

Article for *HOUSEHOLD WORDS* (May 1, 1858) describing a visit to HAMPTON Court on a rainy afternoon. When he is asked to leave his umbrella at the door, the narrator imagines himself like Sterne's Sentimental Traveller and enters into a digressive meditation on what else is left behind when one is asked to leave his umbrella. At an OLD BAILEY trial, he left behind his sense of absurdity, in Parliament his knowledge of the difference between black and white. *Miscellaneous, Journalism*.

"Poetry of Science, The"

Review for the *EXAMINER* (December 9, 1848) of Robert Hunt's *The Poetry of Science, or Studies of the Physical Phenomena of Nature*, a geological treatise to show, in Dickens's words, "that Science, truly expounding Nature, can, like Nature herself, restore in some new form whatever she destroys."

The poetry that science discovers in nature amply compensates for the superstitions it takes away. *Miscellaneous, Journalism*.

Political Squibs from *The Examiner*

Three political verses Dickens contributed anonymously to the *EXAMINER* in 1841 in support of the Liberal cause: "The Fine Old English Gentleman," "The Quack Doctor's Proclamation," and "Subjects for Painters." *Miscellaneous*.

"Poor Man and His Beer"

Article for *ALL THE YEAR ROUND* (April 30, 1859) describing the social experiments of Friar Bacon, who has established a system of garden allotments that entitle the holders to be members of a cooperative club providing beer and social life and to borrow a pound each year to buy a pig. *Miscellaneous, Journalism*.

Characters and Related Entries

Dreary Narrator of "The Poor Man and His Beer."

Philosewers Friend of the narrator who goes with him to inspect the social experiments of Friar Bacon.

"Popular Delusion, A"

An article on BILLINGSGATE Market and the fish trade in England written by Dickens and W. H. WILLS for *HOUSEHOLD WORDS* (June 1, 1850). *Stone*.

"Post-Office Money-Orders"

Article on the history, use, and misuse of postal money orders written by Dickens and W. H. WILLS for HOUSEHOLD WORDS (March 20, 1852). Dickens contributed a lengthy description of the Central Money-order Office in Aldersgate Street. *Stone.*

"Preliminary Word, A"

Dickens's statement of the principles guiding HOUSEHOLD WORDS (March 30, 1850) from the first issue of the magazine. Distinguishing his journal from some of its competitors, he promised "no mere utilitarian spirit, no iron binding of the mind to grim realities." *Household Words* would instead "show to all, that in all familiar things, even those which are repellent on the surface, there is Romance enough, if we will find it out." *Miscellaneous, Journalism.*

Prologue to Westland Marston's play *The Patrician's Daughter*

Dickens wrote the verse prologue to this tragedy, a first play by an unknown playwright, in 1842. The lines, which justify a tragedy of contemporary common life, were spoken by WILLIAM MACREADY on stage.

"Proposals for Amusing Posterity"

A satiric article for HOUSEHOLD WORDS (February 12, 1853) describing some of the ways in which the present age is—by unequal justice, privilege, and hypocrisy—recording jests for the grim amusement of posterity. *Miscellaneous, Journalism.*

"Proposals for a National Jest Book"

Facetious article from HOUSEHOLD WORDS (May 3, 1856) proposing a national jest book that would

record humorous anecdotes from Parliamentary debates, court proceedings, and other public events. A Board of Jokery, composed of "younger sons, nephews, cousins, and cousin-germans, of the Aristocracy" would select the materials to be included, and each householder would be taxed £25 per annum to pay for his copy. Several samples of appropriate materials are included. *Miscellaneous, Journalism.*

Characters and Related Entries

Bull The "Tom Brown" of the National Jest Book, the mediator of the jests.

"The Public Life of Mr. Tulrumble"

See *Mudfog.*

"Railway Dreaming"

Article for HOUSEHOLD WORDS (May 10, 1856), a meditation in a railway carriage about Parisians and their ways of doing things. Thinking of them as inhabitants of the Moon, Dickens wonders at their eating habits and restaurants, and he praises the café as a place where a solitary person becomes part of a "community with the city life of all degrees." He ends with a lengthy description of the PARIS MORGUE. *Miscellaneous, Journalism.*

"Railway Strikes"

Article for HOUSEHOLD WORDS (January 11, 1851) urging the Engine Drivers and Firemen of the North Western Railway to reconsider their decision to strike. Their duties to the public and to other workmen outside the railway are more important, Dickens argues, than loyalty to their fellow railwaymen. The striking workers have been misled by "designing persons" to forget their individual responsibility to carry out their work. He also urges the public to contemplate no harsh measures against the strikers, for the workers will recognize that the strike is a "false step" and return to work with "the steadiness and patriotism of English workmen." *Miscellaneous, Journalism.*

"Rather a Strong Dose"

Article for ALL THE YEAR ROUND (March 21, 1863) ridiculing William Howitt's *History of the Supernatural*. Although Howitt had been an admirer of Dickens's work and a frequent contributor to HOUSEHOLD WORDS, his amiable relationship with Dickens broke down in 1859 when Dickens rejected Howitt's spiritualism. Calling Howitt "the sans-culotte of the Spiritual Revolution," Dickens attacks his acceptance of all sorts of impostors and impossible occurrences and his dismissal of all rational explanations for the events he describes. *Miscellaneous, Journalism.*

"Received, a Blank Child"

Article for HOUSEHOLD WORDS (March 19, 1853) by W. H. WILLS and Dickens describing the history and operations of the FOUNDLING HOSPITAL, a model among charitable institutions. *Stone.*

"Red Tape"

Article for HOUSEHOLD WORDS (February 15, 1851), attacking "Red Tape—the purpose of whose existence is to tie up public questions, great and small, in an abundance of this official article—to make the neatest possible parcels of them, ticket them, and carefully put them away on a top shelf out of human reach— . . . the peculiar curse and nuisance of England." Using the Window Tax as a prime example of such bureaucratic meddling, Dickens describes the ridiculous regulations defining a window and the disastrous effects of poorly lit and badly ventilated buildings, particularly on the health of the poor. *Miscellaneous.*

"Reflections of a Lord Mayor"

Satirical article for HOUSEHOLD WORDS (November 18, 1854). After a state occasion, the lord mayor of London, alone in his dressing room, addresses himself in his mirror on the question whether the lord mayor is an obsolete humbug, as a recent commission has claimed, or an important public figure, as members of the upper classes who attend his dinners proclaim. He decides in favor of the latter, goes to bed, and dreams of being made a baronet. *Miscellaneous.*

"Reopening of the Colosseum, The"

Anonymous news report for the MORNING CHRONICLE (October 13, 1835) expressing disappointment with the new attractions at the Colosseum at its reopening. *Journalism.*

"Report of the Commissioners Appointed to Inquire into the Condition of the Persons Variously Engaged in the University of Oxford"

Satiric article for the EXAMINER (June 3, 1843). In a parody of the Parliamentary report on child labor in the mines and factories, Dickens presents a report on the "Manufacture of Clergymen" at Oxford. He reveals the prevailing ignorance, particularly of "such comprehensive words as justice, mercy, charity, kindness, brotherly love, forbearance, gentleness, and Good Works," and attacks the preoccupation with forms of worship and the church hierarchy associated with the Oxford Movement and High Church Anglicanism. *Miscellaneous, Journalism.*

"Report on the Fire at Hatfield House"

News article for the MORNING CHRONICLE (December 2, 1835) reporting on the fire at the Hertfordshire estate of the Marquess of Salisbury, which destroyed the west wing of his house and in which his mother died. *Journalism.*

"Report on the Northamptonshire Election"

News article for the MORNING CHRONICLE (December 16 and 19, 1835) describing the election at Kettering. Dickens particularly concentrates on the riot caused by conservative supporters riding into the crowd on horses and threatening the Whig supporters. *Journalism.*

Reprinted Pieces

A collection of 31 of Dickens's essays, sketches, and stories from HOUSEHOLD WORDS, first collected into a single volume for the LIBRARY EDITION of Dickens's works in 1858. Five of the articles in the 1858 edition—"A Christmas Tree," "The Poor Relation's Story," "The Child's Story," "The Schoolboy's Story," and "Nobody's Story"—were later included in *Christmas Stories.* The remaining 26 articles are summarized below.

"THE LONG VOYAGE"

The narrator remembers the many stories of sea travel and shipwrecks that have fascinated him from childhood on. He particularly remembers the story of the *Halsewell,* which broke up on the rocks, and the story of a ship's steward who cared for a small boy after their ship was wrecked off the coast of Africa. Originally in HOUSEHOLD WORDS (December 21, 1853).

Characters and Related Entries

Brimer, Mr. Fifth mate of the *Halsewell.*

Macmanus Midshipman on the *Halsewell.*

Mansel, Miss Passenger on the *Halsewell.*

Meriton, Henry Second mate who survives the wreck of the *Halsewell.*

Pierce family Captain of the *Halsewell,* East Indiaman, who perishes along with his two daughters and many others when the ship is wrecked in a storm at sea near Seacombe on the island of Purbeck.

Rogers Third mate of the *Halsewell.*

Schutz, Mr. Passenger on the *Halsewell.*

"THE BEGGING-LETTER WRITER"

In this article for HOUSEHOLD WORDS (May 18, 1850), Dickens catalogs the frauds perpetrated by these "public robbers" who write letters asking for aid. Dickens distinguishes between the poor, who do not write such letters, and those engaged in "one of the most shameless frauds and impositions of this time." At the end of *Chuzzlewit,* Pecksniff becomes a begging-letter writer.

Characters and Related Entries

Southcote Dickens's pseudonym for John Walker, a begging-letter writer who addressed a series of ingenious and lying appeals to Dickens. The novelist took him to court and testified against him, but the magistrate, impressed by "the excellence of his letters," discharged him.

"A CHILD'S DREAM OF A STAR"

Sentimental story of a boy who dreams after his sister dies that she has become an angel. Although he wishes to join her when his younger brother, mother, and his own daughter die, his wish is granted only when he becomes an old man. This story originally appeared in the second issue of HOUSEHOLD WORDS (April 6, 1850). The sister is often taken to refer to Dickens's sister FRANCES.

"OUR ENGLISH WATERING-PLACE"

Sketch of an English seaside town (BROADSTAIRS) during the season. Old-fashioned and outdated, the town at first appears to have been left stranded by the moving tide of history, but by the time the narrator ends the piece, the tide is in and the town is "swelling up with life and beauty." Originally published in HOUSEHOLD WORDS (August 2, 1851) as "Our Watering Place."

Characters and Related Entries

Mills, Julia   Reader who has made marginal notes in the romances in the library at "Our English Watering Place."

Peepy, the Hon. Miss   Reputed to be the "Beauty of her day" in a time long past at "Our English Watering Place."

"OUR FRENCH WATERING-PLACE"

An account of the channel crossing and the accommodations and amusements at a French seaside town (BOULOGNE). Originally published in HOUSEHOLD WORDS (November 4, 1854).

Characters and Related Entries

Bilkins   "The only authority on taste."

Devasseur, Loyal   Landlord who rents two country houses to visitors at the French Watering Place; "a portly, upright, broad-shouldered, brown faced man" and a great admirer of Napoleon.

Féroce   The "gentle and polite" owner of a bathing machine at the French Watering Place.

"BILL-STICKING"

In an interview with the King of the Bill-Stickers, the narrator learns about the history and procedures of the business of poster advertising. Article for HOUSEHOLD WORDS (March 22, 1851).

Characters and Related Entries

"King of the Bill-Stickers"   Purveyor of advertising posters who is interviewed in his van as it circulates, covered with advertisements, in the streets of London.

"BIRTHS. MRS. MEEK, OF A SON"

George Meek's account of the disruptions in his household brought about by the birth of his son, Augustus George, and the presence of his mother-in-law, Mrs. Bigby, and the maternity nurse, Mrs. Prodgit. The sketch originally appeared in HOUSEHOLD WORDS (February 22, 1851).

Characters and Related Entries

Bigby, Mrs.   Mrs. Meeks's mother, "never known . . . to yield any point whatever, to mortal man."

Meek family   George, father of the infant Augustus George, narrates the sketch. He finds his household and his relationship with his wife Mary Jane totally disrupted by the event, especially by the interference of his mother-in-law, Mrs. Bigby, and the nurse, Mrs. Prodgit.

Prodgit, Mrs.   Augustus George Meek's maternity nurse; "she wore a black bonnet of large dimensions, and was copious in figure."

"LYING AWAKE"

Article from HOUSEHOLD WORDS (October 30, 1852) describing the author's abortive attempts to go to sleep. Meanwhile his mind wanders from George III to Niagara Falls, to FREDERICK and MARIA MANNING's execution, to balloon ascents, to the PARIS MORGUE. Finally he gives up trying to sleep and goes for a night walk.

Characters and Related Entries

Winking Charley   "A sturdy vagrant, in one of her Majesty's jails," who is a recurrent figure in the narrator's night thoughts.

"THE GHOST OF ART"

The narrator, a bachelor lawyer and art connoisseur, on a steamship during a thunderstorm meets a man whom he is sure he has met before. The man turns out to be an artist's model whom the narrator has seen in many roles in many paintings. Two years later the model reappears on another stormy night at the narrator's rooms. He announces himself as "The Ghost of Art," and he has resurrected his career by growing a beard, which expresses the characters he now represents in various paintings. Article from HOUSEHOLD WORDS (July 20, 1850).

Characters and Related Entries

Julia Sweetheart of the narrator.

Model, the Artist's model that the narrator meets on a THAMES steamboat.

Parkins, Mrs. Laundress who disregards the requests of the narrator.

"OUT OF TOWN"

Article for HOUSEHOLD WORDS (September 29, 1855) describing Pavilionstone (FOLKESTONE), its great hotel, and the daily activity surrounding the arrivals and departures of the steamboats for France.

"OUT OF THE SEASON"

Stopping at a seaside resort (FOLKESTONE) out of the season, the author finds so many attractions and distractions that he gets no work done on the chapter he intends to write. Originally in HOUSEHOLD WORDS (June 28, 1856).

Characters and Related Entries

Admiral Benbow Inn Hotel at the deserted watering place.

Clocker Grocer in a seaside village who has heard the cry of distress from an emigrant ship.

Wedgington, Mr. and Mrs. B. Acting and singing couple who give a charity performance at the seaside resort out of season.

"POOR MAN'S TALE OF A PATENT, A"

A smith describes the cumbersome and expensive process he went through to patent his invention. It had 35 stages and cost £96 7s. 6d. The article describes in detail the kind of frustrations imposed on Daniel Doyce by the Circumlocution Office in *Dorrit*.

Characters and Related Entries

Bury, George Old John's wife's father, who left his daughter a legacy of £128 10s.

Butcher, William Chartist who explains society's laws regarding the poor to old John the inventor.

Charlotte Old John's daughter whose husband has left her and thus forced her and her three children to live with her parents.

James Son of Old John who is shot in India as a soldier.

John, Old Narrator, an inventor who spends all his money on bureaucratic fees as he tries to secure a patent.

Joy, Thomas A London carpenter who puts up John when he comes to London to seek a patent.

Mary Comfortable daughter of Old John the inventor.

"THE NOBLE SAVAGE"

Article from HOUSEHOLD WORDS (June 11, 1853) challenging the idea of the noble savage, claiming that it is an "enormous superstition" and a "monotonous humbug." Savages from Africa and America of the sort who have been exhibited in London submit to tyrants, mistreat women, and engage in mindless violence. "His virtues are a fable; his happiness is a delusion; his nobility, nonsense."

"A FLIGHT"

Article from HOUSEHOLD WORDS (August 30, 1851) describing a "magic carpet" trip to Paris in a compartment on the South-Eastern Railway, in the company of both French and English travelers.

Characters and Related Entries

Compact Enchantress, the French actress sharing the train compartment with the narrator on a journey from London to Paris.

Demented Traveller Englishman whose faculties are "entirely absorbed in hurry." He is in the narrator's compartment on the train to Paris.

Diego, Don Inventor of a flying machine.

Monied Interest English businessman in the narrator's compartment on the train from London to Paris.

Mystery Older woman companion of the Compact Enchantress on the train from London to Paris.

Zamiel Name given by the narrator to a fellow passenger on the express train for Paris, a "tall, grave, melancholy Frenchman, . . . got up, one thinks, like Lucifer or Mephistopheles, or Zamiel, transformed into a highly genteel Parisian."

"THE DETECTIVE POLICE"

A group of Scotland Yard detectives tell anecdotes of their exploits at a gathering in the offices of HOUSEHOLD WORDS. The names of the policemen thinly conceal actual policemen of the time: Witchem (Whicker) tells of capturing Tally-ho Thompson, a horse thief; Wield (INSPECTOR FIELD) tells of taking Fikey, a forger; Mith (Smith) tells of capturing Shepherdson by disguising himself as a butcher; and Dornton (Thornton) tells of tracing Aaron Mesheck, a con man, to New York. Originally in HOUSEHOLD WORDS (July 27 and August 10, 1850).

Characters and Related Entries

Clarkson Lawyer who defends Shepherdson and his confederates in "The Butcher's Story" narrated by Sergeant Mith.

Dornton, Sergeant Detective policeman from Scotland Yard, "about fifty years of age, with a ruddy face and a high sunburnt forehead," who tells "Adventures of a Carpet Bag."

Dundey, Dr. Irish bank robber whom Sergeant Dornton follows to America.

Fendall, Sergeant A London police inspector, "a prodigious hand at pursuing private inquiries of a delicate nature."

Fikey A forger arrested by Inspector Wield.

Mesheck, Aaron Jewish confidence man who is finally tracked down at the Tombs in New York City by Sergeant Dornton, who describes this adventure in his "Adventures of a Carpet Bag."

Mith, Sergeant Detective policeman from Scotland Yard, "a smooth-faced man with a fresh bright complexion," who tells "The Butcher's Story."

Pigeon, Thomas Alias of Tally Ho Thompson, a horse thief in Sergeant Witchem's story.

Shepherdson Thief arrested by Sergeant Mith in "The Butcher's Story."

Stalker Police inspector who attends a meeting at the offices of HOUSEHOLD WORDS, "a shrewd, hard-headed Scotchman."

Straw, Sergeant A detective police officer from Scotland Yard, "a little wiry Sergeant of meek demeanour and strong sense."

Thompson, Tally-ho (a.k.a. Thomas Pigeon) Horse thief taken by Sergeant Witchem.

Wield, Inspector Charles A London Police inspector, based on INSPECTOR FIELD.

Witchem, Sergeant Detective policeman, "shorter and thicker-set [than Sergeant Dornton], and marked with the small-pox . . . [with] a reserved and thoughtful air, as if he were engaged in deep mathematical calculations."

"THREE 'DETECTIVE' ANECDOTES"

In the first of the three anecdotes, Inspector Wield tells "The Pair of Gloves," about gloves found under the pillow of a murdered woman that nearly incriminate their owner, young Mr. Trinkle. Next Wield tells of arresting on Derby Day at EPSOM a pickpocket, one of the Swell Mob, who had stolen a diamond pin. In the ensuing scuffle, Sergeant Witchem secures the pin by subterfuge, and the thief is convicted and transported. In the third anecdote, Sergeant Dornton tells of arresting a medical student who was stealing from the cloakroom at the teaching hospital. Originally in HOUSEHOLD WORDS (September 14, 1850).

Characters and Related Entries

"Countess, the Nickname of Eliza Grimwood.

Grimwood, Eliza ("the Countess") Murder victim whose case is investigated by Inspector Wield.

Phibbs CHEAPSIDE haberdasher questioned by Inspector Wield about the murder of Eliza Grimwood.

Tatt Friend of Inspector Wield; his diamond pin is stolen, but it is recovered by Sergeant Witchem.

Trinkle Son of a CHEAPSIDE upholsterer whose gloves make him the prime suspect in the murder of Eliza Grimwood; Inspector Wield discovers that he is not guilty of the crime.

"ON DUTY WITH INSPECTOR FIELD"

Article for *HOUSEHOLD WORDS* (June 14, 1851) describing the narrator's night with INSPECTOR FIELD of the Metropolitan Police. Together they tour the thieves' dens and lodging houses in the center of London. They go to ST. GILES, the BOROUGH, the RATCLIFF HIGHWAY, and WHITECHAPEL, observing the poverty, misery, and occasional defiance of the inhabitants of London's underworld.

Characters and Related Entries

Bark Lodging-house keeper and receiver of stolen goods visited by Inspector Field: "a red villain and a wrathful, with a sanguine throat that looks very much as if it were expressly made for hanging."

Blackey A beggar who "stood near London Bridge these five-and-twenty years, with a painted skin to represent disease."

Click Inhabitant of Rats' Castle, a thieves' den in ST. GILES.

Field, Inspector A well-known member of the detective police force.

Green Police constable in WHITECHAPEL.

Haynes, Inspector A police officer in the BOROUGH.

Michael One of the inhabitants of ST. GILES, observed by Inspector Field on his tour of London's criminal slums.

Miles, Bob One of the inhabitants of Rats' Castle, a thieves den in ST. GILES.

O'Donovan Resident, with his wife and child, of an Irish rookery in ST. GILES.

Parker Police officer who accompanies Inspector Field and the narrator to the Old Mint.

Rogers London constable.

Stalker, Mrs. Woman in the slum of ST. GILES who is cautioned by Inspector Field to make herself scarce.

Doré's picture of a police constable shining his bull's-eye lantern on a group of homeless people in the streets of London recalls Dickens's visits to the London slums with Inspector Field.

"Warwick, the Earl of" The name Inspector Field gives to one of the thieves in ST. GILES.

Williams A London constable.

White Police constable who works with Inspector Field.

"DOWN WITH THE TIDE"

An account of a night spent with "Pea," a supervisor of the THAMES Police, on his regular patrol of the river. Pea shows the narrator the haunts of various criminals. They also visit "Waterloo," the toll taker on WATERLOO BRIDGE, who tells them about suicides from the bridge and about the strange people he has seen there.

Characters and Related Entries

Evans, Superintendent Officer of the Thames Police who takes the narrator on an inspection tour of his "beat."

"Peacoat" ("Pea") Officer who leads the narrator on a tour of the THAMES Police. He may be the model for the inspector in *Mutual Friend*.

Steele, Tom Subject of a story told by "Waterloo," the attendant on WATERLOO BRIDGE, an Irishman who jumped to his death from the bridge.

"Waterloo" Toll taker on WATERLOO BRIDGE who describes the suicides and other unusual people he has met on the bridge.

"A WALK IN A WORKHOUSE"

After attending a religious service in a workhouse, Dickens walks through the rest of the institution observing and talking to the inmates. He sees many old people, some of them insane, more of them dispirited, even though their physical needs are reasonably taken care of. Originally in HOUSEHOLD WORDS (May 27, 1850).

Characters and Related Entries

Rogers, Johnny Workhouse inmate.

Walters, Charley A former inmate of the workhouse.

"PRINCE BULL. A FAIRY TALE"

Dickens's allegorical fairy tale about the misconduct in the Crimean War when the red fairy Tape upsets all the plans of Prince Bull. Originally appeared in HOUSEHOLD WORDS (February 17, 1855).

Characters and Related Entries

Bear, Prince Prince Bull's adversary, representative of Russia in Dickens's ALLEGORY of the Crimean War.

Bull, Prince The representative of England and the antagonist to Prince Bear, representing Russia, in Dickens's ALLEGORY of the Crimean War.

Fair Freedom The "lovely princess" who is Prince Bull's wife.

Tape Red fairy godmother who tyrannizes over Prince Bull and disrupts his war against Prince Bear in Dickens's ALLEGORY of the Crimean War.

"PLATED ARTICLE, A"

An article by W. H. WILLS included in *Reprinted Pieces*. Stopping for the night at a dull town in Staffordshire, the narrator is entertained by a plate that describes in detail the processes by which Staffordshire pottery is made. From HOUSEHOLD WORDS (April 24, 1852).

"OUR HONORABLE FRIEND"

Article for HOUSEHOLD WORDS (July 31, 1852) satirizing empty political rhetoric. Dickens describes "the honourable member for Verbosity" (said to be based on BENJAMIN DISRAELI), whose "principles, to sum up all in a word, were Hearths and Altars, Labour and Capital, Crown and Sceptre, Elephant and Castle." The honorable member, "the first to bend sacred matters to electioneering tactics," challenges Tipkisson by making him out to be in favor of "Mosques and Mohammedanism."

Characters and Related Entries

Tipkisson Constituent who heckles and opposes the positions of "Our Honourable Friend."

"OUR SCHOOL"

Article for *HOUSEHOLD WORDS* (October 11, 1851). Dickens relates his memories of WELLINGTON HOUSE ACADEMY, now replaced by the railway. He remembers being first boy and winning a Latin prize; the "Chief, who was considered to know nothing," and the usher, "who was considered to know everything"; several students, Master Mawls, Dumbledon, and Maxby; and Phil, the school handyman, who "had a sovereign contempt for learning: which engenders in us a respect for his sagacity."

Characters and Related Entries

Blinkins The Latin master at "Our School," "a colorless, doubled-up, near-sighted man, with a crutch; who was always cold."

Dumbledon Parlor boarder at "Our School," an "idiotic goggle-eyed boy" whose favored treatment leads his fellow students to believe he is wealthy.

Frost, Miss Mistress at "Our School."

Mawls, Master An "impersonal boy," a pupil at "Our School."

Maxby Pupil at "Our School," favored because one of the ushers is attracted to his sister.

Phil Morose janitor at "Our School" who "had a sovereign contempt for learning," which earns "respect for his sagacity" from the boys.

"OUR VESTRY"

A humorous description of local government, its contentious elections for vestrymen, their insistence on self-government, their disputes over parliamentary procedure, and the debate over water between Tiddypot and Banger that nearly leads to blows. Originally in *HOUSEHOLD WORDS* (August 28, 1852).

Characters and Related Entries

Banger, Captain Vestryman of Wilderness Walk.

Chib Head vestryman, "a remarkably hale old gentleman of eighty-two."

Dogginson Vestryman who thinks that vestrymen Banger and Tiddypot should settle their differences with their fists.

Magg Vestryman who insists that there should be no interference with local self-government.

Tiddypot Vestryman of Gumption House.

Wigsby One of "Our Vestrymen."

"OUR BORE"

Essay in *HOUSEHOLD WORDS* (October 9, 1852) describing a self-absorbed man who bores others with his tedious accounts of his travels, illnesses, and inside knowledge of nearly everything.

Characters and Related Entries

Blanquo, Pierre Our Bore's Swiss mountain guide.

Blumb, R. A. Artist whom Our Bore takes to see "the finest picture in Italy."

Callow Doctor who prescribes "rhubarb and calomel, low diet, and moderate exercise" for Our Bore.

Clatter Physician who diagnoses Our Bore's complaint as "Accumulation of fat about the heart."

Fanchette Daughter of a Swiss innkeeper who nurses Our Bore.

Jilkins Physician who treats Our Bore with sherry and mutton chops.

Moon Physician who has Our Bore treated with "strong acids, cupped, and blistered."

Our Bore Subject of the essay, a "generic" example of "the great bore family."

Parkins Friend and confidante of Our Bore.

Snugglewood Physician who applies leeches to cure Our Bore's brain disorder.

Spine, John Celebrated novelist who reads some of his unpublished manuscript to Our Bore.

"A MONUMENT OF FRENCH FOLLY"

Article for *HOUSEHOLD WORDS* (March 8, 1851) comparing the well-managed and sanitary suburban cattle markets in France with the unsanitary urban markets in London, especially SMITHFIELD. Dickens attacked the stereotypical criticisms of the French practices that those who opposed changes in the English system used to defeat reform measures.

Characters and Related Entries

Doche, Madame Woman selling animals at the Calf Market in Poissy.

François Butcher who is buying calves at the Calf Market in Poissy.

"Restoration of Shakespeare's 'Lear' to the Stage, The"

Review for the EXAMINER (February 4, 1838) of WILLIAM MACREADY's production of *King Lear,* in which he replaced Nahum Tate's standard theatrical version of the play—a version that eliminated the Fool and restored Lear to his throne—with Shakespeare's original text. Although BERTRAM W. MATZ (1908) included this review in *Miscellaneous Papers* as by Dickens, later scholarship has established that the review was by JOHN FORSTER, who probably discussed the production with Dickens. Dickens did write a brief review of Macready's *King Lear* for the *Examiner* (October 27, 1849). *Journalism.*

"Review: A Letter to Lord Ashley, MP, On the Mines and Collieries Bill, by C. W. Vane, Marquess of Londonderry GCB."

A satirical attack on the arguments given by Lord Londonderry for rejecting the recommendations of the Commission on the Employment of Women and Children in the Mines and opposing Lord Shaftesbury's bill regulating working conditions. Dickens damns Londonderry in a Swiftian manner, prais-ing the felicities of the mine owner's literary style and the crudities of his argument. In the MORNING CHRONICLE (October 20, 1842). *Journalism.*

"Review of *Refutation of the Misstatements and Calumnies contained in Mr. Lockhart's Life of Sir Walter Scott, Bart respecting the Messrs Ballantyne. By the Trustees and Son of the late James Ballantyne.*"

Article for the EXAMINER (September 21, 1838) in which Dickens defends John Gibson Lockhart, SIR WALTER SCOTT's biographer, who blamed Scott's publishers for many of Scott's financial difficulties. *Journalism.* Dickens followed this article with two more on the topic for *The Examiner. See* "Scott and His Publishers."

"Robert Keeley"

Tribute in ALL THE YEAR ROUND to the actor ROBERT KEELEY after his death (April 10, 1869), by Dickens and Herman Merivale. Dickens describes Keeley as a comedian who was also a "master of pathos," and he discusses in particular Keeley's performances as Dogberry and Verges in *Much Ado about Nothing* and as Dolly Spanker in DION BOUCICAULT's *London Assurance.* Uncollected.

"Romance"

Song sung by Sam Weller to the coachmen gathered in the tavern opposite the Insolvent Court in Portugal Street (*Pickwick,* 43). The song has been set to music by Sir Frederick Bridge.

"Round of Stories by the Christmas Fire, A"

The extra Christmas number of HOUSEHOLD WORDS, 1852. Dickens contributed two stories: "The Poor Relation's Story" and "A Child's Story." Among the other contributors were ELIZABETH GASKELL and HARRIET MARTINEAU.

"Scott and His Publishers"

Two articles for the EXAMINER (March 31 and September 29, 1839) in which Dickens supports the conclusion of John Gibson Lockhart, SIR WALTER SCOTT's biographer, that the Ballantynes, Scott's publishers, mismanaged Scott's financial affairs. Dickens spells out the many loans that Scott made to the Ballantynes and the many debts that he forgave. He characterizes the Ballantyne family's retaliation on Lockhart and Scott as "pitiful and disgusting." *Miscellaneous*.

"Shakespeare and Newgate"

Article for HOUSEHOLD WORDS (October 4, 1851) by R. H. HORNE and Dickens, describing Samuel Phelps's reforms at Sadler's Wells Theatre, which had declined to the point where it had been taken over by a rowdy audience drawn to the theater by such debased and sensational plays as George Almar's *Jack Ketch*. Phelps cleared out the vendors who worked in the theater, prohibited foul language, and presented a repertory of Shakespeare and other classic dramatists. The new Sadler's Wells has become "a place in which to learn good things." *Stone*.

"Sikes and Nancy"

Dickens's sensational and horrific PUBLIC READING of the murder of Nancy from *Twist*. Although he contemplated this performance piece as early as 1863, he did not perform it until November 14, 1868, when he gave a private reading for an invited audience to secure their advice about whether to include it in his regular program of readings. The reading was sensational, and most of those attending advised him to perform it, but JOHN FORSTER, GEORGE DOLBY, and Dickens's son CHARLES CULLIFORD DICKENS urged him not to. A physician worried about possible hysteria in the audience and about Dickens's own health; Dickens's heartbeat increased during the exhausting performance, but he included it in the repertory of his farewell reading tour in 1869 and performed it regularly, almost compulsively. Legend, at least, blames the strain of performing "Sikes and Nancy" for hastening Dickens's death.

Sketches by Boz. Illustrative of Every-day Life and Every-day People.

Dickens's first book, collecting sketches and tales that he had published in various magazines between 1833 and 1836 and adding three previously unpublished pieces, "A Visit to Newgate," "The Black Veil," and "The Great Winglebury Duel." The First Series, published by JOHN MACRONE in two volumes in February 1836, with 10 illustrations by GEORGE CRUIKSHANK (12 in a second edition), was reprinted in four editions within a year. Macrone published a Second Series, with 16 illustrations by Cruikshank, in 1837 (dated 1836), collecting pieces that had not been collected for the first series and adding one previously unpublished piece, "The Drunkard's Death." Dickens revised many of the sketches before they appeared in *Boz*. CHAPMAN & HALL published the first edition combining the two series in 20 monthly parts between November 1837 and June 1839 and in one volume in 1839. This edition added the previously uncollected "The Tuggses at Ramsgate" and arranged the items into the four sections—"Our Parish," "Scenes," "Characters," and "Tales"—used in subsequent editions.

Cruikshank's frontispiece for the first collection of
Sketches by Boz (1836).

A scholarly edition of *Sketches by Boz* appears
as the first volume in *The Dent Uniform Edition of
Dickens' Journalism,* edited by Michael SLATER and
John Drew. Critical examinations of *Boz* include
Virgil Grillo's (1974) *Charles Dickens'* Sketches by
Boz: *End in the Beginning,* Duane DeVries' (1976)
Dickens's Apprentice Years: The Making of a Novelist,
Kathryn Chittick's (1990) *Dickens and the 1830s,*
and John Drew's (2003) *Dickens the Journalist.*

"OUR PARISH"

The first section of *Sketches by Boz.* In the First
Series the section included "The Beadle. The Par-
ish Engine. The School-master," "The Curate.
The Old Lady. The Half-pay Captain," "The Four

Sisters," "The Election for Beadle," "The Broker's
Man," and "The Ladies' Societies." The last sketch,
"Our Next-Door Neighbour," was added in the
Second Series.

"The Beadle. The Parish Engine.
The School-master"

Opening sketch in *Our Parish,* the first section of
Boz. Originally published in the EVENING CHRON-
ICLE (February 28, 1835) as "Sketches of London
No. 4, The Parish," it mixes satire and humor in
its descriptions of the institutions of local government—the beadle, the fire brigade, and the poor
schoolmaster.

"The Curate. The Old Lady. The Half-pay
Captain"

Second of the sketches comprising "Our Parish" in
Boz, it describes a handsome young curate whose
popularity is effaced by a new clergyman at the
chapel-of-ease, a benevolent old lady, and a retired
naval officer on half-pay. The sketch originally
appeared as "Sketches of London No. 12. Our Parish" in the EVENING CHRONICLE (May 19, 1835).

"The Four Sisters"

First published as "Sketches of London No. 14.
Our Parish" in the EVENING CHRONICLE (June 18,
1835), this sketch tells of the four Willis sisters,
who are so inseparable that when one of them marries, no one in the parish can ascertain which of the
four sisters is the bride. The birth of a child settles
the issue.

"The Election for Beadle"

Originally appeared as "Sketches of London No.
16. Our Parish" in the EVENING CHRONICLE (July
14, 1835). An account of the contest between Bung
and Spruggins for Parish Beadle in which the main
issue is the number of children each man has.

"The Broker's Man"

Three anecdotes in which Mr. Bung describes his
work as an agent for broker Fixem. Originally published as "Sketches of London No. 18, Our Parish"
in the EVENING CHRONICLE (July 28, 1835).

"The Ladies' Societies"

Originally published as "Sketches of London
No. 20. Our Parish" in the EVENING CHRONICLE

(August 20, 1835), this sketch describes the competition between the Child Examination Society and the Bible Distribution Society for dominance in Our Parish.

"Our Next-Door Neighbour"

First published in the MORNING CHRONICLE (March 18, 1836) as "Our Next-Door Neighbours," this sketch describes three parties who inhabit the lodgings in the house next door. The first is a gentleman who disturbs the street with his late-night drinking companions, the next a young man who disappears with the landlord's shirt and bedclothes, the last a widow and her consumptive son, who gradually fails and dies.

Characters in "Our Parish"

Brown, the Misses   Three spinsters who are "enthusiastic admirers of the curate" in "Our Parish." "Ladies' Societies."

Brown, Mrs.   Landlady of one of the parish paupers. "Beadle."

Bung   Former broker's man who is the successful candidate for beadle in "Our Parish." "Election for Beadle."

Dawson, Doctor   Physician in "Our Parish" who delivers Mrs. Robinson's daughter. "Four Sisters."

Fixem   Broker who employed Bung before he became parish beadle. "Broker's Man."

Goat and Boots, the   The inn where Our Curate addresses an antislavery meeting. "Curate."

Gubbins   Former churchwarden who presents Our Curate with an inkstand as a token of the parish's esteem. "The Curate. The Old Lady. The Half-Pay Captain."

Hopkins   Candidate for beadle. "Election for Beadle."

Parker, Mrs. Johnson   "Mother of seven extremely fine girls—all unmarried." "Ladies' Societies."

Purday, Captain   Retired naval officer in "Our Parish" who "always opposes the constituted authorities of the parish."

Robinson   "A gentleman in a public office, with a good salary and a little property of his own," who courts the four Miss Willises in order to marry the youngest of them. "Four Sisters."

Sarah   Servant to the old lady in "Our Parish." "Curate."

Simmons   Beadle in "Our Parish," "the most important member of the local administration." Simmons is often seen as a precursor to Bumble in *Oliver Twist.* "Beadle."

Spruggins, Thomas   Candidate for beadle of the parish who is defeated by Bung, even though he has 10 children to Bung's five. "Election for Beadle."

Timkins   Candidate for beadle whose "nine small children" are insufficient to secure his success in the election. "Election for Beadle."

William   Young man who dies from overwork, copying and translating for the publishers to support his widowed mother. "Neighbour."

Willis, Misses   Four inseparable sisters who become the talk of the parish as to which one has married Mr. Robinson. "Four Sisters."

"SCENES"

"The Streets—Morning"

An hour-by-hour account of London in the Morning, from the empty streets before dawn to the bustle at noon. Originally published as "Sketches of London No. 17" in the EVENING CHRONICLE (July 21, 1835).

"The Streets—Night"

Originally published in BELL'S LIFE IN LONDON (January 17, 1836) as "Scenes and Characters No. 17. The Streets at Night." The sketch describes a "dark, dull, murky winter's night" in suburban streets where the muffin and beer sellers peddle their wares door to door. Later, in a harmonic meeting, theatergoers gather in the small hours of the morning to sing and listen to "glees."

"Shops and Their Tenants"
Originally published in the MORNING CHRONICLE (October 10, 1834) as "Street Sketches No. 2," this sketch describes the series of commercial tenants who occupy the shops in a building that gradually declines from a draper's to a stationer's, to a bonnet maker's and tobacconist's, to a ladies' school, and finally to a dairy.

"Scotland Yard"
Originally published as "Sketches by Boz. New Series No. 2" in the MORNING CHRONICLE (October 4, 1836), this sketch describes the transformation of this area of London from the haunt of coal heavers to the site of fashionable shops and the offices of the Police Commissioners.

"Seven Dials"
Originally "Scenes and Characters No. 1" in BELL'S LIFE IN LONDON (September 27, 1835), this sketch describes the crowded streets in this slum section of London, the women whose dispute ends in blows, the idle young who lean against the lampposts, and the crowded tenement house where the residents quarrel with one another.

"Meditations in Monmouth Street"
Originally published in the MORNING CHRONICLE (September 24, 1836) as "Sketches by Boz. New Series No. 1." At the secondhand clothing shops in Monmouth Street, "the burial-place of the fashions," Boz imagines the former owners of the clothes and shoes that are for sale. In particular he constructs the life story from boyhood to death of one man whose lifetime of suits are hanging together in one of the shops.

"Hackney-coach Stands"
Originally published as "Sketches of London No. 1" in the EVENING CHRONICLE (January 31, 1835). This sketch describes the hackney coach, "a remnant of past gentility ... progressing lower and lower in the scale of four-wheeled degradation, until at last it comes to—*a stand!*"

"Doctors' Commons"
Originally published in the MORNING CHRONICLE (October 11, 1836) as "Sketches by Boz. New Series No. 2," this sketch describes a visit to the Arches Court and the Prerogative Office, where wills are recorded.

"London Recreations"
Originally appeared in the EVENING CHRONICLE (March 17, 1835) as "Sketches of London No. 6." It describes the rich man who takes pride in possessing a garden and directing his gardeners, the retired middle-class couple who spend many hours happily working in their garden, and the working-class family that gathers on a summer afternoon at a suburban public tea garden.

"The River"
Sketch that originally appeared in the EVENING CHRONICLE (June 6, 1835) as "Sketches of London No. 13." It describes boating parties on the THAMES, always marked by some misery or other, and a steam excursion to GRAVESEND.

"Astley's"
Sketch originally published as "Sketches of London No. 11" in the EVENING CHRONICLE (May 5, 1935), recalling the narrator's delight as a child at the performances at ASTLEY'S ROYAL EQUESTRIAN AMPHITHEATRE and describing his observations of a family outing to the theater at the present time.

"Greenwich Fair"
Account of the annual fair at GREENWICH held on Easter Monday, particularly of the itinerant theatrical performance and the temporary ballroom. Originally published in the EVENING CHRONICLE (April 16, 1835) as "Sketches of London No. 9."

"Private Theatres"
Dickens's satiric account of the private theaters in London that allow men of dubious talent to pay for the privilege of performing. The preparations for a particularly disjointed production of *Macbeth* are described in detail. The sketch originally appeared in the EVENING CHRONICLE (August 11, 1835). It foreshadows the accounts of Mr. Wopsle's theatrical adventures in London in *Great Expectations*.

"Vauxhall Gardens by Day"

Originally published as "Sketches by Boz. New Series No. 4" in the MORNING CHRONICLE (October 26, 1836). When Boz goes to VAUXHALL GARDENS in the day, he is disappointed, for the attractions that appear so enchanting by night are tawdry and dingy by day. However, the ascent of two balloons by Mr. Green and his son provides some excitement before the day is over.

"Early Coaches"

Humorous sketch describing the difficulties in taking an early-morning coach. Originally published as "Sketches of London No. 3" in the EVENING CHRONICLE (February 19, 1835).

"Omnibuses"

Originally appeared as "Street Sketches No. 1" in the MORNING CHRONICLE (September 26, 1834). Boz compares the tedium and annoyances of a long coach journey with the variety and amusement on a London omnibus. He describes the "native coolness" of the cad, who competes with the cads on other buses; an officious old man among the passengers; a "stout gentlemen in the white neckcloth"; and the "shabby-genteel man with the green bag," all of whom are regular passengers.

"The Last Cab-driver, and the First Omnibus Cad"

Sketch first published in BELL'S LIFE IN LONDON as "Scenes and Characters No. 6. Some Account of an Omnibus Cad" (November 1, 1835). It describes in particular the "red cab-driver," whose defiance of his fares lands him in COLDBATH FIELDS prison, and William Barker, the first omnibus cad.

"A Parliamentary Sketch"

A tour of Parliament and particularly of Bellamy's, the coffeehouse near the Houses where members gather. This sketch combined two pieces originally in the EVENING CHRONICLE, "The House" (March 7, 1835) and "Bellamy's" (April 11, 1835).

"Public Dinners"

Comic sketch describing the charity dinner for the benefit of the Indigent Orphans' Friends Benevolent Institution. It was originally published in the EVENING CHRONICLE (April 7, 1835).

Cruikshank's illustration for "Public Dinners" in *Sketches by Boz* includes Dickens as the second adult from the left in the procession and Cruikshank himself as the second from the right. Some commentators identify the two stewards leading the procession as Chapman and Hall.

"The First of May"

This sketch from the Second Series of *Boz* first appeared in the LIBRARY OF FICTION, no. 3 (June 1836), as "A Little Talk about Spring and the Sweeps." It laments the changes in the celebrations on the first of May, which have declined from a general celebration of the coming of spring to the parades and dancing of the chimney sweeps, until, today, even the sweeps' festivities have largely disappeared.

"Brokers' and Marine-store Shops"

Survey of the stores dealing in secondhand furniture, clothing, and personal items in various areas of London. Originally in the MORNING CHRONICLE (December 15, 1834) as "Street Sketches No. 5."

"Gin-shops"

Sketch describing "a great vice in England," the gin shops in the slums where the poor seek "temporary oblivion," particularly one such establishment in the ROOKERY OF ST. GILES at the bottom of TOTTENHAM COURT ROAD. Originally published as "Sketches of London No. 2" in the EVENING CHRONICLE (February 7, 1835).

"The Pawnbroker's Shop"

Originally published in the EVENING CHRONICLE (June 30, 1835) as "Sketches of London No. 15," this sketch describes the customers in a lower-class pawnbroker's shop in DRURY LANE: an old woman who regularly pawns and redeems bits of clothing, a drunken carpenter who abuses his wife and child, a mother and daughter who have fallen into poverty, a prostitute, and a drunken old woman.

"Criminal Courts"

Originally published as "Street Sketches No. 3. The Old Bailey" in the MORNING CHRONICLE (October 23, 1834), this sketch describes a boy leaving NEWGATE PRISON in the company of his mother, a trial at the OLD BAILEY in which the accused is found guilty, and the trial of a 13-year-old for picking pockets.

"A Visit to Newgate"

Sketch that first appeared in the first collection of *Sketches by Boz* (1836). On his journey through NEWGATE PRISON, the narrator notes the orderliness of the women's section; the swagger among the boys in the "school," the section for juveniles where he sees "not a wink expressive of anything but the gallows and the hulks"; and the idleness of the male prisoners. As he describes the condemned cells, the most detailed portion of the essay, the narrator imagines himself a condemned felon during his last night on earth, dreaming of freedom and awakening to realize he has only two hours to live. This sketch foreshadows many later scenes in Dickens's novels, especially Pip's visit to Newgate in *Great Expectations,* Fagin in the condemned cell in *Oliver Twist,* and the ending that, according to JOHN FORSTER, Dickens had planned for *Edwin Drood.*

Characters in "Scenes"

Alick "A damp, earthy child in red worsted socks" on the GRAVESEND steam packet. "River."

Barker, William (Bill Boorker, "Aggerwatin' Bill") The first London omnibus conductor, or cad. "Last Cab-Driver."

"Bill, Uncle" "The wit of the party" among a group taking tea in a public tea garden. "London Recreations."

Brown and O'Brien Eligible young men who are passengers on the THAMES excursion. "River."

Bumple Plaintiff in a brawling case being heard in Doctors' Commons (*see* COURTS). The defendant, Sludberry, is accused of using the expression, "You be blowed." "Doctors' Commons."

Captain Member of Parliament and "a very old frequenter of Bellamy's." "Parliamentary Sketch."

Clark, Betsy Flirtatious maid who shows an interest in Mr. Todd's young man. "Streets—Morning."

Collins Policeman keeping order in the House of Commons. "Parliamentary Sketch."

Colosseum Building in Regent's Park in which a panoramic view of London from the top of St. Paul's Cathedral, 64 feet high and covering the circumference of the building, was on display. "Greenwich Fair."

Dando Head boatman at Searles Yard on the THAMES. "River."

Ducrow, Andrew (1793–1842) Famous equestrian performer who became manager of ASTLEYS'S. "Astley's."

Fitz Binkle, Lord and Lady Philanthropic couple who chair the dinner of the Indigent Orphans' Friends' Benevolent Institution. "Public Dinners."

George Eldest son in the family party at ASTLEY'S, a boy of 14 "who was evidently trying to look as if he did not belong to the family." "Astley's."

Green, Charles (1785–1870) Balloonist who made the first ascent in a gas balloon. Of his more than 500 ascents, many were from VAUXHALL, including one in 1836 that covered 480 miles, ending in Nassau, Germany. "Vauxhall."

Harry   Stableman at the GOLDEN CROSS HOTEL. "Early Coaches."

Henry, Mr.   Pawnbroker's assistant, "the gentleman behind the counter, with the curly black hair, diamond ring, and double silver watch guard." "Pawnbroker's."

Hickson   Subscriber who gives one guinea to the Indigent Orphans' Friends' Benevolent Institution. "Public Dinners."

Hobler, Francis   LORD MAYOR's clerk at the MANSION HOUSE Police Court, famous for his jokes at court proceedings. "Last Cab-driver."

Holywell Street   Street running parallel to the Strand on the north, "despised" for its unsavory collection old-clothes dealers. "Monmouth Street."

Jane   Waitress, "the Hebe of Bellamy's." "Parliamentary Sketch."

Jinkins   "An unshaven, dirty, sottish-looking" customer in the pawnbroker's shop. "Pawnbroker's."

Larkins, Jem   Amateur actor, performing under the name Horatio St. Julien, whose specialty is "genteel comedy." "Private Theatres."

Loggins   Actor who plays Macbeth under the stage name Beverly in one of London's private theaters. "Private Theatres."

Mackin, Mrs.   Client in a DRURY LANE pawn shop; "a slipshod woman, with two flat irons in a little basket." "Pawnbroker's."

Macklin, Mrs.   Woman at No. 4 on a street in the suburbs who buys muffins from a street seller on a cold winter evening. "Streets—Night."

Monmouth Street   An extension of St. Martin's Lane through Seven Dials in west London. Dickens describes "the only true and real emporium for

second-hand wearing apparel" in this street. "Monmouth Street."

Nathan   Dresser in a private theater, "a red-headed and red-whiskered Jew." "Private Theatres."

Nicholas   Long-established butler at Bellamy's Coffee House near the Houses of Parliament: "An excellent servant Nicholas is—an unrivalled compounder of salad dressing; an admirable preparer of soda water and lemon; a special mixer of cold grog and punch; and above all an unequalled judge of cheese." "Parliamentary Sketch."

O'Brien   Passenger on the Gravesend packet. "River."

Palmer   Player of many parts in the amateur theaters of London. "Private Theatres."

Peplow, Mrs.   One of the muffin fanciers who spend their evenings at home. She sends her son out to buy muffins from a street seller. "Streets—Night."

St. Julien, Horatio   Jem Larkins's stage name. "Private Theatres."

Sally   Uncle Bill's niece. He teases her about keeping company with a young man. "London Recreations."

Scarton, Charley   Actor in one of the private theaters who "is to take the part of an English sailor, and fight a broadsword combat with six unknown bandits, at one and the same time." "Private Theatres."

Sludberry, Thomas   Defendant in Doctors' Commons (*see* COURTS) accused of brawling at a vestry meeting. "Doctors' Commons."

Sluffen   Cockney orator at the sweeps' annual dinner on the first of May. "First of May."

Smith, M. P.   A new member of Parliament who "seizes both the hands of his gratified constituent, and, after greeting him with the most enthusiastic warmth, darts into the lobby with an extraordinary display of ardor for the public cause." "Parliamentary Sketch."

Smuggins Performer who obliges the harmonic meeting with a comic song. "Streets—Night."

Sulliwin, Mrs. Charwoman in SEVEN DIALS: "Here's poor dear Mrs. Sulliwin, as has five blessed children of her own, can't go out a charing for one afternoon, but what hussies be a comin', and 'ticing away her own 'usband, as she's been married to twelve year come next Easter Monday." "Seven Dials."

Tatham, Mrs. "An old sallow-looking woman" who is a regular customer of a DRURY LANE pawnshop. "Pawnbroker's."

Thompson, Bill Actor at the VICTORIA Theatre. "Streets—Night."

Thomson, Sir John, M.P. Eminent member of Parliament. "Parliamentary Sketch."

Todd's Young Man Baker's assistant who fascinates Betsy Clark. "Streets—Morning."

Tom Hackney coachman. "Hackney."

"Tom, Honest" A Metropolitan representative in Parliament. "Parliamentary Sketch."

Walker Auditor of the charitable society recognized by the senior officer at the public dinner. "Public Dinners."

Walker, Mrs. Resident at No. 5 in the suburban street. "Streets—Night."

Wilson Policeman on duty in the House of Commons. "Parliamentary Sketch."

Woolford, Miss Horse rider who gives a "graceful performance" at ASTLEY'S. "Astley's."

"CHARACTERS"

"Thoughts about People"
Originally published as "Sketches of London No. 10" in the EVENING CHRONICLE (April 23, 1835). Boz describes three types of men that he observes in London: the anonymous clerks who

live a life of routine, misanthropic old fellows who cut themselves off from others, and London apprentices who strut inoffensively in the streets on Sundays.

"A Christmas Dinner"
Sketch describing a family Christmas at the home of Uncle and Aunt George. Originally published as "Scenes and Characters No. 10. Christmas Festivities" in BELL'S LIFE IN LONDON (December 27, 1835).

"New Year, The"
Originally published as "Scenes and Characters No. 11" in BELL'S LIFE IN LONDON (January 3, 1836), this sketch describes the New Year's Eve party hosted by Dobble, a senior civil servant, and the part in it played by Tupple, one of his junior clerks.

"Miss Evans and the Eagle"
Originally appeared in BELL'S LIFE IN LONDON (October 4, 1835) as "Scenes and Characters No. 2." When Miss Jemima Evans and her beau, Samuel Wilkins, spend an evening at the EAGLE INN, they drink a bit too much, and Samuel gets into a brawl with a whiskered young man who seems to him to be paying undue attention to Jemima.

"The Parlour Orator"
Originally entitled "The Parlour," this sketch appeared in BELL'S LIFE IN LONDON (December 13, 1835). It describes a public-house orator, who intimidates the other patrons with his pontificating about liberty and their condition of slavery.

"The Hospital Patient"
Originally published in the CARLTON CHRONICLE (August 6, 1836), this sketch describes a young woman in the hospital from a brutal beating who, just before dying, refuses to identify her lover as the man who beat her.

"The Misplaced Attachment of Mr. John Douce"
Originally published as "Scenes and Characters No. 5. Love and Oysters" in BELL'S LIFE IN LONDON (October 25, 1835), this sketch describes a steady "old boy" widower and his infatuation with a 25-year-old woman in a blue dress who sells oysters. He becomes ridiculous to his longtime male companions, has his proposal turned down by the young lady, and eventually marries his cook.

"The Mistaken Milliner. A Tale of Ambition"

Story of Miss Amelia Martin, a milliner with ambitions to be a singer. Her debut at the WHITE CONDUIT HOUSE, however, is a disaster. Originally published as "Scenes and Characters No. 7. The Vocal Dressmaker" in BELL'S LIFE IN LONDON (November 22, 1835).

"The Dancing Academy"

Originally published as "Scenes and Characters No. 3" in BELL'S LIFE IN LONDON (October 11, 1835), this sketch describes the attempt of naive Augustus Cooper to escape the control of his mother by taking dancing lessons at Signor Billsmethi's Academy. He is set up and sued for breach of contract by Miss Billsmethi and must be rescued by his mother, who supplies a cash settlement of £20 and regains control of her son.

"Shabby-genteel People"

Originally in the MORNING CHRONICLE (November 5, 1834) as "Street Sketches No. 4," this sketch describes Londoners who have fallen into poverty and try to keep up appearances, especially one shabby reader in the British Museum Reading Room.

"Making a Night of It"

Sketch describing two young CITY clerks who celebrate their quarterly payday by getting drunk, going to the theater, being ejected for disrupting the performance, and finally getting arrested for disorderly conduct. It first appeared in BELL'S LIFE IN LONDON, October 18, 1835.

"The Prisoners' Van"

Sketch describing two sisters, 14 and 16, who climb out of the prisoners' van on their way to jail for prostitution. The elder is brazen, the younger tear-

Fred Barnard's illustration for "The Prisoners' Van" in *Sketches by Boz* depicts the contrasting reactions of two young prostitutes as they are taken away by the police.

fully ashamed. It originally appeared in BELL'S LIFE IN LONDON (November 29, 1835).

Characters in "Characters"

Albion, the Public house in Little Russell Street where Potter and Smithers are regulars. "Making a Night of It."

Bella Younger of two sisters detained for prostitution. She hides her face in shame as she climbs into the van. "Prisoner's Van."

Billsmethi (i.e., Bill Smith), Signor The proprietor of a dancing academy in GRAY'S INN LANE who, aided by his son and daughter, extorts £20 from Augustus Cooper by threatening a breach-of-promise suit. "Dancing Academy."

City of London Theatre Theater in Norton Folgate, Spitalfields, where Potter and Smithers drunkenly disturb the performance and are ejected. "Making a Night of It."

Cooper, Augustus Young man "in the oil and colour line" whose mother, "having managed her husband and *his* business in his lifetime, took to managing her son and *his* business after his decease." Augustus, to escape his mother's control, takes dancing lessons at Signor Billsmethi's Academy, is sued for breach of promise by Miss Billsmethi, and is rescued by his mother. "Dancing Academy."

Dobble Host of the New Year's Eve party who is saluted along with his wife, son, and daughters (including especially Julia) by Tuppie, one of his junior clerks. "New Year."

Dounce, John A steady old boy, this widower and retired glove maker makes himself ridiculous by courting a young lady in blue who sells oysters. After she rejects his proposal, he eventually marries his cook. "Dounce."

Ellis An admirer of the parlour orator, "a sharp-nosed, light-haired man in a brown surtout reaching nearly to his heels." "Parlour Orator."

Emily A brazen young prostitute taken off in the prisoner's van with her sister Bella. "Prisoner's Van."

Euston Square Site of the first London railway terminus, built in 1838. Miss Martin's house in Drummond Street next to the square preceded the railway there. "Milliner."

Evans, Jemima ("Jemima Ivins") The young lady of CAMDEN TOWN whose mother and sisters take considerable interest in her courtship by Samuel Wilkins. The couple's excursion to the EAGLE INN, however, ends in a brawl. "Miss Evans."

Exeter Change A building on the north side of the Strand in London that housed a wild animal menagerie until 1828. "Thoughts about People."

Fetter Lane A street running between Holborn and Fleet Street in the City where the residence of Mr. Augustus Cooper is located. "Dancing Academy."

George, Uncle and Aunt Hosts of the family Christmas party. "Christmas Dinner."

Grandpapa and Grandmamma Guests at the Christmas dinner party. "Christmas Dinner."

Harris Law stationer and friend of John Dounce. "Dounce."

Jack Prisoner charged with beating to death the woman with whom he lives. "Hospital Patient."

Jane, Aunt Wife of Uncle Robert, a guest at the Christmas dinner. "Christmas Dinner."

Jennings Robe maker, friend of John Dounce. "Dounce."

Jones Witty barrister's clerk and friend of John Dounce. "Dounce."

Little Russell Street At the Albion Hotel on this street in Bloomsbury, Potter and Smithers celebrate their quarterly payday. "Making a Night of It."

Margaret, Aunt   She married a poor man without her mother's consent, but at the family Christmas celebration, her husband turns out to be a "nice man." "Christmas Dinner."

Martin, Amelia   The mistaken milliner—"pale, tallish, thin, and two-and-thirty"—who attempts to become a singer. "Milliner."

Montague, Julia   Singer who performs "I am a Friar" to an enthusiastic audience at the WHITE CONDUIT. "Mistaken Milliner."

Offley's   A well-known tavern in Covent Garden that is one of the resorts of "old boys." "Dounce."

Potter, Thomas   City clerk who "makes a night of it" with his friend Thomas Smithers. After a good dinner and much drink, they are ejected from the theater for disrupting the performance and end up in prison for disturbing the peace. "Making a Night."

Rainbow Tavern, the   This establishment in Fleet Street, the second-oldest coffeehouse in London, is one of the resorts of the "Old Boys." "Dounce."

Robert, Uncle, and Aunt Jane   Guests at Christmas dinner. "Christmas Dinner."

Rodolph, Mr. and Mrs. Jennings   Singers who perform at the wedding dinner of Miss Martin's friend to the journeyman painter: "To hear them sing separately was divine, but when they went through the tragic duet of 'Red Ruffian, retire!' it was, as Miss Martin afterwards remarked, 'thrilling.'" "Milliner."

Rogers   The parlour orator: "he was smoking a cigar, with his eyes fixed on the ceiling, and had that confident oracular air which marked him as the leading politician, general authority, and universal anecdote-relater, of the place." "Orator."

Smith   London clerk who works at his desk "till five o'clock, working on, all day, as regularly as the dial over the mantel-piece whose loud ticking is as monotonous as his whole existence." "Thoughts about People."

Smithers, Robert   City clerk and friend of Thomas Potter with whom he "makes a night of it" and ends up arrested for disturbing the peace. "Making a Night of It."

Snobee   An unsuccessful candidate for Parliament. "Orator."

Taplin, Harry   Comic entertainer and singer who performs with Miss Amelia Martin at the WHITE CONDUIT. "Milliner."

Tommy   "A little greengrocer with a chubby face" who disagrees with Rogers the orator. "Orator."

Tupple   Guest at the Dobbles' New Year's Eve party who leads the round of toasts. "New Year."

White, Young   Augustus Cooper's more worldly friend, who "had been flaring away like winkin'—going to the theatre—supping at harmonic meetings—eating oysters by the barrel—drinking stout by the gallon—even stopping out all night, and coming home as cool in the morning as if nothing had happened." "Dancing Academy."

Wilkins, Samuel   "Journeyman carpenter of small dimensions" who "kept company" with and eventually marries Jemima Evans. "Evans."

Wilson   The parlour orator's antagonist in the political debates of the Old Street Suburban Representative Discovery Society. "Orator."

"TALES"

"THE BOARDING-HOUSE"

Two sketches, originally published in the MONTHLY MAGAZINE (May and August 1834), describing romantic intrigues in Mrs. Tibb's boarding house in Great Coram Street. In the first, the three male boarders, Mr. Simpson, Mr. Septimus Hicks, and Mr. Calton, each arrange secret marriages to Mrs. Maplestone and her two daughters. In the second, the presence of Mrs. Bloss, a hypochondriac widow, prompts romantic intrigues among the male boarders.

Characters and Related Entries

Agnes   Mrs. Bloss's servant, the object of old Tibbs's affections.

Bloss, Mrs.   The wealthy and vulgar widow who boards at Mrs. Tibbs's. "Having nothing to do, and nothing to wish for," she becomes a hypochondriac, eventually marrying another hypochondriac, Mr. Gobler.

Calton   Superannuated beau, a boarder at Mrs. Tibbs's who "had never been married, but was still on the look-out for a wife with money." He leaves Mrs. Matilda Maplestone at the altar and is sued for breach of promise.

Evenson, John   One of Mrs. Tibbs's boarders, "a thorough radical" who has a running feud with Mr. Wisbottle. He arouses Mrs. Tibbs's suspicions about secret assignations in the maid's storeroom.

Gobler   Hypochondriac who boards at Mrs. Tibbs's and marries Mrs. Bloss, also a hypochondriac.

Great Coram Street   Now known as Coram Street, this is the site in Bloomsbury of Mrs. Tibbs's boarding house.

Hicks, Septimus   "A tallish, white-faced young man, with spectacles, and a black ribbon round his neck," with a passion for Byron, who marries Matilda Maplestone and then deserts her.

James   Servant in Mrs. Tibbs's boarding house.

Maplestone, Mrs. Matilda   Widow who has unsuccessfully made the rounds of the spas for four seasons with her two eligible daughters, Matilda and Julia. Their luck with the gentlemen at Mrs. Tibbs's boarding house is better: Julia marries Mr. Simpson but then elopes six weeks later with a half-pay officer;

Matilda marries Septimus Hicks, who then abandons her; and Mrs. Maplestone, jilted by Mr. Calton, sues him for breach of promise and wins £1000.

O'Bleary, Frederick   An Irish patriot boarding at Mrs. Tibbs's who hopes to better himself by marrying Mrs. Bloss.

Rampart, Sir Charles   Commanding officer of Tibbs's volunteer regiment in 1806.

Robinson   Mrs. Tibbs's maidservant.

Simpson   One of Mrs. Tibbs's boarders, "as empty-headed as the great bell of St. Paul's."

Tibbs, Mr.   Mrs. Tibbs's husband who, inconsequential without her, disappears into the kitchen and never gets to tell about his life in the volunteer corps in 1806. After he engages in a series of romantic intrigues in the boarding house, the Tibbses separate by mutual consent and close the establishment.

Tibbs, Mrs.   "Tidy, fidgety, thrifty" proprietor of a boarding house in Great Coram Street.

Tomkins, Alfred   Clerk for a wine merchant who boards at Mrs. Tibbs's.

Wisbottle   One of Mrs. Tibbs's boarders, "a high Tory . . . [who] knew the Peerage by heart." He feuds with the radical Mr. Evenson.

Wosky, Dr.   Mrs. Bloss's doctor. "He had a very good practice, and plenty of money, which he had amassed by invariably humouring the worst fancies of all the females of all the families he had ever been introduced into."

"MR. MINNS AND HIS COUSIN"

Dickens's first published story. This story appeared under the title "A Dinner at Poplar Walk" in the *Monthly Magazine* (December 1833). It tells of Octavius Budden's unsuccessful attempt to curry favor with his well-to-do cousin Augustus Minns by inviting him to dinner. But Minns, who has an "unmingled horror" of children and dogs, is assaulted by both on the occasion and does not include the Buddens or their son in his will.

Characters and Related Entries

Bill　Coachman who drives Mr. Minns to Stamford Hill.

Brogson　An elderly guest at the Budden's dinner party.

Budden, Octavius　A prosperous corn chandler who retires to a cottage in the country with his wife Amelia and his precocious only son Alexander Augustus Budden. Budden unsuccessfully tries to secure the interest of his cousin Minns for his son.

Flower Pot　Inn in Bishopsgate Street where Minns catches the coach to Stamford Hill.

Jones　Dinner guest of the Buddens, "a little smirking man with red whiskers."

Minns, Augustus　Well-to-do bachelor of 48 who works at SOMERSET HOUSE. He has a "love of order" and an unmingled horror of dogs and children. He spends an uncomfortable evening at the home of his cousin Octavius Budden, whose dog and child both torment him.

Stamford Hill　Suburb north of Islington where Octavius Budden lives at Amelia Cottage, Poplar Walk.

Swan, the　Coach stop in Stamford Hill, north London, where Minns disembarks on his visit to Poplar Walk.

Tavistock Street　In Dickens's time, this street in Covent Garden was residential. Mr. Minns had lodgings here.

"SENTIMENT"

Originally published in BELL'S WEEKLY MAGAZINE (June 7, 1834), this story describes Lavinia Brook Dingwall's brief career at Minerva House, a finishing school where she is sent by her father, a self-

important and fatuous M.P., to "recover" from an unfortunate love affair. Instead she meets her lover at the school dance and elopes with him to live in poverty and misery near BALL'S POND.

Characters and Related Entries

Butler, Theodosius　The conceited young man, author of "Considerations on the Policy of Removing the Duty on Bees'-Wax," who elopes with Lavinia Brook Dingwall. He adopts the alias of Edward M'Neville Walter.

Crumpton, Misses Amelia and Maria　Spinster sisters who operate Minerva House, a finishing school in HAMMERSMITH, where young women acquire "a smattering of everything, and a knowledge of nothing."

Dadson　Writing master at Minerva House who attends the half-yearly ball in "a white waistcoat, black knee-shorts, and ditto silk stockings, displaying a leg large enough for two writing masters." His wife is "in green silk, with shoes and cap-trimmings to correspond."

Dingwall, Cornelius Brook, M.P.　The "haughty, solemn, and portentous" member of Parliament who had "a very great idea of his own abilities, which must have been a great comfort to him, as no one else had." He and his wife place their daughter Lavinia in the Misses Crumpton's school in HAMMERSMITH, and she runs off with Theodosius Butler. Their spoiled infant son Frederick wears "a blue tunic with a black belt a quarter of a yard wide, fastened with an immense buckle—looking like a robber in a melodrama, seen through a diminishing glass."

Hilton　Master of ceremonies at the annual dance of Minerva House School.

James　Brook Dingwall's servant.

Lobskini, Signor　Singing master at Minerva House.

Minerva House　Finishing school for girls in HAMMERSMITH, run by the Misses Crumpton, where the pupils acquire "a smattering of everything and a knowledge of nothing." It has many similarities with Miss Pinkerton's Academy in WILLIAM MAKEPEACE THACKERAY's *Vanity Fair*.

Muggs, Sir Alfred Friend of Cornelius Brook Dingwall who recommends the Misses Crumptons' school to him.

Parsons, Letitia Pupil at Minerva House who performs on the piano.

Smithers, Emily The belle of Minerva House.

Walter, Edward M'Neville Penname of Theodosius Butler.

Wilson, Caroline Pupil at Minerva House, "the ugliest girl in Hammersmith, or out of it."

"THE TUGGSES AT RAMSGATE"

First published in the LIBRARY OF FICTION (April 1836), this story recounts how London grocer Joseph Tuggs, after inheriting £20,000, takes his family to RAMSGATE, where the Waterses, a con man and his wife, entrap young Cymon Tuggs into a compromising relationship with Mrs. Waters and extract £1,500 from Tuggs to hush the matter up.

Characters and Related Entries

Amelia A young girl visiting RAMSGATE.

Cower, Mr. A lawyer who notifies Mr. Tuggs that he has inherited £20,000.

Golding, Mary One of the bathers recognized by Captain Waters at RAMSGATE, who "in her bathing costume, looked as if she were enveloped in a patent mackintosh of scanty dimensions."

Jane A young lady visitor at RAMSGATE.

Mary Anne Girl managing a gambling table at RAMSGATE.

Pegwell Bay Beach resort south of RAMSGATE visited by the Tuggses.

Slaughter, Lieutenant Confederate of Captain and Mrs. Waters who "discovers" Cymon Tuggs hiding behind a curtain.

Thompson, Harry Acquaintance of Captain and Mrs. Waters who is bathing at RAMSGATE.

Tippin, Mr. and Mrs. Musical performers at RAMSGATE.

Tuggs family When London grocer Joseph Tuggs inherits £20,000, he takes Mrs. Tuggs and his two children, Simon and Charlotte (who change their names to Cymon and Carlotta on coming into money) to RAMSGATE. There their näiveté and snobbery make them easy prey to a trio of adventurers.

Waters, Captain Walter and Mrs. Belinda A confidence man and his wife—"a young lady . . . with long black ringlets, large black eyes, brief petticoats, and unexceptionable ankles"—who conspire to entrap Simon Tuggs in a compromising situation and extort £1500 from the Tuggs family.

"HORATIO SPARKINS"

Tale of a draper's assistant who poses as a gentleman and fools the snobbish Maldertons. Originally published in the MONTHLY MAGAZINE (February 1834).

Characters and Related Entries

Barton, Jacob Mrs. Malderton's brother, a grocer who embarrasses his nouveaux riches relatives by frequently speaking of his business.

Delafontaine, Mr. A gentleman in Bedford Square claimed as an acquaintance by Horatio Sparkins.

Fitz-Osborne, the Hon. Augustus Fitz-Edward Fitz-John Flamwell suggests this to be Sparkins's real identity.

Flamwell Name-dropping friend of the Maldertons, "one of those gentlemen of remarkably extensive information whom one occasionally meets in society, who pretend to know everybody, but in reality know nobody."

Gubbleton, Lord   Flamwell claims to be friends with this "devilish good fellow."

John   The Maldertons' manservant who, to impress Sparkins, "had been forced into a white neckerchief and shoes, and touched up, and brushed, to look like a second footman."

Malderton family   Snobbish CAMBERWELL family. Mr. Malderton, who had made his money in a few successful speculations, is "hospitable from ostentation, illiberal from ignorance, and prejudiced from conceit." His wife hopes to marry her two daughters—Teresa, "a very little girl, rather fat," of 28, and Marianne—to high-class suitors. The two sons, Frederick and Thomas, threaten to undermine Theresa's marital prospects with their "low" conversation.

Smith, Samuel   Real name of Horatio Sparkins.

Sparkins, Horatio   Name used by Samuel Smith, a draper's assistant, when he enters the high society of the Maldertons and impresses them with his philosophic banalities and genteel manners.

"THE BLACK VEIL"

Story of a young surgeon whose first patient is a mysterious woman in a black veil. She engages him to come to her house in a remote section of WALWORTH at nine in the morning. There the surgeon is asked to revive the body of her son, a criminal who has just been hanged. Afterward the surgeon becomes a daily visitor to the mother, who has been driven mad by the event. This story's first appearance was in the First Series of *Sketches by Boz.*

Characters and Related Entries

Rose   Fiancée of a struggling young doctor.

Tom   "Corpulent round-headed boy" who delivers messages and medicine for the young surgeon.

"THE STEAM EXCURSION"

Originally in the MONTHLY MAGAZINE (October 1834), this story of an excursion down the river on a steamboat, organized by light-hearted law student Percy Noakes, ends with a rough passage back to London that leaves those in the party exhausted and sick.

Characters and Related Entries

Briggs family   A widow with three daughters, including Julia and Kate, and two sons, Samuel, an attorney, and Alexander, his apprentice. They all go on the steam excursion and seek to outshine their rivals, the Tauntons.

Edkins   "A pale young gentleman in a green stock, and spectacles of the same, a member of the honourable Society of the Inner Temple" who goes on the steam excursion.

Fleetwood family   Mr. and Mrs. Fleetwood and their son are guests on the steam excursion.

Great Marlborough Street   The street in central London running from Regent Street to Soho where the Taunton family lives.

Hardy, Mr.   "Practical joker, immensely popular with married ladies," who plans the steam excursion with Percy Noakes.

Helves, Captain   An uninvited guest brought on the steam excursion by the Tauntons. A braggart and swindler, he entertains the party with exaggerated tales of his military exploits.

Noakes, Percy   Law student and "devilish good fellow" who organizes the steam excursion.

Ram Chowdar Doss Azuph Al Bowlar   East Indian potentate who is the subject of Captain Helves's story on the steam excursion.

Simson   Guest of Percy Noakes on the steam excursion.

Stubbs, Mrs.   Percy Noakes's laundress, "a dirty old woman with an inflamed countenance."

Taunton family   Mrs. Taunton, "a good-looking widow of fifty, with the form of a giantess and the mind of a child," and her two daughters, Emily and

Sophia, attend the steam excursion. They are rivals of the Briggs family, "between whom there existed a degree of implacable hatred."

Wakefield, Mr. and Mrs.   Couple who go, with their daughter, on the steam excursion.

Wizzle   Guest invited to the steam excursion but unable to attend. "Steam Excursion."

"THE GREAT WINGLEBURY DUEL"

When Alexander Trott tries to avoid fighting a duel with Horace Hunter over the hand of Emily Brown by soliciting the influence of the mayor of Winglebury, he inadvertently becomes entangled with Lady Julia Manners and Lord Peter. The duel is averted, but Trott is taken for Lord Peter. When he is bundled off in a carriage with Lady Julia, the two decide to marry, thus allowing Emily Brown to marry Horace Hunter. The story first appeared in *Boz*, First Series. Dickens dramatized the story as *The Strange Gentleman.*

Characters and Related Entries

Blue Lion and Stomach Warmer Inn   Headquarters of the Gentlemen's Whist Club of Winglebury Buffs where Horace Hunter stays.

Brown, Emily   Cause of the Great Winglebury duel.

Cornberry   Rich old man who died, leaving his fiancée, Miss Julia Manners, all his money.

Flair, the Hon. Augustus   Friend of Lord Peter.

Great Winglebury   The fictitious town "exactly forty-two miles from Hyde Park Corner" where the great Winglebury duel takes place. It was based on ROCHESTER.

Hunter, Horace   Emily Brown's lover, who challenges his rival, Alexander Trott, to a duel. He eventually marries Emily.

Manners, Julia   "Buxom, richly-dressed female of about forty" whose planned rendezvous with Lord

Peter gets entangled with the elopement schemes of Alexander Trott. She ends up eloping with Trott.

Overton, Joseph   Mayor of Winglebury who manages to promote the confusion that prevents the duel and leads to the unexpected marriage of Alexander Trott and Miss Julia Manners. He is named Owen Overton in *Strange Gentleman.*

Peter, Lord   Imbecile lord who is courting Julia Manners for her money. He is accidentally displaced by Alexander Trott and then killed in a drunken riding accident.

Thomas   Waiter at the Winglebury Arms.

Trott, Alexander   Young man whose parents want him to marry Emily Brown for her money, but when he is challenged to a duel by her true love, Horace Hunter, Trott is afraid to go through with the wedding. After he solicits the intervention of the mayor of Winglebury, his situation is confused with that of Lord Peter, who is masquerading as a madman to facilitate a rendezvous with Julia Manners. In the end Alexander and Julia marry. In *The Strange Gentleman*, Alexander becomes Walker Trott.

Williamson, Mrs.   Landlady of the Winglebury Arms.

"MRS. JOSEPH PORTER"

The second story published by Dickens, this sketch first appeared as "Mrs. Joseph Porter, 'Over the Way'" in the MONTHLY MAGAZINE (January 1834). It tells of the Gattletons' amateur production of *Othello*, which is disrupted by Mrs. Porter, their jealous and sarcastic neighbor. She encourages Tom Balderstone, who knows Shakespeare by heart, to disrupt the performance with unnecessary promptings, so that she can declare the evening "a complete failure."

Characters and Related Entries

Balderstone, Thomas ("Uncle Tom")   Mrs. Gattleton's rich brother who remembers all of

Shakespeare's plays word for word and disrupts the performance of *Othello* with his unnecessary promptings.

Brown   The violincelloist in the amateur orchestra for the Gattletons' theatricals.

Cape   Violinist in the amateur orchestra for the Gattletons' theatricals.

Evans   "A tall, thin, pale young gentleman with extensive whiskers" who plays Roderigo in the Gattletons' production of *Othello*.

Gattleton family   A stockbroker living comfortably at Rose Villa, Clapham Rise, whose family is "infected with the mania for private theatricals." His "good-tempered, vulgar" wife and his four children, including Caroline, Lucina, and Sempronius, put on *Othello* in their dining room, a production spoiled by their neighbor, Mrs. Joseph Porter.

Glumper, Sir Thomas   One of the guests at the Gattletons' private theatricals.

Harleigh   Musical friend of the Gattletons who is the principal singer in their amateur production of *Masaniello*.

Hickson, Mr. and Mrs.   Couple attending the Gattletons' private theatricals.

Jenkins, Miss   Pianist at the Gattletons' theatricals.

Nixon, Mr. and Mrs.   Members of the audience at the Gattletons' private theatricals.

Porter, Mrs. Joseph   Gossipy and supercilious neighbor of the Gattletons whose talent for "scandal and sarcasm" makes her "courted, and flattered, and caressed, and invited" to her neighbors' amateur theatrical, even though she is, like her daughter Emma, disdainful of the proceedings. After encouraging Tom Balderstone to disrupt the proceedings with unnecessary promptings, she can declare the evening "a complete failure."

Thomas   Pastry cook who caters the Gattletons' party.

Tom   The Gattletons' servant, who plays a fisherman in their theatricals.

Wilson   The Iago of the Gattletons' private theatricals, who is late for the performance because he is detained at the Post Office.

"A PASSAGE IN THE LIFE OF MR. WATKINS TOTTLE"

Story originally published in the MONTHLY MAGAZINE (January and February, 1835), telling of a bachelor of 50 who is too timid and too poor to pursue his "uxorious inclinations." Prompted by his friend Gabriel Parsons, Tottle courts Miss Lillerton and finally proposes when Parsons releases him from his debts on the condition that he be paid back from Miss Lillerton's fortune. However, when Tottle learns that his intended has already accepted the proposal of the Reverend Charles Timson, Parsons abandons him; Tottle takes his own life a few weeks later.

Characters and Related Entries

Cecil Street   Street off the STRAND where Watkins Tottle lives.

Harry   "A genteel-looking young man" locked up for debt in Solomon Jacobs's sponging house.

Ikey   Assistant to Solomon Jacobs, the bailiff who imprisons Watkins Tottle.

Jacobs, Solomon   Bailiff who arrests Watkins Tottle for debt.

Jem   The "sallow-faced red-haired sulky boy" who is the doorkeeper at Solomon Jacobs's sponging house.

Kate   Wife of Harry, a debtor in Solomon Jacobs's sponging house.

Lillerton, Miss   The fastidious woman who is the object of the matrimonial intentions of both Watkins Tottle and the Reverend Timson. She engages the unwitting Tottle to carry a note to Timson setting the date for her wedding to the clergyman.

Martha   Gabriel Parsons's serving maid.

Parsons, Gabriel   Sugar baker and friend of Watkins Tottle who pays Tottle's debts on the condition that Tottle marry Miss Lillerton and pay him back from her estate. He gives up on Tottle when Tottle fails to win Miss Lillerton. His own marriage to his wife Fanny is opposed by her parents, and they marry secretly.

Regent's Canal   Canal—opened in 1820—connecting Paddington with the THAMES at Limehouse. Site of the suicide of Watkins Tottle.

Ross, Frank   Friend of Gabriel Parsons.

Timson, Rev. Charles   Unctuous clergyman and friend of Gabriel Parsons, he is the successful suitor for Miss Lillerton's hand.

Tom   Gabriel Parsons's gardener.

Tottle, Watkins   A timid bachelor of 50 with "uxorious inclinations" who is forced to propose to Miss Lillerton by his friend Gabriel Parsons. Tottle finally proposes, only to learn that Miss Lillerton has already agreed to marry the Reverend Charles Timson.

Walker   A horse dealer from ISLINGTON who is in Solomon Jacobs's sponging house.

Willis, Mr.   "A young fellow of vulgar manners" imprisoned in Solomon Jacobs's sponging house.

"THE BLOOMSBURY CHRISTENING"

Story of the christening of Frederick Charles William Kitterbell, whose godfather, Nicodemus Dumps, "the most miserable man in the world," disrupts the christening party by losing the silver mug he bought for the child and by giving a speech listing the hazards that might afflict the child, thus driving the infant's mother into hysterics. Originally published in the MONTHLY MAGAZINE (April 1834).

Characters and Related Entries

Danton   "Young man of about five-and-twenty, with a considerable stock of impudence, and a very small share of ideas" who attempts to be the life of the Kitterbells' christening party.

Dumps, Nicodemus   Misanthropic bachelor uncle of Charles Kitterbell who disrupts the christening party for the Kitterbells' son by toasting the infant with a list of the dangers he faces in the world. As a result, Dumps is not asked again to sponsor one of his nephew's children.

Great Russell Street   In Bloomsbury, site of Charles Kitterbell's house.

Jane   Maidservant to the Kitterbells.

Kitterbell family   Charles Kitterbell invites his uncle, Nicodemus Dumps, to the christening of his son Frederick Charles William. But Dumps loses the christening cup and casts a pall over the celebration with a misanthropic speech. Jemima, Charles's wife, is "one of those young women who almost invariably . . . recall to one's mind the idea of a cold fillet of veal."

Maxwell, Mrs.   Guest at the Kitterbells' christening party.

St. George's Church, Bloomsbury   Site of the christening of the Kitterbell baby.

Tom   Cad on the omnibus that Dumps takes from PENTONVILLE to Bloomsbury.

Wilson, Mr. and Mrs.   Godparents to the Kitterbells' baby.

"DRUNKARD'S DEATH, THE"

Life story of a drunkard: His wife dies in wretched poverty, his sons are transported or killed, his daughter leaves him, and finally, he drowns himself in the THAMES. This story was written for the Second Series of *Boz*.

Characters and Related Entries

Mary   Daughter of the dying drunkard.

Tom   One of the officers who arrest William Warden.

Warden, William Drunkard whose drinking leads to the degradation of his wife and family and to his own suicide. His wife dies of a broken heart; his son Henry is killed by a gamekeeper; a second son, William, shoots the gamekeeper and is hanged; a third son, John, emigrates to America; and his daughter, Mary, deserts him.

Sketches of Young Couples

A series of facetious sketches of various character types, directed to "The Young Gentlemen of England" to enable them to avert "the dangers" of the leap year and the upcoming marriage of Queen Victoria and to resist the designs of single ladies. The types presented were "The Young Couple," "The Formal Couple," "The Loving Couple," "The Contradictory Couple," "The Couple Who Dote upon Their Children," "The Cool Couple," "The Plausible Couple," "The Nice Little Couple," "The Egotistical Couple," "The Couple Who Coddle Themselves," and "The Old Couple." Published by CHAPMAN & HALL, 1840, with illustrations by HABLOT KNIGHT BROWNE.

Characters and Related Entries

Adams, Jane Young housemaid to the Young Couple who reappears as the devoted old servant to the Old Couple.

Briggs, Mr. and Mrs. Friends of the Egotistical Couple.

Charles and Louisa Cool Couple, who suffer "apathy and dullness" on the rare occasions when they are alone together.

Charlotte Edward's exasperating wife in the Contradictory Couple.

Chirrup, Mr. and Mrs. The Nice Little Couple; "Mr. Chirrup has the smartness, and something of the brisk, quick manner of a small bird. Mrs. Chirrup is the prettiest of all little women." The Chirrups are thought to have been based on Dickens's publisher WILLIAM HALL and his wife.

Chopper, Mrs. Mother of Mrs. Merrywinkle of the Couple Who Coddle Themselves.

Clickit, Mr. and Mrs. Plausible Couple praised by Bobtail Widgers.

Crofts Harvey's barber.

Edward With his wife Charlotte, half of the Contradictory Couple.

Fielding, Emma Described as both a bride in the Young Couple and an old woman in the Old Couple.

Finching, Mrs. Friend of the Plausible Couple, the Widgers.

Fithers Artist friend of Bobtail Widgers.

Glogwog, Sir Chipkins An aristocratic friend of the Egotistical Couple.

Harvey Young man to be married to Miss Emma Fielding.

Jackson, Mr. and Mrs. Friends of the Plausible Couple.

Jenkins Friend of the Contradictory Couple.

Leaver, Augustus and Augusta The Loving Couple, who are totally dependent on each other's attentions.

Louisa Wife of Charles of the Cool Couple, who have very little to do with each other.

Merrywinkle Gentleman whose "name is inseparably connected with his complaints." He and his delicate wife are the Couple Who Coddle Themselves.

Mortimer, Mrs. Friend of Louisa of the Cool Couple.

Parsons, Mrs. Woman whose height is the subject of debate between the Contradictory Couple.

Saunders   Bachelor friend of the Whifflers, the Couple Who Dote upon Their Children; "whatever the attention of Mr. Saunders is called to, Mr. Saunders admires of course."

Scuttlewig, duke of   One of the friends claimed by the name-dropping Egotistical Couple.

Slang, Lord   Friend claimed by the name-dropping Egotistical Couple, Mr. and Mrs. Briggs.

Sliverstone, the Reverend and Mrs.   Egotistical Couple, in which "the lady's egotism is all about her husband and the gentleman's is about his wife."

Slummery   Clever painter praised by the Plausible Couple as a way of pleasing Fithers, who has "forestalled [Slummery] in his department of art, and made it thoroughly and completely his own" and who is in their company.

Snorflerer, Dowager Lady   A friend claimed by the name-dropping Egotistical Couple, Mr. and Mrs. Briggs.

Starling, Mrs.   Friend of the Loving Couple, "a widow lady who lost her husband when she was young, and lost herself about the same time."

Tabblewick, Mrs.   A beautiful woman, once believed by the Plausible Couple to be "the most beautiful woman ever seen."

Whiffler, Mr. and Mrs.   Couple Who Dote upon Their Children—Georgiana, Ned, Dick, Tom, Bob, Mary Anne, Emily, Fanny, Carry, and an unnamed infant on the way.

Widger, Mr. Bobtail and Mrs. Lavinia   The Plausible Couple.

Sketches of Young Gentlemen

Series of facetious sketches of various types of young gentlemen, addressed to "the Young Ladies of the United Kingdom" to correct the libels of the *Sketches of Young Ladies* recently published by Quiz (?Edward Caswell) and illustrated by Phiz (HABLOT KNIGHT BROWNE). Dickens's sketches included "The Bashful Young Gentleman," "The Out-and-out Young Gentleman," "The Very Friendly Young Gentleman," "The Military Young Gentleman," "The Political Young Gentleman," "The Domestic Young Gentleman," "The Censorious Young Gentleman," "The Funny Young Gentleman," "The Theatrical Young Gentleman," "The Poetical Young Gentleman," "The 'Throwing-off' Young Gentleman," and "The Young Ladies' Young Gentleman." Published by CHAPMAN & HALL, 1838, with illustrations by Browne.

Characters and Related Entries

Balim   A Young Ladies' Young Gentleman, "so profusely decked with scarfs, ribands, flowers, and other pretty spoils, that he looked like a lamb . . . adorned for the sacrifice."

Blake, "Warmint"   An Out-and-out Young Gentleman.

Boozle   The temperamental actor who refuses to take over Flimkins's part.

Capper, Mr. and Mrs.   Hosts to Mincin, the Very Friendly Young Gentleman.

Caveton   The Throwing-off Young Gentleman.

Dummins   "Eccentric" and "rather wild" Out-and-out Young Gentleman.

Fairfax, Mr.   The Censorious Young Gentleman, "a remarkably clever person."

Fitz-Sordust, Colonel   The commander of the Military Young Gentlemen.

Flimkins, Mr. and Mrs.   An acting couple at the Surrey Theatre.

Greenwood, Miss   Young woman who speculates on the marital prospects of the Censorious Young Gentleman.

Grey, Misses Amelia and her sister are friends of Felix Nixon, the Domestic Young Gentleman.

Griggins He justifies his characterization as the Funny Young Gentleman by his clowning at Mrs. Brown's party.

Hawkins New Member of Parliament whom the Political Young Gentleman thinks it may be necessary "to bring . . . down on his knees for that vote on the miscellaneous estimates."

Hopkins The Bashful Young Gentleman.

John The Poetical Young Gentleman.

Lambert, Miss Partner of Hopkins, the Bashful Young Gentleman, in the quadrille.

Lowfield, Miss Young woman smitten with Caveton, the Throwing-off Young Gentleman.

Marshall, Miss One of the young ladies who wonders about the mysterious Mr. Fairfax, the Censorious Young Gentleman.

Martin family Particular friends of Mincin, the Very Friendly Young Gentleman.

Milkwash, John The Poetical Young Gentleman: "his countenance is of a plaintive and melancholy cast, his manner is abstracted and bespeaks affliction of the soul: he seldom has his hair cut, and he often talks about being an outcast and wanting a kindred spirit."

Mincin The Very Friendly Young Gentleman.

Nixon, Felix The Domestic Young Gentleman, "lives at home with his mother" and the two chief subjects of his discourse "are himself and his mother."

Thompson, Julia Friend of Felix Nixon, the Domestic Young Gentleman.

Thompson, Mrs. After she asks Mr. Fairfax, the Censorious Young Gentleman, what he thinks of

Mrs. Barker, she agrees with him that the woman has something exceedingly odd in her manner.

Watson, Mrs. and the Misses Friends of Mr. Mincin, the Very Friendly Young Gentleman.

"Sleep to Startle Us, A"

Article for HOUSEHOLD WORDS (March 13, 1852) describing the RAGGED SCHOOL in FIELD LANE and the dormitory for the homeless connected with the school. The narrator visits classes in tailoring, shoemaking, and mathematics, and he observes the 167 occupants of the dormitory as they prepare to sleep after attending the school. He ends by asserting, "An annual sum of money, contemptible in amount as compared with any charges upon any list, freely granted in behalf of these Schools, and shackled with no preposterous Red Tape conditions, would relieve the prisons, diminish the country rates, clear loads of shame and guilt out of the streets, recruit the army and navy, waft to new countries, Fleets full of useful labour, for which their inhabitants would be thankful and beholden to us." *Miscellaneous, Journalism.*

"Slight Depreciation of the Currency, A"

Article for HOUSEHOLD WORDS (November 3, 1855) that deplores the substitution of money for active public service. At a time when duty is especially called for, money alone cannot correct the inequities and injustices in society. *Miscellaneous, Journalism.*

"Slight Question of Fact, A"

Note for ALL THE YEAR ROUND (February 13, 1869) correcting an assertion in the *Pall Mall Gazette* that failed to recognize WILLIAM MACREADY's insistence on public decency in the theaters he managed. Dickens corrects the record. *Miscellaneous*.

"Smuggled Relations"

Humorous article for HOUSEHOLD WORDS (June 23, 1855) describing a number of cases of relations who were kept secret: Cogsford "disguised" his mother as his housekeeper, Mrs. Bean; Benting never acknowledged his globe-trotting brother John; but the narrator and his wife Susannah are the most surprised to learn that their good friend Larver has been married for 10 years without their knowing it. *Miscellaneous*.

"Snoring for the Million"

Satirical article for the EXAMINER (December 24, 1842). Using as his model the popular movement "Singing for the Million"—a movement seeking to discourage "the people from vicious indulgences" by encouraging them to sing—Dickens proposes a movement teaching people to sleep. Then there would be "no more complaints of hunger [and] . . . no fast-widening gulf between the two great divisions of society." *Journalism*.

"Some Account of an Extraordinary Traveller"

Article from HOUSEHOLD WORDS (April 20, 1850) describing the travels of Mr. Booley to America, New Zealand, Australia, Egypt, India, and the Arctic—all through visits to the panoramas on display in London. *Miscellaneous, Journalism*.

Characters and Related Entries
Booley   Retired gentleman from ISLINGTON who has taken an extraordinary series of travels—up the Mississippi, Missouri, Ohio, and Nile rivers; to Australia, New Zealand, India, Egypt; and, most

recently, to the Arctic—all by means of the panoramas on display in London. He describes his travels in lectures to the Social Oysters. Booley also provides an allegorical interpretation of the LORD MAYOR's parade in "Mr. Booley's View of the Last Lord Mayor's Show."

Creeble, Miss   Schoolmistress whom Mr. Booley encounters on some of his travels.

Septimus   Mr. Booley's nephew who accompanies him on his "journey" to the Ohio River.

Social Oysters   HIGHGATE social club to which Mr. Booley reports his extraordinary travels. *Miscellaneous*.

"Some Particulars Concerning a Lion"
See *Mudfog*.

"Spirit Business, The"

Article for HOUSEHOLD WORDS (May 7, 1853), a debunking report of several spiritualist publications from America that prove, Dickens concludes sarcastically, that "the spirit business cannot fail to be regarded by all dispassionate persons as the last great triumph of common sense." *Miscellaneous*.

"The Spirit of Chivalry in Westminster Hall"

Article for DOUGLAS JERROLD's *Shilling Magazine* (August 1845) praising the cartoon "The Spirit of Chivalry," prepared by DANIEL MACLISE, as a proposal for a fresco in the rebuilt House of Lords. *Journalism*.

"Spitalfields"

Article for HOUSEHOLD WORDS (April 5, 1851) by W. H. WILLS and Dickens, describing Spitalfields, an area in east London, east of Bishopsgate, settled by French Huguenots in the 17th century and devoted to the manufacture of silk. The narrators visit a silk warehouse and then go to the homes of two silk weavers. The first is a close and dark abode where the weaver, his wife, and another weaver to whom he rents space struggle to survive. The second, the home of a weaver of patterned silk, is light, airy, and clean, an example of the better opportunities offered in the silk business for students who have attended the School of Design. *Stone.*

"Stores for the First of April"

Article for HOUSEHOLD WORDS (March 7, 1857) in which Dickens calculates "what we have in store" for All Fools' Day. He discusses a number of spiritualist accounts as examples of foolishness, bitterly recounts the reports of bungling and mismanagement in the Crimea and the excuses given by those responsible, and goes on to describe a clergyman who wants to remove an exhibition of the Thugs in India from the British Museum because it encourages crime. *Miscellaneous.*

"Story of Little Dombey, The"

Dickens's PUBLIC READING from *Dombey.* First performed in 1858, it was the first reading he drew from one of the longer novels. It presents the life and death of young Paul Dombey.

"Story of Richard Doubledick"

See *Christmas Stories,* "Seven Poor Travellers."

"'Story without a Beginning, The' (Translated from the German by Boz)"

A fairy tale parodying "The Story without an End," a popular German allegorical tale of the time. Dickens uses his allegorical parody to satirize William IV's conduct in dismissing the Melbourne government. From the MORNING CHRONICLE (December 18, 1834). *Journalism.*

Strange Gentleman, The

A dramatic version of "The Great Winglebury Duel," performed at the ST. JAMES'S THEATRE on September 29, 1836. A strange gentleman arrives at an inn on his way to GRETNA GREEN to marry Emily Brown. He has never met Emily; the marriage has been arranged by his father. His rival for Emily, Horatio Tinkles, challenges him to a duel. Attempting to avoid the duel and to meet Emily, the strange gentleman, Walker Trott, mistakes other guests at the inn and is mistaken by them. In the end he loses Emily to Tinkles, but he gains Miss Julia Dobbs.

Characters and Related Entries

Dobbs, Julia Young woman on her way to GRETNA GREEN to marry a young lord. She gets caught in the mistaken identities and ends up eloping with Walker Trott.

Johnson, John Young man who elopes to GRETNA GREEN with Mary Wilson.

Noakes, Mrs. Landlady at the St. James's Arms.

Overton, Owen Mayor of Winglebury who manages to promote the confusion that prevents the duel and leads to the unexpected marriage of Walker Trott and Julia Dobbs.

Sparks, Tom Boots at the St. James's Arms who delivers the letters from the strange gentleman.

Tinkles, Horatio Walker Trott's rival for Emily Brown. He challenges Trott to a duel and precipitates the disguises and mistaken identities of the play. He is called Horace Hunter in "The Great Winglebury Duel."

Tom Waiter at the St. James's Arms.

Tompkins, Charles Fiancé of Fanny Wilson caught up in the confusion at the St. James's Arms.

Trott, Walker The strange gentleman. To avoid a duel with Horatio Tinkles, his rival for the hand of Emily Brown, Trott attempts to have himself arrested by Mayor Overton, but in the confusion that ensues, he is taken for a madman and loses Emily Brown. In the end he must be satisfied with the hand of heiress Julia Dobbs.

Will Waiter at the St. James's Arms.

Wilson, Fanny and Mary Two sisters on their way to GRETNA GREEN, Fanny is the fiancée of Charles Tomkins, Mary of John Johnson.

"Sucking Pigs"

Article for HOUSEHOLD WORDS (November 8, 1851) adding to the extreme ideologies attacked in an earlier article, "Whole Hogs," the sucking pig of Bloomerism, a movement led by Mrs. Amelia Bloomer, who advocated the wearing of bloomers, pantlike undergarments, as a way of liberating women. The excesses of the Bloomerites in dress, behavior, and rhetoric make them foolish. Bellows, the narrator of the piece, asserts that "if there were anything that we could dispense with in Mrs. Bellows above all other things, we believe it would be a Mission." This article is especially relevant to Dickens's criticism of Mrs. Jellyby and Mrs. Pardiggle in *Bleak House. Miscellaneous, Journalism.*

"Sunday Screw, The"

Article for HOUSEHOLD WORDS (June 22, 1850) discussing a parliamentary bill to eliminate the collec-

tion and delivery of letters on Sunday. Dickens sees this bill as "the beginning of a Sabbatarian Crusade, outrageous to the spirit of Christianity, irreconcilable with the health, the rational enjoyments, and the true religious feeling of the community." He urges LORD SHAFTESBURY, whom he considers "most mischievously deluded on this question," to reconsider lending his influence to a movement which would turn Sunday into "a day of mortification and gloom." *Miscellaneous, Journalism.*

Sunday under Three Heads. As it is; as Sabbath Bills would make it; as it might be made.

Pamphlet published in 1836, under the pseudonym "Timothy Sparks," with three illustrations by HABLOT KNIGHT BROWNE. Prompted by the defeat in Parliament of Sir Andrew Agnew's Sunday Observance Bill, Dickens attacked such legislation for its class bias, pointing out that Agnew's bill would curtail only the recreations of the poor, not those of the rich. In describing Sunday as it is, he follows the activities of the day for both rich and poor, depicting it as the one day on which the poor have meat for their meal and the one day on which they can go out of doors to parks, into the countryside, or to the river for some healthful recreation. The Sabbath bills would turn Sunday into "a day of general gloom and austerity," leaving the poor restless, discontented, and quarrelsome. Sunday might be made a time when the museums were open in the afternoon and when games and outdoor recreations, like those the author had once seen sponsored by a country clergyman, engaged the whole community in healthful activity. "The Sabbath was made for man," Dickens reminds his readers in closing, "not man to serve the Sabbath."

"Supposing"

Under this title Dickens wrote several short articles for HOUSEHOLD WORDS, in each of which he addressed a social or governmental abuse by asking what if the circumstances were changed or what if a different class of people were involved. The articles appeared on April 20, 1850 (on a potpourri of social and political issues); August 10, 1850 (on the misuse of government funds); June 7, 1851 (on class bias in the courts); and February 10, 1855 (on mismanagement during the Crimean War). *Miscellaneous*.

"Tattlesnivel Bleater, The"

Satirical article for ALL THE YEAR ROUND (December 31, 1859) mocking the pretensions of the popular press. The correspondents for the *Tattlesnivel Bleater*, after purveying misinformation on nearly every topic from the state of the queen's health to the subjects of the paintings in the Royal Exhibition, offer the snivelling excuse that there is a conspiracy against them. *Miscellaneous, Journalism*.

"That Other Public"

Satirical article for HOUSEHOLD WORDS (February 3, 1855) calling for "that other public" in both Britain and the United States to rise up against government corruption and mismanagement of the sort evident during the Crimean War in Britain and described as "smart dealing" by the Americans in *Chuzzlewit*. *Miscellaneous, Journalism*.

"Things That Cannot Be Done"

Satirical article for HOUSEHOLD WORDS (October 8, 1853) celebrating the proposition that "Nothing flagrantly wrong can be done, without adequate punishment, under the English law." Dickens decries the light sentences given for acts of brutality and describes at length the example of a ne'er-do-well who has used the law to harass an

heiress and extort money from her. *Miscellaneous, Journalism*.

"Thousand and One Humbugs, The"

Series of satiric articles for HOUSEHOLD WORDS (April 21, April 28, and May 5, 1855), which Dickens described as "new versions of the best known stories" from the *Arabian Nights*. They attack governmental incompetence during the Crimean War and the PALMERSTON administration that took power in February 1855. In the parody the Grand Vizier Parmarstoon (Palmerston) succeeded "Aabbadeen (or The Addled) [Lord Aberdeen], who had for his misdeeds been strangled with a garter." The Vizier's daughter Hansardadade—an allusion to Hansard's, the verbatim record of Parliamentary proceedings—entertains the sultan with the stories of "Scarli Tapa [Red Tape] and the Forty Thieves," in which the cave of riches is entered by the passwords "Debrett's Peerage. Open Sesame!" The other two parodies are "The Story of the Talkative Barber" and "The Story of the Barmacide Feast." *Miscellaneous, Journalism*.

"Threatening Letter to Thomas Hood from an Ancient Gentlemen by Favor of Charles Dickens"

A satirical letter to the editor of HOOD'S MAGAZINE AND COMIC MISCELLANY (May 1844). In the voice of an old curmudgeon, Dickens attacks the decline of the times. Only one judge seems to have the courage to sentence to death a woman who unsuccessfully attempted to drown herself and succeeded only in drowning her child. The popular fascination with dwarfs, inspired by Tom Thumb, and with wild men from the exhibitions of wild Indians are also signs of the times that must be acknowledged in "this ill-fated land." *Journalism*.

"Toady Tree, The"

Article for HOUSEHOLD WORDS (May 26, 1855) denouncing "ruinous gentility and deference to mere rank." Using a series of hypothetical examples, Dickens shows various forms of such destructive deference: Dobbs, who refers to his titled friends by their nicknames; Hobbs, an inventor who has been denied recognition for his work but still kowtows to those in power; Pobbs, who puts his titled acquaintances down as "swells" but depends on their attentions to him. This article is particularly relevant to Doyce, the Meagles, and the Barnacles in *Dorrit*. *Miscellaneous, Journalism*.

"To be Read at Dusk"

In this essay for the KEEPSAKE (1852), the narrator recounts anecdotes of strange occurrences that he overheard some couriers tell at the Great St. Bernard Hospice. A Genoese courier tells of the disappearance of a young bride when she meets Signor Dellombra, a man who possesses a face that has haunted her dreams. A German courier tells of a man who has a premonition of his brother's death.

Characters and Related Entries

Baptista, Giovanni Genoese narrator of the story of Clara and Signor Dellombra.

Carolina Beautiful maid to the English bride haunted by the face in her dreams.

Clara English bride haunted by Signor Dellombra.

Dellombra, Signor "A dark remarkable-looking man, with black hair and a grey moustache," who possesses the evil face that haunts the dreams of the English bride. He kidnaps her and they disappear.

Dodger, the Hon. Ananias Subject of a story about "one of the largest acquisitions of dollars ever made in this country" told by an American traveler to the narrator of "At Dusk."

James Twin brother to John, in business together at Goodman's Fields. He has a premonition of his brother's death.

John James's twin; he appears to his brother as a panthom shortly before his death.

Robert Servant to John in the German courier's tale.

Wilhelm German courier who tells the story of John, the twin who has a ghostly premonition of his brother's death.

"Tooting Farm, The"

Article for the EXAMINER (January 27, 1849) following up "The Paradise at Tooting." Dickens reports that a verdict of manslaughter has justly been returned against Drouet. He asserts that the Board of Guardians, who complained that they were vilified by the press, were also "grossly in the wrong." He goes on to warn that such events as the cholera epidemic at the Tooting baby farm encourage the poor to embrace CHARTISM, and he calls for the abolition of baby farms and the amendment of the POOR LAW. *Miscellaneous*.

"To Working Men"

Article for HOUSEHOLD WORDS (October 7, 1854) written in the wake of the cholera epidemic in London in August and September. Dickens calls on the workingmen whose families suffered most from the outbreak to rise up and demand legislation to improve sanitary conditions and the dwellings of the poor. Only such pressure from the people of the lower and middle classes, Dickens asserts, will make the politicians listen and act. *Miscellaneous, Journalism.*

"Trading in Death"

Article for HOUSEHOLD WORDS (November 27, 1852) on the state funeral for the duke of Wellington. Dickens objects to the expense and commercialization of Wellington's funeral and expresses the hope that it will serve to change the public mind, leading to less costly and more healthful funeral practices. *Miscellaneous, Journalism.*

"Tresses of the Day Star, The"

Article for HOUSEHOLD WORDS (June 21, 1851) by CHARLES KNIGHT, edited with some brief additions by Dickens, describing the new hummingbird exhibit created by John Gould for the Zoological Society. *Stone.*

"'Truly British Judge, A'"

Article in the EXAMINER (August 19, 1848), probably by Dickens, criticizing the "vacillating conduct" of a judge who first sentenced a 10-year-old boy to a month in jail for stealing a purse, then changed the sentence to seven years' transportation, and then changed the sentence again to a year in prison. *Journalism.*

"Two Chapters on Bank Note Forgeries: Chapter II"

Article for HOUSEHOLD WORDS (September 21, 1850) by W. H. WILLS and Dickens describing the history of counterfeit BANK OF ENGLAND notes and the ways in which counterfeiting has been reduced and nearly eliminated. *Stone.*

Uncommercial Traveller, The

A series of sketches Dickens wrote for ALL THE YEAR ROUND in the 1860s. Seventeen of them were first published in volume form in 1861 under the general title *The Uncommercial Traveller*. In later editions more sketches were added: 11 more in the CHEAP EDITION (1865), 8 more in the LIBRARY EDITION (1875), and one final addition in the GADSHILL EDITION (1890). The numbering used to identify particular sketches below is that of the OXFORD ILLUSTRATED EDITION.

1. "His General Line of Business"
The Traveller introduces himself: "Figuratively speaking, I travel for the great house of Human Interest Brothers, and I have rather a large connection in the fancy goods way. Literally speaking, I am always wandering here and there from my rooms in Covent-garden, London—now about the city streets: now, about the country by-roads—seeing many little things, and some great things, which, because they interest me, I think may interest others." The article appeared in ALL THE YEAR ROUND (January 28, 1860) along with "The Shipwreck."

2. "The Shipwreck"
The Traveller describes a visit to the Welsh village of Llanallgo in late December 1859. Only two months before, the Australian trading and passenger ship, the *Royal Charter,* had broken up off the coast near this village, taking at least 500 lives. The Traveller describes the salvage operation, but he has come to the village to observe the selfless dedication of the local clergyman, Stephen Roose Hughes, who has buried the dead and ministered to the living tirelessly since the accident. The article is a tribute to the clergyman's modesty, simplicity, and cheerful earnestness, his "true practical Christianity." The article first appeared in ALL THE YEAR ROUND (January 28, 1860).

3. "Wapping Workhouse"
On a visit to the women's workhouse in Wapping in the East End of London, the Traveller observes the treatment of the physically and mentally ill, the "Refractories" who are required to pick oakum, and the elderly and infirm. Although the institution is

clean and kindly administered, its constrained facilities indicate that the poor rates for supporting such institutions should be equalized rather than based on the wealth or poverty of the local parish. Originally in ALL THE YEAR ROUND (February 18, 1860).

4. "Two Views of a Cheap Theatre"
The Traveller's account of two visits to the Britannia Theatre, Hoxton, a new and spacious building, well ventilated and nicely arranged. On Saturday evening, he sees a PANTOMIME and a melodrama performed there and is especially impressed by the diversity in the audience, its attentiveness, and its enjoyment of the performance. On Sunday evening in the same building, he attends a religious service and notices that the audience is not so mixed as on the evening before; it is made up almost exclusively of "respectable" people. The Traveller suggests that the preacher might attract more working-class people if he was not so condescending in speaking of workingmen, if his stories were more believable, and if he made the New Testament the story that he chose to tell. This article first appeared in ALL THE YEAR ROUND (February 25, 1860).

5. "Poor Merchantile Jack"
The Traveller's account of visiting the slums of LIVERPOOL with a police superintendent and seeing the lodging-house keepers, publicans, and other inhabitants of the area, all of whom are waiting to prey upon visiting seamen. Originally in ALL THE YEAR ROUND (March 10, 1860).

6. "Refreshments for Travellers"
The Traveller laments the refreshments for travelers—watery soup, inedible pastries, and "glutinous lumps of gristle and grease, called pork-pie." The waiters at travelers' hotels show little interest in serving their customers and make no effort to accommodate customers' schedules. Originally in ALL THE YEAR ROUND (March 24, 1860).

7. "Travelling Abroad"
The Traveller's account of a journey from London to Paris, where he is unsettled by a visit to the morgue; to Strasbourg, where he imagines the life of Straudenheim, a merchant he watches from his hotel window; and finally to the mountains of SWITZERLAND. On the way to DOVER, the Traveller

meets a "queer small boy" near the mansion GAD'S HILL PLACE, who has been told by his father—as Dickens himself was—"If you were to be persevering and were to work hard, you might someday come to live in it." Originally in ALL THE YEAR ROUND (April 7, 1860).

8. "*Great Tasmania*'s Cargo, The"
The Traveller's indignant report of a visit to the Liverpool Workhouse, where the discharged soldiers from the *Great Tasmania* were recuperating from a voyage from India on which they had been starved and subjected to disease. Although Pangloss, the government official who accompanies him, takes no responsibility for the diseased and dying men, it is evident to the Traveller that the government has neglected its duty. Originally in ALL THE YEAR ROUND (April 21, 1860).

9. "City of London Churches"
The Traveller tells of a year of making Sunday visits to the dusty old churches in the CITY, which "remain the tombs of the old citizens who lie beneath them and around them, Monuments of another age." Originally in ALL THE YEAR ROUND (May 5, 1860).

10. "Shy Neighbourhoods"
One can know shy neighborhoods—poor neighborhoods in backstreets and byways—by their pets, the birds, donkeys, dogs, cats, and fowl that one encounters while walking through them. Originally in ALL THE YEAR ROUND (May 26, 1860).

12. "Dullborough Town"
The Traveller visits the town where he was a boy and finds it much changed, "mysteriously gone, like my own youth." Then he meets Joe Specks, a boyhood friend, and their shared memories make the visit a rewarding one. Originally in ALL THE YEAR ROUND (June 30, 1860).

13. "Night Walks"
At a time in his life when he has difficulty sleeping, the Traveller takes walks through the streets of London, lasting from midnight until dawn. On these walks he sees the last stragglers in the streets as the pubs close and the city goes to bed. Going from Haymarket to WATERLOO BRIDGE, the narrator meditates on the suicides there; he proceeds

to the empty theaters on the Surrey side of the Thames and then walks past NEWGATE PRISON, KING'S BENCH PRISON, and Bethlehem Hospital. There he meditates on dreams, wondering, "Are not the sane and the insane equal at night as the sane lie dreaming?" Passing the Houses of PARLIAMENT and WESTMINSTER ABBEY, he goes on to COVENT GARDEN Market for some coffee before returning home to sleep as the people return to the streets at dawn. The article first appeared in ALL THE YEAR ROUND (July 21, 1860).

14. "Chambers"
The Traveller describes the loneliness of chambers in the various INNS OF COURT, where single men live in dusty rooms that have never known the liveliness of marriages, children, and family festivals. Originally in ALL THE YEAR ROUND (August 18, 1860).

15. "Nurse's Stories"
The Traveller is drawn to the worlds of Crusoe, Gulliver, and the *Arabian Nights* by pleasant memories; he is also called against his will to remember the dark corners in the ghost stories told to him by his nurse. He especially remembers two such stories: "Captain Murderer," the tale of a serial killer who baked his brides into meat pies, and "Chips," the story of a shipwright who is driven to destruction by a talking rat that he received in a deal with the devil. Originally in ALL THE YEAR ROUND (September 9, 1860).

16. "Arcadian London"
During vacation time, when London is deserted, the city becomes an arcadian wilderness in a golden age. The Traveller goes out into the empty streets from his lodging in BOND STREET to be "soothed by the repose" around him and to celebrate the city, which has become "the abode of love." Originally in ALL THE YEAR ROUND (September 29, 1860).

17. "The Italian Prisoner"
The Traveller recounts a commission given to him by an English friend to deliver a letter to Giovanni Carlavero while on a tour of ITALY. Carlavero, a winemaker, was once a political prisoner who was released through the efforts of the English letter

writer. Carlavero's gratitude is unbounded, and he gives the Traveller a huge bottle of wine to take back to England—a commission that leads to countless difficulties on the return journey. Originally in ALL THE YEAR ROUND (October 13, 1860).

18. "The Calais Night Mail"
The Traveller's account of crossing the Channel from DOVER to CALAIS and boarding the night train to PARIS. Originally in ALL THE YEAR ROUND (May 2, 1863).

19. "Some Recollections of Mortality"
The Traveller is caught up in a crowd in PARIS who observe the body of an old man at the morgue. The incident recalls two earlier experiences in the Traveller's life, first of seeing the body of a woman pulled from the Regent's Canal in London, and then of serving at an inquest into the death of an infant. Originally in ALL THE YEAR ROUND (May 16, 1863).

20. "Birthday Celebrations"
The Traveller remembers many birthday celebrations he has attended: a childhood party, a tedious visit to an Orrery (a precursor to a planetarium) with Olympia Squires, a schooltime celebration with a hamper of food, his 21st birthday, later celebrations of Flipfield's and Mayday's birthdays, and the Dullborough festivity for Shakespeare's birthday. Originally in ALL THE YEAR ROUND (June 6, 1863).

21. "The Short-Timers"
The Traveller's account of a visit to the Limehouse School of Industry, sponsored by the Stepney Union, where the children of the poor are educated for a variety of trades in a very successful educational scheme in which the children attend school for half the normal school hours. Originally in ALL THE YEAR ROUND (June 20, 1862).

22. "Bound for the Great Salt Lake"
The Traveller visits an emigrant ship of 800 Mormons beginning their journey to Utah. He expects "to bear testimony against them," but he is astonished to find their demeanor exemplary and their social arrangements in perfect order. Originally in ALL THE YEAR ROUND (July 4, 1863).

23. "The City of the Absent"
The Traveller's account of his visits to obscure CITY churchyards. Originally in ALL THE YEAR ROUND (July 18, 1863).

24. "An Old Stage-coaching House"
The Traveller stays at the Dolphin's Head, a coaching inn "dying by inches" since the coming of the railway. The town, seven miles from the railway station, is deserted and melancholy, its buildings crumbling; a broken post chaise is even being used as a dwelling. Originally in ALL THE YEAR ROUND (August 1, 1863).

25. "The Boiled Beef of New England"
Article for ALL THE YEAR ROUND (August 15, 1863) describing a visit to a cooperative eating establishment for working people. England is shabbier than almost any other country, the Traveller asserts, and the shabby fashion of the poor often simply imitates that of the rich. One of the qualities of the English workingman, however, is his independence; that quality is apparent in the new "self-supporting Cooking Depot for the Working Classes" in WHITECHAPEL, a gathering place for the creators of a new England.

26. "Chatham Dockyard"
The Traveller's account of daydreaming by the river in CHATHAM and then visiting the dockyard where the warship *Achilles* is under construction. As he meditates on rope making, the Traveller is "spun into a state of blissful indolence, wherein my rope of life seems to be so untwisted by the process as that I can see back to very early days indeed." Originally in ALL THE YEAR ROUND (August 29, 1863).

27. "In the French-Flemish Country"
On a journey to the Flemish area of France, the Traveller goes to a performance of a provincial theater company and to a fair where he sees a ventriloquist and a "face-maker," a mime who makes a thousand faces. Originally in ALL THE YEAR ROUND (September 12, 1863).

28. "Medicine Men of Civilisation"
The procedures of savage medicine men may seem absurd to us, but many "civilized" customs are not far removed from the absurdities of the savages. English funeral customs, for example, are especially absurd, and some savage rituals might improve the way Parliament proceeds. Originally in ALL THE YEAR ROUND (September 26, 1863).

29. "Titbull's Alms-Houses"
The Traveller visits the almshouses established by Sampson Titbull in 1723 in east London. He learns that the inmates resent the neglect of the trustees and are suspicious among themselves, but they are all surprised when Mrs. Mitts, youngest of the women inmates, resigns her place to marry a Greenwich pensioner. Originally in ALL THE YEAR ROUND (October 24, 1863).

30. "The Ruffian"
The Traveller complains that ruffians are taking over the streets because the police tolerate them. As a result of this "constable contemplation," street crime is increasing. The Traveller describes his efforts to have a young woman arrested for using bad language in public and the difficulty he had convincing various authorities that he was seriously pressing charges. Originally in ALL THE YEAR ROUND (October 10, 1868).

31. "Aboard Ship"
Article in ALL THE YEAR ROUND (December 5, 1868). The Traveller's account of sailing on the steamship *Russia* from NEW YORK to LIVERPOOL, his remembrances of other voyages, his constant awareness of the rolling sea and the ship's engine, and his relief on arriving at Queenstown in Ireland and, finally, at Liverpool.

32. "A Small Star in the East"
The Traveller visits a poor neighborhood in RATCLIFF near the river, where underemployed laborers and dockworkers live in "a wilderness of dirt, rags and hunger." He sees a starving Irish family, which includes a young woman suffering from lead poisoning, contracted while working in a nearby lead mill. An unemployed boilermaker's laborer and his wife, who sews pea jackets, have only a loaf of bread and water to eat. The Traveller is so distressed by the starving children of a coal porter and laundress that he cannot continue his observations. However, when he discovers the East London Children's

Hospital, he is heartened to find a dedicated young doctor and his wife caring for the children of their distressed neighborhood. Originally in ALL THE YEAR ROUND (December 19, 1868).

33. "A Little Dinner in an Hour"
The Traveller and his friend Bullfinch endure a dreadful dinner at the Temeraire in Namelesston. Originally in ALL THE YEAR ROUND (January 2, 1869).

34. "Mr. Barlow"
The Traveller remembers, as someone who has blighted his life, his childhood tutor, a pedantic "instructive monomaniac" like the tutor Barlow in *Sanford and Merton,* a popular didactic work for children. Every time he is lectured at, instructed rather than entertained, or talked down to by a condescending letter writer, the narrator remembers the boring Mr. Barlow. Originally in ALL THE YEAR ROUND (January 16, 1869).

35. "On an Amateur Beat"
Walking from his lodgings in COVENT GARDEN to Limehouse, the Traveller imagines himself a police constable on his beat. Near TEMPLE BAR a swarm of ragged street children surround him; farther east he sees a crippled old woman, whose bent form he has often observed before. Then he stops at the CHILDREN'S HOSPITAL and watches the dog Poodles going on his rounds from patient to patient. He ends his walk at a lead mill in Limehouse, where nearly all the workers, in spite of precautions, sooner or later contract lead poisoning. Originally in ALL THE YEAR ROUND (February 27, 1869).

36. "A Fly-leaf in a Life"
The Traveller describes his experiences during a period of withdrawal and rest brought on by exhaustion. He realizes the similarities in his "case" and that of Mr. Merdle in *Dorrit,* they are both victims of "pressure." He also was advised on his spiritual condition by intrusive clergymen and badgered by begging letter writers. The article, first published in ALL THE YEAR ROUND (May 22, 1869), describes Dickens's respite from PUBLIC READINGS in the final months of his life.

37. "A Plea for Total Abstinence"
After observing a temperance march in which the participants grossly overtax the horses pulling their wagons, the Traveller decides that teetotalers are "unable to use [horses] without abusing them," and he declares "total abstinence from horseflesh to be the only remedy of which the case admitted." Originally in ALL THE YEAR ROUND (June 5, 1869).

Characters and Related Entries in *Uncommercial Traveller*

Anderson, Mr. and Mrs. John The neatly dressed and spotless tramps whom the Traveller encounters on the road. John has chalked "hungry" on the spade that he carries (11).

Angelica An old girlfriend of the Traveller (9).

Antonio A guitar-playing Spanish sailor whom the Traveller meets in Megisson's lodging house (5).

Barlow Pedantic tutor in the popular didactic story for children, *Sanford and Merton.* He reminds the Traveller of his own tutor. Every boring lecture, condescending remark, or didactic moment recalls Mr. Barlow (34).

Battens Oldest male resident of Titbull's Alms-Houses, he complains of neglect by the trustees (29).

Bedlam Contracted form of Bethlehem Hospital, the lunatic asylum in London whose name is synonymous with *madhouse.* The Traveller speculates on madness outside the walls of the hospital (13).

Bogles, Mrs. The landlady at the Traveller's London boardinghouse, who is arrested for debt (6).

Boiler, the Rev. Boanerges The tedious preacher from the Traveller's childhood whose "lumbering jocularity" was never amusing to the child (9).

Bones, Banjo and Mrs. Banjo Comic entertainers at a pub for sailors (5).

Brittania Theatre, Hoxton A popular theater, uniting "vastness with compactness," visited by the Traveller (4).

Bullfinch Business advisor to the Traveller who shares a "nasty little dinner" in Namelesston with him (33).

Burlington Arcade A fashionable shopping arcade off Piccadilly (16).

Carlavero, Giovanni Italian winemaker who was once a political prisoner and was released through the efforts of an English visitor (17).

Celia Charity girl who meets her lover, a charity boy, in a deserted CITY churchyard (23).

Chips Shipwright who makes a deal with the devil in one of the ghost stories told to the Traveller by his childhood nurse (15).

Cleverly, William and Susannah Mormon brother and sister on their way to Salt Lake (22).

Cobby The giant tramp who shares a meat pie with the white-haired lady (11).

Cocker, Indignation Patron of the Temeraire who objects to the arithmetic on his restaurant bill, interrupting the waiter who is serving the Traveller (33).

Cook, Captain Commander of the Cunard steamship *Russia,* on which the Traveller sails from NEW YORK to LIVERPOOL (31).

Darby, Mr. and Mrs. Keepers of a disreputable lodging house near the LIVERPOOL docks (5).

Dibble Family Sampson, a blind old man and his wife Dorothy are among the Mormon emigrants to Salt Lake (22).

Dolphin's Head Old coaching inn dying as a result of the coming of the railway (24).

Dullborough The Traveller's version of Chatham, his boyhood home. "Most of us come from Dullborough who come from a country town" (12).

Face-maker, the "A corpulent little man in a large white waistcoat" who performs at a Flemish country fair, changing his face into "a thousand characters" (27).

Flanders, Sally Childhood nurse of the Traveller who took him as a child to her husband's funeral (26).

Flipfield Friend of the Traveller whose birthday celebration is attended by his mother, his sister, and his long-lost brother Tom, who "came to light in foreign parts" (20).

Globson, Bully "A big fat boy, with a big fat head, and a big fat fist," who bullied the Traveller at school (20).

Grazinglands family Alexander, a gentleman of property from the Midlands who comes to London with his wife Arabella to transact some business at the BANK OF ENGLAND. They receive poor service at Jairing's Hotel, and when they complain the waiter tells them that "when indwiduals is not staying in the 'Ouse, their favours is not as a rule looked upon as making it worth Mr. Jairing's while" (6).

Green, Lucy Childhood sweetheart of the Traveller whom he meets as Dr. Specks's wife when he returns to Dullborough (12).

Hughes, Rev. Stephen and Rev. Hugh Historical figures, two brothers who were clergymen in the neighboring parishes of Llanallgo and Penrhos in Wales. Dickens praised their ministry to the survivors and the dead from the shipwreck of the *Royal Charter* on its way from Melbourne to LIVERPOOL on October 26, 1859 (2).

Jack A common sailor as a type described in "Poor Mercantile Jack" (5).

Jack, Dark An African sailor (5).

Jairing's Hotel The London hotel where reputable "families and gentlemen" from the Midlands stay; the Grazinglands eat a desultory meal here served by a waiter who would prefer that they dine somewhere else (6).

Jobson An extensive family of Mormon emigrants beginning their journey from London to Utah (22).

John Unemployed boilermaker visited by the Traveller (32).

Joseph Charity boy whose tryst with Celia in a CITY churchyard is observed by the Traveller (23).

Kinch, Horace Prisoner in the KING'S BENCH PRISON who has succumbed to the "Dry Rot" and who dies in confinement (13).

Kindheart The Traveller's friend in Italy, "an Englishman of an amiable nature, great enthusiasm, and no discretion" (28). He was based on Dickens's friend ANGUS FLETCHER.

Klem Family The summer caretakers of the Traveller's London lodgings. Mrs. Klem is "an elderly woman, laboring under a chronic sniff" and her husband "a meagre and mouldy old man, whom I have never yet seen detached from a flat pint of beer in a pewter pot." Their daughter, Miss Klem, is "apparently ten years older than either of them" (16).

Licensed Victualler, Mr. Host of a LIVERPOOL pub for merchant seamen (5).

Louis The Traveller's servant on his journey to France (7).

Mayday Friend of the Traveller whose birthday celebrations awkwardly bring together guests who do not know each other (20).

Mellows, J. Proprietor who presides over the demise of the Dolphin's Head, an old coaching inn thrown into disuse by the coming of the railway (24).

Mercy Nurse who told horror stories to the Traveller when he was a child (15).

Miggot, Mrs. Laundress at GRAY'S INN (14).

Mitts, Mrs. Youngest woman at Titbull's Alms House, she surprises her fellow inmates by marrying a Greenwich pensioner with one arm (29).

Mormon agent Organizer of the expedition of Mormons from England to the Great Salt Lake; "a compactly-made handsome man in black, rather short, with rich brown hair and beard, and clear bright eyes. From his speech, I should set him down as American" (22).

Murderer, Captain Protagonist of one of the tales told to the Traveller by his nurse. A serial killer who bakes his brides into meat pies, the captain is eventually foiled by a dark twin who avenges her sister's death by taking poison just before she is killed and cooked into a pie (15).

Nan Girl in the Liverpool slums waiting for a mercantile Jack (5).

Oakum-Head One of the "Refractories" in the Wapping Workhouse observed by the Traveller. Her hair is like the oakum that it is her task to pick (3).

Onowenever, Miss The object of a youthful infatuation of the Traveller who "had pervaded every chink and crevice of my mind for three or four years." He remembers writing numerous imaginary letters to the girl's mother, soliciting her daughter's hand in marriage, without "the remotest intention of sending any of those letters" (20).

Pangloss Government official in Liverpool, "lineally descended from the learned doctor of that name," who accompanies the Traveller to see some wounded soldiers from India (8).

Parkle Barrister friend of the Traveller who lives in dusty chambers in GRAY'S INN (14).

Pegg (aka Waterhouse) Liverpool crimp, an agent who traps or tricks men into serving as seamen or soldiers (5).

Poodles Mongrel dog in the East London Children's Hospital who cheers the patients as he makes his rounds from bed to bed (35).

Quickear   One of the policemen who goes with the Traveller to the haunts of sailors in LIVERPOOL (5).

Quinch, Mrs.   Oldest pensioner at Titbull's Almshouses (29).

Royal Charter, The   Ship bound from Melbourne to Liverpool that was wrecked off Llanallgo, Anglesey, on October 26, 1859 (2).

Russia   Cunard steamship on which the Traveller sails from New York to Liverpool (21).

Saggers, Mrs.   Second-oldest inmate at Titbull's Almshouses. She irritates the other residents by leaving a pail outside her door (29).

St. Olave's Church, Hart Street   Church in "the heart of the CITY, described by the Traveller as "Saint Ghastly Grim" because of the skulls that decorate the churchyard gate (23).

Salcy, the Family P.   Theatrical family whose performance the Traveller attends in a French-Flemish town. "The members of the Family P. Salcy were so fat and so like one another—fathers, mothers, sisters, brothers, uncles, and aunts—that I think the local audience were much confused about the plot of the piece under representation" (27).

Sharpeye   Policeman who accompanies the Traveller to the seamen's haunts in the Liverpool slums (5).

Sleek, Dr.   Teacher at the City Free School who proclaims that the Orrery exhibition, a kind of planetarium, is "improving" because it is "devoid of anything that could call a blush to the cheek of a youth" (20).

Specks, Joe   The Traveller's boyhood friend in Dullborough. He has married the Traveller's childhood sweetheart, Lucy Green. The three of them reminisce about the past (12).

"Spirit of the Fort"   The Traveller's name for the "wise boy" who tells him all about the nautical mysteries of CHATHAM (26).

Squires, Olympia   "Most beautiful" girl with whom the Traveller celebrated a birthday during his childhood by going to an Orrery exhibition (20).

Straudenheim   The Traveller imagines the life of this inhabitant of Strasbourg as he watches him from his hotel window (7).

Superintendent   Police inspector who takes the Traveller on a night visit to the slums of Liverpool; "a tall well-looking well-set-up man of a soldierly bearing" (5).

Sweeney, Mrs.   Laundress at GRAY'S INN whose late husband had been a ticket porter for the same institution (14).

Temeraire   Terrible restaurant in Namelesston where the Traveller suffers through a "nasty little dinner" (33).

Testator   Writer who furnishes his rooms in Lyons Inn with furniture he finds in the cellar and is visited by the drunken or spectral former owner of the items (14).

Timpson   Owner of the Dullborough Coach, "Timpson's Blue-Eyed Maid" (12).

Trampfoot   Policeman who accompanies the Traveller on his tour of the Liverpool slums (5).

Uncommercial Traveller   Narrator of a series of sketches Dickens wrote for ALL THE YEAR ROUND in the 1860s. He describes himself in the following terms: "I am both a town traveller and a country traveller, and am always on the road. Figuratively speaking, I travel for the great house of Human Interest Brothers, and have rather a large connection in the fancy goods way" (1).

Ventriloquist, Monsieur the   Performer at the Flemish fair, "thin and sallow and of a weakly aspect" (25).

Victualler, Mr. Licensed   "A sharp and watchful man" who is the host of an establishment for sailors in LIVERPOOL (5).

Waterhouse Alias of PEGG, the LIVERPOOL crimp, or receiver of stolen property (5).

Weedle, Anastasia One of the Mormon emigrants setting out for Utah; "a pretty girl, in a bright Garibaldi, this morning elected by universal suffrage the Beauty of the Ship" (22).

White, Betsy Woman who preys on LIVERPOOL sailors (5).

Wiltshire Family Mormon farmer, a widower who is emigrating to Salt Lake with his son and daughter (22).

"Unsettled Neighbourhood, An"

Article for *HOUSEHOLD WORDS* (November 11, 1854), written from the point of view of an old resident of the neighborhood near the Norwich Railway Terminus Works, describing the turmoil in the neighborhood caused by the railway. This article is similar to the description of the transformation of Stagg's Gardens in *Dombey* (6, 15). *Miscellaneous.*

Characters and Related Entries

Slaughter, Mrs. Greengrocer on Great Twig Street in the "Unsettled Neighbourhood."

Wigzell, J. Pub owner who expands his business into a railway hotel with the coming of the railway. *Miscellaneous.*

"Valentine's Day at the Post Office"

Article for *HOUSEHOLD WORDS* (March 30, 1850) by W. H. WILLS and Dickens, describing the operations of the Post Office. After posting three letters in red, yellow, and green envelopes in FLEET STREET, the authors follow the letters' progress as they are sorted and dispatched at the central office in St. Martin's-le-Grand. *Stone.*

"Verdict for Drouet, The"

Article for the *EXAMINER* (April 21, 1849) continuing Dickens's earlier coverage of the cholera epidemic at the Tooting baby farm begun in "Paradise at Tooting" and continued in "The Tooting Baby Farm." Dickens comments that even though the manslaughter conviction against Drouet has been overturned on a legal technicality, his guilt remains established and "the child-farming system is effectually broken up by this trial." *Miscellaneous.*

Village Coquettes, The

Comic operetta by Dickens with music by JOHN HULLAH, produced at the ST. JAMES'S THEATRE on December 6, 1836. Set in 1729, the story involves two London men-about-town, Squire Norton and Sparkins Flam, who turn the heads of two village girls, Lucy Benson and her cousin Rose. The dandies plan to run off with the girls, but their plan is foiled by a neighboring farmer, Martin Stokes. The squire has a change of heart and blesses Lucy's marriage to her country lover, but Flam is unrepentant and in the end is disowned by his friend. *Miscellaneous.*

Characters and Related Entries

Benson family Lucy, a village coquette, daughter of Old Benson, a small farmer, and sister to Young Benson, flirts for a while with Squire Norton, but she comes to her senses in time and returns to her humble lover, George Edmunds.

Edmunds, George The farm boy who is Lucy Benson's lover.

Flam, the Hon. Sparkins Squire Norton's friend whose plan to abduct Rose is thwarted by the Squire's change of heart.

Maddox, John Farm boy in love with Rose. She briefly deserts him to flirt with Sparkins Flam, a fop from London.

Norton, Squire Villain who attempts to seduce Lucy Benson.

Rose Lucy Benson's cousin, one of the village coquettes.

Stokes, Martin Farmer friend of the Bensons who plays the country bumpkin to expose the schemes of Sparkins Flam and save Lucy Benson from ruin.

"'Virginie' and 'Black-Eyed Susan'"

Dickens's review for the EXAMINER (May 12, 1849) of John Oxenford's English adaptation of Latour de St. Ytres's *Virginie* and the revival of DOUGLAS JERROLD'S *Black-Eyed Susan,* both at the Marylebone Theatre. He has high praise for both plays, particularly the latter. *Miscellaneous, Journalism.*

"Well-Authenticated Rappings"

Facetious article for HOUSEHOLD WORDS (February 20, 1858) describing three instances of unexplained events that have changed the narrator's attitude toward spiritualism. In two instances, a hangover and a case of heartburn are explained as spiritual visitations; in the third, a practical joke becomes a mysterious event. *Miscellaneous, Journalism.*

"Where We Stopped Growing"

Important essay for HOUSEHOLD WORDS (January 1, 1853) meditating on the things from childhood that we never outgrow. Among his childhood reading, Dickens lists *Robinson Crusoe, The Arabian Nights, Bluebeard, Don Quixote,* and *Gil Blas* as unchanging memories. The whole region of COVENT GARDEN and its theaters is still "for me, a dissipated insoluble mystery." The woman in black and the woman in white who roamed the city streets still intrigue him,

as do NEWGATE PRISON and the stories of voyage and travel. "If we can only preserve ourselves from growing up," he concludes, "we shall never grow old, and the young may love us to the last." *Miscellaneous, Journalism.*

"Whole Hogs"

Article for HOUSEHOLD WORDS (August 23, 1851) challenging all-or-nothing teetotalers, pacifists, and vegetarians, who insist that others accept the "whole hog" of their ideologies. Dickens criticizes the intemperance of the teetotalers' rhetoric, the naïveté of the pacifists who would disarm Britain, and the absolutism of the vegetarians. He calls for more moderation in all three movements. *Miscellaneous, Journalism.*

Characters and Related Entries

Scradgers A "rather dirty little gentleman who looks like a converted Hyaena" and is a speaker at temperance rallies.

"Why"

Article for HOUSEHOLD WORDS (March 1, 1856) posing a series of "why" questions that begin facetiously, asking why the young woman at the railway refreshment counter treats him with scorn and why writers speak of "what every schoolboy knows." By the end, the questions are more serious, asking why he does not challenge such lazy characterizations as of the English as money loving and why he believes in the politics of Buffy and Boodle and the procedures of the British judicial system. *Miscellaneous, Journalism.*

"Wind and the Rain, The"

Article for HOUSEHOLD WORDS (May 31, 1851) by HENRY MORLEY and Dickens, explaining the scientific principles behind wind and rain. *Stone.*

"Word in Season, A"

Poem on religious conversion that Dickens wrote for LADY BLESSINGTON's annual THE KEEPSAKE in 1844. *Miscellaneous.*

"Worthy Magistrate, The"

Article for HOUSEHOLD WORDS (August 25, 1855) attacking Mr. Hall, Chief Police Magistrate in the BOW STREET POLICE COURT, for his assertion that the English are a race of drunkards. *Miscellaneous.*

"Young Man from the Country, The"

Article for ALL THE YEAR ROUND (March 1, 1862) in which Dickens reprints several passages from *American Notes* on the corruption in American politics, the suspicion of all who achieve high places, Americans' love of smart dealing, and the slander in the American press. He ends by asking whether things have changed at all in 20 years. *Miscellaneous.*

PART III

Related People, Places, and Topics

Ackroyd, Peter (1949–) English novelist, poet, critic, and biographer. Dickens has a prominent place in Ackroyd's work. His first novel, *The Great Fire of London* (1982), involves a project for filming *Little Dorrit,* and the novel itself is a continuation of Dickens's story. Ackroyd's controversial biography *Dickens* (1990) presents a compelling portrait of the author as a complex and creative personality. Although it lacks scholarly apparatus, its detailed account of Dickens's life, written with a novelist's intuition, makes it the most readable Dickens biography. Ackroyd has also written introductions to paperback editions of most of Dickens's works, an *Introduction to Dickens* (1991) for the general reader, and a short pictorial biography, *Dickens, Public Life and Private Passion* (2002).

Addison, Joseph (1672–1719) One of the 18th-century authors whose works were familiar to Dickens. Although Dickens was not particularly fond of Addison's serious essays, he found his humorous essays "delightful."

Adelphi A residential complex along the THAMES between WATERLOO BRIDGE and Hungerford Bridge, featuring a terrace of houses raised on arches and facing the river. Dickens had lodgings here as a young man. David Copperfield wanders in the dark arches during breaks from Murdstone and Grinby's and later has rooms there in Mrs. Crupp's

house in Buckingham Street (*Copperfield,* 11, 23). Cornelius Brook Dingwall, M.P., has his residence here (*Boz,* 47). Martin Chuzzlewit takes lodgings in a poor public house (*Chuzzlewit,* 13); Mrs. Edson attempts suicide from Adelphi Terrace ("Lirriper's Lodgings"); Arthur Clennam eavesdrops on the meeting between Miss Wade and Rigaud on the terrace (*Dorrit,* II:9). Osborne's, the hotel where Wardle and Pickwick stay, is also in this neighborhood (*Pickwick,* 54, 56).

Adelphi Theatre Theater in the STRAND famous for melodrama and comic sketches. The young Dickens saw CHARLES MATHEWS perform his comic sketches here. Mentioned in *Pickwick* (31).

Adrian, Arthur (1906–1996) Dickens scholar and critic. In *Georgina Hogarth and the Dickens Circle* (1957), Professor Adrian carefully documents Georgina's life with Dickens, answering those who considered her the scheming cause of Dickens's marital troubles. In *Dickens and the Parent-Child Relationship* (1984), Adrian traces four patterns in the parent-child relationships: (1) orphans, (2) unwanted children, (3) children misguided by their parents, (4) children forced to assume parental duties.

Agassiz, Louis (1807–1873) American scientist, naturalist, and professor. Dickens met Agassiz on his trip to America in 1867. Agassiz attended the farewell party for Dickens when the author left BOSTON for NEW YORK.

Ainsworth, William Harrison (1805–1882) Editor, publisher, and novelist, especially of historical and NEWGATE NOVELS. Ainsworth met Dickens in 1834, the year he published his first novel, *Rookwood*. He introduced Dickens to JOHN FORSTER and to his first publisher, JOHN MACRONE. Dickens often attended gatherings of writers at Ainsworth's house and was one of the Trio Club with Ainsworth and Forster. Ainsworth preceded Dickens as editor of *BENTLEY'S MISCELLANY*. His Newgate novel, *Jack Sheppard* (1839), was often compared to *Twist*.

Albany, the Chambers for men of fashion, located on the north side of PICCADILLY. Edward Malderton rests his claim as a man of fashion on knowing a former resident of the Albany (*Boz*, "Sparkins"). Fascination Fledgeby has his rooms here, where he is beaten by Lammle and treated to the pepper plaster by Jenny Wren (*Mutual Friend*, III:8).

Albery, James (1838–1889) Victorian playwright who adapted *Pickwick* for the stage (1871) and whose *Two Roses* (1871) was a popular drama loosely based on *Little Dorrit*.

Albion, the Public house in Little Russell Street where Potter and Smithers are regulars (*Boz*, "Making a Night").

Aldersgate Street The street in London leading north from ST. PAUL'S CATHEDRAL where the warehouse of Chuzzlewit and Son is located. Arthur Clennam comes upon Cavaletto in this street after the foreigner has been run over by a mail coach (*Dorrit*, I:13). Jasper stays in a "hybrid hotel" in a little square behind Aldersgate Street (*Drood*, 23).

Aldgate Pump A London landmark near the corner of LEADENHALL and Fenchurch Streets in the CITY. Mr. Blotton, Pickwick's critic in the Pickwick Club, has his residence in Aldgate High Street (*Pickwick*, 11), which went east from the Pump to Petticoat Lane. Toots, distraught over Walter

Gay's attentions to Florence Dombey, walks back and forth from Leadenhall Street to the Pump to cool himself (*Dombey*, 56).

Alexander, Doris Contemporary scholar at the City University of New York who has written on Eugene O'Neill, Robert Louis Stevenson, Leo Tolstoy, Thomas Mann, and others as well as Dickens. In all her work she is interested in the psychological sources of the creative process. In *Creating Characters with Charles Dickens* (1991), Alexander discusses the ways in which Dickens transformed the people he knew into characters in his novels.

Alexander, Francis (1800–1881) Boston artist who painted Dickens's portrait during his first visit to AMERICA in 1842. The painting was later owned by Dickens's American publisher, JAMES FIELDS.

allegory A narrative that is equated with another story outside of the narrative. Traditionally, allegory was religious, equating, for example, the characters and situations in the story to biblical counterparts. Allegorical characters are often personifications of moral traits or abstract ideas. Unlike symbolism, allegory does not seek to suggest multiple meanings or ambiguities; it establishes a one-to-one relationshp with its referent. The dustheaps in *Mutual Friend*, for example, would be symbolic rather than allegorical, for they suggest several meanings, among them wealth, mortality, pollution, and materialism.

Dickens frequently uses a traditional allegorical motif representing life as a journey. By subtitling *Twist*, "The Parish Boy's Progress," Dickens links his story to an allegorical predecessor, John Bunyan's *Pilgrim's Progress* (1672), in which Christian, the title character, journeys from the City of Destruction to the Celestial City. Master Humphrey says of Little Nell and her journey that she "exist[s] in a kind of allegory," and her story is a kind of progress, ending at the country church where she dies. Dickens's allegorical referent is not so clearly defined as Bunyan's, though *Curiosity Shop* may be the Dickens novel that comes closest to being an allegory.

More often, Dickens uses allegorical elements in the novels. Characters with names that suggest their significance—like Pip (seed), Magwitch (magic + witch?), and Havisham (have a sham? have is sham? have a shame?)—have allegorical roots. The strong oppositions in the novels, like that between Oliver and Fagin, for example, suggest the opposition of innocence and experience, youth and age, good and evil. The parable structure of *Hard Times*, with its allusion to the biblical injunction "as ye sow, so shall ye reap," makes the novel, in part, a retelling of the biblical PARABLE.

Many critics have discussed these allegorical aspects of the novels. JANET L. LARSON (1985) analyzes the ways in which biblical allusion contributes to allegory, especially in the early novels, and she compares *Twist* with *Pilgrim's Progress*. Jonathan Arac (*Commissioned Spirits*, 1979) provides close allegorical readings of the American episodes in *Chuzzlewit* and the opening chapters of *Dorrit*. JULIET MCMASTER (1987) finds allegorical significance in the opposition of light (Ada) and darkness (Vholes) in *Bleak House*. SYLVÈRE MONOD (1968) and GEOFFREY THURLEY (1976) consider the last three novels (*Expectations*, *Friend*, and *Drood*) especially allegorical. Jane Vogel (*Allegory in Dickens*, 1977) offers a reading of all of Dickens's novels as Christian allegories; her interpretations offer some provocative insights into the biblical dimensions of Dickens's vision. Mildred Newcomb (*The Imagined World of Charles Dickens*, 1989) sees all of Dickens's novels as developing an extended "allegory of a nineteenth-century Everyman . . . [who] must find the wisdom to permit the natural processes of life, both for himself and for others whom he touches, the freedom to develop, mature, come to fruition, and decay."

All the Year Round Dickens's second general circulation magazine, successor to HOUSEHOLD WORDS. After quarreling with BRADBURY & EVANS over the publication of a notice regarding his separation from his wife, Dickens returned to CHAPMAN & HALL and began this new magazine on April 30, 1859. Like its predecessor, it appeared in a two-column, unillustrated format at twopence for a weekly number, but besides general-interest articles and stories, it also ran serialized novels. *A Tale of Two Cities* and *Great Expectations* both first appeared here, as did novels by WILKIE COLLINS, EDWARD BULWER LYTTON, ELIZABETH GASKELL, and others. Dickens also contributed to the special Christmas numbers of the magazine (reprinted in *Christmas Stories* 12–20) and published the essays collected in *The Uncommercial Traveller* and other miscellaneous papers there. Dickens acted as editor and publisher of the magazine, hiring W. H. WILLS as his subeditor and CHAPMAN & HALL as his agents.

amateur theatricals From early childhood Dickens was entranced by the theater. In his preface to *The Memoirs of Joseph Grimaldi*, he recalls his excitement at watching the PANTOMIME clowns; before he was nine he wrote a tragedy, *Misnar, Sultan of India*; he spent many hours writing for and performing plays in a toy theater. As a young man, he scheduled an audition at COVENT GARDEN, but illness forced him to cancel it. Although he did not pursue a theatrical career, his theatrical enthusiasm continued throughout his life, especially in the performances of his amateur theatrical groups in the 1840s and 1850s and in the PUBLIC READINGS of the 1860s.

The Dickens family had produced plays at home, performances in which Charles acted, directed, and stage-managed. His first public performances took place in MONTREAL during his American journey in 1842. There, Dickens directed three plays, taking parts in all of them. Between 1845 and 1857, Dickens directed theatrical groups composed of family and friends nearly every year. Regular members of the casts were JOHN FORSTER, DOUGLAS JERROLD, JOHN LEECH, MARK LEMON, AUGUSTUS EGG, FRANK STONE, WILKIE COLLINS, MARY BOYLE, CATHERINE DICKENS, MARY DICKENS, and GEORGINA HOGARTH. Dickens's artist friends designed and constructed sets. Typically the evening included a "serious" play—JONSON's *EVERY MAN IN HIS HUMOUR* or SHAKESPEARE's *Merry Wives of Windsor*, for example—followed by a farce. Dickens directed, managed, and played the leading roles in both plays. Some of the performances were private, for friends and invited guests, like two for QUEEN VICTORIA and Prince Albert, one in 1851 when the group performed EDWARD BULWER LYTTON's *Not So Bad as We Seem*, and the second in 1857, a performance of Collins's *THE FROZEN DEEP*. Public performances

This cartoon from a British magazine on the occasion of Dickens's departure on his American reading tour in 1867 depicts the novelist surrounded by his characters as he bids farewell to John Bull.

were given for charity; the group raised a good deal of money for indigent writers and the GUILD OF LITERATURE AND ART. In the 1850s the group made several tours of England, especially to MANCHESTER, LIVERPOOL, and BIRMINGHAM, on these charitable enterprises.

During a production of *The Frozen Deep* in 1857, Dickens met ELLEN TERNAN, a professional actress hired for the performances in Manchester.

Dickens's favorite roles elicited his histrionic skills. He was said to be "glorious" as the boastful Bobadil in *Every Man in His Humour;* one of the stage carpenters remarked to him, "It was a great loss to the public when you took to writing books!" In a similar vein, Mrs. FREDERICK YATES exclaimed after one of his performances, "Oh Mr. Dickens what a pity it is you can do anything else!"

America   Dickens describes his first American tour, in 1842, in *American Notes.* He also used this American experience in *Chuzzlewit:* Young Martin's journey to the new world becomes a Dantesque descent into the heart of darkness, where the greed and selfishness that are the themes of the novel emerge in exaggerated form on the American frontier.

Dickens's speeches in America calling for an international copyright agreement provoked accusations that he was selfish and greedy. His criticisms of the American character in *Notes*—of sharp dealing, suspiciousness, corrupt politics, slavery, and a slanderous press—enraged his American readers in 1842. In an article in ALL THE YEAR ROUND in 1862, during the American Civil War, he implied that his assessment had not changed in 20 years ("Young Man from the Country").

On his second trip to the United States, between November 9, 1867, and April 22, 1868, Dickens gave an exhausting series of PUBLIC READINGS in 16 eastern cities. He repaired the damage of his earlier visit by his kind remarks on the improvements he found after a quarter century, though he was still caricatured as mercenary for all the money he took back from America to England.

Useful accounts of Dickens's American visits can be found in MICHAEL SLATER's introduction to *Dickens on America and the Americans* (1978), in Sidney P. Moss's *Charles Dickens' Quarrel with America* (1984), and in Jerome Meckier's *Innocent Abroad* (1990).

Amsterdam, Holland After the riots, Lord George Gordon flees here but is refused residence by the "quiet burgomasters" (*Rudge*, 82). After the fall of the House of Clennam, Jeremiah Flintwinch settles in Amsterdam, where he is known as Mynheer van Flyntevynge (*Dorrit*, II:31).

Andersen, Hans Christian (1805–1875) Danish author and writer of *Fairy Tales*, published from 1835 to 1872. A great admirer of Dickens, Andersen first met him on a visit to England in 1847. On a second visit in 1857, Andersen stayed at Dickens's house, remaining for five weeks, far longer than anyone expected. After he left, Dickens put a card in the dressing table mirror in the room where Andersen stayed reading, "Hans Christian Andersen slept in this room for five weeks which seemed to the family ages."

Andrews, Malcolm Professor, University of Kent; editor of *The Dickensian;* president of the Dickens Society. A specialist in Victorian literature and in art history, Andrews has written on landscape painting as well as literary topics. *Dickens on England and the English* (1979) treats Dickens's ambivalent, sometimes contradictory, attitudes toward his country and his fellow Englishmen. In his study of Dickens's treatment of childhood, *Dickens and the Grown-up Child* (1994), Andrews is particularly interested in the relationship between childhood and adulthood and in the "old fashioned" child, like Paul Dombey, precociously adult before his time.

Angel Inn at BURY ST. EDMUNDS where Sam Weller first meets Job Trotter and where Pickwick receives notice that Mrs. Bardell is suing him for breach of promise (*Pickwick*, 15–18). Dickens stayed at the Angel in 1835 while reporting on the parliamentary election.

"Animal Magnetism" Farce by Elizabeth Inchbald (1753–1821) that Dickens read as a child and that he later included in the repertory of his amateur theatrical groups. Dickens, who practiced animal magnetism, or MESMERISM, himself, played a doctor who induced hypnotic spells.

Arabian Nights, The Dickens read these tales as a child, probably in Jonathan Scott's translation (1811), and they became one of his favorite books. He alludes to the tales frequently in his works, often as one of the joys of childhood that represent the realm of FANCY, or imagination. MICHAEL SLATER (1983) remarks that such "allusions are a sure sign that his emotions are deeply stirred; they are a guarantee of the genuineness of his romantic feelings." When Dickens compares the storytelling of his alter ego David Copperfield to that of Scheherazade, he suggests that he consciously connected his own storytelling to the *Arabian Nights* tradition. Slater discusses Dickens's engagement with the *Nights* in "Dickens in Wonderland" (in *The Arabian Nights in English Literature*, ed. Peter L. Caracciolo, 1988).

archetype A term from Jungian psychology for a primordial image or symbol from the "collective unconscious" of the human race that appears repeatedly in MYTHS, dreams, religions, and literature. Such images can awaken the unconscious memories of readers, linking their personal experience to the broader experience of their culture and of humankind. Some of the powerful archetypes that recur in Dickens's works are the city as labyrinth, suggesting that the quest for identity in London is like Theseus' challenge to the Minotaur; the river as both deadly and renewing, producing the drowning/resurrection motif that appears in several novels, particularly *Expectations, Mutual Friend,* and *Drood;* the lost Eden, in which paradise becomes a deadly garden in *Chuzzlewit* and a "ruined garden" at Satis House (*Expectations*); the self as orphan, born to an unknown father like Oliver Twist, to a "posthumous" father like Copperfield, or to a vindictive father like Harmon (*Mutual Friend*); life as a journey, typified by the ways in which the capsule journeys in *Twist* (8) and *Copperfield* (13) become emblematic of the heroes' lives.

aristocracy   The social range in Dickens's novels is sometimes compared to that in WILLIAM MAKEPEACE THACKERAY's works. Thackeray's world stretches from servants through the middle class to the mansions of Lord Steyne, and even to the royal receiving rooms. Dickens, by contrast, starts in society's lower depths—in Fagin's den—and moves on to tell of small tradesmen, professionals (especially lawyers), and gentlemen of the upper-middle class. Far less frequently than Thackeray does he describe the country estates of the landed aristocracy or the mansions of the silver-fork denizens of London.

If the dimensions of Dickens's world were established by his background and experience, they were also influenced by his Radical political views and his sensitivity to the shifts in power during his lifetime. A strong supporter of the Parliamentary REFORM BILL OF 1832 and an opponent of the CORN LAWS in the mid-1840s, Dickens saw the landed aristocracy as obsolete opponents to progress, and, as a disciple of THOMAS CARLYLE, he considered them idle parasites who irresponsibly sapped society's wealth without contributing to it. In their occasional appearances in the early novels, in such figures as Sir Mulberry Hawk (*Nickleby*) or Sir John Chester (*Rudge*), they are villains, but in later works they become increasingly absurd, like the Chuzzlewits, who trace their lineage back to Adam, or the Boodles, Coodles, and Noodles of *Bleak House*, who ritualistically repeat obsolete social rites. More dangerous than old baronets like Sir Leicester Dedlock, who cannot really grasp the significance of the social changes that have made him obsolete, are the middle-class sycophants who kowtow to aristocratic tradition. Mrs. Nickleby nearly sacrifices Kate to Hawk; Turveydrop's dandiacal imitation of the aristocracy imposes on Prince and Caddy (Bleak House).

Dedlock may be an absurd, finally even a pathetic figure, but aristocratic privilege can have destructive implications. The Barnacles, who inherit the Circumlocution Office by traditional right, prevent social progress and ruin individual lives (*Dorrit*), and self-loathing aristocratic idlers like Harthouse (*Hard Times*) and Gowan (*Dorrit*) bring suffering to those around them.

Insofar as aristocratic power was passed into the hands of the merchants and capitalists, England saved itself from a bloodbath like that in France, but by the end of his life, Dickens clearly wondered whether a powerful bourgeoisie is any better than an oppressive aristocracy. Figures like Bounderby (*Hard Times*), Merdle (*Dorrit*), Veneering, and Podsnap (*Mutual Friend*) seem just as destructive in their own ways as the old aristocracy they displaced.

Arundel Street   In the STRAND. The offices of CHAPMAN & HALL, where Dickens bought the issue of the MONTHLY MAGAZINE that contained his first published story, were located here.

Astley's Royal Equestrian Amphitheatre   An outdoor ampitheater for popular entertainment on WESTMINSTER BRIDGE Road in LAMBETH, South London. Its spectacular productions, mixing theater and circus, always included equestrian performances. Dickens provides a detailed description in "Astley's" (*Boz*). Kit Nubbles takes family outings to Astley's (*Curiosity Shop*, 39, 72). George Rouncewell attends an equestrian show and "is much delighted with the horses and the feats of strength; . . . disapproves of the combats, as giving evidences of unskilful swordsmanship; but is touched home by the sentiments" (*Bleak House*, 21).

Athenaeum, The   Chief weekly review of books and cultural affairs in England from 1828 to 1921. *The Athenaeum* was somewhat grudging in its reviews of Dickens's early novels, and during the 1840s it often praised the intent of the novels while faulting their liberties in form and style. By the end of Dickens's career, particularly in HENRY CHORLEY's reviews of *Expectations* and *Mutual Friend*, the magazine acknowledged Dickens's preeminence among English writers; its obituary notice described the novelist as "one of the greatest and most beneficent men of genius England has produced since the days of Shakespeare."

Athenaeum Club   A club for distinguished and learned men, founded in 1824. Dickens was elected to the club in 1838, along with WILLIAM MACREADY, Charles Darwin, and the classical historian George Grote. Among its members during Dickens's time were JOHN FORSTER, THOMAS CARLYLE, WILLIAM MAKEPEACE THACKERAY, BENJAMIN DISRAELI, JOHN RUSKIN, John Stuart Mill, Mathew Arnold, ROBERT BROWNING, and ANTHONY TROLLOPE.

Atlantic Monthly, The   Magazine founded in Boston in 1857 and published by Dickens's American publishers, TICKNOR & FIELDS. "George Silverman's Explanation" appeared here between January and March 1868. Dickens also contributed an article on his friend CHARLES FECHTER, "On Mr. Fechter's Acting" (August 1869), when Fechter, an actor and theater manager, was leaving London to resettle in the United States.

Austin, Henry (d. 1861)   A lifelong friend of Dickens, he married Dickens's sister Letitia in 1837 and was a frequent visitor at the Dickens home. An architect and artist, Austin supervised the remodeling of TAVISTOCK HOUSE and GAD'S HILL PLACE, and he painted portraits of MARIA BEADNELL when Dickens was courting her.

Australia   In the early years of the 19th century, Australia was largely seen as a penal colony to which British convicts had been transported from 1788 on. Magwitch, after he is recaptured on the marshes, is sentenced to transportation, and he makes his fortune as a sheep farmer in Australia (*Expectations*). "Free settlement" of the subcontinent was encouraged from the 1820s, and transportation ceased in 1842. In spite of his dislike of Malthusianism (see MALTHUS, THOMAS), Dickens supported efforts to encourage the poor to emigrate to Australia, and as a director of URANIA COTTAGE, he encouraged some of the women to begin a new life there. This policy also informs the resettlement

of Martha Endell and Little Em'ly in *Copperfield*, who go off to the colony with Daniel Peggotty and the Micawbers (57), where they successfully establish a new life. Dickens encouraged two of his sons, ALFRED and EDWARD DICKENS, to emigrate and take up sheep farming in the outback. Although Dickens never traveled to Australia, he often talked of doing so—even of settling there—and in 1862, he seriously considered making a reading tour of Australia.

autobiography   Dickens was reserved, even secretive, about some parts of his life and never wrote an autobiography. He destroyed some letters from friends and members of his family—especially those from his father—and instructed his heirs to destroy others. He did write a brief account of his childhood experience in the BLACKING FACTORY, which he shared only with JOHN FORSTER. This fragment, reprinted in Forster's biography, is sometimes referred to as "Dickens's Autobiography."

Modern commentators have assumed that Dickens failed to write an autobiography because many of his memories were too painful to commit to paper, but Dickens may not have considered himself a fit subject for such a work. Many Victorian autobiographies, those of John Stuart Mill and Cardinal John Newman, for example, were accounts of intellectual development; others, like ANTHONY TROLLOPE's, were records of achievements. The romantic, confessional mode that Dickens's autobiographical fragment represents was out of fashion.

The novels provided an outlet for Dickens's autobiographical impulses and also enabled Dickens to mask direct personal revelation behind such characters as Pip or David Copperfield, the most directly autobiographical of Dickens's heroes. In their first-person accounts, Dickens could write his life and mask it at the same time, much as ROBERT BROWNING was able to disguise self-revelation behind the characters in his dramatic monologues.

Although *Copperfield* and *Expectations* have often been treated as autobiographical fictions by Dickens critics, nearly all of Dickens's writings are, in a broad sense, autobiographical. They provide a record of the inner life of their author, of the traumas remembered from his childhood, of his repeated attempts to accept his father's irresponsibility and his mother's hard-heartedness, and of his own domestic failures and public successes. Many of Dickens's journalistic writings provide an account of more mundane events in his life: travels; visits to schools, hospitals, and prisons; evenings in the theater and at public entertainments; and observations of people at work or at leisure.

Avignon, France City northwest of MARSEILLE that is the home of Hortense, Lady Dedlock's French maid (*Bleak House*, 12). Cavaletto does odd jobs here (*Dorrit*, I:11). Captain Richard Doubledick recovers from his wounds nearby ("Seven Poor Travellers"). Dickens's visit here is described in *Pictures from Italy*.

Axton, William (1926–) Professor at the University of Louisville and an editor of DICKENS STUDIES NEWSLETTER and *Dickens Studies Annual*. In *Circle of Fire* (1966), Axton discusses Dickens's debt to the popular Victorian theater. His classic article "Keystone Structure in Dickens's Serial Novels" (*University of Toronto Quarterly*, 1967) explores the larger structural patterns in the monthly serials, noting the special importance of parts 5, 10, and 15 in the overall pattern. Axton has also published articles on *Pickwick*, *Dombey*, and other Dickensian topics. *Convivial Dickens* (1983), written with Edward Hewett, describes and supplies recipes for the drinks in Dickens's novels.

Aylmer, Felix (1889–1979) Pen name of Felix Edward Aylmer Jones, English actor and writer. For *Dickens Incognito* (1959), he combed Dickens's diaries to uncover coded references to the author's relationship with ELLEN TERNAN, a project that led to his controversial and later contested discovery of a child born to the couple. In *The Drood Case* (1964), Aylmer argues that Drood was not murdered and that Jasper, though arrested for the crime, was to be exonerated in the conclusion of the novel. His theatrical adaptation of the novel, written with Jane Bacon in 1951, developed dramatically this solution to the Drood mystery.

B

Ball's Pond   A district on the undeveloped north edge of London in Dickens's time. Mr. and Mrs. Theodosious Butler have a house near a brickfield here (*Boz*, "Sentiment"); Mr. Perch, Dombey's messenger, also lives here (*Dombey*, 18).

Baltimore, Maryland   Being served by slaves on his first visit to Baltimore in 1842 left Dickens "with a sense of shame and self-reproach," though he appreciated Barnum's Hotel, the only one in America "where the English traveller will find curtains to his bed." He also spent a memorable evening here with WASHINGTON IRVING, sharing an enormous mint julep. On his second visit in 1868, Dickens found the city still haunted by "the ghost of slavery." Dickens describes his 1842 visit in *Notes* (8–9).

Bank of England   Dickens mentions this CITY landmark in several of his novels. Boz describes an omnibus ride that ends at the bank (*Boz*, "Omnibuses"); the Gordon rioters vainly attack the bank (*Rudge*, 67); and the Traveller meditates on the bank and its treasures during his night walks (*Uncommercial*, 13). The bank is also mentioned in *Nickleby* (35), *Dombey* (13), and *Dorrit* (I:26).

Barbican   District in the CITY of London where Simon Tappertit and the "Prentice Knights" hold their meetings at an inn (*Rudge*, 8). It is also men-

tioned in *Twist* (21), *Chuzzlewit* (37), and *Dorrit* (I:13).

Barham, Richard Harris (1788–1845)   Clergyman and author of the popular collection of tales *The Ingoldsby Legends*, which were originally published in BENTLEY'S MISCELLANY when Dickens was its editor. Examples of Barham's work appear on pages 4, 89, 107, 209, 356, and 432.

Barnard, Frederick (1846–1896)   Illustrator best known for his illustrations to the English HOUSEHOLD EDITION of Dickens's works (1871–79). He also produced a series of character sketches from Dickens in the 1880s.

Barnard Castle   Nicholas Nickleby stops at the King's Head Inn in this market town in Durham on the recommendation of Newman Noggs (*Nickleby*, 7). Dickens and HABLOT KNIGHT BROWNE stayed at the inn in 1838 when they were investigating the Yorkshire Schools.

Barnet, Hertfordshire   In Dickens's time, this town, 11 miles or so north of the CITY, was an important staging point on the route out of London. Oliver Twist meets the Artful Dodger here when he arrives in London (*Twist*, 8). Esther Summerson stops here on her way to Bleak House and during her pursuit of Lady Dedlock with Mr. Bucket (*Bleak House*, 6, 57).

Barnett, C. Z. Victorian playwright, contemporary of Dickens, who produced melodramatic adaptions of *Twist*, *Rudge*, *A Christmas Carol*, and *Cricket* for the stage.

Barnwell, George Hero of *The London Merchant, or the History of George Barnwell*, a domestic tragedy by GEORGE LILLO (1731). It tells the story of a London apprentice who steals from his master and murders his uncle to satisfy the demands of his seductress, Sarah Millwood. When the stolen money gives out, the two give evidence against each other and both are hanged. Dickens alludes to the play in several works, most notably in *Great Expectations*, when Pip attends Wopsle's reading of the play while he is apprenticed to Joe Gargery (15).

Barrow Dickens's mother's family. **Charles** (1759–1826), Dickens's maternal grandfather, was "Chief Conductor of Monies in Town" at the Navy Pay Office, responsible for transferring money to the ports of Plymouth, PORTSMOUTH, Sheerness, and CHATHAM. In 1810 he admitted embezzling money from the office and escaped to the Isle of Man without repaying what he had taken. His daughter ELIZABETH (1789–1863) married JOHN DICKENS in 1809. His son **John Henry** (1796–1869) was a barrister in GRAY'S INN and the founder and editor of the MIRROR OF PARLIAMENT. His younger son **Edward** (1798–1869) was, like Dickens and his father, a shorthand reporter for the paper, which printed verbatim accounts of Parliamentary proceedings. John Henry taught Dickens the Gurney system of shorthand. He was Dickens's subeditor on the DAILY NEWS. Edward's wife, Janet Ross, a painter of miniatures, may have been the original for Miss La Creevy in *Nickleby*. She painted the earliest authenticated portrait of Dickens.

Barrymore, Lionel (1878–1954) American stage and screen actor whose annual portrayal of Scrooge on the radio between 1934 and 1953 made him the American Scrooge of the period and informed his role as Potter, the Scroogelike banker in *It's*

a Wonderful Life. Barrymore also portrayed Daniel Peggotty in George Cukor's 1935 film version of *Copperfield*.

Bart, Lionel (1930–) Playwright of the most popular modern adaptation of *Twist*, the musical *Oliver!*, first produced in 1960 and later made into a film (1968).

Bastille, the Notorious Parisian prison that became a symbol for the tyranny of the ancien régime in France, because many prisoners, like Doctor Manette in *Two Cities*, were held there without trial, simply on the order of a powerful aristocrat. The storming of the Bastille on July 14, 1789, the initial event in the FRENCH REVOLUTION, is described in *A Tale of Two Cities* (II:21). Dickens's description closely follows that of THOMAS CARLYLE in *The French Revolution*.

Bath, Somerset Dickens took the name Pickwick from Moses Pickwick, a coach operator and hotel keeper in this spa town. The Pickwickians spend some time here: Pickwick meets Angelo Cyrus Bantam, the master of ceremonies in the Assembly Rooms; he discovers the manuscript of Prince Bladud, founder of the city, in his rooms on the Royal Crescent; Winkle gets entangled with the Dowlers; and Sam attends the footmen's "swarry" (*Pickwick*, 35–37). Bath is also mentioned as the residence of Volumnia Dedlock (*Bleak House*, 28).

Battle Bridge Old name for King's Cross, site of a bridge over the River Fleet where a battle between the Romans and Britons took place. In *Sketches by Boz*, Dickens describes it as a place inhabited by "proprietors of donkey-carts, boilers of horse-flesh, makers of tiles, and sifters of cinders" ("First of May"). Boffin's Bower and its dust mounds are nearby (*Mutual Friend*). Also mentioned in *Twist* (31) and *Dombey* (31).

Bayham Street, Camden Town In 1823, the Dickens family lived at No. 16, the house that is probably the original of Bob Cratchit's (*Carol*) and

Dickens and his parents lived in this house on Bayham Street in Camden Town after moving to London from Chatham in 1822.

the one occupied by the Micawbers and Traddles (*Copperfield*, 27).

Beadnell, Maria (1810–1886) Youngest daughter of London banker George Beadnell. Dickens fell in love with her in 1830, but her parents objected to the relationship, forbade the courtship, and sent their daughter to school in Paris. The difficult courtship ended in 1833, and Maria subsequently married Henry Winter, a merchant. Dickens portrays the youthful Maria in Dora Spenlow in *Copperfield* and the matronly Mrs. Winter, whom he met again in 1855, in the garrulous Flora Finching in *Little Dorrit*. Maria's older sister Anne married Dickens's friend HENRY KOLLE in 1833.

Beard, Thomas (1807–1891) A journalist and Dickens's lifelong friend. The two worked together as shorthand reporters, and Beard helped Dickens

obtain a position on the MORNING CHRONICLE in 1834. Beard was the best man at Dickens's wedding and godfather to Charley, Dickens's eldest son (*see* DICKENS, CHARLES CULLIFORD). His younger brother, **Dr. Francis Carr Beard** (1814–93), Dickens's regular physician after 1859, attended the author on his deathbed.

Bedford Hotel, Brighton One of the best hotels in BRIGHTON, where Mr. Dombey stays when he visits his son Paul (*Dombey*, 10). Dickens stayed here in 1848, 1849, and 1861.

Bedford Street, Strand When WARREN'S BLACKING was moved from Hungerford Stairs to this street in the STRAND, Dickens was humiliated by having to work in a window in view of those passing by as he pasted labels on the blacking bottles.

Bell's Life in London and Sporting Chronicle A weekly journal to which Dickens contributed 12 "Scenes and Characters" sketches in 1835–36. The sketches were later collected in *Boz*.

David Copperfield is introduced to the captivating Dora Spenlow, a character based on Maria Beadnell.

Bell's Weekly Magazine   Dickens's sketch "Sentiment" (*Boz*) may have originally appeared in this magazine on June 7, 1834.

Bennett, Arnold (1867–1931)   English novelist, one of the realists whose extreme dislike of Dickens characterizes and exaggerates the modernist rejection of the Victorians. In a letter, Bennett wrote: "Of Dickens, dear friend, I know nothing. About a year ago, from idle curiosity, I picked up *The Old Curiosity Shop*, & of all the rotten vulgar un-literary writing . . . ! Worse than George Eliot's."

Bentley, Richard (1794–1871)   Publisher and founder of Richard Bentley & Son. In August 1836, when Dickens was just establishing himself with *Pickwick*, Bentley contracted with him to provide two three-volume novels at £500 each and to edit a new magazine, Bentley's Miscellany. The subsequent success of *Pickwick* and disagreements with Bentley led Dickens to break off his relationship with the publisher in 1839 after only one of the two novels, *Oliver Twist*, had been published. Although there was considerable acrimony between the two men at this time, they later became cordial friends.

Bentley, Thomas (c. 1880–1950)   Actor and film director. After portraying Dickens characters on the stage, Bentley went on to produce and direct many film versions of the novels, among them *Pickwick* (1921), *Twist* (1912), *Chimes* (1914), *Curiosity Shop* (1914), *Rudge* (1915, 1921), and *Hard Times* (1915). His *David Copperfield* (1913) was the first eight-reel British feature film, and his adaptation of *Curiosity Shop* (1935) was the first feature-length sound film based on Dickens.

Bentley's Miscellany   An illustrated monthly magazine started by publisher RICHARD BENTLEY in January 1837. Dickens was its initial editor and GEORGE CRUIKSHANK its illustrator. Dickens continued with the magazine until February 1839, despite frequent disagreements with the publisher. *Oliver Twist* first appeared in 24 serial installments in the magazine. Dickens also contributed "The Mudfog Papers," "The Pantomime of Life," "Some Particulars Concerning a Lion," and "Familiar Epis-

tle from a Parent to a Child Aged Two Years and Two Months" to the *Miscellany*.

Berg Collection   Substantial collection in the New York Public Library containing many Dickens materials, including Dickens's diary for 1867, a memoranda book for 1855–70, manuscripts of several minor works, proof sheets for *Mutual Friend*, and several publishers' agreements. An anthology of Dickens materials in the Berg Collection was edited by Lola L. Szladits in commemoration of the centennial of Dickens's death in 1970.

Berners Street, Oxford Street   A street running north out of Oxford Street where Dickens as a child saw the "White Woman," possibly an original for Miss Havisham ("Where We Stopped Growing").

Bethnal Green   A squalid area in the East End of London where Sikes and Nancy live (*Twist*) and where Eugene Wrayburn leads Bradley Headstone in an aimless pursuit (*Mutual Friend*, III:10).

Beulah Spa, Norwood   A fashionable health spa in the 1830s in southeast London (*Boz*, "Tottle").

Bible   Dickens alludes to the Bible in his novels more than to any other text. Nicholas Bentley, MICHAEL SLATER, and Nina Burgis (1988) provide a list of the main biblical allusions in the novels, and ANDREW SANDERS discusses many of the more important instances in the "Bible" entry in PAUL SCHLICKE (1999). The most frequent are to Genesis and to the Gospels, especially the parables.

Dickens's version of the New Testament for his children, "The Life of Our Lord," tells a simplified version of Jesus's life, emphasizing the parables and moral teachings, for Dickens regarded the New Testament, as he wrote to his son EDWARD DICKENS, as "the best book that ever was or will be known in the world, . . . because it teaches you the best lessons by which any human creature who tries to be truthful and faithful to duty can possibly be guided." He was more dubious about the Old Testament, which he suggested might be "thrown overboard . . . 'to lighten the sinking ship of Christianity.'" Some of his most vindictive characters—Mrs. Clennam in *Dorrit,* for example—base their heartless faith on the Old Testament.

Several critics have written on Dickens's use of the Bible. ALEXANDER WELSH (1971) discusses its role in Dickens's treatment of death and his celebration of the feminine. DENNIS WALDER (1981) discusses his use of the Bible in the broader context of his religion. BERT G. HORNBACK (1972) traces some of the images and symbols from Genesis. Jane Vogel (*Allegory in Dickens,* 1977) finds biblical allegory in all of Dickens's works, centering on the power of a New Testament vision to redeem a world corrupted by Old Testament sins. JANET LARSON (1985), in the most sustained discussion of Dickens's use of the Bible, argues that Dickens, like his fellow Victorians, inherited a "broken scripture," so that he often uses the Bible not as a coherent or simple story but rather as "a paradoxical code that provides him with contradictory interpretations of experience."

bibliography The most important bibliographical resources on Dickens are listed below. Two general bibliographies provide categorized lists of available materials by and about Dickens: the British Museum, *Dickens: An Excerpt from the General Catalogue* (1960), and PHILIP COLLINS, the Dickens section from *The New Cambridge Bibliography of English Literature* (1970).

The most important bibliographies of Dickens's works are J. C. Eckel, *The First Editions of the Writings of Charles Dickens* (1932); Walter E. Smith, *Charles Dickens in the Original Cloth,* 2. vols. (1981; 1983). Two older bibliographies remain the primary resources on Dickens's minor writings: F. G. KITTON, *The Minor Writings of Dickens* (1900), and T. Hatton and A. H. Cleaver, *A Bibliography of the Periodical Works of Dickens* (1933). William Miller's *The Dickens Student and Collector* (1946) remains useful, especially for its coverage of dramatic adaptations, plagiarisms, and other Dickensiana.

Dickens criticism up to 1970 is listed in *Charles Dickens: A Centenary Bibliography* (1971), edited by JOSEPH GOLD. R. C. CHURCHILL's *A Bibliography of Dickensian Criticism, 1836–1975* (1975) annotates its entries and prints excerpts from the critics;

John J. Fenstermaker, in *Charles Dickens, 1940–1975* (1979), provides an index of critical materials indicating which critics discuss various themes and features in each of the novels. Garland Press, beginning in 1981, has been publishing comprehensive annotated bibliographies of Dickens criticism for each of the novels, which are regularly updated in *DICKENS STUDIES ANNUAL.*

bildungsroman Novel describing the maturation of a young man or woman, also known as an apprenticeship novel or a novel of initiation. Derived from such European models as Goethe's *Wilhelm Meister's Apprenticeship* (1796), these novels typically concern a young person from the provinces who, dissatisfied with the social and intellectual restrictions of provincial life, leaves home to make his way in the city. There he is initiated into the truth about the world, often through painful love affairs, and he loses his illusions and accommodates himself to the newly discovered reality. Two of Dickens's novels, *David Copperfield* and *Great Expectations,* are among the English classics of the genre. JEROME H. BUCKLEY (1974) discusses these two works as examples of the bildungsroman in *Season of Youth.* In "Young Man from the Country," Dickens characterizes himself as the typical bildungsroman hero, a young man from the country who went to America and had his idealism dashed by his experiences there. Although the bildungsroman usually has a young man as its protagonist, Dickens's Esther Summerson (*Bleak House*) can be included among the minority of young women in such works.

Billingsgate The fish market in the CITY of London. Mentioned in *Dorrit, Expectations,* and *Uncommercial Traveller.* Slang for foul and vituperative language—such as that heard in a fish market.

Birmingham Dickens visited this city in the industrial MIDLANDS of England many times and gave the first of his PUBLIC READINGS, a performance of *A Christmas Carol,* here in 1853.

Pickwick travels to Birmingham to inform Mr. Winkle of his son's marriage (50). Birmingham is also the original of the factory town that Nell and her Grandfather pass through (*Curiosity Shop*, 43–44). It is the home of John, the poor inventor (*Reprinted*, "Poor Man's Patent"). Birmingham is also mentioned in *Twist* (48), *Nickleby* (27), *Dombey* (20), and *Uncommercial* (25).

Black Country, the Dickens's most surreal account of the industrial north of England appears in his description of Little Nell's journey through the Black Country, based on his own impressions of the area while traveling on the road from BIRMINGHAM to Wolverhampton (*Curiosity Shop* 43–45). He describes a rail journey between the two towns in a winter snowstorm in "Fire and Snow."

Blackfriars Bridge One of the principal bridges across the THAMES in the CITY of London. Built in 1760, its tollhouses were burned and robbed by the Gordon rioters in 1780 (*Rudge*, 67). David Copperfield is robbed of his box of belongings and his money in **Blackfriars Road,** the street leading to the bridge, as he makes his way out of London (*Copperfield*, 12). Mr. George crosses the bridge on his way to visit the Bagnets (*Bleak House*, 27). Clennam and Plornish cross the bridge on their way to visit the MARSHALSEA PRISON (*Dorrit*, I:12), just as Dickens had done as a boy when he went from WARREN'S BLACKING to visit his family in the debtor's prison. The bridge is also mentioned in *Expectations* (46) and *Reprinted*, "Down with the Tide."

Blackheath A village on the outskirts of London, southeast of the city along the DOVER road. David Copperfield's Salem House School is nearby, and he passes through Blackheath on his way to Dover (13). John and Bella Rokesmith settle here after their marriage (*Mutual Friend*, IV:4). The Traveller passes through on his way to the continent (*Uncommercial*, 7).

blacking warehouse Factory for the manufacture of shoe polish. Dickens was sent to work at WARREN'S BLACKING as a boy of 12 while his father was imprisoned for debt in the MARSHALSEA PRISON. In the fragmentary AUTOBIOGRAPHY that he gave to JOHN FORSTER, Dickens described this period in his life as one of "humiliation and neglect." Placed

in a window where he could be observed from the street, Dickens was assigned the task of pasting labels on the blacking bottles. His fellow workers were two working-class boys, Bob Fagin and POLL GREEN, who referred to him as "the young gentleman." Dickens "suffered in secret," humiliated by "this companionship," and despaired that his hopes of a better life had been dashed forever.

This experience in his childhood was so traumatic for Dickens that even as an adult he could not talk about it and he could not go back to Hungerford Stairs, the site of Warren's factory, until after they were torn down. He confided to Forster that "even now, famous and caressed and happy, I often forget in my dreams that I have a dear wife and children; even that I am a man; and wander desolately back to that time of my life."

Most contemporary commentators, following the lead of EDMUND WILSON (1941), consider the blacking warehouse episode the psychic wound that prompted Dickens's creative impulse. It appears only thinly disguised as Murdstone and Grinby's wine-bottling warehouse in *Copperfield*. It has also been considered the source of Pip's apprenticeship in Joe Gargery's forge (*Expectations*) and Oliver's "imprisonment" in Fagin's den (*Twist*).

Blackmore, Edward Junior partner in the law firm of ELLIS AND BLACKMORE for whom Dickens worked as an office boy after leaving school at age 15. A friend of the boy's parents, Blackmore hired Dickens for 13 shillings, sixpence a week and considered him "a bright, clever-looking youth."

Blackwood's Magazine Magazine founded in 1817 in Edinburgh as a Tory rival to the Whig *Edinburgh Review*. During the Victorian period, it became one of the primary venues for serial fiction. Novels by John Galt, Samuel Warren, EDWARD BULWER LYTTON, ANTHONY TROLLOPE, and GEORGE ELIOT appeared in its pages, but in the 1840s it inveighed against "low" novelists like Dickens.

Blessington, Marguerite, countess of (1789–1849) Widowed in her second marriage to Charles John Gardiner, first earl of Blessington, the countess, a friend of Lord Byron, who had lived many years in France, returned to England in 1831 and established one of the most notable salons in Regency London. The scandal surrounding her relationship with ALFRED, COUNT D'ORSAY, both her stepson and her lover, made her house off-limits to many in London society, but artists, writers, dandies, and politicians attended her gatherings at Gore House. In 1836, Dickens was introduced to her salon, where he met WALTER SAVAGE LANDOR, BENJAMIN DISRAELI, EDWARD BULWER LYTTON, WILLIAM MACREADY, and WILLIAM HARRISON AINSWORTH. She wrote novels and memoirs, edited the *Book of Beauty* and *The Keepsake,* and contributed to the DAILY NEWS when it was under Dickens's editorship. Bankrupted in 1849, she fled to Paris with D'Orsay and died there.

Blues and Buffs   The colors of the Whig and Tory parties, respectively, in the Eatanswill election (*Pickwick,* 13). The two inns at Great Winglebury are also Blue and Buff institutions (*Boz,* "Winglebury").

Bonchurch   Town on the Isle of Wight where Dickens spent his summer holiday in 1849.

Bond Street   Fashionable shopping street in the West End of London. The Maldertons shop here (*Boz,* "Sparkins"), and Cousin Feenix stays at Long's Hotel when he comes to England for Edith Granger's wedding (*Dombey,* 31). Bond Street is also mentioned in *Nickleby* (32), *Mutual Friend* (III:8), and *Uncommercial* (16).

Borough, the   Area of London south of LONDON BRIDGE including SOUTHWARK and parts of Bermondsey, LAMBETH, and Rotherhithe. The MARSHALSEA PRISON was situated on the **Borough High Street,** connecting the area with the traumatic period in Dickens's childhood when his father was in the prison. The White Hart Inn, where Pickwick first meets Sam Weller, is located here and was similar to the George Inn in the Borough High Street, the only remaining galleried inn in London today. Bob Sawyer's lodgings are in LANT STREET (*Pickwick,* 10, 32), a street where David Copperfield, like Dickens himself, also had rooms. Much

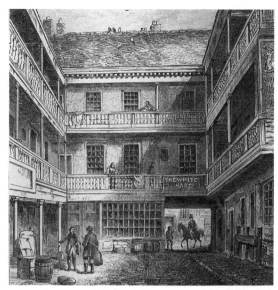

The White Hart Inn in the Borough.

of the first half of *Little Dorrit,* centering in the Marshalsea, takes place in the Borough.

Boston, Massachusetts   Dickens landed in Boston on his first visit to America in 1842, and many of his American friends were members of the Boston intelligentsia that he met at this time—HENRY WADSWORTH LONGFELLOW, CORNELIUS FELTON, RICHARD HENRY DANA, CHARLES SUMNER, and WILLIAM PRESCOTT. He describes his impressions of the city in *Notes* (3). On his reading tour in 1867–68, he gave several readings in Boston and renewed many of his old friendships. He stayed at the Parker House, where he praised the decor and the food but was made ill by the central heating that made the air "like that of a pre-Adamite ironing-day in full blast." He held a dinner at the hotel for his Boston friends—among them JAMES and ANNIE FIELDS, James Russell Lowell, Oliver Wendell Holmes, Longfellow, Charles Eliot Norton, and Thomas Bailey Aldrich.

Boucicault, Dion (1820–1890)   This most prolific of Victorian playwrights, with almost 200 plays to his credit, wrote two popular stage adaptations of Dickens: *Smike: or Nicholas Nickleby* (1859) and *Dot: A Fairy Tale of Home* (1859), an adaptation of

Cricket. He also played Lord Frederick Verisopht in an 1839 production of *Nickleby.*

Boulogne, France A seaport town on the Channel near CALAIS where Dickens frequently went on holiday, described in "Our French Watering Place" (*Reprinted*). It is also mentioned in *Boz* ("Boarding House"), *A Tale of Two Cities* (II:3), and *Reprinted* ("A Flight").

Bowen, John Professor, University of York and University of California. His *Other Dickens: Pickwick to Chuzzlewit* (2000) develops a deconstructive and rhetorical analysis of the early novels. He and ROBERT PATTEN have edited a collection of essays by contemporary scholars, *Palgrave Advances in Charles Dickens Studies* (2005), which presents several topics of current interest in Dickens studies.

Bowes, Yorkshire Site of WILLIAM SHAW's School, the original for Dotheboys Hall, which Dickens visited in 1838 (*Nickleby*).

Bow Street Police Court The main Metropolitan court in London, established in 1749. Here Barnaby Rudge is questioned and one of the rioters hanged (*Rudge*, 58, 77). The trial of the Artful Dodger takes place at Bow Street (*Twist*, 43), as does that of the two girl prostitutes (*Boz*, "Prisoners' Van"). The **Bow Street Runners,** the only detective force until the establishment of the Metropolitan Police in 1829, worked out of the Bow Street Court. Blathers and Duff, the runners who investigate the robbery at Mrs. Maylie's house (*Twist*, 31), are Dickens's fullest description of these officers.

Boyle, Hon. Mary (1810–1890) Niece of MRS. RICHARD WATSON, whom Dickens met at ROCKINGHAM CASTLE in 1849. They were close friends for the rest of his life. She often performed in Dickens's theatricals, usually playing opposite him; he described her as "the very best actress I ever saw off the stage, and immeasurably better than a great many I have seen on it." She was at Gad's Hill when he died.

"Boz" The pen name Dickens used at the beginning of his career. Most of the magazine sketches that would be collected as *Sketches by Boz* were originally published under this pseudonym, as were *The Pickwick Papers* and the early numbers of *Oliver Twist.* The name derived from Dickens's nickname for his younger brother, Augustus, whom he had dubbed Moses in honor of the *Vicar of Wakefield.* The child nasally mispronounced the name as "Boses," and it then was shortened to "Bose" and finally "Boz." When Dickens reappropriated the name for his own pseudonym, he commented, "Boz was a very familiar household word to me, long before I was an author." He was fond of characterizing his works as the spectacular performances of a magician or a theatrical performer, characterizing himself as "The Inimitable Boz."

"Boz's Annual Register and Obituary of Blue Devils" A Christmas book that Dickens agreed to write for CHAPMAN & HALL in 1837. He did not complete the project.

Bradbury, William (1800–1869) Partner in the publishing firm that replaced CHAPMAN & HALL as Dickens's publisher in 1844. There was occasional friction between Dickens and Bradbury, especially when Dickens thought that Bradbury was unnecessarily interfering with his editing of the DAILY NEWS and when Bradbury refused to print in PUNCH Dickens's explanation of his separation in 1858, but the two remained good personal friends in spite of these differences.

Bradbury & Evans Dickens's publishers from 1844 to 1858. With them, Dickens published all his major novels from *Dombey* through *Little Dorrit,* the CHRISTMAS BOOKS from *The Chimes* on, and the weekly magazine HOUSEHOLD WORDS. They were also the publishers of the DAILY NEWS, the paper Dickens edited briefly in 1846. When they refused to publish his explanation of his separation in PUNCH, Dickens left them and returned to CHAPMAN & HALL.

Braham, John (1774?–1856) Tenor and theater manager who sang in Dickens's opera *The Village Coquettes* and acted in two of his farces, *The Strange*

Gentleman and *Is She His Wife?*, which Braham produced at the ST. JAMES'S THEATRE in 1836–37.

Brattin, Joel J. (1956–) Professor, Worcester Polytechnic Institute; textual editor, bibliographer, and critic. In numerous articles, annotated editions of the works, and bibliographical works, Brattin has illuminated the texts of Dickens, Thomas Carlyle, and other Victorian writers.

Brentford, Middlesex A town along the THAMES six miles west of London. Oliver and Sikes pass through on their way to the Maylie robbery (*Twist*, 21). Betty Higden lives in one of "the complicated back settlements of muddy Brentford" (*Mutual Friend*, I:16). Compeyson has a house nearby (*Expectations*, 42).

Bricusse, Leslie (1931–) Lyricist for Wolf Mankowitz's musical adaptation of *Pickwick* (1963) and the writer of the screenplay and lyrics for the musical film *Scrooge* (1970).

Brighton Fashionable seaside resort on the Sussex coast where Dickens was a frequent visitor, usually staying at the Bedford Hotel, where Mr. Dombey stays when visiting his son. Brighton figures most significantly in *Dombey*; young Paul stays at Mrs. Pipchin's establishment here (8) and attends Dr. Blimber's Academy (11). Mr. Turveydrop deports himself near the Pavilion built by his hero and mentor, the Prince Regent (*Bleak House*, 14). Brighton is also mentioned in *Boz* ("Tuggses") and *Nickleby* (50).

Bristol As a young reporter, Dickens was sent to Bristol in 1835 to report on Lord John Russell's election campaign. He stayed at the Bush Inn, where Pickwick and Mr. Winkle stay (*Pickwick*, 38, 48). There the Pickwickians also reconnect with Bob Sawyer, who has set up his medical practice in Bristol; Ben Allen is in the town, and his sister is living outside of Bristol with an aunt when Winkle finds her and proposes.

British Museum As soon as he was 18, Dickens secured a ticket to the old British Museum Reading Room, and he spent many hours as a young man reading there. He describes the place and some of the readers in *Boz*, "Shabby-genteel People."

Brixton A comfortable, middle-class suburb in South London. Wilkins Flasher, the stockbroker, lives here (*Pickwick*, 55), and the Misses Malderton hope to find husbands among the eligible bachelors of Brixton (*Boz*, "Sparkins").

Broadstairs, Kent The coastal resort where Dickens spent many holidays between 1837 and 1851. Dickens describes it in "Our English Watering Place" (*Reprinted*). FORT HOUSE, one of the places where Dickens stayed, has been renamed Bleak House and contains a Dickens museum. An annual Dickens festival is held in Broadstairs.

Brock, Charles E. (1870–1938) Book illustrator and portrait painter, contributor to *PUNCH* and *The Graphic*, who illustrated several of Dickens's novels, including *Pickwick*, *Nickleby*, and *The Christmas Books*. The DICKENSIAN described his work as true to the spirit of Phiz but characterized by humor rather than caricature.

Brook Street A fashionable street in London's West End runnng from BOND STREET to GROSVENOR SQUARE. Feenix's London house, where Mrs. Skewton stays and where Florence last sees Edith, is here (*Dombey*, 61). Mr. Dorrit stays in a hotel on Brook Street when he returns to London from Italy (*Dorrit*, II:16).

Brougham, Henry Peter, Lord (1778–1868) Whig politician, Lord Chancellor 1830–34; prolific writer and social commentator; head of the Society for the Diffusion of Useful Knowledge. His assertion that factory women could hire wet nurses for their infant children and thus had no need for a bill limiting their hours of employment to 10 a day made him the butt of *PUNCH* satire and, perhaps, one of the models for Sir Joseph Bowley in *Chimes*.

Brougham, John (1810–1880) Irish-American actor-manager who played many Dickens roles, among them Crummles, Cratchit, Bagstock, Captain

Bunsby, Micawber, and Turveydrop. He adapted many of the novels for the New York stage, including *Dombey* (1848), *Haunted Man* (1849), *Copperfield* (1851), *Bleak House* (1853), *Dorrit* (1873), *Message from the Sea* (1860), and *Gold Dust* (1871, from *Mutual Friend*). His most famous adaptation was *Little Nell and the Marchioness* (1867), in which Lotte Crabtree played both of the lead female roles, performing a banjo solo as the Marchioness.

Browne, Hablot Knight ("Phiz") (1815–1882) Dickens's chief illustrator, Browne, who took the pseudonym "Phiz" to complement Dickens's "Boz," worked with Dickens on nearly all his major works from *Pickwick* through *A Tale of Two Cities*. He learned his craft as an apprentice at Finden's, prominent steel engravers of the period, and his selection as the illustrator to replace ROBERT SEYMOUR and ROBERT WILLIAM BUSS on *Pickwick*—over WILLIAM MAKEPEACE THACKERAY, who also applied for the position—established his career when he was only

20. The collaboration was successful from the beginning, one of Phiz's first pictures being the memorable "First Appearance of Mr. Samuel Weller." The high points in their collaboration came with the great middle novels, *Dombey*, *Copperfield*, and *Bleak House*, in which Browne's evocative pictures extend the texts. His "dark plates" for *Bleak House*, employing a new technique developed for the novel, are particularly apt in rendering the mood of the work. Dickens dropped Browne after his disappointing illustrations for *Two Cities*, and the two parted with some bitterness, but by 1860 Browne's style, grounded in the graphic-satiric tradition of WILLIAM HOGARTH, was no longer appropriate for the more realistic novels of the period. Browne also worked as an illustrator for many other novelists, including WILLIAM HARRISON AINSWORTH, EDWARD BULWER LYTTON, ANTHONY TROLLOPE, and CHARLES LEVER, and for the major illustrated periodicals of the period. Notable discussions of the collaboration between Browne and Dickens are provided by JOHN

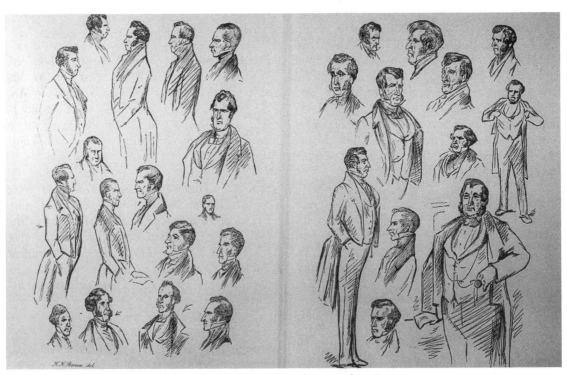

Browne's (Phiz's) suggestions to Dickens for the visual image of Mr. Dombey.

HARVEY (1971), MICHAEL STEIG (1978), and Jane R. Cohen, *Charles Dickens and His Original Illustrators* (1980). Examples of Browne's work appear on pages 23, 86, 104, 166, 175, 193, 229, 325, and 342.

Browning, Robert (1812–1889)   Poet and dramatist, best known for his dramatic monologues and *The Ring and the Book* (1868–69); one of JOHN FORSTER's circle of friends, along with Dickens. Forster also advised Browning on literary matters. Few records of Dickens's friendship with Browning remain. The two met, through Forster and WILLIAM HARRISON AINSWORTH, in the 1830s and occasionally dined or went to the theater together. Dickens admired Browning's plays and was especially moved by the story of Mildred's love and death in *A Blot in the 'Scutcheon* (1843). Although Browning considered vulgar Dickens's penchant for naming his children after famous people and thought him theologically inconsistent, he admired and praised his work in a tribute presented to Dickens before he left on his American reading tour in 1867.

Buckley, Jerome H. (1917–   )   Professor, Harvard; prolific writer on Victorian literature. In *Season of Youth* (1974), Buckley discusses *Copperfield* and *Expectations* as examples of the English BILDUNGSROMAN. *Expectations* is the greater of the two, he suggests, for it offers a much fuller characterization of the narrator, making him a more profound portrait of the author. He also edited the Norton Critical Edition of *David Copperfield* (1992).

Buckstone, John Baldwin (1802–1879)   Actor, theater manager, playwright; friend of Dickens. He adapted "The Bloomsbury Christening" for the stage. As manager of the Theatre Royal, Haymarket, he hired Ellen Ternan, apparently acting on a suggestion from a grateful Dickens.

Bull, the   The Bull and Victoria Inn, more commonly known just as the Bull, figures in several of the novels. It is the site of the Winkle's confrontation with Dr. Slammer (*Pickwick*, 2). It is also the original of the Blue Boar, the inn where Pip stays when he returns home (*Expectations*), and of the Winglebury Arms (*Boz*, "Winglebury").

Bulwer   Edward Bulwer, who added his mother's surname to his own in 1843, is usually known as Lytton, even though he should be properly identified as Bulwer or Bulwer-Lytton. *See* LYTTON.

Burdett-Coutts, Angela Georgina (1814–1906)   Daughter of the radical politician and reformer Francis Burdett, she hyphenated her surname and devoted her life to philanthropy after inheriting the fortune of her maternal grandfather, banker Thomas Coutts, in 1837. Dickens, a member of her father's social circle, which also included Wordsworth and Byron, met her in 1838 or 1839, and the two became lifelong friends. Dickens investigated, recommended, and administered many of her philanthropic projects, including aid to RAGGED SCHOOLS; URANIA COTTAGE, a project to rehabilitate prostitutes; and a slum-clearance, low-cost housing project in BETHNAL GREEN. Baroness Coutts was privy to Dickens's marital troubles and attempted unsuccessfully to reconcile the author and his wife. EDGAR JOHNSON collected many of Dickens's letters to Coutts in *The Heart of Charles Dickens* (1952).

Burnett, Henry (1811–1893)   Singer, music teacher, and husband of Dickens's sister FRANCES ELIZABETH DICKENS. He spent some of his childhood in Brighton, where he sang before George IV at the Pavilion. He met his wife while they were both students at the Royal Academy of Music. They sang several concerts together in 1835–36 and married in 1837. Their sickly, deformed child, **Henry Jr.** (d. 1849), was the inspiration for Tiny Tim and young Paul Dombey. Burnett played Squire Norton in *The Village Coquettes* and for a few years was a member of WILLIAM MACREADY's theatrical company at COVENT GARDEN, before he and Fanny moved to MANCHESTER, where he was a music teacher.

Bury St. Edmunds   The "handsome little town" in Suffolk where Jingle tricks Pickwick into hiding in the courtyard of the girl's school (15, 16). Dr. Chillip, the doctor who delivers David Copperfield, settles down here (60). The Pickwickians stay at the ANGEL Inn (16).

Buss, Robert William (1804–1875)   Graphic artist hired by CHAPMAN & HALL to provide two illustrations for the third number of *Pickwick* after the suicide of ROBERT SEYMOUR. Buss, who had not done any steel engraving before his work for the novel, submitted pictures of the Fat Boy in the arbor and the Muggleton cricket match, which disappointed the publishers. Although they were included in the monthly numbers, the illustrations were later replaced with work by HABLOT KNIGHT BROWNE. Buss was upset by the way Chapman & Hall treated him and by his abrupt dismissal from the project, but he remained a lifelong admirer of Dickens. He produced several paintings on Dickensian subjects for Royal Academy exhibitions. His watercolor "Dickens's Dream," done after the author's death and at the end of Buss's own life, has become a Dickensian icon. It shows the author surrounded by the figures of his imagination, several of them unfinished.

Butt, John (1906–1965)   Professor, University of Edinburgh, scholar of 18th- and 19th-century literature. His pioneering study of Dickens's methods of composition, *Dickens at Work* (1957), done with KATHLEEN TILLOTSON, stresses the importance of the serial form of Dickens's novels and makes use of Dickens's notes, diaries, and number plans to establish his conscious artistic designs.

Byron, George Gordon, Lord (1788–1824)   Although Byron was dead by the time Dickens began his writing career, the rage for the poet and his notoriety were still in force in the 1830s and 1840s. Dickens makes fun of the young men who maintain Byronic poses, like Horatio Sparkins (*Boz*) and Dick Swiveller in *Old Curiosity Shop*, and the hysterical schoolgirls who scream when they see "a complete image of Lord Byron" at Mrs. Jarley's waxworks (*Curiosity Shop*, 29). Dickens treats the Byronic influence more seriously in several of his later characters who inherit the attitude and posture of the Byronic hero: James Steerforth (*Copperfield*), James Harthouse (*Hard Times*), Sydney Carton (*Two Cities*), and Eugene Wrayburn (*Mutual Friend*). JULIET JOHN (2001) discusses Dickens's treatment of these Byronic hero/villains.

C

Cairo, Illinois Illinois town at the junction of the Ohio and Mississippi Rivers that Dickens used as the model for Eden in *Chuzzlewit*. He described the settlement as "a breeding-place of fever, ague, and death. . . . A dismal swamp, on which the half-built houses rot away: . . . teeming, then, with rank unwholesome vegetation, in whose baleful shade the wretched wanderers who are tempted hither, droop, die, and lay their bones" (*Notes* 12).

Calais, France This seaport town on the English Channel across from Dover was a place of refuge for those escaping English justice. Mr. Sparsit retreats to Calais to escape bankruptcy (*Hard Times*, I:7), as do the Veneerings (*Mutual Friend*, IV:17). Clennam and Meagles seek out Miss Wade who has gone into hiding here "in a dead sort of house" (*Dorrit*, II:20). Roger Cly spies on Charles Darnay as he boards the channel boat in Calais (*Two Cities*, II:3). The Traveller gives his impressions of the port and the town (*Uncommercial*, 18).

Camberwell Rural, well-to-do suburb southeast of London. Home of the Maldertons (*Boz*, "Sparkins") and of the brass and copper founder who hires Ruth Pinch as a governess (*Chuzzlewit*, 9). Pickwick has carried out some of his investigations here (*Pickwick*, 1), and Wemmick's marriage to Miss Skiffins takes place in a church near Camberwell Green (*Expectations*, 55).

Camden Town Poor suburb on the northern edge of London where the Dickens family lived at 141 Bayham Street in 1822–23. When John Dickens was imprisoned for debt, Dickens went to live with Elizabeth Roylance in Little College Street. In *Boz*, Camden Town is the home of city clerks ("Streets—Morning"), of Miss Evans, and of the shabby-genteel engraver ("Shabby-Genteel People"). Heyling's despised father-in-law retreats to a run-down lodging in Camden Town (*Pickwick*, 21); Stagg's Gardens, home of the Toodles, is surrounded by railway construction in "Camberling Town" (*Dombey*, 6); and the Micawbers rent a house here, where Traddles sublets a room (*Copperfield*, 27–28).

Canada Dickens visited Canada at the end of his American tour in 1842, going from Niagara Falls to Toronto, Kingston, and Montreal before returning to New York (*Notes*, 14–15). Though he found Canadian hotels vile—Rasco's Hotel in Montreal he described as "the worst in the whole wide world"—he found Canadians' manners more English than those of their southern neighbors. Describing Canada as "full of hope and promise," he praised qualities he found lacking in the United States: "the commerce, roads, and public works, all made *to last*; the respectability and character of the public journals" (*Notes*, 15). The climax of his visit to Canada came in two evenings of theatrical performances in Montreal starring and directed by Dickens. He also visited HALIFAX, Nova Scotia, when his steamship stopped there on its way to BOSTON (*Notes*, 2).

Canterbury, Kent   This cathedral town near GAD'S HILL was one of Dickens's favorite places to take visitors. It has a major role in *Copperfield* as the site of Dr. Strong's school and the home of the Wickfields and Heeps (15–19). Passing through on his way to DOVER, David describes "The sunny streets of Canterbury, dozing as it were in the hot light; and with the sight of its old houses and gateways, and the stately gray Cathedral, with the rooks sailing round the towers" (13).

capital punishment   Over the course of the 19th century the use of capital punishment decreased, as a result of the reduction in the number of crimes considered capital offenses and also as a result of the development of alternative punishments. Dickens could look back on earlier centuries as benighted times that executed for property crimes and minor offenses. After witnessing a public hanging in 1840, Dickens was especially opposed to public executions, which he describes in *Barnaby Rudge,* and he wrote several letters to the DAILY NEWS in 1846 calling for abolition of the death penalty. Later in his life, however, he modified his position, maintaining his opposition to the degrading spectacle of a public execution but no longer opposing all death sentences.

Carey, John (1934–   )   In *The Violent Effigy: A Study of Dickens's Imagination* (1973; published in the U.S. as *Here Comes Dickens: The Imagination of a Novelist*, 1974), Carey, Professor at Merton College, Oxford, considers Dickens as a comic writer who turns the animate inanimate and the inanimate animate, embodying an essentially dualistic vision of the world.

Carey, Lea, and Blanchard   Philadelphia publishing firm that pirated several of Dickens's early works and then made an agreement with the author to buy advance copies of the proofs of his novels from his English publishers.

caricature   A concept from the visual arts in which characteristic features are exaggerated for satiric or comic effect. Dickens was familiar with the work of the English graphic satirists WILLIAM HOGARTH (1697–1764), James Gilray (1757–1815), and Thomas Rowlandson (1756–1827), who used caricature to good effect in their work. The characterization in *Boz* and the physical comedy in the early works owes a good deal to these visual satirists.

Dickens adapted caricature techniques in several ways in his novels. He frequently uses descriptions like the one of the French and English monarchs in the opening chapter of *Two Cities,* which reduces each of the rulers to a single physical marker: "There were a king with a large jaw and a queen with a plain face, on the throne of England; there were a king with a large jaw and a queen with a fair face, on the throne of France." Dickens's characters are often constructed around a few significant visual markers; James Carker's (*Dombey*) feline characteristics place him in the caricature tradition that reduces humans to animals. Working in a verbal medium, Dickens was able to use more than just visual tags; Jingle (*Pickwick*), for example, is characterized by his telegraphic manner of speaking.

Though caricature is traditionally satiric, exaggerating grotesque or ugly features, Dickens did not always employ such exaggeration for ridicule. Mr. Chillip, the doctor who delivers David Copperfield, is made sympathetic by his likeness to a bird who cocks his head to one side, and Peggotty's popping buttons (*Copperfield*) are emblematic of her embracing love for young David. In reviewing the work of JOHN LEECH, an inheritor of the tradition of Hogarth, Dickens praised the artist as "the very first English caricaturist . . . who has considered beauty as being perfectly compatible with his art. He almost always introduces into his graphic sketches some beautiful faces or agreeable forms." Similarly, Dickens used exaggeration for sympathetic and humorous effect as well as for ridicule.

Although Dickens was profoundly influenced early in his career by the graphic satirists and their use of caricature, he moved away from these models later on. MICHAEL STEIG (1978) has traced this movement toward greater realism in Dickens's work. Dickens's use of caricature and his indebtedness to the graphic satire tradition has also been discussed by JOHN HARVEY (1971), Nancy Hill (*A Reformer's Art*, 1981), and Michael Hollington (*Dickens and the Grotesque*, 1984).

Carlisle, Janice   Professor, Yale, specializing in Victorian fiction and Victorian literature generally; an associate director of the DICKENS PROJECT. In *The Sense of an Audience: Dickens, Thackeray, and George Eliot* (1981), Carlisle analyzed several Victorian novels as they revealed the novelists' awareness of and communication with their audiences. *Common Scents: Comparative Encounters in High-Victorian Fiction* (2004) discusses the sense of smell as revealed in many novels of the 1860s. Carlisle has also edited *Great Expectations* (1996) in an edition including critical materials.

Carlton, William J.   (1886–1973)   Dickens scholar and avid Dickensian whose many articles in the *DICKENSIAN* most often concern aspects of Dickens's early life. He was also the author of *Dickens, Short-hand Writer* (1926).

Carlton Chronicle, The   Weekly newspaper in which Dickens first published "The Hospital Patient" (August 6, 1836), (*Boz*).

Carlyle, Thomas   (1795–1881)   Scottish essayist, historian, novelist, and philosopher, he met Dickens in 1840, and the two were lifelong friends. Dickens dedicated *Hard Times* to him. Carlyle's influence is pervasive in Dickens's works. The idealism of *Sartor Resartus* (1833–34), Carlyle's philosophical BILDUNGSROMAN, shaped Dickens's autobiographical novels, *Copperfield* and *Expectations*. The novel's critique of DANDYISM influenced *Bleak House,* and its spiritual and psychological themes helped define Arthur Clennam's personal crisis in *Dorrit*. Carlyle's social philosophy, developed in works like *Chartism* (1839) and *Past and Present* (1843), shaped the critique of Mammonism in *Chuzzlewit* and *Dorrit,* the attacks on UTILITARIANISM in *Hard Times,* and those on aristocratic privilege in *Bleak House* and *Dorrit*. Dickens relied on Carlyle's history *The French Revolution* (1837) for much of the background in *Two Cities*. Dickens valued Carlyle's reactions to his work as

Maclise's portrait of a youthful Carlyle.

well as those of Carlyle's wife, Jane Welsh. Although Carlyle criticized Dickens as a mere entertainer, saying on one occasion, for example, that "Dickens had not written anything which would be found of much use in solving the problems of life," he was more generous on other occasions, describing him after his death as "the good, the gentle, ever friendly noble Dickens,—every inch of him an Honest Man!" Dickens's relationship with Carlyle is treated by MICHAEL GOLDBERG (1972) and by William Oddie (*Dickens and Carlyle: The Question of Influence,* 1972).

Catholic Church   As a liberal Protestant, Dickens had mixed feelings about Roman Catholicism. On the one hand, he attacked religious intolerance; *Rudge* is a testament to his belief that British Catholics had a right to practice their religion without constraint. The Catholic *Dublin Review* noted that the novel opposes "a sturdy, highminded Catholic gentleman, and . . . a mean, vindictive Protestant villain." But Dickens was not so kindly disposed toward Catholicism when it was the dominant religion. In *Child's History* he characterizes Catholic England as benighted, and in *Pictures from Italy* he blames the poverty, oppression, and suffering of the Italian people on corrupt rulers and a reactionary Catholic Church. He sympathized with the Italian revolutionaries and, in Geneva during the 1846 revolution, he supported the overthrow of the Jesuits, commenting in a letter that "I have a sad misgiving that the religion of Ireland lies as deep at the root of all its sorrows, even as English misgovernment and Tory villainy." In an article for HOUSEHOLD WORDS in 1850, after the Pope proposed to elevate Dr. Wiseman to cardinal, Dickens has Mrs. John Bull warn her children against the Bulls of Rome, describing them as "an insolent, audacious, oppressive, intolerable race" that perpetuates "misery, oppression, darkness, and ignorance" ("A Crisis in the Affairs of Mr. John Bull").

Catlin, George (1796–1872)   Ethnographer and artist who lived with various Indian tribes, producing the classic *Illustrations of the Manners, etc. of the North American Indians* (1857). Dickens criticizes him as one of the purveyors of the superstitious idea of the Noble Savage (*Reprinted*, "Noble Savage"). An example of his work appears on page 366.

Cattermole, George (1800–1868)   Watercolorist and illustrator, Dickens's personal friend and husband of Dickens's distant cousin, Clarissa Elderton.

Cattermole's predilection for architectural subjects is illustrated in his rendering of the Maypole Inn for *Barnaby Rudge* (1841).

Cattermole contributed about 40 illustrations for *Master Humphrey's Clock, Curiosity Shop,* and *Rudge*. His work, which concentrated on architectural subjects, especially on romantically depicted old buildings, was particularly apt for the old churches in *Curiosity Shop* and the historic buildings in *Rudge*. Another example of his work appears on page 256 (*Old Curiosity Shop*).

Cavendish Square   Madame Mantalini has her millinery business near this fashionable neighborhood in MARYLEBONE (*Nickleby*). Silas Wegg's post outside the corner house that the Boffins later occupy is near the square (*Mutual Friend*).

Cerebus Club   A drinking club composed of Dickens, JOHN FORSTER, and WILLIAM HARRISON AINSWORTH, with specially designed and engraved goblets, that flourished briefly in 1838 and 1839.

Cervantes Saavedra, Miguel de (1547–1616) Spanish novelist and dramatist; his *Don Quixote* (1605, 1615) has often been considered the first novel in Western literature. Among the treasured books of his childhood, *Quixote* provided Dickens with a model for his own work. Its loosely connected series of adventures that take place on a journey, its use of interpolated tales, and its fundamental opposition of illusion and reality were important features in many of the English novels of the 18th and early 19th centuries. Dickens's early works, especially *Pickwick*, whose hero was described by an early reviewer as "the Cockney Quixote of the nineteenth century," use these Cervantean features. Pickwick's steadfast commitment to principle is similar to Quixote's belief in his chivalric mission, and Pickwick's relationship with Sam Weller echoes that of Quixote and Sancho Panza. In "Dingley Dell and the Fleet," W. H. Auden (*Dyer's Hand*, 1962) compares and contrasts *Quixote* and *Pickwick*. ALEXANDER WELSH (1981) discusses *Pickwick* as a primary example and redefinition of the Quixotic tradition.

Chalk, Kent   Dickens spent his honeymoon at this town in KENT, and it was a regular stop on his walks from GAD'S HILL. With Higham, it served as the model for Pip's village in *Expectations*.

Chancery, Court of   Supreme court in England for the resolution of equity cases, such as those involving contested trusts and legacies; presided over by the LORD CHANCELLOR. Dickens suffered the ineffectiveness of the court when he attempted unsuccessfully to recover damages from a magazine that had pirated *A Christmas Carol*. In *Pickwick*, he describes some long-term prisoners languishing in jail as a result of disputed wills (41, 43). Dickens also attacked court abuses in articles for HOUSEHOLD WORDS. His most extended criticism appears in *Bleak House*, in which the court's delays, obfuscation of issues, and self-serving procedures lead to indolence, despair, and suicide and produce such social ills as festering slums. Dickens's treatment of the court in the novel echoed widespread criticisms in the press in the early 1850s. The court was abolished in 1873 and its functions taken over by the newly established Supreme Court of Justice for England and Wales.

Chancery Lane   This street in the legal area of London where the COURT OF CHANCERY is situated is a major setting in *Bleak House*; Krook's rag and bottle shop, Snagsby's stationer's business, and Sol's Arms are located here. Watkins Tottle is imprisoned for debt in nearby CURSITOR STREET (*Boz*, "Tottle"); Pickwick is confronted by a bail tout here (*Pickwick*, 40); and Rokesmith stops Boffin in Chancery Lane to offer his services as secretary (*Mutual Friend*, I:8).

Chapman, Edward (1804–1880)   Partner in the publishing firm CHAPMAN & HALL. The more literary of the two partners, Chapman conceived the idea for *Pickwick*. In a letter to him in 1839, Dickens described the firm as "the best of booksellers past, present, or to come."

Chapman, Frederic (1823–1895) EDWARD CHAPMAN's cousin who became a partner in CHAPMAN & HALL in 1847, its head in 1864.

Chapman & Hall   Publishing firm founded by EDWARD CHAPMAN and WILLIAM HALL, which, with BRADBURY & EVANS, was one of the two firms that published most of Dickens's works. In 1836, when they contracted with Dickens for *Pickwick,* they gambled their fledgling firm on the innovative idea of serial publication. When the novel became a runaway best seller, they had established the firm and introduced a mode of publication that would be widely adopted by other novelists. They went on to publish *Nickleby* and, in 1840, became Dickens's regular publishers, buying up the rights to *Boz, Twist,* and other early works from JOHN MACRONE and RICHARD BENTLEY. Their relationship with Dickens soured, however, when *Chuzzlewit* and *A Christmas Carol* did not produce the financial returns that Dickens expected, so he moved to BRADBURY & EVANS in 1844, staying with them until 1859. After quarreling with Bradbury & Evans over the publication of his explanation of the separation from his wife, Dickens returned to Chapman & Hall. He published ALL THE YEAR ROUND and the novels of the 1860s with them. Chapman & Hall collaborated with Bradbury & Evans on the CHEAP and LIBRARY EDITIONS of Dickens's works. In 1861 they bought the rights to the novels owned by Bradbury & Evans. Among other Victorian writers published by the firm were THOMAS CARLYLE, EDWARD BULWER LYTTON, ROBERT BROWNING, Elizabeth Barrett Browning, ELIZABETH GASKELL, ANTHONY TROLLOPE, and George Meredith. Dickens's relationship with the firm is discussed at length by ROBERT PATTEN (1978).

characterization   All Dickens criticism is in some way about characterization, for Dickens is known for his characters, many of whom, like Scrooge, Oliver Twist, or Mr. Micawber, are familiar figures in the popular culture. Dickens's gallery of characters is crowded with a wider range of diverse and memorable people than that of any other writer in English since Shakespeare.

Most of Dickens's people are what E. M. FORSTER (1927) described as "flat characters," figures defined by one or two exaggerated traits who "can be expressed in one sentence such as 'I never will desert Mr. Micawber.'" GEORGE ELIOT observed that these defining characteristics were "external traits" and that Dickens "scarcely ever passes from the humorous and external to the emotional and tragic." This method of characterization, JOHN

RUSKIN and other critics have asserted, is that of an entertainer, not that of a serious writer who observes and describes the ways in which experience changes people and enables them to grow. Except for David Copperfield and Pip, these flat characters are said to lack an internal life and remain unchanged by the experiences they go through. "Those who dislike Dickens have an excellent case," Forster admits. "He ought to be bad. He is actually one of our big writers."

The problem for critics, then, has been to explain how Dickens, working primarily with simple, flat characters, was able to create a complex and serious vision of the world. V. S. Pritchett (*The Living Novel,* 1947), suggested an approach that many later critics have followed. For all their eccentricities, Dickens's characters have certain things in common. "The distinguishing quality of Dickens's people," Pritchett argues, "is that they are solitaries. They are people caught living in a world of their own. They soliloquize in it. They do not talk to one another; they talk to themselves. . . . The solitariness of people is paralleled by the solitariness of things. Fog operates as a separate presence, houses quietly rot or boisterously prosper on their own. . . . The people and things of Dickens are all out of touch and out of hearing of each other, each conducting its own inner monologue, grandiloquent or dismaying." Solitary, eccentric, individualized, the world that Dickens's characters inhabit is defined by separation and isolation.

RAYMOND WILLIAMS (*The English Novel from Dickens to Lawrence,* 1970) argues that this dramatic and emphatic use of flat characters expresses a fragmented urban consciousness. It is a "method . . . uniquely capable of expressing the experience of living in cities, . . . a way of seeing men and women that belongs to the street. There is at first an absence of ordinary connection and development. These men and women do not so much relate as pass each other and then sometimes collide. Nor often in the ordinary way do they speak to each other. They speak past each other, each intent above all on defining through his words his own identity and reality." In these collisions, Williams goes on to say, relationships and connections emerge, as if forced to consciousness.

Many critics have explored the ways in which these unfamiliar urban relationships reveal themselves: how characters double, mirror, and repeat each other; how the characters articulate multiple parts of the self that have been separated from one another; how the characters act as projections of each other. Brian Rosenberg (*Little Dorrit's Shadows*, 1996) explores how Dickens uses these techniques to develop the characters in *Dorrit*. Dickens's characters often relate in unusual or grotesque ways, like the figures in a dream rather than real people. TAYLOR STOEHR (1965) and MARK SPILKA (1963) analyze the ways in which they act as parts of a dream or fantasy. Although many of the characters are self-created and self-defined, they are still part of a larger vision, pieces in an imagined world. They have, as James Davies describes it, "a textual life" (*The Textual Life of Dickens's Characters*, 1990). They cannot be removed from their novels without simplification or misrepresentation.

Many Dickensians, especially in the early decades of the 20th century, were engrossed in discovering the ORIGINALS of Dickens's characters, the figures in real life on whom they were based. Although Dickens admittedly drew on real people for many of his characters, he usually transformed them into a different order of being in the novels. DORIS ALEXANDER (*Creating Characters with Charles Dickens*, 1991) reverses the process to study the ways in which the originals are transformed by Dickens's artistic imagination as he gives his characters textual life.

Charing Cross This crossroads in central London adjoining Trafalgar Square is notable in several of the novels. The Pickwickians begin their journeys from the GOLDEN CROSS HOTEL (2), where David Copperfield stays (19); Eugene Wrayburn meets Mr. Dolls in the street near Charing Cross (*Mutual Friend*, III:10).

Charles Dickens Edition Last collected edition of Dickens's works published during his lifetime. Issued by CHAPMAN & HALL in monthly volumes beginning in June 1867, each volume contained eight illustrations. Dickens supplied new prefaces and descriptive headlines for the pages.

Chartism Working-class movement that emerged in 1838 out of the Anti–Poor Law agitation, bringing together several working-class groups. Its name derived from the People's Charter, a document based on six points: universal suffrage, equal electoral districts, payment for members of Parliament, elimination of the property qualification for Parliament, vote by ballot, and annual Parliaments. The Chartists circulated petitions calling for these reforms, and in 1839, 1842, and 1848, they massed in London to present their demands to Parliament, each time without success. The mass meetings and several violent confrontations with authorities led many to fear a violent revolution led by the Chartists. A split in the movement between the "physical force" and the "moral force" factions contributed to the popular perception that many Chartists were dangerous and violent agents of French radicalism.

Dickens supported the radical goals of the Chartists and agreed with THOMAS CARLYLE, who blamed an idle aristocracy and an unresponsive Parliament for the rise of the movement. Dickens's sympathy is probably most directly expressed in *Chimes* in his treatment of Will Fern, a victim of agricultural distress who is radicalized into an incendiary terrorist by the mistreatment he receives from the rich. But Dickens did not endorse the methods or ends of the physical force Chartists, whom he condemns in *Old Curiosity Shop*. *Rudge*, also a response to Chartism, parallels the GORDON RIOTS to the Chartist agitations; its condemnation of mob action can be taken as a warning against physical-force Chartism. In "The Poor Man's Tale of a Patent," an inventor, similar to Daniel Doyce in *Dorrit*, develops sympathy for the Chartists after his frustrating experiences in dealing with the government bureaucracy.

Château des Moulineaux, Boulogne Castle in BOULOGNE that Dickens leased for his summer holidays in 1853 and 1856.

Chatham Seaport town in KENT located at the estuary of the MEDWAY where it meets the THAMES; twin city with ROCHESTER. Pickwick describes the lively seaport town in the following terms: "The principal production . . . appears to be soldiers, sailors, Jews, chalk, shrimps, officers and dockyard men. The commodities chiefly exposed for sale in the public streets are marine stores, hardbake, apples, flat fish and oysters. The streets present a lively and animated appearance, occasioned chiefly by the conviviality of the military" (2). Dickens spent his happiest childhood years here between 1817 and 1823 while his father served as a pay clerk at the naval station. The family lived at 2 Ordinance Terrace, the house where Dickens found his father's library of novels and avidly read the works of HENRY FIELDING, TOBIAS SMOLLETT, MIGUEL DE CERVANTES, and others. His father often walked with his son in the countryside surrounding the town; on one of these walks he advised the boy that if he worked hard he could one day own a house like GAD'S HILL PLACE. Chatham appears as Mudfog and Dullborough (*Uncommercial*, 12, 26); Pickwick's first journey takes him to neighboring Rochester, where he meets Wardle and where Winkle nearly duels with Dr. Slammer (2, 4); David sells some clothes here on his way to DOVER (*Copperfield*, 13). Chatham also appears in "Seven Poor Travellers" and *Reprinted*, "Detective Police."

Cheap Edition First collected edition of Dickens's works, issued by BRADBURY & EVANS and CHAPMAN & HALL in both monthly parts and separate volumes, beginning in 1847. Dickens wrote new prefaces for the novels, and each volume included a frontispiece by a well-known artist but was otherwise unillustrated. These cheap editions were designed to appeal to a new audience rather than to compete with more expensive editions of the novels that were also available at the time.

Cheapside Street near ST. PAUL'S CATHEDRAL in the CITY. Here Pickwick meets Tony Weller for the first time at an inn (20); Mr. Mould lives nearby and listens to the traffic in Cheapside (*Chuzzlewit*, 25). Also mentioned in *Boz*, "Minns" and "Christening"; *Dombey* (13); and *Expectations* (48).

Chelsea Village along the THAMES south of KENSINGTON where Dickens was married at ST. LUKE'S CHURCH and where he often visited THOMAS CAR-

LYLE, the sage of Chelsea. The tearful Job Trotter is compared to the Chelsea Waterworks (*Pickwick*, 28); Swiveller visits Sophy Wackles at her house in Chelsea (*Curiosity Shop*, 8); Gabriel Varden and his regiment march to the Chelsea Bun House (*Rudge*, 42); Mr. Bayham Badger practices medicine here (*Bleak House*, 13); and John stays with Thomas Joy in Chelsea when he comes to London to secure a patent (*Reprinted*, "Poor Man's Tale").

Chertsey Village along the THAMES in Surrey where Bill Sikes takes Oliver to rob Mrs. Maylie's house (*Twist*, 22). Betty Higden passes through on her way up the Thames (*Mutual Friend*, III:8).

Chesterton, G. K. (1874–1936) Novelist; social, political, religious, and literary critic; poet; and journalist. Chesterton, a Londoner like Dickens, challenged the modernist criticisms of Dickens and became the novelist's primary apologist at the beginning of the 20th century. In *Charles Dickens: A Critical Study* (1906), *Appreciations and Criticisms of The Works of Charles Dickens* (1911), *The Victorian Age in Literature* (1913), and numerous introductions to the novels and journalistic essays, Chesterton wrote about the life-affirming, magical world of Dickens. He considered all of Dickens's works part of a single vision revealing an archetypal realm, filled with magic, fantasy, and mystery. Dickens, he claimed, was "the last of the great mythologists."

Chigwell Town in Essex that was a favorite resort of Dickens. The King's Head Inn here, "a delicious old inn," Dickens told JOHN FORSTER, was the original of the Maypole in *Rudge*.

childhood Dickens has a surprising number of child characters, many of them, like Oliver Twist, Tiny Tim, and David Copperfield, among the most memorable figures in his works. This was something new in the novel, as KATHLEEN TILLOTSON (1956) notes: "To put a child at the centre of a novel for adults was virtually unknown when Dickens wrote *Oliver Twist* and *The Old Curiosity Shop*."

Dickens had an essentially romantic view of the child. Like Wordsworth's "best Philosopher," the Dickens child is often more in touch with his immortal origins than are the adults around him. Louisa Gradgrind (*Hard Times*) still sees visions in the fire, in spite of her UTILITARIAN education, as does Lizzie Hexam (*Mutual Friend*), even in the depths of Limehouse Hole. These "philosophical" children have a sensitivity and prescience described in Paul Dombey's case as being "old fashioned." Even in the most oppressive circumstances, they maintain their innocence, as Oliver does in Fagin's den.

Many of Dickens's children are victims of the Victorian world around them. Although Dickens did not write directly about the children laboring in the cotton factories or the mines, he was aware of these exploited children and wrote *Carol* partly as a response to a Parliamentary report describing the cruel abuse of children working in the mines. Tiny Tim is not a factory child, but his maimed legs are caged in iron, symbolic of the oppression brought about by the INDUSTRIAL REVOLUTION. Dickens also writes frequently about the effects of urbanization on the children of his day, children like Jo the crossing sweeper and Charley Neckett (*Bleak House*), who are orphans of the city streets, abandoned to Ignorance and Want—the two specters of childhood revealed to Scrooge by the Spirit of Christmas Present (*Carol*).

Besides these physical and material ills, Dickens's children are often oppressed by hard-hearted, narrow-minded religion, like the Calvinism of the Murdstones (*Copperfield*) or Mrs. Clennam (*Dorrit*) that views children as naturally sinful and in need of harsh treatment to correct their corrupt condition. Such children as Pip (*Expectations*), who is told that all children are "naterally wicious," and Esther Summerson (*Bleak House*), whose birthday is remembered only as a day of shame, are denied their childhoods by this dark and cruel worldview.

Dickens symbolized the situation of the Victorian child in his depiction of the family. The lost childhood is frequently represented as a condition of orphanhood, in which the child must fend for himself and find his own way in the world. In doing so he must give up his childhood and go to work at Murdstone and Grinby like David Copperfield or prepare for a place in the firm of Dombey and Son like young Paul. Even children whose parents are living may be abandoned, as are Jenny Wren (*Mutual Friend*) and Little Nell (*Curiosity Shop*), who must take parental roles with their irresponsible parents. Dickens frequently inverts the child and adult roles as a way of showing the lost childhood in Victorian England.

Frank Donovan (*Dickens and Youth*, 1968) surveys the children in Dickens's novels. ARTHUR ADRIAN (1984) and MALCOLM ANDREWS (1994) write specifically about the relations between parents and children.

Children's Hospital, Great Ormond Street, Bloomsbury   Dickens served as Chairman at a fund-raising dinner for this hospital in 1858 and gave a moving speech on its mission. Betty Higden's great-grandson Johnny dies in the hospital before the Boffins can complete their plan to adopt him (*Mutual Friend*, II:9).

Chisholm, Caroline (1808–1877)   Wife of a captain in the service of the East India Company, Mrs. Chisholm spent time in India and Australia before returning to England in 1848, where she continued and extended her efforts to aid emigrants to the colonies, especially to AUSTRALIA. Dickens aided her work with the Family Colonisation Loan Society, and she provided the letters he reprinted in "A Bundle of Emigrants' Letters." After visiting her home to collect the letters, Dickens wrote to ANGELA BURDETT-COUTTS, "I dream of Mrs. Chisholm, and her housekeeping. The dirty faces of her children are my continual companions." She served as the model for Mrs. Jellyby in *Bleak House*.

Chittick, Kathryn   Professor, Trent University, Ontario; specialist in 20th-century American poetry and Victorian literature. In *Dickens and the 1830s* (1990), Chittick discusses in great detail Dickens's first decade as a reporter, editor, and novelist, especially describing the perception of Dickens and the reception of his work in the periodical press of the period.

Chorley, Henry (1808–1872)   Reviewer for the ATHENAEUM who reviewed many of Dickens's later novels and wrote the magazine's obituary on Dickens. He was a close friend of the novelist during the last two decades of his life, taking part in some of Dickens's theatricals.

Christmas   No writer has been more identified with Christmas than Dickens. Largely on the basis of the *Carol* and the other CHRISTMAS BOOKS, Dickens has been variously described as "Father Christmas" and the "inventor" of Christmas; he deserves some credit for helping rescue the holiday from dour Calvinists, many of whom condemned the traditional Christmas celebrations as pagan rites.

The Dickens Christmas, described in the Pickwickians' celebration at Dingley Dell and in the festivities in the *Carol*, is one of feasting, storytelling, and merrymaking. The exchange of gifts has a secondary role. It is also a time for reflection—especially on the losses of the past year—and for expressing one's common humanity in charity. Scrooge's nephew Fred characterizes Dickens's view of the holiday as "the only time I know of, in the long calendar of the year, when men and women seem by one consent to open their shut-up hearts freely, and to think of people below them as if they really were fellow-passengers to the grave, and not another race of creatures bound on other journeys" (*Carol*, 1).

Storytelling—especially the telling of ghost stories—is one of the traditions celebrated in *Pickwick* and the Christmas books. It was also the basis for the special Christmas numbers of HOUSEHOLD WORDS and ALL THE YEAR ROUND. For these issues, Dickens typically wrote a frame narrative and then collected stories by several other writers to fit the frame. Dickens's contributions to these group efforts are collected as the *Christmas Stories*, even though many of the stories are not about Christmas.

If celebration and feasting predominates in *Pickwick* and the *Carol*, the darker, more reflective side of Christmas is central to some of the other works, particularly the later novels. Redlaw's dark and brooding Christmas (*Haunted Man*) is a prelude to the Christmas season in the later novels: In *Two Cities*, Dr. Manette is kidnapped and forced to tend the victims of the St. Evrémondes' oppression during the Christmas season, an episode that leads to his imprisonment and

to Madame Defarge's revolutionary anger; Pip's meeting with the convict on the marshes that shadows his later life is the dark Christmas story that begins *Expectations*; the mysterious disappearance of Edwin Drood takes place on an apparently murderous Christmas Eve.

Dickens's ideas about Christmas, especially in the early works, are discussed by Paul Davis (*The Lives and Times of Ebenezer Scrooge*, 1990). Katherine Carolan ("Dickens's Last Christmases," *Dalhousie Review*, 1972) considers the dark Christmases of the later novels.

Christmas books   The five stories Dickens wrote for CHRISTMAS between 1843 and 1848: *A Christmas Carol* (1843), *The Chimes* (1844), *The Cricket on the Hearth* (1845), *The Battle of Life* (1846), and *The Haunted Man* (1848). Dickens gave the title *Christmas Books* to the volume in the CHEAP EDITION collecting these tales. Although later editions sometimes use the title *Christmas Stories*, Dickens reserved that title for the stories collected from Christmas numbers of HOUSEHOLD WORDS and ALL THE YEAR ROUND.

Churchill, R. C. (1916–)   Journalist, literary historian and critic. *A Bibliography of Dickensian Criticism, 1836–1975* (1975) provides an annotated bibliography of criticism on each of the novels and on a range of Dickensian topics and includes many apt quotations from the works cited. Churchill's essay "The Genius of Charles Dickens" (in *The New Pelican Guide to English Literature*, ed. B. Ford, 1958; 1982) discusses Dickens as the Shakespeare of the Victorian age, assesses the reasons for his popularity, especially as a comic writer, and summarizes his career from an unusual perspective that judges *Chuzzlewit*, *Bleak House*, and *Dorrit* his "major achievements."

circus   From childhood on, Dickens was fascinated by the circus, a form of popular entertainment that appeared in England in the mid-18th century when Philip Astley opened his circus near WESTMINSTER BRIDGE in 1769. Dickens describes the elaborate equestrian performances at ASTLEY'S ROYAL EQUESTRIAN AMPHITHEATRE in *Boz*. As the young Dickens might have done, Kit Nubbles takes his mother there when he receives his first quarter's pay from the Garlands (*Curiosity Shop*, 39). Dickens reports his delight in clowns in the preface to JOSEPH GRIMALDI's memoirs. The traveling showmen in *Curiosity Shop* and Mr. Chops's career as a performer in *Going into Society* involve entertainments related to the circus, but Dickens's most extensive use of the circus is in *Hard Times*, where it functions as the symbolic counter to Coketown and the school of hard facts. Sleary and company represent the realm of imagination, and they make up a community where the cynicism, opportunism, and exploitation of Coketown is absent. In Coketown, where imagination is suppressed, the serpents and elephants of the circus have been perverted: "It was a town of machinery and tall chimneys, out of which interminable serpents of smoke trailed themselves forever and ever, and never got uncoiled, . . . and where the piston of the steam-engines worked up and down, like the head of an elephant in a state of melancholy madness" (I:5).

Articulating Sleary's—and Dickens's—principle that "people must be amused," the circus also challenges those who wanted to suppress such popular entertainments, particularly on Sundays. Dickens frequently attacked such killjoys.

PAUL SCHLICKE (1985) describes the Victorian circuses that Dickens knew and makes a detailed analysis of the circus in *Hard Times*.

City, the The old City of London as defined by its original boundaries. In the 19th century—and now—the City is largely the financial district in the center of London.

City Road, north London The Micawbers live in Windsor Terrace off this thoroughfare when David boards with them (*Copperfield*, 11). Florence Dombey is kidnapped by old Mrs. Brown in the City Road as Polly is watching for her son to return from school (*Dombey*, 6).

Clapham Residential area in south London where the stockbroker Mr. Gattleton lives at Rose Villa, Clapham Rise (*Boz*, "Porter"). The Poor Relation has lodgings in Clapham Road (*"Poor Relation"*).

Clare Market Slum quarter of HOLBORN noteworthy for its ostentatious gin-shops (*Boz*, "Gin Shops"). The Magpie and Stump was located nearby (*Pickwick*, 20).

Clarendon Edition Definitive scholarly edition of Dickens's works inaugurated in 1966 with KATHLEEN TILLOTSON's edition of *Oliver Twist*. Under the general editorship of JOHN BUTT and Tillotson, the Clarendon provides critical texts of the novels, indicating variations in the manuscript and the editions published during Dickens's lifetime. About half of the novels have been issued in this edition.

Clarke, Joseph Clayton ("Kyd") (c. 1856–1937) Late-Victorian illustrator whose watercolors *Characters from Charles Dickens* (1889) are among the best-known renderings of Dickens in the late 19th century. Kyd also illustrated editions of *Copperfield* and *Expectations* in the 1880s. Examples of his work appear on pages 92 and 332.

Clarke, Mary Cowden (1809–1898) Author of the *Complete Concordance to Shakespeare* (1844–45), she met Dickens in 1848 and joined his theatrical group, playing Dame Quickly in *Merry Wives of Windsor*, Tib in *Every Man in His Humour*, and Mrs. Hilary in *Love, Law, and Physic*. A lifelong friend, she wrote of Dickens and his "indefatigable vivacity, cheeriness, and good humour" in *Recollections of Writers* (1878).

Clerkenwell Area of London north of HOLBORN. The Artful Dodger and Charley Bates pick Mr. Brownlow's pocket at a bookstore near Clerkenwell Green (*Twist*, 10), Gabriel Varden's house and locksmithing business is located here (*Rudge*, 4), Phil Squod works as a tinker in Clerkenwell (*Bleak House*, 26), Jarvis Lorry lives in Clerkenwell when it is still something of a suburb (*Two Cities*, II:6), and Mr. Venus has his taxidermy business in Clerkenwell (*Mutual Friend*, I:7).

Clifford's Inn Oldest of the INNS OF COURT, established in 1345 on the north side of FLEET STREET opposite the TEMPLE. Jack Bamber tells Pickwick the tale of a suicide that occurred here

(*Pickwick,* 21), Melchisedech's offices are located here (*Bleak House,* 34), Tip Dorrit languishes here as a clerk (*Dorrit,* I:7), and Boffin discusses employing Rokesmith as a secretary in the courtyard of the inn (*Mutual Friend,* I:8).

coaches   In the popular imagination, Dickens is often associated with the stagecoach and the inns where the coaches stopped to change horses. This image may be largely derived from *Pickwick,* in which the Pickwickians travel about England by coach, but coach journeys are important in many of the novels, especially those prior to *Dombey.* In retrospective works like *Copperfield* and *Expectations,* coach journeys also play an important role, and the latter novel is structured in "stages" that turn Pip's life into a coach journey. HUMPHRY HOUSE (1941) points out that the age of the coach was largely past by the time Dickens began writing; indeed the transition from the coach to the RAILWAYS symbolized for most Victorians the tumultuous changes wrought by the INDUSTRIAL REVOLUTION. So the coach, even for the Victorians, was a nostalgic reminder of another time. House sums up the special significance of the coach to Dickens and other writers of his generation: "'Coaching' has thus become idealized in the popular memory not merely as a striking and picturesque feature of a vanished world, but because a whole generation, in which there were many writers, caught by admiration of the coaches in their short-lived pride [during their boyhood years], was unable to work off in the boredom of adult experience the glamorous ambitions of boyhood."

Cobham   Village in KENT near GAD'S HILL to which Mr. Tupman retreats after Rachel Wardle runs off with Jingle (*Pickwick,* 11). The Leather Bottle, the inn where Tupman stays, and the town itself were favorite destinations for Dickens and remain sites of Dickensian pilgrimage.

Cochrane and M'Crone   Publishers of the MONTHLY MAGAZINE, in which Dickens published several early sketches.

cockney school, the   Genre of popular fiction at the end of the 19th century, represented by such works as Arthur Morrison's *Tales of Mean Streets* (1894), Arthur St. John Adcock's *East End Idylls* (1897), Somerset Maugham's *Liza of Lambeth* (1897), and the works of EDWIN PUGH and William Pett Ridge. Dickens was an important influence on these writers, both for his depiction of life in London's inner city—as, for example, in Tom All Alone's in *Bleak House* and the Limehouse of *Mutual Friend*—and for such great cockney characters as Sam Weller and Sairey Gamp.

Colburn, Henry (d. 1855)   Publisher and magazine proprietor; partner of RICHARD BENTLEY from 1829 to 1832. He published *The Pic-Nic Papers* (1841).

Coldbath Fields   Middlesex House of Correction in CLERKENWELL, noted for its introduction of the "silent system" in 1834, under which prisoners were required to remain absolutely silent (*Boz,* "Last Cab-Driver").

Colden, David C. (1797–1850)   American lawyer and public servant, son of the Mayor of New York City, he acted as host in NEW YORK on Dickens's first visit to AMERICA in 1842. He first met Dickens in England in 1840.

Collins, Charles Allston (1828–1873)   PRE-RAPHAELITE painter, essayist, and novelist (*Bar Sinister,* 1864); younger brother of WILKIE COLLINS. He was a contributor to HOUSEHOLD WORDS and ALL THE YEAR ROUND; he also designed the cover for *Drood* (see p. 215), but ill health prevented him from illustrating the novel. He married Dickens's daughter KATE MACREADY DICKENS in 1860.

Collins, Philip (1923–)   Professor at the University of Leicester, author of numerous books and articles on Dickens and Victorian literature; perhaps the most important contemporary Dickens scholar. His *Dickens and Crime* (1962) and *Dickens and Education* (1963) were pioneering studies of two areas of Victorian culture that are central in Dickens's novels. In numerous articles, critical essays, and reviews, he has discussed and contributed to nearly every aspect of Dickens studies. As editor of *Dickens: The Critical Heritage* (1971), *The Public Readings of Charles Dickens* (1975), and *Dickens: Interviews and Recollections* (1981), Collins has greatly enlarged our understanding of the cultural and literary context in which Dickens worked. He has also provided important bibliographical studies of Dickens's works and of Dickens scholarship and criticism in *The New Cambridge Bibliography* (1970) and in GEORGE H. FORD's *Victorian Fiction* (1978).

Collins, William Wilkie (1824–1889) Novelist, playwright, and journalist who collaborated with Dickens on several projects and was among Dickens's closest companions during the last two decades of his life. Dickens met Collins in 1851, when Collins was in the company performing EDWARD BULWER LYTTON's *Not So Bad as We Seem*. Twelve years older than Collins, Dickens served as

Wilkie Collins.

a mentor to the younger novelist. Collins joined the staff of HOUSEHOLD WORDS in 1856 and serialized his two best-known novels, *The Woman in White* (1860) and *The Moonstone* (1868), in ALL THE YEAR ROUND. The two novelists collaborated on *The Lazy Tour of Two Idle Apprentices* (1857), on several Christmas numbers of HOUSEHOLD WORDS and ALL THE YEAR ROUND, and on essays for the same periodicals. Dickens produced Collins's plays THE LIGHTHOUSE (1855) and THE FROZEN DEEP (1857). Collins's unconventional and bohemian way of life made him a congenial, accepting colleague, friend, and traveling companion. For a discussion of Collins's possible influence on Dickens as a writer of DETECTIVE STORIES, see T. S. ELIOT's essay "Wilkie Collins and Dickens" (1932; 1951).

Colosseum Building in Regent's Park in which a panoramic view of London from the top of ST. PAUL'S CATHEDRAL 64 feet high and covering the circumference of the building, was on display ("The Colloseum Fête," "The Reopening of the Colloseum," and *Boz*, "Greenwich Fair").

Commercial Road Street in WHITECHAPEL where Captain Cuttle buys the ballad "Lovely Peg" (*Dombey*, 9); also mentioned in *Uncommercial* (3).

Connor, Steven Professor, Birkbeck College, University of London; specializing in 19th- and 20th-century literature, literary theory, and cultural studies. His influential *Charles Dickens* (1985) analyzes several of Dickens's novels using structuralist, deconstructive, or a blend of psychoanalytic and Marxist approaches. Connor has also edited a selection of theoretical essays on Dickens (1996) and editions of *Oliver Twist* (1994) and *Edwin Drood* (1996).

Coolidge, Archibald C. (1928–) Professor, University of Iowa, whose work *Charles Dickens as a Serial Novelist* (1967) was among the early studies of the ways in which serial publication affected the literary qualities of Dickens's novels. He has also written on the gothic influences in Dickens.

Cooling, Kent Village at the edge of the marshes northeast of ROCHESTER that served as one of the models for Pip's village in *Expectations*. Dickens was fond of walking here on his rambles from GAD's HILL, though he reduced the number of "little stone lozenges" that marked the graves of Pip's brothers to five from the 13 such gravestones in Cooling churchyard (*Expectations*, 1).

Cooper, Frederick Fox (1806–1879) Victorian adaptor of Dickens's works for the theater, Cooper turned at least seven of Dickens's novels into plays, most notably *Master Humphrey's Clock* (1840) and *Hard Times* (1854). He was not scrupulous in maintaining fidelity to the original text; in his adaptation of *Two Cities, The Incarcerated Victim of the Bastille* (1860), for example, he spared Carton's life.

copyright As a professional writer who had to support a large family with his pen alone, Dickens was interested in the business of writing and the protection of the writer's intellectual property rights. The English Copyright Act (1709)—the first in the world—was only a little more than a century old when Dickens began writing. He supported the extension of the Act, sponsored by his friend SIR THOMAS NOON TALFOURD, which passed in 1842. His most intense involvement with the issue of copyright, however, came on his American tour in 1842, when he spoke out for an INTERNATIONAL COPYRIGHT agreement between Britain and the United States. American publishers had been pirating the works of Dickens and other English writers. In speeches at Boston and Hartford, Dickens appealed to the self-interest of his American audience, arguing that an American literature would not develop as long as it was cheaper for American publishers to steal the works of foreigners than to pay for the works of Americans. His statements enraged the American newspaper editors—many of them among the pirates—and Dickens was vilified in the press as a money-grubbing, ungrateful guest. Dickens responded with letters on the issue to British journals and with his satire of the American press in *Notes* and *Chuzzlewit*.

Cornhill This thoroughfare in the CITY, running from LEADENHALL Street to the BANK OF ENGLAND, is the site of Dodson and Fogg's offices (*Pickwick*,

20) and the George and Vulture (*Pickwick*, 26). Bob Cratchit slides on the ice on Cornhill on his way home from the office (*Carol*, 1). Bradley Headstone's grudging proposal to Lizzie is delivered in St. Peter's churchyard here (*Mutual Friend*, II:15).

Cornhill, The Monthly periodical established in 1860 and edited by WILLIAM MAKEPEACE THACKERAY. Dickens contributed a memorial to Thackeray in the February 1864 issue.

Corn Laws These tariffs on grain imported into England were supposed to protect British agriculture and stabilize the price of grain, but the Whigs who took power after the REFORM BILL OF 1832 saw the Corn Laws as remnants of privilege for the landed agricultural aristocracy and the most glaring violation of the principle of free trade. The Anti–Corn Law League, formed in 1838 to seek repeal of the tariffs and led by Radicals John Bright and Richard Cobden, was most active during the tumultuous early years of CHARTISM. The anti–Corn Law activists and the Chartists agreed that the Corn Laws raised the price of grain, making food unnecessarily expensive for the poor. A bad grain harvest and the Irish potato famine forced the issue to a crisis in 1845–46, just as Dickens was beginning his brief tenure as editor of the *DAILY NEWS*. He considered repeal one of the central missions of his paper.

courts As a clerk in a law office, a shorthand reporter in Doctors' Commons, and a litigant in the COURT OF CHANCERY, Dickens had numerous opportunities to observe the legal system in action. He describes a number of different courts in his writings. He mentions two debtors' courts: the **Insolvent Debtor's Court,** described by Boz as one of the haunts of shabby-genteel people (*Boz*, "Shabby-genteel"; *Pickwick*, 43; *Dorrit*, I:7), and the **Palace Court,** or **Marshalsea Court,** where Tip Dorrit briefly finds work in an attorney's office (*Dorrit*, I:7). The Insolvent Debtor's Court was abolished in 1861 when personal indebtedness was no longer cause for imprisonment. Tigg compares the **Court of Requests,** a court where the poor could sue for recovery of debts, to the Blue Dragon dunning Chevy Slyme to pay his bill (*Chuzzlewit*, 7). Pickwick is tried for breach of promise in the **Common Pleas Court** (34), the main court for civil actions, which in 1881 would be absorbed into the Queen's Bench Court. David Copperfield trains to become a proctor (23, 33, 39), one of the attorneys practicing in **Doctors' Commons,** a civil court that handled marriage licenses and divorces, as well as ecclesiastical and naval matters. Here Jingle gets a license to marry Rachael Wardle (*Pickwick*, 10), and Tony Weller seeks advice on a will (*Pickwick*, 54). Dickens satirized the court in *Boz* (Doctor's Commons) and clearly regarded it as an institution that had outlived its usefulness. It was abolished in 1857. The COURT OF CHANCERY, supreme court for issues involving legacies, wills, and trusts, is attacked in *Bleak House* as an obsolete, self-serving, and dilatory institution. It was absorbed into the Supreme Court in 1873. Dickens describes the OLD BAILEY, the main criminal court for London, in *Boz* ("Criminal Courts"), as a place where "every trial seems a mere matter of business. There is a great deal of form, but no compassion." Mentioned frequently in the novels, this court is the one in which Charles Darnay is tried for spying (*Two Cities*, II:2).

Coutts, Angela   ANGELA BURDETT-COUTTS, philanthropist and friend of Dickens, is sometimes identified as Miss Coutts. Born Angela Burdett, she added her maternal grandfather's surname, Coutts, to her own name after inheriting his fortune. *See* BURDETT-COUTTS.

Covent Garden   This area of London, west of the CITY and north of the STRAND, where the central fruit and vegetable market was located, was a familiar wandering place for the young Dickens as it was for David Copperfield (12). Several characters have lodgings here, among them Augustus Minns (*Boz*, "Minns"), Arthur Clennam (*Dorrit*, I:13), and the Uncommercial Traveller (1). Copperfield goes to Covent Garden Theatre (19), and Pip takes rooms in Hummums Hotel when Wemmick warns him not to go home (*Expectations*, 45). Job Trotter spends the night in a vegetable basket (*Pickwick*, 47), and Mr. Dolls is tormented by street urchins in Covent Garden (*Mutual Friend*, IV:9).

Coventry   Pickwick and his friends change horses here on their way from BIRMINGHAM to London (*Pickwick*, 51). The city where Nell learns to be a guide for Mrs. Jarley's Waxworks may be based on Coventry (*Curiosity Shop*, 27).

Cox, Constance (1915–1993)   Playwright, actress, and adaptor of many 19th-century novels for the stage. She did the scripts for many of the BBC television serial adaptations of Dickens's novels, among them *Bleak House* (1959), *Twist* (1962), *Curiosity Shop* (1963), *Chuzzlewit* (1964), and *Two Cities* (1965).

crime   Crime fascinated Dickens. From the brutal murders committed by Bill Sikes and Jonas Chuzzlewit to the confidence games of Jingle and Tigg and the white-collar crimes of Uriah Heep and Merdle, there is crime in nearly every novel. Beginning with the FLEET PRISON in *Pickwick*, prisons are omnipresent. NEWGATE PRISON shadows Pip with "the taint of prison and crime" (*Expectations*, 32), and the MARSHALSEA PRISON becomes symbolic of the human condition in *Dorrit*. *Bleak House*, in which Inspector Bucket pursues Lady Dedlock and Tulkinghorn's murderer, is among the first DETECTIVE NOVELS.

Dickens accompanied the police on their rounds and reported on these excursions in articles for his magazines—in "On Duty with Inspector Field" and "Down with the Tide," for example. He visited prisons, witnessed public executions, and walked at night through the crime-ridden areas of London. In observing and writing about crime, Dickens may have been trying to exorcise the taint in his own past, for he seemed to associate his father's imprisonment for debt with criminality. Crime was also a way to represent dramatically the dark side of human nature.

Many critics have written on the thematic significance of the crimes in the various novels. PHILIP COLLINS's *Dickens and Crime* (1962) is a classic on this topic, placing the crimes in the novels into the context of the growing awareness of crime in Victorian England. In *The Novel and the Police* (1988), D. A. Miller makes a deconstructive analysis of crime and public order in several Victorian novels, among them *Bleak House*.

Cross Keys Inn   Inn on WOOD STREET, CHEAP-SIDE, where coaches left for ROCHESTER. Pip, like Dickens, first arrives in London here (*Expectations*, 20). Cavalletto is run over in a nearby street (*Dorrit*, I:13). Also mentioned in *Boz*, "Omnibuses"; *Nickleby* (33); and *Uncommercial* (12).

Crotch, W. Walter (1874–1947)   Editor-in-chief of the International Press Bureau in Paris; editor of the revived HOUSEHOLD WORDS; one of the founding members of the DICKENS FELLOWSHIP in 1902; president of the fellowship from 1915 to 1920. Author of several books on Dickens, including *Charles Dickens, Social Reformer* (1913).

Crowquill, Alfred (1804–1872)   Pen name of writer and illustrator Alfred Henry Forrestier. An associate of GEORGE CRUIKSHANK, Crowquill drew for PUNCH in its early years and wrote for BENTLEY'S MISCELLANY and the New MONTHLY MAGAZINE. He illustrated *Pickwick* (1841) and other novels before concentrating in his later work on illustrations for children's books. An example of his work appears on p. 315.

Cruikshank, George (1792–1878)   Artist, caricaturist, and illustrator, Cruikshank was the preeminent exponent in early Victorian England of the tradition of graphic satire stemming from WILLIAM HOGARTH. Among the nearly 900 works that he illustrated in a long career were several by Dickens. He was Dickens's first illustrator, commissioned by JOHN MACRONE to illustrate *Sketches by Boz*. He also did illustrations for *Mudfog*, *Grimaldi*, and *Bentley's Miscellany* when Dickens was its editor, and, most important, for *Oliver Twist*. His illustrations for *Twist* have sometimes been regarded as the finest original illustrations for any of the novels. Although there were occasional professional disagreements during these projects, Dickens and Cruikshank were close friends socially in the 1840s. Their relationship cooled in the late 1840s when Dickens criticized, in "Frauds on the Fairies," Cruikshank's teetotalism and his retellings of classic fairy tales. By the end of his life, Cruikshank became embittered and implausibly claimed that he originated much of the story and many of the characters in *Oliver Twist*. Dickens's relationship with Cruikshank is discussed by JOHN HARVEY (1971), Jane R. Cohen (*Charles Dickens and His Original Illustrators*, 1980), and at length by ROBERT PATTEN (1992). Examples of Cruikshank's work appear on pages 282 (Fagin), 269 (*Oliver Twist*), and 425 and 428 (*Sketches by Boz*).

Cursitor Street   Street running east from CHANCERY LANE where John Dounce (*Boz*, "Dounce") and Snagsby (*Bleak House*, 10) live. The sponging house where Watkins Tottle is held (*Boz*, "Tottle") and Coavinses (*Bleak House*, 15), the sponging house where Neckett works, are both located here.

Cuttris's Hotel, James Street, Covent Garden   Hotel where Dickens stayed when he returned to London from Italy in 1844 to give a reading of *The Chimes*.

D

Daily News Liberal daily newspaper that began publication on January 21, 1846, with Dickens as editor. The main investors, JOSEPH PAXTON, WILLIAM BRADBURY, and FREDERICK EVANS, capitalized the project with money from railway speculation. Dickens was excited by the opportunites to promote liberal causes like the repeal of the CORN LAWS and, by paying top salaries, to assemble a staff of such first-rate journalists as W. H. WILLS, JOHN FORSTER, W. J. FOX, and DOUGLAS JERROLD. JOHN DICKENS was put in charge of the reporters, a position he held until his death. Dickens found the demands of a daily paper too taxing, and he objected to Bradbury's interference with his direction, so he resigned the editorship on February 9. He did continue to write occasional pieces for the paper.

Daleski, H. M. (1926–) Professor at Hebrew University in Jerusalem who has written on Conrad, Lawrence, and other 19th- and 20th-century writers. In *Dickens and the Art of Analogy* (1970), Daleski discusses repeated patterns (analogies) that act as thematic focal points in the novels. In the analysis of *Great Expectations*, for example, he treats expectation and hidden relationships as the central analogies in the novel.

Dana, Richard Henry, Jr. (1815–1882) American author of *Two Years before the Mast* (1840) and other works, whom Dickens met on his tours to America. Dickens considered Dana "a very nice fellow"; Dana described Dickens as "far from well bred" but "full of life."

dandyism A movement of the Regency period in the 1810s that promoted a male ideal in dress and behavior. Beau Brummel (1778–1840) and the Prince Regent, George IV, were its most notable exemplars; preoccupied with clothes and with their public appearance, they represented the narcissism and dedication to genteel idleness that characterized the dandy. An extravagant and flashy dresser, Dickens, particularly as a young man, was often described as a dandy, but he never affected a posture of idleness.

In *Sartor Resartus* (1833–34), THOMAS CARLYLE defined the dandy as "a Clothes-wearing Man, a man whose trade, office, and existence consists in the wearing of Clothes." He satirically analyzed dandyism as a religion devoted to the worship of self. The dandies in Dickens's novels fit this Carlylean pattern. Steerforth (*Copperfield*), Harthouse (*Hard Times*), and Gowan (*Dorrit*) all cultivate an aristocratic insouciance and boredom and seek only self-gratification. Sydney Carton (*Two Cities*) and Eugene Wrayburn (*Mutual Friend*) are more positive versions of the dandy figure; both transcend their dandiacal tendencies in a concern for others.

Dickens most fully explores dandyism in *Bleak House*. Old Mr. Turveydrop, with his padded clothes and his ideal of "Deportment," is the

Regency dandy surviving into what he calls "degenerate times." His idleness and parasitism, however, are representative of a new "Dandyism of a more mischievous sort, that has got below the surface and is doing less harmless things" (12). The Dedlocks and their aristocratic company represent this new dandyism as they idly perpetuate their own interests and justify their unconcern for anyone else as a rejection of "the Vulgar." Harold Skimpole imitates this mode of being in his irresponsible dilettantism. In its various manifestations, this subsurface dandyism characterizes the self-serving society of *Bleak House.*

Ellen Moers discusses dandyism, Dickens as dandy, and the dandies in his novels in *The Dandy* (1960).

Davenport, Jean (1829–1903) Actress who has been identified as the original of Ninetta Crummles, though this identification has been contested. She went with her parents to America in 1838 and was presented as a child prodigy for several years. She played Dot in several productions of *Cricket.*

Davis, Earle R. (b. 1905) Professor, Kansas State, whose *The Flint and the Flame: The Artistry of Charles Dickens* (1963) provides useful discussions of the influence of Victorian theater on Dickens's novels and of WILKIE COLLINS's influence on Dickens.

Davis, Eliza Wife of the Jewish banker J. P. Davis, who bought TAVISTOCK HOUSE in 1860. She wrote to Dickens in 1863 stating that his portrayal of Fagin in *Twist* had done "a great wrong" to her people. Dickens wrote back defending his portrayal of Fagin, but he was clearly troubled by the suggestion that the novel was anti-Semitic. In *Our Mutual Friend* he included Riah and the circle of Jews who take in Lizzie Hexam partly to redress the balance in his treatment of the Jews. After the later novel appeared, Mrs. Davis sent him a copy of Benisch's Hebrew and English Bible, inscribed: "Presented to Charles Dickens, in grateful and admiring recognition of his having exercised the noblest quality men can possess—that of atoning for an injury as soon as conscious of having inflicted it."

death At the beginning of *Charles Dickens Resurrectionist,* ANDREW SANDERS (1982) takes two pages just to list the more important deaths that occur in Dickens's works, giving substance to the common impression that deaths and deathbed scenes occur frequently in the novels. Dickens was not simply exploiting the sentimental possibilities of such scenes; he was describing a reality of his times. Death was much more frequent in Victorian than in modern England, especially in the cities, and the dying were more present, for people were more likely to die at home than in the hospital. Dickens was probably not guilty of exaggerating the facts about death in Victorian England. The five little stone lozenges on the graves of Pip's five siblings, who died in infancy, in the opening chapter of *Expectations* were based on an actual grave in a country churchyard at CHALK near GAD'S HILL, where there were 13 such markers on one family's plot.

Oscar Wilde's remark that one would need a heart of stone not to laugh at Little Nell's death marks a major change in sensibility between the 19th and 20th centuries. Like Wilde, most modern readers find Dickens's deathbed scenes, particularly those describing the deaths of children, oppressively sentimental and overdone. Yet these were often the scenes most prized by Victorian readers, in both the novels and the stage adaptations. The deaths of Nell, Paul Dombey, and Jo the crossing sweeper (*Bleak House*) moved them to tears and were climactic moments on the stage. The Victorians were much more willing to cry, women and men alike, than modern readers are.

Dickens's SENTIMENTALITY in handling such scenes, particularly the deaths of young women like Little Nell, is often linked to the death of MARY HOGARTH, his sister-in-law, who died at 17. Dickens, who was holding her in his arms at the moment of her death, removed a ring from her finger and wore it for the rest of his life. She became the model for Nell, Florence Dombey, Little Dorrit, and Dickens's other saintly young women. They are, as ALEXANDER WELSH (1971) suggests, angels who act as intermediaries between this world and the next, agents both of death and immortality.

Death also has a didactic role in the novels, for by showing us how to die it teaches us how to live. In an increasingly secular world, death is a reminder of the spiritual dimension in this life and the promise of an afterlife—at least an afterlife in the memories of those who remember the good deeds of the dead. The narrator of the *Carol* expresses this didactic function of the death scenes as Scrooge contemplates his body on its bier:

> Oh cold, cold, rigid, dreadful Death, set up thine altar here, and dress it with such terrors as thou hast at thy command, for this is thy dominion! But of the loved, revered, and honored head, thou canst not turn one hair to thy dread purposes, or make one feature odious. It is not that the hand is heavy, and will fall down when released; it is not that the heart and pulse are still: but that the hand was open, generous, and true, the heart brave, warm, and tender, and the pulse a man's. Strike, Shadow, strike! And see his good deeds springing from the wound, to sow the world with life immortal! (4)

Dickens's theology in this passage seems to suggest that in the death of the good man there is immortality, for his good deeds will be remembered by the living. He makes a similar point about the death of Sydney Carton in *A Tale of Two Cities.*

The most thorough discussion of Dickens's treatment of death is ANDREW SANDERS's (1982). ALEXANDER WELSH (1971) offers several provocative chapters on the idealized young woman as an angel of death and immortality.

debtors' prisons When Dickens was a boy of 12, his father was imprisoned in the MARSHALSEA for debt, an event at the center of the most traumatic episode in Dickens's youth. Although JOHN DICKENS was only held from February 20 to May 28, 1824, Charles was humiliated by the dishonor to the family and by the degrading work he was sent to do at WARREN'S BLACKING warehouse. Dickens used this period in his life as the basis for the episodes in *Copperfield* dealing with Mr. Micawber's imprisonment and David's employment at Murdstone and Grinby's; he wrote about it directly in the fragment of AUTOBIOGRAPHY that he gave to JOHN FORSTER at about the same time.

Personal insolvency was subject to imprisonment during most of Dickens's lifetime, although the penalty was not often exacted in the two decades before it was finally abolished in 1869. During Dickens's youth, however, imprisonment for debt was common. Typically the debtor was arrested and detained for a few days in a sponging house or halfway house—such as that with which Neckett is connected (*Bleak House,* 6)—to allow him time to raise the money to pay the debt. If the debtor was unable (or unwilling, as in *Pickwick*'s case) to pay, he was sent to prison. Dickens writes about each of the three main debtors' prisons in London. Pickwick is imprisoned in the FLEET (*Pickwick,* 41–47), a debtors' prison dating back to the 13th century, which was demolished in 1846. Micawber is held in the KING'S BENCH in SOUTHWARK (*Copperfield,* 11), a prison destroyed during the GORDON RIOTS, rebuilt afterward, and finally demolished in 1880. Mr. Dorrit, like Dickens's father, is imprisoned in the MARSHALSEA, also in Southwark, which was closed in 1842.

Defoe, Daniel (1660–1731) One of the 18th-century writers that Dickens, like David Copperfield, read as a child. *Robinson Crusoe* is frequently mentioned in Dickens's works, most notably in *Pickwick* (7, 30, 44), *Carol* (2), *Chuzzlewit* (5, 21), *Dombey* (4, 39), *Copperfield* (4, 5, 24, 26, 34), *Bleak House* (8), *Dorrit* (I:13, 25), and *Mutual Friend* (IV:17).

De la Rue, Emile (d. 1870) **and Augusta** (d. 1887) Swiss banker and his wife who were neighbors of the Dickenses in GENOA in 1844–45. Dickens attempted through MESMERISM to treat Mrs. De la Rue's psychosomatic maladies that induced sleeplessness and hallucinations. His late-night treatments aroused Catherine's jealousy and engaged Dickens's attentions as "doctor" almost obsessively.

Delmonico's The New York restaurant at which a grand press banquet was held for Dickens during his reading tour in the United States in 1867. In his speech here, Dickens spoke positively about AMERICA and the American press, hoping to heal the wounds caused by his criticisms after his 1842 visit.

Demerara   Colony in British Guiana. Jingle and Job Trotter emigrate there (*Pickwick*, 53), Fred Trent is sent there by his Grandfather (*Curiosity Shop*, 23), and Sol Gills stops there on his journey in search of Walter Gay (*Dombey*, 56).

Deptford   Dock area along the south side of the THAMES east of London. Tony Jobling retreats here to recover financially (*Bleak House*, 20); Toby Magsman tells the story of Chops the dwarf here in "Going into Society."

De Quincey, Thomas (1785–1859)   Romantic essayist and novelist. His *Confessions of an English Opium Eater* (1821), admired by Dickens, influenced the later novelist with its dark vision of urban London and its exploration of the ways in which childhood trauma affected his adult life.

detective story   EDGAR ALLAN POE is usually described as the originator of the detective story: a novel or story in which a crime—usually a murder—is solved by a detective who logically follows a series of clues to discover the identity of the perpetrator. Dickens's *Bleak House* is often listed along with Poe's stories as one of the earliest such novels, but *Bleak House* does not allow the reader to follow along with Inspector Bucket's processes of deduction, and hence it lacks some of the intellectual appeal usually found in such stories. Its plot, as Karen Chase (*Eros and Psyche: The Representation of Personality in Charlotte Bronte, Charles Dickens, and George Eliot*, 1984) points out, does use the techniques of the detective story to unravel the hidden and suppressed identities in the novel.

Some detective figures appear prior to *Bleak House*. The BOW STREET RUNNERS are called in to help solve the robbery at Mrs. Maylie's house in CHERTSEY (*Twist*, 31); Nadgett, a private investigator working for Tigg, uncovers Jonas Chuzzlewit's guilt (51). The most significant detective in the later novels is the Inspector in *Mutual Friend* who solves the Harmon murder.

By including detectives in his novels, Dickens was reflecting the major changes in policing during his lifetime. Robert Peel's Metropolitan Police Force was established in 1829, replacing the army and such semiprivate operations as the Bow Street Runners as keepers of public order. The Detective Department came into being in 1842, so the evolution of the detective in Dickens's novels from Bow Street Runner to private investigator to Department Inspector reflects this historical transition. Several of Dickens's magazine articles describe the work of these new policemen and detectives, most notably "The Detective Police," "Three Detective Anecdotes," "On Duty with Inspector Field," and "Down with the Tide" (*Reprinted*).

Had Dickens finished *Drood*, that novel might have most completely fulfilled the definition of the detective story. Written under the influence of WILKIE COLLINS, it seems to involve a crime in the murder or disappearance of Drood, and Datchery may be a detective in disguise. Ian Ousby (*Bloodhounds of Heaven: The Detective in English Fiction from Godwin to Doyle*, 1976) includes Dickens's detectives among those he discusses.

Devonshire House   Duke of Devonshire's house in PICCADILLY where Dickens and his troupe of actors presented Bulwer-Lytton's *Not So Bad as We Seem* at a benefit for the GUILD OF LITERATURE AND ART, a performance attended by the Queen and Prince Consort on May 16, 1851. After a second performance on May 27, the Duke gave a ball and supper for the actors.

Devonshire Terrace   Dickens lived at number 1 in this street off Marylebone Road, Regent's Park, from 1839 to 1851.

Dexter, Walter (1877–1944)   Author and editor of numerous books relating to Dickens; editor of the DICKENSIAN, 1925–44; leader in the effort to secure the DICKENS HOUSE for a library and museum. Dexter wrote a brief biography of Dickens (1927) and several volumes on Dickensian TOPOGRAPHY; he also made several collections of Dickens's letters, culminating in the collection for the NONESUCH EDITION, the scholarly edition

The house in Devonshire Terrace occupied by Dickens and his family from December 1839 until November 1851.

of the LETTERS recently replaced by the Pilgrim Edition.

Dexter Collection, the J. F. Dickens materials acquired by the British Library in 1969, cataloged in *Charles Dickens: The J. F. Dexter Collection* (1974). The collection includes the manuscripts of two essays, many letters, the preface to *Twist*, proof copies of illustrations by HABLOT KNIGHT BROWNE and GEORGE CRUIKSHANK, and some sets of the novels in parts.

dialect Dickens uses a wide range of regional and class dialects in the novels, usually marking such speech with a few recognizable characteristics rather than attempting to represent a totally accurate transcription. Compare, for example, John Browdie's Yorkshire speech in *Nickleby* with the much fuller rendering of a Yorkshire dialect in Emily Bronte's sometimes unintelligible Joseph in *Wuthering Heights.* Dickens represents class dialects

more fully, especially the languages used by various London subcultures, from the thieves' slang in *Twist* to the upper-class dialect spoken at the Veneering's supper table in *Mutual Friend.* G. L. Brook (*The Language of Dickens,* 1970) and Robert Golding (*Idiolects in Dickens,* 1985) undertake linguistic analyses of the various dialects that appear in the novels.

Diamond Edition American edition of Dickens's works with illustrations by SOLOMON EYTINGE, published by TICKNOR & FIELDS in 1867.

Dickens, Alfred Allen (b. 1813) Dickens's younger brother who died in infancy.

Dickens, Alfred D'Orsay Tennyson (1845–1912) Dickens's fourth son, named for his two godfathers, and nicknamed "Skittles" by his father. He was not suited for the military career that Dickens encouraged, and at age 20, he emigrated to Australia, where he married Jessie Devlin, "the Belle of Melbourne" and had a successful career with the London and Australia Agency Company Ltd. After his father's death, he lectured on Dickens's life and works in England and America. He died in New York on one of his lecture tours. He wrote "My Father and His Friends" (*Nash's Magazine*, 1911).

Dickens, Alfred Lamert (1822–1860)   Dickens's younger brother; a civil engineer and sanitary inspector who left a widow and five children when he died. Dickens aided the family but found his sister-in-law Helen irritating.

Dickens,   Augustus (1827–1866)   Dickens's youngest brother. It was his infant pronounciation of his nickname "Moses" that produced "Boses" and, eventually, "Boz." Although Dickens helped find him a job in London, Augustus deserted his wife and eloped to America with another woman. He died penniless in Chicago. Dickens contributed to the support of his American family and the deserted wife in England.

Dickens, Catherine Hogarth ("Kate") (1815–1879)   Dickens's wife; mother to his ten children; eldest daughter of GEORGE HOGARTH, music critic on the MORNING CHRONICLE and editor of the EVENING CHRONICLE when Dickens as a young man was working as a journalist. She married Dickens on April 2, 1836. An amiable, conventional, and domestic woman, she deferred to her husband, who increasingly found her unresponsive, clumsy, and indolent and an incompetent mother and housekeeper. Some of her duties as housekeeper and hostess were assumed by her younger sister GEORGINA, who moved into the household after the trip to America in 1842. During the 1850s the marriage gradually deteriorated until, in 1857, Charles and Catherine took separate bedrooms, and in 1858 they legally separated. Catherine moved into London with Charley, her oldest child; the other children and Georgina remained at GAD'S HILL with Dickens. Bitter and self-pitying, Catherine nonetheless remained loyal to her husband. Hebe Elsna (*Unwanted Wife: A Defence of Mrs. Charles Dickens*, 1963) describes Catherine's relationship with her husband from Catherine's point of view.

Dickens, Charles Culliford ("Charley") (1837–1896)   Dickens's oldest child. Educated at Eton, he entered a business career, working for Baring's Bank and then going into trade with China. After he went bankrupt in 1868, Dickens made him a subeditor on ALL THE YEAR ROUND. He accompanied his father on the final reading tour and owned GAD'S HILL for a time after Dickens's death. In 1862, he married ELIZABETH ("*Bessie*") EVANS, daughter of Dickens's former publisher. Dickens, who had quarreled with BRADBURY & EVANS, disapproved of the marriage and did not attend the wedding, but he was reconciled with them and his first grandchild, MARY ANGELA, at Christmas 1862. Charley and Bessie had eight children. Charley, who gave public readings of his father's work and lectures about him, published "Dickens as an Editor" (*English Illustrated Magazine*, 1889) and "Glimpses of Charles Dickens" (*North American Review*, 1895). His "Reminiscences of My Father" appeared posthumously in *Windsor Magazine* in 1934.

Dickens, Dora Annie (1850–1851)   Dickens's ninth child, born while *Copperfield* was appearing and named for David's wife. A frail infant, she died at eight months on April 14, 1851.

Dickens, Edward Bulwer Lytton ("Plorn") (1852–1902)   Dickens's 10th and youngest child, a favorite of his father. Sensitive and shy, he did not do well in school and in 1868, at age 17, he was sent by his grieving father to join his brother ALFRED in AUSTRALIA, where he never prospered. He died there in 1902.

Dickens, Elizabeth Ball (1745?–1814)   Dickens's paternal grandmother, a servant in the household of John Crewe, a member of Parliament.

Dickens, Elizabeth Barrow (1789–1863)   Dickens's mother. She married JOHN DICKENS in 1809. Charles was the second of eight children. Although she taught him as a child, he never forgave her for suggesting that he continue to work at WARREN'S BLACKING after her husband was released from prison. He caricatured her as the garrulous Mrs.

Nickleby and used her more sympathetically as the original of Mrs. Micawber (*Copperfield*).

Dickens, Frances Elizabeth ("Fanny") (1810–1848) Dickens's older sister and his fast friend in childhood. Dickens envied her opportunity to study at the Royal Academy of Music while he was working in the BLACKING WAREHOUSE. She received a scholarship and was awarded a silver medal in 1824. She continued at the academy, on and off, until 1834. In 1837 she married HENRY BURNETT, a fellow student at the academy, and they settled in MANCHESTER. Their crippled son, HENRY JR., who died in 1848, was the model for Paul Dombey and Tiny Tim. Fanny appears in the *Carol* as sister Fan, who rescues Scrooge from school, and in "A Child's Dream of a Star." She died of consumption at 38.

Dickens, Francis Jeffrey ("Frank") (1844–1886) Dickens's fifth child, named after his godfather, FRANCIS JEFFREY. He went to India in 1863 and served in the Bengal Mounted Police, returning to England in 1871. Eventually he joined the Canadian Northwest Mounted Police and died in America in 1886.

Dickens, Frederick (1820–1868) Dickens's younger brother. He lived with Dickens and traveled to ITALY with him, but he offended his brother by using Dickens's name to obtain credit and by sponging from him. Dickens may have had him in mind when creating Fred Trent in *Curiosity Shop*. On his death, Dickens remarked, "It was a wasted life, but God forbid that one should be hard upon it, or upon anything in this world that is not deliberately and coldly wrong."

Dickens, Harriet (1819–?) Dickens's sister, fifth child in the family, who died in childhood.

Dickens, Sir Henry Fielding ("Harry") (1849–1933) Dickens's eighth child, the most successful of his children. Educated at BOULOGNE and ROCHESTER, Harry started the GAD'S HILL GAZETTE with his brother EDWARD. Harry went on to Cambridge, won a scholarship and an essay prize, and afterward pursued a distinguished career in the law,

becoming a Queen's Counsel. He was knighted in 1922. In 1876, he married Marie Thérèse Louise Roche; they had seven children. In 1904 he gave public readings of his father's work. He published *Memories of My Father* (1928), "A Chat about my Father" (*Harper's Magazine*, 1914), and *Recollections* (1934).

Dickens, John (1785–1851) Dickens's father. A clerk in the Navy Pay Office, he married ELIZABETH BARROW in 1809. They had eight children. John's work took him from London to PORTSEA, where Charles was born in 1812; back to London in 1815; to CHATHAM in 1817; and finally back to London in 1822. A convivial man but a poor money manager, he was always in debt; in 1824, he was imprisoned in the MARSHALSEA for three months for a debt of £40. His conviviality led to his being chosen the chairman of the prisoners' committee in the short time he was there. After his release, he became a reporter, but he was again arrested for debt in 1834 and rescued by his son. In later years, he traded on Charles's fame to obtain credit, and he became a financial and emotional burden on his son, who deplored his financial irresponsibility. He served as a model, at least in part, for Micawber in *Copperfield* and for William Dorrit.

Dickens, Kate Macready ("Katey") (1839–1929) Dickens's third child, goddaughter of the actor WILLIAM MACREADY. Temperamental and high-spirited, she had a talent for art and studied at Bedford College. She took her mother's side in the separation. In 1858 she married the painter CHARLES ALLSTON COLLINS, prompting her father to conclude that she did so to get away from home. After Collins's death, she married Carlo Perugini, also a painter. Her interviews with GLADYS STOREY many years later gave her version of her father's relationship with ELLEN TERNAN and were the basis of Storey's revelatory book, *Dickens and Daughter* (1939).

Dickens, Laetitia Mary (1816–1893) Dickens's younger sister. She married architect and artist Henry Austin in 1837 and was widowed in 1862.

Acting as her advocate, Dickens secured a government pension for her.

Dickens, Mary ("Mamie") (1838–1896)   Dickens's second child and eldest daughter. Gentle and mild-tempered, she was nicknamed "Mild Glos'ter" by her father, who had named her for MARY HOGARTH, her aunt who died a year before her birth. She remained with Dickens after the separation, serving with GEORGINA HOGARTH as his housekeeper and companion, and she did not visit her mother until after her father's death. She continued to live with Georgina, editing her father's LETTERS with her. She published her reminiscences in *My Father as I Recall Him* (1897).

Dickens, Mary Angela ("Mekitty") (1862–1948)   Dickens's first grandchild, eldest child of CHARLEY. She and the other grandchildren called Dickens "Venerables" as he disliked the title Grandfather. In "My Grandfather as I Knew Him" (*Nash's Magazine*, 1911), she recounts the mixture of awe and fear that she felt in Dickens's presence and the "dreadful moment" of seeing him cry at the final reading of the *Carol*. She was the author of eight novels, including *The Debtor* (1912) and *The Wastrel* (1900).

Dickens, Monica (1915–   )   Dickens's great-granddaughter, grandchild of Henry. Author of numerous works of fiction and nonfiction, she remembers her grandfather's performances of his father's works and discusses her literary inheritance from Dickens in *An Open Book* (1978).

Dickens, Sydney Smith Haldimand (1847–1872)   Dickens's seventh child, nicknamed "Ocean Spectre" for the faraway look in his eyes, as if he were gazing out to sea. Although Dickens was pleased by the boy's choice of a naval career, he was irritated by his extravagance and refused him financial help. Sydney died at sea at age 25 on his way back to England for sick leave.

Dickens, Walter Savage Landor (1841–1863)   Dickens's fourth child, named for his godfather, the poet LANDOR. With the help of ANGELA BURDETT-COUTTS, he was nominated to a cadetship in the East India Company and sailed to India in 1857. He rose to the rank of lieutenant in the 42nd Highlanders and distinguished himself during the Indian Mutiny. Although he was granted sick leave, he died in Calcutta before returning to England, leaving many unpaid debts for his father to settle.

Dickens, William, Jr. (1719–1785)   Dickens's paternal grandfather, a butler at Crewe Hall.

Dickens Fellowship   Organization to promote Dickens's works and preserve his memory. Founded in 1902 and headquartered in London, the fellowship has local branches throughout the world. It administers the DICKENS HOUSE at 48 DOUGHTY STREET as a museum and library and publishes the *DICKENSIAN*, a quarterly devoted to Dickens and his work.

Dickens House   The house at 48 DOUGHTY STREET where Dickens lived from 1837 to 1839 and wrote some of *Pickwick* and *Twist*, all of *Nickleby*, and the beginnings of *Rudge*. It is now the headquarters of the DICKENS FELLOWSHIP and a Dickens museum and library.

Dickensian, The   Journal of the DICKENS FELLOWSHIP, which began publication as a monthly magazine in January 1905 under the editorship of B. W. MATZ. FREDERIC KITTON was originally supposed to edit the journal, but he died before its inception. Matz remained editor until his death in 1925. The journal was published monthly until 1919, when a rise in the cost of paper increased production costs and the journal became a quarterly. CHAPMAN & HALL were its publishers until 1921. Later editors include WALTER DEXTER (1925–44), LESLIE STAPLES (1944–68), MICHAEL SLATER (1968–77), ANDREW SANDERS (1978–86), Margaret Reynolds (1986–91), and MALCOLM ANDREWS (1991–   ). The character of the journal has changed over the years following trends in Dickens studies. In the early years many articles on biographical, topographic, and historical points appeared as well as numerous appreciations of Dickens and his works. As Dickens criticism became more professional in the 1940s and 1950s and Dickens earned greater academic interest, the journal devoted more space to academic criticism. In recent years the journal has become so academic that it has seemed, to some of its readers, too serious, though it remains the best source for information on Dickensiana, biography, and illustrations. Articles by most important Dickens scholars and critics appear in the journal. Among the significant contributors to the journal in its early years, sometimes referred to as the great "amateur scholars" of the early 20th century, were MATZ, J. W. T. LEY, J. CUMING WALTERS, ARTHUR WAUGH, WALTER DEXTER, WILLOUGHBY MATCHETT, J. H. MCNULTY, T. W. HILL, MALCOLM MORLEY, and W. J. CARLTON.

Dickens Project An organization of American teachers, scholars, and other Dickensians, founded by Murray Baumgarten and headquartered at the University of California, Santa Cruz. It sponsors the Dickens Universe, an annual seminar for teachers and others on one of Dickens's novels; an annual scholarly conference on topics relating to Dickens; and various other activities to promote interest in Dickens and his works. It publishes an occasional newsletter, *The Dickens Round.*

Dickens Quarterly Initiated in 1984 as the successor to DICKENS STUDIES NEWSLETTER, this scholarly journal published by the DICKENS SOCIETY contains articles on Dickens, reviews of recent books, a checklist of recent publications, and announcements of Dickensian activities in America and elsewhere.

Dickens Society Founded in 1970 by Robert B. Partlow Jr., the society is dedicated "to conduct, encourage, foster, further, and support research, publication, instruction and general interest in the life, times, and literature of Charles Dickens." It holds an annual meeting and dinner during the convention of the Modern Language Association, publishes the DICKENS QUARTERLY, and sponsors the Robert B. Partlow prize for the best, first article-length publication during the preceding year.

Dickens Studies American academic journal devoted to Dickens, founded and edited by NOEL PEYROUTON and published quarterly from 1965 to 1969.

Dickens Studies Annual Successor to DICKENS STUDIES, this annual collection of articles on Dickens—and, recently, on Victorian literature generally—often includes several articles on a particular novel or topic and has, in recent years, published several papers from the annual conference of the DICKENS PROJECT.

Dickens Studies Newsletter Begun in 1970 as the publication of the American DICKENS SOCIETY, this publication gradually became more of a scholarly journal than a newsletter, becoming the DICKENS QUARTERLY in 1984.

Dilke, Charles Wentworth (1789–1864) Journalist and editor of THE ATHENAEUM, Dilke was a fellow clerk at SOMERSET HOUSE with JOHN DICKENS when Charles was working at WARREN'S BLACKING. When John introduced the boy to his friend, Dilke gave him a half crown and received a very low bow in return. Many years later, when JOHN FORSTER told Dickens of Dilke's memory of this episode, Dickens was deeply disturbed and Forster felt he "had unintentionally touched a painful place in his memory."

Disraeli, Benjamin (1804–1881) Politician and novelist, first earl of Beaconsfield. Although Dickens had known Disraeli in the 1830s as one of the other authors who regularly attended the COUNTESS OF BLESSINGTON's salon, he had never liked him. In the heat of the battle for repeal of the CORN LAWS, Dickens, an advocate of repeal, described Disraeli, leader of the conservative Young England movement and an opponent of repeal, as an "impostor and Humbug." Disraeli is probably the politician satirized as "the honourable member for Verbosity" in Dickens's essay "Our Honourable Friend." As a novelist Disraeli is best known for his trilogy of political novels: *Coningsby* (1844), *Sybil* (1845), and *Tancred* (1847). A leader of the Conservative right, he served as prime minister in 1868 and again from 1874 to 1880.

divorce   Divorces were difficult and very expensive to obtain in Victorian England. They required a decree from the ecclesiastical court in Doctors' Commons (*see* COURTS), followed by a private act of Parliament. The only acceptable grounds were a wife's adultery or a husband's adultery if accompanied by cruelty, incest, bigamy, or bestiality. When Stephen Blackpool asks how much a divorce would cost, Bounderby summarizes the procedure and costs for him: "Why, you'd have to go to Doctors' Commons with a suit, and you'd have to go to a court of Common Law with a suit, and you'd have to go to the House of Lords with a suit, and you'd have to get an Act of Parliament to enable you to marry again, and it would cost you (if it was very plain sailing), I suppose from a thousand to fifteen hundred pound" (*Hard Times*, I:11). Blackpool's frustration at being trapped by the marriage laws has sometimes been seen as representing Dickens's growing unhappiness in his own marriage at the time. In 1850, in "The Murdered Person," he criticized those who supported strict divorce laws for not taking into account those who suffered under such laws.

When Dickens's marriage disintegrated in 1857, he ruled out a divorce as too expensive. He was thinking both of the money an action would cost and of the damage to his reputation and career. Instead of a divorce, Dickens and his wife worked out a separation, with the details negotiated by JOHN FORSTER and MARK LEMON.

In 1857, Parliament passed the Divorce and Matrimonial Causes Act that slightly liberalized the grounds for divorce and moved the action from the ecclesiastical to a civil court. However, the act did not equalize the grounds for men and women, and it did not significantly broaden the grounds for divorce. It did not sanction divorce on grounds of incompatibility, for example, the reason Dickens gave for his own domestic unhappiness.

Dolby, George (d. 1900)   Manager of Dickens's reading tours from 1866 until Dickens's death. Though he began as a servant to the "Chief," he became a trusted friend and companion, "as tender as a woman and as watchful as a doctor." He described his days with Dickens in *Charles Dickens as I Knew Him: The Story of the Reading Tours, 1866–1870* (1885).

doppelgänger   German term for the DOUBLE, especially in romantic literature, in which a ghost, apparition, or dream figure replicates a living person. (*See* DOUBLE.)

D'Orsay, Alfred Count (1801–1852)   French aristocrat and artist who moved to London in the 1820s and became a leader in fashion, the "Prince of Dandies." His scandalous relationship with the COUNTESS OF BLESSINGTON and her husband made him the talk of London. He presided over her fashionable salon at Gore House, where Dickens probably met him in 1840. D'Orsay was godfather to Dickens's sixth child, ALFRED.

Dostoevski, Feodor Mikhailovich (1821–1881)   Russian novelist, author of *Crime and Punishment* (1866), *The Idiot* (1868), *The Brothers Karamazov* (1880), and other novels; a great admirer of Dickens. He knew Dickens's novels well and drew on them for inspiration and as models for his own fiction, most notably in his portrayal of Prince Myshkin in *The Idiot*, based, in part, on Pickwick. Although Dickens's darker novels like *Bleak House* and *Little Dorrit* are often considered "Dostoyevskian," the Russian found Dickens's works "idealistic" and "calming" and was more drawn to the earlier works. Extended studies of the relationship between the two authors include FANGER's (1965), N. M. Lary's *Dostoevsky and Dickens* (1973), and Loralee MacPike's *Dostoevsky's Dickens* (1981).

double   A character who replicates, diametrically contrasts, or represents part of another character. Dickens bases his character thematics on this technique from romantic literature. He sometimes uses doubling as a form of incremental REPETITION, as, for example, with the Cheeryble Brothers (*Nickleby*), the Flintwinch brothers (*Dorrit*), or Charity and Mercy Pecksniff (*Chuzzlewit*). Such characters underscore each other through repetition. Doubles also are often contrasting figures. Their relationship as doubles may be indicated in their physical appearance, their names, or family connections, but in other respects they are opposites to each other, as, for example, are John and James Carker (*Dombey*), Oliver Twist and Monks (*Twist*), or Samuel Pickwick and Sam Weller (*Pickwick*). By combining and mixing repetition and contrast, Dickens can suggest complexity in his characters and ambiguity in theme. Edith Dombey and Alice Marwood, cousins who physically resemble each other and who both have manipulative mothers, appear to be social opposites, one living at the top of society and the other at the bottom, but both are "sold" in the sexual marketplace and both become

Furniss's illustration (1910) of Sydney Carton and Charles Darnay for *A Tale of Two Cities* emphasizes their roles as doubles.

entangled with James Carker (*Dombey*). Their stories both contrast and repeat each other's.

In psychological terms, the double represents an alter ego, a part of the self split from conscious recognition and experienced as other. Dickens's identity plots are often based on this psychological assumption. When David Copperfield asks whether he "shall turn out to be the hero of [his] own life, or whether that station will be held by anybody else" (1), his story frames that question in terms of a series of doubles whom he must recognize and deal with to achieve an integrated sense of himself. Nearly every character in David's account of his life is a partial double to him: Micawber, for example, represents the incompetence David inherits from his father; Murdstone his desire for firmness and order; Heep his ambition and "humbleness"; Steerforth his snobbery. David must connect these parts of himself to overcome the psychological decomposition of his character and to "turn out to be the hero" of his own life. Dickens repeats this mode of characterization and psychological analysis in novel after novel, achieving a greater degree of integration or composition in the later novels.

The doubles in the later novels also articulate the MYTH of the double as described in Freudian terms by Otto Rank (*The Double*, 1971). The stories of Charles Darnay and Sydney Carton or of Eugene Wrayburn and Bradley Headstone, for example, depend on a dynamic where the survival of one of the doubled characters depends on the sacrifice of the other.

LAWRENCE FRANK (1984) discusses Dickens's use of the double in several novels; his analysis of *Copperfield*, while based on similar premises, is markedly different from that offered by Loralee MacPike (*Dostoevsky's Dickens*, 1981). Julian Moynahan's "The Hero's Guilt: The Case of *Great Expectations*" (*Essays in Criticism*, 1960) is the classic analysis of the use of doubling in *Expectations*.

Doughty Street   Dickens lived at No. 48 on this street in Bloomsbury from 1837 to 1839, and he finished *Pickwick* and *Twist*, wrote all of *Nickleby*,

Dickens lived in this house on Doughty Street, now a Dickens museum, from April 1837 to December 1839.

and began *Rudge* here. Since 1921, the house has served as the headquarters of the DICKENS FELLOWSHIP and as a Dickens library and museum.

Dover   Channel port in KENT mentioned frequently in Dickens's novels, most importantly as Betsey Trotwood's home (*Copperfield*, 13). Arthur Clennam returns from China via Dover (*Dorrit*, I:3). Lorry meets Lucie Manette at the Royal George Hotel here (*Two Cities*, I:3). The Traveller passes through Dover on journeys to the Continent (*Uncommercial*, 7, 18).

Dover Road   David's trek to DOVER in search of his Aunt Betsey (*Copperfield*, 13) and Lorry's coach journey on his way to Paris (*Two Cities*, I:2) describe the route between London and Dover.

Doyle, Richard (1824–1883) Illustrator for PUNCH. He contributed illustrations—usually those on the initial page of the separate chapters—for *Chimes, Cricket,* and *Battle*. Dickens did not know Doyle well, and there was little or no consultation between them about the illustrations.

drama   Dickens's fascination with the theater was evident from childhood on. His earliest known work, written when he was just a child, was the tragedy *Misnar, the Sultan of India*. He also wrote several farces that were produced in London during the early years of his writing career: *The Strange Gentleman* (1836), *The Village Coquettes* (1836), *Is She His Wife?* (1837), and *The Lamplighter* (1838). Later, he collaborated with MARK LEMON on *Mr. Nightingale's Diary* (1851) and with WILKIE COLLINS on THE LIGHTHOUSE (1856), THE FROZEN DEEP (1857), and *No Thoroughfare* (1867).

Although Dickens was a mediocre dramatist, his novels adopt many conventions of the theater and the drama to prose narrative. WILLIAM AXTON (1966) discusses the ways in which the Victorian theater influenced Dickens's vision and style. ROBERT GARIS (1965) describes Dickens's novels themselves as theatrical performances.

After illness forced him to cancel an audition at COVENT GARDEN Theatre in 1831, Dickens's ambitions as an actor were satisfied in his AMATEUR THEATRICALS and PUBLIC READINGS. He counted theater people, especially WILLIAM MACREADY and CHARLES FECHTER, among his close friends.

His novels contain many scenes in the theater, from his sketches in *Boz* of private theaters to his hilarious account of Wopsle's *Hamlet* in such a theater (*Expectations*, 31). The episodes describing Crummles's theatrical company are pivotal, both structurally and theatrically, in *Nickleby*. EDGAR and Eleanor JOHNSON's anthology (*The Dickens Theatrical Reader*, 1964) collects many of these passages. In *Dramatic Dickens* (1989), Carol

MacKay has collected a series of papers on various aspects of Dickens's work in relation to the drama.

All of Dickens's novels were adapted for the stage, even before they had completed their serial run. These adaptations are described by MALCOLM MORLEY in a series of articles for the DICKENSIAN (1946–56), by F. Dubrez Fawcett (*Dickens the Dramatist*, 1952), and by H. Philip Bolton (*Dickens Dramatized*, 1987).

dream allegory A common form in medieval literature in which the narrator falls asleep and dreams the allegorical story that the work has to tell. Bunyan used the form in *Pilgrim's Progress*, a work that Dickens alludes to frequently. Dickens employs a version of dream allegory, in which a transforming vision or dream prompts a change of heart, in some of the CHRISTMAS BOOKS. Dickens's dream allegories differ from their medieval predecessors in that the dreams are not those of his narrators.

Drummond Street In this street off Euston Square in northwest London, Dickens and his schoolmates from WELLINGTON HOUSE ACADEMY pretended to be beggars. Miss Amelia Martin maintains her millinery and dressmaking establishment at No. 7 (*Boz*, "Mistaken Milliner").

Drury Lane Street in central London famous for the Drury Lane Theatre, where Miss Petowker of Crummles's theatrical company performed (*Nickleby*, 14). Dick Swiveller's lodgings are located over a tobacconist's shop here (*Curiosity Shop*, 7), and David Copperfield orders beef at an à la mode restaurant here (11), as Dickens himself had done as a boy. The graveyard where Captain Hawdon is buried is nearby (*Bleak House*). Also mentioned in *Boz*, "Astley's," "Broker's," "Gin-shops," "Pawnbroker's," "Shabby-genteel People," *Uncommercial* (4, 25, 35).

Dumas, Alexandre (1802–1870) French novelist and dramatist, author of *The Count of Monte Cristo* (1844) and other works. Dickens visited Dumas in Paris in 1844 with WILLIAM MACREADY and attended a performance of his play *Christine*.

dustheaps Central symbol in *Mutual Friend*, these heaps of rubbish are the source of John Harmon's

The dustheaps in Victorian London provided subsistence for scavengers and made some of their owners rich men, like the elder John Harmon in *Our Mutual Friend*.

wealth and comprise the inheritance he passes on to his son and the Boffins.

Dyson, A. E. (1928–2002) Scholar and literary critic, especially interested in the Christian dimensions of literary works; editor of Dickens criticism (*Dickens: Modern Judgments*, 1968; *Dickens' Bleak House: A Casebook,* 1969) and author of *The Inimitable Dickens* (1970), a celebration of Dickens's works with critical essays on 12 of the novels, especially on Christian thematic elements in them.

Eagle Inn   Famous pleasure garden and tavern in the CITY ROAD in northeast London where musical entertainments were held. Dickens describes it in "Miss Evans and the Eagle" (*Boz*) and in "Amusements of the People."

early Victorian age   Although QUEEN VICTORIA did not take the throne until 1837, the Victorian period is usually dated from 1832, the year of the First REFORM BILL and the death of SIR WALTER SCOTT, and extends to the turn of the century with Victoria's death in 1901. The Early Victorian Period, from 1832 to 1851, the year of the Crystal Palace Exhibition, was characterized by rapid social and political change, vigorous public controversy, and near revolution in the Chartist Movement (*see* CHARTISM) of the 1840s. In literature the period is marked by the emergence of the novel as the dominant literary form. Dickens produced half of his major works during this period; his prolific output, comic exuberance, and social concerns were typical of the novels of the time. G. K. Young's *Victorian England: Portrait of an Age* is a standard history of the period; KATHLEEN TILLOTSON's *Novels of the Eighteen-forties* (1956) is the classic study of the early Victorian novel.

Easthope, John   (1784–1865)   Stockbroker, liberal politician, and publisher of the MORNING CHRONICLE. He took over the paper in 1833 and hired Dickens in 1834. An irascible and peremptory man, he was known as "Blasthope" to his employees. Dickens, during his years working as a reporter on the paper from 1834 to 1836, represented the reporters in a successful negotiation with him.

East India House   Headquarters of the East India Company in LEADENHALL Street in the CITY of London, just around the corner from Dombey and Son. It is a "magnificent" building, "teeming with suggestions of precious stuffs and stones, tigers, elephants, howdahs, hookahs, umbrellas, palm trees, palanquins, and gorgeous princes of a brown complexion sitting on carpets" (*Dombey*, 4). Bob Sawyer and Ben Allen both go abroad on surgical appointments with the East India Company (*Pickwick*, 57).

Edinburgh, Scotland   Dickens went to Edinburgh as a reporter for the MORNING CHRONICLE in 1834 and subsequently set the story "The Bagman's Uncle" in Canongate. A dinner in his honor was held here in 1841. He gave readings here in 1858, 1861, and 1869.

editor, Dickens as   Throughout most of his writing career, Dickens was also engaged as the editor of various periodicals for which he not only wrote himself but also solicited and edited the work of other writers. These editorial enterprises included *BENTLEY'S MISCELLANY* (February 1837–April 1839),

Master Humphrey's Clock (April 4, 1840–December 4, 1841), *DAILY NEWS* (January 21, 1846–February 9, 1846), *HOUSEHOLD WORDS* (March 27, 1850–May 28, 1859), and *ALL THE YEAR ROUND* (April 30, 1859–his death). Although W. H. WILLS served as Dickens's subeditor on the most important of these projects, Dickens was an active copy editor, reworking and even cowriting many of the articles. He was also an active editor in chief, particularly in soliciting materials from other writers and guiding the content of the magazines.

Detailed discussions of Dickens's practices as an editor, particularly of *HOUSEHOLD WORDS*, can be found in the introductions to HARRY STONE (*Uncollected Writings from* Household Words, 1968) and Anne Lohrli's index and reference book on *Household Words* (1973). R. C. Lehman's collection of Dickens's letters to Wills, *Charles Dickens as Editor* (1912), gives some insight into Dickens's role as editor.

education Dickens's own education was limited to a year or so with WILLIAM GILES in CHATHAM and almost three years at WELLINGTON HOUSE ACADEMY after his father was released from the DEBTORS' PRISON. Beyond this he was largely self-educated, teaching himself shorthand to become a parliamentary reporter and reading at the BRITISH MUSEUM, for which he obtained a reader's ticket as soon as he was eligible at age 18. Perhaps because his own education had been so restricted or because he wrote so often about the lives of children, Dickens had a great deal to say about education in his articles and novels, and he depicted schools and teachers in many of his books. PHILIP COLLINS's *Dickens and Education* (1963), the standard work on this topic, takes four pages to list the articles and novels that include schools or remarks on education.

Dickens was a lifelong advocate of national schools, which were not approved by Parliament until 1870, the year of his death. At the same time, he opposed condescending education for the poor, designed to teach them to know their place. He satirized such efforts in the Charitable Grinders School in *Dombey* and in the school where Uriah Heep learned false humility in *Copperfield.*

Many of the schools in the novels exemplify other kinds of educational abuse. Dotheboy's Hall (*Nickleby*) illustrated the neglect and brutality of the Yorkshire schools, where unwanted children were relegated to oblivion. Salem House, Creakle's school in *Copperfield,* based on Dickens's experience at Wellington House, also makes liberal use of corporal punishment and judges its students by their family's social standing. Dr. Blimber's Academy (*Dombey*) is an educational hothouse that forces its students to premature growth—and death—with its heady regimen of classical languages and history. M'Choakumchild's classroom of hard fact in *Hard Times* may be Dickens's most famous school; it offers a satiric version of a UTILITARIAN education, wholly devoted to fact and absolutely opposed to fancy. It has the predictable effect of leaving its graduates incapable of acting on feeling or of making ethical choices. Bradley Headstone's (*Mutual Friend*) preparation as a schoolmaster is similar to that of M'Choakumchild. Both are products of the new teachers' training institutes. Bradley's learning and teaching is "mechanical" and does not enable him to govern his passions.

The most positively presented school in the novels is Doctor Strong's Academy (*Copperfield*). Although Dickens does not give details of the school's curriculum, he does show how David learns from the doctor and his young wife the most important lesson for his own life—the need for "a disciplined heart."

Egg, Augustus (1816–1863) Artist and friend of Dickens who participated in many of Dickens's AMATEUR THEATRICALS, acting and designing costumes. He went to Italy with Dickens and WILKIE COLLINS in 1853. In the mid-1850s, he proposed to Dickens's sister-in-law, GEORGINA HOGARTH, but she refused to marry him.

Eigner, Edwin (1931–) Professor, University of California, Riverside; founding member of the DICKENS PROJECT; scholar and writer on Dickens, Stevenson, and other Victorian writers. *The Metaphysical Novel in England and America: Dickens, Bulwer, Melville, and Hawthorne* (1978) discusses a subgenre in which Dickens and other writers were working. These novels mix romance and realism and are based in an idealistic aesthetic derived from Kant and Hegel rather than in the realistic tradition coming from Locke and Aristotle. In *The Dickens Pantomime* (1989), Eigner explores elements of traditional PANTOMIME in Dickens's novels, especially in *David Copperfield,* where Micawber is a triumphant version of the pantomime clown.

Eisenstein, Sergei (1898–1948) Russian film director and pioneer in cinematography; best known for *Potemkin* (1915) and *Ten Days That Shook the World* (1927–28). He developed the use of MONTAGE as the basic technique of cinematic storytelling. In "Dickens, Griffith, and the Film Today" (in *Film Form*), Eisenstein described Dickens's "head-spinning tempo of changing impressions" as part of the "urbanism" of his work, and he analyzed some scenes from *Twist* for their cinematic qualities, especially for their use of montage. A. L. Zambrano (1977) shows how the rhythm in Eisenstein's films, his use of parallel montage, and his associating of characters with objects derive from Dickens.

elections Dickens is not particularly kind to members of Parliament in the novels. Venal, egotistical, and devoted to humbug, they usually represent established power rather than act as agents of reform. He may have developed this image of politicians as a young man while recording parliamentary proceedings from the press gallery. His famous description of the Eatanswill election in *Pickwick* (13) was based on his experience covering the election in SUDBURY in 1835 for the MORNING CHRONICLE. His account of the contest between the Dedlock forces and Rouncewell the Ironmaster in *Bleak House* (40) dramatizes the shift from landed to industrial power in the years following the REFORM BILL OF 1832. Veneering's "election" (*Mutual Friend*, II:3) is simply a matter of buying the right to represent the borough of Pocket-Breeches, apparently unchanged by reforms in the electoral process. HUMPHRY HOUSE (1941) summed up Dickens's attitude toward the electoral process:

> He saw almost from his boyhood that the imperfections of Parliament were largely caused

by the initial corruption of its members through the very process of election. Influence, whether financial or social, counted for more than merit; the influence was more often than not corruptly exercised; and even when technical corruption did not enter in, the far more subtle corruption of electioneering promises and party propaganda undermined the morale of an M.P. from the start. Nearly all his attacks on Parliament can be reduced to this suspicion of the personal sincerity and independence of its members.

Thus, it was not surprising that when a group of liberal electors from Reading invited Dickens to run for Parliament, he declined to do so on the grounds that he was unwilling to give up his independence.

Eliot, George (Mary Ann Evans) (1819–1880) Though he once described Eliot and GEORGE LEWES as "the ugliest couple in London," Dickens was a great admirer of Eliot's work, especially *Adam Bede,* and he tried unsuccessfully to get her to write for ALL THE YEAR ROUND. Long before she revealed her identity, Dickens, when reading *Scenes of Clerical Life,* identified the author as a woman. On first meeting Dickens, Eliot found his appearance "disappointing—no benevolence in the face and I think little in the head." After dining with him some years later, she discovered "a strain of real seriousness along with his keenness and humour."

Eliot, Thomas Stearns (1888–1965) American poet, playwright, and critic; spokesman for and exemplar of literary modernism; best known for *The Waste Land* (1922). In "Wilkie Collins and Dickens" (1932; 1951), Eliot compared Dickens, preeminently a creator of character, with Collins, a master of plot. He suggested that much could be learned about both writers by studying their collaboration.

When he was working on *The Waste Land,* Eliot was reading *Our Mutual Friend,* and he took the original title for the poem from Betty Higden's remark that "Sloppy is a beautiful reader of the newspaper. He do the Police in different voices" (I:16). Although Eliot later changed the title, his original choice suggests the method of the poem in presenting a series of vignettes in different voices.

Calling *Mutual Friend* "Dickens's Waste Land," EDGAR JOHNSON (1952) compares the poem with the novel, noting the use of dustheaps, the polluted THAMES, and the MYTH of resurrection in both works.

Eliot, William Greenleaf (1811–1887)   Founder of Washington University in ST. LOUIS, grandfather of the poet, T. S. ELIOT, he was Dickens's host in St. Louis on his 1842 tour of AMERICA.

Elliotson, John (1791–1868)   Professor of medicine at the University of London and the leading English theorist of MESMERISM. He was the author of *Human Physiology* (1840) and *On Numerous Cases of Surgical Operations without Pain in the Mesmeric State* (1843) and the founder and editor of *The Zooist*, a journal of mesmerism and phrenology. He was a good friend of Dickens, influencing the novelist's interest and participation in mesmerism.

Ellis and Blackmore   The law firm located in GRAY'S INN to which Dickens was apprenticed in 1827. Dickens found the routine legal work on this job tedious.

Elm Cottage, Petersham   Dickens's summer house in 1839, while he was working on *Nickleby.*

Emerson, Ralph Waldo (1803–1882)   American essayist, poet, and transcendentalist. Dickens dined with him, THOMAS CARLYLE, and JOHN FORSTER in London in 1848. Carlyle, fulminating during the meal on the moral decline of England, shocked Emerson by proclaiming that male chastity was a thing of the past. Dickens continued the joke by assuring Emerson that if his son were "particularly chaste," he would be concerned about his health. After attending one of Dickens's readings in Boston in 1867, Emerson told ANNIE FIELDS, "I am afraid he has too much talent for his genius; it is a fearful locomotive to which he is bound and can never be free from it nor set it at rest. . . . He is too consummate an artist to have a thread of nature left. He daunts me! I have not the key!"

emigration   Dickens's frequent attacks on THOMAS MALTHUS's doctrine of surplus population would suggest that he would reject emigration, one of Malthus's cures for the problem. However, in the novels, in his work with URANIA COTTAGE, and in his journalism, Dickens promoted emigration as a solution to poverty. In "A Bundle of Emigrants' Letters," for example, he wrote, "It is unquestionably melancholy that thousands upon thousands of people, ready and willing to labour, should be wearing away life hopelessly in this island, while within a few months' sail—within a few weeks' when steam communication with Australia shall be established—there are vast tracts of country where no man who is willing to work hard . . . can ever know want." The women at Urania Cottage were encouraged to emigrate and start a new life there, as Em'ly and Martha Endell do in *Copperfield.* Dickens also encouraged his own sons FREDERICK and EDWARD DICKENS to settle in AUSTRALIA.

In the novels, emigration is often a convenient way to dispose of such criminal figures as Monks (*Twist*), Fred Trent (*Curiosity Shop*), or Tom Gradgrind (*Hard Times*). It can also be a test and a way to temper the arrogance of a character like young Martin Chuzzlewit, who is transformed by his time in AMERICA, or Pip, who learns to provide for himself in Egypt (*Expectations*). The novel that most fully exploits emigration as a way to resolve its themes is *Copperfield,* written at the height of Dickens's involvement with Urania Cottage. The Micawbers, Daniel Peggotty, Mrs. Gummidge, Em'ly, Martha Endell, and Mr. Mell all end up successful in Australia and their absence from England conveniently simplifies David's life.

Norris Pope (*Dickens and Charity,* 1978) discusses the controversy about emigration and Dickens's place in it.

"Empty Chair, The"   Famous watercolor painting by LUKE FILDES painted on the day of Dickens's death, showing the novelist's study with an empty chair by the writing desk.

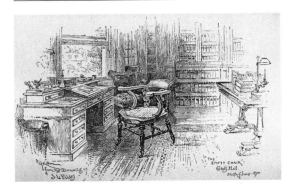

An engraving based on Fildes's painting "The Empty Chair."

Engel, Monroe (1921–) Novelist, critic, and Harvard professor, Engel has written on Dickens's social, political, and aesthetic ideas; in *The Maturity of Dickens* (1959), he makes extensive use of Dickens's journalism to explore these aspects of the novels.

Epping Forest An old-growth forest northeast of London, a destination for holiday excursions like those of the Young Ladies' Young Gentleman (*Young Gentlemen*) and the inmates of Titbull's Almshouses (*Uncommercial*, 29). CHIGWELL, site of the Maypole Inn, is on the south edge of the forest (*Rudge*).

Epsom Races Horse races held on the downs near Epsom, Surrey; the most famous race, the annual Derby, first run in 1780, is described in "Epsom," an article for HOUSEHOLD WORDS. Compeyson met Abel Magwich at the races (*Expectations*, 42). The races are also mentioned in *Reprinted*, "Three Detective Stories."

Evangelicalism Revival movement in the Church of England, stemming from 17th-century Puritanism and reaching fulfillment in the career of John Wesley (1703–91), whose conversion in 1738 is usually considered the beginning of the Evangelical movement. Evangelicals stressed the consciousness of sin; the experience of conversion; rigorous rules of personal conduct; the evangelical mission of the church, both at home and abroad, to convert oth-

ers to Christ; and the responsibility of Christians for social reform. While some Evangelicals left the Church of England to form splinter sects, most notably the Methodists and Wesleyans, others remained within the Anglican Church. Evangelicalism was influential well into the 19th century in giving impetus to movements for prison reform and the abolition of slavery; in promoting temperance, Sunday closing, and strict standards of behavior; and in promoting enthusiastic and participatory forms of worship.

Dickens often allied himself with Evangelicals on issues of social reform, as with LORD SHAFTESBURY on factory reform and the bill to limit the working day to 10 hours. He was strenuously opposed, however, to their sabbatarianism; in *Sunday under Three Heads* (1836), in other essays, and in the novels, he frequently attacked those who wanted to deny necessary amusement to working people.

Nearly all of his portraits of Evangelicals are satiric. Stiggins's Emmanuel Chapel (*Pickwick*), Little Bethel (*Curiosity Shop*), Melchisedech Howler's chapel of the "ranting persuasion" (*Dombey*), and Chadband's congregation (*Bleak House*) are all versions of the enthusiastic meetinghouse that duped susceptible women like Mrs. Weller, Mrs. Garland, Mrs. McStinger, and Mrs. Snagsby into becoming true believers. The enthusiastic preachers are nearly always hypocrites like Stiggins, who professes teetotalism but bears the red nose of drink, or like Chadband, who stuffs himself with muffins as he feeds the starving Jo only with words. Although he is not a clergyman, Pecksniff (*Chuzzlewit*) is the triumphant rendering of this Tartuffian strain in Evangelicalism.

Dickens was harsher in his treatment of the repressive and earnest negativism of the Evangelicals. There is nothing comic in his presentation of Mrs. Clennam (*Dorrit*), whose consciousness of sin and hypocrisy blight Arthur's childhood, produce her paralysis, and lead to her destruction. Even though they are not presented as figures defined by their religion, the Murdstones (*Copperfield*) and the unconverted Scrooge (*Carol*) possess similar repressive Evangelical earnestness.

The best discussion of Dickens and Evangelicalism appears in Norris Pope's *Dickens and Charity* (1978).

Evans, Frederick Mullet (d. 1870) Senior partner in the publishing firm BRADBURY & EVANS. A rotund, good-humoured man, known as "Pater" to the staff of PUNCH. When Evans refused in 1858 to publish in *Punch* Dickens's statement about his marital troubles, Dickens broke with him and two years later, refused to attend the wedding of his son CHARLES CULLIFORD DICKENS to Evans's daughter **Elizabeth ("Bessie") Evans** (d. 1907). Their friendship was never renewed.

Evening Chronicle The newspaper edited by Dickens's father-in-law, GEORGE HOGARTH, to which in 1835 Dickens contributed a number of sketches that were later collected in *Boz*.

Every Man in His Humour The play (1598) by BEN JONSON that Dickens's amateur players performed on numerous occasions, beginning in 1845. Dickens directed the play and performed the role of Bobadil.

Examiner, The Liberal weekly journal of politics and literature founded by John and LEIGH HUNT in 1808. JOHN FORSTER served as its literary editor from 1835 and as its managing editor from 1847 to 1855. Dickens contributed a number of reviews and articles to the paper, most of which are included in *Miscellaneous Papers* and *Journalism*.

Exeter Hall, Strand A meeting hall built in 1830–31, used for conventions and for religious meetings, especially the annual meeting of Evangelicals (*see* EVANGELICALISM) in May. Dickens satirizes it as the Haven of Philanthropy (*Drood*, 17). It is also briefly mentioned in *Nickleby* (5) and *Boz*, "Ladies' Societies."

Eyre, Governor Edward John (1815–1901) Colonial governor in Jamaica whose harsh imposition of martial law to suppress a native rebellion in 1865 provoked intense controversy in Britain. John Stuart Mill's Jamaica Committee attempted unsuccessfully to prosecute Eyre for murder. Dickens, along with THOMAS CARLYLE, JOHN RUSKIN, ALFRED, LORD TENNYSON, and others, joined in the defense of Eyre, arguing that stern measures were called for to prevent further violence.

Eytinge, Solomon (1833–1905) American genre painter and book illustrator who illustrated a number of early American editions of Dickens's works, most notably the DIAMOND EDITION. Dickens said of Eytinge's illustrations, "They are remarkable alike for a delicate perception of beauty, a lively eye for character, a most agreeable absence of exaggeration, and a general modesty and propriety which I greatly like." Examples of his work appear on pages 68, 69, 211, and 361.

F

fairy tales Dickens frequently alludes to fairy tales, traditional folk stories for children in which spirits from an invisible world intervene in the lives of the characters. Dickens treasured such stories from his own childhood; indeed, he credited them with saving him from despair during his dark days in the BLACKING WAREHOUSE. They "kept alive my fancy," he wrote, "and my hope of something beyond that place and time."

Dickens knew well the "Mother Goose" tales retold by CHARLES PERRAULT in France, the folk stories collected by the brothers Grimm in Germany, and similar collections of British tales, many of which first appeared during Dickens's childhood. He was particularly fond of the oriental fairy tales in THE ARABIAN NIGHTS, translated into English in the 18th century, and of James Ridley's mutations of such stories in the *Tales of the Genii* (1764). Allusions to all of these traditional stories appear frequently in nearly all of the novels. Although Dickens also knew the work of such 19th-century fabulists as E. T. A. Hoffmann and HANS CHRISTIAN ANDERSEN, who wrote original fairy tales, he did not draw on their stories as he did on the traditional ones.

So central are these traditional stories to Dickens's work that he developed what HARRY STONE (1979) calls a "fairy tale method," in which particular stories or motifs from fairy tales provide a basis for the symbolism of the novel. Dickens thought these stories nurtured fancy or imagination in the child and reminded the adult of an inner life unconstrained by mundane concerns and expectations. That is why he strenuously objected, in "Frauds on the Fairies," to GEORGE CRUIKSHANK's retelling of traditional tales to promote teetotalism and other versions of such children's stories to teach a moral or serve didactic purposes.

Stone (1979) describes the evolution of Dickens's fairy-tale method from scattered references in the early novels to his conscious intent to give a "higher form" to old nursery stories in the CHRISTMAS BOOKS, to his integrated and systematic use of such materials in the novels from *Dombey* on.

fancy Although Coleridge distinguished the powers of imagination and fancy, Dickens uses the terms interchangeably. His project, as he described it in the "Preliminary Word" to HOUSEHOLD WORDS, was to bring fancy to bear on the grim realities of life: "In the bosoms of the young and old, of the well-to-do and of the poor, we would tenderly cherish that light of Fancy which is inherent in the human breast . . . to show to all, that in all familiar things, even in those which are repellent on the surface, there is Romance enough, if we will find it out:—to teach the hardest workers at this whirling wheel of toil, that their lot is not necessarily a moody, brutal fact, excluded from the sympathies and graces of imagination." The transforming powers of Fancy could create a better world in the imagination and provide an ideal for which to strive. Dickens repeated this idea in the preface to *Bleak House,* in which he said that in the novel he had "purposely dwelt upon the romantic side of familiar things." The function of fancy—or imagination—then, was to transform the real world.

Dickens takes up the opposition of fact and fancy most directly in *Hard Times,* in which Coketown's UTILITARIAN commitment to fact suppresses "the robber Fancy." The lives of both Louisa and Tom Gradgrind are blighted by their inability to imagine the world as different from what it is, to see the romantic possibilities in things.

GARRETT STEWART (1974) traces the effects of imagination on the style of Dickens's novels; ROBERT NEWSOM (1977) discusses dwelling on the "romantic side of familiar things" as a fundamental principle in Dickens's work.

Fanger, Donald (1929–) Professor of Slavic and comparative literature at Harvard. In *Dostoevsky and Romantic Realism* (1965), Fanger considers Balzac, Dickens, and Gogol precursors to FEODOR DOSTOEVSKI, and he labels all of them as "romantic realists" who used the novel form to explore and mythologize the transformation to modernity in the 19th-century cities they all wrote about.

Faraday, Michael (1791–1867)   Leading chemist and physicist of his time, Faraday's most significant achievement was the discovery of electromagnetic induction. Dickens requested Faraday's lecture notes as a source for several scientific articles that appeared in HOUSEHOLD WORDS in 1850. Faraday's remarks on spontaneous combustion there may have bolstered Dickens's position in the debate over Krook's death in *Bleak House:* "It is said that spontaneous combustion does happen sometimes; particularly in great spirit drinkers. I don't see why it should not, if the system were to become too inflammable [sic.]."

Fechter, Charles (1822–1879)   Swiss actor and theater manager, one of Dickens's close friends in the 1860s. He made his name in Paris; when Dickens saw him in *La Dame aux Camélias,* he exclaimed that "a man who can do this can do anything." Fechter moved to London in 1860, and in 1863, with Dickens as his financial backer, he became the lessee of the Lyceum Theatre. Dickens especially praised his performances in *Hamlet* and *Othello* and in 1868, when Fechter moved on to America, contributed an essay to the *Atlantic Monthly,* "On Mr. Fechter's Acting." Fechter played Jules Obenreizer, the leading role in *No Thoroughfare,* a play by WILKIE COLLINS and Dickens that was produced in 1868. The little Swiss chalet that Dickens used as his writing place at GAD'S HILL was a gift from Fechter.

Victorian cartoon of Dickens with his friend and protégé, the actor Charles Fechter.

Felton, Cornelius (1807–1862) Professor of Greek at Harvard whom Dickens met on his American tour in 1842. They became good friends and regular correspondents. Dickens described Felton as "one of the jolliest and simplest of men, and not at all starry, or stripey." Felton reviewed *American Notes* enthusiastically, even though most of his countrymen were disturbed by the book and by Dickens's "ingratitude." Felton called Dickens "the most original and inventive genius since Shakespeare!" He visited Dickens in England in 1853.

Field, Barbara (1935–) Contemporary playwright who adapted *Carol* for the Gutherie Theater in Minneapolis (1975) and *Great Expectations* for the Seattle Children's Theater (1983).

Field, Inspector (1805–1874) Charles F. Field, a well-known member of the detective police force. Dickens describes going on rounds with the policeman in "On Duty with Inspector Field" (*Reprinted*). He also writes about him as Charley Wield in "Detective Police" and "Three Detective Anectotes" (*Reprinted*). Field was also the model for Inspector Bucket in *Bleak House.*

Field, Kate (1838–1896) American journalist, playwright, and lecturer; friend of WALTER SAVAGE LANDOR, ROBERT and Elizabeth Barrett BROWNING, and ANTHONY TROLLOPE. Her *Pen Photographs of Dickens's Readings* (1871) gives a firsthand account of Dickens's public readings in America in 1867–68, "twenty-five of the most delightful and most instructive evenings of my life."

Fielding, Henry (1707–1754) English novelist and playwright, justice of the peace for Middlesex who, with his brother John Fielding, reorganized the police force and established the BOW STREET RUNNERS. Dickens, like David Copperfield (4), read his *Tom Jones* (1749) as a boy. Although Dickens is said to have preferred TOBIAS SMOLLETT to Fielding, he acknowledged his debt to the latter by naming his sixth son for him.

Fielding, Kenneth J. (1924–2005) Prolific scholar, critic, and editor of Dickens. His numerous articles

An engraving of the notorious slum of Field Lane alludes to Dickens with the names "Scrooge" and "Fagan" [sic] on the shop signs.

cover biographical, editorial, critical and historical topics. His *Charles Dickens: A Critical Introduction* (1958; revised 1965) remains one of the best introductions to Dickens's life and works; his edition of *The Speeches of Charles Dickens* (Dickens, 1988) is a model of scholarly editing.

Field Lane One of London's most disreputable slums during Dickens's time, the part of SAFFRON HILL between Charles Street and HOLBORN. Described in *Twist* (26).

Fields, James Thomas and Annie (1817–1881) Dickens's American publisher, senior partner in TICKNOR & FIELDS. As a young man he saw Dickens on his first American tour, and he and his wife Annie (1834–1915) became close friends with the author in 1859 when they visited him at GAD'S HILL. He urged and organized Dickens's reading tour in AMERICA in 1867 and hosted him in BOSTON. The Fields again visited Dickens in England in 1869. On that trip, Dickens took them on several excursions, including one to the opium den in London's East End described in *Drood.* Fields's memories of Dickens are recorded in *Yesterdays with Authors* (1872). Annie's journals, which describe her impressions of Dickens, were published as *Memories of a Hostess* (ed. M. A. De Wolfe Howe, 1923).

Fields, W. C. (1880–1946)   American film actor and comedian, most famous perhaps for his unforgettable portrayal of Mr. Micawber in the 1935 film of *David Copperfield.*

Fildes, Luke (1843–1927)   Painter and illustrator. As a young artist he was recruited by Dickens to do the illustrations for *Drood,* displacing the ailing CHARLES ALLSTON COLLINS, who had done some preliminary sketches. Fildes redesigned the cover that Collins had done and produced 12 pictures for the unfinished novel. After Dickens's death, Fildes painted a watercolor, "The Empty Chair," depicting Dickens's study and writing desk with an empty chair (see p. 517). The picture was engraved for the 1870 Christmas number of *The Graphic* and has become one of the most memorable images associated with the author. Another example of Fildes's work appears on page 222.

films   From the beginning of motion pictures, Dickens's stories have provided material for filmmakers. One of D. W. GRIFFITHS's favorite authors, Dickens suggested techniques of visual storytelling that translated easily from novel to film. SERGEI EISENSTEIN found in Dickens's extensive use

Luke Fildes's picture of the hungry and homeless in the streets of London, an engraving published in the *Graphic* in 1869, depicts a scene similar to those described by Dickens on his night tours of London.

of MONTAGE the fundamental technique of the cinema.

A. L. Zambrano (1977) discusses Dickens's influence on the cinema and many of the film adaptations of his novels. She also provides a checklist of film adaptations. H. Philip Bolton (1987) also catalogs film adaptations. Michael Pointer (*Charles Dickens on the Screen*, 1996) provides a complete filmography for all of the silent and sound film adaptations as well as all television versions of Dickens's novels, and he discusses and evaluates the most important works of each type. John Glavin (*Dickens on Screen*, 2003) also includes a list of film adaptations of the novels.

Finchley In Dickens's time, a village on the northern outskirts of London. The Garlands' Abel Cottage, with its "thatched roof and little spires at the gable ends and pieces of stained glass in some of the windows," is in Finchley (*Curiosity Shop*, 22). Barnaby Rudge escapes to a shed in Finchley (68). Also mentioned in *Dombey* (32). Dickens had lodgings in Finchley while he was writing *Chuzzlewit*.

first-person narrative Mode of narration in which one of the characters tells the story in the first person. Such narration is often contrasted to omniscient narration, in which an unidentified narrator outside the story—often said to be the author or a traditional storyteller—narrates the story from a position of complete knowledge of its events and characters. By contrast, the first-person narrator is limited to his or her own knowledge and understanding of the events in the story.

Dickens frequently wrote his short fiction and journalistic essays using a first-person point of view, as, for example, in the Mrs. Lirriper stories, "The Signal Man's Story," and "George Silverman's Explanation." However, he used first-person narration in only three of the novels. In *Copperfield* and *Expectations*, the narration is appropriate to the autobiographical subject matter. There are moments in *Copperfield* when the demands of first-person narration strain the reader's credulity, as, for example, when David watches Rosa Dartle torment Em'ly without intervening (50). The confessional

mode in *Expectations* makes such scenes less likely. In *Bleak House* the limitations of the first-person narration are used to contrast with the expansiveness of the third-person narration, making evident by contrast the constrictions in Esther's situation and psyche.

Fitzgerald, Percy (1834–1925) Irish author and journalist; frequent contributor to HOUSEHOLD WORDS and ALL THE YEAR ROUND; one of the group of "Mr. Dickens's young men" along with EDMUND YATES, GEORGE AUGUSTUS SALA, and JAMES PAYN. He was a frequent visitor to GAD'S HILL in the 1860s, and Dickens hoped his daughter MARY DICKENS might marry him. Founder of the Boz Club to celebrate Dickens's memory, he wrote several adulatory books and articles about Dickens, among them *History of Pickwick* (1891), *Memoirs of an Author* (1895), *Life of Charles Dickens* (1905), and *Memories of Charles Dickens* (1913).

Fitzroy Street Dickens lived with his parents on this street in MARYLEBONE in 1832–33.

Fleet Market On the present site of Farringdon Street, this meat, fish, and vegetable market "was a long irregular row of wooden sheds and penthouses" that the Gordon rioters use as a stronghold (*Rudge*, 60). Sam Weller tells Pickwick the story of prisoner "number twenty," who longs to go out of the gates of the FLEET PRISON and see the market (*Pickwick*, 41).

Fleet Prison DEBTORS' PRISON in Farringdon Street, east London. The original structure, dating from the 13th century, was burnt down during the GORDON RIOTS in 1780 (*Rudge*, 67). Pickwick is imprisoned in the rebuilt structure that remained in use until 1842 (*Pickwick*, 41–47, 51).

Fleet Street A street that Dickens knew well; there are numerous references to it in the novels. He wandered the street as a child, like David Copperfield, who looks into the windows of food shops on Fleet Street during his lunch hour at Murdstone and Grinby (*Copperfield*, 11). Tellson's Bank (*Two Cities*) is here. The street is also mentioned in *Boz*,

Pickwick, Chuzzlewit, Bleak House, Expectations, and "Holly Tree."

Fletcher, Angus (d. 1862) Scottish sculptor whom Dickens met in London in the 1830s. He produced busts of the famous writers and artists of the time, including one of Dickens in 1841. He acted as the Dickenses' guide on their tour of Scotland in 1841, stayed with them at BROADSTAIRS and Albaro, and amused them with his eccentricities. Dickens nicknamed him "Kindheart." On his death, Dickens remarked: "Poor Kindheart! I think of all that made him so pleasant to us, and am full of grief."

Flint, Kate   Professor, Rutgers University. Flint's *Dickens* (1986) tries several interpretive strategies, both contemporary and more traditional critical approaches, to discover ways of reading Dickens and understanding his relationship to his time. She has also edited *Hard Times, Pictures from Italy,* and *Great Expectations.*

Florence, Italy   Dickens describes this "magnificently stern and sombre" city, one of the last places he visits on his tour of Italy, in *Pictures.*

Florence, William J. (1831–1891) American comic actor famous for his portrayals of Captain Cuttle and Jules Obenreizer in the 1860s.

Folkestone   Dickens had a summer home at this seaside town in KENT in 1855 while he was working on *Dorrit.* Described as Pavilionstone in *Reprinted,* "Out of Town."

Folly Ditch   The ditch separating Jacob's Island from the south bank of the THAMES at Bermondsey. The ditch could be filled at high tide by opening sluice gates. Toby Crackit's house, from which Sikes tries to escape at the end of *Twist,* is situated along the ditch.

Fonblanque,   Albany (1793–1872) Journalist and friend of Dickens. While editor of the EXAMINER, he introduced JOHN FORSTER to *Sketches by Boz* and assigned him to review a performance of

The Village Coquettes. He was a leader writer on the DAILY NEWS when Dickens was editor.

Ford, George H. (1914–1995) Contemporary scholar writing on Dickens's reputation. In numerous articles and in his classic study *Dickens and His Readers: Aspects of Novel Criticism since 1836* (1955), he charts reactions to Dickens's works from his own day to the present. In *The Dickens Critics* (1961), Ford and Lauriat Lane, Jr., collect critical articles representing this changing critical response to Dickens. Ford's edition of *Hard Times,* done with SYLVÈRE MONOD in 1966, is the best available edition of that novel.

Forster, E. M. (1879–1970)   Novelist and critic, best known for *A Passage to India* (1924). As a critic, Forster represents a modernist point of view, largely unsympathetic to Dickens. His well-known distinction between "flat" and "round" characters in *Aspects of the Novel* (1927) assesses Dickens as one-sided:

> Dickens's people are nearly all flat (Pip and David Copperfield attempt roundness, but so diffidently that they seem more like bubbles than solids). Nearly every one can be summed up in a sentence, and yet there is this wonderful feeling of human depth. Probably the immense vitality of Dickens causes his characters to vibrate a little, so that they borrow his life and appear to lead one of their own. It is a conjuring trick; at any moment we may look at Mr. Pickwick edgeways and find him no thicker than a gramophone record.

Forster,   John (1812–1876)   Journalist, biographer, historian; Dickens's closest friend, adviser, literary executor, and first biographer. Son of a Newcastle butcher, Forster came to London, took a degree at University College, and proceeded to make himself a man of letters. When Dickens met him in 1836, he was drama critic for the EXAMINER, a magazine he would edit from 1847 to 1855. There he reviewed Dickens's early plays negatively and *Boz* enthusiastically. Nicknamed "Fuz" by THOMAS CARLYLE and "Beadle of the Universe" by Thorn-

John Forster.

ton Hunt, Forster was a heavy, portentous, and dictatorial man, but he was also a man of great common sense and a true friend to many fellow writers of the time, especially Carlyle, LEIGH HUNT, Charles Lamb, EDWARD BULWER LYTTON, and Dickens. Dickens shared his works in progress with him, and Forster read proof on nearly all the novels. He advised Dickens on financial, literary, and personal matters. Dickens corresponded regularly with him and told him, while he was working on *Copperfield,* the secret of his childhood employment in the BLACKING WAREHOUSE. In the last decade of Dickens's life, when the novelist struck up a close friendship with WILKIE COLLINS, Forster was jealous of Dickens's young friends, and his relationship with the novelist was not as close as it had formerly been. But Forster remained Dickens's Boswell, producing his *Life of Charles Dickens* two years after the author's death. Although he suppressed some facts about Dickens's life, notably about his rela-

tionship with ELLEN TERNAN, his remains one of the great biographies of the period. Besides numerous journalistic essays, Forster also wrote historical works about the 17th century; among his many biographies, those on OLIVER GOLDSMITH, DANIEL DEFOE, Jonathan Swift, and WILLIAM SAVAGE LANDOR are noteworthy. Dickens caricatured his friend in Podsnap in *Our Mutual Friend.* A useful book on Forster is James A. Davies's *John Forster: A Literary Life* (1983).

Forster Collection, Victoria and Albert Museum
The most extensive collection of manuscripts and proof sheets of Dickens's works is that donated by JOHN FORSTER to the Victoria and Albert Museum in London. It includes complete manuscripts for 11 of the novels and for several minor works, as well as proof sheets for many works. The Forster Collection also includes many letters, printed documents, pamphlets, and pictures. A catalog of some of the materials was prepared by the museum for a centenary exhibition in 1970.

Fort House, Broadstairs   One of the houses where Dickens stayed on holidays in BROADSTAIRS. It is now a Dickens museum.

Fort Pitt   A deserted fortification near CHATHAM where Dickens played as a child. The abortive duel between Winkle and Dr. Slammer takes place here (*Pickwick,* 2).

Foundling Hospital   Founded in 1739 by Captain Thomas Coram, a retired merchant seaman, this orphanage took in illegitimate and abandoned children. The building, sometimes called Coram's Hospital, was in Guildford Street, Bloomsbury, in what is now called Coram's Fields. The Meagleses adopt Tattycoram from this institution, giving her an allusive name (*Dorrit,* I:2). *No Thoroughfare* involves a similar adoption.

Fox, W. J.   (1786–1864)   Journalist, Unitarian clergyman, radical UTILITARIAN. He was present in the circle of friends who gathered in 1844 to hear Dickens's prepublication reading of *The Chimes.* He was also a leader writer on the *DAILY NEWS* under

Dickens. His commitments to the repeal of the CORN LAWS and educational reform made him an ally of Dickens politically.

Fox-under-the-Hill, the   A pub along the THAMES that Dickens and David Copperfield visited in their youth.

frame story   A story framing another story or group of stories, as the story of the Canterbury pilgrimage frames the tales in Chaucer's *Canterbury Tales*. Dickens used this convention for many of the CHRISTMAS STORIES in *HOUSEHOLD WORDS* and *ALL THE YEAR ROUND*. Usually, he would write the frame narrative and then recruit other writers to contribute stories to the project.

France   From the time of his first visit to France in 1844, Dickens frequently crossed the Channel to visit or spend extended periods of time there. After an extended stay in Paris in 1846–47, he claimed to be "an accomplished Frenchman," speaking the language like a native. In PARIS he visited several French writers, among them VICTOR HUGO, Eugène Sue, ALEXANDRE DUMAS, Théophile Gautier, Alphonse Lamartine, François-Auguste-René de Chateaubriand, and Eugène Scribe. In 1853, 1854, and 1856, Dickens spent the summers with his family at BOULOGNE, a seaside resort on the Channel southwest of CALAIS, which he describes in "Our French Watering Place." In the 1850s and 1860s, he lived in Paris for several extended visits. He describes the journey from London to Paris in "A Flight." In the mid-1860s, he kept a house at Condette, a village south of Boulogne, where he frequently stayed, often with ELLEN TERNAN.

Dickens describes some of his visits to France in *Pictures from Italy* and in *The Uncommercial Traveller* (7, 18, 27). In the novels, France is most prominent in *Two Cities*. Carker meets Edith in Dijon (*Dombey*, 54); *Dorrit* begins in MARSEILLE, where Clennam is in quarantine on his return from China; and Mrs. Lirriper goes to Sens to meet Jemmy's dying father ("Lirriper's Legacy").

Frank, Lawrence (1933–)   Professor, University of Oklahoma, whose *Charles Dickens and the*

Romantic Self (1984) discusses the self in Dickens's novels as a construct created by the individual and provides psychoanalytic readings of several of the novels.

Freemason's Hall   In Queen Street, HOLBORN. A banquet honoring Dickens was held here on the eve of his departure for AMERICA in 1867.

French Revolution   Dickens's second historical novel, *A Tale of Two Cities* (1859), is set during the French Revolution of 1789. Dickens indicates in his preface to the novel his indebtedness to THOMAS CARLYLE's history, *The French Revolution*, from which he derived many of the incidents for the novel as well as its "philosophy," which found the cause of the conflict in the excesses of the French aristocracy and their treatment of the peasants. Dickens also develops this theme in "Judicial Special Pleading," in which he challenges the notion that the French peasants revolted to secure political rights. "It was," he submits, "a struggle on the part of the people for social recognition and existence. It was a struggle for vengeance against intolerable oppressors. It was a struggle for the overthrow of a system of oppression, which in its contempt of all humanity, decency, and natural rights, and in its systematic degradation of the people, had trained them to be the demons that they showed themselves, when they rose up and cast it down for ever."

Frith, William P. (1819–1909)   Painter often compared to Dickens for his realistic depiction of Victorian life. Several of his works have been used as cover illustrations for recent editions of Dickens. A great admirer of Dickens's work, Frith painted several pictures of Dolly Varden, prompting Dickens to ask him to paint miniatures of Dolly and Kate Nickleby for him. Afterwards the two became friends. Frith asked to be one of the illustrators for the LIBRARY EDITION, for which he provided two illustrations for *Dorrit*. JOHN FORSTER commissioned Frith's famous portrait of Dickens in 1859.

Frozen Deep, The   Play by WILKIE COLLINS based on an idea suggested by Dickens. On a polar expedition, Richard Wardour discovers that the man he has vowed to kill for stealing his love is also a member of the expedition. He contrives to go off into the Arctic wastes with his rival, intending to carry out his revenge, but instead he saves his life and, in the end, dies in the grateful arms of the woman he loves. Dickens's amateur company performed the play with great success at TAVISTOCK HOUSE in January 1857 and in July for the Queen and Prince Albert. Dickens's performance as Wardour was generally acclaimed, and Wardour, who died for love, suggested the character of Sydney Carton to Dickens. In August he took the play to MANCHESTER with three professional actresses—ELLEN TERNAN, her mother, and her sister Maria—in the main female roles.

Frye, Northrop (1912–1991) Canadian literary theorist and critic, especially of English romanticism, whose comprehensive scheme for classifying literary works along archetypal lines has greatly influenced American literary criticism. His most sustained discussion of Dickens appears in "Dickens and the Comedy of Humours" (in *The Stubborn Structure*, 1970), which characterizes the typical Dickens novel in terms of the traditions of classical New Comedy.

Fulham Riverside village west of London where Florence visits Sir Barnet and Lady Skettles (*Dombey*, 24). Arthur Clennam passes through on his way to TWICKENHAM (*Dorrit*, I:16).

Furniss, Harry (1854–1925) Caricaturist, author, lecturer, and illustrator for many London magazines, notably PUNCH. Among his many projects were illustrated complete editions of the works of Dickens and WILLIAM MAKEPEACE THACKERAY. His edition of Dickens (*The Charles Dickens Library*, 1910) contains over 500 of his illustrations and includes a vol-

Harry Furniss, a self-portrait.

ume on the original illustrations to Dickens's works. Examples of Furniss's work appear on pages 139, 155, 270, and 347.

Furnival's Inn One of the INNS OF COURT located in HOLBORN. Its use as a legal community was discontinued in 1818, and the buildings were rented out as chambers. Dickens lived here from 1834 to 1837, writing most of *Pickwick* during his time here. John Westlock has rooms in the inn (*Chuzzlewit*, 36), and Rosa Bud stays in the hotel in the inn (*Drood*, 11, 20). It is also mentioned in *Boz* ("Steam Excursion," "Christening").

G

Gabriel Vardon, the Locksmith of London The first novel that Dickens contracted to write in an agreement with publisher JOHN MACRONE in 1836. He did not fulfill that contract, but the novel he had in mind was eventually published as *Barnaby Rudge* in 1841.

Gadshill Edition First issued by CHAPMAN AND HALL in 1897–98, this edition was edited by B. W. MATZ with introductions by Andrew Lang. The first complete edition of Dickens's works, it included all the original illustrations. In 1903 JOHN FORSTER's *Life of Dickens* was added, and in 1908 B. W. Matz's collection of Dickens's periodical writings, *Miscellaneous Papers*, was added.

Gad's Hill Gazette The family newspaper produced by Dickens's two sons, HENRY and EDWARD DICKENS, started in 1863 and published irregularly over the next few years. It included family news of visitors, excursions, and diversions. Dickens made some joking contributions to it.

Gad's Hill Place Dickens's home for the last decade of his life. Located on a hilltop on the road between GRAVESEND and ROCHESTER, the house was one that Dickens had admired as a boy, his father telling him that if he worked very hard he might live there one day. Dickens purchased the house in 1856 for £1,790, moved there in 1860,

The chalet on the grounds of Gad's Hill that Dickens used as a study. The building was given to the novelist by Charles Fechter and is now housed at the Dickens Museum in Rochester.

and died there in 1870. The house is now a girls' school.

Garden Court   The court in the TEMPLE where Pip and Herbert Pocket have rooms (*Expectations*, 39). Ruth Pinch also waits here to meet Tom and John Westlock (*Chuzzlewit*, 45).

Garis, Robert E. (1925–2001) Professor at Wellesley whose controversial book *The Dickens Theatre* (1965) describes Dickens in his novels as a performer, a master of ceremonies who presents externally described characters who are also performers. Garis suggests that this popular mode separates Dickens from such novelists as Austen and Eliot, who develop more interior worlds in their novels.

Garraway's   Coffeehouse on Change Alley in the CITY, a gathering place for businessmen, where Pickwick writes his "chops and tomata sauce" note to Mrs. Bardell (34), Nadgett keeps watch on Jonas Chuzzlewit (27), and Jeremiah Flintwinch conducts business (*Dorrit*, I:29). The Traveller finds it closed on Sunday (*Uncommercial*, 21).

Garrick Club   A London men's club founded in 1831 that included many theatrical people among its members. The Theatrical Young Gentleman thinks that being a member of the club would be "one of the highest gratifications the world can bestow" (*Young Gentlemen*). Dickens was elected to membership in 1837, but his involvement with the club over the years was sometimes a stormy one. He resigned the first time in 1838 when WILLIAM MACREADY left the club over a personal slight. In 1858, when his friend EDMUND YATES was expelled from the club for not apologizing to WILLIAM MAKEPEACE THACKERAY after publishing an offensive article about him, Dickens defended Yates and enraged Thackeray. The two novelists were not reconciled until shortly before Thackeray's death. Dickens again resigned from the Club in 1865 after W. H. WILLS was turned down for membership.

Gaskell, Elizabeth (1810–1865) MANCHESTER novelist whose first novel, *Mary Barton* (1848), prompted Dickens to place her among the first writers he solicited to contribute to HOUSEHOLD

WORDS; "I do honestly know," he wrote, "that there is no living English writer whose aid I would desire to enlist in preference to the authoress of *Mary Barton* (a book that most profoundly affected and impressed me)." She became a regular contributor to the magazine. "Lizzie Leigh" began in the first issue, and *Cranford* appeared in eight installments between 1851 and 1853. She allowed *North and South* to be serialized in the magazine (1854–55) but objected to the ways in which it was compressed, cut, and adapted for serial publication; she requested that the "novel not be revised, even by Mr. Dickens." She also wrote numerous other stories and articles for HOUSEHOLD WORDS, and even though she disapproved of Dickens's public airing of his marital difficulties, she also contributed some articles to ALL THE YEAR ROUND, but not the novel that Dickens requested. She attended the dinner to launch *Copperfield*. Dickens visited her and her husband, a Unitarian minister, when he was in Manchester.

Geneva, Switzerland   During the month or so that Dickens spent here in 1846, he completed *The Battle of Life* and admired the Swiss revolutionaries who overthrew Catholic rule: "They are a genuine people, these Swiss. . . . They are a thorn in the sides of European despots, and a good wholesome people to live near Jesuit-ridden Kings on the brighter side of the mountains."

Genoa, Italy   Between July 1844 and June 1845, Dickens and his family spent nearly a year, off and on, in Genoa, a seaport town on the northwest coast of Italy. He wrote *The Chimes* here, returning to England in December to read the finished story to his friends. He describes the city, its environs, and its attractions in "Genoa and its Neighbourhood" (*Pictures*). He visited Genoa again in 1853 with WILKIE COLLINS and AUGUSTUS EGG.

genre painting   Popular school of painting during the Victorian period. Genre painters rendered realistic scenes of everyday life in pictures that often implied a story and a moral message. Genre painting had its roots in Dutch domestic realism of the 17th century and was an important influence on such realistic novelists as GEORGE ELIOT, who frequently compared her work to Dutch realistic painting.

Dickens was an admirer of the work of SIR DAVID WILKIE, the Scottish artist whose scenes of the life of the poor influenced such later Victorian artists as WILLIAM FRITH and LUKE FILDES. In a tribute to Wilkie after the artist's death in 1841, Dickens described him as "devoted to all that was true and beautiful, and elevating, in art and nature, . . . who made the cottage hearth his grave theme, and who surrounded the lives, and cares, and daily toils, and occupations of the poor, with dignity and beauty." Dickens's scenes in Daniel Peggotty's boathouse (*Copperfield*) and in Joe Gargery's forge (*Expectations*) are much in the same tradition that he praised in Wilkie's work.

George IV (1762–1830)   Prince Regent, 1811–20, and king, 1820–30. The first of the dandies, he is worshipped by Mr. Turveydrop as the model of deportment (*Bleak House*, 14).

ghost story   Dickens was introduced to this traditional form of storytelling by his childhood nurse, MARY WELLER, whose tales of the macabre and GROTESQUE fascinated and horrified the boy. He describes these "Nurse's Stories" in *Uncommercial* (15). Although he was skeptical of the "truth" of such tales, Dickens knew their appeal. He includes ghost stories among the INTERPOLATED TALES in the early novels. Particularly noteworthy is "The Story of the Goblins Who Stole a Sexton" (*Pickwick*, 29), the first version of his most famous ghost story, *A Christmas Carol* (1843), subtitled "A Ghost Story of Christmas." The CHRISTMAS BOOKS, which blended fantasy and realism to give a "higher form" to old nursery tales, are partly conceived in the tradition of the oral stories—often ghost stories—told to those gathered at the Christmas hearth. *The Haunted Man*, the other ghost story in the series, is based on Dickens's belief that Christmas was an especially appropriate time for the living to remember the dead. Among the ghost stories in the Christmas numbers of Dickens's magazines, "The Signal-Man" (1866) is the most memorable.

Dickens occasionally uses motifs from the ghost story in the longer novels, as in the shadowy presence of Barnaby Rudge's father (*Rudge*), the apparitions that haunt the guilty Lewsome (*Chuzzlewit*, 48), or the vision of the hanging woman that Pip sees on two occasions at Satis House (*Expectations*, 8, 48).

Peter Haining's introduction to *The Complete Ghost Stories of Charles Dickens* (1983) summarizes Dickens's involvement with the genre. STONE (1979) discusses ghost stories as one of the types of children's literature important in Dickens's work.

Giles, William (1798–1856)   Son of a Baptist clergyman in CHATHAM; Dickens's first schoolmaster. He recognized the boy's unusual abilities and gave him individual instruction. When Dickens moved to London at age 11, Giles gave him a copy of Goldsmith's *Bee*, a volume of essays that Dickens treasured. Although his father was a formidable preacher and may have been the model for some of Dickens's unsympathetic portraits of dissenting ministers, young Giles was remembered with great affection by his former pupil.

Gimbel, Colonel Richard (1898–1970)   American merchant, bibliophile, and collector of Dickens materials, including the manuscripts of several minor works. He donated much of his collection to Yale University.

Gissing, George (1857–1903)   Later Victorian novelist and critic, best known for *New Grub Street* (1901). His *Charles Dickens: A Critical Study* (1898) and *Critical Studies of the Works of Charles Dickens* (1924) defend Dickens as a realist against the criticisms of such contemporaries as GEORGE HENRY LEWES and HENRY JAMES. Although Gissing did not celebrate the romantic side of Dickens and his more fanciful inventions, he was profoundly influenced by Dickens's social vision, and he reminds us that much that may seem fantastic in Dickens's work is grounded in careful observation of the social conditions at the time.

Glasgow   Dickens opened the Athenaeum at this Scottish city on December 28, 1847. He also gave several successful public readings of his works in the city, the first in 1858.

Gloucester Place   Dickens lived at no. 57 on this street near HYDE PARK in 1864 when he was beginning work on *Mutual Friend.*

Gold, Joseph (1933–)   Professor, University of Waterloo (Ontario); compiler of *The Stature of Dickens: A Centenary Bibliography* (1971), a list of materials on Dickens and his works from the Victorian period to 1970; author of *Charles Dickens: Radical Moralist* (1972), a provocative introduction to Dickens, with essays on all the novels, emphasizing their moral and, especially, religious themes.

Goldberg, Michael (1930–)   Professor, University of British Columbia; editor and critic of the works of THOMAS CARLYLE, Dickens, and other Victorian and modern writers. He has written on Dickens in relation to D. H. Lawrence, GEORGE BERNARD SHAW, and, especially, Carlyle. In *Carlyle and Dickens* (1972), Goldberg discusses the relationship between the two men and the influence of Carlyle, venerated by Dickens as a literary mentor and hero, on the novelist's work.

Golden Cross Hotel, the   Coaching inn on the present site of Trafalgar Square from which Pickwick begins his travels on May 13, 1827 (*Pickwick,* 2). David Copperfield stays here, "a mouldy sort of establishment in a close neighborhood," when he comes up to London from DOVER (19). Dickens describes the inn on a winter morning in *Boz,* "Early Coaches."

Golden Square   The once-fashionable square in SOHO where many of the old mansions have been turned into lodgings by the time Ralph Nickleby has his office there (*Nickleby,* 2, 4). The home of the Kenwigs is nearby (*Nickleby,* 14). Mr. Peggotty recovers Little Em'ly in the vicinity of the square (*Copperfield,* 50).

Goldsmith, Oliver (1728–1774)   Dramatist, novelist, and essayist; one of the 18th-century authors whom Dickens read as a child. Dickens received a collection of Goldsmith's essays from WILLIAM GILES when he left CHATHAM. His nickname BOZ ultimately derived from *The Vicar of Wakefield,* and Goldsmith was among the writers he read in his course of self-study at the BRITISH MUSEUM. Goldsmith's sentimentality and benevolent characters, like the Reverend Primrose, exerted the greatest influence on Dickens.

Gordon Riots   Disturbances in London in June 1780 stemming from demonstrations to secure the repeal of the Catholic Relief Act of 1778, which had removed some of the civil disabilities against Catholics. Led by Lord George Gordon, who formed the Protestant Association in 1779 to protest the act and deliver a petition to Parliament, the demonstrations assembled a mob of thousands that virtually held London in thrall for a week while Catholic chapels, the homes of Roman Catholics, and several public buildings were pillaged and burned. Gordon was arrested, tried for treason, and acquitted on the grounds that he had no treasonous intent. The Catholic Relief Act was not repealed. In *Rudge,* Dickens writes as if the rioters are trying to prevent passage of the bill. For his readers in 1841, the Gordon Riots had remarkable similarities to the Chartist demonstrations going on in London and other English cities at the time (*see* CHARTISM).

gothic novel   A type of novel popular in the late 18th and early 19th centuries that featured supernatural occurrences, mysterious events and characters, and medieval castles with trapdoors, mysterious passageways, and chambers of horrors. Horace Walpole's *Castle of Otranto* (1764) is usually considered the originator of the form; among its prominent English practitioners were Matthew ("Monk") Lewis, Mary Shelley, and Anne Radcliffe.

Although none of Dickens's novels can be considered a gothic novel, Dickens did use devices and motifs from the gothic in his fiction, such as surrealistic elements of dream, sharp contrasts between light and dark worlds and between country and city, themes of imprisonment and death, and ruined and horrifying houses, such as Satis House (*Expectations*),

Chesney Wold with its Ghost's Walk (*Bleak House*), or Mrs. Clennam's crumbling house (*Dorrit*). Larry Kirkpatrick ("The Gothic Flame of Charles Dickens," *Victorian Newsletter*, 1967) includes these features as part of what he describes as a "gothic substructure" in the novels. ARCHIBALD COOLIDGE (1967) discusses Dickens's use of techniques derived from the gothic novels of Anne Radcliffe. Thomas Loe ("Gothic Plot in *Great Expectations*," *Dickens Quarterly*, 1989) discusses the gothic plot as one of three plotlines in the novel.

Grant, William and Daniel Merchants and manufacturers in MANCHESTER, so famous for their philanthropy that JOHN DICKENS held them up as models to his son. Dickens met them in 1839 and used them as models for the Cheeryble Brothers in *Nickleby*. Although he assured his readers "that the Brothers Cheeryble live; that their liberal charity, their singleness of heart, their noble nature, and their unbounded benevolence, are no creations of the Author's brain," many readers have found them impossible and tiresome and, as Aldous Huxley described them, "gruesome old Peter Pans."

Graves, Robert (1895–1985) English poet and novelist whose *The Real David Copperfield* (1933) is a modernist "rewriting for the ordinary reader." It eliminates repetitions and prolixity of style necessitated by the original serial form, reducing the novel to what Graves calls "its natural length and plot." In doing so, he removes much about David and Agnes and makes the sexual content in David's relationships with Emily and Dora more explicit. Although Graves claimed that he undertook the project because of his admiration for Dickens, most Dickensians have considered his efforts as expressing contempt for the original. GEORGE FORD's (1955) reaction is representative: Graves's "*jeu d'esprit* is about as effective as Pope's attempts to translate Dora's satires into elegant neo-classical verses and will remain an equally amusing specimen for future literary historians."

Gravesend Port on the THAMES estuary in KENT about halfway between London and CHATHAM. The steam excursion boat from London to Gravesend is described in *Boz*, "River." David Copperfield bids farewell to the Australian emigrants at Gravesend (57). Caddy Jellyby spends her honeymoon with Prince here (*Bleak House*, 30). Pip and Herbert row beyond Gravesend as they attempt to smuggle Magwich out of England (*Expectations*, 54).

Gray's Inn One of the INNS OF COURT, located in HOLBORN west of Gray's Inn Road. Dickens worked here in 1827 as a clerk for ELLIS AND BLACKMORE. The Traveller describes the inn as "one of the most depressing institutions in brick and mortar" (*Uncommercial*, 14). Lawyers Perker and Phunkey (*Pickwick*) have their legal offices at the Inn; Percy Noakes (*Boz*, "Excursion") and Tommy Traddles (*Copperfield*) have lodgings here. Flora Finching proposes to meet Arthur Clennam in Gray's Inn Gardens (*Dorrit*, I:13).

Gray's Inn Lane Now called Gray's Inn Road, this street running north from HOLBORN is the site of Signor Billsmethi's dancing academy (*Boz*, "Dancing Academy") and of Micawber's lodgings when he is going under the alias Mortimer (*Copperfield*, 36). Casby lives in a side street off the lane (*Dorrit*, I:13).

Great International Walking Match A 13-mile walking race in Boston refereed by Dickens during his reading tour in the United States in February 1868. The two contestants, Dickens's manager GEORGE DOLBY, representing Great Britain, and the junior partner of his American publishing firm, James Osgood, traveled with Dickens on the tour and engaged in various frivolous competitions. A passionate walker himself, Dickens, who was suffering from a persistent cold, did not participate, but he laid out the course, nicknamed the contestants—"Man of Ross" and "The Boston Bantam"—gave a celebratory dinner for the participants and friends afterward, and wrote up the whole affair in his letters and journals.

Great White Horse, the The "overgrown tavern" in Ipswich where Pickwick and Peter Magnus stay when Pickwick surprises Miss Witherfield by mistaking her room for his own (*Pickwick*, 22).

Dickens stayed at the inn when reporting on the election of 1835.

Greaves, John (1899–1976)   Ardent Dickensian, secretary of the Dickens Fellowship 1948–76, and performer of scenes and characters from Dickens's works. He was the author of numerous articles and books on various points of Dickensian lore, including *Dickens at Doughty Street* (1975), an account of Dickens's early years at the house that is now DICKENS HOUSE; and *Who's Who in Dickens* (1972).

Greeley, Horace (1811–1872)   American journalist, Whig political leader, and editor of the New York *Tribune*. He was one of the few American journalists who supported Dickens's views on COPYRIGHT during Dickens's first visit to AMERICA. He introduced Dickens at the press banquet at Delmonico's in New York during the reading tour in 1868.

Green, Charles (1840–1898)   Artist and illustrator, particularly noted for his pen drawings. He provided the illustrations for *Curiosity Shop* in the English Household Edition (1876). He also did several watercolor paintings of subjects from Dickens and an oil painting of Pickwick addressing the Pickwick Club that is now in the SUZANNET COLLECTION at the DICKENS HOUSE. An example of his work is on p. 252.

Green, Paul (Poll)   One of the boys who worked with Dickens in the BLACKING WAREHOUSE, the son of a fireman who worked at the DRURY LANE Theater.

Greene, Graham (1904–1991)   British novelist and essayist. His classic essay, "The Young Dickens" (1950; reprinted in *The Lost Childhood and Other Essays*, 1951), describes Dickens as a writer of "secret prose" that presents "a mind speaking to itself with no one there to listen" and characterizes the world of *Oliver Twist* as Manichaean, a world without God in which "we can believe in evil-doing, but goodness wilts into philanthropy."

Greenwich   The riverside town east of London where Bella Wilfer and her father run off for a pri-

vate dinner at the Ship Inn (*Mutual Friend*, II:8) and where later Bella and John are married (IV:4). Dickens describes the annual fair held here on Easter Monday in *Boz*, "Greenwich Fair."

Greta Bridge   The town in Yorkshire near Dotheboys Hall where Squeers and his party leave the coach from London (*Nickleby*, 6, 7). Dickens visited the town with HABLOT KNIGHT BROWNE in 1838 when collecting material for the novel.

Gretna Green   This town just over the Scottish border north of Carlisle has traditionally been the destination of runaway lovers, because an immediate marriage could be performed by an innkeeper or a blacksmith. The two couples in "The Great Winglebury Duel" are married by the blacksmith in Gretna Green (*Boz*, "Winglebury"). Harry and Norah are on their way to Gretna Green when they stop at the Holly Tree Inn and meet Edwin and Emmeline, who are on a similar journey ("Holly Tree").

Griffith, D. W. (1875–1948)   American film director, best known for *Birth of a Nation*, often considered the father of film. From Dickens, Griffith's favorite author and the source for many of his cinematic ideas, the filmmaker learned how to place romantic melodrama in a romantic setting, how to use detail to build narrative rhythm and tension, and, especially, how to use the cutback, or parallel cutting, to switch between narrative lines and thereby give rhythm and dynamism to a story.

Grimaldi, Joseph (1778–1837)   Famous clown and star of PANTOMIME during Dickens's childhood years. Dickens edited his memoirs (1838) for RICHARD BENTLEY in 1838. Dickens was eight when he first saw a performance by Grimaldi, "in whose honor I am informed I clapped my hands with great precosity." Throughout his life Dickens was fond of imitating Grimaldi's clowning.

Grosvenor Square   A fashionable square in the West End of London; Mr. Tite Barnacle has his residence at 24 Mews Street, just off the square, where the houses are "abject hangers-on to a fashionable situation" (*Dorrit*, I:10). During the GORDON RIOTS,

Lord Rockingham's house on the square is barricaded against the rioters (*Rudge*, 67).

grotesque, the   The use of exaggeration and fantasy in art and literature to make unfamiliar the familiar and to reveal the tensions and contradictions beneath the surface of things. It emerges in the obsessions of the comedy of humors, in the traditional figures of PANTOMIME on stage, in the exaggerations of visual CARICATURE that reduce humans to animals, and in romantic irony that makes the monstrous simultaneously repellent and attractive. Dickens's use of the grotesque is most apparent in his animation of the material world and his objectification of the human. DOROTHY VAN GHENT (1950) developed the classic description of this aspect of Dickens's work, in which "the course of things demonically possessed is to imitate the human, while the course of human possession is to imitate the inhuman." Michael Hollington (*Dickens and the Grotesque*, 1984) explores the subject in detail. Several of the contributors to John Schad's *Dickens Refigured: Bodies, Desires, and Other Histories* (1996) discuss grotesque elements in Dickens's work.

Guildford   Near this town in Surrey is the site of Dora's birthday picnic (*Copperfield*, 33). Nicholas first meets Crummles as he is traveling from Guildford back to London (*Nickleby*, 22).

Guild of Literature and Art, the   Scheme developed in 1850–51 by Dickens and EDWARD BULWER LYTTON to create an endowment for the support of indigent and deserving artists and writers. Performances by Dickens's theatrical company of Lytton's *Not So Bad as We Seem* were to provide initial funding for the project. Lytton also donated some land on his estate to establish a small artist's colony. Dickens served as chairman of the endowment for several years and gave considerable time to the project, but it failed to generate widespread and substantial support.

Guinness, Sir Alec (1914–2000)   British actor and playwright. His adaptation of *Great Expectations* (1939) for the stage was widely performed in the 1940s. Guinness played Herbert Pocket in the initial production, a role he also performed in DAVID LEAN's masterful film adaptation of the novel (1947). His controversial performance as Fagin in Lean's *Twist* (1948), which exaggerated stereotypical Jewish traits in the character, was significantly edited in early American prints of the film. Guinness has also played Marley in the musical film *Scrooge* (1970) and William Dorrit in the film *Little Dorrit* (1988).

Gurney,   Jeremiah (1812–1886)   American portrait photographer for the New York firm of J. Gurney and Son, which secured exclusive rights to photograph Dickens on his American reading tour in 1868. Dickens was ill at the time the pictures were taken, and the photographs reveal his age and exhaustion.

Guy's Hospital   A teaching hospital in SOUTHWARK where Bob Sawyer is a medical student (*Pickwick*, 30) and where Mrs. Gamp's husband dies (*Chuzzlewit*, 19).

H

Halifax Dickens visited this capital city of Nova Scotia on his American tour in 1841. He describes his "most pleasant impression" of the town and its legislative assembly in *American Notes* (2).

Hall, William (1801–1847) Partner in the publishing firm CHAPMAN & HALL. The business half of the firm, with a head for numbers, Hall sold Dickens the copy of the MONTHLY MAGAZINE that contained Dickens's first published work. Dickens remembered him and the excitement of that moment when he negotiated the terms for *Pickwick*. In 1843, Hall annoyed Dickens by tactlessly suggesting that the poor sales of *Chuzzlewit* might force the firm to reduce the author's payments, prompting Dickens to change publishers to BRADBURY & EVANS.

Halliday, Andrew (1830–1877) Scottish playwright who adapted several of Dickens's novels for the stage, including "Nicholas Nickleby" (1875), "Nell, or; The Old Curiosity Shop" (1871), "Heart's Delight" (*Dombey*, 1873), and "Little Em'ly" (*Copperfield*, 1869), an adaptation praised by Dickens.

Hammersmith A town on the THAMES southwest of London where the Misses Crumpton operate Minerva House, a "finishing establishment for young ladies" (*Boz*, "Sentiment"), and where the Matthew Pocket family reside (*Expectations*, 21).

Oliver passes through Hammersmith on his way to the CHERTSEY robbery (*Twist*, 21).

Hammond, W. J. (1799–1848) Manager and chief comedian at the Strand Theatre in London, famous for his portrayal of Sam Weller in WILLIAM MONCRIEFF's adaptation of *Pickwick*. He toured England in the late 1830s playing his famous Weller character in productions that were only loosely derived from Dickens.

Hampstead Village north of London. Dickens had lodgings here in 1832. After MARY HOGARTH's death, Dickens and his wife rented a cottage at Collins's Farm (now Wylde's Farm) on Hampstead Heath. He and JOHN FORSTER often walked from DOUGHTY STREET to Jack Straw's Castle, an inn near the heath.

Hampstead is mentioned frequently in the novels. Pickwick's fame derived in part from his paper on the source of the Hampstead Ponds (*Pickwick*, 1). Mrs. Bardell is arrested at the Spaniards Inn by the heath as she has tea with some friends (*Pickwick*, 46). Bill Sikes crosses the heath on his way out of London after killing Nancy (*Twist*, 48). Dick Swiveller settles in Hampstead with the Marchioness (*Curiosity Shop*, 73). The Gordon rioters make an abortive expedition to destroy Ken Wood House (*Rudge*, 66). David Copperfield walks out to Hampstead for breakfast (*Copperfield*, 35). Miss

Griffin's school is located near the Hampstead Ponds (*Haunted House*).

Hampton   Mortimer Lightwood and Eugene Wrayburn have a cottage by the THAMES in this village (*Mutual Friend*, I:12). Twist passes through (21); Hawk and Verisopht attend the Hampton races (*Nickleby*, 50).

Hanging-Sword Alley   This narrow alley off WHITEFRIARS Street in east London is the unsavory neighborhood where Jerry Cruncher lives (*Two Cities*, II:1). George Rouncewell notes its military significance as he passes by (*Bleak House*, 27).

Hanover Square   Off Regent Street in Mayfair, the site of the Hanover Square Rooms where Dickens's AMATEUR THEATRICAL company gave several performances of EDWARD BULWER LYTTON's *Not So Bad as We Seem* in 1851 and where he later gave PUBLIC READINGS.

Hardwick, Michael (1924–1991) **and Mollie**   Writers, dramatists, novelists, compilers, and editors, this industrious couple has written radio and TV plays, produced records, and compiled, edited, and written numerous books, many on Victorian topics, several on Dickens. *The Charles Dickens Encyclopedia* (1973) lists the works, characters, places, and people of Dickens and provides a large and well-chosen selection of the most memorable passages in Dickens's works. Their other books on Dickens are *The Charles Dickens Companion* (1965), *Dickens's England* (1970), and *As They Saw Him: Charles Dickens* (1970).

Hardy, Barbara (1924–   )   Contemporary Victorian scholar; Professor at Birkbeck College, University of London, who has written on Austen, Thackeray, Eliot, and Hardy as well as on Dickens. In *The Moral Art of Dickens* (1970), Hardy provides a probing analysis of the moral dimensions of Dickens's characters and the pattern of conversion that underlies most of the novels.

harmonic meeting   These entertainments, held in public houses, combined refreshment with group singing led by professional singers and were the precursors to the later music hall. A typical harmonic meeting is described in *Boz*, "Streets—Night." Harmonic meetings are held regularly at Sol's Arms (*Bleak House*, 33).

Harper and Brothers   New York publishing firm with which Dickens negotiated agreements for the publication of several of his works, in some cases sending them the proof sheets before the English publication so that they could beat the pirates into print. *Great Expectations* and *Edwin Drood* were both published in *Harper's Weekly* from the proof sheets. *Expectations* appeared a week in advance of its appearance in ALL THE YEAR ROUND, making the *Harper's Weekly* serial literally the first published edition of the novel.

Harrisburg, Pennsylvania   A "very cheerful city" where Dickens put up at a "snug hotel" and visited a model prison on his 1842 journey to America (*Notes*, 9).

Harte, Francis Brett (Bret) (1836–1902)   California novelist, humorist, and journalist, often compared to Dickens. According to Mark Twain, Harte described himself as "the best imitator of Dickens in America." Harte's sentimentality, his use of child characters and angelic women, and his method of characterization through peculiarities were aspects of his work most often described as Dickensian.

Dickens read "The Luck of the Roaring Camp" (1868) and "Outcasts of Poker Flat" (1869) shortly before his death, wrote to Harte to tell him how the stories impressed and moved him, and invited Harte to contribute to ALL THE YEAR ROUND. By the time Harte received the letter with Dickens's invitation, Dickens was dead. Harte had written his memorable tribute to his literary mentor, "Dickens in Camp" (July 1870), before Harte received Dickens's letter. The memorial poem described a group of California miners sitting around an open campfire and reading aloud *The Old Curiosity Shop*.

Hartford, Connecticut   Dickens spent four days in this town, "beautifully situated in a basin of green hills," visiting the lunatic asylum and the prison (*Notes*, 5).

Harvard University Harvard's collections contain the manuscripts for several pieces from *The Uncommercial Traveller* and for "George Silverman's Explanation," as well as many letters.

Harvey, J. R. (1942–) Novelist, artist, and printmaker on the faculty of Emmanuel College, Cambridge. In *Victorian Novelists and Their Illustrators* (1971), Harvey analyzes the effect of the graphic satire tradition on Dickens and his illustrators.

Hatfield Town in Hertfordshire to which Sikes escapes after Nancy's murder, but he is driven away from the pub here by a peddler who insists on removing the bloodstain from Sikes's hat (*Twist*, 48). The Lirripers spend their honeymoon here at the Salisbury Arms, where Dickens himself had stayed in 1838 ("Lirriper's Lodgings"). Mrs. Lirriper is buried in the Hatfield churchyard ("Lirriper's Legacy").

Hatton Garden Street in HOLBORN where the police court presided over by Magistrate Fang is located (*Twist*, 11). It is on Phil Squod's beat as a tinker (*Bleak House*, 26). The Jellybys take lodgings here after Mr. Jellyby's bankruptcy (*Bleak House*, 30).

Helps, Sir Arthur (1813–1875) Clerk to the Privy Council, author, and friend of Dickens, especially during the 1860s. He arranged Dickens's audience with QUEEN VICTORIA on March 9, 1870. His obituary tribute to Dickens (*Macmillan's Magazine*, 1870) describes the author as unusually observant, humorous, orderly, disciplined, and attentive.

Henry VIII (1491–1547) King of England, 1509–47, described by Dickens as "a most intolerable ruffian, a disgrace to human nature, and a blot of blood and grease upon the History of England" (*Child's History*).

Hicks, Seymour (1871–1941) British actor, theater manager, and dramatist. He played in every-

thing from music hall to serious drama. He was famous for his portrayal of Scrooge, both in Buckstone's adaptation of the story and in music hall sketches. He played Scrooge in the 1935 film version of the *Carol*.

Highgate Village north of London where Dickens and his parents lived in 1832. His parents and his infant daughter, DORA ANNIE DICKENS, are buried in Highgate Cemetery. The village is significant in *Copperfield*, the novel he was writing when his daughter died. Mrs. Steerforth's house, the retirement cottage of Dr. Strong, and the cottages of Betsey Trotwood and David himself are in Highgate. The village is also mentioned in *Twist* and *Bleak House*.

Hill, T. W. (1866–1953) Active Dickensian; secretary of the DICKENS FELLOWSHIP, 1914–19; and frequent contributor to the DICKENSIAN, most remembered for his explanatory notes to the novels published in that journal.

historical novel A form of the novel developed by SIR WALTER SCOTT, in which historical persons and a historical situation are combined with fictional characters and a fictional story. For Scott, the historical situation usually involved two cultures in conflict, one dying and the other being born, and a period close enough to be within memory of some living persons. In Scott's novels, the fictional characters participate in historical events along with the historic figures. His heroes usually have divided loyalties between the conflicting historical forces.

Influenced by Scott, nearly every major Victorian novelist attempted at least one historical novel; some, like WILLIAM HARRISON AINSWORTH and G. P. R. James, made historical fiction their vocation. The first novel that Dickens planned, *Gabriel Vardon, the Locksmith of London*, was to be a historical novel in the manner of Scott. Although he set aside the project when *Pickwick* became popular, he eventually completed the novel as *Barnaby Rudge* (1841), a story of the GORDON RIOTS in the 1780s. Although Dickens did not employ the elaborate editorial devices that Scott often used to establish the link between his historical subject and the present, *Rudge* had contemporary relevance in 1841, for the Gordon Riots provided an easily recognized parallel to CHARTISM.

Although some of Dickens's shorter stories are set in the past—*The Battle of Life*, for example, takes place in the late 18th century—the only other novel that qualifies as historical is *A Tale of Two Cities* (1859), a novel about the FRENCH REVOLUTION in which Dickens inserted the tale of Charles Darnay, an expatriate French aristocrat, into the revolution, the depiction of which he based mainly on THOMAS CARLYLE's history. Dickens's historical novels are discussed by Avram Fleishman, *The English Historical Novel* (1971) and ANDREW SANDERS (*The Victorian Historical Novel 1840–1880*, 1978).

Hogarth, George (1783–1870)   Dickens's father-in-law. A Scot, educated for the law at Edinburgh, he practiced law for many years in Scotland, acting as SIR WALTER SCOTT's attorney. He was also a violincellist and composer and the music critic for the *Edinburgh Courant*. In 1830, he left the law for journalism and established the *Halifax Guardian*. In 1834, he became music critic for the MORNING CHRONICLE in London. It was there that he met Dickens, who was writing "Street Sketches" for the paper. When he became editor of the newly established EVENING CHRONICLE in 1835, he asked Dickens to contribute sketches to that paper as well. He was hired as music critic for the DAILY NEWS under Dickens's editorship, continuing in that position for 20 years. In 1814 he married Georgina Thomson, daughter of a fellow musician. Three of their daughters had important roles in Dickens's life: Catherine, the eldest, who became his wife (*see* CATHERINE DICKENS); MARY, whose early death deeply affected Dickens; and GEORGINA, Dickens's companion and housekeeper.

Hogarth, Georgina (1827–1917)   Georgina joined the Dickens household after the Dickenses returned from AMERICA in 1842. Gradually she took more and more responsibility for managing the household and, after siding with Dickens during the separation, she remained with him until the end of his life, prompting scandalous and unfounded rumors about Dickens's relationship with her. After his death, she and

MAMIE DICKENS edited the first collection of Dickens's LETTERS (1880–82). ARTHUR ADRIAN (1957) describes Georgina's relationship with Dickens, his family, and his friends.

Hogarth, Mary Scott (1819–1837)   Dickens's sister-in-law. Mary, a pretty and lively girl, four years younger than Catherine (*see* CATHERINE DICKENS), moved into the Dickens's household in 1836, shortly after the marriage of her sister. A year later, on May 6, 1837, she was suddenly taken ill and died the next day in Dickens's arms. Dickens missed a month of *Twist*, ascribing the interruption to "the sudden death of a very dear young relative to whom he was most affectionately attached and whose society had been for a long time the chief solace of his labours." For her tombstone he wrote, "Young, beautiful, and good, God in his mercy numbered her with His angels at the early age of seventeen." He took a ring from her finger and wore it until his own death. Biographers have suggested that Mary was the model for many of Dickens's sweet and innocent young women, particularly Little Nell in *Curiosity Shop*, whose death reminded Dickens of Mary's.

Hogarth, William (1697–1764)   Painter and engraver; graphic satirist and moralist whose works profoundly influenced Dickens; especially important were the progresses, series of narrative pictures telling exemplary stories. Dickens had 48 prints by Hogarth hanging at GAD'S HILL, and he subtitled *Oliver Twist* "The Parish Boy's Progress," indicating his debt to such Hogarth works as "The Harlot's Progress" (1731), "The Rake's Progress" (1735), and "Industry and Idleness" (1747), as well as to John Bunyan's *Pilgrim's Progress* (1678). JOHN HARVEY (1971), Paul Davis ("Imaging *Oliver Twist*: Hogarth, Illustration, and The Part of Darkness," *Dickensian*, 1986), and J. D. Hunt (*Encounters: Essays on Literature and The Visual Arts*, 1971) discuss Dickens's debt to Hogarth.

Hoghton Towers   A deserted mansion on the road between PRESTON and Blackburn that Dickens visited in 1867. George Silverman is sent to the farmhouse to recover his health ("Silverman," 5).

Holborn This section of London and its main thoroughfare, running westward from the CITY to TOTTENHAM COURT ROAD, is frequently mentioned in Dickens's works. Job Trotter runs up Holborn Hill to fetch Perker when Pickwick decides to leave the FLEET PRISON (*Pickwick*, 47); Oliver Twist and Sikes take this route on their way to CHERTSEY (*Twist*, 21). During the GORDON RIOTS, Langdale's distillery on Holborn Hill is burned down (*Rudge*, 68). Mrs. Gamp has rooms in Kingsgate Street off High Holborn, and she and Betsey Prig nurse Lewsome at the Black Bull in Holborn (*Chuzzlewit*, 25). On her arrival in London, Esther Summerson goes to Thavies Inn via Holborn through a thick fog (*Bleak House*, 4).

Holland, Lady Augusta-Mary (1770–1845) Autocratic hostess of a famous literary and Whig political salon at Holland House. Dickens was introduced there in 1838.

Holland, Captain J. B. Proprietor of the MONTHLY MAGAZINE, he was Dickens's first publisher, accepting "A Dinner at Poplar Walk" for the December 1833 issue. Altogether he published nine of Dickens's early sketches in his magazine.

Hollingshead, John (1827–1904) Journalist and, later, theater manager; a frequent contributor to HOUSEHOLD WORDS and ALL THE YEAR ROUND. He described Dickens as "an inspired Cockney" and himself as "a Dickens young man." Dickens is said to have characterized him as "the most ignorant man on the staff [of *Household Words*], but he'll cram up the facts, and won't give us an encyclopaedical article."

Honner, Robert (1809–1852) Actor and theater manager; as manager of Sadler's Wells in the 1840s, he produced and took leading roles in several Dickens adaptations. Among Honner's roles were Fagin, Quilp, Scrooge, the Mysterious Stranger in *Rudge*, and Mrs. Brown in *Dombey*. His wife **Maria** (1812–70) played Oliver, Little Nell, Dot Peerybingle, Clemency Newcome, and Edith Granger.

Hood, Thomas (1799–1845) Poet and wit and a friend of Dickens during first half of the 1840s.

His appreciative review of *Curiosity Shop* in the ATHENAEUM brought Dickens an "unusual glow of pleasure and encouragement." In his 1848 preface to the novel, Dickens goes on to remark, "Long afterwards, and when I had come to know him well, and to see him, stout of heart, going slowly down into his grave, I knew the writer of that essay to be Thomas Hood."

Hood's Magazine and Comic Miscellany One of several literary magazines edited by THOMAS HOOD in the course of his career. He began this journal in 1844, and it continued for three years after his death in 1845. Dickens's essay, "A Threatening Letter to Thomas Hood, from an Ancient Gentleman" appeared in the May 1844 issue (*Miscellaneous, Journalism*).

Hook, Theodore (1788–1841) Tory wit, dramatist, comic writer, and silver-fork novelist, Hook was appointed editor of the *New Monthly Magazine* in 1837, charged to challenge the success of BENTLEY'S MISCELLANY under the editorship of Dickens. Although Hook serialized novels by himself, Frances Eleanor Trollope, and CAPTAIN FREDERICK MARRYAT in the magazine, it did not seriously challenge Bentley's magazine.

Hornback, Bert G. (1935–) Professor, University of Michigan; performer of dramatic readings from Dickens; scholar and critic of Victorian literature, especially Dickens. In *Noah's Arkitecture; A Study of Dickens's Mythology* (1972), Hornback suggests a mythopoeic reading of the novels based largely on the Eden and Noah stories from Genesis. Concentrating on *Copperfield* in "The Hero of My Life" (1981), Hornback explores Dickens's central theme, the function of imagination in creating human wisdom. *Great Expectations: A Novel of Friendship* (1987) offers an introduction to the novel directed to undergraduates.

Horne, Richard Hengist (1803–1884) Poet, journalist, and friend of Dickens, he was on the staff of the DAILY NEWS and HOUSEHOLD WORDS, even though W. H. WILLS was not always satisfied with his work. He performed minor roles in some of Dickens's theatricals, but Dickens thought him "the very worst actor that the world ever saw." He included a long chapter on Dickens in *A New Spirit of the Age* (1844), characterizing the author as "The product of his age . . . a genuine emanation of its aggregate and entire spirit." He emigrated to Australia as a Commissioner of Public Lands in 1852, though he continued to submit occasional essays to Dickens's periodicals. After he returned to England in 1869, Dickens snubbed him, leading Horne to criticize Dickens in his subsequent writings.

Hornsey   An area of north London where Pickwick has carried out "unwearied researches" (*Pickwick*, 1). Betsey Trotwood's husband is buried in the Hornsey churchyard (*Copperfield*, 54).

Horse Guards   The building in WHITEHALL that houses the War Department. Gabriel Varden sets up Sim Tappertit as a shoeblack under an archway near the Horse Guards (*Rudge*, 82). Peggotty takes Mr. Dick to see the guards at the entrance (*Copperfield*, 35). Also mentioned in *Nickleby* (41).

Horsemonger Lane   On this street in the BOROUGH stood the Horsemonger Lane Gaol, where Dickens in 1849 saw the execution of the notorious MANNINGS, which prompted him to write a letter to the *Times* calling for the abolition of public executions. He later based the character of Hortense in *Bleak House* on Mrs. Manning. Mrs. Chivery's tobacco shop is located at 5 Horsemonger Lane (*Dorrit*, I:18).

Horton, Susan (1941–)   Professor, University of Massachusetts, Boston; interested in the ways in which Dickens creates his audience and the ways in which his readers create the novels. Horton explores in *Interpreting Interpreting: Interpreting Dickens's Dombey* (1979) the various ways of reading and interpreting *Dombey and Son*, showing how different interpretive contexts shape the reader's understanding of the novel. *The Reader in the Dickens World* (1981) explores the contradictions in Dickens's rhetorical voice that produce conflicting expectations in the reader.

Houghton, Arthur Boyd (1836–1875)   Painter and illustrator, he provided frontispieces for *Hard Times* and *Mutual Friend* in the CHEAP EDITION.

House, Humphry (1909–1955)   Oxford don and, with EDMUND WILSON, one of the pioneers of contemporary Dickens studies. His classic work, *The Dickens World* (1941), places Dickens in his social and historical contexts and traces his growing awareness of the systematic social problems of Victorian England. The original editor of the Pilgrim Edition of Dickens's LETTERS, his role was assumed by his widow, Madeline House, and GRAHAM STOREY after his early death.

Household Edition   Popular edition of Dickens's works issued in monthly parts by CHAPMAN AND HALL between 1871 and 1879. This edition included JOHN FORSTER's *Life of Dickens*, as well as the novels; it was generously illustrated by several new illustrators, notably James Mahoney, CHARLES GREEN, H. French, F. A. Fraser, A. B. Frost, Gordon Thomson, E. G. Dalziel, and, most significantly, FREDERICK BARNARD, who illustrated nine of the novels. The American Household Edition, issued simultaneously by Harper & Brothers, replaced several of the British illustrators with American artists C. S. Reinhart, Thomas Worth, W. L. Shepperd, E. A. Abbey, and Thomas Nast.

Household Words   Weekly magazine "conducted" and edited by Dickens from March 30, 1850, to May 28, 1859. It took its title from Shakespeare, "Familiar in their mouths as Household Words" (*Henry V*, 4.3.52), and among its stated purposes was "to show to all, that in all familiar things, even in those which are repellant on the surface, there is Romance enough, if we will find it out." The magazine, sold at two shillings for a weekly issue, was also issued in monthly form and in bound annual volumes. Articles were unsigned, and many were edited or coauthored by Dickens or his subeditor, W. H. WILLS. Although serialized novels were not part of the original plan, Dickens ran *Hard Times* in the magazine after the circulation dropped in 1853. Besides the many articles he wrote or collaborated on for the magazine, Dickens wrote the frame narratives and occasional stories for the annual Christmas numbers. After quarreling with BRADBURY & EVANS over the publication of a statement about his separation, Dickens discontinued *Household Words* and incorporated it into ALL THE YEAR ROUND.

Ann Lohrli compiled the contents of the magazine, indentified its contributors, and developed summaries of their work for the magazine (*Household Words*, 1973). Dickens's contributions to the magazine were collected by B. W. MATZ (1908), and his collaborative pieces were collected by HARRY STONE (*Uncollected Writings*, 1968). MICHAEL SLATER (*Dickens's Journalism*, vol. 2, 1996) provides a scholarly edition of the articles for *Household Words*.

Houston, Gail Turley Professor, University of New Mexico, who writes about Victorian cultural history and women's issues during the period, as well as on the novelists, particularly Dickens and Charlotte Brontë. In *Consuming Fictions: Gender, Class, and Hunger in Dickens's Novels* (1994), Houston draws on medical, economic, psychoanalytic, and biographical materials to illuminate several of Dickens's novels. *Royalties: The Queen and Victorian Writers* (1999) is concerned with how Victorian writers, including Dickens, responded to and wrote about the queen and her authority. *From Dickens to Dracula* (2005) studies the gothic strain in Victorian fiction and its use of a transformed language from economics.

Huffam, Christopher (d. 1839) Dickens's godfather, a prosperous naval rigger who lived in Limehouse. Dickens made several memorable visits to him when his family lived in BAYHAM STREET in 1822–23.

Hugo, Victor (1802–1885) French novelist, poet, and dramatist, best known for *The Hunchback of Notre Dame* (1831) and *Les Misérables* (1862); one of the French authors Dickens met on his visit to Paris in 1844. Dickens was sometimes compared to Hugo; both novelists used horror and eccentric characters, and both utilized the serial format.

Hullah, John (1812–1884) Composer who wrote the music for Dickens's comic operetta *The Village Coquettes.*

Hungerford Market A long-established market that had fallen into decay in the early years of the 19th century, when Dickens spent odd hours there while working in the BLACKING WAREHOUSE. A new market replaced the old buildings in 1833, and CHARING CROSS Station was built on the site in 1862. Mr. Dick has rooms in the vicinity of the market (*Copperfield*, 35).

Hungerford Stairs Stairs leading to the THAMES by Hungerford Market. WARREN'S BLACKING was located by the stairs; the Micawbers leave for AUSTRALIA from Hungerford Stairs (*Copperfield*, 57).

Hunt, Leigh (1784–1859) Poet, essayist and editor of literary journals, Hunt was a friend of John Keats, LORD BYRON, Percy Shelley, Thomas Moore, and Charles Lamb. JOHN FORSTER introduced him to Dickens in 1838, and the two became friends. When Dickens based Harold Skimpole on Hunt, however, the friendship was strained. Dickens claimed that only some of Hunt's more delightful characteristics informed the character, but he later admitted that "I suppose that he is the most exact portrait that was ever painted in words! . . . It is an absolute reproduction of a real man."

Hunt, William Holman (1827–1910) Artist and member of the PRE-RAPHAELITE Brotherhood who was the best man at the wedding of CHARLES ALLSTON COLLINS to Dickens's daughter KATE MACREADY DICKENS in 1860.

Huntington Library, California This collection contains the manuscripts of several articles and shorter pieces by Dickens, plus about 1,000 letters.

Hutter, Albert D. (1941–2004) Professor, UCLA; mystery writer; and psychoanalyst. Hutter has written several articles on psychological issues in the novels and their roots in Victorian culture, among

View of Hungerford Stairs by the Thames, where Warren's Blacking Warehouse was located.

them "The High Tower of His Mind: Psychoanalysis and the Reader of *Bleak House*" (*Criticism*, 1977) and "Nation and Generation in *A Tale of Two Cities*" (*PMLA*, 1978). "Dismemberment and Articulation in *Our Mutual Friend*" (*Dickens Studies Annual*, 1983) analyzes the role of Mr. Venus, the taxidermist and articulator of bones, connecting it with the death and resurrection story at the center of the novel, especially in the Harmon murder plot, and with the fragmentation and dismemberment of Victorian society.

Hyde Park   Dickens had lodgings at several addresses in the neighborhood of the park during the 1860s. Oliver and Bill Sikes pass Hyde Park Corner on their way to CHERTSEY (*Twist*, 21).

I

---

illustrations Nearly all of Dickens's novels were illustrated in their serial and first editions. Only *Hard Times* and *Great Expectations*, which first appeared in Dickens's unillustrated magazines, made their first appearance without pictures.

Pickwick, Dickens's first novel, was originally conceived as a series of sporting prints by ROBERT SEYMOUR for which Dickens was to provide editorial copy. Dickens took the opportunity provided by Seymour's suicide to reorient the project, giving more prominence to the verbal narrative. Dickens seems to have thought of *Twist*, which he subtitled "The Parish Boy's Progress," as a narrative in the manner of WILLIAM HOGARTH, whose progresses told stories in series of pictures. Visual narrative, then, had an important place in Dickens's developing idea of the novel. The illustrators with whom Dickens worked on these early novels, HABLOT KNIGHT BROWNE and GEORGE CRUIKSHANK, were both practitioners in the graphic satire tradition descended from Hogarth.

In his standard serial format, each monthly number included two illustrations, so a 20-part novel contained 40 illustrations by the time it was completed. During his career, Dickens worked with 18 illustrators, among them some of the foremost artists of his day, including Cruikshank, JOHN LEECH, DANIEL MACLISE, SIR EDWIN HENRY LANDSEER, and LUKE FILDES. His principal collaborator was Hablot Browne ("PHIZ"), who illustrated most of the novels from *Pickwick* through *Two Cities*.

The illustrations for the later novels are generally considered less successful than those for the earlier books. This decline has been variously attributed to the displacement of visual caricature by more realistic illustration, the increased literacy of Dickens's readers, and Dickens's own diminished interest in the illustrations.

J. R. HARVEY (1971) discusses the Dickens illustrations in relation to the tradition of graphic satire. Jane R. Cohen (*Charles Dickens and His Original Illustrators*, 1980) describes the contributions of each of the 18 original illustrators and the nature of their relationships with Dickens. MICHAEL STEIG (1978) discusses Dickens's collaboration with Browne and the way the illustrations affect the reader's understanding of the novels.

Many later artists have also undertaken to illustrate the novels or to represent the characters. Among the more noteworthy are SOLOMON EYTINGE, FREDERICK BARNARD, J. C. CLARKE ("KYD"), CHARLES GREEN, HARRY FURNISS, C. E. BROCK, and Gordon Ross.

impressionism A technique in writing in which events or scenes are described in terms of how they appear at a precise moment from an individual's point of view. Derived from impressionistic painting, literary impressionism's most notable practitioners were such turn-of-the-century novelists as Stephen Crane and Joseph Conrad. Although Dickens was writing without the example of Monet,

Manet, and their fellow painters to draw on, he made occasional use of impressionistic technique, as in the opening chapter of *Expectations*. There Pip describes the convict picking him up and turning him upside down in the following terms: "The man, after looking at me for a moment, turned me upside down, and emptied my pockets. There was nothing in them but a piece of bread. When the church came to itself—for he was so sudden and strong that he made it go head over heels before me, and I saw the steeple under my feet—when the church came to itself, I say, I was seated on a high tombstone, trembling, while he ate the bread ravenously."

Industrial Revolution Historians usually date the Industrial Revolution from about 1760, when a series of inventions began to transform the manufacture of textiles. The impact of these inventions was not generally recognized, however, until the early 19th century, when the application of steam to power the new machines created a number of new industrial cities in the north of England and railways made them easily accessible from the south. Dickens and other Victorian novelists born during the second decade of the century were the first generation of writers to acknowledge the emergence of industrial England.

The first description of industry in Dickens's works appears in Little Nell's journey through the BLACK COUNTRY in *Curiosity Shop* (43–45), but Dickens's most sustained depiction of industrial England is in *Hard Times*, in which Coketown is based on his observations of life in MANCHESTER and PRESTON. Dickens wrote about these industrial towns as an outsider, a southerner with little day-to-day experience of life there, and he has been criticized for simplifying and misunderstanding the industrial north, especially the labor UNIONS. However, he did not attempt in *Hard Times* to provide a realistic description of the factories or of life in the new industrial cities as ELIZABETH GASKELL, a resident of Manchester, had done in *Mary Barton* (1848). Nor does he take on such issues as child labor or industrial safety. He directs his attention instead to the hard-fact empiricism that produced industrialization and its effects on education and domestic life.

As a novelist of urban life, of the anomie and isolation in the cities and the objectification of the human that turned men into machines, Dickens, more than any other early Victorian novelist, responded to the changes brought about by industrialization. His use of the RAILWAYS in *Dombey* and other novels symbolizes the changes brought about by "steam." RAYMOND WILLIAMS, in his various writings on Dickens, discusses the ways in which Dickens's works responded to industrialization and urbanization.

infant mortality Although the infant mortality rate in Victorian England was lower than that in all but the Scandanavian countries in Europe, it was nevertheless approximately 10 times the current rate. In 1840, the reported rate was 143 of 1,000 live births, and this figure is probably low, since many physicians did not report stillbirths.

The death of a newborn or of the mother was not uncommon. Dickens's daughter Dora died in her first year, not long after the deaths in his novels of Fanny Dombey after the birth of young Paul and of David Copperfield's infant brother. Even though the five little stone lozenges marking the graves of Pip's siblings (*Expectations*, 1) may exaggerate the average figures, they reduced the 13 graves in the churchyard at COOLING that Dickens had in mind to a more believable number.

Victorians often blamed the high infant mortality rate on the practice of baby farming, putting infants in foster facilities like that of Mrs. Mann in *Twist* (2), where Oliver's friend, young Dick, becomes a statistic. Dickens attacked the practice of baby farming in his articles on one such "Paradise at Tooting."

"Inimitable Boz, the" The name Dickens sometimes gave himself, turning his *nom de plume* into the appellation of a theatrical or circus performer. (*See also* "BOZ.")

Inns of Court Located in HOLBORN near the law courts, these institutions were originally the premises of four societies empowered to admit persons to the Bar: GRAY'S INN, LINCOLN'S INN, the Inner TEMPLE, and the Middle Temple. By the middle of the 19th century, chambers in the inns could be rented by people other than barristers and law students. Pip and Herbert Pocket, for example, have rooms in the Temple. There were also several lesser inns, known as the Inns of CHANCERY, that offered such lodgings: Barnard's Inn, CLIFFORD'S INN, FURNIVAL'S INN, Sergeant's Inn, STAPLE INN, and Symond's Inn.

international copyright On his first trip to America in 1842, Dickens raised a considerable controversy when he delivered three speeches—in BOSTON, HARTFORD, and NEW YORK—calling for a system of international copyright. Although copyright laws had been adopted in the 18th century to protect the works of American authors, such protection did not extend to works by foreigners. The works of Dickens and other English authors were commonly reprinted in American papers that specialized in pirating the works of foreigners. Dickens argued that this practice not only denied the authors their rightful reward but also created unfair competition for native writers and discouraged the development of a national literature. His remarks prompted American writers to circulate a petition to Congress urging an international copyright agreement, but his speeches were also attacked as greedy and self-serving in several American newspapers—many of them profiting by piracy. In response, Dickens attacked the American press in *Notes*, satirized it in *Chuzzlewit*, and urged his fellow English writers to deal only with reputable American publishers. An international copyright agreement was not passed until 1891. (*See also* COPYRIGHT.)

interpolated tales Stories inserted or added to a narrative that are not integral to the main plot or story. Dickens modeled his use of interpolated tales on the works of HENRY FIELDING and TOBIAS SMOLLETT, two of his favorite authors as a child. The several interpolated tales in *Pickwick* were long viewed as extraneous to the story, but recent critics have argued that they are necessary to present the dark side of life that the innocent Pickwick otherwise fails to notice. Interpolated tales appear in several of the early novels—*Pickwick*, *Nickleby*, and

Master Humphrey's Clock—but Dickens abandoned the practice in his later, more carefully structured works. Miss Wade's "History of a Self-Tormentor" (*Dorrit*, II:21) has the appearance of an interpolated tale but is organic to the thematic development of the novel.

Irving, Sir Henry (1838–1905) Late-Victorian actor, known for his ability to play many kinds of roles. Among the Dickens characters that he portrayed were Jingle, Bill Sikes, Nicholas Nickleby, Mr. Dombey, John Peerybingle, and Digby Grant, a character based on Mr. Dorrit. He gave performances of Dickens characters for charity. In recognition of his success in these performances, the Dickens family gave him the desk and gas lighting system that Dickens used in his PUBLIC READINGS.

Irving, Washington (1783–1859) American author whose *Sketch-Book* provided an important model for Dickens's *Sketches by Boz*. After corresponding with him, Dickens met Irving on his American tour in 1842. At the Dickens Dinner in New York, Irving supported Dickens's controversial call for an INTERNATIONAL COPYRIGHT agreement when he noted in his toast to the visitor, "It is but fair that those who have laurels for their brows should be permitted to browse on their laurels." Dickens described Irving as "a *great* fellow. We have laughed most heartily together. He is just the man he ought to be."

Islington In the 19th century, this village on the north edge of London was an important way station on the great north road out of London. Either the Angel or the PEACOCK INN is mentioned as a landmark or stopping place in *Boz* ("Prisoners' Van"), *Rudge* (31, 68), *Nickleby* (39), *Twist* (8, 12), and *Bleak House* (59). Potter and Smithers (*Boz*, "Making a Night"), Tom and Ruth Pinch (*Chuzzlewit*, 36, 37), and Mr. Morfin (*Dombey*, 13) live in Islington.

Italy Dickens made two trips to Italy: he spent a year there with his family in 1844–45, first staying at GENOA for several months and later touring the north of Italy, ROME, and NAPLES. The letters he wrote to JOHN FORSTER during this trip provided the basis for *Pictures from Italy* (1846). He went to Italy a second time in 1853 with AUGUSTUS EGG and WILKIE COLLINS, visiting Genoa, Naples—where they climbed Mt. Vesuvius—Rome, FLORENCE, VENICE, and Turin. Dickens was able to appreciate Italy as a tourist because he was not generally recognized as a famous author there and he did not expect it to exemplify his political ideals, as he had expected AMERICA to do. He was unsympathetic to the CATHOLIC CHURCH, however, which he saw as allied with tyranny and oppression, and he described church ceremonies as fraudulent "mummery."

Dickens drew on his Italian experiences for his descriptions of the Dorrit family in Venice and Rome (II:3–7, 11, 14–15, 19). Em'ly flees from Steerforth and hides in a fishing village near Naples (*Copperfield,* 46, 50).

J

Jackson, Thomas A. (1879–1955) In *Charles Dickens: The Progress of a Radical* (1937), a Marxist reading of the novels, Jackson finds many points of agreement between Marx and Engels and Dickens. He describes the late novels from *Bleak House* on as the culmination of Dickens's developing class analysis of his society.

Jaffe, Audrey Contemporary scholar and critic; professor, Ohio State University. In *Vanishing Points: Dickens, Narrative, and the Subject of Omniscience* (1991), Jaffe discusses the NARRATOR and POINT OF VIEW in Dickens's novels, describing his omniscient narrator as occupying a position between a disembodied voice outside the novel and a presence within it, a tension produced by the problematical status of omniscience itself in Victorian England. She also discusses several "semi-omniscient" characters, figures like Florence Dombey, Esther Summerson, David Copperfield, and John Harmon, who mediate between the action in the novel and our consciousness of it, becoming in the process "vanishing points" in the narration. In *Scenes of Sympathy: Identity and Repression in Victorian Fiction* (2000) Jaffe analyzes *A Christmas Carol* as an object designed to convert the reader to sympathy for those like the Cratchits.

James, Henry (1843–1916) American novelist and critic. As a realist and modernist, James is often remembered as antagonistic to Dickens. In his review of *Our Mutual Friend*, written for the *Nation* when he was only 22, he expressed his reservations about Dickens's superficiality and philosophical incoherence and the lack of universal humanity in Dickens's eccentric characters. Nevertheless, in later autobiographical writings, James recalled the powerful hold Dickens had on his childhood imagination and his meeting with "the master" during Dickens's 1867 reading tour in America. GEORGE FORD (1955) discusses James's mixed feelings about his predecessor and speculates about Dickens's influence on James's work, especially on *The Princess Casamassima* (1886).

Jeffrey, Francis (Lord Jeffrey) (1773–1850) Scottish judge, member of Parliament, literary critic, and the editor and founder of the *Edinburgh Review*. An early admirer of Dickens's work, especially *Twist, Curiosity Shop, Carol,* and *Dombey,* Jeffrey became one of Dickens's close friends and a frequent correspondent. Dickens visited him in Scotland in 1841, dedicated *Cricket* to him, and named his fifth child FRANCIS JEFFREY DICKENS after the child's godfather.

Jerdan, William (1782–1869) Editor of the *Literary Gazette* from 1817 to 1850 who urged Dickens, after he introduced Sam Weller into *Pickwick,* to develop his character "to the utmost." Dickens invited him to the dinner celebrating the completion of the novel. Jerdan also contributed to BENTLEY'S MISCELLANY when it was under Dickens's editorship.

Jerrold, Douglas William (1803–1857)   Dramatist, radical satirical journalist, and wit, best known for his play *Black-eyed Susan* (1829). Jerrold, who shared Dickens's political and social views, was one of Dickens's close friends, a man Dickens described as "the gentlest and most affectionate of men." He edited *Douglas Jerrold's Shilling Magazine* and *Douglas Jerrold's Weekly Newspaper*. He worked with Dickens on the DAILY NEWS and on several of the AMATEUR THEATRICALS. After his death Dickens organized several performances of THE FROZEN DEEP for the benefit of Jerrold's widow and family. Jerrold's son, William Blanchard (1826–1884), was a frequent contributor to HOUSEHOLD WORDS.

Jews   The two important Jews in Dickens's novels are Fagin in *Twist* and Riah in *Mutual Friend*. Fagin has often been viewed as an anti-Semitic stereotype and Riah as Dickens's attempt to atone for Fagin. There is a good deal of truth to this characterization, for Dickens was prompted to include Riah in the later novel by ELIZA DAVIS, who complained of his anti-Semitism in *Twist* and urged him to make amends. At the same time, he removed or altered many of the references to "The Jew" in *Oliver Twist* while preparing the text for the CHARLES DICKENS EDITION. Attitudes toward Jews were changing during Dickens's lifetime, and, as HARRY STONE (1959) points out, the treatment of Fagin was representative of the anti-Semitism of its time. By 1865 many of the earlier attitudes toward Jews and the social restrictions placed on them had changed. Riah, then, represents both a change in societal attitudes during the period and Dickens's conscious attempt to right an injustice, however unconscious his earlier anti-Semitism had been.

John, Juliet   Senior lecturer, University of Liverpool. In *Dickens's Villains: Melodrama, Character, Popular Culture* (2001) John discusses both the melodramatic, outward presentation of the villains and their inner psychological complexity. John has

also edited *Cult Criminals* (1998), a set of six Newgate novels from the 1830s, and a source book on *Oliver Twist* (2006).

Johnson, President Andrew (1808–1875)   President of the United States from 1865 to 1868. Dickens met with him in WASHINGTON on February 5, 1868, just a few weeks before Johnson's impeachment. Dickens found him "a man not to be turned or trifled with . . . who must be killed to be got out of the way."

Johnson, Edgar (1912–1995)   Biographer and critic; professor, New York University; Dickens's foremost modern biographer. His *Charles Dickens: His Tragedy and Triumph* (1952) remains a standard scholarly biography. Thoroughly researched and copiously documented, it was reissued in revised and abridged form in 1977. He was the author of numerous articles on Dickens and editor of Dickens's letters to ANGELA BURDETT-COUTTS, *The Heart of Charles Dickens* (1952). With Eleanor Johnson, he also collected a volume of Dickens's writings about the theater, *The Dickens Theatrical Reader* (1964).

Johnson Street   Street in SOMERS TOWN, north London, where the Dickens family lived in 1825 while Charles attended WELLINGTON HOUSE ACADEMY.

Jones, William (1786–1836)   Welsh headmaster of WELLINGTON HOUSE ACADEMY, which Dickens attended between 1824 and 1827. His sadistic treatment of the students, caning them or striking them across the palms with "a bloated mahogany ruler," made him the probable model for Mr. Creakle in *Copperfield*.

Jonson, Ben (1572–1637)   Renaissance playwright, best known for *Volpone* (1606) and *The Alchemist* (1610). A practitioner of the comedy of humors, in which, as Jonson himself described it in *Every Man out of His Humour* (1599), "some one peculiar quality / Doth so possess a man, that it doth draw / All of his affects, his spirits, and his powers, / In their confluctions, all to run one way." Jonson's characters are driven by a single obsession, such as greed, jealousy, or suspiciousness, and at the end of the play, they are called to account for their vices. *Every Man in His Humour* (1598) was a fixture in the repertory of plays performed by Dickens's AMATEUR THEATRICAL groups. Dickens took the role of the boastful coward Bobadil.

The conventions of humors comedy influenced Dickens's flat characters, who are defined by a single central trait; characters' names, which often suggest the moral attributes of the figures who bear them; and his comic plots, which expose the failings of such characters as the hypocritical Pecksniff or the ambitious Uriah Heep. The novel in which the influence of the humors tradition is most apparent is *Chuzzlewit*. NORTHROP FRYE (1968) discusses Dickens in relation to the humors tradition.

journalism   Dickens began his career as a journalist, and throughout his life he was involved in journalistic projects, as a writer, editor, and publisher. Many features of his work as a novelist can be traced to his experience as a journalist: his use of serial form, his close relationship with his audience, his focus on social issues. Although critics have recognized the relevance of Dickens's journalistic writing to the novels, the work, as journalism, has largely been ignored until recently. Dickens's own collections of his journalistic pieces in *Sketches by Boz, Reprinted Pieces, The Uncommercial Traveller,* and *Christmas Stories* have been viewed as minor works, interesting only insofar as they illuminate the novels. MICHAEL SLATER's comprehensive, four-volume scholarly edition, *Dickens' Journalism* (1994–2000), collects most, though not all, of Dickens's journalistic pieces and contextualizes them with explanatory notes. John Drew, who collaborated with Slater on the fourth volume, has provided a scholarly study of these works in *Dickens the Journalist* (2003), which discusses them as journalism rather than as adjuncts to the novels. B. W. MATZ's earlier collection, *Miscellaneous Papers* (1908), lacks scholarly apparatus, but it does include a few pieces not included by Slater. HARRY STONE's *Uncollected Writings from Household Words, 1850–1859* (1968) collects pieces that Dickens collaborated on with other writers or significantly revised.

juvenile crime   There was growing concern in the 1820s and 1830s over the increase in juvenile crime, now generally attributed to the dislocations resulting from industrialization. At the time, no distinction was made between juvenile and adult offenders, and children as young as eight could be imprisoned or transported as adults. The jails, like the criminal rookeries in the slums of the major cities, became schools in criminality where children like Oliver Twist were trained for a life of crime. Dickens was an active supporter of the reform movement, led by Mary Carpenter and LORD SHAFTESBURY, that sought to distinguish juvenile from adult offenders and to provide education for children in hopes of preventing criminal activity. Their efforts led to the Juvenile Offenders Act (1847), which distinguished adult offenders from children under 14 and gave judges the discretionary power to dismiss charges against youthful offenders. In the 1840s and 1850s the reformers also established RAGGED SCHOOLS, reformatory schools, and industrial schools, designed to educate children away from a life of crime. These institutions are generally credited with lowering the juvenile crime rate after 1860.

K

Kafka, Franz (1885–1924)   Novelist and short story writer; born in Prague, he wrote in German. An admirer of Dickens's work, Kafka, especially in *Amerika* (1927), drew on his sense of Dickens, especially *David Copperfield* with its similarly naive and victimized hero. Mark Spilka, whose *Dickens and Kafka* (1963) is the most thorough examination of the connections between the two writers, discusses the relationship of *The Trial* to *Bleak House* and both writers' use of the grotesque.

Kaplan, Fred (1937–)   Professor, City University of New York; scholar of Victorian literature and culture; biographer. Besides his definitive modern biography of THOMAS CARLYLE (1983) and his biographies of Mark Twain, HENRY JAMES, and Gore Vidal, Kaplan has written a scholarly biography of Dickens (1988), particularly revealing in its account of Dickens's personal and family life; *Dickens and Mesmerism* (1975), an account of Dickens's involvement with hypnotism and its effect on his novels; *Sacred Tears: Sentimentality in Victorian Literature* (1987). Kaplan has also edited Dickens's Memorandum Book, which is in the collection of the New York Public Library (1981).

Keeley, Robert (1793–1869)   He and his wife Mary Goward (1806–1899) were actors and theater managers who, in the 1840s, produced many dramas based on Dickens's works. Mrs. Keeley established her reputation as a portrayer of Dickens's children: Oliver, Smike, Nell, and Young Bailey. She also played Meg Veck, Dot Peerybingle, and Clemency Newcome before she gave up Dickensian roles. Her husband was best known for his portrayal of Sairey Gamp. Their daughter Louise played Dot in DION BOUCICAULT's version of *Cricket* (1862). Dickens first met the Keeleys when they were performing in EDWARD STIRLING's adaptation of *Nickleby* in 1839. They remained friends throughout his life. After Robert Keeley's death, Dickens described him as "a master of pathos" onstage and "in private, he had the heart of a child, and the integrity of the noblest man."

Keepsake, The   An illustrated annual edited by the COUNTESS OF BLESSINGTON. Dickens published a verse satire, "A Word in Season" (1843), and a story, "To Be Read at Dusk" (1852), in this annual.

Kenilworth   Medieval castle in Warwickshire, an important setting in SIR WALTER SCOTT's *Kenilworth* (1821), to which Dombey takes Edith Granger during their courtship (*Dombey*, 27). Dickens stayed at the castle with HABLOT KNIGHT BROWNE in 1838.

Kennington   The south London district where Mr. Vholes lives in a country cottage with his three daughters (*Bleak House*, 39). When Jemmy Lirriper gets lost, he is found by the Kennington police ("Lirriper's Lodgings").

Kensington Fashionable suburb of London, south of HYDE PARK, where Gabriel Parsons meets Fanny secretly (*Boz*, "Tottle"); it is the home of Sam Weller's man of principle, who dies from eating crumpets (*Pickwick*, 44). Prince Turveydrop teaches in a Kensington dancing academy (*Bleak House*, 4).

Kent County east of London on the south side of the Thames where Dickens spent some of the happiest years of his childhood in CHATHAM and the last decade of his life at GAD'S HILL PLACE. It provides many settings for the novels, especially Chatham, ROCHESTER, and CANTERBURY. David Copperfield's journey to DOVER in search of Betsey Trotwood follows the Kent Road out of London (*Copperfield*, 13).

Kent, William Charles (1823–1902) Journalist and editor; contributor to HOUSEHOLD WORDS and ALL THE YEAR ROUND. His enthusiastic review of *Dombey* in *The Sun* led to his friendship with Dickens. He organized the reading tour in 1867 and compiled a record of Dickens's readings from papers supplied by the author, published as *Charles Dickens as a Reader* (1872).

Kincaid, James R. (1937–) Professor, University of Southern California; scholar of Victorian literature who has written on Alfred, Lord Tennyson, Anthony Trollope, Lewis Carroll, and, especially, Dickens. *Dickens and the Rhetoric of Laughter* (1971) studies the ways in which Dickens uses laughter to castigate his characters' weaknesses and correct them, producing a world of "freedom, justice, rebirth, flexibility." In *Child Loving: The Erotic Child and Victorian Culture* (1992), which considers the Victorian child figure and its relevance to current concerns about pedophilia and the eroticized child in contempory culture, Kincaid briefly discusses Paul Dombey, Little Nell, David Copperfield, and Oliver Twist. *Annoying the Victorians* (1995) devotes much of its attention to Dickens as it mocks and parodies obsessions of contemporary literary criticism.

King's Bench Prison Last of London's DEBTORS' PRISONS, this prison in SOUTHWARK on the BOROUGH Road became exclusively a debtors' prison in the late 18th century. In 1780 it was burnt down by the Gordon rioters (*Rudge*, 67), but it was later rebuilt. It was demolished in 1869. The Traveller describes the prison in *Uncommercial* (13). Mr. Micawber is imprisoned here while David is staying with the Micawber family (*Copperfield*, 11). Mr. Bray has permission to live in the rules of the prison, that is, to live in an area surrounding the prison, for which he pays a fee (*Nickleby*, 46, 47, 51).

Kingston, Ontario Town in CANADA, visited by Dickens on his 1842 tour of AMERICA, that he described as "a very poor town, rendered still poorer in the appearance of its market-place by the ravages of a recent fire" (*Notes*, 15).

Kingston, Surrey Betty Higden goes through this town along the THAMES on her final journey (*Mutual Friend*, III:8). Magwitch tells of being in jail here (*Expectations*, 42). Gowan sketches here (*Dorrit*, I:17).

Kitton, Frederic G. (1856–1904) Artist and wood-engraver, Dickens bibliographer, compiler, and scholar who illustrated many Dickens subjects and did pioneering work on Dickens's writings and illustrations. He was one of the founders of the DICKENSIAN and was slated to be its first editor, but he died before the magazine made its debut. His library forms part of the collection at DICKENS HOUSE. Among his works on Dickens, *Dickensiana* (1886), *The Minor Writings of Charles Dickens* (1900), *Charles Dickens by Pen and Pencil* (1890), and *Dickens and His Illustrators* (1899) contain some still-useful material.

Knebworth Stately home of SIR EDWARD BULWER LYTTON in Hertfordshire. Lytton invited Dickens's AMATEUR THEATRICAL company to perform *Every Man in His Humour* there in the fall of 1850, and at that time he and Dickens conceived the plan for the GUILD OF LITERATURE AND ART. As part of this scheme, three gothic houses for writers and artists were built on the estate and were dedicated in 1865.

Knight, Charles (1791–1873) Publisher, journalist, regular contributor to *Household Words;* member, with Dickens, of the Shakespeare Society; and one of the organizers of Dickens's AMATEUR THEATRICALS. Dickens shared Knight's passion for educating the common man, and the two celebrated their friendship by dining together each year on Knight's birthday. Knight described his relationship with Dickens in *Passages of a Working Life* (1864).

Knowles, James Sheridan (1784–1862) Dramatist. In 1832 Dickens had an audition for a part in Knowles's play *The Hunchback,* but a cold and a sore throat prevented his keeping the engagement. Dickens was active in charitable efforts to provide Knowles with financial aid during his old age.

Kolle, Henry (1808?–1881) A friend of Dickens's youth, he exchanged letters with the author. He married MARIA BEADNELL's sister Anne.

Kucich, John (1952–) Professor, University of Michigan; psychological critic of Victorian fiction. In a postmodern analysis, *Excess and Restraint in the Novels of Charles Dickens* (1981), Kucich concentrates on the tension between the desire to transcend boundaries and the constraints imposed by society and the human condition. Using this dichotomy, he analyzes the patterns of melodrama in the novels, the nature of villainy, and the ways the endings reconcile this tension. In *Repression in Victorian Fiction: Charlotte Brontë, George Eliot, and Charles Dickens* (1987), Kucich studies the ways in which three Victorian novelists use psychological repression to express the interiority of their characters.

Künstlerroman A subgenre of the BILDUNGSROMAN that describes the maturation of an artist. The most notable example in English is James Joyce's *Portrait of the Artist as a Young Man* (1916). Technically, *David Copperfield* fits this form, but the novel makes little attempt to describe the artist as different from any other successful young man. Indeed, David's success as a novelist seems to be the same as that open to a diligent and disciplined person in any field of endeavor.

"Kyd" Pen name of illustrator JOSEPH CLAYTON CLARKE.

L

Lambeth Slum area south of the THAMES across from Westminster where Peg Sliderskew hides after stealing the papers from Arthur Gride (*Nickleby*, 57). In nearby Walcot Square is the house that Mr. Guppy has taken with the prospect of marrying Esther Summerson (*Bleak House*, 64). The Gordon rioters attack Lambeth Palace, residence of the Archbishop of Canterbury (*Rudge*, 67).

Lamert, James Stepson of Dickens's mother's sister, he lived with the Dickens family in CHATHAM and in CAMDEN TOWN after they moved to London. He built a toy theater for young Charles and introduced him to the theater in Chatham. He also arranged for the boy to work in the BLACKING WAREHOUSE that he managed for his brother-in-law George Lamert. James's father, **Dr. Matthew Lamert** (1774–1848), an army surgeon in Chatham, was probably the model for Dr. Slammer in *Pickwick*.

Lancaster Dickens stayed at the King's Arms Inn in this Lancashire town with WILKIE COLLINS in September 1857 and made it the setting for the ghost story "The Bride's Chamber" in *Lazy Tour*.

Landon, Letitia Elizabeth ("L.E.L") (1802–1838) Poet and historical novelist who used the initials L.E.L. as her nom de plume and, like Byron, had a reputation for scandal. Dickens knew her

as a member of the COUNTESS OF BLESSINGTON's circle at Gore House. She was engaged briefly to JOHN FORSTER and later married George Maclean, governor of the Gold Coast. Three months after her marriage she was found dead of poison under suspicious circumstances.

Landor, Walter Savage (1775–1864) Poet and essayist, friend of Dickens. JOHN FORSTER introduced the young novelist to the old poet in 1840. The two admired each other's work and quickly became friends. On one of his annual birthday visits to Landor at BATH in 1840, Dickens came up with the idea of Little Nell, the character most loved by Landor of all of Dickens's creations. Landor was godfather to Dickens's second son and the model for Boythorn in *Bleak House*, whose hot temper, warm heart, and addiction to superlatives were all characteristic of the poet.

Landseer, Sir Edwin Henry (1802–1873) Painter and sculptor, best known for his paintings of animals and for the lions on Nelson's Monument in Trafalgar Square. He was one of Dickens's many artist friends and a member of "the Portwiners" club along with JOHN FORSTER, WILLIAM MAKEPEACE THACKERAY, EDWARD BULWER LYTTON, WILLIAM MACREADY, MARK LEMON, and DANIEL MACLISE. He provided one illustration, a picture of the dog Boxer, for *Cricket on the Hearth*. He looked after

Landseer's only illustration for Dickens was this picture of John Peerybingle's dog Boxer for *The Cricket on the Hearth.*

Grip, Dickens's pet raven, while the novelist was in Italy and was deeply moved by Dickens's death. He is the artist in "Friend of the Lions."

Langley, Noel (1911–1980)   Novelist, dramatist, screenwriter, and filmmaker who adapted *A Christmas Carol* (1951) and adapted and directed *Pickwick Papers* (1952) for the screen.

Lant Street   On this street in SOUTHWARK Dickens had lodgings while he worked at the BLACKING WAREHOUSE in 1822–23. Bob Sawyer lodges in Mrs. Raddle's house here, where "the majority of the inhabitants either direct their energies to the letting of furnished apartments, or devote themselves to the healthful and invigorating pursuit of mangling" (*Pickwick*, 32).

Larson, Janet L. (1945–)   Professor, Rutgers University; editor-at-large for the *Christian Century* who writes on the relationship between religion and literature. In *Dickens and the Broken Scripture* (1985), she studies the increasingly problematic role of biblical allusion in Dickens's novels as his confidence in biblical texts eroded along with that of his contemporaries.

Laughton, Charles (1899–1962)   British actor who played Pickwick on the London stage (1928), produced a version of *Bleak House* in New York (1953), and was intended for the role of Micaw-

ber in the 1935 MGM film *Copperfield,* a role that established W. C. FIELDS's Dickensian reputation.

Laurence, Samuel (1811–1884)   Artist who did portraits of many literary figures, including THOMAS CARLYLE, WILLIAM MAKEPEACE THACKERAY, and ROBERT BROWNING. He painted portraits of Dickens and his wife in 1837 while Dickens was at work on *Pickwick.*

Laurie, Sir Peter (1808–1877)   London magistrate who mounted a campaign to prevent suicide by sentencing those who tried and failed to the treadmill. Dickens satirized him as Alderman Cute in *The Chimes.* Laurie, who knew Dickens and had taken CATHERINE DICKENS to a LORD MAYOR'S dinner, described the Christmas book as "most disgraceful" and said Dickens was "a dangerous man to meet."

Lausanne   Swiss town on Lake Geneva where Dickens stayed with his family for several months in 1846. He began *Dombey* here and wrote *Battle of Life.* He later drew on his Swiss experiences in describing the Dorrits' journey to Italy.

law terms   The traditional schedule for the law courts in Westminster set four terms in which the courts were open: Hilary, January 11–31; Easter, April 15–May 8; Trinity, May 22–June 12; and Michaelmas, November 2–25. The Long Vacation described the period between Trinity and Michaelmas terms. Although the Judicature Act of 1873 abolished the terms for the courts, they are still informally recognized in various other functions.

Layard, Austen Henry (1817–1894)   Archaeologist who excavated Nineveh and other Middle Eastern sites, writer on art and other subjects, member of Parliament from 1852–57, and friend of Dickens. The novelist met Layard on an ascent of Mt. Vesuvius in 1853. After visiting the Crimea during the Crimean War, Layard formed the Administrative Reform Association to press for changes in the bungling government bureaucracy. Dickens supported his ultimately unsuccessful efforts with several articles in HOUSEHOLD WORDS in 1855. He addressed the association on June 27, 1855.

Leacock, Stephen (1869–1944)   Canadian humorist, essayist, and biographer; political scientist and economist at McGill University. His *Fiction and Reality: A Study of the Art of Charles Dickens* (1916) and *Charles Dickens: His Life and Work* (1933) are the work of a critic who wrote against the modernist denigration of Dickens at the time; they are particularly interesting for their treatment of Dickens as a humorist and caricaturist and for Leacock's comparisons of Dickens with Mark Twain.

Leadenhall Market   In the CITY on **Leadenhall Street.** Sam Weller writes his valentine to Mary at the Blue Boar (*Pickwick,* 33). The fictional Wooden Midshipman is located here, based on the actual marine instrument shop of Norie and Wilson at No. 157 Leadenhall Street (*Dombey*).

Lean, David (1908–1991)   British film director (*Doctor Zhivago, A Passage to India*) whose two adaptations from Dickens, *Great Expectations* (1946) and *Oliver Twist* (1948), are among the most successful film versions of Dickens's novels. Their masterful use of black-and-white photography, montage, and period settings mix realism with fantasy in particularly Dickensian ways.

Leavis, Frank Raymond (1905–1978)   Professor, Cambridge University; founder and editor of *Scrutiny*; literary critic who wrote widely on literary issues, particularly of the 19th and 20th centuries, and established a standard of moral seriousness by which he judged literary works. His controversial discussion of the 19th- and 20th-century novel, *The Great Tradition* (1948), discovered sufficient seriousness in only five major novelists: Jane Austen, GEORGE ELIOT, HENRY JAMES, Joseph Conrad, and D. H. Lawrence. Dickens, described as an "entertainer," achieved such seriousness, Leavis argued, only in *Hard Times,* which Leavis discussed in a note appended to the main text of his work. In 1970 he revised his views, and with his wife, **Queenie Dorothy** (1900–1982), he published *Dickens the Novelist.* Chapters on *Dombey, Copperfield, Bleak House, Hard Times, Dorrit,* and *Expectations* compare Dickens with Tolstoy and Blake and considerably expand the Leavises' view of the serious Dickens canon. Their critical work is characterized by close reading of the text and careful analysis of the psychological and moral situations in the novels. Even when they are wrong, their views are provocative and thoroughly grounded in the text.

Leavis, Q. D.   See LEAVIS, F. R.

Lebanon, Illinois   Town where Dickens stayed when he went out from St. Louis to see the Looking Glass Prairie, "lonely and wild, but oppressive in its barren monotony" (*Notes,* 13).

Lebanon, New York   Site of the "grim" Shaker village that the Dickenses visited in 1842. Afterward, Dickens commented: "I so abhor, and from my soul detest that bad spirit, no matter by what class or sect it may be entertained, which would strip life of its healthful graces, rob youth of its innocent pleasures, pluck from maturity and age their pleasant ornaments, and make existence but a narrow path towards the grave" (*Notes,* 15).

Lee, Jennie (1850–1925)   Stage actress whose fame was largely based on her performance as Jo in *Bleak House,* a role she first performed in the 1870s, giving her last performance in 1921 when she was in her 70s. She was said to play the part "with a realism and a pathos difficult to surpass. . . . [T]he slouching, dejected gait, and the movement of some hunted animal, were admirably exhibited." She was particularly affecting as she recited the Lord's Prayer.

Leech, John (1817–1864)   Illustrator and caricaturist, especially for PUNCH; friend who often dined and occasionally took holidays with Dickens; a participant in the Dickens theatricals. A friend of WILLIAM MAKEPEACE THACKERAY from Charterhouse School and his associate on *Punch,* Leech also applied unsuccessfully to replace ROBERT SEYMOUR as the illustrator for *Pickwick.* He illustrated *A Christmas Carol* and provided some illustrations for all of the other CHRISTMAS BOOKS. Dickens praised the beauty and idealism in his CARICATURES and considered his work "truer to life than even [WILLIAM] HOGARTH." Examples of his work appear on pages 60, 65, and 69.

Leicester Square   Area in west London, "a centre of attraction to indifferent foreign hotels and indifferent foreigners, racket courts, fighting men, swordsmen, old china, gaming houses, exhibitions, and a large medley of shabbiness and shrinking out of sight" (*Bleak House*, 21), where Trooper George has his shooting gallery. Known as Leicester Fields at the time of the GORDON RIOTS, it was the site of the mansion of Sir George Saville, sponsor of the Catholic Relief Bill in Parliament, that was burned by the demonstrators (*Rudge*, 56).

Leigh, Mary Ann   MARIA BEADNELL's closest friend and confidante, the original for Julia Mills, Dora Spenlow's friend in *Copperfield*. She flirted with Dickens, gossiped about his relationship with Maria, and earned his displeasure when some of the gossip got back to him.

Lemon, Mark (1809–1870)   Playwright, novelist, and founding editor of PUNCH from 1841 to 1870. Dickens met Lemon in 1843, and their mutual love of the theater, good company, and conviviality made them close friends. Dickens soon recruited Lemon for his AMATEUR THEATRICAL enterprises, and Lemon acted in most of Dickens's productions, performing especially well as Sir John Falstaff in *The Merry Wives of Windsor* in 1848. Dickens collaborated with Lemon on a farce, *Mr. Nightingale's Diary* (1851), and Lemon adapted for the stage two of Dickens's CHRISTMAS BOOKS, *The Chimes* and *The Haunted Man*. Although he was a regular visitor in Dickens's household and was "Uncle Mark" to the Dickens children, Lemon was rejected by Dickens after he represented CATHERINE DICKENS in the negotiations for the separation in 1858. The two were reconciled at CLARKSON STANFIELD's funeral in 1863, but their close friendship was never resumed.

Lesage, Alain René (1668–1747)   French novelist and dramatist, one of the early practitioners of the PICARESQUE. *Gil Blas* (1715–35; translated by TOBIAS SMOLLETT, 1749) was one of the cherished books of both Copperfield and Dickens. Dickens also refers to Lesage's satirical novel *Le Diable boiteux* (*The Devil upon Two Sticks*, 1707), in which a student releases from captivity Asmodeus, a small, lame demon, and is rewarded by seeing Madrid with all the rooftops pulled away so that he can know the guilty secrets of those living beneath. Dickens alludes to this invention significantly in *Curiosity Shop* (33) and *Dombey* (47).

Leslie, Charles Robert (1794–1859)   Artist, illustrator, and friend of Dickens. Introduced to Dickens by WASHINGTON IRVING, whose books he had illustrated, Leslie was a frequent visitor in Dickens's house. He painted a portrait of Dickens in the role of Bobadil (1846) and did the frontispiece for the CHEAP EDITION of *Pickwick*.

letters   Before he died, Dickens burned many of the letters he had received and requested his correspondents to do likewise, so many of his letters are forever lost. The first collection of his remaining letters, selected and sometimes severely edited by his daughter Mamie (*see* DICKENS, MARY) and GEORGINA HOGARTH appeared in three volumes in 1880–82. The next general selection was done in 1938 by WALTER DEXTER for the NONESUCH EDITION; this collection is the one that has been used until recently by scholars. It has been replaced by the monumental, 12-volume Pilgrim Edition of Dickens's Letters, which includes all the letters and is throughly edited and annotated by Madeline House, GRAHAM STOREY, KATHLEEN TILLOTSON, and others. Several volumes of letters to particular correspondents—among them BEARD, ANGELA BURDETT-COUTTS, MARIA BEADNELL, HENRY KOLLE, W. H. WILLS, and MARK LEMON—have also appeared over the years.

Lettis, Richard (1928–   )   Professor, C. W. Post University; critic of Victorian fiction. Lettis's two volumes on Dickens, *The Dickens Aesthetic* (1989) and *Dickens on Literature* (1990), describe the novelist's writings on literature and aesthetics and are especially useful for their use of Dickens's journalism and editorial advice. Lettis has also made a useful collection of critical materials in *Assessing Great Expectations* (1965; with R. Morris).

Lever, Charles (1806–1872) Irish physician, novelist, and humorist; contributor to HOUSEHOLD WORDS and ALL THE YEAR ROUND; best known for *The Confessions of Harry Lorrequer* (1839) and *Charles O'Malley* (1841). Although Lever's work was often compared to that of Dickens, the two were not close friends, perhaps because the ads for *Lorrequer* suggested that it was superior to *Pickwick*. Nevertheless, Dickens, who admired Lever's work, commissioned a serial from him in 1860 for *All the Year Round*. Unfortunately, the novel, *A Day's Ride*, did not interest readers, and Dickens was forced to serialize *Great Expectations* simultaneously to restore the magazine's circulation. Dickens assuaged Lever's hurt feelings over the episode by helping him negotiate a contract for the novel with CHAPMAN & HALL and by encouraging him to submit more stories and articles to the magazine.

Lewes, George Henry (1817–1878) Author, reviewer, and scientist; he lived with Mary Ann Evans (GEORGE ELIOT) as her husband from 1854 until his death; friend of Dickens. Lewes performed in Dickens's production of *Every Man in His Humour* in 1847. He carried on a public controversy with Dickens over the SPONTANEOUS COMBUSTION in *Bleak House*, which he considered unscientific. After Dickens's death, Lewes enraged JOHN FORSTER with some remarks about Dickens suggesting that the novelist had an "animal intelligence" rather than one that transformed sensations into ideas.

Ley, J. W. T. (1879–1943) Journalist; president of the National Union of Journalists, 1939–40; Dickensian; Honorable Secretary of the DICKENS FELLOWSHIP from 1904 to 1909. He contributed innumerable articles to the DICKENSIAN and stated in 1926 that only six issues of the magazine had appeared that did not include something by him. He edited a still-useful annotated edition of JOHN FORSTER's *Life of Dickens* and authored many books on Dickens, including a volume on Dickens's friendships, *The Dickens Circle* (1918), though much in the latter work has since become outdated.

Library Edition Edition of Dickens's works issued in monthly volumes jointly by BRADBURY & EVANS and CHAPMAN & HALL, beginning in January 1858. Initially unillustrated, it was reissued by Chapman & Hall alone in 1861–62 with the original illustrations.

Library of Fiction, The Monthly periodical edited by Charles Whitehead and published by CHAPMAN & HALL from April 1836 to July 1837. Dickens published two sketches in it that were later included in *Boz*—"Tuggses" and "First of May."

Lighthouse, The Melodrama by WILKIE COLLINS that Dickens produced with his group of amateur players in 1855. Dickens played with great success the role of the lighthouse keeper, Aaron Gurnock, and composed a poetic prologue and "The Song of the Wreck" for the play.

Lillo, George (1693–1739) Dramatist; author of the domestic tragedy *The London Merchant, or The History of George Barnwell* (1731), in which an apprentice is seduced into robbing his employer and murdering his uncle. Dickens frequently alludes to the play, most notably in *Rudge*, where Sim Tappertit compares himself to Barnwell (4), and *Expectations*, where Wopsle reads the play to the apprentice Pip (15).

Lincoln's Inn One of the INNS OF COURT. In 1827, Dickens worked as a clerk in the offices of Molloy, a solicitor here in New Square. Serjeant Snubbin has his chambers in Old Square (*Pickwick*, 31), as do Kenge and Carboy (*Bleak House*, 20). Much of the action of *Bleak House* takes place in the inn and its neighborhood: The COURT OF CHANCERY is held here in **Lincoln's Inn Hall** (1); Tulkinghorn's house, modeled on the house of JOHN FORSTER, is at no. 58, **Lincoln's Inn Fields** (10), a residential square next to the inn. The Gordon rioters gather in the Fields before going on to NEWGATE PRISON (*Rudge*, 63): Betsey Trotwood stays in a hotel here (*Copperfield*, 23).

Linda Dickens's pet St. Bernard who, Dickens wrote to ANNIE FIELDS, on his return to GAD'S HILL after the reading tour in AMERICA, "was greatly excited, weeping profusely, and throwing herself on her back that she might caress [his] foot with her great forepaws."

Lindsay, Jack (1900–1990) Prolific Australian-born poet, novelist, social critic, editor, and translator. His critical biography *Charles Dickens* (1950) approaches its subject from a Marxist and Freudian point of view and offers many original and provocative insights.

Linton, Mrs. Eliza Lynn (1822–1898) Novelist and journalist; regular contributor to HOUSEHOLD WORDS and ALL THE YEAR ROUND. A friend of WALTER SAVAGE LANDOR, who introduced her to Dickens, she earned Dickens's respect for her journal articles: "Good for anything, and thoroughly reliable." In *My Literary Life* (1899), she describes Dickens as "one, who wrote so tenderly, so sentimentally, so gushingly, [yet] had a strain of hardness in his nature which was like a rod of iron in his soul." She sold GAD'S HILL PLACE, which she inherited from her father, to Dickens.

Little College Street Street in CAMDEN TOWN where Dickens boarded with ELIZABETH ROYLANCE in 1824 while his father was in the MARSHALSEA PRISON.

Liverpool Dickens sailed from this port in northwest England when going to AMERICA in 1841 and 1867. Several of his characters also embark for foreign destinations from Liverpool: Lummy Ned (*Chuzzlewit*, 13), Richard Carstone (*Bleak House*, 24), Tom Gradgrind (*Hard Times*, III:7), Tip Dorrit (*Dorrit*, I:7), Captain Jorgan ("Message from the Sea"), Charley ("Holly Tree"), and Captain Ravender ("Golden Mary"). The Traveller describes a visit to the slums near the Liverpool docks where sailors gather (*Uncommercial*, 5). Dickens's theatrical troupe performed in Liverpool in 1847, and Dickens gave several public readings in the city.

Lombard Street Street in east London connecting the BANK OF ENGLAND with Fenchurch Street. MARIA BEADNELL's house was located here, next to the bank of Smith, Payne and Smith, where her father worked. Access to the George and Vulture

through George Yard leads from this street (*Pickwick*, 26); Mr. Merdle's bank (*Dorrit*, II:16) and the offices of Barbox Brothers ("Mugby") are located here. The Traveller speculates about all the money in the banks on the street (*Uncommercial*, 23).

London DONALD FANGER (1965) notes that "the romantic realists—notably Balzac, Dickens and Gogol—were the first fully to realize the potentialities of the metropolis as a subject of fiction." What Paris was to Balzac and Petersburg to Gogol, London was to Dickens. There is now a London, based on the real city of his time, that we think of as "Dickens's London." Maps of this city are available at the DICKENS HOUSE and numerous guide books direct visitors to Dickensian sites.

Much of the work in Dickens TOPOGRAPHY was done around the turn of the century by such Dickensians as FREDERIC KITTON, B. W. MATZ and WALTER DEXTER, though many of the sites they identified no longer exist. *A Dickens Atlas* (1923) by A. A. Hopkins and N. F. Read provides maps of Dickensian sites identified by the topographers and suggests appropriate walking tours. Two recent volumes provide more up-to-date information on Dickens's London: London Transport's centenary guide, *The London of Charles Dickens* (1970), offers an alphabetical listing of Dickensian sites in and around the city; Tony Lynch's *Dickens's England: A Travellers' Companion* (1986) lists sites throughout England that can still be visited. Julian Wolfreys (*Writing London: The Trace of Urban Text from Blake to Dickens*, 1998), in a deconstructive analysis of Dickens's writing about London, argues that Dickens makes his readers participants in creating and interpreting the city. Jacob Korg's *London in Dickens's Day* (1960) collects writings by Dickens and his contemporaries about Victorian London.

London Bridge Two London Bridges appear in Dickens's novels. The old bridge is the one referred to in *Rudge* (5, 8, 16, 43, 49) and *Pickwick* (32) and is the one where David goes during his intervals away from work in the wine-bottling factory (*Copperfield*, 11). The new bridge, opened in 1831 (now in Lake Havasu, Arizona), is the one with the stairs going down to the river where Claypole spies on

Nancy as she talks with Brownlow and Rose Maylie (*Twist*, 46) and where Jonas tosses his bundle of bloody clothes into the river (*Chuzzlewit*, 51).

London Tavern   Public meetings were often held at this institution in Bishopsgate Street. The United Metropolitan Improved Hot Muffin and Crumpet Baking and Punctual Delivery Company organizes here (*Nickleby*, 2). Dickens chaired a meeting of the General Theatrical Fund here in 1836.

London *Times*   Founded in 1785, the *Times* was, by the mid-19th century, the organ of the upper-middle class, the class brought into power by the First REFORM BILL in 1832, which the paper supported. Though it was mildly reformist in the 1820s and 1830s, it was not nearly as liberal as the MORNING CHRONICLE and the DAILY NEWS, two papers with which Dickens was associated. Dickens may have written some penny-a-line pieces for the paper as a boy, but he was unsuccessful in gaining employment with the *Times* as a young man; he worked for the rival *Morning Chronicle* instead, taking great delight in the competition to scoop the rival paper in covering the news. When he started the *Daily News*, the *Times* refused to advertise the new paper and was uneasy with its new radical competitor. Representing its class bias, the *Times* criticized Dickens's vulgarity—in both his writing and his behavior—but it also praised some of his works, especially his early writings. After his death, it called for Dickens to be buried in WESTMINSTER ABBEY.

Dickens wrote letters to the *Times* on January 12, 1861 (asserting the rights of authors to prevent theatrical adaptation of their works); October 8, 1863 (giving his impressions of a recent earthquake); and September 4, 1867 (denying rumors that he was ill).

Long Acre   East-west street running just north of COVENT GARDEN, one of the haunts of young men who idle about the theaters and taverns (*Boz*, "Shabby-genteel"). Dick Swiveller, who has ordered a meal from an establishment in Long Acre and not paid for it, is obliged to put the street on his list of those he cannot enter (*Curiosity Shop*, 8).

Longfellow, Henry Wadsworth (1807–1882) American poet, professor of modern languages at Harvard. Dickens met him on his first American tour in 1842. Longfellow then described Dickens as "a glorious fellow . . . a gay free-and-easy character, with a bright face . . . and withal a slight dash of the Dick Swiveller about him." Dickens thought the poet "a frank accomplished man as well as a fine writer" and invited him to stay with him in London. Longfellow visited Dickens in England in 1842, and his host gave him a night tour of the London slums. He visited again in 1856 and 1868.

Looking-Glass Prairie   Dickens describes his somewhat disappointing visit to this prairie near LEBANON, ILLINOIS, in *Notes* (13).

lord mayor   Title granted to the mayors of major cities, especially the head of the Corporation of London, the group that administers the CITY of London from the Guildhall. The London position, usually held by an important businessman, dates back to 1192. Among the lord mayors of London was DICK WHITTINGTON, who held the position three times, in 1397, 1406, and 1419. His story of a poor boy who makes good in business and rises to become lord mayor is the ARCHETYPAL version of the rags-to-riches tale. Dickens alludes frequently to the Whittington legend, especially in *Dombey*, in which Walter Gay is being groomed for a Whittington-like career.

Louisville   Dickens stopped overnight at this "regular and cheerful" Kentucky town on his way from Cincinnati to ST. LOUIS (*Notes*, 12).

Lowell   Dickens gives an idealized description of this Massachusetts factory town, remarking on the orderly and well-appointed factories, the well-dressed young women who worked in them, and the regimen, which allowed them time for education and for writing for the *Lowell Offering*, their literary magazine. Although he explicitly refrains from comparing these American mills to their European counterparts, he notes that if he did so "it would be between the Good and Evil" (*Notes*, 4).

Lucas, John (1937–) Professor, Loughborough University; writer on many Victorian novelists, especially Dickens, "the greatest novelist in the language." His Marxist reading of the novels in *The Melancholy Man: A Study of Dickens's Novels* (1970) presents Dickens as a truth teller, the conscience of his age, who was at the same time its greatest entertainer. Lucas's Dickens, "far and away the most intelligent of all English novelists," seeks to reconcile these sometimes competing impulses in his art. In *Charles Dickens: The Major Novels* (1992), an introduction to six of Dickens's major works, Lucas again seeks to place the novelist in the context of his time as "the great informant of and for his age, as well as its great conscience."

Ludgate Hill Street running from ST. PAUL'S CATHEDRAL to FLEET STREET. Smike lingers here just before he is captured by Squeers (*Nickleby*, 38). Betsey Trotwood and David are confronted by her husband here (*Copperfield*, 23). The London Coffee House, where Arthur Clennam stays on returning to England, is located here (*Dorrit*, I:3).

Lytton, Edward Bulwer, First Baron Lytton (1803– 1873) Popular novelist, playwright, journalist, and politician. He was a colleague and friend of Dickens, and Dickens named his youngest child for him. Dickens shared his views on political reform and occasionally followed his lead as a novelist. *Oliver Twist* was often linked with Lytton's earlier NEWGATE NOVELS, and Dickens changed the ending of *Expectations* after Lytton objected to the original ending. In 1850, Dickens's theatrical group gave three performances at KNEBWORTH Park, the Lytton estate in Hertfordshire. At that time, the two men conceived the scheme for the GUILD OF LITERATURE AND ART; although some cottages for writers and artists were constructed at Knebworth, the scheme never

Edward Bulwer Lytton in an engraving by Maclise.

gained widespread support. Dickens dedicated *Bleak House*, "as a remembrance of our friendly union, to my companions in the Guild of Literature and Art." Lytton's *A Strange Story* was serialized in ALL THE YEAR ROUND in 1861. Though he thought Dickens incapable of presenting "characters of intellectual depth or refinement," he nonetheless considered him "one of the greatest geniuses in fiction the world has produced."

M

MacKenzie, Norman (1921–) **and Jeanne** (1922– 1986)   Novelist, biographer, and professor, University of Sussex, who collaborated with his wife on several biographical and historical studies of Victorian writers and social thinkers, especially members of the Fabian Society. Their biography *Dickens: A Life* (1979) is a readable account of the author's life that ascribes his energy and artistic productivity to his abandonment by his parents as a young child.

Maclise, Daniel (1806–1870)   Irish-born painter of historical and literary subjects; member of the Royal Academy from 1835; a close friend and companion of Dickens, especially during the 1840s.

In November 1844, Dickens returned to England from Italy to read *The Chimes* to a group of his friends. Maclise's sketch of the occasion identifies those who attended.

Introduced to Dickens by WILLIAM HARRISON AINSWORTH, the artist quickly became one of a nearly inseparable triumvirate with JOHN FORSTER and Dickens. He made several portraits and sketches of Dickens and other members of his family, including the famous frontispiece for *Nicholas Nickleby*, commissioned by CHAPMAN & HALL in 1839. He provided one illustration for *Curiosity Shop* and several for *Chimes, Cricket,* and *Battle,* but the strain of the collaboration also strained the relationship between the two men. In the 1860s, while he was working on his frescoes for the House of Lords, Maclise became remote and reclusive. He died shortly before Dickens, whose last public speech was a tribute to his friend: "the gentlest and most modest of men, . . . incapable of a sordid or ignoble thought, gallantly sustaining the true dignity of his vocation, without one grain of self-ambition, wholesomely natural at the last as at the first, 'in wit a man, simplicity a child.'" Other examples of his work appear on pages 5 (Charles Dickens), 29 (*Battle of Life*), 37 (*Bleak House*), 485 (Carlyle), 560 (Lytton), 565 (Martineau), 617 (Talfourd), and 619 (Thackeray).

Macready, William (1793–1873)   Distinguished actor and theater manager; one of Dickens's closest friends from 1837, when JOHN FORSTER introduced them, until the end of his life. They dined together frequently, traveled together, and were regular correspondents. Macready was a great admirer of

W. C. Macready.

Dickens's work: He was deeply grieved at the death of Little Nell, cried at Dickens's reading of *The Chimes*, and described Dickens's reading of "Sikes and Nancy" as "two Macbeths." He was godfather to Dickens's daughter KATE MACREADY DICKENS. Dickens gave the celebratory speech at Macready's retirement from the stage in 1851 and was a constant friend to the actor and his family until the end of his life. His review of Macready's production of *Lear*, "The Restoration of Shakespeare's 'Lear' to the Stage" (*EXAMINER*, February 4, 1838), commended Macready for abandoning Nahum Tate's revision of the play and restoring Shakespeare's original text, expecially the character of the fool. Dickens also praised "Macready as 'Benedict'" in a review of *Much Ado about Nothing* for the *EXAMINER* (March 4, 1843), challenging those who expected Macready to perform only the great tragic roles (*Miscellaneous, Journalism*).

Macrone, John (1809–1837) Dickens's first publisher. He paid Dickens £100 for the rights to the first series of *Boz*, collected from the various magazines and newspapers in which they had already been published. The success of this production, which he had GEORGE CRUIKSHANK illustrate, prompted Macrone to pay £150 for a second series of sketches and to contract for a three-volume novel, GABRIEL VARDON, THE LOCKSMITH OF LONDON, for £200. These agreements led to some difficult negotiations when Dickens moved to CHAPMAN & HALL, to whom Macrone sold the copyright for *Boz*. After Macrone's untimely death in 1837, Dickens and WILLIAM HARRISON AINSWORTH planned a collection of writings and illustrations to benefit his widow that eventually appeared as *The Pic-nic Papers* (1841), edited by Dickens.

Maiden Lane This street in Holloway, described in *Boz* as "inhabited by proprietors of donkey-carts, boilers of horse-flesh, makers of files, and sifters of cinders" ("First of May"), is where Boffin's Bower and its dustheaps are located (*Mutual Friend*, I:5).

Malthus, Thomas Robert (1766–1834) English clergyman and economist who argued in *An Essay on the Principle of Population* (1798) that as the population grew geometrically, the food supply would increase only arithmetically. His solutions to this problem of "surplus population" were harsh: He advocated sexual abstinence for the poor, emigration, and the denial of charity to the poor, thus forcing them to adopt more prudent ways of life. Although Dickens shared Malthus's belief in emigration as a remedy for poverty, he was outraged by the economist's harsh views on charity. He frequently attacked "philosophers" like Malthus in his broad condemnation of the UTILITARIANS and the school of "hard facts." His most direct attacks on Malthus appear in *Carol* and *Chimes* and in *Hard Times*, in which Gradgrind names one of his children after the economist.

Manchester This Lancashire center of cotton manufacture in the 19th century was often used symbolically to represent industrial England. Coketown is sometimes said to be based on Manchester, but Dickens also connected the town with nearby PRESTON, which he visited during a bitter strike while he was writing *Hard Times*. Dickens's sister FANNY (*see* DICKENS, FRANCES ELIZABETH) lived in

Manchester after her marriage, and Dickens visited her there several times. During one such visit in 1843, he came up with the idea for *A Christmas Carol*, in which Tiny Tim—like the later Paul Dombey—was based on Fanny's sickly son, HENRY BURNETT JR. Dickens and his troupe performed their AMATEUR THEATRICALS in Manchester, and Dickens gave several PUBLIC READINGS in the city on his English tours.

Manchester Buildings A group of houses near WESTMINSTER BRIDGE in London, "a narrow and dirty region, the sanctuary of the smaller members of Parliament" (*Nickleby*, 16), where Nicholas interviews for a position as secretary to Mr. Gregsbury, M.P. Also mentioned in *Boz*, "Parliamentary."

Manheim, Leonard (1902–1983) Professor, University of Hartford; psychoanalytic critic and literary theorist; founder and editor of *Literature and Psychology*; one of the important psychoanalytic critics of Dickens's novels. His articles have appeared in *American Imago* ("The Personal History of *David Copperfield*," 1952; "The Law as Father," 1955), *Texas Studies in Language and Literature* ("Floras and Doras: The Women in Dickens's Novels," 1965), and other journals.

Manning, Frederick George and Maria Notorious murderers who conspired to kill Mrs. Manning's young lover. Dickens attended their public execution in 1849 and wrote two letters to the LONDON TIMES describing the "brutal mirth or callousness" of the crowd there. He proposed that future executions be held secretly within prison walls. He describes being haunted by their execution in "Lying Awake" (*Reprinted*). Mrs. Manning has sometimes been considered the original of Hortense, Lady Dedlock's French maid in *Bleak House*.

Manning, Sylvia (1943–) Chancellor, University of Illinois, Chicago. In *Dickens as Satirist* (1971), Manning does not survey the satiric passages in the novels but rather discusses the profoundly ironic view of life that Dickens reaches in the later novels, in which the characters attempt to survive and grow in "a world somehow dying,

with life and vitality yielding to torpor, rigidity, or death."

Mansion House Official residence of the LORD MAYOR in the CITY of London, it is also the name given to its immediate neighborhood. Nicodemus Dumps sets out from Mansion House for the Kitterbell's Christening (*Boz*, "Christening"); preparations for the lord mayor's Christmas celebration are described in *Carol* (1). Because the lord mayor was chief magistrate, Mansion House was also the site of the London Police Court, where the red cab driver delights the court with his wit (*Boz*, "Last Cab-driver"); Kit Nubbles is taken to this court (*Curiosity Shop*, 60). Haredale petitions the lord mayor to have Mr. Rudge imprisoned during the GORDON RIOTS (*Rudge*, 61).

Marcus, Steven (1928–) Professor, Columbia University, and writer on Victorian cultural and literary history; on Freud, Engels, and other Victorians; and on the psychological and social dimensions of literature. *Dickens: From Pickwick to Dombey* (1965) is one of the most important books on the early novels; although its Freudian approach has been controversial, its thorough grounding in Victorian social history yields insightful and provocative readings of the novels.

Margate The snobbish Tuggses choose RAMSGATE over this competing seaside resort in KENT because they think only tradespeople go to Margate (*Boz*, "Tuggses"). Abel Garland visited Margate as a boy with his schoolmaster (*Curiosity Shop*, 14). During the long vacation, Margate is a destination for "young clerks . . . madly in love" (*Bleak House*, 19). Captain Boldheart seeks out his bride while she is bathing at Margate ("Holiday Romance").

Marryat, Captain Frederick (1792–1848) Prolific popular novelist, particularly of novels about the sea; friend of Dickens during the 1840s who, JOHN FORSTER notes, "was among the first of Dickens's liking." Both were regulars at the COUNTESS OF BLESSINGTON's salon at Gore House. Marryat's critical *Diary in America* (1839) is often compared with *Notes*. He chaired the dinner to welcome Dickens home from America in 1842. Like Dickens, he was profoundly influenced by such PICARESQUE novelists as ALAIN RENÉ LESAGE and TOBIAS SMOLLETT, and his novels often had orphan-waif heroes, who may have influenced such Dickens heroes as Oliver Twist.

Marseille Seaport in southern FRANCE where Arthur Clennam is held in quarantine on his way back to England from China (*Dorrit*, I:1). Dickens passed through Marseille several times during his year in ITALY; he considered the city "a dirty and disagreeable place" with "dust, dust, dust, everywhere" (*Pictures*). Herbert Pocket is in Marseille on business when Magwitch appears at Pip's door in London (*Expectations*, 39).

Marshalsea Prison DEBTORS' PRISON located in the BOROUGH HIGH STREET, SOUTHWARK, where Dickens's father was imprisoned in 1824. Much of the first half of *Dorrit* takes place in the prison, "an

oblong pile of barrack buildings, partitioned off into squalid houses, standing back to back, so that there were no back rooms; environed by a narrow paved yard, hemmed in by high walls duly spiked at the top" (*Dorrit*, I:6). It is also the setting for "The Old Man's Tale about the Queer Client," where "want and misfortune are pent up in the narrow prison; an air of gloom and dreariness seems . . . to hang about the scene, and to impart to it a squalid and sickly hue" (*Pickwick*, 21).

Martineau, Harriet (1802–1876) Novelist, journalist, social philosopher, and autobiographer. One of the first writers whom Dickens recruited for *HOUSEHOLD WORDS*, she contributed many articles and stories to the magazine between 1850 and 1855. Although Dickens subscribed to many of Martineau's radical political and social views, he was not a consistent radical and differed with her on economic issues, especially on the role of government in regulating factories. After *Hard Times* and a series of articles in

The Marshalsea.

Harriet Martineau, in an engraving by Maclise.

HOUSEHOLD WORDS by HENRY MORLEY on accidents in textile mills, she wrote *The Factory Controversy* (1855), a pamphlet in which she attacked Dickens and his magazine as sentimental proponents of "meddling and mischievous" factory legislation. She had become convinced that Dickens and W. H. WILLS were "grievously inadequate to their function [as editors], philosophically and morally." Her contributions to the periodical stopped in 1855; Dickens commented on her attack, "I do suppose that there never was such a wrong-headed woman born—such a vain one—or such a Humbug." In the 1850s, she was widely thought to have been the model for Mrs. Jellyby.

Martin-Harvey, Sir John (1863–1944)   Actor and theater manager who played in London, New York, and many other cities in the late 19th and early 20th century. He played Sam Weller in "Jingle," an 1887 version of *Pickwick* in New York, and in 1935 played Magwitch in two productions of "The Scapegoat," an adaptation of *Expectations*. His greatest Dickensian role, however, was Sydney Carton in "The Only Way," a version of *Two Cities* that MALCOLM MORLEY described

as "the most successful of all plays taken from Dickens." Martin-Harvey performed Carton in numerous stage productions of this play between 1899 and 1923, and in a silent film production in 1926.

Marylebone   Affluent borough northwest of central London. Dickens lived here, on DEVONSHIRE TERRACE, from 1839 to 1851. Next door to his house was the Marylebone Parish Church, usually considered the original of the church where Paul Dombey is christened and Dombey and Edith married.

Matchett, Willoughby (d. 1921)   Regular contributor to the *DICKENSIAN* during its first two decades of publication. He contributed articles on biographical topics, especially on Dickens at WELLINGTON HOUSE ACADEMY; on critical issues in several of the novels, especially *Dombey, Dorrit,* and *Drood;* and on Dickens in relation to various modern authors.

Mathews, Charles J. (1776–1835)   Comic actor, a great favorite of Dickens's during his youth and early manhood. In the early 1830s, Mathews staged a series of "At Homes," one-man shows in which he played all the parts without makeup, using different voices, mannerisms, and gestures to mark the different characters. These performances influenced Dickens's methods of CHARACTERIZATION and, especially, the PUBLIC READINGS later in his career.

Matz, Bertram W. (1865–1925)   First Honorary Secretary of the Dickens Fellowship; editor of the *DICKENSIAN* from its inception until 1925; editor for CHAPMAN & HALL; Dickens collector, bibliographer, and commentator. He wrote, collected, and edited many books and articles on Dickens—and some on other English writers—including the National Edition of Dickens's works (1907–08) and *Miscellaneous Papers* (1908), still a useful collection of Dickens's journalistic essays. He directed the project of making Dickens's DOUGHTY STREET house a Dickens museum. The Matz Collection of Dickens materials forms an important part of the DICKENS HOUSE library.

McMaster, Juliet (1937–) Professor, University of Alberta, who has written on Jane Austen, ANTHONY TROLLOPE, and WILLIAM MAKEPEACE THACKERAY as well as on Dickens. In *Dickens the Designer* (1987), she considers the visual dimensions of seven of Dickens's novels and focuses on the ways in which the physical appearance of the characters articulates their personalities and roles within the novels.

McNulty, J. H. (d. 1954) Early 20th-century journalist, editor of *The Old Lady of Threadneedle Street*, journal of the Bank of England; frequent contributor to the DICKENSIAN from 1916 to 1950. Many of his articles are fantasies taking off from Dickens's novels or characters. Some of his writings on Dickens are collected in *The Dethronement of Shakespeare* (1926), *Concerning Dickens and Other Literary Characters* (1933), and *The Return of Mr. Pickwick* (1936).

Meadows, Kenny (1790–1874) Victorian Illustrator, best known for *The Heads of the People* (1838–40), a series of portraits of literary characters to accompany writings by WILLIAM MAKEPEACE THACKERAY, DOUGLAS JERROLD, and others. In 1838, he also did a series of 24 woodcuts of characters from *Nickleby*, under the title, "Heads from *Nicholas Nickleby*." (See p. 244.)

Meckier, Jerome (1941–) Professor, University of Kentucky; critic of Victorian and modern fiction. In *Hidden Rivalries in Victorian Fiction: Dickens, Realism, and Revaluation* (1987), he pairs novels by Dickens with novels by his contemporaries, showing how the novelists compete with one another by parodying and challenging each other's work. *Innocent Abroad: Charles Dickens's American Engagements* (1990) presents a biographical and historical account of Dickens's two American journeys. In *Dickens's Great Expectations: Misnar's Pavilion versus Cinderella* (2002), Meckier argues that Dickens darkened the Cinderella motif used by other Victorian novelists by recasting the story in terms of the story of Misnar, a popular pseudo-oriental tale.

medievalism Although Dickens was a great admirer of THOMAS CARLYLE and adopted his criticism of industrial England as mechanistic and soulless, he did not share Carlyle's idealization of the Middle Ages. His disdain for the medieval past is implicit in the titles he chose for the false books in his library at GAD'S HILL. Under the general title THE WISDOM OF OUR ANCESTORS, the series included individual volumes entitled *Ignorance, Superstition, The Rack,* and *Disease.* His satiric attack in *The Chimes* on the gentleman who extols the past in terms characteristic of the Young England movement also reveals Dickens's basically progressive, liberal perspective. Dickens's most sympathetic treatment of the Victorian medieval revival probably appears in his humorous description of Wemmick in WALWORTH (*Expectations,* 25), whose small castle in the suburbs offers a refuge from the dehumanizing life of the Victorian city.

Medway, the Chief river in KENT; ROCHESTER and CHATHAM are located near its mouth, where it joins the THAMES. Pickwick meets Dismal Jemmy on a bridge over the river in Rochester (*Pickwick,* 5). Micawber speculates on entering the Medway coal trade (*Copperfield,* 17). The Traveller visits

Victorian engraving of the view across the Medway to Rochester.

the Chatham dockyard on the Medway (*Uncommercial*, 26).

Merivale, Herman Charles (1839–1906) Playwright, novelist, and contributor to ALL THE YEAR ROUND. He acted in Dickens's last theatrical effort, a production of *The Prima Donna* in London on June 2, 1870, just a week before Dickens's death. He described Dickens's active involvement as director and stage manager of the production in a letter to the *Times* (COLLINS, 1981).

mesmerism A therapy developed by Franz Anton Mesmer (1734–1815)—also called animal magnetism—that involved the use of hypnotic trances to effect healing. Mesmer theorized that the process brought cosmic forces to bear on animate bodies. The physician JOHN ELLIOTSON, Dickens's friend, was the foremost British theorist of mesmerism and the founder of its journal, *The Zooist*. During the mesmeric mania of the 1840s and 1850s, Dickens practiced mesmerism on his wife and others, the most celebrated case being his attempt to cure AUGUSTA DE LA RUE in GENOA. Dickens's involvement with mesmerism has been thoroughly explored by FRED KAPLAN (1975).

Midlands Although Dickens was a Londoner and made a literary world that has come to be known as "Dickens's London," he did occasionally write about the Midlands, the area of England beginning roughly at Birmingham and stretching north to Lancashire and Yorkshire. In this section of Britain the INDUSTRIAL REVOLUTION emerged in the first 30 years of the 19th century, as steam power was developed to operate the machines in the textile mills, iron foundries, and the other factories that opened in MANCHESTER, Leeds, BIRMINGHAM, Sheffield, and similar Midlands towns. The Birmingham that Pickwick visits (*Pickwick*, 50) is not described as an industrial city, but Little Nell's journey through the BLACK COUNTRY is an industrial Walpurgisnacht (*Curiosity Shop*, 43–45). In *Bleak House*, Rouncewell's iron foundry is only a short journey to the north from Chesney Wold (63). *Hard Times*, Dickens's most sustained picture of the industrial Midlands,

used PRESTON and MANCHESTER as the prototypes for Coketown.

Mile End Area one mile east of the CITY of London where the tollbooth for the turnpike to the northeast was located. Tony Weller muses on the lives of turnpike keepers as he passes the gate (*Pickwick*, 22). Mrs. Jellyby meets here with "a Society called the East London Branch Aid Ramification" (*Bleak House*, 14).

Millais, Sir John Everett (1829–1896) Painter, one of the founders of the PRE-RAPHAELITE movement in 1848; a protégé of JOHN RUSKIN in the 1850s, his affair with Ruskin's wife Effie led to a scandalous divorce. He married Effie in 1855, settled in Scotland, and later in his career gave up the Pre-Raphaelitism of his earlier work. Dickens attacked his controversial painting "Christ in the Carpenter's Shop," shown in the 1850 Royal Academy Exhibition, as "mean, odious, repulsive, and revolting" ("Old Lamps for New Ones"). Dickens objected to the lack of idealization in the painting and described the realistically depicted boy Jesus as "a hideous wrynecked, blubbery, red-headed boy." Dickens later changed his mind about Pre-Raphaelite art, and he and Millais became friends. Millais recommended LUKE FILDES to Dickens as the illustrator for *Drood*.

Millbank Area along the north side of the Thames between Westminster and CHELSEA. In Dickens's time, much of the area was an undeveloped urban wasteland: "as oppressive, sad, and solitary by night, as any about London. There were neither wharves nor houses on the melancholy waste of road near the great blank Prison. . . . Coarse grass and rank weeds straggled over all the marshy land in the vicinity. In one part, carcases of houses, inauspiciously begun and never finished, rotted away. In another, the ground was cumbered with rusty iron monsters of steam-boilers, wheels, cranks, pipes, furnaces, paddles, anchors, diving-bells, windmill-sails, . . . accumulated by some speculator" (*Copperfield*, 47). The Millbank Penitentiary was erected between 1813 and 1821 on the site of the present Tate Gallery. Bill Barker has spent some time there for his love of handkerchiefs

(*Boz*, Cab-driver). David and Daniel Peggotty follow Martha Endell to this stretch of the river as she contemplates suicide (*Copperfield*, 47). Smith Square, where Lizzie Hexam lives with Jenny Wren, is in the vicinity (*Mutual Friend*, II:1).

Miller, D. A.   Professor, University of California, Berkeley. In his influential Foucaultian analysis of works by WILKIE COLLINS, ANTHONY TROLLOPE, and Dickens, *The Novel and the Police* (1988), Miller studies Victorian fiction as a form of social control. Miller has also written books on Jane Austen and narrative closure.

Miller, J. Hillis (1928–) American scholar, critic, and literary theorist; professor, Yale and University of California, Irvine. Dickens's novels have figured significantly in his work, which ranges broadly over English and American literature, especially of the 19th and 20th centuries. Miller's *Charles Dickens: The World of His Novels* (1958), a phenomenological study concentrating on the language and symbolism in six Dickens novels, has been one of the most influential works of modern Dickens criticism. Miller also discusses Dickens's works in *The Form of Victorian Fiction* (1968), *Charles Dickens and George Cruikshank* (1971), in several of the essays collected in *Victorian Subjects* (1991), and in numerous articles and introductions to editions of the novels.

Mills, John (1908–2005) English actor. His Dickensian roles include Pip in DAVID LEAN's film of *Expectations* (1946), Joe Gargery in a 1975 stage version of the same novel, Jarvis Lorry in a television adaptation of *Two Cities* (1989), and Chuffey in the BBC adaptation of *Chuzzlewit* (1994).

Milnes, Richard Monckton, Lord Houghton (1809–1885) Poet, Conservative politician, bon vivant, bibliophile, friend of Dickens. Known for his wit and repartee, he and Dickens dined at each other's houses. Dickens appreciated his support for Liberal social causes and, especially, his support of copyright legislation.

Mirror of Parliament Newspaper established by Dickens's uncle, John Henry BARROW, in 1828,

which provided verbatim transcripts of parliamentary proceedings. Dickens joined the paper early in 1832. In the two years that he was with the *Mirror*, he developed a reputation as an outstanding parliamentary reporter and rose to become a kind of subeditor. He left the *Mirror* in 1834 to become a parliamentary reporter for the MORNING CHRONICLE.

Mississippi River   Dickens described "the hateful Mississippi" as "an enormous ditch, sometimes two or three miles wide, running liquid mud, six miles an hour" (*Notes*, 12). He located New Eden, the hellish frontier settlement where Martin Chuzzlewit nearly dies from fever, along its banks at what is now CAIRO, ILLINOIS (*Chuzzlewit*, 23).

Mitre Inn, the   At this CHATHAM inn, the boy Charles Dickens was prompted by his father to stand on the dining table and sing duets with his sister. Charley, narrator of "The Holly-Tree," fondly remembers the Mitre from his schooldays in the town.

Mitton, Thomas (1812–1878)   Early friend of Dickens's. They were law clerks together in LINCOLN'S INN in 1828–29. Mitton went on to become a solicitor and represented Dickens for many years.

Moncrieff, William T. (1794–1857)   Theater manager and playwright, best known for *Tom and Jerry*. His adaptation of *Pickwick, Sam Weller, or the Pickwickians*, performed in London in the summer of 1837, did not stage the trial scene. Instead its great moments were the Eatanswill election and a parade at the end celebrating the coronation of Queen Victoria. In 1839, he adapted *Nickleby* as *Nicholas Nickleby and Poor Smike: The Victim of the Yorkshire School*. Moncrieff, believing himself to be the adaptor of novels for the stage whom Dickens attacked in *Nickleby* (48), issued a proclamation that defended his adaptations and asserted, "Having himself *unsuccessfully* tried the drama, there is some excuse for Mr. Dickens's petulance toward its professors." He later collaborated with MALCOLM MORLEY on an article for HOUSEHOLD WORDS, "The Poor Brothers of the Charterhouse" (June 12, 1852).

Monod, Sylvère (1921–) Professor, the Sorbonne; past president of the DICKENS SOCIETY and the DICKENS FELLOWSHIP. *Dickens the Novelist* (1968), an English translation and updating of his earlier *Dickens romancier* (1953), was one of the first works to use Dickens's notes, number plans, diaries, and letters to explore his methods of composition. With GEORGE FORD, Monod has also edited *Bleak House* (1977) and *Hard Times* (1980). His critical introduction to *Chuzzlewit* appeared in 1985.

montage A technique in motion pictures of moving rapidly through a series of brief pictures or cutting between images from parallel or contrasted story lines. D. W. GRIFFITH, who pioneered the technique in film, learned the principle of montage from Dickens. SERGEI EISENSTEIN, in "Dickens, Griffith, and the Film Today," analyzes scenes from *Twist*, breaking them down into their montage images, to show how this fundamental technique of moving pictures was developed by Dickens. A. L. Zambrano (*Dickens and Film*, 1977) discusses Dickens's use of montage.

Monthly Magazine, The Journal in which Dickens's first published story, "A Dinner at Poplar Walk," appeared in the December 1833 issue. The magazine, subtitled "The British Register of Literature, Science, and Belles Lettres" and edited by CAPTAIN J. B. HOLLAND, published eight more sketches by Dickens in 1834–35, all of which were collected in *Boz*. Although the *Monthly*, with a small circulation of about 600, did not pay its contributors, it did effectively start Dickens's literary career by placing a series of his sketches in print.

Montreal Dickens spent two weeks here on his American journey in 1842. He found the Government House superior to the one in KINGSTON and remarked on the "solidity" of the granite quays along the St. Lawrence (*Notes*, 15). Although he appreciated Canadian hospitality, he considered Rosco's Hotel here "the worst in the whole wide world." In *Notes*, he describes at length the emigrants from England and Ireland whom he observed on the boat from Quebec, praising their patience, self-denial, and untiring love for their children (15).

Dickens directed three plays at the THEATRE ROYAL in Montreal, the first of his AMATEUR THEATRICALS. He took parts in all three—Thomas Morton's "A Roland for an Oliver," CHARLES MATHEWS's "Past Two O'Clock in the Morning," and JOHN POOLE's "Deaf as a Post." He was especially pleased by his wife's performance in Mathews's brief interlude.

Monument, the Column designed by Christopher Wren in 1667 commemorating the Great Fire of London in 1666. Located at the spot where the fire broke out, it stands in Fish Street, east London. John Willet recommends sitting at the top of the Monument as the best cheap entertainment in London (*Rudge*, 13). Todgers's is located nearby (*Chuzzlewit*, 8–10). Tom Pinch considers asking directions of the man in the Monument when he first arrives in London (*Chuzzlewit*, 37). The Poor Relation remembers going with Little Frank to look at the outside of the Monument ("Poor Relation's Story").

Moore, Thomas (1779–1852) Popular Irish poet and songwriter of the romantic period, best known for his *Irish Melodies* (1807–35). Dickens was particularly fond of his songs, which he sang to his children and quoted frequently in the novels, especially in the snatches of poetry quoted by Dick Swiveller in *Curiosity Shop*.

Morley, Henry (1822–1894) Journalist, man of letters; professor of English, University of London; editor and staff writer for HOUSEHOLD WORDS and ALL THE YEAR ROUND. Dickens originally recruited Morley in 1850 to write some articles on sanitation; he liked Morley's work so much that he offered him a position on the staff of the magazine. During the next two decades, Morley wrote over 300 pieces for the magazines on a great variety of subjects. Dickens said that "Morley always wants a little screwing up and tightening. It's his habit to write in a loose way," but he appreciated Morley's journalistic skills in researching and putting together a story. Morley, the only university graduate on the staff, said, "Dickens has great genius, but not a trained and cultivated reason."

Morley, Malcolm (1891–1966) Actor, theater manager, playwright, and theater historian. His groundbreaking series of articles on theatrical versions of Dickens's novels, published in the DICKENSIAN between 1946 and 1957, remains some of the most important work on the topic. In another series of articles in the same journal, "The Theatrical TERNANs" (1958–61), Morley told the story of the family of actors and actresses that has such importance to Dickens studies.

Morning Chronicle, The Leading Liberal daily newspaper in the first half of the 19th century, especially under the editorship of JOHN EASTHOPE. Dickens worked as a reporter on the paper from 1834 to 1836, then under the editorship of John Black. He did shorthand reporting of Parliament when it was in session, general reporting and theater reviews during parliamentary recesses. Dickens was fond of recalling the excitement of racing about the country to get a story and then to get it into print before the LONDON TIMES. Dickens also published nine early sketches in the *Chronicle* that would later be collected in *Boz*.

Mudie's Circulating Library Chief circulating library in Victorian England, started in 1842 when Charles Mudie (1818–90) began lending books from his stationer's shop in London. For an annual fee of a guinea, his clients could obtain a year's subscription. Mudie encouraged the publication of novels in a three-volume format because three readers could be simultaneously reading the same book; he also screened the content of the novels, excluding those that might bring a blush to the cheek of a young person. By the 1860s, Mudie's influence on the publishing industry was so great that the three-volume format was nearly universal. Dickens, whose works appeared in serial numbers followed by a single-volume publication and whose subject matter was considered "vulgar" by some Victorian readers, did not conform to the library's standard format, so his novels were not among the "best renters" on Mudie's lists. Toward the end of his career, Dickens made more concessions to the libraries: *Great Expectations* fit exactly the three-volume format; *Mutual Friend* and *Drood* were also circulated by Mudie's. Although Mudie's Library continued in business until 1937, the three-volume format was discontinued in the 1890s.

Murray, Eustace Clare Grenville (1824–1881) Journalist and novelist; member of the British diplomatic service; illegitimate son of Richard Grenville, second Duke of Buckingham and Chandos. He wrote many articles for HOUSEHOLD WORDS and ALL THE YEAR ROUND, most of them as "The Roving Englishman," describing foreign scenes and events while he was in the diplomatic service. He characterized Dickens as "one of the greatest and kindliest public teachers England has ever known."

mystery story Although frequently confused with DETECTIVE STORIES, mystery stories do not always involve detectives; they are an older form, going back to such traditional and folk forms as the GHOST STORY. The mystery story can be defined as any work of prose fiction in which mystery or terror has an important role.

Some of Dickens's earliest writings deal with ghosts, supernatural events, or unexplainable experiences. Although *Boz* is a book devoted to urban realism, "The Black Veil" contains such mysterious elements, and several of the INTERPOLATED TALES in *Pickwick,* such as "The Bagman's Tale" and "The Tale of the Bagman's Uncle," concern supernatural events. In several of the CHRISTMAS BOOKS, Dickens took the ghost story, traditionally told around the hearth on Christmas Eve, and brought it up to date, having the Ghosts of Christmas Past, Present, and Future, for example, visit Scrooge in his city house rather than in some lonely country mansion.

In a broader sense, nearly all of Dickens's novels can be considered mystery stories. As Northrup Frye observed, "there is usually a mystery in Dickens's stories, and this mystery is nearly always the traditional mystery of birth, in sharp contrast to the mystery of death on which the modern whodunit is based." The mysteries at the heart of many Dickens novels involve questions of identity: The resolution to *Twist* entails uncovering the mystery of Oliver's parentage; Amy Dorrit must also learn of her heritage before she can fully understand who she is; Pip must learn the identity of his unknown benefactor, and John Harmon must clear up the mystery of his murder and disappearance. Dickens's last, unfinished novel, *The Mystery of Edwin Drood,* the only one in which "mystery" appears in the title, might have combined the search for a mysterious identity with the solving of a murder, the form that characterizes many modern mystery stories.

In an older sense, mysteries were not things that human agents (detectives) solved but things that religion attempted to explain. The ALLEGORY in some of Dickens's later novels—especially in works like *Expectations,* in which the solution of Pip's identity is connected with the miraculous return of Abel Magwitch, who redeems him from his self-indulgent idleness—seems to rely on this older sense of mystery.

myth   In suggesting that "Dickens was a mythologist rather than a novelist; he was the last of the great mythologists, and perhaps the greatest," G. K. CHESTERTON was stressing the primitive and religious dimensions of Dickens's storytelling. More than just pictures of 19th-century life, the novels use the materials of folklore, fairy tale, and traditional story to explore the mysteries of life and death. Dickens spoke of the CHRISTMAS BOOKS as giving "a higher form" to old nursery tales, essentially turning them into myths of the industrial age in which such larger-than-life heroes as Scrooge learn the meaning of life by confronting a supernatural vision of death.

Myths reach beyond personal issues to address the concerns of a whole society or culture, what psychologist C. G. Jung calls "the race." Much of Dickens's mythological symbolism derives from the BIBLE, especially from Genesis. His Victorian England is an Eden after the fall, a wilderness threatened by Noah's flood and in need of redemption. Dickens uses such ARCHETYPES as the river, the wilderness, the labyrinth, and the prison to express this mythological vision. His biblical imagery has been explored by BERT G. HORNBACK (1972) and JANET LARSON (1985).

NORTHROP FRYE (1970) considers more secular roots for Dickens's mythology in the tradition of New Comedy, a dramatic form from Hellenic Greece available to Dickens in the comedies of Molière and BEN JONSON in which humors characters are driven by dominating obsessions like jealousy or greed. Dickens's characters, hardened by the industrial and urban world in which they find themselves, are also flat figures dominated by singular obsessions. Dickens's heroes, Frye suggests, seek to overcome their situation and connect with a "hidden world of dreams and death, and . . . gain . . . a renewed life and energy."

The mythic impulse in Dickens, as Ian Duncan argues in *Modern Romance and Transformations of the Novel* (1992), defines his difference from SIR WALTER SCOTT. Scott places the melodramatic plot of his novels into historical context, explaining the action as the result of historical forces; Dickens "remythologizes them." In *Two Cities,* for example, he traces the source of the French Revolution to the sexual violation of Madame DeFarge's sister by the Marquis of Evrèmonde.

Dickens's use of myth, as many critics have noted, ultimately serves a serious psychological function. GWEN WATKINS (1987), for example, sees his novels as devoted to a Jungian project, the search for a unified self. Industrialization, social change, and the loss of traditional beliefs and values made self-knowledge and identity problematic in Victorian England. Dickens searches for an underlying story, a myth, that will provide him with a sense of himself. GEOFFREY THURLEY (1976) summarizes this search as follows: "Dickens is at the centre of all his own work. We can describe his entire *oeuvre* in terms of a primal wish-fulfillment fantasy. . . . The elements of this myth can be summarized as follows. The child abandoned by feckless or unfortunate parents climbs out of the abyss of poverty and darkness towards security, peace, and light." In the early novels, Thurley observes, this progress is aided by benevolent uncles and impeded by evil ogres, but in the later novels the hero must take responsibility for his own difficulties and progress, and, by the end of his career, the resolution of the search has become "highly ambiguous." Repeated elements of this mythological search for selfhood include the orphan figure, the journey, and the revelatory or redemptive experience.

N

Nabokov, Vladimir (1899–1977) Russian/American novelist, essayist, and professor of literature. In his course on masters of European fiction at Cornell, Nabokov, at the suggestion of EDMUND WILSON, included *Bleak House* as one of the texts. His lectures on the novel, developing a detailed analysis of its structure, themes, and style, are included in his *Lectures on Literature* (1980), edited by Fredson Bowers and published after Nabokov's death.

Naples The Italian city where Steerforth takes and then abandons Little Em'ly (*Copperfield*, 46, 50). Dickens describes his visit to Naples in *Pictures* (12).

narrator The teller of the story. Dickens's usual narrator is an omniscient observer using a style that is mannered and theatrical. ROBERT GARIS (1965) describes the Dickens narrator as governed by "the constant and overt intention to dazzle us with verbal devices, leading us through our impulse to applaud to a continual awareness of the artificer responsible, a self-exhibiting master of language." KATE FLINT (1986) discovers a more versatile narrator; describing the novels as "dialogic," she shows that the narrator adopts many different voices in the process of telling the story. Thus it might be more appropriate to refer to the Dickens narrators, rather than to a single narrator. AUDREY JAFFE (1991) attempts to mediate these positions by analyzing the different voices adopted by the Dickens narrator, which articulate varying degrees of omniscience and limitation.

Dickens occasionally employed a FIRST-PERSON narration, notably in the autobiographical *Copperfield* and *Expectations,* in Esther Summerson's portion of *Bleak House,* and in several of the CHRISTMAS stories. Commentators on these works have often been interested in the ways in which Dickens modified or failed to modify his usual style to fit his storytelling characters.

Newgate Calendar, The A popular collection of biographies of infamous criminals imprisoned in NEWGATE PRISON. First published in 1773, it was frequently reprinted, expanded, and updated in the subsequent century. Fagin speaks of it as a kind of Who's Who of crime (*Twist,* 43). It is alluded to in several of the novels.

Newgate novel Genre of fiction popular in the 1830s and 1840s that fictionalized the lives of notorious criminals from the NEWGATE CALENDAR. Dickens's friends and fellow novelists EDWARD BULWER LYTTON and WILLIAM HARRISON AINSWORTH were the main practitioners of the form. Lytton's *Eugene Aram* (1832) and *Lucretia* (1846) and Ainsworth's *Rookwood* (1834) and *Jack Sheppard* (1840) prompted a controversy over such fiction. Those attacking the novels claimed that they promoted crime, and they held up as proof a young man named Courvoisier who claimed that

Jack Sheppard had motivated him to murder his master. Although *Oliver Twist* was not about a criminal from the *Newgate Calendar,* it was, like *Sheppard,* illustrated by GEORGE CRUIKSHANK and serialized in BENTLEY'S MISCELLANY, and it was often condemned along with the Newgate novels. Dickens answered these attacks in the preface to the third edition (1841), in which he asserted that rather than crime it was "the principle of Good surviving through every adverse circumstance and triumphing at last" that was the central theme of the novel.

Newgate Prison London's main jail from the 13th century on, it was destroyed during the GOR- DON RIOTS in 1780 (*Rudge,* 64) and rebuilt in 1782. Dickens describes the prison in *Boz,* "Visit to New- gate." Oliver visits Fagin as he awaits execution in Newgate (*Twist,* 52). Wemmick takes Pip to tour the prison, leaving the "taint of Newgate" on him (*Expectations,* 32).

Newlin, George An independent scholar who has produced some monumental reference books on Dickens. His three-volume *Everyone in Dick- ens* (1995) lists, describes, and contextualizes all the people, fictional and real, in Dickens. *Every Thing in Dickens: Ideas and Subjects Discussed by Charles Dickens in His Complete Works, A Topicon* (1996) is a topical index, encyclopedia, anthology that extracts Dickens's comments on a great vari- ety of topics and reprints the great scenes from his works. Newlin has also produced casebooks for *Great Expectations* and *A Tale of Two Cities* that collect materials relevant to the novels.

Newman Street Street running north from OXFORD STREET in central London, one of the "numerous streets which have been devoted time out of mind to professional people, dispensaries, and boarding-houses" (*Boz,* "Dancing Academy"). Mr. Turveydrop's Dancing Academy is located here (*Bleak House,* 14).

New Poor Law The Poor Law Amendment Act of 1834. *See* POOR LAW.

Doré's famous rendering of the exercise yard at Newgate Prison for *London, A Pilgrimage* (1872).

Newsom, Robert (1944–) Professor, Univer- sity of California, Irvine. His influential *Dickens on the Romantic Side of Familiar Things: Bleak House and the Novel Tradition* (1977) analyzes *Bleak House* as representative of both Dickens's work and the novel as a literary form. Beginning with Dickens's assertion that he was concerned with "the roman- tic side of familiar things," Newsom discusses Dick- ens's ability to reveal the unexpected, unfamiliar, and miraculous dimensions of the mundane, and he discovers tensions in the novel between "the famil- iar and the strange, the real and the imaginary, the topical and the mythical, the empirical and the fic- tional, the modern and the ancient." *Bleak House* does not resolve these tensions, which are charac- teristic of many novels of the period, for the instabil- ity in Victorian society that the novel undertakes to present ultimately characterizes the novel itself. In "Embodying Dombey: Whole and in Part" (*Dickens Studies Annual,* 1989), Newsom discusses a similar tension in *Dombey*, but one expressed more primitively in the antithesis of physical wholeness and things falling to pieces. "The Hero's Shame" (*Dickens Studies Annual*, 1983) develops a psychoanalytic reading of the AUTOBIOGRAPHICAL FRAGMENT, its concern with shame rather than guilt, and its ramifications in the novels. Newsom has also written an introduction to Dickens for the general reader, *Charles Dickens Revisited* (2000), and contributed a chapter, "Fictions of Childhood," to *The Cambridge Companion to Charles Dickens* (2001).

New York   On his 1842 journey, Dickens describes the streets—the fashionable people on Broadway, the lack of street entertainers, and the pigs who roam free—and his visits to the Tombs, a lunatic asylum, and a Refuge for the Destitute (*Notes*, 6). Martin Chuzzlewit arrives in New York on the packet ship *Screw* and stays at the Pawkinses' Boarding House (*Chuzzlewit*, 16).

New York Ledger   New York newspaper for which Dickens wrote *Hunted Down* in 1851. He was paid £1,000 for the story.

Niagara Falls   The Dickenses spent 10 days at Niagara Falls on their American journey. The sight of the falls impressed Dickens with "Peace of Mind, tranquillity, calm recollections of the Dead, great thoughts of Eternal Rest and Happiness; nothing of gloom or terror" (*Notes*, 14).

Nisbet, Ada   (1907–1994)   Professor, UCLA; literary scholar, bibliographer, and critic; associate editor of *Nineteenth Century Fiction*, 1960–74; one of the key figures in the postwar generation of Dickens scholars. Nisbet wrote on a variety of Dickensian topics, especially about the reception of the novels, Dickens biography, and Dickens in America. *Dickens and Ellen Ternan* (1952) surveys and evaluates the evidence pertaining to the novelist's relationship with Ellen Ternan. Nisbet's Dickens bibliography in Lionel Stevenson's *Victorian Fiction: A Guide to Research* (1964) presents a comprehensive description of scholarly and critical work on Dickens in English and in other languages; it has

served as the foundation for later bibliographical work on the author. Nisbet's substantial collection of Dickens materials is housed in the Dickens Center at the University of California, Santa Cruz.

Nonesuch Edition   Limited edition of Dickens's works, edited by Arthur Waugh, H. Walpole, WALTER DEXTER, and Thomas Hatton, published in 23 volumes, 1937–38. It reproduced all the original illustrations from the original plates and blocks; included several minor works not included in earlier editions, such as *The Life of Our Lord* and the *Miscellaneous Papers* (as *Collected Papers*); and collected the fullest edition of the LETTERS prior to the Pilgrim Edition. Facsimiles of volumes from this edition have recently been reissued by Barnes and Noble.

Norfolk Street, Marylebone   In this street off Fitzroy Square, the Dickens family had lodgings from 1829 to 1831.

Norwood   Wooded suburb southeast of London where Gabriel Parsons (*Boz*, "Tottle"), James Carker (*Dombey*), and Mr. Spenlow (*Copperfield*) reside.

number plans   Although Dickens apparently improvised his way through his earliest novels, later he kept notes for each of the individual serial parts as he went along (*see* SERIAL PUBLICATION). In these notes he recorded directions for episodes, characters, and motifs that he planned to include in each number. He also noted developments in the plots, tried out names, and raised questions for himself. These plans are fairly complete for all the novels from *Dombey* on, and there are some scattered notes for some of the earlier works. The originals of most of these notes are in the Victoria and Albert Museum; those for *Expectations* are in the Wisbeck and Fenland Museum, Wisbeck, England; those for *Mutual Friend* in the Pierpont Morgan Library, New York. Academic editions of the novels often include the notes in appendices. HARRY STONE (1987) has compiled all the extant notes in a facsimile edition.

Nunn, Trevor (1940–   )   Theater director; executive director, Royal Shakespeare Company. His production of *The Life and Adventures of Nicholas Nickleby* (1980) stands as the most ambitious and experimental theatrical adaptation of any Dickens work. The eight-hour production and the collaborative process developed to produce it are described in Leon Rubin's *The Nicholas Nickleby Story* (1981).

Old Bailey   Central criminal court for London and Middlesex, it was burnt down during the GORDON RIOTS (*Rudge*) and rebuilt in 1809. Dickens describes the court in *Boz*, "Criminal Courts." In the novels, Fagin (*Twist*, 52), Kit Nubbles (*Curiosity Shop*, 63), Charles Darnay (*Two Cities*, II:2), and Magwitch (*Expectations*, 56) are tried at the Old Bailey.

Olympic Theatre   This establishment frequented by the Theatrical Young Gentleman was in Wych Street off the STRAND in London's West End. Madame Vestris managed the theater in the 1830s.

Once a Week   Magazine started in 1859 by BRADBURY & EVANS after Dickens discontinued *HOUSEHOLD WORDS*, which they published, to start *ALL THE YEAR ROUND* with CHAPMAN & HALL. The magazine, which slavishly followed the model of its predecessor, continued in publication for several years.

Onwhyn, Thomas   (1811–1886)   Illustrator and artist, influenced by GEORGE CRUIKSHANK and HABLOT KNIGHT BROWNE. Using the pseudonym "Peter Palette," he illustrated some of the plagiarisms of Dickens's early works in the 1830s. He later became one of the *PUNCH* illustrators.

originals   Many of Dickens's characters were, at least in part, based on real people. Micawber, drawn from Dickens's father, Boythorn from WALTER SAVAGE LANDOR, and Skimpole from LEIGH HUNT are well-known examples. A good deal of effort, particularly around the turn of the century, was devoted to identifying originals. Alex J. Philip and Laurence Gadd (*The Dickens Dictionary*, 1928) include an extensive list of many of the proposed models. Many such attributions are highly speculative and questionable and have little value for furthering an understanding of Dickens and his works, but the study of originals can entail more than source hunting. EDWIN PUGH (*The Charles Dickens Originals*, 1912) studied several examples to show how Dickens transformed particular people into general types. DORIS ALEXANDER (*Creating Characters with Charles Dickens*, 1991) analyzes the psychological complexities in several of Dickens's transformations of real into imagined people.

orphans   Orphans appear in almost all of Dickens's novels; his heroes, from Oliver Twist to Edwin Drood, are almost always orphans or semi-orphans. The number of such children reflects, in part, a social reality of the time; children like Little Dick at Mrs. Mann's baby farm (*Twist*), the Neckett children sustained by the laundry work undertaken by Charley (*Bleak House*), or Jo the crossing sweeper (*Bleak House*) represent social realities of which Dickens, as a supporter of RAGGED SCHOOLS and other charities for children, was particularly aware.

The orphans are also, as many critics have pointed out, mythic figures, relatives of the orphaned children in fairy tales and folklore. Dombey is haunted by fears that his son may become a changeling; Oliver is a kind of holy innocent who remains untouched by the evil world around him; David Copperfield, abandoned at birth by his fairy godmother, Aunt Betsey, must seek to recover his place in that fairy-tale fantasy. GEOFFREY THURLEY (1976) sees the orphan as the central figure in "the Dickens myth," a wish-fulfillment fantasy in which the "orphan is miraculously rescued by magically empowered old gentlemen," a myth that was gradually transformed during Dickens's career to shift the responsibility for rescue to the hero himself. Orphanhood generates the quest for identity that is the central motif in nearly all the novels, and it provides a basis for much of the pathos and sentimentality. It is also essential to the Dickens story, for, as ANNY SADRIN (*Parentage and Inheritance in the Novels of Charles Dickens,* 1994) points out, in the psychological myth that Dickens retells, "fathers must die that their sons shall live."

Orwell, George (1903–1950)   Pen name of Eric Blair, English novelist, essayist, political and social commentator; best known for *Animal Farm* (1946) and *1984* (1949). His essay "Charles Dickens" (1940) is one of the seminal works of Dickens criticism. Orwell describes Dickens as a subversive but not a revolutionary writer, for his criticisms of society showed "no consciousness that the *structure* of society can be changed." From his moral, apolitical point of view, Dickens called for a change of spirit, not a reformation of society. Orwell found Dickens's perspective narrow—that of a 19th-century bourgeois liberal. He has "no ideal of *work*" and sees the world from a consumer's point of view, but he identifies with the underdog and is generously angry on his behalf.

Osborne's Hotel, Adelphi   Hotel, formerly at the corner of John Adam Street, where Wardle holds the celebration for Pickwick's release from the FLEET PRISON (*Pickwick,* 54). Mrs. Edson stays here before moving to Mrs. Lirriper's ("Lirriper's Lodgings").

Our Young Folks   Children's magazine published by TICKNOR & FIELDS, Dickens's American publishers. Dickens published "A Holiday Romance" in the magazine in 1868.

Ouvry, Frederic (1814–1881)   Dickens's friend, solicitor, and adviser. He handled legal matters during the last two decades of Dickens's life, most significantly the separation from Catherine.

Overs, John A. (1808–1844)   London cabinetmaker whom Dickens befriended and encouraged in his writing. Dickens contacted editors on Overs's behalf and wrote a preface for Overs's *Evenings of a Working Man* (1844).

Oxford Illustrated Edition   Edition of Dickens's collected works, issued in 21 volumes between 1947 and 1958, distinctive for its re-engraved images of the original illustrations. Although the texts were not edited for scholarly use, this edition has been the one most often cited in scholarly work prior to the appearance of individual volumes in the CLARENDON EDITION. The introductions in the Oxford Illustrated Edition are by various Dickensians of the postwar era. The edition does not include the miscellaneous papers, plays, or poems.

Oxford Street   Known as Oxford Road in Dickens's day, this street dividing Mayfair to the south and MARYLEBONE to the north is where Gabriel Parsons walks hoping to meet his sweetheart (*Boz,* "Tottle"). Micawber imagines living at the west end facing Hyde Park (*Copperfield,* 28). Jarndyce has London lodgings over an upholsterer's here (*Bleak House,* 13). Clennam and Meagles search for Miss Wade in the side streets in the neighborhood (*Dorrit,* I:27).

Oxford University   Not a university man himself, Dickens seldom mentioned Oxford. He describes some of its undergraduates in London when Steerforth and some of his Oxford acquaintances celebrate David's housewarming (*Copperfield,* 19–20). Dickens attacked Oxford and the Oxford Movement as representative of the narrow ignorance promoted at the university in "Report to the Commissioners . . ." (*Miscellaneous*).

P

Page, Norman (1930–) Professor, University of Nottingham; specialist in Victorian and modern literature. He has written and edited works on Hardy, Austen, Collins, Lawrence, Tennyson, Housman, Kipling, and others. His *Dickens Companion* (1984), a work directed to graduate students and Dickens specialists, describes the resources available for Dickens studies and summarizes the composition, publication, and reception of each of Dickens's works. Page also includes a short critical bibliography for each work and a list of the characters with brief descriptions. His *Dickens Chronology* (1988) provides a year-by-year record of the events in Dickens's life.

Palazzo Peschiere Dickens leased this "palace of the fishponds" during his stay in GENOA in 1844–45.

Pall Mall This fashionable street in central London houses a number of gentlemen's clubs. Here Montague Tigg has his lodgings and his fraudulent insurance company (*Chuzzlewit*, 27–28). Mr. Chops locates here in "Going into Society." Twemlow canvasses for Veneering by spending a whole day sitting in the window of his Pall Mall club (*Mutual Friend*, II:3). Also mentioned in *Boz*, "Winglebury," "Golden Mary," and *Uncommercial* (16).

Palmer, Samuel (1805–1881) Artist engaged by Dickens to provide four sketches for *Pictures from Italy* after CLARKSON STANFIELD withdrew, probably because of what he perceived as anti-Catholic bias in Dickens's text (see p. 412).

Palmerston, Henry John Temple, Viscount (1784–1865) Tory politician, pragmatic, imperialistic, and opportunistic, particularly hated by Dickens. When he became prime minister in the wake of the Crimean debacle of 1855, Dickens attacked him in HOUSEHOLD WORDS as "the Grand Vizier Parmastoon (or Twirling Weathercock)" in a series of articles entitled "The Thousand and One Humbugs" (*Miscellaneous*).

Pancras Road Street in CAMDEN TOWN, north London, where Miss J'mima Ivins and Mr. Samuel Wilkins meet their friends on the way to the EAGLE INN (*Boz*, "Miss Evans"); Heyling, in "The Old Man's Tale about the Queer Client," takes the Pancras Road in his final pursuit of his victim (*Pickwick*, 21); Jerry Cruncher resurrects a body in the St. Pancras Churchyard (*Two Cities*, II:14).

pantomime In Britain, a form of popular theater beginning in the early 18th century and traditionally performed during the Christmas season. The basic pantomime plot revolves around a young lady with two suitors, a wealthy fop chosen by her father to marry her and a poor young man whom she prefers. When she is forced to choose between giving in to her father or running off with her lover, a good fairy transforms the whole group into the characters of traditional pantomime: The young lovers become Harlequin and Columbine, the interfering father Pantaloon, and his servant Clown. In the ensuing pursuit of the runaway couple, the "comic business" of the pantomime, the lovers escape their pursuers through tricks and contrivances until they are finally overtaken and subdued by Pantaloon and Clown. Then the good fairy reappears, secures the father's consent to the marriage, and the play closes with a grand celebration. In articles for his magazines ("The Pantomime of Life," "A Curious Dance around a Curious Tree," and "Paradise Revisited") and in his introduction to the *Memoirs of Grimaldi*, Dickens recounted his childhood pleasure in the pantomime, particularly in the antics of Clown, and he reiterated his belief that the pantomime is "a mirror of life." EDWIN EIGNER (1989) traces this influence in the novels, finding the structure and characters of pantomime as an informing principle in many of the novels.

parables In the *Life of Our Lord*, Dickens's retelling of the gospel story for his children, he placed particular emphasis on Jesus's parables, stories that illustrate a moral or theological teaching and are often ALLEGORICAL. In Jesus's parables, for example, the father usually represents God. Dickens often used New Testament parables in his works. The satire in *Twist*, for example, ironically casts the workhouse and parochial officials as good Samaritans; *Hard Times* is structured on the parable of the sower. *Hard Times* itself is a kind of parable, illustrating the spiritual results of Gradgrind's individualistic materialism. JANET LARSON (1985) discusses both Dickens's use of biblical parables and the parabolic qualities in Dickens's own work.

Paris When Dickens first visited Paris in 1844 on his way to GENOA, he described the city in a letter to ALFRED COUNT D'ORSAY as "the most extraordinary place in the world." He returned for frequent visits to the city, often with friends like WILLIAM MACREADY (1844), DANIEL MACLISE (1850), and WILKIE COLLINS (1855). He describes a cold New Year's Day on one such visit in Paris in "New Year's Day." He was introduced in 1844 to many of the important French writers and artists, among them ALEXANDRE DUMAS, VICTOR HUGO, Théophile Gautier, Eugène Sue, and Eugène Delacroix. He spent several months in Paris with his family during the winter and spring of 1845–46, while he was working on *Dombey*, writing back to JOHN FORSTER that "Paul's death has amazed Paris." During this visit, Dickens went to the **Paris Morgue,** an institution described in *Uncommercial* (7, 19) and in "Railway Dreaming." He also made extended visits to Paris in 1855–56 and 1862–63.

The Dombeys spend a "dull" honeymoon in Paris (*Dombey*, 35), and Lady Dedlock is happy to leave behind the "desolation of Boredom" she finds there (*Bleak House*, 12), but Mrs. Lirriper is enthralled: "And of Paris I can tell you no more my dear than that it's town and country both in one. . . . It's pure enchantment" ("Mrs. Lirriper's Legacy," 1). Revolutionary Paris, the BASTILLE, St. Antoine, and the Monseigneur's palaces are important settings in *Two Cities*.

Parker, David For many years the curator of the DICKENS HOUSE, Parker has facilitated the work of many scholars with his intimate knowledge of Dickens, especially the early Dickens. His *Companion to The Pickwick Papers* (forthcoming) and *The Doughty Street Novels* (2002) discuss the work Dickens did while living in the house that now houses the Dickens Museum.

Park Lane Fashionable street in Mayfair where Nicholas attacks Sir Mulberry Hawk (*Nickleby*, 32); Miss Wade takes Tattycoram to her house in "a labyrinth near Park Lane" (*Dorrit*, II:27).

Parley's Illuminated Library Magazine that specialized in "re-originating" popular works of literature. Dickens sued the magazine for its plagiarism of *Carol* and won the case, but he was unable to collect the damages when the magazine folded.

Parliament In David Copperfield's description of working as a shorthand reporter taking down speeches in Parliament, Dickens drew on his own similar experiences with the MIRROR OF PARLIAMENT and the MORNING CHRONICLE: "Night after night, I record predictions that never come to pass, professions that are never fulfilled, explanations that are only meant to mystify. I wallow in words. . . . I am sufficiently behind the scenes to know the worth of political life. I am quite an Infidel about it, and shall never be converted" (*Copperfield*, 43). Dickens's years as a parliamentary reporter developed his ear for public speech, which he frequently parodied in the novels, and his eye for the absurdities of the proceedings. In the "Parliamentary Sketch" in *Boz* and in gatherings like the Pickwick Club (*Pickwick*, 1) or the meeting of the United Metropolitan Improved Hot Muffin and Crumpet Baking and Punctual Delivery Company (*Nickleby*, 2), he satirized the inflated public rhetoric and the hair splitting that he had observed in Parliament. Nearly all of his M.P.s are presented satrically, from Cornelius Brook Dingwall (*Boz*, "Sentiment") and Mr. Gregsbury (*Nickleby*, 16) to Veneering (*Mutual Friend*). As a member of the Whig Parliament devoted to carrying out investigations and producing blue books full of statistics, Gradgrind's "parliamentary duties" are said to be "sifting for odds and ends" at the "national cinderheap" and "throwing the dust about into the eyes of other people who wanted other odds and ends" (*Hard Times*, II:11), a metaphor Dickens again uses to describe parliamentary activity in *Mutual Friend* (III:8). Dickens satirizes parliamentary ELECTIONS in *Pickwick, Bleak House,* and *Mutual Friend.*

Parliament Street   Street in Westminster where Dickens as a boy went into the Red Lion Pub and ordered a glass of ale. He describes a similar episode in *Copperfield* (11).

Paroissien, David H. (1939–)   Professor, University of Massachusetts; Dickens critic, editor, and historical scholar. He edited and annotated *Pictures from Italy* (1973), *Selected Letters of Charles Dickens* (1984), the Garland bibliography for *Oliver Twist,* an edition of *Edwin Drood,* and the *Companion to Great Expectations* (2000). He has also written numerous articles on Dickensian topics, especially on the early novels. Particularly noteworthy is his survey of Dickens's ideas about literature and art, culled from comments in the letters and articles

("Literature's 'Eternal Duties': Dickens's Professional Creed," in *The Changing World of Charles Dickens,* ed. R. Giddings, 1983). As the general editor of the *Dickens Quarterly,* Paroissien coordinated special issues on several of the novels commemorating the 150th anniversary of their first publication.

Patten, Robert (1939–)   Professor, Rice University. In numerous articles and books, Patten has written on critical, bibliographical, and historical topics relating to Dickens. He is especially interested in Victorian publishing. In *Dickens and His Publishers* (1978) he collects the facts of Dickens's publishing career and discusses how such factors as serial publication affected his work. *George Cruikshank: His Life, Times, and Art* (1992) treats Dickens's connections and collaborations with this important Victorian illustrator. Patten's many articles on Dickensian topics include several on *Pickwick,* especially on the interpolated tales ("Art of *Pickwick*'s Interpolated Tales," *ELH,* 1967); an analysis of the religious dimensions of *Carol* ("Dickens Time and Again," *Dickens Studies Annual,* 1972); and an analysis of the links between *Dombey* and *Vanity Fair* ("The Fight at the Top of the Tree: *Vanity Fair* versus *Dombey and Son,*" *Studies in English Literature,* 1970). Patten has also edited *Pickwick* (1972).

Pavilionstone   Dickens's name for FOLKESTONE, a former fishing village and smuggling town that has been transformed by the trains of the South-Eastern Railway Company bringing travelers on their way to the steamboats for France.

Paxton, Joseph (1803–1865)   Gardener, horticulturalist, designer of the Crystal Palace, member of Parliament. Paxton was the majority financial backer of the DAILY NEWS. Paxton's money came from speculation in railways, and Dickens feared that his financial interests would skew the editorial policy of the paper. He showed Dickens through the Crystal Palace while it was still under construction.

Payn, James (1830–1898)   Novelist, poet, editor, and journalist, best known for *Lost Sir Massingberd* (1864) and *By Proxy* (1878). He published numerous articles in HOUSEHOLD WORDS and described his first meeting with Dickens in 1856 as "an epoch in my existence." Payn was friendly with Dickens, but he did not become one of Dickens's young men. He thought the separation a "sad blot" on Dickens's character and suggested that the novelist "was in a degree intoxicated with universal applause, as well as spoiled by the sycophants who hung about him, and sanctioned his vagaries." His recollections of Dickens appear in *Chambers's Magazine* (1874), which he edited, and in *Some Literary Recollections* (1884).

Peacock Inn   Starting point in ISLINGTON for coaches going north. Nicholas leaves from here on his way to Dotheboys Hall (*Nickleby*, 5); the narrator of the "Holly-Tree" starts from here on his wintry journey to Liverpool.

Pendennis   Autobiographical BILDUNGSROMAN by WILLIAM MAKEPEACE THACKERAY, serialized between 1848 and 1850, which is often compared to Dickens's autobiographical bildungsroman of the same period, *David Copperfield*. The novel tells of the youth and young manhood of Arthur Pendennis (Pen), who survives a disastrous infatuation for an actress, an affair with his housekeeper's daughter, an opportunistic relationship with an heiress, illness, and estrangement from his mother to eventually marry the patient and sensible Laura Bell, a young woman much like Agnes Wickfield.

penny dreadfuls   A form of popular fiction developed in the 1830s and 1840s, these sensational tales written for working-class readers were printed in an eight-page, double-column format; illustrated with crude woodcuts; and sold for a penny. Jo March in Louisa May Alcott's *Little Women* (1868) survives in New York by writing similar tales for the American market. Many of the penny dreadfuls recounted the lives of criminals, as did the NEWGATE NOVELS. Dickens was fascinated with such motifs as the cannibalism in such popular stories as Sweeney Todd, one of the sensational penny dreadfuls. Scenes like the murder of Nancy and the pursuit and death of Sikes contained many

of the elements found in the cheap serials. It is not surprising that several of Dickens's novels were recast by writers like T. P. Prest, who produced *Oliver Twiss* under the pseudonym "Bos" for the penny market.

Pentonville   Fashionable suburb in north London where Nicodemus Dumps rents a "first-floor furnished" (*Boz*, "Christening"), Brownlow has his comfortable house (*Twist*, 12), Guppy has "lowly, but airy" lodgings at Penton Place (*Bleak House*, 9), and Pancks lodges on the second floor of Rugg's agency (*Dorrit*, I:25).

periodicals   Dickens began his writing career as a journalist, and his first publications—stories and sketches later collected in *Boz*—appeared in various magazines and newspapers: MONTHLY MAGAZINE, BELL'S WEEKLY MAGAZINE, MORNING CHRONICLE, EVENING CHRONICLE, and BELL'S LIFE IN LONDON. Throughout his career he also edited and wrote for magazines. Most of his journalistic essays appeared in the EXAMINER, edited by JOHN FORSTER, and in his own magazines: BENTLEY'S MISCELLANY, HOUSEHOLD WORDS, and ALL THE YEAR ROUND. All of the novels were, in a strict sense, periodicals, appearing in either monthly or weekly SERIAL PUBLICATION.

Perrault, Charles   (1628–1703)   French author who collected and retold eight traditional FAIRY TALES that became known in English as "Mother Goose's Tales." This collection, known to Dickens in the cheap chapbooks that circulated in England during his childhood, included "Bluebeard," "Cinderella," "Red Riding Hood," "Sleeping Beauty," "Hop o' My Thumb," and "Puss and Boots," stories to which he alludes frequently in the novels. HARRY STONE (1979) discusses the importance of these stories in Dickens's work.

Perugini, Kate   Married name of KATE DICKENS, Dickens's daughter, whose second husband was Carlo Perugini, a painter. GLADYS STOREY's interviews with her were the basis for *Dickens and Daughter* (1939), one of the works that revealed Dickens's relationship with ELLEN TERNAN.

Peyrouton, Noel C. (1925–1968) Professor, Emerson College, Boston; Dickens scholar; founder and original editor of DICKENS STUDIES. Peyrouton wrote many articles for the DICKENSIAN and DICKENS STUDIES, particularly on Dickens's trips to America and other biographical topics. He was an associate editor for the third volume of the Pilgrim Edition of the LETTERS (1974).

Philadelphia   On his visit to this "handsome, but distractingly regular" city, Dickens found himself succumbing to the Quaker influence: "the collar of my coat appeared to stiffen, and the brim of my hat to expand beneath its quakery influence. My hair shrunk into a sleek short crop, my hands folded themselves upon my breast of their own accord" (*Notes*, 7). He visited the Eastern Penitentiary to observe its system of solitary confinement and concluded that the system's "slow and daily tampering with the mysteries of the brain, to be immeasurably worse than any torture of the body" (*Notes*, 7).

Philadelphia, Dickens Collections   The Free Library of Philadelphia has the manuscript for *The Life of Our Lord,* some other manuscript pages, five shorthand notebooks, and about 900 letters. The Rosenbach Museum and Library has about 100 pages of the manuscript for *Nickleby* and many letters.

philanthropy   One of the most frequent themes in Dickens's work is the need for charity and caring for one's fellow human beings. When Scrooge reforms, he promptly gives money to the charity solicitors he has refused the night before and sends gifts to the Cratchits (*Carol*, 5). In the early novels especially, the hero is aided by benevolent older men like Brownlow (*Twist*) or the Cheeryble brothers (*Nickleby*), but such private philanthropy becomes increasingly problematic in the later novels, for it often has the effect of corrupting the recipients. Magwitch's money makes Pip an ungrateful snob (*Expectations*), and Jarndyce's gifts to Skimpole simply sustain his parasitism (*Bleak House*). Boffin must pretend to be a miser to enable Bella to see the corrupting effect of his kindness to her (*Mutual Friend*).

Dickens reserves his strongest scorn for the professional philanthropists who make a public display of their concern for others. Mrs. Jellyby practices "telescopic philanthropy": She can "see nothing nearer than Africa" (*Bleak House*, 4) and neglects her family while aiding the natives of Borrioboola-Gha. Mrs. Pardiggle, distinguished for her "rapacious benevolence," is a philanthropist who does "a little and ma[kes] a great deal of noise" (*Bleak House*, 8). Mr. Honeythunder's even noisier philanthropy "was of that gunpowderous sort that the difference between it and animosity was hard to determine" (*Drood*, 6).

Dickens, himself an active philanthropist, was aware of the dangers of overzealousness. He lent his name to numerous charitable causes, spoke at their fund-raising events, and wrote about them in his magazines. Two charitable endeavors were particularly important to him: the URANIA COTTAGE project, undertaken with ANGELA BURDETT-COUTTS to rescue girls from the streets and start them in respectable life, and the GUILD OF LITERATURE AND ART, a project founded with EDWARD BULWER LYTTON to provide for needy artists and writers.

philistinism   Matthew Arnold in *Culture and Anarchy* divided British society in his time into three groups: barbarians, philistines, and populace. Philistines, the members of the Victorian middle class, believed that the greatness of Britain derived from its material wealth, and they devoted themselves to the pursuit of money. Dickens satirizes the pursuit of money throughout his novels, though he increasingly seems to think that money has displaced all other measures of value and that, for example, Magwitch believes he can make a gentleman of Pip simply with money (*Expectations*). Dickens's fullest portrait of bourgeois philistinism appears in his attack on "Podsnappery" in *Mutual Friend*. Podsnap swells with monetary pride as he tallies the greatness of England and puts down everything foreign: "Mr. Podsnap was well to do, and stood very high in Mr. Podsnap's opinion. Beginning with a good inheritance, he had married a good inheritance, and had thriven exceedingly in the Marine Insurance way, and was quite satisfied. . . . Mr. Podsnap's world was not a very large world, morally; no, nor even geographically: seeing that although his business was sustained upon commerce with other countries, he considered other countries, with that important reservation, a mistake, and of their manners and customs would conclusively observe, 'Not English!'" (11).

Phillips, Watts (1825–1874) Irish playwright, novelist, and caricaturist. Phillips studied art with GEORGE CRUIKSHANK, wrote some successful plays and some adaptations of Dickens's works for the stage, and wrote serial novels for popular magazines. His play about the French Revolution, *The Dead Heart* (produced in 1859 but written two or three years earlier), uses several plot ideas similar to *A Tale of Two Cities*, including the substitution of another character for the hero on the guillotine. At the time, critics accused Phillips of plagiarizing from Dickens, but Dickens may have read Phillips's play some time before he began his novel. Since the similarities between the two stories can be found in other works of the period treating the French Revolution, it may be that neither Dickens nor Phillips was plagiarizing from the other but were instead working with some of the same story conventions.

Philpotts, Trey Professor, Arkansas Tech; book review editor of *Dickens Quarterly*. His articles on Dickens have appeared in several of the Dickens journals. He is the author of *The Companion to Little Dorrit* (2003).

"Phiz" Pen name of HABLOT KNIGHT BROWNE, Dickens's illustrator.

picaresque novel Genre of realistic prose fiction recounting the adventures of a rogue hero, the picaro, an outsider to respectable society who lives by his wits. Although there are classical rogue stories like *The Satyricon*, the picaresque novel is usually said to begin in 16th-century Spain with *La Vida de Lazarillo de Tormes* (c. 1554). Dickens was especially fond of the work of ALAIN RENÉ LESAGE, a French picaresque novelist of the 18th century, and the English picaresque novels of the 18th century,

especially TOBIAS SMOLLETT's *Roderick Random* and *Peregrine Pickle*. Dickens's early novels, which typically trace a series of loosely related adventures, uses the journey as the basis of plot structure and includes lower-class characters, such as Sam Weller, who live by their wits and are derived from the picaresque tradition; however, Dickens's heroes are not down-and-out lumpen proletarians, and there are few examples in Dickens's novels of the class war that prompts the Continental picaro's acts of trickery and revenge.

Piccadilly Known as Regent's Circus in the mid-19th century, Piccadilly Circus and the surrounding area was a fashionable residential district where Fascination Fledgby has lodgings at the ALBANY (*Mutual Friend*, III:1, 8) and the Lammles are married at St. James Church (*Mutual Friend*, I:10). Esther Summerson first arrives in London at the WHITE HORSE CELLAR in this district (*Bleak House*, 3). Piccadilly is also mentioned in *Nickleby* (64), *Rudge* (67), *Copperfield* (28), and "Somebody's Luggage."

Pierpont Morgan Library, New York This library holds the most significant collection of Dickens materials in the United States, containing the manuscripts of *Our Mutual Friend*, *A Christmas Carol*, *The Cricket on the Hearth*, *The Battle of Life*, and *Sketches of Young Gentlemen*, as well as those for several articles in *Household Words*. The library also has more than 1,300 Dickens letters.

pirated editions Strictly speaking, a pirated edition of a literary work is one that reprints the original work without recognizing or paying the author. In Dickens's day, there were several American publishers who specialized in pirating English works, since there was no international copyright agreement to prevent them from doing so. Although reputable American publishers negotiated for advance copies of foreign works, their payments to the authors were reduced by the activities of the rogue publishers. On his American tour, Dickens spoke out for an INTERNATIONAL COPYRIGHT agreement and was harshly criticized in the American press for doing so.

Even in England, with copyright laws in place, Dickens's works were pirated, or "re-originated" as one of the pirates described it. Such publishers as Edward Lloyd specialized in cheap imitations of popular works; his parts of "Bos's" *Oliver Twiss* followed on the heels of the parts of *Twist*. In exasperation, Dickens finally took one of the pirates to court over a "re-origination" of *Carol*. He won his case, but the pirate declared bankrupcy, leaving Dickens with a moral victory and £500 in legal fees. Dickens learned to tolerate the pirates, as he did the playwrights who put his stories on the stage before they had finished their serial run, but he continued his support for copyright legislation that would protect writers from such thievery, both at home and abroad.

Pisa Dickens describes his visit to this Italian city and its famous leaning tower, "nothing like so high above the wall as I had hoped. It was another of the many deceptions practised by Mr. Harris, Bookseller, at the corner of ST. PAUL's Churchyard, London. *His* Tower was a fiction, but this was a reality—and, by comparison, a short reality" (*Pictures*).

Pittsburgh Dickens visited this industrial city in Pennsylvania on his first trip to the United States in 1841. He compared it to Birmingham in *American Notes* (11).

Plorn Nickname for Dickens's youngest child, EDWARD BULWER LYTTON DICKENS, born in 1852. Dickens sometimes gave the longer version of the name as Plornishmaroon or Plornishmaroontigoonter.

Poe, Edgar Allan (1809–1849) American poet, critic, short-story writer. Poe visited Dickens at his hotel in BALTIMORE in 1842, bringing as a gift his *Tales of the Grotesque and Arabesque* (1840). He admired Dickens's work and was influenced by such stories as "A Madman's Manuscript" in *Pickwick,* and the two spent the afternoon talking about literature. After he returned to England, Dickens sought a publisher for Poe's work. Two years later, Poe was angered when he was slighted in an article on American literature by JOHN FORSTER, whom he thought must have been influenced by Dickens.

Poe's review of *Rudge* (*Graham's Magazine,* 1842) criticized the bifurcation of the murder plot from the GORDON RIOTS plot and suggested that the novel would have been better had Dickens confined the story to London and to a shorter span of time. But Poe praised the atmosphere of the novel. Dickens's raven Grip probably influenced Poe's poem "The Raven."

poetry Dickens published some occasional verse in his periodicals and in some of the novels, such as "The Ivy Green" in *Pickwick* (6). These verses are collected in *Miscellaneous Papers.*

point of view Critical concept describing the vantage point from which an author presents his story. The NARRATOR can write in either a first- or a third-person voice and can be limited in what he or she knows—as is the case, for example, when a character within the story narrates the action—or omniscient, standing outside the action and able to know what all of the characters are doing and thinking. These alternatives describe polar positions on a continuum; there are many possible points of view that are neither fully omniscient nor absolutely limited. Many critics have pointed out that Dickens's first-person narrators like David (*Copperfield*) and Pip (*Expectations*) sometimes know more than we expect them to and share some of the stylistic skills of Dickens's omniscient narrators. AUDREY JAFFE (1991) argues that his omniscient narrator is often less than omniscient.

police During Dickens's lifetime there were major changes in law enforcement and the police. During his childhood, policing was handled by constables, BOW STREET RUNNERS, and, in extreme situations like the GORDON RIOTS or the Peterloo Massacre, by the military. The river police force on the THAMES, described by Dickens in "Down with the Tide," was established early in the century. The Metropolitan Police Act of 1829 created a police force for the area around London, and the Detective Department of the force was begun in 1842. There was substantial resistance to all of these changes, and the police were under a great deal of scrutiny. In magazine articles like "Metropolitan Protectives" and "On Duty with Inspector Field," Dickens described the work of these new police agencies, making them more acceptable to his readers. The police and detectives in the novels, from the soldiers who pursue the escaped convicts at the beginning of *Expectations* to the BOW STREET RUNNERS Blathers and Duff in *Twist* (31) to Bucket (*Bleak House*) and the Police Inspector (*Mutual Friend*), reflect these changes and the growing professionalism in the police forces of the time.

political economy   The principles of classical economics, known as political economy in Britain, were a subject of intense debate during Dickens's lifetime, particularly in the 1830s and 1840s. Following the REFORM BILL OF 1832, the Whigs took power after decades of Conservative rule; they introduced many measures to limit or end government interference in the economy, to establish free trade and a free market for labor. The economic philosophy behind this legislation, variously referred to as political economy, laissez-faire, and UTILITARIANISM, broadly reflected the ideas of such economists as Adam Smith, David Ricardo, and THOMAS ROBERT MALTHUS and such utilitarian philosophers as Jeremy Bentham. These ideas were popularized at the time by writers like HARRIET MARTINEAU, whose *Illustrations of Political Economy* (1832–34) emphasized the principles in story form. Although Dickens supported some of the principles of the economists, especially free trade and the abolition of the CORN LAWS, he did not do so for reasons of economic principle. His concerns were humanitarian (getting bread for the poor) and political (opposing aristocratic privilege). He opposed the economists' cold-hearted rationalism, which dehumanized factory workers and turned them into "hands," allowed the exploitation of women and children under the guise of supporting a free market, and made the market rather than economic justice the determinant of a fair wage. He attacked the political economists as "philosophers" in *Twist*, satirized them through Filer and his associates in *Chimes*, and exposed the moral emptiness of the "hard facts school" in Gradgrind and Bounderby in *Hard Times*.

Pompeii   Dickens describes his visit to this city buried in the eruption of Mount Vesuvius in A.D. 79 in *Pictures*. Mr. Meagles includes "morsels of tesselated pavement" from Pompeii among the souvenirs of his travels (*Dorrit*, I:16).

Poole, John   (1786?–1872)   Playwright, author of popular theatrical farces, one of which, *Deaf as a Post*, Dickens directed and performed in at MONTREAL in 1842. Toward the end of his life, Poole, wasted by alcohol, retired to Paris, where he lived in poverty. Dickens provided money for him from the performances of some of his benefit theatricals.

Poor Law   The Poor Law Amendment Act of 1834 (also called the New Poor Law) was one of the first major pieces of legislation passed by the Whig Parliament that took power after the REFORM BILL OF 1832. The act centralized welfare by grouping parishes throughout England and Wales into 21 unions and building workhouses for the poor in each. The law eliminated "outdoor relief"—receiving aid while remaining out of the workhouse—and it provided that conditions in the workhouse be such as to discourage paupers from seeking aid except as a last resort. The workhouses quickly became known as "Poor Law Bastilles," and many stories circulated of paupers like Betty Higden who chose death outside to the privations and indignities within the workhouse. Dickens satirizes the workhouses and attacks the Poor Law in the opening chapters of *Twist* (1–7), in the account of Mr. Nandy (*Dorrit*, I:31), and in the story of Betty Higden (*Mutual Friend*, I:17, II:14, III:8).

Portland Place   Fashionable residential street in MARYLEBONE. Mr. Dombey's house was nearby in a "dark, dreadfully genteel Street" (*Dombey*, 3). The extensive Tapkins family is "at Home, Wednesdays" at their residence in Portland Place (*Mutual Friend*, I:17).

Portsmouth   Dickens was born in this seaport on the English Channel in Hampshire, southwest England, on February 7, 1812. The Dickenses' house at 1 Mile End Terrace, **Portsea** (now 393 Commercial Road), is now the Dickens Museum. The family left Portsmouth for London in 1838. Nicholas Nickleby and Smike appear with Crummles's theatrical company during their run in Portsmouth (*Nickleby*, 22–25).

Pre-Raphaelite art   School of painting established in 1848 by seven young artists and poets, the most noteworthy being Dante Gabriel Rossetti, William Holman Hunt, and JOHN EVERETT MILLAIS. Through their work and their magazine, *The Germ,* they promoted an art that closely observed nature and expressed ideas, qualities they found in medieval and Renaissance art prior to Raphael. By 1850 their work had become controversial, its medieval and religious subject matter suggesting that they were philosophically allied to the Tractarians. In "Old Lamps for New Ones," Dickens attacked MILLAIS'S painting "Christ in the House of His Parents" for its degrading realism. He later altered his opinion of Millais's work and the two became friends, but he remained opposed to reactionary Victorian MEDIEVALISM.

Prescott, William H. (1796–1859)   American historian, author of *Conquest of Mexico* and other works. He was one of the group of American friends that Dickens made on his American tour in 1842. Prescott visited Dickens in England in 1849.

Preston   Dickens visited this textile manufacturing town in Lancashire in January 1854 during a long and bitter strike of the factory workers. His article about his trip, "On Strike," appeared in HOUSEHOLD WORDS, February 11, 1854 (*Miscellaneous*). Preston was one of the sources for Coketown in *Hard Times.* George Silverman's "infant home was a cellar in Preston" ("Silverman").

Priestley, J. B. (1894–1984)   Novelist, playwright; author and editor of numerous works of nonfiction; broadcaster and stage producer; president of the DICKENS FELLOWSHIP, 1970. Priestley's lower-middle class characters and urban settings in his novels have been compared to those of Dickens, a novelist with whom Priestley is often connected. In advising young writers, Priestley urged them to "write for the common man and woman—like Hemingway, Dick-

ens, Twain, and Poe did—for they are the ones who will keep your work alive long after you're gone." Priestley's pictorial biography of Dickens (1961) tells Dickens's life from a fellow Londoner's point of view. He stresses the comic side of Dickens and illustrates the general proposition, stated in *The English Novel* (1935), that Dickens's "later stories are better novels than the earlier ones, but they are not better Dickens." His analyses of Micawber and Swiveller in *English Comic Characters* (1925) offer sympathetic insight into Dickens's comedy, as does his centennial essay ("The Great Inimitable" in *Charles Dickens 1812–1870*, ed. E. W. F. Tomlin, 1969), which seeks to describe the "inimitable" qualities in Dickens's work. Priestley also prepared an edition of selected *Sketches by Boz* (1948) and wrote the general introduction to the Centennial Edition of Dickens's Works (1970).

prisons   Biographers suggest that Dickens's interest in prisons stemmed from the traumatic months in his childhood when his father was imprisoned in the MARSHALSEA for debt. DEBTORS' PRISONS and criminal prisons appear in many of his works. In "A Visit to Newgate," Boz describes the prison and imagines himself a condemned prisoner awaiting execution, foreshadowing many of the prison scenes in the later novels: Pickwick's imprisonment in the FLEET (*Pickwick*, 40); Fagin's condemned cell in NEWGATE (*Twist*, 51); the storming of Newgate by the Gordon rioters (*Rudge*, 64); Micawber's imprisonment for debt (*Copperfield*, 11); the symbolic Marshalsea of *Dorrit*, representing the physical and mental prisons that confine the human spirit; the BASTILLE, where Doctor Manette is buried for 17 years (*Two Cities*); and the Newgate that Pip visits with Wemmick, which leaves a "taint" upon him as he meets Estella in London (*Expectations*, 32). According to JOHN FORSTER, he planned to end his last novel with Jasper's meditations in his condemned cell.

Dickens visited prisons himself and entered into the controversies over prison reform in his journalistic writings and novels, as in his account of Heep and Littimer as "model prisoners" (*Copperfield*, 61), a satirical attack on the experimental PENTONVILLE Prison. Dickens joined the prison controversy of the 1840s with a chapter in *American Notes* (7), where he described the Eastern Penitentiary in PHILADELPHIA, an institution that used a system of solitary confinement, known as the separate system, to reform its inmates. Dickens criticized the system as cruel and unnatural and supported its alternative, the silent system, in which prisoners associated with their fellow prisoners but were not allowed to communicate with them. Attacked for his advocacy of the silent system, Dickens defended himself and reiterated his arguments against the separate system in "Pet Prisoners," a controversial article for HOUSEHOLD WORDS that criticized the application of silent principles at Pentonville. PHILIP COLLINS (1962) provides a comprehensive account of Dickens's ideas on prison reform and concludes that "it is impossible . . . to discover a consistent attitude, or a clear development in Dickens's various pronouncements on penal discipline. The most that one can say is that, throughout his career, he approved of severe penal measures, and inclined more towards a deterrent than a curative policy, and that the inclination became stronger, and was more vehemently expressed, the older he grew."

Procter, Bryan Waller (1787–1874) Lawyer, poet, and dramatist who wrote under the pen name "Barry Cornwall." Friend of Lord Byron, LEIGH HUNT, and Charles Lamb, Procter wrote one tragedy, *Mirandola*, and *The Life of Edmund Kean*. He was, with Dickens, a member of the COUNTESS OF BLESSINGTON's literary salon at Gore House, and the two were lifelong friends. Procter's work appeared in both HOUSEHOLD WORDS and ALL THE YEAR ROUND. His daughter, the immensely popular poet **Adelaide Anne Procter** (1825–64), also published in both of Dickens's magazines. She submitted her poems to Dickens under the pseudonym "Mary Berwick," and he accepted them not knowing who had written them. He wrote an introduction for a posthumous edition of her *Legends and Lyrics* (1866).

progress, the A literary form describing a journey that moves forward in distinct stages or steps. The English model for a progress narrative is Bunyan's *Pilgrim's Progress* (1673), next to the Bible the best-known literary work in Victorian England. Dickens and the other Victorian novelists allude to it frequently; Dickens makes his most extensive use of it in *Curiosity Shop,* in which Nell's allegorical journey recalls Christian's, and such scenes as the escape from the city and passage through a wicket gate (16) allude explicitly to scenes in Bunyan's narrative.

In subtitling *Twist* "The Parish Boy's Progress," Dickens probably had in mind the progresses of WILLIAM HOGARTH, who turned Bunyan's narrative on its head in a series of visual narratives that described the downward movement of their protagonists. "The Harlot's Progress" (1732), for example, described the corruption of a country girl who comes to London, and "The Rake's Progress" (1735) the dissolution into dissipation and madness of a young man-about-town. Although Oliver's story is predicted to follow a similar progress to the gallows, it takes a counter direction, prompting some critics to see Bunyan rather than Hogarth as Dickens's inspiration, but in the course of *Twist,* Oliver is displaced by Fagin as the central character of the progress, and Fagin completes the predicted progress to the gallows.

Dickens also described Esther Summerson's autobiographical narrative as a progress (*Bleak House*), and even though Esther's story has an upward movement, the story of Lady Dedlock has many of the elements of one of Hogarth's progresses. Commentators have described several other novels as progresses, especially *Pickwick,* with its peregrinations throughout England, and *Expectations,* in which Pip's life story is broken into "stages."

prostitution Of the three common Victorian attitudes toward prostitution—condemnation, acceptance with regulation, and reformation—Dickens adopted the third. He nearly always portrays the prostitute as a victim of economic necessity or duplicity, pities her as a remorseful creature outside the bounds of domestic happiness, and seeks her reformation. His work at URANIA COTTAGE was founded on a commitment to changing the lives of the women there, but Dickens was also a realist who knew that such efforts were not always successful.

Prostitutes appear in his earliest work, Boz's realistic sketches of urban life, in the two girls being taken away in "The Prisoners' Van," the gaudy but ravaged woman in "The Pawnbroker's Shop," and the battered woman in "The Hospital Patient." These women represented the many prostitutes on the London streets at the time, who constituted a social problem that engaged Victorian reformers like Dickens and shocked foreign visitors. Although we never see Nancy, Sikes's doxy in *Twist*, on the streets, Dickens identified her as a prostitute in a canceled sentence in the 1846 preface, and Brownlow's proposal to remove her from her degradation moves the remorseful girl, even though she rejects his offer. The economic necessity that drives these women into the streets also explains Lilian Fern's fall in the vision of the future in *The Chimes* (3) and the remorse of the prostitute who warns Little Dorrit off the streets (*Dorrit*, I:14). While Alice Marwood was driven to the streets to survive, her story also embodies the cherished Victorian tale of the poor girl seduced and then abandoned to prostitution by the rich man (*Dombey*, 34). Little Em'ly is Dickens's fullest development of this story, even though Em'ly is saved from the streets by Daniel Peggotty and by the example of her counterpart, Martha Endell (*Copperfield*, 47, 50). Dickens's most probing treatment of the theme of prostitution comes in the story of Edith Dombey, the rich and respectable lady who is doubled with her cousin, the prostitute Alice Marwood. By paralleling the two women, Dickens suggests that mercenary marriage is a form of prostitution, something Edith herself recognizes when she tells her mother that Dombey has "bought" her (*Dombey*, 27). MICHAEL SLATER (1983) surveys Dickens's treatment of prostitution and his attitude toward the prostitute.

protagonist   Chief character in a novel, play, or story. In the novel, the term is often preferred to *hero*, for the novel's central figure is usually an average person who is not faced with extraordinary tests or called upon to perform extraordinary deeds. ANGUS WILSON (1962) has said that "to examine the heroes and heroines of Dickens is to dwell on weaknesses and failures." Indeed, the central character in a Dickens novel has often been considered the least interesting figure in the book: conventional, with good intentions and without serious flaws, and less clearly defined than the characters around him. This accounting may describe fairly

well such early Dickens protagonists as Nicholas Nickleby, but, as Beth Herst (*The Dickens Hero: Selfhood and Alienation in the Dickens World*, 1990) has shown, the later Dickens heroes are much more complex figures who become the heroes of their own lives and achieve self-integration only by alienating themselves from society.

psychological novel   A novel emphasizing interior characterization, focusing on the personal history, circumstances, and motives that prompt its characters to act. Among Victorian novelists, GEORGE ELIOT is usually considered the major practitioner in this form. Commentators who stress the dramatic side of Dickens's work or his realistic depiction of Victorian society tend to describe his works as SOCIOLOGICAL NOVELS, and they often ignore their psychological dimensions.

Although they do not employ an analytic narration similar to Eliot's, Dickens's works, as many recent critics have shown, are intensely psychological. His use of first-person narration and his understanding of personal history in *Copperfield*, *Bleak House*, *Great Expectations*, and such stories as "George Silverman's Explanation" is pre-Freudian. The central theme in all of his work—the search for an integrated sense of self—is fundamentally psychological. Although his plots are dramatic and focus on external events and his people are individualized through physical traits, gestures, and mannerisms, these markers externalize an interior drama. The uncanny coincidences in the plots and such devices as REPETITION and DOUBLING in characterization convey the psychological import of the story. Among the critics who have analyzed the psychological dimensions of Dickens's work are LEONARD MANHEIM (1952, 1955, 1965), TAYLOR STOEHR (1965), MARK SPILKA (1963), Karen Chase (*Eros and Psyche: The Representation of Personality in Charlotte Bronte, Charles Dickens, and George Eliot*, 1984), LAWRENCE FRANK (1984), Dirk den Hartog (*Dickens and Romantic Psychology*, 1987), ALBERT HUTTER (1977, 1983), and GWEN WATKINS (1987).

public readings   Just after Christmas 1853, Dickens gave a reading of *Carol* in Birmingham for charity, the first of many public readings of his works. He had previously given private readings of his CHRIST-MAS BOOKS or of parts of his novels in progress for friends and family members, the best-known being his reading of the *Chimes* in 1844. Several more charity readings in the mid-1850s were a prelude to a career as a professional reader that began in 1858 and continued—with almost annual seasons in London, regular provincial tours, and the famous American tour in 1867–68—until his death.

Dickens prepared performance texts for the readings, condensing the shorter pieces or extracting passages from the longer novels. His most frequent and popular readings were "The Trial from Pickwick," performed 164 times, and "A Christmas Carol," performed 127 times. The most notorious selection, "Sikes and Nancy," introduced into his repertory in 1868, recounted the murder of Nancy and the death of Sikes from *Twist*. It was sensational theater that horrified some of his listeners and so excited the performer that his doctor

advised him against doing it. However, Dickens did not follow his doctor's advice, and he continued to perform "Sikes and Nancy" and other pieces until a few months before his death. The strain of the performances is believed to have hastened his demise.

The readings were really performances rather than readings. Dickens knew his texts and played the different characters in different voices. KATE FIELD (1871) described many of the performances that she attended during Dickens's American tour. PHILIP COLLINS (1975) provides an account of the readings and the performance texts. EMLYN WILLIAMS has re-created the public readings for modern audiences; recordings of several of his performances are available.

publishers   For most of his career Dickens worked with two publishers, CHAPMAN & HALL and BRADBURY & EVANS. As he was establishing himself and developing a reputation, he changed publishers frequently to take advantage of growing opportunities. His first publisher was JOHN MACRONE, who issued both series of *Sketches by Boz*. Impressed with the success of the sketches, Chapman & Hall engaged Dickens to write the copy for the monthly numbers of *Pickwick*. RICHARD BENTLEY published *Twist* after it appeared in BENTLEY'S MISCELLANY, his magazine that Dickens was editing. He was promised a second novel, but Dickens turned that project over to Chapman & Hall, who became his regular publishers with *Nickleby* and *Master Humphrey's Clock*. When they talked of reducing his monthly payments when *Chuzzlewit* failed to meet expectations, Dickens moved to Bradbury & Evans. They published the novels from *Dombey* through *Dorrit* as well as HOUSEHOLD WORDS. When they refused to include Dickens's statement, "Personal," regarding his marital separation in PUNCH, another of their publications, Dickens returned to Chapman & Hall, publishing with them the remaining novels and ALL THE YEAR ROUND, the magazine he created to break his magazine contract with Bradbury & Evans. Several of the collected editions of Dickens's works published during his lifetime were published cooperatively by Chapman & Hall and Bradbury & Evans. Dickens published with several American firms; from 1867 on, his official Ameri-

Dickens at his reading desk for his final performance on March 15, 1870.

Punch often ran cartoons that parodied the famous original illustrations for Dickens's works. Here Tenniel, in an 1893 cartoon, recalls Leech's illustration for Christmas Present in *A Christmas Carol* (for the original, see the illustration on page 65), as he shows Sadstone [Gladstone] facing a Spirit of Christmas Present holding the torch of anarchy and surrounded by explosive political issues.

can publisher was TICKNOR & FIELDS. The standard work on the subject is *Dickens and His Publishers*, by ROBERT PATTEN (1978).

Pugh, Edwin (1874–1930)   Novelist and critic; a member of the COCKNEY SCHOOL whose novels (e.g., *Man of Straw*, 1897; *Tony Drum, A Cockney Boy*, 1898) realistically described the life of the London poor. An avowed follower of Dickens, he wrote *Charles Dickens: The Apostle of the People* (1908), characterizing the novelist as a protosocialist, and *The Charles Dickens Originals* (1912), an account of the real people who were transformed into Dickens characters.

Punch   Weekly magazine featuring satiric commentary, caricature, and parody, the most influential and long-standing of many Victorian comic magazines and miscellanies. Begun in 1841 by MARK LEMON, who edited the magazine until 1870, and published by BRADBURY & EVANS, *Punch* included many of Dickens's friends and associates among its staff and regular contributors. W. H. WILLS and DOUGLAS JERROLD were among its founding group; JOHN LEECH, WILLIAM MAKEPEACE THACKERAY, JOHN TENNIEL, and LEIGH HUNT were among its regular contributors.

Punch and Judy   Popular puppet play performed by street performers in Britain since the late 17th century. The usual version of the story has Punch, an irascible, humpbacked creature, kill his child in a fit of anger. When his wife Judy attacks him with a stick, he takes it from her and beats her to death. He goes on to bludgeon his dog and the doctor, trick the hangman who is to execute him

Doré's vignette of a Punch and Judy performance in the streets of London.

for his crimes into hanging himself, and, finally, trick even the devil. Dickens makes fullest use of Punch and Judy in *Curiosity Shop:* Nell travels with a pair of Punch and Judy performers, and Quilp has many Punch-like qualities. PAUL SCHLICKE (1985) discusses the Punch shows, Dickens's interest in them, and his use of the story in *Curiosity Shop.*

Putnam, George Washington (1812–1896) Dickens's faithful secretary on his first American trip in 1842. Putnam amused the Dickenses with his good humor and tall stories, and he was absolutely efficient in handling Dickens's correspondence and traveling arrangements. Putnam published his reminiscences of his time with Dickens in the *Atlantic Monthly* (1870).

Putney Suburban village on the Surrey side of the THAMES west of London where Dora Spenlow's aunts live. David and Dora are married in the parish church of St. Mary (*Copperfield,* 41–43). Arthur Clennam crosses Putney Heath on his way to visit the Meagleses at TWICKENHAM (*Dorrit,* I:16).

Pykett, Lyn Pro-vice chancellor, University of Wales, Aberystwyth; Victorian scholar; editor of the *Journal of Victorian Culture.* Pykett has written books on Emily Brontë, WILKIE COLLINS, and the sensation novel, as well as a contemporary introduction to the critical issues in Dickens's work, *Charles Dickens* (2002).

Q, R

Quarterly Review The major Tory quarterly journal, founded in 1809 to respond to the Whig *Edinburgh Review*. The *Quarterly* tended to regard Dickens as a mere popular entertainer beneath serious notice, a view made explicit in John Wilson Croker's unsigned review commenting on Dickens's vulgarity in the March 1843 issue. Abraham Hayward's review essay in the October 1837 issue, however, was a generally favorable assessment of Dickens's work, and Dickens noted that it contained "a great deal that I know to be true." He was bothered, however, by Hayward's famous prophesy: "The fact is, Mr Dickens writes too often and too fast. . . . If he persists much longer in this course, it requires no gift of prophesy to foretell his fate—he has risen like a rocket, and he will come down like a stick."

Quebec Dickens describes his visit to this "place not to be forgotten or mixed up in the mind with other places" in *American Notes* (15).

Rackham, Arthur (1867–1939) English watercolorist and illustrator, known in particular for his mystical and fantastic illustrations to children's books. He illustrated *Carol* (1915).

Rae, Dr. John (1813–1893) Surgeon and arctic explorer. Rae was a member of the expeditions in 1848–49 and 1851 to search for Sir John Frank-

Scrooge meets "Old Scratch" in Rackham's fanciful illustration for Stave 4 of *A Christmas Carol* (1915).

lin and his crews. Rae's report to the Admiralty in 1854 concluded, from information obtained from some Eskimo, that the surviving members of

Franklin's crew had resorted to cannibalism before dying of starvation. Dickens challenged Rae's conclusions in "The Lost Arctic Voyagers." Rae's reply to Dickens's article appeared in two installments in HOUSEHOLD WORDS: "The Lost Arctic Voyagers" (December 2, 1854) and "Dr. Rae's Report" (December 30, 1854). Rae's report to the Hudson Bay Company of his 1853–54 expedition to learn of Franklin's fate also appeared in HOUSEHOLD WORDS (February 3, 1855).

ragged schools   Free schools for inner-city children created by a movement that was begun early in the century but became particularly active in the 1840s with the establishment of the Ragged School Union in 1844. Dickens and ANGELA BURDETT-COUTTS were active supporters of the schools; Dickens wrote a letter praising their work in the DAILY NEWS in February 1846, and he devoted many articles to their work in the early years of HOUSEHOLD WORDS. His article "A Sleep to Startle Us" (March 13, 1852) describes a visit to the ragged school at FIELD LANE. Although he disagreed with the Evangelical zeal of many in the movement (see EVANGELICALISM), he thought these schools, by offering education rather than punishment, were taking a reasonable approach to the problems of juvenile crime and delinquency. His disagreements with the Evangelicals, however, dampened his interest, and in later years he was no longer convinced that the schools could change things. His satirical account of such a school in Mutual Friend (II:1) indicates his disillusionment with their work. Norris Pope (Dickens and Charity, 1978) surveys Dickens's involvement with these schools.

railways   For the Victorians, the railway was the emblem of change and progress, the visible manifestation of the age of steam. It arrived suddenly and seemed to displace the old England of coaches and coaching inns almost overnight. This transformation occurred in the middle of Dickens's writing career and can be traced as trains replace coaches in the novels. Pickwick's world is defined by the coach, but when Tony Weller reappears a few years later in Master Humphrey's Clock, he inveighs against "the rail [as] unconstitootonal and

an inwaser o' priwileges . . . a nasty, wheezin', creakin', gaspin', puffin', bustin' monster, always out o' breath, like a unpleasant beetle in that 'ere gas magnifier" (3). In Dombey, the railway becomes an important symbol. The building of the railway creates a turmoil that divides the city and transforms CAMDEN TOWN (6). Dombey's journey to Leamington after his son's death describes a railway journey in sensuous detail, and Carker's death by train makes the railway itself an actor in the plot of the novel (55).

The railway's importance in Dombey, as HUMPHRY HOUSE (1941) has pointed out, coincided with the railway boom of the mid-1840s. In 1840 there were 1,857 miles of railway in Britain, and by 1850 there were 6,621. After Dombey, railways routinely appear in the novels of contemporary life—Bleak House, Mutual Friend, and Drood. They have prominence in some of the shorter fiction: The two Idle Apprentices travel by train and spend some time in a railway station (Lazy Tour). Mugby Junction has a railway station as its major setting, and its final chapter, "No. 1 Branch Line: The Signal-Man," tells a railway ghost story. Although Dickens is often associated with coaches, "his understanding of the sensual and social effects of the whole railway revolution," House points out, "was deeper and wider than that of his contemporaries."

Dickens frequently described railway journeys in his journalistic essays and travel books. "Railway Dreaming" describes the reveries of a passenger on a train as he observes the passing countryside, "Fire and Snow" a winter rail journey through the BLACK COUNTRY. In "An Unsettled Neighbourhood," Dickens describes the transformation of an urban district into a railway town; "An Old Stage-Coaching House" depicts a country village deserted when the railway replaces the coaches that used to stop in the town. "A Narrative of Extraordinary Suffering" is a facetious account of Mr. Lost, befuddled in his imaginary journeys via Bradshaw's railway schedule.

One of the more traumatic experiences in Dickens's life was the STAPLEHURST RAILWAY ACCIDENT when the train on which he was returning from France with ELLEN TERNAN and her mother derailed on a trestle, killing 10 and injuring 50. He managed to get himself and his traveling companions safely out of the upset carriage, and he rescued several other passengers and aided the injured and dying. Although he is somewhat facetious in describing his experience in the afterword to *Mutual Friend,* he was very shaken by it. His son reported that afterward even a slight jolt on a railway journey would cause him to panic and grip the seat with both hands.

Ramsgate   A popular seaside resort on the north coast of KENT. Dickens visited here when vacationing at BROADSTAIRS. The Tuggses are typical of the Londoners who took the steamboat down to Ramsgate for their holiday (*Boz,* "Tuggses").

Ratcliff   THAMES-side slum notorious for crime in the East End of London. Nancy has moved from Ratcliff to FIELD LANE, an equally notorious district (*Twist,* 13). Bunsby's boat, the *Cautious Clara,* is lying in Ratcliff when Florence visits with Cuttle (*Dombey,* 23). The Ratcliff Highway is described in *Boz,* "Broker's," and by the Traveller (*Uncommercial,* 30).

Rathbone, Basil (1892–1967)   American screen actor, famous for his portrayals of Sherlock Holmes and such villains as Sir Guy of Gisbourne in *Robin Hood* (1938). His Dickensian roles included Murdstone in the MGM *David Copperfield* (1935), St. Evrémonde in the MGM *A Tale of Two Cities* (1935), and Scrooge in a 1957 television production of *Carol.*

Reade, Charles (1814–1880)   Popular and controversial novelist and dramatist and friend of Dickens, his SENSATION NOVELS followed a formula that combined a melodramatic plot with an issue of social reformation. *Hard Cash* (1863), serialized in ALL THE YEAR ROUND, exposed abuses under the insanity laws and in private mental institutions. *It Is Never Too Late to Mend* (1856), written at the same time as *Little Dorrit,* attempted to reveal the inhumanity of imprisonment. Some of Reade's work, *Cream* (1859), for example, was too sexually suggestive to be included in MUDIE'S CIRCULATING LIBRARY.

realism   In the broadest sense, realism describes simply the attempt to represent faithfully in a work of literature or art the real world, in other words, to create verisimilitude. In regard to the 19th century, the term more specifically refers to the practice of writers, mainly novelists, who appeared around the middle of the century and called themselves realists—writers like Gustave Flaubert and Guy de Maupassant in France and GEORGE ELIOT and ANTHONY TROLLOPE in England. By describing the lives of common people as representative of the wider social life, the realists attempted to convince their readers of the truth of their pictures and to create sympathy for the people they wrote about. To these ends, many chose a style and technique that effaced the author or narrator and made the details of setting and story speak for themselves.

From the beginning of his career, well before the appearance of doctrinal realism, Dickens pursued some of the goals of the realists. His concern to represent accurately life in London in the 1830s informed *Sketches by Boz* and is an important element in the novels. He also chose as subjects of his stories the common urban dwellers favored by the later realists. But in style and technique, Dickens did not subscribe to the canons of realism. His narrator is visibly present in the narrative, and the early works in particular are advertised as the unique work of "the Inimitable Boz." Dickens also stresses the peculiarities of his characters and the bizarre and surprising turns in his stories, insisting in his prefaces that truth is stranger than fiction. The tendency to heighten reality and to exaggerate the peculiar, uncanny, and bizarre are characteristics that DONALD FANGER (1965) describes as those of "romantic realists," writers like Honoré de Balzac, Nikolay Gogol, and FEODOR DOSTOEVSKI, whose historical position places them in a transitional period between ROMANTICISM and realism. Besides realistic verisimilitude, these writers sought to project a personal myth, creating their particular visions of London, Paris, or St. Petersburg, and, by heightening and intensifying the physical data from the world around them, to impose on it a Manichaean worldview, pitting good against evil, light against darkness, spirit against the material.

By the end of Dickens's career, realism was established as the dominant mode for serious fiction, and his later novels, particularly *Great Expectations,* are more realistic in style and technique; their tone of disillusionment is also characteristic of realistic fiction. John Romano (*Dickens and Reality,* 1978), by stressing these qualities in Dickens's later work, particularly in *Our Mutual Friend,* attempts to shift the balance in Dickens criticism away from its focus on the mythic and romantic to the realistic elements in his work.

Red 'Us This THAMES-side pub in Battersea was a popular cockney resort (*Boz,* "River").

Reed, John Professor, Wayne State University; poet, critic, social and historical commentator on Victorian literature. Reed writes about Victorian literature in its social contexts. *Victorian Conventions* (1975), a typological study of recurrent motifs, themes, and character types, draws heavily on Dickens's works and includes particular discussions of his treatment of the convict's return, the orphan, and disguise. *Dickens and Thackeray: Punishment and Forgiveness* (1995) traces its themes through all the major novels of both Dickens and WILLIAM MAKEPEACE THACKERAY.

Reform Bill of 1832 One of the most important legislative actions of the century, the Reform Bill—sometimes referred to as the First Reform Bill to distinguish it from later bills in 1867 and 1884—reapportioned Parliament by reducing the property qualifications for electors, eliminating many pocket boroughs, and creating new electoral districts, particularly in the industrial north of England. At the time, the bill was often viewed as the dividing line between past and present, for it was passed only after much public pressure had forced reluctant members of Parliament to respond to the will of the populace. Furthermore, it unseated the long-standing Tory majority in favor of the reform-minded Whigs, thus opening up the political process for the reforms of the 1830s and 1840s. Its passage can be described as the political beginning of the Victorian age.

Dickens was a Parliamentary reporter during the final stages of the effort to secure passage of the bill. Although his sympathies were clearly on the side of the Whig reformers, he did not find the reformed Parliament much more democratic than the old Tory House of Commons. His satires of the Boodles, Coodles, and Doodles who govern (*Bleak House*) or the Veneerings and their compatriots (*Mutual Friend*) suggest that a few powerful families still controlled the reins of power, even after reform.

Regent's Park Dickens lived near Regent's Park at 1 DEVONSHIRE TERRACE during the 1840s. He had furnished lodgings at 3 Hanover Terrace in the spring and summer of 1861.

religion Dickens's religion has been a topic of considerable controversy. Zealots in his own time accused him of blasphemy, and modern readers have sometimes found his religious views mere sentimental piety.

The novels are clear about the religious attitudes and practices that Dickens disliked. He frequently attacked Evangelical (*see* EVANGELICALISM) and Dissenting pietism: the pious hypocrisies of Stiggins (*Pickwick*), the ranting of Melchisedek Howler (*Dombey*), the oily self-righteousness of Chadband (*Bleak House*). In *Sunday under Three Heads* he attacked the negative Sabbatarianism that blighted the Clennam household (*Dorrit*) and denied innocent Sunday recreation to the poor. He also disliked formalistic religion, criticizing the Puseyites for their emphasis on ritual and Roman Catholicism for its superstitious mummery (*Pictures from Italy*). He blamed the CATHOLIC CHURCH for the deplorable poverty and oppression in the Catholic nations of southern Europe.

Rejecting both the extremes of Dissenting pietism and Catholic or high-Anglican formalism, Dickens's religious ideas were closest to those of Broad Church Anglicanism. Although he was drawn to UNITARIANISM for a few years around the time he was working on *Dombey,* he remained orthodox in his belief in Christ's divinity, redemption, and resurrection, themes of central importance in the late novels from *Two Cities* on. He described himself as a New Testament Christian, rejecting the rigid and negative doctrines of Protestant sects that stressed the Old Testament, as the Calvinistic Mrs. Clennam does. In *The Life of Our Lord,* his retelling of the Gospels for his children, he stressed the moral teachings and parables in the New Testament.

PETER ACKROYD (1990) offers a good summary of Dickens's religious views. DENNIS WALDER (1981) treats them at greater length, tracing their implications for the novels. JANET LARSON (1985) considers Dickens's uses of the BIBLE. Critics who discuss religious themes in the novels include A. E. DYSON (1970), JOSEPH GOLD (1972), and ANDREW SANDERS (1982).

Religious Hiccoughs The title Dickens gave privately to CHAUNCY HARE TOWNSHEND's *Religious Opinions* (1868), a volume Dickens edited for publication as Townshend's literary executor.

repetition Dickens frequently uses stylistic repetition as a way of heightening the effect of his prose or emphasizing particular themes. The repetitions of *fog* in the opening paragraphs of *Bleak House* or the series of antitheses at the beginning of *Two Cities* are well-known examples of stylistic repetitions that introduce important themes. The repetition of the biblical quotation "I am the resurrection and the life, saith the Lord" at the end of *Two Cities* prepares for Carton's sacrifice and underscores its significance. Some of Dickens's repetitions were prompted by the serial form in which he worked. Repeating certain character traits or patterns of speech was a way to remind his readers of the identity of a character they might not have encountered for several months. SYLVÈRE MONOD (1967) discusses Dickens's use of repetition. J. HILLIS MILLER (*Fiction and Repetition,* 1982) analyzes several novels—though none by Dickens—to show how repetition develops meaning in fiction.

resurrection men Grave robbers who, like Jerry Cruncher, dug up the bodies of the recently dead to sell to surgeons and medical students. These "honest tradesmen" were not always as honest as Cruncher makes them out to be. They sometimes obtained their specimens without the arduous task of digging, resorting in extreme cases to murder to obtain their bodies. Dickens uses Cruncher's

unusual avocation to parody the resurrection theme in the main story of *Two Cities* (II:14).

Reynolds, Frank (1876–1953) Painter; illustrator for PUNCH and other magazines. Reynolds did colored illustrations for editions of *Pickwick* (1910), *Copperfield* (1911), and *Curiosity Shop* (1913). He produced a series of paintings on Dickensian subjects in 1912–13 that were reproduced as a portfolio of prints and distributed by the Old Black Swan Distillery.

Reynolds, G. W. M. (1814–1879) Popular novelist, editor, radical journalist, and Chartist leader, best known for his *Mysteries of London,* an English imitation of Eugène Sue's *Mysteries of Paris.* His plagiaristic *Pickwick Abroad, or The Tour in France* (1839) continued Dickens's novel by taking Pickwick on a continental grand tour.

Richardson's Show The entertainment at the "heart" of Greenwich Fair that mixed "a melodrama (with three murders and a ghost), a pantomime, a comic song, an overture, and some incidental music, all done in five-and-twenty minutes" (*Boz,* "Greenwich Fair").

Richmond Town on the Surrey side of the THAMES west of London where Tupman settles down after the perigrinations of the Pickwick Club have ended (*Pickwick,* 57). Estella stays here at the home of Mrs. Brandley when she is coming out in London (*Expectations,* 33, 38).

Roche, Louis (d. 1849) French native who was Dickens's "Brave courtier" on his trips to Italy in 1844 and to Switzerland in 1846, "a most faithful, affectionate, and devoted man."

Rochester, Kent Sister town to CHATHAM where Dickens spent the happiest and most memorable years of his childhood between 1817 and 1822. GAD'S HILL PLACE, the house that Dickens purchased in 1856 and occupied from 1860 until the end of his life, is two miles outside of town on the GRAVESEND Road. Rochester is a major setting in several of the novels: The BULL Inn is the first stop on the travels of the Pickwickians (*Pickwick*, 2–4). It is the market town in *Great Expectations* where Satis House and Pumblechook's shop are located. It is Cloisterham in *Drood*. It is also the setting of "Seven Poor Travellers" and the original of Winglebury (*Boz*, "Winglebury") and Dullborough (*Uncommercial*, 12).

Rockingham Castle Castle in Northamptonshire, home of Dickens's friends the WATSONS, which he visited several times, in 1847, 1849, and 1852, and used as the original of Chesney Wold in *Bleak House.*

romanticism A movement in literature, the arts, philosophy, and politics of the late 18th and early 19th centuries that revolted against neoclassical formalism, objectivity, and established rules and conventions, celebrating instead subjectivity, imagination, and spiritual freedom. Living when he did, Dickens was profoundly influenced by romanticism and was, in many ways, a romantic himself. The romantic writers who most influenced him were not the poets but rather the prose essayists—Charles Lamb, Thomas De Quincey, and, especially, THOMAS CARLYLE.

Dickens's romanticism is probably most evident in his interest in personal growth and his belief in subjectivity and imagination. The importance of memory in David Copperfield's personal history or in Pip's inner awareness of his bad faith with himself and Joe (*Expectations*) makes these first-person narratives personal histories of the mental and emotional growth of their narrators. Like his romantic predecessors who sought the child in the man, Dickens, as Peter Coveney (*Poor Monkey, The Child in Literature*, 1957) points out, was "the central figure in the transference of the romantic child into Victorian literature." His heroes, like David Copperfield, Arthur Clennam, and Pip, are shaped in childhood, while child victims like Oliver Twist and Paul Dombey represent different versions of Wordsworth's "prison house" closing in on the growing boy.

For Dickens, as for the romantics, imagination provided the power to enable the child—or the man—to survive in the world. He attacked the schools of hard facts, the UTILITARIANISM and literalism that stunted fancy and nurtured only material self-interest. He celebrated the power of imagination to create the self and to change the world. GARRETT STEWART (1974) discusses at length the role of imagination in Dickens's work.

Dickens did not accept all of the romantic assumptions. His celebrations of nature are, for the most part, perfunctory. He was a creature of the city; his values and perceptions were urban, not pastoral. The common people whose language he adopted were city dwellers. He did not accept romantic primitivism and usually found little nobility among savages. Although he wrote ghost stories, was interested in bizarre and mysterious events, and practiced MESMERISM, Dickens was fundamentally a rationalist about such issues. He rejected most supernatural explanations as superstition. Similarly, he rejected the romantic celebration of the past, especially the MEDIEVALISM of the PRE-RAPHAELITES and others.

Donald Stone (*The Romantic Impulse in Victorian Fiction*, 1980) includes Dickens among the novelists he treats. Stewart (1974) offers the most sustained and provocative analysis of the romantic core in Dickens's works. Dirk den Hartog (*Dickens and Romantic Psychology*, 1987) discusses the influence of Wordsworth and other romantics on Dickens's ideas about the self.

Rome Dickens's account of his trip to Rome appears in *Pictures* (11). The Dorrit family's journey to Italy ends in Rome, where both Frederick and William die (*Dorrit*, II:19).

Rookery of St. Giles One of the most notorious slums in London in the 1830s and 1840s. Much of the Rookery was cleared during the construction of New OXFORD STREET in 1844–45. Dickens describes "the filth and miserable appearance of this part of London" in *Boz*, "Gin-Shops," and again in *Reprinted*, "Inspector Field." The Rookery has sometimes been suggested as the original of Tom-All-Alone's in *Bleak House.*

Royal Exchange, the ('Change) Dickens describes wandering in the CITY of London as a child: "I found myself on 'Change, and saw the shabby people sitting under placards about ships. I settled that they were misers, who had embarked all their wealth to go and buy gold dust or something of that sort, and were waiting for their respective captains to come and tell them they were ready to set sail" (*Miscellaneous*, "Gone Astray"). These shabby figures outside the Exchange reappear in several of the works: *Boz*, "Shabby-genteel People"; *Curiosity Shop* (4); and *Expectations* (22). Located at CORNHILL and Threadneedle Street, the old Exchange burned in 1838 and was rebuilt in 1842. In Dickens's time it served as a center for trading activity.

Royal Literary Fund   A charity devoted to providing aid to impoverished authors and their families. Dickens was active in the organization for many years. During the late 1850s, he, JOHN FORSTER, and Charles Dilke spearheaded a movement to reform the institution, which they claimed spent too much money on administrative expenses and played favorites in choosing beneficiaries. Their demands for changes, however, were largely unsuccessful.

Roylance, Elizabeth   The "reduced old lady" with whom Dickens had lodgings while the rest of his family was in the MARSHALSEA PRISON in 1824. She served as the model for Mrs. Pipchin in *Dombey*.

Ruskin, John (1819–1894)   Art and architectural critic; social critic. Although Ruskin and Dickens were not personally acquainted, Ruskin admired Dickens's work, and he was one of the few Victorians who praised *Hard Times*. He had reservations about Dickens's use of exaggeration and caricature in his novels, but, Ruskin concluded, "He is entirely right in his main drift and purpose in every book he has written; and all of them, but especially in *Hard Times*, should be studied with close and earnest care by all persons interested in social questions."

Russell, Lord John (1792–1878)   Whig/Liberal politician; one of the architects of the REFORM BILL OF 1832; prime minister (1846–52, 1865–66). Dickens admired Russell and was, according to Russell's daughter, "a very great friend, and was always very welcome at any time."

S

Sabbatarianism Throughout his life, Dickens opposed efforts to turn Sunday into an enforced day of inactivity. He saw such Sunday laws as doubly harsh upon the poor, whose only time for recreation and amusement was the one day of the week when they were not working. He was particularly annoyed when proposed legislation exempted servants from restrictions so that they could provide for the comforts of their masters. He attacked such laws especially in "Sunday under Three Heads" (1836) and in his descriptions of the depressing Sundays under the dark dispensation of Mrs. Clennam's dour EVANGELICALISM in *Little Dorrit* (I:3).

Sadleir, John (1814–1856) Irish member of Parliament, banker, and swindler. When his financial schemes collapsed in 1856, while Dickens was working on *Dorrit*, he killed himself and became the unwitting model for Merdle.

Sadrin, Anny (1935–2001) French scholar, translator, and editor; president of the DICKENS SOCIETY. *Parentage and Inheritance in the Novels of Charles Dickens* (1994) traces its themes in *Twist, Dombey, Bleak House, Little Dorrit, Great Expectations,* and *Mutual Friend.* A collection of essays, *Dickens, Europe, and the New World* (1999), deals broadly with Dickens in other cultures, in translation, and away from home.

Saffron Hill Street in HOLBORN, between Leather Lane and Farringdon Road, that was a notorious criminal district until 1867 when the area was altered by the construction of the Holborn Viaduct. Fagin's den of thieves is located here (*Twist*), and Phil Squod has worked here as a tinker (*Bleak House,* 26).

St. Albans Old Roman town in Hertfordshire where Dickens locates Jarndyce's Bleak House (6). Bill Sikes passes through the town when he is running from the murder of Nancy (*Twist,* 48).

St. Andrew's Church Church designed by Sir Christopher Wren in 1686, located near the HOLBORN Viaduct. On the way to the CHERTSEY robbery, Sikes notes the time on St. Andrew's clock as he and Oliver pass by (*Twist,* 21). Snagsby's partner Peffer is buried in the churchyard (*Bleak House,* 10).

St. Bartholomew's Hospital (Bartholomew's) Hospital in SMITHFIELD in the CITY where Jack Hopkins studies surgery with Doctor Slasher (*Pickwick,* 32) and Betsey Prig works as an occasional nurse (*Chuzzlewit,* 49). Arthur Clennam takes Cavalletto to Bartholomew's after he is injured in the street (*Dorrit,* I:13).

St. Dunstan's Church in FLEET STREET, also known as St. Dunstan's-in-the-West. The old church, torn down in 1831, was one of the sights of London. Its clock had a large gilt dial with two figures that struck the hours on a bell. As a child wandering in the CITY, Dickens stopped to watch "those obliging monsters strike upon the bells" (*Miscellaneous*, "Gone Astray"). Maypole Hugh also watches the figures (*Rudge*, 40), as do David and his aunt (*Copperfield*, 23). The new church, designed by John Shaw in 1831, is the church in *The Chimes* where Trotty Veck keeps his post.

St. Giles   Church at the center of a notorious slum area in London that included the ROOK-ERY and SEVEN DIALS, places that Dickens visited when touring the underworld with INSPECTOR FIELD (*Reprinted*, "Inspector Field"). Fascinated with the area and its criminal population, Dickens also describes it in *Boz* ("Seven Dials"). Sampson and Sally Brass are banished to St. Giles (*Curiosity Shop*, 73).

St. James's Park   Royal park south of PALL MALL, next to Buckingham Palace. Brooker confronts Ralph Nickleby in the park during a rainstorm (*Nickleby*, 44). Martin Chuzzlewit bids farewell to Mary Graham here as he prepares to set out for America (*Chuzzlewit*, 14). Meagles, Doyce, and Arthur Clennam discuss their troubles with the Circumlocution Office at a meeting in the park (*Dorrit*, I:10). Sally Brass is rumored to have "enlisted as a private in the second regiment of the Foot Guards and . . . been seen in uniform, and on duty, to wit, leaning on her musket and looking out of a sentry-box in St. James's Park" (*Curiosity Shop*, 73).

St. James's Square   Fashionable square off PALL MALL, near St. James's Palace. The Gordon rioters threw valuables, including the keys to NEW-GATE PRISON, into the pond in the center of the square (*Rudge*, 70). Twemlow "devoted many anxious hours . . . in the cold gloom, favorable to meditation, of St. James's Square" trying to figure out his relationship with Veneering (*Mutual Friend*, I:2).

St. James's Street   In this street in central London, off ST. JAMES'S SQUARE, the narrator of "To Be Taken with a Grain of Salt" has his lodgings (*Marigold*, 2); Josiah Bounderby stays in a hotel here (*Hard Times*, III:3); "Our Bore" meets William the Fourth while walking here (*Reprinted*).

St. James's Theatre   Theater on ST. JAMES'S SQUARE where many of the plays Dickens wrote as a young man were produced. In 1836, *The Strange Gentleman* opened the season on September 29 and *The Village Coquettes* opened on December 9. In 1837, *Is She His Wife?* opened on March 6.

St. Louis, Missouri   Dickens describes the French influence in the town and wonders about the climate: "I think it must rather dispose to fever, in the summer and autumnal seasons. . . . It is very hot, lies among great rivers, and has vast tracts of undrained swampy land around it" (*Notes*, 12).

St. Luke's Church, Chelsea   Church where Dickens married CATHERINE HOGARTH DICKENS, April 2, 1836.

St. Mark's Cathedral, Venice   In his "Italian Dream" of Venice in *Pictures*, Dickens describes the cathedral as "A grand and dreamy structure, of immense proportions; golden with old mosaics; redolent of perfumes; dim with the smoke of incense; costly in treasure of precious stones and metals, glittering through iron bars; holy with the bodies of deceased saints; rainbow-hued with windows of stained glass; dark with carved woods and coloured marbles; obscure in its vast heights, and lengthened distances; shining with silver lamps and winking lights; unreal, fantastic, solemn, inconceivable throughout" ("An Italian Dream").

St. Martin's-in-the-Fields   On the steps of this church on Trafalgar Square, the Traveller is surprised on one of his night walks by "a beetle-browed hair-lipped youth of twenty, and it had a loose bundle of rags on, which it held together with one of its hands." When the Traveller reaches out to touch him on the shoulder, "it twisted out of its garment . . . and left me standing alone with its rags in my hands" (*Uncommercial*, 13). David meets Daniel Peggotty on the steps of the church when the fisherman is searching for his runaway niece (*Copperfield*, 40). Earlier David describes a pudding shop behind the church where he purchased currant puddings when he was working at Murdstone and Grinby (*Copperfield*, 11).

St. Mary-le-Strand Church Eighteenth-century church by James Gibbs in the STRAND where JOHN DICKENS and ELIZABETH BARROW DICKENS were married in 1807. He was a clerk in nearby SOMERSET HOUSE at the time.

St. Pancras Church The clock on the new church, erected in 1819–22, informs Mrs. Tibbs of the time (*Boz*, "Boarding House"). Roger Cly is "buried" in the churchyard of the old church, where Jerry Cruncher goes on his "fishing" expedition (*Two Cities*, II:14).

St. Paul's Cathedral Main London cathedral, rebuilt by Sir Christopher Wren in 1697, after the Great Fire. This London landmark is mentioned frequently in the novels. On one of its more notable appearances, it prompts John Browdie's remark, "Ecod, he be a soizable 'un be he" (*Nickleby*, 39). Lord George Gordon stops at the church on his way into London (*Rudge*, 37). Captain Cuttle, when he prepares the bower at the top of the Wooden Midshipman for Florence, tells her, "You're as safe here as if you was at the top of St. Paul's Cathedral, with the ladder cast off" (*Dombey*, 48). David Copperfield takes Peggotty to visit the cathedral, but she finds it does not compare in all particulars with the picture of the building on the lid of her workbox (*Copperfield*, 33). The cathedral is also mentioned in *Boz*, "Shops and Their Tenants"; *Twist* (18); *Nickleby* (3, 45); *Chuzzlewit* (38); *Copperfield* (23); *Bleak House* (19); *Dorrit* (I:3, II:34); and *Mutual Friend* (I:8).

St. Peter's Cathedral, Rome Although Dickens appreciated the beauty and majesty of the cathedral, he was put off by some of the decoration: "the pillars of stately marble were swathed in some impertinent frippery of red and yellow," which had the effect of making the building look like "the opening scenes in a very lavish pantomime." He found "a much greater sense of mystery and wonder" in SAINT MARK's Cathedral at Venice (*Pictures*, "Rome").

Sala, George Augustus (1828–1896) Journalist and novelist; frequent contributor to HOUSEHOLD WORDS and ALL THE YEAR ROUND whose work in these magazines was sometimes mistaken for that of Dickens; one of the most conspicuous of "Dickens's young men" who followed and imitated the novelist. Son of an actress who played in some of Dickens's AMATEUR THEATRICALS, he pleased the novelist with his conscientiousness and earnestness. He served for many years as a special correspondent for the London *Daily Telegraph*. Dickens sent him to Russia following the Crimean War as a special correspondent for *Household Words*, but the two quarreled about the resulting articles, and their friendship was broken off between 1856 and 1858. In his writings about Dickens in his autobiography, his memoir of Dickens (1870), and *Things I Have Known* (1894), Sala credits the novelist's "friendship and encouragement" with making him a journalist and writer of books.

Sand, George Pen name of Amantine-Lucile-Aurore Dupin (1804–76); French novelist, feminist, and radical; she advocated free love and was famous in her own time for her many love affairs, most memorably with the musician Chopin. Dickens met her in 1860 in Paris and described her in a letter to W. H. WILLS as "a chubby, matronly, swarthy, black-eyed" woman "whom you might suppose to be the Queen's monthly nurse," with "nothing of the blue-stocking about her, except a little final way of settling all your opinions with hers."

Sanders, Andrew (1946–) Professor, University of Durham; scholar and editor of Victorian fiction; editor of the DICKENSIAN, 1978–86. His wide-ranging survey, *The Victorian Historical Novel 1840–1880* (1978), discusses *Rudge* and *Two Cities* along with works by other novelists, major and minor. His *Companion to "A Tale of Two Cities"* (1988) provides a useful introduction to the text and backgrounds of that novel. In *Charles Dickens Resurrectionist* (1982), Sanders considers Dickens's personal religious beliefs about death and resurrection and analyzes the deaths in the novels as they embody these beliefs. In *Dickens and the Spirit of the Age* (2001), Sanders writes of Dickens as an embodiment of the important features of his time. He takes a similar point of view in *Charles Dickens* (2003), an introduction for the general reader. Sanders has also prepared editions of *Dombey*, *David Copperfield*, *Bleak House*, and *A Tale of Two Cities*.

sanitary reform   Under this general rubric, a number of related reform issues were brought together: slum living conditions, water supplies and the handling of sewage, overcrowded living conditions, the ventilation of houses, and the diseases caused by these environmental conditions, especially cholera, typhus, and smallpox. The leading reformer on these issues was Edwin Chadwick, whose *Report on the Sanitary Condition of the Labouring Population* (1842) prompted debate and legislative action, especially the Public Health Act of 1848. But this bill was seriously flawed, for it excluded London from its provisions and hence sparked even more intense activity on the part of the reformers. In an 1850 speech to the Metropolitan Sanitary Association, an organization devoted to extending the provisions of the law to include London, Dickens said that the act was even worse than the tragedy of *Hamlet* with Hamlet left out: "the existence of a Public Health Act with the metropolis excluded from its operation suggested . . . the representation of *Hamlet* with nothing in it but the gravedigger."

HOUSEHOLD WORDS, begun during the years of intense debate to have London included in the act, crusaded on issues of sanitary reform, running numerous articles on various aspects of the topic. In an 1849 preface to *Chuzzlewit*, Dickens wrote, "In all my writings I hope I have taken every possible opportunity of showing the want of sanitary improvements in the neglected dwellings of the poor." From Boz's descriptions of slum conditions to the hovels in the Limehouse of *Mutual Friend*, Dickens exposed the unhealthy sanitary conditions and disease in poor neighborhoods. His most focused attack appears in *Bleak House* in his description of Tom-All-Alone's and the disease carried by Jo from the inner city out to the suburbs.

satire   Although there is a good deal of incidental satire in Dickens's novels and journalistic essays, he is not usually thought of as a satirist. His satire criticizes its targets not as irrational, a common satiric point of view, but rather as inhumane. He attacks rationalists, like the "philosophers" who know all about the poor but have no sympathy for their condition. Dickens's alternative to the rationalism of the UTILITARIANS was a deep-felt concern for one's fellow man.

Sustained satires in the novels include the attacks on POLITICAL ECONOMISTS, the "philosophers" of the POOR LAW in *Twist*, and the hard facts school in *Hard Times;* the satire of American greed and selfishness (*Chuzzlewit*), a journey that reads like the fifth voyage of Gulliver; and the attacks on the COURT OF CHANCERY (*Bleak House*), government red tape, and aristocratic privilege in the Circumlocution Office (*Dorrit*); and the pretentious Podsnappery and PHILISTINISM of the nouveaux riches (*Mutual Friend*). He satirized many of the same social ills in articles for *HOUSEHOLD WORDS* and *ALL THE YEAR ROUND*, especially the failure of government to address the needs of the poor. J. B. PRIESTLEY characterized the satiric Dickens in a speech to the DICKENS FELLOWSHIP in 1970: "Dickens is, in a way, the boy who saw the Emperor was not wearing any new clothes and that is why you find Dickens's enemies are the pillars of the Establishment, particularly the legal pillars, and senior academics, and all those who have been surrounding themselves for years by a cocoon of humbug and cant and pretense. Dickens went clean through that to the heart of the matter." The standard work on the subject is *Dickens as Satirist*, by SYLVIA MANNING (1971).

Saturday Review, The   Conservative weekly review of "Politics, Literature, Science and Art," established by A. J. Beresford-Hope in 1855. Its anonymous reviews of fiction were often harsh, especially Fitzjames Stephen's reviews of Dickens. He attacked Dickens as a purveyor of "light literature" and was particularly offended by Dickens's satire of the Circumlocution Office. Reviewing *Dorrit*, Stephen wrote, "The production among such readers [who will think little, and cultivate themselves still less] of false impressions of the system of which they form a part—especially if the falsehood tends to render them discontented with and disaffected to the institutions under which they live—cannot but be a serious evil, and must often involve great moral deliquency."

Schlicke, Paul   Contemporary professor, University of Aberdeen, specializing in the role of popular entertainment in Dickens's works. In *Dickens and Popular Entertainment* (1985), he surveys the role of popular theater, street performers, circuses, and other entertainments in Dickens's novels and journalism. He analyzes the role of such performances in three novels: *Nickleby*, *Curiosity Shop*, and *Hard Times*. He has also prepared an annotated bibliography for *Curiosity Shop* (with Priscilla Schlicke, 1988), an edition of *Hard Times* (1989), and the comprehensive *Oxford Reader's Companion to Dickens* (1999).

Schor, Hilary   Professor, University of Southern California; feminist critic, especially interested in women's narratives. She has written on the law in Victorian England, on Elizabeth Gaskell, and on other Victorian topics, as well as on Dickens. In *Dickens and the Daughter of the House* (1999), Schor revisits Dickens's women, studying the daughters in the novels and the stories they tell. She finds richer and more complex views of women and their situations than Dickens is often credited with.

Schwarzbach, F. S. (1949–)   Professor, Washington University, St. Louis. Schwarzbach specializes in the Victorian city and in Dickens as a novelist responding to the urbanization of life in the 19th century. In *Dickens and the City* (1979), he finds an underlying mythic structure in the novels that describes a fall, mirroring Dickens's own experience, from a rural paradise into the urban hell of London. Schwarzbach has also edited, with Ira Bruce Nadel, a collection of essays, *Victorian Artists and the City* (1980).

Scott, Sir Walter (1771–1832)   Historical novelist, poet; known as "the author of *Waverley*" (1814) and of the many Waverley novels that followed it; definitive novelist of the generation immediately preceding Dickens. He influenced Dickens and nearly every other Victorian novelist to write historical novels and to include a broad social panorama in their works. His efforts to embody historical forces in the lives of individuals and to connect public issues with the private lives of his characters inform the Victorian novel and shape even those novels without historical subjects.

Scott was also important to Dickens as a model of the professional writer who had been victimized during his career by unscrupulous publishers and by the lack of adequate copyright protection. In his speeches on COPYRIGHT in America, Dickens used Scott's writing himself to death as an example of the cruel results from the lack of a copyright law. Had there been such a law, Dickens told his listeners, "Scott might not have sunk beneath the mighty pressures on his brain, but might have lived to add new creatures of his fancy to the crowd which swarm about you in your summer walks and gather round your winter evening hearths."

Searle, Ronald (1920–)   Illustrator for PUNCH and other magazines; book illustrator; famous for his St. Trinian's cartoons of fiendish schoolgirls. He illustrated *Carol* (1961), *Expectations* (1962), and *Twist* (1962). He also did cartoons for the 1970 film *Scrooge*.

Senior, Nassau (1790–1864)   Professor of POLITICAL ECONOMY at Oxford, frequent contributor to the *Edinburgh Review* and QUARTERLY REVIEW. In his review of RICHARD HENGIST HORNE's *New Spirit of the Age* in the *Westminster Review* (1844), he commented on the economics of *Carol*: "The process whereby poor men are to be enabled to earn good wages, wherewith to buy turkeys for themselves, does not enter into the account; indeed it would quite spoil the dénouement and all the generosity. Who went without turkey and punch in order that Bob Cratchit might get them—for, unless there were turkey and punch in surplus, some one must go without—is a disagreeable reflection kept wholly out of sight." The satire in *The Chimes* involving Trotty's bowl of tripe is a response to this criticism.

sensation novel   Subgenre of the English novel in the 1860s; its main practitioners were WILKIE COLLINS, CHARLES READE, and Mrs. Henry Wood. Sensation novels, modeled in many ways on the novels of Dickens, dealt with topical issues or scandals, used the conventions of melodrama to provide a sequence of sensational incidents, and employed the serial form to enhance the mysteries and suspense in their plots. Dickens's attacks on the POOR LAW (*Twist*) and the COURT OF CHANCERY (*Bleak House*) suggested ways to address topical issues in fiction that Reade in particular would exploit in such novels as *Hard Cash* (1863), which dealt with abuses in the treatment of the insane. Collins's mystery "novels with a secret," in turn, influenced Dickens, suggesting the unknown benefactor in *Expectations* or the Harmon mystery in *Mutual Friend*. The concentration of sensational incidents in such fiction appears in Dickens in such sequences as the revelation of Magwitch's identity, the burning of Miss Havisham, and Orlick's capture of Pip in *Expectations*. Although Dickens cannot be strictly described as one of the sensation novelists, his close association with Collins and Reade and the publication of their work in ALL THE YEAR ROUND clearly influenced him.

sentimentality   From a modernist point of view, sentimentality has been defined as emotion in excess of the facts. The works of Dickens and other Victorians have often been judged by this modernist standard, and their portrayal of children, death, and especially of dying children has been dismissed as grossly sentimental. Certainly Dickens and his contemporaries—and indeed 20th-century writers on occasion—were not without moments of false or overindulgent emotion, but the modern assessment of sentimentality often fails to take into account the 19th-century context in which Dickens was writing. The facts of infant mortality, child labor, limited educational opportunity, and poverty were more extreme than we often imagine. The suffering of children was a fact, not just the imaginings of exaggerated feeling.

Philosophical assumptions of the time also shaped Victorian sentimentality. Inheriting the romantic belief in the imagination, the Victorians idealized the power to imagine themselves in another's place. Shared feeling and a sympathetic understanding were considered defining human traits that led to emotional responses different from those conditioned by a cynical and rational modernism. Such "sentimentalism" was sought by the Victorians as a way of preserving traditional values in the face of a corrosive empiricism and rationalism. The imagination stifled by the hard facts school, Dickens believed, included the power to sympathize with others and envision the way things might otherwise be. FRED KAPLAN (1987) traces the backgrounds and historical context of Victorian sentimentalism.

serial publication   Although occasional novels had been published in serial form before the Vic-

torian age, Dickens's *Pickwick Papers* was responsible for setting the fashion for later novels and for defining the standard form of the Victorian serial. Although *Pickwick* began as 24 pages of letterpress and four illustrations for each monthly part, Dickens revised the format after ROBERT SEYMOUR's death to 32 pages of text accompanied by two illustrations. This revised plan allowed for more sustained development of the narrative, something essential in transforming the anecdotal sketch into a continuing novel. *Pickwick* was completed in 20 parts over 19 months, the last part constituting a double number. Dickens followed this format in all of his monthly serials except *Twist* (which ran in BENTLEY'S MISCELLANY and had 24 somewhat irregular installments) and *Drood*, which was planned for 12 parts.

The weekly serials, all of which ran in Dickens's magazines, had much shorter installments, typically only one or two short chapters, and were sometimes unillustrated, as was the case with *Hard Times* and *Expectations*. This tighter format had the effect of concentrating the narrative on fewer plotlines and condensing the style.

Although suspense and cliff-hanging endings are assumed to be the major narrative characteristics of the serial, Dickens made rather sparing use of such devices. He saw the serial, instead, as an opportunity for sustained familiarity with a large number of characters, for developing parallel narratives with complex interconnections, and for shaping the narrative to the changing expectations of his audience. He did not write the novel and then cut it up into parts. Rather, he thought of the novel in terms of its monthly numbers and, from *Dombey* on, kept NUMBER PLANS in which he plotted out each part and made memoranda of what he wanted to include. WILLIAM AXTON (1967) has also shown that he thought of the structure of the whole novel in terms of part divisions, making the fifth, 10th, and 15th numbers climactic turning points in the development of the story.

Michael Lund, in numerous articles and in *The Victorian Serial* (1991, with Linda K. Hughes), has done the most work on Victorian serial publication. Several Dickens scholars have studied the serial parts and analyzed the ways in which the serial form affected Dickens's methods of composition and novelistic form. See especially JOHN BUTT and KATHLEEN TILLOTSON (1957), ARCHIBALD

COOLIDGE (1967), SYLVÈRE MONOD (1968), and ROBERT PATTEN (1978).

setting The physical and temporal context in which the action of a narrative takes place. Physically, the setting includes particular houses or rooms, like Bleak House or Miss Havisham's dining room with its decaying wedding feast. More broadly, it includes cities or countries: the France of *Two Cities* or the Coketown of *Hard Times*. Dickens's great setting is, of course, London, which he transformed in his imagination. He often adapted actual London streets and districts to fit the thematic requirements of his stories. Ralph Nickleby, a usurer, for example, lives on GOLDEN SQUARE and Jaggers's office (*Expectations*) is located on Little Britain, an actual street in the CITY that Dickens uses to suggest Jaggers's world as a microcosm of the nation. There are numerous books and atlases devoted to Dickensian TOPOGRAPHY, identifying the places that Dickens used in his novels, both those he used literally and those he adopted as models for fictional settings.

Temporally, the setting includes the time period in which the action occurs, its distance from or closeness to the time of narration, and the season of the year or time of day. The first chapter of *Mutual Friend,* for example, begins by establishing that the time is the present, autumn, and twilight, a setting symbolically relevant to an analysis of a civilization in "decline and fall." HUMPHRY HOUSE (1941) has shown that Dickens typically wrote about a vague period 10 or 15 years before the time of composition, though he was often inconsistent in particular historical details.

Seven Dials In Dickens's day, a notorious slum district surrounding ST. GILES Circus where seven streets came together. Boz describes the area in "Seven Dials" as "streets of dirty, straggling houses, with now and then an unexpected court composed

Gustave Doré's picture of a street in Seven Dials.

of buildings as ill-proportioned and deformed as the half-naked children that wallow in the kennels." The area is also described in *Boz*, "Monmouth Street." Mr. Mantalini descends to operating a mangle in this district (*Nickleby*, 64).

Seymour, Robert (1798–1836)   Artist and illustrator, famous for his prints of amateur sportsmen ineptly engaged in hunting and fishing. His proposal to do a series of such prints involving a club of inept sportsmen was the generating idea that eventually became *Pickwick*. Seymour interested CHAPMAN & HALL in the proposal, and they sought a writer to provide copy for the illustrations. After being turned down by William Clarke, they approached Dickens, who agreed to the proposal but broadened the subject matter from its sporting emphasis. In effect, Dickens insisted on having at least an equal role with the artist in determining the direction of the work. By the second number, he had, in "The Stroller's Tale" of the dying clown, introduced subject matter far afield from Seymour's original conception, a change that was especially troubling to Seymour, who suffered from periodic bouts of depression. Dickens insisted that Seymour redraw the first version of the plate illustrating the tale. After he completed the illustrations for the second number, Seymour shot himself. His lack of self-confidence and history of mental illness clearly were the primary causes of his suicide, but the stresses in working with Dickens probably contributed to it as well.

Many years later, Mrs. Seymour and her son contended that Seymour had originated *Pickwick* and that Dickens did not give the artist proper credit or reward. Dickens challenged their claims, which were largely discredited, in the preface to the CHARLES DICKENS EDITION of his works, 1867. An example of Seymour's work appears on page 329.

Shadwell   Just a month before he died, Dickens took his American publisher, J. T. FIELDS, to visit an opium den in this dockside area of east London, which Fields described as follows: "In a miserable court, at night, we found a haggard old woman blowing at a kind of pipe made of an old ink bottle; and the words that Dickens puts into the mouth of this wretched creature in *Edwin*

Drood we heard her croon as we leaned over the tattered bed in which she was lying." In the novel, this old woman becomes the Princess Puffer, who croons a description of her business as she coaxes her clients to take another pipe of the opium she has prepared: "I makes my pipes of old penny ink-bottles, ye see, deary . . . and I fits in a mouth-piece, this way, and I takes my mixter out of this thimble with this little horn spoon; and so I fills, deary" (*Drood*, 1).

Shaftesbury, Lord (Anthony Ashley Cooper) (1801–1885)   Member of Parliament; prominent Evangelical (*see* EVANGELICALISM); leader in issues of social reform, particularly in industrial and sanitary legislation; president of the RAGGED SCHOOL Union. Though Dickens did not share Lord Shaftesbury's narrow religious convictions (see, for example, his disagreement about Sunday closing in "The Sunday Screw"), he supported nearly all of Shaftesbury's reforms. The two men were friends and occasionally dined together. Shaftesbury was said to be without a sense of humor, and there is no indication that he read Dickens's novels, but he did read JOHN FORSTER's *Life of Dickens*, remarking in his journal, "The man was a phenomenon, an exception, a special production. Nothing like him ever preceded. Nature isn't such a tautologist as to make another to follow him."

Shakespeare, William (1564–1616)   Dickens knew Shakespeare's plays well, both from reading them and from seeing them performed in the London theaters. Some of Dickens's earliest articles were reviews for the EXAMINER of productions of Shakespeare. Nicholas Bentley, MICHAEL SLATER, and Nina Burgis list nearly two full pages of allusions to Shakespeare in *The Dickens Index* (1988); the most frequently mentioned plays are *Hamlet*, *Julius Caesar*, *Macbeth*, and *Othello*. Dickens is frequently compared to Shakespeare, particularly as a creator of character. The eminent Shakespearean Alfred B. Harbage explored the connections between the two writers in *A Kind of Power: The Shakespeare-Dickens Analogy* (1975). Valerie Gager (*Dickens and Shakespeare: The Dynamics of Influence*, 1996) discusses the influence of Shakespeare on Dickens.

Shanklin   The seaside resort on the Isle of Wight visited by Dickens in 1849. The Lammles spend their disillusioning honeymoon here (*Mutual Friend*, I:10).

Shaw, George Bernard (1856–1950)   Irish dramatist, critic, novelist, and social commentator; a great admirer of Dickens and, like him, a prolific comic writer who devoted his works to correcting social ills. At a time when most Dickensians celebrated the comic Dickens of the early novels, Shaw praised the late Dickens of the dark social novels. He published introductions for *Hard Times* (1913) and *Great Expectations* (1937) and frequently derived characters and situations in his plays from Dickens. In *Shaw on Dickens* (1985), Dan H. Laurence and Martin Quinn collect Shaw's writings on Dickens and discuss Shaw's indebtedness to the novelist.

Shaw, William   One-eyed schoolmaster at BOWES Academy, YORKSHIRE, who served as the model for Squeers in *Nickleby*. Pretending to represent a prospective client, Dickens interviewed Shaw, who was already notorious and who had been accused of abusing and maiming some of his charges.

Shepherd's Bush   URANIA COTTAGE, the refuge for fallen women sponsored by ANGELA BURDETT-COUTTS and directed by Dickens, was located on Acton Road in this section of west London.

Sheridan, Richard Brinsley (1751–1816)   Sentimental comic dramatist, best known for *School for Scandal* (1777). Dickens knew and admired Sheridan's plays, alluding to them on several occasions, most notably perhaps in "Finches of the Grove" (*Expectations*, 34), taken from *The Critic*.

Sherman, Captain   Commander of the steamboat *Burlington* on Lake Champlain, the boat Dickens described as "superior . . . to any other in the world." Dickens attributed its "graceful comfort and beautiful contrivance" solely to its captain (*Notes*, 15).

Shooter's Hill   Hill on the DOVER ROAD near BLACKHEATH. Tony Weller retires to "an excel-

lent public house near Shooter's Hill, where he is quite reverenced as an oracle" (*Pickwick*, 57). Jerry Cruncher catches up with the Dover Mail as it is laboring up the hill (*Two Cities*, I:2). The Elmses, where Master Harry Walmers's father lived, is nearby ("Holly Tree").

short story, the   Although he was writing at the time when EDGAR ALLAN POE was defining the concentration and unity of effect that characterizes the modern short story, Dickens seems to take little interest in these technical issues. Some of his ghost stories in *Pickwick* may have influenced Poe, but Dickens held to a looser and more traditional notion of the short story than his American counterpart did. DEBORAH THOMAS (1982) suggests that the feature distinguishing Dickens's idea of the short story was the "concept of oral narration." He connected such stories with those told aloud in the family circle or around the Christmas hearth.

His stories often fit into traditional forms like the GHOST STORY or the autobiographical narrative. In general terms, the stories are differentiated from SKETCHES by the presence of characters and plot, but many of Dickens's shorter pieces fall into a gray area in which sketches and familiar essays use some of the techniques of story, and stories take on the didactic or illustrative qualities of the essay.

Several of Dickens's shorter works are remarkable examples of the oral and traditional storytelling form. Sam Weller's anecdotes, such as the story of "The Man as Killed His-self on Principle" (*Pickwick*, 44), are delightful examples of tall tales and legends. "Mrs. Lirriper's Lodgings," "Mrs. Lirriper's Legacy," and "Doctor Marigold" are humorous personal narratives revealing the characters of their first-person cockney narrators. "George Silverman's Explanation" and Miss Wade's "History of a Self-Tormentor" are confessional narratives, exposing the neuroses of their narrators through the personal histories they relate. "The Schoolboy's Story," one of ALFRED, LORD TENNYSON's favorites, is an evocative character sketch of a teacher by a former student that reveals the kindness of the teacher, Old Cheeseman, and the growth in the narrator. Among Dickens's many ghost stories are two of his most successful shorter works, "No. 1 Branch

Line: The Signalman" and the perfect *A Christmas Carol*, one of the most memorable short stories in any language.

Most of Dickens's stories are collected in *Boz, Christmas Books, Christmas Stories,* and *Reprinted Pieces.* The standard critical work on the short stories is by DEBORAH THOMAS (1982). She has also edited a collection of the stories (1976).

sketch, the   A traditional literary form, analogous to the visual art form from which it takes its name; the sketch is usually a short piece describing a character or a place or evoking a mood. In traditional character sketches, the characters are types, representative rather than individualized figures. By combining the type with the individual, Dickens modified the convention and brought tension into his characters. The portrayal of Scrooge, for example, complicates the traditional miser by giving him a zestful, self-seeking vitality, a paradoxical conception that enables Dickens to turn the character sketch into a conversion story.

In *Boz,* Dickens distinguished sketches from stories, the sketches lacking the plot and character development of the SHORT STORIES. The most immediate models for Dickens's sketches were those of WASHINGTON IRVING, whose *Sketch Book* influenced Dickens's early work in particular.

Slater, Michael (1936–) Contemporary scholar and critic; professor, Birkbeck College, University of London; editor of the DICKENSIAN, 1968–77; chairman of the trustees of the Dickens House Museum; president of the DICKENS FELLOWSHIP. Slater is the author of *Dickens on America and the Americans* (1978), an illustrated account of Dickens's travels in America; *Dickens and Women* (1983), a biographical and critical account of the women in Dickens's life and the women characters in his novels; *The Dickens Index* (with Nicholas Bentley and Nina Burgis, 1988), a reference guide to Dickens, especially useful for its explanations of references, allusions, quotations, and topicalities in the novels; and *Intelligent Person's Guide to Dickens* (2000), an introduction to Dickens for the general reader. He has also edited the four-volume collection *Dickens' Journalism* (1994–2000), an edition that contextual-

izes and annotates the articles. Slater has also edited and provided substantial introductions to editions of *The Christmas Books, Nicholas Nickleby, Martin Chuzzlewit, Hard Times,* and *Our Mutual Friend.* He also edited *Dickens 1970* (1970), a centenary collection of essays by major British scholars, and compiled and edited *The Catalogue of the Suzannet Charles Dickens Collection* (1975).

slavery   Dickens altered the chronological organization of *American Notes* to devote a chapter to the issue of slavery, which he saw as the issue above all others defining American society. In doing so, as JEROME MECKIER (1990) points out, he challenged other British travel writers, particularly HARRIET MARTINEAU, who explained slavery as an anomaly in an otherwise progressive nation. Dickens stressed the ways in which slavery brutalized all Americans and determined the character of the nation, and he then provided a catalog of particular instances of cruelty and inhumanity.

In *Chuzzlewit* Dickens illustrates the brutality of the system through a former slave who was "shot in the leg; gashed in the arm; scored in his live limbs, like a crimped fish; beaten out of shape; had his neck gulled with an iron collar, and wore iron rings upon his wrists and ankles" (17). The contradiction of slavery in a free society is represented by the Norris family, abolitionists who assert the necessity of separating the races (17), and by the Watertoast Association, which dissolves when its members learn that an Irish politician they have supported is an advocate of emancipation (21).

An article written with HENRY MORLEY for HOUSEHOLD WORDS in 1852, "North American Slavery," while just as opposed to slavery, takes a somewhat more positive view of the chances for abolition and the opportunities for America "to do what is right."

Smith, Albert (1816–1860)   Novelist, playwright, comic writer, editor; brother of ARTHUR SMITH. Smith's novels, especially such comic PICARESQUE serials as *The Adventures of the Scattergood Family* (1845) and *The Struggles and Adventures of Christopher Tadpole* (1847), were strongly influenced by Dickens's early works. Married to a daughter of

ROBERT and MARY KEELEY, Smith shared Dickens's love of the theater. He dramatized *Cricket* and *Battle of Life* with Dickens's approval. In the 1850s, he gave public performances of his work, perhaps suggesting the idea to Dickens.

Smith, Arthur (d. 1861) Business manager for Dickens's public readings from 1858 to 1861; brother of ALBERT SMITH. Dickens described him as "the best man of business I know." When he died in 1861, Dickens felt his loss deeply.

Smith, Grahame (1933–) Professor, Stirling University; critic, historical scholar, editor of Dickens. In *Dickens, Money, and Society* (1968), Smith traces the connection between Dickens's psychological concerns and his social analysis that concluded that money had become the glue holding together a society no longer bound by other ties. A biography, *Charles Dickens: A Literary Life* (1996), concentrates on Dickens's professional life as a writer. *Dickens and the Dream of Cinema* (2003) explores the visual elements in Dickens's style and his links to the cinema.

Smith, O. (Richard John Smith) (1768–1855) One of the leading actors at the ADELPHI THEATRE. Famous for his portrayals of villains, he took the stage name "O" after playing a character named Obi in 1829. Smith performed in many of the Adelphi's adaptations of Dickens's works, playing Sikes, Newman Noggs, Hugh the Maypole hostler, Toby Veck, and John Peerybingle. He was best known for his portrayal of Scrooge in EDWARD STIRLING's adaptation.

Smith, Sydney (1771–1845) Liberal clergyman; canon of ST. PAUL'S; famous wit; one of the founders of the *Edinburgh Review;* friend of Dickens. His *Lectures on Moral Philosophy* was one of Dickens's favorite books. The two men met in the 1830s, probably at the COUNTESS OF BLESSINGTON's salon. Although Smith was "deterred by the Vulgarity" of the pen name "Boz," he thought the *Sketches* "written with great power. . . . The soul of Hogarth has migrated into the body of Mr. Dickens." He especially praised *Nickleby* and *Chuzzlewit.* Dickens named his seventh child after Smith.

Smith, Dr. Thomas Southwood (1788–1861) Unitarian minister, medical doctor, Poor Law Commissioner; energetic advocate of factory and SANITARY REFORM; one of the founders of the *Westminster Review,* the Society for the Diffusion of Useful Knowledge, and the Health of Towns Association. He sent Dickens the *Report of the Children's Employment Commission* in 1843 that sparked Dickens's indignation and led to *A Christmas Carol.* Smith was especially influential on Dickens's views regarding sanitary reform.

Smithfield London's wholesale meat market in the CITY. Oliver passes by the confusion of the market, "a stunning and bewildering scene," on his way to the CHERTSEY robbery (*Twist,* 21). Pip, on his first day in London, observes the "shameful place, being all asmear with filth and fat and blood and foam" (*Expectations,* 20). Dickens called for removing the market from the center of London in "A Monument of French Folly" (*Reprinted*). The market is also mentioned in *Nickleby* (4), *Rudge* (18), and *Dorrit* (I:13).

Smollett, Tobias George (1721–1771) Novelist, editor, and translator of CERVANTES and ALAIN RENÉ LESAGE. Like David Copperfield, Dickens read Smollett's novels as a child. The influence of *Roderick Random* (1748) and *Peregrine Pickle* (1751) is especially evident in the loose PICARESQUE structure, physical comedy, alliterative titles, and young heroes of Dickens's early novels. Smollett's *Sir Launcelot Greaves* (1760–62), the first serialized novel in English, may have suggested that mode of publication to Dickens.

Snow Hill Steep and busy street leading from HOLBORN down to Farringdon Street. The Saracen's Head, where Squeers stays in London, was located on the hill (*Nickleby,* 4). Also mentioned in *Boz,* "Christening"; *Rudge* (67); *Twist* (26); and *Dorrit* (I:13).

social problem novel A subgenre of British fiction that emerged in the 1830s, also known as the "condition of England novel," "fiction with a purpose," and the industrial novel. Influenced by

Old Smithfield Market, London. Dickens mentions the market in many of his works, including *Oliver Twist, Great Expectations,* and *Nicholas Nickleby.* Dickens called for removing the market from the center of London in his essay "A Monument of French Folly."

the propaganda novels of William Godwin and the social philosophy of THOMAS CARLYLE, novelists like Frances Trollope (*Michael Armstrong, the Factory Boy,* 1839), BENJAMIN DISRAELI (*Coningsby, Sybil, Tancred,* 1844–47), and ELIZABETH GASKELL (*Mary Barton,* 1848) addressed the social issues of the day, particularly those brought about by the INDUSTRIAL REVOLUTION. Many of Dickens's novels were influenced by this thesis fiction. *Oliver Twist* and, especially, *Hard Times,* in which the condition of England and particular issues of social reform are central to the purpose, are examples of the genre.

sociological novel   A type of novel that defines its characters in terms of social class and broad social categories and assumes that society influences or determines the ways in which human

beings act. Dickens's treatment of such social issues as the POOR LAW, EDUCATION, and industrialization; his close observation of the social world; and his many characters described in networks of social relationships to one another have led commentators to characterize him as a sociological novelist. Philosophically, however, he was more an idealist than a realist (*see* REALISM), and he was inconsistent on the ways social forces shaped individuals and controlled behavior. His external rendering of his characters is often better described as a dramatic than a sociological technique.

Soho   Area surrounding Soho Square in the West End of London. Esther Summerson meets Caddy Jellyby in the square (*Bleak House,* 23). Doctor Manette's London house is near the square (*Two*

Cities, II:6), as is the house of Jules Obenreizer ("No Thoroughfare").

Soloman Bell the Raree Showman   Title for a children's book that Dickens agreed to write for Christmas 1836 but that he was forced to abandon because of the pressures of other commitments.

Somerset House   In Dickens's time this building in the STRAND housed government offices, including those of the POOR LAW commissioners. Dickens's father and his uncle, Thomas BARROW, were clerks in the building, as is Minns (*Boz,* "Minns").

Somers Town   Area in northwest London, north of Euston Station. The Dickens family lived in the Polygon in Somers Town in the 1820s when many foreigners, Spanish refugees, and artists lived in the area. Boz describes it as the dwelling place of CITY clerks ("Streets—Morning"). Snawley's house, where Smike is held after Squeers captures him, is located here (*Nickleby,* 38). Skimpole occupies a dilapidated dwelling in the Polygon (*Bleak House,* 43).

Southwark   Area south of the Thames in London, usually referred to as the BOROUGH. **Southwark Bridge,** also called the Iron Bridge, is Little Dorrit's place of refuge.

"Sparks, Timothy"   Pseudonym under which Dickens published *Sunday under Three Heads.*

speeches   Dickens was an outstanding public speaker, described by EDMUND YATES as "by far the best after-dinner speaker I have ever heard." His many speeches, particularly at the dinners of civic and philanthropic societies, have been collected and edited in an outstanding scholarly edition by KENNETH J. FIELDING (*Dickens,* 1988).

Spilka, Mark (1925–)   Professor, Brown University; Freudian critic who has written extensively on Lawrence, Hemingway, and literary theory as well as on Dickens. In *Dickens and Kafka, A Mutual Interpretation* (1963), Spilka is not interested so much in Dickens's influence on Kafka as he is in the ways in which the similarities and differences

between them illuminate the two writers. His comparison with Kafka did a great deal to open up the dark side of Dickens's work.

sporting novels   Popular genre of comic writing in the 1830s. Its chief practitioners were Pierce Egan (1772–1849), whose *Life in London* (1821–28) recounted the adventures of Tom and Jerry, cockney devotees of the turf, and R. S. SURTEES (1805–64), who in 1831 created Jorrocks, a cockney grocer, squire, and follower of the hunt. These works were important predecessors to *Pickwick.* Originally planned as a series of sketches of sporting misadventures, *Pickwick* was to be another in this popular genre of comic writing. Protesting that he was not a sportsman, Dickens broadened the proposed subject matter for the novel, but the original idea is implicit in some of the early scenes and in the character of Winkle.

Stanfield, Clarkson (1793–1867)   Marine and landscape painter, described by Dickens as "the Natural Historian of [England's] speciality, the Sea." He met Dickens in 1838, toured Cornwall with him in 1842, provided some illustrations for *Battle of Life* and *Haunted Man,* and painted scenery for several of Dickens's amateur theatrical productions. Although he agreed to illustrate *Pictures from Italy,* he withdrew from the project when he was offended by the anti-Catholic bias in the work. Dickens's obituary tribute to "Stanny" appeared in ALL THE YEAR ROUND (June 1, 1867) and in *Miscellaneous.*

Stanley, Edward, Lord, Earl of Derby (1799–1869)   Whig politician; chief Secretary for Ireland, 1830–33; Secretary for War and the Colonies, 1833–34, 1841–45. When Dickens was a parliamentary reporter, Stanley was especially impressed by the accuracy of Dickens's transcription of one of his speeches, and he asked Dickens to retranscribe a speech that other journalists had misreported. Dickens first met THOMAS CARLYLE at Stanley's house in 1840.

Staplehurst railway accident   On June 9, 1865, while returning from FRANCE with ELLEN TERNAN and her mother, Dickens was involved in a railway accident on the tidal train from FOLKESTONE to London. The train was traveling near Staplehurst in KENT when it derailed at a gap in the tracks on a bridge where some repair work was going on. The workmen had misread the schedule and did not expect the train for another two hours. Several cars went off the bridge; the car in which Dickens was traveling was left hanging off the bridge, still coupled to the car behind it. Shaken but unhurt, Dickens escaped through a window and managed to get his traveling companions out of the wreck. Then, for the next few hours, he ministered to the injured and dying. Ten people were killed in the accident and about 50 were injured. Dickens was heroic in his efforts to aid them. Only after he was no longer needed did he remember the manuscript of *Mutual Friend,* on which he was working at the time. He climbed back into the compartment to get it. Although he was cool and collected during the accident, he was in shock afterward. Weakened and nervous during the rest of the summer, he never again felt easy about train travel.

Staple Inn   One of the INNS OF COURT, dating from the 16th century and located in GRAY'S INN Road. Snagsby walks here in summer "to observe how countrified the sparrows and the leaves are" (*Bleak House,* 10). Grewgious's chambers are in the inn, as are those he secures for Neville Landless (*Drood,* 11).

A newspaper picture showing Dickens tending the injured during the Staplehurst railway accident.

Staples, Leslie C. (1896–1980)   Secretary of the DICKENS FELLOWSHIP during World War II; editor of the DICKENSIAN from 1944 to 1968; president of the fellowship, 1968. Staples began publishing articles in the *Dickensian* in 1917 on biographical, bibliographical, and topographic topics. A collector of Dickens materials, particularly of the plagiarisms and piracies of Dickens's novels, Staples donated his collection to the DICKENS HOUSE Library.

Steig, Michael (1936–)   Professor, Simon Fraser University; Freudian critic of Victorian literature; reader-response theorist and critic. Steig's *Dickens and Phiz* (1978) is the standard work on Dickens's relationship with HABLOT KNIGHT BROWNE. He establishes their relation as a collaborative one and discusses Phiz's illustrations as the first interpretations of Dickens's novels, analyzing in illuminating detail many of Browne's pictures. In numerous articles, Steig has offered psychological and, more recently, reader-response discussions of Dickens's novels. Particularly interesting is the analysis of *Copperfield* in *Stories of Reading: Subjectivity and Literary Understanding* (1989) and a series of articles on *Curiosity Shop*.

Stephen, James Fitzjames (1829–1894)   Lawyer, authority on legal history, reviewer, and social commentator; brother of philosopher and editor Leslie Stephen. He wrote several reviews of Dickens's novels for the *Saturday Review*, objecting to Dickens's use of fantasy and exaggeration. Stephen was particularly incensed by the attack on the Circumlocution Office in *Dorrit* and may have been spurred to attack by the rumor that Tite Barnacle was based on his own father, an important civil servant. He charged Dickens with irresponsibility and with writing just for the money. He repeated and enlarged his criticisms in an anonymous article for the *Edinburgh Review*, "The License of Modern Novelists" (July 1857), prompting Dickens, uncharacteristically, to respond in an article for *Household Words*, "Curious Misprint in the Edinburgh Review" (August 1, 1857).

Stewart, Garrett (1945–)   Professor, University of Iowa. *Dickens and the Trials of Imagina-*tion (1974) employs stylistic analysis to explore the important theme of imagination in Dickens's novels, especially *Pickwick, Curiosity Shop, Chuzzlewit,* and *Mutual Friend.* In *Death Sentences: Styles of Dying in British Fiction* (1984), Stewart discusses death scenes in 19th- and 20th-century novels, beginning with a substantial chapter on Dickens. *Dear Reader: The Conscripted Audience in Nineteenth-Century Fiction* (1996) considers the reader's role in novels throughout the period.

Stirling, Edward (1809–1894)   Playwright, theater manager, actor. He wrote more than 200 plays, many of them adaptations and many of those from Dickens. His adaptations of *Pickwick, Twist, Nickleby, Curiosity Shop,* and *Chuzzlewit* were on the boards well before the novels completed their serial runs; this haste to produce led to such absurdities as Smike's inheriting a fortune in Stirling's version of *Nickleby.* After attending a performance of Stirling's *Nickleby* at the behest of ADELPHI THEATRE manager FREDERICK YATES, Dickens commented: "My general objection to the adaptation of any unfinished work of mine simply is that being badly done and worse acted, it tends to vulgarize the characters, to destroy or weaken the minds of those who see the impressions I have endeavoured to create. . . . No such objection can exist where the thing is as admirably done in every respect as you have done in this instance." Dickens saw several of Stirling's adaptations and, though occasionally unhappy with them, was usually quite positive. Stirling adapted several of the CHRISTMAS BOOKS for the stage as well as the early novels. He played Noggs in *Nickleby.*

Stoehr, Taylor (1931–)   Professor, University of Massachusetts, Boston; critic; editor of the works of Paul and Percival Goodman. His *Dickens: The Dreamer's Stance* (1965) analyzes the style in Dickens's last six novels as characteristic of dream translations, illustrating Dickens's "dream manner" or "supernaturalism." Using some of the techniques of dream analysis, Stoehr finds a characteristic plot with apparent and hidden strands that produce a series of discoveries leading to the hero's rebirth.

Stone, Frank (1800–1859) Painter, illustrator, close friend of Dickens, his neighbor when he lived at TAVISTOCK HOUSE. Stone was a prominent member of Dickens's theatrical troupe. He did three illustrations for *Haunted Man* and a frontispiece for the CHEAP EDITION of *Chuzzlewit*. He also painted some portraits of Dickens's children.

Stone, Harry (1926–) Professor, California State University, Northridge; Dickens scholar and editor who has made important contributions to understanding Dickens's minor writings and his use of fairy tale and fantasy. In *Dickens and the Invisible World* (1979), Stone discusses Dickens's use of fairy tales, legends, and other folk and fantasy materials, arguing that by the later novels, beginning with *Dombey*, Dickens had developed a "fairy-tale method" that he used as the underlying structure for his novels. In *The Night Side of Dickens: Cannibalism, Passion, Necessity* (1994), Stone exhaustively analyzes three areas of Dickens's psyche as it emerges in metaphors and suggestions of cannibalism, instances of "consuming passion that leads to misery and self-destruction," and characters who are the inevitable products of earlier acts and events. In *Uncollected Writings from Household Words, 1850–1859* (1968), Stone collects and annotates Dickens's contributions to articles that he coauthored or significantly edited. Stone has also edited the facsimile edition *Dickens' Working Notes for his Novels* (1987) and several editions of minor works by Dickens. Important among his many articles are "Dickens and Harriet Beecher Stowe" (*Nineteenth Century Fiction*, 1957), "Dickens and the Jews" (*Victorian Studies*, 1959), "Dickens's Woman in White" (*Victorian Newsletter*, 1968) on Miss Havisham in *Expectations*, and "The Love Pattern in Dickens's Novels" (in *Dickens the Craftsman*, ed. Partlow, 1970).

Stone, Marcus (1840–1921) Artist, illustrator, one of the young men at GAD'S HILL in the 1860s. After FRANK STONE died in 1859, Dickens became a second father to his son Marcus and the rest of the family. J. W. T. LEY (1918) describes Marcus as "Dickens's favorite among all the young men that worshipped him in the last decade of his life."

Marcus was often invited to stay at Gad's Hill, and he frequently accompanied Dickens on his walks. Dickens employed him to illustrate *Mutual Friend* and the LIBRARY EDITION of *Expectations*, which had not been previously illustrated. Stone also illustrated *Pictures from Italy, American Notes*, and *A Child's History of England* for the Library Edition, and he drew frontispieces for the CHEAP EDITIONS of *Drood* and *Two Cities*. Stone described Dickens as "the best man I ever knew. He was such a good man that you put his greatness in second place when you knew him. He occupied himself daily in some sort of work for somebody." Examples of his work appear on pages 160 and 290.

Storey, Gladys (1897–1964) Her biographical *Dickens and Daughter* (1939), based on interviews with Dickens's daughter KATE, was one of the first books to reveal Dickens's relationship with ELLEN TERNAN.

Storey, Graham (1922–2005) Reader in English, Cambridge. With Madeline House, Storey served as the general editor of the Pilgrim Edition of the letters of Charles Dickens, begun in 1965 and completed in 2002.

Stowe, Mrs. Harriet Elizabeth Beecher (1811–1896) American novelist, best known for *Uncle Tom's Cabin* (1852). She sent Dickens a presentation copy of that novel in 1852, and in "North American Slavery" he described it as "a noble work" but criticized its "overstrained conclusions and violent extremes." The two met a year later when she was touring England, but they did not establish an ongoing friendship. By the end of his life, Dickens was less charitable toward Stowe; when she published an article in 1869 on Lord Byron's affair with Augusta Leigh, Dickens wrote to JAMES FIELDS, his American publisher, "wish Mrs. Stowe was in the pillory." HARRY STONE (1957) provides a detailed account of the relationship between the two novelists.

Strand, the One of the main commercial thoroughfares in London, connecting the CITY with the West End. Hungerford Stairs, where Dickens worked as a boy at WARREN'S BLACKING, was located off the Strand, as were the offices of the MORNING CHRONICLE. Miss La Creevy's house, "halfway down the crowded thoroughfare," advertised her paintings with a "large gilt frame upon the street door" (*Nickleby*, 3). Martin Chuzzlewit has lodgings in the Strand (*Chuzzlewit*, 48). Dick Swiveller has "only one avenue to the Strand left open"; his creditors occupy all the other routes (*Curiosity Shop*, 8). The street is mentioned frequently in Dickens's works.

Sucksmith, Harvey Peter Contemporary literary scholar, whose important study of Dickens's conscious artistry, *The Narrative Art of Charles Dickens* (1970), challenges the notion of Dickens as an unconscious artist with detailed analyses of the rhetorical devices he used to achieve certain effects.

Sudbury Dickens reported a by-election in this Suffolk town for the MORNING CHRONICLE in July 1834 and then used it as the model for Eatanswill in *Pickwick* (13). The Swan Inn in Sudbury is the original of the Peacock, where the Buffs have their headquarters.

Sullivan, Francis L. (1903–1956) British character actor, famous for his screen roles as Crisparkle in *Edwin Drood* (1935), Bumble in DAVID LEAN's *Oliver Twist* (1948), and Jaggers in both the Universal production (1934) and Lean's (1946) version of *Great Expectations*.

Sumner, Charles (1811–1874) American lawyer, writer, law professor at Harvard, leader in the antislavery campaign. He served as Dickens's principal escort in Boston during the 1842 journey, and Dickens dined with him in Washington during his 1867 reading tour. He described Dickens in 1842 as "a most delightful person, overflowing with genius, cordiality & kindliness. Under *thirty* (he will be 30 next month) & a more than conqueror of the world."

Surrey Theatre At this theater in BLACKFRIAR'S ROAD, Dickens attended a performance of *Twist* in 1838 that so distressed him that he "laid himself down upon the floor in a corner of the box and

never rose from it until the drop-scene fell." This theater was also probably the one where Frederick Dorrit plays the clarinet and Fanny Dorrit works as a dancer (*Dorrit*, I:7, 20).

Surtees, Robert Smith (1805–1864) Sporting novelist, best known for Jorrocks, a cockney grocer, huntsman, and squire whose "jaunts and jollities" Surtees described in the *New Sporting Magazine*, which he edited from 1831 to 1836. Jorrocks's popularity contributed to ROBERT SEYMOUR's scheme for a series of comic sporting plates that ultimately became *Pickwick*. A huntsman himself, Surtees continued to publish sporting novels centered on Jorrocks in the 1840s, among them *Handley Cross* (1843) and *Hillingdon Hall* (1845). JOHN LEECH illustrated several of his books.

Suzannet Collection Extensive collection of Dickens materials compiled by the Comte Alain de Suzannet (1882–1950), including editions of the novels, Dickens's reading texts, texts of Dickens's speeches, many letters and manuscripts, pictures and drawings, and miscellaneous Dickensiana. He and his wife donated many items from this collection to the DICKENS HOUSE MUSEUM. Other items were sold at auction after his death. MICHAEL SLATER (1975) edited a descriptive catalog of the collection.

Swinburne, Algernon C. (1837–1909) Poet, critic. In GENOA in 1844–45, the Dickens children played with the "golden-haired son of the Swinburnes," who was home from his first term at Eton. Swinburne became an enthusiast for Dickens's work while he was at Eton and was an ardent Dickensian throughout his life. In a posthumously published essay on Dickens (1913), he shared his appreciation for the novels and provided several unusual insights into them, particularly into some of the incidental characters.

Switzerland Dickens traveled through Switzerland in 1845 and spent the summer of 1846 with his family there. David Copperfield recuperates from the loss of Dora in Switzerland (*Copperfield*, 58). The Dorrits pass through on their way to Italy (*Dorrit*, I:2). The narrator of "The Holly Tree" remembers a little Swiss inn, "a very homely place, in a village of one narrow zigzag street, among mountains," where a murder occurred while he was staying there (1). The Traveller describes a journey to Switzerland (*Uncommercial*, 7). In the Swiss Alps, Vendale discovers his true identity and Obenreizer meets his death ("No Thoroughfare").

T

Talfourd, Sir Thomas Noon (1795–1854) Jurist and author; member of Parliament for Reading; judge. A friend of William Wordsworth, Samuel Taylor Coleridge, and Charles Lamb, he introduced Dickens to the literary circles of London at Gore House and Holland House and nominated him for membership in the ATHENAEUM CLUB. Dickens dedicated *Pickwick* to him, gratefully acknowledging Talfourd's efforts for the copyright bill. Talfourd represented Dickens in his suit against the pirates who plagiarized *Carol*. He is usually regarded as the original of Traddles in *Copperfield*. Dickens's obituary for Talfourd appeared in HOUSEHOLD WORDS (March 25, 1854).

Tauchnitz, Baron Christian Bernard (1816–1895) German publisher who issued cheap reprints of English novels for continental readers. Tauchnitz often contracted to buy advance proofs of the novels; his standard payment was £50. Dickens's dealings with him were very friendly.

Taunton, Vale of Rural area in Somerset where Mrs. Nickleby visited the Hawkinses while she was in school (*Nickleby*, 35). Vholes has a habit of telling people, "I have the privilege of supporting an aged father in the Vale of Taunton—his native place—and I admire that country very much" (*Bleak House*, 37).

Thomas Noon Talfourd, said to be the original of Traddles in *David Copperfield. Illustration by Daniel Maclise.*

619

Tavistock House, the Dickens family home from November 1851 to September 1860.

Tavistock House   House in Bloomsbury on Tavistock Square that the Dickens family occupied from 1851 to 1860. Dickens purchased the lease from FRANK STONE, who moved into a neighboring house. The building was sizable, providing ample space for the large family; its spacious schoolroom could be converted into a theater for Dickens's theatrical productions.

Temple, the   Area in London between FLEET STREET and the THAMES. Owned by the Knights Templar in the Middle Ages, it later became the site of two INNS OF COURT, the Inner Temple and the Middle Temple. Sir John Chester's apartment is located in the Paper Buildings here (*Rudge*, 15). The library that Tom Pinch is employed to man-age is located in some dusty rooms in the Temple (*Chuzzlewit*, 39), John Westlock courts Ruth Pinch in Fountain Court (*Chuzzlewit*, 45), and Stryver's chambers are in the Temple (*Two Cities*, II:5). Pip and Herbert Pocket have rooms on an upper story in GARDEN COURT (*Expectations*, 39). Eugene Wrayburn and Mortimer Lightwood (*Mutual Friend*, I:8), Charley ("Holly-Tree"), Slinkton ("Hunted Down"), and the bachelor in "The Ghost of Art" (*Reprinted*) all have chambers here.

Temple Bar   In Dickens's day, prior to the installation of the Griffin in 1880, it was an arched gateway to the CITY, dividing FLEET STREET from the STRAND. Dickens described it in *Bleak House* as "that leaden-headed old corporation: Temple Bar" (1). The 'Prentice Knights took an oath not "to damage or in any way disfigure Temple Bar, which was strictly constitutional, and always to be approached with reverence" *Rudge* (8). It is also mentioned in *Chuzzlewit* (45), *Copperfield* (46), *Two Cities* (I:12; II:12, 24), and *Mutual Friend* (III:2; IV:10).

Tennent, Sir James Emerson (1804–1869)   Liberal politician, supporter of the REFORM BILL OF 1832 and the abolition of the CORN LAWS; author; long-time friend of Dickens. A traveler and writer of travel books, Tennent climbed Vesuvius with Dickens and traveled around Italy with him in 1853. Dickens dedicated *Our Mutual Friend* to him.

Tenniel, John (1820–1914)   Painter and illustrator, famous for his illustrations for *PUNCH* and for Lewis Carroll's Alice books. Tenniel and Dickens became friends when the artist was employed to provide five illustrations for *Haunted Man*. Later he acted in several of Dickens's AMATEUR THEATRICALS. As the political cartoonist for *Punch*, Tenniel frequently used Dickens characters in his cartoons, as on p. 590 (*Punch*). See also p. 159.

Tennyson, Alfred (Lord Tennyson) (1809–1892)   Poet laureate, friend. Dickens met Tennyson in the early 1840s, probably through JOHN FORSTER. Their relationship was most active in the 1840s, before Tennyson's marriage. Dickens invited Tennyson to vacation with his family in Switzerland. Although the poet declined the invitation, he did visit Dickens in Lausanne. Tennyson particularly admired *Pickwick* and Old Cheeseman in "The Schoolboy's Story." Dickens thought *Idylls of the King* "the noblest" of Tennyson's works.

Ternan, Ellen Lawless ("Nelly") (1839–1914) Dickens's mistress, an actress from a theatrical family. With her mother, Frances Eleanor Jarman, and her sister Maria, Ellen was hired for the Manchester performances of Dickens's production of THE FROZEN DEEP in August 1857. Infatuated with the young actress, Dickens went to Doncaster, where Ellen was playing in December, a trip obliquely described in *Idle Tour*. This was the beginning of a secret relationship that continued until Dickens's death. The sparse documentary evidence of the relationship has caused a great deal of speculation about whether Ellen was, in fact, Dickens's mistress, whether they had a child, and just how responsive Ellen was to Dickens's attentions. The heroines of the late novels are sometimes taken as proof that Ellen scorned and tormented Dickens as Estella does Pip (*Expectations*).

Ellen often traveled with Dickens to France, and she was with him in the STAPLEHURST RAILWAY ACCIDENT. He left her £1000 in his will. In 1876, after Dickens's death, Ellen married George W. Robinson, a clergyman and later headmaster of a school in MARGATE. By all accounts, she never mentioned her relationship with Dickens during her later life.

Dickens's relationship with Ellen was first revealed by Thomas Wright (*Life of Charles Dickens*, 1935) and by Dickens's daughter KATE MACREADY DICKENS in interviews with GLADYS STOREY (1939). The most useful accounts of the relationship are provided by ADA NISBET (1952), FRED KAPLAN (1988), PETER ACKROYD (1990), and Claire Tomalin (*The Invisible Woman: The Story of Nelly Ternan and Charles Dickens*, 1991).

Thackeray, William Makepeace (1811–1863) Novelist, comic illustrator, essayist, and lecturer; Dickens's friend and great rival. Their novels were often compared. On publishing *Vanity Fair* in 1848, Thackeray described himself as "all but at the top of the tree, . . . and having a great fight up there with Dickens." *Vanity Fair* was often compared with *Dombey,* especially in its treatment of businessmen, and the autobiographical PENDENNIS with *Copperfield.* The two authors first met in 1836, when Thackeray applied to take over for ROBERT SEYMOUR as the illustrator for *Pickwick.* Son of a colonial administrator in India and university educated, Thackeray thought Dickens "abominably coarse," but he admired and was occasionally awed by his work. Dickens especially admired *Vanity Fair* among Thackeray's works. In 1858 the two men quarreled over an attack on Thackeray by EDMUND YATES. This GARRICK CLUB affair estranged Dickens and Thackeray until 1863, when the two were reconciled just a few weeks before Thackeray's death.

William Makepeace Thackeray, a portrait by Maclise.

Dickens's obituary tribute to Thackeray appeared in the *Cornhill* in February 1864.

Thames, River   The River Thames is so constant a presence in Dickens's work as to be taken for granted. From such early sketches as "The River" and "The Steam Excursion" (*Boz*) to *Mutual Friend*, in which the polluted Thames is one of the controlling symbols, the river holds an important place in Dickens's work. It is used symbolically in three novels in particular. In *Dombey*, the Thames links London to the sea, providing the avenue for Dombey's business and, for young Paul, the connection to the sea of immortality he associates with the golden waves on the wall of his room. In *Expectations*, the river connects London with Pip's home country and links his childhood and later life. The climactic struggle between Magwitch and Compeyson on the river recalls their earlier struggle on the marshes and has the effect of bringing Pip's childhood and adulthood together. The polluted river in *Mutual Friend* acts both as an extension of the wasteland symbolized by the dustheaps and as a source of life and renewal.

Thames Street   Street running from BLACKFRIARS to the TOWER OF LONDON. Joe Willet goes to "some deep cellars hard by Thames Street" to pay the Maypole's bill (*Rudge*, 13). Mrs. Clennam's house is in this street or nearby (*Dorrit*).

Theatre Royal, Montreal   On his 1842 journey to America, Dickens acted in and directed an evening of theater at this venue in MONTREAL. It was the first of his AMATEUR THEATRICAL productions.

Theatrical Fund   Charity founded in 1839 to provide pensions for actors and actresses and other theatrical performers. Dickens served as one of the trustees for the fund for many years and addressed its meetings on several occasions. KENNETH J. FIELDING (*Dickens*, 1988) includes 13 speeches given at various meetings of this charity, which Dickens actively supported throughout his life.

Thomas, Deborah A. (1943–) Professor, Villanova University, who has written on both Dickens

and Thackeray. *Dickens and the Short Story* (1982) identifies and analyzes the many short stories by Dickens, a part of his work neglected by most other critics. Thomas discusses both those stories published in his collections of short fiction and those inserted into the novels. She has also edited a collection of Dickens's short fiction (1976). *"Hard Times": A Fable of Fragmentation and Wholeness* (1997) is a critical introduction to the novel.

Thompson, John   Dickens's manservant. When he was dismissed for dishonesty in 1867, after more than 20 years' service, Dickens set him up in business.

Thurley, Geoffrey (1936–) Professor, University of Essex; poet, critic, translator, novelist. In *The Dickens Myth: Its Genesis and Structure* (1976), Thurley discusses Dickens's works from *Twist* through *Expectations* as a mythic response to the social uncertainties of Victorian England, in which the individual is beset by the danger of falling into poverty and the obligations imposed by rising into affluence. The epitome of this myth is *Expectations*.

Thurtell, John (1794–1824)   Notorious murderer who was executed in 1824 for the murder of William Weare. An account of his crime was included in THE NEWGATE CALENDAR in 1828. Dickens cites him as an example of a murderer who maintained remarkable composure during his trial (*Miscellaneous*, "Demeanour of Murderers").

"Tibbs"   Pen name used by Dickens for a series of sketches, under the general title *Scenes and Characters*, that appeared in BELL'S LIFE IN LONDON between September 27, 1835, and January 17, 1836. These sketches were later collected in *Boz*.

Ticknor & Fields   Dickens's American publishing firm in which JAMES FIELDS was the senior partner. The firm published the DIAMOND EDITION of Dickens's works in 1867, illustrated by SOLOMON EYTINGE, and the American CHARLES DICKENS EDITION. They also published the texts of Dickens's PUBLIC READINGS during his American tour. Dickens wrote occasional pieces for their magazine, ATLANTIC MONTHLY ("George Silverman's Explanation" and "On Mr. Fechter's Acting"), and for their children's magazine, OUR YOUNG FOLKS ("Holiday Romance").

Tillotson, Kathleen (1906–2001) Professor, University of London, whose pioneering work on Dickens and other Victorian novelists set the direction for much later scholarship. *Novels of the Eighteen-forties* (1956) surveys the social and intellectual context for the novel boom in the decade and analyzes in detail four novels—including *Dombey*—as representative of the period. In *Dickens at Work* (with JOHN BUTT, 1957), she establishes methods of studying Dickens as a serial novelist, using manuscripts, proof sheets, and Dickens's working notes and placing the novels into the immediate historical context of the time in which they were written. Tillotson edited the first volume in the CLARENDON EDITION, *Twist* (1966), and served as general editor for the project. She also edited several volumes of the Pilgrim Edition of the LETTERS.

Tobin, Daniel Dickens's closest friend at WELLINGTON HOUSE ACADEMY. The two boys staged plays and performed boyish pranks together. After their schooldays, according to JOHN FORSTER, Tobin worked as an occasional amanuensis for Dickens, but his requests for money finally exasperated the novelist, who broke off their relationship.

Toole, J. L. (1830–1906) Late-Victorian actor famous for his many Dickensian roles: Buzfuz, Artful Dodger, Bob Cratchit, Caleb Plummer, Trotty Veck, Ben Britain, and Tetterby. He was especially famous for his portrayal of the Dodger, which he played more than 3,000 times. Dickens praised his acting, and Toole responded with the comment: "To know from his own lips that he approved of my efforts to realize some of his creations on the stage has always given me great satisfaction."

Topham, Francis William (1808–1877) Painter, illustrator, and engraver. Topham was a member of Dickens's amateur acting troupe before Dickens asked him to provide the frontispieces for the three

volumes of *A Child's History of England* (see p. 369). Topham also did several watercolor paintings of scenes from *Curiosity Shop* and *Rudge*.

topography Dickens often made use of actual places as the SETTINGS for his novels and stories, so that particular streets and buildings can be identified as the ones Dickens had in mind. On other occasions he mixes the fictional with the real, placing imaginary streets, houses, or inns into real towns or neighborhoods. These practices, of course, have prompted many ardent Dickensians to visit the actual places mentioned in the novels and to seek out the originals of the fictional places, identifying, for example, the Uncommercial Traveller's Dullborough as ROCHESTER and the country village where Nell dies as Tong in Shropshire. These topographic identifications are often disputed, and the methods for arriving at them are various and, sometimes, questionable. Coketown, for example, has been identified as both MANCHESTER and PRESTON, obscuring, perhaps, Dickens's intent to create an imaginary factory town to meet the thematic demands of his story. It is important to remember that even "real" places became fictional when Dickens chose to make them part of his story.

Topographic activity was particularly intense in the early decades of the 20th century, but many of the settings identified during those years have since disappeared. Alex Philip and Laurence Gadd include a useful index of the attributions made during this period in *The Dickens Dictionary* (1928). Two useful guides to Dickensian places are London Transport's *The London of Charles Dickens* (1970) and Tony Lynch's *Dickens's England: A Traveller's Companion* (1986).

Tottenham Court Road Street running north from ST. GILES Circus, in Dickens's time the site of many drapers' shops. Horatio Sparkins is a clerk in such a shop (*Boz*, "Sparkins"). Boz also describes a wedding party in this road ("Hackney-Coach"). Miss Knag's brother Mortimer has a stationer's shop here (*Nickleby*, 18). Peggotty recovers Traddles's table and flower stand from a shop at the upper end of the street (*Copperfield*, 34).

Tower of London   Quilp's domicile is located nearby on Tower Hill (*Curiosity Shop*, 4). Lord George Gordon (*Rudge*, 73) and Charles Darnay (*Two Cities*, II:6) are both imprisoned in the Tower.

Townshend, the Reverend Chauncy Hare (1798–1868)   Clergyman; proponent of MESMERISM and author of *Facts in Mesmerism* (1840); devoted friend of Dickens. A gentle, affectionate man, Townshend has been said to be the original of both Cousin Feenix (*Dombey*) and Twemlow (*Mutual Friend*). He died while Dickens was on his reading tour in America. On hearing of his death, Dickens wrote to GEORGINA HOGARTH, "It is not a light thing to lose such a friend, and I truly loved him." Townshend named Dickens his literary executor and left him the task of editing and publishing his *Religious Opinions*, published with an introduction by Dickens in 1869.

"Tringham, Mr."   Pseudonym used by Dickens to conceal his identity in his relationship with ELLEN TERNAN.

Trollope, Anthony (1815–1882)   Prolific novelist, best known for his series of Barsetshire novels; civil servant with the Postal Service; son of the novelist Frances Trollope and brother of THOMAS ADOLPHUS TROLLOPE. Although Trollope admired Dickens's success, he thought his novels pandered to the public and were deficient artistically. In *The Warden* (1855), the first of the Barsetshire novels, he satirized Dickens as Mr. Popular Sentiment, "a very powerful man" who used his novels to address social issues and who preferred "ridicule" to "convincing argument," used simplification and exaggeration as his tools, and knew that "the artist who paints for the million must use glaring colours." Trollope praised Dickens on many occasions, but he harbored reservations about the artistic qualities of his work, and in his *Autobiography* (1883) he

ranked Dickens below both WILLIAM MAKEPEACE THACKERAY and GEORGE ELIOT while acknowledging his immense popularity.

Trollope, Thomas Adolphus (1810–1892)   Journalist, novelist; contributor to ALL THE YEAR ROUND; brother of ANTHONY TROLLOPE. Tom Trollope spent most of his adult life in Italy, working as an Italian correspondent for British newspapers. He first met Dickens in Italy in 1845 and thought him "a dandified, pretty-boy-looking sort of figure," but after he knew Dickens better, he described him as "a strikingly manly man, not only in appearance but in bearing" and "perhaps the largest-hearted man I ever knew." Trollope's second wife was Frances Eleanor Ternan, sister of ELLEN TERNAN. Although Dickens did not like her, he published two of her novels in *All the Year Round*.

True Sun   Newspaper begun in 1832 with Samuel Laman Blanchard as editor. For a few months in 1832 Dickens worked as a general reporter for the paper, while he was also writing for the MIRROR OF PARLIAMENT as a parliamentary reporter. The exact length of his tenure with the paper is uncertain.

Tunbridge Wells   Fashionable spa in KENT where Mr. Finching, "on a donkey," proposed to Flora Casby (*Dorrit*, I:24) and where "Foolish Mr. Porters" reputedly proposed to Miss Twinkleton (*Drood*, 3).

"Turnham, Mr."   One of the pseudonyms Dickens used to keep his identity secret in his relationship with ELLEN TERNAN.

Twickenham   Country village on the north side of the Thames, west of HAMMERSMITH, where Lord Frederick Verisopht is killed by Sir Mulberry Hawk in a duel (*Nickleby*, 50). Arthur Clennam visits the Meagleses in their cottage near the river here (*Dorrit*, I:16, 17, 26, 28).

U

unions, labor What Dickens thought of labor unions is usually derived from *Hard Times*. In that novel Slackbridge, the unconvincing labor organizer, is, as GEORGE BERNARD SHAW (1985) described him, "a mere figment of the middle-class imagination. . . . Even at their worst trade union organizers are not a bit like Slackbridge." Dickens's failure with Slackbridge is usually taken as an indication that he did not understand unions and simply accepted the middle-class prejudice that unions were unnecessary and dangerous.

Dickens's position on unions, as developed in *Hard Times* and his journal articles—especially "On Strike," "Railway Strikes," and "To Working Men"—is much more ambivalent. Stephen Blackpool's "muddle" in the novel suggests that Dickens shared THOMAS CARLYLE's view that laissez-faire capitalism left workers without leadership from those above them in society, vulnerable to demagogues like Slackbridge. In other instances, however, as in the essay "To Working Men," he calls on members of the working class to take the initiative themselves to right the injustices that beset them. Though he attacks the outside agitators like Slackbridge and Gruffshaw ("On Strike"), he does not discount the workers' grievances. Blackpool is at least as wronged by Bounderby as he is by Slackbridge. In spite of all the factory owners' statements about the interests of workers and owners being identical, Bounderby shows no recognition of any common bonds with Blackpool, an irony underscored as Dickens shows both of them to be the victims of failed marriages.

Dickens was also aware of the imbalance of power in the relations of owners and workers, a recognition that informs his ironic presentation of Mrs. Sparsit's views on the issue: "It is much to be regretted," she comments to Bitzer, ". . . that the united masters allow of such combinations. . . . Being united themselves, they ought one and all to set their faces against employing any man who is united with any other man" (*Hard Times,* II:1). Somewhat naively, perhaps, Dickens continued to believe that the issues between workers and masters could be settled through arbitration, for the interests of the two groups were linked, but he thought that the workers might have to take the initiative to make those above them recognize their common lot. JACK LINDSAY (1950) comes much closer to describing Dickens's views than most other commentators when he writes, "Dickens reveals an ambivalent attitude; he wants the workers to unite and insists that the people will take for themselves the rights that will never be given to them by Parliament, but at the same time he feels something frightening in the fact of mass organizations. He advocates trade unionism and shrinks from its results."

Unitarianism After returning from AMERICA in 1842, perhaps influenced by the religious liberalism of the New England Unitarians he met there, Dickens began attending a Unitarian chapel in London.

He was drawn to Unitarianism by its emphasis on the moral teachings in the New Testament rather than the theology. It was the theological contentiousness in the Church of England at the time, particularly the quarrels between the Evangelicals (*see* EVANGELICALISM) and the Puseyites, that made Unitarianism attractive to Dickens. He attended the Unitarian chapel for most of the 1840s, while he was writing *Chuzzlewit, Dombey,* and, significantly, *The Life of Our Lord* for his children. The latter has sometimes been described as a "Unitarian gospel," but as DENNIS WALDER (1981) points out, "This is to read into it a theological significance, hardly applicable, unless this simply means having a moral emphasis."

United States   See AMERICA.

Urania Cottage   An asylum for former prostitutes in SHEPHERD'S BUSH, founded by ANGELA BURDETT-COUTTS in 1847. Dickens was involved in the project from the start, acting as planner and administrator, and took an active role in the day-to-day operation of the facility from 1846 to 1858. His "Appeal to Fallen Women" (1850) states his aims for the project; Alice Marwood in *Dombey,* Martha Endell and Little Em'ly in *Copperfield,* and the prostitute whom Little Dorrit meets on the streets (*Dorrit,* I:14) are indications in Dickens's novels of his involvement with the issue of PROSTITUTION during this period.

utilitarianism   An empirical and individualistic moral and social philosophy that was especially influential in the mid-Victorian period. Also known as Philosophical Radicalism or Benthamism—after its founder Jeremy Bentham (1748–1832)—utilitarianism was grounded in the assumption that human beings sought to minimize pain and maximize pleasure, and it set as its social goal "the greatest happiness of the greatest number." Although Dickens was sympathetic to the radicals' goals of reforming and rationalizing social and political institutions, he distrusted their use of statistics, their preference for the abstract generalization over the individual case, and their favoring of rationality over imagination. His most direct attacks on utilitarianism in the novels appear in his critique of the "philosophers" behind the NEW POOR LAW in *Twist,* his attack on the statistical political economist Filer in *Chimes,* and his exposé of the moral emptiness of the school of fact in *Hard Times.*

V

Vale, Sam (1797–1848) Comic actor whose popular portrayal of the cockney Simon Spatterdash in *The Boarding House* at the DRURY LANE Theatre in 1822 is thought to be the original inspiration for the character of Sam Weller.

Valentine Vox, the Ventriloquist Popular serial novel by Henry Cockton, published in 1839–40, that shows the influence of both *Pickwick* and *Nickleby*. Its loose series of adventures and its sketches of London life recall Dickens's early work in a general way; the story of Valentine's friend Goodman, who is kidnapped and imprisoned in a lunatic asylum, recalls in particular the story of Nicholas and Smike.

Van Ghent, Dorothy (1907–1967) Professor, University of Buffalo; poet; critic of the English and American novel. Her two influential essays on Dickens, "The Dickens World: The View from Todgers's" (*Sewanee Review*, 1950) and "On *Great Expectations*" (in *The English Novel: Form and Function*, 1953), include telling discussions of Dickens's use of animism and objectification. These related processes, in which the physical world comes alive and the human world is objectified, are at the heart of Dickens's vision of industrial England and crucial to his techniques of characterization.

Vauxhall Bridge The bridge across the THAMES connecting Westminster and Kennington. Charley Hexam and Bradley Headstone meet Eugene Wrayburn here (*Mutual Friend*, II:1). The bridge is also mentioned in *Boz*, "River" and "Somebody's Luggage."

Vauxhall Gardens This famous pleasure ground of the 18th and early 19th century—it was closed in 1859—was situated on the south side of the THAMES by VAUXHALL BRIDGE. Dickens describes it in *Boz*, "Vauxhall."

Venice, Italy Dickens describes his impressions of the city in *Pictures* (8). After gaining their riches, the Dorrits travel to Venice, where Fanny meets Sparkler once again and Amy longs for London (*Dorrit*, II:3–7).

Victoria, Queen (1819–1901) When Victoria married Prince Albert in 1840, Dickens carried on a facetious fantasy with JOHN FORSTER and DANIEL MACLISE in which he pretended to be heartbroken that she had given her heart to another and not recognized his love for her.

The Queen attended benefit performances given by Dickens's AMATEUR THEATRICAL troupe of *Every Man in His Humour* in 1848, *Not So Bad as We Seem* in 1851, and *The Frozen Deep* in 1857. Although the Queen sent for him after the 1857 performance, Dickens begged to be excused from appearing before her, since he was still "in my Farce dress." He did have an audience with the Queen at Buckingham Palace on March 9, 1870. She found him "very agreeable, with a pleasant voice and manner."

Victoria, the   The Old Vic Theatre in Waterloo Road on the south bank of the THAMES was famous in the 19th century for its melodramas. The the-ater is described in *Sketches of Young Gentlemen* and "Amusements of the People."

Villa Bagnarello, Albaro   The Villa di Bella Vista, the house that Dickens rented for his fam-ily on their trip to Italy in 1844. He described the overgrown and ill-cared-for building as a "pink jail" and moved his family to the PALAZZO PESCHIERE in GENOA after only two and a half months in Albaro.

Walder, Dennis (1943–) Professor, Open University; South African scholar and writer who has written on the drama of Athol Fugard and other literary topics. *Dickens and Religion* (1981) discusses the religious elements in each of the novels, relating them to Dickens's own religious development. Walder has also edited *Sketches by Boz* and *Dombey*.

Walters, J[ohn] Cuming (d. 1933) Journalist, editor of the *Manchester City News*; president of the DICKENS FELLOWSHIP. One of the active Dickensians in the early years of the 20th century, Walters wrote two books on *Drood* (1905 and 1912), arguing the thesis, controversial at the time, that Edwin was dead, murdered by Jasper, and that Datchery was Helena Landless in disguise. He also wrote a biographical study, *The Phases of Dickens* (1911).

Walworth The semirural suburb south of London where Wemmick has his castle and retreats from the public life in the city (*Expectations*, 24). The "back part of Walworth" at the turn of the century is described as "a dreary waste" in *Boz*, "Black Veil." Mr. Tibbs retires to Walworth after separating from Mrs. Tibbs (*Boz*, "Boarding House"). The Traveller describes the high winds at Walworth in *Uncommercial* (6).

Wapping This dockside area in east London is mentioned in *Mutual Friend* (II:12). The Wapping Workhouse is described in *Uncommercial* (3).

Wardour, Richard Hero of WILKIE COLLINS's play *THE FROZEN DEEP*, who gives up his life to save the life of his rival for the woman he loves. Dickens was very moved when he played the role in 1857 and was inspired to develop a similar situation in Sydney Carton's story in *Two Cities*.

Warren, Jonathan Early 19th-century businessman, proprietor of the BLACKING WAREHOUSE where Dickens worked as a boy in 1824. He claimed to have invented the blacking recipe that his more famous brother Robert used to develop WARREN'S BLACKING. Jonathan established a blacking business at 30 Hungerford Stairs to challenge his brother's business, located at 30 STRAND. When JAMES LAMERT became a manager in Jonathan's firm, he suggested that Dickens might be employed there.

Warren's Blacking A manufacturer of blacking. In 1824, when Dickens worked in the BLACKING WAREHOUSE, there were two firms claiming to possess Warren's original recipe for the product. The first, owned by Robert Warren and located at 30 STRAND, was later described by Dickens as "the famous one." The other, which had been sold by JONATHAN WARREN to George Lamert and was located at 30 Hungerford Stairs, was the firm in which Dickens worked as a boy.

Washington, D.C. Dickens describes the city, the Congress, and his meeting with President Tyler in 1842 in *Notes* (8): "Take the worst parts of the City Road in Pentonville, or the straggling outskirts of Paris, where the houses are smallest, preserving all their oddities, but especially the small shops and dwellings, occupied in Pentonville (but not in Washington) by furniture-brokers, keepers of poor eating-houses, and fanciers of birds. Burn the whole down; build it up again in wood and plaster; widen it a little; throw in part of St. John's Wood; put green blinds outside all the private houses, with a red curtain and a white one in every window; plough up all the roads; plant a great deal of coarse turf in every place where it ought *not* to be; erect three handsome buildings in stone and marble, anywhere, but the more entirely out of everyone's way the better; call one the Post Office, one the Patent Office, and one the Treasury; make it scorching hot in the morning, and freezing cold in the afternoon, with an occasional tornado of wind and dust; leave a brick-field without the bricks, in all central places where a street may naturally be expected; and that's Washington."

Waterloo Bridge   This bridge over the THAMES, between BLACKFRIARS BRIDGE and WESTMINSTER BRIDGE, was completed in 1817. The arches under the bridge provided "unfurnished lodgings" for the homeless, as they did for a fortnight for Sam Weller (*Pickwick*, 16). The drunkard Warden commits suicide by drowning under the bridge (*Boz*, "Drunkard's Death"). Dickens describes the bridge, its inhabitants and suicides, in *Reprinted*, "Down with the Tide."

Watkins, Gwen (1923–)   Critic, biographer; wife of Welsh poet Vernon Watkins. Much of her writing is about the life and work of her late husband. *Dickens in Search of Himself* (1987) treats Dickens as a psychological writer, discussing his works as documents in a self-exploration or as translations, in a psychoanalytic sense, of his subconscious life and experience.

Watson, Hon. Mr. Richard (1800–1852) **and Mrs. Lavinia** (1816–1888)   Dickens met the Watsons when he was in Lausanne in 1846 and subsequently visited them at ROCKINGHAM CAS-

TLE, their home in Northamptonshire, in 1849 and 1851. There he met MARY BOYLE, Mrs. Watson's niece, and organized AMATEUR THEATRICALS. On Watson's death in 1852, Dickens wrote, "I loved him as my heart, and cannot think of him without tears." Chesney Wold in *Bleak House* is based on Rockingham Castle.

Waugh, Arthur (1866–1943)   Chairman of CHAPMAN & HALL; journalist; author; father of Alec and Evelyn Waugh; one of the founders of the DICKENS FELLOWSHIP and its president, 1909–10. He wrote on ALFRED, LORD TENNYSON, ROBERT BROWNING, and other Victorian writers as well as on Dickens. Described by the DICKENSIAN as "an authority [on Dickens] who does not labour or cavil over a minor bibliographical or topographical detail as some of us do," Waugh sometimes irritated other Dickensians with his critical judgments in his introductions to the Biographical Edition of Dickens (1902–3).

Webster, Thomas (1800–1886)   Artist who furnished the frontispiece for the CHEAP EDITION of *Nickleby*.

Weller, Christiana (1825–1910)   Young woman pianist whom Dickens met in 1844 when he introduced her at a performance at the LIVERPOOL Mechanics Institute. He was immediately infatuated with her, seeing "an angel's message in her face . . . that smote me to the heart." He seemed to connect her innocence with that of MARY HOGARTH, for he wrote to T. J. Thompson, "I cannot joke about Miss Weller; for she is too good; and interest in her (spiritual young creature that she is, and destined to an early death, I fear) has become a sentiment with me." When Thompson confessed his love for the girl, a shocked Dickens encouraged him to propose to her, and he reconciled the couple twice during their engagement. But when Dickens visited the Thompsons in Lausanne in 1846, he was disappointed with Christiana, who seemed "to have a whimpering, pouting temper." Her younger sister Anna married Dickens's brother FREDERICK DICKENS over the objections both of her parents and of Dickens.

Weller, Mary Dickens's nurse when the family lived in CHATHAM between 1817 and 1822. Dickens remembers the terrifying stories she told him as a child, particularly the tale of Captain Murderer, recounted in "Nurse's Stories" (*Uncommercial*, 15). In later life, Mary Weller recalled the recitations and songs performed by her young charge. She has usually been considered the original of Mary, the Nupkinses' maid in *Pickwick*, and Clara Peggotty in *Copperfield*.

Wellington House Academy The school in Hampstead Road, North London, that Dickens attended after leaving WARREN'S BLACKING. The sadistic headmaster of the school, WILLIAM JONES, would become the model for Creakle of Salem House in *Copperfield*, but Dickens's two years there were largely happy ones. His fellow students remembered him as high-spirited and involved in amateur theatrical performances, and he did well enough academically to win a Latin prize.

Wellington Street The offices of both *HOUSE-HOLD WORDS* and *ALL THE YEAR ROUND* were located in this street off the STRAND.

Welsh, Alexander (1933–) Professor, Yale University; scholar and critic of Victorian fiction who has written on Sir WALTER SCOTT, GEORGE ELIOT, and WILLIAM MAKEPEACE THACKERAY as well as on Dickens. *The City of Dickens* (1971) relates several central issues and historical concerns in Dickens's work: the city as both historical fact and spiritual ideal, the heroines as representatives of hearth and home and as angels of death, and the endings of the novels as they relate to the ending of life. *From Copyright to Copperfield: The Identity of Dickens* (1987) offers a biographical interpretation of the middle novels from *Chuzzlewit* through *Copperfield*, identifying a midcareer crisis, beginning with the American journey, as the source of the heroes and issues in these novels. *Dickens Redressed* (2000) analyzes *Bleak House* and *Hard Times*. In *Hamlet in His Modern Guises* (2001), Welsh devotes a quarter of the book to a discussion of *Great Expectations*, drawing out the similarities between Pip and the Prince of Denmark. In *Reflec-*

tions on the Hero as Quixote (1981) Welsh traces the influence of CERVANTES on subsequent fiction, particularly on *Pickwick*.

Westminster Abbey Britain's national church, located on Parliament Square across from the Houses of Parliament. Although Dickens requested to be buried in a private funeral in ROCHESTER, his family acceded to the wishes of Dean Stanley and the larger public, who requested that he be buried in the Poets' Corner in the Abbey. His body was interred there in an unannounced, private ceremony on June 14, 1870.

Two political young gentlemen discuss the policy of charging an admission fee to the Abbey (*Young Gentlemen*). The "poet" Slum compares himself to some lesser poets buried in the Poets' Corner in the Abbey (*Curiosity Shop*, 28). Daniel Peggotty and David pass the Abbey as they follow Martha Endell through the streets of London (*Copperfield*, 47). Pip and Herbert Pocket attend services at the Abbey (*Expectations*, 22). Miss Abbey Potterson is thought by some regulars at her pub to be named after the Abbey (*Mutual Friend*, I:6). The Traveller spends a quarter of an hour in the "fine gloomy society" of the Abbey on one of his night walks (*Uncommercial*, 13).

Westminster Bridge This bridge connecting LAMBETH with Westminster by the Houses of Parliament is where Barnaby Rudge first meets the crowds of demonstrators when he enters London with his mother (*Rudge*, 47). The bridge is also mentioned in *Boz*, "River"; *Mutual Friend* (II:1); and *Uncommercial* (13).

Westminster Hall Part of the original complex of the Houses of Parliament that was not destroyed in the fire of 1834. Here Geoffrey Haredale meets Lord George Gordon during the prelude to the riots (*Rudge*, 43). The Jarndyce case is heard in the old courts here (*Bleak House*, 19). John Harmon, disguised as Julius Handford, gives his address at the Exchequer Coffee House in this complex of buildings (*Mutual Friend*, I:3).

Whitechapel District in east London, site of many coaching inns in Dickens's time. Pickwick sets out for Ipswich from the Bull Inn (*Pickwick*, 20, 22); Joe Willet has dinner at the Black Lion (*Rudge*, 13); David first arrives in London at the Blue Boar (*Copperfield*, 5). Oliver is taken to a house in Whitechapel after being recaptured by Nancy and Sikes (*Twist*, 19).

White Conduit House   This popular resort in PENTONVILLE was the site of the annual dinner for the chimney sweeps (*Boz*, "First of May"). Miss Amelia Martin makes her disastrous debut as a singer here (*Boz*, "Mistaken Milliner").

Whitefriars   A slum in Dickens's time, this area between FLEET STREET and the TEMPLE was one of the places where the drunkard lived (*Boz*, "Drunkard's Death"). Jerry Cruncher's lodgings are in HANGING-SWORD ALLEY (*Two Cities*, II:1). Pip gets Wemmick's warning not to go home at the Whitefriars gate to the Temple (*Expectations*, 44).

Whitehall   Street running from Trafalgar Square to Parliament Square. Jingle alludes to the beheading of King Charles I as the coach passes Whitehall Palace (*Pickwick*, 2). John Harmon sees a notice announcing the discovery of his body at the Metropolitan Police Headquarters in Whitehall Place (*Mutual Friend*, II:13).

Whitehead, Charles (1804–1862)   Novelist, poet, literary editor, friend of Dickens. His burlesque novel, *The Autobiography of Jack Ketch* (1834), brought him recognition and an invitation from CHAPMAN & HALL, which he declined, to be part of the project that eventually became *Pickwick Papers*. He recognized the quality of Dickens's early sketches and asked him to write for the LIBRARY OF FICTION, a monthly periodical he edited for Chapman & Hall. Dickens contributed "The Tuggses at Ramsgate." Whitehead later published in BENTLEY'S MISCELLANY the novel *Richard Savage* (1842), a book much admired by Dickens.

White Horse Cellar   Coaching inn in PICCADILLY where the Pickwickians depart for BATH (*Pickwick*, 35) and where Esther Summerson arrives from Reading (*Bleak House*, 3).

Doré's rendering of Dick Whittington listening to the Bow Bells calling him back to the City of London.

Whittington, Richard (Dick) (d. 1423)   LORD MAYOR of London who is associated with the legend of Dick Whittington and his cat. According to the story, Dick, while working as a servant to Mr. Fitzwarren, sent his cat, the only thing he owned, on one of his master's trading vessels. The cat saved the king of Barbary from a plague of rats and was purchased for an enormous sum, but meanwhile Dick had run away from mistreatment as a servant in Fitzwarren's kitchen. Stopping to rest at HIGHGATE, he heard the Bow Bells ringing, calling him to "turn again" and go back to Fitzwarren's house. He did so, received payment for his cat, and became a wealthy businessman and eventually lord mayor.

Dickens refers to this legend frequently in the novels; it is central to the story of Walter Gay, who is compared to Whittington in his employment and whose story resembles Whittington's (*Dombey*, 4, 6, 9). See also *Curiosity Shop* (50), *Rudge* (31), *Chuzzlewit* (7), *Copperfield* (48), *Bleak House* (6, 31), and *Dorrit* (II:12).

Wilkie, Sir David (1785–1841) Scottish genre and portrait painter; godfather of WILKIE COLLINS; friend of Dickens. Dickens was often compared to Wilkie, an artist known for his renderings of common people in their everyday lives. He had at least one of Wilkie's paintings at GAD'S HILL PLACE. In a tribute to Wilkie on the painter's death, Dickens spoke of him as one "who made the cottage hearth his grave theme, and who surrounded the lives, and cares, and daily toils, and occupations of the poor, with dignity and beauty."

Williams, Bransby (1870–1961) British actor, playwright, music hall performer. Williams began his career performing Dickens characters in music hall sketches in the 1890s and continued performing in these sketches and in numerous other Dickensian theatrical roles until the 1950s. Among the many Dickensian roles that he played on stage were Fagin (1909), Micawber and Daniel Peggotty (1921), and Magwitch (1947). In silent films he played Buzfuz in THOMAS BENTLEY's *Adventures of Mr. Pickwick* (1921) and Gradgrind in Bentley's *Hard Times* (1915). He was the English LIONEL BARRYMORE, playing Scrooge almost annually on BBC radio. He did readings of the *Carol* in which he performed all the roles, and he played Scrooge on BBC television (1946, 1950). As a playwright, he adapted plays from *Rudge*, *Dombey*, *Two Cities*, *Twist*, and *Copperfield*. In 1925, he founded the Tabard Players, a professional troupe devoted to the production of Dickens on stage.

Williams, Emlyn (1905–1987) Welsh actor, director, and writer, whose one-man show playing Dickens performing the PUBLIC READINGS began in 1951. He said of his inspiration for the performance, "I got the idea from Charles Dickens in 1951. . . . I was reading his autobiography [proba-

bly JOHNSON's biography], and I suddenly thought I'll dress up as Dickens and do what he did—tell a story from one of his books." In 1952 he wrote and performed a version of *Bleak House* in which he played all 35 characters. Williams later developed performances from Dickens's reading texts and from readings he himself extracted from the novels. By 1979 he had performed Dickens almost 2,000 times.

Williams, Raymond (1921–1988) Professor, Cambridge; Marxist critic and theorist, best known for *Culture and Society, 1780–1950* (1951) and *Keywords* (1976). In *The English Novel from Dickens to Lawrence* (1970), Williams saw Dickens, who developed characters and a literary form particularly adapted to express a new urban consciousness, as the defining figure in the novel as it responded to industrialization and urbanization. Williams also discussed Dickens in *The Country and the City* (1973) and wrote introductions to *Dombey* (1970) and *Hard Times* (1966).

Williams, Samuel (1788–1853) Wood engraver and illustrator who contributed one illustration for *Curiosity Shop*, "The child in her gentle slumber," and engraved illustrations by HABLOT KNIGHT BROWNE and GEORGE CATTERMOLE.

Samuel Williams's illustration "The Child in Her Gentle Slumber" for the opening number of *The Old Curiosity Shop* foreshadowed Cattermole's later picture of Nell on her deathbed (see illustration on page 256).

Wills, William Henry (1810–1880) Journalist and editor, Wills contributed to BENTLEY'S MIS-CELLANY when Dickens was editor and became Dickens's secretary at the DAILY NEWS. He served as the "sub-editor" and part owner of both HOUSE-HOLD WORDS and ALL THE YEAR ROUND, taking responsibility for the day-to-day operation of both periodicals. Dickens described him as having "no genius, and [being], in literary matters, sufficiently commonplace to represent a very large proportion of our readers." The two complemented each other nicely and became intimate friends as well as business associates. Wills, who was privy to Dickens's affair with ELLEN TERNAN, was a loyal and discreet friend who fully deserved Dickens's tribute: "we doubt whether any two men can have gone on more happily, and smoothly, or with greater trust and confidence in each other."

Wilson, Angus (1913–1991) British novelist, critic; best known for *Hemlock and After* (1952) and *Anglo-Saxon Attitudes* (1956). His fiction is often compared to Dickens's, especially its characters. In "Charles Dickens: A Haunting" (*Critical Quarterly*, 1960), Wilson describes the hold his childhood reading of Dickens had on his imagination. His critical introduction to *The World of Charles Dickens* (1970) discusses Dickens's career chronologically, fitting its perceptive commentaries on the individual novels into a broad and sympathetic treatment of Dickens's life and career. His introductions to the Penguin *Twist* (1966) and *Drood* (1974) and the Signet *Expectations* (1963) similarly combine solid information about the author and texts with sympathetic and sharp criticism. Noteworthy among Wilson's many essays on Dickens and his works are "Dickens on Children and Childhood" (in *Dickens 1970*, edited by MICHAEL SLATER, 1970), "Heroes and Heroines of Dickens" (*Dickens and the Twentieth Century*, edited by John Gross and Gabriel Pearson, 1962), and "Dickens and Dostoyevsky" (*Dickensian*, 1970).

Wilson, Edmund (1895–1972) American literary critic, novelist, playwright, poet, and social commentator. Wilson's essay "Dickens: The Two Scrooges" (a 1939 lecture, printed in *The Wound and the Bow*, 1941) established the modern critical

approaches to Dickens and, as ADA NISBET (1964) points out, made it "customary to refer to individual critics as pre- or post-Wilsonian." Wilson challenged the modernists, who viewed Dickens as a vulgar entertainer, with a Dostoevskian Dickens, divided between bourgeois optimism and deep personal pain and social despair. Wilson found this dualism, engendered by Dickens's childhood experiences in the BLACKING WAREHOUSE, running through his works but most profoundly expressed in the dark later novels.

Windsor, Berkshire Esther Summerson's unhappy childhood home (*Bleak House*, 1); site of some of John Podger's 17th-century adventures in Pickwick's tale (*Humphrey*).

Winter, Mrs. Henry Married name of MARIA BEADNELL.

Winterbourne House at BONCHURCH, Isle of Wight, where Dickens spent the summer of 1849.

Wisdom of Our Ancestors General title for a series of fake books that Dickens had constructed for his library at GAD'S HILL PLACE. The individual volumes were entitled I. Ignorance, II. Superstition, III. The Block, IV. The Stake, V. The Rack, VI. Dirt, VII. Disease.

wood engraving Technique for printing illustrations that became increasingly widespread during Dickens's career. Dickens's primary illustrators—HABLOT KNIGHT BROWNE and GEORGE CRUIKSHANK—had their drawings etched onto steel plates from which they were printed, a technique widely used in the 1830s. Beginning in the 1840s, etching on steel was gradually replaced by wood engraving, in which the picture was cut into the end grain of a hardwood like boxwood or peartree. Firms of engravers like Dalziel Brothers, who produced the engravings for the HOUSEHOLD EDITION, could quickly produce the blocks from an artist's drawings.

Wooden Midshipman, the Wooden figure that acts as the sign for Sol Gill's nautical instrument shop (*Dombey*). Dickens based the effigy in his novel on one outside a shop in LEADENHALL STREET, which can now be seen in the DICKENS HOUSE MUSEUM. The latter figure is mentioned by the Traveller in *Uncommercial* (3).

Wood Street   Street in the CITY where the CROSS KEYS INN is located. This coaching inn was the terminal for coaches to and from ROCHESTER. Pip arrives in London and leaves again from this inn (*Expectations*, 20, 32). Cavaletto is run down by a fast mail coach in this street (*Dorrit*, I:13).

workhouse   Institution for housing the poor, often referred to as Union Workhouses after the NEW POOR LAW of 1834, which divided the country into several districts, each uniting several parishes into a single unit with one workhouse.

Wright's Inn   Hotel next to the BULL INN in ROCHESTER, described by Jingle as "very dear—half-a-crown in the bill if you look at the waiter" (*Pickwick*, 2). It is the original of the Crozier in Cloisterham in *Drood* (18).

Y

Yale University The Yale Dickens collection includes manuscripts for *Mudfog Papers*, several short articles and sketches, and several hundred letters.

Yates, Edmund (1831–1894) Journalist, novelist, and dramatist; contributor to ALL THE YEAR ROUND. Yates met Dickens in 1854 and became an intimate friend and protégé of the novelist. His nomination to the GARRICK CLUB led to Dickens's dispute with WILLIAM MAKEPEACE THACKERAY. With B. R. Brough, Yates wrote a parody of *Hard Times*. In 1872, Yates toured America giving lectures that included his reminiscences of Dickens.

Yates, Frederick (1797–1842) Actor, theater owner, manager and director at the ADELPHI THEATRE; father of EDMUND YATES; friend of Dickens. He directed and acted in several early adaptations of Dickens's novels, playing Pickwick, Mantalini, Fagin, Quilp, and Sir John Chester. **Mrs. Yates,** Frederick's wife, an actress who played Nancy in *Twist*, Dolly Varden, and the widow Rudge, said after seeing Dickens perform in *The Lighthouse*, "O Mr Dickens what a pity it is you can do anything else!"

York Setting for the tale "The Five Sisters of York" (*Nickleby*, 6). John Chivery goes to York when he is seeking information on the Dorrit family fortune (*Dorrit*, I:25).

Yorkshire Dickens stayed at the George and New Inn at GRETA BRIDGE in 1838 when he was in Yorkshire with HABLOT KNIGHT BROWNE gathering information on YORKSHIRE SCHOOLS for *Nickleby*. The inn serves as the coach stop for Dotheboys Hall (*Nickleby*, 6) and was probably also the model for the Holly Tree Inn. Allan and Esther Woodcourt's new Bleak House is also located in Yorkshire (64).

Yorkshire schools These notorious schools charged cheap fees and were used as dumping grounds for illegitimate and unwanted children. The schools garnered such children by advertising "no extra charges" and "no vacations." At the 1823 trial of WILLIAM SHAW for the gross neglect of students at his school at Bowes, where two children had become totally blind from infection, testimony revealed that the boys were served maggoty food, beaten, denied medical treatment, and housed five to a bed. Dickens began *Nickleby* with the idea of exposing such schools through the example of Dotheboys Hall. He traveled to YORKSHIRE and, posing as a client, interviewed Shaw while preparing to write the novel.

PART IV

Appendices

CHRONOLOGY OF DICKENS'S LIFE AND MAJOR WORKS

Publication dates are those for the first complete editions.

1812
Dickens born at Portsmouth.

1814
John Dickens, the novelist's father, transferred to London.

1817
John Dickens transferred to Chatham in Kent, where Charles spent the happiest years of his boyhood.

1821
Charles begins his education at William Giles's school in Chatham.

1822
John Dickens transferred to London.

1824
John Dickens arrested for debt and imprisoned in the King's Bench and then the Marshalsea prisons. Dickens employed at the blacking warehouse. After his father's release from prison, Dickens enters Wellington House Academy.

1827
When his father again gets into financial difficulty, Dickens is withdrawn from Wellington House. He goes to work for the firm of Ellis and Blackmore as a solicitor's clerk.

1829
Dickens learns shorthand and works as a freelance court reporter at Doctor's Commons.

1830
After his 18th birthday, Dickens secures a reader's ticket to the British Museum. He meets Maria Beadnell.

1831
Dickens works as a parliamentary reporter for *Mirror of Parliament*.

1832
Dickens works as a reporter for the *True Sun*. Illness prevents him from attending an audition at Covent Garden Theatre. He courts Maria Beadnell.

1833
Dickens breaks off his romance with Maria Beadnell. In December, his first story, "A Dinner at Poplar Walk," is published in the *Monthly Magazine*.

1834
Dickens goes to work as a reporter on the *Morning Chronicle* and continues to publish stories and sketches in various London papers and magazines. He meets Catherine Hogarth.

1835
Dickens contributes series of sketches to the *Evening Chronicle* and *Bell's Life in London*. He is engaged to Catherine Hogarth.

1836

Sketches by Boz, first and second series. In March, *Pickwick* begins its serial run. Dickens and Catherine are married in April. Two short plays by Dickens, *The Strange Gentleman* and *The Village Coquettes,* are produced at the St. James's Theatre. Dickens meets John Forster.

1837

The Pickwick Papers. Bentley's Miscellany begins publication with Dickens as editor. Dickens's first child, Charles Culliford Boz, is born. The Dickens family moves to 48 Doughty Street. In May, Mary Hogarth dies and Dickens suspends publication of the monthly numbers of *Pickwick* and *Twist* for the month of June. Dickens is elected to the Garrick Club.

1838

Oliver Twist; Sketches of Young Gentlemen; Memoirs of Grimaldi. Dickens and Hablot Knight Browne make an expedition to investigate Yorkshire schools. Dickens is elected to the Athenaeum Club.

1839

Nicholas Nickleby. Dickens resigns as editor of *Bentley's Miscellany.* The Dickens family takes its first holiday at Broadstairs and, in December, moves to Devonshire Terrace.

1840

Master Humphrey's Clock, vol. I; *Sketches of Young Couples.*

1841

Master Humphrey's Clock, vol. II; *The Old Curiosity Shop; Barnaby Rudge.* Dickens declines an invitation to run for Parliament as the Liberal candidate for Reading. Dickens and Catherine tour Scotland. In October, Dickens falls ill and undergoes an operation for a fistula.

1842

American Notes. Dickens and Catherine tour America, leaving in January and returning to England in July.

1843

A Christmas Carol. In October, Dickens presides at the inauguration of the Athenaeum Club in Manchester. While he is there, he conceives the idea for *Carol.*

1844

Martin Chuzzlewit; The Chimes. Dickens changes publishers from Chapman & Hall to Bradbury & Evans. In July, the Dickens family travels to Genoa, Italy, for a stay of nearly a year. In December, Dickens returns to London to read *The Chimes* to a gathering of friends.

1845

The Cricket on the Hearth. The Dickens family returns to England in June. The first of Dickens's amateur theatricals, a production of Ben Jonson's *Every Man in His Humour,* is staged at Frances Kelly's theater in September.

1846

Pictures from Italy; The Battle of Life. Dickens briefly serves as editor of a new Liberal newspaper, the *Daily News.* The Dickens family spends the summer and autumn in Switzerland and France. Dickens writes *The Life of Our Lord* for his children.

1847

The Cheap Edition, the first collected edition of Dickens's works, begins publication in monthly parts and separate volumes, published jointly by Chapman & Hall and Bradbury & Evans. The Dickens family returns to London from Paris in February. The amateur theatrical troupe tours to Manchester and Liverpool.

1848

Dombey and Son; The Haunted Man. In April the theatrical troupe gives several performances in London to benefit the effort to preserve Shakespeare's birthplace. From April to July, they tour several towns in the north of England and Scotland. Dickens's sister Frances (Fanny) dies.

1849

Dickens conceives the idea for a weekly magazine. He and his family spend the summer at

Broadstairs and then at Bonchurch on the Isle of Wight.

1850

David Copperfield. The first issue of *Household Words* appears in March. Dickens and Lytton create the Guild of Literature and Art, and the first theatrical performances to benefit the group are held at Knebworth.

1851

Catherine Dickens suffers a nervous breakdown in March; Dickens's father dies at the end of that month, and his infant daughter, Dora Annie, dies in April. The Dickens family moves to Tavistock House from Devonshire Terrace.

1852

A Child's History of England, vol. I; *Christmas Books* collected for the first time for the Cheap Edition. The theatrical troupe tours the Midlands performing Lytton's *Not So Bad as We Seem.* The Dickenses take their first holiday at Boulogne.

1853

Bleak House; A Child's History of England, vol. II. Dickens spends the summer at Boulogne; in the autumn he tours Italy with Wilkie Collins and Augustus Egg. In December he gives his first public reading, a benefit performance of *Carol* in Birmingham.

1854

Hard Times; A Child's History of England, vol. III. In January, Dickens visits Preston in preparation for writing about industrial England.

1855

Dickens visits Paris with Collins in February and returns to that city in November with his family to spend six months there. He has a disillusioning reunion with Maria Beadnell, now the garrulous and middle-aged Mrs. Winter.

1856

Dickens purchases Gad's Hill Place.

1857

Little Dorrit; The Lazy Tour of Two Idle Apprentices. Dickens's personal life is troubled by growing marital discord. Dickens takes possession of Gad's Hill Place. After performing in Collins's *The Frozen Deep* at Tavistock House in January, Dickens takes the play to Manchester in August using professional actresses, among them Ellen Ternan. In September, Dickens and Collins tour through the north of England, a trip described in *The Lazy Tour.*

1858

Reprinted Pieces, a collection of articles from *Household Words,* first appears as a volume in the Library Edition of Dickens's works. In May, Dickens and Catherine separate. Dickens quarrels with Bradbury & Evans when they refuse to publish his statement "Personal." Dickens begins public readings for his own benefit, first in London in April and, later in the year, on a tour of Britain, giving 87 readings at 44 different sites.

1859

A Tale of Two Cities; Hunted Down. Dickens leaves Bradbury & Evans and returns to Chapman & Hall, suspending publication of *Household Words* and beginning a new weekly magazine, *All the Year Round.* Dickens moves to Gad's Hill with his younger children and with Georgina Hogarth as his housekeeper.

1861

Great Expectations; The Uncommercial Traveller, first collection. Dickens makes an extensive reading tour throughout England during the fall. His son Charley marries Bessie Evans, daughter of his former publisher.

1862

Dickens gives a series of readings in London in June. He goes to Paris with Georgina Hogarth and his daughter Mamie for the winter.

1863

Dickens is saddened by the deaths of his mother, William Makepeace Thackeray, and his son Walter.

1865

Our Mutual Friend; The Uncommercial Traveller, second collection. Dickens suffers from lameness in his left foot. Returning from a holiday in Paris with Ellen Ternan, Dickens escapes injury in the Staplehurst railway accident.

1866

Although suffering from pain and exhaustion, Dickens makes an extensive reading tour during the spring and early summer.

1867

The first volumes in the Charles Dickens Edition of Dickens's works appear, an edition containing new prefaces and headlines for the pages and the last edition published during Dickens's lifetime. After an exhausting provincial reading tour in the winter and spring, Dickens agrees, against the advice of Forster, to undertake an American reading tour late in the year. Early in November, he sets out from Liverpool for Boston.

1868

Troubled by a persistent cold and worn down by travel, Dickens nonetheless makes a triumphant tour of America, returning to England in May. On an English reading tour in the fall, he gives his first performance of "Sikes and Nancy."

1869

Although his doctor urges him to discontinue the readings, particularly the performances of "Sikes and Nancy," Dickens persists until April, when illness forces him to return home.

1870

The Mystery of Edwin Drood. Despite failing health, Dickens undertakes a farewell series of readings at the beginning of the year. On March 9, he is received by Queen Victoria at Buckingham Palace; a week later, on March 15, he gives his final reading, a performance of *Carol.* On June 8, after working on the sixth number of *Edwin Drood,* Dickens falls ill and dies the next day. He is buried in the Poets' Corner in Westminster Abbey on June 14.

1872–74

Forster publishes *The Life of Charles Dickens.*

1874

Christmas Stories, the collection containing the Christmas writings of Dickens for *Household Words* and *All the Year Round,* appears as a volume in the Charles Dickens Edition.

1880

The Mudfog Papers, a collection of stories, sketches, and essays originally published in *Bentley's Miscellany.*

1908

Miscellaneous Papers, ed. B. W. Matz, two vols., a collection of Dickens's periodical essays, plays, and poems, assembled for the Gadshill Edition of Dickens's works.

Dickens's Major Works

(Listed chronologically; date of first edition.)

Sketches by Boz, 1836
Pickwick Papers, 1837
Oliver Twist, 1838.
Sketches of Young Gentlemen, 1838
Nicholas Nickleby, 1839
Sketches of Young Couples, 1840
The Old Curiosity Shop, 1841
Barnaby Rudge, 1841
Master Humphrey's Clock, 1841
American Notes, 1842
A Christmas Carol, 1843
Martin Chuzzlewit, 1844
The Chimes, 1844
The Cricket on the Hearth, 1845
Pictures from Italy, 1846
The Battle of Life, 1846
Dombey and Son, 1848
The Haunted Man, 1848
David Copperfield, 1850
Christmas Books, 1852
Bleak House, 1853
A Child's History of England, 1854

Hard Times, 1854
Little Dorrit, 1857
Lazy Tour of Two Idle Apprentices, 1857 (with Wilkie Collins)
Reprinted Pieces, 1858
A Tale of Two Cities, 1859
The Uncommercial Traveller, 1860
Great Expectations, 1861
Our Mutual Friend, 1867
No Thoroughfare, 1867 (with Wilkie Collins)
George Silverman's Explanation, 1868
Holiday Romance, 1868
The Mystery of Edwin Drood, 1870
Christmas Stories, 1871
Miscellaneous Papers, Plays and Poems, 1908 (edited by B. W. Matz)
Speeches of Charles Dickens, 1960 (edited by K. J. Fielding)
Uncollected Writings from "Household Words" 1850–1859, 1968 (edited by Harry Stone)
The Letters of Charles Dickens, 1965–2002 (edited by House, Storey, and Tillotson)
Dickens' Journalism, 1992–1998 (edited by Slater and Drew)

SECONDARY SOURCE BIBLIOGRAPHY

Ackroyd, Peter. *Dickens*. Sinclair-Stevenson, 1990. [biography]

———. *Dickens: Public Life and Private Passion*. London: BBC, 2003. [biography]

———. *Introduction to Dickens*. London: Sinclair-Stevenson, 1991.

Adrian, Arthur. *Dickens and the Parent-Child Relationship*. Athens: Ohio University Press, 1984.

———. *Georgina Hogarth and the Dickens Circle*. London: Oxford University Press, 1957. [biography]

Alexander, Doris. *Creating Characters with Charles Dickens*. University Park: Pennsylvania State University Press, 1991.

Allen, Michael. *Charles Dickens' Childhood*. London: Macmillan, 1988. [biography]

Allingham, Philip V. "The Names of Dickens's American Originals in *Martin Chuzzlewit*," *Dickens Quarterly*, 7 (September 1990): 329–337.

Altick, Richard. "Education, Print and Paper in *Our Mutual Friend*." In *Nineteenth-Century Literary Perspectives: Essays in Honor of Lionel Stevenson*, edited by Clyde de L. Ryals, 237–254. Durham, N.C.: Duke University Press, 1974.

Andrews, Malcolm. *Dickens and the Grown-Up Child*. Iowa City: University of Iowa Press, 1994.

———. *Dickens on England and the English*. New York: Barnes and Noble, 1979.

Arac, Jonathan. *Commissioned Spirits: The Shaping of Social Motion in Dickens, Carlyle, Melville, and Hawthorne*. New Brunswick, N.J.: Rutgers University Press, 1979.

Auden, W. H. "Dingley Dell and the Fleet." In *The Dyer's Hand*, 407–428. New York: Random House, 1962.

Auerbach, Nina. "Dickens and Dombey, a Daughter after All," *Dickens Studies Annual*, 5 (1976): 49–67.

———. *Woman and the Demon*. Cambridge, Mass.: Harvard University Press, 1982.

Axton, William. *Circle of Fire*. Lexington: University of Kentucky Press, 1966.

———. "Keystone Structure in Dickens's Serial Novels," *University of Toronto Quarterly* 37 (1967): 31–50.

Aylmer, Felix. *Dickens Incognito*. London: Rupert Hart-Davis, 1959.

———. *The Drood Case*. London: Rupert Hart-Davis, 1964.

Barret, Edwin B. "*Little Dorrit* and the Disease of Modern Life," *Nineteenth Century Fiction* 25 (1970): 199–215.

Baumgarten, Murray. "Writing the Revolution," *Dickens Studies Annual* 12 (1983): 161–176.

Bayley, John. "*Oliver Twist*: 'Things as they really are.'" In *Dickens and the Twentieth Century*, edited by John Gross and Gabriel Pearson, 49–64. London: Routledge, 1962.

Bentley, Nicholas, Michael Slater, and Nina Burgis. *The Dickens Index*. New York: Oxford University Press, 1988.

Bergonzi, Bernard. "*Nicholas Nickleby*." In *Dickens and the Twentieth Century*, edited by John Gross and Gabriel Pearson, 65–76. London: Routledge, 1963.

Bloom, Harold, ed. *Bleak House: Modern Critical Interpretations*. New York: Chelsea, 1987.

———, ed. *Great Expectations: Modern Critical Interpretations*. New York: Chelsea, 2000.

Blout, Trevor. "Dickens and Mr. Krook's Spontaneous Combustion," *Dickens Studies Annual* 1 (1970): 183–211.

Bolton, H. Philip. *Dickens Dramatized*. Boston: G. K. Hall, 1987. [bibliography]

Bowen, John. *Other Dickens: Pickwick to Chuzzlewit*. New York: Oxford University Press, 2000.

Bowen, John, and Robert Patten, eds. *Palgrave Advances in Charles Dickens Studies*. Basingstoke, England: Palgrave Macmillan, 2006.

Brook, G. L. *The Language of Dickens*. London: Andre Deutsch, 1970.

Brooks, Chris. *Signs for the Times*. London: Allen and Unwin, 1984.

Brooks, Peter. "Repetition, Repression, and Returns: The Plotting of *Great Expectations*." In *Reading for the Plot: Design and Intention in Narrative*, 113–142. New York: Knopf, 1984.

Buckley, Jerome. *Season of Youth*. Cambridge, Mass.: Harvard University Press, 1974.

Budd, Dona. "Language Couples in *Bleak House*," *Nineteenth Century Literature* 49 (1994): 196–220.

Butt, John, and Kathleen Tillotson. *Dickens at Work*. London: Methuen, 1957.

Carey, John. *The Violent Effigy: A Study in Dickens' Imagination*. London: Faber and Faber, 1973.

Carlisle, Janice. *Common Scents: Comparative Encounters in High-Victorian Fiction*. Oxford: Oxford University Press, 2004.

———, ed. *Great Expectations*. New York: Bedford/St. Martin's, 1996.

———. *The Sense of an Audience: Dickens, Thackeray, and George Eliot*. Athens: University of Georgia Press, 1987.

Carlton, William J. *Dickens, Shorthand Writer*. London: Palmer, 1926.

Carolan, Katherine. "Dickens' Last Christmases," *Dalhousie Review* 52 (1972): 373–383.

Chase, Karen. *Eros and Psyche: The Representation of Personality in Charlotte Bronte, Charles Dickens, and George Eliot*. New York: Methuen, 1984.

Chesterton, G. K. *Appreciations and Criticisms of the Works of Charles Dickens*. London: Dent, 1911.

———. *Charles Dickens*. London: Hodder and Stoughton, 1903.

———. *Charles Dickens: A Critical Study*. London: Methuen, 1906.

Chittick, Kathryn. *Dickens and the 1830s*. New York: Cambridge University Press, 1990.

Churchill, R. C. *A Bibliography of Dickensian Criticism, 1836–1975*. New York: Garland, 1975. [bibliography]

———. "The Genius of Charles Dickens." In *The New Pelican Guide to English Literature* [1958]. Vol.

6: *From Dickens to Hardy*, edited by Boris Ford, 117–138. London: Penguin, 1982.

Cohen, Jane R. *Charles Dickens and His Original Illustrators*. Columbus: Ohio State University Press, 1980.

Collins, Philip. "Charles Dickens." In *New Cambridge Bibliography of English Literature*. Cambridge: Cambridge University Press, 1969. [bibliography]

———. "Charles Dickens." In *Victorian Fiction: A Second Guide to Research*, edited by George H. Ford. New York: Modern Language Association of America, 1978. [bibliography]

———. *Charles Dickens: David Copperfield*. London: Edward Arnold, 1977.

———. *Dickens and Crime*. London: Macmillan, 1962.

———. *Dickens and Education*. London: Macmillan, 1963.

———, ed. *Dickens: Interviews and Recollections*. 2 vols. London: Macmillan, 1981.

———, ed. *Dickens: The Critical Heritage*. London: Routledge & Kegan Paul, 1971.

———, ed. *The Public Readings*. Oxford: Clarendon Press, 1975.

———. "Some Narrative Devices in *Bleak House*," *Dickens Studies Annual* 19 (1990): 125–146.

———, and Edward Guiliano, eds. *The Annotated Dickens*. 2 vols. New York: Potter, 1986.

Connor, Steven, ed. *Charles Dickens*. London; New York: Longman, 1996.

———. *Charles Dickens*. Rereading Literature. New York: Blackwell, 1985.

———. "Dead? or Alive? *Edwin Drood* and the Work of Mourning," *Dickensian* 89 (1993): 85–102.

———. "'They're All in One Story': Public and Private Narratives in *Oliver Twist*," *Dickensian* 85 (1989): 3–16.

Coolidge, Archibald C. *Dickens as a Serial Novelist*. Ames: Iowa State University Press, 1967.

Cotsell, Michael A. *Critical Essays on Charles Dickens's A Tale of Two Cities*. New York: Gale, 1998.

Coveney, Peter. *Poor Monkey, the Child in Literature*. London: Barrie and Rockliff, 1957.

Crotch, W. Walter. *Charles Dickens, Social Reformer*. London: Chapman and Hall, 1913.

Dabney, Ross H. *Love and Property in the Novels of Dickens*. Berkeley: University of California Press, 1967.

Daldry, Graham. *Charles Dickens and the Form of the Novel.* Totowa, N.J.: Barnes and Noble, 1987.

Daleski, H. M. *Dickens and the Art of Analogy.* London: Faber and Faber, 1970.

David, Deirdre. *Rule Britannia: Women, Empire, and Victorian Writing.* Ithaca, N.Y.: Cornell University Press, 1995.

Davies, James A. *John Forster: A Literary Life.* Totowa, N.J.: Barnes and Noble, 1983.

———. *The Textual Life of Dickens's Characters.* New York: Barnes and Noble, 1990.

Davis, Earle R. *The Flint and the Flame: The Artistry of Charles Dickens.* Columbia: University of Missouri Press, 1963.

Davis, Paul. "Imaging Oliver Twist: Hogarth, Illustration, and the Part of Darkness," *Dickensian* 82 (1986): 158–176.

———. *The Lives and Times of Ebenezer Scrooge.* New Haven, Conn.: Yale University Press, 1990.

DeVries, Duane. *Dickens's Apprentice Years: The Making of a Novelist.* New York: Barnes and Noble, 1976.

Dickens, Charles. *The Speeches of Charles Dickens.* Edited by K. J. Fielding. Oxford: Clarendon Press, 1960. Hemel Hempstead, England: Harvester, Wheatsheaf, 1988.

Dolby, George. *Charles Dickens as I Knew Him: The Story of the Reading Tours, 1866–1870.* London: Fisher Unwin, 1885.

Donoghue, Denis. "The English Dickens and *Dombey and Son*," *Nineteenth Century Fiction* 24 (1970): 383–403.

Donovan, Frank. *Dickens and Youth.* New York: Dodd, Mead, 1968.

Drew, John. *Dickens the Journalist.* New York: Palgrave Macmillan, 2003.

Duffield, Howard. "John Jasper—Strangler," *American Bookman* 70 (1930): 581–588.

Duncan, Ian. *Modern Romance and Transformations of the Novel.* Cambridge: Cambridge University Press, 1992.

Dunn, Richard J. *Oliver Twist: Whole Heart and Soul.* New York: Twayne, 1993.

Dyson, A. E., ed. *Dickens' Bleak House: A Casebook.* London: Macmillan, 1969.

———, ed. *Dickens: Modern Judgements.* London: Macmillan, 1968.

———. *The Inimitable Dickens.* London: Macmillan, 1970.

Eckel, J. C. *The First Editions of the Writings of Charles Dickens.* London: Chapman and Hall, 1932. [bibliography]

Eigner, Edwin. *The Dickens Pantomime.* Berkeley: University of California Press, 1989.

———. *The Metaphysical Novel in England and America: Dickens, Bulwer, Melville, and Hawthorne.* Berkeley: University of California Press, 1978.

Eisenstein, Sergei. "Dickens, Griffith, and the Film Today." In *Film Form.* New York: Harcourt, 1949.

Eliot, T. S. "Wilkie Collins and Dickens" [1932]. In *Selected Essays*, 460–470. London: Faber and Faber, 1951.

Elsna, Hebe. *Unwanted Wife: A Defence of Mrs. Charles Dickens.* London: Jarrolds, 1963.

Engel, Monroe. *The Maturity of Dickens.* Cambridge, Mass.: Harvard University Press, 1959.

Epstein, Norrie. *The Friendly Dickens.* New York: Viking, 1998.

Fanger, Donald. *Dostoevsky and Romantic Realism.* Cambridge, Mass.: Harvard University Press, 1965.

Fawcett, F. Dubrez. *Dickens the Dramatist.* London: Allen, 1952.

Fenstermaker, John J. *Charles Dickens, 1940–1975: An Analytical Subject Index to Periodical Criticism of the Novels and Christmas Books.* Boston: G. K. Hall, 1979. [bibliography]

Fielding, K. J. "Benthamite Utilitarianism and *Oliver Twist*: A Novel of Ideas," *Dickens Quarterly* 4 (1987): 49–65.

———. *Charles Dickens: A Critical Introduction.* 1958. 2nd ed. London: Longman's, Green, 1965.

Findlater, Richard, ed. *Memoirs of Grimaldi, by Charles Dickens.* London: Macgibbon and Kee, 1968.

Fleishman, Avrom. *The English Historical Novel.* Baltimore: Johns Hopkins University Press, 1971.

Flint, Kate. *Dickens.* Brighton, Sussex: Harvester, 1986.

Ford, George. *Dickens and His Readers: Aspects of Novel Criticism since 1836.* Princeton, N.J.: Princeton University Press, 1955.

———, and Lauriat Lane Jr., eds. *The Dickens Critics.* Ithaca, N.Y.: Cornell University Press, 1961.

————, and S. Monod, eds. *Bleak House*. New York: Norton, 1977.

————, and S. Monod, eds. *Hard Times*. New York: Norton, 1966.

Forster, E. M. *Aspects of the Novel*. New York: Harcourt, 1927.

Forster, John. *The Life of Charles Dickens*. London: Chapman and Hall, 1872–74.

Forsyte, Charles. *The Decoding of Edwin Drood*. New York: Scribner's, 1980.

Fowler, Roger. "The Politics of Barnaby Rudge." In *The Changing World of Charles Dickens*, edited by R. Giddings, 51–74. London: Routledge, 1989.

Frank, Lawrence. *Charles Dickens and the Romantic Self*. Lincoln: University of Nebraska Press, 1984.

Fruttero, Carlo, and Franco Lucentini. *The D. Case or the Truth about The Mystery of Edwin Drood*. New York: Harcourt, 1992.

Frye, Northrop. "Dickens and the Comedy of Humours." In *The Stubborn Structure*, 218–240. Ithaca, N.Y.: Cornell University Press, 1970.

Furbank, P. N. Introduction to *Martin Chuzzlewit*. Harmondsworth, U.K.: Penguin, 1968.

Gager, Valerie. *Dickens and Shakespeare: The Dynamics of Influence*. Cambridge: Cambridge University Press, 1996.

Garfield, Leon. *The Mystery of Edwin Drood Concluded*. New York: Pantheon, 1980.

Garis, Robert. *The Dickens Theatre*. Oxford: Clarendon Press, 1965.

Giddings, Robert, ed. *The Changing World of Charles Dickens*. New York: Barnes and Noble, 1983.

Gilbert, Elliot, ed. *Critical Essays on Charles Dickens's Bleak House*. London: Macmillan, 1989.

Gilmour, Robin. "The Gradgrind School: Political Economy in the Classroom," *Victorian Studies* 11 (1967): 207–224.

Gissing, George. *Charles Dickens: A Critical Study*. London: Blackie, 1898.

Gitter, Elisabeth G. "The Blind Daughter in Charles Dickens's *Cricket on the Hearth*," *Studies in English Literature, 1500–1900*, 39 (1999): 675–689.

Glancy, Ruth. *A Tale of Two Cities: Dickens's Revolutionary Novel*. New York: Twayne, 1991.

Glavin, John, ed. *Dickens on Screen*. Cambridge: Cambridge University Press, 2003.

Gold, Joseph. *Charles Dickens: Radical Moralist*. Minneapolis: University of Minnesota Press, 1972.

————, comp. *The Stature of Dickens: A Centenary Bibliography*. Toronto: University of Toronto Press, 1971.

Goldberg, Michael. *Carlyle and Dickens*. Athens: University of Georgia Press, 1972.

Golding, Robert. *Idiolects in Dickens: The Major Techniques and Chronological Development*. London: Macmillan, 1985.

Greaves, John. *Dickens at Doughty Street*. London: Elm Tree, 1975.

————. *Who's Who in Dickens*. London: Elm Tree, 1972.

Greene, Graham. Introduction to *Oliver Twist*. Reprinted as "The Young Dickens," in *The Lost Childhood and Other Essays*. London: Eyre and Spottiswoode, 1951, 51–57.

Grillo, Virgil. *Charles Dickens' Sketches by Boz: End in the Beginning*. Boulder: Colorado Associated University Press, 1974.

Gross, John, and Gabriel Pearson, eds. *Dickens and the Twentieth Century*. London: Routledge, 1962.

Guerard, Albert J. *The Triumph of the Novel: Dickens, Dostoevsky, Faulkner*. New York: Oxford University Press, 1976.

Guida, Fred. *A Christmas Carol and Its Adaptations: Dickens's Story on Screen and Television*. Jefferson, N.C.: McFarland, 2000.

Haining, Peter, ed. *The Complete Ghost Stories of Charles Dickens*. New York: Franklin Watts, 1983.

Harbage, Alfred B. *A Kind of Power: The Shakespeare-Dickens Analogy*. Philadelphia: American Philosophical Society, 1975.

Hardwick, Michael, and Mollie Hardwick. *The Charles Dickens Encyclopedia*. Reading, U.K.: Osprey, 1973.

————. *As They Saw Him … Charles Dickens: The Great Novelist as Seen through the Eyes of His Family, Friends and Contemporaries*. London: Harrap, 1970.

————. *The Charles Dickens Companion*. London: J. Murray, 1965.

————. *Dickens's England*. London: J. M. Dent, 1970.

Hardy, Barbara. *The Moral Art of Dickens*. London: Athlone Press, 1970.

Hartog, Dirk den. *Dickens and Romantic Psychology*. London: Macmillan, 1987.

Harvey, John. *Victorian Novelists and Their Illustrators.* London: Sidgewick and Jackson, 1971.

Hatton, T., and A. H. Cleaver. *A Bibliography of the Periodical Works of Dickens.* London: Chapman and Hall, 1933.

Hayward, Arthur L. *The Dickens Encyclopedia.* London: Routledge, 1924.

Herst, Beth. *The Dickens Hero; Selfhood and Alienation in the Dickens World.* London: Weidenfield and Nicolson, 1990.

Hewett, Edward, and W. F. Axton. *Convivial Dickens: The Drinks of Dickens and His Times.* Athens: Ohio University Press, 1983.

Hibbert, Christopher. *The Making of Charles Dickens.* New York: Harper and Row, 1967.

Holbrook, David. *Charles Dickens and the Image of Woman.* New York: New York University Press, 1993.

Hollington, Michael. *Dickens and the Grotesque.* London: Croom Helm, 1984.

Holloway, John. "*Hard Times*: A History and a Criticism." In *Dickens and the Twentieth Century,* edited by John Gross and Gabriel Pearson, 159–174. London: Routledge, 1962.

Holoch, George. "Consciousness and Society in *Little Dorrit,*" *Victorian Studies* 21 (1978): 335–351.

Hornback, Bert G. *Great Expectations: A Novel of Friendship.* New York: Twayne, 1987.

———. *"The Hero of My Life": Essays on Dickens.* Athens: Ohio University Press, 1981.

———. *Noah's Arkitecture: A Study of Dickens's Mythology.* Athens: Ohio University Press, 1972.

Horton, Susan. *Interpreting Interpreting: Interpreting Dickens's Dombey.* Baltimore: Johns Hopkins University Press, 1979.

———. *The Reader in the Dickens World: Style and Response.* Pittsburgh: University of Pittsburgh Press, 1981.

———. "Swivellers and Snivellers: Competing Epistemologies in *The Old Curiosity Shop,*" *Dickens Quarterly* 7 (1990): 212–217.

House, Humphry. *The Dickens World.* Oxford: Oxford University Press, 1941.

Houston, Gail Turley. *Consuming Fictions: Gender, Class, and Hunger in Dickens's Novels.* Carbondale: Southern Illinois University Press, 1994.

———. *From Dickens to Dracula: Gothic, Economics, and Victorian Fiction.* Cambridge; New York: Cambridge University Press, 2005.

———. *Royalties: The Queen and Victorian Writers.* Charlottesville: University Press of Virginia, 1999.

Hughes, Linda K., and Michael Lund. *The Victorian Serial.* Charlottesville: University Press of Virginia, 1991.

Hughes, Winifred. *The Maniac in the Cellar: Sensation Novels of the 1860s.* Princeton, N.J.: Princeton University Press, 1980.

Hunt, John Dixon. *Encounters: Essays on Literature and the Visual Arts.* New York: Norton, 1971.

Hutter, Albert D. "Dismemberment and Articulation in *Our Mutual Friend,*" *Dickens Studies Annual* 11 (1983): 135–175.

———. "The High Tower of His Mind: Psychoanalysis and the Reader of *Bleak House,*" *Criticism* 19 (1977): 296–316.

———. "Nation and Generation in *A Tale of Two Cities,*" *PMLA* 93 (1978): 448–462.

Jackson, Thomas A. *Charles Dickens: The Progress of a Radical.* London: Lawrence and Wishart, 1937.

Jacobson, Wendy S. *Companion to The Mystery of Edwin Drood.* London: Allen and Unwin, 1986.

Jaffe, Audrey. *Scenes of Sympathy: Identity and Repression in Victorian Fiction.* Ithaca, N.Y.: Cornell University Press, 2000.

———. *Vanishing Points: Dickens, Narrative, and the Subject of Omniscience.* Berkeley: University of California Press, 1991.

John, Juliet. *Charles Dickens's Oliver Twist: A Sourcebook.* New York: Routledge, 2005.

Johnson, Edgar. *Charles Dickens: His Tragedy and Triumph.* 2 vols. New York: Simon and Schuster, 1952. Reissued revised and abridged. New York: Viking, 1977. [biography]

———, ed. *The Heart of Charles Dickens, as Revealed in His Letters to Angela Burdett-Coutts.* New York: Sloan and Pearce, 1952.

———, and Eleanor Johnson. *The Dickens Theatrical Reader.* London: Victor Gollancz, 1964.

Jordan, John O., ed. *The Cambridge Companion to Charles Dickens.* New York: Cambridge University Press, 2001.

Kaplan, Fred. *Dickens.* New York: William Morrow, 1988. [biography]

———. *Dickens and Mesmerism.* Princeton, N.J.: Princeton University Press, 1975.

———. *Sacred Tears: Sentimentality in Victorian Fiction.* Princeton, N.J.: Princeton University Press, 1987.

Kettle, Arnold. *"Our Mutual Friend."* In *Dickens and the Twentieth Century,* edited by John Gross and Gabriel Pearson. London: Routledge, 1962: 213–226.

Kincaid, James R. *Annoying the Victorians.* New York: Routledge, 1995.

———. *Child Loving: The Erotic Child and Victorian Culture.* New York: Routledge, 1992.

———. *Dickens and the Rhetoric of Laughter.* Oxford: Clarendon Press, 1971.

Kirkpatrick, Larry. "The Gothic Flame of Charles Dickens," *Victorian Newsletter* 31 (1967): 20–24.

Kitton, Frederic G. *Charles Dickens by Pen and Pencil.* London: F. T. Sabin, 1890.

———. *Dickens and His Illustrators.* London: G. Redway, 1899.

———. *Dickensiana.* London: G. Redway, 1886. New York: Haskell House, 1971.

———. *The Minor Writings of Charles Dickens.* London: E. Stock, 1900. New York: AMS Press, 1975.

Korg, Jacob, ed. *London in Dickens's Day.* New York: Prentice Hall, 1960.

———, ed. *Twentieth-Century Interpretations of Bleak House.* New York: Prentice Hall, 1966.

Kucich, John. *Excess and Restraint in the Novels of Charles Dickens.* Athens: University of Georgia Press, 1981.

———. *Repression in Victorian Fiction: Charlotte Brontë, George Eliot, and Charles Dickens.* Berkeley: University of California Press, 1987.

Lankford, William T. "'The Parish Boy's Progess': The Evolving Form of *Oliver Twist,*" *PMLA* 93 (1978): 20–32.

Larson, Janet L. *Dickens and the Broken Scripture.* Athens: University of Georgia Press, 1985.

Lary, N. M. *Dostoevsky and Dickens.* London: Routledge, Kegan Paul, 1973.

Leacock, Stephen. *Charles Dickens: His Life and Work.* Garden City, N.Y.: Doubleday, Doran, 1933.

Leavis, F. R. *The Great Tradition.* London: Chatto and Windus, 1948.

Leavis, F. R., and Q. D. Leavis. *Dickens the Novelist.* London: Chatto and Windus, 1970.

Lehman, R. C. *Charles Dickens as Editor.* London: Macmillan, 1912.

Lettis, Richard. *The Dickens Aesthetic.* New York: AMS, 1989.

———. *Dickens on Literature.* New York: AMS, 1990.

Lettis, Richard, and R. Morris, eds. *Assessing Great Expectations.* San Francisco: Chandler, 1965.

Ley, J. W. T. *The Dickens Circle.* New York: Dutton, 1918. [biography]

Lindsay, Jack. *Charles Dickens: A Biographical and Critical Study.* London: Andrew Dakers, 1950. [biography]

Loe, Thomas. "Gothic Plot in *Great Expectations,*" *Dickens Quarterly* 6 (1989): 102–110.

Lohrli, Anne. *Household Words … Table of Contents, List of Contributors and Their Contributions.* Toronto: University of Toronto Press, 1973. [bibliography]

London Transport. *The London of Charles Dickens.* London: London Transport, 1970.

Lucas, John. *Charles Dickens: The Major Novels.* London: Penguin, 1992.

———. *The Melancholy Man: A Study of Dickens's Novels.* London: Methuen, 1970.

Lynch, Tony. *Dickens's England: A Traveller's Companion.* New York: Facts On File, 1986.

MacKay, Carol, ed. *Dramatic Dickens.* New York: Palgrave Macmillan, 1989.

MacKenzie, Norman, and Jeanne MacKenzie. *Dickens: A Life.* New York: Oxford University Press, 1979.

MacPike, Loralee. *Dostoevsky's Dickens.* Totowa, N.J.: Barnes and Noble, 1981.

———. "'The Old Curiosity Shape': Changing Views of Little Nell," *Dickens Studies Newsletter* 12 (1981): 33–38, 70–76.

Magnet, Myron. *Dickens and the Social Order.* Philadelphia: University of Pennsylvania Press, 1985.

Manheim, Leonard. "Floras and Doras: The Women in Dickens's Novels," *Texas Studies in Language and Literature* 7 (1965): 181–200.

———. "The Law as Father," *American Imago* 12 (1955): 17–23.

———. "The Personal History of *David Copperfield*: A Study in Psychoanalytic Criticism," *American Imago* 9 (1952): 21–43.

Manning, Sylvia. *Dickens as Satirist.* New Haven, Conn.: Yale University Press, 1971.

Marcus, Steven. *Dickens: From Pickwick to Dombey.* London: Chatto and Windus, 1965.

Marlow, James. *Charles Dickens: The Uses of Time.* Selinsgrove, Pa.: Susquehauna University Press, 1994.

Matz, Bertram W., ed. *Miscellaneous Papers.* National Edition of the Works of Charles Dickens. London: Chapman and Hall, 1908.

Matz, Bertram W. "*The Mystery of Edwin Drood:* A Bibliography," *Dickensian* 7 (May 1911): 130–133.

Matz, Winifred, comp. "A Bibliography of *Edwin Drood,*" *Dickensian* 24 (Summer 1928): 236; (Autumn 1928): 301–302; 25 (Winter 1928–29): 42–44; 26 (Spring 1929): 185–187.

McKnight, Natalie. *Idiots, Madmen, and Other Prisoners in Dickens.* New York: St. Martin's, 1993.

McMaster, Juliet. *Dickens the Designer.* London: Macmillan, 1987.

Meckier, Jerome. *Dickens's Great Expectations: Misnar's Pavilion versus Cinderella.* Lexington: University Press of Kentucky, 2002.

———. *Hidden Rivalries in Victorian Fiction: Dickens, Realism, and Revaluation.* Lexington: University Press of Kentucky, 1987.

———. *Innocent Abroad: Charles Dickens's American Entanglements.* Lexington: University Press of Kentucky, 1990.

Metz, Nancy Aycock. "Dickens, *Punch,* and Pecksniff," *Dickens Quarterly* 10 (March 1993): 6–17.

Miller, D. A. *The Novel and the Police.* Berkeley: University of California Press, 1988.

Miller, J. Hillis. Afterword to *Our Mutual Friend,* 901–911. New York: New American Library, 1964.

———, ed. *Charles Dickens and George Cruikshank.* Los Angeles: Clark Memorial Library, 1971.

———. *Charles Dickens: The World of His Novels.* Cambridge, Mass.: Harvard University Press, 1958.

———. *Fiction and Repetition: Seven English Novels.* Cambridge, Mass.: Harvard University Press, 1982.

———. *The Form of Victorian Fiction.* South Bend, Ind.: University of Notre Dame Press, 1968.

———. Introduction to *The Adventures of Oliver Twist.* New York: Holt, Rinehart and Winston, 1962.

———. "The Topography of Jealousy in *Our Mutual Friend.*" In *Dickens Refigured: Bodies, Desires and Other Histories,* edited by John Schad. Manchester: Manchester University Press, 1996.

———. *Victorian Subjects.* Durham, N.C.: Duke University Press, 1991.

Miller, William. *The Dickens Student and Collector: A List of Writings Relating to Charles Dickens and His Works, 1836–1945.* London: Chapman and Hall, 1946. [bibliography]

———. "Imitations of *Pickwick,*" *Dickensian* 32 (Winter 1935–36): 4–5.

Mitchell, Charles. "*The Mystery of Edwin Drood:* The Interior and Exterior of Self," *ELH* 33 (1966): 228–246.

Moers, Ellen. *The Dandy.* New York: Viking, 1960.

Moncrieff, Scott. "The *Cricket* in the Study," *Dickens Studies Annual* 22 (1993): 137–153.

Monod, Sylvère. *Dickens the Novelist.* Norman: University of Oklahoma Press, 1968.

———. *Martin Chuzzlewit.* London: Allen and Unwin, 1985.

Morgan, Nicholas H. *Secret Journeys: Theory and Practice in Reading Dickens.* Rutherford, N.J.: Fairleigh Dickinson University Press, 1992.

Moss, Sidney P. *Charles Dickens' Quarrel with America.* New York: Whitston, 1984.

Moynahan, Julian. "Dealings with the Firm of Dombey and Son: Firmness versus Wetness." In *Dickens and the Twentieth Century,* edited by John Gross and Gabriel Pearson, 121–131. London: Routledge, 1962.

———. "The Hero's Guilt: The Case of *Great Expectations,*" *Essays in Criticism* 10 (1960): 60–79.

Nabokov, Vladimir. "Charles Dickens, *Bleak House.*" In *Lectures on Literature,* edited by Fredson Bowers, 63–124. New York: Harcourt, 1980.

Needham, Gwendolyn. "The Undisciplined Heart of David Copperfield," *Nineteenth Century Fiction* 9 (1954): 81–107.

Nelson, Harland S. *Charles Dickens.* Boston: Twayne, 1981.

Newcomb, Mildred. *The Imagined World of Charles Dickens.* Columbus: Ohio State University Press, 1989.

Newlin, George, ed. *Everyone in Dickens.* Westport, Conn.: Greenwood Press, 1995.

———, ed. *Every Thing in Dickens: Ideas and Subjects Discussed by Charles Dickens in His Complete Works, a Topicon.* Westport, Conn.: Greenwood Press, 1996.

Newman, S. J. *Dickens at Play.* New York: St. Martin's, 1981.

Newsom, Robert. *Charles Dickens Revisited.* New York: Twayne, 2000.

———. *Dickens on the Romantic Side of Familiar Things: Bleak House and the Novel Tradition.* New York: Columbia University Press, 1977.

———. "Embodying Dombey: Whole and in Part," *Dickens Studies Annual* 18 (1989): 192–219.

———. "Fictions of Childhood." In *The Cambridge Companion to Charles Dickens,* edited by John O. Jordan, 92–105. Cambridge: Cambridge University Press, 2001.

———. "The Hero's Shame" *Dickens Studies Annual* 11 (1983): 1–24.

Nisbet, Ada. "The Autobiographical Matrix of *Great Expectations,*" *Victorian Newsletter,* 15 (1959): 10–13.

———. "Charles Dickens." In *Victorian Fiction: A Guide to Research,* edited by Lionel Stevenson. Cambridge, Mass.: Harvard University Press, 1964. [bibliography]

———. *Dickens and Ellen Ternan.* Berkeley: University of California Press, 1952. [biography]

———, and Blake Nevius, eds. *Dickens Centennial Essays.* Berkeley: University of California Press, 1971.

Oddie, William. *Dickens and Carlyle: The Question of Influence.* London: Centenary, 1972.

Orwell, George. "Charles Dickens." In *Essays of George Orwell,* 55–111. New York: Doubleday, 1954.

Ousby, Ian. *Bloodhounds of Heaven: The Detective in English Fiction from Godwin to Doyle.* Cambridge, Mass.: Harvard University Press, 1976.

Page, Norman. *Bleak House: A Novel of Connections.* New York: Twayne, 1990.

———. *A Dickens Chronology.* Boston: G. K. Hall, 1988.

———. *A Dickens Companion.* London: Macmillan, 1984.

Palmer, William. *Dickens and the New Historicism.* New York: St. Martin's, 1997.

Paris, Bernard J. *Imagined Human Beings: A Psychological Approach to Character and Conflict in Literature.* New York: New York University Press, 1997.

Parker, David. *The Companion to The Pickwick Papers.* Robertsbridge, England: Helm, 2003.

———. *The Doughty Street Novels.* New York: AMS Press, 2002.

Paroissien, David H. *Companion to Great Expectations.* Westport, Conn.: Greenwood, 2000.

———.*Companion to Oliver Twist.* Edinburgh: Edinburgh University Press, 1992.

———. "Literature's 'Eternal Duties': Dickens's Professional Creed." In *The Changing World of Charles Dickens,* edited by Robert Giddings, 21–50. Totowa, N.J.: Barnes and Noble, 1983.

———, ed. *Selected Letters of Charles Dickens.* New York: Twayne, 1984.

Partlow, Robert B. "The Moving I: A Study of Point of View in *Great Expectations,*" *College English* 23 (1961): 122–131.

Patten, Robert. "Art of *Pickwick*'s Interpolated Tales," *ELH* 34 (1967): 349–66.

———. *Charles Dickens and His Publishers.* Oxford: Clarendon Press, 1978. [biography]

———. "Dickens Time and Again," *Dickens Studies Annual* 2 (1972): 163–196.

———. "The Fight at the Top of the Tree: *Vanity Fair* versus *Dombey and Son,*" *Studies in English Literature* 10 (1970): 759–772.

———. *George Cruikshank's Life, Times, and Art.* New Brunswick, N.J.: Rutgers, 1992.

———. Introduction to *The Pickwick Papers.* Harmondsworth, U.K.: Penguin, 1972.

Pearson, Gabriel. "*The Old Curiosity Shop.*" In *Dickens and the Twentieth Century,* edited by John Gross and Gabriel Pearson, 77–90. London: Routledge, 1962.

Philpotts, Trey. *The Companion to Little Dorrit.* Robertsbridge, England: Helm, 2003.

Pointer, Michael. *Charles Dickens on the Screen.* Lanham, Md.: Scarecrow, 1996.

Pope, Norris. *Dickens and Charity.* New York: Columbia University Press, 1978.

Priestley, J. B. *Charles Dickens: A Pictorial Biography.* New York: Viking, 1961. [biography]

———. *English Comic Characters.* New York: Dodd, Mead, 1925.

———. "The Great Inimitable." In *Charles Dickens 1812–1870,* edited by E. W. F. Tomlin, 13–31. New York: Simon and Schuster, 1969.

Pritchett, V. S. *The Living Novel.* New York: Random House, 1947.

Pugh, Edwin. *The Charles Dickens Originals.* New York: Scribner's, 1912.

———. *Charles Dickens: The Apostle of the People.* London: New Age Press, 1908.

Pykett, Lyn. *Charles Dickens.* Houndmills, U.K.: Palgrave, 2002.

Rank, Otto. *The Double.* Chapel Hill: University of North Carolina Press, 1971.

Reed, John. *Dickens and Thackeray: Punishment and Forgiveness.* Athens: Ohio University Press, 1995.

———. *Victorian Conventions.* Athens: Ohio University Press, 1975.

Reid, J. C. *Charles Dickens: Little Dorrit.* London: Edward Arnold, 1967.

Rice, Thomas J. "The Politics of Barnaby Rudge." In *The Changing World of Charles Dickens,* edited by R. Giddings, 51–74. London: Routledge, 1989.

Robson, W. W. "*The Mystery of Edwin Drood.* The Solution?" *Times Literary Supplement,* 11 November 1983, p. 1,246.

Romano, John. *Dickens and Reality.* New York: Columbia University Press, 1978.

Rosenberg, Brian. *Little Dorrit's Shadows: Character and Contradiction in Dickens.* Columbia: University of Missouri Press, 1996.

Rosenberg, Edgar, ed. *Great Expectations.* New York: Norton, 1999.

Rubin, Leon. *The Nicholas Nickleby Story.* New York: Penguin, 1981.

Sadoff, Dianne. F. *Monsters of Affection: Dickens, Eliot, and Brontë on Fatherhood.* Baltimore: Johns Hopkins University Press, 1982.

Sadrin, Anny, ed. *Dickens, Europe, and the New Worlds.* New York: St. Martin's, 1999.

———. *Great Expectations.* London: Unwin, 1988.

———. *Parentage and Inheritance in the Novels of Charles Dickens.* Cambridge: Cambridge University Press, 1994.

Sanders, Andrew. *Charles Dickens.* Authors in Context. Oxford: Oxford University Press, 2003.

———. *Charles Dickens Resurrectionist.* London: Macmillan, 1982.

———. *The Companion to A Tale of Two Cities.* London: Unwin Hyman, 1988.

———. *Dickens and the Spirit of the Age.* Oxford: Clarendon, 2001.

———. *The Victorian Historical Novel 1840–1880.* London: Macmillan, 1978.

Schad, John, ed. *Dickens Refigured: Bodies, Desires, and Other Histories.* Manchester: Manchester University Press, 1996.

———. *The Reader in the Dickensian Mirrors.* London: Macmillan, 1992.

Schlicke, Paul. *Dickens and Popular Entertainment.* London: Allen and Unwin, 1985.

Schlicke, Paul, ed. *Oxford Reader's Companion to Dickens.* New York: Oxford University Press, 1999.

———. "The True Pathos of *The Old Curiosity Shop,*" *Dickens Quarterly* 7 (1990): 189–199.

Schor, Hilary. *Dickens and the Daughter of the House.* Cambridge: Cambridge University Press, 1999.

Schwarzbach, F. S. *Dickens and the City.* London: Athlone, 1979.

———, and Ira Bruce Nadel, eds. *Victorian Artists and the City.* New York: Pergamon, 1980.

Scott, P. J. M. *Reality and Comic Confidence in Charles Dickens.* New York: Barnes and Noble, 1979.

Sedgwick, Eve Kosofsky. *Between Men: English Literature and Male Homosocial Desire.* New York: Columbia University Press, 1985.

Shaw, George Bernard. Preface to *Great Expectations.* Edinburgh: R. and R. Clark, 1937.

———. *Shaw on Dickens.* Edited by Dan H. Laurence and Martin Quinn. New York: Frederick Ungar, 1985.

Simpson, Margaret. *Companion to Hard Times.* Westport, Conn.: Greenwood, 1997.

Slater, Michael. "Dickens (and Forster) at Work on *The Chimes,*" *Dickens Studies* 2 (1966): 106–140.

———. *Dickens and Women.* London: J. M. Dent, 1983.

———. *Intelligent Person's Guide to Dickens.* London: Duckworth, 2000.

———. Introduction to *The Christmas Books.* Harmondsworth, U.K.: Penguin, 1971.

———, ed. *Dickens' Journalism.* 4 vols; vol. 4 edited with John Drew. Columbus: Ohio State University Press, 1994–2000.

———. "Dickens in Wonderland." In *The Arabian Nights in English Literature,* edited by Peter L. Caracciolo. New York: St. Martin's, 1988.

———. *Dickens 1970*. London: Chapman & Hall, 1970.

———, ed. *Dickens on America and the Americans*. Austin: University of Texas Press, 1978.

———. "On Reading *Oliver Twist*," *Dickensian* 70 (1974): 75–81.

———, ed. *Nicolas Nickleby*. Facsimile ed. Philadelphia: University of Pennsylvania Press, 1982.

Smith, Grahame. *Charles Dickens: A Literary Life*. London: Macmillan, 1996.

———. *Dickens and the Dream of Cinema*. Manchester: Manchester University Press, 2003.

———. *Dickens, Money, and Society*. Berkeley: University of California Press, 1968.

Smith, Walter E. *Charles Dickens in the Original Cloth*. 2 vols. Los Angeles: Heritage Bookshop, 1981–83. [bibliographies]

Solomon, Pearl. *Dickens and Melville in Their Time*. New York: Columbia University Press, 1975.

Spilka, Mark. *Dickens and Kafka, a Mutual Interpretation*. Bloomington: Indiana University Press, 1963.

Steig, Michael. "Abuse and the Comic Grotesque in *The Old Curiosity Shop*: Problems of Response," *Dickens Quarterly* 11 (1994): 103–114.

———. *Dickens and Phiz*. Bloomington: Indiana University Press, 1978.

———. *Stories of Reading: Subjectivity and Literary Understanding*. Baltimore: Johns Hopkins University Press, 1989.

Stewart, Garrett. *Dear Reader: The Conscripted Audience in Nineteenth-Century British Fiction*. Baltimore: Johns Hopkins University Press, 1996.

———. *Death Sentences: Styles of Dying in British Fiction*. Cambridge, Mass.: Harvard University Press, 1984.

———. *Dickens and the Trials of Imagination*. Cambridge, Mass.: Harvard University Press, 1974.

Stoehr, Taylor. *Dickens: The Dreamer's Stance*. Ithaca, N.Y.: Cornell University Press, 1965.

Stone, Donald. *The Romantic Impulse in Victorian Fiction*. Cambridge, Mass.: Harvard University Press, 1980.

Stone, Harry. "Dickens and Harriet Beecher Stowe," *Nineteenth Century Fiction* 12 (1957): 188–202.

———. *Dickens and the Invisible World*. Bloomington: Indiana University Press, 1979.

———. "Dickens and the Jews," *Victorian Studies* 2 (1959): 223–253.

———. "Dickens' Artistry and *The Haunted Man*," *South Atlantic Quarterly* 61 (1962): 492–505.

———. "Dickens's Woman in White," *Victorian Newsletter* 33 (1968): 5–8.

———, ed. *Dickens' Working Notes for His Novels*. Chicago: University of Chicago Press, 1987.

———. "The Love Pattern in Dickens's Novels." In *Dickens the Craftsman*, edited by Robert B. Partlow. Carbondale: Southern Illinois University Press, 1970.

———. *The Night Side of Dickens: Cannibalism, Passion, Necessity*. Columbus: Ohio State University Press, 1994.

———, ed. *Uncollected Writings from Household Words, 1850–1859*. 2 vols. Bloomington: Indiana University Press, 1968.

Storey, Gladys. *Dickens and Daughter*. London: Muller, 1939.

Storey, Graham. *David Copperfield: Interweaving Truth and Fiction*. New York: Twayne, 1991.

———. *Dickens Bleak House*. Landmarks of World Literature Series. Cambridge: Cambridge University Press, 1987.

Sucksmith, Harvey Peter. "The Dustheaps in *Our Mutual Friend*," *Essays in Criticism* 23 (1973): 206–212.

———. *The Narrative Art of Charles Dickens*. Oxford: Clarendon Press, 1970.

Swinburne, Algernon C. *Dickens*. London: Chatto and Windus, 1913.

Tambling, Jeremy. *Bleak House: Charles Dickens*. New Casebooks. New York: Palgrave Macmillan, 1998.

———. *Dickens, Violence and the Modern State: Dreams of the Scaffold*. London: Macmillan, 1995.

Thacker, John. *Edwin Drood: Antichrist in the Cathedral*. New York: St. Martin's, 1990.

Thomas, Deborah A. *Dickens and the Short Story*. Philadelphia: University of Pennsylvania Press, 1982.

———. *Hard Times: A Fable of Fragmentation and Wholeness*. New York: Twayne; London: Prentice Hall, 1997.

Thurley, Geoffrey. *The Dickens Myth*. New York: St. Martin's, 1976.

Tick, Stanley. "Autobiographical Impulses in *The Haunted Man*," *Dickens Quarterly* 18 (2001): 62–69.

Tillotson, Kathleen. *Novels of the Eighteen-forties.* Oxford: Clarendon Press, 1954.

Tomalin, Claire. *The Invisible Woman: The Story of Nelly Ternan and Charles Dickens.* New York: Alfred A. Knopf, 1991. [biography]

Trilling, Lionel. "Little Dorrit." In *The Opposing Self,* 50–65. New York: Viking, 1955.

Van Ghent, Dorothy. "The Dickens World: The View from Todgers's," *Sewanee Review* 58 (1950): 419–438.

———. "On *Great Expectations.*" In *The English Novel: Form and Function,* 125–138. New York: Rinehart, 1953.

Vogel, Jane. *Allegory in Dickens.* Tuscaloosa: University of Alabama Press, 1977.

Walder, Dennis. *Dickens and Religion.* London: Allen and Unwin, 1981.

Watkins, Gwen. *Dickens in Search of Himself.* London: Macmillan, 1987.

Welsh, Alexander. *The City of Dickens.* Oxford: Clarendon Press, 1971.

———. *Dickens Redressed.* New Haven, Conn.: Yale University Press, 2000.

———. *From Copyright to Copperfield: The Identity of Dickens.* Cambridge, Mass.: Harvard University Press, 1987.

———. *Reflections on the Hero as Quixote.* Princeton, N.J.: Princeton University Press, 1981.

Westland, Ella. "Little Nell and the Marchioness: Some Functions of Fairy Tale in *The Old Curiosity Shop,*" *Dickens Quarterly* 7 (1991): 68–75.

Whipple, Edward. *Charles Dickens.* Boston: Houghton Mifflin, 1912.

Williams, Raymond. *The Country and the City.* New York: Oxford University Press, 1973.

———. *The English Novel from Dickens to Lawrence.* London: Chatto and Windus, 1970.

———. Introduction to *Dombey and Son.* Harmondsworth, U.K.: Penguin, 1970.

Wilson, Angus. "Charles Dickens: A Haunting," *Critical Quarterly* 2 (1960): 101–108.

———. "Dickens and Dostoyevsky." In *Diversity and Depth in Fiction: Selected Critical Writings of Angus Wilson,* edited by Kerry McSweeney, 64–87. New York: Viking, 1984.

———. "Dickens on Children and Childhood." In *Dickens 1970,* edited by Michael Slater, 195–227. London: Chapman and Hall, 1970.

———. "Heroes and Heroines of Dickens." In *Dickens and the Twentieth Century,* edited by John Gross and Gabriel Pearson, 3–11. London: Routledge, 1962.

———. Introduction to *Oliver Twist.* Harmondsworth, England: Penguin, 1966.

———. *The World of Charles Dickens.* New York: Viking, 1970.

Wilson, Edmund. "Dickens: The Two Scrooges," *New Republic,* March 1940. Reprinted in *The Wound and the Bow,* 1–93. Boston: Houghton Mifflin, 1941.

Wolfreys, Julian. *Writing London: The Trace of the Urban Text from Blake to Dickens.* New York: St. Martin's, 1998.

Woodward, Kathleen. "Passivity and Passion in *Little Dorrit,*" *Dickensian* 71 (1975): 140–148.

Young, G. M. *Victorian England: Portrait of an Age.* London: Oxford University Press, 1936.

Zambrano, A. L. *Dickens and Film.* New York: Gordon, 1977.

Zemka, Sue. "From the Punchmen to Pugin's Gothics: The Broad Road to a Sentimental Death in *The Old Curiosity Shop,*" *Nineteenth Century Literature* 48 (1993): 291–309.

Bibliographies for individual novels are available in the series The Garland Bibliographies (Garland Publishing).

Volumes of notes on individual novels are available in The Dickens Companion series (Unwin Hyman).

INDEX